Gillette®

LEAGUE
Publications Ltd

RUGBY LEAGUE 2003-04
Out of the Ashes

League Publications Ltd

First published in Great Britain in 2003 by
League Publications Ltd
Wellington House
Briggate
Brighouse
West Yorkshire HD6 1DN

A CIP catalogue record for this book is available from the British Library
ISBN 1-901347-12-5

Designed and Typeset by League Publications Limited
Printed by ColourBooks Ltd, Dublin, Eire

Contributing Editor	Tim Butcher
Contributors	Gareth Walker
	Tony Hannan
	Malcolm Andrews
	Mike Latham
	John Drake
	Raymond Fletcher
	Steve Kilgallon
Statistics, production and design	Daniel Spencer
Pictures	Andy Howard
	Varley Picture Agency
	Action Photographics, Australia
	Graham Lynch
	Dave Williams
	Sig Kasatkin
	Max Flego
	Gordon Clayton
	Simon Wilkinson
	Trevor Smith

CONTENTS

ACKNOWLEDGEMENTS

Rugby League 2003/2004 is the eighth in League Publications Ltd's annual series of Rugby League Yearbooks and this is the first year of its production with the backing of world-leading company Gillette.

Once again the yearbook relies on the hard work and dedication of all the contributors to Rugby Leaguer & Rugby League Express and Rugby League World magazine who provide such a tremendous service to the game of Rugby League.

The statistical review was put together meticulously, as always, by Daniel Spencer, who has also single-handedly designed the book again.

As always we are lucky to be able to include some wonderful action photography provided by, in particular, Rugby Leaguer & League Express staff photographer Andy Howard, Varley Picture Agency and Col Whelan of Action Photographics in Sydney.

Special mentions for Gareth Walker, Malcolm Andrews, Raymond Fletcher and Mike Latham, who have contributed so much to the writing of this book; to Opta Index, who compiled the Opta Index Analysis in our mind-boggling statistical section; and to John Drake, the man responsible for the excellent totalrl.com website, who proofed many pages of this book.

Tim Butcher
Editor
Rugby League 2003/2004

FOREWORD

What might have been.

This yearbook's record of the Ashes Series of 2003 is titled "The Nearly Men", and as we produce this book in the hours after the third Test at the McAlpine Stadium, the disappointment that ran through the British game in the wake of the 3-0 series defeat by the Australians was still strong.

Just how bad will it seem when you sit down to read this book? Watching Luke Ricketson run in that try on the final whistle at Huddersfield, just a couple of minutes after Craig Fitzgibbon had levelled the match with that touchline kick, was for me like watching my house burn down to the ground - a feeling of complete disbelief.

Great Britain were so close, leading in all three Tests going into the last ten minutes in every game...

Despite the loss it would be hard to put together a credible case to support the argument that British Rugby League is not catching up with Antipodean game. Great Britain were not outclassed, as they had been so many times in the past 30 years. Every game was a true Test, won by the best team, just, on the night.

GB coach David Waite's claims that international Rugby League had grown in stature on the back the series was on the button.

British Rugby League had shown signs even before 2003 had begun that it was producing players of a very high calibre, with more and more young faces gradually appearing in Super League, not just to make up the numbers, but to become stars in their own right.

England Academy's 2-nil series win over the Australian Schoolboys last December was hailed as a sign of things to come. The British youngsters beat the Aussies for the first time for 30 years, and followed that up by beating them again a week later. Those who witnessed the wins will not have been surprised that some of those Academy players became big operators in Super League VIII.

Luke Robinson performed in those games as he was going to in Wigan's remarkable season. Gareth Hock - who wasn't to make his senior Warriors debut until the Challenge Cup - was also obviously something special. Richard Mathers showed all the poise that would make him one of Leeds' best performers by the end of the season. His teammate Ryan Bailey would surely have been a Great Britain player at the end of the year but for a moment of madness that interrupted his glittering career. Bradford's Jamie Langley showed maturity beyond his tender years to lead his side to a magnificent victory. Tom Saxton of Castleford Tigers and Graeme Horne were established and accomplished Super League players by the time the domestic season ended.

And the generation above them isn't in bad shape either. The young England A side that pushed the Kangaroos so close at Brentford in October contained some magnificent prospects, some of whom should maybe have already been given their Great Britain spurs - Leeds halfbacks Danny McGuire and Rob Burrow just two real stars for the very near future.

The development of young players has taken a quantum leap over the past few years - and for that David Waite in one of his other roles as Performance Director, must take the credit. It's important that the game backs him to make sure the gains aren't lost.

To sum it up in a few words, Rugby League in 2003 has been another year of ups and downs, but that is the nature of sport.

Every supporter of every club in the land will have enjoyed highs and suffered lows during the year.

2003 was the year of the Bulls, who on their return to Odsal collected the Powergen Challenge Cup - played for the first time under a closed roof in Cardiff - the Minor Premiership and the Super League Championship. They couldn't have achieved much more but even they had lows - remember the three-match losing home run with defeats to London, Wigan and St Helens? All that could be forgotten as coach of the year Brian Noble steered his side to all the glittering prizes.

Champions St Helens might have lost their crown, as well a getting a hiding in the World Club Challenge, but there were some great times at Knowsley Road - and one unforgettable night at Odsal also springs to mind.

Wigan's run to the Grand Final was an amazing story; Leeds Rhinos could never find a win against the Bulls all season, despite some of the closest local derbies ever between the two - including the heartstopping Cup final in Cardiff - but still led the Super League for big chunks of the season.

The Super League play-offs featured Warrington and London for the first time after the most compelling of run-ins. Castleford, Widnes and Huddersfield were all in with a chance until the penultimate round. And Hull fans certainly had a great season despite an incredible slide from third spot as the weight of the club's injury run finally got the better of them. And the Kingston Communications Stadium established itself very quickly as many fans' favourite League venue.

Wakefield Trinity Wildcats also provided some great memories, with the stunning win at St Helens prominent among them, while Halifax fans, despite their team's relegation to the National League, could take comfort from the club emerging from its CVA by the end of the year.

Super League will welcome back Salford next season, who weren't quite as invincible as the Giants the year before, but nevertheless proved themselves the best in the division when it mattered.

National Leagues One and Two created an extremely competitive environment which will see more good young players emerge over the next few years. As will the National League Three and the expanding TotalRL.com Conference below it.

Expansion was a keyword for 2003, which brings us back to the international scene, as 2003 saw Australia, Russia and Lebanon stage international tournaments, and New Caledonia, Serbia & Montenegro and Greece become new names on the list of League-playing nations.

Which leaves us all looking forward with great excitement to next year, which will have already kicked off with the early rounds of the Challenge Cup by the time you read this book.

And the RFL had yet to finalise its broadcasting arrangements as the Ashes series came to a close, but an improved deal was on the table to give Rugby League firm foundations for the future.

With a year as entertaining and enthralling as 2003, we're in for a very healthy future. We hope you enjoy the read.

Rugby League 2003-2004 is the eighth annual yearbook produced by the game's biggest selling newspaper. It has an in-depth statistical section, featuring every team in the Rugby Football League, chapters on all the major competitions both here and abroad and a record of every game in Super League and the NFP.

It is illustrated with over 200 full colour and black and white photographs.

It covers the professional game in Great Britain, as well as giving details of the international season, and the Australian NRL season. It gives you the match facts for every Super League, Challenge Cup games involving professional teams, National League One and Two and Arriva Trains Cup game, so that you can recall the achievements of your favourite team or player.

And we have selected five individuals who we judge to have made the biggest impact on Rugby League in 2003.

This book contains a whole host of information that no serious Rugby League fan can afford to be without.

League Publications produces the weekly newspaper 'Rugby Leaguer & Rugby League Express', as well as the monthly glossy magazine 'Rugby League World' and the website 'totalrugbyleague.com'.

We hope you enjoy looking back over the year 2003 with us. 2004 is almost upon us, and you can find your club's fixtures for next season at the back of this yearbook.

Tim Butcher
Editor
Rugby League 2003/2004

1
PERSONALITIES OF 2003

Adrian Morley

It was certainly an eventful year for Adrian Morley.

The former Leeds second-rower started it by playing his full part in Sydney Roosters' comprehensive 38-0 World Club Challenge victory over St Helens at the Reebok Stadium in February.

And the 26 year old then went on to enhance his growing reputation as one of the world's best forwards with another outstanding season Down Under in the NRL.

Morley was a tower of strength in a Roosters pack that took them all the way to the Grand Final, though Ricky Stuart's side fell just short of a Premiership double by losing out to Penrith Panthers.

Morley was in tears after the game. And things quickly went from bad to worse.

Returning to these shores as a hero figure following his exploits in the NRL, Morley was seen as the man to lead Great Britain's forwards into battle in the Ashes.

But in the very first tackle of the series, the Salford-born hard man caught Robbie Kearns with a reckless high tackle, and with just 12 seconds on the clock, was dismissed by referee Steve Ganson.

It will go down as the quickest red card in Test history, and although the Lions rallied bravely in that Wigan encounter, they slid to a crucial First Test defeat.

Morley escaped suspension and returned for the second Test at Hull - creating the first try with the pass of the series, a brilliant flicked effort for Terry Newton.

But it wasn't enough to prevent the Ashes returning Down Under, much to the disappointment of Morley and his teammates. And he was felt fortunate by some when he escaped disciplinary punishment again after a second-half high tackle on Aussie winger Matt Sing.

One thing's for sure - Adrian Morley will never forget 2003.

Jamie Peacock

Jamie Peacock took home just about every award available to him in 2003 after a season of consistent achievement with the Bulls.

Placed alongside his Challenge Cup winners' medal and Grand Final ring, were prizes for Man of Steel, Rugby League Writers' Player of the Year and Super League Players' Player of the Year.

Peacock also came within a vote of clinching the Lance Todd Trophy - just losing out to Leeds' Gary Connolly, and he may have won it had the ballot taken place at the end of the game rather than 15 minutes before the final hooter.

Peacock's exploits appeared to have taken their toll during the Ashes series, when - after a mighty performance in the First Test that helped compensate for the early dismissal of teammate Adrian Morley - he faded a little.

But Peacock has still come a long way since being loaned out by the Bulls to Featherstone Rovers and spending a year playing country football in Australia.

Now he is one of the most respected forwards in world Rugby League - held in high esteem by players and coaches alike.

The second-rower was also named as a Personality of the Year in 2000 after another terrific campaign with the Bulls - though it is 2003 that will go down as the Year of the Peacock.

Gavin Clinch

Salford City Reds were always going to need an on-field general to guide their return to Super League. In Gavin Clinch, they found the ideal man.

Australian Clinch was quickly earmarked by coach Karl Harrison as the player to spearhead the Reds' National League One campaign, and the former Halifax, Wigan and Huddersfield number seven did not disappoint.

Clinch formed an outstanding halfback partnership with Cliff Beverley, playing a significant role in the New Zealander finishing the season as the game's leading tryscorer in all competitions.

Clinch himself was a regular try scorer too - crossing the line 12 times.

But it was his creativity in the middle of the field that was most influential.

Unsurprisingly, he was named as the NL1 Player of the Year, and Players' Player, after a season of tormenting defences with his darting runs, intelligent play-making and varied kicking game.

His trademark one-on-one steals were also in evidence throughout a campaign where he was consistently targeted by opposition defences for special attention. Clinch probably took more late hits than any player in the game during 2003.

But arguably his biggest contribution to the Reds cause was his ability to perform in the biggest matches.

Clinch was the Man of the Match in both the Arriva Trains Cup Final and the NL1 Grand Final, and also stood up in most of the seven clashes against nearest rivals Leigh Centurions.

Now he looks set to be the Reds' key man on their return to Super League in 2004.

This is the second time Clinch has been named among the Five Personalities of the Year, having earned a place in 1998 for his exploits in helping to guide Halifax to third place in Super League.

Brian Carney

2003 was the year that Brian Carney emerged as a world class Rugby League player.

The former law student and Gaelic footballer from Dublin had certainly made an impression on the game during his time with Gateshead, Hull and in his first two years with Wigan.

But it was Super League VIII that Carney really stamped his mark on the sport.

Carney was in fantastic form for Wigan as their late-season charge took them to within 40 minutes of Grand Final glory.

One game in particular marked the progress that the Irishman has made in recent seasons.

The Warriors were outsiders going into their Final Eliminator against second-placed Leeds Rhinos at Headingley.

But Carney scored two breathtaking long-distance tries to help Wigan to a memorable 23-22 success.

His second was most people's try of the season.

There looked to be nothing on when Carney took a regulation drive deep inside his own quarter. But the winger blasted through the first line of defence, beat two more players immediately, and then won a thrilling race to the line that covered virtually the entire length of the field.

Such was Carney's late season form that he was an automatic choice for David Waite's Great Britain squad for the Ashes - and his club form soon translated to the International stage.

Carney scored two well-taken tries on debut at Wigan, and impressed throughout the series with his combative, all-action style.

It even led to speculation linking him with a move to NRL Champions Penrith Panthers - though Carney himself was quick to play down the stories.

And it wasn't just his performances on the field that marked him out as one of the game's leading personalities.

Carney's likeable, articulate manner made him popular with media and spectators alike, and he looks set for a bright future in Rugby League.

17

Gareth Hock

In a year where a host of talented young stars shot to prominence in Super League, none shone brighter than Wigan's Gareth Hock.

After first catching the eye with his displays in England Academy's historic wins over the Australian Schoolboys last winter, Hock forced his way into first team reckoning at the Warriors and ended the season as a key member of the European Nations Cup winners England A.

Hock was also deservedly crowned Super League's Young Player of the Year at the Man of Steel awards, beating off competition from the likes of Leeds stand-off Danny McGuire and his own Wigan teammate Luke Robinson.

Hock made his Wigan debut by scoring two tries in a comprehensive Challenge Cup win at Doncaster, and

was rarely out of the picture after that.

He missed just four games for the Warriors, and scored 11 tries in all competitions.

A tall, long-striding player whose strength defies his build, Hock is also an excellent ball player, and looks set to make it all the way to full International honours.

There is also an interesting story behind Hock's progression to becoming one of the country's best young players. As a junior, Hock - then called Gareth Charnock - found himself in a "little bit of trouble", according to Wigan's respected Head of Youth Development Brian Foley, when interviewed by Rugby League World magazine in July.

He then went missing for a few weeks before returning as Gareth Hock, and declaring "Fresh start Brian".

He hasn't looked back since, and the multi-talented Hock should be around for a good few years to come.

2
THE 2003 SEASON

DECEMBER 2002
Catch up time

THE drawn series with the Kiwis - and with it the winning of the Baskerville Shield - had finished off the 2002 season on a high note. But that wasn't the end of it - there was much more feelgood to come before the turn of the year.

The formidable Combined Australian High Schools arrived in late November for a tour that would culminate with two Tests against the England Academy.

The young Aussies came with a proud 30-year record - they had never been defeated in the northern hemisphere and the record looked likely to remain intact when they defeated the Academic Lion Cubs in Tottenham, 32-0 and the BARLA Young Lions three times by 44-4, 54-9 and 28-4. The third Test at South Leeds Stadium had been a reasonable effort by the British amateurs, with two Londoners, Rob Worrincy and Alex Rowe, the pick of the home side.

But, against all expectation, England Academy defeated the Aussies 28-22 in the first Test at Knowsley Road, St Helens. Leeds' Richard Mathers was adjudged gamestar alongside another top performer, Wigan scrum-half Luke Robinson, with Leeds winger Matt Gardner scoring two tries in a memorable win.

The Mike Gregory-coached Academy was expected to feel the backlash the following Friday at Headingley, but instead of resting on their laurels, they gave the Aussies a bigger beating, this time by 22-12

The 2,119 people at Headingley that night witnessed history - it was the first time the Aussies had ever lost a series, but they could have no complaints after being outplayed for the second time in the space of five days.

Leeds Rhinos prop Ryan Bailey and Wigan loose forward Gareth Hock, who was voted the player of the series, were brilliant in a superb performance. Wakefield winger Matty Wray and Wigan fullback Chris Melling each got a pair of tries, but it was essentially a great team performance, with coach Gregory deserving huge plaudits.

"The boys know when to put it on," he said after the second Test. "There were some brains out there, a

Sunday 8th December 2002

ENGLAND ACADEMY 28 COMBINED AUSTRALIAN HIGH SCHOOLS 20

ENGLAND ACADEMY: 1 Chris Melling (Wigan Warriors); 2 Matt Gardner (Leeds Rhinos); 3 Dwayne Barker (Leeds Rhinos); 4 Chris Bridge (Bradford Bulls); 5 Matthew Wray (Wakefield Trinity Wildcats); 6 Richard Mathers (Leeds Rhinos); 7 Luke Robinson (Wigan Warriors); 8 Ryan Bailey (Leeds Rhinos); 9 Bob Beswick (Wigan Warriors); 10 Craig Barton (Wigan Warriors); 11 Jon Wilkin (St Helens); 12 Jamie Langley (Bradford Bulls) (C); 13 Gareth Hock (Wigan Warriors). Subs (all used): 14 Tommy Gallagher (Leeds Rhinos); 15 Bruce Johnson (St Helens); 16 Tom Saxton (Castleford Tigers); 17 Graeme Horne (Hull FC).
Tries: Barker (7), Hock (11), Gardner (29, 46), Gallagher (37);
Goals: Melling 4.
AUSTRALIAN SCHOOLBOYS: 1 Ben Farrell (St Mary's College, Toowoomba); 2 Dimitri Pelo (Palm Beach Currumbin); 3 Steven Ross (Kiama High School); 4 Jesse Caine (Woolooware High School); 5 Jermaine Ale (Lambton High School); 6 Russ Aitken (Cronulla High School); 7 Tim Smith (Coombabah High School); 8 Michael Weyman (Erindale College) (C); 9 Stephen Goodhew (Kirwan State High School); 10 Tom Learoyd (Farrer Memorial Agricultural School); 11 Ashton Sims (Kirwan State High School); 12 Ben Hannant (Palm Beach Currumbin); 13 Liam Fulton (Westfields Sports High School). Subs (all used): 14 Luke Mercer (Hunter Sports High School); 15 Jacob Lillyman (Kirwan State High School); 16 Justin Poore (Endeavour Sports High School); 17 Ryan Hoffman (St Gregory's College, Campbelltown).
Tries: Pelo (20, 42), Ross (26, 63); **Goals:** Smith 3.
Sin bin: Goodhew (24) - dissent.
Rugby Leaguer & League Express Men of the Match:
England: Luke Robinson; *Australia:* Michael Weyman.
Penalty count: 12-6; **Half-time:** 16-10; **Referee:** Karl Kirkpatrick (England); **Attendance:** 1,236 *(at Knowsley Road, St Helens).*

lot of tough players who see the situations and read the game. That's exactly what they did. They're smart. We just give them ideas and they go out there and do their stuff.

"All 17 had decided what the jersey meant. The future of our game, the quality of our players is such that maybe in five or six years we'll be able to say we are the world champions at senior level.

"We said it was the start of a journey when we went to New Zealand and Australia last year and everyone involved in that tour did a wonderful job. We have got to follow it on. It's one series' win and we'll take the credit. Now we have got to take it to the next stage.

Friday 13th December 2002

ENGLAND ACADEMY 22 COMBINED AUSTRALIAN HIGH SCHOOLS 12

ENGLAND ACADEMY: 1 Chris Melling (Wigan Warriors); 2 Matt Gardner (Leeds Rhinos); 3 Dwayne Barker (Leeds Rhinos); 4 Chris Bridge (Bradford Bulls); 5 Matthew Wray (Wakefield Trinity Wildcats); 6 Richard Mathers (Leeds Rhinos); 7 Luke Robinson (Wigan Warriors); 8 Ryan Bailey (Leeds Rhinos); 9 Bob Beswick (Wigan Warriors); 10 Craig Barton (Wigan Warriors); 11 Jon Wilkin (St Helens); 12 Jamie Langley (Bradford Bulls) (C); 13 Gareth Hock (Wigan Warriors). Subs (all used): 14 Tommy Gallagher (Leeds Rhinos); 15 Bruce Johnson (St Helens); 16 Tom Saxton (Castleford Tigers); 17 Graeme Horne (Hull FC).
Tries: Wray (26, 47), Melling (30, 33); **Goals:** Melling 3.
AUSTRALIAN SCHOOLBOYS: 1 Ben Farrell (St Mary's College, Toowoomba); 5 Jermaine Ale (Lambton High School); 3 Steven Ross (Kiama High School); 4 Jesse Caine (Woolooware High School); 2 Dimitri Pelo (Palm Beach Currumbin); 6 Russ Aitken (Cronulla High School); 7 Stephen Goodhew (Kirwan State High School); 8 Michael Weyman (Erindale College) (C); 9 Heath L'Estrange (Terra Sancta College, Quakers Hill); 10 Ashton Sims (Kirwan State High School); 11 Tom Learoyd (Farrer Memorial Agricultural School); 12 Justin Poore (Endeavour Sports High School); 13 Liam Fulton (Westfields Sports High School). Subs (all used): 14 Tim Smith (Coombabah High School); 15 Ryan Hoffman (St Gregory's College, Campbelltown); 16 Ben Hannant (Palm Beach Currumbin); 17 Jacob Lillyman (Kirwan State High School).
Tries: Goodhew (7), Learoyd (51); **Goals:** Farrell, Smith.
Rugby Leaguer & League Express Men of the Match:
England: Ryan Bailey; *Australia:* Michael Weyman.
Penalty count: 13-12; **Half-time:** 14-6; **Referee:** Richard Silverwood (England); **Attendance:** 2,119 *(at Headingley Stadium, Leeds).*

"But these 18 year olds have put us back on the map."

Australia coach Chris Anderson admitted that the Junior Lions' series win over the Australian Schoolboys was "a good thing for Rugby League". Anderson told the Sydney Sunday Telegraph the defeat was not a reflection on declining standards in Australia, but rather an indication that the British game was improving at junior level.

"It's a reflection of the fact that England are getting their act together," he said. "It's the first positive sign that they are making progress over there."

Meanwhile Wigan Chairman Maurice Lindsay - whose club held more young riches than most - laughed off reports in the Sydney press that he was interested in the Brisbane Broncos chief executive position.

"I only have to have lunch with Wayne Bennett and they have me as chief executive of Brisbane," said Lindsay. "There is absolutely nothing in it.

"My whole life is committed to seeing our current crop of young players come through at Wigan, like the crop we had in the late eighties.

I get great satisfaction from seeing those kids, and I'm not chasing a full time job anywhere."

A daunting prospect awaited a more senior emerging star when Bradford Bulls and Great Britain star Leon Pryce appeared before Bradford Magistrates court charged with an offence of assault occasioning grievous bodily harm with intent.

Pryce was scheduled to face Bradford Crown Court on January 2 over an allegation that he glassed a man in a city night-club on September 14 that year.

Bradford were strongly linked with Karl Pratt, who had been told he didn't figure in Leeds coach Daryl Powell's plans for the 2003 season. Pratt had to take the Rhinos to a tribunal to earn free-agent status and pave the way for a move to Odsal.

Hull secured the future of their Great Britain star Richard Horne until the end of the 2006 season after he signed a three-year extension to his current deal, which still had twelve months remaining on it.

And the following year's World Club Challenge was put in jeopardy when the Rugby Football League put a block on the Sydney Roosters taking on Widnes Vikings at the Halton Stadium only days before playing Super League champions St Helens. The Vikings had negotiated a warm-up game with the Roosters, and were angry when RFL officials intervened to rule out the game, claiming that they didn't want to divert attention from the big game itself. Saints coach Ian Millward's proposal to play the game in Australia fell on deaf ears at the Roosters.

Off the field, the move towards unification of the amateur and professional arms of the game was on hold as RFL Executive Chairman Richard Lewis made a dramatic plea to stalling BARLA officials to give the plan the green light. Lewis had offered BARLA three places on the RFL's supreme decision-making body, the RFL Council.

In the wider world, former Wigan and New Zealand coach Frank Endacott called on the Rugby League International Federation to consider awarding the 2005 Rugby League World Cup to New Zealand when it met in Sydney in February.

And New Zealand captain Stacey Jones was named as the winner of the Rugby League World Golden Boot for 2003.

Strela Kazan made history at Hull Kingston Rovers' Craven Park ground, then they became the first Russian team to play in the Rugby League Challenge Cup - branded as the TXU Energi Challenge Cup, although a corporate takeover later caused a re-branding as "Powergen".

The team from Tatarstan went down 20-16 to their hosts Embassy in the second round, having fought back from 20-6 down in the second half, loose forward Maxim Romanov scoring a hat-trick of tries.

"The game was very tough, and the conditions made it very difficult for us," said Kazan fullback Oleg Sokolov. "We had prepared for the game in Dubai, where it was very hot, and certainly it wasn't like Dubai out there today.

"We had a difficult trip here, flying from Dubai back to Moscow, where we spent all night in Moscow Airport, before flying to England. But we tried our best, and are determined to win next time. This is great encouragement for Rugby League in Kazan, where the strength of the game builds every day."

The result meant that Embassy became one of five Hull clubs set to appear in the third round, the others being East Hull, Skirlaugh, Cottingham and Hull KR.

In round one, Bradford side Birkenshaw had proved too strong for the Dublin City Exiles, running out 56-0 victors in the Emerald Isle. Cardiff Demons also stumbled out of season to a 56-12 defeat at Shaw Cross Sharks, while Edinburgh's Eagles put up a much more competitive effort before going down 26-8 at home to Oulton Raiders.

There was controversy as North East Cup winners Newcastle were unable to find enough players to send a team to Coventry, while Siddal easily accounted for the students of Leeds Met 78-0.

The Army, RAF and Royal Navy all fell at the first hurdle, with Hunslet Warriors, Crosfields and Cottingham Tigers respectively all making the second round.

TXU ENERGI CHALLENGE CUP FIRST ROUND

Saturday 30th November 2002
Heworth 4 Thornhill Trojans 24; Woolston Rovers 20 Saddleworth Rangers 10; Dudley Hill 12 Huddersfield Syngenta 4; Leigh East 46 Eccles 4; East Hull 36 Normanton Knights 4; Wigan St Patricks 17 Oldham St Annes 20; Waterhead 16 Hull Dockers 12; Castleford Panthers 4 Walney Central 11; Coventry Bears - walk over v Newcastle Knights; Millom 20 Embassy 26; Hensingham 4 Halton Simms Cross 9; West Bowling 28 Rochdale Mayfield 0; Wath Brow Hornets 12 East Leeds 0; Thatto Heath Crusaders 12 Castleford Lock Lane 19; The Army 10 Hunslet Warriors 22; Milford Marlins 16 Widnes St Maries 8; Redhill 24 York Acorn 12; Cottingham Tigers 34 Royal Navy 2; Sheffield Hillsborough Hawks 8 Skirlaugh 24; Siddal 78 Leeds Metropolitan University 0; Elland 12 Sharlston Rovers 8; Featherstone Lions 16 Ince Rosebridge 8; Eastmoor Dragons 18 Wigan St Judes 26; Leigh Miners Rangers 20 West Hull 6; Askam 2 Ideal Isberg 12; Dublin City Exiles 0 Birkenshaw 56.

Sunday 1st December 2002
Edinburgh Eagles 8 Oulton Raiders 26; RAF 2 Crosfields 5; Shaw Cross Sharks 56 Cardiff Demons 12.

TXU ENERGI CHALLENGE CUP SECOND ROUND

Saturday 14 December 2002
Waterhead 4 Shaw Cross Sharks 18; Walney Central 2 Halton Simms Cross 12; Siddal 14 Ideal Isberg 0; Wigan St Judes 16 Oulton Raiders 24; Hunslet Warriors 18 Woolston Rovers 30; Castleford Lock Lane 8 Thornhill 18; Birkenshaw 0 West Bowling 14; Wath Brow Hornets 66 Milford Marlins 6; Leigh Miners Rangers 68 Crosfields 8; Leigh East 20 Skirlaugh 28; Featherstone Lions 10 Oldham St Annes 12; Elland 4 Redhill 13; East Hull 48 Coventry Bears 8; Cottingham Tigers 17 Bradford Dudley Hill 4.

Sunday 15 December 2002
Embassy 20 Strela Kazan 16.

JANUARY
New horizons

The second week of January 2003 provided a boost for supporters who yearned to see Rugby League expand its frontiers.

It was the week the Rugby Football League, at the Palace of Westminster, announced a nationwide expansion of its Rugby League Conference competition, sponsored once again by TotalRL.com, to 52 clubs, along with the names of the ten clubs who would do battle in the new National League Three competition to begin later in the year.

And the following day, international Rugby League received a significant boost, with the official formation of the European Rugby League Federation in Paris.

The launch co-incided with a fact-finding mission to the south of France by a four-man RFL delegation looking into the Super League bids from three French clubs.

The Hotel La Fayette Concorde, at the top of the Champs Elysées, was the venue for the historic ERLF announcement, with a full-time administrator based in the French capital, to be appointed (although by the end of the year no appointment had been made).

Great Britain and France were the Federation's two founder members, and seven other European countries - Scotland, Wales, Ireland, Italy, Russia, Serbia and Holland - were invited to apply for membership, along with Lebanon and Morocco. Representatives of nine of the eleven nations were present at the meeting, with Wales and Serbia sending apologies for their absence. The general assembly was to meet at least twice a year.

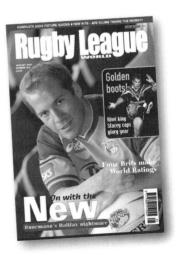

MEPs Terry Wynn and Brian Simpson flew in from Brussels to attend and pledge European Parliament support for the fledgling organisation, with financial assistance possible from the European Union for developing League nations such as Serbia, Holland and the North African and Asian countries.

A healthy 20 members of the French media were present - around half the number expected after the French Rugby Union hastily organised a last-minute Paris press conference of their own on the same morning.

The European Federation's first public act

was to announce a provisional international calendar for 2003, with the launch of a new biennial, six-country European Nations Cup - featuring England 'A', Scotland, Ireland, Wales, France and Russia - the first to be staged in November 2003.

After the huge success of the Russia/Tatarstan v USA matches in Moscow and Kazan the previous September, 2003 was also to see the launch of the four-nation Victory Cup (between Russia, BARLA (GB), France and the USA) to be held in May at Moscow's giant 85,000 capacity Luzhniki Stadium.

The Arriva Trains Cup, involving the National League One and Two sides kicked off on Sunday 19 January.

York City Knights chief executive Steve Ferres declared the club's first-ever fixture a huge success, despite his team going down 36-26 to Hull KR at the Huntington Stadium.

Cheered on by a 3,105 crowd, the Knights led for large parts of the game, but a lack of match practice cost them dear as they buckled under a late Rovers onslaught.

The game's other debutant club, London Skolars, also showed tremendous promise in their first match before going down 10-22 at home to Dewsbury Rams.

"Today was the culmination of many years of hard work by a lot of people at the club," said Skolars' coach and managing director Mark Croston after the game. "It has all come together, it is a new start and a lot of good things happened, but we are determined to move on and improve each week."

In a highly-encouraging opening round of ATC clashes, over 3,000 saw the games at Salford and Leigh, where the home teams beat Swinton and Oldham respectively.

Union Treiziste Catalane learned that they would be invited to apply for entry into Super League from 2005 the week before they played Gateshead Thunder in the third round of the Challenge Cup at the Thunderdome.

UTC, based in Perpignan, would have to satisfy a detailed set of entry criteria and, in addition, satisfy the same criteria as any National League 1 club applying for promotion, including a requirement to provide guarantees relating to capital and future stadium development work, as well as future cash flow forecasts.

The Rugby Football League was to assist the club in developing a business plan, and bringing up their playing squad and their club infrastructure to Super League standards.

"It's been a surprise for us all," said UTC Chairman Bernard Guasch.

"I don't know for sure why UTC was chosen, but the Roussillon area and [neighbouring] Aude, with clubs like Carcassonne, Limoux and Lézignan, are the heartland of Rugby League today. This is where there is the greatest potential for spectator support, not to mention the proximity to Spain, where we could also play in places like Gerona. Perpignan and St Estève councils support this project because it is important for the tourism and economy of the area."

The decision came as a shock to Toulouse officials, who were favourites to be the first French club to enter Super League since Paris St Germain withdrew in 1997. "The news that we hadn't been selected came like a hammer blow," said Toulouse Chairman Carlos Zalduendo, the prime mover behind his club's revival over the past seven years. Toulouse had put forward their dossier to the RFL in October, and were considered as the front-runners because of their business links and location.

In the Cup, UTC made short work of Thunder in a 38-4 win, while Toulouse put up a good show in a 26-10 defeat at NL1 favourites Salford Reds.

The other French sides were also knocked out, Pia losing 28-18 at Hunslet, and Villeneuve being edged 26-22 at Featherstone.

Villeneuve's exit was cloaked in controversy as a war of words erupted after the final whistle.

The Leopards hit out at referee Peter Taberner, who penalised them seven times in the first ten minutes, with Jason Webber and Vincent Wulf being sin-binned, while ex-Kiwi captain Quentin Pongia's tackle on Andy Bailey was placed on report after the intervention of a touch judge. The final penalty count was 17-5 in Featherstone's favour.

Villeneuve Chairman Pierre Soubiran, who the previous Monday had written to the RFL requesting to be allowed into National Division One next season after the club's Super League application was rejected, was livid with anger.

"That's the last time we come here," he said. "Finished!"

But Featherstone coach Andy Kelly had accusations of his own.

" We finished with eleven head injuries and we were putting injured players on for injured players, and if that's the spirit of the game then I have missed something along the line," said Kelly.

The two shock results of the third round were victories for amateur clubs Wath Brow Hornets and Halton Simms Cross.

Wath Brow defeated their Cumbrian neighbours Workington Town 13-12 at Whitehaven's Recreation Ground on the Friday night, thanks to a late winning field goal from Carl Rudd, in front of 3,017 spectators. Halton Simms Cross defeated London Skolars 15-8 at the Halton Stadium thanks to a stunning try by fullback Brian Capewell on 57 minutes.

Freezing weather wiped out the four senior friendlies that had been scheduled for the first weekend of 2003. But London Broncos had no problem with the weather when they went down 18-12 to West Tigers in their warm-up in Gosford, though a series of injuries picked up in training camp down under meant they had to field ten guest players from the local Central Coast competition.

Back in the UK, hundreds of aspiring Super League players took part in the second stage of the Broncos' 'Prop Idol' project, the club's search for a Rugby League star, at centres in London, Bristol, Nottingham, Liverpool and Croydon.

England A coach John Kear was confirmed as the new first team coach of

Hull FC, with Shaun McRae remaining as Director of Rugby. "My role doesn't change - it still incorporates being head coach, and I would stress that the buck still stops with me," said McRae.

Kear experienced a Hull derby as Hull KR and Hull FC met for the first time since 1998 when they clashed in the inaugural Clive Sullivan Memorial Trophy match at Craven Park. The five-year break was the longest in the 103 years of the cross-city derby as Hull had to fight hard to gain a 10-0 victory.

Kear's assistant's job at Wigan was filled by the promotion of Mike Gregory, who this month guided the Warriors on a training camp in Cyprus. England Academy coach Gregory was previously in charge of the club's under-21s side, and Denis Betts moved up from the under-17s to assume that role.

Betts finally laid his playing boots to rest at the end of his Testimonial fixture - a 20-16 Wednesday night defeat by Widnes Vikings at the JJB Stadium. Betts had officially retired following Wigan's record Grand Final defeat by the Bulls in 2001, but he had always harboured a hope that he could play one last game at the JJB Stadium before he officially called it a day.

Huddersfield Giants confirmed the appointment of Brian McDermott to their coaching staff on a one-year contact to work under coach Tony Smith.

Halifax reached agreements with Brett Goldspink and Robbie Beckett as both players formally left the club, and Leon Pryce's court case was adjourned until March 3.

Things didn't quite go according to plan on the last Monday night in January at Knowsley Road, when St Helens were narrowly defeated 41-39 by rugby union club Sale Sharks.

The Sharks ran up their 41 points with seven tries and three conversions playing rugby union in the first half. Saints replied with seven tries and two conversions in the second half under League rules, with Sean Long's last-minute conversion attempt sailing wide, denying Saints the draw.

Widnes Vikings, in South Africa on a pre-season training camp, were also discussing a possible cross-code challenge against the Pretoria Blue Bulls. One player who wasn't with the squad in South Africa was Australian Steve Carter, who stayed at home with an ankle injury, and was due to see a specialist to determine whether he needed major surgery.

And on Sunday 26 January 2003 the British Amateur Rugby League Association voted to accept unification with the Rugby Football League after almost 30 years of independence. "This decision is a massive step forward for the sport of Rugby League at all levels and everybody involved in the game should be delighted," said RFL Executive Chairman Richard Lewis.

"Unification means that grassroots Rugby League will, for the first time, have a clearly defined and expanded role in the sport and a greater influence within the game in general."

FEBRUARY
World vision?

International Rugby League was back on the agenda as the World Sevens in Sydney were revived on the first weekend of February.

England beat Tonga, Australian Aboriginals, France and Manly on the way to the final but their hopes of emulating the 1992 Wigan side in lifting the title were dashed amid a first-half blitz from Parramatta Eels. Mike Gregory's side were trailing 28-6 by the interval, as a Nathan Hindmarsh-inspired and Brian Smith-coached Parramatta side powered their way to the trophy.

Hindmarsh crossed for two tries, and was later deservedly named Player of the Tournament, while pacy backs Luke Burt and Steve Witt also recorded try doubles.

Parramatta (and former Bradford Bulls) coach Smith dedicated his side's win in the World Sevens on Sunday to his old friend Peter Deakin, who that Saturday morning died after a long illness.

"The World Sevens epitomised everything about Rugby League that Peter liked. He would have enjoyed being here," said Smith. "I got a lot of credit for our success with the Bulls - but really it was down to Peter. It was his energy and perception that created Bullmania. He changed the pace of marketing. He showed how it should be done."

The two-day 24-team Sevens tournament saw around 2,000 points scored, with a total of more than 50,000 spectators turning up at Aussie Stadium, the Sydney Football Stadium renamed after a massive sponsorship from a company called Aussie Home Loans.

The most moving moment was when the Coogee Dolphins and the USA Tomahawks lined up before taking part in an exhibition match. The Dolphins watched as a tribute to their colleagues who died in the Bali terrorism blast was played on the big screen. Then everyone stood in silence in memory of the American astronauts who had died a few hours earlier that day.

Leeds centre Keith Senior finished as the competition's joint top tryscorer, with eight from five games, while Richard Horne, Lee Gilmour and Andy Farrell were among others to impress through the course of the tournament.

The England side that flew out to Sydney

was: Danny Orr, Richard Horne, Rob Smyth, Phil Cantillon, Lee Gilmour, Keith Senior, Andy Farrell (C), Marcus St Hilaire, Gareth Ellis and Andrew Brocklehurst.

The Bowl final was won by North Queensland Cowboys, who beat Fiji 18-8, and the Plate by the Bulldogs with a 24-18 final win over NZ Warriors.

The International Federation meeting in Sydney that week agreed to play a Tri-Nations tournament between Great Britain, Australia and New Zealand in the UK in the months of October and November 2004.

The format was to involve the nations playing each other twice, culminating in a final to determine the tournament's champions. Matches involving Australia and New Zealand were to commence in October, fixtures involving Great Britain to begin two weeks after the Tetley's Super League Grand Final. The tournament was likely to be repeated in 2005, with the Federation putting the World Cup, originally scheduled for 2005, on the backburner.

The weekend of the Powergen Rugby League Challenge Cup fourth round was over-shadowed by tragedy when news emerged that two young Wigan players, both related to major figures associated with the club, were tragically killed in a motor vehicle accident on the Saturday night.

Billy-Joe Edwards, brother of Wigan legend Shaun Edwards, and Craig Johnson, the brother of current Wigan star Paul Johnson, were both thought to have been killed outright in the accident - both players were 19 years old. Paul Johnson had been selected to play in the Powergen Challenge Cup against amateurs Halton Simms Cross the following day, but stood down from the team.

"Ours was a very quiet dressing room today, both before and after," said Wigan coach Stuart Raper after the game, which Wigan won 82-3. A minute's silence was held before kick-off in memory of the two players.

Hunslet Hawks provided the shock of the round, when they defeated Huddersfield Giants 18-14 at the South Leeds Stadium, bringing to an end a 29-match unbeaten run by the Giants, and spoiling the Giants' chances of creating what would have been a new Rugby League record of 30 games without defeat.

Hull attracted a crowd of 15,310 to a highly atmospheric opening of their new ground, the Kingston Communications Stadium. They beat off a determined challenge from Halifax, emerging victorious 22-16, despite having two players dismissed by referee Steve Ganson. Hull skipper Jason Smith was dismissed after just 28 seconds of the match, while Richard Fletcher was sent off five minutes into the second half, both for high tackles. Smith and Fletcher were suspended for one and two games respectively.

In another blow for Hull, new threequarter Dwayne West looked certain to miss the entire Super League VIII season, needing a knee reconstruction after rupturing his ligaments in the match. It was West's first appearance for the club since joining them from Saints during the close season.

The second amateur club - Wath Brow Hornets - went out of the competition, beaten by only 18-6 by Batley Bulldogs at Whitehaven on the Saturday night.

The only French club remaining in the competition - UTC of Perpignan, who had already been provisionally accepted into Super League for 2005 - went down 2-70 at home to St Helens.

And in the Saturday TV game Wakefield knocked out Castleford Tigers 20-18, Ryan Hudson being sent off in the first half after throwing a punch at Wildcats' new signing Matt Seers. Hudson received a one-match suspension and Seers was out of the Super League opener after breaking his hand in the dust-up.

Leeds set off to Lanzarote after their 46-6 home Cup win over Whitehaven to make their final preparations for Super League VIII as British fans steeled themselves for the World Club Challenge showdown between St Helens and Sydney Roosters.

For the second time in three years, Saints flattered to deceive as the Aussie champions hammered them 38-0 in sub-zero temperatures at the Reebok Stadium.

Roosters coach Ricky Stuart had been a spectator at Wilderspool the previous Saturday as Bradford Bulls beat Warrington Wolves 38-12 in the Cup, and had been perturbed at the performance of referee Bob Connolly. "I just had a very good chat with Stuart Cummings (RFL Technical Executive). I'm worried about the interpretations of the referee, but Stuart said he was trying to get them as close as possible to the Australian game," said Stuart.

Stuart was right - a refereeing interpretation was the major talking point of the game.

Cummings had to defend Russell Smith's decision to allow the Roosters a controversial try after what appeared to be a knock-on by Roosters halfback Brett Finch. With 54 minutes gone and St Helens 0-18 down and on the attack, Sean Long offloaded the ball as Finch moved in to effect a tackle. The ball hit Finch's right hand and fell to the ground. Finch reacted quickest and scooped the ball up to send Todd Byrne racing away for a crucial try.

Saints appealed for the knock-on, and

WORLD CLUB CHALLENGE

Friday 14th February 2003

ST HELENS 0 SYDNEY ROOSTERS 38

SAINTS: 5 Darren Albert; 19 Ade Gardner; 3 Martin Gleeson; 4 Paul Newlove; 2 Anthony Stewart; 20 Tommy Martyn; 7 Sean Long; 8 Darren Britt; 6 Jason Hooper; 12 John Stankevitch; 11 Chris Joynt (C); 16 Darren Smith; 13 Paul Sculthorpe. Subs (all used): 10 Barry Ward; 15 Tim Jonkers; 14 Mick Higham; 18 Mark Edmondson.
ROOSTERS: 1 Anthony Minichiello; 2 Todd Byrne; 4 Justin Hodges; 3 Chris Flannery; 5 Shannon Hegarty; 6 Brad Fittler (C); 9 Craig Wing; 8 Jason Cayless; 17 Michael Crocker; 10 Peter Cusack; 11 Adrian Morley; 12 Craig Fitzgibbon; 13 Luke Ricketson. Subs (all used): 14 Ned Catic; 15 Todd Payten; 16 Chad Robinson; 7 Brett Finch.
Tries: Fitzgibbon (36), Morley (40), Byrne (54), Fittler (57), Payten (78); **Goals:** Fitzgibbon 9/9.
Rugby Leaguer & League Express Men of the Match:
Saints: Darren Albert; *Roosters:* Craig Fitzgibbon.
Penalty count: 6-8; **Half-time:** 0-18;
Referee: Russell Smith (England);
Attendance: 19,807 *(at The Reebok Stadium, Bolton).*

Brett Finch weaves past Darren Britt during Sydney Roosters' World Club Challenge win over St Helens

referee Russell Smith called for assistance from video referee David Campbell, who awarded the try in accordance with a recently introduced amendment to the knock-on rule.   In a pre-season announcement, Cummings had confirmed the British game would follow the same interpretations of the knock-on rule that have existed in Australia for two years. " It was absolutely the correct decision," said Cummings.

It wasn't the only controversy as Jason Hooper had an early try disallowed for the most marginal of forward passes from Tommy Martyn to Paul Newlove. From then on it wasn't going to be Saints' night as second row Craig Fitzgibbon scored 22 points - from nine goals from as many attempts as well, as scoring his side's opening try.

The rangy Fitzgibbon was to become even better known to British fans late in the year, and by co-incidence that week the Kangaroos itinerary for the autumn was unveiled, with Moscow mooted as a possibility for a warm-up match en route.

February

Super League VIII had its earliest ever start when St Helens and Bradford Bulls clashed at Knowsley Road on Friday 21 February, and the Bulls were expected to take full revenge for their Super League Grand Final defeat at the hands of Saints the previous October. Saints after all had been humiliated seven days earlier by the Roosters.

But as League Express reporter Mike Latham reflected: "Saints poured scorn on those who had come to write their early season epitaph, with a stunning eight-try rejoinder to the Bulls' hopes".

Sean Long, whose kicking game had been so disappointing against the Roosters, was back to his brilliant, mesmerising best, as Saints roared into a 40-10 lead before the hour-mark. Two-try Paul Sculthorpe was also in inspirational form as Saints ran out 46-22 winners

On a murky evening, with the temperature having risen considerably, Saints made a late change when Darren Albert withdrew with gastro-enteritis. John Kirkpatrick, who scored two sharply taken tries, proved an able replacement. Paul Wellens was not ready to return after injury, so Anthony Stewart, who left the field late in the game with a wrist injury, filled the fullback berth. The injured Keiron Cunningham and departed Peter Shiels were also missing from their Grand Final team.

The Bulls were missing Michael Withers, Tevita Vaikona and the departed Brandon Costin and Brian McDermott from their Grand Final team of four months ago - as Saints blitzed the Bulls, going in at half-time 28-4.

The Rhinos marketed Super League VIII by asking their fans to 'Believe Leeds' and, after a thoroughly competent seven-try performance to dispose of Widnes Vikings by 32-12 at Headingley on the Sunday, optimism in Leeds was rife.

Daniel Frame worked tirelessly for the Vikings and new signing, former Leeds player Dean Lawford, marshalled well from the stand-off position. But the Vikings lacked the guile of Kevin Sinfield - who kicked magnificently in general play - the awesome power of Wayne McDonald, and the ruthless finishing of Mark Calderwood, who scored his second hat-trick in his 50th start for Leeds which had seen him bag an incredible 39 tries.

The Vikings - hit by a spinal injury to Andrew Isherwood on training camp in South Africa and the early return to Australia of Craig Weston and Steve Carter before the season started - tried that month to entice Henry Paul from rugby union, although nothing came of the move.

Steve Prescott made a triumphant return to Belle Vue with a classy hat-trick as Hull began their challenge for a top-four spot by overcoming a gritty Wildcats side 28-14. It took late tries by prop Craig Greenhill and Toa Kohe-Love to finally give the visitors a comfortable winning margin.

Tony Smith, captain for the day with namesake Jason suspended, was an expert pivot for a Hull side that had unsung heroes in the pack in Scott Logan and Adam Maher. And there were glimpses of superb attacking flair from Richie Barnett and Colin Best.

Huddersfield Giants' return to Super League was ruined by a combination of their own mistakes and a workmanlike performance from steely Warrington in the Saturday TV game.

The Giants contributed to their own downfall with a series of crucial handling errors and vital lapses in discipline, and despite an improved second-half display and no lack of endeavour, they failed to overturn a 16-0 half-time deficit, going down 20-8.

Andrew Brocklehurst grounded by London's Tony Martin as Halifax shock the Broncos

Warrington, with busy halfbacks Nathan Wood and Lee Briers prompting a work-hungry pack, built a match-winning advantage on two tries from Australian three-quarter Brent Grose and the accurate boot of Briers. The Wolves stand-off finished with six goals from as many attempts and also had a spell on the sidelines after taking two late, high shots from first Darren Fleary and then Stanley Gene in the space of three second-half minutes. Both incidents were placed on report, while Fleary and Ben Cooper were also sin-binned for the Giants. Fleary was found guilty of illegal use of the forearm and suspended for three matches and Gene guilty of striking the same player. He copped two matches.

Castleford Tigers caused an early shock when they beat Wigan Warriors 19-10 at the Jungle, scoring three tries to nil. All Wigan's points came from penalties and they never overcame the early loss through injury of captain Andrew Farrell, just after the quarter-mark, and Mick Cassidy, after only eight minutes. They also finished with only 12 men after Paul Johnson was sent off for a high tackle on Jamie Thackray two minutes from time. Johnson got a two-match ban.

Danny Orr was an inspiring captain for Castleford, and he popped over a field goal at a crucial stage in the second half, though only two tries in the last four minutes - from Darren Rogers and Waine Pryce - secured the win.

But the major shock of the weekend came in the capital as Halifax - with the Blue Sox moniker dropped - stunned the Broncos with a 26-22 success, having confidently been predicted to go through the season without a win. Chris Birchall dived through a mass of players to touch down a Martin Moana kick just before the hourmark to secure the points. "At 1000-1 I'm not going to be stupid enough to put money on us to win the league," said Fax coach Tony Anderson.

SUPER LEAGUE TABLE - *Sunday 23rd February*

	P	W	D	L	F	A	D	PTS
St Helens	1	1	0	0	46	22	24	2
Leeds Rhinos	1	1	0	0	32	12	20	2
Hull FC	1	1	0	0	28	14	14	2
Warrington Wolves	1	1	0	0	20	8	12	2
Castleford Tigers	1	1	0	0	19	10	9	2
Halifax	1	1	0	0	26	22	4	2
London Broncos	1	0	0	1	22	26	-4	0
Wigan Warriors	1	0	0	1	10	19	-9	0
Huddersfield Giants	1	0	0	1	8	20	-12	0
Wakefield T Wildcats	1	0	0	1	14	28	-14	0
Widnes Vikings	1	0	0	1	12	32	-20	0
Bradford Bulls	1	0	0	1	22	46	-24	0

MARCH
Talks with Auntie

The Powergen Challenge Cup resumed as news leaked out that the BBC had asked the Rugby Football League to consider switching the Challenge Cup final to an autumn timeslot, after the existing deal ran out in 2004. RFL boss Richard Lewis and a representative of TWI, the company recently appointed to advise on the RFL's media strategy, met Pat Younge, the BBC's Head of Programming, and his colleagues to discuss the basis of any future BBC contract.

"My response was that we didn't want to consider the final in isolation," said Lewis. "There are many other issues to consider too, not least the relationship between the final and the earlier rounds. The whole thing has to be considered as a package. We want the BBC to tell us their plans for staging a Super League highlights programme nationally, and we want them to look at making a bid to screen our international programme. We want them to show a year-round commitment to the sport, not one that subsides after the Challenge Cup finishes."

In the weekend's fifth round ties, only Swinton Lions were able to upset opponents from a higher league, when the National League 2 club shocked Featherstone Rovers from National League 1, beating them 22-10 at Moor Lane.

Elsewhere there were some big scores against the smaller clubs, with Hull running up an 88-0 scoreline against Sheffield Eagles at the Kingston Communications Stadium, Bradford defeating Hunslet Hawks 82-0 at Headingley, and Wigan registering a 50-10 verdict over Doncaster at Belle Vue.

Adrian Lam pulled the strings and Craig Smith provided the steel as Wigan eased through a potentially tricky tie against the spirited Dragons. Lam frequently launched the star-studded Warriors backline, while Smith shouldered a huge workload as one of only two Wigan props in their 17. Both players had willing allies, with Lam's halfback partner Julian O'Neill heavily involved in several tries and Danny Sculthorpe supporting Smith up front. Brian Carney helped himself to a first-half hat-trick, and teenager Gareth Hock - on debut - impressed with a brace of tries.

Two of the National League One promotion favourites fought out a tremendous encounter on the Friday evening, despite the atrocious weather conditions, as Salford City Reds edged Hull KR at Craven Park by 12-2. St Helens had Steve Rowlands and Jon Wilkin on debut as they beat a spirited Batley Bulldogs side at Knowsley Road by 38-12 on the same soggy night.

Widnes had to thank Adam Hughes for two spectacular tries that took them to a 22-12 win at Wakefield.   It was enough to clinch him the man of the match award, although he was pushed close for honours by Dean Lawford.

And in the Saturday TV game London Broncos, with young British halves Rob Purdham and Chris Thorman the standouts, went out of the Cup as Leeds Rhinos won 21-12 at Headingley.

That week reports from Australia confirmed that the Rugby League International Federation was ready to postpone the World Cup indefinitely.

The 2005 World Cup, which had already been scaled back to eight teams, was to be replaced by a Tri-Nations Series between Great Britain, Australia and New Zealand, with no plans to reschedule it at a later date.

"I would suggest there won't be a World Cup in 2005 - although that could change," ARL chief executive Geoff Carr told the Sydney Morning Herald. "The priority is - let's get the Tri-Nations up and running and make that a success. My guess is that we will have a World Cup. But we might go back to what we were doing in the early 1990s, where you accumulate points in international series and the two highest nations play off."

For the first time since the launch of Super League in 1996, a single round of matches broke through the 10,000 average crowd barrier.

A total of 61,982 supporters watched Super League matches over the weekend of 7-9 March, breaking the previous six-match record of 55,374 fans set in 2000. And the figure would have been much higher if it hadn't been for the wet and cold weather that dampened attendances.

Bradford Bulls led the way, with 20,283 fans turning up at Odsal to see the Bulls' emotional homecoming against Wakefield Trinity Wildcats, as local pop idol Gareth Gates ceremonially kicked off the game.

There were 12,901 at the Kingston Communications Stadium on the Friday night to watch Hull go down 4-10 to London Broncos, while Wigan attracted 8,187 against Huddersfield Giants and Halifax drew 4,388 on the same night against Castleford Tigers.

On the Saturday evening Widnes and St Helens attracted 7,518 to Halton Stadium, while Warrington drew an impressive 8,705 against Leeds Rhinos in the first Super League game of the club's final season at Wilderspool.

The Bulls were disrupted by the loss of Robbie Paul (neck) and Jamie Peacock (broken hand), both injured in the Cup win over Hunslet going into the game with Wakefield, and picked up several more injuries during the afternoon. A young, almost unknown called Stuart Reardon made his debut off the bench as they scraped a 22-10 win over the Wildcats, who had boom prop Michael Korkidas on report for starting a melee late in the game. Korkidas was later found guilty of a reckless high tackle and suspended for two matches. James Lowes was suspended for one match for striking, although teammate Stuart Fielden escaped a ban and was only fined for the same offence. Lee Gilmour settled the game with a superb individual try on 70 minutes.

London Broncos ruined Hull FC's hopes of celebrating their first Super League match at the new stadium with one of the best defensive displays ever seen producing a 10-4 victory in the Friday TV game.

Broncos' new winger Andrew King, signed from South Sydney Rabbitohs, played a key role, less than two days after arriving in this country.

King, 27, who played for Keighley Cougars in the 1996 season, played for the full 80 minutes and made an immediate impact on the game, tackling Hull winger Colin Best as the Hull winger attempted to pass the ball over his own line to Hull fullback Steve Prescott after a Jim Dymock bomb. The ball went loose, and London fullback Nigel Roy swooped to score the only try of the match.

More bad news for Hull was that forward Warren Jowitt, signed from Salford City Reds at the end of the previous season, needed surgery on a pelvic injury, after already undergoing a hernia operation. He was expected to be out for another four months.

St Helens adapted superbly to difficult conditions at Halton Stadium to grind out a 22-4 win against Widnes Vikings and maintain their unbeaten start to Super League VIII. With Sean Long a key figure in the middle of the park, Ian Millward's side showed a willingness to move the ball wide in the rain and mud, and were rewarded with tries to impressive wingmen Ade Gardner, who bagged a pair, and Darren Albert. Long grabbed the other, the opening score that put Saints in the driving seat for almost the entire match. Widnes coach Neil Kelly wasn't too disappointed with his side's effort, after another outstanding performance from Dean Lawford - filling in for stomach virus-victim Ryan Sheridan at scrum-half.

Wigan Warriors maintained their 100 per cent record over the Giants in Super League on a cold and drizzly night at the JJB Stadium with a 33-22 win. Late Wigan tries by Danny Sculthorpe and Martin Aspinwall cushioned the fitful Warriors in the face of a stirring Giants performance, easily their best in nine Super League games against Wigan. The visitors twice narrowed the margin to seven points after looking well on the way to a heavy defeat at the break.

The Giants were missing five first-choice players with Stanley Gene and Darren Fleary suspended after their indiscretions in the opening game against Warrington and Jeff Wittenberg, Paul Reilly and Jamie Bloem on the injured list. Matt Calland, playing in the second row, sustained a fractured cheekbone, which ended his Super League career.

A quickfire 12-point haul midway through the second half maintained Castleford's unbeaten start to the season, but only after Halifax had once again proved their critics wrong with another gutsy display at the Shay. Michael Smith's strong running constantly punched holes in the Fax defence, and set up the Tigers' match-winning try from Wayne Godwin on the hourmark. Halifax's Shayne McMenemy was later that week suspended for one match for a careless high tackle on Damian Gibson.

Leeds picked up a fine 32-22 victory after overcoming brave Warrington at Wilderspool, who did it tough all afternoon following the dismissal of former Rhino Nick Fozzard just before the half-time hooter. Referee Steve Ganson's decision to give Fozzard his marching orders came on the intervention of a touch judge who had allegedly seen the huge Wolves prop head-butt Barrie McDermott. It was the end of an eventful afternoon for Fozzard, who had already been placed on-report in the first half for a high tackle. On the following Tuesday Fozzard was found guilty of the reckless high tackle and suspended for one match. But stunningly he was found not guilty of head-butting. The Rhinos' Matt Adamson was found to have no case to answer after being put on report for a high tackle on Fozzard!

The "big four" - Bradford Bulls, Leeds Rhinos, St Helens and Wigan - made up the quartet of teams that went into the hat for the Powergen Challenge Cup semi-final draw held at the Millennium Stadium in Cardiff, made by Welsh legends Jonathan Davies and Scott Gibbs.

After watching his side run in 48 unanswered second-half points against Salford after being held 6-6 at the break, St Helens coach Ian Millward was relishing the big clubs going up against each other. "You only get so many chances to play in the semi-finals of a Challenge Cup, and we can't wait for the opportunity," Millward said. "It's great for Rugby League that these four sides are involved in the semis.

"I just think it's part of the real momentum in Rugby League at the moment. From the Grand Final last year to the Test series with New Zealand, to the Academy beating Australia and then the way the season has started with such good crowds. It's going to be hard to pick a winner out of the four, and that's great. It will be a super semi-final weekend and I'm excited about it now."

St Helens' quarter-final win included the 100th try of Paul Sculthorpe's career, when he crossed for his first of a try double in the first half at the Willows.

A second-half power performance saw Bradford Bulls overcome an enterprising Widnes Vikings side 38-28 on a heavily-sanded pitch. Trailing 22-12 at the interval after a superb opening 40 minutes from the home side, the Bulls grasped the nettle from the first minute of the second half and finally sealed an entertaining encounter late on. The Vikings were still in the game right up until Scott Naylor's last minute try, though in truth the Bulls had much the better of the second period. Missing five first-choice players, including four of their pack, the Bulls were led from the front by two-try loose forward Mike Forshaw and Great Britain prop Stuart Fielden, who put in a massive 80-minute performance. Out wide, the left-wing partnership of Shontayne Hape and Lesley Vainikolo caused numerous problems, notably after the break, while Leon Pryce also made some crucial contributions. The Vikings had their fair share of impressive individuals too, Dean Lawford again a bundle of creativity in the middle of the park, Daniel Frame a strong runner from stand-off and Julian O'Neill and Adam Hughes handfuls.

Wigan won through with an eventually comfortable 70-12 win over Swinton, who had agreed a set fee of £17,500 from the Warriors to switch the quarter-final to the JJB Stadium.

Amazingly Swinton took a shock lead in the ninth minute when Chris Hough sent up a huge bomb towards Kris Radlinski. Simon Knox managed to pat the ball back in mid-air, and loose forward Rob Russell followed up to collect and side-step two Wigan defenders to touch down by the posts. But Wigan led 30-6 at half-time and the result was never in doubt.

Matt Adamson and two-try David Furner were the stars of Leeds' 41-18 home win over Hull as the Rhinos qualified for their tenth semi-final in eleven seasons.

Hull were in the news as it was announced they would be meeting Castleford Tigers in a challenge match in Jacksonville, Florida on Saturday 17 January 2004 to promote Rugby League in America.

And Gateshead Thunder again faced an uncertain future following the unexpected decision of Chairman and owner Mike Jeffels to leave the club at the end of the season. All seven of the Australians were set to depart for home less than two months after linking up with Gateshead. RFL officials were set to travel to Tyneside for crisis talks with Jeffels, and the following week Thunder fell to two defeats to Salford City Reds in the Arriva Trains Cup, by 90-8 and 100-12.

St Helens won the clash of two unbeaten sides in Round Three of Super League as they hammered Castleford Tigers 54-12 at Knowsley Road. Sean Long collected 30 points and passed the career milestone of 100 tries as Saints produced a cavalier attacking performance to delight the majority of the 10,000-plus crowd.

Long scored three tries and kicked nine goals from as many attempts as Saints blitzed a Tigers side for whom Aussie Paul Mellor finally made an injury-delayed debut off the bench.

That left Leeds Rhinos as the only other 100 per cent side after they beat Huddersfield Giants 42-28 at Headingley on the same Friday night. It took a near faultless opening to the second half, which saw them rack up 24 points in as many minutes, to salvage the their unbeaten start after Huddersfield had looked likely to end one of Rugby League's leanest spells.

The Giants had to go back to 1959 for their last league victory at Headingley but their desire - exemplified by Mick Slicker, Brandon Costin, Jarrod O'Doherty and the returning Stanley Gene - saw them race into a worthy 8-18 lead, before falling to a sucker punch just before the break, which seemed to sap their momentum. Steve McNamara had just kicked his fifth goal, in a performance of stunning accuracy from both touchlines, when Eorl Crabtree fumbled the re-start on his own ten-metre line. Barrie McDermott re-gathered and although Julian Bailey pulled off a beautiful tackle on his own line to deny the storming Keith Senior, Andrew Dunemann spotted the smallest of holes at dummy-half to plunge over.

A gap of only four points as the teams turned around was scant reward for

Sean O'Loughlin gets in between London duo Chris Thorman and Jim Dymock as London stun Wigan

the visitors' tireless efforts and angled running, their deflation evident as they succumbed to the remorseless Rhinos charge. Chev Walker was the gamestar as he collected two tries.

A 90-metre special from Toa Kohe-Love finally helped see off a resilient Widnes Vikings to give Hull FC their first win in Super League at their new home. The 38-18 success - with Steve Prescott helping himself to a personal tally of 22 points from a try and nine goals - condemned the Vikings to bottom place in the Super League table.

Lee Briers was Warrington Wolves' inspiration as they chalked up a second win in three games - a 29-8 win at London.

Bradford Bulls hammered local rivals Halifax 62-22 at Odsal as James Lowes returned from a one-match suspension and sparked the Bulls into life after a slow start, scoring two opportunist first-half tries and creating another for returning-from-injury captain Robbie Paul.

Gareth Hock was the pick of the Wigan youngsters as they rose to a big challenge to snatch a late 34-29 victory in an end-to-end thriller at Wakefield. Missing several first team regulars, especially in the pack, Wigan kept battling back each time the Wildcats looked set to gain their first Super League win over them.   It was Hock's long-striding breakaway that finished off Wakefield in the 73rd minute when he tore down the left before sending in David Hodgson for the match-winning try.

As Wigan's injury-list lengthened, chairman Maurice Lindsay denied reports that the Warriors had signed Gorden Tallis.

A Round Four weekend of massive shocks got underway at the JJB Stadium on the Friday night as London Broncos stunned Wigan with a 34-30 win.

It was the Broncos' first ever success at Wigan, and all the more remarkable considering their dreadful start. They looked to be set for a hiding as Wigan, confident and composed early on, ran in 16 points in the opening 14 minutes.

March

Broncos coach Tony Rea's satisfaction was increased by the indication that the Broncos' policy of introducing more English players was bearing fruit. Eight English players were in the Broncos side, including former Wigan juniors Rob Jackson and Neil Budworth. And injuries ruled out three English players - Paul Sykes, Rob Purdham and Dom Peters - all of whom might have featured.

But Australian lock Jim Dymock emerged as the Broncos' hero, hauling his side back into contention with a brace of tries before displaying his superb creative skills. "It was a bit of a shock," said Wigan coach Stuart Raper, who as well as missing skipper Andrew Farrell was without Jamie Ainscough and Julian O'Neill. Mick Cassidy's return from injury was ruined when he left the field in the 24th minute with a strained calf and suspected broken hand.

On Saturday night Wakefield Wildcats got their season up and running with a surprise 20-14 win at Castleford. Trinity's victory was the result of youthful exuberance and invaluable experience, personified in the performances of Gareth Ellis and Brad Davis. Ellis confirmed his growing status as one of the game's brightest centre prospects while Davis - at 35 Super League's oldest player - came up with a great performance and secured the points with a converted try just before the hourmark.

The biggest shock of them all came on the Sunday at the McAlpine Stadium as Huddersfield Giants pulled off a fully-deserved 36-22 over previously unbeaten St Helens. Halfback Brandon Costin ended a week of media pressure in the perfect manner - by guiding the Giants to a memorable first win of the season - and over the Super League Champions. (Costin had been at the centre of a re-opened controversy relating to his challenge on Sean Long two years ago, which resulted in Long suffering a knee injury that ended his 2001 season).

Widnes Vikings were the only team left without a league point as they lost at home to Bradford Bulls by 26-18. The Vikings matched the Bulls try-for-try, but whereas Adam Hughes missed with four kicks at goal for the home side, Paul Deacon capped an authoritative personal display with an unerring five-goal haul.

A solid performance proved enough for a 27-14 Hull victory at Wilderspool against a Warrington side that lacked a cutting edge after Lee Briers' last-minute withdrawal. Russell Smith awarded no less than 21 penalties in the contest, which saw Richard Fletcher sin-binned and Jason Smith (suspected high tackle) and Graham Appo (alleged trip) placed on-report, though neither was found to have a case to answer.

St Helens' stunning defeat left Leeds Rhinos as the only undefeated team in Super League, clear at the top of the table after a hard fought 20-14 win at Halifax on the Friday night, with Halifax fullback Lee Finnerty being suspended for one match after being put on report for a reckless high tackle on Willie Poching.

The Rhinos faced a mouthwatering clash against St Helens at Knowsley Road on the first Saturday night in April.

SUPER LEAGUE TABLE - *Sunday 30th March*

	P	W	D	L	F	A	D	PTS
Leeds Rhinos	4	4	0	0	126	76	50	8
St Helens	4	3	0	1	144	74	70	6
Hull FC	4	3	0	1	97	56	41	6
Bradford Bulls	4	3	0	1	132	96	36	6
Warrington Wolves	4	2	0	2	85	75	10	4
Wigan Warriors	4	2	0	2	107	104	3	4
London Broncos	4	2	0	2	74	89	-15	4
Castleford Tigers	4	2	0	2	65	94	-29	4
Huddersfield Giants	4	1	0	3	94	117	-23	2
Wakefield T Wildcats	4	1	0	3	73	98	-25	2
Halifax	4	1	0	3	72	124	-52	2
Widnes Vikings	4	0	0	4	52	118	-66	0

APRIL
Rhinos rumble on

As Super League moved into April, Rugby Football League Technical Executive Stuart Cummings joined the call for the media to focus less on referees and more on the game itself.

"With so many cracking games, I can't understand why commentators want to talk about what the referees are doing," Cummings told 'Rugby Leaguer & League Express'.

Cummings had also advised his referees to cut out excessive familiarity with players on the field - at least in televised games. "It is bang out of order for referees to use nicknames when addressing players," said Cummings. "It can give the impression that they are too close to particular players, and obviously we would like the public to recognise that they are not. I believe that first names should be used."

Wayne McDonald certainly deflected the focus from officials as he settled a belting match at Knowsley Road on the Saturday evening, as Leeds stayed top of the table with five wins out of five. McDonald brought the house down with a stunning 70-metre try with eight minutes remaining to seal a 24-16 win for the Rhinos.

The Rhinos were just 20-16 ahead when McDonald took matters into his own hands. Collecting David Furner's offload, he swatted off Paul Wellens' challenge and, his huge legs pumping, gathered pace. He evaded the clutches of Darren Albert and Chris Joynt and, ignoring the screaming Keith Senior and Francis Cummins on his outside, charged through down the left.

With Barry Ward injured, Saints had only one recognised prop in the admirable Darren Britt and they struggled to contain the physical Rhinos "four-pack", with coach Daryl Powell cleverly switching Barrie McDermott and Danny Ward with McDonald and Chris Feather.

Furner had a big game in the second row, recovering from a missed tackle in the lead-up to Saints' first try to produce a punishing defensive effort, while skipper Kevin Sinfield capped a mature captain's display with the gamestar rating.

Sean Long, Saints' attacking inspiration, left the field seven minutes into the second half, suffering from a virus, and Darren Smith also limped off just after the midway point of the first half.

Julian O'Neill landed back in Widnes that weekend, almost ten years after he last donned the famous black and white shirt. The Australian stand-off played twelve games for the club in 1993, including jetting back to England to figure in their Challenge Cup final defeat at Wembley, ironically to Wigan, the club now offloading him.

On his second debut for Widnes, O'Neill capped an impressive debut with a five-goal haul and a hand in two tries after coming on as substitute late in the first half, as the Vikings got off the mark and relegated Halifax to the bottom of the table with a 44-16 win at the Halton Stadium.

Vikings coach Neil Kelly was delighted with the debut of O'Neill and showed his sense of humour by sending in Widnes's other Julian O'Neill, the Kiwi prop, for the post-match press conference. The majority of the 7,135 crowd, including a good number from Halifax, represented Widnes's best gate of the season so far.

Tony Anderson, the Halifax coach, was far from pleased by his side's performance and also unhappy with referee Colin Morris. "I haven't seen him at this level for three years and hopefully won't see him for another three years," was his post-match comment. Former Saints teammates Julian O'Neill, the prop, and Halifax's Paul Davidson were involved in a punch-up early in the second half. Both were sin-binned.

A disputed late match-winning try by Alex Wilkinson, although coach Tony Smith attributed it to debutant Jamie Bloem after the game, snatched Huddersfield Giants a 14-10 victory at Wakefield, in a battle of the previous week's giant-killers that failed to live up to expectations.

The controversial match-winning try came in the 71st minute, with Wakefield claiming it followed a forward pass, although the ball was deflected by a home player.

Hull moved into third spot in the table with an excellent 20-4 Friday night home win over Wigan, still missing captain Andy Farrell and the experience of Mick Cassidy, in front of 11,536 people. Prop forward Scott Logan - who with Craig Greenhill had set the platform for the win - broke his leg in the 52nd minute. Hull skipper Jason Smith also suffered a sternum injury and centre Toa Kohe-Love a shoulder injury.

Wigan, already hit by an injury crisis, and facing a Powergen Challenge Cup tie against Bradford Bulls at the McAlpine Stadium the following Sunday, also suffered more injuries. Forward Stephen Wild incurred ankle ligament damage, Brett Dallas a hamstring tear, hooker Mark Smith damaged his shoulder, and Danny Sculthorpe suffered a sternum injury.

The Bulls blasted a shell-shocked Wolves side with four tries and 20-unanswered points in the opening 12 minutes of their Sunday evening clash at Odsal, eventually emerging 32-8 winners. They were without Mike Forshaw, with an arm injury, and Shontayne Hape and Jamie Peacock, but welcomed back Tevita Vaikona, playing only his third game of the season, and second row dynamo Danny Gartner. Gartner suffered a calf injury which was to keep him out of the Cup semi-final the week after, while Michael Withers picked up a stomach injury.

Warrington centre Ben Westwood was helped from the field and found to have broken a leg, while Sid Domic suffered a broken thumb. Wolves skipper Lee Briers, who didn't play, was to see a specialist that week about his shoulder problem.

Castleford came away from Griffin Park with a 24-12 win. Tony Rea's squad had also been ravaged by injuries and had to draft in Austin Buchanan, Damien

Kennedy and Karl Long on loan, as well as give a debut to Jamie Fielden.

Cumbrian prop forward Mark Cox had been ruled out for the season after being involved in a serious car accident in the capital the previous weekend. Cox suffered a broken leg and serious facial injuries.

But the Broncos still provided a stiff test for the Wayne Bartrim-led Tigers, who jumped above Wigan and Warrington into the top five.

That weekend there was better news for Gateshead Thunder, who recorded their first victory in 48 games over Workington Town in the Arriva Trains Cup. The morale-boosting 48-12 win - their first since defeating York 30-12 on 20 May 2001 - was achieved at their temporary Gateshead rugby union club base.

And the Rugby Football League confirmed the dates and venues for this season's Origin match and the Australian tour of Great Britain, with Hull officials celebrating that the Kingston Communications Stadium would host the second Ashes Test.

Leeds chief executive Gary Hetherington rated the goal kicked by Rhinos skipper Kevin Sinfield right on full-time of the Powergen Challenge Cup semi-final against St Helens at the McAlpine Stadium as the most important kick in the history of the club.

And many League fans rate the game, which the Rhinos eventually won 33-26, as the greatest ever.

"For almost unbearable tension-packed drama this has to go down as one of the most memorable of all Challenge Cup semi-finals," wrote Rugby Leaguer & League Express match reporter Raymond Fletcher. "It was climax on top of climax. The first 80 minutes were exciting enough, and then they crammed in another 20 with the same amazing finish. Unbelievable!"

Sinfield's conversion from the right touchline enabled the Rhinos to draw level, and take the game into extra time.

Leeds had the hero in young Danny McGuire. Sent on as a 58th substitute, the outstanding 20 year old prospect produced the stunning last-minute try that Sinfield coolly converted to bring the score to 26-all, and then scored an even better match-clinching touchdown with just over a minute left.

McGuire had been preferred on the substitutes' bench to his teammate Rob Burrow. "I found out on Thursday that I would be playing," said McGuire. "It was my dream as a kid, growing up and supporting Leeds, to play in big games for the club. It will be a great honour to go to Cardiff and represent Leeds."

Leeds skipper Kevin Sinfield leads the celebrations following the Rhinos' thrilling win over St Helens

It was one game that did not deserve a loser. Both teams were left with only one replacement each out of the dozen allowed when they went into extra time and uncharted territory.

Leeds showed nerves of steel in the closing stages of the first 80 minutes, when defeat stared them in the face. Darren Smith seemed to have clinched victory for St Helens when he went in for his second try to make it 26-20 to the Saints. Although Paul Sculthorpe failed with the conversion attention from wide out, there were only three minutes left when Leeds restarted play. But St Helens knocked on at the short kick-off, and Leeds were thrown a lifeline.

After winning the scrum, five play-the-balls took them close to the opposition line, where McGuire put in a short kick. Smith fumbled it, and Tim Jonkers picked it up in an offside position. Leeds took a tap penalty, survived another two tackles, and then a quick dummy by McGuire enabled him to sneak into the corner for a touchdown confirmed by the video referee.

After just 47 seconds of extra-time Sean Long booted the ball nearly 50 metres into the Leeds in-goal, where Francis Cummins slipped and Mike Bennett came tearing up to touch down. Saints went wild, but the video referee had been called on and after several looks decided the Saints player was offside. With just a few seconds of the first ten-minute session left, the ever-cool Sinfield edged Leeds in front with a close range field-goal.

The tension increased with every passing minute of the next period, building up to another dramatic finish. With just over two minutes left Mick Higham went agonisingly close to grabbing the match-winning try for St Helens, as he was buried under a mass of defenders. It resulted in a handover, and Leeds set themselves for one last victory surge. After four play-the-balls had brought them clear of their line, David Furner fed Sinfield 60 metres out, and he split the defence down the middle before handing on to McGuire. He took his chance in classic style to swerve round Darren Albert and dive over in the corner with Smith wrapped round his legs. There was another long video delay before the try was given, and Sinfield banged over another great goal to deny St Helens one last throw of the dice.

St Helens had been beaten at their own game. The Saints had pulled off many similar late victories, and now they were on the receiving end. Paul Sculthorpe did all he could to pull another one out of the bag with a try and six goals, while Higham was the most penetrative forward on the field with his sharp dashes. Sean Long, who was not fully fit, was pushed into action perhaps a little earlier than intended, when Leeds threatened to run away with the game in the first half, but he still made his mark.

As a painful cameo, Matt Adamson was hoping to make the Cup final, despite fracturing his cheekbone. Adamson sustained the injury in the opening minutes but stayed on until the interval.

Anyone who thought the Bulls were over the top had that theory dispelled the following day at the same stadium, as James Lowes was the star of the 36-22 win over Wigan.

The 32 year old Bulls hooker, playing what he revealed was his last Cup semi-final, was again outstanding as he and another senior citizen, Mike Forshaw, spearheaded the Bulls' march to Cardiff and a repeat of the 2000 final against the Rhinos. The power of the Bulls props Joe Vagana and Stuart Fielden was also crucial.

The Bulls settled the game with a devastating 20-minute spell after half-time, after the spirited Warriors had recovered from 12-2 down to go in with a 16-12 interval lead.

Wigan, already fielding a patched-up side with five players requiring needles in order to play and, lacking five regulars through injury, with Brett Dallas, Jamie Ainscough, Mick Cassidy and Stephen Wild joining captain Andrew Farrell on the sidelines, suffered further anxieties. Kris Radlinski was stretchered off to hospital in a neck brace with what turned out to be a whiplash injury, and David Hodgson (dislocated shoulder) and Craig Smith (suspected broken finger) joined Gareth Hock (leg injury) on the lengthy casualty list. And in the days after the game it emerged that Academy International Luke Robinson had broken his hand and required surgery.

Jamie Peacock made a surprise return from a broken hand for the Bulls after successfully coming through a midweek Alliance game, and earned special praise from his coach Brian Noble afterwards for a huge effort.

Brian Carney summed up Wigan's determination with a terrific solo try nine minutes from time, taking on four would-be tacklers as he drove over from dummy half.

It was a late Easter in 2003 and two rounds were sandwiched in between the Powergen Challenge Cup semi-finals and final.

It looked a tall order for Wigan, on the back of their Cup exit, as they faced St Helens at the JJB on Good Friday.

But, deprived of nine first-team players through injury and fielding four debutants, the Warriors produced a stirring performance, recovering from a 22-12 half-time deficit and then holding on in the desperate, gripping late stages for a 24-22 win.

Wigan had four youngsters on debut - former Academy winger Jon Whittle, signed for his one and only appearance from sister union club Orrell - David Allen, Kevin Brown and Mark Roberts.

Veteran props Terry O'Connor and Craig Smith were outstanding, relentlessly taking their side forward. Their young apprentice Danny Sculthorpe had arguably his best game in a Wigan shirt and was a key figure in the Warriors wrestling the second-half advantage from Saints.   At scrum-half, Adrian Lam prompted and probed in typical style, while on the right wing Brian Carney was a constant source of danger, as well as defending superbly.

Fullback Shaun Briscoe was the pick of the young guns with a display of tremendous composure at the back, closely followed by the courageous Mark Smith, playing with several pain-killing injections but contributing fully from loose forward. But the pick of them all was Wigan-born hooker Terry Newton, who grabbed two vital tries and kept the Warriors pack rolling forward through a compelling contest.

For St Helens, it was a fourth defeat in a row.

The night before, Leeds equalled their best ever start to a season (in 1972-73) with a tenth successive Cup and League win, thanks to the "ugliest drop goal ever" that set up a 15-14 win at Castleford. That was coach Daryl Powell's description of Andrew Dunemann's 77th minute match winner. Rob Burrow went on as a replacement and made a terrific break that set up the position for Dunemann's winning goal. The Tigers suffered a blow with a broken arm injury to Jamie Thackray, as they slid out of the top-six.

They were overtaken by the Giants, who on the Saturday narrowly won 21-20 at Halifax, who had former Giant Andrew Frew on debut. It was Huddersfield's third successive victory, and first on Halifax soil since 1977. The manner of the victory, achieved with a towering field goal by skipper Brandon Costin with just 38 seconds left on the clock, suggested the Giants were at last finding their feet at the top level.

After romping into a 20-8 lead after 49 minutes they were holding on desperately in the face of a stirring Halifax fight-back until, with the scores level, they still had the composure to set up Costin for his match-winner. It sealed only the Giants' second win over 'Fax in 12 attempts in Super League and sparked bitter recriminations from home coach Tony Anderson. "Not many of my blokes will be able to please their wives tonight, not many will be able to use their wedding tackle," Anderson said after accusing the Giants of continually lifting in the tackle and hitting his players in the groin area.

A devastating six-try second-half performance from Bradford made sure of a 48-24 win over Hull in front of another 15,000-plus crowd at Odsal. The Bulls' eighth successive win put them clear in second place, hot on the heels of leaders Leeds.

Coach Brian Noble, already with a question mark over the fitness of prop Joe Vagana, lost Stuart Fielden, who tore a post cruciate ligament in the 20th minute. The following Tuesday, Fielden was banned for two matches for "ungentlemanly conduct" - after being found guilty of lifting his knees in the tackle in the incident in which Hull skipper Jason Smith dislocated his shoulder.

The suspension would have ruled him out of the following Saturday's Powergen Challenge Cup final against Leeds, but he was injured anyway. Fellow

Bulls prop Richard Moore escaped with a warning letter from the RFL after being put on report for a similar offence in the 33rd minute, when Hull loose forward Chris Chester tore stomach muscles. And Richard Fletcher, like Smith only playing after passing a late fitness test, twice needed attention to a sternum injury before also coming off in the second half.

Warrington - with captain Lee Briers back - moved into the top-six with a 35-20 home win over Wakefield in a cracking game. Wakefield lost a concussed Brad Davis after 17 minutes and had two controversial no-try calls against them in the second period.

And Widnes Vikings got their second win of the Super League season - a 32-20 home success over London Broncos that owed much to the skill and opportunism of stand-in fullback Paul Atcheson. The Welsh international celebrated his first start of the season, deputising for injured skipper Stuart Spruce, with a brace of tries, including the match-winner just three minutes from the end. Marvin Golden made his debut on the wing for the Vikings.

With Cup finalists Leeds and Bradford calling off their Round Seven fixtures on Easter Monday, injury-blighted third-placed Hull took the opportunity to close the points gap with a 46-18 win over Halifax.

Former winger Gareth Raynor made a shock return after leaving the Airlie Birds at the end of the previous season in a big money move to rugby union. Leicester agreed to allow Raynor to re-join Hull for a limited period. Hull also had Liam Higgins making his only appearance of the season off the bench that day. Raynor scored two first-half tries and Richie Barnett - standing in as skipper in the absence of Jason Smith - two more after the break.

Castleford Tigers jumped back into the play-off positions as they got back to winning form with a 29-16 win over the Giants at the McAlpine Stadium.

Ryan Hudson scored a try, had a hand in another and was a constant irritation to Huddersfield, as Francis Maloney's 76th minute field goal gave Castleford a vital seven-point lead, before Andy Lynch sealed it with a late try.

A one-sided ten-try romp at Knowsley Road ended Saints' four-match losing run in style as Warrington were thrashed 56-6. Saints had Tommy Martyn back from a broken arm, with the Wolves again missing Lee Briers.

And on the Tuesday night Widnes made it three wins from three games to move into the top-six with a convincing 26-6 win at Wakefield. Two quick-fire Lawford field goals, in the 65th and 70th minutes, gave the Vikings breathing space and the Australian Julian O'Neill - the inspiration for the win - blasted over from Lawford's inside pass to settle the issue. Paul Atcheson added a close-range try - his third of the Easter programme - to send the visiting fans home happy. And unsung hooker Shane Millard was rewarded for his part in Widnes's revival by being named Rugby League World magazine's Player of the Month for April.

SUPER LEAGUE TABLE - *Tuesday 22nd April*

	P	W	D	L	F	A	D	PTS
Leeds Rhinos	6	6	0	0	165	106	59	12
Bradford Bulls	6	5	0	1	212	128	84	10
Hull FC	7	5	0	2	187	126	61	10
St Helens	7	4	0	3	238	128	110	8
Castleford Tigers	7	4	0	3	132	137	-5	8
Widnes Vikings	7	3	0	4	154	160	-6	6
Wigan Warriors	6	3	0	3	135	146	-11	6
Huddersfield Giants	7	3	0	4	145	176	-31	6
Warrington Wolves	7	3	0	4	134	183	-49	6
London Broncos	6	2	0	4	106	145	-39	4
Wakefield T Wildcats	7	1	0	6	109	173	-64	2
Halifax	7	1	0	6	126	235	-109	2

CHALLENGE CUP FINAL
Indoor football

Welsh Rugby League legends David Watkins and John Bevan led the battle to take the Powergen Challenge Cup Final back to the Millennium Stadium after Bradford Bulls secured the first silverware of the season with a tense 22-20 victory.

The 2003 Challenge Cup Final will be remembered for its magnificent surroundings - the first to be played 'indoors', with the stadium roof closed to keep out the elements. And for Leeds skipper Kevin Sinfield's decision not to take a shot at goal after being awarded a penalty almost in front of the Bradford sticks, with just minutes remaining and his side two points in arrears.

Sinfield, a hero of the epic semi-final win over St Helens just two weeks earlier, chose instead to run the ball at a tiring Bulls defence, sensing the opportunity for an outright win rather than a potential replay at Elland Road. But it was a perfect opportunity for Sinfield to level the scores, and perhaps an opportunity for a winning field goal.

Instead, the Bulls stayed calm, and their defence held, even when Robbie Paul misread a grubber and almost allowed Mark Calderwood to pounce. From that drop-out, Leeds launched a final raid down the left, but Keith Senior's pass to Francis Cummins sailed into touch, and the Rhinos' chance of winning went with it.

The scoreline reflected the closeness of a titanic struggle that contained many heroes. Matt Adamson played despite breaking a cheekbone in the semi-final two weeks earlier, and with the added distraction of his daughter being hospitalised after breaking an arm in an accident in Cardiff on Friday. "It wasn't a risk or a gamble," said Adamson. "I spoke to the surgeon and specialist, and he said that the worst case scenario was that it would fracture again, and would need an operation."

For the Bulls, Jamie Peacock, whose only game since he broke a hand in the Cup game against Hunslet had been in the semi-final win over Wigan, was within one vote of being voted man of the match.

But the ultimate accolade went to losing fullback Gary Connolly, who was a thoroughly deserving winner of the Lance Todd Trophy. From the earliest minutes, when he struck back to score a converted equalising try, until the closing stages, when he strove desperately to turn the game back Leeds' way, Connolly set a marvellous example.

But for the first time in the trophy's 57-year history, it was presented on the field before the Challenge Cup itself had been handed to the winning captain. The distraught Connolly trooped up to receive the trophy but failed to acknowledge the congratulations of the chief guest Neil Kinnock, the Vice President of the European Commission, or other members of the platform party. Instead Connolly carried the trophy back to his waiting Leeds teammates.

Leeds were hit early by a disputed Robbie Paul try, to which Paul Deacon added the goal to put them 6-0 down after only five minutes. The Rhinos needed a quick response to prevent the Bulls getting on a roll, and Connolly provided it. First he brought relief when Bradford tried to maintain the pressure by kicking into the Leeds in-goal area. Connolly was quick to react, and ran the ball out, just managing to avoid a drop-out, with a hint of a double movement, as he lunged a few inches into the field of play.

Leeds then worked their way to the Bradford line, where a similar lunge just got him over for a terrific try. Leaving his fullback post, he had again seized the initiative by going to acting half-back at a play-the-ball 15 metres from the Bulls' line. A snap dummy bamboozled a clutch of defenders, and a determined burst took him over the line, with Peacock hanging round his legs and Deacon wrapped round his head. Connolly was actually grounded just short of the line, and it needed the video referee to decide that his momentum had taken him over.

But despite Leeds providing the stories of the day, Bradford - without Stuart Fielden and Michael Withers, who had to withdraw on the morning of the game with a groin problem, missing - were worthy victors.

They began with all cylinders firing. With less than two minutes gone a three-man tackle on Ryan Bailey forced the ball loose, Lee Radford scooped it up and sprinted away, with only David Furner giving chase, but video referee Geoff Berry decided the ball had been stolen.

Clever Bulls kicking and strong chasing forced successive drop-outs by the Rhinos, and eventually their lines were broken when Tevita Vaikona stepped past Furner to make the initial burst, before sending Robbie Paul over the line with a suspiciously forward looking pass.

Deacon's conversion put the Bulls 6-0 ahead, but within minutes Connolly was stretching out to score at the opposite end after good approach play from Adamson, and Sinfield popped over the conversion.

The huge Leeds support was cheering again moments later when David Furner went over in the corner, but his effort was ruled out for crossing. The penalty gave the initiative back to the Bulls, and they launched an all-out raid.

Challenge Cup Final

Just as it seemed the Rhinos had weathered the storm, Barrie McDermott was penalised, on the last tackle, for taking out Daniel Gartner in back play, and Deacon's conversion edged the Bulls back in front at 8-6.

It was a short-lived advantage. Bailey forced the ball loose with a big hit on Joe Vagana, and when James Lowes was penalised for ball-stealing on the next tackle - and then marched a further ten metres for dissent - Sinfield levelled the game. While that was happening, Adamson was receiving treatment for his damaged cheek, and continued to make signals to a worried Leeds bench.

Paul Anderson came off the bench for the Bulls, but spilt the ball with his first touch. Despite Bradford claims for a two-man steal, Leeds played to the whistle and responded with a clinical attack that ended with Sinfield hoisting the ball into the corner. Lesley Vainikolo and Calderwood both rose to take the catch, but missed, allowing the supporting Chris McKenna to gratefully take the bouncing ball. Shontayne Hape did his best to hold up the big Aussie centre, but after another lengthy video debate the try was awarded.

POWERGEN CHALLENGE CUP FINAL

Saturday 26th April 2003

BRADFORD BULLS 22 LEEDS RHINOS 20

BULLS: 1 Robbie Paul (C); 2 Tevita Vaikona; 20 Scott Naylor; 4 Shontayne Hape; 5 Lesley Vainikolo; 3 Leon Pryce; 7 Paul Deacon; 8 Joe Vagana; 9 James Lowes; 11 Daniel Gartner; 18 Lee Radford; 12 Jamie Peacock; 13 Mike Forshaw. Subs (all used): 10 Paul Anderson; 14 Lee Gilmour; 27 Robert Parker; 15 Karl Pratt.
Tries: Paul (6), Vainikolo (39), Peacock (43);
Goals: Deacon 5/5.
RHINOS: 18 Gary Connolly; 2 Mark Calderwood; 3 Chris McKenna; 4 Keith Senior; 1 Francis Cummins; 13 Kevin Sinfield (C); 14 Andrew Dunemann; 19 Ryan Bailey; 9 Matt Diskin; 10 Barrie McDermott; 5 Chev Walker; 12 Matt Adamson; 11 David Furner. Subs (all used): 8 Danny Ward; 17 Wayne McDonald; 7 Rob Burrow; 16 Willie Poching.
Tries: Connolly (10), McKenna (22), Furner (60);
Goals: Sinfield 4/4.
Rugby Leaguer & League Express Men of the Match:
Bulls: Jamie Peacock; *Rhinos:* Gary Connolly.
Penalty count: 9-5; **Half time:** 14-14;
Referee: Russell Smith (Castleford);
Attendance: 71,212 *(at The Millennium Stadium, Cardiff).*

Then, just two minutes from half-time, Rob Burrow took a heavy knock in a tackle by Lee Gilmour, and was helped from field. Without the other hero of Leeds' semi-final win, Danny McGuire, on the bench, the Rhinos were temporally disorganised, and the Bulls produced a strong set of six that ended with Vainikolo diving on to a Deacon chip to the corner for the try of the game, after a long Pryce pass to the left had created the space. Again, the video referee was called into action, but the half ended with the try being awarded, and Deacon kicking a magnificent conversion from the touchline to again level the scores at 14-14.

The teams turned round to face their own fans, and the early action was at the Bulls fans' end, Vaikona failing to get on the end of a high kick to the corner before Peacock crashed over in the corner to give Geoff Berry another headache in the video van. It was difficult to see whether the Bulls second row had been held up in a three-man Rhinos tackle, but the try was awarded, and Deacon kicked another touchline goal. In effectively four minutes of play either side of the break, the Bulls had gone from 8-14 down to 20-14 ahead.

Now chasing the game, Leeds launched into all-out attack. There was a moment of controversy when Sinfield kicked early for Calderwood to chase, and having seemingly beaten Vainikolo for pace the big Bradford winger stumbled and brought down the Leeds man at the same time. The Rhinos fans screamed for a penalty, but had to be content with a drop-out, and the Bulls held their ground.

A Deacon penalty on 51 minutes stretched the Bulls lead to eight points, and another try would almost certainly have ended any Leeds hopes. But a

Robbie Paul all wrapped up by Matt Diskin, with help from Barrie McDermott and Chev Walker

moment of madness from Gilmour gifted Senior an interception. Although Gilmour got back to make amends with a great tackle, the Bulls were on the back foot, and McDermott ran across the face of the defence to bring Furner running onto a good angle to go over unopposed. Sinfield's conversion brought the Rhinos back to within two points entering the final quarter, and the Bulls seemed to have little left in the tank.

But then came that crucial penalty decision by Sinfield in those unbearably tense final moments before chaotic scenes when the stadium clock flashed up the 80th minute and someone in the crowd blew a klaxon. Not realising it wasn't the official clock, the Bulls players threw their arms in the air in celebration, and workmen carried staging onto the pitch - not realising the official hooter had yet to sound. With over a minute of play remaining, the Bulls had to quickly refocus as Leeds threw everything into a frantic finale before the siren eventually sounded.

In the aftermath, Leeds threatened to register a formal complaint about the performance of referee Russell Smith. "I am bitterly disappointed at the way the game was refereed today. It seemed every 50-50 decision went against us, and there were others that I felt were more than 50-50 in favour of us but still didn't come our way," said coach Daryl Powell.

"I think, in the cold light of day, Daryl will look at the performance of the referee and video referee and see that there were calls for both camps that could have gone either way," responded Bulls coach Brian Noble.

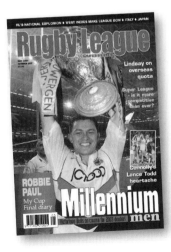

MAY
Warriors turn corner

Leeds Rhinos, despite the heartache of the narrow defeat at the hands of their biggest rivals in Cardiff, still topped the Super League table as April turned to May.

And they had two home games over the first weekend of the new month to give them to chance to stretch clear of Bradford, who themselves faced a formidable post-Cup Final test at Wigan on the Friday.

Leeds' game the same night looked to be straightforward, but it took another Andrew Dunemann's field goal as the clock deemed injury time to seal a 13-12 win over Wakefield Trinity Wildcats at Headingley and preserve the Rhinos' undefeated Super League record.

"If it was an 'ugly' one-pointer which secured the points at the Jungle a fortnight ago then this snap effort with the final play of a match dominated by endeavour rather than skill, could only be described as hideous, the ball wavering in the driving rain as it struggled to mount the crossbar," wrote Phil Caplan in Rugby Leaguer & League Express.

It sickened the Wildcats, who had matched the league leaders throughout, skipper Adrian Vowles and tireless hooker David March epitomising their never-say-die attitude with heroic tackling and vigorous running out of dummy-half.

Five days later, the Rhinos welcomed Wigan to Headingley in the Round Seven game postponed from Easter Monday, and though they remained unbeaten, dropped a point as a majestic game finished in a 24-all draw.

In terms of spectacle - all four of the Rhinos tries were classic strikes from distance - and raw courage, Danny Sculthorpe making a Herculean contribution as Wigan's injury nightmare saw them restricted to one fit prop, this was a titanic clash.

The Warriors, with Nick Graham, in his second game for Wigan, to the fore, dictated the tempo and width in a mesmerising first half begun when Barrie McDermott pulverised best mate Terry O'Connor in the second minute. In a desperate finish, Adrian Lam and Andrew Dunemann both missed field goals either side of an effort that went tantalisingly close from Danny McGuire.

When Dunemann shaped for a field goal two minutes from time Leeds fans were thinking third time lucky after the Rhinos' last two one-point league wins, but Wigan's scrambling to deny him space summed up their exceptional effort.

It was indeed a mighty effort from Wigan, as, on the previous Friday, the Bulls came down from what their coach, Brian Noble, described as the "emotional high" of winning the Challenge Cup to stun the Warriors, with Leon Pryce's late winning try securing a 14-8 win at the JJB.

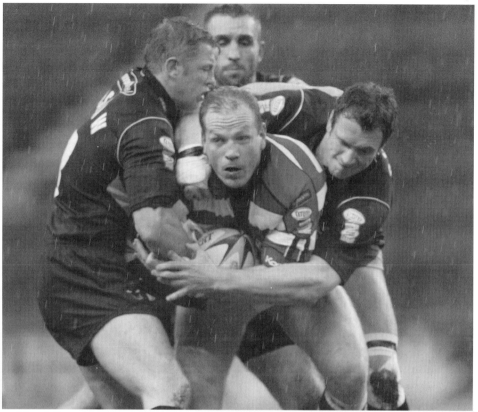

Wigan's Terry O'Connor held up by Bradford's Mike Forshaw and Jamie Peacock in Round Eight

Wigan coach Stuart Raper, who gave a debut to Nick Graham, signed from his old club Cronulla, refused to blame the club's massive injury list - lengthened by the medial ligament injury that forced the impressive Craig Smith out of the action early in the second half.

Raper did point out, though, that the Bulls made their breakthrough soon after Smith's departure left the admirable Terry O'Connor as the sole Wigan player seemingly capable of making ground against the huge Bulls pack.

With the scores level at 8-all, Wigan had two great opportunities to set up a winning one-pointer as Adrian Lam's effort after his side's first attack in ages hardly got off the floor. Then two Bulls players were caught out at a play-the-ball after Brian Carney's run, but Tickle, with a monster 74th-minute penalty effort from two metres inside the Bradford half, saw his effort fall agonisingly under the crossbar. O'Loughlin was then well wide with a 35-metre field-goal attempt.

But Pryce made the vital breakthrough in a pulsating finish to a terrific game. With the Wigan defence expecting a field-goal attempt on the last tackle, James Lowes caught them napping. The Bulls' inspiration chipped through, right-footed, and Pryce just beat Radlinski to the loose ball before romping over jubilantly. Deacon's first successful conversion wrapped up their seventh successive win over the Warriors.

Also in Round Eight, Warrington ended the Vikings' three-match winning run in some style as they hammered their neighbours 34-6. The Wolves had Lee

Briers back after a shin problem forced him to miss the heavy defeat at St Helens, and Sid Domic returned, a month after dislocating a thumb at Bradford.

"That display must rank amongst the best since my return, and it was all about learning our lesson from what happened to us at St Helens," said Wolves coach Paul Cullen.

The Broncos followed up their wins at Hull and Wigan with their third success on the road in Super League VIII - a 30-22 win over Huddersfield at the McAlpine Stadium.

Andrew King, Tony Martin and Austin Buchanan each scored two tries as the Broncos inflicted a second successive home defeat on the Giants.

Cash-strapped Halifax remain firmly rooted to the foot of the table after St Helens made light of incessant rain and a waterlogged pitch to run in seven tries and 38-unanswered points at the Shay.

On the Mayday Bank Holiday Monday, in one of the most astonishing finishes in Super League history, Castleford Tigers snatched a point at the Jungle that even their coach Graham Steadman said they did not deserve, drawing 26-all with Hull.

Hull were leading 26-8 when Danny Orr touched down on 70 minutes. The next converted Tigers try, by Michael Eagar, came on 75 minutes. Then Damian Gibson scored with 79 minutes and six seconds on the clock, with Wayne Bartrim's equalising conversion being followed immediately by the final hooter.

Chris Chester, back from injury, was the key figure in Hull's first-half dominance, producing the final pass for Steve Prescott's opening try and putting in Richie Barnett for a couple more. The 14-8 interval lead was soon extended, with Richard Horne dodging in for a try to which Prescott added the goal and a penalty a few minutes later. When Colin Best swept in for their fifth try after 58 minutes to make it 26-8 to Hull, it began to look embarrassing for Castleford. But it was Hull who finished with red faces.

A major blow for the visitors was a broken leg sustained by Matt Crowther, a day before his 29th birthday and in his first match after missing five with a calf injury. On a brighter note, Australian recruit Dean Treister made a promising start as a 33rd minute substitute only 48 hours after the Cronulla hooker landed from Australia.

The first weekend of May was also significant for the launch of National League Three, with South London and Coventry allaying fears that there was going to be a north-south divide in the ten-team competition. The Bears beat title favourites Warrington-Woolston 16-13 and the Storm - who came into the competition late after the withdrawal of Crawley Jets, beat Huddersfield-Underbank Rangers 24-16. Teesside Steelers made the bold decision to fly down from Newcastle Airport to their opening fixture with St Albans Centurions, and were rewarded with a last-minute 20-16 win.

The Bulls were unable to agree a date with London Broncos for the Cup final-deferred Round Seven match at Griffin Park, which left the Rhinos three points clear at the top of Super League.

In Round Nine the Bulls sent Castleford Tigers tumbling out of the play-off places with a 30-10 victory at Odsal. But Bradford had to weather the 32nd minute dismissal of Leon Pryce to secure a memorable 11th successive victory.

The character of the Challenge Cup winners was tested to the full by the numerical disadvantage, yet the incident concerned – an impetuous and unnecessary late challenge on Danny Orr - seemed only to galvanise them. Orr was concussed and left the field and on the following Tuesday Pryce was suspended for two matches.

The win kept Bradford above Hull, who that afternoon had easily accounted for the Giants at the KC Stadium by 34-6, in a game riddled with penalties, with match referee Ronnie Laughton issuing some 31, mainly for technical offences. And the persistent lying on or holding down resulted in Dean Treister, Jim Gannon and Darren Turner all being sent to the bin in separate incidents.

The Giants were without Steve McNamara who had a tendon operation the previous Friday, but Hull welcomed back Tony Smith. Treister made his home debut and he managed to make it a try-scoring one. Huddersfield gave Graham Holroyd a debut off the bench, as they started a search for a back-rower after Anthony Colella was forced to retire from the game with a serious knee injury.

When Wigan officials look back at the first half of Super League VIII in years to come, they may conclude that the injury crisis that engulfed the Warriors was one of the best things that could have happened to the club. Missing established stars such as Andy Farrell, Mick Cassidy and Brett Dallas left the Warriors outside the top six, and with an almighty battle on to emulate their league finishes of recent seasons.

A typically-involved display from skipper Adrian Lam, opportunism from hooker Terry Newton, who delayed a knee operation indefinitely to help the club over their shortage of personnel, and big efforts from props Danny Sculthorpe and Terry O'Connor saw Wigan build on the midweek point they earned at Leeds with a 22-18 win at Widnes. A controversial Jamie Ainscough try and Danny Tickle penalty had Wigan 16-12 in front and the hard-working Newton sealed it by plunging over from dummy-half eight minutes from time for a converted try.

Shane Millard followed suit for the Vikings with three minutes to go to cap another impressive personal performance, but time ran out on a brave Vikings effort.

On the Friday night the Rhinos - missing Gary Connolly, David Furner, Chev Walker and Matt Diskin, plus long-term injury absentee Matt Adamson - won in the capital 32-14, with Danny McGuire collecting two tries.

Broncos coach Tony Rea was upset with referee Richard Silverwood for a decision to disallow a second-half Austin Buchanan effort which would have brought his side level with the kick to come. It was a hammer blow for the Broncos as the Rhinos powered home with 14 points in the final seven minutes of the contest.

The Broncos had two Leeds loan players in their side - Buchanan and second-rower Damien Kennedy, and that week took another, in Academy international forward Tommy Gallagher.

Warrington consolidated their play-off place with a 38-8 success at the Shay, with Graham Appo scoring a hat-trick of well-taken tries. Halifax's eighth successive defeat was made worse on that Friday night as new filtered through that Wakefield had pulled off the shock of the season, winning 16-10 at St Helens

- their first win at Knowsley Road for 23 years - with halfback Jamie Rooney the star.

Off the field, the RFL was coming under pressure from Super League clubs to agree a TV contract - with the current BSkyB deal set to run out at the end of the season. Clubs claimed, with some justification, they were unable to agree player contracts for the following year if they didn't know what their income would be.

There could never be a more dramatic return.

Andy Farrell's field goal just seconds from time earned Wigan the priceless league points in the clash against neighbours Warrington, who had looked odds on to win the Round 10 contest at the JJB as the game approached its closing stages.

Farrell's Super League season had been limited to 23 minutes of Round One action after he picked up a knee injury in the defeat at Castleford. His comeback was nicely timed as another Great Britain international, Kris Radlinski, was forced to have surgery on a nagging wrist injury.

Having led 6-12 at the break, Paul Cullen's men had done a fine job on the Warriors and with eight minutes of the game to play they still led 18-20.

However, Farrell was to prove the catalyst for a late Wigan rally and, having squared the match on 76 minutes with a penalty goal, he subsequently landed the all important one-pointer to leave the brave Wolves devastated.

Castleford kept Wigan in sixth spot as they demolished Widnes Vikings 40-2 at the Jungle, with on-loan from Leeds halfback Jon Hepworth making his debut from the bench.

There were several outstanding performances, with the most awesome by Andy Lynch. The young forward made a massive impact after going on as a 23rd minute substitute, setting up two tries and powering in for another himself. The even younger fullback, Tom Saxton, was another standout.

Jamie Rooney was again the key as Wakefield ground out a 22-18 home win over Halifax - leaving them two points adrift at the bottom of the table. Rooney twice spliced open the much-criticised Halifax defence, which otherwise scrambled well throughout a feisty encounter that blew up in the first half. Michael Korkidas was cleared by the disciplinary after Halifax prop Chris Birchall was badly concussed in a tackle, and Matt Seers, who had been put on report for possible use of the knees in a tackle, was also deemed not guilty. Dallas Hood had worse luck as he was banned for a match for striking after being cited by the League's executive.

All talk at the final whistle of another nerve-jangling clash at Headingley was referee Steve Ganson's decision to give a 79th minute penalty to Hull, serenely dispatched by Steve Prescott - in his 100th appearance for Hull - which saw both sides emerge with a point from a 10-10 draw.

The award was against Francis Cummins who collected a ball clearly knocked forward by Keith Senior, but tipped back by Paul Cooke, who had originally been attempting to send a pass wide to the wing in one last hurrah to save the game.

Instead of a scrum, for which there would not have been time for the sides to pack down, Prescott was offered the chance to square the match which he duly took, an outcome Hull deserved, their right to it obscured by the ensuing pandemonium. Tony Smith became Hull's third broken leg victim of the season.

Leeds' dropped point put the Bulls two points behind with a game in hand after a routine 52-6 win at Huddersfield. With hooker James Lowes rested, 20 year old Aaron Smith made his debut for the Bulls, while ex-Halifax junior Gareth Greenwood made his Giants bow off the bench.

Skipper Robbie Paul led the way for the Bulls with three of his side's nine tries with the Giants' main consolation being the bumper 8,297 crowd, their second biggest in Super League.

And it was back to business as normal at Knowsley Road as Saints hammered London 62-16, with Keiron Cunningham delighted to be back in the starting line-up, playing the third game of his comeback since the elbow dislocation he suffered against the Kiwis in the first Test the previous autumn that threatened his career, and scoring three fine tries. And Mick Higham underlined his own superb skills by coming off the bench to fire his own three-try salvo.

Then all of a sudden, Leeds Rhinos, unbeaten until Round 11, found themselves in second spot, with their modern-day nemesis Bradford Bulls sitting above them.

Almost 22,000 crammed into Odsal on the Friday night to see Bradford emerge 48-22 winners - 13 successive wins in all matches by Bradford, while the defeat left Leeds one short of the club's record of 11 unbeaten matches from the start of a league season.

Bradford - who that night opened their impressive new hospitality stand - were 38-6 ahead before Leeds scored their first try in the 56th minute. There was pace and power throughout the Bradford side, particularly on the wings where Tevita Vaikona and Lesley Vainikolo both charged in for two tries. Robbie Paul highlighted an impressive match at fullback with his 100th Super League try, putting him just one behind career leader Kris Radlinski's 101 for Wigan Warriors.

Another example of Bradford's awesome power came with Paul Anderson's try when Paul Deacon sent the massive prop on a 20-metre charge, completing his run with a ram-rod hand off of Gary Connolly.

Castleford Tigers cemented their play-off spot with a 32-16 win over the resurgent Wolves at Wilderspool, going three points clear of their rivals after their Round Ten hammering of Widnes at the Jungle.

And the comprehensive victory was all the more notable taking into account the Tigers' injury crisis, which was highlighted by Dean Sampson's appearance from the bench.

Sampson had announced his retirement from the game at the end of the previous year but answered an SOS from coach Graham Steadman, rewarding him with a try on 29 minutes which really gave the visitors the upper hand.

Deon Bird celebrated his return from a broken jaw with a match-winning hat-trick and Jules O'Neill produced another fine individual display as the Vikings prevailed 42-30 over Huddersfield in a 12-try thriller at the Halton Stadium.

The Giants held the lead on four separate occasions but the Vikings staged a late revival with 18 points in the last eight minutes to earn the spoils, Bird sealing the win with a 60-metre interception try in injury time. The following Tuesday Huddersfield announced they had signed Ben Roarty - a tryscorer in Melbourne Storm's Australian Grand Final win in 1999 - from Penrith Panthers.

A spectacular Dennis Moran hat-trick sent London on their way to a 36-12 win at Wakefield. Super League VII's top try-scorer, who had missed a large chunk of this season recovering from a knee operation, proved both his fitness and his adaptability, mopping up at fullback and making three incisive bursts to the line, which ripped the heart out of Trinity's challenge.

Andy Farrell's 30 points from a hat-trick and nine goals, all hit in succession after he had missed with his first two shots, and an exciting hat-trick from teenager Kevin Brown highlighted Wigan's ten-try 58-12 romp over hapless Halifax at the JJB Stadium.

The hat-trick marked Brown's first senior tries, all scored in a devastating 12-minute spell in the second half. Wigan duly extended Brown's contract until the end of 2005.

And on the Spring Bank Holiday Monday, Hull went three points clear of Wigan in third place with a stunning 30-6 win over St Helens at the KC Stadium. Two-try Colin Best, Richie Barnett, Craig Greenhill and Paul King all had big games in a superb 17-man display - loan signing, Leeds prop Ewan Dowes, making his Hull debut - and Steve Prescott's combined contribution in attack and defence epitomised Hull's never-say-die performance.

On the last Thursday of May, Hull and Saints were informed, along with Halifax, that they were to be deducted two points for salary cap breaches during 2002. The three clubs had 14 days in which to lodge an appeal.

Also that week, Martin Moana of Halifax and Dominic Peters of London were banned by the RFL following Doping Control Panel hearings. Peters was suspended for 12 months after being found guilty of providing a urine sample containing stanozolol, and had his contract cancelled by the Broncos. Moana was suspended from playing for 28 days after being found guilty of providing a urine sample containing ephedrine

An un-named third player had been charged with providing a sample containing a banned substance, but after taking into consideration mitigating evidence, the independent panel handed down a 12-month suspended sentence and fined him £2,500.

The RFL refused to comment further.

SUPER LEAGUE TABLE - *Monday 26th May*

	P	W	D	L	F	A	D	PTS
Bradford Bulls	10	9	0	1	356	174	182	18
Leeds Rhinos	11	8	2	1	266	214	52	18
Hull FC	11	7	2	2	287	174	113	16
Wigan Warriors	11	6	1	4	268	234	34	13
Castleford Tigers	11	6	1	4	240	211	29	13
St Helens	11	6	0	5	378	166	164	12
Warrington Wolves	11	5	0	6	242	250	-8	10
Widnes Vikings	11	4	0	7	222	286	-64	8
London Broncos	10	4	0	6	202	273	-71	8
Wakefield T Wildcats	11	3	0	8	171	250	-79	6
Huddersfield Giants	11	3	0	8	209	334	-125	6
Halifax	11	1	0	10	164	391	-227	2

JUNE
Salary cap bites

The salary cap was the major issue in the game going into June, with Halifax's two-point deduction for transgressions in 2002 particularly cruel, leaving them looking dead in the water, six points adrift at the bottom of the table.

Hull looked fairly comfortable five points clear of the seventh-placed team, Warrington, even with two points deducted, and with a much better points difference, but St Helens were now only sixth because of a better points difference than the Wolves.

The story of Round 12 was Dennis Moran and the London Broncos. Moran, who had scored a hat-trick of tries the previous week at Wakefield, scored another hat-trick as the Broncos shocked the Bulls 22-12 at Odsal. And in between the two games, the Australian made a dramatic return journey around the world from England to Australia and back to attend to a family bereavement.

Moran had only arrived back at Heathrow mid-morning, immediately getting a connecting flight to Leeds-Bradford Airport in time for the Bulls game.

Salary cap victims Halifax and Hull played out a game without either team conceding a single penalty at The Shay on the Friday night, when Hull defeated their hosts 60-10. Hull coach Shaun McRae and Halifax boss Tony Anderson joined forces to praise Huddersfield whistler Colin Morris after the game, thought to be the first on record to be played without a penalty being awarded.

Halifax had loan signing from St Helens, John Kirkpatrick, on debut and also signed former Warrington and Leeds prop Neil Harmon, who had agreed to join Chorley Lynx, but was allowed to move to play in Super League again.

Prop Darrell Griffin became the first Super League player to come from the TotalRL.com Rugby League Conference when he made his debut for Wakefield Trinity Wildcats at the Halton Stadium on the Saturday night. Griffin began his career in League as a winger at Oxford Cavaliers when the nation-wide summer competition was inaugurated in 1998. He moved on to the London Broncos' Academy, and had impressed Wakefield coach Shane McNally, who needed a replacement for Australian Clinton O'Brien, who had returned home. The Wildcats turned down the chance to sign new St Helens recruit Keith Mason because they couldn't

afford him. They had first call on the Welsh International as part of the deal that saw him leave the club to join Melbourne Storm in 2001. Wakefield subsequently signed Griffin after two trial matches.

The stunning London win at Bradford gave Leeds the chance to go top again and they duly took it with a 30-20 win in a marvellous game at Wigan, which the Rhinos won by overcoming a 14-0 deficit, with skipper Kevin Sinfield setting an inspiring lead. A wonderful 80-metre try from Mark Calderwood just before half-time got the Rhinos back in the game and set up the win.

Castleford Tigers leapt over Wigan into fourth spot with a 32-18 win over Huddersfield at the Jungle. Jon Hepworth, the 20 year old halfback or hooker on loan from Leeds Rhinos until the end of the season, was outstanding, as was centre Michael Eagar, scorer of two tries.

There was nothing between the Wolves and St Helens at Wilderspool as a bumper crowd witnessed a 30-30 draw. A sun-drenched crowd was treated to a wonderful game of fluctuating fortunes, chock-full of controversy and incident, with Saints fighting back from 24-10 down early in the second half to lead 30-24 before Lee Penny's try and Lee Briers' fifth conversion earned the home side a deserved share of the spoils.

On the weekend of Round 13, Rugby Leaguer & League Express revealed that a new five-year deal from BSkyB worth £53 million for Super League and international coverage was on then table at RFL headquarters at Red Hall. But the offer would only stand if the Challenge Cup Final was not put back to September, the BBC's preferred option.

St Helens centre Paul Newlove was ruled out of action for ten weeks after dislocating his thumb attempting a tackle during the Friday night 34-38 loss to Wigan Warriors at Knowsley Road.

Newlove, 31, was in the final year of his contract at St Helens, and had been told, along with teammate Tommy Martyn, that he would not be retained at the end of the season. There was thought to be considerable interest from other Super League clubs in Newlove's availability, with Castleford Tigers heading the queue for his services.

Keith Mason made his Saints debut but he was upstaged by Luke Robinson, who came off the bench with Wigan 14-0 down and turned the game on its head with a try hat-trick as Saints slipped out of the top six.

Hull forward Richard Fletcher was dismissed for the second time in the season by senior referee Steve Ganson at the KC Stadium in the Airlie Birds' 26-20 home defeat by Bradford in front of 19,549 supporters, the second highest Super League crowd of the season so far.

Fletcher, who became the sixth Super League player to be sent off in 2003 - coincidentally all by Ganson - was dismissed in the 54th minute following the intervention of a touch judge. Fletcher was alleged to have kick Bradford stand-off Karl Pratt just prior to crossing the line for what appeared to be a crucial try. But he had the score disallowed and was immediately sent off.

Fletcher was later found guilty of kicking by the RFL but was not suspended, the Disciplinary Committee deciding that his dismissal was sufficient punishment.

Hull's Kirk Yeaman takes on Bradford's Karl Pratt during Round Thirteen's big clash

Hull fullback Steve Prescott signed a two-year deal that tied him to Hull until 2005 while news leaked out that Brisbane's New Zealand hooker Richard Swain had signed with the Black & Whites for 2004 - leaving former Cronulla Shark hooker Dean Treister open to other offers.

London Broncos came out on top in Super League's foray into Wales as they defeated Widnes Vikings 40-18 in front of 3,128 supporters at Aberavon RUFC. The Broncos, who were leading 34-6 at half-time, comfortably accounted for the Vikings in a match that was the climax of a Festival of Rugby League that was staged throughout the weekend at the Aberavon club. Broncos' star Dennis

61

June

Moran narrowly failed to score his third hat-trick in as many weeks, touching down just two times.

Halifax coach Tony Anderson insisted his side could still avoid relegation following a 28-26 defeat at Huddersfield, Brandon Costin's try and conversion on 71 minutes putting two scores between the local rivals. Prop Jeff Wittenberg that week became the third Giants player to announce his retirement from the game due to injury. The 30 year old had a knee operation in February, but the injury had not responded to the rehabilitation process. The Giants made enquiries with St Helens about taking forwards Mark Edmondson and John Stankevitch on loan.

Fax were cast eight points adrift at the foot of Super League by the Wildcats' resounding 32-12 home in over Warrington. A tremendous second-half display clinched the victory for a makeshift Wakefield side missing three or four regulars and others being forced to play out of position, including Gareth Ellis switched from centre to second row.

And the Rhinos stayed two points clear at the top with a 39-26 home win over the Tigers in a 12-try Saturday night extravaganza that was only settled by Rob Burrow's field goal seven minutes from time. Cas prop Nathan Sykes had to withdraw from the game to be at his wife's bedside for the birth of their first child at the end of week in which captain Danny Orr was announced as the captain of the Yorkshire Origin side.

Halifax slumped to their 13th consecutive defeat - a club record - 20-48 at home to Widnes, and now looked certainties to be relegated to National League One at the end of the season, with speculation rife at the Shay that the club was about release a number of high-profile players as a cost-cutting measure. Coach Tony Anderson admitted that his bid to bring fans favourite Fereti Tuilagi back to the Shay had failed.

St Helens were on a downward path too as they sank to eight position after a 20-14 defeat at Headingley. Andrew Dunemann was the star, with crucial tackles, a hand in two of the three Leeds tries, and a fine kicking game. Saints, for whom two-try Keiron Cunningham was outstanding, suffered another blow in the pack as captain Chris Joynt broke his nose 32 minutes into the game.

Bradford only just kept Leeds in their sights as they edged a tight game at Wilderspool 24-20. The Wolves, with three minutes remaining, were leading 20-14. Even when Mike Forshaw forced his way over for a try, that Paul Deacon goaled superbly from the touchline to tie the scores, it seemed that the Wolves would still welcome a share of the spoils.

But then Deacon's long, raking kick down field for a 40/20 was chased back by the hapless Dean Gaskell, and his despairing dive to try and avoid the head and feed for Bradford turned into a disaster. Gaskell only succeeded in turning the ball back into the in-goal area and the ball stopped tantalisingly before the dead-ball line as the youngster desperately tried to scramble to his feet and recover. Scott Naylor had never given up the chase and, as Gaskell attempted to close the gap to the ball, it was Naylor who won the race for the match-winning touchdown.

David Hodgson, one of ten players aged 21 or under in the Warriors side, scored a brace of tries, including the clincher 12 minutes from the end, to earn Wigan a 28-14 win over Hull at the JJB. It was the Warriors' fifth win in their last six games and saw them leapfrog over Hull into third place at Super League's half-way point.

London Broncos climbed into the play-off positions with a 28-16 win at Castleford. The Broncos made it four successive wins on their travels with a tremendous fightback that shattered the Tigers' hopes of returning to the top four. Cas - who that week had tied prop Andy Lynch to a new three-year contract - were looking full value for their 16-8 lead going into the last 15 minutes when London hit them with a three-try scoring burst. The first two comeback tries went to Tony Martin to crown an eventful match by the centre. He had also pulled off a try-saving tackle in the first half and had a spell in the sin bin. Dennis Moran also stood out with two tries to take his total to ten in London's last four matches.

And Huddersfield won the battle of tenth v 11th, beating Wakefield 26-4 on a glorious sun-lit summer evening at the McAlpine. Paul Reilly, playing only his fourth game back after a nine-month lay-off with a broken leg, pressed his Origin claims with a superb display from fullback, but then ruined his evening's work when he was sent off for alleged striking in the last minute after Richard Newlove finally broke the Wildcats' duck in the corner.

Another fans' favourite, Kumul Stanley Gene, returned after a one-match lay-off with a rib injury to spearhead the victory charge. Reilly was banned for one game but was able to play in the Giants' next first-grade game - a visit to Warrington Wolves in Round 16. That weekend's game in London has been postponed because of pitch maintenance over-running at Griffin Park, but the Giants had a Senior Academy game against Salford on the Thursday, which counted against the suspension.

The Saturday night after the RFL rejected BSkyB's 53 million pound offer and started negotiations with the BBC for international rights, Wigan threw Super League into turmoil with an incredible 35-22 win at Odsal.

It was Wigan's first win in Bradford since their previous trip to Odsal in 2000 and Bradford had now lost two successive home matches for the first time in a Super League season, leaving them four points adrift of leaders Leeds Rhinos.

Andy Farrell was back to his international best, and he highlighted an outstanding performance with his 100th try for the club and eight goals for a 20-point haul for Wigan, who learned that week that Aussie centre Jamie Ainscough was returning to Australia because of the arm injury that had dogged his season.

The previous evening the Rhinos had little trouble in dispensing with Wakefield at Belle Vue by 48-12. Slick Leeds shrugged off an early 12-point deficit to consolidate their position at the top of the table and send local rivals Wakefield crashing to their heaviest defeat of the season. Rob Burrow and Mark Calderwood each scored try-doubles.

Hull kept up with the chasing pack with a 22-14 win over play-off rivals Castleford, in a thrilling TV game that wasn't decided until Hull prop Paul King crashed over in the dying seconds to finally confirm Hull's first win in their last three starts. More injury worries for Shaun McRae though as Chris Chester was added to the injury list with an ankle problem and Richie Barnett aggravated a neck injury early on.

Hull had signed Bradford threequarter Alex Wilkinson - who made his debut against Cas - and Leeds stand-off Peter Lupton on loan. Wilkinson had already had similar loan spells with London Broncos, last season, and Huddersfield Giants in 2003.

Warrington leapfrogged Widnes Vikings with their second win over them of the year - a 32-28 win at the Halton Stadium. Graham Appo was the Wolves hero with a dramatic match-winning try two minutes from the end of an outstanding derby that see-sawed to keep an 8,531 crowd on the edge of their seats till the end. There was still one sting in the tail as the Vikings mounted a last-gasp recovery act, but Shane Millard agonisingly knocked-on with the line open in the first minute of injury-time.

On the Friday night St Helens, who had signed Kiwi Willie Talau on a three-year contract from the start of 2004, rediscovered the winning feeling, running in ten tries to demolish Halifax at Knowsley Road and end a worrying sequence of just one point from their previous four games.

Stand-in skipper Paul Sculthorpe, deputising for the injured Chris Joynt, scored four second-half tries as Saints, 22-2 ahead at the break, ruthlessly turned the screw on the back of an incredible 14-1 penalty count, while Sean Long amassed 22 points from a try and nine goals.

Halifax, who that week had released Kiwi forward Anthony Seuseu "by mutual consent" had young stand-off Simon Grix on debut off the bench.

The Bulls were still the bookies' favourites to win the Grand Final, despite their stunning 35-0 home defeat by St Helens at Odsal on the Friday night of a Super League Round 16 brought forward from Sunday to accommodate the following Wednesday's Origin match. Bradford had now suffered three successive home defeats and lost their skipper Robbie Paul, who broke his arm in the 53rd minute of a game played in teeming rain.

In the week leading up to the game the Rugby Football League announced that James Lowes' behaviour towards referee Karl Kirkpatrick in the game between Bradford and Wigan at Odsal should be the subject of an investigation by the RFL's new Disciplinary Commissioner, former senior police officer Gary Haigh.

But the RFL backed down, apparently when it realised it had no authority to pursue any additional charges against Lowes after the referee had penalised him for dissent, but had then taken no further action.

Bulls coach Brian Noble criticised the Bradford supporters who booed his team at Odsal. The Bulls' players left the field to a chorus of boos at half-time and full-time.

Sean Long's last-minute field goal was the bullet in the head for suffering Bradford who were given a lesson in wet-weather football. Regular hooker Mick Higham started his second successive game at scrum-half and looked a natural. He stood out with two first-half tries as Saints led 22-0 at half-time.

Leeds Rhinos missed a chance to go six points clear at the top as the Vikings saved their best of the season for a 29-14 win at the Halton Stadium. Local winger Paul Devlin was the hero, scoring two second-half tries.

Devlin's coup de grace came with 12 minutes remaining as he fielded Kevin Sinfield's downtown kick and evaded two chasers before burning down the left touchline, warding off Rob Burrow's challenge, then Chev Walker and David Furner, for a try that brought the house down.

Wigan - who debuted former Kiwi skipper Quentin Pongia, and were linked with a move for Aussie Test centre Mark Gasnier, after Brett Dallas was tipped to sign for Cronulla Sharks for 2004 - moved to within a point of Bradford with a 24-10 home win over Castleford.

Only when the lively David Hodgson took things into his own hands, breaking away from close to halfway and evading the trailing cover defence for a memorable solo try 14 minutes from time, were the Warriors safe. Paul Johnson's late try, created by a 40-metre burst by Luke Robinson and then some deft handling by Pongia, was cruel on the Tigers, giving the final scoreline a lopsided look.

Leeds loanee Peter Lupton made his Hull debut in a one-sided 44-4 thrashing of Wakefield - missing first-choice halves Brad Davis and Jamie Rooney - on the Thursday night at the KC Stadium. Gareth Raynor made his second appearance of the season after moving back permanently from rugby union and helped himself to a try.

The Wolves and Giants played out an enthralling contest at an exhilarating pace at Wilderspool on the Saturday afternoon. The game could have gone either way after Rob Smyth's 76th minute touchdown looked to have sewn the game up for the Wolves.

But after Brandon Costin went in a minute from time the visitors only trailed by four points and they got a chance to have a further crack at the Wolves when Paul March stole possession from Dean Gaskell. Giants' wingman Hefin O'Hare subsequently went close to the Wolves line but from the resulting play-the-ball Ben Roarty knocked on - as the Wolves defence appeared to be offside - and the full-time hooter soon sounded.

SUPER LEAGUE TABLE - *Sunday 29th June*

	P	W	D	L	F	A	D	PTS
Leeds Rhinos	16	12	2	2	417	315	102	26
Bradford Bulls	15	11	0	4	440	306	134	22
Wigan Warriors	16	10	1	5	413	344	69	21
Hull FC *	16	10	2	4	447	256	191	20
London Broncos	14	8	0	6	342	335	7	16
St Helens *	16	8	1	7	525	280	245	15
Castleford Tigers	16	7	1	8	338	342	-4	15
Warrington Wolves	16	7	1	8	368	392	-24	15
Widnes Vikings	16	7	0	9	379	398	-19	14
Huddersfield Giants	15	5	0	10	309	428	-119	10
Wakefield T Wildcats	16	4	0	12	229	414	-185	8
Halifax *	16	1	0	15	238	635	-397	0

* two points deducted for 2002 salary cap breach

The win meant a chasing pack of London Broncos, St Helens, Castleford, the Wolves and Widnes Vikings were separated by just two points going into July

* May was also the month when it was decided Cardiff's Millennium Stadium would stage the Powergen Challenge Cup final for a second successive year, on Saturday 15 May 2004.

"We are due to return to Wembley in 2006, but we have built into this new agreement the option of playing at the Millennium Stadium in 2005 and 2006, should Wembley's rebuilding run into any unforeseen delays," said RFL Executive Chairman Richard Lewis.

JULY
Bulls back on top

BSkyB raised their offer for TV coverage of Super League and internationals to £55 million, but with the RFL still negotiating with the BBC, clubs were still unsure of their budgets for 2004, in the week the transfer window opened.

Clubs feared they would inadvertently exceed the salary cap - ironically in a week where St Helens, Halifax and Hull were preparing their appeals against salary cap points deductions.

One player whose future was publicly up for grabs was Castleford captain Danny Orr, with the Tigers moving heaven and earth to try and keep him at the Jungle.

After Cas had beaten Halifax 38-12 at the Jungle on the first Sunday in July to move back into sixth, Tigers supporters were of the opinion they already had a replacement for Orr, strongly tipped to leave at the end of the season, as Jon Hepworth - a local product from Castleford Panthers on loan from the Rhinos - highlighted a good all-round display with two outstanding solo tries. Halifax were the Tigers' equals for almost an hour. Then they were shot down by a five-try blitz that sent them to their 16th successive defeat. Tony Anderson's men had hit back in great style after going 10-0 down in ten minutes to lead 12-10 midway through the first half and be level with 24 points shared at half-time.

Leeds stayed four points clear of Bradford at the top with a 30-20 win over the Wolves at Headingley. In the comparative match the previous season, Lee Briers' last-gasp field goal clinched victory and his two touchdowns in four minutes around the hour mark nearly salvaged this seemingly lost cause.

Briers' excellent contribution made an interesting comparison with that of his opposite number Danny McGuire, starting in his favoured position of stand-off, for the first time in tandem with Rob Burrow. The Leeds prodigy showed some excellent touches up to his withdrawal for Kevin Sinfield in the 47th minute, his pass to put Keith Senior clear for Francis Cummins' try a gem.

When McGuire left the fray, Leeds were 22-8 ahead - which soon became 28-8 when Chris McKenna crossed. In the end, after Briers' heroics, the league leaders secured the points courtesy of a late David Furner penalty.

Bradford Bulls awoke from the nightmare of three comprehensive home defeats to reassert their position among the front-runners for the Minor Premiership with an ultimately comfortable 30-18 victory at Belle Vue. Fullback Leon Pryce's break from halfway, immediately after the restart, gave the Bulls the belief and momentum that has recently been missing, and inspired two tries shortly afterwards which opened up a decisive 26-12 advantage.

Brett Dallas put weeks of frustration behind him with a sensational return to

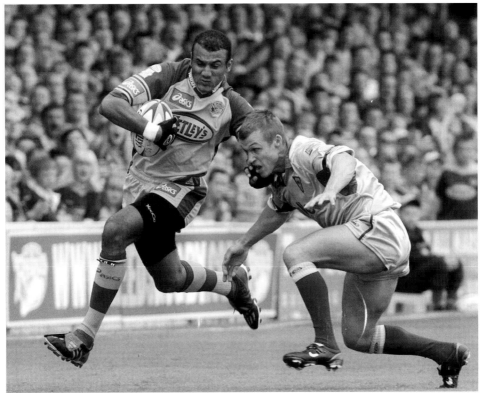

Leeds' Mark Calderwood fends off Warrington's Dean Gaskell as the Rhinos see off the brave Wolves

action after injury at the McAlpine Stadium but the Giants ruined his day with an outstanding 32-24 victory, their first over Wigan for 22 years.

Dallas returned to the Warriors ranks after a hamstring injury, determined to win another contract at the JJB after turning down the chance to return to the NRL with Cronulla, scoring a brilliant hat-trick, as well as creating Wigan's opening try.

But the Giants, with stand-out performances by two-try Brandon Costin, Stanley Gene and Paul March, earned perhaps their best win of the Super League era.

St Helens coach Ian Millward confessed he felt "victimised" after being censured twice in a week by Rugby Football League bosses. Millward was reprimanded for leaving his seat in the stand to go to the touchline during recent Super League matches. The RFL told Millward any coach who wants to go to the dugout at any stage of the game must be named in the ten staff permitted to sit on the touchline on the official teamsheet. And then his team were fined £300 - £100 a minute - for a late kick-off against Halifax.

Nevertheless Saints gave the Vikings a first-half lesson in finishing on the Friday night of Round 17 as they continued their revival with a third successive win - by 32-18 - at Knowsley Road.

The reigning Champions moved into a decisive 24-0 interval lead on the back of some ruthless execution, while the Vikings had nothing to show for several spells of sustained pressure. Though Widnes had the better of the second half, re-creating some of the momentum of their splendid win over Leeds, the damage had been done.

And in the Saturday TV game London Broncos, having lost their fight to keep Australian centre Tony Martin, who was joining New Zealand Warriors for next season, got their first point of the season on their home ground, Griffin Park. But London, and most of the TV audience, thought they deserved more from a 20-20 draw with Hull.

With the scores tied and time running out, Dennis Moran chased his own kick with the Hull line, and glory, at his mercy. Colin Best - slotting in at fullback after skipper Richie Barnett, carrying a knock into the game, left the fray, and who played a major part in nearly every scoring incident - clearly gave Moran's shirt a tug. To everyone's amazement, referee Steve Ganson waved away appeals for what surely would have been a match-winning penalty with only seconds left on the clock.

Broncos scrum-half Chris Thorman was once again a bag of tricks, showing some wonderful individual touches to celebrate his call-up that week to the Great Britain squad on the back of his whirlwind performance in Yorkshire's 56-6 Origin win.

Hull suffered another injury blow in their 46-10 Round 18 defeat at Widnes Vikings, when their new signing from Halifax, Shayne McMenemy, suffered a dislocated elbow on his debut.

And fullback Steve Prescott, who had been in sensational form with 13 tries and 71 goals from 16 games, was injured in the Origin Game at the start of the month, originally diagnosed as suffering a dislocated knee-cap. The club found that Prescott had in fact broken his knee-cap and was out for the season.

The Vikings left Super League's best defensive record in tatters with a red-hot attacking display as Jules O'Neill put on a master-class of the stand-off's art, collecting 18 points from another wonderful individual performance, in a 46-10 win. Adam Hughes scored two tries as the Vikings put injury-hit Hull to the sword, romping into an unassailable 34-6 interval lead.

The only blot on a wonderful afternoon for the Vikings came with six minutes remaining when Anthony Farrell was sent off for a high tackle on Dean Treister. Farrell was found guilty but escaped a ban.

At the McAlpine Stadium, the Giants claimed another big four scalp as a 79th minute Brandon Costin try sealed their first win over Leeds for 38 years, by 30-24. Huddersfield should have been home and dry at 24-12 with 13 minutes to play, before scores from Wayne McDonald and David Furner threw the Rhinos a late lifeline. Then Costin - after seeing a field-goal attempt charged down moments earlier - took on the Rhinos defence and reached out to score despite a two-man tackle.

The Bulls moved within two points of the Rhinos - with the Round 7 game at London still in hand - as they hammered Halifax at the Shay 60-12. Injury-hit Fax had suffered another blow with the news that young halfback Simon Grix broke his wrist and were considering taking disciplinary action against stay-away centre Danny Halliwell.

Wigan took advantage of Hull's fall from grace by beating Wakefield 38-12.

The Warriors' defeat at Huddersfield had gone down badly in the corridors of power at the JJB, just like the defeats at London and Salford that spelt the end of Frank Endacott's coaching reign the previous year.

As if to prove the point, club owner Dave Whelan made an extraordinary on-pitch address to the Wigan players during the warm-up. Whelan walked down the tunnel and across to the far corner of the well-manicured JJB Stadium pitch, gathered the players around him for a brief moment while he said a few words, and then walked off again.

When the Wildcats fought back from 16-0 down to trail only 16-12 early in the second half, some of the Warriors faithful were getting edgy. But a three-try scoring flurry saw Wigan stretch away before the outstanding Adrian Lam scored the only try of a scrappy final quarter. Lam, so often the try creator, bagged a brace, as did Brett Dallas, who took his tally to five in his last two games since returning from a troublesome hamstring.

In a game expected to be too tight to call, the Lee Briers-inspired Wolves wiped the floor with London in a 50-8 win. The Wolves ran in eight tries with Darren Burns, Rob Smyth and Briers all bagging braces, whilst Briers also booted nine goals in his gamestar performance.

But after the game, X-rays revealed that Briers had broken his left wrist five minutes into the second half and was expected to be sidelined for eight weeks.

Warrington were back in the top-six as Castleford had been beaten at home by St Helens the previous Friday. Danny Orr gave Castleford Tigers fans something extra to remember him by with a superb performance that included the first hat-trick of his career, even though Saints won 46-32.

Only 48 hours earlier Orr had admitted he would not be playing for Cas next year after being lured away by another top Super League club, which turned out to be Wigan, and not Hull, who had also tried to entice him. But he showed he was still totally committed to the Tigers' cause by turning in one of his best ever displays. With six goals for a total of 24 points plus a big say in another try, even those who jeered him at the start were cheering him long before the finish.

Orr's supreme effort was all in vain as St Helens produced a much greater team display with a spectacular eight-try onslaught that stretched their winning run to four matches. Their poor form of a few weeks ago was a distant memory. Although Orr took all the headlines, Sean Long ran him very close for match honours in a captivating stand-off duel. A 55-metre interception try and seven goals was Long's scoring haul, but he produced much more, including setting up the first try for halfback partner Mick Higham. The Saints' winning run had begun when the pair was brought together for the first time and they now looked inseparable. Higham's switch to scrum-half meant he had conceded the hooker role to Keiron Cunningham, but they were working well together. Never better than when Cunningham thundered 30 metres before passing inside for Higham to notch his second try.

Saints fullback Paul Wellens gave Great Britain coach David Waite another nudge after being left out of his initial Test squad with a couple of well-taken tries that would have stretched to a hat-trick but for a video call going against him.

July

Wigan coach Stuart Raper denied he would be leaving Wigan after his side had won a terrific 28-12 Round 19 victory in the Friday night game in London.

"I'm not going to comment on something that keeps on coming up because I'm just about sick of it. I stand by everything that I said in the week and I still expect to be at Wigan next season," he said.

But on the bus back from the capital, Raper told his stunned players he was leaving. And by Saturday, Wigan had admitted Raper was to go. Chairman Maurice Lindsay was keen to avoid talking about who could take over from Raper. "Stuart is the hardest working coach I've ever known, and he still has plenty of time to go with us before the end of the season," said Lindsay.

Speculation was mounting that former Wigan favourite Ellery Hanley could be in line for the job.

Adrian Lam led from the front as the Warriors chalked up their second successive victory, himself still due to make a decision about his future. Meanwhile the Broncos were still looking for their first home win of the season. Brett Dallas had flown home to Australia to be with his seriously ill mother, as Wigan confirmed they had withdrawn their offer for Australian Test centre Mark Gasnier and signed 21 year old threequarter Martin Aspinwall to a two year deal.

The top-five teams all won their games. Leaders Leeds had no trouble beating Halifax 54-6 at Headingley, with Wayne McDonald celebrating his new two-year deal at the club with a towering performance. David Furner had also agreed a one year extension to his contract.

Fax - with young loan players from St Helens, Jon Hill and Chris Maye, on debut - had set a new unwanted record - 18 successive Super League defeats.

Bradford signalled their intentions of making Odsal a fortress again with a 40-8 victory that dented the resurgent Vikings' play-off aspirations. Lesley Vainikolo's awesome power saw him score two tries, with Paul Deacon producing a superb display at halfback behind a tremendous pack, in which Paul Anderson, Joe Vagana, Daniel Gartner and two-try Lee Radford were especially impressive.

Hull skipper Jason Smith - making his first team return following a three-month injury lay-off - was the victim of a big Paul Noone hit after only his second touch of the ball in the home tie with Warrington. Smith was stretchered off less than a minute after he took the field, and Hull fans were fuming when referee Russell Smith decided to only place Noone on report. It was the correct decision as Noone was later found to have no case to answer. Hull went on to win 38-14.

And the weekend following the rejection of their appeal against the salary cap points deduction, St Helens farewelled Tommy Martyn and then staged the kind of dramatic late, late show of which their departed hero would have been proud, securing a 22-18 win over the Giants.

Martyn was afforded a wonderful pre-match send-off from the Knowsley Road fans and a fine speech from Chairman Eamonn McManus to mark his honour-laden ten-year Saints career that had ended with his recent move to Leigh.

Saints' fifth successive win was achieved in heart-stopping fashion and matched almost any of their famous last-gasp recovery bids of recent times. Paul Wellens was the Saints hero this time around, stretching over to score in the left corner with just two minutes remaining of a pulsating match, after Sean Long and Keiron Cunningham provided the opening with deft passing. Long's touchline conversion rubbed salt in the Giants wounds. It was the first time they had trailed in the match.

A still under-strength Castleford ran in six tries, with young hooker Wayne Godwin grabbing two in three minutes late on, to win 32-4 at Wakefield. The Tigers were inspired by Ryan Hudson in his first match as club captain.

That week the RFL named Keiron Cunningham of St Helens and Matt Calland as the un-named players who had appeared at Doping Control hearings but had not subsequently named after being found guilty.

Cunningham was found guilty of having provided a sample containing traces of hormone substance HCG. The Panel, which is independent of the RFL, fined him £2,500 and gave him a one-year ban suspended for one year. The panel accepted there were mitigating circumstances, which were a factor in determining the punishment.

Calland was found guilty of providing a sample containing nandrolone. He received a six-month suspended ban which expired at the end of December 2003. Calland denied knowingly taking the substance.

Cunningham himself explained the 'mitigating circumstances' surrounding his positive test. He had been administered the substance in June 2002 by a dietician employed by the RFL, who had also been recommended to his club. The substance was given as a purported fat burner to keep his weight down whilst recovering from a broken hand.   "I was under pressure to be fit for the one-off test against Australia, and was told that the substance was natural and approved," Cunningham said.

The 'News of the World' alleged that the dietician, Mike Sutherland, employed full-time as a fireman in Bolton, had been given a 12-month contract by the RFL in October 2002, but without any checks being taken on his qualifications. Sutherland had first been involved with Great Britain for the 2001 Ashes series against Australia. RFL Executive Chairman Richard Lewis admitted that the RFL had been at fault.

Cunningham took on the vice-captaincy at Belle Vue, where St Helens were 36-15 winners over Wakefield, after Trinity - with three Academy players on debut, Mark Field, Matthew Blake and Darren Jordan - led 14-0 early on.

The Broncos had to play two games in four days, with their Round 15 catchup game against Huddersfield on the Tuesday - which they won 32-16 to register their first home success in the capital for ten months, thanks in the main to a brilliant display from Chris Thorman.

And on the Friday - with Wood Green youngster Joe Mbu looking assured on his debut and Dennis Moran scoring two tries - they went down 27-22 at Headingley, Andrew King's disputed try three minutes from time putting only a converted score between the sides. Leeds announced that week they had signed Papua New Guinea Test winger Marcus Bai, all-time leading tryscorer at his current club Melbourne Storm, on a two-year deal.

Hull slipped out of the top four as the Giants registered a fifth successive home success - a 30-14 win at the McAlpine. Steve McNamara was the pivotal figure against his home-town club, justifying his decision to carry on his playing

Widnes' Deon Bird tackled by Wigan's Gareth Hock and Terry Newton during Stuart Raper's last game

career after the Giants' promotion season last year.

Giants coach Tony Smith said he would decide that week whether he was prepared to sign a new contract to stay at the McAlpine Stadium for another year.

Widnes's first success on Wigan soil for over 13 years and their first win over Wigan in 18 attempts, proved to be the last straw for Warriors boss Stuart Raper.

Halfbacks Ryan Sheridan and Jules O'Neill were the Widnes stars in the 22-18 win, alongside hooker Shane Millard. Sheridan returned after a five-match absence with an ankle injury to replace Dean Lawford, who now entered hospital for surgery on a double hernia.

Raper was sacked the following Monday and replaced, on a temporary basis, by his assistant Mike Gregory.

A dejected Tony Anderson couldn't face the after-match press conference following Halifax's 66-6 mauling at Wilderspool, instead favouring an early return to the team bus. Graham Appo's 34 points included four tries. To deepen the gloom at the Shay, Martin Moana left to join NL1 favourites Salford City Reds.

Danny Orr looked like he had played his last match for Castleford Tigers after it was thought he had broken an arm in two places in a 40-20 home defeat by Bradford. However, after X-rays, the injury proved to be a broken metacarpal.

And on the Wednesday in the Round 7 catch-up game, Leon Pryce was in unstoppable form, finishing with a four-try haul in a 60-6 mauling of London at Brentford. The result put Bradford at the top of the table thanks to their superior points difference over the Rhinos.

SUPER LEAGUE TABLE - *Wednesday 30th July*

	P	W	D	L	F	A	D	PTS
Bradford Bulls	20	16	0	4	670	370	300	32
Leeds Rhinos	20	15	2	3	552	393	159	32
Wigan Warriors	20	12	1	7	521	422	99	25
St Helens *	20	12	1	7	661	363	298	23
Hull FC *	20	11	3	6	529	366	163	23
Warrington Wolves	20	9	1	10	518	474	44	19
Castleford Tigers	20	9	1	10	460	444	16	19
London Broncos	20	9	1	10	442	536	-94	19
Widnes Vikings	20	9	0	11	473	498	-25	18
Huddersfield Giants	20	8	0	12	435	544	-109	16
Wakefield T Wildcats	20	4	0	16	278	550	-272	8
Halifax *	20	1	0	19	274	853	-579	0

* two points deducted for 2002 salary cap breach

AUGUST
High summer drama

It was a busy week for coaching appointments. As well as Mike Gregory's promotion at Wigan, Tony Smith was appointed new boss at Leeds Rhinos for 2004 and 2005, with current coach Daryl Powell moving upstairs, to become Director of Rugby.

Saints assistant Jon Sharp was duly unveiled as Huddersfield Giants coach for 2004.

London's Chris Thorman also sprung a surprise when he announced that he had turned down Hull to join Parramatta Eels in the NRL in 2004.

But those stories were overshadowed by the shock jailing of Leeds duo Ryan Bailey and Chev Walker - both of whom were in David Waite's initial GB squad - along with Rochdale fullback Paul Owen, after they pleaded guilty to violent disorder.

The severity of the sentences stunned the players, their clubs and the whole world of Rugby League. Walker and Bailey eventually decided not to appeal against the decision by Paul Batty QC to jail them for 18 months and nine months respectively at Leeds Crown Court for what the judge called "mindless, dangerous and drunken violence", following a fight between the two players and their fellow Rhinos player Dwayne Barker, who received 150 hours community service, and Owen, who was hit with 15-month jail sentence.

The turmoil made Leeds' must-win Round 21 game at Hull on the Saturday night all the more important and they showed great resolve to emerge with a 26-12 win that put them two points clear of Bradford - at least until the Bulls' 30-16 win over Huddersfield on the Sunday.

Hull went into the match with 13 first-team squad players unavailable because of injury and at least seven of them would have been in the starting line-up. Yet the Airlie Birds pushed Leeds all the way and were still in with a chance of a shock victory until they conceded two late tries.

After the game Hull - looking nervous in fifth place with a stiff run-in - placed a bizarre media ban on reporting injury news at the club.

Paul Deacon led the way as the Bulls tuned up for their Round 22 summit clash at Headingley the following Friday by regaining the Super League leadership, beating the Giants 30-16 on a glorious summer's evening at Odsal. Deacon underlined his recent golden spell of form with two tries and five goals from six attempts to lead the Bulls' first-half demolition of a Giants side searching fruitlessly for their first win at Odsal for nearly 34 years.

The Giants still had an outside chance of the play-offs, at the back of a queue headed by Widnes Vikings, with the Wolves, Tigers and Broncos in between.

Widnes took their turn in sixth spot after beating the Tigers 27-16 at Halton Stadium. The Vikings had given their worst display of the season when losing 40-2 at the Jungle in mid-May and so the win was especially satisfying, as tries by Adam Hughes, Paul Devlin (his second of the game) and Dan Potter in the last 17 minutes saw Widnes recover from a Mitch Healey-inspired Tigers lead of 16-12. That week Castleford revealed that Newcastle Knights stand-off Sean Rudder would join them for 2004 and 2005.

Mike Gregory got his first-grade coaching career off to a fine start as Wigan won an excellent game at Warrington - where Gregory had spent 15 years as a player - 18-16.

Craig Smith proved the difference, his 73rd minute try bringing the visitors level and leaving Andy Farrell, Wigan's best, with a simple conversion to win the game.

Saints registered their seventh straight win - by 30-18 after staging a second-half revival in London against the weary Broncos, with Ian Millward's side coming from behind to run in 18-unanswered points in a ten-minute spell. The Broncos, still tired from their humiliation against Bradford Bulls only four days before, managed a much-improved performance.

And Halifax were left ten points adrift at the bottom with just seven games to play after they went down to Wakefield at the Shay in a Friday night game.

Injury-depleted Wakefield ended their own run of seven consecutive defeats and clinched their first win since June 8. They were missing prop Michael Korkidas, serving a one-match suspension after his send-off in the home defeat against St Helens, but halfbacks Ben Jeffries - back to form after a nervy few weeks - and Jamie Rooney exploited every opening to the full.

At the end of a week when Danny Halliwell became the latest Fax player to jump from the sinking ship.

In a strange press conference after his side's 28-18 victory over Hull on the Saturday of Round 22, Saints coach Ian Millward swore 30 times in under five minutes, alleged the "powers that be" were conspiring against his club, and declared Saints had no chance of winning Super League.

Jon Wilkin had scored two long-range second-half tries as St Helens made it eight consecutive wins with a gutsy, if unspectacular victory. But Millward, missing five key players in Paul Sculthorpe, Darren Smith, Martin Gleeson, Chris Joynt and Paul Newlove lost prop Darren Britt with a serious face injury inside the first minute.

And that was the reason for Millward's black mood. Already understrength at prop, Millward had been trying to persuade the experienced Aussie to sign for one more season, but the 34 year old was forced to retire from the game when the extent of his injury became clear.

Saints were looking safe in fourth, but Hull were left only two points clear of Warrington, who struck a significant blow as they beat Castleford on their own patch. Three tries in four minutes either side of half-time put a Nathan Wood-inspired Warrington on the way to a 29-16 victory.

The Wolves leapt over Widnes, who managed a 30-30 draw at Huddersfield.

Huddersfield were dealt a blow beforehand with the news that inspirational stand off Brandon Costin - who received his award as Rugby Leaguer & League Express Super League player of the Month for July at half-time - was to be deprived of his opportunity to break Super League's scoring run due to a shoulder problem. If he had crossed he would have scored in the last ten of the Giants' Super League fixtures, beating the record of nine held by Paul Newlove, Anthony Sullivan and Paul Sterling. Giants boss Tony Smith handed a debut to former Bradford Bull Craig McDowell, whilst England Student international Chris Plume was an unused substitute.

Wakefield snatched their first home point for over two months with a dramatic Michael Korkidas try in the dying seconds of a pulsating 26-all draw with the Broncos in tortuously hot conditions at Belle Vue.

Wigan warmed up for their upcoming clashes with Leeds and Bradford with a comfortable 40-0 victory over National League-bound Halifax in Mike Gregory's first home game in charge.

The game was effectively over when the Warriors ran in three tries in ten minutes midway through the first half through Stephen Wild, two, and Brett Dallas, and Andy Farrell and Shaun Briscoe added two more scores to secure an interval lead of 30-0.

However dogged resistance from Halifax - who had three players on debut in Byron Smith, Wayne Corcoran and on-loan from Huddersfield Rikki Sheriffe - restricted the Warriors to just 10 points in the second half.

But the big game of the weekend was the Leeds-Bradford clash at Headingley on the Friday night, a pulsating game that the Bulls edged 18-16 in front of over 23,000 spellbound supporters.

Stuart Reardon had a stormer at fullback and his fearsome tackle that pushed the breaking Danny McGuire into touch just before half-time was the gamebreaking moment. A Leeds try then would have given them a 16-6 lead at the break, Gary Connolly - playing his 500th senior game - and Keith Senior scoring first-half tries.

But the Bulls battled back and sealed the win, despite a try from the fizzing Rob Burrow, with tries straight after the break from Rob Parker and Mike Forshaw.

The Bulls were two points clear at the top of the table.

The decision of the Super League clubs two season before to bolt on six more fixtures at the end of the season had its critics, but the quality of the games ensured some healthy crowds and TV audiences.

Leeds and Wigan played out their second 24-all draw of the season at Headingley. With Wigan leading 24-20 and barely a minute left, Andrew Dunemann instigated a runaround in his own quarter with the colossal Keith Senior, before shooting through a gap and bursting to half way with Danny McGuire on his outside. Electing to kick, his accuracy and weight on the ball was near perfect, the young prodigy showing astonishing pace, balance and presence to burn off the cover, gather at speed and touch down wide out. Kevin Sinfield's missed conversion, to go with a failed penalty attempt in the 41st minute, meant that honour was satisfied.

Lesley Vainikolo pulled Bradford Bulls through 36-22 as battling Hull threatened register a shock victory at Odsal on the Saturday night. The Super League leaders trailed 22-16 going into the last 24 minutes as Vainikolo who powered in for two tries to complete his hat-trick. Vainikolo also launched sub Lee Gilmour on the way to the second of his two tries. The attendance of 10,478 was Super League's record-extending 40th five-figure crowd of the season.

The shake-up for the top-six became even more exciting as London Broncos beat Warrington 19-12 at Griffin Park. London skipper Jim Dymock - who had signed a new one-year contract midweek - was the star man. Dennis Moran was also tied to a new three-year deal in the week, as the Broncos also gave a debut to Wests Tigers prop Steve Trindall.

A 30-28 Widnes home win over Wakefield saw them replace Warrington in sixth. In the end, the Vikings were grateful for three tries either side of the interval - two from Anthony Farrell and one from Andy Hay which had pushed the home side into a seemingly unassailable lead, before a Jamie Rooney-inspired Wakefield launched an amazing comeback from 30-10 down to trail by just two points for a tense last nine minutes, with Rooney netting a try hat-trick and six goals.

Castleford were looking increasingly adrift after a 26-10 defeat at St Helens on the Friday night. Saints fans paid tribute to retiring prop Darren Britt, but it was the surprise return of another hero, Paul Newlove - out since dislocating his thumb against Wigan on June 6th - that proved decisive in sparking Saints' ninth win in a row.

Cas were missing a posse of players too, as Darren Rogers, Lee Harland, Danny Orr, Jamie Thackray, Mark Lennon, Jon Hepworth and Paul Jackson all sat out the game.

Halifax were condemned to National League One rugby as Huddersfield hammered them 54-12 at the Shay. The Giants were still not out of the play-off reckoning and when Stanley Gene stepped through for his hat-trick try on the hooter, and Jamie Bloem converted, it brought up the club's highest ever Super League score.

With Daryl Cardiss joining Warrington Wolves, and with Stuart Donlan (thumb ligaments), Heath Cruckshank (shoulder), Dane Dorahy (dead leg) and Andrew Frew (groin) on the injured list, Tony Anderson was forced to name no fewer than twelve players under the age of 21, including seven teenagers. Brad Attwood came off the bench for his debut, while Rikki Sheriffe, Byron Smith and Wayne Corcoran made their home bows.

The match was the last attended by Stephen Pearson, the leader of the advisory committee running Halifax and the acting chief executive of the club, who was facing a battle for his life after being diagnosed with cancer of the kidneys. Pearson, the man responsible for saving the club from financial ruin, attended in a wheelchair, and was given an emotional reception by the home supporters. He died the following week, only ten days after his illness as diagnosed.

London Broncos were back in sixth spot as they picked up a 26-12 win at the Shay. At the end of a dreadful few days in which 'Fax were mathematically relegated; handed a £1,000 suspended fine and told to pay £270 costs by an RFL Advisory Panel hearing for a programme article earlier in the year which attacked Bradford as the "retards" from "Odslum"; and then suffered the tragic loss of Stephen Pearson - a minute's silence was held that Friday night in his memory - coach Tony Anderson, who signed a new contract in the week, saw his youthful charges put in a performance which provided Fax with their first scent of possible success since a two-point defeat at Huddersfield in early June. Until Jim Dymock steadied the Broncos ship and Dennis Moran and Tony Martin scored late tries. London gave a debut on the wing to new signing Joel Caine from Wests Tigers and also signed former St Helens hooker Dave McConnell from Chorley Lynx.

After the game Anderson slammed some of his Super League rivals, who he accused of poaching some of his club's brightest young stars throughout the season.

Castleford Tigers had a must-win game at home to Leeds and five tries in the first 33 incredible minutes left Leeds trailing 24-0, mesmerised by the wiles of Mitch Healey and crushed by the power of Castleford's forwards. Leeds gave a debut to union winger Liam Botham, who had trialled with Bradford and interested London earlier in the season but he made little impact as the Tigers ran out 28-20 winners.

The Rhinos' stumble gave Bradford a chance to move five points clear at the top on the Bank Holiday Monday but Kris Radlinski - returning from a 14-week absence - inspired Wigan to a 26-12 win at the JJB stadium. And Andy Farrell pronounced himself fit and played a classic captain's role, scoring a 59th minute try that quickly dispelled any Bradford thoughts of a quick comeback after they trailed 10-0 at the break.

The previous Saturday, Warrington made it three derby wins on the trot against their oldest foes from Widnes, who having built up a ten-point lead then fell off the pace as the Wolves ended 30-16 winners.

Warrington had come under fire from Widnes fans for an official promotional poster for the game featuring a cartoon drawing of the Widnes skyline, adorned with clouds of smoke and green slime suggestive of chemical waste - an idea reinforced by images of a three-eyed fish and a barrel of toxic waste.   B e n Westwood's try three minutes from time finally settled an exciting affair.

Hull had to beat St Helens at the KC Stadium to avoid dropping to sixth spot. And after a 42-18 defeat ended St Helens nine-match winning run, coach Ian Millward declared that Saints could not win Super League this year. One high point for St Helens was the debut of Willie Talau, who had sacrificed his New Zealand Test spot to join St Helens six months ahead of schedule.

And Huddersfield Giants continued their challenge for a play-off spot by completing a hat-trick of victories over the Wildcats in Super League VIII on a sunny Sunday evening at the McAlpine Stadium.

Despite losing the inspirational Brandon Costin for the rest of the campaign with a shoulder injury, the Giants looked confident and committed from the off and hometown hero Darren Turner, celebrating his benefit year, grabbed a rare share of the limelight with two tries as his side built an 18-4 lead just after the half-hour mark of a fiercely contested game.

With games to come against fellow play-off contenders Castleford, Widnes, Warrington and London, the Giants were outside bets for the play-offs.

The Giants stumbled at the first hurdle as the Tigers beat them 26-28 in the Friday TV game at the Jungle. Huddersfield who were left licking their wounds, most notably a suspected fractured cheekbone sustained by Stanley Gene.

They also suffered a self-inflicted blow when Jim Gannon was sent off in the 67th minute for a high tackle, although he escaped a ban, and Craig Huby's penalty goal gave Castleford an 18-12 lead. Until then Huddersfield always looked capable of snatching victory.

The Broncos remained in sixth, despite going down heavily for the second time in a month to the Bulls. London's Steele Retchless touched down on his club record equalling 171st appearance to give them a lead but the Bulls scored nine tries, six of which came after the break.

Warrington's chance to move into the top-six had gone in a 34-26 defeat at Headingley on the Friday night. Graham Appo was in magnificent form in the third rip-roaring encounter of the season between the sides. Andrew Dunemann's late try ensured the Rhinos' victory.

St Helens maintained their 100 per cent record over the Vikings in Super League with a superb 40-4 win at Halton Stadium to consolidate their top-four place. After earning a hard fought 4-0 lead at the break, courtesy of a Keiron Cunningham try, Saints cut loose to post six second-half tries, all converted by stand-in skipper Sean Long, in a derby played in front of Widnes's biggest Super League crowd, 9,457.

Wigan kept in third place and their hopes of finishing higher with the expected landslide victory at hapless Halifax, 68-12. Danny Tickle helped turn the screw and pile on the agony with ten goals and a 24-point personal haul against his old team.

And in the Saturday TV game Hull's play-off hopes were struck a blow when Wakefield beat them 35-28 at Belle Vue.

SUPER LEAGUE TABLE - *Sunday 31st August*

	P	W	D	L	F	A	D	PTS
Bradford Bulls	25	20	0	5	820	462	358	40
Leeds Rhinos	25	17	3	5	672	501	171	37
Wigan Warriors	25	16	2	7	697	486	211	34
St Helens *	25	16	1	8	803	455	348	31
Hull FC *	25	12	3	10	651	509	142	25
London Broncos	25	11	2	12	543	670	-127	24
Warrington Wolves	25	11	1	13	631	577	54	23
Castleford Tigers	25	11	1	13	556	564	-8	23
Widnes Vikings	25	11	1	13	580	642	-62	23
Huddersfield Giants	25	10	1	14	579	656	-77	21
Wakefield T Wildcats	25	6	1	18	411	678	-267	13
Halifax *	25	1	0	24	328	1071	-743	0

* two points deducted for 2002 salary cap breach

A difficult week had seen the Wildcats release player-coach Adrian Vowles and experienced squad members Matt Seers and Waisale Sovatabua; Jon Wells sign for London; Brad Davis set to decide on an offer to go to Villeneuve; and the future of Trinity football manager Shane McNally was still up in the air. But Michael Korkidas set the lead up front and Jamie Rooney provided the craft in an enthusiastic performance that featured a try-scoring trialist's debut from French international Sylvain Houles.

SEPTEMBER
Too close to call

Bradford Bulls duly secured the Minor Premiership with a thrilling last-gasp 22-21 victory in Round 26 over the Rhinos on a memorable Sunday evening at Odsal. The Rhinos were left to look anxiously over their shoulders at resurgent Wigan with two games to go.

The Bulls' fourth win of the season over the Rhinos, including the Challenge Cup Final, was watched by another huge Odsal crowd of 21,102, their third 20,000 plus home gate of the campaign - a new Super League record.

Leeds looked to be in the driving seat when Joe Vagana was deemed guilty of reefing in a two-man tackle on Barrie McDermott as the Leeds prop tried to offload. Kevin Sinfield's penalty made it 14-14 as James Lowes, stand-in skipper in the continuing absence of the injured Robbie Paul, made his way to the sin bin after voicing his disapproval of the decision to referee Steve Ganson. Sinfield received then potted a close-range field goal, via the bar. But with Lowes sitting, arms folded, on the bench Anderson briefly took over his role at dummy-half and passed for Deacon to tie the scores with a firmly-struck field goal from in front of the posts, with 14 minutes remaining. Lesley Vainikolo and Sinfield swapped tries and Sinfield kept his nerve to tie the scores again with the conversion, with five minutes left.

But there was one more twist and when McDermott lost the ball 20 metres from his own line, his coach's face on the big screen told a thousand words. The Bulls kept their nerve and worked the position for Deacon to send the match-winning 20-metre field goal soaring through the night sky, with 139 seconds left on the clock.

St Helens were almost assured of fourth spot even though they lost for the third time in the season to Wigan, the Warriors winning 28-4 winners at Knowsley Road on the Friday to ensure they'd finish at least third, with two games to go and a point behind the Rhinos. Wigan, back to full strength, seized the initiative from the off to exploit Saints' lack of a recognised prop forward - Keith Mason staring on the bench. Craig Smith and Quentin Pongia took full advantage, both players putting in hugely influential displays in a tough front row that featured another top display from Terry Newton, with Terry O'Connor making a big impact as a sub.

The Warriors' win was especially pleasing for coach Mike Gregory, as it was achieved largely without the help of Adrian Lam and skipper Andrew Farrell. Lam, returning after four weeks out with ankle trouble, was forced out of the action at half-time to allow Luke Robinson another opportunity to reveal his huge talent, while Farrell managed just 24 minutes of first-half action in two spells before succumbing to a knee injury.

Six clubs were still vying for the remaining two play-off spots.

Two of them, Hull and Castleford, met at the KC Stadium, with the home side hanging on in fifth position with a 32-12 win. Paul Cooke - the club's third-choice kicker in the absence of injured duo Matt Crowther and Steve Prescott - landed seven goals from eight attempts.

Hull duo Sean Ryan and Craig Greenhill, and Michael Eagar of Cas all lined up against the clubs they were to join the following season, while Danny Orr was roundly booed by the home fans after choosing Wigan over the Airlie Birds earlier this year.

One player not lacking support was Adrian Vowles - given a hero's welcome by the considerable travelling Castleford contingent on his Tigers return.

The Giants leapfrogged Widnes on points difference after beating them 25-22 at the McAlpine, as Widnes coach Neil Kelly admitted his side's play-off chances had all but vanished; Warrington beat Halifax 40-18; and Dennis Moran scored his second hat-trick of the season against Wakefield - his fourth of the year - in a 38-14 home win.

And in a piece of history, Bridgend Blue Bulls, led by former Great Britain internationals Kevin Ellis and Allan Bateman, defeated Carlisle Centurions 33-26 in the final of the Harry Jepson Trophy, to become the first Welsh champions of the TotalRL.com Conference.

On their own insistence, the Bulls were presented with the new League Leaders Shield after their final regular season Round 27 home game against Castleford Tigers.

But if the Bulls fans had thought that the Tigers would prove to be accommodating guests, they were sadly mistaken as Cas ran out 28-12 winners, Andy Lynch giving another eye-catching display at prop and Danny Orr, in his penultimate game for the club, a hugely important influence. Skipper Ryan Hudson, the lively Wayne Godwin and the experienced war horses Mitch Healey and Adrian Vowles were other stand-outs for the Tigers.

Wins for Warrington on the Friday and London the following day meant it was all in vain for Cas. Huddersfield and Widnes also saw their play-off hopes finally dashed.

Widnes were booed from the field and their coach Neil Kelly said he was "ashamed" after conceding 38 second-half points to lose 40-0 to the Broncos at the Halton Stadium.

"In the space of 80 minutes, the Vikings were transformed from play-off contenders into a club on the brink of crisis," wrote Mike Latham in Rugby Leaguer & League Express.

Two-nil at the break became 40-0 as Joel Caine scored a hat-trick and Chris Thorman kicked eight goals.

Warrington's win over Huddersfield at the McAlpine ended the Giants' rousing eight-match unbeaten home record. Huddersfield had four men sin-binned in their bad-tempered 25-12 defeat. Six players were sin-binned and the game was reduced to 11-a-side on two occasions. Mark Hilton was put on report for a high tackle on Paul Reilly in the fourth minute, and was suspended for three matches by the RFL Disciplinary the following Tuesday.

Wigan and Leeds were locked in a battle for second spot and Wigan kept up the heat with a 28-6 Friday night win over Hull, Luke Robinson again put on a dazzling show as the Warriors brought down their home programme in style, and Leeds produced the comeback of Super League history at Headingley on the same night.

An ill-advised PA announcement that season tickets for 2004 were now on sale, served only to infuriate Rhinos fans as they trailed St Helens 20-0 on the hourmark. Incredibly, tries to Rob Burrow, Mark Calderwood, Gary Connolly, Richard Mathers and Willie Poching took Leeds to a 30-20 victory.

In the only dead rubber of the round, Wakefield compounded Halifax's fate with a 68-6 thrashing at Belle Vue.

Going into the last round of the season, the last two spots in the play-offs were being contested by London (28 points), Hull (27) and Warrington (27), while Leeds and Wigan could yet exchange second and third spots, although St Helens were secure in fourth place.

To put it simply, it was complicated.

A Hull win over the Rhinos at the KC Stadium would allow Wigan, if they could beat Castleford, to leapfrog Leeds into second, allowing them a second bite of the cherry in the play-offs.

That meant sixth-placed Hull were under the most pressure, with a tougher ask than the seventh-placed Wolves, who hosted Wakefield in the final Super League game at Wilderspool. Hull had a points difference 51 points better than Warrington's, which should have been decisive if London (fifth) won their home game with Huddersfield, and Hull and Warrington both won or lost.

On the Saturday night the Rhinos secured second spot and un-nerved al Hull fans with a 28-12 win at the KC Stadium, with a crowd of almost 15,000 watching on.

Hull shrugged off the late withdrawal of centre Richie Barnett, and the loss of Sean Ryan, playing his final game for the black and whites, after only three minutes with a shoulder injury, to more than match the visitors during a very competitive first half but Willie Poching's converted try just before the interval left Hull with just too much to do.

Warrington said a fond farewell to 108-year-old Wilderspool with a superb 52-12 win over the Wildcats in front of a sell-out crowd that saw them qualify for the play-offs for the first time. The Wolves never looked in trouble from the moment fans favourite Sid Domic crashed over on four minutes and so it was to prove as they had the game signed, sealed and delivered by the half-time hooter, going in 32-0 up. Not for the first time this season Graham Appo was the star for the home side as he crossed for a scorching hat-trick, and booted a perfect ten

Rikki Sheriffe loses possession against Widnes during Halifax's final Super League game

goals from as many attempts.

Warrington were sixth and London made the play-offs too when they secured fifth position after a 22-12 win over the Giants. The Broncos - who lost in-form Bill Peden with a knee ligament injury -had to withstand a massive physical test from the Giants who were waving farewell to coach Tony Smith and club skipper Steve McNamara, who was retiring as a player to join the Bulls' coaching staff.

Halifax bade a sad farewell to Super League with a 48-20 home defeat to Widnes. Phil Cantillon made his final appearance for the Vikings, with Anthony Farrell playing his last club game before bringing the curtain down on a distinguished 17-year career.

Halifax gave a first-team debut to halfback Danny Jones, aged 17 years and 200 days, one of the youngest players to represent the club and following in the recent footsteps of Danny Tickle, Simon Grix, Chris Chester, David Hodgson and Ryan Clayton, who all made a Super League bow for the club before reaching their 18th birthday.

Fax's losing run extended to a club record 27 consecutive games and, for the first time in their history they were unable to earn a home victory during a season. Their opening day win in the capital against the Broncos was indeed a false dawn.

Wigan knew they could only finish third after Leeds' win the night before as they beat Castleford Tigers at the Jungle 23-18. Adrian Lam, who had missed five of the last six matches, led Wigan's victory charge when he came on as a 30th minute substitute.

And the Bulls ended a run of three consecutive defeats against Saints on a Friday night of farewells at Knowsley Road. Though the result was meaningless in terms of final placings, tries by wing pair Tevita Vaikona and Lesley Vainikolo either side of the interval and the clincher from Leon Pryce 25 minutes from time, gave the Bulls a timely response to two heavy league defeats at Saints' hands this season.

Worrying for Saints was the sight of one their two remaining prop forwards Keith Mason leaving the field minutes into the game with a torn calf muscle.

For the Bulls, another big night at Odsal with Leeds Rhinos after a week off, while Saints awaited London Broncos, with Wigan Warriors set to host a Warrington club riding high on the crest of a wave.

FINAL SUPER LEAGUE TABLE - *Sunday 21st September*

	P	W	D	L	F	A	D	PTS
Bradford Bulls	28	22	0	6	878	529	349	44
Leeds Rhinos	28	19	3	6	751	555	196	41
Wigan Warriors	28	19	2	7	776	512	264	40
St Helens *	28	16	1	11	845	535	310	31
London Broncos	28	14	2	12	643	696	-53	30
Warrington Wolves	28	14	1	13	748	619	129	29
Hull FC *	28	13	3	12	701	577	124	27
Castleford Tigers	28	12	1	15	612	633	-21	25
Widnes Vikings	28	12	1	15	640	727	-87	25
Huddersfield Giants	28	11	1	16	628	715	-87	23
Wakefield T Wildcats	28	7	1	20	505	774	-269	15
Halifax *	28	1	0	27	372	1227	-855	0

* two points deducted for 2002 salary cap breach

3
SUPER LEAGUE
PLAY-OFFS 2003

WEEK ONE - ELIMINATION PLAY-OFFS

WIGAN WARRIORS 25 ....**WARRINGTON WOLVES 12**
ST HELENS 24 ....**LONDON BRONCOS 6**

No side from outside the top-two had ever won the Super League title in the play-off era.

But the way that Wigan had finished the regular season had many tipping them to be the first to achieve it.

As the Warriors faced up to meet Warrington in the Saturday play-off, they were coming off the back of an eight-match unbeaten run, a sequence that had begun with Mike Gregory's first game in charge after the premature exit of Stuart Raper - a narrow 18-16 win at Wilderspool on the 3rd August.

The Wolves' winning run was more modest - three games - but it included a feisty 25-12 victory at Huddersfield in the penultimate round, which demonstrated what a tough combination coach Paul Cullen had assembled - despite the continued absence of captain Lee Briers with a scaphoid injury. Stand-in stand-off Graham Appo was one of the form players, voted by League supporters as the Rugby Leaguer & League Express Player of the Month for September.

"The scenes we witnessed at the end of an enthralling Elimination Play-off game at the JJB would have been considered highly unlikely little more than 12 months ago," wrote Mike Latham after the Warriors' 25-12 win.

"The Wolves, having secured sixth place instead of their usual battle against relegation, had given everything in their first venture into the play-offs and their wonderful fans, bedecked in primrose and blue, saluted their favourites' efforts before the gesture was reciprocated."

An outstanding fullback display from Kris Radlinski was the key to Wigan's win, after the Wolves held a deserved 12-6 lead at the interval, and stayed in contention until just seven minutes from the end when a field goal from Luke Robinson put Wigan in the comfort zone.

Radlinski pulled off some marvellous tackles and then showed his attacking

capabilities with the crucial assist for Brett Dallas's second-half try that helped turn the tide Wigan's way.

"Proud doesn't sum up the effort and quality of the display of the players," said Cullen at the end. "We made an absolute mockery of the three or four million pounds that is separating the budgets of the two sides. We have seen the best performance from Wigan all season - they needed that to beat us. The pace was breathtaking and it was an exceptional game of Rugby League - one that would have done justice to a Grand Final."

With a move to a new home - the Halliwell Jones Stadium - for the 2004 season on schedule, a tide of optimism washed over the town of Warrington, despite elimination at their first bite at a play-off series.

Cullen's side had been worthy leaders at half-time. Appo's penalty, after Wigan prop Quentin Pongia was sin-binned for holding on too long after making a try-saving tackle on Daryl Cardiss, gave the Wolves a deserved lead. Cardiss then latched onto a Nat Wood chip but lost the ball as he tried to ground it over the Wigan line in the force of a double-tackle by Adrian Lam and Radlinski, video referee Steve Cross rightly disallowing the score.

But Warrington moved into an 8-0 lead after 15 minutes following a sensational 80-metre counter-attack sparked by Brent Grose after he had

Darren Burns gets to grips with Andy Farrell

intercepted Lam's pass. Grose exchanged passes with the supporting Appo and was then hauled down just short of the line by Radlinski. But the quick-thinking Appo sent Darren Burns over from first receiver and then added the conversion.

Warrington finally cracked after 26 minutes when Terry Newton ran across the face of the defence before producing a delicate chip that was gathered by Lam for a try converted by Andy Farrell. But Paul Johnson became Wigan's second player to be yellow carded after obstructing Wolves winger Dean Gaskell in back-play, as Radlinski's brilliant cover tackle foiled Sid Domic's left wing break.

The Wolves again took full advantage of their brief numerical advantage when Nat Wood brilliantly anticipated a Lam chip and plucked the ball out of the evening sky before racing 80 metres to the left corner for a sensational try that opened up that shock interval lead.

Wigan's recovery bid was underway when Danny Tickle fought his way over from dummy-half following a rampaging run by Craig Smith, who was outstanding in the second half. Tickle's angled conversion tied the scores after 48 minutes.

Johnson returned from the bin to pull off an outstanding close-range tackle on Burns, after Appo and Nat Wood made the opening, as both sides went for broke in a white-hot atmosphere.

The Warriors finally took the lead for the first time just before the midway point of the second half when Robinson, called into the England A squad that week, calmly potted a 20-metre penalty after he was tackled high by Nat Wood just four minutes after taking the field.

Wigan moved six points clear with 14 minutes left, keeping the ball alive mercilessly to punish a tiring Wolves defence, with Radlinski linking into the attack down the left and brilliantly committing three defenders before ushering Dallas over.

Robinson received from Newton and put distance between the sides with a calmly potted field goal seven minutes from the end, with Smith's late barnstorming effort, after taking Newton's pass from dummy-half and crashing over, cruel justice on a terrific Wolves effort.

In the aftermath, there were major doubts surrounding the fitness of captain Farrell. Struggling also against illness and a hip problem in the lead-up to the game, Farrell eventually quit the action six minutes before half-time with a recurrence of a knee injury.

Wigan now faced an enthralling tie against arch rivals and defending Super League champions St Helens at the JJB the following Friday.

On the evening before Wigan's win over the Wolves, Saints had accounted for London Broncos - also in their first play-off series, but crucially missing Bill Peden with a medial knee ligament injury sustained in the previous week's win over Huddersfield - at Knowsley Road by 24-6.

The win left Saints coach Ian Millward, who had written off his side's chances completely earlier in an injury-ravaged season, in bullish mood: "We'll be there, don't worry. Get down to the bookies - we're flying."

The return of Paul Sculthorpe from a nagging hamstring injury was the main factor behind his confidence after an end-of-season slump when they lost four of their last five regular-season games. And with Sculthorpe restored to the side, Sean Long enjoyed one of his most influential games of the season.

Long, who retained the captaincy despite the return of Chris Joynt, ended an eight-game try-scoring drought when he at last got the try he needed to reach the 100-try landmark for Saints. That set his side on the way, and he followed it up with another as Saints took control in the first half, building a decisive 20-6

Paul Sculthorpe tackled by Neil Budworth

lead by the break, Long weighing in with the assist for Willie Talau's crucial try just before the break.

Millward played down a 50th-minute incident that was placed on report by referee Karl Kirkpatrick, with Talau and Mark Edmondson involved in alleged lifting in a double-tackle on Broncos captain Jim Dymock. The pair were found to have no case to answer by RFL disciplinary chiefs. As was a similar incident involving Dennis Moran and Rob Purdham.

It was a landmark night for Long, who finished with a 16-point haul, as he became only the third player in Saints history to reach the career double of 100 tries and 100 goals for the club, following Len Killeen and his old halfback partner Tommy Martyn. Millward was also delighted with the contribution of Talau who capped a fine display with his first Saints try.

WEEK TWO - ELIMINATION SEMI-FINAL

WIGAN WARRIORS 40..ST HELENS 24

Wigan coach Mike Gregory put Gareth Hock on stand-by to take over Andy Farrell's loose forward role in the week leading up to the game. But it was going to take more than a knee injury to keep Farrell out of the Elimination Semi-final at the JJB Stadium that Friday night.

For the champions Great Britain centre Martin Gleeson came through a calf injury scare - but the absence of injury victims Darren Britt and Keith Mason - left them threadbare in the front row. In the only change, Anthony Stewart came on to the left wing for Darren Albert, who suffered a groin injury against the Broncos the previous week.

A 40-24 win - watched by a bumper 21,790 crowd, the biggest for a Warriors game at the JJB - left the Warriors faithful - after four games and

Brian Carney celebrates his try with Brett Dallas

four wins against the old enemy in 2003 - dreaming of Old Trafford.

The Warriors put together a near-perfect first half to ensure their progress to the Final Eliminator - building a 34-6 interval lead on the back of the power and presence of Craig Smith, Quentin Pongia and Terry O'Connor and the superb skills of Terry Newton.

The only negatives for the Warriors concerned Smith and Adrian Lam. Smith faced a worrying couple of days after being accused of raising his knee in a tackle by John Stankevitch in the first half, although he avoided punishment, instead receiving a letter from the League advising him to change his running style.

Two-try Lam had to quit the action late in the first half with a knee injury, which later was diagnosed as needing surgery, ruling him out of the rest of the play-offs.

Saints coach Ian Millward was consoled by his side's outstanding second-half revival: "We won the second half 18-6 and that is indicative of what could have happened had we played differently in the first half."

The best try of the night came 21 seconds from half-time as Brian Carney clawed a Paul Newlove kick out of the air and embarked on a blistering 75-metre run down the right, burning off Jason Hooper's despairing cover tackle for a superb try.

Incredibly, after a ten-match unbeaten run, Wigan coach Mike Gregory had still not been handed the job permanently.

BRADFORD BULLS 30 ....**LEEDS RHINOS 14**

The following night Bradford Bulls beat Leeds for the fifth time in 2003, a 30-14 final scoreline not reflecting the closeness of another rip-roaring encounter between the two local rivals.

The Rhinos produced a tremendous first-half defensive effort to be only 8-4 down at the interval, despite being under constant pressure. Two second-half touchdowns helped them to a 14-12 lead and, having scored three tries to one, they looked to be heading for victory.

Then Leon Pryce came up with the match-breaking try. Sent on as a substitute to do something special, he did just that as he went on his own to leave a trail of defenders in his wake before stretching out for the touchdown. Paul Deacon added the goal to make it 18-14 and there was no way back for Leeds as Mike Forshaw produced a quick one-two to leave Leeds stunned.

James Lowes set up the first in the 71st minute with a neat kick to the corner and Forshaw won the race to touch down. Three minutes later the loose forward struck again with a strong solo effort that saw him power over after a short burst.

Another big factor in the Bradford victory was the superb kicking of Paul Deacon, both tactically and for goal. The scrum-half never put a foot wrong as he kicked seven goals from as many attempts, with the first bringing him his 1,000th point for Bradford.

David Furner worked non-stop in the second row for Leeds and it was his sudden burst from a play-the-ball that put Leeds 14-12 in front, after Kevin Sinfield added the goal in the 64th minute. But the extra spark behind the pack was missing, with halfbacks Andrew Dunemann and Rob Burrow both carefully marked.

Poor discipline also let Leeds down at crucial times, with three of Deacon's goals coming from penalties. Two came in rapid succession just when Leeds should have been pushing ahead after a Mark Calderwood try put them level at 8-8 in the 47th minute. The penalties were for high tackles with captain Kevin Sinfield placed on report for the second, which put a doubt over his availability for the eliminator against Wigan Warriors the following Friday, although on the Monday the RFL's executive committee decided he had no case to answer.

Bradford took a gamble by giving Michael Withers his first game since being injured in April, although a specialist advised against Robbie Paul making a comeback after his long injury lay-off.

Lesley Vainikolo opened the scoring after only nine minutes to maintain his record of touching down in all five matches against Leeds in 2003. His try came when he inter-passed with Daniel Gartner to go over on the left. The pair both claimed another try in the 20th minute after chasing a kick but the video referee ruled neither had touched down.

The video referee also disallowed a Calderwood touchdown, but Leeds emerged from a long period under pressure with a try for Francis Cummins off Sinfield's wide pass in the 32nd minute.

Jamie Peacock evades the challenge of Rob Burrow

A Deacon penalty goal was the only other score before the interval and Leeds could be satisfied with being only four points behind, after Bradford had dominated territorially.

They were more than satisfied after only seven minutes of the second half when swift cross-field passing ended with Calderwood going over in the right corner - the winger's 26th try of the season.

Although two more penalty goals from Deacon regained Bradford the lead, Furner's converted try edged the Rhinos back in front and it looked like being a fourth nail-biting finish involving these two fierce rivals this season, with possibly Leeds hanging on for a rare victory. Then Pryce came along with his try and Forshaw doubled them up.

Bulls coach Brian Noble hadn't ruled out the pair meeting for a sixth time – in the Grand Final - although they had to overcome Wigan, whose winning habit looked unbreakable. "They've shown all year they can bounce back from adversity," said Noble. "Their team spirit is intact, which is the main thing, and they are very strong at Headingley."

WEEK THREE - FINAL ELIMINATOR

LEEDS RHINOS 22 WIGAN WARRIORS 23

The showdown at Headingley produced the most dramatic Final Eliminator in the competition's history.

Wigan rewrote the record books by becoming the first side from outside the top two to qualify for the Grand Final, as Danny Tickle's sweetly-struck left-foot field goal three minutes from time secured a 23-22 win for the Warriors.

It was just enough to separate two sides that had produced four majestic clashes in 2003 - two of them ending in draws - all of them strewn with unyielding defence, searing attack and spectacular touchdowns.

Even then there was so nearly one last sting in the tail as the Rhinos launched their final long-range foray of Daryl Powell's reign, Tickle and Kris Radlinski producing stunning tackles on Francis Cummins and Kevin Sinfield before Richard Mathers, on the last play, was crowded out just short of the try-line by magnificent scrambling cover, led, inevitably, by skipper supreme Andy Farrell.

Both sides could justifiably claim that they deserved the glory, Wigan's desire and drive to claw back from ten and then eight-point deficits in each half a testimony to their self-belief under Mike Gregory and Leeds unfortunate not to be further ahead at the break after their best half of a spirited year.

The difference was Brian Carney, whose two length-of-the-field touchdowns to start and finish the try-scoring deserved the ultimate accolade.

"The Irishman's combination of evasive power, indefatigable will and raw pace shattered Headingley hopes and will have raised Australian eyebrows," wrote match reporter Phil Caplan.

The winger's stunning contributions – first in tandem with Radlinski and then with all his own work – confirmed him as one of the game's hottest properties.

Carney's opening effort was even better than his spectacular touchline burst that destroyed Saints the week before, taking Andrew Dunemann's capriciously bouncing kick near his own line and weaving clear before linking with Radlinski, another master of composure, who gloriously sent him on the inside to the whitewash.

Just after the hour, when skipper Sinfield had put Leeds 20-16 ahead with a penalty and penned the visitors back on their line with a last-tackle grubber, Carney struck again to devastating effect.

Radlinski was again instrumental clearing his lines, and Mick Cassidy's quick play-the-ball created a glimmer of space allowing Carney to pounce from dummy-half. He charged and twisted away from David Furner and Keith Senior before evading the clutches of Wayne McDonald and a desperate Richard Mathers, in a breathtaking burst which provided the perfect tonic for his ailing coach Gregory who had been laid low during the week by a bug.

It was left to Gregory's assistant Denis Betts to sum up Carney's exceptional efforts in a wonderful contest. "There's no other winger in the world who could have scored that second try," he said.

If Carney was the obvious hero, the catalyst for Wigan's 11-match glory run had been Quentin Pongia, the former Kiwi skipper's mid-season arrival the fulcrum around which the Warriors had found their edge and consistency.

Leeds could justifiably point to a contentious decision to award a scrum when Willie Poching was impeded by Mark Smith and Tickle when attempting to play the ball, which

Terry O'Connor knocked back by Matt Diskin as Chris Feather moves in

led to the position for the decisive one point. But that should not detract from the fact that Wigan outscored them by four tries to three.

Daryl Powell's decision to bring in Danny McGuire - ostensibly at fullback - paid rich dividends, the youngster's roving commission adding an extra dimension to the Rhinos attack and his exhilarating combination with Rob Burrow accounting for all the wonderfully-crafted home tries. It was only the fourth occasion they started together in Super League VIII.

Mathers had been a revelation since being given an extended run, and although it was felt to be too soon to bring back Ryan Bailey - released from a young offenders' institute the previous Monday, but tagged as part of an electronic curfew order - props Barrie McDermott, Wayne McDonald, Danny Ward and Chris Feather all saved their most consistent displays for last.

For the devastated Powell, in his last match in charge before his two-year sabbatical, the ultimate prize had remained tantalisingly out of reach.

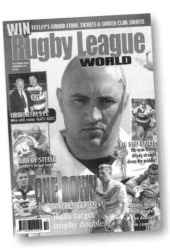

But for Warriors' caretaker boss Mike Gregory there was a timely boost as he prepared for the Grand Final. The following Tuesday the club announced that he and assistant Betts had signed two-year deals to keep them in charge at the JJB Stadium until the end of the 2005 season.

SUPER LEAGUE GRAND FINAL
Bulls double top

Stuart Reardon completed a remarkable season which he began as an unknown reserve by collecting the Harry Sunderland Trophy as the Bulls became the first club to win the Challenge Cup and a Super League Grand Final in the same season.

The 22 year old fullback had been loaned out for most of 2002, first to National League One Featherstone Rovers and then Salford City Reds. But he got his big break when Brian Noble's two first choice fullbacks Michael Withers and Robbie Paul became long-term injury victims. Reardon had taken his chance so well that, although the duo were passed fit for the final, he kept his fullback spot and they were accommodated elsewhere. Withers himself had won the Harry Sunderland Trophy with an outstanding fullback display against Wigan two years before when he scored three tries. Reardon scored only one in the 2003 climax, but it was the try that put Bradford on the way to their 25-12 victory.

The scores were locked at 6-6 after 53 minutes, with Bradford's only scores coming from Paul Deacon penalties. Then Joe Vagana - who seemed to physically grow as the game wore on - charged forward from 20 metres out. Reardon followed him, and was ready when the prop slipped out a pass. Despite stumbling, he burst away from a clutch of defenders before lunging over the line with another hanging on to him. Deacon tagged on the goal and Bradford never looked back.

Deacon, who kicked six goals from six attempts, as well as a crucial field goal that stretched the Bulls lead to seven points after 70 minutes, was another man of the match contender, with Stuart Fielden, Jamie Peacock and Lesley Vainikolo also playing starring roles.

One game too far for Wigan as Bulls grab Grand Final glory

There was also a trademark try at the end from James Lowes - his 99th for the Bulls - when he shot over from acting halfback to finally put the issue beyond doubt. It was a fitting way for Lowes to bring down the curtain on a career that started at Hunslet in 1987.

Daniel Gartner, heading back to Australia, and Warrington-bound Mike Forshaw were also

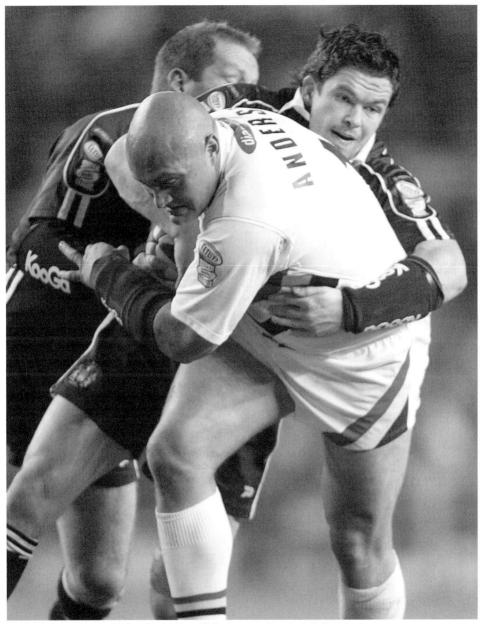

Andy Farrell and Terry O'Connor combine to halt Paul Anderson

playing their last games in Bradford colours.

The Super League VIII Grand Final was the first to sell out in advance and 65,537 League fans crammed into Old Trafford to soak up another electric atmosphere on a clear, dry and still evening. A myriad of club shirts, fancy dress and assorted flags gave the event a Challenge Cup Final feel.

Reardon's try and one from Shontayne Hape, in a decisive eight-minute spell just before the hour, turned the game the Bulls' way as brave Wigan found it half a game too far.

93

The Warriors were eventually dominated by the sheer force and momentum created by an impressive Bulls pack, not helping their cause with a nervy completion rate after a first quarter which they dominated.

"This was a rough, tough, almost old-fashioned match played in good spirits with the best team winning, but with the losers showing that they too are building an exciting team for the future," reflected Rugby League World magazine editor Tony Hannan.

The Warriors fielded the same 17 as beat Leeds at Headingley the week before, Brian Carney surviving a late fitness scare after a training injury, while Robbie Paul made his expected return to the Bulls bench after over three months out with a broken arm. Paul only played a total of 25 minutes but made an important contribution. Karl Pratt was given the starting stand-off role, with Leon Pryce on the bench. Rob Parker, St Helens-bound Lee Gilmour and Scott Naylor - who returned to Salford the following month - were the unlucky players to miss out for the Bulls, with Jamie Langley ruled out with an ankle injury.

The Warriors, all in black, knew their first task was to withstand the Bulls' onslaught and prevent a first-half humiliation similar to the 2001 Grand Final. Then, with Withers notching a first-half hat-trick, the Bulls established a game-sealing 26-0 interval lead on their way to a 37-6 win. That they succeeded in that aim was down to a huge effort by the pack, props Quentin Pongia and Craig Smith, and Mick Cassidy rising to the challenge against the Bulls' mighty pack.

The Warriors looked the more composed side as the early exchanges were played at a punishing pace. The first clean break came on 12 minutes, Kris Radlinski sending Hodgson streaking around Withers and through down the left, only for the impressive Reardon to halt his 40-metre run with a solid cover tackle.

Two minutes later, the Warriors had the chance to break the tense deadlock after Lowes felled Luke Robinson with a high tackle, but captain Andrew Farrell's 15-metre angled kick rebounded off an upright into the grateful arms of Vagana.

But Wigan had the initiative and took the lead on 17 minutes, as Danny Tickle showed twinkling footwork to elude the challenges of Deacon and Hape, and broke clear 40 metres down the right channel for a fine try that Farrell smoothly converted for his 100th goal of the season.

Briefly, the Bulls looked rattled as Robinson twice pushed the them back with raking kicks and, as they tried to break back, Lowes put a kick through down the left and then followed through with a second high tackle that felled Carney.

Farrell and Brett Dallas were both pulled down five metres short of the Bulls line, before Robinson spoilt the position with a diagonal kick that ran dead. For the rest of the half, Wigan hardly completed a set satisfactorily.

The Bulls had got their first points after 26 minutes when Deacon potted a penalty from 30 metres, after Paul, with his first touch after replacing Lowes at hooker, was robbed by Terry Newton in a one-on-one tackle, only for the ball to rebound to the offside Gareth Hock.

Robinson's deep kick-off forced a Bulls drop-out, but the position was spoilt when Hodgson, receiving from Radlinski after a sweeping attack, was bundled into touch by a double-tackle involving Pratt and Vaikona.

Paul had given his side fresh impetus and, after Reardon straightened up a faltering attack, Deacon hoisted a precise high kick to the corner where the airborne Vainikolo challenged Carney. The ball rebounded, Vainikolo grabbed the ball out of Robinson's despairing clutches and claimed the touchdown.

Video referee Steve Cross faced the hardest of tasks before, after endless replays, he decided that Vainikolo had knocked on and disallowed the score.

Two penalties piggybacked the Warriors downfield and Newton was held up on the last in a massed tackle. But the Bulls were soon back on the attack and, after Martin Aspinwall pulled off a great tackle on Hape, Paul Johnson gave away a penalty for a hand in the tackle and Deacon potted the 18-metre angled penalty.

But the Warriors still went in with a 6-4 interval lead, just as they had in the inaugural Grand Final five years before against Leeds, after Radlinski ended Gartner's 40-metre break and then, with 26 seconds on the clock, Reardon was held up close to the line, again by Radlinski.

The Bulls set the tone for their second-half bombardment as the heroic Radlinski was twice forced to retrieve perfect long, raking kicks by Pratt and then Deacon. Then Deacon kicked through on a planned move but Tevita Vaikona was offside as he challenged Radlinski to the ball 20 metres out.

Lowes came back on for Paul, and Pryce replaced Pratt eight minutes after the re-start as the Bulls continued to turn the screw.

Deacon broke through down the left channel and threw out a pass, intended for the supporting Gartner who Mr Kirkpatrick deemed was held back by Robinson. Deacon brought the scores level on 50 minutes with the 17-metre angled kick.

Carney was then carried off on a stretcher after a double-tackle involving Gartner and Pryce, who came in to complete Gartner's tackle after the Irish winger brought the ball up from a defensive position and appeared to slam Carney's head into the turf.

Referee Karl Kirkpatrick, after advice from the video referee, decided the

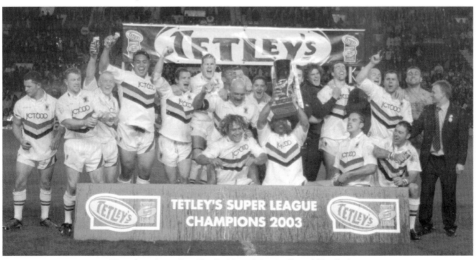

The victorious Bradford side celebrate Grand Final glory

injury was caused accidentally and waved play on.

To make matters worse for the Warriors, they lost possession in the incident, allowing the Bulls to set up the position for Reardon's try. Deacon converted that for a 12-6 lead after 51 minutes.

As the Bulls pounded the Wigan line, Brett Dallas was forced to concede a drop-out under pressure from Withers, after Lee Radford kicked through with his first touch.

And in the next attack, just before the hour-mark, the Wigan defence cracked again as Pryce and Deacon swept the ball to the left for Hape to scythe over. Deacon was again on target with the conversion.

Radlinski was again the Wigan hero with a last-ditch tackle on Lowes, who had cleverly combined with Forshaw, before halting Hape's long break with another tackle out of the top drawer. Deacon, though, ensured that the Bulls got something from the attack, potting a 20-metre field goal to extend his side's lead to 19-6 with ten minutes remaining.

TETLEY'S SUPER LEAGUE GRAND FINAL

Saturday 18th October 2003

BRADFORD BULLS 25 WIGAN WARRIORS 12

BULLS: 17 Stuart Reardon; 2 Tevita Vaikona; 6 Michael Withers; 4 Shontayne Hape; 5 Lesley Vainikolo; 15 Karl Pratt; 7 Paul Deacon; 8 Joe Vagana; 9 James Lowes; 29 Stuart Fielden; 11 Daniel Gartner; 12 Jamie Peacock; 13 Mike Forshaw. Subs (all used): 10 Paul Anderson; 18 Lee Radford; 3 Leon Pryce; 1 Robbie Paul (C).
Tries: Reardon (51), Hape (59), Lowes (75);
Goals: Deacon 6/6; **Field goal:** Deacon.
WARRIORS: 1 Kris Radlinski; 5 Brian Carney; 18 Martin Aspinwall; 14 David Hodgson; 2 Brett Dallas; 15 Sean O'Loughlin; 20 Luke Robinson; 30 Quentin Pongia; 9 Terry Newton; 10 Craig Smith; 11 Mick Cassidy; 12 Danny Tickle; 13 Andy Farrell (C). Subs (all used): 4 Paul Johnson; 8 Terry O'Connor; 23 Gareth Hock; 17 Mark Smith.
Tries: Tickle (17), Radlinski (72); **Goals:** Farrell 2/3.
Rugby Leaguer & League Express Men of the Match:
Bulls: Stuart Reardon; *Warriors:* Kris Radlinski.
Penalty count: 7-6; **Half-time:** 4-6;
Referee: Karl Kirkpatrick (Warrington);
Attendance: 65,537 *(at Old Trafford, Manchester).*

Wigan, lacking nothing in guts or spirit, pulled back six points from nowhere.

Aspinwall, one of the success stories of their season, fashioned the score with a startling break after receiving a pass from Robinson from a scrum 15 metres from the Wigan line. Aspinwall ducked under the attempted tackles of Pratt and Reardon, rounded the covering Vainikolo and showed great awareness to send the supporting Radlinski racing over from just over 20 metres out as Pratt chased back. Farrell converted to cut the deficit to 12-19 after 72 minutes.

But Tickle knocked-on Deacon's deep re-start and the Bulls set up the position for the clinching try. Forshaw and then Fielden were held up close to the line before Lowes drove over from dummy-half for his 99th and final try for the Bulls. Deacon added his sixth goal.

Paul returned for the closing three minutes and made one final contribution, tackling Hodgson into touch by the corner flag, just before the Warriors centre planted the ball over the line.

"Ultimately, we lost the ball game because Bradford were bigger and stronger in collision," was Wigan coach Mike Gregory's post-match summation.

"But I've got to give credit to the players, they have been strong for the last month and, to get here from third place, I am very proud of what they have achieved."

Gregory had tasted defeat for the first time since taking over the coaching reins, as the Warriors' 11-match unbeaten run came to an end. But with ten Wigan-born players in their ranks, and nine players who had come up through the club's youth ranks, the future looked bright.

2003 SUPER LEAGUE SEASON

ROUND BY ROUND

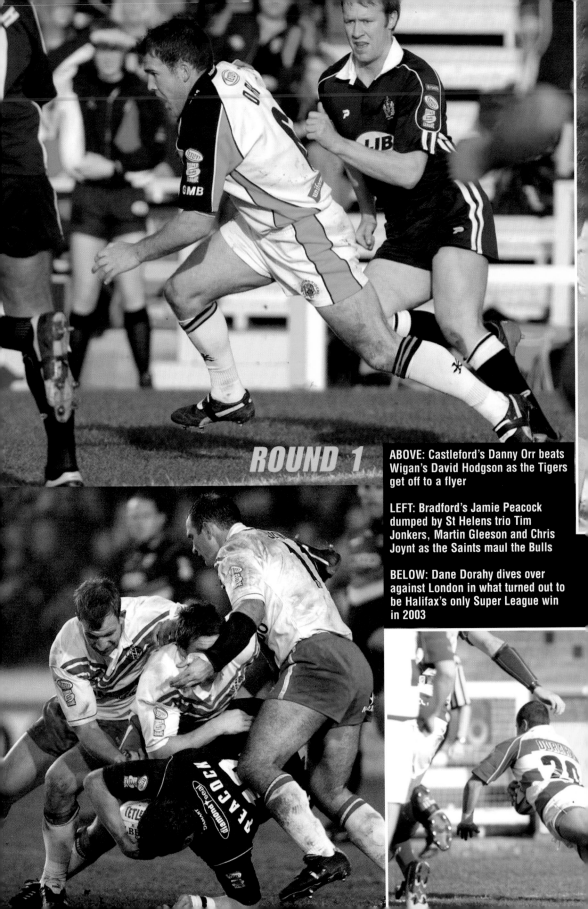

ROUND 1

ABOVE: Castleford's Danny Orr beats Wigan's David Hodgson as the Tigers get off to a flyer

LEFT: Bradford's Jamie Peacock dumped by St Helens trio Tim Jonkers, Martin Gleeson and Chris Joynt as the Saints maul the Bulls

BELOW: Dane Dorahy dives over against London in what turned out to be Halifax's only Super League win in 2003

ROUND 2

ROUND 3

ROUND 4

LEFT: London's Russell Bawden loses the ball under pressure from Paul King and Adam Maher as the Broncos upset Hull at the first Super League game at KC Stadium

RIGHT: Wigan's David Hodgson races away to score against Wakefield as the Warriors edge a Belle Vue thriller

Huddersfield's Darren Fleary surrounded as the Giants get off the mark with a stunning win at home to champions St Helens

CHALLENGE CUP

ROUND 4

SEMI FINALS

ROUND 5

QUARTER FINALS

Leeds' Danny McGuire leaves St Helens' Darren Smith trailing as he races away to score the match-winning try in extra time of a pulsating Challenge Cup semi final

TOP LEFT: Hunslet coach Roy Sampson and Phil Hasty celebrate the Hawks' shock win over Huddersfield

LEFT: Richie Barnett on the charge as Hull take apart Sheffield

RIGHT: Bradford's Lesley Vainikolo looks for a way through during the Bulls' semi-final win over Wigan

BELOW: Sean Long dives in as St Helens march past Salford

Wigan's Adrian Lam rolls over to score during a big win against Swinton

ROUND 5

No way through the St Helens defence for Leeds' Matt Adamson as the Rhinos edge Saints at Knowsley Road following a Wayne McDonald wonder try

Danny Tickle looks to break free as injury-hit Wigan defeat St Helens on Good Friday

ROUND 6

Gary Connolly tackled by Adrian Lam as Leeds and Wigan fight out the first of two Headingley 24-all draws

Huddersfield's Brandon Costin dumped by Andy Hobson and Daryl Cardiss as the Giants defeat Halifax by a point

ROUND 7

CHALLENGE CUP FINAL

BRADFORD BULLS 22
LEEDS RHINOS....................20

ABOVE: Tevita Vaikona comes face to face with Ryan Bailey and Matt Adamson

BELOW: Jamie Peacock grounded by Chev Walker and David Furner

James Lowes and Paul Deacon celebrate Bradford's Challenge Cup Final win over Leeds

Chris McKenna scores despite the attentions of Shontayne Hape

No way through for Barrie McDermott

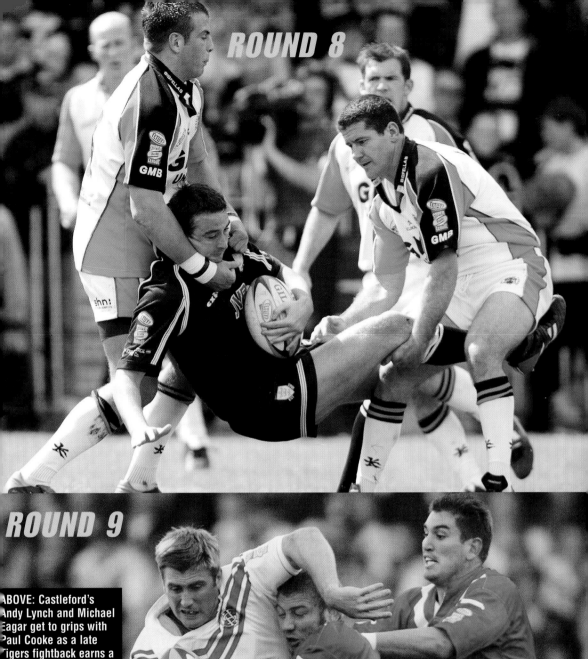

ROUND 8

ROUND 9

ABOVE: Castleford's Andy Lynch and Michael Eagar get to grips with Paul Cooke as a late Tigers fightback earns a draw against Hull

RIGHT: Wakefield duo David March and Dallas Hood combine to halt Mark Edmondson as the Wildcats stun the Saints

RIGHT: Warrington's Darren Burns takes on Wigan's Danny Tickle as a late Andy Farrell field goal earns the Warriors victory

ROUND 10

ROUND 11

Bradford's Mike Forshaw tries to escape the clutches of Leeds' Chev Walker as the Bulls charge past the Rhinos

ROUND 12

London duo Tony Martin and Dennis Moran celebrate the Broncos' victory over Bradford at Odsal

ROUND 13

ROUND 15

ABOVE: Terry O'Connor halted against Bradford as Wigan win at Odsal

BELOW: St Helens' Martin Gleeson takes on Lee Gilmour as the Saints hand Bradford a third successive home defeat

Warrington's Nick Fozzard looks for support as Bradford score two late tries at Wilderspool to deny the Wolves the spoils

ROUND 14

ROUND 16

Hull's Toa Kohe-Love held up by Bradford duo Rob Parker and Jamie Peacock as the Bulls edge it at a packed KC Stadium

Widnes' Robert Relf knocked down by Leeds' David Furner as the Vikings halt the Rhinos

ROUND 18

Huddersfield's Julian Bailey wrapped up by Leeds' Mark Calderwood and Chris McKenna as the Giants claim another big win

ROUND 20

Widnes' Julian O'Neill collared by Wigan's Craig Smith as the Vikings defeat the Warriors at JJB Stadium to end the coaching reign of Stuart Raper

Wigan's Gareth Hock looks to get the ball away under pressure from Huddersfield's Hefin O'Hare as the Giants cut down the Warriors

ROUND 17

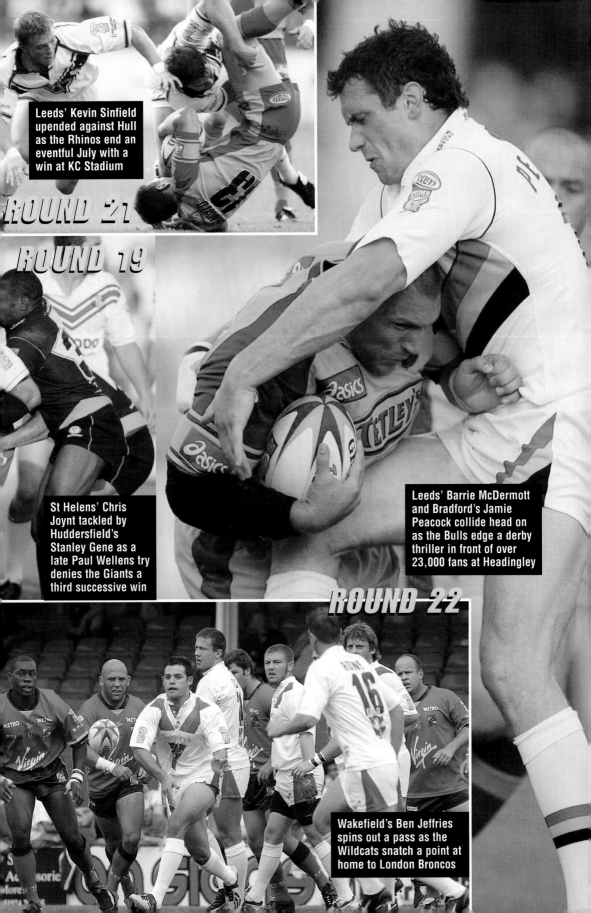

Leeds' Kevin Sinfield upended against Hull as the Rhinos end an eventful July with a win at KC Stadium

ROUND 21

ROUND 19

St Helens' Chris Joynt tackled by Huddersfield's Stanley Gene as a late Paul Wellens try denies the Giants a third successive win

Leeds' Barrie McDermott and Bradford's Jamie Peacock collide head on as the Bulls edge a derby thriller in front of over 23,000 fans at Headingley

ROUND 22

Wakefield's Ben Jeffries spins out a pass as the Wildcats snatch a point at home to London Broncos

LEFT: Leeds' Keith Senior takes on Wigan duo Shaun Briscoe and Martin Aspinwall as the Rhinos earn a 24-all draw thanks to a dramatic last-minute Danny McGuire try

ROUND 23

ABOVE: London's Dennis Moran caught by Warrington's Mark Hilton as the Broncos edge the battle of the play-off chasers

ROUND 24

Dejected Halifax fans leave the Shay following their side's 12-54 loss to Huddersfield, a defeat that confirmed relegation

ABOVE: Castleford's Paul Mellor grounds Leeds debutant Liam Botham as the Tigers stun the Rhinos at The Jungle

BELOW: Wakefield's Sylvain Houles defies the challenge of Gareth Raynor to score as the Wildcats put a massive dent in Hull's play-off hopes

ROUND 25

Warrington's Nathan Wood celebrates with fans as the Wolves take apart Wakefield to reach the play-offs

ROUND 28

BELOW: London's Rob Purdham on the charge against Huddersfield as the Broncos grab a play-off spot

BELOW RIGHT: Leeds' Wayne McDonald tackled by Sean Long as the Rhinos produce a sensational comeback against St Helens

ROUND 26

ABOVE LEFT: Wigan's Brian Carney races away to score a stunning try as the Warriors defeat St Helens for a third time in Super League VIII

LEFT: Bradford's Lesley Vainikolo celebrates scoring against Leeds as the Bulls inflict another narrow defeat on the Rhinos

ROUND 27

ELIMINATION SEMI-FINAL

ABOVE: Wigan's Craig Smith pushed back by the St Helens defence as the Warriors dash their fiercest rivals' hopes of retaining their Super League crown

BELOW: Warrington's Nick Fozzard skips past Wigan's David Hodgson as the battling Wolves bow out

BELOW RIGHT: London's Francis Stephenson halted by St Helens' John Stankevitch and Keiron Cunningham as the Broncos fall at Knowsley Road

ELIMINATION PLAY-OFFS

ichael Withers
e of Leeds
Cummins, Rob
Keith Senior as
tch their 2003
Rhinos to
h their third
rand Final

QUALIFYING SEMI-FINAL

FINAL ELIMINATOR

RIGHT: Wigan skipper Andy Farrell on the burst during the Warriors' breathtaking one-point victory over Leeds at Headingley

LEFT: Wayne McDonald, Rob Burrow and Kevin Sinfield show the agony of defeat as the Rhinos' rollercoaster season comes to an end

GRAND FINAL

BRADFORD BULLS 25
WIGAN WARRIORS 12

CLOCKWISE, FROM TOP LEFT:
Stuart Reardon tackled by Kris Radlinski; Joe Vagana halted by Terry Newton; Mick Cassidy looks for support; Quentin Pongia looks to break through; Shontayne Hape celebrates scoring

4
NATIONAL LEAGUE 2003

THE NATIONAL LEAGUE SEASON
Expanded horizons

The competitions outside Super League underwent a major make-over in 2003 with the decision to split the old NFP into two divisions. It proved a resounding success, certainly on the field. The increased competitiveness in both National League One and Two ensured a wealth of keenly-contested matches, and the make-up of the top sixes in both divisions was not settled until the closing weeks of the season.

NATIONAL LEAGUE ONE

As the relegated team from Super League VII, **SALFORD CITY REDS** were widely predicted to make an immediate return to the top flight. And despite a couple of early stutters, Karl Harrison's side proved they were a class above the rest by taking out the three pieces of silverware on offer.

Andy Coley

The Reds were crowned Arriva Trains Cup winners, NL1 Minor Premiers, and most importantly won the Grand Final in a season of success at the Willows.

Early-season draws against Leigh (in the ATC Cup) and Whitehaven (league), plus an NL1 defeat at Featherstone, indicated that they would not prove the unstoppable force that Huddersfield had been the year before.

But they were too good for any of their nearest rivals - particularly Leigh, who they beat in the other six meetings between the two clubs in 2003.

Harrison had a wealth of top-drawer performers within his ranks - most notably wily scrum-half and NL1 Player of the Year Gavin Clinch and halfback

Cliff Beverley

partner Cliff Beverley, who finished as the game's top tryscorer, with 39 in all competitions.

In the pack, Andy Coley set an impressive lead, and was supported by the consistent Malcolm Alker, Neil Baynes, Paul Highton, Simon Baldwin and Dave Highton. Substitute prop Gareth Haggerty also made some telling contributions, particularly late in the season.

In the backs, veteran Alan Hunte crossed for 32 tries in his final season, and was closely followed by Stuart Littler (30), impressive loanee Andy Kirk (24) and rock-solid fullback Jason Flowers (17).

Damian Munro

The Reds' nearest rivals for the majority of the season were **LEIGH CENTURIONS**, who again fell just short of realising their Super League goal.

Under Australian coach Paul Terzis, they reached the final of the ATC, and finished second in the table for the second consecutive year.

But that wasn't enough to save Terzis's job, and in amazing circumstances, he was sacked by the club just a week before the end of the regular season and was replaced by Leigh legend Alex Murphy, who became director of rugby.

It was hoped that the move - along with the previous signing of St Helens stand-off Tommy Martyn - would inspire the Centurions to glory, but they fell short in the final showdown against Salford - their third defeat in the Grand Final in four years,

It wasn't all gloom and doom of course - as for much of the year Leigh yet again proved to be one of the shining lights outside the top flight.

Hooker Paul Rowley, winger Damian Munro and Mr Consistency, Adam Bristow, all deservedly gained selection for the NL1 Team of the Year. Munro finished with a remarkable 32 tries from as many appearances, with Rowley notching 20 and Bristow 17.

When he fully recovered from a back injury that has dogged him in recent years, fullback Neil Turley again proved a points-machine, while Australian Pat Weisner, Samoan Willie Swann and halfback John Duffy all had their moments in an entertaining side.

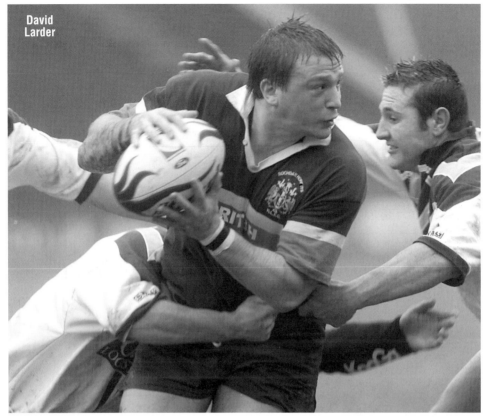

David
Larder

ROCHDALE HORNETS finished in third place for the third consecutive season under coach Martin Hall, who was deservedly rewarded with the NL1 Coach of the Year prize.

But again Hornets fell just short in the play-offs - this time in the most heart-breaking circumstances, to a breakaway last-minute try to Hull Kingston Rovers at Spotland.

Hall was served by several outstanding performers, including NL1 Player of the Year nominee Paul Smith, who sealed a move to Super League with Huddersfield. Smith formed an outstanding second-row partnership with David Larder, with the pair scoring a remarkable 35 tries between them, and both were named in the NL1 Team of the Year, along with hard-working prop Paul Southern.

Loose forward Damian Ball and prop Gareth Price were other foundations of a superb pack whilst, in the backs, Mick Nanyn broke the club record for points in a season, in his first year at Spotland.

Halfbacks Ian Watson and Radney Bowker also had top seasons, after Bowker joined on loan from rivals Salford.

The club's hopes of challenging the top two were hit with a quickfire double blow in mid-season, when form fullback Paul Owen was imprisoned in the nightclub incident that saw Leeds' pair Chev Walker and Ryan Bailey also jailed, and hooker John Hamilton broke a leg.

And with Hall having one of the smallest squads in the competition, the loss of two key players hit them hard in the closing weeks.

Makali
Aizue

HULL KINGSTON ROVERS were undoubtedly one of the success stories of 2003, and fell just one game short of a shock Grand Final appearance.

With a large close-season turnover of players and a new coach in Australian Steve Linnane, the Robins stuttered somewhat at the start, and were as low as eighth in the table in late May.

But they put together a stunning run during the second half of the season and, after memorable play-off wins against Oldham and Rochdale, ended up crashing out at the Final Eliminator when they were well beaten at Leigh.

That late run was sparked by Latham Tawhai and Paul Mansson at halfback, the Kiwi duo re-uniting a partnership that helped Hunslet to the title in 1999.

Prop or second-rower Jon Aston was among the most consistent performers in the competition, while Papua New Guinean International Makali Aizue and Australian Anthony Seibold also made significant impacts after their arrivals.

Winger Alasdair McClarron finished as top tryscorer with 19 and made the NL1 Team of the Year, while fullback Lynton Stott and veteran super-sub Paul Fletcher also made telling contributions.

And perhaps the biggest positive for this famous club was the emergence of several talented youngsters on the first team scene - headed by workaholic hooker Paul Pickering.

Phil
Farrell

OLDHAM sealed a play-off place for the fourth consecutive year - but only on the last day of an up-and-down campaign.

Just two wins from their opening nine games saw the Roughyeds languishing in eighth, though they did pick up to clinch fifth place with a final day win at Featherstone.

The return to playing in the town at Boundary Park was another major positive, though on reflection, this was something of a transitional season for the club under respected player-coach Steve Molloy.

The coach was a virtual ever-present in a pack that had big efforts from back-rower Chris Morley and Australian Dane Morgan, along with the consistent Phil Farrell.

Promising youngsters Gavin Dodd and Lee Doran finished as joint top tryscorers with 14, closely followed by halfback Gareth Barber.

And the form of ex-Castleford Academy player Jon Goddard was also a highlight, particularly after he moved to fullback.

The Roughyeds bucked a National League trend by increasing their crowds significantly - largely due to their move back to Boundary Park - but they will be fully aware that they would rise considerably again should they mount a genuine Super League push in 2004.

David
Fatialofa

WHITEHAVEN promised to break into the very top echelons on NL1 after a promising Arriva Trains Cup campaign and an early-season draw with favourites Salford.

But they never quite achieved their potential, although this was certainly another season of progress at the Recreation Ground, both on and off the field, earning them the National League Community Award at the end of the campaign.

That they didn't finish higher than seventh was largely down to the remarkable statistic that they drew five of their 18 league games - including two stalemates with the Reds.

Coach Steve McCormack continued the work started by Paul Cullen at the Recreation Ground, and was well served by a team made up of committed locals and a sprinkling of talented Kiwis.

Of the New Zealand contingent, stand-off Leroy Joe ran in 26 tries, while David Fatialofa was one of the competition's best front-rowers, and hooker Aaron Lester typically influential.

Centres Howard Hill and David Seeds both contributed significantly, sharing 33 tries, while fullback Gary Broadbent deservedly made the NL1 Team of the Year after an outstanding first season at the club.

And just as importantly, the Haven board continued to stir interest among the local community, increasing their average crowds and attracting over 4,000 to the much-anticipated Cumbria versus New Zealand A game in October.

FEATHERSTONE ROVERS were in the top six for the entire campaign - apart from when it mattered most, on the last day of the season.

A last-day home defeat to Oldham saw Rovers slide down to seventh, and miss out on the play-offs for the first time since their introduction in 1998.

That effectively cost coach Andy Kelly his job, as he departed soon after, though there were several achievements during his tenure.

The main one was the continued emergence of a wealth of youngsters - headed by brilliant stand-off Richard Whiting, whose debut season at first team level ended with the NL1 Young Player of the Year prize and a move to Super League with Hull.

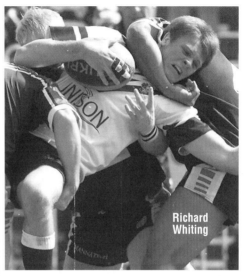

Richard Whiting

He will be joined at the KC Stadium by second-rower Andy Bailey, who also impressed under Kelly with his strong running.

Among the more established players, Richard Chapman and Jamie Stokes both passed 100 career tries for the club, while Stuart Dickens enhanced his reputation with another season of commitment and consistency.

Two more to stand out of a weekly basis were fullback Nathan Graham and evergreen Australian centre Brendan O'Meara, while Ian Tonks had his moments in the front row.

DONCASTER DRAGONS were another club to fall below pre-season expectations, and were forced to see off Batley in the controversial relegation play-off to ensure their NL1 status.

Not that there weren't bright spots for the Dragons and their long-serving coach St John Ellis - particularly the late-season arrival of Graham Holroyd on loan from Huddersfield.

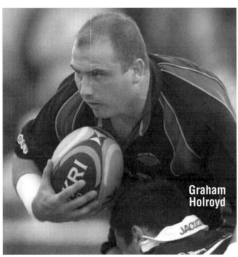

Graham Holroyd

The experienced stand-off helped compensate for the mid-season loss of Paul Mansson to Hull Kingston Rovers, and finished the year by signing a five-year contract at the club.

Other pluses included the week-to-week displays of second-rower Peter Green and prop Gareth Handford, and the extended first-team experience given to youngsters such as winger Alex Muff and utility Dean Colton.

And there was also the fact that the Dragons remain one of the more financially stable clubs in the game - thanks principally to the investment of their chairman John Wright.

BATLEY BULLDOGS' end to the 2002 season had promised much for their future, but the loss of key halfbacks Dean Lawford and Glen Tomlinson hit them hard, and like Doncaster they had to endure the relegation play-off, eventually seeing off Sheffield Eagles, the losers from the NL2 Grand Final.

Barry Eaton

They did improve towards the end of the season once their side had settled, but were rocked by the resignation of popular coach Paul Storey, who will be replaced for next season by his assistant Gary Thornton.

Their star man was undoubtedly scrum-half Barry Eaton - an ever present who also scored in every game for the Bulldogs. Eaton had the added satisfaction of setting a new mark of 38 consecutive goal kicks, surpassing the records set by Henry Paul and Hazem El Masri.

Fullback Craig Lingard was yet again the Bulldogs' top try scorer with 20, and is now within sight of Tomlinson's all-time club record, whilst youngster Mark Toohey emerged as one for the future and represented the National League under-21s.

Centre Danny Maun had another excellent season out wide and was named in the NL1 Team of the Year, while there were unsung heroes in the shape of Ryan Horsley and Andy Spink.

DEWSBURY RAMS finished bottom of the pile and were relegated to National League Two after a disappointing season.

And early home win against Featherstone promised much more, but it would be 11 games before they won again - by which time they were already virtually down.

That late-season win at Doncaster, plus a draw at home to Whitehaven and spirited displays against Oldham and Featherstone, showed that the Rams didn't go down without a fight under player-coach Andy Fisher.

But there was still much disappointment at the Ram Stadium.

Positives included the form of sprightly halfback or hooker Jim Elston and eye-catching winger Michael Wainwright, who finished with a creditable 13 tries.

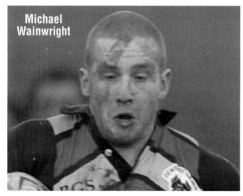

Michael Wainwright

Prop Frank Watene was a tower of strength throughout in the front row, and fellow packmen Simon Hicks and Billy Kershaw deserved better.

But for too long the Rams lacked a cutting edge - hardly helped by an injury to one of their leading strike players, Danny Wood - though the arrival of Frenchman Sylvain Houles did add some late sparkle to an otherwise gloomy campaign.

NATIONAL LEAGUE TWO

SHEFFIELD EAGLES finished top of National League Two on points difference after a season of achievement under player coach Mark Aston.

The Eagles legend decided to pull the boots on for one more season - and help guide a team full of talented young players to the inaugural NL2 Minor Premiership.

Unfortunately, they fell just short of ultimate success in the Grand Final against Keighley. But there were still many positives to reflect on.

The biggest of which was undoubtedly the progression of those young players, led by second-rower Andy Raleigh, who finished the season a target for almost half the clubs in Super League.

Prop Mitchell Stringer was another starlet to stand out, along with fellow front-rower Jack Howieson and centre Nick Turnbull.

Aston was also indebted to an almighty effort up front from veteran prop Jon Bruce, who was deservedly nominated for the competition's Player of the Year award.

And Eagles stalwarts Andy Poynter and Gavin Brown were also prominent, along with PNG International Tom O'Reilly, who arrived mid-season from France, and free-scoring Australian winger Tony Weller.

The Eagles ended the season with a disappointing 36-14 defeat at Batley in the much talked-about promotion play-off - a game that brought down the curtain on Aston's playing career. But 2003 yielded a lot to be optimistic about for the South Yorkshire club.

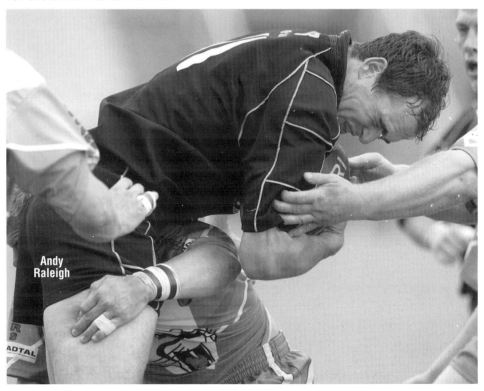

Andy Raleigh

Craig
Dean

CHORLEY LYNX were undoubtedly the success story of National League Two - and perhaps the entire Rugby League.

Strugglers for so long, the Lynx enjoyed a new lease of life under rookie boss Darren Abram, who deservedly went on to clinch the competition's Coach of the Year award.

Abram was indebted to his two first choice halfbacks, Mick Coates and Craig Dean, who guided the team around the field superbly.

Hooker or back-rower Dave McConnell had an outstanding campaign that resulted in a late-season move to Super League with London Broncos, while loose forward Ian Hodson was equally consistent.

Centre Anton Garcia ended the year with 16 tries, while fullback Mark McCully was among the game's leading points scorers.

And winger Eric Andrews - on a season-long loan from Leigh - almost wrote his own piece of Rugby League history when he scored tries in 15 consecutive games, just two short of the all-time record.

As with Sheffield, Chorley's season ended in disappointment, with consecutive play-off defeats to the Eagles and then Keighley, plus the departure of Abram to Leigh, with former St Helens and Salford player Mark Lee taking up the reins at Victory Park.

But it remained one of the most successful campaigns in the club's history.

Level with Sheffield and Chorley on points were **KEIGHLEY COUGARS**, the division's pace-setters for much of the year until a mid-season slump.

Four defeats in six games in June and July saw Gary Moorby's side drop from first place to fourth, before a recovery ended with them in third place.

And they kicked on from there with superb play-off wins over Hunslet, Barrow and Chorley before defeating the Eagles in a pulsating NL2 Grand Final.

That proved a fitting end to a glorious career in a Keighley shirt for Jason Ramshaw, who called time on 11 years at Cougar Park and played his full part throughout 2003, missing just two games.

Second-rower Oliver Wilkes was an ever-present, and outstanding throughout, earning a place in the NL2 Team of the Year. His back-row partner Ian Sinfield was an unsung hero, along with evergreen prop Phil Stephenson and hard working centre David Foster.

His namesake Matt finished as the Cougars' top tryscorer, with 19 in all competitions, closely followed by consistent scrum-half Matt Firth.

Simeon Hoyle was again a revelation at hooker and named Man of the Match in the Grand Final, while stand-off Paul Ashton finished the season with a flourish and was superb throughout the play-offs.

125

Richie Hayes

YORK CITY KNIGHTS' first season in the professional game ended with a highly creditable fourth-place finish - though with the squad they recruited at the beginning of the year, even greater things were expected.

But Paul Broadbent's side was hit by constant injury problems, many of them serious. Broadbent himself had to undergo a knee reconstruction, while Chris Smith, Scott Rhodes and George Mack all spent long spells on the sidelines.

When Rhodes did play, he formed a formidable halfback partnership with fellow ex-Dewsbury player Danny Brough, who finished the season as the NL2 Young Player of the Year.

Veteran prop Richie Hayes was as consistent as ever, while Australian loose forward Trevor Krause made a big impact in his first season in the country.

Krause was joint leading tryscorer along with Darren Callaghan, with Alex Godfrey, Mark Cain and Neil Law not far behind.

Broadbent ended the season by retiring as coach due to personal reasons, and he has been replaced for the new campaign by former Featherstone assistant Richard Agar.

An up-and-down season at BARROW RAIDERS ended with Cameron Bell's side in fifth position.

The play-offs saw them record a superb shock win at York, before going out at Keighley the following week.

Having lost several key members of their 2002 squad, the Raiders were always up against it, but yet again proved a match for any side when on form, particularly at Craven Park.

They had prolific tryscorers in the threequarters in Jamie Marshall and Paul Jones, while Adam Pate's emergence in the second half of the year was also a major plus.

Tau Liku

Kiwi halfback Tane Manihera was again a major influence, while in the pack, Tau Liku was as consistent as anyone, along with impressive Australian James King, who enjoyed a fine debut year and was rewarded with a call-up by Ireland for the Euro Nations.

Bell's two year charge at the Raiders ended by mutual agreement at the end of the season, with Peter Roe stepping into the vastly experience New Zealander's shoes.

HUNSLET HAWKS' year started in amazing circumstances with an unbelievable Challenge Cup win over Huddersfield Giants, and although that proved to be their peak, there were still more positives than negatives at the South Leeds Stadium.

That famous 18-14 win over the full-time Giants shook the Rugby League world at the time, and provided the Hawks faithful with something to cherish for years to come.

Coach Roy Sampson also helped them into a play-off place, though their Grand Final dreams were ended at the first hurdle at Keighley.

Sampson was another coach to battle against almost constant injury problems, which stretched his limited squad.

But he did have NL2's best player in his ranks in scrum-half Phil Hasty - crowned the competition's Player of the Year before securing a move to Hull KR.

Winger Bryn Powell will also be playing at a higher level in 2004 - in Super

Bryn Powell

League with Salford - after another boom season that yielded 24 tries, while George Rayner was also a regular scorer.

Consistent performers for the Hawks included second-rower Wayne Freeman, the ageless Mick Coyle and Steve Pryce, and solid centre Iain Higgins.

Former Castleford hooker Jamaine Wray also emerged as a major talent, though one of the major disappointments of the year was that Craig Ibbetson's season was cut short when he dislocated his shoulder playing for the National League under-21s.

127

SWINTON LIONS were another side to hit their major high in the Challenge Cup - with a stirring home win over NL1 side Featherstone.

But despite taking points from all but two of the top six, their inconsistency cost them dearly in the final shake-up.

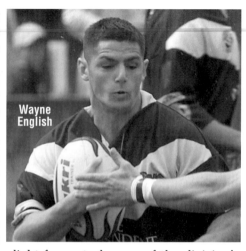

Wayne English

A league double over Minor Premiers Sheffield showed they were capable of beating the best, but narrow defeats against Keighley (both by less than one score) proved crucial.

Coach Peter Roe had several stand-outs though - none more so than fullback Wayne English, who defied his slight frame to be one of the division's top performers.

Goalkicking halfback Chris Hough was also a cornerstone of the Swinton side, as was prop Simon Knox - nominated for the NL2 Player of the Year award.

Jason Roach was top tryscorer with 17 in all competitions, closely followed by Lee Hudson and Australian import Kris Tassell.

Roe was another coach to depart at the end of the campaign, with his assistant Paul Kidd taking over, along with former Swinton favourite Les Holliday, who will be director or rugby.

It was a difficult start to the year for **WORKINGTON TOWN**, with dwindling crowds accompanied by just a handful of players turning up for training and one match - against local rivals Whitehaven - played with just 16 men.

That led to the exit of coach Paul Penrice early in the season, and he was eventually replaced by Billy McGinty, who ignited something of a revival.

Unfortunately for the Cumbrians, McGinty left at the end of the season to become assistant coach at Huddersfield Giants.

But while McGinty was in charge, Town enjoyed some improved performances, sparked by the arrival of Lancashire-based stand-off Shaun

Jamie Beaumont

Boylan and, later, former Salford halfback Neil Alexander.

Of the long-standing Town players, second-rower or centre Jamie Beaumont, winger Graeme Lewthwaite and centre Brett McDermott all made an impact.

Matt Tunstall and Hitro Okesene were pillars of strength in the front row, while Anthony Murray put in some excellent displays after signing from Oldham. And second-rower Gareth Dean - another McGinty recruit - was arguably their player of the year.

GATESHEAD THUNDER avoided the wooden spoon in a year of peaks and troughs for the North East club.

Yusuf Sozi

The beginning of the season included the arrival of a host of Australian players along with coach Bill Ryan as an advisor.

But financial restraints soon resulted in their departure, and the Arriva Trains Cup saw them concede 190 points in four days against full-time Salford in a bizarrely-arranged cross-group fixture - defeats that almost prompted respected coach Paul Fletcher to quit.

But Fletcher stuck it out to the end of the season, and Thunder shocked NL2 by recording wins at York and Swinton in their first two away league fixtures.

Unfortunately, they won just once more - against London Skolars - and also suffered the indignation of being the only team to lose to the capital outfit, in August.

That result did end with Fletcher resigning, and Seamus McCallion will take the coaching hot seat next season.

He will have a host of brilliant youngsters at his disposal, notably halfbacks Paul and Neil Thorman. They were among the top performers of 2003, along with free-scoring centre Damien Reid, Hull-bound winger Richie Barnett, tough prop Yusuf Sozi and fullback Kevin Neighbour.

LONDON SKOLARS' debut year in professional Rugby League ended with 28 defeats and a playing roster as big as many of the scores posted against them.

But a late-season victory over Gateshead, financial stability, and extensive off-field work in the community ensured that the campaign provided a valuable and solid stepping stone for their future progression.

Coach Mark Croston stepped into the breach relatively late prior to the season, combining his role with a full-time position as managing director at the club, and used 72 players during an experimental year.

There were some stand-out performers among them however, especially South African second rower Rubert Jonker, whose blockbusting displays earned him selection for the NL2 side to take on New Zealand A in October.

Huy Le

Goal kicker Jake Johnstone was also a near ever-present, along with talented prop Glen Osborn and outside back Charlie Oyebade.

The Skolars also had the distinction of fielding what is believed to be the first Vietnamese-born player to figure at first team level in this country. Stand-off Huy Le caught the eye on several occasions in what was a fascinating first year for the capital's latest club.

ARRIVA TRAINS CUP FINAL
Reds lay down marker

Salford City Reds lifted the Arriva Trains Cup after a gritty and accomplished win in an incident-packed Arriva Trains Cup Final at Rochdale's Spotland Stadium.

The Reds weathered an early Leigh storm before hitting them with four well-executed tries in a decisive 14 minutes just before half-time.

And they kept their heads in an increasingly heated second half that spilled over on more than one occasion, and ended with the dismissal of Phil Kendrick for a late elbow on Man of the Match Gavin Clinch.

"I thought we toughed it out," Salford coach Karl Harrison said.

"We were extremely patient, didn't panic and stuck to the script I'd wrote. Some of my players took some real cheap shots out there and showed some resolve by not retaliating."

His counterpart Paul Terzis admitted: "That ten, 15 minutes before half-time was such a crucial period of the game.

"We were on the front foot, but after that we were up against it.

"I thought at times we stuck to a gameplan, did really well and had them on the back foot. But the thing about Salford is that they are a very patient team."

Leigh had started brightly, and led 5-0 after the opening quarter, courtesy of a stunning individual try to Leroy Rivett and a Neil Turley field goal.

But four Salford tries in that crucial 14 minutes - all created by either Clinch or Cliff Beverley - had Salford in command at the break, 20-5 up. Props Gareth Haggerty and Andy Coley both crossed, as well as Stuart Littler and Andy Kirk.

Leigh battled on, and tries to Willie Swann and Damian Munro hinted at a comeback.

But the Reds were never in real danger of losing after the break, and tries to Danny Arnold and Alan Hunte confirmed their win, despite a late Turley effort.

ARRIVA TRAINS CUP FINAL

Sunday 6th July 2003

LEIGH CENTURIONS 19 SALFORD CITY REDS 36

CENTURIONS: 1 Neil Turley; 2 Damian Munro; 3 Alan Hadcroft; 4 Phil Kendrick; 5 Leroy Rivett; 6 Patrick Weisner; 7 John Duffy; 8 Sonny Nickle; 9 Paul Rowley; 10 Rob Ball; 11 Sean Richardson; 12 Bryan Henare; 13 Adam Bristow. Subs (all used): 14 David Bradbury; 15 Dale Cardoza; 16 Willie Swann; 17 Paul Norman.
Tries: Rivett (13), Swann (45), Munro (57), Turley (73);
Goal: Turley; **Field goal:** Turley.
Dismissal: Kendrick (78) - late tackle.
Sin bin: Nickle (70) - fighting.
On report: Brawl (70).
CITY REDS: 1 Jason Flowers; 2 Danny Arnold; 3 Stuart Littler; 4 Alan Hunte; 5 Andy Kirk; 6 Cliff Beverley; 7 Gavin Clinch; 8 Neil Baynes; 9 Malcolm Alker; 10 Andy Coley; 11 Simon Baldwin; 12 Paul Highton; 13 Chris Charles. Subs: 14 Steve Blakeley; 15 David Highton; 16 Mick Berne (not used); 17 Gareth Haggerty.
Tries: Haggerty (24), Coley (30), Littler (34), Kirk (37), Arnold (48), Hunte (64); **Goals:** Charles, Blakeley 5.
Sin bin: Hunte (70) - fighting.
On report: Brawl (70).
Rugby Leaguer & League Express Men of the Match:
Centurions: Neil Turley; *City Reds:* Gavin Clinch.
Penalty count: 10-8; **Half-time:** 5-20;
Referee: Peter Taberner (Wigan);
Attendance: 6,486 *(at Spotland, Rochdale).*

NATIONAL LEAGUE PLAY-OFFS
Top six thrillers

NATIONAL LEAGUE ONE

Oldham and Whitehaven were the first two casualties of the NL1 play-offs, as they crashed out on the opening weekend in high-scoring affairs at Hull KR and Rochdale respectively.

The Roughyeds were always up against it at Craven Park, and particularly after tries by Paul Parker and Craig Poucher just before half-time put the Robins in command at 26-12 at the break.

With Paul Mansson outstanding, Steve Linnane's side eased to a 38-24 victory in the second half, though Oldham never gave up fighting and scored last through Chris Percival.

It was a closer affair at Spotland, where Rochdale Hornets eventually ran out 40-38 against 'Haven in a real thriller.

Hull KR's Paul Fletcher looks for support under pressure from Rochdale's Paul Southern

Hornets led virtually throughout the contest, but weren't in the next round until Dave Larder crossed five minutes from the end, making Leroy Joe's late score a consolation.

The second weekend saw the clash of the top two at the Willows - where an amazing game unfolded between Salford and Leigh.

A tight first half saw the Reds go in 12-8 at the interval, before two minutes of madness turned the game on its head. First Ricky Bibey and then Paul Rowley were dismissed for Leigh within moments of each other, and with Adam Bristow still in the sin bin, they were temporarily down to ten men.

But they rallied remarkably, and gave Salford a genuine shock before going down 26-18. Karl Harrison's Reds, however, had booked their place in the Grand Final

131

It was an even more exciting finish at Rochdale, where Hull KR came through a titanic match to extend their late-season run.

The sides were locked at 26-all inside the last minute after a pulsating game, when Rochdale's Ian Watson lined up a match-winning field goal.

But it was charged down by Lynton Stott, Latham Tawhai scooped the loose ball up, and sent Paul Parker on a length of the field sprint for a remarkable gamebreaking try.

That 30-26 win gave the Robins an away trip to Leigh for the chance to join Salford in the Grand Final.

But they were ruthlessly brushed aside 42-12 by a Centurions side with yet another sniff of Super League.

The game was over at half-time, as a Paul Rowley-inspired Leigh side raced into a 32-4 lead, Leroy Rivett scoring twice.

The Robins did regain some pride after the break, but it was not enough to prevent the Centurions booking their Grand Final date with destiny.

NATIONAL LEAGUE TWO

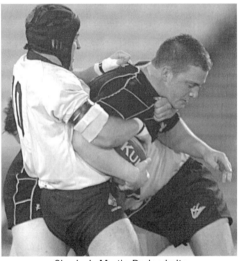

Chorley's Martin Roden halts
Sheffield's Jack Howieson

Barrow Raiders produced the shock of the opening weekend when they stunned highly-fancied York City Knights 50-30 at the Huntington Stadium.

A superb performance from Australian scrum-half Andy Henderson and 26 points from winger Adam Pate sealed the Raiders win, and ended York hopes of promotion in their first season.

The result at Cougar Park went to form, with Keighley beating Hunslet 25-12, with Paul Ashton's eight goals from as many attempts crucial.

That gave the Cougars a home game against Barrow - and Jason Ramshaw the chance to say goodbye to the Keighley faithful ahead of his retirement.

He did so in style, as the Cougars roared into a commanding 35-6 lead before four late Barrow tries made the scoreline respectable. Ashton was again the gamestar in the 35-26 win.

In the day's other play-off game, Sheffield Eagles booked their Grand Final place with an assured 31-14 defeat of second place Chorley.

Halfbacks Gavin Brown and Mark Aston played key roles, while the game also marked the end of Eric Andrews' 15-match try scoring run for the Lynx.

Defeat for Darren Abram's side meant a daunting home clash with in-form Keighley, and the Cougars proved too strong, running out 45-12, with stand off Ashton yet again influential.

Ashton - described as a "maverick" by coach Gary Moorby after the game - scored 25 points as the Cougars' swept into the Grand Final.

NATIONAL LEAGUE GRAND FINALS
Reds, Cougars grab glory

NATIONAL LEAGUE ONE GRAND FINAL

Salford City Reds secured an immediate return to Super League as Leigh once again imploded on the big stage.

The Reds - by some distance the best side in the competition all season - again showed their class with a quality all-round performance, but they were aided by a Centurions team that lacked discipline and made mistakes at crucial stages.

It was sixth time that Salford had beaten Leigh during the course of another marathon season, ensuring their stint in National League One was the briefest possible.

In the end, the "Alex Murphy factor" just didn't pay off for Leigh - neither did the sacking of coach Paul Terzis just weeks before the end of the season.

"I thought Salford deserved to win - they had a lot more discipline that we had," was Murphy's assessment of the game.

"They looked like a Super League side, like they'd trained together all year. We've had a nightmare, making decisions and doing the basic things wrong.

"We got ourselves back into the game but pressed the self-destruct button again, doing some stupid things.

"Bad discipline cost us dear, and we're not happy about that."

The Reds built a commanding early 16-0 lead.

Alan Hunte touched down brilliantly from Man of the Match Gavin Clinch's kick in the third minute, after Leroy Rivett had hesitated. And then Clinch split the Leigh defence up the middle before handing onto the game's leading

NATIONAL LEAGUE ONE GRAND FINAL

Sunday 5th October 2003

LEIGH CENTURIONS 14 SALFORD CITY REDS 31

CENTURIONS: 1 Neil Turley; 2 Damian Munro; 3 Alan Hadcroft; 4 Danny Halliwell; 5 Leroy Rivett; 6 John Duffy; 7 Tommy Martyn; 8 Sonny Nickle; 9 Patrick Weisner; 10 Paul Norman; 11 Sean Richardson; 12 Willie Swann; 13 Adam Bristow. Subs (all used): 14 David Bradbury; 15 Lee Sanderson; 16 Bryan Henare; 17 Ricky Bibey.
Tries: Richardson (33), Halliwell (38), Swann (65);
Goal: Turley.
On report: Nickle (60) - late tackle on Clinch.
CITY REDS: 1 Jason Flowers; 2 Danny Arnold; 3 Stuart Littler; 4 Alan Hunte; 5 Andy Kirk; 6 Cliff Beverley; 7 Gavin Clinch; 8 Neil Baynes; 9 Malcolm Alker; 10 Andy Coley; 11 Simon Baldwin; 12 Paul Highton; 13 Chris Charles. Subs (all used): 14 Steve Blakeley; 15 David Highton; 16 Martin Moana; 17 Gareth Haggerty.
Tries: Hunte (3, 52), Beverley (23), Littler (73);
Goals: Charles 6, Blakeley; **Field goal:** Blakeley.
Rugby Leaguer & League Express Men of the Match:
Centurions: Willie Swann; *City Reds:* Gavin Clinch.
Penalty count: 10-10; **Half-time:** 10-16;
Referee: Richard Silverwood (Dewsbury);
Attendance: 9,186 *(at Halton Stadium, Widnes).*

Alan Hunte tries to break free from Neil Turley

tryscorer, Cliff Beverley. Two conversions and two penalties from Chris Charles put the Reds in total control.

But Leigh fought back well before half-time.

First Sean Richardson touched down after Tommy Martyn almost went over close to the line, and then Neil Turley's brilliant flick pass created a try for Danny Halliwell. Turley's conversion made it 16-10 at the break.

But then the Centurions self-destructed. Charles kicked a needlessly-conceded penalty, and Hunte scored his second after another Clinch kick. Steve Blakeley added a field goal, and a fourth Charles penalty made it 25-10.

Willie Swann did respond for Leigh, but Stuart Littler's 73rd minute score - from a wild Rivett pass - sealed matters late on.

Soon after the game, a champagne-soaked Karl Harrison was asked to contrast his emotions with those he felt at this time last season - just after the Reds' relegation.

"We set a plan out and started training November 4th last year," Harrison said.

"For it all to come to fruition on a day like this shows that the plan has worked out. It's a real emotional time for me right now after the disappointments of last year.

"It's a great turnaround for the Salford club.

"It's not down to me - it's down to the guys out there, they've performed all season. They deserve the accolades, they've taken all the shots out there.

"Leigh have been dangerous every time we've played them this season, and have some quality Rugby League players out there.

"We got a little bit loose and gave them too much football. But at half-time we spoke about composure.

"I don't think it was a fluent performance from us by any means, but in semi-finals and finals it's all about the result and not the performance."

NATIONAL LEAGUE TWO GRAND FINAL

The closest imaginable video referee decision finally settled an enthralling battle and sealed Keighley Cougars' promotion to National League One.

When winger Andy Robinson crashed over in the left corner with less than six minutes remaining, it was impossible to tell with the naked eye whether he had grounded the ball before taking out the corner flag and sliding into touch.

Such was the tension, that Keighley coach Gary Moorby could not bear to watch the big screen decision.

But video referee Gerry Kershaw awarded the try after several viewings, to send the Cougars and their travelling army into raptures.

The game was still not safe, and the Eagles launched one late bid for glory. But when Tony Weller was hauled down by a brilliant tackle from David Foster and James Rushforth and then lost the ball, Sheffield's hopes were gone.

"We came here with that underdog tag, but we were very confident we could

The champagne flows as Keighley celebrate National League Two Grand Final glory

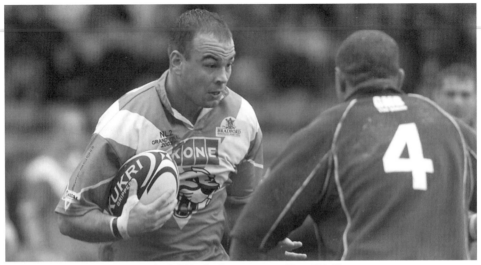

Ian Sinfield looks for a way past Tom O'Reilly

do a job on Sheffield," said Cougars coach Gary Moorby.

"It was a close game, we showed a lot of character and came up with the right plays when it really mattered.

"We knew they had a good forward pack, and were missing Jonny Bruce, but we more than matched them. We had to work hard in the ruck area, we had to stop their go-forward, and for most of the game we did that. Our completion rate was good, and we didn't cough up any cheap ball. I'm delighted."

Mark Aston's side had led for the majority of the second half, after Tom O'Reilly's 51st minute try and Peter Reilly's one-pointer put them 11-9 ahead.

They also took an early lead through Gavin Brown's penalty, before a Matt Foster try, two Paul Ashton goals and a Matt Firth field goal helped the Cougars to a 9-4 interval lead.

The second half was a highly-tense affair before Robinson's try settled matters. It also provided a fitting end to a glorious career for Cougar legend Jason Ramshaw.

Eagles assistant coach Howard Cartwright had no complaints.

"The officials called Robinson's try a try, and we have to accept that," he said. "Keighley did well, they forced four sets back-to-back and we helped them by making basic errors. That was the killer for us.

"The weather was a leveller, and the game became a bit of an arm-wrestle. But we let ourselves down a little bit. We didn't control the ball well, and when we did get on top and hit the front, our handling let us down. We shot ourselves in the foot."

NATIONAL LEAGUE TWO GRAND FINAL

Sunday 5th October 2003

KEIGHLEY COUGARS 13 SHEFFIELD EAGLES 11

COUGARS: 1 Matt Foster; 2 Max Tomlinson; 3 David Foster; 4 James Rushforth; 5 Andy Robinson; 6 Paul Ashton; 7 Matt Firth; 8 Phil Stephenson; 9 Simeon Hoyle; 10 Danny Ekis; 11 Oliver Wilkes; 12 Ian Sinfield; 13 Lee Patterson. Subs (all used): 14 Chris Wainwright; 15 Richard Mervill; 16 Mick Durham; 17 Jason Ramshaw.
Tries: M Foster (7), Robinson (74);
Goals: Ashton 2; **Field goal:** Firth.
EAGLES: 1 Andy Poynter; 2 Tony Weller; 3 Richard Goddard; 4 Tom O'Reilly; 5 Greg Hurst; 6 Gavin Brown; 7 Mark Aston; 8 Jack Howieson; 9 Gareth Stanley; 10 Dale Laughton; 11 Andy Raleigh; 12 Craig Brown; 13 Wayne Flynn. Subs (all used): 14 Peter Reilly; 15 Simon Tillyer; 16 Nick Turnbull; 17 Mitchell Stringer.
Try: O'Reilly (51); **Goals:** G Brown 3; **Field goal:** Reilly.
Rugby Leaguer & League Express Men of the Match:
Cougars: Simeon Hoyle; *Eagles:* Andy Raleigh.
Penalty count: 6-8; **Half-time:** 9-4; **Referee:** Peter Taberner (Wigan).*(At Halton Stadium, Widnes).*

5
INTERNATIONAL YEAR

ASHES SERIES 2003
The nearly men

The history books will show the 20th Kangaroos scored their first 3-0 Ashes series win in 2003 since the Unbeatables of 1986.

Before they left for the northern hemisphere, coach Chris Anderson - who was to wait until the end of the tour before sorting out his uncertain future with the Cronulla Sharks - drummed into his injury-depleted squad the need to uphold the great tradition of Australian sides that had not lost a Test series to any country in the world for a quarter of a century.

The last time Australia lost a series was in the shock two-Tests to nil defeat of the Bob Fulton-led Kangaroos by France in 1978. The British Lions hadn't won an Ashes series since 1970.

"The Kangaroos are vulnerable with so many experienced stars missing," Anderson admitted. "If anything, we're a bit short of depth in the centres. But we have got plenty of utility players who can cover that for us. It will be a tough tour.'

Around 20 stars were unavailable for the Kangaroo squad. They included the pair who captained Australia in the past two years, Andrew Johns and Gorden Tallis.

Seven from the squad that humiliated New Zealand in the July Trans-Tasman Test were ruled out. They included Johns, centres Brent Tate (Broncos) and Jamie Lyon (Eels) as well as stand-off Shaun Timmins and prop Luke Bailey (both Dragons), who were all injured or recovering from surgery. Tallis decided to quit the representative arena while Bryan Fletcher (Rabbitohs) planned his marriage at the same time as the tour.

Other internationals out injured included the Dragons' Jason Ryles, Mark Gasnier and Trent Barrett, Newcastle's Matthew Gidley, Ben Kennedy and Timana Tahu, Sharks' prop Jason Stevens and Melbourne stand-off Scott Hill.

Their absence opened the way for several newcomers, especially a couple of rookie forwards from the Premiership-winning Penrith Panthers. Three of these rookies – winger/centre Luke Lewis, and props Joel Clinton and Trent Waterhouse - were among six players yet to make their Test debuts. The others were Michael De Vere (Broncos), Michael Crocker (Roosters) and Richard Villasanti (Warriors).

Penrith provided five of the Kangaroos. The others were Panthers captain Craig Gower, to cover the two halfback positions and hooker, and veteran centre Ryan Girdler, back in the international arena after two years.

In the absence of Johns and Tallis, Darren Lockyer had been handed the captaincy. He was only the fourth Queenslander to be Kangaroo skipper, after Tom Gorman (1929-30), Wally Lewis (1986) and Mal Meninga (1990 and 1994).

There was a big shock when David Waite named his Great Britain squad after the Super League Grand Final.

Waite revealed his squad to the media on the Monday afternoon - and only minutes before, as journalists headed into the David Lloyd centre in north Leeds to hear the announcement, Waite was on his mobile in a corridor, frantically trying to convince Warrington's Paul Wood he'd really been selected.

After failing to get hold of Wolves coach Paul Cullen to break the news more gently, Waite was left to persuade Wood - after less than 50 first-grade games - he really had made it into the squad, which left for a week's warm-weather training in Spain the following Wednesday morning.

The other uncapped selections were Wigan's Ireland winger Brian Carney, Wakefield centre Gareth Ellis and Castleford skipper Ryan Hudson. Bradford fullback Stuart Reardon was called into the squad on the day it flew to La Manga as cover for Terry Newton, who was given compassionate leave to be with his wife, experiencing late complications to her pregnancy. Keiron Cunningham was unavailable after undergoing knee and ankle operations at the end of the domestic season. Reardon had been named in, and trained with, the England 'A' squad only the day before.

Waite's most surprising omission, St Helens fullback Paul Wellens, had tonsillitis, while Bradford star Leon Pryce - who pleaded guilty at Teesside Crown Court on the same day to a wounding charge - had been excluded because he "had no guarantee he could travel with the team to train."

Captain Andy Farrell delayed his long-standing knee injury to take part in the series and the door was left open for any outstanding performers in the England A squad to be drafted into the squad. "I'm not in the situation where I have to blood people," said Waite, "[but] some of those very talented young players may be given the opportunity to play against the world's best and impress."

GREAT BRITAIN SQUAD: Paul Anderson (Bradford Bulls); Brian Carney (Wigan Warriors); Gary Connolly (Leeds Rhinos); Paul Deacon (Bradford Bulls); Gareth Ellis (Wakefield Trinity Wildcats); Andy Farrell (Wigan Warriors) (c); Stuart Fielden (Bradford Bulls); Mike Forshaw (Bradford Bulls); Lee Gilmour (Bradford Bulls); David Hodgson (Wigan Warriors); Richard Horne (Hull FC); Ryan Hudson (Castleford Tigers); Sean Long (St Helens); Barrie McDermott (Leeds Rhinos); Adrian Morley (Sydney Roosters); Terry Newton (Wigan Warriors); Jamie Peacock (Bradford Bulls); Kris Radlinski (Wigan Warriors); Stuart Reardon (Bradford Bulls); Paul Sculthorpe (St Helens); Keith Senior (Leeds Rhinos); Kevin Sinfield (Leeds Rhinos); Paul Wood (Warrington Wolves)

AUSTRALIA SQUAD: Darren Lockyer (Broncos) (c); Robbie Kearns (Storm) (vc); Matt Sing (Cowboys); Anthony Minichiello (Roosters); Luke Lewis (Panthers); Michael De Vere (Broncos); Shannon Hegarty (Roosters); Ryan Girdler (Panthers); Craig Wing (Roosters); Craig Gower (Panthers); Brett Kimmorley (Sharks); Phil Bailey (Sharks); Joel Clinton (Panthers); Danny Buderus (Knights); Luke Ricketson (Roosters); Craig Fitzgibbon (Roosters); Michael Crocker (Roosters); Petero Civoniceva (Broncos); Steve Simpson (Knights); Shane Webcke (Broncos); Willie Mason (Bulldogs); Richard Villasanti (Warriors); Trent Waterhouse (Panthers).

FIRST ASHES TEST

GREAT BRITAIN 18 AUSTRALIA 22

Great Britain's Ashes dreams were shattered in one moment of madness at the JJB Stadium as Adrian Morley's dismissal, 12 seconds into the game, left the home side facing a battle against simple mathematics.

Despite a heroic display, the Lions' hopes of a winning start to the three-match series effectively ended as Morley walked shamefaced down the tunnel, with the Kangaroos just having enough spark and opportunism from their key players to decide a pulsating, tough and typically engrossing Test.

Morley was given the red card for his reckless forearm smash on Robbie Kearns' chin as the Aussie prop made the first hit-up of the game after Sean Long's deep kick-off. With Kearns on the deck receiving treatment, referee Steve Ganson had plenty of time to ponder his options, and was not short of advice from touch-judge Steve Wright and video referee David Campbell.

Nine years before at Wembley, Great Britain lost skipper Shaun Edwards in a 25th-minute dismissal after pole-axing Bradley Clyde, yet still held out to win the first Test, 8-4. But with the whole game to play short-handed, history was not to repeat itself.

Debates will rage for a long time about whether Great Britain could have won the game had they retained their full complement of players. Certainly the game showed that the Kangaroos weren't short of the winning ethos.

GREAT BRITAIN: 1 Kris Radlinski (Wigan Warriors); 2 Brian Carney (Wigan Warriors); 3 Gary Connolly (Leeds Rhinos); 4 Keith Senior (Leeds Rhinos); 5 Richard Horne (Hull FC); 6 Paul Sculthorpe (St Helens); 7 Sean Long (St Helens); 8 Stuart Fielden (Bradford Bulls); 9 Terry Newton (Wigan Warriors); 10 Adrian Morley (Sydney Roosters); 11 Jamie Peacock (Bradford Bulls); 12 Andy Farrell (Wigan Warriors) (C); 13 Mike Forshaw (Bradford Bulls). Subs (all used): 14 Paul Anderson (Bradford Bulls); 15 Barrie McDermott (Leeds Rhinos); 16 Paul Deacon (Bradford Bulls); 17 Lee Gilmour (Bradford Bulls).
Tries: Carney (19, 71), Senior (50);
Goals: Long 2/4, Deacon 1/1.
Dismissal: Morley (1) - swinging arm.
AUSTRALIA: 1 Darren Lockyer (Brisbane Broncos) (C); 2 Anthony Minichiello (Sydney Roosters); 4 Phil Bailey (Cronulla Sharks); 3 Craig Wing (Sydney Roosters); 5 Shannon Hegarty (Sydney Roosters); 6 Craig Gower (Penrith Panthers); 7 Brett Kimmorley (Cronulla Sharks); 8 Shane Webcke (Brisbane Broncos); 9 Danny Buderus (Newcastle Knights); 10 Robbie Kearns (Melbourne Storm); 11 Steve Simpson (Newcastle Knights); 12 Craig Fitzgibbon (Sydney Roosters); 13 Luke Ricketson (Sydney Roosters). Subs (all used): 14 Petero Civoniceva (Brisbane Broncos); 15 Willie Mason (Bulldogs); 16 Trent Waterhouse (Penrith Panthers); 17 Michael Crocker (Sydney Roosters).
Tries: Bailey (11), Waterhouse (31), Gower (69), Lockyer (75); **Goals:** Gower 0/2, Fitzgibbon 3/3.
Sin bin: Crocker (47) - striking.
Rugby Leaguer & League Express Men of the Match:
Great Britain: Keith Senior; *Australia:* Darren Lockyer.
Penalty count: 7-4; **Half-time:** 4-8; **Referee:** Steve Ganson (England); **Attendance:** 24,614 *(at JJB Stadium, Wigan).*

And the tourists retained an effective spine to their team, no matter how rough they looked around the edges. Skipper Darren Lockyer, brilliant halfback Brett Kimmorley, and the front row of Kearns, Shane Webcke and Danny Buderus carried the Green and Golds home.

Kimmorley was effectively playing on one leg for most of the second half, after suffering a corked thigh, but such is his importance to the team there was no suggestion of him coming off.

And with just five minutes remaining - and the Lions leading 18-16 after Brian Carney scored his second try in the right corner - the gamble paid off for Australia. Kimmorley's long pass sparked their attack from 40 metres out,

Keith Senior stretches out to score Great Britain's second try

and Lockyer joined the line to send Craig Wing on the incisive break through the left centre that broke British hearts. Lockyer popped up on the inside, and jubilantly crossed for the try that decided the Test.

The Lions took huge heart from the sterling performances of several players. Skipper Andrew Farrell typically led from the front in a pack forced to work overtime to cover for Morley's absence. Stuart Fielden slugged it out down the middle and never took a backward step, and Mike Forshaw and Jamie Peacock produced heroic tackling stints.

Down the left Keith Senior looked the game's most dangerous attacker, Richard Horne fully justified his selection - on the left wing - with a mature display, Gary Connolly produced some rock-solid defence out of the top drawer in the right centre, and Carney marked his Test bow with two finely taken tries.

The kick-off was delayed for 15 minutes on a clear, cold evening in Wigan, after horrendous problems on the motorway system. The Australians had just four players from their third Test triumph at the JJB two years ago - Lockyer, Buderus, Kearns and Petero Civoniceva. Ten of the Lions players had played that day, and 13 in the game at Wigan against the Kiwis the previous year, when a famous victory squared the series.

At first it looked as though the Kangaroos would run riot, as they dominated possession and eventually stretched the Great Britain defence, for Craig Gower and Lockyer to link superbly and send makeshift centre Phil Bailey slicing in at the right corner for the opening try. Kimmorley, with a 40-metre run, and Kearns, with a huge drive for the line, had sucked in the British defence. Star goalkicker

141

Craig Fitzgibbon was laid low in back play after being clobbered by Terry Newton, and stand-in Gower missed the shot at goal.

The home crowd was hollering for retribution as Anthony Minichiello caught Horne high after a Farrell chip, but it more a reaction than malicious challenge, and the winger stayed on the field. Great Britain ran the penalty, and then were awarded another for Trent Waterhouse's interference on Peacock. This time Sean Long took a shot at goal, but pulled his angled effort wide of the upright.

But the Lions now held the initiative, and pulled level just before the midway point of the first half. Another move down the increasingly productive left channel was ended by Lockyer's smart tackle on Horne, but Paul Sculthorpe, Long and Connolly quickly took advantage of the momentum of that attack. Connolly showed great hands and awareness to send Carney over on the opposite flank to complete a flowing move, although Long's conversion attempt was off-target.

Willie Mason had claims for a try chalked off by the video referee after kicking through a loose ball, when Peacock was unable to gather. In the lead-up Lockyer, in attempting to kick through, ricocheted the ball off referee Ganson before Mason got his chance. The scrum was put down with the Australians getting the put-in.

Great Britain survived a Long knock-on close to his own line. Connolly made a cast-iron tackle on Wing, and Civoniceva went close before the move ended with a loose Luke Ricketson offload. And the British then broke away in thrilling fashion as Sculthorpe ran the ball on the last, only for the supporting Senior to send his pass behind Horne as he threw it out to the wing.

And after Newton needlessly conceded a penalty for a dig at Wing in the tackle, the Kangaroos took the opportunity to regain the lead. Waterhouse marked his Test debut with a try from Lockyer's angled, low kick that eluded Long's grasp. Gower was again off-target with the conversion attempt, though. Lockyer then showed great positional play to clear the danger posed by Long's testing kick as a rugged and compelling half ended with the Kangaroos just in front.

Within seven minutes of the re-start the numbers were briefly evened up. Michael Crocker was sin-binned for striking Carney after a melee following Kimmorley's kick to the corner flag. In the scramble Kris Radlinski made a superb tackle to prevent Kimmorley diving over the line.

With Kimmorley now clearly struggling, and taking up a defensive position on the wing, Great Britain spied their chance. A Lockyer fumble under his own posts, from a Long kick, showed the Kangaroos skipper was only human and set up the position. From the scrum Senior collected Sculthorpe's sharp pass, evaded Bailey's tackle and slammed the ball over the line as Minichiello came across. The stadium erupted, and Long kept his nerve to land the testing conversion for a 10-8 lead after 50 minutes.

Horne briefly switched to hooker as Lee Gilmour came on the wing with Newton rested. The Lions then had a great chance to move further ahead as Senior seized on a through the legs Ricketson offload ten-metres from his own line and hared off down the left. As three men converged on him, Senior threw a difficult inside pass to the supporting Radlinski that the fullback was agonisingly just unable to gather 40 metres from the Australian line, and the chance was gone.

But on the hour mark Long cleverly gained a penalty after scooting from dummy-half, running at Buderus, who had not got back in the defensive line, and then potting the resulting 33-metre kick straight and true.

The Kangaroos counter-attacked after Newton conceded another penalty, for "afters" in a tackle on Shannon Hegarty, after Paul Deacon's long raking kick. On the last tackle of the resulting attack, from ten-metres out, Kimmorley, from dummy-half, threw out a wonderful pass that took out three defenders, and Gower sliced over for a try. Fitzgibbon, who had only just returned to the action, kicked the conversion for a 14-12 lead.

But Gower then knocked on from Deacon's deep re-start kick, and the Lions ruthlessly took advantage. Long, taking on the line, had the ball reefed out in a two-man tackle by Civoniceva, but Ganson sensibly waved "play-on" and Sculthorpe's great vision saw him throw out a flat pass to Carney, ten-metres out, on the wing. The Wigan crowd favourite sensibly kept his body low to the ground, and did remarkably well to ground the ball in the corner before the tackle of three Australians sent the flag flying. Video referee Mr Campbell agreed, and Deacon landed the touch-line conversion to send British hopes soaring.

But Lockyer's try, with Wing - another player out of his normal position - playing the decisive role, was a cruel blow. Fitzgibbon landed the conversion that put his side back in front and, with a minute left, added a penalty after Deacon sent a goal-line drop-out straight into touch after Radlinski had been pressurised by Kimmorley's kick.

SECOND ASHES TEST

"We blew it". Coach David Waite went on to elaborate at greater length why Great Britain's best chance in 33 years of winning an Ashes series had gone. But those three little words summed it up precisely. "It's as simple as that," he added.

With Britain leading 20-12 at half-time it was odds on them levelling the series and going on to win the Ashes. They had played brilliantly, and needed only to stick to the same game plan to clinch victory. But everything they did right in the first half they did wrong in the second.

When the Kangaroos went 20-8 down after 23 minutes it looked as if they were going to suffer a hiding. But in their hour of need, up stepped Brett

Saturday 15th November 2003

GREAT BRITAIN 20 AUSTRALIA 23

GREAT BRITAIN: 1 Kris Radlinski (Wigan Warriors); 2 Brian Carney (Wigan Warriors); 3 Gary Connolly (Leeds Rhinos); 4 Keith Senior (Leeds Rhinos); 5 Richard Horne (Hull FC); 6 Paul Sculthorpe (St Helens); 7 Paul Deacon (Bradford Bulls); 8 Stuart Fielden (Bradford Bulls); 9 Terry Newton (Wigan Warriors); 10 Barrie McDermott (Leeds Rhinos); 11 Jamie Peacock (Bradford Bulls); 12 Adrian Morley (Sydney Roosters); 13 Andy Farrell (Wigan Warriors) (C). Subs: 14 Sean Long (St Helens) (not used); 15 Kevin Sinfield (Leeds Rhinos); 16 Mike Forshaw (Bradford Bulls); 17 Paul Anderson (Bradford Bulls).
Tries: Newton (4), Radlinski (17), Connolly (23);
Goals: Deacon 4/4.
On report: Morley (61) - high tackle.
AUSTRALIA: 1 Darren Lockyer (Brisbane Broncos) (C); 2 Anthony Minichiello (Sydney Roosters); 3 Craig Wing (Sydney Roosters); 4 Michael De Vere (Brisbane Broncos); 5 Matt Sing (North Queensland Cowboys); 6 Craig Gower (Penrith Panthers); 7 Brett Kimmorley (Cronulla Sharks); 8 Shane Webcke (Brisbane Broncos); 9 Danny Buderus (Newcastle Knights); 10 Robbie Kearns (Melbourne Storm); 11 Steve Simpson (Newcastle Knights); 12 Craig Fitzgibbon (Sydney Roosters); 13 Luke Ricketson (Sydney Roosters). Subs (all used): 14 Petero Civoniceva (Brisbane Broncos); 15 Willie Mason (Bulldogs); 16 Trent Waterhouse (Penrith Panthers); 17 Michael Crocker (Sydney Roosters).
Tries: Lockyer (10), Fitzgibbon (37), Kimmorley (47);
Goals: Fitzgibbon 5/6; **Field goal:** Kimmorley.
Rugby Leaguer & League Express Men of the Match:
Great Britain: Paul Deacon; *Australia:* Brett Kimmorley.
Penalty count: 2-8; **Half-time:** 12-20; **Referee:** Tim Mander (Australia); **Attendance:** 25,147 *(At KC Stadium, Hull).*

Kimmorley. Kimmorley had run the show, dominating the first Test before being injured and doing the same for the full 80 minutes at Hull, despite being unable to train all week.

If anything, Kimmorley had been even more impressive than Andrew Johns two years before. With less obvious talent around him he has taken the initiative and produced the deadliest of touches when most needed. With Australia desperate for a quick score to turn around an eight-point half-time deficit, it was Kimmorley who provided it. There was a wall of Britons in front of him when he got the ball 10 metres out, yet a shimmy and a dummy took him effortlessly through to the posts.

And when the scores were locked at 20-20 with five minutes to go, he popped up with the vital field goal after Britain had spurned their chance of a one-pointer.

The Cronulla halfback had already come to Australia's rescue in the first half, when Britain threatened to pull clear. Immediately after Britain had taken a 6-2 lead he struck back with a perfectly-placed short kick behind the posts that Darren Lockyer touched down. Craig Fitzgibbon added the goal to make it 6-8.

Then, when Britain looked to be heading for an unbelievable 20-8 half-time lead, it was that man again who had a crucial midfield role in the dazzling move that ended with Craig Fitzgibbon scoring a vital try three minutes before the interval. That was the Gamebreaker.

Ironically, Britain's best player at Hull was the man opposite Kimmorley. Paul Deacon did not have the same impact overall, but he was a key figure in Britain's early dominance, and fully justified his promotion from the substitutes' bench. Brought in for his all-round kicking skills, the Bradford Bulls scrum-half hacked on for Kris Radlinski to score a try, and had a 100 per cent success with his four goal kicks. He also supported well to make one of Britain's longest clear breaks in the first half, before being more subdued as the home forwards lost their early authority.

Sean Long was on the bench and inexplicably was never brought on, despite Britain needing a new spark in the second half. Barrie McDermott was in the starting line up, Mike Forshaw on the bench, Adrian Morley moving from prop to second row.

Morley made a proper early impact, in contrast to his seven-second blow that earned him a sensational dismissal in the first Test. This time he was Britain's hero after only four minutes, scooping up Andrew Farrell's short kick and hooking out a superb pass for Terry Newton to touch down.

Morley resorted to type late in the game, when a reckless one-armed head tackle laid out Matt Sing and put the Sydney Rooster forward on report. He was cleared yet again to play in the next Test.

The high tackle was a rare bad incident in a fierce but well disciplined match of only ten penalties. Only two went against the Kangaroos, who did not concede one in the last hour and were awarded seven in the same spell, from which

Kris Radlinski and Jamie Peacock show the pain of Ashes defeat

Fitzgibbon landed two all-important goals. But there were no serious arguments with Australian referee Tim Mander's handling of the game.

Apart from the occasional lapses, Britain's tackling was often magnificent, never more so than late in the second half, when they repelled a sustained siege by the Aussies. With the advantage of three scrums in their favour, plus three penalties, the Kangaroos went through 14 play-the-balls before being forced to spill the ball by Britain's smothering defence.

Considering Britain matched Australia's three tries, and two of Fitzgibbon's five goals went in off a post, perhaps they deserved at least a draw. But, such was the disappointment at the failure to build on their early supremacy, nobody in the British camp was pushing the claim.

Australia looked nervous in the opening minutes, and made an early blunder. After Fitzgibbon kicked the first of his three penalty goals, they failed to stop the restart going dead, and from the position gained Newton scored the

145

first try. Deacon's goal made it 6-2, but that was soon wiped out by Lockyer's converted try.

Australia's Fitzgibbon and Anthony Minichiello both had tries rejected by the video referee on either side of Lockyer's try after trying to touch down kicks, and Britain went back on the attack.

More Australian hesitancy led to another British try when Paul Sculthorpe's kick was hacked on by Deacon and Radlinski won the chase to touch down. This time the video referee ruled in Britain's favour. Deacon tagged on the goal, added a penalty three minutes later, and sent Britain's hopes soaring when he converted Gary Connolly's first ever Great Britain try in 31 Test and World Cup matches.

It followed another error by the dithering Aussies when they lost the ball, and Britain maintained the pressure for Paul Anderson to do well to push out the pass from which Connolly slipped through from close range to force his way over. The 12-point lead after only 23 minutes was beyond expectations, but that was as good as it got for Britain.

Australia became increasingly more menacing, and they struck back with a typical long-distance raid. Sing began it with a long, winding run before Danny Buderus took over and kicked ahead. There was a kind deflection, and Kimmorley linked with Craig Gower before Fitzgibbon dived over in the corner. Fitzgibbon was unable to add the goal, his only miss on the tour. But the second row forward was bang on target with his conversion of Kimmorley's try and two second-half penalties to make it 24 out of 25.

The smallest of consolations for Britain was that their 20 points was the most they have scored in losing an Ashes Test.

THIRD ASHES TEST

There could be nothing but disbelief about the sensational closing stages of the Third Test at the McAlpine Stadium.

Three times in as many weeks Britain had held leads inside the last quarter of the game, only to see the never-say-die Australians climb off the canvas to snatch victory.

The latest instalment of what had been an enthralling trilogy was arguably the cruellest on the Lions. Again Britain had led the game for most of the second half – after Paul Sculthorpe's 52nd minute try. But then, on 76 minutes, the Kangaroos secured one of several repeat sets of tackles when Craig Wing's attempted offload in a frantic finish struck the

Saturday 22nd November 2003

GREAT BRITAIN 12 AUSTRALIA 18

GREAT BRITAIN: 1 Kris Radlinski (Wigan Warriors); 2 Brian Carney (Wigan Warriors); 3 Martin Gleeson (St Helens); 4 Lee Gilmour (Bradford Bulls); 5 Richard Horne (Hull FC); 6 Paul Sculthorpe (St Helens); 7 Paul Deacon (Bradford Bulls); 8 Stuart Fielden (Bradford Bulls); 9 Terry Newton (Wigan Warriors); 10 Adrian Morley (Sydney Roosters); 11 Jamie Peacock (Bradford Bulls); 12 Andy Farrell (Wigan Warriors) (C); 13 Mike Forshaw (Bradford Bulls). Subs (all used): 14 Sean Long (St Helens); 15 Barrie McDermott (Leeds Rhinos); 16 Kevin Sinfield (Leeds Rhinos); 17 Gareth Ellis (Wakefield Trinity Wildcats).
Tries: Radlinski (25), Sculthorpe (52);
Goals: Deacon 1/2, Long 1/1.
On report: Newton (2) - high tackle on Kearns.
AUSTRALIA: 1 Darren Lockyer (Brisbane Broncos) (C); 2 Anthony Minichiello (Sydney Roosters); 3 Craig Wing (Sydney Roosters); 4 Michael De Vere (Brisbane Broncos); 5 Matt Sing (North Queensland Cowboys); 6 Michael Crocker (Sydney Roosters); 7 Brett Kimmorley (Cronulla Sharks); 8 Shane Webcke (Brisbane Broncos); 9 Danny Buderus (Newcastle Knights); 10 Robbie Kearns (Melbourne Storm); 11 Steve Simpson (Newcastle Knights); 12 Craig Fitzgibbon (Sydney Roosters); 13 Luke Ricketson (Sydney Roosters). Subs (all used): 14 Petero Civoniceva (Brisbane Broncos); 15 Willie Mason (Bulldogs); 16 Trent Waterhouse (Penrith Panthers); 17 Darren Smith (St Helens).
Tries: Ricketson (22, 79), De Vere (76); **Goals:** Fitzgibbon 3/3.
Rugby Leaguer & League Express Men of the Match:
Great Britain: Kris Radlinski; *Australia:* Shane Webcke.
Penalty count: 8-5; **Half-time:** 6-6;
Referee: Russell Smith (England);
Attendance: 24,163 *(at McAlpine Stadium, Huddersfield)*.

146

hand of Kevin Sinfield as he attempted the tackle.

Referee Russell Smith, who had just before penalised Martin Gleeson for an improper play-the-ball just inside his own half when he was being pulled down by Michael Crocker, hesitantly waved six more tackles as the Australians gained possession.

It was a harsh call on Britain, who had withstood wave after wave of attacks with sheer guts and determination.

In the same set of six, the Australians struck when, with a long pass to the right, their brilliant captain Darren Lockyer crafted a try for Michael de Vere in the right corner.

Still the Kangaroos trailed by two points, with the touchline conversion from Craig Fitzgibbon to come. The Sydney Roosters second-rower - who started the year by winning the Man of the Match in the World Club Challenge against St Helens - displayed nerves of steel to slot home the kick.

There was yet more drama to come with two minutes left and a possible set apiece to come.

From the restart Australia worked their way to the halfway line, and Lockyer set himself for what would have been an unlikely field-goal attempt, over 60 metres out.

But when the pass went to ground, Lockyer spotted a gap and accelerated through it. He was hauled down by Adrian Morley, but just managed to flick a pass out that was picked off the floor by Craig Wing, who in turn found Brett Kimmorley with a desperate offload.

Kimmorley carried the ball a further 20 metres before standing in Radlinski's tackle and handing on to Lockyer, and it was his pass out of Andy Farrell and Lee Gilmour's desperate cover tackle that put Luke Ricketson over for the stunning late winner. Great Britain's players slumped to the ground

There had been several outstanding Lions performers. In the pack, Stuart Fielden and Andy Farrell - despite his injury - had played the entire 240 minutes of the series. Brian Carney continued his emergence as a genuine world class winger, while fullback Kris Radlinski didn't put a foot wrong, constantly positioning himself superbly in defence and scoring an excellent try.

The Huddersfield contest started in explosive fashion, with Terry Newton's high tackle on Robbie Kearns - which earned the hooker a one-match suspension - one of several bone-shuddering hits.

Newton's shot was correctly judged illegal, although not initially by referee Russell Smith. But it was the Wigan number nine whose guile helped Britain open the scoring. In trademark style, Newton targeted the offside Webcke at a play-the-ball, earning a penalty that Paul Deacon slotted home with ease.

Australia soon found their feet, with Kimmorley's short-range kicking game again causing problems and forcing a line drop-out.

And it was predictably the little scrum-half who laid on the game's first try. The Kangaroos earned another back-to-back set when Fielden reefed the ball one-on-one from Willie Mason, who quickly regathered. Two tackles later, Kimmorley's wide pass put Ricketson on the outside of Paul Sculthorpe and over the line. Fitzgibbon made no mistake with the extras.

But Britain responded immediately. Again it was a Mason handling error that led to the try - the mighty Australian substitute this time dropping the ball cold inside his own quarter.

Britain took full advantage, as Radlinski took Sean Long's well-timed pass and carried Ricketson over the line with him for a try awarded by video referee Gerry Kershaw.

Deacon this time missed the kick, and it remained 6-all at half-time.

The Lions started the second half the brighter, with impressive centre Lee Gilmour scything through down the left before cutting across field and launching an attack on the right.

Both Gilmour and Martin Gleeson had excellent games in the centres, after being called up to replace the injured Keith Senior and Gary Connolly. Another newcomer, Wakefield's Gareth Ellis, also had a significant impact when he came off the bench.

It was a high tackle on Gilmour, by Ricketson, that led to Britain's second try.

After a rampaging run from official Man of the Match Adrian Morley, Newton timed his flat pass perfectly for Sculthorpe to charge onto, and reach out and score.

But from then on, it was the Australians who started to build pressure, in line with their performances during the first Two Tests.

Lockyer glided through and handed onto Kearns, who was only hauled down by a desperate but legitimate last-ditch tackle from Newton.

Then Radlinski produced a superb tackle on his own line to help prevent Crocker from scoring. The Wigan fullback also swept up a dangerous Lockyer grubber.

But British mistakes inside their own half, and sure Australian handling, were beginning to take their toll.

And when referee Smith harshly awarded six more tackles to Australia when that loose ball deflected off Sinfield, the Kangaroos had the position to create De Vere's leveller.

Then it was all about that man Lockyer, who twice had a hand in Ricketson's late, late winner.

That one play - which encompassed skill, desire and most importantly belief - summed up the entire 2003 Ashes series.

"It's about finishing the games off," reflected Australian coach Chris Anderson, who had courted controversy by drafting Saints' veteran Darren Smith into his side ahead of young tourist Luke Lewis.

"We came over here an under-rated team. Whether it's an Australian quality or not, I don't know, but we showed the quality of being able to hang in there and stay positive.

"That's a belief as much as anything. It's not a skill, it's a belief that the team has. It's a belief that the senior blokes of this squad have built into this team

Paul Sculthorpe touches down to put Great Britain in front

over the series, and it's a great thing.

"It was a good series, and I was on the edge of my seat for the three matches. In all three games it went right down to the wire.

"It was a really good spectacle - one of the old fashioned, tough games. It was tough throughout the game, and opportunities weren't there often, and when they were we just had that little bit of class to take them, as we showed at the end."

Great Britain coach David Waite - expected to step down from his position - was in more positive mood than after the Hull defeat, though he could not hide his obvious disappointment.

"We have improved dramatically and they still believe in themselves, but we have fallen short on three occasions," Waite said.

"You've got to make the tackles for 80 minutes, and we didn't do that. We didn't quite build pressure and when they needed to find support they did.

"At this level, the method needs to be better, we just missed out in little moments. We take enough out of them when we had the chance, we only completed 70 per cent and didn't get a line drop out.

"They are an honest, tenacious and improving team, and we have to regroup for what should be an incredible Tri-Series. There are so many positive things to talk about."

Ashes Series 2003

The absence of the likes of Andrew Johns and Gorden Tallis should in no way detract from the ability of those who toured - and conquered.

The 2003 Kangaroos had at least four players who would grace any Australian side from any era.

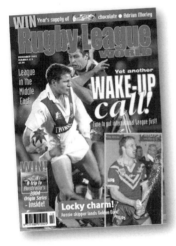

Man of the Series - and winner of the Alan Prescott medal – Brett Kimmorley was outstanding in both of the first two Tests, and particularly in Hull, when his virtuoso performance secured the Ashes. He again helped lay on two tries in the third Tests at the McAlpine. People forget that it was Kimmorley wearing the number seven shirt when Australia won the 2000 World Cup, not Johns, who was at hooker.

Fullback Lockyer was the kind of player everyone will tell their grandchildren about. A graceful runner who could conjure magic every time he touched the ball. It was the Kangaroo captain who produced two moments of brilliance to win the third Test.

Two days after the series he was named as Rugby League World magazine Golden Boot winner for 2003 as the outstanding player in the world.

Prop Shane Webcke was immense up front throughout - none more so than at Huddersfield, where his constant charges punched holes in the British defence. His on-going battle with Stuart Fielden was fascinating to watch.

And Craig Fitzgibbon was the complete second-rower - dangerous with the ball and a magnificent defender. His near flawless goal kicking - he missed just one goal in three matches and his nerveless touchline effort set up the third Test win - made him a contender for Man of the Series.

With Wing and Ricketson also providing big contributions, this was not a team that should go down in history as a second string outfit.

The 2003 Kangaroos were a class side that showed immeasurable levels of character. But that was of little consolation to a British public left deflated by three games which Great Britain could have won.

Great Britain coach David Waite came in for criticism for his team selections and tactical approach and appeared to confirm that he would hand over the coaching reins.

"We weren't quite good enough this time, for a number of little reasons," he said. "We were unfortunate, I think, in a couple of circumstances.

"But the reality is, it's in the paper tomorrow, and we lost 3-0."

On a positive note the Rugby Football League was looking forward to paying off its debts by the end of 2003 on the back of three sell-out crowds for the Ashes series.

"We are obviously disappointed with the results of the three Tests, but in terms of their financial return we are very happy," said RFL boss Richard Lewis.

"We had planned for full stadiums, but what is particularly pleasing is how well we did with the corporate market too. The financial returns are coming in ahead of budget, and we are on track to clearing our inherited debt by the end of the year."

AUSTRALIAN TOUR GAMES

French Test coach Gilles Dumas backed Great Britain to win back the Ashes after the Australians had to fight hard for a 34-10 victory over his "Les Bleus XIII" invitational side in Carcassonne.

The scoreline was almost identical to the one registered by the previous year's Kiwis against the full French Test team - the same New Zealand tourists who drew their series in Great Britain.

And Dumas said the Roos reminded him of Gary Freeman's squad.

Saturday 25th October 2003

FRENCH SELECTION 10 AUSTRALIA 34

FRENCH SELECTION: 1 Julien Gerin (Toulouse); 2 Dmitri Pero (Burleigh); 3 Sylvain Houles (Wakefield Trinity Wildcats); 4 Teddy Saddaoui (Carcassonne); 5 Frederic Zitter (Toulouse); 6 Frederic Banquet (Carcassonne); 7 Julien Rinaldi (UTC); 8 Olivier Pramil (Toulouse); 9 Cederic Gay (Toulouse); 10 Jerome Guisset (Warrington Wolves) (C); 11 Daniel Dumas (Cronulla Sharks); 12 Djamel Fakir (UTC); 13 John Wiagafa (Limoux). Subs (all used): 14 Abde El Khalouki (Villefranche); 15 Marc Faumuina (Villefranche); 16 Pierre Sabatie (Villeneuve); 17 Artie Shead (Toulouse).
Try: Rinaldi (78); **Goals:** Rinaldi 3/3.
AUSTRALIA: 1 Anthony Minichiello (Sydney Roosters); 2 Luke Lewis (Penrith Panthers); 3 Shannon Hegarty (Sydney Roosters); 4 Michael De Vere (Brisbane Broncos); 5 Matt Sing (North Queensland Cowboys); 6 Craig Wing (Sydney Roosters); 7 Craig Gower (Penrith Panthers); 8 Petero Civoniceva (Brisbane Broncos); 9 Michael Crocker (Sydney Roosters); 10 Robbie Kearns (Melbourne Storm) (C); 11 Willie Mason (Bulldogs); 12 Trent Waterhouse (Penrith Panthers); 13 Phil Bailey (Cronulla Sharks). Subs (all used): 14 Joel Clinton (Penrith Panthers); 15 Shane Webcke (Brisbane Broncos); 16 Richard Villasanti (New Zealand Warriors); 17 Brett Kimmorley (Cronulla Sharks).
Tries: Crocker (10, 65), Sing (15, 62), Waterhouse (54), Minichiello (75); **Goals:** De Vere 5/6.
Rugby Leaguer & League Express Men of the Match:
French Selection: Julien Rinaldi; *Australia:* Michael Crocker.
Penalty count: 9-1; **Half-time:** 4-12; **Referee:** Richard Frileux (France); **Attendance:** 7,813 *(at Stade Albert Domec, Carcassonne).*

"I think the Lions have a big chance because they are a new (Australian) team - very young with not a lot of experience," said Dumas.

French Federation chairman Jean-Paul Ferré's gamble of sending half the Test side to Lebanon instead of playing a full international against the Aussies failed to pay off. France was beaten 26-18 by Lebanon a few hours before the game in Carcassonne kicked off.

More bad news for the French was a badly broken leg to Wakefield centre Sylvain Houles.

Hooker Michael Crocker scored two tries on debut as Matt Sing's second try guaranteed the Australians a comfortable victory - but it didn't come until the 62nd minute.

Tuesday 28th October 2003

ENGLAND 'A' 22 AUSTRALIA 26

ENGLAND 'A': 1 Shaun Briscoe (Wigan Warriors); 2 Mark Calderwood (Leeds Rhinos); 3 Martin Gleeson (St Helens); 4 Martin Aspinwall (Wigan Warriors); 5 Ade Gardner (St Helens); 6 Chris Thorman (London Broncos); 7 Rob Burrow (Leeds Rhinos); 8 Andy Lynch (Castleford Tigers); 9 Matt Diskin (Leeds Rhinos); 10 Robert Parker (Bradford Bulls); 11 Danny Tickle (Wigan Warriors); 12 Lee Radford (Bradford Bulls); 13 Sean O'Loughlin (Wigan Warriors) (C). Subs (all used): 14 Danny McGuire (Leeds Rhinos); 15 Gareth Hock (Wigan Warriors); 16 Mick Higham (St Helens); 17 Danny Sculthorpe (Wigan Warriors).
Tries: Gardner (18), Aspinwall (52), Gleeson (60), Lynch (74);
Goals: Thorman 3/4.
Sin bin: Sculthorpe (69) - fighting.
AUSTRALIA: 1 Darren Lockyer (Brisbane Broncos) (C); 2 Matt Sing (North Queensland Cowboys); 3 Shannon Hegarty (Sydney Roosters); 4 Michael De Vere (Brisbane Broncos); 5 Luke Lewis (Penrith Panthers); 6 Craig Gower (Penrith Panthers); 7 Brett Kimmorley (Cronulla Sharks); 15 Joel Clinton (Penrith Panthers); 9 Danny Buderus (Newcastle Knights); 10 Petero Civoniceva (Brisbane Broncos); 11 Steve Simpson (Newcastle Knights); 12 Craig Fitzgibbon (Sydney Roosters); 13 Luke Ricketson (Sydney Roosters). Subs (all used): 14 Michael Crocker (Sydney Roosters); 18 Robbie Kearns (Melbourne Storm); 16 Trent Waterhouse (Penrith Panthers); 17 Willie Mason (Bulldogs).
Tries: Buderus (15), Sing (28), Kearns (43), Crocker (47);
Goals: Fitzgibbon 5/5.
Sin bin: Gower (69) - fighting.
Rugby Leaguer & League Express Men of the Match:
England 'A': Rob Burrow; *Australia:* Brett Kimmorley.
Penalty count: 3-7; **Half-time:** 6-14; **Referee:** Glen Black (New Zealand); **Attendance:** 6,817 *(at Griffin Park, Brentford).*

Australia got the English leg of their tour off to a winning start in London on a Tuesday night - but it was the stirring, skilful performance of John Kear's young charges that will linger in the memory.

England 'A', with their eldest player just 24 and with only one full Great Britain International - Martin Gleeson - in their ranks, shook the Kangaroos to their core and almost snatched a stunning late win.

After only seven minutes of the second half, the home side was staring at a heavy loss, 6-26 down and with the Green and Gold machine clicking slowly into gear.

But, inspired by the invention and

persistence of will-o-the-wisp scrum-half Rob Burrow, and the second-half introduction of Danny McGuire, Kear's side came within a whisker of a famous victory.

In the end, the Australians held on - the 20-point cushion that they had established proving to be just enough. There were plenty of flashes of brilliance, most often from scrum-half Brett Kimmorley and captain Darren Lockyer. But the game was only won when Lockyer cleared Chris Thorman's dangerous late chip.

And Gleeson showed the kind of form that earned him his Lions place last year - displaying brilliant footwork on more than one occasion.

Brett Kimmorley issued another warning sign of his enormous talent six days ahead of the Ashes Test series with a typically authoritative display as the Kangaroos warmed up in impressive style at the Brewery Field, Bridgend.

The linchpin of the Kangaroos attack scored one try and was involved in the other four as his side romped into a 30-0 lead after only 27 minutes, on their way to their highest ever score against Wales in a dozen internationals stretching back to 1911.

He went on to add a second try, as all seven of the Kangaroos starting back-line got in on the scoring act, forming an effective midfield triangle with the equally impressive Craig Gower and Danny Buderus.

Australia's win was easily their highest against Wales, surpassing their 51-19 victory at Wembley in 1933, while Craig Fitzgibbon, with 11 goals from as many attempts, set new records for goals and points in the fixture.

The Kangaroos' only concern was a recurrence of the calf injury suffered by Ryan Girdler, who limped off midway through the first half.

Sunday 2nd November 2003

WALES 4 AUSTRALIA 76

WALES: 1 Paul Atcheson (Widnes Vikings) (C); 2 Hefin O'Hare (Huddersfield Giants); 3 Kris Tassell (Swinton Lions); 4 Adam Hughes (Widnes Vikings); 5 Damian Gibson (Castleford Tigers); 6 Aled James (Widnes Vikings); 7 Mark Lennon (Castleford Tigers); 8 Robert Roberts (unattached); 9 Ian Watson (Rochdale Hornets); 10 Anthony Farrell (Widnes Vikings); 11 Jon Aston (Hull Kingston Rovers); 12 Chris Morley (Oldham); 13 Kevin Ellis (Bridgend Blue Bulls). Subs (all used): 14 Allan Bateman (Bridgend Blue Bulls); 15 David Mills (Widnes Vikings); 16 Gareth Price (Rochdale Hornets); 17 Jordan James (Sheffield Eagles).
Try: Tassell (36); **Goals:** Lennon 0/1.
AUSTRALIA: 1 Darren Lockyer (Brisbane Broncos) (C); 2 Anthony Minichiello (Sydney Roosters); 3 Ryan Girdler (Penrith Panthers); 4 Phil Bailey (Cronulla Sharks); 5 Shannon Hegarty (Sydney Roosters); 6 Craig Gower (Penrith Panthers); 7 Brett Kimmorley (Cronulla Sharks); 8 Shane Webcke (Brisbane Broncos); 9 Danny Buderus (Newcastle Knights); 10 Petero Civoniceva (Brisbane Broncos); 11 Steve Simpson (Newcastle Knights); 12 Craig Fitzgibbon (Sydney Roosters); 13 Luke Ricketson (Sydney Roosters). Subs (all used): 14 Richard Villasanti (New Zealand Warriors); 15 Willie Mason (Bulldogs); 16 Trent Waterhouse (Penrith Panthers); 17 Craig Wing (Sydney Roosters).
Tries: Girdler (4), Bailey (7), Simpson (13), Kimmorley (19, 46), Lockyer (27), Buderus (39, 78), Hegarty (57), Wing (61), Minichiello (73, 80), Gower (75); **Goals:** Fitzgibbon 11/11, Kimmorley 0/1, Gower 1/1.
Rugby Leaguer & League Express Men of the Match:
Wales: Ian Watson; *Australia:* Brett Kimmorley.
Penalty count: 4-6; **Half-time:** 4-36; **Referee:** Karl Kirkpatrick (England); **Attendance:** 3,112 *(at Brewery Field, Bridgend).*

TRANS-TASMAN TESTS
Kiwis bounce back

What a contrast the two Trans-Tasman Tests of 2003 provided. In July it was an international humiliation of the Kiwis. Three months later the New Zealanders had their revenge with a convincing victory over the Kangaroos on the first leg of the Australians' tour.

The former almost certainly rang down the curtain on Test matches staged mid-season, with neither New Zealand nor Britain willing to endure another post-Origin ambush. The latter breathed new life into the sport at international level. It proved the world champions were not unbeatable.

First the July encounter in Sydney. A year after the Australians inflicted the biggest defeat in history on the British Lions (64-10) they were at it again at the same venue (Aussie Stadium). It was the Kiwis' turn to suffer the ignominy of a 48-6 thrashing.

The New Zealand coach Daniel Anderson later revealed that, in the lead-up to the Test, he had received an email from Britain's coach David Waite warning him of what awaited his lads.

"He said he wasn't coming back for the post-Origin ambush after what happened last year," Anderson said. "It's not good for international football."

When Australia led 30-nil at half-time it seemed as if the scoreline of 12 months earlier could be topped. But for much of the second half, the New Zealanders managed to stem the tide.

The Kiwis began well enough. Just three and a half minutes into the game back-rower Logan Swann grabbed a loose ball 20 metres from the line and planted the ball down between the posts. However, the video refereeing team of Allan Caddy (New Zealand) and Phil Cooley (Australia) replayed the incident in which Matt Sing lost the ball over and over again before deciding Swann had stripped the ball illegally. It was later revealed that Cooley had overruled his New Zealand counterpart, who had believed the strip was fair. Most of the fans in the crowd of 30,605 thought so, too.

The video decision seemed to cut at the heart of the Kiwis. From then on they were never really in with a chance.

Sing struck the first blow. He took a clever inside pass from centre Brent Tate, juggled the ball for a moment before taking control and touching down for the first try of the evening. Six minutes later it was Tate who scored himself, winning the race for a wonderful cross-field chip kick from Andrew Johns.

As the first half drew to a close the Australians let loose in typical fashion.

A sensational offload by Shane Webcke sent young Jamie Lyon, the baby of the 2001 Kangaroo tour, on a 55-metre run to the line to score. Another

No way past Paul Rauhihi for Willie Mason during July's Trans-Tasman Test

wonderful pass, this time from Petero Civoniceva, saw big Willie Mason thunder across for a try. Then back-rowers Luke Ricketson and Bryan Fletcher combined to give Lyon a clear run to the tryline for his second touchdown of the evening.

It was 30-nil at half-time and the Kiwis were shell-shocked.

They regrouped at the break and Nigel Vagana was unlucky not to have scored in the first minute of the second stanza.

Then, against the run of play, Tate took off from dummy-half and ran 95 metres to score. And when playmaker Stacey Jones and stop-gap fullback David Vaealiki departed with injuries it was a case of just how big the Australian score was going to be.

Hull recruit Richard Swain scored a consolation try for the Kiwis and converted it himself before the Australians ran in another three four-pointers.

Australia's coach Chris Anderson was in awe of his players: "The lopsided score was because we were really on our game. It would be cruel not to acknowledge the quality of the football. You never expect to win by that score. But when we get on a roll like that, it's hard for anyone to stop us."

It was to be two very different line-ups for the return match at Auckland's North Harbour Stadium, a fortnight after the NRL grand final.

The Kangaroos were decimated by the unavailability of some 18 stars through injury or retirement. The absentees included Australia's most recent two captains – Andrew Johns, who had suffered a career-threatening neck injury, and Gorden Tallis, who had decided to quit the representative arena. Also missing from the ranks of those who played in July were centres Brent Tate and Jamie Lyon, stand-off Shaun Timmins and prop Luke Bailey, all for medical reasons. Dane Carlaw wasn't selected, Bryan Fletcher was getting married and Petero Civoniceva was under suspension.

The Kiwis also had their share of injury problems – most notably to playmaker Stacey Jones. David Vaealiki, Paul Rauhihi, Richard Swain and Stephen Kearney were all injured. Willie Talau had gone to England to join St Helens and Matt Utai was not considered because coach Anderson reckoned he hadn't shown enough mental commitment to the Kiwi cause in July.

With the new-look sides came a new look on the scoreboard.

And a new genuine pride in the Kiwi camp. Players' pride in representing New Zealand. Pride in the Kiwi strip they were wearing. And that pride destroyed the Kangaroos in the 100th Test between the two southern hemisphere neighbours, with the New Zealanders posting their first win over Australia in four years.

"We had a call when the going got tough – Kiwi!" New Zealand's captain Ruben Wiki explained. "We had our names on our jerseys and the silver fern over our hearts. We just looked at that and it paid off."

Hat-trick hero Clinton Toopi agreed: "Kiwi called us through. We said it at the times we were down and out or fatigued. Kiwi! When we heard the word, it got us back on track."

At first it looked as if a repeat of the July thrashing was on the cards.

After 13 minutes the Kangaroos led 10-nil. With just five minutes on the clock, scrum half Brett Kimmorley, in his first outing in six weeks, started a backline movement. And when winger Matt Sing, flung the ball back inside to avoid going into touch, Kimmorley backed up to score the opening try. The Kangaroos then capitalised on two consecutive penalties. Lockyer broke the defensive line off a typically flat Kimmorley pass and second-rower Steve Simpson came back inside to score.

But the expected Australian tryfest never occurred as, suddenly, everything started to go right for the New Zealanders. Their big forwards began steamrolling their way through the rucks. And the backs took full advantage.

After a penalty against Kimmorley for going high on the 18 year old newcomer Thomas Leuluai, the Kiwis kept the ball alive in the tradition of the Harlem Globetrotters. Nigel Vagana was collared centimetres short of the line, but in the next movement he popped a miracle ball to hooker Monty Betham who, in turn, found centre Vinnie Anderson unmarked out wide. Debutant Anderson touched down to give the Kiwis new hope. In the 28th minute Henry Fa'afili was over and Sione Faumuina's conversion levelled the scores.

Then came a concerted Australian push. Centre Shannon Hegarty was tackled within a whisker of the tryline. The next tackle Willie Mason was also

155

grounded tantalisingly short.

Lockyer tried to send a cut-out pass to the unmarked Sing. In the flicker of an eyelid Kiwi winger Francis Meli had gathered the ball in an intercept just a metre or so from his line. Sing managed to slow him, then Lockyer reeled him in. But Meli's pass found Clinton Toopi with a clear 30-metre run to score.

The Kiwis were looking good with a half-time lead of 14-10.

It was a fired-up Kangaroos outfit that returned for the second half. Mason was almost over the line in the first minute. But, tackled by Toopi, he lost the ball.

Nigel Vagana went close to scoring twice within a minute before making a trysaving tackle on Lockyer at the other end of the field. But the Australians were not to be denied. Lockyer put in a kick along the ground. The ball ricocheted off Anthony Minichiello's left boot, Shane Webcke grabbed it with glee and touched down.

The Aussies were almost in another couple of times. Lockyer's pass to Sing a metre from the tryline was knocked down by the defence and then Lockyer himself lost the ball on the tryline. Luck was deserting the visitors.

There was a wonderful break by Joe Galuvao, carrying on from where he left off in helping Penrith to Premiership success. In the next tackle, Monty Betham, Leuluai and Francis Meli all handled before Toopi was over to score his second try. Three minutes later he made it a hat-trick after Faumuina, Leuluai and Vagana all handled.

To rub salt into the wound, Toopi attracted two defenders, leaving the way open for Anderson to grab his second touchdown as the clock wound down to full-time.

Kiwi coach Daniel Anderson was elated: "It's a nice way to cap off the year. I thought every player showed their best form. Everyone had a dig, right across the park."

His opposite number, Chris Anderson, was circumspect: "We just didn't take the opportunities when we had them. It was a good, tough game of footy and, in a game as close as that, when your opportunities come, you need to take them."

TRANS-TASMAN TESTS

Friday 25th July 2003

AUSTRALIA 48 NEW ZEALAND 6

AUSTRALIA: Anthony Minichiello (Sydney Roosters), Shannon Hegarty (Sydney Roosters), Brent Tate (Brisbane Broncos), Jamie Lyon (Parramatta Eels), Matt Sing (North Qld Cowboys), Shaun Timmins (St Geo Illawarra Dragons), Andrew Johns (Newcastle Knights) (c); Shane Webcke (Brisbane Broncos), Danny Buderus (Newcastle Knights), Luke Bailey (St Geo Illawarra Dragons), Gorden Tallis (Brisbane Broncos), Dane Carlaw (Brisbane Broncos), Luke Ricketson (Sydney Roosters). Subs: Bryan Fletcher (Souths Rabbitohs), Craig Wing (Sydney Roosters), Willie Mason (Bulldogs), Petero Civoniceva (Brisbane Broncos).
Tries: Sing (16, 57), Tate (21, 43), Lyon (30, 38), Mason (32), Hegarty (70), Wing (77); **Goals:** Johns 6
NEW ZEALAND: David Vaealiki (Parramatta Eels), Matt Utai (Bulldogs), Nigel Vagana (Bulldogs), Clinton Toopi (NZ Warriors), Francis Meli (NZ Warriors), Willie Talau (Bulldogs), Stacey Jones (NZ Warriors); Paul Rauhihi (North Qld Cowboys), Richard Swain (Brisbane Broncos), Ruben Wiki (Canberra Raiders) (c), Stephen Kearney (Melbourne Storm), Logan Swann (NZ Warriors), Awen Guttenbeil (NZ Warriors). Subs: Tony Puletua (Penrith Panthers), Monty Betham (NZ Warriors), Jerry Seuseu (NZ Warriors), Joe Galuvao (Penrith Panthers).
Try: Swain (52); **Goal:** Swain
Rugby Leaguer & League Express Men of the Match:
Australia: Shane Webcke; *New Zealand:* Paul Rauhihi.
Half-time: 30-0; **Referee:** Bill Harrigan (Australia);
Attendance: 30,605 *(at Aussie Stadium, Sydney)*

(Brisbane's Darren Lockyer was chosen for Australia but withdrew through injury and was replaced by Hegarty while the Warrior's Ali Lauiti'iti was in New Zealand's squad but missed the Test through suspension. Galuvao was his replacement)

Saturday 18th October 2003

NEW ZEALAND 30 AUSTRALIA 16

NEW ZEALAND: Motu Tony (NZ Warriors); Henry Fa'afili (NZ Warriors); Vinnie Anderson (NZ Warriors); Clinton Toopi (NZ Warriors); Francis Meli (NZ Warriors); Nigel Vagana (Bulldogs); Sione Faumuina (NZ Warriors); Jason Cayless (Sydney Roosters); Monty Betham (NZ Warriors); Nathan Cayless (Parramatta Eels); Joe Galuvao (Penrith Panthers); Tony Puletua (Penrith Panthers); Ruben Wiki (Canberra Raiders) (c). Subs: Thomas Leuluai (NZ Warriors); Awen Guttenbeil (NZ Warriors); Jerry Seuseu (NZ Warriors); Ali Lauiti'iti (NZ Warriors).
Tries: Anderson (19; 77), Fa'afili (28), Toopi (37; 67; 70);
Goals: Faumuina 3
AUSTRALIA: Darren Lockyer (Brisbane Broncos) (c); Anthony Minichiello (Sydney Roosters); Shannon Hegarty (Sydney Roosters); Michael De Vere (Brisbane Broncos); Matt Sing (North Qld Cowboys); Craig Wing (Sydney Roosters); Brett Kimmorley (Cronulla Sharks); Shane Webcke (Brisbane Broncos); Danny Buderus (Newcastle Knights); Robbie Kearns (Melbourne Storm); Steve Simpson (Newcastle Knights); Craig Fitzgibbon (Sydney Roosters); Luke Ricketson (Sydney Roosters). Subs: Willie Mason (Bulldogs); Richard Villasanti (NZ Warriors); Phil Bailey (Cronulla Sharks). Craig Gower (Penrith Panthers).
Tries: Kimmorley (5), Simpson (12), Webcke (52); **Goals:** Fitzgibbon 2
Rugby Leaguer & League Express Men of the Match:
New Zealand: Clinton Toopi; *Australia:* Shane Webcke.
Half-time: 14-10; **Referee:** Sean Hampstead;
Attendance: 21,296 *(at North Harbour Stadium, Auckland)*

(Penrith's Paul Whatuira, the Roosters' Andrew Lomu and the Warriors' Tevita Latu and Wairangi Koopu were also in the Kiwis' provisional 21-man squad)

OTHER INTERNATIONALS
A vote for the Euro

EUROPEAN NATIONS CUP

England lifted the European Nations Cup at a canter, by 68-6, against an injury-ravaged French side in the final at Wilderspool.

Gilles Dumas was without 11 of his first-choice players, and had only one of his preferred pack in the side, skipper Pascal Jampy. The injury list was the only possible explanation for how a French selection had so tested the Kangaroos the previous month, yet so limply allowed England to stride into a 16-0 lead after just 11 minutes.

Poor fringe defence from the French contributed to all three, as Gareth Hock shot through after Ade Gardner ran around some scrappy tackling on the left and Matt Diskin ran hard through similar efforts on the right to send in Rob Burrow.

Sandwiched in between, England showed enterprise as Danny McGuire kicked from a scrum on his own line for Mark Calderwood to rush 65 metres and hack the ball from the grasp of French winger Fourcade Abasse, then go on to touch down. It looked, briefly, as if the game remained a contest when France scored their only try on 16 minutes, as Freddy Banquet's bomb was spilled by Calderwood, and Teddy Saddaoui got a hand to the ball.

But five tries before half-time killed the game. A nice McGuire drop-off cut open the French defence for Burrow's second score, while a Burrow chip on his own 30-metre line launched a bout of interpassing that ended with Andy Lynch fending off Abasse to score.

But the best of the five was Calderwood's second, as he bravely dived over Abasse's back, caught a McGuire kick with his fingertips and kept control to touch down.

That added up to 44-6, and the best spell of French resistance followed - only for England to again produce a spectacular effort, as Gardner shot 80 metres down the wing and interpassed with Calderwood.

Calderwood's generosity was well rewarded, as he bagged two of the three remaining tries.

England had seen off Wales and Russia - who had met in the first of the ties - in the two pool games.

Wales ran in 14 tries against the out-classed Russians in Aberavon by 74-4. Adam Hughes and Lenny Woodard each scored hat-tricks, although the gamestar was Bears centre Igor Gavrilin, who put in a superb performance in defeat.

The young England team made short work of Russia at Odsal, winning 102-0. Wigan prop Danny Sculthorpe was the stand-out player, throwing some superlative balls out of the tackle. His combination down the English left flank with official man of the match Danny Tickle and winger Mark Calderwood always had the Russians perplexed.

In the Pool decider, watched by just over 2,000 at a chilly Headingley, England beat Wales 22-4 in a lacklustre game.

Matt Diskin and Danny Tickle were deservedly singled out by their coach John Kear, but there was little free-flowing football. Wales spilled the ball from the kick-off, and Rob Burrow's fifth-tackle grubber caused a scramble that left Hefin O'Hare flat on his back and Diskin dabbing the ball down for a 6-0 lead - with 60 seconds gone.

As the home halfbacks struggled to create space, it took until the 15th minute for another scoring opportunity, when Tickle landed a penalty for a high shot by Chris Morley. Ade Gardner tore in at the flag two minutes later off a long Jamie Rooney pass, but 12-0 was never enough of a cushion for England. The Welsh held them for the rest of the first half, while adding a score of their own, when the busy Ian Watson kicked through for Mark Lennon to score his final try before flying back to Australia to join Manly.

Wales began the second period the stronger side, with David Mills' charge sending Jordan James close to the line. But former Royal Marine James was then involved in the punch-up that had been brewing for some time, and while the Wales defence rushed to join in, England substitute Danny McGuire weaved his way through their increasingly thinning ranks for the decisive 60-metre score. Then, just before the hourmark Bridgend winger Lenny Woodard made a mess of a simple kick return and Diskin scored a simple second try.

France had won their pool on points difference only after beating Ireland 26-18 in their opener at Dalymount Park, Dublin. Up 26-0 at half-time and looking for all the world like they could threaten England for the first Euro Nations title, the Tricolours' resolve was washed away in the rain that descended on a bitterly cold stadium at the interval.

Ireland's inability to convert any of their four second-half tries was the only thing that prevented them giving the French a real fright.

Ireland had got up late the previous week in Glasgow, a Karl Fitzpatrick try pinching a 24-22 win over Scotland, just 35 seconds from the end. Fitzpatrick, who was Gavin Clinch's understudy at Salford, ironically got his chance after Clinch withdrew from the Irish squad through injury. The 21 year old, whose grandparents were born in County Mayo, was one of 13 players on debut in a new-look Irish squad.

The outcome of the two games meant Scotland could still qualify for the final by beating France by five or more points, but in wet and windswept Narbonne they edged an exciting game only 8-6. Danny Arnold, Joe Berry, Nathan Graham and captain Wayne McDonald were the only survivors from Scotland's 42-20 win over France in Lezignan in July 2001, but Billy McGinty's new-look side pushed hard for the try that would take them to Wilderspool. But when Michael Van Snick defused a last-gasp Andrew Henderson bomb, France were through.

Sunday 26th October 2003

SCOTLAND 22 IRELAND 24

SCOTLAND: 1 Lee Penny (Warrington Wolves); 2 Jason Roach (Swinton Lions); 4 PJ Solomon (Doncaster Dragons); 3 Damien Reid (Gateshead Thunder); 5 Danny Arnold (Salford City Reds); 6 John Duffy (Leigh Centurions); 7 Andrew Henderson (Barrow Raiders); 8 Joe Berry (Batley Bulldogs); 9 Dave McConnell (Chorley Lynx); 10 Wayne McDonald (Leeds Rhinos) (C); 11 Iain Morrison (Huddersfield Giants); 12 Simon Knox (Swinton Lions); 13 Oliver Wilkes (Keighley Cougars). Subs (all used): 14 Nathan Graham (Featherstone Rovers); 15 Spencer Miller (Whitehaven); 16 Matthew Tunstall (Workington Town); 17 Jack Howieson (Sheffield Eagles).
Tries: Penny (10, 19), Arnold (55), Roach (67); **Goals:** Duffy 3.
IRELAND: 1 Francis Cummins (Leeds Rhinos); 2 Rob Smyth (Warrington Wolves); 3 Lee Doran (Oldham); 4 Anthony Stewart (St Helens); 5 Dean Gaskell (Warrington Wolves); 6 Paul Handforth (Wakefield Trinity Wildcats); 7 Neil Roden (Oldham); 8 Richard Marshall (London Broncos); 9 Phil Cantillon (Widnes Vikings) (C); 10 Mick Slicker (Huddersfield Giants); 11 Phil Farrell (Oldham); 12 James King (Barrow Raiders); 13 Tommy Gallagher (Leeds Rhinos). Subs (all used): 14 Karl Fitzpatrick (Salford City Reds); 15 Chris Maye (St Helens); 16 David Bates (Gateshead Thunder); 17 Martin McLoughlin (Oldham).
Tries: Cantillon (30), King (38), Fitzpatrick (52, 80); **Goals:** Handforth 2, Fitzpatrick 2.
Rugby Leaguer & League Express Men of the Match: *Scotland:* Andrew Henderson; *Ireland:* Karl Fitzpatrick.
Penalty count: 6-10; **Half-time:** 12-12; **Referee:** Thierry Alibert (France); **Attendance:** 1,123 *(at Old Anniesland).*

Saturday 1st November 2003

IRELAND 18 FRANCE 26

IRELAND: 1 Francis Cummins (Leeds Rhinos); 2 Rob Smyth (Warrington Wolves); 3 Lee Doran (Oldham); 4 Anthony Stewart (St Helens); 5 Dean Gaskell (Warrington Wolves); 6 Karl Fitzpatrick (Salford City Reds); 7 Neil Roden (Oldham); 8 Mick Slicker (Huddersfield Giants); 9 Phil Cantillon (Widnes Vikings); 10 Richard Marshall (London Broncos); 11 Chris Maye (St Helens); 12 James King (Barrow Raiders); 13

Tommy Gallagher (Leeds Rhinos). Subs (all used): 14 Carl De Chenu (Sheffield Eagles); 15 Paul Handforth (Wakefield Trinity Wildcats); 16 David Bates (Gateshead Thunder); 17 Martin McLoughlin (Oldham).
Tries: Stewart (45), King (51), Cummins (67), Cantillon (75); **Goal:** Fitzpatrick.
FRANCE: 1 Frederic Banquet (Carcassonne); 2 Michael Van Snick (Villeneuve); 3 Claude Sirvent (St Gaudens); 4 Teddy Saddaoui (Carcassonne); 5 Fourcade Abasse (St Gaudens); 6 Laurent Frayssinous (UTC); 7 Julien Rinaldi (UTC); 8 Olivier Pramil (Toulouse); 9 Cederic Gay (Toulouse); 10 Jerome Guisset (Warrington Wolves) (C); 11 Pascal Jampy (UTC); 12 Artie Shead (Toulouse); 13 Laurent Carrasco (Villeneuve). Subs (all used): 14 Julien Gerin (Toulouse); 15 Rachid Hechiche (Lyon); 16 John Wiagafa (Limoux); 17 Sebastien Raguin (Toulouse).
Tries: Banquet (6), Jampy (15), Sirvent (27, 33), Frayssinous (38); **Goals:** Frayssinous 2, Banquet.
Rugby Leaguer & League Express Men of the Match: *Ireland:* Anthony Stewart; *France:* Claude Sirvent.
Penalty count: 7-7; **Half-time:** 26-0; **Referee:** Glen Black (New Zealand); **Attendance:** 1,082 *(at Dalymount Park, Dublin).*

Sunday 2nd November 2003

ENGLAND 'A' 102 RUSSIA 0

ENGLAND 'A': 1 Paul Sykes (London Broncos); 2 Mark Calderwood (Leeds Rhinos); 3 Shaun Briscoe (Wigan Warriors); 4 Ian Sibbit (Warrington Wolves); 5 Waine Pryce (Castleford Tigers); 6 Danny McGuire (Leeds Rhinos); 7 Jamie Rooney (Wakefield Trinity Wildcats); 8 Danny Sculthorpe (Wigan Warriors); 9 Matt Diskin (Leeds Rhinos) (C); 10 Robert Parker (Bradford Bulls); 11 Danny Tickle (Wigan Warriors); 12 Gareth Hock (Wigan Warriors); 13 Rob Purdham (London Broncos). Subs (all used): 14 Rob Burrow (Leeds Rhinos); 15 Andy Lynch (Castleford Tigers); 16 Ryan Clayton (Halifax); 17 Ade Gardner (St Helens).
Tries: Calderwood (13, 33, 76), Rooney (17, 34), Tickle (20, 38), McGuire (29), Parker (39, 67), Purdham (43), Clayton (54, 58), Burrow (63, 72), Sykes (65), Gardner (70, 74, 80); **Goals:** Tickle 11, Rooney 2.
RUSSIA: 1 Oleg Lougonov; 25 Rinat Chamsoutdinov; 15 Sergei Dobrynin; 4 Raphael Yakubov; 19 Denis Korolev; 6 Victor Netchaev; 23 Igor Gavrilin; 8 Alexander Lysenkov; 20 Roman Outchinikov; 10 Evgeny Bojoukov; 11 Aidar Akhmetsin; 12 Kirill Koulemin; 13 Robert Ilyasov. Subs (all used): 14 Oleg Sokolov; 15 Andrei Zhukov; 16 Alexei Makovetsky; 17 Ian Gvozdev.
Rugby Leaguer & League Express Men of the Match: *England 'A':* Danny Sculthorpe; *Russia:* Roman Outchinikov.
Penalty count: 6-4; **Half-time:** 38-0; **Referee:** Richard Silverwood (England); **Attendance:** 1,576 *(at Odsal Stadium, Bradford).*

Sunday 9th November 2003

FRANCE 6 SCOTLAND 8

FRANCE: 1 Frederic Banquet (Carcassonne); 2 Michael Van Snick (Villeneuve); 3 Claude Sirvent (St Gaudens); 4 Teddy Saddaoui (Carcassonne); 5 Fourcade Abasse (St Gaudens); 6 Laurent Frayssinous (UTC); 7 Julien Rinaldi (UTC); 8 Rachid Hechiche (Lyon); 9 David Berthezene (UTC); 10 Olivier Pramil (Toulouse); 11 Pascal Jampy (UTC) (C); 12 John Wiagafa (Limoux); 13 Laurent Carrasco (Villeneuve). Subs (all used): 14 Julien Gerin (Toulouse); 15 Marc Faumuina (Villefranche); 16 Pierre Sabatie (Villeneuve); 17 Sebastien Azema (Carcassonne).
Goals: Frayssinous 3.
SCOTLAND: 1 Lee Penny (Warrington Wolves); 2 Jason Roach (Swinton Lions); 3 PJ Solomon (Doncaster Dragons); 4 Oliver Wilkes (Keighley Cougars); 5 Danny Arnold (Salford City Reds); 6 Lee Kiddie (Whitehaven); 7 Andrew Henderson (Barrow Raiders); 8 Joe Berry (Batley Bulldogs); 9 Dave McConnell (Chorley Lynx); 10 Wayne McDonald (Leeds Rhinos) (C); 11 Iain Morrison (Huddersfield Giants); 12 Simon Knox (Swinton

Lions); 13 Nathan Graham (Featherstone Rovers). Subs (all used): 14 Spencer Miller (Whitehaven); 15 James Houston (Featherstone Rovers); 16 Jack Howieson (Sheffield Eagles); 17 Matthew Tunstall (Workington Town).
Try: Henderson (34); **Goals:** Wilkes 2.
Rugby Leaguer & League Express Men of the Match: *France:* Frederic Banquet; *Scotland:* Jason Roach.
Penalty count: 7-13; **Half-time:** 0-6; **Referee:** Richard Silverwood (England); **Attendance:** 2,200 *(at Parc Des Sports, Narbonne).*

ENGLAND 'A' 22 WALES 4

ENGLAND 'A': 1 Paul Sykes (London Broncos); 2 Waine Pryce (Castleford Tigers); 3 Martin Aspinwall (Wigan Warriors); 4 Stuart Reardon (Bradford Bulls); 5 Ade Gardner (St Helens); 6 Jamie Rooney (Wakefield Trinity Wildcats); 7 Rob Burrow (Leeds Rhinos); 8 Andy Lynch (Castleford Tigers); 9 Matt Diskin (Leeds Rhinos); 10 Robert Parker (Bradford Bulls); 11 Danny Tickle (Wigan Warriors); 12 Gareth Hock (Wigan Warriors); 13 Sean O'Loughlin (Wigan Warriors) (C). Subs (all used): 14 Danny McGuire (Leeds Rhinos); 15 Ian Sibbit (Warrington Wolves); 16 Ryan Clayton (Halifax); 17 Danny Sculthorpe (Wigan Warriors).
Tries: Diskin (1, 58), Gardner (17), McGuire (47); **Goals:** Tickle 3.
WALES: 1 Damian Gibson (Castleford Tigers); 2 Hefin O'Hare (Huddersfield Giants); 3 Kris Tassell (Swinton Lions); 4 Adam Hughes (Widnes Vikings); 5 Lenny Woodard (Bridgend Blue Bulls); 6 Aled James (Widnes Vikings); 7 Mark Lennon (Castleford Tigers); 8 Robert Roberts (unattached); 9 Ian Watson (Rochdale Hornets); 10 Anthony Farrell (Widnes Vikings); 11 Justin Morgan (Toulouse); 12 Paul Atcheson (Widnes Vikings) (C); 13 Chris Morley (Oldham). Subs (all used): 14 Jon Aston (Hull Kingston Rovers); 15 David Mills (Widnes Vikings); 16 Gareth Price (Rochdale Hornets); 17 Jordan James (Sheffield Eagles).
Try: Lennon (31).
Rugby Leaguer & League Express Men of the Match: *England 'A':* Matt Diskin; *Wales:* Adam Hughes.
Penalty count: 11-5; **Half-time:** 12-4; **Referee:** Thierry Alibert (France); **Attendance:** 2,124 *(at Headingley Stadium, Leeds).*

Sunday 16th November 2003

ENGLAND 'A' 68 FRANCE 6

ENGLAND 'A': 1 Shaun Briscoe (Wigan Warriors); 2 Mark Calderwood (Leeds Rhinos); 3 Stuart Reardon (Bradford Bulls); 4 Martin Aspinwall (Wigan Warriors); 5 Ade Gardner (St Helens); 6 Danny McGuire (Leeds Rhinos); 7 Rob Burrow (Leeds Rhinos); 8 Andy Lynch (Castleford Tigers); 9 Matt Diskin (Leeds Rhinos); 10 Robert Parker (Bradford Bulls); 11 Danny Tickle (Wigan Warriors); 12 Gareth Hock (Wigan Warriors); 13 Sean O'Loughlin (Wigan Warriors) (C). Subs (all used): 14 Jamie Rooney (Wakefield Trinity Wildcats); 15 Danny Sculthorpe (Wigan Warriors); 16 Rob Purdham (London Broncos); 17 Ian Sibbit (Warrington Wolves).
Tries: Hock (2, 26), Calderwood (7, 37, 63, 74), Burrow (11, 24), Aspinwall (31), Lynch (34), Gardner (57), Parker (71); **Goals:** Tickle 9, Rooney.
FRANCE: 1 Frederic Banquet (Carcassonne); 2 Michael Van Snick (Villeneuve); 3 Fabrice Estebanez (Limoux); 4 Teddy Saddaoui (Carcassonne); 5 Fourcade Abasse (St Gaudens); 6 Laurent Frayssinous (UTC); 7 Julien Rinaldi (UTC); 8 Marc Faumuina (Villefranche); 9 David Berthezene (UTC); 10 Olivier Pramil (Toulouse); 11 Pascal Jampy (UTC) (C); 12 John Wiagafa (Limoux); 13 Laurent Carrasco (Villeneuve). Subs (all used): 14 Julien Gerin (Toulouse); 15 Rachid Hechiche (Lyon); 16 Pierre Sabatie (Villeneuve); 17 Sebastien Azema (Carcassonne).
Try: Saddaoui (16); **Goal:** Frayssinous.
Rugby Leaguer & League Express Men of the Match: *England 'A':* Mark Calderwood; *France:* Fourcade Abasse.
Penalty count: 7-7; **Half-time:** 44-6; **Referee:** Karl Kirkpatrick (England); **Attendance:** 2,536 *(at Wilderspool, Warrington).*

WALES 74 RUSSIA 4

WALES: 1 Paul Atcheson (Widnes Vikings) (C); 2 Hefin O'Hare (Huddersfield Giants); 3 Kris Tassell (Swinton Lions); 4 Adam Hughes (Widnes Vikings); 5 Lenny Woodard (Bridgend Blue Bulls); 6 Aled James (Widnes Vikings); 7 Mark Lennon (Castleford Tigers); 8 Robert Roberts (unattached); 9 Ian Watson (Rochdale Hornets); 10 Justin Morgan (Toulouse); 11 Jordan James (Sheffield Eagles); 12 Chris Morley (Oldham); 13 Kevin Ellis (Bridgend Blue Bulls). Subs (all used): 14 Damian Gibson (Castleford Tigers); 15 Allan Bateman (Bridgend Blue Bulls); 16 Damien Hudd (Torfaen Tigers); 17 Gareth Price (Rochdale Hornets).
Tries: Hughes (1, 69, 73), O'Hare (6), Lennon (9), Roberts (18), Watson (28), Ellis (31), Woodard (37, 57, 76), Bateman (42), Price (62), J James (67); **Goals:** Watson, Hughes 2, Lennon 6.
RUSSIA: 1 Oleg Sokolov; 2 Rinat Chamsoutdinov; 3 Igor Gavrilin; 4 Vladimir Ovtchinnikov; 5 Sergei Dobrynin; 6 Victor Netchaev; 7 Denis Nikolski; 8 Petr Sokolov; 9 Roman Outchinikov; 10 Alexander Lysenkov; 11 Robert Ilyasov; 12 Kirrill Koulemin; 13 Evgeny Bojoukov. Subs (all used): 14 Aidar Akhmetsin; 15 Jan Gvozdev; 16 Andrei Zhukov; 17 Rouslan Izmailov.
Try: Dobrynin (13).
Dismissal: Chamsoutdinov (72) - lying on.
Rugby Leaguer & League Express Men of the Match: *Wales:* Adam Hughes; *Russia:* Igor Gavrilin.
Penalty count: 7-7; **Half-time:** 34-4; **Referee:** Glen Black (New Zealand); **Attendance:** 1,100 *(at Talbot Athletic Ground, Aberavon).*

159

Other Internationals

MEDITERRANEAN CUP

Bulldogs star Hazem El Masri lent his voice to the growing clamour for a Rugby League World Cup in Australia in 2008. El Magic scored a try and kicked five goals as Lebanon beat France 26-18 in Tripoli to retain the Mediterranean Cup in October.

The four-team tournament - which also included Morocco and Serbia & Montenegro - saw three double headers staged over seven days in the Middle East.

While the earlier games were characterised by one-sided scorelines and low crowds, over 4,000 enthusiastic people turned up for the nationally televised final match, the result of which was in doubt until El Masri's brother and Lebanese winger Wissam El Masri scored an interception try one minute before time.

KIWI A TOUR

The New Zealand Residents headed home with their heads held high, despite no wins from their gruelling five games in 14-days schedule on their first tour to the UK.

A thrilling opening clash with Cumbria at Whitehaven saw the Kiwis fire back from being 24-nil down with 12 minutes remaining to snatch a draw. Over 4,000 fans packed into Whitehaven's Recreation Ground after the kick-off was delayed.

The second game was probably the most disappointing, as the Kiwis crashed 27-8 at Keighley to a National Two side coached by Peter Roe. Seven

---

NEW ZEALAND 'A' TOUR 2003

Sunday 19th October 2003

CUMBRIA 24 NEW ZEALAND 'A' 24

CUMBRIA: 1 Gary Broadbent (Whitehaven); 2 Matt Gardner (Leeds Rhinos); 3 Brett McDermott (Whitehaven); 4 David Seeds (Whitehaven); 5 Ade Gardner (St Helens); 6 Peter Lupton (Hull FC); 7 Rob Purdham (London Broncos); 8 Ryan McDonald (Widnes Vikings); 9 Carl Sice (Whitehaven); 10 Ewan Dowes (Hull FC); 11 Craig Chambers (Whitehaven); 12 Graeme Morton (Whitehaven); 13 Howard Hill (Whitehaven). Subs (all used): 14 Paul Davidson (Halifax); 15 Marc Jackson (Whitehaven); 16 Craig Walsh (Whitehaven); 17 Jon Roper (Rochdale Hornets). **Tries:** Dowes (11), Broadbent (24), Hill (37, 50); **Goals:** Lupton 4.
NEW ZEALAND 'A': 1 Lusi Sione; 2 Nigel Taumoli; 3 Vila Apu'ula; 4 Hale Va'asa; 5 Ricky Henry; 6 Gavin Bailey; 7 Steve Buckingham; 8 George Tuakura; 9 Shane Beyers; 10 Sinave Faitala; 11 Jesse Royal; 12 Tyrone Pau; 13 Karl Edmondson. Subs (all used): 14 Aoterangi Herangi; 15 Wayne McDade; 16 Jonny Limmer; 17 Taylor Pelenise.
Tries: Pelenise (68), Henry (73), Sione (76), Va'asa (78); **Goals:** Buckingham 4.
Rugby Leaguer & League Express Men of the Match: *Cumbria:* Peter Lupton; *New Zealand 'A':* Shane Beyers.
Penalty count: 7-6; **Half-time:** 18-0;
Referee: Robert Connolly (Wigan); **Attendance:** 4,124 *(at The Recreation Ground, Whitehaven).*

Wednesday 22nd October 2003

NATIONAL LEAGUE TWO 27 NEW ZEALAND 'A' 8

NATIONAL LEAGUE TWO: 1 Wayne English (Swinton Lions); 2 Mark McCully (Chorley Lynx); 3 David Foster (Keighley Cougars); 4 Matt Foster (Keighley Cougars); 5 Richie Barnett (Gateshead Thunder); 6 Chris Hough (Swinton Lions); 7 Matt Firth (Keighley Cougars); 8 Phil Stephenson (Keighley Cougars); 9 Lee Jackson (York City Knights); 10 Yusuf Sozi (Gateshead Thunder); 11 Andy Raleigh (Sheffield Eagles); 12 Wayne Freeman (Hunslet Hawks); 13 Jason Ramshaw (Keighley Cougars). Subs (all used): 14 Ian Sinfield (Keighley Cougars); 15 Rubert Jonker (London Skolars); 16 Simeon Hoyle (Keighley Cougars); 17 Mitchell Stringer (Sheffield Eagles).
Tries: Barnett (27), McCully (43), Hough (65); **Goals:** Hough 7; **Field goal:** Hough.
NEW ZEALAND 'A': 1 Paul Fisiiahi; 2 Tame Tupou; 3 Nigel Taumoli; 4 Hale Va'asa; 5 Vila Apu'ula; 6 Gavin

used): 14 Terry Newton (Wigan Warriors); 15 Paul Deacon (Bradford Bulls); 8 Paul Wood (Warrington Wolves); 17 Paul Anderson (Bradford Bulls).
Tries: Radlinski (8, 62, 77), Ellis (18), Hudson (26), Senior (35), Anderson (41), Sinfield (47), Hodgson (67); **Goals:** Long 5, Sinfield 3.
NEW ZEALAND 'A': 1 Lusi Sione; 2 Vila Apu'ula; 3 Nigel Taumoli; 4 Hale Va'asa; 5 Tame Tupou; 6 Gavin Bailey; 7 Steve Buckingham; 15 Wayne McDade; 9 Jonny Limmer; 17 Tyrone Pau; 11 Jesse Royal; 12 Lance Poka; 13 Hami Lauaki. Subs (all used): 14 Karl Edmondson; 8 George Tuakura; 16 Walter Mackie; 10 Sinave Faitala.
Tries: Sione (22, 31, 53); **Goals:** Buckingham 3.
Rugby Leaguer & League Express Men of the Match: *Great Britain:* Kris Radlinski; *New Zealand 'A':* Lusi Sione.
Penalty count: 4-3; **Half-time:** 24-12;
Referee: Steve Ganson (St Helens);
Attendance: 5,217 *(at Headingley Stadium, Leeds).*

Sunday 2nd November 2003

NATIONAL LEAGUE ONE 40 NEW ZEALAND 'A' 28

NATIONAL LEAGUE ONE: 1 Neil Turley (Leigh Centurions); 2 Alasdair McClarron (Hull Kingston Rovers); 3 Stuart Littler (Salford City Reds); 4 Alan Hadcroft (Leigh Centurions); 5 Jason Lee (Doncaster Dragons); 6 Radney Bowker (Salford City Reds); 7 John Duffy (Leigh Centurions); 8 Neil Baynes (Salford City Reds); 9 Malcolm Alker (Salford City Reds); 10 Andy Coley (Salford City Reds); 11 Simon Baldwin (Salford City Reds); 12 Sean Richardson (Leigh Centurions); 13 Chris Charles (Salford City Reds). Subs (all used): 14 Gareth Haggerty (Salford City Reds); 15 Andy Spink (Batley Bulldogs); 16 David Highton (Salford City Reds); 17 Danny Halliwell (Leigh Centurions).
Tries: Turley (4, 43), Bowker (7), Littler (18), Alker (24), Baldwin (31), Haggerty (66); **Goals:** Turley 6.
NEW ZEALAND 'A': 1 Lusi Sione; 2 Vila Apu'ula; 3 Nigel Taumoli; 4 Hale Va'asa; 5 Paul Fisiiahi; 6 Aoterangi Herangi; 7 Steve Buckingham; 8 George Tuakura; 9 Jonny Limmer; 10 Sinave Faitala; 11 Jesse Royal; 12 Lance Poka; 13 Hami Lauaki. Subs (all used): 14 Taylor Pelenise; 15 Wayne McDade; 16 Walter Mackie; 17 Tyrone Pau.
Tries: Fisiiahi (28), Va'asa (41, 52), Taumoli (72), Limmer (75); **Goals:** Buckingham 4.
Rugby Leaguer & League Express Men of the Match: *National League One:* John Duffy; *New Zealand 'A':* Hale Va'asa.
Penalty count: 7-7; **Half-time:** 28-4;
Referee: Colin Morris (Huddersfield);
Attendance: 1,429 *(at The Coliseum, Leigh).*

Bailey; 7 Steve Buckingham; 8 George Tuakura; 9 Shane Beyers; 10 Walter Mackie; 11 Jesse Royal; 12 Lance Poka; 13 Jonny Limmer. Subs (all used): 14 Aoterangi Herangi; 15 Sinave Faitala; 16 Taylor Pelenise; 17 Tyrone Pau.
Tries: Apu'ula (20), Limmer (61).
Sin bin: Limmer (10) - lying on; Tuakura (39), (76) - persistent interference.
Rugby Leaguer & League Express Men of the Match: *National League Two:* Chris Hough; *New Zealand 'A':* Jonny Limmer.
Penalty count: 18-8; **Half-time:** 11-4;
Referee: Ronnie Laughton (Barnsley);
Attendance: 1,326 *(at Cougar Park, Keighley).*

Sunday 26th October 2003

WARRINGTON WOLVES 28 NEW ZEALAND 'A' 26

WOLVES: 1 Nick Owen (D); 2 Richard Varkulis (D); 3 Steve Warburton (D); 4 Ben Westwood; 5 Phil Berry (D); 6 Gary Hulse; 7 Jamie Durbin; 8 Warren Stevens; 9 Shane Williams (D); 10 Danny Heaton (D); 11 Darren Burns; 12 Paul Noone; 13 Mike Govin (D). Subs (all used): 14 Dave Pennington (D); 15 Dave Saxton (D); 16 Tommy Grundy (D); 17 Matt Wilson (D).
Tries: Govin (8), Warburton (21), Owen (27), Grundy (39), Durbin (54); **Goals:** Owen 4.
NEW ZEALAND 'A': 1 Lusi Sione; 2 Tame Tupou; 3 Vila Apu'ula; 4 Ricky Henry; 5 Paul Fisiiahi; 6 Aoterangi Herangi; 7 Steve Buckingham; 8 George Tuakura; 9 Shane Beyers; 10 Sinave Faitala; 11 Jesse Royal; 12 Lance Poka; 13 Karl Edmondson. Subs (all used): 14 Jonny Limmer; 15 Hami Lauaki; 16 Wayne McDade; 17 Taylor Pelenise.
Tries: Apu'ula (4), Sione (42), Limmer (61), Fisiiahi (76, 78); **Goals:** Buckingham 3.
Rugby Leaguer & League Express Men of the Match: *Wolves:* Gary Hulse; *New Zealand 'A':* Jonny Limmer.
Penalty count: 7-6; **Half-time:** 22-4;
Referee: Ian Smith (Oldham);
Attendance: 3,409 *(at Wilderspool, Warrington).*

Wednesday 29th October 2003

GREAT BRITAIN 52 NEW ZEALAND 'A' 18

GREAT BRITAIN: 1 Kris Radlinski (Wigan Warriors) (C); 2 Stuart Reardon (Bradford Bulls); 3 Richard Horne (Hull FC); 4 Keith Senior (Leeds Rhinos); 5 David Hodgson (Wigan Warriors); 6 Kevin Sinfield (Leeds Rhinos); 7 Sean Long (St Helens); 16 Stuart Fielden (Bradford Bulls); 9 Ryan Hudson (Castleford Tigers); 10 Barrie McDermott (Leeds Rhinos); 11 Adrian Morley (Sydney Roosters); 12 Gareth Ellis (Wakefield Trinity Wildcats); 13 Lee Gilmour (Bradford Bulls). Subs (all

160

goals from 11 attempts for Swinton's Chris Hough ensured that a three tries to two advantage was turned into a considerably bigger return.

Next it was to a low key Warrington and another late surge from the Kiwis, as two Paul Fisiiahi tries almost snatched a draw, before the young Wolves held on for a 28-26 success.

The result against Great Britain was never in doubt but fullback Luisi Sione came up with a hat-trick of tries in the honourable 52-18 defeat at Headingley.

The final game saw midweek endeavours take their toll as a National League One XIII beat the tourists 40-28 at Leigh.

MISCELLANEOUS

Months of planning came to fruition when the Ionio Cup between Italy and Greece was staged before a crowd of 4,000 at Oki Jubilee Oval on September 27.

A last-minute try by captain Paul Dezolt gave the Italians a 26-24 win.

The BARLA Great Britain Lions outshone a talented French side by 12-6 at the Recreation Ground in September. The winning score came in the 58th minute when work-horse loose forward and captain Tommy Goulden broke to put in the eager Matt Rogers.

Paul Toole's conversion put the British lads in the driving seat and the Blackbrook centre enhanced that position six minutes later with his fourth goal of the night.

France beat the hosts Russia 29-12 in the final of the Victory Cup in Moscow in May in front of 10,000 Russian fans.

France had beaten BARLA 30-24 and Russia were victorious against the USA 44-14 on the way to the final. BARLA beat Russia in the Bowl 70-10.

The National League under-21s team put on a brave performance on the final day of the Lapérouse Challenge at Albi in October before losing 28-22 to the competition winners, the French regional side Midi-Pyrenees-Aquitaine.

And Featherstone Rovers' outstanding stand-off prospect Richard Whiting earlier played a starring role in the under-21s' first match against the other French regional side in the tournament, Languedoc-Roussillon, a game they lost 48-26.

In the opening match of the tournament, Midi-Pyrenees-Aquitaine beat the touring New Zealand Maori 24-18.

The New Zealanders put on a much stronger display in their second game with a 56-36 victory over Languedoc-Roussillon, finishing as competition runners-up on points difference.

The Welsh Dragons retained the amateur Home Nations Championship with a 28-18 win over England at Aberavon in September.

The New Zealand Kiwi Ferns won the nine-team women's World Cup in October in fine style with a ten try 54-0 demolition of their Maori colleagues, after seeing off the brave Great Britain Lionesses in the semi-final.

At least Great Britain had the satisfaction of keeping New Zealand to their lowest score of the tournament in the semi-final, 38-0. They beat Samoa 28-12,

Other Internationals

Tonga 54-0 on the way to the semi-final, drawing with the Cook Islands 20-20 and were edged by the Maori 10-8.

Samoa won the Plate, beating the Cooks 28-18, and Tokelau the Bowl with a 26-12 victory over Tonga.

The Australian Combined Services finished their three-match tour of the UK with a last-gasp 7-6 defeat against their British counterparts.

A field goal 90 seconds from time by Royal Navy scrum-half Scott Partis sealed the one-point win for the British at Hull KR's Craven Park. A week before the CASRL had fallen to a 46-32 defeat against a strong BARLA under-23s side at Robin Park in Wigan. But they avoided going home without a win by virtue of a 22-10 midweek victory over the Army at Ram Stadium - stand-off and captain Brian Jones impressing for the tourists.

Great Britain Police whitewashed the Australian Police in their three-match series. After an opening 32-20 win at Featherstone, they clinched the series with a 13-6 win at Ram Stadium.

And the British showed no mercy in the third and final Test, as they recorded a 16-6 win, with recently retired Keighley legend Jason Ramshaw among the try scorers.

The touring Manly district side completed their brief tour of the UK with a 28-4 defeat at Whitehaven.

It brought the curtain down on a four-match tour that saw them play an exhibition game against the Australian Legends, then defeat Yorkshire BARLA (40-14) and Oldham (27-26), before the loss at Whitehaven.

French side Lezignan won the second York International 9's in June, involving 26 teams, beating York Ironsides 18-10 in an exciting Fairfax Cup Final. It was second time lucky for the Frenchmen, who went down narrowly to London Koogas in the previous year's inaugural event.

The Army won the 2003 NAAFI Inter Services Challenge, beating the RAF 32-22 and the Royal Navy 24-20.

INTERNATIONAL SCOREBOARD

MEDITERRANEAN CUP FINAL

France 18 ....Lebanon 26

Other results

France 120.....................Serbia & Montenegro 0
Lebanon 60 ....Morocco 0
France 72..Morocco 0
Lebanon 102....................Serbia & Montenegro
Morocco 58 ....Serbia & Montenegro 4

FRANCE

French Championship - Elite 1

	P	W	D	L	F	A	D	Pts
Villeneuve	20	16	1	3	751	309	442	53
Pia	20	16	1	3	718	354	364	53
UTC	20	16	0	4	798	328	470	52
Limoux	20	13	0	7	615	328	287	46
Toulouse	20	10	2	8	535	367	168	42
St-Gaudens	20	10	0	10	588	439	149	40
Lézignan	20	9	1	10	409	506	-97	39
Villefranche	20	8	1	11	437	507	-70	37
Carpentras	20	5	0	15	262	657	-395	30
Carcassonne	20	4	0	16	323	666	-343	28
Paris-Chatillon	20	0	0	20	183	1158	-975	20

Play-offs

Championship quarter-final play-offs

Villeneuve 52 ....Villefranche 6 (agg. 86-12)
Pia 40 ....Lézignan 11 (agg. 45-49)
UTC 18 ....St Gaudens 19 (agg. 36-43)
Limoux 40 ....Toulouse 30 (agg. 77-62)

Championship semi-finals, first leg

Lézignan 22..............................St Gaudens 24
Limoux 18 ....Villeneuve 12

Second leg

Villeneuve 33.................Limoux 17 (agg. 45-35)
St Gaudens 40 ....Lézignan 16 (agg. 64-38)

Championship final

St Gaudens 18.............................Villeneuve 31
at Stade de l'Amitié, Narbonne

Coupe de France final

Pia 14 ....Villeneuve 16

NEW ZEALAND

Bartercard Cup Grand Final

CANTERBURY BULLS 32 (Clint Newton 2, Shane Beyers, Jimmy O'Brien, Vince Whare, Toby Wallace tries; O'Brien 4 goals) d. MARIST RICHMOND BROTHERS 28 (Harry Kapi, Ben Collins, Sonny Lavea, Henry Turua, Steve Matai, Karl Guttenbeil tries; Tony Esera, Matai goals). Referee: Andy Cook.

162

COUNTY OF ORIGIN
The last hurrah?

Yorkshire - cheered on by a vociferous, parochial crowd at Odsal on a Wednesday night in early July - may have helped kill off the three year old County of Origin concept as they wiped the floor with their Red Rose rivals by 56-6.

The series - reduced at short notice from two games to a single fixture at short notice - was shelved when the Super League IX fixtures were announced at the end of the year.

David Waite was treating the match as a trial before the autumn's Ashes series, but it was more of an ordeal as he watched a Lancashire side, 10 to 3 on favourites, and fielding ten Great Britain players, give a pitiful performance.

On the positive side, Yorkshire were a delight to watch. They lit up a miserable wet evening to equal their highest ever score and achieve a record winning margin. All their starting backs scored tries, and Chris Thorman marked his county debut with a 20-point haul, from a try and eight goals, that equalled the Yorkshire record against Lancashire.

Although Yorkshire included seven Test players it was non-international Thorman who took the match honours on his county debut,

winning the Roy Powell Medal as the man of the match. Brought in as a replacement for injured captain Danny Orr, the 22 year old London Broncos stand-off grabbed the opportunity to impress Waite with an outstanding all-round game.

Ryan Hudson pushed Thorman close for match honours with a performance full of passion and leadership qualities that belied the fact that he was only the stand-in captain for club colleague Orr. The highlight of an impressive display was his setting up of Gareth Ellis's try when he broke from a scrum near the centre spot and strode clear, before passing inside for the Wakefield centre to complete the 50-metre raid.

Lancashire could do little more than stand and admire. The late withdrawal of Paul Sculthorpe with a hamstring injury was a blow, but they still had enough experience to put on a much better show. They started well enough, but after failing to turn early pressure into points they collapsed.

Although Lancashire captain Andrew Farrell did not hit his best form, he tried hard to set the right example but received little response. Farrell's conversion of Sean O'Loughlin's try clocked up his 3,000th career point, and the magnificent achievement deserved a more fitting occasion.

It was Yorkshire's first win in four Origin matches, and put them level with Lancashire's 44 victories in all meetings between the two counties.

The first of what was scheduled to be two matches between the National League under-21s and their Super League counterparts was played at Leigh in June, with the full-timers running out 52-12 winners.

Despite a one-sided second half and picking up a spate of injuries during the game, the National League side could take much from their performance against a skilful Super League outfit.

Steve Crooks' charges were strong favourites before the game, and - a 20-minute period in the first half aside - never looked like losing.

In Bradford pair Chris Bridge

Tuesday 10th June 2003

NATIONAL LEAGUE UNDER-21S 12 SUPER LEAGUE UNDER-21S 52

NATIONAL LEAGUE: 1 Nathan Batty (Dewsbury Rams); 2 Mick Nanyn (Rochdale Hornets); 3 Damian Reed (Gateshead Thunder); 4 Richard Whiting (Featherstone Rovers); 5 David Alstead (Leigh Centurions); 6 Lee Marsh (Salford City Reds); 7 Lee Sanderson (Leigh Centurions) (C); 8 Jamie Bovill (Hull Kingston Rovers); 9 Paul Pickering (Hull Kingston Rovers); 10 Gary Smith (Whitehaven); 11 Andy Bailey (Featherstone Rovers); 12 Craig Ibbetson (Hunslet Hawks); 13 Mark Toohey (Batley Bulldogs). Subs (all used): 14 Danny Ekis (Keighley Cougars); 15 Gareth Haggerty (Salford City Reds); 16 Jon Goddard (Oldham); 17 Paul Thorman (Gateshead Thunder).
Tries: Whiting (20), Reed (29); **Goals:** Nanyn 2/2.
SUPER LEAGUE: 1 Steve Rowlands (St Helens); 2 Steve Maden (St Helens); 3 Stuart Reardon (Bradford Bulls); 4 Chris Bridge (Bradford Bulls); 5 Matthew Wray (Wakefield Trinity Wildcats); 6 Peter Lupton (Leeds Rhinos); 7 Richard Mathers (Leeds Rhinos) (C); 8 Richard Moore (Bradford Bulls); 9 Aaron Smith (Bradford Bulls); 10 Steve Snitch (Wakefield Trinity Wildcats); 11 Jason Netherton (Leeds Rhinos); 12 Dwayne Barker (Leeds Rhinos); 13 Richard Blakeway (Castleford Tigers). Subs (all used): 14 Joe Mbu (London Broncos); 15 Craig Farrimond (Warrington Wolves); 16 Jaymes Chapman (Halifax); 17 Tommy Gallagher (Leeds Rhinos).
Tries: Bridge (3, 39, 78), Rowlands (5), Maden (51, 54), Reardon (61), Lupton (65), Farrimond (69); **Goals:** Bridge 8/9.
Rugby Leaguer & League Express Men of the Match:
National League: Richard Whiting; *Super League:* Chris Bridge.
Penalty count: 6-7; **Half-time:** 12-18; **Referee:** Richard Silverwood (Dewsbury); **Attendance:** 690 *(at The Coliseum, Leigh).*

and Richard Moore they had the game's two outstanding performers; Bridge collecting 28 points from a hat-trick of tries and Moore proving a considerable handful during his two spells.

But the National League side were certainly not shamed, and the end scoreline didn't quite justify their efforts. They held their top-flight counterparts at 12-all just minutes before half-time, before the Super League outfit's superior strength and fitness shone through.

NL coach Steve McCormack picked out Hull KR hooker Paul Pickering, Featherstone centre Richard Whiting and Leigh scrum-half Lee Sanderson as eye-catching individuals, while there were also notable contributions from Lee Marsh and substitute props Gareth Haggerty and Danny Ekis.

The anticipated return match - a curtain raiser to the Origin match - was postponed at late notice because of concerns over damage to a rain-soaked Odsal pitch.

SEASON DOWN UNDER
Zeroes to heroes

Fairytales can come true...it can happen to you...

Just ask coach John Lang and his Panthers' outfit.

Two years ago, before he joined the club that nestles at the foot of the Blue Mountains, they were holders of the wooden spoon. Hardly something the players would one day boast about to their grandchildren.

Now they are the NRL Premiers. A case of 'From Worst To First'!

How satisfying for Lang – shown the door by the Cronulla Sharks for allegedly failing to instil a winning culture at that club.

A winning culture? The three or four days of non-stop celebrations at Penrith after the Panthers' Grand Final success showed just what Lang instilled among a team of three or four hard-headed veterans and a host of enthusiastic youngsters.

As coaching guru Jack Gibson, known for his pithy comments on Rugby League, once said: "All clubs need a good administration – before anything else."

And that was Penrith's first step towards redemption - the appointment of former Cronulla, Gateshead and Hull boss (and good mate of Lang) Shane Richardson as chief executive.

But it didn't all fall into place immediately.

It was a tough first year, with the Panthers losing their first eight outings in 2002 under Lang's tutelage before showing some hope for the future. But their seven victories in 2002 meant that only South Sydney (with five) had won fewer games.

However Lang had been blooding a few young kids who were to show their true mettle in 2003. Wingers Luke Rooney and Luke Lewis. Props Joel Clinton and Trent Waterhouse. All were 20 years old or younger.

The Panthers lost their opening two games in 2003.

But in Round Three they showed their true colours, snatching a 23-22 victory over the reigning Premiers, the Sydney Roosters.

In the words of the cliché, the rest is history.

The Panthers methodically went ahead with the task at hand. Their tough forward pack laid the foundations. There were the two Kiwi second-rowers Tony Puletua and Joe Galuvao, variously dubbed 'The Bruise Brothers' and 'The Hair Bears'. Veteran Scott Sattler, rewarded with his first Origin selection at the age of 31). Scheming hooker Luke Priddis, the only player in the club to have experienced Premiership success (with the Broncos in 2000). And Clinton and Waterhouse.

A clever backline then took full advantage.

Captain and scrum-half Craig Gower, later to be robbed of recognition for his efforts as the finest player in the NRL competition by the cancellation of the Dally M Awards night, because of a revolt by the Players' Association.   T h e will-o'-the-wisp stand-off Preston Campbell, the 2001 Dally M Player of the Year, who was given free rein to exploit his talents by Lang. Exciting fullback Rhys Wesser, who was to top the NRL tryscoring lists with 25. The two Lukes, who also had a field day every weekend (Lewis with 18 tries and Rooney with 17). And the unrecognised centre Paul Whatuira, whose consistent efforts were to gain him recognition in the Kiwi Test squad (even though he didn't make the final 17 to play Australia in the October Trans-Tasman Test).

If Lang was happy with the way his protégés were going, his characteristic poker face never showed it.

Against all predictions, the Panthers took out the Minor Premiership.

But the critics were still predicting a Roosters v Warriors Grand Final.

In the play-offs, the Panthers accounted for Brisbane 28-18, after they had trailed the Broncos 18-4 late in the first half. After a fortnight's rest, they beat the Warriors 28-20 in a match that was much more one-sided than the final scores suggest.

Meanwhile the Roosters were showing the form that had won them the 2002 Grand Final. They hammered Newcastle 36-8. But they slackened off after an almost perfect first half, after which they had led 30-2. After their two-week break, they ensured their place in the Grand Final with a 28-18 victory over the Bulldogs, with British Test forward Adrian Morley giving an inspirational exhibition of powerhouse rugby.

All was set for a crackerjack grand final. East versus West. And the first involving two Sydney clubs in the history of the NRL.

The players did not disappoint. Most of those who watched – the 81,166 that packed Telstra Stadium and the 4.5 million others who watched on television around Australia – reckoned it was the most stirring finale to a season in decades.

Canberra's 1989 victory over Balmain (24-12 in extra time) was quoted by many as the most recent to stir the blood. Others suggested you had to go back 40 years to St George's 8-3 success over Western Suburbs in the game immortalised by 'The Gladiators' photo of Norm Provan and Arthur Summons to find a grand final of comparable tension.

Whatever your choice, the Penrith-Roosters clash had everyone on the edge of their seats to the final whistle.

In torrential rain, Penrith humbled the Sydney Roosters in decisive fashion 18-6.

And hooker Priddis, the man who won the Clive Churchill Medal as Man of the Match, summed it up perfectly: "Wooooo! Unreal. It's been our best game of the year. Woooo!"

Woooo, indeed!

The media had persuaded all but the diehard Penrith fans to believe that the Roosters only had to turn up at the Olympic headquarters and take home the trophy.

But the Roosters had frail wings. Brad Fittler couldn't pass properly

Penrith's Martin Lang collared by Sydney Roosters' Craig Fitzgibbon

because of an injured shoulder. Craig Fitzgibbon had miraculously recovered from an injury that had looked like ending his season, before breaking a thumb in the penultimate finals' match. And there were others feeling a bit crook – as the old Aussie expression so wonderfully describes malaises.

The first half was 40 minutes of the most gripping Rugby League seen in years, from two sides showing total commitment. The bone-crushing defence had the fans shuddering every time contact was made. The precious few line-breaks that were made were cut down by last-ditch tackles.

There was but one try in the first 40 minutes. Priddis made a break from ten metres inside his own half and there was no way the Roosters would fully recover. He drew fullback Andrew Minichiello as he made it to the Roosters' 20-metre line. And big Rooney loomed up outside to take the pass and score.

That first try, ten minutes before the break, broke a nil-all deadlock. It had the fans looking at their watches, for that first half-hour had seemed to pass with no more than a twinkling of an eyelid. Such was the excitement.

Seven minutes into the second half, Roosters utility star Craig Wing weaved some magic. He collared Wesser near the Panthers' tryline in a tackle that dislodged the ball.

It was all legitimate. Moments later a reverse pass from Roosters' sub Chris Flannery sent Test centre Shannon Hegarty over for a try. The conversion from Fitzgibbon hit the right-hand upright and bounced over. Suddenly the two sides were all square once again. And the Roosters looked to be on a roll. But they couldn't produce a winning move.

Almost 54 minutes into proceedings Fittler found that little touch of genius we expect of the former Australian captain. He flicked the ball to winger Todd Byrne who sped down the left wing unopposed for what looked to be the wining

167

Penrith Panthers - 2003 NRL Grand Final Winners

try. But Sattler had other ideas. He sped across the pitch on what most thought was a futile attempt to collar Byrne. Suddenly the ageing legs found a metre or two of extra pace and Byrne found himself floundering over the touchline.

It was the defining point of the game.

"That's what grand finals are all about," said Sattler. "You don't give up. You'll do anything on a day like this."

Some 33 years ago his father John Sattler became part of Rugby League folklore by playing through almost an entire grand final with a badly shattered jaw – in the days when there were no replacements for any reason – to lead South Sydney to victory.

With that tackle, Scott Sattler – like his Dad – became part of grand final folklore.

The tackle seemed to lift the Panthers. They defended even more ferociously – if that was at all possible. And with 15 minutes remaining, Priddis turned the tide. He darted from dummy half, waltzed around Fitzgibbon and scored.

Significantly it was left to Priddis and Rooney to seal the victory, the hooker firing a long pass to the unmarked Rooney who touched down for his second try of the evening.

"Everyone wrote us off all year," Scott Sattler explained. "They were waiting for us to fall down. But we had faith in ourselves."

And Wesser summed it up succinctly: "I'm so proud to be a Panther."

A day later, five Panthers found themselves selected in Australia's squad for the Kangaroo tour of New Zealand, France and Britain – Lewis, Ryan Girdler, Gower, Clinton and Waterhouse. But several of Penrith's 2003 heroes – not the least Priddis, Campbell, Wesser and Rooney – were overlooked. Three others – Puletua, Galuvao and Whatuira – were chosen in the New Zealand Test squad.

The Panthers had certainly come a long way in such a short time!

HERE'S how the other clubs fared:

SYDNEY ROOSTERS: The 2002 Premiers were again the yardstick by which the others judged their performances. And six of their players ended up in Australia's Kangaroo squad (fullback Anthony Minichiello, centre Shannon Hegarty, utility stars Craig Wing and Michael Crocker and back-rowers Craig Fitzgibbon and Luke Ricketson. And centre Justin Hodges and utility Chris Flannery would have been in contention but for injuries. Jason Cayless played for the New Zealand Kiwis and Adrian Morley for Great Britain. And captain Brad Fittler was again inspirational.

NEW ZEALAND WARRIORS: After a mixed season, they came home under a wet sail only to falter on the penultimate week of the Premiership. Fourteen of their players were capped for the Kiwis during 2003 – wingers Francis Meli (the club's Player of the Year) and Henry Fa'afili, centres Clinton Toopi and Vinnie Anderson, halves Stacey Jones, Lance Hohaia and Thomas Leuluai, utility stars Motu Tony and Sione Faumuina, hooker Monty Betham and

Brad Fittler

fellow-forwards Jerry Seuseu, Ali Lauiti'iti, Awen Guttenbeil and Logan Swann – while two others – hooker Tevita Latu and utility Wairangi Koopu – were in the provisional Kiwi squad for the October Test. Prop Richard Villasanti became the first Auckland-based player to be chosen for Australia, while PJ Marsh was in the running until a season-ending neck injury.

BULLDOGS: The Bulldogs, eager to make amends for the disappointment of the 2001 salary cap scandal, were favourites for much of the year to win the Premiership. But they fell apart at season's end. They lost in the first week of the finals to the Warriors (48-22), before beating the Storm 30-0. However, they were no match for the Roosters, going down 28-18 in their

Sione Faumuina

Steve
Price

preliminary final. Best of the bunch was their inspirational captain Steve Price, who won Rugby League Week's Player of the Year award.

MELBOURNE STORM: The Victorian side surprised many critics by getting so far. Much of the credit must go to rookie coach Craig Bellamy who instilled a new spirit in the Storm. One of the finds of the year was rookie fullback Billy Slater, a former jockey, who scored 19 tries. The halves Matt Orford and Matt Geyer must have gone close to Kangaroo selection, while prop Robbie Kearns was named captain of the touring side. Stephen Kearney played for the Kiwis in the July Trans-Tasman Test.

CANBERRA RAIDERS: Former Bradford Bulls coach Matthew Elliott steered the Raiders into the finals, against all predictions. But they were crushed by Melbourne in the first week of the play-offs. The Raiders had a team of virtual no-names. But Player of the Year Ruben Wiki was to captain the Kiwis in their two Tests against Australia and fullback Clinton Schifcofske was ever-consistent and winger Joel Monaghan snared 21 tries in as many matches.

NEWCASTLE KNIGHTS: The Novocastrians suffered from a spate of injuries to key personnel – especially a career-threatening neck injury to inspirational captain Andrew Johns. Others to spend time on the sidelines included internationals Ben Kennedy, Steve Simpson and Adam MacDougall. Without Johns they were bundled out of the play-offs, beaten 36-8 by the Roosters on the first weekend.

BRISBANE BRONCOS: It was a season in which they achieved an unwanted record. At one stage, early in the proceedings, the Broncos were on top and looking good. Then came the usual mid-season slump that coincided with the Origin duties for the Broncos' players. But this year they never recovered. They scraped into the play-

Billy
Slater

offs. But when beaten 28-18 by Penrith on the first weekend it was their eighth straight loss – a club record. And a side that had ten internationals on its books could manage just four in the Kangaroo squad (Darren Lockyer, Shane Webcke, Petero Civoniceva and Michael De Vere – and De Vere was making his debut in the green and gold).

PARRAMATTA EELS: Yet another disappointing season from a side that should have done better. Injuries to captain Nathan Cayless and rugged second-rower Nathan Hindmarsh didn't help the Eels' cause. Centre Jamie Lyon managed to make the July Test side. And David Vaealiki played fullback as the Kiwis were hammered in that Trans-Tasman Test.

ST GEORGE-ILLAWARRA DRAGONS: Another team that underachieved, under new coach Nathan Brown. They never really found the answer to the absence of injured captain Trent Barrett. Prop Luke Bailey came of age to make the Test side for the July encounter. But, for only the second time in history there wasn't a Dragon in the Kangaroo side.

NORTH QUEENSLAND COWBOYS: It was their best season since joining the big league in 1995, but some woeful performances late in the year robbed them of a first appearance in the play-offs. It was a vintage season for veteran winger Matt Sing, who topped the club's tryscoring with 21 tries in 20 matches. He also grabbed a hat-trick for Queensland in Origin III. Centre Josh Hannay made his Origin debut and rewrote the club record books with the most points in a season (230) and most in a career (478).

CRONULLA SHARKS: A disappointing season led to a bitter off-field wrangle between the board and coach Chris Anderson, which still had not been resolved when this yearbook went to press. Anderson had promised to bring a winning ethic to the club. But the Sharks could manage just eight successes all year. Scrum-half Brett Kimmorley and utility star Phil Bailey made the Kangaroo touring squad.

WESTS TIGERS: Once again among the cellar-dwellers. Few highlights, except the discovery of a super goal-kicking talent in Luke Covell, who booted two-pointers at an 80 per cent success rate. Also making a big impression, in a couple of late season games, was schoolboy half Benji Marshall, an undoubted superstar of the future. Coach Tim Sheens has bought a handful of veterans, including Penrith grand final hero Scott Sattler, in an effort to show his youngsters in 2004 how to achieve success.

MANLY SEA EAGLES: A run of sub-standard performances saw coach Peter Sharp announce his impending departure well before the season ended. He will be succeeded by one of Manly's favourite sons, former Test half Des Hasler. A clear-out of deadwood gives Sea Eagles supporters a glimmer of hope for 2004.

SOUTH SYDNEY RABBITOHS: For the second year since winning their legal fight for a return to the fray, the Rabbitohs won fewer matches than any other club. And they were racked by turmoil. Club chairman George Piggins headed off a palace coup by stepping aside, but before he did so he presided over the sacking of coach Craig Coleman and his replacement by former international Paul Langmack. But the changes did no good with Souths winning only five games and collecting the wooden spoon.

171

NRL SCOREBOARD

FINAL NRL PREMIERSHIP TABLE

	P	W	L	B	F	A	Pts
Penrith Panthers	24	18	6	2	659	527	40
Sydney Roosters	24	17	7	2	680	445	38
Bulldogs	24	16	8	2	702	419	36
Canberra Raiders	24	16	8	2	620	463	36
Melbourne Storm	24	15	9	2	564	486	34
New Zealand Warriors	24	15	9	2	545	510	34
Newcastle Knights	24	14	10	2	632	635	32
Brisbane Broncos	24	12	12	2	497	464	28
Parramatta Eels	24	11	13	2	570	582	26
St George-Illawarra Dragons	24	11	13	2	548	593	26
North Queensland Cowboys	24	10	14	2	606	629	24
Cronulla Sharks	24	8	16	2	497	704	20
Wests Tigers	24	7	17	2	470	598	18
Manly Sea Eagles	24	7	17	2	557	791	18
South Sydney Rabbitohs	24	3	21	2	457	758	8

QUALIFYING FINALS

CANBERRA RAIDERS 18 ....MELBOURNE STORM 30
Raiders: T- Joel Monaghan (14), Jamaal Lolesi (21),
Michael Monaghan (80); G - Clinton Schifcofske 3
Storm: T- Marcus Bai (25, 67), Matt Orford (28), Fifita Moala (32),
Matt Geyer (47), Craig Smith (63); G - Matt Orford 3
Half-time: 12-16; Referee: Tim Mander
Attendance: 14,094 At Canberra Stadium (September 12)

BULLDOGS 22 ....NZ WARRIORS 48
Bulldogs: T- Nigel Vagana (27), Hazem El Masri (47), Mark O'Meley (47), Matt Utai (68); G - Hazem El Masri 3
Warriors: T - Francis Meli (2, 10, 49, 54, 75), Brent Webb (36, 62),
Motu Tony (58), Sione Faumuina (64); G - Brent Webb 5, Sione Faumuina
Half-time: 4-16; Referee: Bill Harrigan
Attendance: 18,312 at Sydney Showground (September 13)

SYDNEY ROOSTERS 36 ....NEWCASTLE KNIGHTS 8
Roosters: T - Craig Wing (3), Ned Catic (12), Ryan Cross (15),
Todd Byrne (19), Chris Flannery (40, 65);
G - Michael Crocker 3, Craig Fitzgibbon 3
Knights: T - Matthew Gidley (45); G - Daniel Abraham 2
Half-time: 30-2; Referee: Sean Hampstead
Attendance: 23,853 at Aussie Stadium (September 13)

PENRITH PANTHERS 28 ....BRISBANE BRONCOS 18
Panthers: T- Luke Lewis (15, 48), Ben Ross (38), Ryan Girdler (51),
Scott Sattler (65); G - Ryan Girdler 4
Broncos: T - Stu Kelly (1, 13), Scott Minto (29); G- Michael De Vere 3
Half-time: 10-18; Referee: Steve Clark
Attendance: 18,534 at Penrith Football Stadium (September 14)

SEMI-FINALS

NZ WARRIORS 17 ....CANBERRA RAIDERS 16
Warriors: T - Logan Swann (25), Clinton Toopi (35), Henry Fa'afili (45);
G - Brent Webb 2; FG - Stacey Jones
Raiders: T - Simon Woolford (7), Luke Davico (56);
G - Clinton Schifcofske 4
Half-time: 10-10; Referee: Tim Mander
Attendance: 31,616 at Aussie Stadium (September 20)

MELBOURNE STORM 0 ....BULLDOGS 30
Bulldogs: T - Nigel Vagana (8, 69), Corey Hughes (29), Willie Mason
(46), Adam Perry (75); G - Hazem El Masri 4; FG - Braith Anasta 2
Half-time: 0-13; Referee: Bill Harrigan
Attendance: 19,637 at Aussie Stadium (September 21)

PRELIMINARY FINALS

SYDNEY ROOSTERS 28 ....BULLDOGS 18
Roosters: T - Shannon Hegarty (17), Chris Walker (24), Chris Flannery
(45, 60); G - Craig Fitzgibbon 5, Michael Crocker
Bulldogs: T – Mark O'Meley (37), Matt Utai (52, 69); G - Hazem El Masri 3
Half-time: 16-6; Referee: Bill Harrigan
Attendance: 41,123 at Aussie Stadium (September 27)

PENRITH PANTHERS 28 ....NZ WARRIORS 20
Panthers: T - Luke Lewis (11), Rhys Wesser (30), Luke Priddis (44),
Ryan Girdler (52), Joe Galuvao (62); G - Ryan Girdler 4
Warriors: T - Logan Swann (22), Richard Villasanti (36),
Clinton Toopi (58), Brent Webb (66); G – Brett Webb 2
Half-time: 10-10; Referee: Tim Mander
Attendance: 43,174 at Telstra Stadium (September 28)

GRAND FINAL

PENRITH PANTHERS 18 ....SYDNEY ROOSTERS 6
Panthers: T - Rooney (30, 73), Priddis (65); G - Girdler, Campbell 2
Roosters: T - Hegarty (48); G - Fitzgibbon

Panthers: Rhys Wesser, Luke Lewis, Ryan Girdler, Paul Whatuira, Luke Rooney, Preston Campbell, Craig Gower (c), Joel Clinton, Luke Priddis, Martin Lang, Joe Galuvao, Tony Puletua, Scott Sattler. Subs: Ben Ross, Trent Waterhouse, Shane Rodney, Luke Swain. Coach: John Lang.
Roosters: Anthony Minichiello, Todd Byrne, Ryan Cross, Shannon Hegarty, Chris Walker, Brad Fittler (c), Craig Wing, Jason Cayless, Michael Crocker, Ned Catic, Adrian Morley, Craig Fitzgibbon, Luke Ricketson. Subs: Brett Finch, Andrew Lomu, Chad Robinson, Chris Flannery.
Referee: Bill Harrigan; **Video referees:** Phil Cooley & Steve Clark;
Half-time: 6-0; **Penalties:** 3-1
Clive Churchill Medal: Luke Priddis
Attendance: 81,166 at Telstra Stadium (October 5)
Rugby Leaguer & League Express Men of the Match
Panthers: Luke Priddis; *Roosters:* Adrian Morley

TOP POINTSCORERS

	T	G	FG	Pts
Hazem El Masri (Bulldogs)	9	130	-	294
Josh Hannay (Cowboys)	10	95	-	230
Clinton Schifcofske (Raiders)	8	94	2	222
Michael De Vere (Broncos)	12	69	-	186
Matt Orford (Storm)	8	74	-	180
Mark Riddell (Dragons)	7	69	-	166
Preston Campbell (Panthers)	12	56	-	164

TOP TRYSCORERS

Rhys Wesser (Panthers)	25
Francis Meli (Warriors)	23
Nigel Vagana (Bulldogs)	22
Scott Donald (Sea Eagles)	21
Matt Sing (Cowboys)	21
Joel Monaghan (Raiders)	21
Matt Utai (Bulldogs)	21

MINOR GRAND FINALS

PREMIER LEAGUE

CANBERRA RAIDERS 31 ....ST MARY'S-PENRITH COUGARS 6
Raiders: T – Phil Graham 3, Jason Bulgarelli, Matthew Gafa;
G - Matthew Gafa 3, Jace Van Dijk; FG – Michael Monaghan
Cougars: T – Anthony Amour; G – Daniel Russell
Half-time: 13-0
Referee: Tony Archer

JIM BEAM CUP

THE ENTRANCE TIGERS 14 .............WENTWORTHVILLE MAGPIES 10
Tigers: T – Brett Blaker, Jamie Forbes; G – Brett Westwood 3
Magpies: T – Daniel Bell, Scott Ella; G – Craig Parke
Half-time: 6-4
Referee: Jason Robinson

GOLDEN POINT KILLS OFF DRAWS

BEFORE the 2003 season kicked off, the NRL unilaterally decided to eliminate draws by introducing the so-called 'golden point'.

The first match decided on the golden point was in Round 10. Manly and Parramatta were locked at 34-all when the full-time siren sounded. Manly (and former Leeds Rhinos) stand-off Ben Walker booted the 'golden point' penalty goal that broke the deadlock, some eight minutes into extra time. Walker had previously missed with two field goal attempts and Parramatta half Michael Witt with an attempt at a one-pointer.

Later in the season there were three other golden point results. The golden point resulted in Brisbane sneaking into the finals series and Parramatta missing the playoffs. Had draws still been allowed the two sides would have swapped positions on the final League ladder.

Every season the fans watch the State of Origin Series in unabashed awe. Inevitably, they think they've witnessed the greatest series in history.

Twelve months later they go through the same procedure and wonder if there is any limit to the talent, the defensive ferocity, the attacking skill on show before them.

The 2003 Series was no different. The three matches had each and every Rugby League scribe reporting the encounters reaching for his or her thesaurus, searching for superlatives with which to describe the exploits of the players.

History will show how after a couple of years in Queensland hands the Origin Shield returned to New South Wales – thanks largely to magnificent displays in the first two encounters by Newcastle's freakish scrum-half Andrew Johns. Then, with the series already lost, the Maroons turned the sport on its head with their biggest victory on record, setting the scene for yet another spine-chilling series next season.

Joey Johns was in the headlines even before the Origin Series kicked-off. There was a much-publicised feud between the NSW captain and his coach Phil Gould, culminating in a threat by Johns to pack up and go home to Newcastle. Of course, saner heads prevailed. And both Johns and Gould were glad they did bury the hatchet.

The opening clash, at the rebuilt Suncorp Stadium (a magnificent edifice that now bears little resemblance to the old Lang Park except in the fervour of the fans) could be described as the Andrew Johns Show. Such was his dominance!

NSW prop Luke Bailey, coming off the bench, was named official Man of the Match by the Nine Television Network commentary team. But the 52,420 fans that packed the new 'Cauldron' knew otherwise. Joey Johns was the difference between the two sides. He set up three of the NSW tries with deft passes. He kicked a field goal to put the Blues in an almost unbeatable position. And he scored his side's only other try in the closing minutes, thus hammering the final nail in the coffin.

He was most certainly the dominant figure on the pitch, though Queensland fullback Darren Lockyer had matched him in the first half. And it was fitting that he should post the first score of the evening - a weaving run from 20 metres out made the defence appear non-existent. He converted his own try and the xenophobic Queensland crowd was in raptures.

But Anthony Minichiello, who had been having a difficult time at fullback for the Blues, suddenly clicked, running onto a Johns' pass to touch down for the equaliser 19 minutes into the game.

He was to score again not too many minutes later - but only after a touch judge's decision had cost the Queenslanders dearly. Shannon Hegarty was adjudged to have touched the ball as he watched it bounce into touch. Video replays showed he was nowhere near the ball. NSW got the scrum feed in good field position. Johns threw a dummy that fooled the defence, opening up a gap for Minichiello to score again.

In the final minute before half-time, Minichiello was involved once more. This time it was in a trysaving tackle on a rampaging Andrew Gee that bounced the ball loose as the Queenslander was crossing the tryline between the posts.

The Queenslanders could have gone to the break on equal terms. Instead they trailed by six.

That quickly changed when Gorden Tallis took four defenders with him as he scored three minutes into the second half. Eight minutes later it appeared Tallis had scored again as he juggled the ball before touching down. But replays persuaded the video referee that while Tallis was juggling, the ball hit the head of NSW winger Timana Tahu. Technically it was knock-on by Tallis, even though the Raging Bull regathered the ball.

By this time the Maroons were without centres Justin Hodges and Paul Bowman. And they were tiring fast in the brutal encounter.

The video referee denied Luke Bailey a try (off a Johns' kick along the ground). Then another Johns dummy fooled everyone, and opened a gap for Craig Wing to dance his way to the line.

The Maroons still refused to capitulate. So Johns snapped a field goal before scoring his own try.

It was a fitting conclusion to a savage clash.

It was another vintage display from Johns when the two sides moved south to the Olympic stadium in Sydney for Origin II. He carved up the Queenslanders to inspire victory in not just the match but the Origin series.

And Wally Lewis, the man who had dominated so many Origin encounters in the past, shook his head in admiration: "He's just the best player in the world."

The Blues led 17-0 at half-time and refused to let the visitors back into the game in the second stanza.

Sadly for the massive crowd of 79,132, the encounter did not quite live up to the excitement of Origin I, but the partisan NSW fans were rewarded as the Blues squared up the ledger. Each state had now won 33 matches and 10 series.

Never once did the Maroons get the slightest sniff of a possible win.

A lucky bounce of a Johns' banana kick off the left-hand post, leaving Queensland fullback Darren Lockyer going the wrong way, gave NSW loose-forward Ben Kennedy the first try of the match in the 12th minute. Seven minutes later centre Matthew Gidley ran 20 metres from dummy-half to extend the lead.

Then came a touch of luck for NSW. After advice from the video referees, Bill Harrigan placed Kennedy on report for a high tackle on Steve Price that left the Queensland prop reeling around like a drunken sailor (and subsequently earned the Novocastrian a four-match suspension). But Harrigan did not award a penalty, instead sticking to his previous ruling of a scrum feed to the Blues. And immediately NSW prop Bryan Fletcher made the break that resulted in a try for fullback Anthony Minichiello.

Right on the half-time siren there was a bit more of Andrew Johns' magic. Sensing there was nothing to be gained by running the ball, Johns snapped a field goal for the New South Welshmen to lead 17-0.

Johns stretched the lead with a penalty goal early in the second half. Moments later NSW stand-off Shaun Timmins put a kick along the ground and

Timana Tahu and Gidley dived to touch down almost simultaneously. Tahu was adjudged to have scored. He added a second try in the closing minutes off a remarkable Gidley flick pass, scooping the ball off the ground in a wonderful display of agility.

Queensland's only points came from a suspect try by debutant hooker Michael Crocker.

"They were just too good," said Maroons fullback Darren Lockyer.

Back in Brisbane for Origin III, the Maroons rediscovered the Queensland spirit in a rousing and at times brutal display, restoring their pride with a 36-6 hammering of the New South Welshmen.

"We played like Queenslanders," the Maroons captain Gorden Tallis explained. "This is what the [Queensland] jersey is all about. In Game One we were competitive, but a few dodgy decisions went against us. In Game Two we were beaten by the better side - we were embarrassed. In Game Three we had a bit more to play for."

And the xenophobic supporters in the full house of more than 52,000 fans fully understood this as they took up the chant of 'Queenslander, Queenslander, Queenslander' when the Maroons began to establish their superiority.

Johns said the game was one of the most physical he had ever played.

And it was obvious from the opening whistle.

The Queensland forwards, so timid in Origin II, had fire in their bellies - smashing their opponents with ferocious tackles.

Johns returned the compliment in the second minute of proceedings with a bone-crusher that left Brisbane Broncos centre Brent Tate wondering where he was. And there was 'Mate against Mate' as in the classic Origins of the past, with Tonie Carroll placed on report for an alleged high tackle on Broncos' teammate

2003 STATE OF ORIGIN SERIES

ORIGIN I

QUEENSLAND 12 ....**NEW SOUTH WALES 25**
Queensland: T - Lockyer (15), Tallis (43); G - Lockyer 2
NSW: T - Minichiello (19, 25), Wing (62), Johns (73); G - Johns 4; FG - Johns

Queensland: Darren Lockyer (Broncos), Shannon Hegarty (Roosters), Brent Tate (Broncos), Justin Hodges (Roosters), Matt Sing (Cowboys), Ben Ikin (Broncos), Shaun Berrigan (Broncos); Shane Webcke (Broncos), PJ Marsh (Warriors), Petero Civoniceva (Broncos), Gorden Tallis (Broncos) (c), Dane Carlaw (Broncos), Tonie Carroll (Broncos). Subs: Steve Price (Bulldogs), Chris Flannery (Roosters), Andrew Gee (Broncos), Paul Bowman (Cowboys).
NSW: Anthony Minichiello (Roosters), Timana Tahu (Knights), Matthew Gidley (Knights), Jamie Lyon (Eels), Michael De Vere (Broncos), Shaun Timmins (Dragons), Andrew Johns (Knights) (c); Robbie Kearns (Storm), Danny Buderus (Knights), Jason Ryles (Dragons), Craig Fitzgibbon (Roosters), Ben Kennedy (Knights), Luke Ricketson (Roosters). Subs: Luke Bailey (Dragons), Craig Wing (Roosters), Josh Perry (Knights), Phil Bailey (Sharks).
Referee: Bill Harrigan; **Video referee:** Eddie Ward
Rugby Leaguer & League Express Men of the Match
Qld: Darren Lockyer; *NSW:* Andrew Johns
Half-time: 6-12; **Attendance:** 52,420 at Suncorp Stadium (June 11)

ORIGIN II

NEW SOUTH WALES 27 ....**QUEENSLAND 4**
NSW: T - Kennedy (12), Gidley (19), Minichiello (26), Tahu (49, 72); G - Johns 3; FG - Johns
Queensland: T – Crocker (69)

NSW: Anthony Minichiello (Roosters), Timana Tahu (Knights), Matthew Gidley (Knights), Jamie Lyon (Eels), Michael De Vere (Broncos), Shaun Timmins (Dragons), Andrew Johns (Knights) (c); Robbie Kearns (Storm), Danny Buderus (Knights), Jason Ryles (Dragons), Craig Fitzgibbon (Roosters), Ben Kennedy (Knights), Luke Ricketson (Roosters). Subs: Luke Bailey (Dragons), Craig Wing (Roosters), Bryan Fletcher (Rabbitohs), Phil Bailey (Sharks).
Queensland: Darren Lockyer (Broncos), Matt Sing (Cowboys), Brent Tate (Broncos), Tonie Carroll (Broncos), Shannon Hegarty (Roosters), Ben Ikin (Broncos), Shaun Berrigan (Broncos); Shane Webcke (Broncos), Michael Crocker (Roosters), Steve Price (Bulldogs), Gorden Tallis (Broncos) (c), Petero Civoniceva (Broncos), Dane Carlaw (Broncos). Subs: Travis Norton (Bulldogs), Andrew Gee (Broncos), Scott Sattler (Panthers), Matt Bowen (Cowboys).
Referee: Bill Harrigan; **Video referees:** Steve Clark & Phil Cooley
Rugby Leaguer & League Express Men of the Match
NSW: Andrew Johns; *Qld:* Darren Lockyer
Half-time: 17-0; **Attendance:** 79,132 at Telstra Stadium (June 25)

ORIGIN III

QUEENSLAND 36 ....**NEW SOUTH WALES 6**
Queensland: T - Tate (5, 64), Sing (13, 16, 75), Smith (70), Crocker (78); G - Hannay 4
NSW: T - Tahu (47); G – Johns

Queensland: Darren Lockyer (Broncos), Shannon Hegarty (Roosters), Brent Tate (Broncos), Josh Hannay (Cowboys), Matt Sing (Cowboys), Ben Ikin (Broncos), Shaun Berrigan (Broncos); Shane Webcke (Broncos), Cameron Smith (Storm), Petero Civoniceva (Broncos), Gorden Tallis (Broncos) (c), Dane Carlaw (Broncos), Tonie Carroll (Broncos). Subs: Steve Price (Bulldogs), Michael Crocker (Roosters), Travis Norton (Bulldogs), Matt Bowen (Cowboys).
NSW: Anthony Minichiello (Roosters), Timana Tahu (Knights), Matthew Gidley (Knights), Jamie Lyon (Eels), Michael De Vere (Broncos), Shaun Timmins (Dragons), Andrew Johns (Knights) (c); Robbie Kearns (Storm), Danny Buderus (Knights), Jason Ryles (Dragons), Bryan Fletcher (Rabbitohs), Luke Ricketson (Roosters), Braith Anasta (Bulldogs). Luke Bailey (Dragons), Craig Wing (Roosters), Willie Mason (Bulldogs), Phil Bailey (Sharks).
Referee: Bill Harrigan; **Video referees:** Tim Mander & Eddie Ward:
Rugby Leaguer & League Express Men of the Match
Qld: Matt Sing; *NSW:* Andrew Johns
Half-time: 16-0; **Attendance:** 52,130 at Suncorp Stadium (July 16)

Queensland's Dane Carlaw hauls down New South Wales' Andrew Johns during Origin II

Michael De Vere (Carroll was later exonerated).

Tate shook off the cobwebs to score the first try of the evening. Stand-off Ben Ikin, so maligned by the media for his kicking display in the first two matches, put up a superb cross-field bomb. Veteran Cowboy Matt Sing leaped high and batted the ball back to a trailing Tate who fell on it for a four-pointer.

It was certainly Sing's night. Seven minutes later he brought the ball back into the field of play from a seemingly impossible position, refusing to be trapped behind his own tryline. And within half a minute he had scored at the other end of the field.

Darren Lockyer had begun the movement by spinning out of a couple of tackles. Then half Shaun Berrigan, Ikin and 20 year old rookie hooker Cameron Smith took the ball some 50 metres. It was left to Berrigan to torpedo a pass some 30 metres across the pitch to an unmarked Sing, who had an unrestricted passage to the line.

Just three minutes later and Sing was in again, this time off an incredible long pass from Lockyer. The Queenslanders led 16-0 after as many minutes and a cricket score was in the offing.

However, the score remained unchanged until half-time.

The Blues seemed to lift after the break. When Timana Tahu beat Lockyer to the ball after a kick along the ground by Braith Anasta, the visitors were back in the game at 16-6. But that was as good as it got for NSW, with Tate scoring his second try to snuff out any hopes of a Blues' revival.

Exciting young Aboriginal utility back Matt Bowen came off the bench with 11 minutes remaining. With his first touch of the ball he danced some 70 metres downfield. And the movement finished with Lockyer sending Smith over for a try - a worthy reward for the debutant, who had given superb service to his outside backs and had defended stoutly.

In the space of the next eight minutes, Sing scored his third try and was then involved (with Ikin and Lockyer) in the lead-up to Queensland's final try, to substitute Michael Crocker.

At 36-6, it equalled the Maroons' biggest Origin success, posted in the third match of the 1989 series.

As the beaming former Test star Kevin Walters noted on national television later: "Isn't it great to be a Queenslander!"

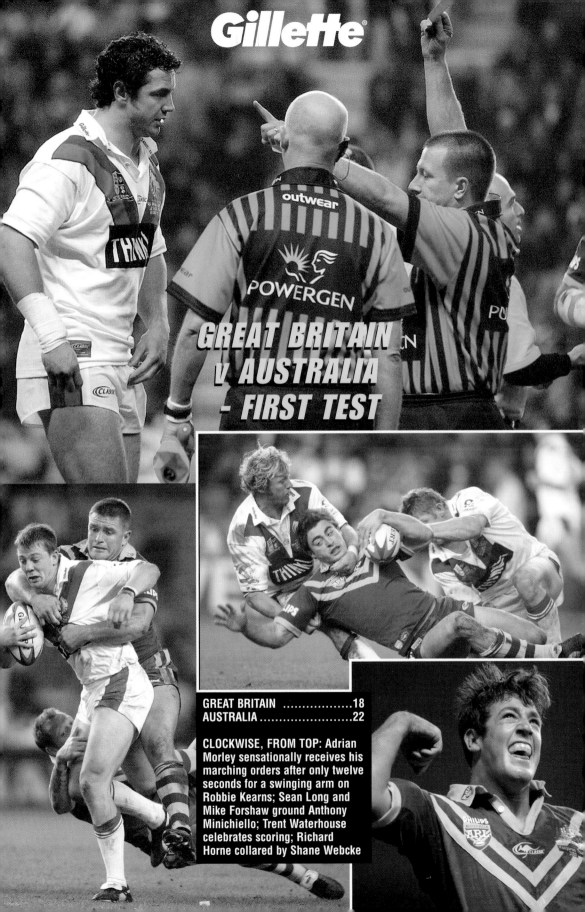

Gillette®

GREAT BRITAIN v AUSTRALIA - FIRST TEST

GREAT BRITAIN 18
AUSTRALIA 22

CLOCKWISE, FROM TOP: Adrian Morley sensationally receives his marching orders after only twelve seconds for a swinging arm on Robbie Kearns; Sean Long and Mike Forshaw ground Anthony Minichiello; Trent Waterhouse celebrates scoring; Richard Horne collared by Shane Webcke

GREAT BRITAIN v AUSTRALIA - SECOND TEST

GREAT BRITAIN 20
AUSTRALIA 23

CLOCKWISE, FROM TOP:
Adrian Morley gets an amazing pass away to set up a try for Terry Newton; Gary Connolly crashes over to score for his first Great Britain try; Darren Lockyer celebrates Australia's Test Series win; A dejected Andy Farrell leads the Great Britain side from the field

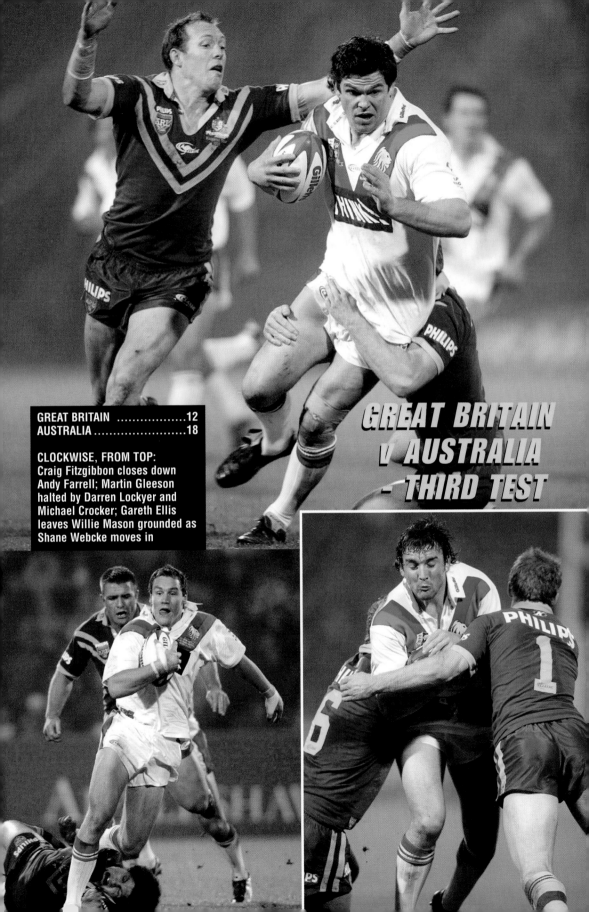

GREAT BRITAIN 12
AUSTRALIA 18

CLOCKWISE, FROM TOP:
Craig Fitzgibbon closes down
Andy Farrell; Martin Gleeson
halted by Darren Lockyer and
Michael Crocker; Gareth Ellis
leaves Willie Mason grounded as
Shane Webcke moves in

GREAT BRITAIN
v AUSTRALIA
- THIRD TEST

ABOVE: Chris Thorman kicks ahead as a brave England 'A' side push Australia all the way

BELOW RIGHT: Richard Villasanti tackled by David Mills as Australia sweep aside Wales

AUSTRALIAN TOUR

LEFT: Awen Guttenbeil on the charge as New Zealand defeat Australia in October

BELOW: Jamie Lyon races away to score as the Kangaroos down the Kiwis in July

TRANS-TASMAN TESTS

WORLD CLUB CHALLENGE

ST HELENS 0
SYDNEY ROOSTERS.............38

TOP: St Helens' Paul Sculthorpe looks for a way through

LEFT: Paul Newlove and Chris Joynt combine to halt Brad Fittler

RIGHT: Adrian Morley celebrates the Roosters' World Club Challenge win

LEFT: Keith Senior bursts through against Tonga in February's World Sevens in Sydney. England lost out to Parramatta Eels in the tournament's final

WORLD SEVENS

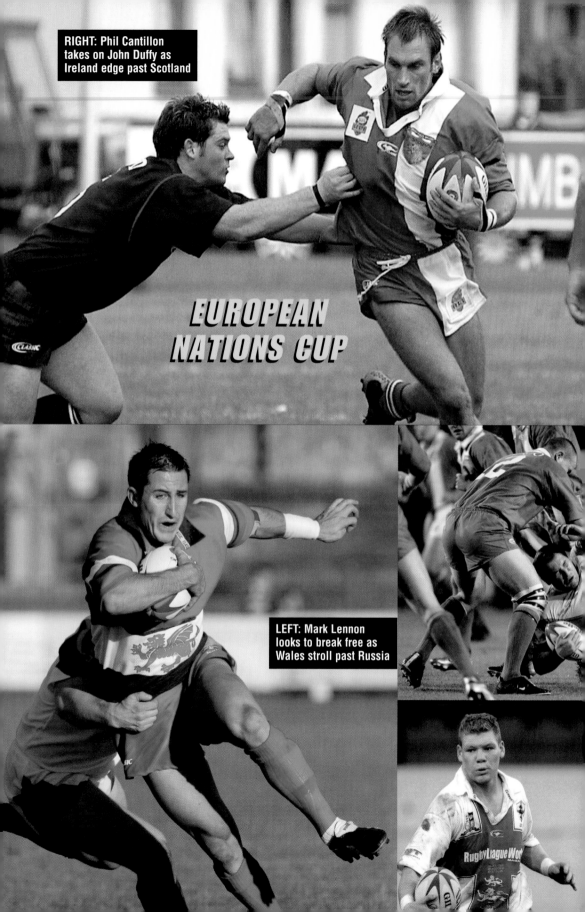

RIGHT: Phil Cantillon takes on John Duffy as Ireland edge past Scotland

EUROPEAN NATIONS CUP

LEFT: Mark Lennon looks to break free as Wales stroll past Russia

RIGHT: Gareth Hock feels the force of Kris Tassell and Aled James as England see off Wales

LEFT: Rachid Hechiche grounded as France defeat Ireland

BELOW: Danny Tickle slips through as England pass the century mark against Russia

RIGHT: Danny McGuire bursts through the French defence as England win the European Nations Cup

LEFT: Andrew Henderson weaves through as Scotland sneak past France

THE ORIGIN GAME

RIGHT: Matt Diskin defies the challenge of Mike Forshaw to score a try as Yorkshire take apart Lancashire

INSET: Ryan Hudson celebrates Origin success

NEW ZEALAND A TOUR

CLOCKWISE FROM ABOVE LEFT: The Kiwis perform the Haka at Warrington; Cumbria's Rob Purdham looks for a way through; National League One's Radney Bowker on the charge; Vila Apu'ula offloads under pressure from Great Britain's Gareth Ellis

INSET: National League Two's Phil Stephenson held up

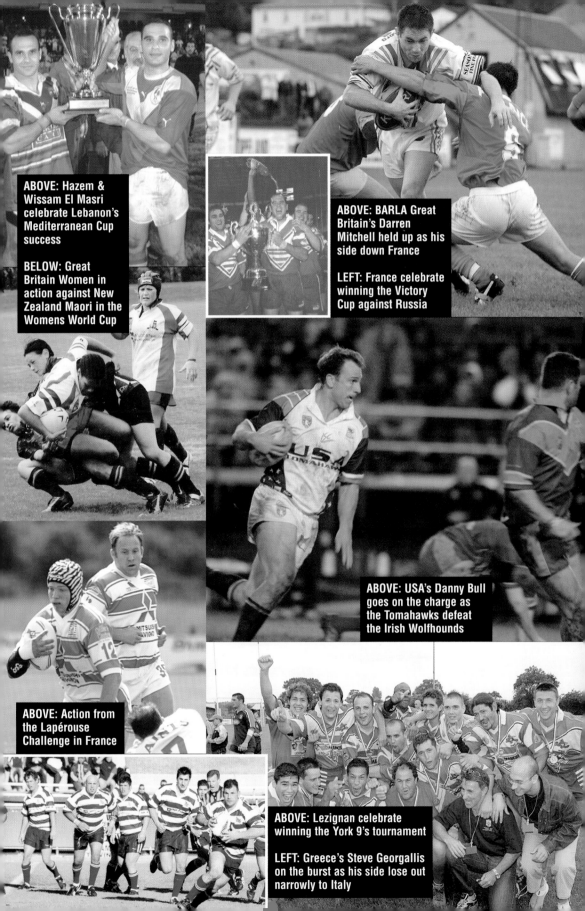

ABOVE: Hazem & Wissam El Masri celebrate Lebanon's Mediterranean Cup success

BELOW: Great Britain Women in action against New Zealand Maori in the Womens World Cup

ABOVE: BARLA Great Britain's Darren Mitchell held up as his side down France

LEFT: France celebrate winning the Victory Cup against Russia

ABOVE: USA's Danny Bull goes on the charge as the Tomahawks defeat the Irish Wolfhounds

ABOVE: Action from the Lapérouse Challenge in France

ABOVE: Lezignan celebrate winning the York 9's tournament

LEFT: Greece's Steve Georgallis on the burst as his side lose out narrowly to Italy

NRL SEASON

ABOVE: Newcastle's Kurt Gidley goes airborne to score against Parramatta

ABOVE: Bulldogs' Luke Patten leaps over St George-Illawarra's Mark Riddell to claim a high ball

BELOW: Manly's Steve Menzies grounded against South Sydney

LEFT: Brisbane's Casey McGuire scores against Parramatta

BELOW: Sydney Roosters' Anthony Minichiello tackled against Newcastle in the play-offs

St George-Illawarra's Reece Simmonds shows his delight at scoring against Parramatta

BELOW: New Zealand Warrior Francis Meli crosses for one of his five tries against the Bulldogs in the play-offs

LEFT: Parramatta's Daniel Heckenberg loses the ball under a heavy challenge from Newcastle's Matthew Kennedy

NRL GRAND FINAL

CLOCKWISE, FROM ABOVE: Scott Sattler and Craig Gower celebrate Penrith's Grand Final win over Sydney Roosters with the Panthers' fans; Luke Rooney touches down; Rhys Wesser in the thick of the action

STATE OF ORIGIN

BELOW: New South Wales' Andrew Johns celebrates scoring in Origin I with Robbie Kearns. The Blues went on to clinch a 2-1 series victory

ABOVE LEFT: Darren Lockyer dives over to score for Queensland

ABOVE: Hull KR's Harvey Howard takes on Whitehaven's Howard Hill

ABOVE: Rochdale's Matt Calland looks to escape the clutches of Whitehaven's David Seeds during the play-offs

ABOVE: Oldham's Gavin Dodd looks for a gap against Hull KR

BELOW: Leigh's Tommy Martyn celebrates a try against Oldham

NATIONAL LEAGUE: ONE SEASON

ABOVE: Featherstone's Richard Chapman leaves the Leigh defence trailing

LEFT: Doncaster's Marvin Golden attempts to break free against Batley

RIGHT: Dewsbury's Billy Kershaw takes on Batley's Mark Toohey

LEIGH CENTURIONS..............14
SALFORD CITY REDS 31

RIGHT: Alan Hunte, Gareth Haggerty, Stuart Littler and Cliff Beverley celebrate Salford's return to Super League

BELOW: Paul Highton gets to grips with Leigh's Lee Sanderson

NATIONAL LEAGUE ONE GRAND FINAL

BELOW: No way past Adam Bristow and Danny Halliwell for Andy Coley

NATIONAL LEAGUE CUP FINAL

LEFT: Stuart Littler beats Neil Turley to score as Salford win the National League Cup by defeating Leigh

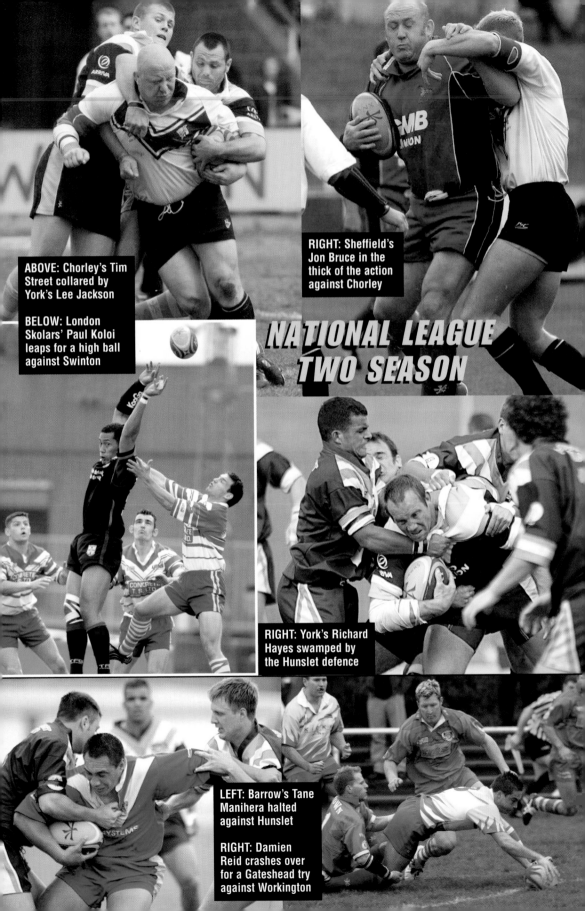

ABOVE: Chorley's Tim Street collared by York's Lee Jackson

BELOW: London Skolars' Paul Koloi leaps for a high ball against Swinton

RIGHT: Sheffield's Jon Bruce in the thick of the action against Chorley

NATIONAL LEAGUE TWO SEASON

RIGHT: York's Richard Hayes swamped by the Hunslet defence

LEFT: Barrow's Tane Manihera halted against Hunslet

RIGHT: Damien Reid crashes over for a Gateshead try against Workington

KEIGHLEY COUGARS 13
SHEFFIELD EAGLES 11

RIGHT: Andy Robinson heads for the line on his way to scoring Keighley's winning try

BELOW: James Rushforth and retiring Cougar legend Jason Ramshaw lift the National League Two trophy

NATIONAL LEAGUE TWO GRAND FINAL

ABOVE: Keighley's Matt Firth ducks under the challenge of Sheffield's Richard Goddard

NATIONAL LEAGUE THREE GRAND FINAL

LEFT: Warrington-Woolston celebrate as they defeat Teesside to win the first ever National League Three Grand Final

RIGHT: Mark Wallington races clear

TOTALRL.COM CONFERENCE FINAL

MAIN PICTURE: Bridgend's Kevin Ellis leads his team on a lap of honour at Wilderspool following the Blue Bulls' Grand Final win over Carlisle

LEFT: Allan Bateman held up

TOP: Bolton-Le-Moors celebrate their Shield Final win over Torfaen

NATIONAL CONFERENCE GRAND FINAL

ABOVE: The victorious Siddal side celebrates winning the National Conference Grand Final by defeating West Hull

RIGHT: Liam Walsh on the charge

NATIONAL CUP FINAL

LEFT: Kieron, Michael & Chris Deakin show their delight following Oldham St Annes' National Cup win over West Hull

RIGHT: St Annes' Martin Taylor looks for support under pressure

6
STATISTICAL REVIEW

PLAYER	CLUB	YEAR	APP	TRIES	GOALS	FG	PTS
Darren Abram	Oldham	1996-97	25(2)	11	0	0	44
Darren Adams	Paris	1996	9(1)	1	0	0	4
Guy Adams	Huddersfield	1998	1(2)	0	0	0	0
Matt Adamson	Leeds	2002-03	43(2)	9	0	0	36
Phil Adamson	St Helens	1999	(1)	0	0	0	0
Jamie Ainscough	Wigan	2002-03	30(2)	18	0	0	72
Glen Air	London	1998-2001	57(13)	27	0	1	109
Darren Albert	St Helens	2002-03	55	36	0	0	144
Paul Alcock	Widnes	2003	1(3)	0	0	0	0
Neil Alexander	Salford	1998	(1)	0	0	0	0
Malcolm Alker	Salford	1997-2002	119(1)	26	0	1	105
Chris Allen	Castleford	1996	(1)	0	0	0	0
David Allen	Wigan	2003	(1)	0	0	0	0
Gavin Allen	London	1996	10	0	0	0	0
John Allen	Workington	1996	20(1)	6	0	0	24
Ray Allen	London	1996	5(3)	3	0	0	12
Richard Allwood	Gateshead	1999	(4)	0	0	0	0
Sean Allwood	Gateshead	1999	3(17)	1	0	0	4
David Alstead	Warrington	2000-02	23(10)	3	0	0	12
Asa Amone	Halifax	1996-97	32(7)	10	0	0	40
Grant Anderson	Castleford	1996-97	15(6)	3	0	0	12
Paul Anderson	Bradford	1997-2003	66(90)	29	0	0	116
	Halifax	1996	5(1)	1	0	0	4
Paul Anderson	Sheffield	1999	3(7)	1	0	0	4
	St Helens	1996-98	2(28)	4	1	0	18
Eric Anselme	Halifax	1997	(2)	0	0	0	0
Graham Appo	Warrington	2002-03	34(4)	26	62	0	228
	Huddersfield	2001	7	4	0	0	16
Colin Armstrong	Workington	1996	11(2)	1	0	0	4
Richard Armswood	Workington	1996	5(1)	1	0	0	4
Danny Arnold	Salford	2001-02	26(13)	13	0	0	52
	Huddersfield	1998-2000	55(7)	26	0	0	104
	Castleford	2000	(4)	0	0	0	0
	St Helens	1996-97	40(1)	33	0	0	132
Martin Aspinwall	Wigan	2001-03	33(12)	12	0	0	48
Mark Aston	Sheffield	1996-99	67(6)	6	243	6	516
Paul Atcheson	Widnes	2002-03	11(29)	4	0	0	16
	St Helens	1998-2000	58(4)	18	0	0	72
	Oldham	1996-97	40	21	0	0	84
David Atkins	Huddersfield	2001	26(1)	4	0	0	16
Brad Attwood	Halifax	2003	(3)	0	0	0	0
Warren Ayres	Salford	1999	2(9)	1	2	0	8
Jerome Azema	Paris	1997	(1)	0	0	0	0
David Baildon	Hull	1998-99	26(2)	4	0	0	16
Julian Bailey	Huddersfield	2003	28	9	0	0	36
Ryan Bailey	Leeds	2002-03	15(13)	0	0	0	0
Simon Baldwin	Sheffield	1999	7(15)	2	0	0	8
	Halifax	1996-98	41(15)	16	0	1	65
Rob Ball	Wigan	1998-2000	3(4)	0	0	0	0
Michael Banks	Bradford	1998	(1)	0	0	0	0
Frederic Banquet	Paris	1996	16(2)	7	4	0	36
Lee Bardauskas	Castleford	1996-97	(2)	0	0	0	0
Craig Barker	Workington	1996	(2)	0	0	0	0
Dwayne Barker	Hull	2003	(1)	0	0	0	0
Mark Barlow	Wakefield	2002	(1)	0	0	0	0
Danny Barnes	Halifax	1999	2	0	0	0	0
Richie Barnett	Hull	2003	22	12	0	0	48
	London	2001-02	31(4)	13	0	0	52
David Barnhill	Leeds	2000	20(8)	5	0	0	20
Paul Barrow	Warrington	1996-97	1(10)	1	0	0	4
Scott Barrow	St Helens	1997-2000	9(13)	1	0	0	4
Steve Barrow	London	2000	2	0	0	0	0
	Hull	1998-99	4(17)	1	0	0	4
	Wigan	1996	(8)	3	0	0	12
Ben Barton	Huddersfield	1998	1(6)	1	0	0	4
Danny Barton	Salford	2001	1	0	0	0	0
Wayne Bartrim	Castleford	2002-03	41(2)	9	157	0	350
Greg Barwick	London	1996-97	30(4)	21	110	2	306
David Bastian	Halifax	1996	(2)	0	0	0	0
David Bates	Castleford	2001-02	(4)	0	0	0	0
	Warrington	2001	1(2)	0	0	0	0
Nathan Batty	Wakefield	2001	1(1)	0	0	0	0

PLAYER	CLUB	YEAR	APP	TRIES	GOALS	FG	PTS
Russell Bawden	London	1996-97,					
		2002-03	50(47)	15	0	0	60
Neil Baxter	Salford	2001	1	0	0	0	0
Neil Baynes	Salford	1999-2002	68(18)	6	0	0	24
	Wigan	1996-98	(10)	1	0	0	4
Robbie Beazley	London	1997-99	48(15)	13	0	0	52
Robbie Beckett	Halifax	2002	27	15	0	0	60
Dean Bell	Leeds	1996	1	1	0	0	4
Ian Bell	Hull	2003	(1)	0	0	0	0
Mark Bell	Wigan	1998	22	12	0	0	48
Paul Bell	Leeds	2000	1	0	0	0	0
Troy Bellamy	Paris	1997	5(10)	0	0	0	0
Adrian Belle	Huddersfield	1998	10(2)	0	0	0	0
	Oldham	1996	19	8	0	0	32
Jamie Benn	Castleford	1998, 2000	3(8)	1	15	0	34
Andy Bennett	Warrington	1996	6(5)	1	0	0	4
Mike Bennett	St Helens	2000-03	29(31)	4	0	0	16
John Bentley	Huddersfield	1999	13(4)	3	0	0	12
	Halifax	1996, 1998	22(3)	24	0	0	96
Phil Bergman	Paris	1997	20(1)	14	0	0	56
Joe Berry	Huddersfield	1998-99	25(14)	3	0	0	12
Colin Best	Hull	2003	28	19	0	0	76
Roger Best	London	1997-98	1(5)	1	0	0	4
Mike Bethwaite	Workington	1996	17(3)	1	0	0	4
Denis Betts	Wigan	1998-2001	82(24)	33	0	0	132
Ricky Bibey	Wigan	2001-03	5(29)	0	0	0	0
Chris Birchall	Halifax	2002-03	24(22)	4	0	0	16
	Bradford	2000	(1)	0	0	0	0
Deon Bird	Widnes	2003	18	7	0	0	28
	Wakefield	2002	10(1)	1	0	0	4
	Hull	2000-02	37(22)	20	0	0	80
	Gateshead	1999	19(3)	13	0	0	52
	Paris	1996-97	30	12	2	0	52
Richie Blackmore	Leeds	1997-2000	63	25	0	0	100
Matthew Blake	Wakefield	2003	(3)	0	0	0	0
Steve Blakeley	Salford	1997-2002	103(5)	26	241	2	588
	Warrington	2000	4(3)	1	9	0	22
Richard Blakeway	Castleford	2002-03	1(13)	0	0	0	0
Ian Blease	Salford	1997	(1)	0	0	0	0
Jamie Bloem	Huddersfield	2003	18(4)	3	11	0	34
	Halifax	1998-2002	82(25)	25	100	2	302
Vea Bloomfield	Paris	1996	4(14)	3	0	0	12
Pascal Bomati	Paris	1996	17(1)	10	0	0	40
Simon Booth	Hull	1998-99	15(9)	2	0	0	8
	St Helens	1996-97	10(4)	1	0	0	4
Steve Booth	Huddersfield	1998-99	16(4)	2	3	0	14
Alan Boothroyd	Halifax	1997	2(3)	0	0	0	0
John Boslem	Paris	1996	(5)	0	0	0	0
Liam Botham	Leeds	2003	(1)	0	0	0	0
Frano Botica	Castleford	1996	21	5	84	2	190
Hadj Boudebza	Paris	1996	(2)	0	0	0	0
David Boughton	Huddersfield	1999	26(1)	4	0	0	16
David Bouveng	Halifax	1997-99	66(2)	19	0	0	76
Tony Bowes	Huddersfield	1998	3(2)	0	0	0	0
Radney Bowker	St Helens	2001	(1)	0	0	0	0
David Boyle	Bradford	1999-2000	36(13)	15	0	1	61
David Bradbury	Hudds-Sheff	2000	21(2)	1	0	0	4
	Salford	1997-99	23(10)	6	0	0	24
	Oldham	1996-97	19(6)	9	0	0	36
John Braddish	St Helens	2001-02	1(1)	0	3	0	6
Graeme Bradley	Bradford	1996-98	62(1)	29	0	0	116
Darren Bradstreet	London	1999-2000	1(3)	0	0	0	0
Liam Bretherton	Wigan	1999	(5)	2	0	0	8
	Warrington	1997	(2)	0	0	0	0
Johnny Brewer	Halifax	1996	4(2)	2	0	0	8
Chris Bridge	Bradford	2003	(3)	0	0	0	0
Lee Briers	Warrington	1997-2003	146(11)	47	419	37	1063
	St Helens	1997	3	0	11	0	22
Carl Briggs	Salford	1999	8(5)	3	0	1	13
	Halifax	1996	5(3)	1	0	0	4
Mike Briggs	Widnes	2002	1(2)	1	0	0	4

PLAYER	CLUB	YEAR	APP	TRIES	GOALS	FG	PTS
Shaun Briscoe	Wigan	2002-03	23(5)	11	0	0	44
Darren Britt	St Helens	2002-03	41	3	0	0	12
Gary Broadbent	Salford	1997-2002	117(2)	22	0	0	88
Paul Broadbent	Wakefield	2002	16(5)	0	0	0	0
	Hull	2000-01	40(9)	3	0	0	12
	Halifax	1999	26(1)	2	0	0	8
	Sheffield	1996-98	63(1)	6	0	0	24
Andrew Brocklehurst							
	Halifax	2001-03	37(8)	2	0	0	8
Justin Brooker	Wakefield	2001	25	9	0	0	36
	Bradford	2000	17(4)	11	0	0	44
Darren Brown	Salford	1999-2001	47(9)	11	6	0	56
Gavin Brown	Leeds	1996-97	5(2)	1	2	0	8
Kevin Brown	Wigan	2003	4(8)	6	0	0	24
Lee Brown	Hull	1999	(1)	0	0	0	0
Michael Brown	London	1996	(2)	0	0	0	0
Todd Brown	Paris	1996	8(1)	2	0	0	8
Adrian Brunker	Wakefield	1999	17	6	0	0	24
Justin Bryant	Paris	1996	4(1)	0	0	0	0
	London	1996	7(8)	1	0	0	4
Austin Buchanan	London	2003	3(1)	2	0	0	8
Neil Budworth	London	2002-03	32(7)	2	0	0	8
James Bunyan	Huddersfield	1998-99	8(7)	2	0	0	8
Andy Burgess	Salford	1997	3(12)	0	0	0	0
Darren Burns	Warrington	2002-03	50(2)	13	0	0	52
Gary Burns	Oldham	1996	6	1	0	0	4
Paul Burns	Workington	1996	5(2)	1	0	0	4
Rob Burrow	Leeds	2001-03	29(43)	26	25	1	155
Dean Busby	Warrington	1999-2002	34(34)	7	0	0	28
	Hull	1998	8(6)	0	0	0	0
	St Helens	1996-98	1(7)	0	0	0	0
Ikram Butt	London	1996	5(1)	0	0	0	0
Shane Byrne	Huddersfield	1998-99	1(5)	0	0	0	0
Didier Cabestany	Paris	1996-97	20(6)	2	0	0	8
Joel Caine	London	2003	6	4	1	0	18
Mark Calderwood							
	Leeds	2001-03	73(9)	52	0	0	208
Mike Callan	Warrington	2002	(4)	0	0	0	0
Matt Calland	Huddersfield	2003	2	0	0	0	0
	Hull	1999	1	0	0	0	0
	Bradford	1996-98	44(5)	24	0	0	96
Dean Callaway	London	1999-2000	26(24)	12	0	0	48
Laurent Cambres	Paris	1996	(1)	0	0	0	0
Chris Campbell	Warrington	2000	7(1)	2	0	0	8
Logan Campbell	Hull	1998-99,					
		2001	70(13)	14	0	0	56
	Castleford	2000	14(2)	3	0	0	12
	Workington	1996	7(1)	1	0	0	4
Blake Cannova	Widnes	2002	(1)	0	0	0	0
Phil Cantillon	Widnes	2002-03	27(21)	18	0	0	72
	Leeds	1997	(1)	0	0	0	0
Daryl Cardiss	Warrington	2003	7	2	2	0	12
	Halifax	1999-2003	91(8)	39	4	0	164
	Wigan	1996-98	12(6)	4	0	0	16
Dale Cardoza	Warrington	2002	5	1	0	0	4
	Halifax	2001	3	1	0	0	4
	Huddersfield	2000-01	20(9)	11	0	0	44
	Sheffield	1998-99	11(7)	3	0	0	12
Paul Carige	Salford	1999	24(1)	7	0	0	28
Jim Carlton	Huddersfield	1999	3(11)	2	0	0	8
Brian Carney	Wigan	2001-03	68(9)	35	0	0	140
	Hull	2000	13(3)	7	0	0	28
	Gateshead	1999	3(2)	2	0	0	8
Martin Carney	Warrington	1997	(1)	0	0	0	0
Paul Carr	Sheffield	1996-98	45(5)	15	0	0	60
Bernard Carroll	London	1996	2(1)	1	0	0	4
Mark Carroll	London	1998	15(3)	1	0	0	4
Tonie Carroll	Leeds	2001-02	42(2)	30	0	0	120
Darren Carter	Workington	1996	10(3)	0	1	0	2
Steve Carter	Widnes	2002	14(7)	4	0	0	16
John Cartwright	Salford	1997	9	0	0	0	0
Garreth Carvell	Hull	2001-03	13(48)	7	0	0	28
	Leeds	1997-2000	(4)	0	0	0	0
	Gateshead	1999	4(4)	1	0	0	4
Garen Casey	Salford	1999	13(5)	3	23	0	58
Mick Cassidy	Wigan	1996-2003	175(24)	29	0	0	116
Chris Causey	Warrington	1997-99	(18)	1	0	0	4
Arnaud Cervello	Paris	1996	4	4	0	0	16
Gary Chambers	Warrington	1996-2000	65(28)	2	0	0	8
Pierre Chamorin	Paris	1996-97	27(3)	8	3	0	38
Chris Chapman	Leeds	1999	(1)	0	0	0	0
Damien Chapman							
	London	1998	6(2)	3	4	1	21
David Chapman	Castleford	1996-98	24(6)	8	0	0	32
Jaymes Chapman							
	Halifax	2002-03	5(8)	1	0	0	4
Richard Chapman							
	Sheffield	1996	1	2	0	0	8
Chris Charles	Castleford	2001	1(4)	1	0	0	4
Andy Cheetham	Huddersfield	1998-99	30	11	0	0	44
Kris Chesney	London	1998	1(2)	0	0	0	0
Chris Chester	Hull	2002-03	5(7)	6	0	0	24
	Wigan	1999-2001	21(22)	5	0	0	20
	Halifax	1996-99	47(14)	16	15	1	95
Lee Chilton	Workington	1996	10(3)	6	0	0	24
Gary Christie	Bradford	1996-97	4(7)	1	0	0	4
Dean Clark	Leeds	1996	11(2)	3	0	0	12
Des Clark	St Helens	1999	4	0	0	0	0
	Halifax	1998-99	35(13)	6	0	0	24
Greg Clarke	Halifax	1997	1(1)	0	0	0	0
John Clarke	Oldham	1996-97	27(4)	5	0	0	20
Jon Clarke	Warrington	2001-03	70(2)	12	1	0	50
	London	2000-01	19(11)	2	0	0	8
	Wigan	1997-99	13(10)	3	0	0	12
Ryan Clayton	Halifax	2000,					
		2002-03	28(12)	6	0	0	24
Gavin Clinch	Halifax	1998-99,					
		2001-02	88(2)	26	45	5	199
	Hudds-Sheff	2000	18(2)	5	0	1	21
	Wigan	1999	10(2)	4	12	0	40
Bradley Clyde	Leeds	2001	7(5)	1	0	0	4
Evan Cochrane	London	1996	5(1)	1	0	0	4
Anthony Colella	Huddersfield	2003	5(1)	2	0	0	8
Andy Coley	Salford	2001-02	18(24)	5	0	0	20
Steve Collins	Hull	2000	28	17	0	0	68
	Gateshead	1999	20(4)	13	0	0	52
Wayne Collins	Leeds	1997	21	3	0	0	12
Gary Connolly	Leeds	2003	25	5	0	0	20
	Wigan	1996-2002	156(4)	69	5	0	286
Mick Cook	Sheffield	1996	9(10)	2	0	0	8
Paul Cook	Huddersfield	1998-99	11(6)	2	13	0	34
	Bradford	1996-97	14(8)	7	38	1	105
Paul Cooke	Hull	1999-2003	88(27)	18	56	1	185
Ben Cooper	Huddersfield	2000-01,					
		2003	27(9)	3	0	0	12
Ged Corcoran	Halifax	2003	1(11)	0	0	0	0
Wayne Corcoran	Halifax	2003	4(2)	0	0	0	0
Mark Corvo	Salford	2002	7(5)	0	0	0	0
Brandon Costin	Huddersfield	2001, 2003	47	34	52	2	242
	Bradford	2002	20(1)	8	0	0	32
Wes Cotton	London	1997-98	12	3	0	0	12
Phil Coussons	Salford	1997	7(2)	3	0	0	12
Alex Couttet	Paris	1997	1	0	0	0	0
Nick Couttet	Paris	1997	1	0	0	0	0
Jamie Coventry	Castleford	1996	1	0	0	0	0
Jimmy Cowan	Oldham	1996-97	2(8)	0	0	0	0
Will Cowell	Warrington	1998-2000	6(8)	1	0	0	4
Neil Cowie	Wigan	1996-2001	116(27)	10	0	1	41
Mark Cox	London	2003	(3)	0	0	0	0
Eorl Crabtree	Huddersfield	2001, 2003	4(15)	1	0	0	4
Andy Craig	Halifax	1999	13(7)	1	3	0	10
	Wigan	1996	5(5)	2	0	0	8
Scott Cram	London	1999-2002	65(7)	4	0	0	16
Steve Craven	Hull	1998-2003	53(42)	4	0	0	16
Nicky Crellin	Workington	1996	(2)	0	0	0	0
Jason Critchley	Wakefield	2000	7(1)	4	0	0	16
	Castleford	1997-98	27(3)	11	0	0	44
Martin Crompton	Salford	1998-2000	30(6)	11	6	2	58
	Oldham	1996-97	36(1)	16	0	3	67
Paul Crook	Oldham	1996	4(9)	0	3	0	6
Lee Crooks	Castleford	1996-97	27(2)	2	14	0	36
Alan Cross	St Helens	1997	(2)	0	0	0	0
Kevin Crouthers	Warrington	2001-03	12(1)	4	0	0	16
	London	2000	6(4)	1	0	0	4
	Wakefield	1999	4(4)	1	0	0	4
	Bradford	1997-98	3(9)	2	0	0	8
Matt Crowther	Hull	2001-03	48	20	166	0	412
	Hudds-Sheff	2000	10(4)	5	22	0	64
	Sheffield	1996-99	43(4)	22	10	0	108
Heath Cruckshank							
	Halifax	2003	19(1)	0	0	0	0
	St Helens	2001	1(12)	0	0	0	0
Paul Cullen	Warrington	1996	19	3	0	0	12
Francis Cummins							
	Leeds	1996-2003	198(8)	116	26	2	518
Keiron Cunningham							
	St Helens	1996-2003	191(5)	89	0	0	356
Andy Currier	Warrington	1996-97	(2)	1	0	0	4
Joe Dakuitoga	Sheffield	1996	6(3)	0	0	0	0
Brett Dallas	Wigan	2000-03	79	50	0	0	200
Paul Darbyshire	Warrington	1997	(6)	0	0	0	0
Maea David	Hull	1998	1	0	0	0	0
Paul Davidson	Halifax	2001-03	22(30)	10	0	0	40
	London	2000	6(10)	4	0	0	16
	St Helens	1998-99	27(16)	7	0	0	28
	Oldham	1996-97	17(18)	14	0	1	57
Gareth Davies	Warrington	1996-97	1(6)	0	0	0	0
Wes Davies	Wigan	1998-2001	22(22)	11	0	0	44
Brad Davis	Wakefield	2001-03	15(12)	15	22	5	109
	Castleford	1997-2000	83	26	41	9	195
Matt Daylight	Hull	2000	17(1)	7	0	0	28
	Gateshead	1999	30	25	0	0	100
Paul Deacon	Bradford	1998-2003	108(43)	35	369	12	890
	Oldham	1997	(2)	0	0	0	0
Craig Dean	Halifax	1996-97	25(11)	12	1	1	51
Gareth Dean	London	2000	(4)	0	0	0	0
Yacine Dekkiche	Hudds-Sheff	2000	11(3)	3	0	0	12
Jason Demetriou	Widnes	2002-03	47(1)	15	1	0	62

195

Super League Players 1996-2003

PLAYER	CLUB	YEAR	APP	TRIES	GOALS	FG	PTS
Martin Dermott	Warrington	1997	1	0	0	0	0
David Despin	Paris	1996	(1)	0	0	0	0
Fabien Devecchi	Paris	1996-97	17(10)	2	0	0	8
Paul Devlin	Widnes	2002-03	24	14	0	0	56
Matt Diskin	Leeds	2001-03	59(10)	9	0	0	36
Paul Dixon	Sheffield	1996-97	5(9)	1	0	0	4
Gareth Dobson	Castleford	1998-2000	(10)	0	0	0	0
Michael Docherty							
	Hull	2000-01	(6)	0	0	0	0
Sid Domic	Warrington	2002-03	41(4)	17	0	0	68
Glen Donkin	Hull	2002-03	(10)	1	0	0	4
Stuart Donlan	Halifax	2001-03	65(2)	22	0	0	88
Jason Donohue	Bradford	1996	(4)	0	0	0	0
Jeremy Donougher							
	Bradford	1996-99	40(21)	13	0	0	52
Justin Dooley	London	2000-01	37(18)	2	0	0	8
Dane Dorahy	Halifax	2003	20	7	45	0	118
	Wakefield	2000-01	16(2)	4	19	1	55
Ewan Dowes	Hull	2003	3(15)	3	0	0	12
	Leeds	2001-03	1(9)	0	0	0	0
Adam Doyle	Warrington	1998	9(3)	4	0	0	16
Rod Doyle	Sheffield	1997-99	52(10)	10	0	0	40
Damien Driscoll	Salford	2001	23(1)	1	0	0	4
John Duffy	Salford	2000	3(11)	0	1	1	3
	Warrington	1997-99	12(12)	0	0	0	0
Andrew Duncan	London	1997	2(4)	2	0	0	8
	Warrington	1997	(1)	0	0	0	0
Andrew Dunemann							
	Leeds	2003	27	4	0	2	18
	Halifax	1999-2002	68	19	0	1	77
Matt Dunford	London	1997-98	18(20)	3	0	0	13
Jamie Durbin	Warrington	2003	(1)	0	0	0	0
James Durkin	Paris	1997	(5)	0	0	0	0
Bernard Dwyer	Bradford	1996-2000	65(10)	14	0	0	56
Jim Dymock	London	2001-03	77(1)	13	0	0	52
Leo Dynevor	London	1996	8(11)	5	7	0	34
Jason Eade	Paris	1997	9	4	0	0	16
Michael Eagar	Castleford	1999-2003	130(2)	60	0	0	240
	Warrington	1998	21	6	0	0	24
Barry Eaton	Widnes	2002	25	2	49	4	110
	Castleford	2000	1(4)	0	3	0	6
Greg Ebrill	Salford	2002	15(6)	1	0	0	4
Cliff Eccles	Salford	1997-98	30(5)	1	0	0	4
Chris Eckersley	Warrington	1996	1	0	0	0	0
Steve Edmed	Sheffield	1997	15(1)	0	0	0	0
Mark Edmondson							
	St Helens	1999-2003	15(46)	4	0	0	16
Diccon Edwards	Castleford	1996-97	10(5)	1	0	0	4
Peter Edwards	Salford	1997-98	35(2)	4	0	0	16
Shaun Edwards	London	1997-2000	32(8)	16	1	0	66
	Bradford	1998	8(2)	4	0	0	16
	Wigan	1996	17(3)	12	1	0	50
Danny Ekis	Halifax	2001	(1)	0	0	0	0
Abi Ekoku	Bradford	1997-98	21(4)	6	0	0	24
	Halifax	1996	15(1)	5	0	0	20
Olivier Elima	Wakefield	2003	1(5)	0	0	0	0
	Castleford	2002	(1)	1	0	0	4
Abderazak Elkhalouki							
	Paris	1997	(1)	0	0	0	0
Gareth Ellis	Wakefield	1999-2003	59(17)	14	2	0	60
Danny Ellison	Castleford	1998-99	7(16)	6	0	0	24
	Wigan	1996-97	15(1)	13	0	0	52
Patrick Entat	Paris	1996	22	2	0	0	8
Jason Erba	Sheffield	1997	1(4)	0	0	0	0
Paul Evans	Paris	1997	18	8	0	0	32
Wayne Evans	London	2002	11(6)	2	0	0	8
Richie Eyres	Warrington	1997	2(5)	0	0	0	0
	Sheffield	1997	2(3)	0	0	0	0
Esene Faimalo	Salford	1997-99	23(25)	2	0	0	8
	Leeds	1996	3(3)	0	0	0	0
Joe Faimalo	Salford	1998-2000	23(47)	7	0	0	28
	Oldham	1996-97	37(5)	7	0	0	28
Karl Fairbank	Bradford	1996	17(2)	4	0	0	16
David Fairleigh	St Helens	2001	26(1)	8	0	0	32
Jim Fallon	Leeds	1996	10	5	0	0	20
Danny Farrar	Warrington	1998-2000	76	13	0	0	52
Andy Farrell	Wigan	1996-2003	204	69	922	13	2133
Anthony Farrell	Widnes	2002-03	24(22)	4	1	0	18
	Leeds	1997-2001	99(13)	18	0	0	72
	Sheffield	1996	14(5)	5	0	0	20
Craig Farrell	Hull	2000-01	1(3)	0	0	0	0
Abraham Fatnowna							
	London	1997-98	7(2)	2	0	0	8
	Workington	1996	5	2	0	0	8
Vince Fawcett	Wakefield	1999	13(1)	2	0	0	8
	Warrington	1998	4(7)	1	0	0	4
	Oldham	1997	5	3	0	0	12
Danny Fearon	Huddersfield	2001	(1)	0	0	0	0
	Halifax	1999-2000	5(6)	0	0	0	0
Chris Feather	Leeds	2003	(26)	2	0	0	8
	Wakefield	2001-02	13(20)	6	0	0	24
Luke Felsch	Hull	2000-01	46(6)	7	0	0	28
	Gateshead	1999	28(1)	2	0	0	8
Leon Felton	Warrington	2002	4(2)	0	0	0	0
	St Helens	2001	1(1)	0	0	0	0
Jamie Field	Wakefield	1999-2003	89(38)	9	0	0	36
	Huddersfield	1998	15(5)	0	0	0	0
	Leeds	1996-97	3(11)	0	0	0	0
Mark Field	Wakefield	2003	(3)	1	0	0	4
Jamie Fielden	London	2003	(1)	0	0	0	0
	Huddersfield	1998-2000	4(8)	0	0	0	0
Stuart Fielden	Bradford	1998-2003	65(76)	26	0	0	104
Lafaele Filipo	Workington	1996	15(4)	3	0	0	12
Salesi Finau	Warrington	1996-97	16(15)	8	0	0	32
Liam Finn	Halifax	2002-03	16(5)	2	30	1	69
Lee Finnerty	Halifax	2003	18(2)	5	2	0	24
Phil Finney	Warrington	1998	1	0	0	0	0
Simon Finnigan	Widnes	2003	8(11)	1	0	0	4
Matt Firth	Halifax	2000-01	12(2)	0	0	0	0
Andy Fisher	Wakefield	1999-2000	31(8)	4	0	0	16
Darren Fleary	Huddersfield	2003	24(2)	4	0	0	16
	Leeds	1997-2002	98(9)	3	0	0	12
Greg Fleming	London	1999-2001	64(1)	40	2	0	164
Richard Fletcher	Hull	1999-2003	10(48)	5	0	0	20
Greg Florimo	Halifax	2000	26	6	4	0	32
	Wigan	1999	18(2)	7	1	0	30
Jason Flowers	Halifax	2002	24(4)	4	0	0	16
	Castleford	1996-2001	119(19)	33	0	1	133
Stuart Flowers	Castleford	1996	(3)	0	0	0	0
Adrian Flynn	Castleford	1996-97	19(2)	10	0	0	40
Wayne Flynn	Sheffield	1997	3(5)	0	0	0	0
Adam Fogerty	Warrington	1998	4	0	0	0	0
	St Helens	1996	13	1	0	0	4
Paul Forber	Salford	1997-98	19(12)	4	0	0	16
Mike Ford	Castleford	1997-98	25(12)	5	0	3	23
	Warrington	1996	3	0	0	0	0
Jim Forshaw	Salford	1999	(1)	0	0	0	0
Mike Forshaw	Bradford	1997-2003	162(7)	32	0	0	128
	Leeds	1996	11(3)	5	0	0	20
Mark Forster	Warrington	1996-2000	102(1)	40	0	0	160
David Foster	Halifax	2000-01	4(9)	0	0	0	0
Nick Fozzard	Warrington	2002-03	43(11)	2	0	0	8
	Huddersfield	1998-2000	24(8)	2	0	0	8
	Leeds	1996-97	6(16)	3	0	0	12
David Fraisse	Workington	1996	8	0	0	0	0
Daniel Frame	Widnes	2002-03	55	13	0	0	52
Andrew Frew	Halifax	2003	17	5	0	0	20
	Wakefield	2002	21	8	0	0	32
	Huddersfield	2001	26	15	0	0	60
Dale Fritz	Castleford	1999-2003	120(4)	9	0	0	36
David Furner	Leeds	2003	27	4	12	0	40
	Wigan	2001-02	51(2)	21	13	0	110
David Furness	Castleford	1996	(1)	0	0	0	0
Tommy Gallagher							
	London	2003	1(9)	1	0	0	4
Mark Gamson	Sheffield	1996	3	0	0	0	0
Jim Gannon	Halifax	1999-2003	108(6)	17	0	0	68
Steve Garces	Salford	2001	(1)	0	0	0	0
Jean-Marc Garcia							
	Sheffield	1996-97	35(3)	22	0	0	88
Ade Gardner	St Helens	2002-03	23(10)	12	0	0	48
Steve Gartland	Oldham	1996	1(1)	0	1	0	2
Daniel Gartner	Bradford	2001-03	74(1)	26	0	0	104
Dean Gaskell	Warrington	2002-03	21	1	0	0	4
Richard Gay	Castleford	1996-2002	94(16)	39	0	0	156
Andrew Gee	Warrington	2000-01	33(1)	4	0	0	16
Stanley Gene	Huddersfield	2001, 2003	33(2)	17	0	0	68
	Hull	2000-01	5(23)	6	0	0	24
Steve Georgallis	Warrington	2001	5(1)	2	0	0	8
Shaun Geritas	Warrington	1997	(5)	1	0	0	4
Anthony Gibbons							
	Leeds	1996	9(4)	2	0	1	9
David Gibbons	Leeds	1996	3(4)	2	0	0	8
Scott Gibbs	St Helens	1996	9	3	0	0	12
Damian Gibson	Castleford	2003	20(2)	3	0	0	12
	Salford	2002	28	3	0	0	12
	Halifax	1998-2001	104(1)	39	0	0	156
	Leeds	1997	18	3	0	0	12
Ian Gildart	Oldham	1996-97	31(7)	0	0	0	0
Chris Giles	Widnes	2003	14	6	0	0	24
	St Helens	2002	(1)	0	0	0	0
Peter Gill	London	1996-99	75(6)	20	0	0	80
Carl Gillespie	Halifax	1996-99	47(36)	13	0	0	52
Michael Gillett	London	2001-02	23(21)	12	0	0	52
Simon Gillies	Warrington	1999	28	6	0	0	24
Lee Gilmour	Bradford	2001-03	44(31)	20	0	0	80
	Wigan	1997-2000	44(39)	22	0	0	88
Marc Glanville	Leeds	1998-99	43(3)	5	0	0	20
Eddie Glaze	Castleford	1996	1	0	0	0	0
Paul Gleadhill	Leeds	1996	4	0	0	0	0
Mark Gleeson	Warrington	2000-03	5(21)	5	0	0	20
Martin Gleeson	St Helens	2002-03	48(1)	22	0	0	88
	Huddersfield	1999-2001	47(9)	18	0	0	72
Jonathan Goddard							
	Castleford	2000-01	(2)	0	0	0	0
Richard Goddard	Castleford	1996-97	11(3)	2	0	10	28
Brad Godden	Leeds	1998-99	47	15	0	0	60
Wayne Godwin	Castleford	2001-03	8(31)	12	0	0	48
Marvin Golden	Widnes	2003	4	1	0	0	4
	London	2001	17(2)	1	0	0	4
	Halifax	2000	20(2)	5	0	0	20
	Leeds	1996-99	43(11)	19	0	0	76

PLAYER	CLUB	YEAR	APP	TRIES	GOALS	FG	PTS
Brett Goldspink	Halifax	2000-02	64(5)	2	0	0	8
	Wigan	1999	6(16)	1	0	0	4
	St Helens	1998	19(4)	2	0	0	8
	Oldham	1997	13(2)	0	0	0	0
Luke Goodwin	London	1998	9(2)	3	1	1	15
	Oldham	1997	16(4)	10	17	2	76
Andy Gorski	Salford	2001-02	(2)	0	0	0	0
Bobbie Goulding	Salford	2001-02	31(1)	2	56	4	124
	Wakefield	2000	12	3	25	3	65
	Huddersfield	1998-99	27(1)	3	65	4	146
	St Helens	1996-98	42(2)	9	210	4	460
James Graham	St Helens	2003	(1)	0	0	0	0
Nathan Graham	Bradford	1996-98	17(28)	4	0	1	17
Nick Graham	Wigan	2003	13(1)	2	0	0	8
Jon Grayshon	Huddersfield	2003	2(10)	0	0	0	0
Brett Green	Gateshead	1999	10(2)	0	0	0	0
Toby Green	Huddersfield	2001	3(1)	1	0	0	4
Craig Greenhill	Hull	2002-03	56	3	2	0	16
Brandon Greenwood	Halifax	1996	1	0	0	0	0
Gareth Greenwood	Huddersfield	2003	(1)	0	0	0	0
	Halifax	2002	1	0	0	0	0
Lee Greenwood	Halifax	2000-03	38(2)	17	0	0	68
	Sheffield	1999	1(1)	0	0	0	0
Darrell Griffin	Wakefield	2003	13(4)	1	0	0	4
Jonathan Griffiths	Paris	1996	(4)	1	0	0	4
Andrew Grima	Workington	1996	2(9)	2	0	0	8
Tony Grimaldi	Hull	2000-01	56(1)	14	0	0	56
	Gateshead	1999	27(2)	10	0	0	40
Danny Grimley	Sheffield	1996	4(1)	1	0	0	4
Simon Grix	Halifax	2003	2(4)	0	0	0	0
Brett Grogan	Gateshead	1999	14(7)	3	0	0	12
Brent Grose	Warrington	2003	29	15	0	0	60
Jerome Guisset	Warrington	2000-03	55(47)	14	0	0	56
Reece Guy	Oldham	1996	3(4)	0	0	0	0
Gareth Haggerty	Widnes	2002	1(2)	1	0	0	4
Andy Haigh	St Helens	1996-98	20(16)	11	0	0	44
Carl Hall	Leeds	1996	7(2)	3	0	0	12
Martin Hall	Halifax	1998	2(10)	0	0	0	0
	Hull	1999	7	0	0	0	0
	Castleford	1998	4	0	0	0	0
	Wigan	1996-97	31(5)	7	6	0	40
Steve Hall	London	2002-03	35(3)	10	0	0	40
	St Helens	1999-2001	36(22)	19	0	0	76
Graeme Hallas	Huddersfield	2001	1	0	0	0	0
	Hull	1998-99	30(10)	6	39	1	103
	Halifax	1996	11(4)	5	0	0	20
Danny Halliwell	Halifax	2000-03	17(8)	4	0	0	16
	Warrington	2002	9(1)	8	0	0	32
	Wakefield	2002	3	0	0	0	0
Colum Halpenny	Wakefield	2003	28	7	0	0	28
	Halifax	2002	22	12	0	0	48
Jon Hamer	Bradford	1996	(1)	0	0	0	0
Andrew Hamilton	London	1997, 2003	1(20)	3	0	0	12
John Hamilton	St Helens	1998	3	0	0	0	0
Karle Hammond	Halifax	2002	10(2)	2	14	0	36
	Salford	2001	2(3)	1	0	0	4
	London	1999-2000	47	23	2	3	99
	St Helens	1996-98	58(8)	28	0	4	116
Anthony Hancock	Paris	1997	8(6)	1	0	0	4
Michael Hancock	Salford	2001-02	12(24)	7	0	0	28
Gareth Handford	Castleford	2001	7(2)	0	0	0	0
	Bradford	2000	1(1)	0	0	0	0
Paul Handforth	Wakefield	2000-03	17(30)	7	3	0	34
Paddy Handley	Leeds	1996	1(1)	2	0	0	8
Dean Hanger	Warrington	1999	7(11)	3	0	0	12
	Huddersfield	1998	20(1)	5	0	0	20
Lee Hansen	Wigan	1997	10(5)	0	0	0	0
Shontayne Hape	Bradford	2003	29	11	0	0	44
Lionel Harbin	Wakefield	2001	(1)	0	0	0	0
Ian Hardman	St Helens	2003	(1)	0	0	0	0
Jeff Hardy	Hudds-Sheff	2000	20(5)	6	0	1	25
	Sheffield	1999	22(4)	7	0	0	28
Spencer Hargrave	Castleford	1996-99	(6)	0	0	0	0
Lee Harland	Castleford	1996-2003	130(32)	19	0	0	76
Neil Harmon	Halifax	2003	13(3)	0	0	0	0
	Salford	2001	6(5)	0	0	0	0
	Bradford	1998-2000	15(13)	2	0	0	8
	Huddersfield	1998	12	1	0	0	4
	Leeds	1996	10	1	0	0	4
Iestyn Harris	Leeds	1997-2001	111(7)	57	490	6	1214
	Warrington	1996	16	4	63	2	144
Karl Harrison	Hull	1999	26	2	0	0	8
	Halifax	1996-98	60(2)	2	0	0	8
Carlos Hassan	Bradford	1996	6(4)	2	0	0	8
Phil Hassan	Wakefield	2002	9(1)	0	0	0	0
	Halifax	2000-01	25(4)	3	0	0	12
	Salford	1998	15	2	0	0	8
	Leeds	1996-97	38(4)	12	0	0	48
Tom Haughey	London	2003	2(2)	0	0	0	0
	Wakefield	2001-02	5(12)	0	0	0	0
Simon Haughton	Wigan	1996-2002	63(46)	32	0	0	128

PLAYER	CLUB	YEAR	APP	TRIES	GOALS	FG	PTS
Andy Hay	Widnes	2003	25(1)	5	0	0	20
	Leeds	1997-2002	112(27)	43	0	0	172
	Sheffield	1996-97	17(3)	5	0	0	20
Adam Hayes	Hudds-Sheff	2000	2(1)	0	0	0	0
Joey Hayes	Salford	1999	9	2	0	0	8
	St Helens	1996-98	11(6)	7	0	0	28
Mitch Healey	Castleford	2001-03	68(1)	10	16	0	72
Ricky Helliwell	Salford	1997-99	(2)	0	0	0	0
Bryan Henare	St Helens	2000-01	4(12)	1	0	0	4
Richard Henare	Warrington	1996-97	28(2)	24	0	0	96
Brad Hepi	Castleford	1999, 2001	9(21)	3	0	0	12
	Salford	2000	3(5)	0	0	0	0
	Hull	1998	15(1)	3	0	0	12
Jon Hepworth	Castleford	2003	4(10)	3	0	0	12
	Leeds	2003	(1)	0	0	0	0
	London	2002	(2)	0	0	0	0
Ian Herron	Hull	2000	9	1	17	0	38
	Gateshead	1999	25	4	105	0	226
Jason Hetherington	London	2001-02	37	9	0	0	36
Gareth Hewitt	Salford	1999	2(1)	0	0	0	0
Andrew Hick	Hull	2000	9(9)	1	0	0	4
	Gateshead	1999	12(5)	2	0	0	8
Paul Hicks	Wakefield	1999	(1)	0	0	0	0
Darren Higgins	London	1998	5(6)	2	0	0	8
Iain Higgins	London	1997-98	1(7)	2	0	0	8
Liam Higgins	Hull	2003	(1)	0	0	0	0
Mick Higham	St Helens	2001-03	29(41)	22	0	0	88
Chris Highton	Warrington	1997	1(1)	0	0	0	0
David Highton	Salford	2002	4(5)	2	0	0	8
	Warrington	1998-2001	18(14)	2	0	0	8
Paul Highton	Salford	1998-2002	69(47)	9	0	0	36
	Halifax	1996-97	12(18)	2	0	0	8
Andy Hill	Huddersfield	1999	(4)	0	0	0	0
	Castleford	1999	(4)	0	0	0	0
Howard Hill	Oldham	1996-97	22(12)	4	0	0	16
John Hill	St Helens	2003	(1)	0	0	0	0
	Halifax	2003	1(2)	0	0	0	0
	Warrington	2001-02	(4)	0	0	0	0
Mark Hilton	Warrington	1996-2000, 2002-03	95(27)	4	0	0	16
Andy Hobson	Halifax	1998-2003	51(85)	8	0	0	32
Gareth Hock	Wigan	2003	7(22)	8	0	0	32
Andy Hodgson	Wakefield	1999	14(2)	2	1	0	10
	Bradford	1997-98	8(2)	4	0	0	16
David Hodgson	Wigan	2000-03	81(14)	41	0	0	164
	Halifax	1999	10(3)	5	0	0	20
Darren Hogg	London	1996	(1)	0	0	0	0
Michael Hogue	Paris	1997	5(7)	0	0	0	0
Chris Holden	Warrington	1996-97	2(1)	0	0	0	0
Stephen Holgate	Halifax	2000	1(10)	0	0	0	0
	Hull	1999	1	0	0	0	0
	Wigan	1997-98	11(26)	2	0	0	8
	Workington	1996	19	3	0	0	12
Martyn Holland	Wakefield	2000-03	52(3)	6	0	0	24
Graham Holroyd	Huddersfield	2003	3(5)	0	0	0	0
	Salford	2000-02	40(11)	8	75	5	187
	Halifax	1999	24(2)	3	74	5	165
	Leeds	1996-98	40(26)	22	101	8	298
Dallas Hood	Wakefield	2003	17(2)	1	0	0	4
Jason Hooper	St Helens	2003	20(4)	8	0	0	32
Sean Hoppe	St Helens	1999-2002	69(16)	32	0	0	128
Graeme Horne	Hull	2003	6(13)	4	0	0	16
Richard Horne	Hull	1999-2003	111(9)	42	12	0	192
John Hough	Warrington	1996-97	9	2	0	0	8
Sylvain Houles	Wakefield	2003	4	1	0	0	4
	London	2001-02	17(10)	11	0	0	44
	Hudds-Sheff	2000	5(2)	1	0	0	4
Harvey Howard	Wigan	2001-02	25(27)	1	0	0	4
	Bradford	1998	4(2)	1	0	0	4
	Leeds	1996	8	1	0	0	4
Kim Howard	London	1997	4(5)	0	0	0	0
Stuart Howarth	Workington	1996	(2)	0	0	0	0
Phil Howlett	Bradford	1999	5(1)	2	0	0	8
Craig Huby	Castleford	2003	(9)	0	3	0	6
Ryan Hudson	Castleford	2002-03	46(6)	13	0	0	52
	Wakefield	2000-01	42(9)	11	0	1	45
	Huddersfield	1998-99	12(7)	0	0	0	0
Adam Hughes	Widnes	2002-03	54(1)	31	51	0	226
	Halifax	2001	8(8)	8	0	0	32
	Wakefield	1999-2000	43(3)	21	34	0	152
	Leeds	1996-97	4(5)	4	0	0	16
Ian Hughes	Sheffield	1996	9(8)	4	0	0	16
Steffan Hughes	London	1999-2001	1(13)	1	0	0	4
David Hulme	Salford	1997-99	53(1)	5	0	0	20
	Leeds	1996	8(1)	2	0	0	8
Paul Hulme	Warrington	1996-97	23(1)	2	0	0	8
Gary Hulse	Warrington	2001-03	10(19)	4	0	0	16
Alan Hunte	Salford	2002	19(2)	9	0	0	36
	Warrington	1999-2001	83	49	0	0	196
	Hull	1998	21	7	0	0	28
	St Helens	1996-97	30(2)	28	0	0	112
Nick Hyde	Paris	1997	5(5)	1	0	0	4
Andy Ireland	Hull	1998-99	22(15)	0	0	0	0
	Bradford	1996	1	0	0	0	0

Super League Players 1996-2003

PLAYER	CLUB	YEAR	APP	TRIES	GOALS	FG	PTS
Kevin Iro	St Helens	1999-2001	76	39	0	0	156
	Leeds	1996	16	9	0	0	36
Andrew Isherwood							
	Wigan	1998-99	(5)	0	0	0	0
Olu Iwenofu	London	2000-01	2(1)	0	0	0	0
Chico Jackson	Hull	1999	(4)	0	0	0	0
Lee Jackson	Hull	2001-02	37(9)	12	1	0	50
	Leeds	1999-2000	28(24)	7	0	0	28
Michael Jackson	Sheffield	1998-99	17(17)	2	0	0	8
	Halifax	1996-97	27(6)	11	0	0	44
Paul Jackson	Castleford	2003	1(7)	0	0	0	0
	Wakefield	1999-2002	57(41)	2	0	0	8
	Huddersfield	1998	(11)	0	0	0	0
Rob Jackson	London	2002-03	16(10)	5	0	0	20
Wayne Jackson	Halifax	1996-97	17(5)	2	0	0	8
Aled James	Widnes	2003	3	0	0	0	0
Andy James	Halifax	1996	(4)	0	0	0	0
Pascal Jampy	Paris	1996-97	3(2)	0	0	0	0
Ben Jeffries	Wakefield	2003	19(6)	8	1	0	34
Mick Jenkins	Hull	2000	24	2	0	0	8
	Gateshead	1999	16	3	0	0	12
Ed Jennings	London	1998-99	1(2)	0	0	0	0
Matthew Johns	Wigan	2001	24	3	0	1	13
Andy Johnson	Castleford	2002-03	32(16)	11	0	0	44
	London	2000-01	24(21)	12	0	0	48
	Huddersfield	1999	1	1	0	0	4
	Wigan	1996-99	24(20)	19	0	0	76
Jason Johnson	St Helens	1997-99	2	0	0	0	0
Mark Johnson	Salford	1999-2000	22(9)	16	0	0	64
	Hull	1998	10(1)	4	0	0	16
	Workington	1996	12	4	0	0	16
Nick Johnson	London	2003	(1)	0	0	0	0
Paul Johnson	Wigan	1996-2003	74(46)	54	0	0	216
Danny Jones	Halifax	2003	1	0	0	0	0
David Jones	Oldham	1997	14(1)	5	0	0	20
Mark Jones	Warrington	1996	8(11)	2	0	0	8
Phil Jones	Wigan	1999-2001	14(7)	6	25	0	74
Stuart Jones	St Helens	2003	(18)	2	0	0	8
	Wigan	2002	5(3)	1	0	0	4
Jamie Jones-Buchanan							
	Leeds	1999-2003	5(32)	4	0	0	16
Tim Jonkers	St Helens	1999-2003	40(64)	12	0	0	48
Darren Jordan	Wakefield	2003	(1)	0	0	0	0
Warren Jowitt	Hull	2003	(2)	0	0	0	0
	Salford	2001-02	17(4)	2	0	0	8
	Wakefield	2000	19(3)	8	0	0	32
	Bradford	1996-99	13(25)	5	0	0	20
Chris Joynt	St Helens	1996-2003	182(12)	66	0	0	264
Gregory Kacala	Paris	1996	7	1	0	0	4
Damon Keating	Wakefield	2002	7(17)	1	0	0	4
Shaun Keating	London	1996	1(3)	0	0	0	0
Mark Keenan	Workington	1996	3(4)	1	0	0	4
Tony Kemp	Wakefield	1999-2000	15(5)	2	0	1	9
	Leeds	1996-98	23(2)	5	0	2	22
Damien Kennedy	London	2003	5(11)	1	0	0	4
Shane Kenward	Wakefield	1999	28	6	0	0	24
	Salford	1998	1	0	0	0	0
Jason Keough	Paris	1997	2	1	0	0	4
Martin Ketteridge							
	Halifax	1996	7(5)	0	0	0	0
Ronnie Kettlewell							
	Warrington	1996	(1)	0	0	0	0
David Kidwell	Warrington	2001-02	14(12)	9	0	0	36
Andrew King	London	2003	23(1)	15	0	0	60
Dave King	Huddersfield	1998-99	11(17)	2	0	0	8
Paul King	Hull	1999-2003	74(41)	12	0	1	49
Andy Kirk	Leeds	2001-02	4(4)	0	0	0	0
John Kirkpatrick	St Helens	2001-03	10(11)	10	0	0	40
	Halifax	2003	4	1	0	0	4
Wayne Kitchin	Workington	1996	11(6)	3	17	1	47
Ian Knott	Wakefield	2002-03	34(5)	7	79	0	186
	Warrington	1996-2001	68(41)	24	18	0	132
Matt Knowles	Wigan	1996	(3)	0	0	0	0
Phil Knowles	Salford	1997	1	0	0	0	0
Simon Knox	Halifax	1999	(6)	0	0	0	0
	Salford	1998	1(1)	0	0	0	0
	Bradford	1996-98	9(19)	7	0	0	28
Toa Kohe-Love	Hull	2002-03	42	19	0	0	76
	Warrington	1996-2001	114(2)	69	0	0	276
Paul Koloi	Wigan	1997	1(2)	1	0	0	4
Michael Korkidas							
	Wakefield	2003	22(3)	5	0	0	20
David Krause	London	1996-97	22(1)	7	0	0	28
Ben Kusto	Huddersfield	2001	21(4)	9	0	1	37
Adrian Lam	Wigan	2001-03	83(1)	34	1	8	146
Mark Lane	Paris	1996	(2)	0	0	0	0
Allan Langer	Warrington	2000-01	47	13	4	0	60
Kevin Langer	London	1996	12(4)	2	0	0	8
Chris Langley	Huddersfield	2000-01	18(1)	3	0	0	12
Jamie Langley	Bradford	2002-03	1(16)	2	0	0	8
Andy Last	Hull	1999-2003	15(9)	4	0	0	16
Dale Laughton	Warrington	2002	15(1)	0	0	0	0
	Huddersfield	2000-01	36(2)	4	0	0	16
	Sheffield	1996-99	48(22)	5	0	0	20
Jason Laurence	Salford	1997	1	0	0	0	0
Graham Law	Wakefield	1999-2002	34(30)	6	40	0	104
Neil Law	Wakefield	1999-2002	83	39	0	0	156
	Sheffield	1998	1(1)	1	0	0	4
Dean Lawford	Widnes	2003	15(1)	5	2	4	28
	Halifax	2001	1(1)	0	0	0	0
	Leeds	1997-2000	15(8)	2	3	0	14
	Huddersfield	1999	6(1)	0	6	1	13
	Sheffield	1996	9(5)	2	1	1	11
Johnny Lawless	Halifax	2001-03	73(1)	10	0	0	40
	Hudds-Sheff	2000	19(6)	3	0	0	12
	Sheffield	1996-99	76(4)	11	0	0	44
Leroy Leapai	London	1996	2	0	0	0	0
Jim Leatham	Hull	1998-99	20(18)	4	0	0	16
	Leeds	1997	(1)	0	0	0	0
Andy Leathem	Warrington	1999	2(8)	0	0	0	0
	St Helens	1996-98	2(1)	1	0	0	4
Danny Lee	Gateshead	1999	16(2)	0	0	0	0
Jason Lee	Halifax	2001	10(1)	2	0	0	8
Mark Lee	Salford	1997-2000	25(11)	1	0	4	8
Robert Lee	Hull	1999	4(3)	0	0	0	0
Matthew Leigh	Salford	2000	(6)	0	0	0	0
Jim Lenihan	Huddersfield	1999	19(1)	10	0	0	40
Mark Lennon	Castleford	2001-03	30(21)	10	21	0	82
Gary Lester	Hull	1998-99	46	17	0	0	68
Stuart Lester	Wigan	1997	1(3)	0	0	0	0
Afi Leuila	Oldham	1996-97	17(3)	2	0	0	8
Simon Lewis	Castleford	2001	4	3	0	0	12
Jon Liddell	Leeds	2001	1	0	0	0	0
Jason Lidden	Castleford	1997	15(1)	7	0	0	28
Stuart Littler	Salford	1998-2002	73(12)	20	0	0	80
Peter Livett	Workington	1996	3(1)	0	0	0	0
Scott Logan	Hull	2001-03	27(20)	5	0	0	20
David Lomax	Huddersfield	2000-01	45(9)	4	0	0	16
	Paris	1997	19(2)	1	0	0	4
Dave Long	London	1999	(1)	0	0	0	0
Karl Long	London	2003	(1)	0	0	0	0
	Widnes	2002	4	1	0	0	4
Sean Long	St Helens	1997-2003	133(6)	81	534	7	1399
	Wigan	1996-97	1(5)	0	0	0	0
Davide Longo	Bradford	1996	1(3)	0	0	0	0
Gary Lord	Oldham	1996-97	28(12)	3	0	0	12
Paul Loughlin	Huddersfield	1998-99	34(2)	4	4	0	24
	Bradford	1996-97	36(4)	15	8	0	76
Karl Lovell	Hudds-Sheff	2000	14	5	0	0	20
	Sheffield	1999	22(4)	8	0	0	32
James Lowes	Bradford	1996-2003	205	84	2	2	342
Laurent Lucchese							
	Paris	1996	13(5)	2	0	0	8
Peter Lupton	Hull	2003	4(7)	1	0	0	4
	London	2000-02	10(15)	2	2	0	12
Andy Lynch	Castleford	1999-2003	55(45)	12	0	0	48
Brad Mackay	Bradford	2000	24(2)	8	0	0	32
Graham Mackay	Hull	2002	27	18	24	0	120
	Bradford	2001	16(3)	12	1	0	50
	Leeds	2000	12(8)	10	2	0	44
Steve Maden	Warrington	2002	3	0	0	0	0
Mateaki Mafi	Warrington	1996-97	7(8)	7	0	0	28
Brendan Magnus	London	2000	3	1	0	0	4
Mark Maguire	London	1996-97	11(4)	7	13	0	54
Adam Maher	Hull	2000-03	88(4)	24	0	0	96
	Gateshead	1999	21(5)	3	0	0	12
Lee Maher	Leeds	1996	4(1)	0	0	0	0
Shaun Mahony	Paris	1997	5	0	0	0	0
David Maiden	Hull	2000-01	32(10)	11	0	0	44
	Gateshead	1999	5(16)	8	0	0	32
Craig Makin	Salford	1999-2001	24(20)	2	0	0	8
Brady Malam	Wigan	2000	5(20)	1	0	0	4
Francis Maloney	Castleford	1998-99, 2003	54(7)	22	22	1	133
	Salford	2001-02	45(1)	26	5	0	114
	Wakefield	2000	11	1	1	0	6
	Oldham	1996-97	39(2)	12	91	2	232
George Mann	Warrington	1997	14(5)	1	0	0	4
	Leeds	1996	11(4)	2	0	0	8
David March	Wakefield	1999-2003	89(13)	24	0	0	96
Paul March	Huddersfield	2003	22(4)	7	0	0	28
	Wakefield	1999-2001	32(23)	14	18	0	92
Nick Mardon	London	1997-98	14	2	0	0	8
Oliver Marns	Halifax	1996-2002	54(19)	23	0	0	92
Paul Marquet	Warrington	2002	23(2)	0	0	0	0
Iain Marsh	Salford	1998-2001	1(4)	0	0	0	0
Lee Marsh	Salford	2001-02	3(4)	0	0	0	0
Richard Marshall	London	2002-03	33(11)	1	0	0	4
	Huddersfield	2000-01	35(14)	1	0	0	4
	Halifax	1996-99	38(34)	2	0	0	8
Jason Martin	Paris	1997	15(2)	3	0	0	12
Scott Martin	Salford	1997-99	32(18)	8	0	0	32
Tony Martin	London	1996-97, 2001-03	97(1)	36	170	1	485
Mick Martindale	Halifax	1996	(4)	0	0	0	0
Tommy Martyn	St Helens	1996-2003	125(20)	87	63	12	486
Dean Marwood	Workington	1996	9(6)	0	22	0	44
Martin Masella	Warrington	2001	10(14)	5	0	0	20
	Wakefield	2000	14(8)	4	0	0	16
	Leeds	1997-1999	59(5)	1	0	0	4

PLAYER	CLUB	YEAR	APP	TRIES	GOALS	FG	PTS
Colin Maskill	Castleford	1996	8	1	1	0	6
Keith Mason	St Helens	2003	11(5)	1	0	0	4
	Wakefield	2000-01	5(17)	0	0	0	0
Vila Matautia	St Helens	1996-2001	31(68)	9	0	0	36
Barrie-Jon Mather							
	Castleford	1998, 2000-02	50(12)	21	0	0	84
Richard Mathers	Leeds	2002-03	14(2)	2	0	0	8
	Warrington	2002	4(3)	0	0	0	0
Jamie Mathiou	Leeds	1997-2001	31(82)	3	0	0	12
Terry Matterson	London	1996-98	46	15	90	6	246
Casey Mayberry	Halifax	2000	1(1)	0	0	0	0
Chris Maye	Halifax	2003	3(4)	0	0	0	0
Joe Mbu	London	2003	4(4)	0	0	0	0
Danny McAllister	Gateshead	1999	3(3)	1	0	0	4
	Sheffield	1996-97	33(7)	10	0	0	40
John McAtee	St Helens	1996	2(1)	0	0	0	0
Nathan McAvoy	Bradford	1998-2002	67(22)	45	0	0	180
	Salford	1997-98	36	15	0	0	60
Dave McConnell	London	2003	(4)	0	0	0	0
	St Helens	2001-02	3(2)	4	0	0	16
Robbie McCormack							
	Wigan	1998	24	2	0	0	8
Steve McCurrie	Widnes	2002-03	44(6)	7	0	0	28
	Warrington	1998-2001	69(26)	31	0	0	124
Barrie McDermott							
	Leeds	1996-2003	148(28)	20	0	0	80
Brian McDermott							
	Bradford	1996-2002	138(32)	33	0	0	132
Wayne McDonald							
	Leeds	2002-03	21(30)	9	0	0	36
	St Helens	2001	7(11)	4	0	0	16
	Hull	2000	5(8)	4	0	0	16
	Wakefield	1999	9(17)	8	0	0	32
Ryan McDonald	Widnes	2002-03	6(4)	0	0	0	0
Craig McDowell	Huddersfield	2003	(1)	0	0	0	0
	Warrington	2002	(1)	0	0	0	0
	Bradford	2000	(1)	0	0	0	0
Wes McGibbon	Halifax	1999	1	0	0	0	0
Billy McGinty	Workington	1996	1	0	0	0	0
Danny McGuire	Leeds	2001-03	20(20)	20	0	1	81
Gary McGuirk	Workington	1996	(4)	0	0	0	0
Richard McKell	Castleford	1997-98	22(7)	2	0	0	8
Chris McKenna	Leeds	2003	20(1)	4	0	0	16
Phil McKenzie	Workington	1996	4	0	0	0	0
Chris McKinney	Oldham	1996-97	4(9)	2	0	0	8
Shayne McMenemy							
	Hull	2003	3(2)	2	0	0	8
	Halifax	2001-03	63	11	0	0	44
Andy McNally	Castleford	2001, 2003	2(5)	1	0	0	4
Steve McNamara	Huddersfield	2001, 2003	41(9)	3	134	1	281
	Wakefield	2000	15(2)	2	32	0	72
	Bradford	1996-99	90(3)	14	348	7	759
Neil McPherson	Salford	1997	(1)	0	0	0	0
Duncan McRae	London	1996	11(2)	3	0	1	13
Derek McVey	St Helens	1996-97	28(4)	6	1	0	26
Dallas Mead	Warrington	1997	2	0	0	0	0
Robert Mears	Leeds	2001	23	6	0	0	24
Paul Medley	Bradford	1996-98	6(35)	9	0	0	36
Paul Mellor	Castleford	2003	17(3)	3	0	0	12
Craig Menkins	Paris	1997	4(5)	0	0	0	0
Gary Mercer	Castleford	2002	(1)	0	0	0	0
	Leeds	1996-97, 2001	40(2)	9	0	0	36
	Warrington	2001	18	2	0	0	8
	Halifax	1998-2001	73(2)	16	0	0	64
Tony Mestrov	London	1996-97, 2001	59(8)	4	0	0	16
	Wigan	1998-2000	39(39)	3	0	0	12
Keiran Meyer	London	1996	4	1	0	0	4
Simon Middleton	Castleford	1996-97	19(3)	8	0	0	32
Shane Millard	Widnes	2003	28	10	0	0	40
	London	1998-2001	72(14)	11	1	0	46
David Mills	Widnes	2002-03	3(44)	5	0	0	20
Lee Milner	Halifax	1999	(1)	0	0	0	0
John Minto	London	1996	13	4	0	0	16
Martin Moana	Halifax	1996-2001, 2003	126(22)	62	0	1	249
	Wakefield	2002	19(2)	10	0	0	40
	Huddersfield	2001	3(3)	2	0	0	8
Steve Molloy	Huddersfield	2000-01	26(20)	3	0	0	12
	Sheffield	1998-99	32(17)	3	0	0	12
Chris Molyneux	Huddersfield	2000-01	1(18)	0	0	0	0
	Sheffield	1999	1(2)	0	0	0	0
Adrian Moore	Huddersfield	1998-99	1(4)	0	0	0	0
Danny Moore	London	2000	7	0	0	0	0
	Wigan	1998-99	49(3)	18	0	0	72
Jason Moore	Workington	1996	(5)	0	0	0	0
Richard Moore	Bradford	2002-03	1(16)	0	0	0	0
	London	2002	(7)	2	0	0	8
Dennis Moran	London	2001-03	79(2)	56	1	5	231
Willie Morganson							
	Sheffield	1997-98	18(12)	5	3	0	26
Paul Moriarty	Halifax	1996	3(2)	0	0	0	0

PLAYER	CLUB	YEAR	APP	TRIES	GOALS	FG	PTS
Adrian Morley	Leeds	1996-2000	95(14)	25	0	0	100
Chris Morley	Salford	1999	3(5)	0	0	0	0
	Warrington	1998	2(8)	0	0	0	0
	St Helens	1996-97	21(16)	4	0	0	16
Iain Morrison	Huddersfield	2003	8(11)	0	0	0	0
	London	2001	(1)	0	0	0	0
Gareth Morton	Leeds	2001-02	1(1)	0	0	0	0
Wilfried Moulinec							
	Paris	1996	1	0	0	0	0
Mark Moxon	Huddersfield	1998-2001	20(5)	1	0	1	5
Brett Mullins	Leeds	2001	5(3)	1	0	0	4
Damian Munro	Widnes	2002	8(2)	1	0	0	4
	Halifax	1996-97	9(6)	8	0	0	32
Matt Munro	Oldham	1996-97	26(5)	8	0	0	32
Craig Murdock	Salford	2000	(2)	0	0	0	0
	Hull	1998-99	21(6)	8	0	2	34
	Wigan	1996-98	18(17)	14	0	0	56
Doc Murray	Warrington	1997	(2)	0	0	0	0
	Wigan	1997	6(2)	0	0	0	0
David Mycoe	Sheffield	1996-97	12(13)	1	0	0	4
Rob Myler	Oldham	1996-97	19(2)	6	0	0	24
Stephen Myler	Widnes	2003	2(3)	2	6	0	20
Vinny Myler	Bradford	2003	(1)	0	0	0	0
Matt Nable	London	1997	2(2)	1	0	0	4
Brad Nairn	Workington	1996	14	4	0	0	16
Frank Napoli	London	2000	14(6)	2	0	0	8
Carlo Napolitano	Salford	2000	(3)	1	0	0	4
Jim Naylor	Halifax	2000	7(6)	2	0	0	8
Scott Naylor	Bradford	1999-2003	127(1)	51	0	0	204
	Salford	1997-98	23(1)	9	0	0	36
Mike Neal	Salford	1998	(1)	0	0	0	0
	Oldham	1996-97	6(4)	3	0	0	12
Jonathan Neill	Huddersfield	1998-99	20(11)	0	0	0	0
	St Helens	1996	1	0	0	0	0
Jason Netherton	London	2003	3	0	0	0	0
	Halifax	2002	2(3)	0	0	0	0
	Leeds	2001	(3)	0	0	0	0
Paul Newlove	St Helens	1996-2003	162	106	0	0	424
Richard Newlove	Wakefield	2003	17(5)	8	0	0	32
Terry Newton	Wigan	2000-03	110(6)	39	0	0	156
	Leeds	1996-1999	55(14)	4	0	0	16
Gene Ngamu	Huddersfield	1999-2000	29(2)	9	67	0	170
Sonny Nickle	St Helens	1999-2002	86(18)	14	0	0	56
	Bradford	1996-98	25(16)	9	0	0	36
Jason Nicol	Salford	2000-02	52(7)	11	0	0	44
Tawera Nikau	Warrington	2000-01	51	7	0	0	28
Rob Nolan	Hull	1998-99	20(11)	6	0	0	24
Paul Noone	Warrington	2000-03	30(40)	5	1	0	22
Chris Norman	Halifax	2003	13(3)	2	0	0	8
Paul Norman	Oldham	1996	(1)	0	0	0	0
Andy Northey	St Helens	1996-97	8(17)	2	0	0	8
Danny Nutley	Warrington	1998-2001	94(1)	3	0	0	12
Tony Nuttall	Oldham	1996-97	1(7)	0	0	0	0
Clinton O'Brien	Wakefield	2003	(2)	0	0	0	0
Matt O'Connor	Paris	1997	11(4)	1	26	2	58
Terry O'Connor	Wigan	1996-2003	164(36)	9	0	0	36
Jarrod O'Doherty	Huddersfield	2003	26	3	0	0	12
David O'Donnell	Paris	1997	21	3	0	0	12
Martin Offiah	Salford	2000-01	41	20	0	2	82
	London	1996-99	29(3)	21	0	0	84
	Wigan	1996	8	7	0	0	28
Hefin O'Hare	Huddersfield	2001, 2003	33(1)	16	0	0	64
Hitro Okesene	Hull	1998	21(1)	0	0	0	0
Anderson Okiwe	Sheffield	1997	1	0	0	0	0
Jamie Olejnik	Paris	1997	11	8	0	0	32
Kevin O'Loughlin	Halifax	1997-98	2(4)	0	0	0	0
	St Helens	1997	(3)	0	0	0	0
Sean O'Loughlin	Wigan	2002-03	32(18)	8	0	0	32
Julian O'Neill	Widnes	2002-03	29(22)	2	0	0	8
	Wakefield	2001	24(1)	2	0	0	8
	St Helens	1997-2000	95(8)	5	0	0	20
Julian O'Neill	Widnes	2003	20(1)	5	84	2	190
	Wigan	2002-03	29(1)	12	72	0	192
Steve O'Neill	Gateshead	1999	1(1)	0	0	0	0
Tom O'Reilly	Warrington	2001-02	8(6)	1	0	0	4
Chris Orr	Huddersfield	1998	19(3)	2	0	0	8
Danny Orr	Castleford	1997-2003	150(18)	65	279	3	821
Jason Palmada	Workington	1996	12	2	0	0	8
Junior Paramore	Castleford	1996	5(5)	3	0	0	12
Paul Parker	Hull	1999-2002	23(18)	9	0	0	36
Robert Parker	Bradford	2000, 2002-03	3(39)	6	0	0	24
	London	2001	9	1	0	0	4
Wayne Parker	Halifax	1996-97	12(1)	0	0	0	0
Ian Parry	Warrington	2001	(1)	0	0	0	0
Jules Parry	Paris	1996	10(2)	0	0	0	0
Regis Pastre-Courtine							
	Paris	1996	4(3)	4	0	0	16
Andrew Patmore	Oldham	1996	8(5)	3	0	0	12
Henry Paul	Bradford	1999-2001	81(5)	29	350	6	822
	Wigan	1996-98	60	37	23	0	194
Junior Paul	London	1996	3	1	0	0	4
Robbie Paul	Bradford	1996-2003	159(15)	106	1	0	426
Danny Peacock	Bradford	1997-99	32(2)	15	0	0	60

Super League Players 1996-2003

PLAYER	CLUB	YEAR	APP	TRIES	GOALS	FG	PTS
Jamie Peacock	Bradford	1999-2003	101(25)	25	0	0	100
Martin Pearson	Wakefield	2001	21(1)	3	60	3	135
	Halifax	1997-98, 2000	55(6)	24	181	0	458
	Sheffield	1999	17(6)	9	36	2	110
Jacques Pech	Paris	1996	16	0	0	0	0
Mike Pechey	Warrington	1998	6(3)	2	0	0	8
Bill Peden	London	2003	21(3)	7	0	0	28
Sean Penkywicz	Halifax	2000-03	29(27)	8	0	0	32
Julian Penni	Salford	1998-99	4	0	0	0	0
Lee Penny	Warrington	1996-2003	140(5)	54	0	0	216
Paul Penrice	Workington	1996	11(2)	2	0	0	8
Chris Percival	Widnes	2002-03	26	6	0	0	24
Apollo Perelini	St Helens	1996-2000	103(16)	27	0	0	108
Mark Perrett	Halifax	1996-97	15(4)	4	0	0	16
Adam Peters	Paris	1997	16(3)	0	0	0	0
Dominic Peters	London	1998-2003	58(11)	12	0	0	48
Mike Peters	Warrington	2000	2(12)	1	0	0	4
	Halifax	2000	1	0	0	0	0
Willie Peters	Wigan	2000	29	15	5	6	76
	Gateshead	1999	27	11	1	6	52
Adrian Petrie	Workington	1996	(1)	0	0	0	0
Rowland Phillips	Workington	1996	22	1	0	0	4
Nathan Picchi	Leeds	1996	(1)	0	0	0	0
Ian Pickavance	Hull	1999	4(2)	2	0	0	8
	Huddersfield	1999	3(14)	0	0	0	0
	St Helens	1996-98	12(44)	6	0	0	24
James Pickering	Castleford	1999	1(19)	0	0	0	0
Nick Pinkney	Salford	2000-02	64	29	0	0	116
	Halifax	1999	26(2)	13	0	0	52
	Sheffield	1997-98	33	10	0	0	40
Michal Piscuonov	Paris	1996	1(1)	1	0	0	4
Darryl Pitt	London	1996	2(16)	4	0	1	17
Andy Platt	Salford	1997-98	20(3)	1	0	0	4
Michael Platt	Salford	2001-02	3	1	0	0	4
Willie Poching	Leeds	2002-03	26(30)	17	0	0	68
	Wakefield	1999-2001	65(4)	20	0	0	80
Quentin Pongia	Wigan	2003	10(6)	0	0	0	0
Dan Potter	Widnes	2002-03	34(2)	6	0	0	24
	London	2001	1(3)	1	0	0	4
Craig Poucher	Hull	1999-2002	31(5)	5	0	0	20
Daio Powell	Sheffield	1999	13(1)	2	0	0	8
	Halifax	1997-98	30(3)	17	0	0	68
Daryl Powell	Leeds	1998-2000	49(30)	12	0	2	50
Karl Pratt	Bradford	2003	16(5)	7	0	0	28
	Leeds	1999-2002	62(12)	33	0	0	132
Steve Prescott	Hull	1998-99, 2001-03	99	46	191	3	569
	Wakefield	2000	22(1)	3	13	0	38
	St Helens	1996-97	32	15	17	0	94
Lee Prest	Workington	1996	(1)	0	0	0	0
Gareth Price	Salford	2002	(2)	0	0	0	0
	London	2002	2(2)	3	0	0	12
	St Helens	1999	(11)	2	0	0	8
Gary Price	Wakefield	1999-2001	55(13)	11	0	0	44
Richard Price	Sheffield	1996	1(2)	0	0	0	0
Tony Priddle	Paris	1997	11(7)	3	0	0	12
Karl Pryce	Bradford	2003	(1)	0	0	0	0
Leon Pryce	Bradford	1998-2003	109(22)	66	0	0	264
Waine Pryce	Castleford	2000-03	66(12)	35	0	0	140
Andrew Purcell	Castleford	2000	15(5)	3	0	0	12
	Hull	1999	27	4	0	0	16
Rob Purdham	London	2002-03	29(9)	2	1	1	11
Scott Quinnell	Wigan	1996	6(3)	1	0	0	4
Lee Radford	Bradford	1999-2003	27(59)	12	12	0	72
	Hull	1998	(7)	2	0	0	8
Kris Radlinski	Wigan	1996-2003	189	110	1	0	442
Adrian Rainey	Castleford	2002	4(7)	1	0	0	4
Jean-Luc Ramondou	Paris	1996	1(1)	1	0	0	4
Craig Randall	Halifax	1999	8(11)	4	0	0	16
	Salford	1997-98	12(18)	4	0	0	16
Scott Ranson	Oldham	1996-97	19(2)	7	0	0	28
Aaron Raper	Castleford	1999-2000	48(4)	4	2	1	21
Ben Rauter	Wakefield	2001	15(6)	4	0	0	16
Gareth Raynor	Hull	2001-03	63	34	0	0	136
	Leeds	2000	(3)	0	0	0	0
Tony Rea	London	1996	22	4	0	0	16
Stuart Reardon	Bradford	2003	14(6)	5	0	0	20
	Salford	2002	7(1)	3	0	0	12
Mark Reber	Wigan	1999-2000	9(9)	5	0	0	20
Alan Reddicliffe	Warrington	2001	1	0	0	0	0
Tahi Reihana	Bradford	1997-98	17(21)	0	0	0	0
Paul Reilly	Huddersfield	1999-2001, 2003	68(5)	15	0	0	60
Robert Relf	Widnes	2002-03	54(2)	5	0	0	20
Steve Renouf	Wigan	2000-01	55	40	0	0	160
Steele Retchless	London	1998-2003	152(6)	11	0	0	44
Scott Rhodes	Hull	2000	2	0	0	0	0
Phillipe Ricard	Paris	1996-97	2	0	0	0	0
Andy Rice	Huddersfield	2000-01	2(13)	1	0	0	4
Basil Richards	Huddersfield	1998-99	28(17)	1	0	0	4
Craig Richards	Oldham	1996	1	0	0	0	0
Andy Richardson	Hudds-Sheff	2000	(2)	0	0	0	0
Sean Richardson	Widnes	2002	2(18)	1	0	0	4
	Wakefield	1999	5(1)	0	0	0	0
	Castleford	1996-97	3(8)	1	0	0	4
Shane Rigon	Bradford	2001	14(11)	12	0	0	48
Craig Rika	Halifax	1996	2	0	0	0	0
Peter Riley	Workington	1996	7(5)	0	0	0	0
Julien Rinaldi	Wakefield	2002	(3)	1	0	0	4
Leroy Rivett	Warrington	2002	9	1	0	0	4
	Hudds-Sheff	2000	5(1)	1	0	0	4
	Leeds	1996-2000	39(15)	21	0	0	84
Jason Roach	Warrington	1998-99	29(7)	15	0	0	60
	Castleford	1997	7	4	0	0	16
Ben Roarty	Huddersfield	2003	16	2	0	0	8
Mark Roberts	Wigan	2003	(3)	0	0	0	0
Robert Roberts	Huddersfield	2001	(1)	0	0	0	0
	Halifax	2000	(3)	0	0	0	0
	Hull	1999	24(2)	4	13	4	46
Jason Robinson	Wigan	1996-2000	126(1)	87	0	1	349
Jeremy Robinson	Paris	1997	10(3)	1	21	0	46
John Robinson	Widnes	2003	1	0	0	0	0
Luke Robinson	Wigan	2002-03	10(17)	5	6	1	33
Will Robinson	Hull	2000	22	4	0	0	16
	Gateshead	1999	28	9	0	0	36
Carl Roden	Warrington	1997	1	0	0	0	0
Matt Rodwell	Warrington	2002	10	3	0	0	12
Darren Rogers	Castleford	1999-2003	136	72	0	0	288
	Salford	1997-98	42	16	0	0	64
Jamie Rooney	Wakefield	2003	16(2)	10	64	4	172
	Castleford	2001	2(1)	0	6	0	12
Jonathan Roper	Castleford	2001	13	7	12	0	52
	Salford	2000	1(4)	1	3	0	10
	London	2000	4	0	0	0	0
	Warrington	1996-2000	75(8)	33	71	0	274
Scott Roskell	London	1996-97	30(2)	16	0	0	64
Steve Rosolen	London	1996-98	25(9)	10	0	0	40
Adam Ross	London	1996	(1)	0	0	0	0
Paul Round	Castleford	1996	(3)	0	0	0	0
Steve Rowlands	St Helens	2003	(1)	0	0	0	0
Paul Rowley	Huddersfield	2001	24	3	0	0	12
	Halifax	1996-2000	107(3)	27	1	3	113
Nigel Roy	London	2001-03	81	31	0	0	124
Chris Rudd	Warrington	1996-98	31(17)	10	16	0	72
James Rushforth	Halifax	1997	(4)	0	0	0	0
Danny Russell	Huddersfield	1998-2000	50(13)	8	0	0	32
Ian Russell	Oldham	1997	1(3)	1	0	0	4
	Paris	1996	3	0	0	0	0
Richard Russell	Castleford	1996-98	37(4)	2	0	0	8
Robert Russell	Salford	1998-99	2(1)	0	1	0	2
Chris Ryan	London	1998-99	44(3)	17	10	0	88
Sean Ryan	Hull	2002-03	53	8	0	0	32
Matt Salter	London	1997-99	14(34)	8	0	0	32
Ben Sammut	Hull	2000	20	4	67	0	150
	Gateshead	1999	26(2)	6	17	0	58
Dean Sampson	Castleford	1996-2003	124(28)	24	0	0	96
Paul Sampson	Wakefield	2000	17	8	0	0	32
Jason Sands	Paris	1996-97	28	0	0	0	0
Lokeni Savelio	Halifax	2000	2(11)	0	0	0	0
	Salford	1997-98	18(20)	0	0	0	0
Tom Saxton	Castleford	2002-03	16(10)	5	0	0	20
Jonathan Scales	Halifax	2000	1	0	0	0	0
	Bradford	1996-98	46(4)	24	0	0	96
Andrew Schick	Castleford	1996-98	45(13)	10	0	0	40
Garry Schofield	Huddersfield	1998	(2)	0	0	0	0
Gary Schubert	Workington	1996	(1)	0	0	0	0
Matt Schultz	Hull	1998-99	23(9)	2	0	0	8
	Leeds	1996	2(4)	0	0	0	0
John Schuster	Halifax	1996-97	31	9	127	3	293
Nick Scruton	Leeds	2002	1	0	0	0	0
Danny Sculthorpe	Wigan	2002-03	8(17)	4	0	0	16
Paul Sculthorpe	St Helens	1998-2003	151(1)	73	230	4	756
	Warrington	1996-98	40	6	0	0	24
Mick Seaby	London	1997	3(2)	1	0	0	4
Danny Seal	Halifax	1996-99	8(17)	3	0	0	12
Matt Seers	Wakefield	2003	11(1)	2	0	0	8
Anthony Seibold	London	1999-2000	33(19)	5	0	0	20
Keith Senior	Leeds	1999-2003	113(1)	62	0	0	248
	Sheffield	1996-99	90(2)	40	0	0	160
Fili Seru	Hull	1998-99	37(1)	13	0	0	52
Anthony Seuseu	Halifax	2003	1(11)	1	0	0	4
Darren Shaw	Salford	2002	5(9)	1	0	0	4
	London	1996, 2002	22(8)	3	0	0	12
	Castleford	2000-01	50(6)	1	0	0	4
	Sheffield	1998-99	51(1)	3	0	1	13
Mick Shaw	Halifax	1999	5	1	0	0	4
	Leeds	1996	12(2)	7	0	0	28
Phil Shead	Paris	1996	3(2)	0	0	0	0
Richard Sheil	St Helens	1997	(1)	0	0	0	0
Kelly Shelford	Warrington	1996-97	25(3)	4	2	2	18
Ryan Sheridan	Widnes	2003	14(3)	2	0	0	8
	Leeds	1997-2002	123(7)	46	0	1	185
	Sheffield	1996	9(3)	5	0	1	21
Rikki Sheriffe	Halifax	2003	6(1)	3	0	0	12

PLAYER	CLUB	YEAR	APP	TRIES	GOALS	FG	PTS
Ian Sherratt	Oldham	1996	5(3)	1	0	0	4
Peter Shiels	St Helens	2001-02	44(3)	11	0	0	44
Gary Shillabeer	Huddersfield	1999	(2)	0	0	0	0
Ian Sibbit	Warrington	1999-2001, 2003	51(9)	21	0	0	84
Mark Sibson	Huddersfield	1999	2	2	0	0	8
Jon Simms	St Helens	2002	(1)	0	0	0	0
Craig Simon	Hull	2000	23(2)	8	0	0	32
	Gateshead	1999	25(4)	6	0	0	24
Darren Simpson	Huddersfield	1998-99	17(1)	5	0	0	20
Robbie Simpson	London	1999	6(7)	0	0	0	0
Kevin Sinfield	Leeds	1997-2003	108(25)	22	185	3	461
Wayne Sing	Paris	1997	18(1)	2	0	0	8
Fata Sini	Salford	1997	22	7	0	0	28
Ben Skerrett	Castleford	2003	(1)	0	0	0	0
Kelvin Skerrett	Halifax	1997-99	31(6)	2	0	0	8
	Wigan	1996	1(8)	0	0	0	0
Troy Slattery	Wakefield	2002-03	33(5)	4	0	0	16
	Huddersfield	1999	3	1	0	0	4
Mick Slicker	Huddersfield	2001, 2003	9(34)	1	0	0	4
	Sheffield	1999	(3)	1	0	0	4
	Halifax	1997	2(5)	0	0	0	0
Ian Smales	Castleford	1996-97	10(8)	5	0	0	20
Aaron Smith	Bradford	2003	3	0	0	0	0
Byron Smith	Halifax	2003	6(1)	0	0	0	0
Chris Smith	Hull	2001-02	12	3	0	0	12
	St Helens	1998-2000	62(9)	26	0	0	104
	Castleford	1996-97	36(1)	12	0	0	48
Craig Smith	Wigan	2002-03	51(1)	5	0	0	20
Damien Smith	St Helens	1998	21(1)	8	0	0	32
Danny Smith	Paris	1996	10(2)	1	15	0	34
	London	1996	2(1)	1	0	0	4
Darren Smith	St Helens	2003	25(1)	14	0	0	56
Gary Smith	Castleford	2001	(1)	0	0	0	0
Hudson Smith	Bradford	2000	8(22)	2	0	0	8
	Salford	1999	23(2)	5	0	0	20
James Smith	Salford	2000	23(3)	6	0	0	24
Jamie Smith	Hull	1998-99	24(6)	6	12	0	48
	Workington	1996	5(3)	0	1	0	2
Jason Smith	Hull	2001-03	58(2)	13	0	1	53
Kris Smith	London	2001	(1)	0	0	0	0
	Halifax	2001	(1)	0	0	0	0
Leigh Smith	Workington	1996	9	4	0	0	16
Mark Smith	Wigan	1999-2003	28(58)	6	0	0	24
Michael Smith	Castleford	1998, 2001-03	67(31)	28	0	0	112
	Hull	1999	12(6)	3	0	0	12
Paul Smith	Warrington	2001	(1)	0	0	0	0
	Castleford	1997-2000	6(37)	3	0	0	12
Paul Smith	London	1997	7(1)	2	0	0	8
Peter Smith	Oldham	1996	2	0	0	0	0
Richard Smith	Wakefield	2001	8(1)	1	0	0	4
	Salford	1997	(1)	1	0	0	4
Tony Smith	Hull	2001-03	43(5)	26	0	0	104
	Wigan	1997-2000	66(5)	46	0	0	184
	Castleford	1996-97	18(2)	10	0	0	40
Tony Smith	Workington	1996	9	1	0	0	4
Rob Smyth	Warrington	2000-03	65	35	20	0	180
	London	1998-2000	32(2)	9	15	0	66
	Wigan	1996	11(5)	16	0	0	64
Steve Snitch	Wakefield	2002-03	4(21)	1	0	0	4
Bright Sodje	Wakefield	2000	15	4	0	0	16
	Sheffield	1996-99	54	34	0	0	136
Alfred Songoro	Wakefield	1999	8(5)	4	0	0	16
Romain Sort	Paris	1997	(1)	0	0	0	0
Paul Southern	Salford	1997-2002	79(33)	6	13	0	50
	St Helens	2002	1(1)	0	0	0	0
Roy Southernwood							
	Wakefield	1999	1	0	0	0	0
	Halifax	1996	2	0	0	0	0
Waisale Sovatabua							
	Wakefield	2001-03	44(3)	19	0	0	76
	Hudds-Sheff	2000	23(1)	8	0	0	32
	Sheffield	1996-99	56(17)	19	0	1	77
Yusef Sozi	London	2000-01	(5)	0	0	0	0
Andy Speak	Castleford	2001	4(4)	0	0	0	0
	Wakefield	2000	6(5)	2	0	0	8
	Leeds	1999	4	1	0	0	4
Tim Spears	Castleford	2003	(3)	0	0	0	0
Ady Spencer	London	1996-99	8(36)	5	0	0	20
Robert Spicer	Wakefield	2002-03	6(6)	1	0	0	4
Stuart Spruce	Widnes	2002-03	45(4)	19	0	0	76
	Bradford	1996-2001	107(2)	57	0	0	228
Lee St Hilaire	Castleford	1997	4(2)	0	0	0	0
Marcus St Hilaire	Huddersfield	2003	27	8	0	0	32
	Leeds	1996-2002	59(33)	31	0	0	124
Dylan Stainton	Workington	1996	2(3)	0	0	0	0
Mark Stamper	Workington	1996	(1)	0	0	0	0
John Stankevitch	St Helens	2000-03	64(35)	19	0	0	76
Gareth Stanley	Bradford	2000	1	1	0	0	4
Graham Steadman							
	Castleford	1996-97	11(17)	5	0	0	20
Jamie Stenhouse	Warrington	2000-01	9(3)	3	0	0	12
Gareth Stephens	Sheffield	1997-99	23(6)	2	0	0	8
David Stephenson							
	Hull	1998	11(7)	3	0	0	12
	Oldham	1997	10(8)	2	0	0	8
Francis Stephenson							
	London	2002-03	28(21)	5	0	0	20
	Wigan	2001	2(9)	0	0	0	0
	Wakefield	1999-2000	50(1)	6	0	0	24
Paul Sterling	Leeds	1997-2000	79(12)	50	0	0	200
Paul Stevens	Oldham	1996	2(1)	0	0	0	0
	London	1996	(1)	0	0	0	0
Warren Stevens	Warrington	1996-99, 2002-03	17(44)	0	0	0	0
	Salford	2001	(8)	0	0	0	0
Anthony Stewart	St Helens	1997-2003	93(23)	44	0	0	176
Troy Stone	Widnes	2002	18(6)	1	0	0	4
	Huddersfield	2001	12(1)	1	0	0	4
Lynton Stott	Wakefield	1999	21	4	6	1	29
	Sheffield	1996-98	40(4)	15	0	0	60
Graham Strutton	London	1996	9(1)	2	0	0	8
Matt Sturm	Warrington	2002-03	1(17)	0	0	0	0
	Huddersfield	1998-99	46	8	0	0	32
Anthony Sullivan	St Helens	1996-2001	137(2)	105	0	0	420
Phil Sumner	Warrington	1996	(5)	0	0	0	0
Simon Svabic	Salford	1998-2000	13(5)	3	19	0	50
Anthony Swann	Warrington	2001	3	1	0	0	4
Willie Swann	Warrington	1996-97	25(2)	6	0	0	24
Nathan Sykes	Castleford	1996-2003	153(37)	3	0	0	12
Paul Sykes	London	2001-03	41(1)	9	38	1	113
	Bradford	1999-2002	5(4)	2	3	0	14
Wayne Sykes	London	1999	(2)	0	0	0	0
Whetu Taewa	Sheffield	1997-98	33(7)	8	0	0	32
Alan Tait	Leeds	1996	3(3)	1	0	0	4
Willie Talau	St Helens	2003	6(1)	1	0	0	4
Ian Talbot	Wakefield	1999	9(5)	2	31	0	70
	Wigan	1997	3	1	0	0	4
Gael Tallec	Halifax	2000	5(19)	3	0	0	12
	Castleford	1998-99	19(21)	3	0	0	12
	Wigan	1996-97	8(12)	3	0	0	12
Joe Tamani	Bradford	1996	11(3)	4	0	0	16
Andrew Tangata-Toa							
	Huddersfield	1999	15	2	0	0	8
Kris Tassell	Wakefield	2002	24	10	0	0	40
	Salford	2000-01	35(10)	12	0	0	48
Shem Tatupu	Wigan	1996	(3)	0	0	0	0
Tony Tatupu	Wakefield	2000-01	20	2	0	0	8
	Warrington	1997	21(1)	6	0	0	24
Joe Taylor	Paris	1997	9(5)	2	0	0	8
Lawrence Taylor	Sheffield	1996	(1)	0	0	0	0
Frederic Teixido	Sheffield	1999	(4)	0	0	0	0
	Paris	1996-97	2(3)	1	0	0	4
Jason Temu	Hull	1998	13(2)	1	0	0	4
	Oldham	1996-97	25(3)	1	0	0	4
Paul Terry	London	1997	(1)	0	0	0	0
Jamie Thackray	Castleford	2003	1(7)	1	0	0	4
	Halifax	2000-02	10(38)	3	0	0	12
Adam Thaler	Castleford	2002	(1)	0	0	0	0
Giles Thomas	London	1997-99	1(2)	0	0	0	0
Steve Thomas	Warrington	2001	2	0	0	0	0
Alex Thompson	Sheffield	1997	4(11)	0	0	0	0
Bobby Thompson							
	Salford	1999	28	5	2	0	24
Chris Thorman	London	2003	26(1)	7	81	1	191
	Huddersfield	2000-01	38(13)	10	2	0	44
	Sheffield	1999	5(13)	2	8	1	25
Tony Thorniley	Warrington	1997	(5)	0	0	0	0
Danny Tickle	Wigan	2002-03	30(15)	14	50	1	157
	Halifax	2000-02	25(17)	10	91	2	224
Kris Tickle	Warrington	2001	(1)	0	0	0	0
John Timu	London	1998-2000	57(3)	11	0	0	44
Kerrod Toby	London	1997	2(2)	0	0	0	0
Tulsen Tollett	London	1996-2001	105(5)	38	49	1	251
Glen Tomlinson	Wakefield	1999-2000	41(5)	8	0	0	32
	Hull	1998	5	1	0	0	4
	Bradford	1996-97	27(13)	12	0	0	48
Ian Tonks	Castleford	1996-2001	32(50)	11	13	0	70
Paul Topping	Oldham	1996-97	23(10)	1	19	0	42
Patrick Torreilles	Paris	1996	9(1)	1	25	0	54
Mat Toshack	London	1998-2003	117(20)	24	0	0	96
Darren Treacy	Salford	2002	24(1)	6	1	0	26
Dean Treister	Hull	2003	16(1)	3	0	0	12
Steve Trindall	London	2003	(7)	0	0	0	0
George Truelove	Wakefield	2002	2	1	0	0	4
	London	2000	5	1	0	0	4
Va'aiga Tuigamala							
	Wigan	1996	21	10	3	0	46
Fereti Tuilagi	St Helens	1999-2000	43(15)	21	0	0	84
	Halifax	1996-98	55(3)	27	0	0	108
Sateki Tuipulotu	Leeds	1996	6(3)	1	2	0	8
Darren Turner	Huddersfield	2000-01, 2003	37(13)	10	0	0	40
	Sheffield	1996-99	41(29)	15	0	0	60
Ian Turner	Paris	1996	1(1)	1	0	0	4
Gregory Tutard	Paris	1996	1(1)	0	0	0	0

Super League Players 1996-2003

PLAYER	CLUB	YEAR	APP	TRIES	GOALS	FG	PTS
Brendon Tuuta	Warrington	1998	18(2)	4	0	0	16
	Castleford	1996-97	41(1)	3	0	0	12
Mike Umaga	Halifax	1996-97	38(1)	16	5	0	74
Kava Utoikamanu							
	Paris	1996	6(3)	0	0	0	0
Joe Vagana	Bradford	2001-03	86(1)	8	0	0	32
Nigel Vagana	Warrington	1997	20	17	0	0	68
Tevita Vaikona	Bradford	1998-2003	139(2)	84	0	0	336
Lesley Vainikolo	Bradford	2002-03	43(4)	32	0	0	128
Eric Van Brussell	Paris	1996	2	0	0	0	0
Marcus Vassilakopoulos							
	Sheffield	1997-99	15(11)	3	10	2	34
	Leeds	1996-97	1(3)	0	0	0	0
Phil Veivers	Huddersfield	1998	7(6)	1	0	0	4
	St Helens	1996	(1)	1	0	0	4
Eric Vergniol	Paris	1996	14(1)	6	0	0	24
Adrian Vowles	Castleford	1997-2001, 2003	125(1)	29	1	1	119
	Wakefield	2002-03	24(3)	6	1	0	26
	Leeds	2002	14(3)	2	0	0	8
Mike Wainwright	Warrington	1996-99, 2003	75(13)	10	0	0	40
	Salford	2000-02	72(3)	9	0	0	36
Ben Walker	Leeds	2002	23(1)	8	100	0	232
Chev Walker	Leeds	1999-2003	68(16)	35	0	0	140
Matt Walker	Huddersfield	2001	3(6)	0	0	0	0
Anthony Wall	Paris	1997	9	3	3	0	18
Mark Wallace	Workington	1996	14(1)	3	0	0	12
Kerrod Walters	Gateshead	1999	10(12)	2	1	0	10
Kevin Walters	Warrington	2001	1	0	0	0	0
Barry Ward	St Helens	2002-03	4	0	0	0	16
Danny Ward	Leeds	1999-2003	32(36)	5	0	1	21
Phil Waring	Salford	1997-99	6(8)	2	0	0	8
Brett Warton	London	1999-2001	49(7)	14	133	0	322
Kyle Warren	Castleford	2002	13(14)	3	0	0	12
Frank Watene	Wakefield	1999-2001	24(37)	6	0	0	24
Dave Watson	Sheffield	1998-99	41(4)	4	0	0	16
Ian Watson	Salford	1997, 2002	24(17)	8	3	5	43
	Workington	1996	4(1)	1	15	0	34
Kris Watson	Warrington	1996	11(2)	2	0	0	8
Michael Watts	Warrington	2002	3	0	0	0	0
Jason Webber	Salford	2000	25(1)	10	0	0	40
Paul Wellens	St Helens	1998-2003	122(23)	49	15	1	227
Jon Wells	Wakefield	2003	22(1)	1	0	0	4
	Castleford	1996-2002	114(14)	49	0	0	196
Dwayne West	St Helens	2000-02	8(16)	6	0	0	24
	Wigan	1999	1(1)	0	0	0	0
Craig Weston	Widnes	2002	19(5)	2	1	2	12
	Huddersfield	1998-99	46(1)	15	15	0	90
Ben Westwood	Warrington	2002-03	29(1)	14	0	0	56
	Wakefield	1999-2002	31(7)	8	1	0	34
Andrew Whalley	Workington	1996	(2)	0	0	0	0
Matt Whitaker	Huddersfield	2003	2(12)	0	0	0	0
David White	Wakefield	2000	(1)	0	0	0	0
Josh White	Salford	1998	18(3)	5	5	1	31
	London	1997	14(2)	8	0	1	33
Paul White	Huddersfield	2003	2(5)	3	5	0	22
Danny Whittle	Warrington	1998	(2)	0	0	0	0
David Whittle	St Helens	2002	1(2)	0	0	0	0
	Warrington	2001	1(2)	0	0	0	0
Jon Whittle	Wigan	2003	1	0	0	0	0
Stephen Wild	Wigan	2001-03	17(13)	9	0	0	36
Oliver Wilkes	Huddersfield	2000-01	1(6)	0	0	0	0
	Sheffield	1998	(1)	0	0	0	0
Jon Wilkin	St Helens	2003	5(4)	3	0	0	12
Alex Wilkinson	Hull	2003	11(1)	1	0	0	4
	Huddersfield	2003	8	4	0	0	16
	London	2002	5(1)	0	0	0	0
	Bradford	2000-01	3(3)	1	0	0	4
Bart Williams	London	1998	5(3)	1	0	0	4
Craig Wilson	Hull	2000	2(16)	1	0	1	5
	Gateshead	1999	17(11)	5	0	1	21
George Wilson	Paris	1996	7(2)	3	0	0	12
Richard Wilson	Hull	1998-99	(13)	0	0	0	0
Scott Wilson	Warrington	1998-99	23(2)	6	0	0	24
Johan Windley	Hull	1999	2(2)	1	0	0	4
Paul Wingfield	Warrington	1997	5(3)	6	1	0	26
Michael Withers	Bradford	1999-2003	90(4)	68	8	2	290
Jeff Wittenberg	Huddersfield	1998	18(1)	1	0	0	4
	Bradford	1997	8(9)	4	0	0	16
Martin Wood	Sheffield	1997-98	24(11)	4	18	2	54
Nathan Wood	Warrington	2002-03	42	12	0	2	50
	Wakefield	2002	11	2	0	0	8
Paul Wood	Warrington	2000-03	25(49)	11	0	0	44
David Woods	Halifax	2002	18(2)	8	0	0	32
Matthew Wray	Wakefield	2002-03	13(3)	2	0	0	8
David Wrench	Wakefield	2002-03	15(26)	3	0	0	12
	Leeds	1999-2001	7(17)	0	0	0	0
Craig Wright	Castleford	2000	1(9)	0	0	0	0
Nigel Wright	Huddersfield	1999	4(6)	1	0	0	4
	Wigan	1996-97	5(5)	2	0	1	9
Ricky Wright	Sheffield	1997-99	2(13)	0	0	0	0
Vincent Wulf	Paris	1996	13(4)	4	0	0	16
Andrew Wynyard	London	1999-2000	34(6)	4	0	0	16
Bagdad Yaha	Paris	1996	4(4)	2	4	0	16
Malakai Yasa	Sheffield	1996	1(3)	0	0	0	0
Kirk Yeaman	Hull	2001-03	20(15)	9	0	0	36
Grant Young	London	1998-99	22(2)	2	0	0	8
Ronel Zenon	Paris	1996	(4)	0	0	0	0
Nick Zisti	Bradford	1999	6(1)	0	0	0	0

SUPER LEAGUE VIII
Club by Club

11 September 2002 - Brandon Costin leaves for Huddersfield

25 September 2002 - New Zealand Warriors centre Shontayne Hape signs from Down Under

15 October 2002 - James Lowes shelves plans for retirement to sign a new one-year contract

24 October 2002 - Bulls assistant coach Darrell Shelford quits to join Saracens RU club

26 November 2002 - Leon Pryce arrested and charged with assault occasioning grievous bodily harm with intent after an incident in a nightclub

9 December 2002 - England A International Stuart Reardon agrees a two-year extension to his contract

10 December 2002 - Robbie Paul signs a contract extension until the end of the 2006 season

11 December 2002 - Nathan McAvoy set to leave after failing to agree a new deal

19 December 2002 - Former Leeds and current Great Britain international Karl Pratt moves to Odsal

3 January 2003 - Great Britain prop Stuart Fielden signs a new five-year deal

27 February 2003 - Chief Executive Abi Ekoku set to depart in April after three years with the club

9 March 2003 - Over 20,000 supporters welcome the Bulls back to Odsal and witness a hard-fought 22-10 victory over Wakefield

18 March 2003 - Leon Pryce's court date is put back until after the Grand Final in October

1 April 2003 - New Zealand winger Lesley Vainikolo signs a new two-year contract with the club with an option for a third year

KEY DATES - BRADFORD BULLS

13 April 2003 - James Lowes is the inspiration as the Bulls beat Wigan 36-22 in the Challenge Cup semi-final to set up a final meeting with Leeds

26 April 2003 - The Bulls lift the Powergen Challenge Cup Final after a thrilling 22-20 win over Leeds in Cardiff

23 May 2003 - Bulls win the battle of Super League's top two, beating Leeds 48-22 in front of 21,784 fans at Odsal

1 June 2003 - Shock 22-12 defeat by London ends ten-game winning run

15 June 2003 - Last minute Scott Naylor try helps beat Warrington 24-20 and stay within two points of Leeds at the top

27 June 2003 - Suffer an unprecedented third successive home defeat, failing to score a point in 35-0 defeat by Saints

30 July 2003 - Go top of the table after a comprehensive 60-6 victory over a tired London side, with Leon Pryce scoring four tries

8 August 2003 - Move two points clear at the top of the table after beating Leeds 18-16 at Headingley

7 September 2003 - Clinch the Minor Premiership after 21-20 defeat of Leeds in thriller at Odsal

14 September 2003 – Presented with League Leaders Shield at Odsal despite 14-28 loss to Castleford in their last home game of regular season

29 September 2003 – Lesley Vainikolo and Jamie Peacock are named in the Super League Dream Team

4 October 2003 – Reach the Grand Final after two late Mike Forshaw tries inspire the Bulls to a 30-14 victory over Leeds at Odsal

13 October 2003 – The Bulls claim a hat-trick of awards as Jamie Peacock scoops the coveted Man of Steel award, Brian Noble walks away with Coach of the Year and Lesley Vainikolo receives the Top Metre Gainer award

18 October 2003 – The Bulls become the first team to win the Challenge Cup and Grand Final in the same season by defeating Wigan Warriors 25-12 at Old Trafford

20 October 2003 - Leon Pryce pleads guilty to unlawful wounding in an incident in a Bradford bar last year

21 October 2003 – Logan Swann signs on a one-year contract

23 October 2003 – Bradford announce the signing of Hull centre Toa Kohe-Love on a three-year contract

BRADFORD BULLS

DATE	FIXTURE	RESULT	SCORERS	LGE	ATT
8/2/03	Warrington (a) (CCR4)	W12-38	t:Vainikolo(2),Paul,L Pryce,Naylor,Hape g:Deacon(7)	N/A	5,869
21/2/03	St Helens (a)	L46-22	t:L Pryce(2),Radford g:Deacon(5)	12th	12,217
2/3/03	Hunslet (a) (CCR5) ●	W0-82	t:Vainikolo(3),Pratt(2),L Pryce(2),Vaikona(2),Fielden,Gartner,Parker, Gilmour,Radford,Hape g:Deacon(11)	N/A	5,685
9/3/03	Wakefield (h)	W22-10	t:Pratt,L Pryce,Gilmour,Hape g:Radford(3)	9th	20,283
15/3/03	Widnes (a) (CCQF)	W28-38	t:Forshaw(2),Hape,L Pryce,Paul,Naylor g:Deacon(7)	N/A	4,129
23/3/03	Halifax (h)	W62-22	t:Lowes(3),Paul(3),L Pryce,Hape,Deacon,Pratt,Reardon g:Deacon(7),Lowes(2)	3rd	15,557
30/3/03	Widnes (a)	W18-26	t:Paul,Withers,Naylor,Anderson g:Deacon(5)	4th	6,420
6/4/03	Warrington (h)	W32-8	t:Vainikolo,Withers,Lowes,L Pryce,Deacon,Vaikona g:Deacon(4)	2nd	15,157
13/4/03	Wigan (CCSF) ●●	W36-22	t:Radford(2),Lowes,Hape,Deacon,Vaikona g:Deacon(6)	N/A	15,359
18/4/03	Hull (h)	W48-24	t:L Pryce(2),Pratt(2),Vaikona,Hape,Vainikolo,Lowes g:Deacon(8)	2nd	15,182
26/4/03	Leeds (CCF) ●●●	W22-20	t:Paul,Vainikolo,Peacock g:Deacon(5)	N/A	71,212
2/5/03	Wigan (a)	W8-14	t:L Pryce(2),Vainikolo g:Deacon	2nd	10,281
11/5/03	Castleford (h)	W30-10	t:Vaikona(2),Vagana,Deacon g:Deacon(7)	2nd	14,749
18/5/03	Huddersfield (a)	W6-52	t:Paul(3),Vaikona(2),Naylor,Pratt,Peacock,Vainikolo g:Radford(5),Deacon(3)	2nd	8,297
23/5/03	Leeds (h)	W48-22	t:Vaikona(2),Vainikolo(2),Gartner,Anderson,Paul,Pratt g:Deacon(8)	1st	21,784
1/6/03	London (h)	L12-22	t:Naylor,Parker g:Deacon(2)	2nd	10,835
8/6/03	Hull (a)	W20-26	t:Pratt,Hape,Vainikolo g:Deacon(7)	2nd	19,549
15/6/03	Warrington (a)	W20-24	t:Gartner,Paul,Forshaw,Naylor g:Deacon(4)	2nd	7,507
21/6/03	Wigan (h)	L22-35	t:Paul,Deacon,Vagana,Gartner g:Deacon(3)	2nd	15,732
27/6/03	St Helens (h)	L0-35	No Scorers	2nd	11,127
6/7/03	Wakefield (a)	W18-30	t:Hape(2),Vagana,Vainikolo,Gartner,Lowes g:Deacon(3)	2nd	4,658
11/7/03	Halifax (a)	W12-60	t:Parker(2),Gartner(2),Vainikolo(2),Naylor,Anderson,Deacon,Radford, L Pryce g:Deacon(8)	2nd	4,555
20/7/03	Widnes (h)	W40-8	t:Vainikolo(2),Radford(2),Hape,Vaikona,Reardon g:Deacon(6)	2nd	12,116
27/7/03	Castleford (a)	W20-40	t:Deacon,L Pryce,Radford,Naylor,Gartner,Gilmour,Vaikona g:Deacon(6)	2nd	9,081
30/7/03	London (a)	W6-60	t:L Pryce(4),Vainikolo(2),Anderson,Naylor,Vaikona,Langley,Lowes g:Deacon(8)	1st	3,651
3/8/03	Huddersfield (h)	W30-16	t:Deacon(2),Reardon,Vainikolo,Radford g:Deacon(5)	1st	11,368
8/8/03	Leeds (a)	W16-18	t:Vainikolo,Parker,Forshaw g:Deacon(3)	1st	23,035
16/8/03	Hull (h)	W36-22	t:Vainikolo(3),Gilmour(2),Anderson,Langley g:Radford(4)	1st	10,478
25/8/03	Wigan (a)	L26-12	t:Vagana,Vaikona g:Deacon(2)	1st	14,714
31/8/03	London (a)	W12-54	t:Peacock(2),Vaikona(2),Radford,Hape,Lowes,Parker,Vagana g:Deacon(9)	1st	3,910
7/9/03	Leeds (h)	W22-21	t:Deacon,Reardon,Vainikolo g:Deacon(4) fg:Deacon(2)	1st	21,102
14/9/03	Castleford (h)	L14-28	t:Hape,L Pryce g:Deacon(3)	1st	13,628
19/9/03	St Helens (a)	W18-22	t:Hape,Vaikona,Vainikolo,L Pryce g:Deacon(3)	1st	8,432
4/10/03	Leeds (h) (QSF)	W30-14	t:Forshaw(2),Vainikolo,L Pryce g:Deacon(7)	N/A	19,786
18/10/03	Wigan (GF) ●●●●	W25-12	t:Reardon,Hape,Lowes g:Deacon(6) fg:Deacon	N/A	65,537

● Played at Headingley Stadium, Leeds
●● Played at McAlpine Stadium, Huddersfield
●●● Played at Millennium Stadium, Cardiff
●●●● Played at Old Trafford, Manchester

		APP		TRIES		GOALS		FG		PTS	
	D.O.B.	ALL	SL	ALL	SL	ALL	SL	ALL	SL	ALL	SL
Paul Anderson	25/10/71	12(20)	12(16)	5	5	0	0	0	0	20	20
Chris Bridge	5/7/84	(3)	(3)	0	0	0	0	0	0	0	0
Paul Deacon	13/2/79	34	29	10	9	173	137	3	3	389	313
Stuart Fielden	14/9/79	15(4)	11(4)	1	0	0	0	0	0	4	0
Mike Forshaw	5/10/70	31(1)	26(1)	6	4	0	0	0	0	24	16
Daniel Gartner	15/10/72	28	24	8	7	0	0	0	0	32	28
Lee Gilmour	12/3/78	13(20)	12(16)	5	4	0	0	0	0	20	16
Shontayne Hape	30/1/82	34	29	15	11	0	0	0	0	60	44
Jamie Langley	21/12/83	1(15)	1(14)	2	2	0	0	0	0	8	8
James Lowes	11/10/69	30	27	10	9	2	2	0	0	44	40
Richard Moore	2/2/81	1(8)	1(7)	0	0	0	0	0	0	0	0
Vinny Myler	20/3/83	(1)	(1)	0	0	0	0	0	0	0	0
Scott Naylor	2/2/72	31	27	9	7	0	0	0	0	36	28
Robert Parker	5/9/81	4(28)	3(24)	6	5	0	0	0	0	24	20
Robbie Paul	3/2/76	18(2)	14(1)	13	10	0	0	0	0	52	40
Jamie Peacock	14/12/77	28	24	4	3	0	0	0	0	16	12
Karl Pratt	18/7/80	19(7)	16(5)	9	7	0	0	0	0	36	28
Karl Pryce	27/7/86	(1)	(1)	0	0	0	0	0	0	0	0
Leon Pryce	9/10/81	27(3)	22(3)	22	18	0	0	0	0	88	72
Lee Radford	26/3/79	13(20)	11(17)	10	7	12	12	0	0	64	52
Stuart Reardon	13/10/81	15(6)	14(6)	5	5	0	0	0	0	20	20
Aaron Smith	10/9/82	3	3	0	0	0	0	0	0	0	0
Joe Vagana	21/1/75	32	28	5	5	0	0	0	0	20	20
Tevita Vaikona	18/8/74	29	26	18	15	0	0	0	0	72	60
Lesley Vainikolo	4/5/79	32	27	28	22	0	0	0	0	112	88
Michael Withers	16/5/76	5(1)	3(1)	2	2	0	0	0	0	8	8

LEAGUE RECORD
P28-W22-D0-L6
(1st, SL/Grand Final Winners,
Champions)
F878, A529, Diff+349
44 points.

CHALLENGE CUP
Winners

ATTENDANCES
Best - v Leeds (SL - 21,784)
Worst - v Hull (SL - 10,478)
Total (SL, inc play-offs) - 228,884
Average (SL, inc play-offs) - 15,259
(Up by 3,735 on 2002)

TOP TACKLES
James Lowes 666

TOP CARRIES
Lesley Vainikolo 431

TOP METRES
Lesley Vainikolo 3677

TOP BREAKS
Lesley Vainikolo 35

TOP OFFLOADS
Tevita Vaikona 59

TOP BUSTS
Lesley Vainikolo 146

5 September 2002 - Hooker Wayne Godwin signs new two-year deal

12 September 2002 - Darren Rogers renews contract for a further two years

17 October 2002 - Halifax forward Jamie Thackray joins the Tigers on a two-year deal

18 October 2002 - Australian halfback Mitch Healey signs a new one-year contract

28 October 2002 - Tigers sign promising young fullback or winger Tom Saxton on a full-time contract

31 October 2002 - Centre Francis Maloney returns to the club from Salford City Reds

5 November 2002 - Australian utility back Damian Gibson joins from Salford

7 November 2002 - Coach Graham Steadman and assistant Gary Mercer agree new two and one-year contracts with the club

19 November 2002 - Tigers sign Cronulla centre Paul Mellor on a two-year deal

7 January 2003 - GMB Trade Union announced as new main shirt sponsor

8 February 2003 - Knocked out of the Challenge Cup in a 20-18 defeat at Wakefield

17 April 2003 - Leeds defeat Cas in a 15-14 nail biter

21 April 2003 - Cas bounce back with 29-16 victory over in-form Huddersfield at the McAlpine

5 May 2003 - Wayne Bartrim's conversion with the last kick of the game earns a dramatic 26-all draw with Hull

KEY DATES - CASTLEFORD TIGERS

15 May 2003 - Sign stand-off or hooker Jon Hepworth on a month loan deal from Leeds

18 May 2003 - Move up to fifth with 40-2 win over Widnes at The Jungle

24 May 2003 - Prop Dean Sampson answers Graham Steadman's SOS after an injury crisis at the club, and comes out of retirement to score a vital try in a 32-16 win over Warrington

5 June 2003 - Tom Saxton signs a new extended contract to stay until the end of 2005

12 June 2003 - Prop Andy Lynch agrees a new three-year contract

10 July 2003 - Wigan-bound Danny Orr turns down highest contract ever offered by the club. Jon Hepworth signs on a permanent deal after loan spell from Leeds

31 July 2003 - Announce the signing of Newcastle Knights star stand-off Sean Rudder for the next two seasons

12 August 2003 - Confirm that Mitch Healey and Andy Johnson will be released at the end of the season

14 August 2003 - Tigers announce the signing of Hull prop Craig Greenhill on a one-year contract for 2004

22 August 2003 - Mitch Healey stars as Cas claim stunning 28-20 win over Leeds

1 September 2003 - Tigers confirm utility back Mark Lennon will leave at the end of the season to join NRL side Manly

5 September 2003 - Former skipper Adrian Vowles puts pen to paper on a short-term deal, almost two years since he played his last match for the club

18 September 2003 – Confirm the signing of Widnes scrum-half Ryan Sheridan for the 2004 season

21 September 2003 – A 16-23 defeat to Wigan on the final day means that Cas just miss out on the play-offs and finish the 2003 season in eighth place

26 September 2003 – GMB Union will again be the clubs shirts sponsors for the 2004 season

28 September 2003 – Prop Andy Lynch is named in the Super League Dream Team

8 October 2003 - Paul Newlove will play for the Tigers next year after being released by St Helens

Andy Lynch

CASTLEFORD TIGERS

DATE	FIXTURE	RESULT	SCORERS	LGE	ATT
8/2/03	Wakefield (a) (CCR4)	L20-18	t:Lennon(2),Orr g:Bartrim(3)	N/A	4,125
23/2/03	Wigan (h)	W19-10	t:Rogers(2),Pryce g:Bartrim(3) fg:Orr	5th	8,462
7/3/03	Halifax (a)	W10-20	t:Maloney,Gibson,Godwin g:Bartrim(2),Orr(2)	3rd	4,388
21/3/03	St Helens (a)	L54-12	t:Lynch g:Bartrim(4)	7th	10,292
29/3/03	Wakefield (h)	L14-20	t:Eagar,Lennon g:Bartrim(3)	8th	6,883
6/4/03	London (a)	W12-24	t:Lennon,Pryce,Eagar g:Bartrim(6)	5th	3,013
17/4/03	Leeds (h)	L14-15	t:Lynch g:Bartrim(5)	8th	10,655
21/4/03	Huddersfield (a)	W16-29	t:Smith(2),Hudson,Lynch g:Orr(6) fg:Maloney	5th	5,139
5/5/03	Hull (h)	D26-26	t:Orr(2),Eagar,Gibson g;Bartrim(5)	5th	8,713
11/5/03	Bradford (a)	L30-10	t:Smith g:Bartrim(3)	7th	14,749
18/5/03	Widnes (h)	W40-2	t:Rogers(2),Hudson,Saxton,Lynch,McNally,Hepworth g:Bartrim(5),Orr	5th	6,516
24/5/03	Warrington (a)	W16-32	t:Hudson(2),Sampson,Pryce,Saxton g:Bartrim(5),Orr	5th	6,090
30/5/03	Huddersfield (h)	W32-18	t:Eagar(2),Orr,Rogers,Bartrim,Johnson g:Bartrim(4)	4th	5,682
7/6/03	Leeds (a)	L39-26	t:Pryce(2),Eagar,Orr,Rogers g:Bartrim(3)	4th	14,488
15/6/03	London (h)	L16-28	t:Eagar,Rogers g:Bartrim(4)	5th	5,630
20/6/03	Hull (a)	L22-14	t:Orr,Eagar,Pryce g:Bartrim	5th	10,703
27/6/03	Wigan (a)	L24-10	t:Orr,Mellor g:Orr	7th	9,884
6/7/03	Halifax (h)	W38-12	t:Hepworth(2),Orr,Mellor,Smith,Johnson,Thackray g:Healey(3),Orr(2)	6th	5,444
11/7/03	St Helens (h)	L32-46	t:Orr(3),Saxton,Smith g:Orr(6)	7th	6,320
19/7/03	Wakefield (a)	W4-32	t:Godwin(2),Pryce,Fritz,Rogers,Hudson g:Orr(3),Healey	6th	4,094
27/7/03	Bradford (h)	L20-40	t:Pryce(2),Rogers,Eagar g:Orr,Healey	7th	9,081
1/8/03	Widnes (h)	L27-16	t:Healey(2) g:Healey(4)	8th	5,698
10/8/03	Warrington (h)	L16-29	t:Mellor,Johnson,Godwin g:Healey(2)	9th	5,940
15/8/03	St Helens (a)	L26-10	t:Saxton,Pryce g:Healey	9th	8,041
22/8/03	Leeds (h)	W28-20	t:Healey,Rogers,Lynch,Fritz,Maloney,Eagar g:Healey(2)	9th	8,281
29/8/03	Huddersfield (h)	W26-18	t:Pryce(2),Gibson,Eagar g:Huby(3),Healey(2)	8th	5,289
7/9/03	Hull (a)	L32-12	t:Maloney,Lynch g:Orr(2)	8th	10,631
14/9/03	Bradford (a)	W14-28	t:Orr,Godwin,Lynch,Saxton g:Orr(6)	8th	13,628
21/9/03	Wigan (h)	L16-23	t:Pryce,Johnson,Orr g:Orr(2)	8th	7,886

		APP		TRIES		GOALS		FG		PTS	
	D.O.B.	ALL	SL	ALL	SL	ALL	SL	ALL	SL	ALL	SL
Wayne Bartrim	9/10/71	15(1)	14(1)	1	1	56	53	0	0	116	110
Richard Blakeway	22/7/83	1(11)	1(11)	0	0	0	0	0	0	0	0
Michael Eagar	15/8/73	25(2)	24(2)	11	11	0	0	0	0	44	44
Dale Fritz	18/11/69	26	25	2	2	0	0	0	0	8	8
Damian Gibson	14/5/75	21(2)	20(2)	3	3	0	0	0	0	12	12
Wayne Godwin	13/3/82	6(14)	6(14)	5	5	0	0	0	0	20	20
Lee Harland	4/9/74	7(7)	7(6)	0	0	0	0	0	0	0	0
Mitch Healey	11/5/71	23	22	3	3	16	16	0	0	44	44
Jon Hepworth	25/12/82	4(10)	4(10)	3	3	0	0	0	0	12	12
Craig Huby	21/5/86	(9)	(9)	0	0	3	3	0	0	6	6
Ryan Hudson	20/11/79	27	26	5	5	0	0	0	0	20	20
Paul Jackson	29/9/78	1(8)	1(7)	0	0	0	0	0	0	0	0
Andy Johnson	14/6/74	14(11)	14(11)	4	4	0	0	0	0	16	16
Mark Lennon	17/8/80	5(2)	4(2)	4	2	0	0	0	0	16	8
Andy Lynch	20/10/79	25(2)	24(2)	7	7	0	0	0	0	28	28
Francis Maloney	26/5/73	11(3)	11(3)	3	3	0	0	1	1	13	13
Andy McNally	9/1/82	2(1)	2(1)	1	1	0	0	0	0	4	4
Paul Mellor	21/8/74	17(3)	17(3)	3	3	0	0	0	0	12	12
Danny Orr	17/5/78	24(1)	23(1)	13	12	33	33	1	1	119	115
Waine Pryce	3/10/81	29	28	13	13	0	0	0	0	52	52
Darren Rogers	6/5/74	28	27	10	10	0	0	0	0	40	40
Dean Sampson	27/6/67	1(3)	1(3)	1	1	0	0	0	0	4	4
Tom Saxton	3/10/83	15(5)	15(5)	5	5	0	0	0	0	20	20
Ben Skerrett	21/10/80	(1)	(1)	0	0	0	0	0	0	0	0
Michael Smith	10/5/76	21(4)	20(4)	5	5	0	0	0	0	20	20
Tim Spears	27/7/84	(3)	(3)	0	0	0	0	0	0	0	0
Nathan Sykes	8/9/74	26(1)	25(1)	0	0	0	0	0	0	0	0
Jamie Thackray	30/9/79	1(8)	1(7)	1	1	0	0	0	0	4	4
Adrian Vowles	30/5/71	2(1)	2(1)	0	0	0	0	0	0	0	0

LEAGUE RECORD
P28-W12-D1-L15
(8th, SL)
F612, A633, Diff-21
25 points.

CHALLENGE CUP
Round Four

ATTENDANCES
Best - v Leeds (SL - 10,655)
Worst - v Huddersfield (SL - 5,289)
Total (SL only) - 100,782
Average (SL only) - 7,199
(Up by 285 on 2002)

TOP TACKLES
Nathan Sykes 665

TOP CARRIES
Andy Lynch 470

TOP METRES
Andy Lynch 3172

TOP BREAKS
Danny Orr 38

TOP OFFLOADS
Andy Lynch 90

TOP BUSTS
Michael Smith 112

19 September 2002 - Financial problems force the club to make nine of their backroom staff redundant and offer players reduced contracts

21 October 2002 - Kiwi Martin Moana re-signs from Wakefield

14 November 2002 - Gavin Clinch leaves for Salford City Reds

18 November 2002 - Australian forward Heath Cruckshank joins on a six-week trial

28 November 2002 - The club drops their Blue Sox nickname and revert back to Halifax RLFC

10 December 2002 - Australian duo Brett Goldspink and Robbie Beckett are suspended without pay for failing to report for pre-season training

12 December 2002 - Sign Bradford prop Chris Birchall and Aussie Heath Cruckshank

7 January 2003 - Brett Goldspink and Robbie Beckett officially leave the club

14 January 2003 - Australian halfback Dane Dorahy signs on a three-month trial

22 January 2003 - Kiwi back Lee Finnerty joins on a three-month trial

9 February 2003 - Crash out of the Challenge Cup at Hull despite the home side having two men sent off

KEY DATES - HALIFAX

23 February 2003 - Fax pull off the shock of the opening round of Super League VIII with a 26-22 victory at London

6 March 2003 - Australian utility back Andrew Frew signs

12 March 2003 - Halifax set up a new CVA (Corporate Voluntary Agreement) and a new company structure to run the club

28 March 2003 - Dane Dorahy signs a permanent, one-year contract

6 April 2003 - Go bottom of the table after a 44-16 hammering by Widnes Vikings

18 April 2003 - Remain at the foot of the table after a last-minute Huddersfield field goal condemns them to a 20-21 defeat

27 May 2003 - Martin Moana suspended for 28 days after being found guilty by RFL Doping Control Panel of providing a urine sample containing ephedrine

29 May 2003 - Docked their only two league points with immediate effect for breaching the salary cap in 2002

30 May 2003 - Sign veteran prop Neil Harmon and take St Helens winger John Kirkpatrick on loan

3 June 2003 - Aussie Scott MacDougall signs on a one-month trial from Gateshead Thunder

8 June 2003 - Eight points adrift at the foot of the table after losing their 12th consecutive game 28-26 at Huddersfield

14 June 2003 - Another home defeat, to Widnes, in front of the lowest Super League crowd of the season - 1,919

20 June 2003 - Terminate the contract of Kiwi forward Anthony Seuseu "by mutual consent"

1 July 2003 - Release Aussie back-rower Shayne McMenemy, who joins Hull

15 July 2003 - Sign St Helens youngsters John Hill and Chris Maye on loan

29 July 2003 - Martin Moana leaves to join Salford City Reds

11 August 2003 - Chris Birchall leaves to join Glasgow RU

15 August 2003 - 54-12 defeat by Huddersfield Giants officially condemns Fax to relegation

21 August 2003 - Club devastated by the death from cancer of acting chief executive Stephen Pearson, leader of the advisory group responsible for saving club from extinction

27 August 2003 - Australian winger Andrew Frew heads home after walking out

9 September 2003 - Fax appoint their former player Paul Dixon as football manager

11 September 2003 - The club officially comes out of its Corporate Voluntary Arrangement

21 September 2003 – Halifax say goodbye to Super League after 12 years in the top flight with a final day defeat to Widnes

28 September 2003 – Centre Stuart Donlan joins Huddersfield on loan for the 2004 season with winger Rikki Sheriffe staying at the Shay for an extra year

6 October 2003 – Fax announce the sponsorship by Halifax Home Insurance. Paul Davidson signs a 12-month deal to stay at Halifax

13 October 2003 – Coach Tony Anderson announces that the club will not have any full-time players for the National League season

16 October 2003 – Sean Penkywicz leaves for Huddersfield

20 October 2003 – Jamie Bloem and Oli Marns rejoin the club

21 October 2003 – Widnes hooker Phil Cantillon signs for the 2004 season

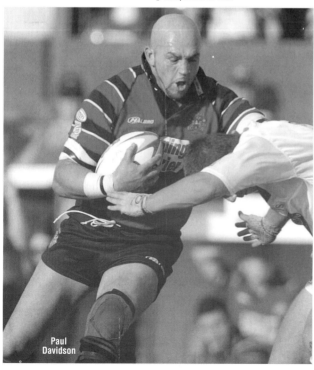

Paul Davidson

HALIFAX

DATE	FIXTURE	RESULT	SCORERS	LGE	ATT
9/2/03	Hull (a) (CCR4)	L24-16	t:Dorahy,Greenwood g:Dorahy(4)	N/A	15,310
23/2/03	London (a)	W22-26	t:Finnerty,Dorahy,Brocklehurst,Birchall g:Dorahy(5)	6th	3,022
7/3/03	Castleford (h)	L10-20	t:Dorahy g:Dorahy(3)	8th	4,388
23/3/03	Bradford (a)	L62-22	t:Moana,Clayton,Greenwood,Dorahy g:Dorahy(3)	9th	15,557
28/3/03	Leeds (h)	L14-20	t:Donlan,Dorahy g:Dorahy(3)	11th	4,073
6/4/03	Widnes (a)	L44-16	t:Cardiss,Seuseu,Dorahy g:Dorahy(2)	12th	7,135
18/4/03	Huddersfield (h)	L20-21	t:Clayton,Davidson,Donlan g:Dorahy(4)	12th	4,616
21/4/03	Hull (a)	L46-18	t:Frew,Dorahy,Clayton g:Dorahy(3)	12th	9,070
2/5/03	St Helens (h)	L0-38	No Scorers	12th	3,372
9/5/03	Warrington (h)	L8-38	t:Cardiss g:Dorahy(2)	12th	3,174
16/5/03	Wakefield (a)	L22-18	t:Penkywicz,Finn,Greenwood g:Dorahy(2),Finn	12th	2,806
23/5/03	Wigan (a)	L58-12	t:Birchall,Chapman g:Dorahy,Finnerty	12th	7,393
30/5/03	Hull (h)	L10-60	t:Frew,Lawless g:Dorahy	12th	3,143
8/6/03	Huddersfield (a)	L28-26	t:Penkywicz,Finn,Davidson,Frew g:Dorahy(5)	12th	3,980
14/6/03	Widnes (h)	L20-48	t:Finnerty,Norman,Penkywicz g:Finn(3),Finnerty	12th	1,919
20/6/03	St Helens (a)	L58-2	g:Finn	12th	7,891
28/6/03	London (h)	L16-50	t:Clayton,Kirkpatrick,Frew g:Dorahy(2)	12th	1,781
6/7/03	Castleford (a)	L38-12	t:Frew,Dorahy g:Dorahy(2)	12th	5,444
11/7/03	Bradford (h)	L12-60	t:Clayton,Hobson g:Dorahy(2)	12th	4,555
18/7/03	Leeds (a)	L54-6	t:Greenwood g:Dorahy	12th	10,019
27/7/03	Warrington (a)	L66-6	t:Birchall g:Dorahy	12th	5,291
1/8/03	Wakefield (h)	L18-30	t:Greenwood(2),Penkywicz g:Dorahy(3)	12th	2,274
10/8/03	Wigan (a)	L40-0	No Scorers	12th	7,409
15/8/03	Huddersfield (h)	L12-54	t:Finnerty,Greenwood g:Finn(2)	12th	2,473
22/8/03	London (h)	L12-26	t:Sheriffe,Penkywicz g:Finn(2)	12th	1,276
31/8/03	Wigan (h)	L12-68	t:Greenwood,Finnerty g:Finn(2)	12th	2,543
7/9/03	Warrington (a)	L40-18	t:Sheriffe,Finnerty g:Finn(3)	12th	5,761
14/9/03	Wakefield (a)	L68-6	t:Hobson g:Finn	12th	3,112
21/9/03	Widnes (h)	L20-48	t:Greenwood(2),Norman,Brocklehurst g:Finn(2)	12th	2,088

		APP		TRIES		GOALS		FG		PTS	
	D.O.B.	ALL	SL	ALL	SL	ALL	SL	ALL	SL	ALL	SL
Brad Attwood	24/11/84	(3)	(3)	0	0	0	0	0	0	0	0
Chris Birchall	25/3/81	15(7)	14(7)	3	3	0	0	0	0	12	12
Andrew Brocklehurst	6/3/83	27(2)	26(2)	2	2	0	0	0	0	8	8
Daryl Cardiss	13/7/77	13(3)	13(3)	2	2	0	0	0	0	8	8
Jaymes Chapman	17/12/83	5(7)	5(7)	1	1	0	0	0	0	4	4
Ryan Clayton	22/11/82	25(2)	25(2)	5	5	0	0	0	0	20	20
Ged Corcoran	28/3/83	1(11)	1(11)	0	0	0	0	0	0	0	0
Wayne Corcoran	10/7/85	4(2)	4(2)	0	0	0	0	0	0	0	0
Heath Cruckshank	28/6/76	20(1)	19(1)	0	0	0	0	0	0	0	0
Paul Davidson	1/8/69	4(19)	4(18)	2	2	0	0	0	0	8	8
Stuart Donlan	29/8/78	18	17	2	2	0	0	0	0	8	8
Dane Dorahy	17/12/77	21	20	8	7	49	45	0	0	130	118
Liam Finn	2/11/83	11(6)	11(5)	2	2	17	17	0	0	42	42
Lee Finnerty	30/4/78	19(2)	18(2)	5	5	2	2	0	0	24	24
Andrew Frew	9/3/75	17	17	5	5	0	0	0	0	20	20
Lee Greenwood	28/9/80	28	27	10	9	0	0	0	0	40	36
Simon Grix	28/9/85	2(4)	2(4)	0	0	0	0	0	0	0	0
Danny Halliwell	23/3/81	5(5)	4(5)	0	0	0	0	0	0	0	0
Neil Harmon	9/1/69	13(3)	13(3)	0	0	0	0	0	0	0	0
John Hill	10/10/81	1(2)	1(2)	0	0	0	0	0	0	0	0
Andy Hobson	26/12/78	18(7)	17(7)	2	2	0	0	0	0	8	8
Danny Jones	6/3/86	1	1	0	0	0	0	0	0	0	0
John Kirkpatrick	3/1/79	4	4	1	1	0	0	0	0	4	4
Johnny Lawless	3/11/74	28	27	1	1	0	0	0	0	4	4
Chris Maye	28/2/84	3(4)	3(4)	0	0	0	0	0	0	0	0
Shayne McMenemy	19/7/76	11	10	0	0	0	0	0	0	0	0
Martin Moana	13/8/73	17	16	1	1	0	0	0	0	4	4
Chris Norman	22/1/83	14(3)	13(3)	2	2	0	0	0	0	8	8
Sean Penkywicz	18/5/82	18(9)	18(8)	5	5	0	0	0	0	20	20
Anthony Seuseu	24/3/79	1(12)	1(11)	1	1	0	0	0	0	4	4
Rikki Sheriffe	5/5/84	6(1)	6(1)	3	3	0	0	0	0	12	12
Byron Smith	5/3/84	6(1)	6(1)	0	0	0	0	0	0	0	0

LEAGUE RECORD
P28-W1-D0-L27
(12th, SL)
F372, A1227, Diff-855
0 points. *(two points deducted for 2002 salary cap breach)*

CHALLENGE CUP
Round Four

ATTENDANCES
Best - v Huddersfield (SL - 4,616)
Worst - v London (SL - 1,276)
Total (SL only) - 41,675
Average (SL only) - 2,977
(Down by 1,103 on 2002)

TOP TACKLES
Johnny Lawless 695

TOP CARRIES
Andy Hobson 288

TOP METRES
Andy Hobson 2028

TOP BREAKS
Lee Finnerty 21

TOP OFFLOADS
Paul Davidson 36

TOP BUSTS
Lee Finnerty 65

KEY DATES - HUDDERSFIELD GIANTS

20 January 2003 - Giants complete the signing of Leeds prop Darren Fleary

30 January 2003 - Steve McNamara named as skipper and Chris Bridge signs on loan from Bradford

4 February 2003 - Jamie Bloem is ruled out for three months with a broken leg

9 February 2003 - Hunslet Hawks shock Huddersfield, sending them crashing out of the Challenge Cup 18-14 in the fourth round

4 March 2003 - Alex Wilkinson signs on a one-month loan from Bradford

11 March 2003 - Centre Matt Calland joins the injury list with a fractured eye socket

17 March 2003 - Calland announces his retirement after medical advice

30 March 2003 - The Giants shock St Helens 36-22 to record their first Super League win of the season

4 April 2003 - Giants take former Leeds and Halifax halfback Graham Holroyd on a ten-day trial

6 April 2003 - Huddersfield record their second consecutive win with a nail biting 14-10 victory over Wakefield

18 April 2003 - Brandon Costin kicks a last minute field goal to clinch a 21-20 win over Halifax

23 April 2003 - Formally complete the signing of Graham Holroyd

8 May 2003 - Australian forward Anthony Colella has to retire because of a knee injury

27 May 2003 - Sign Aussie back-rower Ben Roarty from Penrith Panthers

4 September 2002 - Giants sign New Zealand Warriors fullback Ivan Cleary

9 September 2002 - Brandon Costin returns after a year with Bradford Bulls

24 October 2002 - Paul March and Darren Turner agree new contracts

29 October 2002 - Prop Jeff Wittenberg re-signs on a one-year contract

31 October 2002 - Skipper Steve McNamara re-signs on a one-year contract

4 November 2002 - Club shocked by new signing Ivan Cleary's decision to accept a coaching role with Sydney Roosters

5 November 2002 - Sign South Sydney forward Anthony Colella on a two-year contract

8 November 2002 - Newcastle Knights' second row Jarrod O'Doherty joins

15 November 2002 - Jamie Bloem signs from local rivals Halifax

10 January 2003 - Welsh international Robert Roberts released due to "internal disciplinary matters"

2 June 2003 - Prop Jeff Wittenberg becomes the third Giants player to retire after failing to recover fully from a knee operation

3 June 2003 - Promising young forward Jon Grayshon signs a three-year contract

6 July 2003 - Stun Wigan 32-24 at the McAlpine Stadium

12 July 2003 - Last-minute Brandon Costin try seals a 30-24 win over Leeds, the first for 38 years

18 July 2003 - Paul Wellens' try two minutes from time prevents Giants claiming a league double over St Helens for first time in half a century

28 July 2003 - Coach Tony Smith announces his decision to quit the club at the end of the season to join Leeds

4 August 2003 - Confirm Saints assistant Jon Sharp as new head coach on a three-year contract

12 August 2003 - Australian forward Jarrod O'Doherty to return home at end of the season

18 August 2003 - Giants complete the signing of Rochdale second-rower Paul Smith

21 September 2003 – A final day 22-12 defeat at London means the Giants finish the season in tenth place. The game also marks the end of Steve McNamara's playing career to take up a coaching role at Bradford Bulls

28 September 2003 – Announce the signing of centre Stuart Donlan on a year-long loan from Halifax

7 October 2003 – Confirm the signing of 22 year old Chris Nero from St George-Illawarra

9 October 2003 – Brandon Costin signs a one year extension to keep him at the McAlpine until the end of 2005

16 October 2003 – Sean Penkywicz joins from Halifax

Brandon Costin

HUDDERSFIELD GIANTS

DATE	FIXTURE	RESULT	SCORERS	LGE	ATT
9/2/03	Hunslet (a) (CCR4)	L18-14	t:Costin(2),St Hilaire g:Costin	N/A	1,256
22/2/03	Warrington (h)	L8-20	t:O'Hare,St Hilaire	9th	4,104
7/3/03	Wigan (a)	L33-22	t:Wilkinson,Turner,Colella,Gannon g:Costin(2),McNamara	10th	8,187
21/3/03	Leeds (a)	L42-28	t:O'Hare,Wilkinson,Costin g:McNamara(6)	11th	10,357
30/3/03	St Helens (h)	W36-22	t:Cooper,Colella,Turner,March,Bailey,O'Hare,Costin g:Costin(4)	9th	5,835
6/4/03	Wakefield (a)	W10-14	t:Gannon,Wilkinson g:McNamara(3)	8th	4,109
18/4/03	Halifax (a)	W20-21	t:McNamara,Bailey,St Hilaire g:McNamara(4) fg:Costin	7th	4,616
21/4/03	Castleford (h)	L16-29	t:Costin,O'Hare,Bloem g:McNamara,Costin	8th	5,139
4/5/03	London (h)	L22-30	t:March,Wilkinson,Turner,St Hilaire g:McNamara(3)	10th	3,046
11/5/03	Hull (a)	L34-6	t:Gene g:Costin	10th	8,337
18/5/03	Bradford (h)	L6-52	t:Bailey g:Bloem	11th	8,297
25/5/03	Widnes (a)	L42-30	t:Costin(2),Bailey,St Hilaire,Reilly g:McNamara(3),Costin,Bloem	11th	4,946
30/5/03	Castleford (a)	L32-18	t:Gene,Bailey,March g:McNamara(3)	11th	5,682
8/6/03	Halifax (h)	W28-26	t:Roarty,Reilly,Turner,O'Hare,Costin g:Costin(4)	11th	3,980
15/6/03	Wakefield (h)	W26-4	t:Roarty,Reilly,Costin,St Hilaire,Bailey g:McNamara(3)	10th	3,989
28/6/03	Warrington (a)	L32-28	t:Fleary,Gene,March,Costin g:McNamara(4),Costin(2)	10th	5,689
6/7/03	Wigan (h)	W32-24	t:Costin(2),Gannon,St Hilaire,Reilly,March g:McNamara(3),Costin	10th	4,802
12/7/03	Leeds (h)	W30-24	t:Gene(2),Costin(2) g:McNamara(5),Costin(2)	10th	6,340
18/7/03	St Helens (a)	L22-18	t:Costin(2) g:McNamara(4),Costin	10th	9,288
22/7/03	London (a)	L32-16	t:Costin(2),O'Hare g:McNamara(2)	10th	2,679
27/7/03	Hull (h)	W30-14	t:Reilly,St Hilaire,March,Fleary,Costin g:McNamara(5)	10th	4,821
3/8/03	Bradford (a)	L30-16	t:Costin,Fleary,White g:McNamara(2)	10th	11,368
10/8/03	Widnes (h)	D30-30	t:St Hilaire,O'Hare,Gene,Bailey,Reilly g:White(5)	10th	4,140
15/8/03	Halifax (a)	W12-54	t:Gene(3),O'Hare(2),Fleary,Costin,Bailey,White,O'Doherty g:McNamara(5),Bloem(2)	10th	2,473
24/8/03	Wakefield (h)	W26-14	t:Turner(2),O'Doherty,McNamara g:Bloem(3),McNamara(2)	10th	3,621
29/8/03	Castleford (a)	L26-18	t:O'Hare,Crabtree g:Bloem(3),McNamara(2)	10th	5,289
7/9/03	Widnes (h)	W25-12	t:Reilly,O'Hare,Bloem,March g:McNamara(3),Bloem fg:McNamara	9th	3,555
12/9/03	Warrington (h)	L12-25	t:O'Doherty,Bloem g:McNamara(2)	9th	4,443
21/9/03	London (a)	L22-12	t:White,Bailey g:McNamara(2)	10th	3,286

		APP		TRIES		GOALS		FG		PTS	
	D.O.B.	ALL	SL	ALL	SL	ALL	SL	ALL	SL	ALL	SL
Julian Bailey	17/11/78	29	28	9	9	0	0	0	0	36	36
Jamie Bloem	26/5/71	18(4)	18(4)	3	3	11	11	0	0	34	34
Matt Calland	20/8/71	3	2	0	0	0	0	0	0	0	0
Anthony Colella	12/7/75	5(1)	5(1)	2	2	0	0	0	0	8	8
Ben Cooper	8/10/79	10(7)	9(7)	1	1	0	0	0	0	4	4
Brandon Costin	23/6/72	23	22	21	19	20	19	1	1	125	115
Eorl Crabtree	2/10/82	5(11)	4(11)	1	1	0	0	0	0	4	4
Darren Fleary	2/12/72	25(2)	24(2)	4	4	0	0	0	0	16	16
Jim Gannon	16/6/77	26(2)	25(2)	3	3	0	0	0	0	12	12
Stanley Gene	11/5/74	21(1)	21(1)	9	9	0	0	0	0	36	36
Jon Grayshon	10/5/83	2(10)	2(10)	0	0	0	0	0	0	0	0
Gareth Greenwood	14/1/83	(1)	(1)	0	0	0	0	0	0	0	0
Graham Holroyd	25/10/75	3(5)	3(5)	0	0	0	0	0	0	0	0
Paul March	25/7/79	23(4)	22(4)	7	7	0	0	0	0	28	28
Craig McDowell	5/11/81	(1)	(1)	0	0	0	0	0	0	0	0
Steve McNamara	18/9/71	15(8)	15(8)	2	2	68	68	1	1	145	145
Iain Morrison	6/5/83	8(12)	8(11)	0	0	0	0	0	0	0	0
Jarrod O'Doherty	16/9/77	27	26	3	3	0	0	0	0	12	12
Hefin O'Hare	2/6/79	29	28	12	12	0	0	0	0	48	48
Paul Reilly	10/5/76	17	17	7	7	0	0	0	0	28	28
Ben Roarty	5/2/75	16	16	2	2	0	0	0	0	8	8
Mick Slicker	16/8/78	9(20)	8(20)	0	0	0	0	0	0	0	0
Marcus St Hilaire	26/1/77	28	27	9	8	0	0	0	0	36	32
Darren Turner	13/10/73	22(6)	22(5)	6	6	0	0	0	0	24	24
Matt Whitaker	6/3/82	2(13)	2(12)	0	0	0	0	0	0	0	0
Paul White	7/12/82	3(5)	2(5)	3	3	5	5	0	0	22	22
Alex Wilkinson	9/10/82	8	8	4	4	0	0	0	0	16	16
Jeff Wittenberg	19/3/73	(1)	0	0	0	0	0	0	0	0	0

LEAGUE RECORD
P28-W11-D1-L16
(10th, SL)
F628, A715, Diff-87
23 points.

CHALLENGE CUP
Round Four

ATTENDANCES
Best - v Bradford (SL - 8,297)
Worst - v London (SL - 3,046)
Total (SL only) - 66,112
Average (SL only) - 4,722
(Up by 2,152 on 2002, NFP)

TOP TACKLES
Mick Slicker 556

TOP CARRIES
Stanley Gene 417

TOP METRES
Stanley Gene 3228

TOP BREAKS
Brandon Costin 33

TOP OFFLOADS
Jarrod O'Doherty 42

TOP BUSTS
Stanley Gene 111

1 October 2002 - Warren Jowitt joins on two-year contract from Salford

3 October 2002 - Hooker Lee Jackson released

22 November 2002 - Richard Fletcher signs a new one-year contract extension

5 December 2002 - Richard Horne agrees a new contract until the end of 2006

6 January 2003 - John Kear confirmed as new first team coach, with Shaun McRae becoming director of rugby

12 January 2003 - Hull beat Hull KR, the first derby clash for five years, in the Clive Sullivan Memorial Match at Craven Park

9 February 2003 - Claim a narrow Challenge Cup victory over Halifax despite having Jason Smith and Richard Fletcher sent off, in the first game to be held at the Kingston Communications Stadium

25 February 2003 - Dwayne West to miss the entire season after rupturing knee ligaments

7 March 2003 - First Super League game at the KC Stadium ends in disappointment as London grind out a 10-4 win

13 March 2003 - Warren Jowitt to undergo a career-saving operation on his pelvis

16 March 2003 - Hull's Challenge Cup run is ended at the quarter-final stage by Leeds

4 April 2003 - Convincing 20-4 win over Wigan at home takes Hull briefly to the top of the table

7 April 2003 - Prop Scott Logan out for the season after breaking his leg against Wigan

18 April 2003 - Injury crisis takes its toll as Hull are hammered 48-24 by Bradford

KEY DATES - HULL F.C.

21 April 2003 - Former winger Gareth Raynor returns on loan from Leicester Tigers RU and scores two tries as Hull beat Halifax

28 April 2003 - Confirm the short-term signing of Cronulla Sharks hooker Dean Treister

5 May 2003 - Draw 26-all with Castleford despite holding an 18-point lead at one stage

6 May 2003 - Matt Crowther's career in danger after news that he has snapped both tibia and fibula bones in Cas game

20 May 2003 - Move to ease severe injury crisis with the signing of prop Ewan Dowes from Leeds on a month's loan

26 May 2003 - Stun Saints 30-6 to go three points clear of Wigan in third place

29 May 2003 - Docked two league points with immediate effect for breaching the salary cap

12 June 2003 - Fullback Steve Prescott signs a two-year contract extension

17 June 2003 - Sign Bradford threequarter Alex Wilkinson and Leeds stand-off Peter Lupton on loan

25 June 2003 - Gareth Raynor signs on a permanent two-year deal after Leicester RU agree to release him

26 June 2003 - Go back to third with a 44-4 win over Wakefield

1 July 2003 - Confirm the capture of New Zealand International hooker Richard Swain for 2004 season

2 July 2003 - Sign former Halifax forward Shayne McMenemy for rest of season

15 July 2003 - Release Tony Smith from his contract due to a severe leg injury

24 July 2003 - Extend the loan periods of Alex Wilkinson, Peter Lupton and Ewan Dowes for a further month

30 July 2003 - Sign Leeds prop Ewan Dowes on a permanent two-year deal

6 August 2003 - Richard Fletcher signs a new three-year deal

7 August 2003 - Sign Castleford centre Michael Eagar on a two-year deal for next season

11 August 2003 - Second-rower Adam Maher announces his retirement at end of season

24 August 2003 - Hammer Saints 42-18 at KC Stadium in a return to form

30 August 2003 - Suffer a shock 35-28 defeat by Wakefield to dent their top-six hopes

7 September 2003 – Back to winning ways with a 32-12 defeat of Castleford at the KC

15 September 2003 – Complete the signings of Aussie Paul McNicholas and Gateshead winger Richie Barnett

20 September 2003 – Lose their final game of the season 12-28 at home to Leeds to miss out on the play-offs

23 October 2003 – Toa Kohe-Love leaves to join Bradford

4 November 2003 - Alex Wilkinson signs permanent two-year deal

HULL F C

HULL F.C.

DATE	FIXTURE	RESULT	SCORERS	LGE	ATT
9/2/03	Halifax (h) (CCR4)	W24-16	t:Best,Barnett,Kohe-Love g:Crowther(6)	N/A	15,310
23/2/03	Wakefield (a)	W14-28	t:Prescott(3),Greenhill,Kohe-Love g:Crowther(4)	3rd	5,645
2/3/03	Sheffield (a) (CCR5) ●	W0-88	t:Barnett(4),Prescott(3),G Horne(2),Crowther,Cooke,Kohe-Love,		
			R Horne,Ryan,Best g:Crowther(14)	N/A	11,729
7/3/03	London (h)	L4-10	g:Crowther(2)	4th	12,901
16/3/03	Leeds (a) (CCQF)	L41-18	t:Prescott(2),T Smith g:Crowther(2),Prescott	N/A	11,420
23/3/03	Widnes (h)	W38-18	t:J Smith,R Horne,Prescott,Kohe-Love,Logan g:Prescott(9)	4th	8,743
30/3/03	Warrington (a)	W14-27	t:Best,Barnett,Kohe-Love,Prescott g:Prescott(5) fg:J Smith	3rd	6,784
4/4/03	Wigan (h)	W20-4	t:Best,Maher,Yeaman g:Prescott(4)	3rd	11,536
18/4/03	Bradford (a)	L48-24	t:Barnett(2),Last g:Prescott(6)	3rd	15,182
21/4/03	Halifax (h)	W46-18	t:Best(2),Raynor(2),Barnett(2),Prescott,R Horne g:Prescott(7)	3rd	9,070
5/5/03	Castleford (a)	D26-26	t:Barnett(2),Prescott,R Horne,Best g:Prescott(3)	3rd	8,713
11/5/03	Huddersfield (h)	W34-6	t:Kohe-Love,Treister,T Smith,R Horne,Best,Prescott g:Prescott(5)	3rd	8,337
17/5/03	Leeds (a)	D10-10	t:Best g:Prescott(3)	3rd	11,273
26/5/03	St Helens (h)	W30-6	t:Best(2),Yeaman,Prescott,Donkin,Kohe-Love g:Prescott(3)	3rd	12,490
30/5/03	Halifax (a)	W10-60	t:Barnett(2),Prescott(2),Chester(2),Maher,Yeaman,Dowes,Best		
			g:Prescott(10)	3rd	3,143
8/6/03	Bradford (h)	L20-26	t:Barnett,R Horne,Best g:Prescott(4)	3rd	19,549
13/6/03	Wigan (a)	L28-14	t:Chester,R Horne g:Prescott(3)	4th	11,278
20/6/03	Castleford (h)	W22-14	t:Treister(2),Yeaman,King g:Prescott(3)	4th	10,703
26/6/03	Wakefield (a)	W44-4	t:Prescott(2),R Horne,Raynor,Dowes,Best,Ryan,G Horne g:Prescott(6)	4th	9,575
5/7/03	London (a)	D20-20	t:Best(2),Wilkinson g:Cooke(4)	3rd	4,151
13/7/03	Widnes (a)	L46-10	t:Maher,Yeaman g:Cooke	4th	6,707
20/7/03	Warrington (a)	W38-14	t:Best(2),G Horne(2),Fletcher,Ryan g:Cooke(7)	4th	9,835
27/7/03	Huddersfield (a)	L30-14	t:Carvell,Last,Best g:Cooke	5th	4,821
2/8/03	Leeds (h)	L12-26	t:G Horne g:Cooke(4)	5th	13,081
9/8/03	St Helens (a)	L28-18	t:Maher,Greenhill,Yeaman g:Cooke(3)	5th	8,019
16/8/03	Bradford (a)	L36-22	t:Last,Best,R Horne,Raynor g:Cooke(3)	5th	10,478
24/8/03	St Helens (h)	W42-18	t:Raynor(2),Barnett(2),Chester,Cooke,Best,Lupton g:Cooke(5)	5th	11,212
30/8/03	Wakefield (a)	L35-28	t:J Smith(2),Raynor,R Horne,McMenemy g:Cooke(4)	5th	3,689
7/9/03	Castleford (a)	W32-12	t:Raynor,Dowes,McMenemy,R Horne g:Cooke(7),Greenhill	5th	10,631
12/9/03	Wigan (a)	L28-6	t:Yeaman g:Cooke	6th	11,115
20/9/03	Leeds (h)	L12-28	t:Cooke,Raynor g:Cooke(2)	7th	14,706

● Played at KC Stadium

		APP		TRIES		GOALS		FG		PTS		
	D.O.B.	ALL	SL	ALL	SL	ALL	SL	ALL	SL	ALL	SL	
Dwayne Barker	21/9/83	(1)	(1)	0	0	0	0	0	0	0	0	
Richie Barnett	21/4/72	25	22	17	12	0	0	0	0	68	48	
Ian Bell	28/1/83	(1)	(1)	0	0	0	0	0	0	0	0	
Colin Best	22/11/78	31	28	21	19	0	0	0	0	84	76	
Garreth Carvell	21/4/80	3(19)	3(18)	1	1	0	0	0	0	4	4	
Chris Chester	8/10/78	22(3)	21(2)	4	4	0	0	0	0	16	16	
Paul Cooke	17/4/81	29(2)	28	3	2	42	42	0	0	96	92	
Steve Craven	9/4/72	1(6)	(5)	0	0	0	0	0	0	0	0	
Matt Crowther	6/5/74	6	3	1	0	28	6	0	0	60	12	
Glen Donkin	16/9/82	(5)	(5)	1	1	0	0	0	0	4	4	
Ewan Dowes	4/3/81	3(15)	3(15)	3	3	0	0	0	0	12	12	
Richard Fletcher	17/5/81	5(13)	3(13)	1	1	0	0	0	0	4	4	
Craig Greenhill	14/2/72	30(1)	28	2	2	1	1	0	0	10	10	
Liam Higgins	19/7/83	(2)	(1)	0	0	0	0	0	0	0	0	
Graeme Horne	22/3/85	6(14)	6(13)	6	4	0	0	0	0	24	16	
Richard Horne	16/7/82	31	28	11	10	0	0	0	0	44	40	
Warren Jowitt	9/9/74	(2)	(2)	0	0	0	0	0	0	0	0	
Paul King	28/6/79	20(9)	18(8)	1	1	0	0	0	0	4	4	
Toa Kohe-Love	2/12/74	17	14	7	5	0	0	0	0	28	20	
Andy Last	25/3/81	12(5)	9(5)	3	3	0	0	0	0	12	12	
Scott Logan	22/6/76	8(2)	5(2)	1	1	0	0	0	0	4	4	
Peter Lupton	7/3/82	4(7)	4(7)	1	1	0	0	0	0	4	4	
Adam Maher	2/8/72	23(1)	22	4	4	0	0	0	0	16	16	
Shayne McMenemy	19/7/76	3(2)	3(2)	2	2	0	0	0	0	8	8	
Steve Prescott	26/12/73	19	16	18	13	72	71	0	0	216	194	
Gareth Raynor	24/2/78	11	11	9	9	0	0	0	0	36	36	
Sean Ryan	23/8/73	29(1)	28	3	2	0	0	0	0	12	8	
Jason Smith	14/3/72	11(2)	9(2)	3	3	0	0	1	1	13	13	
Tony Smith	16/7/70	9	7	2	1	0	0	0	0	8	4	
Dean Treister	19/12/75	16(1)	16(1)	3	3	0	0	0	0	12	12	
Dwayne West	8/6/80	(1)	0	0	0	0	0	0	0	0	0	
Alex Wilkinson	9/10/82	11(1)	11(1)	1	1	0	0	0	0	4	4	
Kirk Yeaman	15/9/83	18(8)	18(8)	7	7	0	0	0	0	28	28	

LEAGUE RECORD
P28-W13-D3-L12
(7th, SL)
F701, A577, Diff+124
27 points. *(two points deducted for 2002 salary cap breach)*

CHALLENGE CUP
Quarter Finalists

ATTENDANCES
Best - v Bradford (SL - 19,549)
Worst - v Huddersfield (SL - 8,337)
Total (SL only) - 162,369
Average - SL only) - 11,598
(Up by 4,670 on 2002)

TOP TACKLES
Paul Cooke 696

TOP CARRIES
Craig Greenhill 531

TOP METRES
Craig Greenhill 3594

TOP BREAKS
Colin Best 38

TOP OFFLOADS
Sean Ryan 51

TOP BUSTS
Colin Best 139

28 October 2002 - Rhinos sign halfback Andrew Dunemann from Halifax and young prop Chris Feather from Wakefield

26 November 2002 - Scrum-half Ryan Sheridan released from the final year of his contract

27 November 2002 - Andy Hay becomes the second Great Britain international to leave the club in as many days

3 December 2002 - Kevin Sinfield is appointed new captain of the Rhinos

5 December 2002 - Karl Pratt seeks to win release from his contract at a tribunal after being told he has no future at Headingley

6 December 2002 - Prop Danny Ward agrees new two-year contract

12 December 2002 - RFL tribunal allows Karl Pratt to leave as a free agent

26 December 2002 - Rhinos announce signing of Great Britain international Gary Connolly after his release from Wigan Warriors

All roads head to Odsal for 'biggest game of season'
- FAZ MAKES A POINT ON RETURN!
- BULLDOGS STUN ROBINS TO MAKE LAST FOUR

23 February 2003 - Mark Calderwood scores a hat-trick as the Rhinos start the Super League season with a comprehensive 32-12 win over Widnes

16 March 2003 - Into Challenge Cup semi-finals after a resounding 41-18 victory over Hull

28 March 2003 - A narrow 20-14 victory over Halifax sees Leeds maintain their 100 per cent start to the season as they top the table

12 April 2003 - Captain Kevin Sinfield and two-try Danny McGuire inspire Leeds to a classic 33-26 Challenge Cup semi-final win over St Helens after extra-time

17 April 2003 - Need an Andrew Dunemann field goal two minutes from time to claim a 15-14 victory over Castleford

KEY DATES - LEEDS RHINOS

26 April 2003 - Gary Connolly wins Lance Todd Trophy but is on the losing side as Leeds are defeated 22-20 by Bradford at the Millennium Stadium

6 May 2003 - Remain undefeated after a 24-all draw with Wigan

23 May 2003 - Suffer their first Super League defeat of the season, 48-22 at Bradford

8 June 2003 - Move four points clear at the top of the table after coming from behind to beat Castleford Tigers 39-26

28 June 2003 - Lose only their second game of the season after being outclassed by Widnes in a 29-14 defeat at the Halton Stadium

30 June 2003 - Andrew Dunemann signs two-year contract extension

16 July 2003 - David Furner agrees one-year extension to his contract

18 July 2003 - Wayne McDonald agrees new two-year contract

23 July 2003 - Winger Francis Cummins signs a one-year contract extension

24 July 2003 - Papua New Guinean winger Marcus Bai signs on a two-year deal from Melbourne Storm from next season

29 July 2003 - Ryan Bailey and Chev Walker are jailed and will serve nine and 18-month terms at a young offenders institution for their part in a fight outside a nightclub last year. Dwayne Barker given community service

30 July 2003 - Huddersfield Giants coach Tony Smith to join as head coach at the end of the season, with current coach Daryl Powell becoming director of football

2 August 2003 - Go back to the top of the table with 26-12 victory at Hull

8 August 2003 - Lose a thrilling top of the table clash 18-16 to Bradford, watched by over 23,000 fans at Headingley

15 August 2003 - Last-minute Danny McGuire try earns Rhinos a 24-all draw with Wigan

Leeds end topsy turvy week with Hull win

22 August 2003 - Liam Botham makes his Rugby League debut but can't prevent Rhinos suffering 28-20 defeat at Castleford

5 September 2003 - Richard Mathers agrees a new one-year contract

7 September 2003 – The Rhinos lose another thriller at Odsal, 22-21

20 September 2003 – Leeds earn a final game win at Hull to seal second spot

4 October 2003 – Leeds lose 30-14 away to Bradford in the Qualifying semi-final

10 October 2003 – The Rhinos' season is over after a dramatic 23-22 loss at home to Wigan in the Final Eliminator

LEEDS RHINOS

DATE	FIXTURE	RESULT	SCORERS	LGE	ATT
9/2/03	Whitehaven (h) (CCR4)	W46-6	t:Burrow(2),McDonald,McKenna,Sinfield,Furner,Cummins,Connolly, Calderwood g:Furner(5)	N/A	7,535
23/2/03	Widnes (h)	W32-12	t:Calderwood(3),McKenna,Cummins,Senior,Dunemann g:Furner,Sinfield	2nd	13,013
1/3/03	London (h) (CCR5)	W21-12	t:Senior,Calderwood,Sinfield g:Furner(4) fg:Sinfield	N/A	6,717
9/3/03	Warrington (a)	W22-32	t:Walker(2),Calderwood,Connolly,Adamson,Senior g:Furner(4)	2nd	8,705
16/3/03	Hull (h) (CCQF)	W41-18	t:Furner(2),Senior,McDermott,Calderwood,Cummins,McGuire g:Furner(6) fg:Sinfield	N/A	11,420
21/3/03	Huddersfield (h)	W42-28	t:Calderwood(3),Walker(2),Cummins,Dunemann,Diskin g:Sinfield(3),Furner(2)	2nd	10,357
28/3/03	Halifax (a)	W14-20	t:Feather,McDermott,Walker g:Sinfield(4)	1st	4,073
5/4/03	St Helens (a)	W16-24	t:Senior(2),Poching,McDonald g:Sinfield(4)	1st	10,785
12/4/03	St Helens (CCSF) ●	W33-26 (aet)	t:Calderwood(2),McGuire(2),Cummins g:Sinfield(6) fg:Sinfield	N/A	19,118
17/4/03	Castleford (a)	W14-15	t:McGuire,Poching,Walker g:Sinfield fg:Dunemann	1st	10,655
26/4/03	Bradford (CCF) ●●	L22-20	t:Connolly,McKenna,Furner g:Sinfield(4)	N/A	71,212
2/5/03	Wakefield (a)	W13-12	t:McGuire g:Sinfield(4) fg:Dunemann	1st	10,740
6/5/03	Wigan (h)	D24-24	t:Calderwood,Cummins,McGuire,Burrow g:Sinfield(4)	1st	11,115
9/5/03	London (a)	W14-32	t:McGuire(2),Burrow,Calderwood,Dunemann,Cummins g:Sinfield(4)	1st	5,666
17/5/03	Hull (h)	D10-10	t:Poching,McKenna g:Sinfield	1st	11,273
23/5/03	Bradford (a)	L48-22	t:Walker,Calderwood,Sinfield g:Sinfield(5)	2nd	21,784
30/5/03	Wigan (a)	W20-30	t:Cummins,Calderwood,McGuire,Burrow,Connolly g:Sinfield(5)	1st	11,386
7/6/03	Castleford (h)	W39-26	t:Cummins(2),McDonald,Calderwood,McGuire,Burrow,Senior g:Sinfield(5) fg:Burrow	1st	14,488
13/6/03	St Helens (h)	W20-14	t:Walker,Connolly,Cummins g:Sinfield(4)	1st	14,073
20/6/03	Wakefield (a)	W12-48	t:Calderwood(2),Burrow(2),McGuire,Senior,Cummins,Walker,Poching g:Sinfield(6)	1st	6,678
28/6/03	Widnes (a)	L29-14	t:Poching,Adamson g:Sinfield(3)	1st	6,837
6/7/03	Warrington (h)	W30-20	t:Poching(2),Cummins,Furner,McKenna g:Furner(5)	1st	13,498
12/7/03	Huddersfield (a)	L30-24	t:Sinfield,McGuire,McDonald,Furner g:Sinfield(4)	1st	6,340
18/7/03	Halifax (h)	W54-6	t:Cummins(2),Calderwood(2),McKenna,Burrow,Feather,Jones-Buchanan,Walker g:Sinfield(6),Burrow(3)	1st	10,019
25/7/03	London (h)	W27-22	t:McDonald,Walker,McGuire,Poching g:Sinfield(5) fg:Sinfield	1st	8,231
2/8/03	Hull (a)	W12-26	t:McGuire,Cummins,Poching g:Sinfield(7)	2nd	13,081
8/8/03	Bradford (h)	L16-18	t:Connolly,Senior,Burrow g:Sinfield(2)	2nd	23,035
15/8/03	Wigan (h)	D24-24	t:Senior,Furner,Adamson,McGuire g:Sinfield(4)	2nd	14,019
22/8/03	Castleford (a)	L28-20	t:Calderwood,Senior,McGuire,Adamson g:Sinfield(2)	2nd	8,281
29/8/03	Warrington (h)	W34-26	t:Sinfield,Diskin,McGuire,Cummins,Dunemann g:Sinfield(7)	2nd	10,750
7/9/03	Bradford (a)	L22-21	t:McDonald,Poching,Sinfield g:Sinfield(4) fg:Sinfield	2nd	21,102
12/9/03	St Helens (h)	W30-20	t:Burrow,Calderwood,Connolly,Mathers,Poching g:Sinfield(5)	2nd	15,273
20/9/03	Hull (a)	W12-28	t:Senior,Calderwood,Poching,Burrow g:Sinfield(6)	2nd	14,706
4/10/03	Bradford (a) (QSF)	L30-14	t:Cummins,Calderwood,Furner g:Sinfield	N/A	19,786
10/10/03	Wigan (h) (FE)	L22-23	t:Burrow(2),McGuire g:Sinfield(5)	N/A	17,264

● Played at McAlpine Stadium, Huddersfield
●● Played at Millennium Stadium, Cardiff

		APP		TRIES		GOALS		FG		PTS	
	D.O.B.	ALL	SL	ALL	SL	ALL	SL	ALL	SL	ALL	SL
Matt Adamson	14/8/72	27(1)	22(1)	4	4	0	0	0	0	16	16
Ryan Bailey	11/11/83	15(6)	10(6)	0	0	0	0	0	0	0	0
Liam Botham	26/8/77	1	1	0	0	0	0	0	0	0	0
Rob Burrow	26/9/82	16(17)	13(16)	14	12	3	3	1	1	63	55
Mark Calderwood	25/10/81	33	28	25	20	0	0	0	0	100	80
Gary Connolly	22/6/71	30	25	7	5	0	0	0	0	28	20
Francis Cummins	12/10/76	35	30	18	15	0	0	0	0	72	60
Matt Diskin	27/1/82	34	29	2	2	0	0	0	0	8	8
Ewan Dowes	4/3/81	(4)	(3)	0	0	0	0	0	0	0	0
Andrew Dunemann	10/6/76	32	27	4	4	0	0	2	2	18	18
Chris Feather	7/12/81	(28)	(26)	2	2	0	0	0	0	8	8
David Furner	6/2/70	32	27	8	4	27	12	0	0	86	40
Jon Hepworth	25/12/82	(1)	(1)	0	0	0	0	0	0	0	0
Jamie Jones-Buchanan	1/8/81	1(10)	1(10)	1	1	0	0	0	0	4	4
Richard Mathers	24/10/83	10(2)	10(2)	1	1	0	0	0	0	4	4
Barrie McDermott	22/7/72	27(6)	25(4)	2	1	0	0	0	0	8	4
Wayne McDonald	3/9/75	17(14)	14(12)	6	5	0	0	0	0	24	20
Danny McGuire	6/12/82	19(14)	19(10)	18	15	0	0	0	0	72	60
Chris McKenna	29/10/74	24(1)	20(1)	6	4	0	0	0	0	24	16
Willie Poching	30/8/73	13(19)	13(16)	12	12	0	0	0	0	48	48
Keith Senior	24/4/76	32	27	12	10	0	0	0	0	48	40
Kevin Sinfield	12/9/80	34(1)	29(1)	6	4	122	112	5	2	273	242
Chev Walker	9/10/82	17(4)	14(2)	11	11	0	0	0	0	44	44
Danny Ward	15/6/80	6(12)	6(9)	0	0	0	0	0	0	0	0

LEAGUE RECORD
P28-W19-D3-L6
(2nd, SL/Final Eliminator)
F751, A555, Diff+196
41 points.

CHALLENGE CUP
Runners Up

ATTENDANCES
Best - v Bradford (SL - 23,035)
Worst - v London (CC - 6,717)
Total (SL, inc play-offs) - 197,148
Average (SL, inc play-offs) - 13,143
(Up by 951 on 2002)

TOP TACKLES
Matt Diskin 681

TOP CARRIES
Barrie McDermott 378

TOP METRES
Wayne McDonald 2934

TOP BREAKS
Danny McGuire 37

TOP OFFLOADS
Kevin Sinfield 46

TOP BUSTS
Willie Poching 89

2 September 2002 - Steele Retchless signs a new one-year deal

6 September 2002 - Jim Dymock pens a new one-year contract

11 September 2002 - Broncos announce that they are remaining at Griffin Park for the 2003 season

12 September 2002 - Nigel Roy signs new two-year deal

24 October 2002 - Broncos sign props Jamie Fielden, from Doncaster, and Mark Cox, from Whitehaven, both on two-year contracts

12 November 2002 - Wigan youngsters Neil Budworth and Rob Jackson sign two-year contracts

23 December 2002 - Newcastle Knights forward Bill Peden joins the club

13 February 2003 - Jim Dymock becomes new club captain, taking over from the injured Jason Hetherington

27 February 2003 - Winner of the Prop Idol competition James Hersey signs a professional playing contract with the Broncos

1 March 2003 - London miss out on a place in the Challenge Cup quarter-finals after a 21-12 defeat by Leeds

6 March 2003 - South Sydney centre Andrew King signs on a one-year deal

KEY DATES - LONDON BRONCOS

28 March 2003 - London record their first ever Super League win at Wigan, 34-30

31 March 2003 - Prop Mark Cox ruled out for the season after been involved in a serious car accident

4 April 2003 - Karl Long and Leeds Academy star Austin Buchanan sign on short term deals

9 April 2003 - Prop Jamie Fielden quits the club to rejoin Doncaster Dragons

27 May 2003 - Winger Dominic Peters suspended for 12 months after being found guilty by the RFL Doping Control Panel of providing a urine sample containing stanozolol

29 May 2003 - Broncos terminate the contract of Dominic Peters

1 June 2003 - Dennis Moran scores a stunning hat-trick as the Broncos shock Bradford Bulls 22-12 at Odsal

26 June 2003 - Sign young Leeds forward Jason Netherton on a month's loan deal

28 June 2003 - Dennis Moran scores third hat-trick in five games as Broncos crush Halifax 50-16

5 July 2003 - Miss out on their first home win in ten months as Hull battle back for a 20-all draw

7 July 2003 - Centre Tony Martin to leave the club at the end of the season and join New Zealand Warriors

8 July 2003 - Confirmation that hooker Jason Hetherington has retired after failing to recover from shoulder surgery

21 July 2003 - Sign youngster Joe Mbu for 2004

22 July 2003 - Finally break their Griffin Park duck with 32-16 victory over Huddersfield Giants

31 July 2003 - Chris Thorman signs for NRL side Parramatta Eels for next season

14 August 2003 - Captain Jim Dymock agrees new one-year contract extension, and Dennis Moran pens three-year deal

15 August 2003 - Wests Tigers prop Steve Trindall joins on a short-term deal

17 August 2003 - Win crucial game against Warrington 19-12 to enhance play-off hopes

25 August 2003 - Sign Chorley hooker Dave McConnell and Wests Tigers fullback Joel Caine on short-term deals

4 September 2003 - London re-sign club captain Mat Toshack on a two-year deal

13 September 2003 - Joel Caine scores a second-half hat-trick as Broncos beat Widnes 40-0 at the Halton Stadium

21 September 2003 - Beat Huddersfield 22-12 to seal fifth place and their first ever play-off place

26 September 2003 - The Broncos are eliminated at the first hurdle of the play-offs at St Helens

9 October 2003 – Sign John Kirkpatrick from St Helens and Jon Wells from Wakefield on two-year contracts

13 October 2003 – Francis Stephenson signs a new two-year contract

Dennis Moran

LONDON BRONCOS

DATE	FIXTURE	RESULT	SCORERS	LGE	ATT
9/2/03	Oldham (h) (CCR4)	W42-12	t:Hall(2),Jackson(2),Peters,Thorman,Roy,Martin g:Martin(5)	N/A	1,514
23/2/03	Halifax (h)	L22-26	t:Hall,Peden,Martin g:Martin(5)	7th	3,022
1/3/03	Leeds (a) (CCR5)	L21-12	t:Peden,Dymock g:Martin(2)	N/A	6,717
7/3/03	Hull (a)	W4-10	t:Roy g:Martin(3)	7th	12,901
22/3/03	Warrington (h)	L8-29	t:King g:Martin(2)	8th	3,105
28/3/03	Wigan (a)	W30-34	t:Dymock(2),King,Thorman,Martin,Jackson g:Martin(5)	7th	8,375
6/4/03	Castleford (h)	L12-24	t:Martin,King g:Martin(2)	9th	3,013
18/4/03	Widnes (a)	L32-20	t:Hall,Roy,Stephenson,Martin g:Martin(2)	10th	5,708
4/5/03	Huddersfield (a)	W22-30	t:King(2),Buchanan(2),Martin(2) g:Martin(3)	8th	3,046
9/5/03	Leeds (h)	L14-32	t:King,Hall g:Martin(3)	9th	5,666
16/5/03	St Helens (a)	L62-16	t:Peters,Stephenson g:Thorman(4)	10th	7,602
25/5/03	Wakefield (a)	W12-36	t:Moran(2),Thorman,Bawden,Roy g:Thorman(6)	9th	3,305
1/6/03	Bradford (a)	W12-22	t:Moran(3),Toshack g:Thorman(3)	9th	10,835
8/6/03	Widnes (h) ●	W40-18	t:Sykes(2),Moran(2),Peden,Thorman,Gallagher g:Thorman(6)	6th	3,128
15/6/03	Castleford (a)	W16-28	t:Moran(2),Martin(2) g:Thorman(6)	6th	5,630
28/6/03	Halifax (a)	W16-50	t:Moran(3),Martin(2),Budworth,Jackson,Thorman,Purdham g:Martin(4),Thorman(3)	5th	1,781
5/7/03	Hull (h)	D20-20	t:Roy,Martin,Hall g:Thorman(4)	7th	4,151
13/7/03	Warrington (a)	L50-8	t:Peden g:Thorman(2)	8th	5,562
18/7/03	Wigan (h)	L12-28	t:Sykes,Peden g:Thorman(2)	8th	3,984
22/7/03	Huddersfield (h)	W32-16	t:King(2),Thorman,Retchless,Thorman g:Thorman(6)	7th	2,679
25/7/03	Leeds (a)	L27-22	t:Moran(2),Kennedy,King g:Thorman(3)	8th	8,231
30/7/03	Bradford (h)	L6-60	t:Peden g:Thorman	8th	3,651
3/8/03	St Helens (h)	L18-30	t:King,Dymock,Moran g:Thorman(3)	9th	4,214
10/8/03	Wakefield (a)	D26-26	t:Roy(2),King(2),Peden g:Thorman(3)	8th	2,415
17/8/03	Warrington (h)	W19-12	t:Roy,Sykes g:Thorman(5) fg:Thorman	7th	2,916
22/8/03	Halifax (a)	W12-26	t:Moran(2),Sykes,Martin g:Thorman(5)	6th	1,276
31/8/03	Bradford (h)	L12-54	t:Retchless,King g:Sykes,Caine	6th	3,910
7/9/03	Wakefield (h)	W38-14	t:Moran(3),Roy,Martin,King,Caine g:Thorman(5)	6th	2,916
13/9/03	Widnes (a)	W0-40	t:Caine(3),Moran,Peden,Thorman g:Thorman(8)	5th	5,009
21/9/03	Huddersfield (h)	W22-12	t:Sykes,Moran,Thorman g:Thorman(5)	5th	3,286
26/9/03	St Helens (a) (EPO)	L24-6	t:King g:Thorman	N/A	7,188

● Played at Talbot Athletic Ground, Port Talbot

	D.O.B.	APP ALL	SL	TRIES ALL	SL	GOALS ALL	SL	FG ALL	SL	PTS ALL	SL
Russell Bawden	24/7/73	19(12)	19(10)	1	1	0	0	0	0	4	4
Austin Buchanan	22/5/84	3(1)	3(1)	2	2	0	0	0	0	8	8
Neil Budworth	10/3/82	27(3)	25(3)	1	1	0	0	0	0	4	4
Joel Caine	18/9/78	6	6	4	4	1	1	0	0	18	18
Mark Cox	22/1/78	1(3)	(3)	0	0	0	0	0	0	0	0
Jim Dymock	4/4/72	29	27	4	3	0	0	0	0	16	12
Jamie Fielden	9/5/78	(2)	(1)	0	0	0	0	0	0	0	0
Tommy Gallagher	10/9/83	1(9)	1(9)	1	1	0	0	0	0	4	4
Steve Hall	10/7/79	19(2)	17(2)	6	4	0	0	0	0	24	16
Andrew Hamilton	17/10/72	(15)	(13)	0	0	0	0	0	0	0	0
Tom Haughey	30/1/82	4(2)	2(2)	0	0	0	0	0	0	0	0
Rob Jackson	4/9/81	14(5)	12(5)	4	2	0	0	0	0	16	8
Nick Johnson	16/4/83	(3)	(1)	0	0	0	0	0	0	0	0
Damien Kennedy	2/6/83	5(11)	5(11)	1	1	0	0	0	0	4	4
Andrew King	3/7/73	23(1)	23(1)	15	15	0	0	0	0	60	60
Karl Long	18/11/80	(1)	(1)	0	0	0	0	0	0	0	0
Richard Marshall	9/10/75	10(8)	8(8)	0	0	0	0	0	0	0	0
Tony Martin	10/7/78	26	24	14	13	36	29	0	0	128	110
Joe Mbu	6/11/83	4(4)	4(4)	0	0	0	0	0	0	0	0
Dave McConnell	25/3/81	(4)	(4)	0	0	0	0	0	0	0	0
Dennis Moran	22/1/77	25(2)	25(2)	24	24	0	0	0	0	96	96
Jason Netherton	5/10/82	3	3	0	0	0	0	0	0	0	0
Bill Peden	10/2/70	22(3)	21(3)	8	7	0	0	0	0	32	28
Dominic Peters	11/12/78	3	2	2	1	0	0	0	0	8	4
Rob Purdham	14/4/80	19(8)	17(8)	1	1	0	0	0	0	4	4
Steele Retchless	16/6/71	30(1)	28(1)	2	2	0	0	0	0	8	8
Nigel Roy	15/3/74	30	28	9	8	0	0	0	0	36	32
Francis Stephenson	20/1/76	17(12)	16(12)	2	2	0	0	0	0	8	8
Paul Sykes	11/8/81	17	17	6	6	1	1	0	0	26	26
Chris Thorman	26/9/80	28(1)	26(1)	8	7	81	81	1	1	195	191
Mat Toshack	18/2/73	18(3)	18(2)	1	1	0	0	0	0	4	4
Steve Trindall	23/4/73	(7)	(7)	0	0	0	0	0	0	0	0

LEAGUE RECORD
P28-W14-D2-L12
(5th, SL/Elimination Play Off)
F643, A696, Diff-53
30 points.

CHALLENGE CUP
Round Five

ATTENDANCES
Best - v Leeds (SL - 5,666)
Worst - v Oldham (CC - 1,514)
Total (SL only) - 49,641
Average (SL only) - 3,546
(Down by 214 on 2002)

TOP TACKLES
Steele Retchless 843

TOP CARRIES
Steele Retchless 508

TOP METRES
Steele Retchless 3369

TOP BREAKS
Dennis Moran 49

TOP OFFLOADS
Russell Bawden 56

TOP BUSTS
Dennis Moran 91

KEY DATES - ST HELENS

14 February 2003 - Saints hammered 38-0 by Sydney City Roosters in the World Club Challenge

21 February 2003 - Saints bounce back from WCC defeat to crush Bradford 46-22 in Super League opener

4 March 2003 - Tommy Martyn joins Keiron Cunningham on the sidelines after breaking an arm

12 April 2003 - Saints lose to Leeds in heart-breaking circumstances after extra-time in Challenge Cup semi-final

18 April 2003 - Lose an unprecedented fourth game in a row, 24-22 at Wigan

21 April 2003 - End four-game losing streak with comprehensive 56-6 defeat of Warrington

9 May 2003 - Suffer shock 16-10 home defeat by Wakefield

29 May 2003 - Club docked two league points with immediate effect for breaching salary cap and announce that Tommy Martyn will leave at the end of the season

30 May 2003 - Sign Welsh international prop Keith Mason from Melbourne Storm

5 June 2003 - Announce that Paul Newlove will not be offered a new contract with the club

7 June 2003 - Shocked by an amazing Wigan comeback and lose 38-34 at home

9 June 2003 - Paul Newlove ruled out for ten weeks after dislocating his thumb

17 June 2003 - Confirm the signing of Canterbury Bulldogs centre Willie Talau on a three-year contract

27 June 2003 - Emerge from recent run of poor form to hammer Bradford 35-0 at Odsal

18 July 2003 - Second-half comeback gives Saints a 22-18 win over Huddersfield and their fifth consecutive win

25 July 2003 - Confirm the signing of Warrington prop Nick Fozzard for next season

5 August 2003 - Mark Edmondson signs new two-year contract

9 August 2003 - Make it eight wins in a row and go third after 28-18 home win over Hull

12 August 2003 - Withdraw from Middlesex Sevens rugby union tournament due to growing injury crisis

14 August 2003 - Prop Darren Britt announces his retirement after bad facial injury

9 September 2003 - Barry Ward announces his decision to retire at the end of the season

12 September 2003 – Saints blow a 20-point lead in the last 20 minutes to lose 30-20 away to Leeds Rhinos

16 September 2003 - Appoint former prop Apollo Perelini as strength and conditioning coach

26 September 2003 – Saints ease past London 24-6 in the play-offs at Knowsley Road

4 October 2003 – Saints are eliminated by bitter rivals Wigan, 40-24, at JJB Stadium

24 October 2003 – Dave Rotheram is announced as the new assistant coach to replace Huddersfield-bound Jon Sharp

26 October 2003 - Confirm capture of Lee Gilmour and Ricky Bibey

15 October 2002 - Paul Sculthorpe signs five-year deal, ending speculation about a possible move to rugby union

24 October 2002 - Stuart Jones signs from Wigan

31 October 2002 - Australian forward Peter Shiels announces his retirement

5 November 2002 - Former Australian international Darren Smith joins from the Bulldogs

12 November 2002 - Saints to stay at Knowsley Road after proposed move to new stadium at Ravenhead Park falls through

18 November 2002 - Keiron Cunningham out for six months after sustaining serious elbow injury playing for Great Britain

28 January 2003 - Saints beaten 39-41 by Sale Sharks in a Cross Code Challenge match, losing the first half of union 41-0 before scoring 39 points without reply in the League half

1 February 2003 - Sean Long signs a new five-year contract

Sean Long

ST HELENS

DATE	FIXTURE	RESULT	SCORERS	LGE	ATT
8/2/03	Union Treiziste Catalane (a) (CCR4)	W6-70	t:Long(4),Stewart(2),Hooper(2),Gardner,Gleeson,Smith,Stankevitch,Albert g:Long(9)	N/A	2,700
14/2/03	Sydney Roosters (WCC) ●	L0-38	No Scorers	N/A	19,807
21/2/03	Bradford (h)	W46-22	t:Kirkpatrick(2),Sculthorpe(2),Ward,Hooper,Gardner,Higham g:Long(7)	1st	12,217
28/2/03	Batley (h) (CCR5)	W38-12	t:Jonkers(2),Martyn,Ward,Maden,Edmondson,Kirkpatrick g:Long(4),Martyn	N/A	5,002
8/3/03	Widnes (a)	W4-22	t:Gardner(2),Long,Albert g:Long(3)	1st	7,518
16/3/03	Salford (a) (CCQF)	W6-54	t:Sculthorpe(2),Smith(2),Newlove,Stewart,Albert,Long,Britt,Gardner g:Long(7)	N/A	5,717
21/3/03	Castleford (h)	W54-12	t:Long(3),Newlove(2),Albert,Jonkers,Higham,Jones g:Long(9)	1st	10,292
30/3/03	Huddersfield (a)	L36-22	t:Albert,Smith,Jones,Long g:Long(2),Sculthorpe	2nd	5,835
5/4/03	Leeds (h)	L16-24	t:Smith,Sculthorpe,Gleeson g:Long,Sculthorpe	4th	10,785
12/4/03	Leeds (CCSF) ●●	L33-26 (aet)	t:Smith(2),Newlove,Sculthorpe g:Sculthorpe(5)	N/A	19,118
18/4/03	Wigan (h)	L24-22	t:Albert(2),Higham,Hooper g:Sculthorpe(3)	4th	15,607
21/4/03	Warrington (h)	W56-6	t:Hooper(2),Gleeson(2),Sculthorpe,Higham,Newlove,Smith,Gardner,Martyn g:Sculthorpe(8)	4th	8,963
2/5/03	Halifax (a)	W0-38	t:Stewart(3),Martyn,Long,Stankevitch,Sculthorpe g:Sculthorpe(5)	4th	3,372
9/5/03	Wakefield (h)	L10-16	t:Gleeson,Albert g:Sculthorpe	4th	8,569
16/5/03	London (h)	W62-16	t:Cunningham(3),Higham(3),Sculthorpe,Smith,Wilkin,Bennett,Gleeson g:Sculthorpe(7),Long(2)	4th	7,602
26/5/03	Hull (a)	L30-6	t:Joynt g:Sculthorpe	6th	12,490
1/6/03	Warrington (a)	D30-30	t:Sculthorpe(2),Bennett,Gardner,Long,Newlove g:Sculthorpe(3)	6th	8,590
6/6/03	Wigan (h)	L34-38	t:Smith(2),Gleeson,Wellens,Ward,Gardner g:Sculthorpe(5)	7th	12,827
13/6/03	Leeds (a)	L20-14	t:Cunningham(2),Wellens g:Long	8th	14,073
20/6/03	Halifax (h)	W58-2	t:Sculthorpe(4),Britt,Albert,Wellens,Long,Gleeson,Higham g:Long(9)	7th	7,891
27/6/03	Bradford (a)	W0-35	t:Higham(2),Albert,Joynt,Sculthorpe,Hooper g:Long(5) fg:Long	6th	11,127
4/7/03	Widnes (h)	W32-18	t:Hooper,Smith,Gardner,Gleeson,Cunningham g:Long(5),Wellens	5th	10,028
11/7/03	Castleford (a)	W32-46	t:Higham(2),Wellens(2),Gleeson(2),Albert,Long g:Long(7)	5th	6,320
18/7/03	Huddersfield (h)	W22-18	t:Albert(2),Cunningham,Wellens g:Long(3)	5th	9,288
27/7/03	Wakefield (a)	W15-36	t:Long(2),Albert(2),Stankevitch,Wellens g:Long(6)	4th	4,210
3/8/03	London (a)	W18-30	t:Higham,Wellens,Albert,Gardner,Stankevitch g:Long(5)	4th	4,214
9/8/03	Hull (h)	W28-18	t:Wilkin(2),Stankevitch,Wellens g:Long(6)	4th	8,019
15/8/03	Castleford (h)	W26-10	t:Gardner(2),Stankevitch,Newlove g:Long(5)	4th	8,041
24/8/03	Hull (a)	L42-18	t:Higham,Stewart,Cunningham g:Long(3)	4th	11,212
31/8/03	Widnes (a)	W4-40	t:Albert(2),Cunningham,Wellens,Mason,Higham,Smith g:Long(6)	4th	9,457
5/9/03	Wigan (h)	L4-28	t:Smith	4th	14,508
12/9/03	Leeds (a)	L30-20	t:Smith,Cunningham,Stewart g:Long(4)	4th	15,273
19/9/03	Bradford (h)	L18-22	t:Hooper,Albert,Smith g:Long(3)	4th	8,432
26/9/03	London (h) (EPO)	W24-6	t:Long(2),Talau,Smith g:Long(4)	N/A	7,188
3/10/03	Wigan (a) (ESF)	L40-24	t:Smith(2),Hooper,Cunningham,Newlove g:Long(2)	N/A	21,790

● Played at The Reebok Stadium, Bolton
●● Played at McAlpine Stadium, Huddersfield

		APP		TRIES		GOALS		FG		PTS	
	D.O.B.	ALL	SL	ALL	SL	ALL	SL	ALL	SL	ALL	SL
Darren Albert	28/2/76	28	24	19	17	0	0	0	0	76	68
Mike Bennett	9/5/80	17(10)	17(6)	2	2	0	0	0	0	8	8
Darren Britt	9/10/69	24	20	2	1	0	0	0	0	8	4
Keiron Cunningham	28/10/76	21(2)	21(2)	11	11	0	0	0	0	44	44
Mark Edmondson	3/11/79	7(15)	6(11)	1	0	0	0	0	0	4	0
Ade Gardner	24/6/83	24(6)	21(5)	12	10	0	0	0	0	48	40
Martin Gleeson	28/5/80	24	21	11	10	0	0	0	0	44	40
James Graham	10/9/85	(1)	(1)	0	0	0	0	0	0	0	0
Ian Hardman	8/2/84	(1)	(1)	0	0	0	0	0	0	0	0
Mick Higham	18/9/80	19(14)	15(13)	15	15	0	0	0	0	60	60
John Hill	10/10/81	(1)	(1)	0	0	0	0	0	0	0	0
Jason Hooper	14/10/77	23(5)	20(4)	10	8	0	0	0	0	40	32
Stuart Jones	7/12/81	(19)	(18)	2	2	0	0	0	0	8	8
Tim Jonkers	3/7/81	15(15)	11(14)	3	1	0	0	0	0	12	4
Chris Joynt	7/12/71	19(6)	15(5)	2	2	0	0	0	0	8	8
John Kirkpatrick	3/1/79	2(4)	1(4)	3	2	0	0	0	0	12	8
Sean Long	24/9/76	33(2)	29(1)	18	13	118	98	1	1	309	249
Steve Maden	13/9/82	1	0	1	0	0	0	0	0	4	0
Tommy Martyn	4/6/71	5(1)	2(1)	3	2	1	0	0	0	14	8
Keith Mason	20/1/82	11(5)	11(5)	1	1	0	0	0	0	4	4
Paul Newlove	10/8/71	24	19	8	6	0	0	0	0	32	24
Steve Rowlands	9/9/84	1(1)	(1)	0	0	0	0	0	0	0	0
Paul Sculthorpe	22/9/77	23	20	16	13	40	35	0	0	144	122
Darren Smith	8/12/68	30(1)	25(1)	19	14	0	0	0	0	76	56
John Stankevitch	6/11/79	23(4)	18(4)	6	5	0	0	0	0	24	20
Anthony Stewart	5/3/79	27(5)	23(5)	8	5	0	0	0	0	32	20
Willie Talau	25/1/76	6(1)	6(1)	1	1	0	0	0	0	4	4
Barry Ward	13/1/71	15(13)	14(9)	3	2	0	0	0	0	12	8
Paul Wellens	27/2/80	28(2)	26(2)	10	10	1	1	0	0	42	42
Jon Wilkin	11/1/83	5(5)	5(4)	3	3	0	0	0	0	12	12

LEAGUE RECORD
P28-W16-D1-L11
(4th, SL/Elimination Semi Finalists)
F845, A535, Diff+310
31 points. *(two points deducted for 2002 salary cap breach)*

CHALLENGE CUP
Semi Finalists

ATTENDANCES
Best - v Wigan (SL - 14,508)
Worst - v Batley (CC - 5,002)
Total (SL, inc play-offs) - 144,650
Average (SL, inc play-offs) - 9,643
(Down by 937 on 2002)

TOP TACKLES
Mick Higham 636

TOP CARRIES
Paul Wellens 445

TOP METRES
Paul Wellens 2781

TOP BREAKS
Darren Albert 33

TOP OFFLOADS
Keiron Cunningham 55

TOP BUSTS
Keiron Cunningham 82

27 September 2002 - Brad Davis to stay at the club until November 2003

10 October 2002 - Wildcats sign Castleford duo Jon Wells and Olivier Elima and re-sign Jamie Field and Troy Slattery

29 October 2002 - Australian centre Kris Tassell released

31 October 2002 - Wildcats sign Aussie duo Clinton O'Brien and Ben Jeffries. Threequarter Richard Newlove is snapped up from Featherstone Rovers and Ian Knott and David Wrench re-sign.

8 November 2002 - Prop Michael Korkidas signs from Sydney City Roosters

20 November 2002 - Centre or fullback Matt Seers signs from Wests Tigers on a one-year deal

3 December 2002 - Jamie Rooney signs from Featherstone Rovers

18 December 2002 - England A star Gareth Ellis extends his contract to 2005

14 January 2003 - Former Halifax star Colum Halpenny signs to become the Wildcats' tenth close season signing. Yorkshire Academy star Rob Spicer is promoted to the first team squad.

5 February 2003 - Wildcats confirm that food retailer Sainsbury's are to continue as their main club and shirt sponsor

2 March 2003 - A late try from Steve McCurrie sees Wakefield knocked out of the Challenge Cup fifth round by Widnes

29 March 2003 - Ex-Castleford star Brad Davis scores a crucial try to give the Wildcats their first win of the season, 20-14 at The Jungle

KEY DATES - WAKEFIELD TRINITY WILDCATS

31 March 2003 - Australian prop Clinton O'Brien retires

9 May 2003 - Record one of the biggest shocks of the Super League era with a stunning 16-10 win at St Helens

16 May 2003 - Jamie Rooney stars as Wildcats win battle of the bottom clubs, beating Halifax 22-18

8 June 2003 - Get season back on track, scoring 22 unanswered second-half points in 32-12 win over Warrington

11 June 2003 - Sign former London Broncos junior Darrell Griffin on an 18-month full-time deal

15 July 2003 - Young French forward Olivier Elima signs two-year contract extension to stay until the end of 2005

17 August 2003 - Jamie Rooney scores 24 points but Wildcats still lose 30-28 to Widnes

18 August 2003 - Sign trio David Wrench, Robert Spicer and youngster Mark Field on extended contracts

25 August 2003 - French international Sylvain Houles joins on a week's trial

27 August 2003 - Wakefield confirm that player-coach Adrian Vowles has left the club

28 August 2003 - Both Waisale Sovatabua and Matt Seers leave the club, though Frenchman Sylvain Houles is signed permanently

30 August 2003 - Wakefield dent Hull's play-off aspirations with a stunning 35-28 win at Belle Vue

8 September 2003 - Confirm the signing of Parramatta Eels and Samoan international forward David Solomona

14 September 2003 - Wildcats heap further misery on Halifax with a thumping 68-6 win, Jamie Rooney and Colum Halpenny both scoring hat-tricks

22 September 2003 – Coach Shane McNally signs a new two-year contract to stay with the Wildcats until the end of 2005

26 September 2003 - Announce the capture of loose forward Sid Domic from Warrington

17 October 2003 - Aussie threequarter Jason Demetriou signs from Widnes

3 November 2003 - Confirm the departure of Ian Knott, Martyn Holland, Matt Wray and Richard Newlove

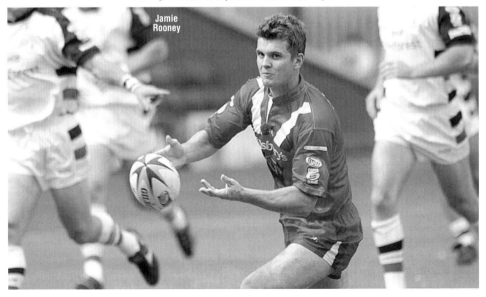

Jamie Rooney

WAKEFIELD T WILDCATS

DATE	FIXTURE	RESULT	SCORERS	LGE	ATT
8/2/03	Castleford (h) (CCR4)	W20-18	t:Ellis,Jeffries,Sovatabua g:Knott(4)	N/A	4,125
23/2/03	Hull (h)	L14-28	t:Jeffries,Handforth g:Knott(3)	10th	5,645
2/3/03	Widnes (h) (CCR5)	L12-22	t:Ellis g:Knott(4)	N/A	2,625
9/3/03	Bradford (a)	L22-10	t:Vowles,Ellis g:Jeffries	11th	20,283
23/3/03	Wigan (h)	L29-34	t:Newlove,Wells,Davis,Holland g:Knott(6) fg:Davis	10th	4,496
29/3/03	Castleford (a)	W14-20	t:Ellis,Seers,Davis g:Knott(4)	10th	6,883
6/4/03	Huddersfield (h)	L10-14	t:Ellis g:Knott(3)	10th	4,109
18/4/03	Warrington (a)	L35-20	t:Seers,Korkidas,Vowles,Knott g:Knott(2)	11th	6,323
22/4/03	Widnes (h)	L6-26	t:J Field g:Rooney	11th	3,411
2/5/03	Leeds (a)	L13-12	t:Sovatabua g:Rooney(4)	11th	10,740
9/5/03	St Helens (a)	W10-16	t:Newlove,Sovatabua g:Rooney(3) fg:Rooney(2)	11th	8,569
16/5/03	Halifax (h)	W22-18	t:Davis(2),Newlove g:Rooney(5)	8th	2,806
25/5/03	London (h)	L12-36	t:Knott g:Rooney(4)	10th	3,305
31/5/03	Widnes (a)	L34-6	t:Jeffries g:Knott	10th	5,179
8/6/03	Warrington (h)	W32-12	t:Davis(2),Halpenny,March,Vowles,Jeffries g:Davis(4)	10th	3,612
15/6/03	Huddersfield (a)	L26-4	t:Newlove	11th	3,989
20/6/03	Leeds (h)	L12-48	t:Halpenny,March g:Rooney(2)	11th	6,678
26/6/03	Hull (a)	L44-4	t:J Field	11th	9,575
6/7/03	Bradford (h)	L18-30	t:Jeffries,Halpenny,Rooney g:Rooney(3)	11th	4,658
11/7/03	Wigan (a)	L38-12	t:Halpenny,March g:Rooney(2)	11th	8,073
19/7/03	Castleford (h)	L4-32	g:Rooney(2)	11th	4,094
27/7/03	St Helens (h)	L15-36	t:Jeffries,Rooney g:Rooney(3) fg:Rooney	11th	4,210
1/8/03	Halifax (a)	W18-30	t:Rooney,Jeffries,Newlove,Knott g:Rooney(7)	11th	2,274
10/8/03	London (h)	D26-26	t:Newlove(2),Rooney,Korkidas g:Rooney(5)	11th	2,415
17/8/03	Widnes (a)	L30-28	t:Rooney(3),M Field g:Rooney(6)	11th	5,697
24/8/03	Huddersfield (a)	L26-14	t:Jeffries,Hood g:Handforth(3)	11th	3,621
30/8/03	Hull (h)	W35-28	t:Korkidas,Wrench,March,Houles,Wray g:Rooney(7) fg:Rooney	11th	3,689
7/9/03	London (a)	L38-14	t:Jeffries,Wray,March g:Rooney	11th	2,916
14/9/03	Halifax (h)	W68-6	t:Rooney(3),Halpenny(3),Griffin,Wrench,March,Korkidas,Newlove, Knott,Snitch g:Rooney(7),Davis	11th	3,112
21/9/03	Warrington (a)	L52-12	t:Spicer,Korkidas g:Rooney(2)	11th	9,261

		APP		TRIES		GOALS		FG		PTS	
	D.O.B.	ALL	SL	ALL	SL	ALL	SL	ALL	SL	ALL	SL
Matthew Blake	17/3/83	(3)	(3)	0	0	0	0	0	0	0	0
Brad Davis	13/3/68	18(6)	16(6)	6	6	5	5	1	1	35	35
Olivier Elima	19/5/83	1(6)	1(5)	0	0	0	0	0	0	0	0
Gareth Ellis	3/5/81	29	27	5	3	0	0	0	0	20	12
Jamie Field	12/12/76	24(2)	24(2)	2	2	0	0	0	0	8	8
Mark Field	21/3/84	(3)	(3)	1	1	0	0	0	0	4	4
Darrell Griffin	19/6/81	13(4)	13(4)	1	1	0	0	0	0	4	4
Colum Halpenny	25/4/79	30	28	7	7	0	0	0	0	28	28
Paul Handforth	6/10/81	7(13)	7(11)	1	1	3	3	0	0	10	10
Martyn Holland	21/3/77	17(2)	15(2)	1	1	0	0	0	0	4	4
Dallas Hood	11/12/77	19(2)	17(2)	1	1	0	0	0	0	4	4
Sylvain Houles	3/8/81	4	4	1	1	0	0	0	0	4	4
Ben Jeffries	4/9/80	21(6)	19(6)	9	8	1	1	0	0	38	34
Darren Jordan	18/3/84	(1)	(1)	0	0	0	0	0	0	0	0
Ian Knott	2/10/76	18(4)	16(4)	4	4	27	19	0	0	70	54
Michael Korkidas	12/1/81	24(3)	22(3)	5	5	0	0	0	0	20	20
David March	25/7/79	28(1)	26(1)	6	6	0	0	0	0	24	24
Richard Newlove	18/7/78	18(5)	17(5)	8	8	0	0	0	0	32	32
Clinton O'Brien	16/1/74	1(3)	(2)	0	0	0	0	0	0	0	0
Jamie Rooney	17/3/80	16(2)	16(2)	10	10	64	64	4	4	172	172
Matt Seers	28/6/74	12(1)	11(1)	2	2	0	0	0	0	8	8
Troy Slattery	6/8/73	12(4)	11(3)	0	0	0	0	0	0	0	0
Steve Snitch	22/2/83	4(18)	4(18)	1	1	0	0	0	0	4	4
Waisale Sovatabua	26/6/73	6(4)	6(3)	3	2	0	0	0	0	12	8
Robert Spicer	22/9/84	5(6)	5(6)	1	1	0	0	0	0	4	4
Adrian Vowles	30/5/71	20(2)	18(2)	3	3	0	0	0	0	12	12
Jon Wells	23/9/78	24(1)	22(1)	1	1	0	0	0	0	4	4
Matthew Wray	15/5/84	9(2)	9(2)	2	2	0	0	0	0	8	8
David Wrench	3/1/79	10(16)	10(14)	2	2	0	0	0	0	8	8

LEAGUE RECORD
P28-W7-D1-L20
(11th, SL)
F505, A774, Diff-269
15 points.

CHALLENGE CUP
Round Five

ATTENDANCES
Best - v Leeds (SL - 6,678)
Worst - v London (SL - 2,415)
Total (SL only) - 56,240
Average (SL only) - 4,017
(Up by 127 on 2002)

TOP TACKLES
David March 770

TOP CARRIES
Michael Korkidas 393

TOP METRES
Michael Korkidas 3063

TOP BREAKS
Gareth Ellis 22

TOP OFFLOADS
Jamie Field 75

TOP BUSTS
Gareth Ellis 73

5 September 2002 - Wolves sign former player Warren Stevens from Whitehaven

26 September 2002 - One-year option taken up on his contract by utility back Graham Appo

27 September 2002 - Complete signing of ex-player Mike Wainwright from Salford

1 October 2002 - Six players released - Tommy O'Reilly, Jon Hill, Dave Alstead, Leon Felton, Steve Maden and Craig Johnson

3 October 2002 - South Sydney centre or winger Brent Grose signed on one-year contract

31 October 2002 - Wolves re-sign former player Ian Sibbit from NRL side Melbourne Storm

25 November 2002 - Hooker Mark Gleeson re-signs on a one-year contract

5 December 2002 - Leroy Rivett is released less than 12 months into his two-year contract

6 December 2002 - Wolves given the go-ahead to build new 14,000-capacity stadium in time for the 2004 season

KEY DATES - WARRINGTON WOLVES

23 January 2003 - Dale Laughton and Dean Busby both released after long-term injury problems

8 February 2003 - Warrington crash out of the Challenge Cup against Bradford

28 February 2003 - Hooker Mark Gleeson extends his contract with the club to 2005

22 March 2003 - Move into the top three after a 29-8 win at London backs up their opening day victory over Huddersfield

18 April 2003 - First home win of the season - 35-20 over Wakefield

9 May 2003 - Graham Appo scores a hat-trick in a comfortable 38-8 win over Halifax

1 June 2003 - Late Lee Penny try gives Wolves a share of the spoils in a 30-all draw with St Helens

15 June 2003 - Suffer heartbreak as last-gasp try by Bradford earns them a 24-20 win at Wilderspool

22 June 2003 - Win derby clash with Widnes 32-28 thanks to a late Graham Appo try

28 June 2003 - Play-off push continues with 32-28 win over Huddersfield

13 July 2003 - Move into top six with sensational 50-8 win over London

15 July 2003 - Lee Briers out for at least two months after breaking his wrist against London

7 August 2003 - Sign St George Illawarra Dragons prop Chris Leikvoll on a two-year deal from next season

14 August 2003 - Confirm the signing of Daryl Cardiss from Halifax until the end of the 2004

23 August 2003 - Make it three wins out of three against Widnes, winning derby clash 30-16 at Wilderspool

7 September 2003 – Survive a shock 16-18 half-time deficit to finish off relegated Halifax 40-18

13 September 2003 – Daryl Cardiss inspires Warrington to a 25-12 win over Huddersfield in a heated match at the McAlpine

21 September 2003 – The Wolves say goodbye to Wilderspool after 108 years in style by thrashing Wakefield 52-12 and securing a play-off place

24 September 2003 – Graham Appo named in the Super League Dream Team

27 September 2003 – The Wolves bow out of their first ever play-offs, 25-12 to Wigan, after leading 6-12 at half-time

2 October 2003 - Announce the re-signings of Graham Appo, Brent Grose, Nat Wood, Mark Gleeson, Warren Stevens, Paul Noone, Dean Gaskell, Darren Burns and Gary Hulse, and release Lee Penny and Rob Smyth

24 October 2003 – Warrington sign Great Britain international Mike Forshaw from Bradford on a one-year contract

WARRINGTON WOLVES

DATE	FIXTURE	RESULT	SCORERS	LGE	ATT
8/2/03	Bradford (h) (CCR4)	L12-38	t:Burns g:Briers(4)	N/A	5,869
22/2/03	Huddersfield (a)	W8-20	t:Grose(2) g:Briers(6)	4th	4,104
9/3/03	Leeds (h)	L22-32	t:Appo(2),Domic g:Briers(5)	6th	8,705
22/3/03	London (a)	W8-29	t:Domic,Grose,Westwood,Sibbit,Appo g:Briers(4) fg:Briers	5th	3,105
30/3/03	Hull (h)	L14-27	t:Clarke g:Appo(5)	5th	6,784
6/4/03	Bradford (a)	L32-8	t:Hilton,Domic	7th	15,157
18/4/03	Wakefield (h)	W35-20	t:Sibbit,Penny,N Wood,Smyth,Clarke,Fozzard g:Briers(4),Smyth fg:Briers	5th	6,323
21/4/03	St Helens (a)	L56-6	t:Penny g:Smyth	9th	8,963
3/5/03	Widnes (h)	W34-6	t:Grose(2),Smyth,Guisset,Appo,Sibbit,P Wood g:Briers(3)	6th	7,264
9/5/03	Halifax (a)	W8-38	t:Appo(3),N Wood,P Wood,Domic,Wainwright g:Briers(5)	5th	3,174
16/5/03	Wigan (a)	L21-20	t:Domic,Grose,Briers g:Briers(3) fg:Briers(2)	7th	11,224
24/5/03	Castleford (h)	L16-32	t:Burns,Briers,Smyth g:Briers(2)	7th	6,090
1/6/03	St Helens (h)	D30-30	t:Grose(2),Clarke,Guisset,Penny g:Briers(5)	7th	8,590
8/6/03	Wakefield (a)	L32-12	t:Smyth,Grose g:Briers(2)	8th	3,612
15/6/03	Bradford (h)	L20-24	t:Smyth,Appo,Grose g:Appo(4)	9th	7,507
22/6/03	Widnes (a)	W28-32	t:Appo(2),Smyth,N Wood,Grose,Hulse g:Briers(4)	8th	8,531
28/6/03	Huddersfield (h)	W32-28	t:Smyth(2),Appo,Briers,Sibbit,Hilton g:Briers(4)	8th	5,689
6/7/03	Leeds (a)	L30-20	t:Briers(2),P Wood g:Briers(4)	8th	13,498
13/7/03	London (h)	W50-8	t:Burns(2),Briers(2),Smyth(2),Guisset,Sibbit g:Briers(9)	6th	5,562
20/7/03	Hull (a)	L38-14	t:Appo,Grose g:Appo(2),Smyth	7th	9,835
27/7/03	Halifax (h)	W66-6	t:Appo(4),Grose(2),Burns(2),Clarke,Smyth,N Wood,Hulse g:Appo(9)	6th	5,291
3/8/03	Wigan (h)	L16-18	t:N Wood,Appo g:Appo(4)	7th	8,705
10/8/03	Castleford (a)	W16-29	t:P Wood,N Wood,Domic,Grose g:Appo(6) fg:N Wood	6th	5,940
17/8/03	London (a)	L19-12	t:N Wood,Appo g:Appo(2)	8th	2,916
23/8/03	Widnes (h)	W30-16	t:P Wood,Cardiss,Domic,Appo,N Wood,Westwood g:Appo(2),Cardiss	7th	6,902
29/8/03	Leeds (a)	L34-26	t:Westwood(2),Domic,Appo,N Wood g:Appo(3)	7th	10,750
7/9/03	Halifax (h)	W40-18	t:Westwood(2),Burns(2),Penny,Gaskell,Gleeson g:Appo(6)	7th	5,761
12/9/03	Huddersfield (a)	W12-25	t:Cardiss,P Wood g:Appo(7),Cardiss fg:N Wood	7th	4,443
21/9/03	Wakefield (h)	W52-12	t:Appo(3),Domic(2),Westwood(2),Noone g:Appo(10)	6th	9,261
27/9/03	Wigan (a) (EPO)	L25-12	t:Burns,N Wood g:Appo(2)	N/A	14,154
26/10/03	New Zealand 'A' (h)	W28-26	t:Govin,Warburton,Owen,Grundy,Durbin g:Owen(4)	N/A	3,409

		APP		TRIES		GOALS		FG		PTS	
	D.O.B.	ALL	SL	ALL	SL	ALL	SL	ALL	SL	ALL	SL
Graham Appo	11/7/74	29(1)	29	23	23	62	62	0	0	216	216
Phil Berry	17/12/85	1	0	0	0	0	0	0	0	0	0
Lee Briers	14/6/78	15	14	7	7	64	60	4	4	160	152
Darren Burns	17/5/74	27(2)	25(2)	9	8	0	0	0	0	36	32
Daryl Cardiss	13/7/77	7	7	2	2	2	2	0	0	12	12
Jon Clarke	14/6/78	29	28	4	4	0	0	0	0	16	16
Kevin Crouthers	3/1/76	2	2	0	0	0	0	0	0	0	0
Sid Domic	8/2/75	21(3)	20(3)	10	10	0	0	0	0	40	40
Jamie Durbin	7/9/84	1(1)	(1)	1	0	0	0	0	0	4	0
Nick Fozzard	22/7/77	26(1)	25(1)	1	1	0	0	0	0	4	4
Dean Gaskell	12/4/83	20	20	1	1	0	0	0	0	4	4
Mark Gleeson	16/6/82	2(18)	2(17)	1	1	0	0	0	0	4	4
Mike Govin	5/11/84	1	0	1	0	0	0	0	0	4	0
Brent Grose	11/9/79	30	29	15	15	0	0	0	0	60	60
Tommy Grundy	17/4/85	(1)	0	1	0	0	0	0	0	4	0
Jerome Guisset	29/8/78	8(18)	8(18)	3	3	0	0	0	0	12	12
Danny Heaton	19/4/81	1	0	0	0	0	0	0	0	0	0
Mark Hilton	31/3/75	26(1)	25(1)	2	2	0	0	0	0	8	8
Gary Hulse	20/1/81	3(16)	2(16)	2	2	0	0	0	0	8	8
Paul Noone	22/4/81	13(14)	12(14)	1	1	0	0	0	0	4	4
Nick Owen	16/10/84	1	0	1	0	4	0	0	0	12	0
Dave Pennington	26/11/84	(1)	0	0	0	0	0	0	0	0	0
Lee Penny	24/9/74	13	12	4	4	0	0	0	0	16	16
Dave Saxton	26/5/86	(1)	0	0	0	0	0	0	0	0	0
Ian Sibbit	15/10/80	21(1)	20(1)	5	5	0	0	0	0	20	20
Rob Smyth	22/2/77	18	17	11	11	3	3	0	0	50	50
Warren Stevens	4/10/78	2(23)	1(22)	0	0	0	0	0	0	0	0
Matt Sturm	13/12/72	1(5)	1(5)	0	0	0	0	0	0	0	0
Richard Varkulis	21/5/82	1	0	0	0	0	0	0	0	0	0
Mike Wainwright	25/2/75	21(3)	20(3)	1	1	0	0	0	0	4	4
Steve Warburton	9/3/82	1	0	1	0	0	0	0	0	4	0
Ben Westwood	25/7/81	18(1)	16(1)	8	8	0	0	0	0	32	32
Shane Williams	3/6/83	1	0	0	0	0	0	0	0	0	0
Matt Wilson	3/12/84	(1)	0	0	0	0	0	0	0	0	0
Nathan Wood	24/1/72	29	28	10	10	0	0	2	2	42	42
Paul Wood	10/10/81	14(12)	14(11)	6	6	0	0	0	0	24	24

LEAGUE RECORD
P28-W14-D1-L13
(6th, SL/Elimination Play Off)
F748, A619, Diff+129
29 points.

CHALLENGE CUP
Round Four

ATTENDANCES
Best - v Wakefield (SL - 9,261)
Worst - v New Zealand 'A' (3,409)
Total (SL only) - 98,434
Average (SL only) - 7,031
(Up by 878 on 2002)

TOP TACKLES
Jon Clarke 584

TOP CARRIES
Darren Burns 389

TOP METRES
Darren Burns 2782

TOP BREAKS
Graham Appo 40

TOP OFFLOADS
Nathan Wood 54

TOP BUSTS
Graham Appo 99

223

KEY DATES - WIDNES VIKINGS

7 January 2003 - Forward Gareth Haggerty released

21 January 2003 - Andy Isherwood suffers a serious back injury during training with the team in South Africa

27 January 2003 - Vikings shocked as Australian stand-off Craig Weston resigns from his contract to return home

20 February 2003 - Australian second-row forward Simon Finnigan signs

15 March 2003 - Widnes go down 38-28 to Bradford in the Challenge Cup quarter-final, despite leading 22-12 at half-time

3 September 2002 - Sign Deon Bird from Wakefield

3 October 2002 - Five players released - Barry Eaton, Sean Richardson, Damian Munro, Mike Briggs and Blake Cannavo

11 November 2002 - Vikings sign second row forward Andrew Isherwood from Leigh Centurions and take Australian Simon Finnigan on a trial from Penrith Panthers

12 November 2002 - Vikings agree £200,000 sponsorship deal with Finnforest

28 November 2002 - Ryan Sheridan joins the club after being released by Leeds Rhinos

9 December 2002- Andy Hay becomes second released Leeds Rhinos player to join the Vikings

23 March 2003 - Vikings slump to the bottom of the table after defeat by Hull at the KC Stadium

3 April 2003 - Sign centre Marvin Golden from National League One team Doncaster Dragons

5 April 2003 - Complete the signing of stand-off Julian O'Neill from Wigan

6 April 2003 - New signing Julian O'Neill kicks five goals on his debut in a 44-16 win at home against Halifax

3 May 2003 - Three-game winning run halted in 34-6 defeat to Warrington

25 May 2003 - Join the top-six race after 42-30 victory in see-saw clash with Huddersfield Giants

31 May 2003 - Move level on points with sixth-placed Saints after easy 34-6 win over Wakefield

14 June 2003 - Move into the top six with 48-20 win at Halifax

28 June 2003 - Outstanding performance sees Vikings claim 29-14 win over league leaders Leeds Rhinos

13 July 2003 - A superb team performance sees them beat Hull 46-10

18 July 2003 - Deon Bird agrees one-year extension to his contract

19 July 2003 - Adam Hughes signs new two-year contract and Stuart Spruce and Chris Giles sign one-year deals

1 August 2003 - Move into top six with tough 27-16 win over Castleford

4 August 2003 - Sign senior Academy star stand-off Stephen Myler on a two-year deal

12 August 2003 - Daniel Frame rejects Huddersfield to sign a new two year contract

2 September 2003 - Hooker Shane Millard and prop Julian O'Neill sign two-year contract extensions and utility player Paul Atcheson one year

4 September 2003 - Simon Finnigan agrees a two-year contract

7 September 2003 – Lose 25-12 away to Huddersfield

13 September 2003 – The Vikings are thumped 0-40 against London

21 September 2003 – The departing Phil Cantillon scores two tries in his last game for Widnes in the 20-48 defeat of Halifax

23 September 2003 – The Vikings announce the signing of Manly scrum-half Jason Ferris for the 2004 season

29 October 2003 - Jason Ferris stuns the Vikings by performing a U-turn and retiring

30 October 2003 - Halifax prop Andy Hobson signed on one-year deal

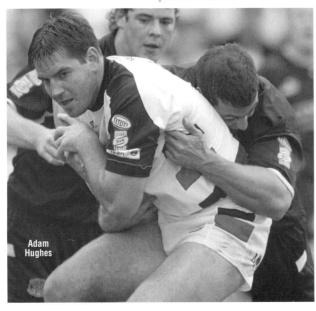

Adam Hughes

WIDNES VIKINGS

DATE	FIXTURE	RESULT	SCORERS	LGE	ATT
9/2/03	Dewsbury (h) (CCR4)	W48-6	t:Percival(2),Lawford,Hay,Hughes,Cantillon,Potter,Sheridan,Demetriou g:Hughes(6)	N/A	3,196
23/2/03	Leeds (a)	L32-12	t:Demetriou,Frame g:Hughes(2)	11th	13,013
2/3/03	Wakefield (a) (CCR5)	W12-22	t:Hughes(2),Lawford,McCurrie g:Hughes(3)	N/A	2,625
8/3/03	St Helens (h)	L4-22	t:Hughes	12th	7,518
15/3/03	Bradford (h) (CCQF)	L28-38	t:Demetriou,Spruce,Lawford,Hughes,Cantillon g:Hughes(3),Lawford	N/A	4,129
23/3/03	Hull (a)	L38-18	t:Spruce,Demetriou,Mills g:Hughes(3)	12th	8,743
30/3/03	Bradford (h)	L18-26	t:Potter,Millard,Giles,Finnigan g:Lawford	12th	6,420
6/4/03	Halifax (h)	W44-16	t:Giles(2),Lawford(2),Frame(2),Hay,Hughes g:O'Neill(A)(5),Lawford	11th	7,135
18/4/03	London (h)	W32-20	t:Atcheson(2),McCurrie,Hay,Millard g:O'Neill(A)(6)	9th	5,708
22/4/03	Wakefield (a)	W6-26	t:Lawford,Golden,O'Neill(A),Atcheson g:O'Neill(A)(4) fg:Lawford(2)	6th	3,411
3/5/03	Warrington (a)	L34-6	t:Hay g:O'Neill(A)	9th	7,264
10/5/03	Wigan (h)	L18-22	t:Hughes,Millard g:O'Neill(A)(5)	8th	6,307
18/5/03	Castleford (a)	L40-2	g:O'Neill(A)	9th	6,516
25/5/03	Huddersfield (h)	W42-30	t:Bird(3),Hughes(2),Frame,Sheridan g:O'Neill(A)(7)	8th	4,946
31/5/03	Wakefield (h)	W34-6	t:Frame,Giles,O'Neill(NZ),Devlin,Sheridan,Bird g:O'Neill(A)(3),Hughes(2)	8th	5,179
8/6/03	London (a) ●	L40-18	t:Millard(2),Cantillon g:O'Neill(A)(3)	9th	3,128
14/6/03	Halifax (a)	W20-48	t:Giles(2),Millard,Relf,Lawford,Frame,Demetriou,Hughes g:O'Neill(A)(7) fg:O'Neill(A),Lawford	7th	1,919
22/6/03	Warrington (h)	L28-32	t:Cantillon,Bird,Millard,Lawford g:O'Neill(A)(6)	9th	8,531
28/6/03	Leeds (h)	W29-14	t:Devlin(2),O'Neill(NZ),Hughes,Spruce g:O'Neill(A)(4) fg:Lawford	9th	6,837
4/7/03	St Helens (a)	L32-18	t:Cantillon(2),Devlin g:O'Neill(A)(3)	9th	10,028
13/7/03	Hull (h)	W46-10	t:Hughes(2),Devlin,Millard,Spruce,Cantillon,O'Neill(A),Demetriou g:O'Neill(A)(7)	9th	6,707
20/7/03	Bradford (a)	L40-8	t:Hughes g:O'Neill(A)(2)	9th	12,116
26/7/03	Wigan (a)	W18-22	t:Bird,Hay,Millard,Potter g:O'Neill(A)(3)	9th	8,600
1/8/03	Castleford (h)	W27-16	t:Devlin(2),Frame,Hughes,Potter g:O'Neill(A)(3) fg:O'Neill(A)	6th	5,698
10/8/03	Huddersfield (a)	D30-30	t:Devlin(2),Cantillon(2),Demetriou g:O'Neill(A)(5)	7th	4,140
17/8/03	Wakefield (h)	W30-28	t:O'Neill(A)(2),Farrell(2),Hay g:O'Neill(A)(5)	6th	5,697
23/8/03	Warrington (a)	L30-16	t:Relf,Spruce g:O'Neill(A)(4)	8th	6,902
31/8/03	St Helens (h)	L4-40	t:Devlin	9th	9,457
7/9/03	Huddersfield (a)	L25-12	t:Hughes,Demetriou g:Myler(2)	10th	3,555
13/9/03	London (h)	L0-40	No Scorers	10th	5,009
21/9/03	Halifax (a)	W20-48	t:Myler(2),Cantillon(2),Spruce,Bird,O'Neill(A),Hughes,Millard g:Myler(4),Farrell,Demetriou	9th	2,088

● Played at Talbot Athletic Ground, Port Talbot

	D.O.B.	APP ALL	APP SL	TRIES ALL	TRIES SL	GOALS ALL	GOALS SL	FG ALL	FG SL	PTS ALL	PTS SL
Paul Alcock	12/11/82	1(3)	1(3)	0	0	0	0	0	0	0	0
Paul Atcheson	17/5/73	8(11)	8(9)	3	3	0	0	0	0	12	12
Deon Bird	27/1/76	21	18	7	7	0	0	0	0	28	28
Phil Cantillon	2/6/76	1(24)	1(21)	11	9	0	0	0	0	44	36
Jason Demetriou	13/1/76	26(1)	23(1)	8	6	1	1	0	0	34	26
Paul Devlin	19/2/81	20	19	10	10	0	0	0	0	40	40
Anthony Farrell	17/1/69	5(24)	5(21)	2	2	1	1	0	0	10	10
Simon Finnigan	8/12/81	8(11)	8(11)	1	1	0	0	0	0	4	4
Daniel Frame	7/6/75	31	28	7	7	0	0	0	0	28	28
Chris Giles	26/12/76	14	14	6	6	0	0	0	0	24	24
Marvin Golden	21/12/76	4	4	1	1	0	0	0	0	4	4
Andy Hay	5/11/73	28(1)	25(1)	6	5	0	0	0	0	24	20
Adam Hughes	1/10/77	30(1)	27(1)	17	13	19	7	0	0	106	66
Aled James	17/2/82	3	3	0	0	0	0	0	0	0	0
Dean Lawford	9/5/77	18(1)	15(1)	8	5	3	2	4	4	42	28
Steve McCurrie	1/6/73	19(6)	16(6)	2	1	0	0	0	0	8	4
Ryan McDonald	24/2/78	(3)	(2)	0	0	0	0	0	0	0	0
Shane Millard	30/7/75	31	28	10	10	0	0	0	0	40	40
David Mills	1/6/81	(22)	(20)	1	1	0	0	0	0	4	4
Stephen Myler	21/7/84	2(3)	2(3)	2	2	6	6	0	0	20	20
Julian O'Neill (A)	14/10/72	20(1)	20(1)	5	5	84	84	2	2	190	190
Julian O'Neill (NZ)	24/7/73	26(4)	23(4)	2	2	0	0	0	0	8	8
Chris Percival	25/12/79	5	3	2	2	0	0	0	0	8	0
Dan Potter	8/11/78	12(2)	11(1)	4	3	0	0	0	0	16	12
Robert Relf	29/1/71	31	28	2	2	0	0	0	0	8	8
John Robinson	18/12/83	1	1	0	0	0	0	0	0	0	0
Ryan Sheridan	24/5/75	16(3)	14(3)	3	2	0	0	0	0	12	8
Stuart Spruce	1/1/71	22(2)	19(2)	6	5	0	0	0	0	24	20

LEAGUE RECORD
P28-W12-D1-L15
(9th, SL)
F640, A727, Diff-87
25 points.

CHALLENGE CUP
Quarter Finalists

ATTENDANCES
Best - v St Helens (SL - 9,457)
Worst - v Dewsbury (CC - 3,196)
Total (SL only) - 91,149
Average (SL only) - 6,511
(Down by 73 on 2002)

TOP TACKLES
Shane Millard 856

TOP CARRIES
Shane Millard 488

TOP METRES
Shane Millard 3274

TOP BREAKS
Adam Hughes 31

TOP OFFLOADS
Daniel Frame 58

TOP BUSTS
Daniel Frame 70

KEY DATES - WIGAN WARRIORS

24 October 2002 - Warriors sign three of their young stars - Shaun Briscoe, Gareth Hock and David Allen - on full time contracts

2 January 2003 - Assistant coach John Kear leaves the club to join Hull FC. Wigan immediately appoint under-21s coach Mike Gregory as Stuart Raper's right hand man.

9 February 2003 - An 82-3 Challenge Cup victory over Halton Simms Cross is marred by tragedy, as two of their under-21 stars Billy-Joe Edwards and Craig Johnson are killed in a car crash that weekend

23 February 2003 - Andy Farrell suffers a knee injury in a 19-10 opening day Super League defeat at Castleford

16 March 2003 - Wigan ease into the Challenge Cup semi-finals with a 70-12 win over Swinton Lions

4 April 2003 - Warriors suffer a 20-4 defeat at Hull

13 April 2003 - Injuries take their toll as Wigan crash out of the Challenge Cup in the semi-finals, 36-22 to Bradford

18 April 2003 - A patched-up Warriors side fielding four Academy debutants defeat St Helens 24-22 at the JJB Stadium

24 April 2003 - Ease the injury situation by signing Cronulla Sharks loose forward Nick Graham on a six-month deal

6 May 2003 - Late try from Danny Sculthorpe earns the Warriors a 24-all draw at table-topping Leeds

13 May 2003 - Great Britain fullback Kris Radlinski ruled out for three months with recurring wrist injury

16 May 2003 - Andy Farrell scores a late field goal in his comeback game to give Warriors a 21-20 victory over Warrington

23 May 2003 - Warriors move up to fourth place in the table after 58-12 win over Halifax

29 May 2003 - Extend young star Kevin Brown's contract until the end of 2005

7 June 2003 - Luke Robinson scores a superb hat-trick as Wigan beat Saints 38-34 at Knowsley Road

17 June 2003 - Jamie Ainscough retires after failing to recover from a freak arm injury

19 June 2003 - New Zealand Test prop Quentin Pongia joins Warriors for rest of season

21 June 2003 - Andy Farrell inspires Wigan to a 35-22 win at Bradford

27 June 2003 - Good form continues as a 24-10 victory over Castleford takes Wigan third

6 July 2003 - Brett Dallas hat-trick not enough as the Warriors crash to 32-24 defeat at Huddersfield

14 July 2003 - Confirm the signing of Great Britain stand-off Danny Orr on a four-year deal from next season

19 July 2003 - Announce that coach Stuart Raper will leave at the end of the season

29 July 2003 - Assistant coach Mike Gregory takes charge with immediate effect as Stuart Raper leaves

15 August 2003 - Battle out second 24-all draw with Leeds at Headingley

28 August 2003 - Prop Quentin Pongia signs until the end of 2004

11 September 2003 - Grant early contract release to Nick Graham

21 September 2003 – Wigan finish off the weekly rounds with a 23-16 win at Castleford and third place

27 September 2003 – Wigan come back from a half-time deficit to defeat Warrington 25-12 in the play-offs

4 October 2003 – Eliminate bitter rivals St Helens with a 40-24 victory

10 October 2003 – Injury-time Danny Tickle field goal sends Wigan to Old Trafford after a nail-biting 23-22 victory at Leeds

11 October 2003 – Gareth Hock wins the Super League Young Player of the Year

14 October 2003 – Mike Gregory signs two-year contract as coach

18 October 2003 - Wigan miss out on the title with a 25-12 loss against Bradford in the Grand Final at Old Trafford

3 November 2003 - Brett Dallas signs one-year deal, but doubts hang over the career of Adrian Lam, who requires knee surgery

Gareth Hock

WIGAN WARRIORS

DATE	FIXTURE	RESULT	SCORERS	LGE	ATT
9/2/03	Halton Simms Cross (h) (CCR4)	W82-3	t:Radlinski(3),Newton(2),Farrell(2),O'Loughlin(2),Aspinwall,Hodgson, Ainscough,Bibey,Wild,Carney g:Farrell(11)	N/A	3,790
23/2/03	Castleford (a)	L19-10	g:O'Neill(4),Farrell	8th	8,462
2/3/03	Doncaster (a) (CCR5)	W10-50	t:Carney(3),Hock(2),Ainscough,Hodgson,O'Neill,Newton g:O'Neill(7)	N/A	3,653
7/3/03	Huddersfield (h)	W33-22	t:O'Loughlin,Dallas,Hodgson,Ainscough,Sculthorpe,Aspinwall g:O'Neill(4) fg:Lam	5th	8,187
16/3/03	Swinton (a) (CCQF) ●	W12-70	t:Hodgson(2),Dallas(2),Robinson,Hock,Johnson,Ainscough,Bibey, M Smith,Lam,Aspinwall,O'Loughlin g:O'Neill(7),Robinson(2)	N/A	5,114
23/3/03	Wakefield (a)	W29-34	t:Hodgson(2),Lam(2),O'Neill,Aspinwall g:O'Neill(3),Tickle(2)	6th	4,496
28/3/03	London (h)	L30-34	t:Tickle,Hodgson,Johnson,Hock,Carney g:Tickle(4),Robinson	6th	8,375
4/4/03	Hull (a)	L20-4	t:Hock	6th	11,536
13/4/03	Bradford (CCSF) ●●	L36-22	t:Newton,Sculthorpe,Carney g:Tickle(5)	N/A	15,359
18/4/03	St Helens (h)	W24-22	t:Newton(2),Tickle,Briscoe g:Tickle(4)	6th	15,607
2/5/03	Bradford (h)	L8-14	t:Ainscough g:Tickle(2)	7th	10,281
6/5/03	Leeds (a)	D24-24	t:Sculthorpe(2),Ainscough,Tickle g:Tickle(4)	7th	11,115
10/5/03	Widnes (a)	W18-22	t:Carney,Aspinwall,Ainscough,Newton g:Tickle(3)	6th	6,307
16/5/03	Warrington (h)	W21-20	t:Briscoe(2),Lam g:Farrell(4) fg:Farrell	6th	11,224
23/5/03	Halifax (h)	W58-12	t:Farrell(3),Brown(3),Hodgson,Newton,Johnson,Ainscough g:Farrell(9)	4th	7,393
30/5/03	Leeds (a)	L20-30	t:Briscoe(2),Aspinwall g:Farrell(4)	5th	11,386
6/6/03	St Helens (a)	W34-38	t:Robinson(3),Brown(2),Hodgson g:Farrell(7)	5th	12,827
13/6/03	Hull (h)	W28-14	t:Hodgson(2),Hock,Aspinwall g:Farrell(6)	3rd	11,278
21/6/03	Bradford (a)	W22-35	t:Graham(2),Farrell,Tickle g:Farrell(8) fg:Lam(3)	3rd	15,732
27/6/03	Castleford (h)	W24-10	t:Aspinwall,Hodgson,Johnson g:Farrell(6)	3rd	9,884
6/7/03	Huddersfield (a)	L32-24	t:Dallas(3),Hodgson g:Farrell(4)	4th	4,802
11/7/03	Wakefield (h)	W38-12	t:Dallas(2),Lam(2),Farrell,Cassidy,Briscoe g:Farrell(5)	3rd	8,073
18/7/03	London (a)	W12-28	t:Lam,Briscoe,Aspinwall,Hodgson g:Farrell(6)	3rd	3,984
26/7/03	Widnes (h)	L18-22	t:Hodgson,Robinson,Brown g:Farrell(3)	3rd	8,600
3/8/03	Warrington (a)	W16-18	t:Hock,Dallas,C Smith g:Farrell(3)	3rd	8,705
10/8/03	Halifax (h)	W40-0	t:Wild(2),Dallas,Farrell,Briscoe,C Smith,Sculthorpe g:Farrell(5),Tickle	3rd	7,409
15/8/03	Leeds (a)	D24-24	t:Tickle(2),Carney,Hock g:Farrell(3),Robinson	3rd	14,019
25/8/03	Bradford (h)	W26-12	t:Dallas,Radlinski,Aspinwall,Carney,Farrell g:Farrell(3)	3rd	14,714
31/8/03	Halifax (a)	W12-68	t:Dallas(3),Radlinski(2),Carney(2),Hock,Tickle,Hodgson,Robinson,Johnson g:Tickle(10)	3rd	2,543
5/9/03	St Helens (a)	W4-28	t:Carney(2),Hock,Johnson g:Tickle(3),Farrell(2),Robinson	3rd	14,508
12/9/03	Hull (h)	W28-6	t:Hodgson(2),Tickle,Hock g:Tickle(5),Robinson	3rd	11,115
21/9/03	Castleford (a)	W16-23	t:O'Connor,Dallas,Hodgson,Tickle g:Farrell(3) fg:Lam	3rd	7,886
27/9/03	Warrington (h) (EPO)	W25-12	t:Lam,Tickle,Dallas,C Smith g:Tickle(2),Farrell,Robinson fg:Robinson	N/A	14,154
3/10/03	St Helens (h) (ESF)	W40-24	t:Lam(2),Tickle,Cassidy,O'Loughlin,Carney,Radlinski g:Tickle(4),Lam,Robinson	N/A	21,790
10/10/03	Leeds (a) (FE)	W22-23	t:Carney(2),O'Loughlin(2) g:Farrell(3) fg:Tickle	N/A	17,264
18/10/03	Bradford (GF) ●●●	L25-12	t:Tickle,Radlinski g:Farrell(2)	N/A	65,537

● Played at JJB Stadium
●● Played at McAlpine Stadium, Huddersfield
●●● Played at Old Trafford, Manchester

	D.O.B.	APP		TRIES		GOALS		FG		PTS	
		ALL	SL	ALL	SL	ALL	SL	ALL	SL	ALL	SL
Jamie Ainscough	20/7/71	12	9	8	5	0	0	0	0	32	20
David Allen	15/9/85	(1)	(1)	0	0	0	0	0	0	0	0
Martin Aspinwall	21/10/81	29(5)	26(4)	10	8	0	0	0	0	40	32
Ricky Bibey	22/9/81	3(9)	2(7)	2	0	0	0	0	0	8	0
Shaun Briscoe	23/2/83	14(5)	13(5)	8	8	0	0	0	0	32	32
Kevin Brown	2/10/84	4(8)	4(8)	6	6	0	0	0	0	24	24
Brian Carney	23/7/76	31	28	16	11	0	0	0	0	64	44
Mick Cassidy	8/7/73	23(2)	21(2)	2	2	0	0	0	0	8	8
Brett Dallas	18/10/74	21	19	16	14	0	0	0	0	64	56
Andy Farrell	30/5/75	24	23	9	7	99	88	1	1	235	205
Nick Graham	1/10/74	13(1)	13(1)	2	2	0	0	0	0	8	8
Gareth Hock	5/9/83	9(23)	7(22)	11	8	0	0	0	0	44	32
David Hodgson	8/8/81	35	31	20	16	0	0	0	0	80	64
Paul Johnson	25/11/78	18(10)	16(10)	6	5	0	0	0	0	24	20
Adrian Lam	25/8/70	28(1)	24(1)	10	9	1	1	5	5	47	43
Terry Newton	7/11/78	28(3)	25(2)	8	4	0	0	0	0	32	16
Terry O'Connor	13/10/71	20(7)	19(7)	1	1	0	0	0	0	4	4
Sean O'Loughlin	24/11/82	28(5)	27(2)	7	4	0	0	0	0	28	16
Julian O'Neill	14/10/72	4(2)	2(1)	2	1	25	11	0	0	58	26
Quentin Pongia	9/7/70	10(6)	10(6)	0	0	0	0	0	0	0	0
Kris Radlinski	9/4/76	21	17	8	5	0	0	0	0	32	20
Mark Roberts	9/11/82	(3)	(3)	0	0	0	0	0	0	0	0
Luke Robinson	25/7/84	9(15)	8(14)	6	5	8	6	1	1	41	33
Danny Sculthorpe	8/9/79	11(12)	8(11)	5	4	0	0	0	0	20	16
Craig Smith	31/10/71	30	26	3	3	0	0	0	0	12	12
Mark Smith	18/8/81	9(16)	8(13)	1	0	0	0	0	0	4	0
Danny Tickle	10/3/83	25(6)	22(6)	12	12	49	44	1	1	147	137
Jon Whittle	9/9/82	1	1	0	0	0	0	0	0	0	0
Stephen Wild	26/4/81	4(8)	4(5)	3	2	0	0	0	0	12	8

LEAGUE RECORD
P28-W19-D2-L7
(3rd, SL/Grand Final Runners Up)
F776, A512, Diff+264
40 points.

CHALLENGE CUP
Semi Finalists

ATTENDANCES
Best - v St Helens (ESF - 21,790)
Worst - v Halton Simms Cross
(CC - 3,790)
Total (SL, inc play-offs) - 179,470
Average (SL, inc play-offs) - 11,217
(Up by 737 on 2002)

TOP TACKLES
Sean O'Loughlin 541

TOP CARRIES
Brian Carney 363

TOP METRES
Brian Carney 3359

TOP BREAKS
Adrian Lam 34

TOP OFFLOADS
Danny Sculthorpe 43

TOP BUSTS
Brian Carney 149

SUPER LEAGUE VIII
Round by Round

ROUND 1

Friday 21st February 2003

ST HELENS 46 BRADFORD BULLS 22

SAINTS: 2 Anthony Stewart; 19 Ade Gardner; 3 Martin Gleeson; 4 Paul Newlove; 21 John Kirkpatrick; 13 Paul Sculthorpe; 7 Sean Long; 8 Darren Britt; 6 Jason Hooper; 10 Barry Ward; 12 John Stankevitch; 11 Chris Joynt (C); 16 Darren Smith. Subs (all used): 17 Mike Bennett; 15 Tim Jonkers; 14 Mick Higham; 20 Tommy Martyn.
Tries: Ward (3), Kirkpatrick (16, 49), Sculthorpe (18, 77), Hooper (22), Gardner (27), Higham (58);
Goals: Long 7/10.
BULLS: 3 Leon Pryce; 15 Karl Pratt; 20 Scott Naylor; 4 Shontayne Hape; 5 Lesley Vainikolo; 1 Robbie Paul (C); 7 Paul Deacon; 8 Joe Vagana; 9 James Lowes; 29 Stuart Fielden; 11 Daniel Gartner; 12 Jamie Peacock; 13 Mike Forshaw. Subs (all used): 14 Lee Gilmour; 18 Lee Radford; 27 Robert Parker; 10 Paul Anderson.
Tries: Radford (41), L Pryce (60, 68); **Goals:** Deacon 5/5.
Rugby Leaguer & League Express Men of the Match: *Saints:* Sean Long; *Bulls:* Leon Pryce.
Penalty count: 11-9; **Half-time:** 28-4;
Referee: Ian Smith (Oldham); **Attendance:** 12,217.

Saturday 22nd February 2003

HUDDERSFIELD GIANTS 8 WARRINGTON WOLVES 20

GIANTS: 3 Ben Cooper; 2 Hefin O'Hare; 20 Matt Calland; 4 Julian Bailey; 34 Marcus St Hilaire; 33 Stanley Gene; 6 Brandon Costin; 8 Mick Slicker; 15 Darren Turner; 25 Darren Fleary; 10 Jim Gannon; 7 Jarrod O'Doherty; 13 Steve McNamara (C). Subs (all used): 5 Matthew Whitaker; 9 Paul March; 12 Anthony Colella (D); 11 Eorl Crabtree.
Tries: O'Hare (45), St Hilaire (62);
Goals: McNamara 0/1, Costin 0/1.
Sin bin: Fleary (54) - late, high shot on Briers; Cooper (74) - holding down.
On report: Fleary (54) - late, high shot on Briers; Gene (57) - high tackle on Briers.
WOLVES: 5 Graham Appo; 2 Rob Smyth; 12 Ian Sibbit; 4 Ben Westwood; 3 Brent Grose; 6 Lee Briers (C); 7 Nathan Wood; 8 Nick Fozzard; 9 Jon Clarke; 10 Mark Hilton; 11 Darren Burns; 23 Mike Wainwright; 13 Sid Domic. Subs (all used): 14 Mark Gleeson; 18 Paul Noone; 16 Paul Wood; 15 Jerome Guisset.
Tries: Grose (9, 37); **Goals:** Briers 6/6.
Sin bin: Westwood (80) - dissent.
Rugby Leaguer & League Express Men of the Match: *Giants:* Brandon Costin; *Wolves:* Nathan Wood.
Penalty count: 11-9; **Half-time:** 0-16;
Referee: Russell Smith (Castleford); **Attendance:** 4,104.

Sunday 23rd February 2003

LEEDS RHINOS 32 WIDNES VIKINGS 12

RHINOS: 18 Gary Connolly; 2 Mark Calderwood; 3 Chris McKenna; 4 Keith Senior; 1 Francis Cummins; 14 Andrew Dunemann; 7 Rob Burrow; 17 Wayne McDonald; 9 Matt Diskin; 19 Ryan Bailey; 11 David Furner; 12 Matt Adamson; 13 Kevin Sinfield (C). Subs (all used): 10 Barrie McDermott; 8 Danny Ward; 6 Danny McGuire; 5 Chev Walker.
Tries: McKenna (7), Calderwood (10, 22, 56), Cummins (29), Senior (45), Dunemann (50);
Goals: Furner 1/6, Sinfield 1/2.
Sin bin: Bailey (68) - fighting.
VIKINGS: 1 Stuart Spruce; 21 Chris Percival; 4 Adam Hughes; 3 Deon Bird; 5 Jason Demetriou; 18 Dean Lawford; 7 Ryan Sheridan (C); 8 Robert Relf; 9 Shane Millard; 10 Julian O'Neill (NZ); 12 Steve McCurrie; 11 Andy Hay; 13 Daniel Frame. Subs (all used): 17 Anthony Farrell; 19 Paul Atcheson; 23 David Mills; 22 Phil Cantillon.
Tries: Demetriou (23), Frame (33); **Goals:** Hughes 2/3.
Sin bin: Relf (68) - fighting.
Rugby Leaguer & League Express Men of the Match: *Rhinos:* Wayne McDonald; *Vikings:* Daniel Frame.
Penalty count: 6-8; **Half-time:** 18-12; **Referee:** Colin Morris (Huddersfield); **Attendance:** 13,013.

LONDON BRONCOS 22 HALIFAX 26

BRONCOS: 3 Nigel Roy; 21 Rob Jackson; 4 Tony Martin; 11 Mat Toshack; 5 Steve Hall; 13 Jim Dymock (C); 23 Chris Thorman; 8 Francis Stephenson; 14 Neil Budworth; 10 Richard Marshall; 12 Steele Retchless; 17 Tom Haughey; 9 Bill Peden (D). Subs (all used): 6 Rob Purdham; 19 Nick Johnson; 22 Andrew Hamilton; 24 Russell Bawden.
Tries: Hall (32), Peden (40), Martin (76);
Goals: Martin 5/5.
Sin bin: Roy (22) - fighting.
HALIFAX: 5 Lee Finnerty; 2 Lee Greenwood; 3 Stuart Donlan; 4 Danny Halliwell; 21 Chris Norman; 6 Martin Moana; 20 Dane Dorahy; 8 Andy Hobson; 9 Johnny Lawless (C); 16 Chris Birchall; 11 Heath Cruckshank; 12 Andrew Brocklehurst; 13 Shayne McMenemy. Subs: 7 Sean Penkywicz (not used); 10 Paul Davidson; 15 Ryan Clayton; 17 Anthony Seuseu.
Tries: Finnerty (9), Dorahy (12), Brocklehurst (51), Birchall (57); **Goals:** Dorahy 5/5.
Sin bin: Finnerty (22) - fighting.
Rugby Leaguer & League Express Men of the Match: *Broncos:* Jim Dymock; *Halifax:* Shayne McMenemy.
Penalty count: 8-7; **Half-time:** 14-12;
Referee: Robert Connolly (Wigan); **Attendance:** 3,022.

CASTLEFORD TIGERS 19 WIGAN WARRIORS 10

TIGERS: 22 Mark Lennon; 2 Waine Pryce; 1 Damian Gibson; 3 Michael Eagar; 5 Darren Rogers; 6 Danny Orr (C); 7 Mitch Healey; 8 Nathan Sykes; 9 Wayne Bartrim; 10 Andy Lynch; 23 Michael Smith; 12 Dale Fritz; 11 Lee Harland. Subs (all used): 19 Wayne Godwin; 17 Paul Jackson; 18 Jamie Thackray; 20 Tom Saxton.
Tries: Rogers (5, 76), Pryce (79); **Goals:** Bartrim 3/5;
Field goal: Orr.
WARRIORS: 1 Kris Radlinski; 5 Brian Carney; 4 Paul Johnson; 14 David Hodgson; 3 Jamie Ainscough; 6 Julian O'Neill; 7 Adrian Lam; 16 Danny Sculthorpe; 9 Terry Newton; 10 Craig Smith; 11 Mick Cassidy; 13 Andy Farrell (C); 15 Sean O'Loughlin. Subs (all used): 18 Martin Aspinwall; 12 Danny Tickle; 17 Mark Smith; 19 Stephen Wild.
Goals: Farrell 1/1, O'Neill 4/5.
Dismissal: Johnson (78) - high tackle on Thackray.
Rugby Leaguer & League Express Men of the Match: *Tigers:* Danny Orr; *Warriors:* Kris Radlinski.
Penalty count: 8-10; **Half-time:** 6-4;
Referee: Steve Ganson (St Helens); **Attendance:** 8,462.

WAKEFIELD TRINITY WILDCATS 14 HULL FC 28

WILDCATS: 1 Martyn Holland; 5 Jon Wells; 3 Gareth Ellis; 17 Richard Newlove (D); 24 Colum Halpenny; 6 Ben Jeffries; 14 Paul Handforth; 18 Michael Korkidas; 9 David March; 10 Dallas Hood; 11 Troy Slattery; 15 Ian Knott; 13 Adrian Vowles (C). Subs (all used): 8 Clinton O'Brien; 2 Waisale Sovatabua; 19 Olivier Elima (D); 20 David Wrench.
Tries: Jeffries (31), Handforth (56); **Goals:** Knott 3/3.
HULL: 1 Steve Prescott; 2 Colin Best; 4 Toa Kohe-Love; 3 Richie Barnett; 5 Matt Crowther; 6 Richard Horne; 7 Tony Smith (C); 8 Craig Greenhill; 22 Andy Last; 12 Scott Logan; 11 Adam Maher; 14 Sean Ryan; 16 Paul Cooke. Subs (all used): 17 Chris Chester; 23 Ian Bell (D); 15 Steve Craven; 10 Paul King.
Tries: Prescott (21, 26, 48), Greenhill (65), Kohe-Love (76); **Goals:** Crowther 4/7.
Sin bin: R Horne (38) - lying on.
Rugby Leaguer & League Express Men of the Match: *Wildcats:* Ben Jeffries; *Hull:* Steve Prescott.
Penalty count: 10-8; **Half-time:** 8-10; **Referee:** Richard Silverwood (Dewsbury); **Attendance:** 5,645.

ROUND 2

Friday 7th March 2003

HALIFAX 10 CASTLEFORD TIGERS 20

HALIFAX: 5 Lee Finnerty; 2 Lee Greenwood; 3 Stuart Donlan; 15 Ryan Clayton; 21 Chris Norman; 6 Martin Moana; 20 Dane Dorahy; 8 Andy Hobson; 9 Johnny Lawless (C); 16 Chris Birchall; 11 Heath Cruckshank; 12 Andrew Brocklehurst; 13 Shayne McMenemy. Subs (all used): 1 Daryl Cardiss; 7 Sean Penkywicz; 10 Paul Davidson; 17 Anthony Seuseu.
Try: Dorahy (7); **Goals:** Dorahy 3/3.
On report: McMenemy (60) - high tackle.
TIGERS: 1 Damian Gibson; 2 Waine Pryce; 3 Michael Eagar; 14 Andy Johnson; 5 Darren Rogers; 6 Danny Orr (C); 22 Mark Lennon; 8 Nathan Sykes; 9 Wayne Bartrim; 10 Andy Lynch; 23 Michael Smith; 12 Dale Fritz; 13 Ryan Hudson. Subs (all used): 16 Francis Maloney (D2); 17 Paul Jackson; 18 Jamie Thackray; 19 Wayne Godwin.
Tries: Maloney (31), Gibson (55), Godwin (60);
Goals: Bartrim 2/4, Orr 2/2.
Rugby Leaguer & League Express Men of the Match: *Halifax:* Shayne McMenemy; *Tigers:* Michael Smith.
Penalty count: 8-7; **Half-time:** 8-8; **Referee:** Richard Silverwood (Dewsbury); **Attendance:** 4,388.

HULL FC 4 LONDON BRONCOS 10

HULL: 1 Steve Prescott; 2 Colin Best; 3 Richie Barnett; 4 Toa Kohe-Love; 5 Matt Crowther; 6 Richard Horne; 7 Tony Smith (C); 8 Craig Greenhill; 22 Andy Last; 12 Scott Logan; 11 Adam Maher; 14 Sean Ryan; 16 Paul Cooke. Subs (all used): 10 Paul King; 13 Jason Smith; 17 Chris Chester; 20 Garreth Carvell.
Goals: Crowther 2/2.
BRONCOS: 3 Nigel Roy; 5 Steve Hall; 4 Tony Martin; 21 Rob Jackson; 25 Andrew King (D); 13 Jim Dymock (C); 23 Chris Thorman; 8 Francis Stephenson; 14 Neil Budworth; 10 Richard Marshall; 11 Mat Toshack; 12 Steele Retchless; 17 Tom Haughey. Subs (all used): 6 Rob Purdham; 15 Mark Cox; 22 Andrew Hamilton; 24 Russell Bawden.
Try: Roy (6); **Goals:** Martin 3/3.
Rugby Leaguer & League Express Men of the Match: *Hull:* Paul King; *Broncos:* Nigel Roy.
Penalty count: 8-6; **Half-time:** 4-8; **Referee:** Russell Smith (Castleford); **Attendance:** 12,901.

WIGAN WARRIORS 33 HUDDERSFIELD GIANTS 22

WARRIORS: 1 Kris Radlinski; 5 Brian Carney; 3 Jamie Ainscough; 14 David Hodgson; 2 Brett Dallas; 6 Julian O'Neill; 7 Adrian Lam (C); 16 Danny Sculthorpe; 9 Terry Newton; 10 Craig Smith; 19 Stephen Wild; 12 Danny Tickle; 15 Sean O'Loughlin. Subs (all used): 17 Mark Smith; 18 Martin Aspinwall; 23 Gareth Hock; 21 Ricky Bibey.
Tries: O'Loughlin (16), Dallas (31), Hodgson (41), Ainscough (48), Sculthorpe (67), Aspinwall (79);
Goals: O'Neill 4/6, Tickle 0/1; **Field goal:** Lam.
GIANTS: 34 Marcus St Hilaire; 2 Hefin O'Hare; 4 Julian Bailey; 3 Ben Cooper; 16 Alex Wilkinson (D); 13 Steve McNamara (C); 6 Brandon Costin; 8 Mick Slicker; 15 Darren Turner; 10 Jim Gannon; 20 Matt Calland; 12 Anthony Colella; 7 Jarrod O'Doherty. Subs (all used): 9 Paul March; 5 Matthew Whitaker; 18 Jon Grayshon; 11 Eorl Crabtree.
Tries: Wilkinson (39), Turner (57), Colella (60), Gannon (71); **Goals:** McNamara 1/2, Costin 2/2.
Rugby Leaguer & League Express Men of the Match: *Warriors:* Kris Radlinski; *Giants:* Darren Turner.
Penalty count: 7-6; **Half-time:** 13-4; **Referee:** Karl Kirkpatrick (Warrington); **Attendance:** 8,187.

Saturday 8th March 2003

WIDNES VIKINGS 4 ST HELENS 22

VIKINGS: 1 Stuart Spruce (C); 2 Paul Devlin; 20 Dan Potter; 4 Adam Hughes; 5 Jason Demetriou; 13 Daniel Frame; 18 Dean Lawford; 8 Robert Relf; 9 Shane Millard; 10 Julian O'Neill (NZ); 11 Andy Hay; 12 Steve McCurrie; 3 Deon Bird. Subs (all used): 23 David Mills; 19 Paul Atcheson; 22 Phil Cantillon; 17 Anthony Farrell.
Try: Hughes (76); **Goals:** Hughes 0/2, Lawford 0/1.
SAINTS: 2 Anthony Stewart; 5 Darren Albert; 16 Darren Smith; 4 Paul Newlove; 19 Ade Gardner; 13 Paul Sculthorpe; 7 Sean Long; 8 Darren Britt; 11 Chris Joynt (C); 10 Barry Ward; 15 Tim Jonkers; 12 John Stankevitch; 6 Jason Hooper. Subs: 14 Mick Higham; 22 Stuart Jones; 18 Mark Edmondson; 21 John Kirkpatrick (not used).
Tries: Long (13), Albert (43), Gardner (50, 80);
Goals: Long 3/5.
Sin bin: Stewart (6) - holding down; Smith (74) - professional foul.
Rugby Leaguer & League Express Men of the Match: *Vikings:* Dean Lawford; *Saints:* Sean Long.
Penalty count: 8-9; **Half-time:** 0-6;
Referee: Ian Smith (Oldham); **Attendance:** 7,518.

Sunday 9th March 2003

BRADFORD BULLS 22 WAKEFIELD TRINITY WILDCATS 10

BULLS: 3 Leon Pryce; 2 Tevita Vaikona; 20 Scott Naylor; 4 Shontayne Hape; 5 Lesley Vainikolo; 15 Karl Pratt; 7 Paul Deacon; 8 Joe Vagana; 9 James Lowes (C); 29 Stuart Fielden; 11 Daniel Gartner; 14 Lee Gilmour; 13 Mike Forshaw. Subs (all used): 18 Lee Radford; 17 Stuart Reardon (D); 27 Robert Parker; 10 Paul Anderson.
Tries: Pratt (8), L Pryce (50), Gilmour (70), Hape (72);
Goals: Deacon 0/1, Radford 3/4.
On report: Incident leading to fight (74).
WILDCATS: 1 Martyn Holland; 5 Jon Wells; 3 Gareth Ellis; 17 Richard Newlove; 24 Colum Halpenny; 6 Ben Jeffries; 7 Brad Davis; 18 Michael Korkidas; 9 David March; 10 Dallas Hood; 15 Ian Knott; 19 Olivier Elima; 13 Adrian Vowles (C). Subs (all used): 12 Jamie Field; 14 Paul Handforth; 2 Waisale Sovatabua; 20 David Wrench.
Tries: Vowles (14), Ellis (29); **Goals:** Jeffries 1/3.
Sin bin: Korkidas (30) - dissent.
On report: Incident leading to fight (74).
Rugby Leaguer & League Express Men of the Match: *Bulls:* Karl Pratt; *Wildcats:* Adrian Vowles.
Penalty count: 10-4; **Half-time:** 4-8;
Referee: Robert Connolly (Wigan); **Attendance:** 20,283.

WARRINGTON WOLVES 22 LEEDS RHINOS 32

WOLVES: 5 Graham Appo; 3 Brent Grose; 12 Ian Sibbit; 4 Ben Westwood; 20 Dean Gaskell; 6 Lee Briers (C); 7 Nathan Wood; 8 Nick Fozzard; 9 Jon Clarke; 10 Mark Hilton; 11 Darren Burns; 23 Mike Wainwright; 13 Sid Domic. Subs (all used): 14 Mark Gleeson; 18 Paul Noone; 15 Jerome Guisset; 16 Paul Wood.
Tries: Domic (6), Appo (43, 65); **Goals:** Briers 5/7.
Dismissal: Fozzard (36) - headbutt on McDermott.
On report: Fozzard (22) - high tackle on Sinfield.
RHINOS: 18 Gary Connolly; 2 Mark Calderwood; 5 Chev Walker; 4 Keith Senior; 1 Francis Cummins; 14 Andrew Dunemann; 7 Rob Burrow; 19 Ryan Bailey; 9 Matt Diskin; 17 Wayne McDonald; 11 David Furner; 12 Matt Adamson; 13 Kevin Sinfield (C). Subs (all used): 20 Jamie Jones-Buchanan; 16 Willie Poching; 10 Barrie McDermott; 15 Chris Feather.
Tries: Calderwood (20), Connolly (25), Adamson (35), Senior (55), Walker (59, 70);
Goals: Furner 4/6, Sinfield 0/1.
On report: Adamson (30) - high shot on Fozzard.
Rugby Leaguer & League Express Men of the Match: *Wolves:* Sid Domic; *Rhinos:* Chev Walker.
Penalty count: 10-5; **Half-time:** 8-18;
Referee: Steve Ganson (St Helens); **Attendance:** 8,705.

ROUND 3

Friday 21st March 2003

LEEDS RHINOS 42 HUDDERSFIELD GIANTS 28

RHINOS: 18 Gary Connolly; 2 Mark Calderwood; 5 Chev Walker; 4 Keith Senior; 1 Francis Cummins; 14 Andrew Dunemann; 7 Rob Burrow; 17 Wayne McDonald; 9 Matt Diskin; 10 Barrie McDermott; 11 David Furner; 12 Matt Adamson; 13 Kevin Sinfield (C). Subs (all used): 15 Chris Feather; 24 Ewan Dowes; 6 Danny McGuire; 16 Willie Poching.
Tries: Calderwood (8, 46, 62), Cummins (11), Dunemann (39), Walker (52, 65), Diskin (77);
Goals: Furner 2/6, Sinfield 3/4.

GIANTS: 3 Ben Cooper; 2 Hefin O'Hare; 4 Julian Bailey; 16 Alex Wilkinson; 34 Marcus St Hilaire; 13 Steve McNamara (C); 6 Brandon Costin; 8 Mick Slicker; 15 Darren Turner; 10 Jim Gannon; 12 Anthony Colella; 7 Jarrod O'Doherty; 33 Stanley Gene. Subs (all used): 9 Paul March; 25 Darren Fleary; 11 Eorl Crabtree; 18 Jon Grayshon.
Tries: O'Hare (2, 74), Wilkinson (36), Costin (79); **Goals:** McNamara 6/7.
Rugby Leaguer & League Express Men of the Match: *Rhinos:* Chev Walker; *Giants:* Jarrod O'Doherty.
Penalty count: 10-7; **Half time:** 14-18; **Referee:** Ronnie Laughton (Barnsley); **Attendance:** 10,357.

ST HELENS 54 CASTLEFORD TIGERS 12

SAINTS: 1 Paul Wellens; 2 Anthony Stewart; 16 Darren Smith; 4 Paul Newlove; 5 Darren Albert; 13 Paul Sculthorpe; 7 Sean Long; 8 Darren Britt; 14 Mick Higham; 15 Tim Jonkers; 11 Chris Joynt (C); 12 John Stankevitch; 6 Jason Hooper. Subs (all used): 19 Ade Gardner; 22 Stuart Jones; 17 Mike Bennett; 18 Mark Edmondson.
Tries: Albert (22), Jonkers (24), Long (30, 49, 56), Newlove (47, 66), Higham (60), Jones (68);
Goals: Long 9/9.
TIGERS: 1 Damian Gibson; 2 Waine Pryce; 14 Andy Johnson; 3 Michael Eagar; 5 Darren Rogers; 6 Danny Orr (C); 22 Mark Lennon; 8 Nathan Sykes; 9 Wayne Bartrim; 10 Andy Lynch; 23 Michael Smith; 12 Dale Fritz; 13 Ryan Hudson. Subs (all used): 16 Francis Maloney; 17 Paul Jackson; 11 Lee Harland; 4 Paul Mellor (D).
Try: Lynch (5); **Goals:** Bartrim 4/4.
Rugby Leaguer & League Express Men of the Match: *Saints:* Sean Long; *Tigers:* Andy Lynch.
Penalty count: 8-5; **Half-time:** 18-12;
Referee: Ian Smith (Oldham); **Attendance:** 10,292.

Saturday 22nd March 2003

LONDON BRONCOS 8 WARRINGTON WOLVES 29

BRONCOS: 3 Nigel Roy; 25 Andrew King; 4 Tony Martin; 21 Rob Jackson; 5 Steve Hall; 23 Chris Thorman; 7 Dennis Moran; 8 Francis Stephenson; 14 Neil Budworth; 10 Richard Marshall; 12 Steele Retchless; 11 Mat Toshack; 13 Jim Dymock (C). Subs (all used): 15 Mark Cox; 17 Tom Haughey; 22 Andrew Hamilton; 24 Russell Bawden.
Try: King (30); **Goals:** Martin 2/3.
WOLVES: 5 Graham Appo; 3 Brett Grose; 12 Ian Sibbit; 4 Ben Westwood; 20 Dean Gaskell; 6 Lee Briers (C); 7 Nathan Wood; 8 Nick Fozzard; 9 Jon Clarke; 10 Mark Hilton; 11 Darren Burns; 23 Mike Wainwright; 13 Sid Domic. Subs (all used): 14 Mark Gleeson; 15 Jerome Guisset; 16 Paul Wood; 18 Paul Noone.
Tries: Domic (18), Grose (26), Westwood (54), Sibbit (58), Appo (78); **Goals:** Briers 4/6; **Field goal:** Briers.
Sin bin: N Wood (66) - professional foul.
Rugby Leaguer & League Express Men of the Match: *Broncos:* Steele Retchless; *Wolves:* Lee Briers.
Penalty count: 9-8; **Half-time:** 8-14; **Referee:** Richard Silverwood (Dewsbury); **Attendance:** 3,105.

Sunday 23rd March 2003

HULL FC 38 WIDNES VIKINGS 18

HULL: 6 Richard Horne; 2 Colin Best; 4 Toa Kohe-Love; 3 Richie Barnett; 1 Steve Prescott; 16 Paul Cooke; 13 Jason Smith (C); 8 Craig Greenhill; 7 Tony Smith; 12 Scott Logan; 11 Adam Maher; 14 Sean Ryan; 17 Chris Chester. Subs (all used): 10 Paul King; 19 Richard Fletcher; 24 Kirk Yeaman; 26 Graeme Horne.
Tries: J Smith (7), R Horne (16), Prescott (47), Kohe-Love (67), Logan (72); **Goals:** Prescott 9/10.
Sin bin: Barnett (60) - holding down.
VIKINGS: 1 Stuart Spruce (C); 24 Chris Giles (D); 5 Jason Demetriou; 4 Adam Hughes; 21 Chris Percival; 13 Daniel Frame; 18 Dean Lawford; 8 Robert Relf; 9 Shane Millard; 10 Julian O'Neill (NZ); 20 Dan Potter; 12 Steve McCurrie; 3 Deon Bird. Subs (all used): 23 David Mills; 19 Paul Atcheson; 25 Simon Finnigan (D); 17 Anthony Farrell.
Tries: Spruce (14), Demetriou (20), Mills (29);
Goals: Hughes 3/5.
Sin bin: Frame (52) - holding down;
Percival (62) - interference.
Rugby Leaguer & League Express Men of the Match: *Hull:* Adam Maher; *Vikings:* Dean Lawford.
Penalty count: 12-7; **Half-time:** 18-16;
Referee: Russell Smith (Castleford); **Attendance:** 8,743.

WAKEFIELD TRINITY WILDCATS 29
WIGAN WARRIORS 34

WILDCATS: 1 Martyn Holland; 5 Jon Wells; 3 Gareth Ellis; 17 Richard Newlove; 24 Colum Halpenny; 6 Ben Jeffries; 7 Brad Davis; 12 Jamie Field; 14 Paul Handforth; 10 Dallas Hood; 11 Troy Slattery; 15 Ian Knott; 13 Adrian Vowles (C). Subs (all used): 16 Jamie Rooney (D); 8 Clinton O'Brien; 2 Waisale Sovatabua; 20 David Wrench.
Tries: Newlove (6), Wells (28), Davis (31), Holland (66); **Goals:** Knott 6/7; **Field goal:** Davis.
WARRIORS: 1 Kris Radlinski; 2 Brett Dallas; 18 Martin Aspinwall; 14 David Hodgson; 3 Jamie Ainscough; 15 Sean O'Loughlin; 7 Adrian Lam (C); 16 Danny Sculthorpe; 17 Mark Smith; 10 Craig Smith; 12 Danny Tickle; 4 Paul Johnson; 23 Gareth Hock. Subs (all used): 21 Ricky Bibey; 20 Luke Robinson; 19 Stephen Wild; 6 Julian O'Neill.
Tries: Hodgson (18, 73), Lam (20, 71), O'Neill (45), Aspinwall (49); **Goals:** Tickle 2/3, O'Neill 3/5.
Rugby Leaguer & League Express Men of the Match: *Wildcats:* Martyn Holland; *Warriors:* Adrian Lam.
Penalty count: 6-7; **Half-time:** 19-12;
Referee: Steve Ganson (St Helens); **Attendance:** 4,496.

BRADFORD BULLS 62 HALIFAX 22

BULLS: 1 Robbie Paul (C); 15 Karl Pratt; 20 Scott Naylor; 4 Shontayne Hape; 5 Lesley Vainikolo; 3 Leon Pryce; 7 Paul Deacon; 8 Joe Vagana; 9 James Lowes; 29 Stuart Fielden; 18 Lee Radford; 14 Lee Gilmour; 13 Mike Forshaw. Subs (all used): 17 Stuart Reardon; 19 Jamie Langley; 27 Robert Parker; 10 Paul Anderson.
Tries: Lowes (8, 24, 78), Paul (18, 59, 80), L Pryce (29), Hape (43), Deacon (48), Pratt (55), Reardon (76);
Goals: Deacon 7/8, Lowes 2/3.
HALIFAX: 5 Lee Finnerty; 4 Danny Halliwell; 15 Ryan Clayton; 3 Stuart Donlan; 2 Lee Greenwood; 6 Martin Moana; 20 Dane Dorahy; 8 Andy Hobson; 9 Johnny Lawless (C); 10 Paul Davidson; 11 Heath Cruckshank; 12 Andrew Brocklehurst; 13 Shayne McMenemy. Subs (all used): 1 Daryl Cardiss; 7 Sean Penkywicz; 16 Chris Birchall; 17 Anthony Seuseu.
Tries: Moana (6), Clayton (34), Greenwood (66), Dorahy (71); **Goals:** Dorahy 3/4.
Sin bin: Davidson (62) - striking in the tackle.
Rugby Leaguer & League Express Men of the Match: *Bulls:* James Lowes; *Halifax:* Martin Moana.
Penalty count: 13-7; **Half-time:** 24-10; **Referee:** Karl Kirkpatrick (Warrington); **Attendance:** 15,557.

ROUND 4

Friday 28th March 2003

HALIFAX 14 LEEDS RHINOS 20

HALIFAX: 5 Lee Finnerty; 2 Lee Greenwood; 3 Stuart Donlan; 15 Ryan Clayton; 4 Danny Halliwell; 6 Martin Moana; 20 Dane Dorahy; 8 Andy Hobson; 9 Johnny Lawless (C); 16 Chris Birchall; 11 Heath Cruckshank; 12 Andrew Brocklehurst; 13 Shayne McMenemy. Subs (all used): 1 Daryl Cardiss; 7 Sean Penkywicz; 10 Paul Davidson; 17 Anthony Seuseu.
Tries: Donlan (7), Dorahy (75); **Goals:** Dorahy 3/4.
Sin bin: Davidson (45) - interference.
RHINOS: 18 Gary Connolly; 2 Mark Calderwood; 5 Chev Walker; 4 Keith Senior; 1 Francis Cummins; 14 Andrew Dunemann; 7 Rob Burrow; 10 Barrie McDermott; 9 Matt Diskin; 17 Wayne McDonald; 12 Matt Adamson; 16 Willie Poching; 13 Kevin Sinfield (C). Subs (all used): 6 Danny McGuire; 15 Chris Feather; 20 Jamie Jones-Buchanan; 24 Ewan Dowes.
Tries: Feather (18), McDermott (47), Walker (61);
Goals: Sinfield 4/6.
Sin bin: Jones-Buchanan (69) - obstruction.
Rugby Leaguer & League Express Men of the Match: *Halifax:* Martin Moana; *Rhinos:* Wayne McDonald.
Penalty count: 12-8; **Half-time:** 6-8;
Referee: Steve Ganson (St Helens); **Attendance:** 4,073.

WIGAN WARRIORS 30 LONDON BRONCOS 34

WARRIORS: 1 Kris Radlinski; 5 Brian Carney; 4 Paul Johnson; 14 David Hodgson; 2 Brett Dallas; 15 Sean O'Loughlin; 7 Adrian Lam (C); 8 Terry O'Connor; 17 Mark Smith; 10 Craig Smith; 11 Mick Cassidy; 12 Danny Tickle; 23 Gareth Hock. Subs (all used): 21 Ricky Bibey; 16 Danny Sculthorpe; 9 Terry Newton; 20 Luke Robinson.
Tries: Tickle (2), Hodgson (6), Johnson (14), Hock (54), Carney (80); **Goals:** Tickle 4/6, Robinson 1/1.
BRONCOS: 3 Nigel Roy; 5 Steve Hall; 4 Tony Martin; 21 Rob Jackson; 25 Andrew King; 23 Chris Thorman; 7 Dennis Moran; 8 Francis Stephenson; 14 Neil Budworth; 10 Richard Marshall; 11 Mat Toshack; 12 Steele Retchless; 13 Jim Dymock (C). Subs (all used): 24 Russell Bawden; 17 Tom Haughey; 15 Mark Cox; 22 Andrew Hamilton.
Tries: Dymock (24, 38), King (40), Thorman (42), Martin (65), Jackson (77); **Goals:** Martin 5/6.
Rugby Leaguer & League Express Men of the Match: *Warriors:* Mark Smith; *Broncos:* Jim Dymock.
Penalty count: 12-7; **Half-time:** 16-18; **Referee:** Ronnie Laughton (Barnsley); **Attendance:** 8,375.

Saturday 29th March 2003

CASTLEFORD TIGERS 14
WAKEFIELD TRINITY WILDCATS 20

TIGERS: 1 Damian Gibson; 2 Waine Pryce; 3 Michael Eagar; 4 Paul Mellor; 5 Darren Rogers; 6 Danny Orr (C); 16 Francis Maloney; 8 Nathan Sykes; 9 Wayne Bartrim; 10 Andy Lynch; 23 Michael Smith; 12 Dale Fritz; 13 Ryan Hudson. Subs (all used): 14 Andy Johnson; 17 Paul Jackson; 11 Lee Harland; 22 Mark Lennon.
Tries: Eagar (3), Lennon (67); **Goals:** Bartrim 3/3.
Sin bin: Maloney (14) - fighting.
WILDCATS: 24 Colum Halpenny; 5 Jon Wells; 3 Gareth Ellis; 4 Matt Seers; 17 Richard Newlove; 6 Ben Jeffries; 7 Brad Davis; 12 Jamie Field; 9 David March; 18 Michael Korkidas; 11 Troy Slattery; 15 Ian Knott; 13 Adrian Vowles (C). Subs (all used): 14 Paul Handforth; 19 Olivier Elima; 21 Steve Snitch; 20 David Wrench.
Tries: Ellis (19), Seers (38), Davis (57);
Goals: Knott 4/6.
Sin bin: Seers (9) - obstruction; Davis (14) - fighting.
Rugby Leaguer & League Express Men of the Match: *Tigers:* Damian Gibson; *Wildcats:* Brad Davis.
Penalty count: 7-10; **Half-time:** 8-10; **Referee:** Karl Kirkpatrick (Warrington); **Attendance:** 6,883.

Sunday 30th March 2003

HUDDERSFIELD GIANTS 36 ST HELENS 22

GIANTS: 34 Marcus St Hilaire; 2 Hefin O'Hare; 4 Julian Bailey; 3 Ben Cooper; 16 Alex Wilkinson; 9 Paul March; 6 Brandon Costin (C); 25 Darren Fleary; 15 Darren Turner; 10 Jim Gannon; 33 Stanley Gene; 12 Anthony Colella; 7 Jarrod O'Doherty. Subs (all used): 8 Mick Slicker; 11 Eorl Crabtree; 18 Jon Grayshon; 5 Matthew Whitaker.
Tries: Cooper (5), Colella (16), Turner (29), March (32), Bailey (59), O'Hare (70), Costin (79); **Goals:** Costin 4/7.
SAINTS: 1 Paul Wellens; 2 Anthony Stewart; 16 Darren Smith; 4 Paul Newlove; 5 Darren Albert; 13 Paul Sculthorpe; 7 Sean Long; 8 Darren Britt; 14 Mick Higham; 12 John Stankevitch; 15 Tim Jonkers; 11 Chris Joynt (C); 6 Jason Hooper. Subs (all used): 19 Ade Gardner; 22 Stuart Jones; 17 Mike Bennett; 23 Jon Wilkin.
Tries: Albert (1), Smith (37), Jones (41), Long (62);
Goals: Long 2/3, Sculthorpe 1/1.
Rugby Leaguer & League Express Men of the Match: *Giants:* Anthony Colella; *Saints:* Darren Smith.
Penalty count: 5-5; **Half-time:** 20-10;
Referee: Robert Connolly (Wigan); **Attendance:** 5,835.

WARRINGTON WOLVES 14 HULL FC 27

WOLVES: 5 Graham Appo; 3 Brent Grose; 12 Ian Sibbit; 4 Ben Westwood; 20 Dean Gaskell; 18 Paul Noone; 7 Nathan Wood (C); 8 Nick Fozzard; 9 Jon Clarke; 10 Mark Hilton; 11 Darren Burns; 23 Mike Wainwright; 13 Sid Domic. Subs (all used): 14 Mark Gleeson; 16 Paul Wood; 15 Jerome Guisset; 21 Matt Sturm.
Tries: Clarke (15); **Goals:** Appo 5/5.
On report: Appo (80) - alleged trip on Kohe-Love.
HULL: 6 Richard Horne; 2 Colin Best; 3 Richie Barnett; 4 Toa Kohe-Love; 1 Steve Prescott; 16 Paul Cooke; 13 Jason Smith (C); 12 Scott Logan; 7 Tony Smith; 8 Craig Greenhill; 11 Adam Maher; 14 Sean Ryan; 17 Chris Chester. Subs (all used): 24 Kirk Yeaman; 26 Graeme Horne; 19 Richard Fletcher; 10 Paul King.
Tries: Best (20), Barnett (25), Kohe-Love (51), Prescott (60); **Goals:** Prescott 5/8; **Field goal:** J Smith.
Sin bin: Fletcher (44) - professional foul on Sibbit.
On report: J Smith (8) - high tackle on Hilton.
Rugby Leaguer & League Express Men of the Match: *Wolves:* Graham Appo; *Hull:* Toa Kohe-Love.
Penalty count: 11-10; **Half-time:** 14-14;
Referee: Russell Smith (Castleford); **Attendance:** 6,784.

WIDNES VIKINGS 18 BRADFORD BULLS 26

VIKINGS: 1 Stuart Spruce (C); 20 Dan Potter; 5 Jason Demetriou; 4 Adam Hughes; 24 Chris Giles; 13 Daniel Frame; 18 Dean Lawford; 8 Robert Relf; 9 Shane Millard; 10 Julian O'Neill (NZ); 11 Andy Hay; 12 Steve McCurrie; 3 Deon Bird. Subs (all used): 23 David Mills; 25 Simon Finnigan; 17 Anthony Farrell; 19 Paul Atcheson.
Tries: Potter (15), Millard (25), Giles (66), Finnigan (71);
Goals: Lawford 1/1, Hughes 0/4.
BULLS: 1 Robbie Paul (C); 15 Karl Pratt; 20 Scott Naylor; 4 Shontayne Hape; 5 Lesley Vainikolo; 3 Leon Pryce; 7 Paul Deacon; 8 Joe Vagana; 9 James Lowes; 29 Stuart Fielden; 14 Lee Gilmour; 18 Lee Radford; 13 Mike Forshaw. Subs (all used): 10 Paul Anderson; 27 Robert Parker; 19 Jamie Langley; 6 Michael Withers.
Tries: Paul (35), Withers (45), Naylor (50), Anderson (69); **Goals:** Deacon 5/5.
Rugby Leaguer & League Express Men of the Match: *Vikings:* Shane Millard; *Bulls:* Paul Deacon.
Penalty count: 4-3; **Half-time:** 8-8;
Referee: Peter Taberner (Wigan); **Attendance:** 6,420.

ROUND 5

Friday 4th April 2003

HULL FC 20 WIGAN WARRIORS 4

HULL: 6 Richard Horne; 1 Steve Prescott; 3 Richie Barnett; 4 Toa Kohe-Love; 2 Colin Best; 16 Paul Cooke; 13 Jason Smith (C); 8 Craig Greenhill; 7 Tony Smith; 12 Scott Logan; 11 Adam Maher; 14 Sean Ryan; 17 Chris Chester. Subs (all used): 10 Paul King; 19 Richard Fletcher; 24 Kirk Yeaman; 26 Graeme Horne.
Tries: Best (37), Maher (42), Yeaman (68);
Goals: Prescott 4/6.
WARRIORS: 1 Kris Radlinski; 5 Brian Carney; 18 Martin Aspinwall; 14 David Hodgson; 2 Brett Dallas; 15 Sean O'Loughlin; 7 Adrian Lam (C); 8 Terry O'Connor; 17 Mark Smith; 10 Craig Smith; 4 Paul Johnson; 12 Danny Tickle; 23 Gareth Hock. Subs (all used): 22 Shaun Briscoe; 16 Danny Sculthorpe; 9 Terry Newton; 19 Stephen Wild.
Try: Hock (62); **Goal:** Tickle 0/1.
Rugby Leaguer & League Express Men of the Match: *Hull:* Craig Greenhill; *Warriors:* Adrian Lam.
Penalty count: 6-5; **Half-time:** 10-0; **Referee:** Karl Kirkpatrick (Warrington); **Attendance:** 11,536.

Saturday 5th April 2003

ST HELENS 16 LEEDS RHINOS 24

SAINTS: 2 Anthony Stewart; 5 Darren Albert; 3 Martin Gleeson; 4 Paul Newlove; 19 Ade Gardner; 13 Paul Sculthorpe; 7 Sean Long; 8 Darren Britt; 15 Tim Jonkers; 18 Mark Edmondson; 16 Darren Smith; 12 John Stankevitch; 6 Jason Hooper. Subs (all used): 1 Paul Wellens; 14 Mick Higham; 22 Stuart Jones; 11 Chris Joynt (C).

Tries: Smith (2), Sculthorpe (42), Gleeson (64);
Goals: Long 1/1, Sculthorpe 1/2.
RHINOS: 18 Gary Connolly; 2 Mark Calderwood; 3 Chris McKenna; 4 Keith Senior; 1 Francis Cummins; 14 Andrew Dunemann; 7 Rob Burrow; 10 Barrie McDermott; 9 Matt Diskin; 8 Danny Ward; 12 Matt Adamson; 11 David Furner; 13 Kevin Sinfield (C). Subs (all used): 6 Danny McGuire; 15 Chris Feather; 16 Willie Poching; 17 Wayne McDonald.
Tries: Senior (7, 28), Poching (53), McDonald (72);
Goals: Sinfield 4/6.
Rugby Leaguer & League Express Men of the Match: *Saints:* Paul Sculthorpe; *Rhinos:* Kevin Sinfield.
Penalty count: 11-8; **Half-time:** 6-14;
Referee: Ian Smith (Oldham); **Attendance:** 10,785.

Sunday 6th April 2003

LONDON BRONCOS 12 CASTLEFORD TIGERS 24

BRONCOS: 3 Nigel Roy; 18 Austin Buchanan (D); 25 Andrew King; 4 Tony Martin; 5 Steve Hall; 13 Jim Dymock (C); 7 Dennis Moran; 24 Russell Bawden; 14 Neil Budworth; 8 Francis Stephenson; 12 Steele Retchless; 11 Mat Toshack; 6 Rob Purdham. Subs (all used): 10 Richard Marshall; 16 Jamie Fielden (D); 26 Damien Kennedy (D); 29 Karl Long (D).
Tries: Martin (3), King (8); **Goals:** Martin 2/4.
TIGERS: 1 Damian Gibson; 2 Waine Pryce; 3 Michael Eagar; 4 Paul Mellor; 5 Darren Rogers; 6 Danny Orr (C); 22 Mark Lennon; 8 Nathan Sykes; 9 Wayne Bartrim; 10 Andy Lynch; 23 Michael Smith; 12 Dale Fritz; 13 Ryan Hudson. Subs (all used): 19 Wayne Godwin; 14 Andy Johnson; 11 Lee Harland; 16 Francis Maloney.
Tries: Lennon (23), Pryce (43), Eagar (77);
Goals: Bartrim 6/8.
Rugby Leaguer & League Express Men of the Match: *Broncos:* Russell Bawden; *Tigers:* Wayne Bartrim.
Penalty count: 5-7; **Half-time:** 12-10;
Referee: Peter Taberner (Wigan); **Attendance:** 3,013.

WIDNES VIKINGS 44 HALIFAX 16

VIKINGS: 1 Stuart Spruce (C); 21 Chris Percival; 5 Jason Demetriou; 4 Adam Hughes; 24 Chris Giles; 13 Daniel Frame; 18 Dean Lawford; 8 Robert Relf; 9 Shane Millard; 10 Julian O'Neill (NZ); 11 Andy Hay; 12 Steve McCurrie; 25 Simon Finnigan. Subs (all used): 23 David Mills; 22 Phil Cantillon; 17 Anthony Farrell; 26 Julian O'Neill (A) (D2).
Tries: Giles (5, 72), Hay (10), Lawford (18, 43), Frame (61, 76), Hughes (63);
Goals: Lawford 1/3, O'Neill (A) 5/5.
Sin bin and on report: O'Neill (NZ) (42) - fighting.
HALIFAX: 1 Daryl Cardiss; 2 Lee Greenwood; 15 Ryan Clayton; 3 Stuart Donlan; 21 Chris Norman; 6 Martin Moana; 20 Dane Dorahy; 8 Andy Hobson; 9 Johnny Lawless (C); 16 Chris Birchall; 11 Heath Cruckshank; 12 Andrew Brocklehurst; 13 Shayne McMenemy. Subs (all used): 7 Sean Penkywicz; 10 Paul Davidson; 17 Anthony Seuseu; 14 Liam Finn.
Tries: Cardiss (32), Seuseu (52), Dorahy (79);
Goals: Dorahy 2/3.
Sin bin and on report: Davidson (42) - fighting.
Rugby Leaguer & League Express Men of the Match: *Vikings:* Adam Hughes; *Halifax:* Martin Moana.
Penalty count: 5-3; **Half-time:** 14-6; **Referee:** Colin Morris (Huddersfield); **Attendance:** 7,135.

WAKEFIELD TRINITY WILDCATS 10 HUDDERSFIELD GIANTS 14

WILDCATS: 1 Martyn Holland; 24 Colum Halpenny; 3 Gareth Ellis; 4 Matt Seers; 5 Jon Wells; 6 Ben Jeffries; 7 Brad Davis; 10 Dallas Hood; 9 David March; 18 Michael Korkidas; 11 Troy Slattery; 15 Ian Knott; 13 Adrian Vowles (C). Subs (all used): 14 Paul Handforth; 19 Olivier Elima; 12 Jamie Field; 20 David Wrench.
Try: Ellis (21); **Goals:** Knott 3/5.
GIANTS: 34 Marcus St Hilaire; 2 Hefin O'Hare; 4 Julian Bailey; 33 Stanley Gene; 16 Alex Wilkinson; 9 Paul March; 6 Brandon Costin; 25 Darren Fleary; 15 Darren Turner; 8 Mick Slicker; 13 Steve McNamara (C); 18 Jon Grayshon; 7 Jarrod O'Doherty. Subs: 26 Jamie Bloem (D); 11 Eorl Crabtree; 10 Jim Gannon; 5 Matthew Whitaker (not used).
Tries: Gannon (62), Wilkinson (71);
Goals: McNamara 3/4.
Rugby Leaguer & League Express Men of the Match: *Wildcats:* Gareth Ellis; *Giants:* Steve McNamara.
Penalty count: 12-13; **Half-time:** 10-4; **Referee:** Richard Silverwood (Dewsbury); **Attendance:** 4,109.

BRADFORD BULLS 32 WARRINGTON WOLVES 8

BULLS: 6 Michael Withers; 2 Tevita Vaikona; 20 Scott Naylor; 3 Leon Pryce; 5 Lesley Vainikolo; 1 Robbie Paul (C); 7 Paul Deacon; 8 Joe Vagana; 9 James Lowes; 29 Stuart Fielden; 18 Lee Radford; 11 Daniel Gartner; 14 Lee Gilmour. Subs (all used): 17 Stuart Reardon; 19 Jamie Langley; 27 Robert Parker; 10 Paul Anderson.
Tries: Vainikolo (3), Withers (5), Lowes (9), L Pryce (11), Deacon (36), Vaikona (49); **Goals:** Deacon 4/6.
Sin bin: Lowes (74) - fighting.
WOLVES: 5 Graham Appo; 2 Rob Smyth; 3 Brent Grose; 4 Ben Westwood; 24 Kevin Crouthers; 19 Gary Hulse; 7 Nathan Wood (C); 8 Nick Fozzard; 9 Jon Clarke; 10 Mark Hilton; 11 Darren Burns; 21 Matt Sturm; 13 Sid Domic. Subs (all used): 18 Paul Noone; 16 Paul Wood; 15 Jerome Guisset; 17 Warren Stevens.
Tries: Hilton (16), Domic (32); **Goals:** Appo 0/2.
Sin bin: N Wood (74) - fighting.
Rugby Leaguer & League Express Men of the Match: *Bulls:* James Lowes; *Wolves:* Graham Appo.
Penalty count: 3-4; **Half-time:** 26-8;
Referee: Robert Connolly (Wigan); **Attendance:** 15,157.

ROUND 6

Thursday 17th April 2003

CASTLEFORD TIGERS 14 LEEDS RHINOS 15

TIGERS: 1 Damian Gibson; 2 Waine Pryce; 4 Paul Mellor; 11 Lee Harland; 5 Darren Rogers; 3 Michael Eagar; 6 Danny Orr (C); 8 Nathan Sykes; 9 Wayne Bartrim; 10 Andy Lynch; 23 Michael Smith; 12 Dale Fritz; 13 Ryan Hudson. Subs: 19 Wayne Godwin; 20 Tom Saxton (not used); 17 Paul Jackson; 18 Jamie Thackray.
Try: Lynch (12); **Goals:** Bartrim 5/6, Orr 0/1.
RHINOS: 18 Gary Connolly; 2 Mark Calderwood; 5 Chev Walker; 4 Keith Senior; 1 Francis Cummins; 6 Danny McGuire; 14 Andrew Dunemann; 10 Barrie McDermott; 9 Matt Diskin; 19 Ryan Bailey; 11 David Furner; 16 Willie Poching; 13 Kevin Sinfield (C). Subs (all used): 7 Rob Burrow; 20 Jamie Jones-Buchanan; 15 Chris Feather; 17 Wayne McDonald.
Tries: McGuire (23), Poching (57), Walker (72);
Goals: Sinfield 1/4; **Field goal:** Dunemann.
Rugby Leaguer & League Express Men of the Match: *Tigers:* Ryan Hudson; *Rhinos:* Chev Walker.
Penalty count: 8-5; **Half-time:** 10-4; **Referee:** Richard Silverwood (Dewsbury); **Attendance:** 10,655.

Friday 18th April 2003

WIGAN WARRIORS 24 ST HELENS 22

WARRIORS: 22 Shaun Briscoe; 5 Brian Carney; 18 Martin Aspinwall; 4 Paul Johnson; 27 Jon Whittle (D); 15 Sean O'Loughlin; 7 Adrian Lam (C); 8 Terry O'Connor; 9 Terry Newton; 10 Craig Smith; 21 Ricky Bibey; 12 Danny Tickle; 17 Mark Smith. Subs (all used): 24 David Allen (D); 25 Kevin Brown (D); 26 Mark Roberts (D); 16 Danny Sculthorpe.
Tries: Newton (16, 58), Tickle (35), Briscoe (46);
Goals: Tickle 4/5.
SAINTS: 1 Paul Wellens; 19 Ade Gardner; 3 Martin Gleeson; 16 Darren Smith; 5 Darren Albert; 13 Paul Sculthorpe; 7 Sean Long; 8 Darren Britt; 14 Mick Higham; 10 Barry Ward; 11 Chris Joynt (C); 12 John Stankevitch; 6 Jason Hooper. Subs (all used): 18 Mark Edmondson; 22 Stuart Jones; 15 Tim Jonkers; 2 Anthony Stewart.
Tries: Albert (10, 40), Higham (18), Hooper (27);
Goals: Sculthorpe 3/5.
Rugby Leaguer & League Express Men of the Match: *Warriors:* Terry Newton; *Saints:* Mick Higham.
Penalty count: 7-3; **Half-time:** 12-22; **Referee:** Karl Kirkpatrick (Warrington); **Attendance:** 15,607.

WARRINGTON WOLVES 35 WAKEFIELD TRINITY WILDCATS 20

WOLVES: 1 Lee Penny; 2 Rob Smyth; 12 Ian Sibbit; 3 Brent Grose; 5 Graham Appo; 6 Lee Briers (C); 7 Nathan Wood; 8 Nick Fozzard; 9 Jon Clarke; 10 Mark Hilton; 15 Jerome Guisset; 23 Mike Wainwright; 11 Darren Burns. Subs (all used): 19 Gary Hulse; 18 Paul Noone; 21 Matt Sturm; 17 Warren Stevens.
Tries: Sibbit (2), Penny (14), N Wood (36), Smyth (47), Clarke (71), Fozzard (74); **Goals:** Briers 4/5, Smyth 1/1;
Field goal: Briers.
WILDCATS: 24 Colum Halpenny; 2 Waisale Sovatabua; 3 Gareth Ellis; 4 Matt Seers; 5 Jon Wells; 6 Ben Jeffries; 7 Brad Davis; 18 Michael Korkidas; 9 David March; 10 Dallas Hood; 15 Ian Knott; 12 Jamie Field; 13 Adrian Vowles (C). Subs (all used): 14 Paul Handforth; 17 Richard Newlove; 19 Olivier Elima; 20 David Wrench.
Tries: Seers (26), Korkidas (55), Vowles (61), Knott (77); **Goals:** Knott 2/4.
Rugby Leaguer & League Express Men of the Match: *Wolves:* Mike Wainwright; *Wildcats:* Michael Korkidas.
Penalty count: 1-5; **Half-time:** 18-6; **Referee:** Colin Morris (Huddersfield); **Attendance:** 6,323.

WIDNES VIKINGS 32 LONDON BRONCOS 20

VIKINGS: 19 Paul Atcheson; 14 Marvin Golden (D); 5 Jason Demetriou; 4 Adam Hughes; 24 Chris Giles; 26 Julian O'Neill (A); 18 Dean Lawford; 8 Robert Relf; 9 Shane Millard; 10 Julian O'Neill (NZ); 11 Andy Hay; 12 Steve McCurrie (C); 13 Daniel Frame. Subs (all used): 23 David Mills; 7 Ryan Sheridan; 17 Anthony Farrell; 25 Simon Finnigan.
Tries: McCurrie (19), Atcheson (26, 77), Hay (74), Millard (80); **Goals:** O'Neill (A) 6/7.
Sin bin: Mills (40) - interference.
BRONCOS: 25 Andrew King; 5 Steve Hall; 4 Tony Martin; 21 Rob Jackson; 18 Austin Buchanan; 23 Chris Thorman; 7 Dennis Moran; 12 Steele Retchless; 14 Neil Budworth; 24 Russell Bawden; 3 Nigel Roy; 11 Mat Toshack; 13 Jim Dymock (C). Subs (all used): 9 Bill Peden; 8 Francis Stephenson; 6 Rob Purdham; 26 Damien Kennedy.
Tries: Hall (9), Roy (32), Stephenson (40), Martin (44);
Goals: Martin 2/5.
Sin bin: Peden (39) - interference;
King (66) - interference.
Rugby Leaguer & League Express Men of the Match: *Vikings:* Paul Atcheson; *Broncos:* Neil Budworth.
Penalty count: 10-13; **Half-time:** 16-16;
Referee: Russell Smith (Castleford); **Attendance:** 5,708.

BRADFORD BULLS 48 HULL FC 24

BULLS: 1 Robbie Paul (C); 2 Tevita Vaikona; 20 Scott Naylor; 4 Shontayne Hape; 5 Lesley Vainikolo; 3 Leon Pryce; 7 Paul Deacon; 10 Paul Anderson; 9 James Lowes; 29 Stuart Fielden; 18 Lee Radford; 14 Lee Gilmour; 13 Mike Forshaw. Subs (all used): 15 Karl Pratt; 19 Jamie Langley; 27 Robert Parker; 30 Richard Moore.
Tries: Vaikona (29), L Pryce (40, 79), Hape (46), Pratt (55, 73), Vainikolo (58), Lowes (65); **Goals:** Deacon 8/9.
On report: Moore (33) - leading with a knee running into tackle.
HULL: 6 Richard Horne; 1 Steve Prescott; 3 Richie Barnett; 24 Kirk Yeaman; 2 Colin Best; 16 Paul Cooke; 13 Jason Smith (C); 8 Craig Greenhill; 22 Andy Last; 10 Paul King; 11 Adam Maher; 14 Sean Ryan; 17 Chris Chester. Subs (all used): 20 Garreth Carvell; 19 Richard Fletcher; 15 Steve Craven; 26 Graeme Horne.
Tries: Barnett (8, 80), Last (68); **Goals:** Prescott 6/6.
Rugby Leaguer & League Express Men of the Match: *Bulls:* Lesley Vainikolo; *Hull:* Craig Greenhill.
Penalty count: 10-11; **Half-time:** 14-10;
Referee: Ian Smith (Oldham); **Attendance:** 15,182.

HALIFAX 20 HUDDERSFIELD GIANTS 21

HALIFAX: 1 Daryl Cardiss; 33 Andrew Frew (D); 15 Ryan Clayton; 3 Stuart Donlan; 2 Lee Greenwood; 6 Martin Moana; 20 Dane Dorahy; 8 Andy Hobson; 9 Johnny Lawless (C); 16 Chris Birchall; 11 Heath Cruckshank; 12 Andrew Brocklehurst; 13 Shayne McMenemy. Subs (all used): 4 Danny Halliwell; 7 Sean Penkywicz; 10 Paul Davidson; 17 Anthony Seuseu.
Tries: Clayton (45), Davidson (57), Donlan (66);
Goals: Dorahy 4/4.
Sin bin: Birchall (5) - interference.
GIANTS: 34 Marcus St Hilaire; 2 Hefin O'Hare; 4 Julian Bailey; 26 Jamie Bloem; 16 Alex Wilkinson; 6 Brandon Costin; 13 Steve McNamara (C); 10 Jim Gannon; 15 Darren Turner; 8 Mick Slicker; 7 Jarrod O'Doherty; 12 Anthony Colella; 33 Stanley Gene. Subs (all used): 3 Ben Cooper; 9 Paul March; 18 Jon Grayshon; 25 Darren Fleary.
Tries: McNamara (25), Bailey (38), St Hilaire (49);
Goals: McNamara 4/4; **Field goal:** Costin.
Rugby Leaguer & League Express Men of the Match: *Halifax:* Daryl Cardiss; *Giants:* Brandon Costin.
Penalty count: 6-10; **Half-time:** 2-14;
Referee: Steve Ganson (St Helens); **Attendance:** 4,616.

ROUND 7

Monday 21st April 2003

HULL FC 46 HALIFAX 18

HULL: 1 Steve Prescott; 28 Gareth Raynor (D2); 24 Kirk Yeaman; 3 Richie Barnett (C); 2 Colin Best; 16 Paul Cooke; 6 Richard Horne; 8 Craig Greenhill; 22 Andy Last; 10 Paul King; 11 Adam Maher; 20 Garreth Carvell; 14 Sean Ryan. Subs (all used): 15 Steve Craven; 26 Graeme Horne; 27 Liam Higgins; 25 Glen Donkin.
Tries: Best (15, 70), Raynor (18, 21), Barnett (58, 79), Prescott (65), R Horne (68); **Goals:** Prescott 7/11.
Sin bin: Yeaman (62) - fighting.
HALIFAX: 1 Daryl Cardiss; 33 Andrew Frew; 15 Ryan Clayton; 3 Stuart Donlan; 5 Lee Finnerty; 20 Dane Dorahy; 7 Sean Penkywicz; 17 Anthony Seuseu; 9 Johnny Lawless (C); 10 Paul Davidson; 11 Heath Cruckshank; 12 Andrew Brocklehurst; 6 Martin Moana. Subs (all used): 4 Danny Halliwell; 8 Andy Hobson; 16 Chris Birchall; 23 Ged Corcoran (D).
Tries: Frew (35), Dorahy (53), Clayton (78);
Goals: Dorahy 3/4.
Sin bin: Finnerty (62) - fighting.
Rugby Leaguer & League Express Men of the Match: *Hull:* Richie Barnett; *Halifax:* Dane Dorahy.
Penalty count: 13-10; **Half-time:** 20-8; **Referee:** Ronnie Laughton (Barnsley); **Attendance:** 9,070.

HUDDERSFIELD GIANTS 16 CASTLEFORD TIGERS 29

GIANTS: 34 Marcus St Hilaire; 2 Hefin O'Hare; 4 Julian Bailey; 3 Ben Cooper; 16 Alex Wilkinson; 6 Brandon Costin; 13 Steve McNamara (C); 25 Darren Fleary; 9 Paul March; 8 Mick Slicker; 26 Jamie Bloem; 7 Jarrod O'Doherty; 33 Stanley Gene. Subs (all used): 15 Darren Turner; 11 Eorl Crabtree; 18 Jon Grayshon; 5 Matthew Whitaker.
Tries: Costin (24), O'Hare (27), Bloem (44);
Goals: McNamara 1/1, Costin 1/3.
Sin bin: Bailey (18) - obstruction.
TIGERS: 1 Damian Gibson; 2 Waine Pryce; 4 Paul Mellor; 5 Darren Rogers; 20 Tom Saxton; 6 Danny Orr (C); 16 Francis Maloney; 8 Nathan Sykes; 13 Ryan Hudson; 10 Andy Lynch; 23 Michael Smith; 12 Dale Fritz; 11 Lee Harland. Subs (all used): 19 Wayne Godwin; 14 Andy Johnson; 17 Paul Jackson; 21 Richard Blakeway.
Tries: Smith (18, 36), Hudson (59), Lynch (77);
Goals: Orr 6/6; **Field goal:** Maloney.
Rugby Leaguer & League Express Men of the Match: *Giants:* Brandon Costin; *Tigers:* Ryan Hudson.
Penalty count: 8-10; **Half-time:** 12-14;
Referee: Robert Connolly (Wigan); **Attendance:** 5,139.

ST HELENS 56 WARRINGTON WOLVES 6

SAINTS: 1 Paul Wellens; 6 Jason Hooper; 3 Martin Gleeson; 4 Paul Newlove; 19 Ade Gardner; 13 Paul Sculthorpe; 20 Tommy Martyn; 8 Darren Britt; 15 Tim Jonkers; 18 Mark Edmondson; 12 John Stankevitch; 16 Darren Smith; 11 Chris Joynt (C). Subs (all used): 14 Mick Higham; 22 Stuart Jones; 7 Sean Long; 10 Barry Ward.
Tries: Hooper (3, 33), Sculthorpe (7), Gleeson (14, 65), Higham (31), Newlove (40), Smith (44), Gardner (76), Martyn (78); **Goals:** Sculthorpe 8/10.
Sin bin: Wellens (56) - holding down.

WOLVES: 1 Lee Penny; 2 Rob Smyth; 3 Brent Grose; 24 Kevin Crouthers; 5 Graham Appo; 19 Gary Hulse; 7 Nathan Wood (C); 8 Nick Fozzard; 9 Jon Clarke; 10 Mark Hilton; 15 Jerome Guisset; 23 Mike Wainwright; 11 Darren Burns. Subs (all used): 16 Paul Wood; 18 Paul Noone; 21 Matt Sturm; 17 Warren Stevens.
Try: Penny (25); **Goal:** Smyth 1/1.
Rugby Leaguer & League Express Men of the Match: *Saints:* Tommy Martyn; *Wolves:* Mike Wainwright.
Penalty count: 7-9; **Half-time:** 34-6;
Referee: Ian Smith (Oldham); **Attendance:** 8,963.

Tuesday 22nd April 2003

WAKEFIELD TRINITY WILDCATS 6 WIDNES VIKINGS 26

WILDCATS: 24 Colum Halpenny; 2 Waisale Sovatabua; 3 Gareth Ellis; 4 Matt Seers; 5 Jon Wells; 6 Ben Jeffries; 7 Brad Davis; 10 Dallas Hood; 9 David March; 18 Michael Korkidas; 12 Jamie Field; 15 Ian Knott; 13 Adrian Vowles (C). Subs (all used): 16 Jamie Rooney; 21 Steve Snitch; 19 Olivier Elima; 11 Troy Slattery.
Try: J Field (16); **Goals:** Rooney 1/1, Knott 0/2.
VIKINGS: 19 Paul Atcheson; 14 Marvin Golden; 13 Daniel Frame; 4 Adam Hughes; 24 Chris Giles; 26 Julian O'Neill (A); 18 Dean Lawford; 8 Robert Relf; 9 Shane Millard; 10 Julian O'Neill (NZ); 11 Andy Hay; 12 Steve McCurrie (C); 25 Simon Finnigan. Subs (all used): 7 Ryan Sheridan; 17 Anthony Farrell; 5 Jason Demetriou; 27 Paul Alcock (D).
Tries: Lawford (27), Golden (45), O'Neill (A) (74), Atcheson (77); **Goals:** O'Neill (A) 4/5;
Field goals: Lawford 2.
Rugby Leaguer & League Express Men of the Match: *Wildcats:* David March; *Vikings:* Julian O'Neill (A).
Penalty count: 10-5; **Half-time:** 4-8;
Referee: Steve Ganson (St Helens); **Attendance:** 3,411.

Tuesday 6th May 2003

LEEDS RHINOS 24 WIGAN WARRIORS 24

RHINOS: 18 Gary Connolly; 2 Mark Calderwood; 3 Chris McKenna; 4 Keith Senior; 1 Francis Cummins; 14 Andrew Dunemann; 6 Danny McGuire; 19 Ryan Bailey; 9 Matt Diskin; 10 Barrie McDermott; 11 David Furner; 5 Chev Walker; 13 Kevin Sinfield (C). Subs (all used): 8 Danny Ward; 15 Chris Feather; 16 Willie Poching; 7 Rob Burrow.
Tries: Calderwood (3), Cummins (17), McGuire (49), Burrow (65); **Goals:** Sinfield 4/6.
WARRIORS: 1 Kris Radlinski; 5 Brian Carney; 18 Martin Aspinwall; 14 David Hodgson; 3 Jamie Ainscough; 15 Sean O'Loughlin; 7 Adrian Lam (C); 8 Terry O'Connor; 9 Terry Newton; 16 Danny Sculthorpe; 4 Paul Johnson; 12 Danny Tickle; 28 Nick Graham. Subs (all used): 23 Gareth Hock; 17 Mark Smith; 22 Shaun Briscoe; 26 Mark Roberts.
Tries: Sculthorpe (11, 69), Ainscough (21), Tickle (32);
Goals: Tickle 4/4, Lam 0/1.
Rugby Leaguer & League Express Men of the Match: *Rhinos:* Rob Burrow; *Warriors:* Nick Graham.
Penalty count: 8-5; **Half time:** 8-18;
Referee: Steve Ganson (St Helens); **Attendance:** 11,115.

Wednesday 30th July 2003

LONDON BRONCOS 6 BRADFORD BULLS 60

BRONCOS: 1 Paul Sykes; 25 Andrew King; 4 Tony Martin; 21 Rob Jackson; 3 Nigel Roy; 6 Rob Purdham; 23 Chris Thorman; 24 Russell Bawden; 14 Neil Budworth; 12 Steele Retchless; 9 Bill Peden; 26 Damien Kennedy; 13 Jim Dymock (C). Subs (all used): 5 Steve Hall; 7 Dennis Moran; 8 Francis Stephenson; 31 Joe Mbu.
Try: Peden (20); **Goal:** Thorman 1/1.
BULLS: 17 Stuart Reardon; 2 Tevita Vaikona; 20 Scott Naylor; 4 Shontayne Hape; 5 Lesley Vainikolo; 3 Leon Pryce; 7 Paul Deacon; 8 Joe Vagana; 9 James Lowes (C); 10 Paul Anderson; 12 Jamie Peacock; 18 Lee Radford; 13 Mike Forshaw. Subs (all used): 14 Lee Gilmour; 19 Jamie Langley; 26 Chris Bridge; 27 Robert Parker.
Tries: Anderson (2), L Pryce (9, 12, 34, 50), Vainikolo (23, 37), Naylor (29), Vaikona (40), Langley (62), Lowes (65); **Goals:** Deacon 8/11.
Rugby Leaguer & League Express Men of the Match: *Broncos:* Joe Mbu; *Bulls:* Leon Pryce.
Penalty count: 9-8; **Half-time:** 6-42;
Referee: Ian Smith (Oldham); **Attendance:** 3,651.

ROUND 8

Friday 2nd May 2003

HALIFAX 0 ST HELENS 38

HALIFAX: 1 Daryl Cardiss; 2 Lee Greenwood; 4 Danny Halliwell; 3 Stuart Donlan; 5 Lee Finnerty; 6 Martin Moana; 20 Dane Dorahy; 8 Andy Hobson; 9 Johnny Lawless (C); 16 Chris Birchall; 11 Heath Cruckshank; 12 Andrew Brocklehurst; 13 Shayne McMenemy. Subs (all used): 10 Paul Davidson; 14 Liam Finn; 15 Ryan Clayton; 17 Anthony Seuseu.
SAINTS: 1 Paul Wellens; 2 Anthony Stewart; 3 Martin Gleeson; 4 Paul Newlove; 5 Darren Albert; 20 Tommy Martyn; 7 Sean Long; 8 Darren Britt; 15 Tim Jonkers; 18 Mark Edmondson; 11 Chris Joynt (C); 16 Darren Smith; 13 Paul Sculthorpe. Subs (all used): 9 Keiron Cunningham; 10 Barry Ward; 12 John Stankevitch; 22 Stuart Jones.
Tries: Stewart (6, 45, 63), Martyn (29), Long (47), Stankevitch (73), Sculthorpe (79); **Goals:** Sculthorpe 5/8.
Rugby Leaguer & League Express Men of the Match: *Halifax:* Daryl Cardiss; *Saints:* Anthony Stewart.
Penalty count: 5-7; **Half-time:** 0-12; **Referee:** Richard Silverwood (Dewsbury); **Attendance:** 3,372.

LEEDS RHINOS 13 WAKEFIELD TRINITY WILDCATS 12

RHINOS: 18 Gary Connolly; 2 Mark Calderwood; 3 Chris McKenna; 4 Keith Senior; 1 Francis Cummins; 14 Andrew Dunemann; 6 Danny McGuire; 19 Ryan Bailey; 9 Matt Diskin; 10 Barrie McDermott; 11 David Furner; 16 Willie Poching; 13 Kevin Sinfield (C). Subs (all used): 8 Danny Ward; 15 Chris Feather; 20 Jamie Jones-Buchanan; 21 Richard Mathers.
Try: McGuire (39); **Goals:** Sinfield 4/4;
Field goal: Dunemann.
WILDCATS: 24 Colum Halpenny; 2 Waisale Sovatabua; 3 Gareth Ellis; 4 Matt Seers; 5 Jon Wells; 16 Jamie Rooney; 7 Brad Davis; 18 Michael Korkidas; 9 David March; 10 Dallas Hood; 15 Ian Knott; 12 Jamie Field; 13 Adrian Vowles (C). Subs (all used): 11 Troy Slattery; 21 Steve Snitch; 6 Ben Jeffries; 20 David Wrench.
Try: Sovatabua (50); **Goals:** Rooney 4/4.
Sin bin: Halpenny (58) – holding down.
Rugby Leaguer & League Express Men of the Match: *Rhinos:* Keith Senior; *Wildcats:* David March.
Penalty count: 9-9; **Half-time:** 12-4; **Referee:** Karl Kirkpatrick (Warrington); **Attendance:** 10,740.

WIGAN WARRIORS 8 BRADFORD BULLS 14

WARRIORS: 1 Kris Radlinski; 5 Brian Carney; 18 Martin Aspinwall; 14 David Hodgson; 3 Jamie Ainscough; 15 Sean O'Loughlin; 7 Adrian Lam (C); 8 Terry O'Connor; 17 Mark Smith; 10 Craig Smith; 12 Danny Tickle; 4 Paul Johnson; 28 Nick Graham (D). Subs (all used): 16 Danny Sculthorpe; 22 Shaun Briscoe; 23 Gareth Hock; 25 Kevin Brown.
Try: Ainscough (1); **Goals:** Tickle 2/4.
BULLS: 1 Robbie Paul (C); 2 Tevita Vaikona; 20 Scott Naylor; 4 Shontayne Hape; 5 Lesley Vainikolo; 3 Leon Pryce; 7 Paul Deacon; 8 Joe Vagana; 9 James Lowes; 11 Daniel Gartner; 18 Lee Radford; 12 Jamie Peacock; 13 Mike Forshaw. Subs (all used): 10 Paul Anderson; 27 Robert Parker; 14 Lee Gilmour; 30 Richard Moore.
Tries: L Pryce (46, 77), Vainikolo (62); **Goals:** Deacon 1/4.
Rugby Leaguer & League Express Men of the Match: *Warriors:* Terry O'Connor; *Bulls:* James Lowes.
Penalty count: 6-5; **Half-time:** 6-0;
Referee: Ian Smith (Oldham); **Attendance:** 10,281.

Saturday 3rd May 2003

WARRINGTON WOLVES 34 WIDNES VIKINGS 6

WOLVES: 1 Lee Penny; 2 Rob Smyth; 3 Brent Grose; 12 Ian Sibbit; 5 Graham Appo; 6 Lee Briers (C); 7 Nathan Wood; 8 Nick Fozzard; 9 Jon Clarke; 10 Mark Hilton; 15 Jerome Guisset; 23 Mike Wainwright; 11 Darren Burns. Subs (all used): 13 Sid Domic; 16 Paul Wood; 18 Paul Noone; 17 Warren Stevens.
Tries: Grose (6, 43), Smyth (8), Guisset (21), Appo (30), Sibbit (38), P Wood (67); **Goals:** Briers 3/8.
VIKINGS: 1 Stuart Spruce (C); 14 Marvin Golden; 5 Jason Demetriou; 4 Adam Hughes; 24 Chris Giles; 26 Julian O'Neill (A); 18 Dean Lawford; 8 Robert Relf; 9 Shane Millard; 10 Julian O'Neill (NZ); 11 Andy Hay; 12 Steve McCurrie; 13 Daniel Frame. Subs (all used): 7 Ryan Sheridan; 17 Anthony Farrell; 19 Paul Atcheson; 27 Paul Alcock.
Try: Hay (13); **Goal:** O'Neill (A) 1/1.
Sin bin: Frame (33) - ball stealing.
On report: Relf (72) - altercation with Appo.
Rugby Leaguer & League Men of the Match: *Wolves:* Nathan Wood; *Vikings:* Robert Relf.
Penalty count: 13-12; **Half-time:** 24-6; **Referee:** Ronnie Laughton (Barnsley); **Attendance:** 7,264.

Sunday 4th May 2003

HUDDERSFIELD GIANTS 22 LONDON BRONCOS 30

GIANTS: 34 Marcus St Hilaire; 2 Hefin O'Hare; 4 Julian Bailey; 33 Stanley Gene; 16 Alex Wilkinson; 6 Brandon Costin; 13 Steve McNamara (C); 10 Jim Gannon; 9 Paul March; 25 Darren Fleary; 26 Jamie Bloem; 12 Anthony Colella; 7 Jarrod O'Doherty. Subs (all used): 8 Mick Slicker; 15 Darren Turner; 3 Ben Cooper; 18 Jon Grayshon.
Tries: March (6), Wilkinson (48), Turner (55), St Hilaire (75); **Goals:** McNamara 3/3, Costin 0/1.
BRONCOS: 3 Nigel Roy; 25 Andrew King; 4 Tony Martin; 21 Rob Jackson; 18 Austin Buchanan; 6 Rob Purdham; 7 Dennis Moran; 24 Russell Bawden; 9 Bill Peden; 12 Steele Retchless; 11 Mat Toshack; 26 Damien Kennedy; 13 Jim Dymock (C). Subs (all used): 5 Steve Hall; 14 Neil Budworth; 8 Francis Stephenson; 23 Chris Thorman.
Tries: King (13, 35), Buchanan (21, 71), Martin (30, 42);
Goals: Martin 3/7.
Rugby Leaguer & League Express Men of the Match: *Giants:* Paul March; *Broncos:* Tony Martin.
Penalty count: 4-6; **Half-time:** 6-20;
Referee: Russell Smith (Castleford); **Attendance:** 3,046.

Monday 5th May 2003

CASTLEFORD TIGERS 26 HULL FC 26

TIGERS: 1 Damian Gibson; 2 Waine Pryce; 4 Paul Mellor; 14 Andy Johnson; 5 Darren Rogers; 6 Danny Orr (C); 7 Mitch Healey; 8 Nathan Sykes; 9 Wayne Bartrim; 10 Andy Lynch; 11 Lee Harland; 12 Dale Fritz; 13 Ryan Hudson. Subs (all used): 17 Paul Jackson; 3 Michael Eagar; 21 Richard Blakeway; 20 Tom Saxton.
Tries: Orr (14, 70), Eagar (75), Gibson (79);
Goals: Bartrim 5/5.
HULL: 1 Steve Prescott; 2 Colin Best; 3 Richie Barnett (C); 4 Toa Kohe-Love; 5 Matt Crowther; 16 Paul Cooke; 6 Richard Horne; 8 Craig Greenhill; 22 Andy Last; 10 Paul King; 14 Sean Ryan; 11 Adam Maher; 17 Chris Chester. Subs (all used): 9 Dean Treister (D); 15 Steve Craven; 20 Garreth Carvell; 24 Kirk Yeaman.
Tries: Prescott (8), Barnett (17, 25), R Horne (43), Best (58); **Goals:** Prescott 3/7.
Rugby Leaguer & League Express Men of the Match: *Tigers:* Danny Orr; *Hull:* Chris Chester.
Penalty count: 6-10; **Half-time:** 8-14;
Referee: Robert Connolly (Wigan); **Attendance:** 8,713.

ROUND 9

Friday 9th May 2003

HALIFAX 8 WARRINGTON WOLVES 38

HALIFAX: 1 Daryl Cardiss; 2 Lee Greenwood; 15 Ryan Clayton; 3 Stuart Donlan; 33 Andrew Frew; 6 Martin Moana; 20 Dane Dorahy; 8 Andy Hobson; 9 Johnny Lawless (C); 16 Chris Birchall; 11 Heath Cruckshank; 12 Andrew Brocklehurst; 13 Shayne McMenemy. Subs (all used): 10 Paul Davidson; 4 Danny Halliwell; 7 Sean Penkywicz; 17 Anthony Seuseu.
Try: Cardiss (58); **Goals:** Dorahy 2/2.
WOLVES: 1 Lee Penny; 2 Rob Smyth; 3 Brent Grose; 12 Ian Sibbit; 5 Graham Appo; 6 Lee Briers (C); 7 Nathan Wood; 8 Nick Fozzard; 9 Jon Clarke; 10 Mark Hilton; 11 Darren Burns; 23 Mike Wainwright; 13 Sid Domic. Subs (all used): 14 Mark Gleeson; 16 Paul Wood; 18 Paul Noone; 17 Warren Stevens.
Tries: N Wood (14), P Wood (20), Appo (25, 64, 79), Domic (49), Wainwright (53); **Goals:** Briers 5/7.
Rugby Leaguer & League Express Men of the Match: *Halifax:* Andy Hobson; *Wolves:* Sid Domic.
Penalty count: 9-2; **Half-time:** 2-16;
Referee: Peter Taberner (Wigan); **Attendance:** 3,174.

LONDON BRONCOS 14 LEEDS RHINOS 32

BRONCOS: 3 Nigel Roy; 25 Andrew King; 21 Rob Jackson; 4 Tony Martin; 5 Steve Hall; 23 Chris Thorman; 7 Dennis Moran; 12 Steele Retchless; 9 Bill Peden; 24 Russell Bawden; 11 Mat Toshack; 26 Damien Kennedy; 13 Jim Dymock (C). Subs (all used): 6 Rob Purdham; 8 Francis Stephenson; 14 Neil Budworth; 18 Austin Buchanan.
Tries: King (33), Hall (39); **Goals:** Martin 3/3.
RHINOS: 21 Richard Mathers; 2 Mark Calderwood; 3 Chris McKenna; 4 Keith Senior; 1 Francis Cummins; 6 Danny McGuire; 14 Andrew Dunemann; 19 Ryan Bailey; 7 Rob Burrow; 10 Barrie McDermott; 16 Willie Poching; 20 Jamie Jones-Buchanan; 13 Kevin Sinfield (C). Subs (all used): 27 Jon Hepworth (D); 24 Ewan Dowes; 15 Chris Feather; 8 Danny Ward.
Tries: Burrow (10), Calderwood (17), McGuire (30, 74), Dunemann (44), Cummins (79); **Goals:** Sinfield 4/7.
Rugby Leaguer & League Express Men of the Match: *Broncos:* Chris Thorman; *Rhinos:* Danny McGuire.
Penalty count: 7-5; **Half-time:** 12-14; **Referee:** Richard Silverwood (Dewsbury); **Attendance:** 5,666.

ST HELENS 10 WAKEFIELD TRINITY WILDCATS 16

SAINTS: 1 Paul Wellens; 5 Darren Albert; 3 Martin Gleeson; 16 Darren Smith; 2 Anthony Stewart; 13 Paul Sculthorpe; 7 Sean Long; 10 Barry Ward; 14 Mick Higham; 18 Mark Edmondson; 15 Tim Jonkers; 12 John Stankevitch; 11 Chris Joynt (C). Subs (all used): 17 Mike Bennett; 9 Keiron Cunningham; 22 Stuart Jones; 19 Ade Gardner.
Tries: Gleeson (36), Albert (45); **Goals:** Sculthorpe 1/3.
WILDCATS: 1 Martyn Holland; 24 Colum Halpenny; 17 Richard Newlove; 3 Gareth Ellis; 2 Waisale Sovatabua; 16 Jamie Rooney; 7 Brad Davis; 18 Michael Korkidas; 9 David March; 10 Dallas Hood; 11 Troy Slattery; 12 Jamie Field; 13 Adrian Vowles (C). Subs (all used): 14 Paul Handforth; 21 Steve Snitch; 6 Ben Jeffries; 20 David Wrench.
Tries: Newlove (16), Sovatabua (67); **Goals:** Rooney 3/4;
Field goals: Rooney 2.
Sin bin: Newlove (35) - deliberate offside.
Rugby Leaguer & League Express Men of the Match: *Saints:* Keiron Cunningham; *Wildcats:* Jamie Rooney.
Penalty count: 8-6; **Half-time:** 6-8; **Referee:** Karl Kirkpatrick (Warrington); **Attendance:** 8,569.

Saturday 10th May 2003

WIDNES VIKINGS 18 WIGAN WARRIORS 22

VIKINGS: 1 Stuart Spruce (C); 14 Marvin Golden; 5 Jason Demetriou; 4 Adam Hughes; 24 Chris Giles; 18 Dean Lawford; 7 Ryan Sheridan; 8 Robert Relf; 9 Shane Millard; 10 Julian O'Neill (NZ); 11 Andy Hay; 13 Daniel Frame; 26 Julian O'Neill (A). Subs (all used): 15 Ryan McDonald; 17 Anthony Farrell; 19 Paul Atcheson; 27 Paul Alcock.
Tries: Hughes (50), Millard (77); **Goals:** O'Neill (A) 5/6.
WARRIORS: 1 Kris Radlinski; 5 Brian Carney; 18 Martin Aspinwall; 14 David Hodgson; 3 Jamie Ainscough; 4 Paul Johnson; 7 Adrian Lam (C); 8 Terry O'Connor; 9 Terry Newton; 16 Danny Sculthorpe; 23 Gareth Hock; 12 Danny Tickle; 28 Nick Graham. Subs (all used): 17 Mark Smith; 22 Shaun Briscoe; 26 Mark Roberts; 25 Kevin Brown.
Tries: Carney (18), Aspinwall (36), Ainscough (60), Newton (72); **Goals:** Tickle 3/5.

Rugby Leaguer & League Express Men of the Match: *Vikings:* Shane Millard; *Warriors:* Adrian Lam.
Penalty count: 8-5; **Half-time:** 4-10;
Referee: Russell Smith (Castleford); **Attendance:** 6,307.

Sunday 11th May 2003

HULL FC 34 HUDDERSFIELD GIANTS 6

HULL: 6 Richard Horne; 2 Colin Best; 4 Toa Kohe-Love; 3 Richie Barnett; 1 Steve Prescott; 16 Paul Cooke; 7 Tony Smith (C); 8 Craig Greenhill; 9 Dean Treister; 10 Paul King; 11 Adam Maher; 14 Sean Ryan; 17 Chris Chester. Subs (all used): 15 Steve Craven; 20 Garreth Carvell; 24 Kirk Yeaman; 26 Graeme Horne.
Tries: Kohe-Love (1), Treister (7), T Smith (13), R Horne (28), Best (62), Prescott (67);
Goals: Prescott 5/6, Cooke 0/1.
Sin bin: Treister (25) - holding down.
GIANTS: 34 Marcus St Hilaire; 2 Hefin O'Hare; 4 Julian Bailey; 26 Jamie Bloem; 16 Alex Wilkinson; 6 Brandon Costin (C); 9 Paul March; 8 Mick Slicker; 15 Darren Turner; 25 Darren Fleary; 7 Jarrod O'Doherty; 18 Jon Grayshon; 33 Stanley Gene. Subs (all used): 10 Jim Gannon; 5 Matthew Whitaker; 11 Eorl Crabtree; 17 Graham Holroyd (D).
Try: Gene (53); **Goal:** Costin 1/1.
Sin bin: Gannon (27) – interference;
Turner (66) – holding down.
Rugby Leaguer & League Express Men of the Match: *Hull:* Chris Chester; *Giants:* Eorl Crabtree.
Penalty count: 19-12; **Half-time:** 24-0; **Referee:** Ronnie Laughton (Barnsley); **Attendance:** 8,337.

BRADFORD BULLS 30 CASTLEFORD TIGERS 10

BULLS: 1 Robbie Paul (C); 2 Tevita Vaikona; 20 Scott Naylor; 4 Shontayne Hape; 5 Lesley Vainikolo; 3 Leon Pryce; 7 Paul Deacon; 8 Joe Vagana; 9 James Lowes; 30 Richard Moore; 12 Jamie Peacock; 11 Daniel Gartner; 14 Lee Gilmour. Subs (all used): 15 Karl Pratt; 18 Lee Radford; 27 Robert Parker; 10 Paul Anderson.
Tries: Vaikona (20, 23), Vagana (54), Deacon (60);
Goals: Deacon 7/8.
Dismissal: Pryce (32) - late tackle on Orr.
TIGERS: 20 Tom Saxton; 2 Waine Pryce; 1 Damian Gibson; 3 Michael Eagar; 5 Darren Rogers; 6 Danny Orr (C); 7 Mitch Healey; 8 Nathan Sykes; 13 Ryan Hudson; 17 Paul Jackson; 23 Michael Smith; 12 Dale Fritz; 9 Wayne Bartrim. Subs (all used): 19 Wayne Godwin; 14 Andy Johnson; 21 Richard Blakeway; 29 Ben Skerrett (D).
Try: Smith (11); **Goal:** Bartrim 3/4.
Rugby Leaguer & League Express Men of the Match: *Bulls:* James Lowes; *Tigers:* Wayne Bartrim.
Penalty count: 11-10; **Half-time:** 16-8;
Referee: Steve Ganson (St Helens); **Attendance:** 14,749.

ROUND 10

Friday 16th May 2003

ST HELENS 62 LONDON BRONCOS 16

SAINTS: 1 Paul Wellens; 5 Darren Albert; 3 Martin Gleeson; 4 Paul Newlove; 2 Anthony Stewart; 13 Paul Sculthorpe; 7 Sean Long; 8 Darren Britt; 9 Keiron Cunningham; 11 Chris Joynt (C); 17 Mike Bennett; 23 Jon Wilkin; 16 Darren Smith. Subs (all used): 14 Mick Higham; 12 John Stankevitch; 10 Barry Ward; 19 Ade Gardner.
Tries: Cunningham (7, 13, 72), Sculthorpe (20), Smith (24), Higham (37, 68, 76), Wilkin (45), Bennett (55), Gleeson (60); **Goals:** Sculthorpe 7/9, Long 2/2.
BRONCOS: 5 Steve Hall; 6 Rob Purdham; 11 Mat Toshack; 21 Rob Jackson; 2 Dominic Peters; 23 Chris Thorman; 7 Dennis Moran; 24 Russell Bawden; 9 Bill Peden; 10 Richard Marshall; 12 Steele Retchless; 26 Damien Kennedy; 13 Jim Dymock (C). Subs: 14 Neil Budworth; 4 Tony Martin (not used); 8 Francis Stephenson; 29 Tommy Gallagher (D).
Tries: Peters (40), Stephenson (48); **Goals:** Thorman 4/4.
Sin bin: Hall (36) - holding down.
Rugby Leaguer & League Express Men of the Match: *Saints:* Keiron Cunningham; *Broncos:* Bill Peden.
Penalty count: 10-11; **Half-time:** 28-10;
Referee: Ronnie Laughton (Barnsley); **Attendance:** 7,602.

WAKEFIELD TRINITY WILDCATS 22 HALIFAX 18

WILDCATS: 1 Martyn Holland; 2 Waisale Sovatabua; 3 Gareth Ellis; 17 Richard Newlove; 24 Colum Halpenny; 16 Jamie Rooney; 7 Brad Davis (C); 18 Michael Korkidas; 9 David March; 10 Dallas Hood; 11 Troy Slattery; 12 Jamie Field; 15 Ian Knott. Subs (all used): 4 Matt Seers; 6 Ben Jeffries; 20 David Wrench; 21 Steve Snitch.
Tries: Davis (17, 63), Newlove (38); **Goals:** Rooney 5/6.
On report: Seers (28) - use of knees in tackle.
HALIFAX: 5 Lee Finnerty; 33 Andrew Frew; 3 Stuart Donlan; 15 Ryan Clayton; 2 Lee Greenwood; 20 Dane Dorahy; 7 Sean Penkywicz; 8 Andy Hobson; 9 Johnny Lawless (C); 10 Paul Davidson; 11 Heath Cruckshank; 12 Andrew Brocklehurst; 6 Martin Moana. Subs (all used): 4 Danny Halliwell; 14 Liam Finn; 16 Chris Birchall; 17 Anthony Seuseu.
Tries: Penkywicz (23), Finn (71), Greenwood (75);
Goals: Dorahy 2/2, Finn 1/2.
Rugby Leaguer & League Express Men of the Match: *Wildcats:* Jamie Rooney; *Halifax:* Sean Penkywicz.
Penalty count: 7-7; **Half-time:** 12-8;
Referee: Robert Connolly (Wigan); **Attendance:** 2,806.

WIGAN WARRIORS 21 WARRINGTON WOLVES 20

WARRIORS: 22 Shaun Briscoe; 5 Brian Carney; 18 Martin Aspinwall; 14 David Hodgson; 3 Jamie Ainscough; 28 Nick Graham; 7 Adrian Lam; 8 Terry O'Connor; 9 Terry Newton; 16 Danny Sculthorpe; 4 Paul Johnson; 12 Danny Tickle; 13 Andy Farrell (C). Subs (all used): 11 Mick Cassidy; 21 Ricky Bibey; 17 Mark Smith; 23 Gareth Hock.
Tries: Lam (25), Briscoe (47, 50); **Goals:** Farrell 4/4;
Field goal: Farrell.
WOLVES: 1 Lee Penny; 5 Graham Appo; 12 Ian Sibbit; 3 Brent Grose; 2 Rob Smyth; 6 Lee Briers (C); 11 Darren Burns; 8 Nick Fozzard; 9 Jon Clarke; 10 Mark Hilton; 13 Sid Domic; 23 Mike Wainwright; 15 Jerome Guisset. Subs (all used): 14 Mark Gleeson; 16 Paul Wood; 18 Paul Noone; 17 Warren Stevens.
Tries: Domic (18), Grose (34), Briers (55);
Goals: Briers 3/3; **Field goal:** Briers 2.
Rugby Leaguer & League Express Men of the Match: *Warriors:* Adrian Lam; *Wolves:* Lee Briers.
Penalty count: 6-5; **Half-time:** 6-12; **Referee:** Richard Silverwood (Dewsbury); **Attendance:** 11,224.

Saturday 17th May 2003

LEEDS RHINOS 10 HULL FC 10

RHINOS: 18 Gary Connolly; 2 Mark Calderwood; 3 Chris McKenna; 4 Keith Senior; 1 Francis Cummins; 14 Andrew Dunemann; 6 Danny McGuire; 19 Ryan Bailey; 9 Matt Diskin; 10 Barrie McDermott; 11 David Furner; 16 Willie Poching; 13 Kevin Sinfield (C). Subs (all used): 17 Wayne McDonald; 12 Matt Adamson; 7 Rob Burrow; 20 Jamie Jones-Buchanan.
Tries: Poching (50), McKenna (59); **Goals:** Sinfield 1/3.
HULL: 6 Richard Horne; 2 Colin Best; 4 Toa Kohe-Love; 24 Kirk Yeaman; 1 Steve Prescott; 16 Paul Cooke; 7 Tony Smith (C); 8 Craig Greenhill; 9 Dean Treister; 10 Paul King; 11 Adam Maher; 14 Sean Ryan; 17 Chris Chester. Subs (all used): 26 Graeme Horne; 25 Glen Donkin; 20 Garreth Carvell; 22 Andy Last.
Try: Best (9); **Goals:** Prescott 3/3.
Rugby Leaguer & League Express Men of the Match: *Rhinos:* Mark Calderwood; *Hull:* Steve Prescott.
Penalty count: 7-6; **Half time:** 0-8;
Referee: Steve Ganson (St Helens); **Attendance:** 11,273.

Sunday 18th May 2003

CASTLEFORD TIGERS 40 WIDNES VIKINGS 2

TIGERS: 20 Tom Saxton; 2 Waine Pryce; 1 Damian Gibson; 3 Michael Eagar; 5 Darren Rogers; 6 Danny Orr (C); 7 Mitch Healey; 8 Nathan Sykes; 13 Ryan Hudson; 23 Michael Smith; 14 Andy Johnson; 12 Dale Fritz; 9 Wayne Bartrim. Subs (all used): 27 Jon Hepworth (D); 28 Andy McNally (D2); 21 Richard Blakeway; 10 Andy Lynch.
Tries: Hudson (16), Saxton (28), Rogers (42, 53), Lynch (58), McNally (75), Hepworth (79);
Goals: Bartrim 5/6, Orr 1/1.
VIKINGS: 19 Paul Atcheson; 5 Jason Demetriou; 13 Daniel Frame; 4 Adam Hughes; 24 Chris Giles; 18 Dean Lawford; 7 Ryan Sheridan (C); 8 Robert Relf; 9 Shane Millard; 10 Julian O'Neill (NZ); 11 Andy Hay; 12 Steve McCurrie; 26 Julian O'Neill (A). Subs (all used): 15 Ryan McDonald; 17 Anthony Farrell; 22 Phil Cantillon; 20 Dan Potter.
Goal: O'Neill (A) 1/1.
Rugby Leaguer & League Express Men of the Match: *Tigers:* Andy Lynch; *Vikings:* Ryan Sheridan.
Penalty count: 7-5; **Half-time:** 12-2;
Referee: Peter Taberner (Wigan); **Attendance:** 6,516.

HUDDERSFIELD GIANTS 6 BRADFORD BULLS 52

GIANTS: 3 Ben Cooper; 2 Hefin O'Hare; 26 Jamie Bloem; 4 Julian Bailey; 34 Marcus St Hilaire; 6 Brandon Costin (C); 17 Graham Holroyd; 25 Darren Fleary; 9 Paul March; 10 Jim Gannon; 7 Jarrod O'Doherty; 11 Eorl Crabtree; 15 Darren Turner. Subs (all used): 33 Stanley Gene; 8 Mick Slicker; 22 Gareth Greenwood (D); 19 Iain Morrison.
Try: Bailey (77); **Goal:** Bloem 1/1.
BULLS: 1 Robbie Paul (C); 2 Tevita Vaikona; 20 Scott Naylor; 4 Shontayne Hape; 5 Lesley Vainikolo; 15 Karl Pratt; 7 Paul Deacon; 8 Joe Vagana; 24 Aaron Smith (D); 11 Daniel Gartner; 14 Lee Gilmour; 12 Jamie Peacock; 13 Mike Forshaw. Subs (all used): 17 Stuart Reardon; 18 Lee Radford; 27 Robert Parker; 10 Paul Anderson.
Tries: Vaikona (2, 26), Paul (11, 58, 69), Naylor (15), Pratt (38), Peacock (68), Vainikolo (72);
Goals: Deacon 3/4, Radford 5/5.
Rugby Leaguer & League Express Men of the Match: *Giants:* Eorl Crabtree; *Bulls:* Tevita Vaikona.
Penalty count: 4-3; **Half-time:** 0-28;
Referee: Ian Smith (Oldham); **Attendance:** 8,297.

ROUND 11

Friday 23rd May 2003

BRADFORD BULLS 48 LEEDS RHINOS 22

BULLS: 1 Robbie Paul (C); 2 Tevita Vaikona; 20 Scott Naylor; 4 Shontayne Hape; 5 Lesley Vainikolo; 15 Karl Pratt; 7 Paul Deacon; 8 Joe Vagana; 9 James Lowes; 11 Daniel Gartner; 18 Lee Radford; 12 Jamie Peacock; 13 Mike Forshaw. Subs (all used): 17 Stuart Reardon; 14 Lee Gilmour; 27 Robert Parker; 10 Paul Anderson.
Tries: Vaikona (3, 75), Gartner (29), Anderson (33), Paul (38), Vainikolo (41, 62), Pratt (46); **Goals:** Deacon 8/10.
RHINOS: 18 Gary Connolly; 2 Mark Calderwood; 3 Chris McKenna; 5 Chev Walker; 1 Francis Cummins; 6 Danny McGuire; 14 Andrew Dunemann; 19 Ryan Bailey; 9 Matt Diskin; 10 Barrie McDermott; 11 David Furner; 12 Matt Adamson; 13 Kevin Sinfield (C). Subs (all used): 17 Wayne McDonald; 16 Willie Poching; 7 Rob Burrow; 8 Danny Ward.
Tries: Walker (56), Calderwood (60), Sinfield (72);
Goals: Sinfield 5/6.
Rugby Leaguer & League Express Men of the Match: *Bulls:* Tevita Vaikona; *Rhinos:* Matt Adamson.
Penalty count: 4-4; **Half-time:** 24-6; **Referee:** Karl Kirkpatrick (Warrington); **Attendance:** 21,784.

WIGAN WARRIORS 58 HALIFAX 12

WARRIORS: 22 Shaun Briscoe; 5 Brian Carney; 4 Paul Johnson; 14 David Hodgson; 3 Jamie Ainscough; 28 Nick Graham; 7 Adrian Lam; 16 Danny Sculthorpe; 9 Terry Newton; 21 Ricky Bibey; 11 Mick Cassidy; 12 Danny Tickle; 13 Andy Farrell (C). Subs (all used): 25 Kevin Brown; 23 Gareth Hock; 18 Martin Aspinwall; 17 Mark Smith.
Tries: Hodgson (12), Newton (19), Farrell (23, 56, 64), Johnson (40), Brown (50, 59, 61), Ainscough (68);
Goals: Farrell 9/11.
Sin bin: Newton (54) - fighting.
HALIFAX: 5 Lee Finnerty; 33 Andrew Frew; 15 Ryan Clayton; 3 Stuart Donlan; 2 Lee Greenwood; 20 Dane Dorahy; 7 Sean Penkywicz; 8 Andy Hobson; 9 Johnny Lawless (C); 16 Chris Birchall; 11 Heath Cruckshank; 12 Andrew Brocklehurst; 6 Martin Moana. Subs (all used): 4 Danny Halliwell; 10 Paul Davidson; 18 Jaymes Chapman; 17 Anthony Seuseu.
Tries: Birchall (72), Chapman (79);
Goals: Dorahy 1/1, Finnerty 1/2.
Sin bin: Davidson (26) - dissent, (54) - fighting; Birchall (36) - holding down.
Rugby Leaguer & League Express Men of the Match: *Warriors:* Andy Farrell; *Halifax:* Johnny Lawless.
Penalty count: 6-8; **Half-time:** 22-2;
Referee: Russell Smith (Castleford); **Attendance:** 7,393.

Saturday 24th May 2003

WARRINGTON WOLVES 16 CASTLEFORD TIGERS 32

WOLVES: 1 Lee Penny; 2 Rob Smyth; 3 Brent Grose; 12 Ian Sibbit; 5 Graham Appo; 6 Lee Briers (C); 7 Nathan Wood; 8 Nick Fozzard; 9 Jon Clarke; 10 Mark Hilton; 15 Jerome Guisset; 23 Mike Wainwright; 13 Sid Domic. Subs (all used): 14 Mark Gleeson; 11 Darren Burns; 16 Paul Wood; 17 Warren Stevens.
Tries: Burns (15), Briers (39), Smyth (59);
Goals: Briers 2/3.
TIGERS: 20 Tom Saxton; 2 Waine Pryce; 1 Damian Gibson; 3 Michael Eagar; 5 Darren Rogers; 6 Danny Orr (C); 7 Mitch Healey; 8 Nathan Sykes; 13 Ryan Hudson; 10 Andy Lynch; 14 Andy Johnson; 12 Dale Fritz; 9 Wayne Bartrim. Subs (all used): 27 Jon Hepworth; 21 Richard Blakeway; 23 Michael Smith; 36 Dean Sampson.
Tries: Hudson (21, 76), Sampson (29), Pryce (37), Saxton (54); **Goals:** Bartrim 5/5, Orr 1/1.
Rugby Leaguer & League Express Men of the Match: *Wolves:* Nick Fozzard; *Tigers:* Andy Lynch.
Penalty count: 6-3; **Half-time:** 10-18;
Referee: Ian Smith (Oldham); **Attendance:** 6,090.

Sunday 25th May 2003

WIDNES VIKINGS 42 HUDDERSFIELD GIANTS 30

VIKINGS: 19 Paul Atcheson; 2 Paul Devlin; 3 Deon Bird; 4 Adam Hughes; 24 Chris Giles; 26 Julian O'Neill (A); 7 Ryan Sheridan (C); 8 Robert Relf; 9 Shane Millard; 17 Anthony Farrell; 11 Andy Hay; 12 Steve McCurrie; 13 Daniel Frame. Subs: 14 Marvin Golden (not used); 10 Julian O'Neill (NZ); 23 David Mills; 22 Phil Cantillon.
Tries: Bird (19, 58, 80), Hughes (27, 76), Frame (38), Sheridan (72); **Goals:** O'Neill (A) 7/7.
GIANTS: 1 Paul Reilly; 2 Hefin O'Hare; 26 Jamie Bloem; 4 Julian Bailey; 34 Marcus St Hilaire; 6 Brandon Costin; 13 Steve McNamara (C); 25 Darren Fleary; 9 Paul March; 10 Jim Gannon; 7 Jarrod O'Doherty; 11 Eorl Crabtree; 33 Stanley Gene. Subs (all used): 15 Darren Turner; 8 Mick Slicker; 18 Jon Grayshon; 19 Iain Morrison.
Tries: Bailey (2), St Hilaire (30), Reilly (35), Costin (52, 68); **Goals:** McNamara 3/3, Costin 1/2, Bloem 1/1.
Rugby Leaguer & League Express Men of the Match: *Vikings:* Julian O'Neill (A); *Giants:* Stanley Gene.
Penalty count: 6-4; **Half-time:** 18-18;
Referee: Steve Ganson (St Helens); **Attendance:** 4,946.

WAKEFIELD TRINITY WILDCATS 12 LONDON BRONCOS 36

WILDCATS: 1 Martyn Holland; 24 Colum Halpenny; 3 Gareth Ellis; 17 Richard Newlove; 2 Waisale Sovatabua; 16 Jamie Rooney; 7 Brad Davis; 18 Michael Korkidas; 9 David March; 12 Jamie Field; 11 Troy Slattery; 15 Ian Knott; 13 Adrian Vowles (C). Subs (all used): 14 Paul Handforth; 20 David Wrench; 21 Steve Snitch; 5 Jon Wells.
Try: Knott (14); **Goals:** Rooney 4/4.
BRONCOS: 7 Dennis Moran; 2 Dominic Peters; 4 Tony Martin; 3 Nigel Roy; 5 Steve Hall; 6 Rob Purdham; 23 Chris Thorman; 8 Francis Stephenson; 14 Neil Budworth; 29 Tommy Gallagher; 9 Bill Peden; 11 Mat Toshack; 13 Jim Dymock (C). Subs (all used): 22 Andrew Hamilton; 10 Richard Marshall; 12 Steele Retchless; 24 Russell Bawden.
Tries: Thorman (6), Moran (18, 60, 78), Bawden (23), Roy (66); **Goals:** Thorman 6/8.

Rugby Leaguer & League Express Men of the Match: *Wildcats:* Paul Handforth; *Broncos:* Dennis Moran.
Penalty count: 7-5; **Half-time:** 8-18; **Referee:** Richard Silverwood (Dewsbury); **Attendance:** 3,305.

Monday 26th May 2003

HULL FC 30 ST HELENS 6

HULL: 1 Steve Prescott; 2 Colin Best; 4 Toa Kohe-Love; 3 Richie Barnett (C); 24 Kirk Yeaman; 16 Paul Cooke; 6 Richard Horne; 8 Craig Greenhill; 9 Dean Treister; 10 Paul King; 14 Sean Ryan; 11 Adam Maher; 17 Chris Chester. Subs (all used): 20 Garreth Carvell; 30 Ewan Dowes (D); 26 Graeme Horne; 25 Glen Donkin.
Tries: Yeaman (4), Prescott (15), Donkin (32), Best (49, 67), Kohe-Love (60); **Goals:** Prescott 3/6.
Sin bin: Kohe-Love (44) - obstruction.
ST HELENS: 1 Paul Wellens; 5 Darren Albert; 3 Martin Gleeson; 4 Paul Newlove; 2 Anthony Stewart; 13 Paul Sculthorpe; 7 Sean Long; 8 Darren Britt; 9 Keiron Cunningham; 11 Chris Joynt (C); 17 Mike Bennett; 23 Jon Wilkin; 16 Darren Smith. Subs (all used): 15 Tim Jonkers; 14 Mick Higham; 18 Mark Edmondson; 10 Barry Ward.
Try: Joynt (56); **Goal:** Sculthorpe 1/1.
Rugby Leaguer & League Express Men of the Match: *Hull:* Steve Prescott; *Saints:* Paul Wellens.
Penalty count: 4-3; **Half time:** 14-0;
Referee: Robert Connolly (Wigan); **Attendance:** 12,490.

ROUND 12

Friday 30th May 2003

CASTLEFORD TIGERS 32 HUDDERSFIELD GIANTS 18

TIGERS: 20 Tom Saxton; 2 Waine Pryce; 1 Damian Gibson; 3 Michael Eagar; 5 Darren Rogers; 6 Danny Orr (C); 7 Mitch Healey; 8 Nathan Sykes; 13 Ryan Hudson; 10 Andy Lynch; 23 Michael Smith; 14 Andy Johnson; 9 Wayne Bartrim. Subs (all used): 27 Jon Hepworth; 19 Wayne Godwin; 21 Richard Blakeway; 36 Dean Sampson.
Tries: Eagar (5, 11), Orr (38), Rogers (46), Bartrim (53), Johnson (57); **Goals:** Bartrim 4/7.
GIANTS: 1 Paul Reilly; 2 Hefin O'Hare; 3 Ben Cooper; 4 Julian Bailey; 34 Marcus St Hilaire; 6 Brandon Costin; 33 Stanley Gene; 25 Darren Fleary; 9 Paul March; 10 Jim Gannon; 7 Jarrod O'Doherty; 19 Iain Morrison; 13 Steve McNamara (C). Subs (all used): 15 Darren Turner; 8 Mick Slicker; 26 Jamie Bloem; 17 Graham Holroyd.
Tries: Gene (23), Bailey (67), March (71);
Goals: McNamara 3/3.
Rugby Leaguer & League Express Men of the Match: *Tigers:* Michael Eagar; *Giants:* Brandon Costin.
Penalty count: 11-7; **Half-time:** 18-6;
Referee: Peter Taberner (Wigan); **Attendance:** 5,682.

HALIFAX 10 HULL FC 60

HALIFAX: 5 Lee Finnerty; 2 Lee Greenwood; 15 Ryan Clayton; 33 Andrew Frew; 19 John Kirkpatrick (D); 20 Dane Dorahy; 7 Sean Penkywicz; 8 Andy Hobson; 9 Johnny Lawless (C); 16 Chris Birchall; 11 Heath Cruckshank; 12 Andrew Brocklehurst; 14 Liam Finn. Subs (all used): 10 Paul Davidson; 17 Anthony Seuseu; 18 Jaymes Chapman; 21 Chris Norman.
Tries: Frew (47), Lawless (76);
Goals: Dorahy 1/1, Finn 0/1.
HULL: 1 Steve Prescott; 2 Colin Best; 4 Toa Kohe-Love; 24 Kirk Yeaman; 3 Richie Barnett (C); 6 Richard Horne; 16 Paul Cooke; 8 Craig Greenhill; 9 Dean Treister; 10 Paul King; 11 Adam Maher; 14 Sean Ryan; 17 Chris Chester. Subs (all used): 30 Ewan Dowes; 26 Graeme Horne; 20 Garreth Carvell; 25 Glen Donkin.
Tries: Barnett (2, 19), Prescott (13, 37), Maher (22), Yeaman (54), Dowes (59), Chester (61, 73), Best (66);
Goals: Prescott 10/10.
Rugby Leaguer & League Express Men of the Match: *Halifax:* Johnny Lawless; *Hull:* Steve Prescott.
Penalty count: 0-0; **Half-time:** 0-30;
Referee: Colin Morris (Huddersfield); **Attendance:** 3,143.

WIGAN WARRIORS 20 LEEDS RHINOS 30

WARRIORS: 22 Shaun Briscoe; 2 Brett Dallas; 4 Paul Johnson; 14 David Hodgson; 3 Jamie Ainscough; 15 Sean O'Loughlin; 7 Adrian Lam; 8 Terry O'Connor; 9 Terry Newton; 16 Danny Sculthorpe; 11 Mick Cassidy; 13 Andy Farrell (C); 28 Nick Graham. Subs (all used): 17 Mark Smith; 18 Martin Aspinwall; 21 Ricky Bibey; 12 Danny Tickle.
Tries: Briscoe (14, 18), Aspinwall (45); **Goals:** Farrell 4/4.
Sin bin: Newton (73) - fighting.
RHINOS: 18 Gary Connolly; 2 Mark Calderwood; 3 Chris McKenna; 4 Keith Senior; 1 Francis Cummins; 6 Danny McGuire; 14 Andrew Dunemann; 17 Wayne McDonald; 9 Matt Diskin; 10 Barrie McDermott; 11 David Furner; 5 Chev Walker; 13 Kevin Sinfield (C). Subs (all used): 7 Rob Burrow; 19 Ryan Bailey; 16 Willie Poching; 15 Chris Feather.
Tries: Cummins (26), Calderwood (40), McGuire (50), Burrow (62), Connolly (65); **Goals:** Sinfield 5/5.
Sin bin: Bailey (73) - fighting.
Rugby Leaguer & League Express Men of the Match: *Warriors:* Shaun Briscoe; *Rhinos:* Kevin Sinfield.
Penalty count: 9-3; **Half-time:** 14-12;
Referee: Ian Smith (Oldham); **Attendance:** 11,386.

Saturday 31st May 2003

WIDNES VIKINGS 34 WAKEFIELD TRINITY WILDCATS 6

VIKINGS: 19 Paul Atcheson; 2 Paul Devlin; 3 Deon Bird; 4 Adam Hughes; 24 Chris Giles; 26 Julian O'Neill (A); 7 Ryan Sheridan (C); 8 Robert Relf; 9 Shane Millard; 17 Anthony Farrell; 11 Andy Hay; 12 Steve McCurrie; 13 Daniel Frame. Subs (all used): 1 Stuart Spruce; 10 Julian O'Neill (NZ); 23 David Mills; 22 Phil Cantillon.
Tries: Frame (6), Giles (18), O'Neill (NZ) (36), Devlin (56), Sheridan (68), Bird (73);
Goals: O'Neill (A) 3/5, Hughes 2/2.
WILDCATS: 4 Matt Seers; 24 Colum Halpenny; 3 Gareth Ellis; 17 Richard Newlove; 5 Jon Wells; 6 Ben Jeffries; 7 Brad Davis (C); 18 Michael Korkidas; 14 Paul Handforth; 10 Dallas Hood; 11 Troy Slattery; 21 Steve Snitch; 15 Ian Knott. Subs (all used): 1 Martyn Holland; 9 David March; 23 Robert Spicer; 25 Darrell Griffin (D).
Try: Jeffries (79); **Goal:** Knott 1/2, Davis 0/1.
Rugby Leaguer & League Express Men of the Match: *Vikings:* Shane Millard; *Wildcats:* Gareth Ellis.
Penalty count: 3-8; **Half-time:** 16-0; **Referee:** Karl Kirkpatrick (Warrington); **Attendance:** 5,179.

Sunday 1st June 2003

BRADFORD BULLS 12 LONDON BRONCOS 22

BULLS: 1 Robbie Paul (C); 2 Tevita Vaikona; 20 Scott Naylor; 4 Shontayne Hape; 5 Lesley Vainikolo; 15 Karl Pratt; 7 Paul Deacon; 8 Joe Vagana; 9 James Lowes; 11 Daniel Gartner; 18 Lee Radford; 12 Jamie Peacock; 13 Mike Forshaw. Subs (all used): 3 Leon Pryce; 19 Jamie Langley; 27 Robert Parker; 10 Paul Anderson.
Tries: Naylor (32), Parker (37); **Goals:** Deacon 2/2.
BRONCOS: 7 Dennis Moran; 1 Paul Sykes; 3 Nigel Roy; 4 Tony Martin; 5 Steve Hall; 6 Rob Purdham; 23 Chris Thorman; 24 Russell Bawden; 14 Neil Budworth; 12 Steele Retchless; 9 Bill Peden; 11 Mat Toshack; 13 Jim Dymock (C). Subs (all used): 26 Damien Kennedy; 10 Richard Marshall; 8 Francis Stephenson; 29 Tommy Gallagher.
Tries: Moran (5, 37, 51), Toshack (20);
Goals: Thorman 3/4.
Rugby Leaguer & League Express Men of the Match: *Bulls:* Jamie Peacock; *Broncos:* Dennis Moran.
Penalty count: 3-2; **Half-time:** 12-16;
Referee: Robert Connolly (Wigan); **Attendance:** 10,835.

WARRINGTON WOLVES 30 ST HELENS 30

WOLVES: 1 Lee Penny; 2 Rob Smyth; 3 Brent Grose; 12 Ian Sibbit; 5 Graham Appo; 6 Lee Briers (C); 7 Nathan Wood; 8 Nick Fozzard; 9 Jon Clarke; 10 Mark Hilton; 11 Darren Burns; 23 Mike Wainwright; 13 Sid Domic. Subs (all used): 18 Paul Noone; 14 Mark Gleeson; 15 Jerome Guisset; 17 Warren Stevens.
Tries: Grose (4, 17), Clarke (26), Guisset (42), Penny (75); **Goals:** Briers 5/5.
SAINTS: 2 Anthony Stewart; 5 Darren Albert; 3 Martin Gleeson; 4 Paul Newlove; 19 Ade Gardner; 13 Paul Sculthorpe; 7 Sean Long; 8 Darren Britt; 9 Keiron Cunningham; 11 Chris Joynt (C); 17 Mike Bennett; 12 John Stankevitch; 16 Darren Smith. Subs (all used): 1 Paul Wellens; 14 Mick Higham; 10 Barry Ward; 22 Stuart Jones.
Tries: Bennett (13), Sculthorpe (23, 47), Gardner (51), Long (53), Newlove (64); **Goals:** Sculthorpe 3/6.
Rugby Leaguer & League Express Men of the Match: *Wolves:* Lee Briers; *Saints:* Ade Gardner.
Penalty count: 4-4; **Half-time:** 18-10; **Referee:** Richard Silverwood (Dewsbury); **Attendance:** 8,590.

ROUND 13

Friday 6th June 2003

ST HELENS 34 WIGAN WARRIORS 38

SAINTS: 1 Paul Wellens; 19 Ade Gardner; 3 Martin Gleeson; 4 Paul Newlove; 2 Anthony Stewart; 13 Paul Sculthorpe; 7 Sean Long; 8 Darren Britt; 9 Keiron Cunningham; 26 Keith Mason (D); 11 Chris Joynt (C); 17 Mike Bennett; 16 Darren Smith. Subs (all used): 6 Jason Hooper; 14 Mick Higham; 10 Barry Ward; 22 Stuart Jones.
Tries: Gleeson (1), Wellens (9), Ward (24), Gardner (60), Smith (70, 80); **Goals:** Sculthorpe 5/7.
Sin bin: Jones (35) - fighting.
WARRIORS: 22 Shaun Briscoe; 4 Paul Johnson; 18 Martin Aspinwall; 25 Kevin Brown; 14 David Hodgson; 15 Sean O'Loughlin; 7 Adrian Lam; 10 Craig Smith; 9 Terry Newton; 8 Terry O'Connor; 11 Mick Cassidy; 26 Nick Graham; 13 Andy Farrell (C). Subs (all used): 20 Luke Robinson; 16 Danny Sculthorpe; 23 Gareth Hock; 17 Mark Smith.
Tries: Hodgson (31), Robinson (38, 46, 56), Brown (43, 50); **Goals:** Farrell 7/7.
Sin bin: O'Loughlin (15) - obstruction;
Sculthorpe (35) - fighting.
Rugby Leaguer & League Express Men of the Match: *Saints:* Paul Sculthorpe; *Warriors:* Luke Robinson.
Penalty count: 6-8; **Half-time:** 20-12;
Referee: Russell Smith (Castleford); **Attendance:** 12,827.

Saturday 7th June 2003

LEEDS RHINOS 39 CASTLEFORD TIGERS 26

RHINOS: 18 Gary Connolly; 2 Mark Calderwood; 5 Chev Walker; 4 Keith Senior; 1 Francis Cummins; 14 Andrew Dunemann; 6 Danny McGuire; 17 Wayne McDonald; 9 Matt Diskin; 10 Barrie McDermott; 11 David Furner; 16 Willie Poching; 13 Kevin Sinfield (C). Subs (all used): 15 Chris Feather; 19 Ryan Bailey; 7 Rob Burrow; 20 Jamie Jones-Buchanan.
Tries: McDonald (13), Cummins (19, 28), Calderwood (35), McGuire (57), Burrow (59), Senior (78);
Goals: Sinfield 5/8; **Field goal:** Burrow.
TIGERS: 20 Tom Saxton; 2 Waine Pryce; 1 Damian Gibson; 3 Michael Eagar; 5 Darren Rogers; 6 Danny Orr (C); 7 Mitch Healey; 36 Dean Sampson; 13 Ryan Hudson; 10 Andy Lynch; 23 Michael Smith; 14 Andy Johnson; 9 Wayne Bartrim. Subs (all used): 19 Wayne Godwin; 26 Craig Huby (D); 27 Jon Hepworth; 21 Richard Blakeway.
Tries: Eagar (5), Orr (9), Pryce (39, 41), Rogers (62);
Goals: Bartrim 3/5.
Rugby Leaguer & League Express Men of the Match: *Rhinos:* Andrew Dunemann; *Tigers:* Ryan Hudson.
Penalty count: 6-4; **Half-time:** 20-16; **Referee:** Richard Silverwood (Dewsbury); **Attendance:** 14,488.

Sunday 8th June 2003

LONDON BRONCOS 40 WIDNES VIKINGS 18

BRONCOS: 7 Dennis Moran; 1 Paul Sykes; 3 Nigel Roy; 4 Tony Martin; 5 Steve Hall; 6 Rob Purdham; 23 Chris Thorman; 24 Russell Bawden; 14 Neil Budworth; 12 Steele Retchless; 11 Mat Toshack; 9 Bill Peden; 13 Jim Dymock (C). Subs (all used): 10 Richard Marshall; 22 Andrew Hamilton; 25 Andrew King; 29 Tommy Gallagher.
Tries: Peden (13), Thorman (16), Sykes (19, 34), Gallagher (32), Moran (36, 78); **Goals:** Thorman 6/6.
VIKINGS: 19 Paul Atcheson; 2 Paul Devlin; 3 Deon Bird; 4 Adam Hughes; 24 Chris Giles; 26 Julian O'Neill (A); 7 Ryan Sheridan (C); 8 Robert Relf; 9 Shane Millard; 17 Anthony Farrell; 11 Andy Hay; 12 Steve McCurrie; 13 Daniel Frame. Subs (all used): 22 Phil Cantillon; 23 David Mills; 10 Julian O'Neill (NZ); 1 Stuart Spruce.
Tries: Millard (4, 69), Cantillon (59);
Goals: O'Neill (A) 3/3.
Rugby Leaguer & League Express Men of the Match: *Broncos:* Jim Dymock; *Vikings:* Shane Millard.
Penalty count: 5-4; **Half-time:** 34-6;
Referee: Ian Smith (Oldham); **Attendance:** 3,128
(at Talbot Athletic Ground, Port Talbot).

HULL FC 20 BRADFORD BULLS 26

HULL: 1 Steve Prescott; 2 Colin Best; 4 Toa Kohe-Love; 24 Kirk Yeaman; 3 Richie Barnett (C); 16 Paul Cooke; 6 Richard Horne; 8 Craig Greenhill; 9 Dean Treister; 10 Paul King; 11 Adam Maher; 14 Sean Ryan; 17 Chris Chester. Subs (all used): 20 Garreth Carvell; 30 Ewan Dowes; 26 Graeme Horne; 19 Richard Fletcher.
Tries: Barnett (45), R Horne (67), Best (79);
Goals: Prescott 4/5.
Dismissal: Fletcher (54) – kicking.
Sin bin: Treister (62) – fighting.
BULLS: 1 Robbie Paul (C); 2 Tevita Vaikona; 3 Leon Pryce; 4 Shontayne Hape; 5 Lesley Vainikolo; 15 Karl Pratt; 7 Paul Deacon; 8 Joe Vagana; 9 James Lowes; 27 Robert Parker; 11 Daniel Gartner; 12 Jamie Peacock; 13 Mike Forshaw. Subs (all used): 17 Stuart Reardon; 14 Lee Gilmour; 18 Lee Radford; 30 Richard Moore.
Tries: Pratt (27), Hape (55), Vainikolo (66);
Goals: Deacon 7/8.
Sin bin: Peacock (13) - obstruction;
Radford (62) - fighting.
Rugby Leaguer & League Express Men of the Match: *Hull:* Craig Greenhill; *Bulls:* Paul Deacon.
Penalty count: 10-13; **Half-time:** 4-8;
Referee: Steve Ganson (St Helens); **Attendance:** 19,549.

WAKEFIELD TRINITY WILDCATS 32 WARRINGTON WOLVES 12

WILDCATS: 1 Martyn Holland; 24 Colum Halpenny; 4 Matt Seers; 5 Jon Wells; 17 Richard Newlove; 14 Paul Handforth; 7 Brad Davis; 12 Jamie Field; 9 David March; 10 Dallas Hood; 11 Troy Slattery; 3 Gareth Ellis; 13 Adrian Vowles (C). Subs (all used): 6 Ben Jeffries; 21 Steve Snitch; 23 Robert Spicer; 25 Darrell Griffin.
Tries: Davis (18, 73), Halpenny (21), March (50), Vowles (60), Jeffries (68); **Goals:** Davis 4/6.
WOLVES: 5 Graham Appo; 2 Rob Smyth; 3 Brent Grose; 12 Ian Sibbit; 20 Dean Gaskell; 6 Lee Briers (C); 7 Nathan Wood; 8 Nick Fozzard; 9 Jon Clarke; 10 Mark Hilton; 11 Darren Burns; 23 Mike Wainwright; 13 Sid Domic. Subs (all used): 18 Paul Noone; 14 Mark Gleeson; 15 Jerome Guisset; 17 Warren Stevens.
Tries: Smyth (33), Grose (40); **Goals:** Briers 2/3.
Rugby Leaguer & League Express Men of the Match: *Wildcats:* David March; *Wolves:* Lee Briers.
Penalty count: 9-8; **Half-time:** 10-12;
Referee: Peter Taberner (Wigan); **Attendance:** 3,612.

HUDDERSFIELD GIANTS 28 HALIFAX 26

GIANTS: 1 Paul Reilly; 2 Hefin O'Hare; 26 Jamie Bloem; 4 Julian Bailey; 34 Marcus St Hilaire; 6 Brandon Costin; 17 Graham Holroyd; 25 Darren Fleary (C); 9 Paul March; 10 Jim Gannon; 7 Jarrod O'Doherty; 23 Ben Roarty (D); 15 Darren Turner. Subs (all used): 8 Mick Slicker; 19 Iain Morrison; 3 Ben Cooper; 5 Matthew Whitaker.
Tries: Roarty (9), Reilly (17), Turner (39), O'Hare (55), Costin (71); **Goals:** Costin 4/6.
HALIFAX: 1 Daryl Cardiss; 19 John Kirkpatrick; 33 Andrew Frew; 15 Ryan Clayton; 2 Lee Greenwood; 20 Dane Dorahy; 7 Sean Penkywicz; 8 Andy Hobson; 9 Johnny Lawless (C); 16 Chris Birchall; 13 Shayne McMenemy; 12 Andrew Brocklehurst; 14 Liam Finn. Subs (all used): 5 Lee Finnerty; 11 Heath Cruckshank; 10 Paul Davidson; 25 Neil Harmon (D).
Tries: Penkywicz (26), Finn (35), Davidson (60), Frew (79); **Goals:** Dorahy 5/5.
Rugby Leaguer & League Express Men of the Match: *Giants:* Darren Turner; *Halifax:* Dane Dorahy.
Penalty count: 9-5; **Half-time:** 18-12;
Referee: Robert Connolly (Wigan); **Attendance:** 3,980.

ROUND 14

Friday 13th June 2003

LEEDS RHINOS 20 ST HELENS 14

RHINOS: 18 Gary Connolly; 2 Mark Calderwood; 5 Chev Walker; 4 Keith Senior; 1 Francis Cummins; 14 Andrew Dunemann; 6 Danny McGuire; 17 Wayne McDonald; 9 Matt Diskin; 10 Barrie McDermott; 11 David Furner; 12 Matt Adamson; 13 Kevin Sinfield (C). Subs (all used): 19 Ryan Bailey; 15 Chris Feather; 16 Willie Poching; 7 Rob Burrow.
Tries: Walker (2), Connolly (18), Cummins (26);
Goals: Sinfield 4/6.
SAINTS: 1 Paul Wellens; 2 Anthony Stewart; 3 Martin Gleeson; 5 Darren Albert; 19 Ade Gardner; 13 Paul Sculthorpe; 7 Sean Long; 8 Darren Britt; 9 Keiron Cunningham; 26 Keith Mason; 11 Chris Joynt (C); 17 Mike Bennett; 16 Darren Smith. Subs (all used): 10 Barry Ward; 15 Tim Jonkers; 6 Jason Hooper; 14 Mick Higham.
Tries: Cunningham (3, 31), Wellens (46);
Goals: Long 1/3.
On report: Hooper (60) - late challenge on Sinfield.
Rugby Leaguer & League Express Men of the Match: *Rhinos:* Andrew Dunemann; *Saints:* Paul Wellens.
Penalty count: 7-6; **Half time:** 16-10; **Referee:** Karl Kirkpatrick (Warrington); **Attendance:** 14,073.

WIGAN WARRIORS 28 HULL FC 14

WARRIORS: 22 Shaun Briscoe; 18 Martin Aspinwall; 15 Sean O'Loughlin; 25 Kevin Brown; 14 David Hodgson; 28 Nick Graham; 7 Adrian Lam; 8 Terry O'Connor; 9 Terry Newton; 10 Craig Smith; 11 Mick Cassidy; 23 Gareth Hock; 13 Andy Farrell (C). Subs (all used): 20 Luke Robinson; 12 Danny Tickle; 17 Mark Smith; 21 Ricky Bibey.
Tries: Hodgson (15, 68), Hock (20), Aspinwall (44);
Goals: Farrell 6/7.
HULL: 6 Richard Horne; 2 Colin Best; 4 Toa Kohe-Love; 24 Kirk Yeaman; 1 Steve Prescott; 16 Paul Cooke (C); 26 Graeme Horne; 8 Craig Greenhill; 9 Dean Treister; 10 Paul King; 14 Sean Ryan; 11 Adam Maher; 17 Chris Chester. Subs (all used): 22 Andy Last; 30 Ewan Dowes; 20 Garreth Carvell; 19 Richard Fletcher.
Tries: Chester (29), R Horne (49); **Goals:** Prescott 3/3.
Sin bin: R Horne (74) - holding down.
Rugby Leaguer & League Express Men of the Match: *Warriors:* Andy Farrell; *Hull:* Sean Ryan.
Penalty count: 5-5; **Half-time:** 12-8; **Referee:** Richard Silverwood (Dewsbury); **Attendance:** 11,278.

Saturday 14th June 2003

HALIFAX 20 WIDNES VIKINGS 48

HALIFAX: 5 Lee Finnerty; 2 Lee Greenwood; 15 Ryan Clayton; 33 Andrew Frew; 19 John Kirkpatrick; 14 Liam Finn; 1 Daryl Cardiss; 8 Andy Hobson; 9 Johnny Lawless (C); 16 Chris Birchall; 11 Heath Cruckshank; 12 Andrew Brocklehurst; 13 Shayne McMenemy. Subs (all used): 7 Sean Penkywicz; 10 Paul Davidson; 21 Chris Norman; 25 Neil Harmon.
Tries: Finnerty (17), Norman (35), Penkywicz (69);
Goals: Finn 3/4, Finnerty 1/1.
VIKINGS: 1 Stuart Spruce; 2 Paul Devlin; 5 Jason Demetriou; 4 Adam Hughes; 24 Chris Giles; 26 Julian O'Neill (A); 7 Ryan Sheridan (C); 8 Robert Relf; 9 Shane Millard; 17 Anthony Farrell; 27 Paul Alcock; 12 Steve McCurrie; 13 Daniel Frame. Subs (all used): 11 Andy Hay; 18 Dean Lawford; 22 Phil Cantillon; 23 David Mills.
Tries: Millard (2), Relf (10), Giles (27, 38), Lawford (52), Frame (60), Demetriou (74), Hughes (79);
Goals: O'Neill (A) 7/9; **Field goals:** O'Neill (A), Lawford.
Rugby Leaguer & League Express Men of the Match: *Halifax:* Paul Davidson; *Vikings:* Adam Hughes.
Penalty count: 8-4; **Half-time:** 12-21;
Referee: Steve Ganson (St Helens); **Attendance:** 1,919.

Sunday 15th June 2003

WARRINGTON WOLVES 20 BRADFORD BULLS 24

WOLVES: 5 Graham Appo; 2 Rob Smyth; 3 Brent Grose; 18 Paul Noone; 20 Dean Gaskell; 7 Nathan Wood (C); 9 Jon Clarke; 8 Nick Fozzard; 14 Mark Gleeson; 10 Mark Hilton; 16 Paul Wood; 23 Mike Wainwright; 11 Darren Burns. Subs (all used): 15 Jerome Guisset; 21 Matt Sturm; 17 Warren Stevens; 19 Gary Hulse.
Tries: Smyth (14), Appo (39), Grose (53);
Goals: Appo 4/5.
On report: N Wood (46) - high tackle.
BULLS: 1 Robbie Paul (C); 2 Tevita Vaikona; 20 Scott Naylor; 4 Shontayne Hape; 15 Karl Pratt; 3 Leon Pryce; 7 Paul Deacon; 8 Joe Vagana; 24 Aaron Smith; 27 Robert Parker; 11 Daniel Gartner; 12 Jamie Peacock; 13 Mike Forshaw. Subs (all used): 14 Lee Gilmour; 18 Lee Radford; 10 Paul Anderson; 30 Richard Moore.
Tries: Gartner (8), Paul (46), Forshaw (78), Naylor (80);
Goals: Deacon 4/5.
Rugby Leaguer & League Express Men of the Match: *Wolves:* Nathan Wood; *Bulls:* Paul Deacon.
Penalty count: 8-7; **Half-time:** 14-6;
Referee: Russell Smith (Castleford); **Attendance:** 7,507.

CASTLEFORD TIGERS 16 LONDON BRONCOS 28

TIGERS: 20 Tom Saxton; 2 Waine Pryce; 1 Damian Gibson; 3 Michael Eagar; 5 Darren Rogers; 6 Danny Orr (C); 7 Mitch Healey; 8 Nathan Sykes; 13 Ryan Hudson; 10 Andy Lynch; 23 Michael Smith; 14 Andy Johnson; 9 Wayne Bartrim. Subs (all used): 4 Paul Mellor; 36 Dean Sampson; 27 Jon Hepworth; 21 Richard Blakeway.
Tries: Eagar (6), Rogers (58); **Goals:** Bartrim 4/4.
BRONCOS: 7 Dennis Moran; 1 Paul Sykes; 3 Nigel Roy; 4 Tony Martin; 5 Steve Hall; 6 Rob Purdham; 23 Chris Thorman; 24 Russell Bawden; 14 Neil Budworth; 12 Steele Retchless; 11 Mat Toshack; 9 Bill Peden; 13 Jim Dymock (C). Subs (all used): 10 Richard Marshall; 8 Francis Stephenson; 26 Damien Kennedy; 29 Tommy Gallagher.
Tries: Moran (30, 79), Martin (65, 68);
Goals: Thorman 6/7.
Sin bin: Martin (13) - interference.
Rugby Leaguer & League Express Men of the Match: *Tigers:* Ryan Hudson; *Broncos:* Tony Martin.
Penalty count: 8-9; **Half-time:** 8-8;
Referee: Robert Connolly (Wigan); **Attendance:** 5,630.

HUDDERSFIELD GIANTS 26 WAKEFIELD TRINITY WILDCATS 4

GIANTS: 1 Paul Reilly; 2 Hefin O'Hare; 6 Brandon Costin; 4 Julian Bailey; 34 Marcus St Hilaire; 33 Stanley Gene; 9 Paul March; 25 Darren Fleary (C); 15 Darren Turner; 10 Jim Gannon; 23 Ben Roarty; 7 Jarrod O'Doherty; 26 Jamie Bloem. Subs (all used): 13 Steve McNamara; 8 Mick Slicker; 19 Iain Morrison; 17 Graham Holroyd.
Tries: Roarty (20), Reilly (28), Costin (31), St Hilaire (39), Bailey (60); **Goals:** Costin 0/1, McNamara 3/4.
Dismissal: Reilly (80) - alleged striking.
On report: Brawl (80) - after Newlove's try.
WILDCATS: 1 Martyn Holland; 24 Colum Halpenny; 4 Matt Seers; 5 Jon Wells; 17 Richard Newlove; 14 Paul Handforth; 7 Brad Davis; 12 Jamie Field; 9 David March; 10 Dallas Hood; 11 Troy Slattery; 3 Gareth Ellis; 13 Adrian Vowles (C). Subs (all used): 6 Ben Jeffries; 18 Michael Korkidas; 21 Steve Snitch; 25 Darrell Griffin.
Try: Newlove (80).
On report: Brawl (80) - after Newlove's try.
Rugby Leaguer & League Express Men of the Match: *Giants:* Paul Reilly; *Wildcats:* Matt Seers.
Penalty count: 7-11; **Half-time:** 22-0;
Referee: Ashley Klein (London); **Attendance:** 3,989.

ROUND 15

Friday 20th June 2003

HULL FC 22 CASTLEFORD TIGERS 14

HULL: 1 Steve Prescott; 2 Colin Best; 3 Richie Barnett (C); 24 Kirk Yeaman; 32 Alex Wilkinson (D); 16 Paul Cooke; 6 Richard Horne; 8 Craig Greenhill; 9 Dean Treister; 10 Paul King; 14 Sean Ryan; 11 Adam Maher; 17 Chris Chester. Subs (all used): 20 Garreth Carvell; 30 Ewan Dowes; 26 Graeme Horne; 19 Richard Fletcher.
Tries: Yeaman (17), Treister (34, 48), King (79);
Goals: Prescott 3/4.
Sin bin: R Horne (76) - holding down.
TIGERS: 1 Damian Gibson; 2 Waine Pryce; 16 Francis Maloney; 3 Michael Eagar; 5 Darren Rogers; 6 Danny Orr (C); 7 Mitch Healey; 8 Nathan Sykes; 13 Ryan Hudson; 10 Andy Lynch; 23 Michael Smith; 12 Dale Fritz; 9 Wayne Bartrim. Subs (all used): 11 Lee Harland; 14 Andy Johnson; 27 Jon Hepworth; 4 Paul Mellor.
Tries: Orr (28), Eagar (54), Pryce (60);
Goals: Bartrim 1/2, Orr 0/1.
Rugby Leaguer & League Express Men of the Match: *Hull:* Dean Treister; *Tigers:* Danny Orr.
Penalty count: 8-9; **Half time:** 10-6;
Referee: Ashley Klein (London); **Attendance:** 10,703.

ST HELENS 58 HALIFAX 2

SAINTS: 2 Anthony Stewart; 5 Darren Albert; 3 Martin Gleeson; 1 Paul Wellens; 19 Ade Gardner; 7 Sean Long; 14 Mick Higham; 8 Darren Britt; 9 Keiron Cunningham; 10 Barry Ward; 23 Jon Wilkin; 17 Mike Bennett; 13 Paul Sculthorpe (C). Subs (all used): 22 Stuart Jones; 15 Tim Jonkers; 26 Keith Mason; 16 Darren Smith.
Tries: Britt (5), Albert (13), Wellens (16), Long (30), Gleeson (45), Sculthorpe (51, 62, 76, 79), Higham (56);
Goals: Long 9/10.
HALIFAX: 1 Daryl Cardiss; 5 Lee Finnerty; 33 Andrew Frew; 21 Chris Norman; 2 Lee Greenwood; 14 Liam Finn; 7 Sean Penkywicz; 25 Neil Harmon; 9 Johnny Lawless (C); 10 Paul Davidson; 11 Heath Cruckshank; 12 Andrew Brocklehurst; 15 Ryan Clayton. Subs (all used): 8 Andy Hobson; 16 Chris Birchall; 22 Simon Grix (D); 23 Ged Corcoran.
Goals: Finn 1/1.
Rugby Leaguer & League Express Men of the Match: *Saints:* Keiron Cunningham; *Halifax:* Sean Penkywicz.
Penalty count: 14-1; **Half-time:** 22-2;
Referee: Peter Taberner (Wigan); **Attendance:** 7,891.

WAKEFIELD TRINITY WILDCATS 12 LEEDS RHINOS 48

WILDCATS: 1 Martyn Holland; 24 Colum Halpenny; 3 Gareth Ellis; 4 Matt Seers; 5 Jon Wells; 16 Jamie Rooney; 7 Brad Davis; 18 Michael Korkidas; 9 David March; 25 Darrell Griffin; 11 Troy Slattery; 12 Jamie Field; 13 Adrian Vowles (C). Subs (all used): 20 David Wrench; 6 Ben Jeffries; 17 Richard Newlove; 21 Steve Snitch.
Tries: Halpenny (7), March (14);
Goals: Rooney 2/2, Davis 0/1.
Sin bin: March (76) - interference.
RHINOS: 21 Richard Mathers; 2 Mark Calderwood; 5 Chev Walker; 4 Keith Senior; 1 Francis Cummins; 14 Andrew Dunemann; 6 Danny McGuire; 17 Wayne McDonald; 9 Matt Diskin; 10 Barrie McDermott; 11 David Furner; 12 Matt Adamson; 13 Kevin Sinfield (C). Subs (all used): 7 Rob Burrow; 19 Ryan Bailey; 16 Willie Poching; 15 Chris Feather.
Tries: Calderwood (22, 58), Burrow (32, 43), McGuire (34), Senior (51), Cummins (65), Walker (70), Poching (78); **Goals:** Sinfield 6/10.
Rugby Leaguer & League Express Men of the Match: *Wildcats:* David March; *Rhinos:* Andrew Dunemann.
Penalty count: 9-8; **Half-time:** 12-16; **Referee:** Richard Silverwood (Dewsbury); **Attendance:** 6,678.

Saturday 21st June 2003

BRADFORD BULLS 22 WIGAN WARRIORS 35

BULLS: 1 Robbie Paul (C); 2 Tevita Vaikona; 20 Scott Naylor; 4 Shontayne Hape; 5 Lesley Vainikolo; 3 Leon Pryce; 7 Paul Deacon; 8 Joe Vagana; 9 James Lowes; 11 Daniel Gartner; 14 Lee Gilmour; 12 Jamie Peacock; 13 Mike Forshaw. Subs (all used): 15 Karl Pratt; 18 Lee Radford; 27 Robert Parker; 30 Richard Moore.
Tries: Paul (27), Deacon (43), Vagana (50), Gartner (68);
Goals: Deacon 3/4.
WARRIORS: 22 Shaun Briscoe; 5 Brian Carney; 15 Sean O'Loughlin; 18 Martin Aspinwall; 14 David Hodgson; 28 Nick Graham; 7 Adrian Lam; 10 Craig Smith; 9 Terry Newton; 8 Terry O'Connor; 11 Mick Cassidy; 23 Gareth Hock; 13 Andy Farrell (C). Subs (all used): 12 Danny Tickle; 20 Luke Robinson; 16 Danny Sculthorpe; 25 Kevin Brown.
Tries: Graham (6, 80), Farrell (11), Tickle (31);
Goals: Farrell 8/9; **Field goals:** Lam 3.
Sin bin: Sculthorpe (26) – interference at the play-the-ball.
Rugby Leaguer & League Express Men of the Match: *Bulls:* Paul Deacon; *Warriors:* Adrian Lam.
Penalty count: 7-7; **Half-time:** 6-24; **Referee:** Karl Kirkpatrick (Warrington); **Attendance:** 15,732.

Sunday 22nd June 2003

WIDNES VIKINGS 28 WARRINGTON WOLVES 32

VIKINGS: 1 Stuart Spruce (C); 2 Paul Devlin; 3 Deon Bird; 4 Adam Hughes; 5 Jason Demetriou; 26 Julian O'Neill (A); 18 Dean Lawford; 8 Robert Relf; 9 Shane Millard; 17 Anthony Farrell; 11 Andy Hay; 12 Steve McCurrie; 13 Daniel Frame. Subs (all used): 22 Phil Cantillon; 10 Julian O'Neill (NZ); 23 David Mills; 25 Simon Finnigan.
Tries: Cantillon (34), Bird (37), Millard (51), Lawford (75); **Goals:** O'Neill (A) 6/6.
WOLVES: 5 Graham Appo; 20 Dean Gaskell; 3 Brent Grose; 12 Ian Sibbit; 2 Rob Smyth; 6 Lee Briers (C); 7 Nathan Wood; 8 Nick Fozzard; 9 Jon Clarke; 10 Mark Hilton; 16 Paul Wood; 18 Paul Noone; 11 Darren Burns. Subs (all used): 19 Gary Hulse; 15 Jerome Guisset; 14 Mark Gleeson; 17 Warren Stevens.
Tries: Smyth (7), N Wood (12), Grose (26), Appo (55, 78), Hulse (69); **Goals:** Briers 4/6.
Rugby Leaguer & League Express Men of the Match: *Vikings:* Julian O'Neill (A); *Wolves:* Nathan Wood.
Penalty count: 10-6; **Half-time:** 14-16;
Referee: Ian Smith (Oldham); **Attendance:** 8,531.

Tuesday 22nd July 2003

LONDON BRONCOS 32 HUDDERSFIELD GIANTS 16

BRONCOS: 7 Dennis Moran; 1 Paul Sykes; 4 Tony Martin; 3 Nigel Roy; 25 Andrew King; 6 Rob Purdham; 23 Chris Thorman; 10 Richard Marshall; 14 Neil Budworth; 8 Francis Stephenson; 12 Steele Retchless; 9 Bill Peden; 13 Jim Dymock (C). Subs (all used): 24 Russell Bawden; 26 Damien Kennedy; 29 Tommy Gallagher; 21 Rob Jackson.
Tries: Moran (2), Retchless (45), King (60, 71), Thorman (65); **Goals:** Thorman 6/7.
GIANTS: 1 Paul Reilly; 34 Marcus St Hilaire; 4 Julian Bailey; 6 Brandon Costin; 2 Hefin O'Hare; 9 Paul March; 17 Graham Holroyd; 25 Darren Fleary (C); 13 Steve McNamara; 10 Jim Gannon; 19 Iain Morrison; 23 Ben Roarty; 26 Jamie Bloem. Subs (all used): 3 Ben Cooper; 8 Mick Slicker; 5 Matt Whitaker; 18 Jon Grayshon.
Tries: Costin (15, 52), O'Hare (79);
Goals: McNamara 2/3.
Rugby Leaguer & League Express Men of the Match: *Broncos:* Chris Thorman; *Giants:* Ben Roarty.
Penalty count: 11-8; **Half-time:** 8-6;
Referee: Robert Connolly (Wigan); **Attendance:** 2,679.

ROUND 16

Thursday 26th June 2003

HULL FC 44 WAKEFIELD TRINITY WILDCATS 4

HULL: 1 Steve Prescott; 28 Gareth Raynor (D3); 2 Colin Best; 24 Kirk Yeaman; 32 Alex Wilkinson; 16 Paul Cooke (C); 6 Richard Horne; 8 Craig Greenhill; 9 Dean Treister; 10 Paul King; 14 Sean Ryan; 11 Adam Maher; 31 Peter Lupton (D). Subs (all used): 20 Garreth Carvell; 30 Ewan Dowes; 26 Graeme Horne; 19 Richard Fletcher.
Tries: Prescott (8, 34), R Horne (11), Raynor (35), Dowes (47), Best (62), Ryan (71), G Horne (79);
Goals: Prescott 6/7, R Horne 0/1, Cooke 0/1.
WILDCATS: 1 Martyn Holland; 5 Jon Wells; 4 Matt Seers; 23 Robert Spicer; 24 Colum Halpenny; 14 Paul Handforth; 6 Ben Jeffries; 18 Michael Korkidas; 9 David March; 25 Darrell Griffin; 12 Jamie Field; 3 Gareth Ellis; 13 Adrian Vowles (C). Subs (all used): 22 Matthew Wray; 17 Richard Newlove; 21 Steve Snitch; 20 David Wrench.
Try: J Field (19); **Goals:** Handforth 0/1.
Rugby Leaguer & League Express Men of the Match: *Hull:* Craig Greenhill; *Wildcats:* Ben Jeffries.
Penalty count: 10-8; **Half-time:** 24-4;
Referee: Russell Smith (Castleford); **Attendance:** 9,575.

Friday 27th June 2003

BRADFORD BULLS 0 ST HELENS 35

BULLS: 1 Robbie Paul (C); 2 Tevita Vaikona; 20 Scott Naylor; 4 Shontayne Hape; 5 Lesley Vainikolo; 3 Leon Pryce; 7 Paul Deacon; 8 Joe Vagana; 9 James Lowes; 29 Stuart Fielden; 11 Daniel Gartner; 12 Jamie Peacock; 13 Mike Forshaw. Subs (all used): 15 Karl Pratt; 18 Lee Radford; 14 Lee Gilmour; 10 Paul Anderson.
SAINTS: 1 Paul Wellens; 2 Anthony Stewart; 3 Martin Gleeson; 6 Jason Hooper; 5 Darren Albert; 7 Sean Long; 14 Mick Higham; 8 Darren Britt; 9 Keiron Cunningham; 26 Keith Mason; 16 Darren Smith; 17 Mike Bennett; 13 Paul Sculthorpe (C). Subs (all used): 19 Ade Gardner; 11 Chris Joynt; 10 Barry Ward; 15 Tim Jonkers.
Tries: Higham (12, 15), Albert (33), Joynt (37), Sculthorpe (42), Hooper (48); **Goals:** Long 5/7;
Field goal: Long.
Rugby Leaguer & League Express Men of the Match: *Bulls:* Jamie Peacock; *Saints:* Mick Higham.
Penalty count: 10-8; **Half-time:** 0-22;
Referee: Ian Smith (Oldham); **Attendance:** 11,127.

WIGAN WARRIORS 24 CASTLEFORD TIGERS 10

WARRIORS: 22 Shaun Briscoe; 5 Brian Carney; 18 Martin Aspinwall; 4 Paul Johnson; 14 David Hodgson; 15 Sean O'Loughlin; 7 Adrian Lam; 8 Terry O'Connor; 9 Terry Newton; 10 Craig Smith; 11 Mick Cassidy; 28 Nick Graham; 13 Andy Farrell (C). Subs (all used): 16 Danny Sculthorpe; 30 Quentin Pongia (D); 20 Luke Robinson; 23 Gareth Hock.
Tries: Aspinwall (21), Hodgson (66), Johnson (77);
Goals: Farrell 6/8.
TIGERS: 5 Darren Rogers; 2 Waine Pryce; 4 Paul Mellor; 16 Francis Maloney; 28 Andy McNally; 6 Danny Orr (C); 7 Mitch Healey; 23 Michael Smith; 13 Ryan Hudson; 8 Nathan Sykes; 14 Andy Johnson; 12 Dale Fritz; 11 Lee Harland. Subs (all used): 21 Richard Blakeway; 26 Craig Huby; 27 Jon Hepworth; 10 Andy Lynch.
Tries: Orr (16), Mellor (35); **Goals:** Orr 1/4.
Rugby Leaguer & League Express Men of the Match: *Warriors:* David Hodgson; *Tigers:* Lee Harland.
Penalty count: 7-4; **Half-time:** 8-10; **Referee:** Ronnie Laughton (Barnsley); **Attendance:** 9,884.

Saturday 28th June 2003

WARRINGTON WOLVES 32 HUDDERSFIELD GIANTS 28

WOLVES: 5 Graham Appo; 2 Rob Smyth; 3 Brent Grose; 12 Ian Sibbit; 20 Dean Gaskell; 6 Lee Briers (C); 7 Nathan Wood; 8 Nick Fozzard; 9 Jon Clarke; 10 Mark Hilton; 18 Paul Noone; 11 Darren Burns; 13 Sid Domic. Subs (all used): 14 Mark Gleeson; 17 Warren Stevens; 21 Matt Sturm; 19 Gary Hulse.
Tries: Appo (10), Briers (26), Smyth (31, 76), Sibbit (55), Hilton (70); **Goals:** Briers 4/7.
On report: Fozzard (35) - alleged elbow on Gannon.
GIANTS: 1 Paul Reilly; 2 Hefin O'Hare; 4 Julian Bailey; 6 Brandon Costin; 34 Marcus St Hilaire; 33 Stanley Gene; 9 Paul March; 25 Darren Fleary (C); 15 Darren Turner; 10 Jim Gannon; 23 Ben Roarty; 7 Jarrod O'Doherty; 26 Jamie Bloem. Subs (all used): 13 Steve McNamara; 8 Mick Slicker; 19 Iain Morrison; 17 Graham Holroyd.
Tries: Fleary (6), Gene (36), March (44), Costin (79);
Goals: Costin 2/2, McNamara 4/5.
Sin bin: Bailey (47) - professional foul on Burns.
Rugby Leaguer & League Express Men of the Match: *Wolves:* Mark Hilton; *Giants:* Stanley Gene.
Penalty count: 8-5; **Half-time:** 14-14;
Referee: Steve Ganson (St Helens); **Attendance:** 5,689.

WIDNES VIKINGS 29 LEEDS RHINOS 14

VIKINGS: 1 Stuart Spruce (C); 20 Dan Potter; 5 Jason Demetriou; 4 Adam Hughes; 2 Paul Devlin; 26 Julian O'Neill (A); 18 Dean Lawford; 8 Robert Relf; 9 Shane Millard; 10 Julian O'Neill (NZ); 11 Andy Hay; 13 Daniel Frame; 3 Deon Bird. Subs (all used): 22 Phil Cantillon; 12 Steve McCurrie; 23 David Mills; 25 Simon Finnigan.
Tries: O'Neill (NZ) (9), Hughes (15), Spruce (26), Devlin (51, 68); **Goals:** O'Neill (A) 4/5; **Field goal:** Lawford.
RHINOS: 21 Richard Mathers; 2 Mark Calderwood; 5 Chev Walker; 4 Keith Senior; 1 Francis Cummins; 14 Andrew Dunemann; 6 Danny McGuire; 17 Wayne McDonald; 9 Matt Diskin; 10 Barrie McDermott; 11 David Furner; 12 Matt Adamson; 13 Kevin Sinfield (C). Subs (all used): 7 Rob Burrow; 19 Ryan Bailey; 16 Willie Poching; 15 Chris Feather.
Tries: Poching (20), Adamson (65); **Goals:** Sinfield 3/3.
Rugby Leaguer & League Express Men of the Match: *Vikings:* Julian O'Neill (NZ); *Rhinos:* Kevin Sinfield.
Penalty count: 4-3; **Half-time:** 16-8; **Referee:** Colin Morris (Huddersfield); **Attendance:** 6,837.

HALIFAX 16 LONDON BRONCOS 50

HALIFAX: 20 Dane Dorahy; 2 Lee Greenwood; 15 Ryan Clayton; 33 Andrew Frew; 19 John Kirkpatrick; 22 Simon Grix; 7 Sean Penkywicz; 8 Andy Hobson; 9 Johnny Lawless (C); 25 Neil Harmon; 11 Heath Cruckshank; 12 Andrew Brocklehurst; 6 Martin Moana. Subs (all used): 5 Lee Finnerty; 10 Paul Davidson; 21 Chris Norman; 16 Chris Birchall.
Tries: Clayton (9), Kirkpatrick (23), Frew (47);
Goals: Dorahy 2/3.
On report: Finnerty (74) - high tackle.
BRONCOS: 7 Dennis Moran (C); 25 Andrew King; 3 Nigel Roy; 4 Tony Martin; 5 Steve Hall; 6 Rob Purdham; 23 Chris Thorman; 8 Francis Stephenson; 14 Neil Budworth; 12 Steele Retchless; 30 Jason Netherton (D); 26 Damien Kennedy; 9 Bill Peden. Subs (all used): 21 Rob Jackson; 10 Richard Marshall; 24 Russell Bawden; 29 Tommy Gallagher.
Tries: Moran (4, 29, 31), Martin (13, 39), Budworth (43), Jackson (65), Thorman (71), Purdham (75);
Goals: Martin 4/6, Thorman 3/3.
Rugby Leaguer & League Express Men of the Match: *Halifax:* Andrew Frew; *Broncos:* Bill Peden.
Penalty count: 3-6; **Half-time:** 10-26;
Referee: Robert Connolly (Wigan); **Attendance:** 1,781.

ROUND 17

Friday 4th July 2003

ST HELENS 32 WIDNES VIKINGS 18

SAINTS: 1 Paul Wellens; 19 Ade Gardner; 3 Martin Gleeson; 5 Darren Albert; 2 Anthony Stewart; 7 Sean Long (C); 14 Mick Higham; 8 Darren Britt; 9 Keiron Cunningham; 26 Keith Mason; 17 Mike Bennett; 16 Darren Smith; 6 Jason Hooper. Subs (all used): 15 Tim Jonkers; 23 Jon Wilkin; 11 Chris Joynt; 18 Mark Edmondson.
Tries: Hooper (7), Smith (13), Gardner (33), Gleeson (36), Cunningham (78); **Goals:** Long 5/5, Wellens 1/1.
Sin bin: Long (73) - fighting.
VIKINGS: 19 Paul Atcheson; 5 Jason Demetriou; 20 Dan Potter; 4 Adam Hughes; 2 Paul Devlin; 26 Julian O'Neill (A) (C); 18 Dean Lawford; 8 Robert Relf; 9 Shane Millard; 10 Julian O'Neill (NZ); 11 Andy Hay; 25 Simon Finnigan; 13 Daniel Frame. Subs (all used): 22 Phil Cantillon; 23 David Mills; 12 Steve McCurrie; 30 Stephen Myler (D).
Tries: Devlin (53), Cantillon (70, 75);
Goals: O'Neill (A) 3/3.
Sin bin: Millard (73) - fighting.
Rugby Leaguer & League Express Men of the Match: *Saints:* Keiron Cunningham; *Vikings:* Dean Lawford.
Penalty count: 8-8; **Half-time:** 24-0;
Referee: Russell Smith (Castleford); **Attendance:** 10,028.

Saturday 5th July 2003

LONDON BRONCOS 20 HULL FC 20

BRONCOS: 7 Dennis Moran (C); 25 Andrew King; 3 Nigel Roy; 4 Tony Martin; 5 Steve Hall; 6 Rob Purdham; 23 Chris Thorman; 8 Francis Stephenson; 14 Neil Budworth; 24 Russell Bawden; 30 Jason Netherton; 12 Steele Retchless; 9 Bill Peden. Subs (all used): 10 Richard Marshall; 21 Rob Jackson; 26 Damien Kennedy; 29 Tommy Gallagher.
Tries: Roy (7), Martin (23), Hall (52);
Goals: Thorman 4/4.
HULL: 2 Colin Best; 28 Gareth Raynor; 24 Kirk Yeaman; 32 Alex Wilkinson; 3 Richie Barnett (C); 16 Paul Cooke; 6 Richard Horne; 8 Craig Greenhill; 9 Dean Treister; 10 Paul King; 11 Adam Maher; 14 Sean Ryan; 31 Peter Lupton. Subs (all used): 19 Richard Fletcher; 20 Garreth Carvell; 26 Graeme Horne; 30 Ewan Dowes.
Tries: Best (19, 74), Wilkinson (59); **Goals:** Cooke 4/5.
Rugby Leaguer & League Express Men of the Match: *Broncos:* Nigel Roy; *Hull:* Colin Best.
Penalty count: 6-6; **Half-time:** 12-8;
Referee: Steve Ganson (St Helens); **Attendance:** 4,151.

Sunday 6th July 2003

LEEDS RHINOS 30 WARRINGTON WOLVES 20

RHINOS: 21 Richard Mathers; 2 Mark Calderwood; 3 Chris McKenna; 4 Keith Senior; 1 Francis Cummins; 6 Danny McGuire; 7 Rob Burrow; 17 Wayne McDonald; 9 Matt Diskin; 10 Barrie McDermott (C); 16 Willie Poching; 12 Matt Adamson; 11 David Furner. Subs (all used): 19 Ryan Bailey; 15 Chris Feather; 5 Chev Walker; 13 Kevin Sinfield.
Tries: Cummins (21), Poching (28, 44), Furner (32), McKenna (49); **Goals:** Furner 5/7.
WOLVES: 5 Graham Appo; 2 Rob Smyth; 3 Brent Grose; 4 Ben Westwood; 20 Dean Gaskell; 6 Lee Briers (C); 7 Nathan Wood; 8 Nick Fozzard; 9 Jon Clarke; 10 Mark Hilton; 18 Paul Noone; 12 Ian Sibbit; 13 Sid Domic. Subs: 16 Paul Wood; 15 Jerome Guisset; 17 Warren Stevens; 19 Gary Hulse (not used).
Tries: P Wood (36), Briers (59, 63); **Goals:** Briers 4/4.
Rugby Leaguer & League Express Men of the Match: *Rhinos:* Willie Poching; *Wolves:* Lee Briers.
Penalty count: 10-7; **Half time:** 16-8; **Referee:** Ronnie Laughton (Barnsley); **Attendance:** 13,498.

CASTLEFORD TIGERS 38 HALIFAX 12

TIGERS: 3 Michael Eagar; 2 Waine Pryce; 4 Paul Mellor; 16 Francis Maloney; 5 Darren Rogers; 6 Danny Orr (C); 27 Jon Hepworth; 8 Nathan Sykes; 7 Mitch Healey; 10 Andy Lynch; 12 Dale Fritz; 21 Richard Blakeway; 14 Andy Johnson. Subs (all used): 20 Tom Saxton; 19 Wayne Godwin; 23 Michael Smith; 18 Jamie Thackray.
Tries: Orr (7), Mellor (10), Smith (53), Hepworth (61, 70), Johnson (64), Thackray (74);
Goals: Healey 3/4, Orr 2/4.
HALIFAX: 1 Daryl Cardiss; 2 Lee Greenwood; 3 Stuart Donlan; 33 Andrew Frew; 21 Chris Norman; 20 Dane Dorahy; 7 Sean Penkywicz; 16 Chris Birchall; 9 Johnny Lawless (C); 25 Neil Harmon; 15 Ryan Clayton; 12 Andrew Brocklehurst; 6 Martin Moana. Subs (all used): 8 Andy Hobson; 18 Jaymes Chapman; 22 Simon Grix; 23 Ged Corcoran.
Tries: Frew (14), Dorahy (20); **Goals:** Dorahy 2/3.
Rugby Leaguer & League Express Men of the Match: *Tigers:* Jon Hepworth; *Halifax:* Dane Dorahy.
Penalty count: 8-5; **Half-time:** 12-12;
Referee: Ian Smith (Oldham); **Attendance:** 5,444.

WAKEFIELD TRINITY WILDCATS 18 BRADFORD BULLS 30

WILDCATS: 1 Martyn Holland; 17 Richard Newlove; 24 Colum Halpenny; 4 Matt Seers; 5 Jon Wells; 6 Ben Jeffries; 16 Jamie Rooney; 18 Michael Korkidas; 9 David March; 25 Darrell Griffin; 3 Gareth Ellis; 12 Jamie Field; 13 Adrian Vowles (C). Subs (all used): 20 David Wrench; 21 Steve Snitch; 22 Matthew Wray; 14 Paul Handforth.
Tries: Jeffries (2), Halpenny (26), Rooney (78);
Goals: Rooney 3/3.
BULLS: 3 Leon Pryce; 2 Tevita Vaikona; 20 Scott Naylor; 4 Shontayne Hape; 5 Lesley Vainikolo; 15 Karl Pratt; 7 Paul Deacon; 8 Joe Vagana; 9 James Lowes (C); 29 Stuart Fielden; 11 Daniel Gartner; 12 Jamie Peacock; 18 Lee Radford. Subs (all used): 19 Jamie Langley; 27 Robert Parker; 14 Lee Gilmour; 10 Paul Anderson.
Tries: Vagana (11), Hape (16, 67), Vainikolo (40), Gartner (43), Lowes (49); **Goals:** Deacon 3/6.
Rugby Leaguer & League Express Men of the Match: *Wildcats:* Adrian Vowles; *Bulls:* Leon Pryce.
Penalty count: 7-8; **Half-time:** 12-14;
Referee: Robert Connolly (Wigan); **Attendance:** 4,658.

HUDDERSFIELD GIANTS 32 WIGAN WARRIORS 24

GIANTS: 1 Paul Reilly; 2 Hefin O'Hare; 6 Brandon Costin; 4 Julian Bailey; 34 Marcus St Hilaire; 33 Stanley Gene; 9 Paul March; 25 Darren Fleary (C); 15 Darren Turner; 10 Jim Gannon; 23 Ben Roarty; 7 Jarrod O'Doherty; 26 Jamie Bloem. Subs (all used): 8 Mick Slicker; 13 Steve McNamara; 19 Iain Morrison; 17 Graham Holroyd.
Tries: Costin (10, 45), Gannon (23), St Hilaire (34), Reilly (60), March (68); **Goals:** Costin 1/4, McNamara 3/4.
Sin bin: Turner (32) - interference.
WARRIORS: 22 Shaun Briscoe; 5 Brian Carney; 4 Paul Johnson; 14 David Hodgson; 2 Brett Dallas; 25 Kevin Brown; 7 Adrian Lam; 8 Terry O'Connor; 17 Mark Smith; 10 Craig Smith; 11 Mick Cassidy; 23 Gareth Hock; 13 Andy Farrell (C). Subs (all used): 30 Quentin Pongia; 20 Luke Robinson; 16 Danny Sculthorpe; 15 Sean O'Loughlin.
Tries: Hodgson (4), Dallas (42, 52, 57); **Goals:** Farrell 4/4.
On report: C Smith (65) - alleged high tackle.
Rugby Leaguer & League Express Men of the Match: *Giants:* Brandon Costin; *Warriors:* Brett Dallas.
Penalty count: 10-7; **Half-time:** 14-6; **Referee:** Richard Silverwood (Dewsbury); **Attendance:** 4,802.

ROUND 18

Friday 11th July 2003

HALIFAX 12 BRADFORD BULLS 60

HALIFAX: 1 Daryl Cardiss; 2 Lee Greenwood; 3 Stuart Donlan; 15 Ryan Clayton; 33 Andrew Frew; 20 Dane Dorahy; 7 Sean Penkywicz; 25 Neil Harmon; 9 Johnny Lawless (C); 16 Chris Birchall; 11 Heath Cruckshank; 12 Andrew Brocklehurst; 6 Martin Moana. Subs (all used): 8 Andy Hobson; 18 Jaymes Chapman; 22 Simon Grix; 23 Ged Corcoran.
Tries: Clayton (33), Hobson (61); **Goals:** Dorahy 2/3.
Sin bin: Donlan (67) - persistent interference.
BULLS: 17 Stuart Reardon; 2 Tevita Vaikona; 20 Scott Naylor; 4 Shontayne Hape; 5 Lesley Vainikolo; 3 Leon Pryce; 7 Paul Deacon; 8 Joe Vagana; 9 James Lowes (C); 27 Robert Parker; 11 Daniel Gartner; 12 Jamie Peacock; 13 Mike Forshaw. Subs (all used): 10 Paul Anderson; 14 Lee Gilmour; 18 Lee Radford; 26 Chris Bridge (D).
Tries: Parker (6, 68), Gartner (13, 80), Naylor (18), Anderson (23), Vainikolo (27, 38), Deacon (49), Radford (63), L Pryce (73); **Goals:** Deacon 8/11.
Rugby Leaguer & League Express Men of the Match: *Halifax:* Jaymes Chapman; *Bulls:* Robert Parker.
Penalty count: 5-8; **Half-time:** 6-34;
Referee: Steve Ganson (St Helens); **Attendance:** 4,555.

CASTLEFORD TIGERS 32 ST HELENS 46

TIGERS: 20 Tom Saxton; 5 Darren Rogers; 4 Paul Mellor; 16 Francis Maloney; 2 Waine Pryce; 6 Danny Orr (C); 7 Mitch Healey; 8 Nathan Sykes; 27 Jon Hepworth; 23 Michael Smith; 14 Andy Johnson; 12 Dale Fritz; 13 Ryan Hudson. Subs (all used): 3 Michael Eagar; 19 Wayne Godwin; 11 Lee Harland; 18 Jamie Thackray.
Tries: Orr (19, 29, 77), Saxton (52), Smith (58);
Goals: Orr 6/6.
SAINTS: 1 Paul Wellens; 5 Darren Albert; 3 Martin Gleeson; 6 Jason Hooper; 2 Anthony Stewart; 7 Sean Long; 14 Mick Higham; 8 Darren Britt; 9 Keiron Cunningham; 26 Keith Mason; 17 Mike Bennett; 16 Darren Smith; 13 Paul Sculthorpe (C). Subs (all used): 15 Tim Jonkers; 21 John Kirkpatrick; 11 Chris Joynt; 18 Mark Edmondson.
Tries: Higham (14, 66), Wellens (22, 32), Gleeson (36, 46), Albert (44), Long (71); **Goals:** Long 7/9.
Rugby Leaguer & League Express Men of the Match: *Tigers:* Danny Orr; *Saints:* Sean Long.
Penalty count: 2-5; **Half-time:** 14-24; **Referee:** Richard Silverwood (Dewsbury); **Attendance:** 6,320.

WIGAN WARRIORS 38
WAKEFIELD TRINITY WILDCATS 12

WARRIORS: 22 Shaun Briscoe; 5 Brian Carney; 18 Martin Aspinwall; 14 David Hodgson; 2 Brett Dallas; 28 Nick Graham; 7 Adrian Lam; 8 Terry O'Connor; 9 Terry Newton; 30 Quentin Pongia; 11 Mick Cassidy; 4 Paul Johnson; 13 Andy Farrell (C). Subs (all used): 23 Gareth Hock; 20 Luke Robinson; 21 Ricky Bibey; 15 Sean O'Loughlin.
Tries: Dallas (7, 51), Farrell (13), Cassidy (24), Briscoe

(55), Lam (60, 80); **Goals:** Farrell 5/7.
WILDCATS: 24 Colum Halpenny; 5 Jon Wells; 3 Gareth Ellis; 23 Robert Spicer; 17 Richard Newlove; 6 Ben Jeffries; 16 Jamie Rooney; 18 Michael Korkidas; 9 David March; 25 Darrell Griffin; 20 David Wrench; 12 Jamie Field; 13 Adrian Vowles (C). Subs (all used): 7 Brad Davis; 10 Dallas Hood; 21 Steve Snitch; 15 Ian Knott.
Tries: Halpenny (30), March (42); **Goals:** Rooney 2/3.
Rugby Leaguer & League Express Men of the Match: *Warriors:* Adrian Lam; *Wildcats:* David March.
Penalty count: 11-11; **Half-time:** 16-8;
Referee: Ashley Klein (London); **Attendance:** 8,073.

Saturday 12th July 2003

HUDDERSFIELD GIANTS 30 LEEDS RHINOS 24

GIANTS: 1 Paul Reilly; 2 Hefin O'Hare; 6 Brandon Costin; 4 Julian Bailey; 34 Marcus St Hilaire; 33 Stanley Gene; 9 Paul March; 25 Darren Fleary (C); 15 Darren Turner; 10 Jim Gannon; 7 Jarrod O'Doherty; 23 Ben Roarty; 26 Jamie Bloem. Subs (all used): 13 Steve McNamara; 8 Mick Slicker; 19 Iain Morrison; 5 Matt Whitaker.
Tries: Gene (1, 27), Costin (62, 79);
Goals: Costin 2/3, McNamara 5/5.
Sin bin: Roarty (43) - holding down.
RHINOS: 18 Gary Connolly; 2 Mark Calderwood; 5 Chev Walker; 3 Chris McKenna; 1 Francis Cummins; 13 Kevin Sinfield (C); 7 Rob Burrow; 8 Danny Ward; 9 Matt Diskin; 10 Barrie McDermott; 12 Matt Adamson; 16 Willie Poching; 11 David Furner. Subs (all used): 15 Chris Feather; 6 Danny McGuire; 20 Jamie Jones-Buchanan; 17 Wayne McDonald.
Tries: Sinfield (23), McGuire (50), McDonald (67), Furner (75); **Goals:** Sinfield 4/4.
Sin bin: Furner (44) - lifting leg of opponent while in possession; Diskin (45) - off the ball tackle.
Rugby Leaguer & League Express Men of the Match: *Giants:* Brandon Costin; *Rhinos:* David Furner.
Penalty count: 7-9; **Half-time:** 16-6;
Referee: Russell Smith (Castleford); **Attendance:** 6,340.

Sunday 13th July 2003

WARRINGTON WOLVES 50 LONDON BRONCOS 8

WOLVES: 5 Graham Appo; 2 Rob Smyth; 3 Brent Grose; 12 Ian Sibbit; 20 Dean Gaskell; 6 Lee Briers (C); 7 Nathan Wood; 16 Paul Wood; 9 Jon Clarke; 15 Jerome Guisset; 11 Darren Burns; 18 Paul Noone; 13 Sid Domic. Subs (all used): 14 Mark Gleeson; 4 Ben Westwood; 17 Warren Stevens; 8 Nick Fozzard.
Tries: Burns (1, 53), Guisset (11), Briers (15, 57), Sibbit (26), Smyth (32, 43); **Goals:** Briers 9/11.
BRONCOS: 7 Dennis Moran; 1 Paul Sykes; 3 Nigel Roy; 25 Andrew King; 5 Steve Hall; 6 Rob Purdham; 23 Chris Thorman; 24 Russell Bawden; 14 Neil Budworth; 12 Steele Retchless; 30 Jason Netherton; 9 Bill Peden; 13 Jim Dymock (C). Subs (all used): 21 Rob Jackson; 8 Francis Stephenson; 10 Richard Marshall; 29 Tommy Gallagher.
Try: Peden (79); **Goals:** Thorman 2/2.
Rugby Leaguer & League Express Men of the Match: *Wolves:* Lee Briers; *Broncos:* Jim Dymock.
Penalty count: 6-6; **Half-time:** 32-2;
Referee: Ian Smith (Oldham); **Attendance:** 5,562.

WIDNES VIKINGS 46 HULL FC 10

VIKINGS: 1 Stuart Spruce (C); 20 Dan Potter; 5 Jason Demetriou; 4 Adam Hughes; 2 Paul Devlin; 26 Julian O'Neill (A); 18 Dean Lawford; 8 Robert Relf; 9 Shane Millard; 10 Julian O'Neill (NZ); 11 Andy Hay; 25 Simon Finnigan; 13 Daniel Frame. Subs (all used): 22 Phil Cantillon; 17 Anthony Farrell; 23 David Mills; 12 Steve McCurrie.
Tries: Devlin (4), Hughes (14, 69), Millard (29), Spruce (32), Cantillon (35), O'Neill (A) (39), Demetriou (48);
Goals: O'Neill (A) 7/9.
Dismissal: Farrell (74) - high tackle.
HULL: 2 Colin Best; 28 Gareth Raynor; 24 Kirk Yeaman; 32 Alex Wilkinson; 26 Graeme Horne; 16 Paul Cooke (C); 6 Richard Horne; 8 Craig Greenhill; 9 Dean Treister; 30 Ewan Dowes; 11 Adam Maher; 14 Sean Ryan; 33 Shayne McMenemy (D). Subs (all used): 19 Richard Fletcher; 20 Garreth Carvell; 31 Peter Lupton; 22 Andy Last.
Tries: Maher (10), Yeaman (76); **Goals:** Cooke 1/2.
Rugby Leaguer & League Express Men of the Match: *Vikings:* Julian O'Neill (A); *Hull:* Dean Treister.
Penalty count: 5-7; **Half-time:** 34-6;
Referee: Robert Connolly (Wigan); **Attendance:** 6,707.

ROUND 19

Friday 18th July 2003

LEEDS RHINOS 54 HALIFAX 6

RHINOS: 18 Gary Connolly; 2 Mark Calderwood; 3 Chris McKenna; 5 Chev Walker; 1 Francis Cummins; 6 Danny McGuire; 7 Rob Burrow; 17 Wayne McDonald; 9 Matt Diskin; 19 Ryan Bailey; 16 Willie Poching; 12 Matt Adamson; 13 Kevin Sinfield (C). Subs (all used): 10 Barrie McDermott; 15 Chris Feather; 20 Jamie Jones-Buchanan; 21 Richard Mathers.
Tries: McKenna (9), Burrow (16), Feather (28), Cummins (30, 48), Calderwood (40, 57), Jones-Buchanan (67), Walker (70); **Goals:** Sinfield 6/7, Burrow 3/3.
Sin bin: Mathers (63) - obstruction.
HALIFAX: 1 Daryl Cardiss; 2 Lee Greenwood; 3 Stuart Donlan; 15 Ryan Clayton; 33 Andrew Frew; 20 Dane Dorahy; 7 Sean Penkywicz; 25 Neil Harmon; 9 Johnny Lawless (C); 16 Chris Birchall; 11 Heath Cruckshank; 18 Jaymes Chapman; 6 Martin Moana. Subs (all used): 8 Andy Hobson; 26 John Hill (D); 27 Chris Maye (D); 12 Andrew Brocklehurst.
Try: Greenwood (75); **Goal:** Dorahy 1/1.
Sin bin: Penkywicz (43) - interference.
Rugby Leaguer & League Express Men of the Match: *Rhinos:* Willie Poching; *Halifax:* Daryl Cardiss.
Penalty count: 9-4; **Half-time:** 26-0;
Referee: Robert Connolly (Wigan); **Attendance:** 10,019.

LONDON BRONCOS 12 WIGAN WARRIORS 28

BRONCOS: 3 Nigel Roy; 1 Paul Sykes; 21 Rob Jackson; 4 Tony Martin; 25 Andrew King; 6 Rob Purdham; 23 Chris Thorman; 10 Richard Marshall; 14 Neil Budworth; 12 Steele Retchless; 24 Russell Bawden; 9 Bill Peden; 13 Jim Dymock (C). Subs (all used): 7 Dennis Moran; 8 Francis Stephenson; 26 Damien Kennedy; 29 Tommy Gallagher.
Tries: Sykes (5), Peden (31); **Goals:** Thorman 2/3.
WARRIORS: 22 Shaun Briscoe; 5 Brian Carney; 18 Martin Aspinwall; 15 Sean O'Loughlin; 14 David Hodgson; 28 Nick Graham; 7 Adrian Lam; 8 Terry O'Connor; 9 Terry Newton; 10 Craig Smith; 11 Mick Cassidy; 12 Danny Tickle; 13 Andy Farrell (C). Subs (all used): 20 Luke Robinson; 30 Quentin Pongia; 25 Kevin Brown; 23 Gareth Hock.
Tries: Lam (19), Briscoe (47), Aspinwall (50), Hodgson (76); **Goals:** Farrell 6/6.
Rugby Leaguer & League Express Men of the Match: *Broncos:* Jim Dymock; *Warriors:* Adrian Lam.
Penalty count: 6-2; **Half-time:** 12-10; **Referee:** Karl Kirkpatrick (Warrington); **Attendance:** 3,984.

ST HELENS 22 HUDDERSFIELD GIANTS 18

SAINTS: 1 Paul Wellens; 5 Darren Albert; 3 Martin Gleeson; 6 Jason Hooper; 2 Anthony Stewart; 7 Sean Long; 14 Mick Higham; 8 Darren Britt; 9 Keiron Cunningham; 26 Keith Mason; 11 Chris Joynt (C); 17 Mike Bennett; 13 Paul Sculthorpe. Subs (all used): 21 John Kirkpatrick; 15 Tim Jonkers; 22 Stuart Jones; 18 Mark Edmondson.
Tries: Albert (47, 64), Cunningham (52), Wellens (78);
Goals: Long 3/4.
Sin bin: Wellens (16) - ball stealing.
GIANTS: 1 Paul Reilly; 2 Hefin O'Hare; 4 Julian Bailey; 6 Brandon Costin; 34 Marcus St Hilaire; 33 Stanley Gene; 9 Paul March; 25 Darren Fleary (C); 15 Darren Turner; 10 Jim Gannon; 7 Jarrod O'Doherty; 23 Ben Roarty; 13 Steve McNamara. Subs (all used): 8 Mick Slicker; 19 Iain Morrison; 5 Matt Whitaker; 18 Jon Grayshon.
Tries: Costin (8, 21); **Goals:** McNamara 4/4, Costin 1/1.
Rugby Leaguer & League Express Men of the Match: *Saints:* Darren Albert; *Giants:* Brandon Costin.
Penalty count: 7-4; **Half-time:** 0-14;
Referee: Ian Smith (Oldham); **Attendance:** 9,288.

Saturday 19th July 2003

WAKEFIELD TRINITY WILDCATS 4 CASTLEFORD TIGERS 32

WILDCATS: 24 Colum Halpenny; 5 Jon Wells; 3 Gareth Ellis; 23 Robert Spicer; 22 Matthew Wray; 6 Ben Jeffries; 16 Jamie Rooney; 18 Michael Korkidas; 9 David March; 10 Dallas Hood; 15 Ian Knott; 12 Jamie Field; 13 Adrian Vowles (C). Subs (all used): 7 Brad Davis; 25 Darrell Griffin; 21 Steve Snitch; 20 David Wrench.
Goals: Rooney 2/2.
Sin bin: Davis (66) - holding down.
TIGERS: 5 Darren Rogers; 1 Damian Gibson; 4 Paul Mellor; 3 Michael Eagar; 2 Waine Pryce; 6 Danny Orr; 7 Mitch Healey; 18 Jamie Thackray; 19 Wayne Godwin; 10 Andy Lynch; 23 Michael Smith; 12 Dale Fritz; 13 Ryan Hudson (C). Subs (all used): 14 Andy Johnson; 8 Nathan Sykes; 11 Lee Harland; 27 Jon Hepworth.
Tries: Pryce (2), Fritz (18), Rogers (23), Hudson (52), Godwin (69, 72); **Goals:** Orr 3/7, Healey 1/1.
Sin bin: Hudson (41) - holding down.
On report: Fritz (78) - high tackle.
Rugby Leaguer & League Express Men of the Match: *Wildcats:* David March; *Tigers:* Ryan Hudson.
Penalty count: 18-10; **Half-time:** 2-14;
Referee: Steve Ganson (St Helens); **Attendance:** 4,094.

Sunday 20th July 2003

BRADFORD BULLS 40 WIDNES VIKINGS 8

BULLS: 17 Stuart Reardon; 2 Tevita Vaikona; 20 Scott Naylor; 4 Shontayne Hape; 5 Lesley Vainikolo; 3 Leon Pryce; 7 Paul Deacon; 8 Joe Vagana; 9 James Lowes (C); 10 Paul Anderson; 11 Daniel Gartner; 12 Jamie Peacock; 13 Mike Forshaw. Subs (all used): 14 Lee Gilmour; 19 Jamie Langley; 18 Lee Radford; 27 Robert Parker.
Tries: Hape (26), Vainikolo (29, 56), Radford (38, 74), Vaikona (60), Reardon (63); **Goals:** Deacon 6/7.
VIKINGS: 1 Stuart Spruce (C); 5 Jason Demetriou; 20 Dan Potter; 4 Adam Hughes; 2 Paul Devlin; 26 Julian O'Neill (A); 18 Dean Lawford; 8 Robert Relf; 9 Shane Millard; 10 Julian O'Neill (NZ); 11 Andy Hay; 25 Simon Finnigan; 13 Daniel Frame. Subs (all used): 22 Phil Cantillon; 17 Anthony Farrell; 23 David Mills; 12 Steve McCurrie.
Try: Hughes (12); **Goals:** O'Neill (A) 2/2.
Rugby Leaguer & League Express Men of the Match: *Bulls:* Paul Deacon; *Vikings:* Stuart Spruce.
Penalty count: 7-5; **Half-time:** 16-6;
Referee: Ashley Klein (London); **Attendance:** 12,116.

HULL FC 38 WARRINGTON WOLVES 14

HULL: 6 Richard Horne; 2 Colin Best; 4 Toa Kohe-Love; 3 Richie Barnett (C); 32 Alex Wilkinson; 16 Paul Cooke; 26 Graeme Horne; 8 Craig Greenhill; 9 Dean Treister; 30 Ewan Dowes; 14 Sean Ryan; 11 Adam Maher; 17 Chris Chester. Subs (all used): 13 Jason Smith; 24 Kirk Yeaman; 19 Richard Fletcher; 20 Garreth Carvell.
Tries: Best (32, 43), G Horne (38, 53), Fletcher (51), Ryan (74); **Goals:** Cooke 7/9.
WOLVES: 5 Graham Appo; 2 Rob Smyth; 3 Brent Grose; 4 Ben Westwood; 20 Dean Gaskell; 9 Jon Clarke; 7 Nathan Wood (C); 16 Paul Wood; 11 Darren Burns; 15 Jerome Guisset; 12 Ian Sibbit; 18 Paul Noone; 13 Sid Domic. Subs (all used): 10 Mark Hilton; 19 Gary Hulse; 17 Warren Stevens; 23 Mike Wainwright.
Tries: Appo (27), Grose (63);
Goals: Smyth 1/2, Appo 2/3.
Sin bin: Appo (50) - professional foul.
On report: Noone (36) - high tackle.
Rugby Leaguer & League Express Men of the Match: *Hull:* Paul Cooke; *Wolves:* Sid Domic.
Penalty count: 11-8; **Half time:** 14-8;
Referee: Russell Smith (Castleford); **Attendance:** 9,835.

ROUND 20

Friday 25th July 2003

LEEDS RHINOS 27 LONDON BRONCOS 22

RHINOS: 18 Gary Connolly; 2 Mark Calderwood; 5 Chev Walker; 4 Keith Senior; 1 Francis Cummins; 6 Danny McGuire; 14 Andrew Dunemann; 17 Wayne McDonald; 9 Matt Diskin; 19 Ryan Bailey; 11 David Furner; 12 Matt Adamson; 13 Kevin Sinfield (C). Subs (all used): 15 Chris Feather; 16 Willie Poching; 7 Rob Burrow; 3 Chris McKenna.
Tries: McDonald (2), Walker (12), McGuire (34), Poching (73); **Goals:** Sinfield 5/5; **Field goal:** Sinfield.
BRONCOS: 7 Dennis Moran; 1 Paul Sykes; 21 Rob Jackson; 3 Nigel Roy; 25 Andrew King; 13 Jim Dymock (C); 23 Chris Thorman; 8 Francis Stephenson; 14 Neil Budworth; 10 Richard Marshall; 12 Steele Retchless; 9 Bill Peden; 6 Rob Purdham. Subs (all used): 24 Russell Bawden; 22 Andrew Hamilton; 31 Joe Mbu (D); 26 Damien Kennedy.
Tries: Moran (21, 68), Kennedy (52), King (77);
Goals: Thorman 3/4.
Sin bin: Jackson (24) - interference.
Rugby Leaguer & League Express Men of the Match: *Rhinos:* Matt Adamson; *Broncos:* Dennis Moran.
Penalty count: 6-10; **Half-time:** 20-6; **Referee:** Richard Silverwood (Dewsbury); **Attendance:** 8,231.

Saturday 26th July 2003

WIGAN WARRIORS 18 WIDNES VIKINGS 22

WARRIORS: 14 David Hodgson; 5 Brian Carney; 18 Martin Aspinwall; 15 Sean O'Loughlin; 25 Kevin Brown; 28 Nick Graham; 7 Adrian Lam; 8 Terry O'Connor; 9 Terry Newton; 10 Craig Smith; 11 Mick Cassidy; 12 Danny Tickle; 13 Andy Farrell (C). Subs (all used): 20 Luke Robinson; 30 Quentin Pongia; 19 Stephen Wild; 23 Gareth Hock.
Tries: Hodgson (42), Robinson (76), Brown (80);
Goals: Farrell 3/3.
VIKINGS: 19 Paul Atcheson; 20 Dan Potter; 5 Jason Demetriou; 4 Adam Hughes; 2 Paul Devlin; 26 Julian O'Neill (A) (C); 7 Ryan Sheridan; 8 Robert Relf; 9 Shane Millard; 10 Julian O'Neill (NZ); 11 Andy Hay; 13 Daniel Frame; 3 Deon Bird. Subs (all used): 22 Phil Cantillon; 17 Anthony Farrell; 25 Simon Finnigan; 12 Steve McCurrie.
Tries: Bird (5), Hay (10), Millard (27), Potter (34);
Goals: O'Neill (A) 3/4.
Rugby Leaguer & League Express Men of the Match: *Warriors:* Craig Smith; *Vikings:* Ryan Sheridan.
Penalty count: 11-4; **Half-time:** 0-22;
Referee: Ian Smith (Oldham); **Attendance:** 8,600.

Sunday 27th July 2003

WARRINGTON WOLVES 66 HALIFAX 6

WOLVES: 1 Lee Penny; 2 Rob Smyth; 3 Brent Grose; 12 Ian Sibbit; 20 Dean Gaskell; 5 Graham Appo; 7 Nathan Wood (C); 8 Nick Fozzard; 9 Jon Clarke; 10 Mark Hilton; 15 Jerome Guisset; 16 Paul Wood; 18 Paul Noone. Subs (all used): 19 Gary Hulse; 11 Darren Burns; 23 Mike Wainwright; 17 Warren Stevens.
Tries: Clarke (1), Grose (9, 58), Smyth (18), Burns (25, 35), Appo (30, 41, 71, 79), N Wood (38), Hulse (50);
Goals: Appo 9/12.
HALIFAX: 1 Daryl Cardiss; 33 Andrew Frew; 15 Ryan Clayton; 3 Stuart Donlan; 2 Lee Greenwood; 20 Dane Dorahy; 7 Sean Penkywicz; 8 Andy Hobson; 9 Johnny Lawless (C); 26 John Hill; 11 Heath Cruckshank; 12 Andrew Brocklehurst; 6 Martin Moana. Subs (all used): 14 Liam Finn; 16 Chris Birchall; 25 Neil Harmon; 23 Ged Corcoran.
Try: Birchall (43); **Goals:** Dorahy 1/1.
On report:
Hobson & Brocklehurst (17) - high tackle on Fozzard.
Rugby Leaguer & League Express Men of the Match: *Wolves:* Graham Appo; *Halifax:* Daryl Cardiss.
Penalty count: 5-5; **Half-time:** 36-0; **Referee:** Colin Morris (Huddersfield); **Attendance:** 5,291.

CASTLEFORD TIGERS 20 BRADFORD BULLS 40

TIGERS: 20 Tom Saxton; 5 Darren Rogers; 4 Paul Mellor; 3 Michael Eagar; 2 Waine Pryce; 6 Danny Orr; 7 Mitch Healey; 8 Nathan Sykes; 19 Wayne Godwin; 10 Andy Lynch; 23 Michael Smith; 12 Dale Fritz; 13 Ryan Hudson (C). Subs (all used): 14 Andy Johnson; 18

Jamie Thackray; 27 Jon Hepworth; 30 Tim Spears (D).
Tries: Rogers (19), Eagar (21), Pryce (25, 66);
Goals: Orr 1/2, Healey 1/2.
BULLS: 17 Stuart Reardon; 2 Tevita Vaikona; 20 Scott Naylor; 4 Shontayne Hape; 5 Lesley Vainikolo; 3 Leon Pryce; 7 Paul Deacon; 8 Joe Vagana; 9 James Lowes (C); 10 Paul Anderson; 11 Daniel Gartner; 12 Jamie Peacock; 13 Mike Forshaw. Subs (all used): 14 Lee Gilmour; 19 Jamie Langley; 18 Lee Radford; 27 Robert Parker.
Tries: Deacon (15), L Pryce (34), Radford (40), Naylor (42), Gartner (51), Gilmour (69), Vaikona (72);
Goals: Deacon 6/7.
Rugby Leaguer & League Express Men of the Match:
Tigers: Michael Smith; *Bulls:* Paul Deacon.
Penalty count: 7-7; **Half-time:** 16-18;
Referee: Steve Ganson (St Helens); **Attendance:** 9,081.

WAKEFIELD TRINITY WILDCATS 15 ST HELENS 36

WILDCATS: 5 Jon Wells; 22 Matthew Wray; 24 Colum Halpenny; 3 Gareth Ellis; 23 Robert Spicer; 6 Ben Jeffries; 16 Jamie Rooney; 18 Michael Korkidas; 9 David March; 25 Darrell Griffin; 12 Jamie Field; 20 David Wrench; 15 Ian Knott. Subs (all used): 7 Brad Davis (C); 27 Mark Field (D); 28 Matthew Blake (D); 29 Darren Jordan (D).
Tries: Jeffries (6), Rooney (19); **Goals:** Rooney 3/3;
Field goal: Rooney.
Dismissal: Korkidas (54) - punching.
SAINTS: 5 Darren Albert; 2 Anthony Stewart; 1 Paul Wellens; 6 Jason Hooper; 19 Ade Gardner; 7 Sean Long (C); 14 Mick Higham; 10 Barry Ward; 9 Keiron Cunningham; 26 Keith Mason; 17 Mike Bennett; 15 Tim Jonkers; 23 Jon Wilkin. Subs (all used): 27 Steve Rowlands; 22 Stuart Jones; 18 Mark Edmondson; 12 John Stankevitch.
Tries: Stankevitch (26), Long (32, 70), Wellens (40), Albert (41, 74); **Goals:** Long 6/6.
Sin bin: Jones (56) - holding down;
Jonkers (61) - holding down.
On report: Wilkin (16) - high tackle.
Rugby Leaguer & League Express Men of the Match:
Wildcats: David Wrench; *Saints:* Sean Long.
Penalty count: 10-9; **Half-time:** 15-18;
Referee: Russell Smith (Castleford); **Attendance:** 4,210.

HUDDERSFIELD GIANTS 30 HULL FC 14

GIANTS: 1 Paul Reilly; 2 Hefin O'Hare; 6 Brandon Costin; 4 Julian Bailey; 34 Marcus St Hilaire; 9 Paul March; 33 Stanley Gene; 25 Darren Fleary (C); 15 Darren Turner; 10 Jim Gannon; 23 Ben Roarty; 5 Matt Whitaker; 26 Jamie Bloem. Subs (all used): 3 Ben Cooper; 19 Iain Morrison; 8 Mick Slicker; 13 Steve McNamara.
Tries: Reilly (25), St Hilaire (30), March (52), Fleary (56), Costin (77); **Goals:** McNamara 5/6, Costin 0/1.
HULL: 6 Richard Horne; 2 Colin Best; 4 Toa Kohe-Love; 3 Richie Barnett (C); 32 Alex Wilkinson; 16 Paul Cooke; 26 Graeme Horne; 8 Craig Greenhill; 22 Andy Last; 30 Ewan Dowes; 19 Richard Fletcher; 14 Sean Ryan; 17 Chris Chester. Subs (all used): 10 Paul King; 20 Garreth Carvell; 24 Kirk Yeaman; 31 Peter Lupton.
Tries: Carvell (42), Last (60), Best (72);
Goals: Cooke 1/3.
Rugby Leaguer & League Express Men of the Match:
Giants: Steve McNamara; *Hull:* Andy Last.
Penalty count: 13-8; **Half-time:** 14-0; **Referee:** Karl Kirkpatrick (Warrington); **Attendance:** 4,821.

ROUND 21

Friday 1st August 2003

HALIFAX 18 WAKEFIELD TRINITY WILDCATS 30

HALIFAX: 1 Daryl Cardiss; 2 Lee Greenwood; 3 Stuart Donlan; 33 Andrew Frew; 21 Chris Norman; 20 Dane Dorahy; 7 Sean Penkywicz; 8 Andy Hobson; 9 Johnny Lawless (C); 25 Neil Harmon; 11 Heath Cruckshank; 15 Ryan Clayton; 27 Chris Maye. Subs (all used): 12 Andrew Brocklehurst; 14 Liam Finn; 16 Chris Birchall; 26 John Hill.
Tries: Greenwood (69, 79), Penkywicz (75);
Goals: Dorahy 3/5.
WILDCATS: 5 Jon Wells; 22 Matthew Wray; 24 Colum Halpenny; 3 Gareth Ellis; 17 Richard Newlove; 16 Jamie Rooney; 6 Ben Jeffries; 25 Darrell Griffin; 9 David March; 21 Steve Snitch; 20 David Wrench; 12 Jamie Field; 15 Ian Knott. Subs (all used): 7 Brad Davis (C); 27 Mark Field; 28 Matthew Blake; 23 Robert Spicer.
Tries: Rooney (22), Jeffries (33), Newlove (39), Knott (66); **Goals:** Rooney 7/8.
Rugby Leaguer & League Express Men of the Match:
Halifax: Daryl Cardiss; *Wildcats:* Ben Jeffries.
Penalty count: 9-12; **Half-time:** 4-22; **Referee:** Ronnie Laughton (Barnsley); **Attendance:** 2,274.

WIDNES VIKINGS 27 CASTLEFORD TIGERS 16

VIKINGS: 1 Stuart Spruce (C); 20 Dan Potter; 3 Deon Bird; 4 Adam Hughes; 2 Paul Devlin; 26 Julian O'Neill (A); 7 Ryan Sheridan; 8 Robert Relf; 9 Shane Millard; 10 Julian O'Neill (NZ); 11 Andy Hay; 12 Steve McCurrie; 13 Daniel Frame. Subs (all used): 22 Phil Cantillon; 17 Anthony Farrell; 19 Paul Atcheson; 25 Simon Finnigan.
Tries: Devlin (31, 67), Frame (47), Hughes (63), Potter (77); **Goals:** O'Neill (A) 3/7; **Field goal:** O'Neill (A).
Sin bin: O'Neill (NZ) (58) - fighting.
TIGERS: 5 Darren Rogers; 1 Damian Gibson; 4 Paul Mellor; 3 Michael Eagar; 2 Waine Pryce; 27 Jon Hepworth; 7 Mitch Healey; 23 Michael Smith; 13 Ryan Hudson (C); 10 Andy Lynch; 11 Lee Harland; 12 Dale Fritz; 14 Andy Johnson. Subs (all used): 20 Tom Saxton; 18 Jamie Thackray; 26 Craig Huby; 19 Wayne Godwin.
Tries: Healey (24, 58); **Goals:** Healey 4/4.
Sin bin: Healey (34) - persistent interference;
Fritz (58) - fighting.
Rugby Leaguer & League Express Men of the Match:
Vikings: Daniel Frame; *Tigers:* Mitch Healey.
Penalty count: 9-7; **Half-time:** 6-8;
Referee: Robert Connolly (Wigan); **Attendance:** 5,698.

Saturday 2nd August 2003

HULL FC 12 LEEDS RHINOS 26

HULL: 6 Richard Horne; 2 Colin Best; 24 Kirk Yeaman; 32 Alex Wilkinson; 28 Gareth Raynor; 16 Paul Cooke (C); 26 Graeme Horne; 8 Craig Greenhill; 9 Dean Treister; 20 Garreth Carvell; 19 Richard Fletcher; 14 Sean Ryan; 31 Peter Lupton. Subs (all used): 10 Paul King; 30 Ewan Dowes; 25 Glen Donkin; 22 Andy Last.
Try: G Horne (74); **Goals:** Cooke 4/5.
Sin bin: Last (59) – persistent offside.
RHINOS: 18 Gary Connolly; 2 Mark Calderwood; 3 Chris McKenna; 4 Keith Senior; 1 Francis Cummins; 6 Danny McGuire; 14 Andrew Dunemann; 17 Wayne McDonald; 9 Matt Diskin; 10 Barrie McDermott; 11 David Furner; 12 Matt Adamson; 13 Kevin Sinfield (C). Subs (all used): 15 Chris Feather; 16 Willie Poching; 8 Danny Ward; 7 Rob Burrow.
Tries: McGuire (4), Cummins (66), Poching (79);
Goals: Sinfield 7/9.
Sin bin: McKenna (29) – persistent offside.
Rugby Leaguer & League Express Men of the Match:
Hull: Richard Horne; *Rhinos:* Kevin Sinfield.
Penalty count: 13-10; **Half-time:** 6-10; **Referee:** Russell Smith (Castleford); **Attendance:** 13,081.

Sunday 3rd August 2003

LONDON BRONCOS 18 ST HELENS 30

BRONCOS: 1 Paul Sykes; 5 Steve Hall; 4 Tony Martin; 3 Nigel Roy; 25 Andrew King; 7 Dennis Moran; 23 Chris Thorman; 8 Francis Stephenson; 14 Neil Budworth; 12 Steele Retchless; 9 Bill Peden; 31 Joe Mbu; 13 Jim Dymock (C). Subs (all used): 24 Russell Bawden; 22 Andrew Hamilton; 21 Rob Jackson; 26 Damien Kennedy.
Tries: King (24), Dymock (32), Moran (70);
Goals: Thorman 3/4.
SAINTS: 5 Darren Albert; 2 Anthony Stewart; 1 Paul Wellens; 16 Darren Smith; 19 Ade Gardner; 7 Sean Long (C); 14 Mick Higham; 8 Darren Britt; 9 Keiron Cunningham; 18 Mark Edmondson; 17 Mike Bennett; 15 Tim Jonkers; 6 Jason Hooper. Subs (all used): 21 John Kirkpatrick; 26 Keith Mason; 12 John Stankevitch; 10 Barry Ward.
Tries: Higham (21), Wellens (40), Albert (45), Gardner (51), Stankevitch (75); **Goals:** Long 5/6.
Rugby Leaguer & League Express Men of the Match:
Broncos: Paul Sykes; *Saints:* Darren Albert.
Penalty count: 8-6; **Half-time:** 12-10; **Referee:** Karl Kirkpatrick (Warrington); **Attendance:** 4,214.

WARRINGTON WOLVES 16 WIGAN WARRIORS 18

WOLVES: 1 Lee Penny; 3 Brent Grose; 12 Ian Sibbit; 4 Ben Westwood; 20 Dean Gaskell; 7 Nathan Wood (C); 5 Graham Appo; 10 Mark Hilton; 9 Jon Clarke; 17 Warren Stevens; 11 Darren Burns; 16 Paul Wood; 18 Paul Noone. Subs (all used): 26 Jamie Durbin (D); 19 Gary Hulse; 23 Mike Wainwright; 15 Jerome Guisset.
Tries: N Wood (52), Appo (58); **Goals:** Appo 4/4.
Sin bin: N Wood (77) - fighting.
On report: N Wood (77) - fighting.
WARRIORS: 14 David Hodgson; 5 Brian Carney; 18 Martin Aspinwall; 4 Paul Johnson; 2 Brett Dallas; 15 Sean O'Loughlin; 7 Adrian Lam; 8 Terry O'Connor; 9 Terry Newton; 10 Craig Smith; 12 Danny Tickle; 19 Stephen Wild; 13 Andy Farrell (C). Subs (all used): 30 Quentin Pongia; 23 Gareth Hock; 25 Kevin Brown; 20 Luke Robinson.
Tries: Hock (29), Dallas (65), C Smith (73);
Goals: Farrell 3/3.
Sin bin: C Smith (77) - fighting.
On report: C Smith (77) - fighting.
Rugby Leaguer & League Express Men of the Match:
Wolves: Darren Burns; *Warriors:* Andy Farrell.
Penalty count: 8-7; **Half-time:** 2-6; **Referee:** Richard Silverwood (Dewsbury); **Attendance:** 8,705.

BRADFORD BULLS 30 HUDDERSFIELD GIANTS 16

BULLS: 17 Stuart Reardon; 14 Lee Gilmour; 20 Scott Naylor; 4 Shontayne Hape; 5 Lesley Vainikolo; 3 Leon Pryce; 7 Paul Deacon; 8 Joe Vagana; 24 Aaron Smith; 10 Paul Anderson; 11 Daniel Gartner; 12 Jamie Peacock (C); 13 Mike Forshaw. Subs (all used): 26 Chris Bridge; 19 Jamie Langley; 18 Lee Radford; 27 Robert Parker.
Tries: Reardon (7), Deacon (13, 20), Vainikolo (25), Radford (40); **Goals:** Deacon 5/6.
GIANTS: 3 Ben Cooper; 2 Hefin O'Hare; 6 Brandon Costin; 4 Julian Bailey; 5 Matt Whitaker; 9 Paul March; 33 Stanley Gene; 25 Darren Fleary (C); 15 Darren Turner; 10 Jim Gannon; 19 Iain Morrison; 23 Ben Roarty; 7 Jarrod O'Doherty. Subs (all used); 8 Mick Slicker; 13 Steve McNamara; 18 Jon Grayshon; 21 Paul White.
Tries: Costin (39), Fleary (59), White (68);
Goals: McNamara 2/3.
Rugby Leaguer & League Express Men of the Match:
Bulls: Paul Deacon; *Giants:* Ben Roarty.
Penalty count: 14-6; **Half-time:** 30-6;
Referee: Ashley Klein (London); **Attendance:** 11,368.

ROUND 22

Friday 8th August 2003

LEEDS RHINOS 16 BRADFORD BULLS 18

RHINOS: 18 Gary Connolly; 2 Mark Calderwood; 3 Chris McKenna; 4 Keith Senior; 1 Francis Cummins; 13 Kevin Sinfield (C); 14 Andrew Dunemann; 8 Danny Ward; 9 Matt Diskin; 10 Barrie McDermott; 11 David Furner; 12 Matt Adamson; 16 Willie Poching. Subs (all used): 15 Chris Feather; 17 Wayne McDonald; 6 Danny McGuire; 7 Rob Burrow.
Tries: Connolly (34), Senior (37), Burrow (59);
Goals: Sinfield 2/4.
BULLS: 17 Stuart Reardon; 2 Tevita Vaikona; 20 Scott Naylor; 4 Shontayne Hape; 5 Lesley Vainikolo; 3 Leon Pryce; 7 Paul Deacon; 8 Joe Vagana; 9 James Lowes (C); 10 Paul Anderson; 18 Lee Radford; 12 Jamie Peacock; 13 Mike Forshaw. Subs (all used): 27 Robert Parker; 29 Stuart Fielden; 19 Jamie Langley; 14 Lee Gilmour.
Tries: Vainikolo (18), Parker (44), Forshaw (53);
Goals: Deacon 3/3.
Rugby Leaguer & League Express Men of the Match:
Rhinos: Keith Senior; *Bulls:* Stuart Reardon.
Penalty count: 5-6; **Half-time:** 10-6; **Referee:** Karl Kirkpatrick (Warrington); **Attendance:** 23,035.

Saturday 9th August 2003

ST HELENS 28 HULL FC 18

SAINTS: 5 Darren Albert; 2 Anthony Stewart; 1 Paul Wellens; 6 Jason Hooper; 19 Ade Gardner; 7 Sean Long (C); 14 Mick Higham; 8 Darren Britt; 9 Keiron Cunningham; 10 Barry Ward; 12 John Stankevitch; 17 Mike Bennett; 15 Tim Jonkers. Subs (all used): 18 Mark Edmondson; 26 Keith Mason; 23 Jon Wilkin; 21 John Kirkpatrick.
Tries: Stankevitch (33), Wellens (39), Wilkin (50, 77);
Goals: Long 6/6.
Sin bin: Ward (74) - fighting.
HULL: 6 Richard Horne; 2 Colin Best; 32 Alex Wilkinson; 3 Richie Barnett (C); 28 Gareth Raynor; 16 Paul Cooke; 26 Graeme Horne; 8 Craig Greenhill; 9 Dean Treister; 20 Garreth Carvell; 11 Adam Maher; 14 Sean Ryan; 17 Chris Chester. Subs (all used): 10 Paul King; 30 Ewan Dowes; 24 Kirk Yeaman; 19 Richard Fletcher.
Tries: Maher (5), Greenhill (66), Yeaman (80);
Goals: Cooke 3/4.
Sin bin: Greenhill (74) - fighting.
Rugby Leaguer & League Express Men of the Match:
Saints: Jon Wilkin; *Hull:* Dean Treister.
Penalty count: 11-9; **Half-time:** 16-8;
Referee: Ian Smith (Oldham); **Attendance:** 8,019.

Sunday 10th August 2003

WIGAN WARRIORS 40 HALIFAX 0

WARRIORS: 22 Shaun Briscoe; 5 Brian Carney; 18 Martin Aspinwall; 14 David Hodgson; 2 Brett Dallas; 15 Sean O'Loughlin; 20 Luke Robinson; 10 Craig Smith; 9 Terry Newton; 30 Quentin Pongia; 12 Danny Tickle; 19 Stephen Wild; 13 Andy Farrell (C). Subs (all used): 23 Gareth Hock; 25 Kevin Brown; 16 Danny Sculthorpe; 17 Mark Smith.
Tries: Wild (11, 16), Dallas (21), Farrell (32), Briscoe (35), C Smith (46), Sculthorpe (62);
Goals: Farrell 5/5, Tickle 1/2.
HALIFAX: 5 Lee Finnerty; 2 Lee Greenwood; 3 Stuart Donlan (C); 33 Andrew Frew; 21 Chris Norman; 14 Liam Finn; 20 Dane Dorahy; 25 Neil Harmon; 7 Sean Penkywicz; 29 Byron Smith (D); 15 Ryan Clayton; 12 Andrew Brocklehurst; 27 Chris Maye. Subs (all used): 18 Jaymes Chapman; 23 Ged Corcoran; 24 Wayne Corcoran (D); 30 Rikki Sheriffe (D).
Sin bin: G Corcoran (52, 73) - holding down.
Rugby Leaguer & League Express Men of the Match:
Warriors: Craig Smith; *Halifax:* Sean Penkywicz.
Penalty count: 9-8; **Half-time:** 30-0;
Referee: Russell Smith (Castleford); **Attendance:** 7,409.

CASTLEFORD TIGERS 16 WARRINGTON WOLVES 29

TIGERS: 5 Darren Rogers; 4 Paul Mellor; 16 Francis Maloney; 3 Michael Eagar; 2 Waine Pryce; 27 Jon Hepworth; 7 Mitch Healey; 8 Nathan Sykes; 13 Ryan Hudson (C); 10 Andy Lynch; 23 Michael Smith; 12 Dale Fritz; 11 Lee Harland. Subs (all used): 14 Andy Johnson; 19 Wayne Godwin; 20 Tom Saxton; 26 Craig Huby.
Tries: Mellor (4), Johnson (57), Godwin (69);
Goals: Healey 2/3.
WOLVES: 1 Lee Penny; 3 Brent Grose; 12 Ian Sibbit; 4 Ben Westwood; 20 Dean Gaskell; 5 Graham Appo; 7 Nathan Wood (C); 10 Mark Hilton; 9 Jon Clarke; 8 Nick Fozzard; 11 Darren Burns; 16 Paul Wood; 23 Mike Wainwright. Subs (all used): 13 Sid Domic; 19 Gary Hulse; 17 Warren Stevens; 15 Jerome Guisset.
Tries: P Wood (37), N Wood (40), Domic (41), Grose (72); **Goals:** Appo 6/8; **Field goal:** N Wood.
Rugby Leaguer & League Express Men of the Match:
Tigers: Wayne Godwin; *Wolves:* Nathan Wood.
Penalty count: 7-9; **Half-time:** 4-14;
Referee: Ashley Klein (London); **Attendance:** 5,940.

WAKEFIELD TRINITY WILDCATS 26 LONDON BRONCOS 26

WILDCATS: 5 Jon Wells; 22 Matthew Wray; 24 Colum Halpenny; 3 Gareth Ellis (C); 17 Richard Newlove; 16 Jamie Rooney; 6 Ben Jeffries; 21 Steve Snitch; 9 David March; 25 Darrell Griffin; 12 Jamie Field; 20 David

Wrench; 15 Ian Knott. Subs (all used): 7 Brad Davis; 13 Adrian Vowles; 18 Michael Korkidas; 23 Robert Spicer.
Tries: Newlove (10, 56), Rooney (65), Korkidas (79);
Goals: Rooney 5/6.
BRONCOS: 7 Dennis Moran; 25 Andrew King; 3 Nigel Roy; 21 Rob Jackson; 1 Paul Sykes; 6 Rob Purdham; 23 Chris Thorman; 24 Russell Bawden; 14 Neil Budworth; 12 Steele Retchless; 9 Bill Peden; 31 Joe Mbu; 13 Jim Dymock (C). Subs (all used): 26 Damien Kennedy; 8 Francis Stephenson; 22 Andrew Hamilton; 11 Mat Toshack.
Tries: Roy (19, 48), Peden (27), King (31, 34);
Goals: Thorman 3/6.
Rugby Leaguer & League Express Men of the Match:
Wildcats: Jamie Rooney; *Broncos:* Jim Dymock.
Penalty count: 4-1; **Half-time:** 10-20;
Referee: Robert Connolly (Wigan); **Attendance:** 2,415.

HUDDERSFIELD GIANTS 30 WIDNES VIKINGS 30

GIANTS: 1 Paul Reilly; 2 Hefin O'Hare; 3 Ben Cooper; 4 Julian Bailey; 34 Marcus St Hilaire; 33 Stanley Gene; 21 Paul White; 25 Darren Fleary (C); 15 Darren Turner; 10 Jim Gannon; 19 Iain Morrison; 23 Ben Roarty; 7 Jarrod O'Doherty. Subs: 8 Mick Slicker; 26 Jamie Bloem; 24 Craig McDowell (D); 27 Chris Plume (not used).
Tries: St Hilaire (2), O'Hare (6), Gene (14), Bailey (19), Reilly (39); **Goals:** White 5/6.
VIKINGS: 1 Stuart Spruce (C); 20 Dan Potter; 5 Jason Demetriou; 4 Adam Hughes; 2 Paul Devlin; 26 Julian O'Neill (A); 7 Ryan Sheridan; 8 Robert Relf; 9 Shane Millard; 10 Julian O'Neill (NZ); 13 Daniel Frame; 12 Steve McCurrie; 3 Deon Bird. Subs (all used): 22 Phil Cantillon; 25 Simon Finnigan; 17 Anthony Farrell; 19 Paul Atcheson.
Tries: Devlin (11, 44), Cantillon (25, 31), Demetriou (70); **Goals:** O'Neill (A) 5/5.
Rugby Leaguer & League Express Men of the Match:
Giants: Stanley Gene; *Vikings:* Julian O'Neill (A).
Penalty count: 7-6; **Half-time:** 30-18; **Referee:** Richard Silverwood (Dewsbury); **Attendance:** 4,140.

ROUND 23

Friday 15th August 2003

HALIFAX 12 HUDDERSFIELD GIANTS 54

HALIFAX: 5 Lee Finnerty; 2 Lee Greenwood; 21 Chris Norman; 15 Ryan Clayton; 30 Rikki Sheriffe; 14 Liam Finn; 7 Sean Penkywicz; 25 Neil Harmon; 9 Johnny Lawless (C); 29 Byron Smith; 18 Jaymes Chapman; 12 Andrew Brocklehurst; 24 Wayne Corcoran. Subs (all used): 10 Paul Davidson; 23 Ged Corcoran; 27 Chris Maye; 31 Brad Attwood (D).
Tries: Finnerty (4), Greenwood (33); **Goals:** Finn 2/2.
GIANTS: 1 Paul Reilly; 2 Hefin O'Hare; 6 Brandon Costin; 4 Julian Bailey; 34 Marcus St Hilaire; 33 Stanley Gene; 21 Paul White; 25 Darren Fleary (C); 13 Steve McNamara; 10 Jim Gannon; 19 Iain Morrison; 23 Ben Roarty; 7 Jarrod O'Doherty. Subs (all used): 8 Mick Slicker; 15 Darren Turner; 26 Jamie Bloem; 11 Eorl Crabtree.
Tries: Fleary (10), Costin (13), Bailey (15), White (25), O'Doherty (30), O'Hare (38, 43), Gene (48, 55, 80);
Goals: McNamara 5/8, Bloem 2/2.
Rugby Leaguer & League Express Men of the Match:
Halifax: Sean Penkywicz; *Giants:* Stanley Gene.
Penalty count: 7-7; **Half-time:** 12-32;
Referee: Ian Smith (Oldham); **Attendance:** 2,473.

LEEDS RHINOS 24 WIGAN WARRIORS 24

RHINOS: 18 Gary Connolly; 2 Mark Calderwood; 3 Chris McKenna; 4 Keith Senior; 1 Francis Cummins; 13 Kevin Sinfield (C); 14 Andrew Dunemann; 8 Danny Ward; 9 Matt Diskin; 10 Barrie McDermott; 11 David Furner; 12 Matt Adamson; 16 Willie Poching. Subs (all used): 6 Danny McGuire; 15 Chris Feather; 17 Wayne McDonald; 7 Rob Burrow.
Tries: Senior (12), Furner (26), Adamson (76), McGuire (79); **Goals:** Sinfield 4/6.
WARRIORS: 22 Shaun Briscoe; 5 Brian Carney; 18 Martin Aspinwall; 14 David Hodgson; 2 Brett Dallas; 15 Sean O'Loughlin; 20 Luke Robinson; 8 Terry O'Connor; 9 Terry Newton; 10 Craig Smith; 11 Mick Cassidy; 19 Stephen Wild; 13 Andy Farrell (C). Subs (all used): 4 Paul Johnson; 30 Quentin Pongia; 12 Danny Tickle; 23 Gareth Hock.
Tries: Carney (16), Tickle (33, 46), Hock (68);
Goals: Farrell 3/3, Robinson 1/1.
Sin bin: Aspinwall (39) – professional foul.
Rugby Leaguer & League Express Men of the Match:
Rhinos: Keith Senior; *Warriors:* Luke Robinson.
Penalty count: 9-5; **Half-time:** 14-12;
Referee: Ashley Klein (London); **Attendance:** 14,019.

ST HELENS 26 CASTLEFORD TIGERS 10

SAINTS: 1 Paul Wellens; 2 Anthony Stewart; 4 Paul Newlove; 6 Jason Hooper; 19 Ade Gardner; 7 Sean Long (C); 23 Jon Wilkin; 26 Keith Mason; 9 Keiron Cunningham; 10 Barry Ward; 12 John Stankevitch; 17 Mike Bennett; 15 Tim Jonkers. Subs (all used): 31 John Hill (D); 30 James Graham (D); 22 Stuart Jones; 28 Ian Hardman (D).
Tries: Stankevitch (24), Newlove (28), Gardner (59, 78);
Goals: Long 5/5.
TIGERS: 20 Tom Saxton; 2 Waine Pryce; 3 Michael Eagar; 4 Paul Mellor; 28 Andy McNally; 16 Francis Maloney; 7 Mitch Healey; 8 Nathan Sykes; 19 Wayne Godwin; 10 Andy Lynch; 12 Dale Fritz; 14 Andy Johnson; 13 Ryan Hudson (C). Subs (all used): 1 Damian Gibson; 9 Wayne Bartrim; 26 Craig Huby; 30 Tim Spears.
Tries: Saxton (8), Pryce (65); **Goals:** Healey 1/2.
Rugby Leaguer & League Express Men of the Match:
Saints: Sean Long; *Tigers:* Ryan Hudson.
Penalty count: 10-7; **Half-time:** 14-6;
Referee: Robert Connolly (Wigan); **Attendance:** 8,041.

Saturday 16th August 2003

BRADFORD BULLS 36 HULL FC 22

BULLS: 17 Stuart Reardon; 2 Tevita Vaikona; 20 Scott Naylor; 4 Shontayne Hape; 5 Lesley Vainikolo; 13 Mike Forshaw; 15 Karl Pratt; 8 Joe Vagana; 9 James Lowes (C); 10 Paul Anderson; 11 Daniel Gartner; 12 Jamie Peacock; 18 Lee Radford. Subs (all used): 27 Robert Parker; 29 Stuart Fielden; 19 Jamie Langley; 14 Lee Gilmour.
Tries: Vainikolo (5, 66, 77), Anderson (11), Gilmour (56, 63), Langley (73); **Goals:** Radford 4/8, Lowes 0/1.
HULL: 32 Alex Wilkinson; 2 Colin Best; 3 Richie Barnett (C); 24 Kirk Yeaman; 28 Gareth Raynor; 16 Paul Cooke; 6 Richard Horne; 8 Craig Greenhill; 22 Andy Last; 10 Paul King; 11 Adam Maher; 14 Sean Ryan; 17 Chris Chester. Subs (all used): 34 Dwayne Barker (D); 30 Ewan Dowes; 31 Peter Lupton; 19 Richard Fletcher.
Tries: Last (1), Best (16), R Horne (27), Raynor (47);
Goals: Cooke 3/4.
Rugby Leaguer & League Express Men of the Match:
Bulls: Lesley Vainikolo; *Hull:* Richard Horne.
Penalty count: 8-4; **Half-time:** 12-16; **Referee:** Richard Silverwood (Dewsbury); **Attendance:** 10,478.

Sunday 17th August 2003

LONDON BRONCOS 19 WARRINGTON WOLVES 12

BRONCOS: 7 Dennis Moran; 25 Andrew King; 4 Tony Martin; 3 Nigel Roy; 1 Paul Sykes; 6 Rob Purdham; 23 Chris Thorman; 24 Russell Bawden; 14 Neil Budworth; 12 Steele Retchless; 31 Joe Mbu; 9 Bill Peden; 13 Jim Dymock (C). Subs (all used): 8 Francis Stephenson; 32 Steve Trindall (D); 22 Andrew Hamilton; 26 Damien Kennedy.
Tries: Roy (3), Sykes (41); **Goals:** Thorman 5/8;
Field goal: Thorman.
WOLVES: 1 Lee Penny; 20 Dean Gaskell; 4 Ben Westwood; 3 Brent Grose; 28 Daryl Cardiss (D); 5 Graham Appo; 7 Nathan Wood (C); 10 Mark Hilton; 9 Jon Clarke; 8 Nick Fozzard; 11 Darren Burns; 23 Mike Wainwright; 16 Paul Wood. Subs (all used): 19 Gary Hulse; 18 Paul Noone; 13 Sid Domic; 15 Jerome Guisset.
Tries: N Wood (32), Appo (72); **Goals:** Appo 2/2.
On report: Appo (38) - high tackle on Hamilton.
Rugby Leaguer & League Express Men of the Match:
Broncos: Paul Sykes; *Wolves:* Lee Penny.
Penalty count: 8-7; **Half-time:** 14-6;
Referee: Russell Smith (Castleford); **Attendance:** 2,916.

WIDNES VIKINGS 30
WAKEFIELD TRINITY WILDCATS 28

VIKINGS: 1 Stuart Spruce (C); 5 Jason Demetriou; 3 Deon Bird; 4 Adam Hughes; 2 Paul Devlin; 26 Julian O'Neill (A); 7 Ryan Sheridan; 8 Robert Relf; 22 Phil Cantillon; 10 Julian O'Neill (NZ); 11 Andy Hay; 9 Shane Millard; 13 Daniel Frame. Subs (all used): 25 Simon Finnigan; 17 Anthony Farrell; 19 Paul Atcheson; 12 Steve McCurrie.
Tries: O'Neill (A) (9, 15), Farrell (38, 46), Hay (42);
Goals: O'Neill (A) 5/5.
WILDCATS: 5 Jon Wells; 22 Matthew Wray; 24 Colum Halpenny; 3 Gareth Ellis (C); 17 Richard Newlove; 16 Jamie Rooney; 7 Brad Davis; 21 Steve Snitch; 9 David March; 25 Darrell Griffin; 12 Jamie Field; 20 David Wrench; 15 Ian Knott. Subs (all used): 27 Mark Field; 13 Adrian Vowles; 18 Michael Korkidas; 23 Robert Spicer.
Tries: Rooney (19, 67, 71), M Field (53);
Goals: Rooney 6/6.
Rugby Leaguer & League Express Men of the Match:
Vikings: Julian O'Neill (A); *Wildcats:* Jamie Rooney.
Penalty count: 8-9; **Half-time:** 18-10;
Referee: Steve Ganson (St Helens); **Attendance:** 5,697.

ROUND 24

Friday 22nd August 2003

HALIFAX 12 LONDON BRONCOS 26

HALIFAX: 5 Lee Finnerty; 2 Lee Greenwood; 21 Chris Norman; 33 Andrew Frew; 30 Rikki Sheriffe; 14 Liam Finn; 7 Sean Penkywicz; 25 Neil Harmon; 9 Johnny Lawless (C); 29 Byron Smith; 15 Ryan Clayton; 12 Andrew Brocklehurst; 24 Wayne Corcoran. Subs (all used): 10 Paul Davidson; 18 Jaymes Chapman; 23 Ged Corcoran; 31 Brad Attwood.
Tries: Sheriffe (21), Penkywicz (60); **Goals:** Finn 2/2.
BRONCOS: 1 Paul Sykes; 25 Andrew King; 3 Nigel Roy; 4 Tony Martin; 33 Joel Caine (D); 23 Chris Thorman; 7 Dennis Moran; 24 Russell Bawden; 14 Neil Budworth; 12 Steele Retchless; 31 Joe Mbu; 9 Bill Peden; 13 Jim Dymock (C). Subs (all used): 8 Francis Stephenson; 22 Andrew Hamilton; 11 Mat Toshack; 32 Steve Trindall.
Tries: Sykes (10), Moran (37, 78), Martin (69);
Goals: Thorman 5/6.
Rugby Leaguer & League Express Men of the Match:
Halifax: Rikki Sheriffe; *Broncos:* Jim Dymock.
Penalty count: 7-9; **Half-time:** 6-16; **Referee:** Karl Kirkpatrick (Warrington); **Attendance:** 1,276.

CASTLEFORD TIGERS 28 LEEDS RHINOS 20

TIGERS: 20 Tom Saxton; 2 Waine Pryce; 1 Damian Gibson; 3 Michael Eagar; 5 Darren Rogers; 16 Francis Maloney; 7 Mitch Healey; 8 Nathan Sykes; 19 Wayne Godwin; 10 Andy Lynch; 4 Paul Mellor; 12 Dale Fritz; 13 Ryan Hudson (C). Subs: 30 Tim Spears; 27 Jon Hepworth; 26 Craig Huby; 31 Chris Elliott (not used).
Tries: Healey (6), Rogers (13), Lynch (20), Fritz (26), Maloney (33), Eagar (68); **Goals:** Healey 2/6.
RHINOS: 21 Richard Mathers; 2 Mark Calderwood; 1 Francis Cummins; 4 Keith Senior; 28 Liam Botham (D); 6 Danny McGuire; 14 Andrew Dunemann; 8 Danny Ward; 9 Matt Diskin; 10 Barrie McDermott; 11 David Furner; 12 Matt Adamson; 13 Kevin Sinfield (C). Subs (all used): 7 Rob Burrow; 16 Willie Poching; 15 Chris Feather; 17 Wayne McDonald.
Tries: Calderwood (39), Senior (47), McGuire (61), Adamson (77); **Goals:** Sinfield 2/3, Burrow 0/1.
Rugby Leaguer & League Express Men of the Match:
Tigers: Mitch Healey; *Rhinos:* Danny McGuire.
Penalty count: 8-7; **Half-time:** 24-4;
Referee: Ian Smith (Oldham); **Attendance:** 8,281.

Saturday 23rd August 2003

WARRINGTON WOLVES 30 WIDNES VIKINGS 16

WOLVES: 28 Daryl Cardiss; 4 Ben Westwood; 3 Brent Grose; 12 Ian Sibbit; 20 Dean Gaskell; 5 Graham Appo; 7 Nathan Wood (C); 8 Nick Fozzard; 9 Jon Clarke; 10 Mark Hilton; 11 Darren Burns; 16 Paul Wood; 13 Sid Domic. Subs (all used): 19 Gary Hulse; 14 Mark Gleeson; 15 Jerome Guisset; 17 Warren Stevens.
Tries: P Wood (30), Cardiss (35), Domic (42), Appo (44), N Wood (52), Westwood (77);
Goals: Appo 2/4, Cardiss 1/1, Clarke 0/1.
VIKINGS: 1 Stuart Spruce (C); 2 Paul Devlin; 4 Adam Hughes; 5 Jason Demetriou; 20 Dan Potter; 26 Julian O'Neill (A); 7 Ryan Sheridan; 8 Robert Relf; 9 Shane Millard; 10 Julian O'Neill (NZ); 11 Andy Hay; 13 Daniel Frame; 3 Deon Bird. Subs (all used): 22 Phil Cantillon; 25 Simon Finnigan; 17 Anthony Farrell; 23 David Mills.
Tries: Relf (10), Spruce (70); **Goals:** O'Neill (A) 4/4.
Rugby Leaguer & League Express Men of the Match:
Wolves: Mark Hilton; *Vikings:* Robert Relf.
Penalty count: 5-4; **Half-time:** 10-10;
Referee: Russell Smith (Castleford); **Attendance:** 6,902.

Sunday 24th August 2003

HULL FC 42 ST HELENS 18

HULL: 6 Richard Horne; 2 Colin Best; 24 Kirk Yeaman; 3 Richie Barnett; 28 Gareth Raynor; 16 Paul Cooke; 13 Jason Smith (C); 8 Craig Greenhill; 22 Andy Last; 10 Paul King; 19 Richard Fletcher; 14 Sean Ryan; 17 Chris Chester. Subs (all used): 20 Garreth Carvell; 30 Ewan Dowes; 32 Alex Wilkinson; 31 Peter Lupton.
Tries: Chester (3), Raynor (5, 67), Barnett (9, 11), Cooke (25), Best (31), Lupton (57); **Goals:** Cooke 5/8.
ST HELENS: 1 Paul Wellens; 2 Anthony Stewart; 4 Paul Newlove; 6 Jason Hooper; 19 Ade Gardner; 7 Sean Long (C); 14 Mick Higham; 26 Keith Mason; 9 Keiron Cunningham; 10 Barry Ward; 12 John Stankevitch; 17 Mike Bennett; 16 Darren Smith. Subs (all used): 15 Tim Jonkers; 23 Jon Wilkin; 22 Stuart Jones; 32 Willie Talau (D).
Tries: Higham (14), Stewart (49), Cunningham (63);
Goals: Long 3/3.
Rugby Leaguer & League Express Men of the Match:
Hull: Paul Cooke; *St Helens:* Mick Higham.
Penalty count: 3-8; **Half-time:** 32-6;
Referee: Ashley Klein (London); **Attendance:** 11,212.

HUDDERSFIELD GIANTS 26
WAKEFIELD TRINITY WILDCATS 14

GIANTS: 1 Paul Reilly; 2 Hefin O'Hare; 4 Julian Bailey; 26 Jamie Bloem; 34 Marcus St Hilaire; 33 Stanley Gene; 9 Paul March; 25 Darren Fleary (C); 15 Darren Turner; 10 Jim Gannon; 19 Iain Morrison; 23 Ben Roarty; 7 Jarrod O'Doherty. Subs (all used): 8 Mick Slicker; 13 Steve McNamara; 21 Paul White; 11 Eorl Crabtree.
Tries: Turner (3, 22), O'Doherty (32), McNamara (80);
Goals: Bloem 3/4, McNamara 2/2.
WILDCATS: 1 Martyn Holland; 17 Richard Newlove; 3 Gareth Ellis; 24 Colum Halpenny; 22 Matthew Wray; 14 Paul Handforth; 6 Ben Jeffries; 18 Michael Korkidas; 9 David March; 25 Darrell Griffin; 12 Jamie Field; 20 David Wrench; 13 Adrian Vowles (C). Subs (all used): 10 Dallas Hood; 11 Troy Slattery; 21 Steve Snitch; 23 Robert Spicer.
Tries: Jeffries (14), Hood (36);
Goals: Jeffries 0/1, Handforth 3/4.
Rugby Leaguer & League Express Men of the Match:
Giants: Ben Roarty; *Wildcats:* David March.
Penalty count: 12-16; **Half-time:** 18-10;
Referee: Robert Connolly (Wigan); **Attendance:** 3,621.

Monday 25th August 2003

WIGAN WARRIORS 26 BRADFORD BULLS 12

WARRIORS: 1 Kris Radlinski; 2 Brett Dallas; 14 David Hodgson; 18 Martin Aspinwall; 5 Brian Carney; 15 Sean O'Loughlin; 20 Luke Robinson; 10 Craig Smith; 9 Terry Newton; 30 Quentin Pongia; 11 Mick Cassidy; 12 Danny Tickle; 13 Andy Farrell (C). Subs (all used): 4 Paul Johnson; 8 Terry O'Connor; 16 Danny Sculthorpe; 23 Gareth Hock.
Tries: Dallas (23), Radlinski (38), Aspinwall (46), Carney (52), Farrell (59); **Goals:** Farrell 3/6.
BULLS: 17 Stuart Reardon; 2 Tevita Vaikona; 20 Scott

Naylor; 4 Shontayne Hape; 5 Lesley Vainikolo; 3 Leon Pryce; 7 Paul Deacon; 8 Joe Vagana; 9 James Lowes (C); 10 Paul Anderson; 11 Daniel Gartner; 12 Jamie Peacock; 13 Mike Forshaw. Subs (all used): 27 Robert Parker; 29 Stuart Fielden; 18 Lee Radford; 14 Lee Gilmour.
Tries: Vagana (57), Vaikona (65); **Goals:** Deacon 2/2.
Rugby Leaguer & League Express Men of the Match:
Warriors: Martin Aspinwall; *Bulls:* Stuart Reardon.
Penalty count: 5-6; **Half time:** 10-0;
Referee: Steve Ganson (St Helens); **Attendance:** 14,714.

ROUND 25

Friday 29th August 2003

CASTLEFORD TIGERS 26 HUDDERSFIELD GIANTS 18

TIGERS: 20 Tom Saxton; 2 Waine Pryce; 1 Damian Gibson; 3 Michael Eagar; 5 Darren Rogers; 16 Francis Maloney; 7 Mitch Healey; 8 Nathan Sykes; 19 Wayne Godwin; 10 Andy Lynch; 4 Paul Mellor; 12 Dale Fritz; 13 Ryan Hudson (C). Subs (all used): 6 Danny Orr; 23 Michael Smith; 26 Craig Huby; 14 Andy Johnson.
Tries: Gibson (25), Pryce (44, 61), Eagar (73);
Goals: Huby 3/3, Healey 2/3, Orr 0/1.
GIANTS: 1 Paul Reilly; 2 Hefin O'Hare; 4 Julian Bailey; 26 Jamie Bloem; 34 Marcus St Hilaire; 33 Stanley Gene; 9 Paul March; 25 Darren Fleary (C); 15 Darren Turner; 10 Jim Gannon; 19 Iain Morrison; 23 Ben Roarty; 7 Jarrod O'Doherty. Subs (all used): 8 Mick Slicker; 13 Steve McNamara; 3 Ben Cooper; 11 Eorl Crabtree.
Tries: O'Hare (28), Crabtree (77);
Goals: Bloem 3/3, McNamara 2/3.
Dismissal: Gannon (67) - high tackle.
Rugby Leaguer & League Express Men of the Match:
Tigers: Mitch Healey; *Giants:* Stanley Gene.
Penalty count: 9-9; **Half-time:** 8-12; **Referee:** Karl Kirkpatrick (Warrington); **Attendance:** 5,289.

LEEDS RHINOS 34 WARRINGTON WOLVES 26

RHINOS: 18 Gary Connolly; 21 Richard Mathers; 3 Chris McKenna; 4 Keith Senior; 1 Francis Cummins; 6 Danny McGuire; 14 Andrew Dunemann; 8 Danny Ward; 9 Matt Diskin; 12 Matt Adamson; 11 David Furner; 16 Willie Poching; 13 Kevin Sinfield (C). Subs (all used): 10 Barrie McDermott; 15 Chris Feather; 7 Rob Burrow; 20 Jamie Jones-Buchanan.
Tries: Sinfield (24), Diskin (33), McGuire (47), Cummins (65), Dunemann (78); **Goals:** Sinfield 7/7.
WOLVES: 28 Daryl Cardiss; 20 Dean Gaskell; 3 Brent Grose; 18 Paul Noone; 4 Ben Westwood; 5 Graham Appo; 7 Nathan Wood (C); 8 Nick Fozzard; 9 Jon Clarke; 10 Mark Hilton; 23 Mike Wainwright; 16 Paul Wood; 13 Sid Domic. Subs (all used): 17 Warren Stevens; 15 Jerome Guisset; 14 Mark Gleeson; 19 Gary Hulse.
Tries: Westwood (5, 55), Domic (38), Appo (58), N Wood (74); **Goals:** Appo 3/5.
Rugby Leaguer & League Express Men of the Match:
Rhinos: Kevin Sinfield; *Wolves:* Graham Appo.
Penalty count: 5-5; **Half-time:** 14-10; **Referee:** Richard Silverwood (Dewsbury); **Attendance:** 10,750.

Saturday 30th August 2003

WAKEFIELD TRINITY WILDCATS 35 HULL FC 28

WILDCATS: 5 Jon Wells; 22 Matthew Wray; 30 Sylvain Houles (D); 24 Colum Halpenny; 17 Richard Newlove; 6 Ben Jeffries; 16 Jamie Rooney; 18 Michael Korkidas; 9 David March; 25 Darrell Griffin; 10 Dallas Hood (C); 20 David Wrench; 12 Jamie Field. Subs (all used): 21 Steve Snitch; 1 Martyn Holland; 14 Paul Handforth; 28 Matthew Blake.
Tries: Korkidas (15), Wrench (18), March (22, pen), Houles (33), Wray (47); **Goals:** Rooney 7/8;
Field goal: Rooney.
HULL: 32 Alex Wilkinson; 2 Colin Best; 3 Richie Barnett; 24 Kirk Yeaman; 28 Gareth Raynor; 16 Paul Cooke; 6 Richard Horne; 8 Craig Greenhill; 22 Andy Last; 10 Paul King; 14 Sean Ryan; 17 Chris Chester; 13 Jason Smith (C). Subs (all used): 20 Garreth Carvell; 30 Ewan Dowes; 31 Peter Lupton; 33 Shayne McMenemy.
Tries: J Smith (9, 37), Raynor (40), R Horne (58), McMenemy (61); **Goals:** Cooke 4/5.
Sin bin: J Smith (23) - obstruction, (54) - interference.
Rugby Leaguer & League Express Men of the Match:
Wildcats: Michael Korkidas; *Hull:* Jason Smith.
Penalty count: 7-5; **Half-time:** 24-18;
Referee: Russell Smith (Castleford); **Attendance:** 3,689.

Sunday 31st August 2003

HALIFAX 12 WIGAN WARRIORS 68

HALIFAX: 5 Lee Finnerty; 2 Lee Greenwood; 21 Chris Norman; 15 Ryan Clayton; 30 Rikki Sherriffe; 14 Liam Finn; 7 Sean Penkywicz; 25 Neil Harmon; 9 Johnny Lawless (C); 29 Byron Smith; 18 Jaymes Chapman; 12 Andrew Brocklehurst; 24 Wayne Corcoran. Subs (all used): 10 Paul Davidson; 23 Ged Corcoran; 27 Chris Maye; 31 Brad Attwood.
Tries: Greenwood (2), Finnerty (45); **Goals:** Finn 2/2.
WARRIORS: 1 Kris Radlinski; 5 Brian Carney; 18 Martin Aspinwall; 14 David Hodgson; 2 Brett Dallas; 15 Sean O'Loughlin; 20 Luke Robinson; 30 Quentin Pongia; 17 Mark Smith; 10 Craig Smith (C); 4 Paul Johnson; 12 Danny Tickle; 23 Gareth Hock. Subs (all used): 11 Mick Cassidy; 19 Stephen Wild; 28 Nick Graham; 22 Shaun Briscoe.
Tries: Hock (6), Tickle (11), Dallas (18, 34, 67), Hodgson (23), Robinson (26), Radlinski (37, 79), Carney

ROUND 26 - Huddersfield's Steve McNamara held up against Widnes

(49, 53), Johnson (76); **Goals:** Tickle 10/12.
Rugby Leaguer & League Express Men of the Match:
Halifax: Lee Finnerty; *Warriors:* Danny Tickle.
Penalty count: 5-6; **Half-time:** 6-42;
Referee: Ashley Klein (London); **Attendance:** 2,543.

LONDON BRONCOS 12 BRADFORD BULLS 54

BRONCOS: 1 Paul Sykes; 25 Andrew King; 4 Tony Martin; 3 Nigel Roy; 33 Joel Caine; 6 Rob Purdham; 7 Dennis Moran; 8 Francis Stephenson; 14 Neil Budworth; 24 Russell Bawden; 11 Mat Toshack; 12 Steele Retchless; 13 Jim Dymock (C). Subs (all used): 9 Bill Peden; 32 Steve Trindall; 34 Dave McConnell (D); 22 Andrew Hamilton.
Tries: Retchless (10), King (73);
Goals: Sykes 1/2, Caine 1/1.
BULLS: 17 Stuart Reardon; 2 Tevita Vaikona; 20 Scott Naylor; 14 Lee Gilmour; 4 Shontayne Hape; 15 Karl Pratt; 7 Paul Deacon; 8 Joe Vagana; 9 James Lowes (C); 10 Paul Anderson; 11 Daniel Gartner; 12 Jamie Peacock; 13 Mike Forshaw. Subs (all used): 19 Jamie Langley; 18 Lee Radford; 27 Robert Parker; 29 Stuart Fielden.
Tries: Peacock (15, 33), Radford (35), Hape (46), Lowes (52), Parker (57), Vaikona (61, 65), Vagana (70);
Goals: Deacon 9/10.
Rugby Leaguer & League Express Men of the Match:
Broncos: Steele Retchless; *Bulls:* Karl Pratt.
Penalty count: 7-8; **Half-time:** 6-18;
Referee: Robert Connolly (Wigan); **Attendance:** 3,910.

WIDNES VIKINGS 4 ST HELENS 40

VIKINGS: 1 Stuart Spruce (C); 5 Jason Demetriou; 28 Aled James (D); 4 Adam Hughes; 2 Paul Devlin; 13 Daniel Frame; 7 Ryan Sheridan; 8 Robert Relf; 9 Shane Millard; 10 Julian O'Neill (NZ); 11 Andy Hay; 25 Simon Finnigan; 3 Deon Bird. Subs (all used): 17 Anthony Farrell; 22 Phil Cantillon; 23 David Mills; 30 Stephen Myler.
Try: Devlin (72); **Goals:** Myler 0/1.
SAINTS: 1 Paul Wellens; 5 Darren Albert; 32 Willie Talau; 4 Paul Newlove; 19 Ade Gardner; 7 Sean Long (C); 14 Mick Higham; 10 Barry Ward; 9 Keiron Cunningham; 12 John Stankevitch; 16 Darren Smith; 17 Mike Bennett; 6 Jason Hooper. Subs (all used): 15 Tim Jonkers; 26 Keith Mason; 22 Stuart Jones; 2 Anthony Stewart.
Tries: Cunningham (23), Wellens (49), Mason (56), Higham (62), Albert (67, 79), Smith (77);
Goals: Long 6/7.
Rugby Leaguer & League Express Men of the Match:
Vikings: Julian O'Neill (NZ); *Saints:* Keiron Cunningham.
Penalty count: 7-7; **Half-time:** 0-4;
Referee: Ian Smith (Oldham); **Attendance:** 9,457.

ROUND 26

Friday 5th September 2003

ST HELENS 4 WIGAN WARRIORS 28

SAINTS: 1 Paul Wellens; 5 Darren Albert; 3 Martin Gleeson; 4 Paul Newlove; 19 Ade Gardner; 7 Sean Long (C); 14 Mick Higham; 12 John Stankevitch; 9 Keiron Cunningham; 17 Mike Bennett; 16 Darren Smith; 32 Willie Talau; 6 Jason Hooper. Subs (all used): 15 Tim Jonkers; 26 Keith Mason; 2 Anthony Stewart; 22 Stuart Jones.
Try: Smith (63); **Goals:** Long 0/1.
Sin bin: Hooper (30) - obstruction.
WARRIORS: 1 Kris Radlinski; 5 Brian Carney; 18 Martin Aspinwall; 14 David Hodgson; 2 Brett Dallas; 15 Sean O'Loughlin; 7 Adrian Lam; 30 Quentin Pongia; 9 Terry Newton; 10 Craig Smith; 11 Mick Cassidy; 12 Danny Tickle; 13 Andy Farrell (C). Subs (all used): 4 Paul Johnson; 8 Terry O'Connor; 20 Luke Robinson; 23 Gareth Hock.
Tries: Carney (13, 38), Hock (35), Johnson (60);
Goals: Tickle 3/3, Farrell 2/2, Radlinski 0/1, Robinson 1/1.
Rugby Leaguer & League Express Men of the Match:
Saints: Sean Long; *Warriors:* Craig Smith.
Penalty count: 11-10; **Half-time:** 0-20; **Referee:** Russell Smith (Castleford); **Attendance:** 14,508.

Sunday 7th September 2003

LONDON BRONCOS 38 WAKEFIELD TRINITY WILDCATS 14

BRONCOS: 1 Paul Sykes; 33 Joel Caine; 3 Nigel Roy; 4 Tony Martin; 25 Andrew King; 23 Chris Thorman; 7 Dennis Moran; 12 Steele Retchless; 14 Neil Budworth; 8 Francis Stephenson; 11 Mat Toshack; 9 Bill Peden; 13 Jim Dymock (C). Subs (all used): 32 Steve Trindall; 24 Russell Bawden; 31 Joe Mbu; 6 Rob Purdham.
Tries: Moran (16, 52, 60), Roy (31), Martin (37), King (56), Caine (74); **Goals:** Thorman 5/8.
WILDCATS: 5 Jon Wells; 22 Matthew Wray; 3 Gareth Ellis; 30 Sylvain Houles; 24 Colum Halpenny; 16 Jamie Rooney; 6 Ben Jeffries; 18 Michael Korkidas; 9 David March; 25 Darrell Griffin; 10 Dallas Hood (C); 12 Jamie Field. Subs (all used): 14 Paul Handforth; 21 Steve Snitch; 15 Ian Knott; 17 Richard Newlove.
Tries: Jeffries (19), Wray (39), March (79);
Goals: Rooney 1/3.
Rugby Leaguer & League Express Men of the Match:
Broncos: Dennis Moran; *Wildcats:* Dallas Hood.
Penalty count: 4-2; **Half-time:** 16-8; **Referee:** Karl Kirkpatrick (Warrington); **Attendance:** 2,916.

WARRINGTON WOLVES 40 HALIFAX 18

WOLVES: 1 Lee Penny; 4 Ben Westwood; 3 Brent Grose; 28 Daryl Cardiss; 20 Dean Gaskell; 5 Graham Appo; 7 Nathan Wood (C); 16 Paul Wood; 9 Jon Clarke; 10 Mark Hilton; 11 Darren Burns; 23 Mike Wainwright; 13 Sid Domic. Subs (all used): 19 Gary Hulse; 14 Mark Gleeson; 18 Paul Noone; 17 Warren Stevens.
Tries: Penny (1), Westwood (18, 71), Burns (30, 56), Gaskell (63), Gleeson (66); **Goals:** Appo 6/7.
HALIFAX: 5 Lee Finnerty; 2 Lee Greenwood; 27 Chris Maye; 21 Chris Norman; 30 Rikki Sheriffe; 14 Liam Finn; 7 Sean Penkywicz; 25 Neil Harmon; 9 Johnny Lawless (C); 29 Byron Smith; 18 Jaymes Chapman; 12 Andrew Brocklehurst; 15 Ryan Clayton. Subs (all used): 8 Andy Hobson; 10 Paul Davidson; 23 Ged Corcoran; 24 Wayne Corcoran.
Tries: Sheriffe (9, 12), Finnerty (26); **Goals:** Finn 3/3.
Sin bin: Chapman (58) – flopping on in the tackle.
Rugby Leaguer & League Express Men of the Match: *Wolves:* Darren Burns; *Halifax:* Johnny Lawless.
Penalty count: 12-4; **Half-time:** 16-18;
Referee: Ian Smith (Oldham); **Attendance:** 5,761.

HULL FC 32 CASTLEFORD TIGERS 12

HULL: 6 Richard Horne; 2 Colin Best; 3 Richie Barnett; 24 Kirk Yeaman; 28 Gareth Raynor; 16 Paul Cooke; 13 Jason Smith (C); 8 Craig Greenhill; 9 Dean Treister; 10 Paul King; 11 Adam Maher; 14 Sean Ryan; 17 Chris Chester. Subs (all used): 20 Garreth Carvell; 30 Ewan Dowes; 31 Peter Lupton; 33 Shayne McMenemy.
Tries: Raynor (18), Dowes (39), McMenemy (75), R Horne (79); **Goals:** Cooke 7/8, Greenhill 1/1.
TIGERS: 20 Tom Saxton; 2 Waine Pryce; 3 Michael Eagar; 16 Francis Maloney; 5 Darren Rogers; 6 Danny Orr; 7 Mitch Healey; 8 Nathan Sykes; 19 Wayne Godwin; 10 Andy Lynch; 4 Paul Mellor; 12 Dale Fritz; 13 Ryan Hudson (C). Subs (all used): 23 Michael Smith; 1 Damian Gibson; 24 Adrian Vowles (D2); 14 Andy Johnson.
Tries: Maloney (31), Lynch (44); **Goals:** Orr 2/3.
Rugby Leaguer & League Express Men of the Match: *Hull:* Richard Horne; *Tigers:* Andy Lynch.
Penalty count: 9-6; **Half-time:** 16-4; **Referee:** Richard Silverwood (Dewsbury); **Attendance:** 10,631.

HUDDERSFIELD GIANTS 25 WIDNES VIKINGS 12

GIANTS: 1 Paul Reilly; 2 Hefin O'Hare; 26 Jamie Bloem; 4 Julian Bailey; 34 Marcus St Hilaire; 13 Steve McNamara; 9 Paul March; 25 Darren Fleary (C); 15 Darren Turner; 10 Jim Gannon; 16 Eorl Crabtree; 23 Ben Roarty; 7 Jarrod O'Doherty. Subs (all used): 8 Mick Slicker; 19 Iain Morrison; 21 Paul White; 5 Matt Whitaker.
Tries: Reilly (12), O'Hare (43), Bloem (64), March (80); **Goals:** McNamara 3/4, Bloem 1/1; **Field goal:** McNamara.
VIKINGS: 1 Stuart Spruce (C); 5 Jason Demetriou; 28 Aled James; 4 Adam Hughes; 2 Paul Devlin; 13 Daniel Frame; 7 Ryan Sheridan; 8 Robert Relf; 9 Shane Millard; 10 Julian O'Neill (NZ); 11 Andy Hay; 25 Simon Finnigan; 3 Deon Bird. Subs (all used): 17 Anthony Farrell; 23 David Mills; 22 Phil Cantillon; 30 Stephen Myler.
Tries: Hughes (9), Demetriou (58);
Goals: Hughes 0/1, Myler 2/2.
Rugby Leaguer & League Express Men of the Match: *Giants:* Paul March; *Vikings:* Shane Millard.
Penalty count: 8-9; **Half-time:** 8-6;
Referee: Ashley Klein (London); **Attendance:** 3,555.

BRADFORD BULLS 22 LEEDS RHINOS 21

BULLS: 17 Stuart Reardon; 2 Tevita Vaikona; 20 Scott Naylor; 4 Shontayne Hape; 5 Lesley Vainikolo; 15 Karl Pratt; 7 Paul Deacon; 8 Joe Vagana; 9 James Lowes (C); 10 Paul Anderson; 11 Daniel Gartner; 19 Jamie Peacock; 13 Mike Forshaw. Subs (all used): 18 Lee Radford; 27 Robert Parker; 14 Lee Gilmour.
Tries: Deacon (12), Reardon (45), Vainikolo (69);
Goals: Deacon 4/4; **Field goal:** Deacon 2.
Sin bin: Lowes (56) - dissent.
RHINOS: 18 Gary Connolly; 2 Mark Calderwood; 3 Chris McKenna; 4 Keith Senior; 1 Francis Cummins; 6 Danny McGuire; 14 Andrew Dunemann; 10 Barrie McDermott; 9 Matt Diskin; 12 Matt Adamson; 11 David Furner; 16 Willie Poching; 13 Kevin Sinfield (C). Subs (all used): 8 Danny Ward; 17 Wayne McDonald; 7 Rob Burrow; 20 Jamie Jones-Buchanan.
Tries: McDonald (23), Poching (53), Sinfield (75);
Goals: Sinfield 4/4; **Field goal:** Sinfield.
Rugby Leaguer & League Express Men of the Match: *Bulls:* Paul Deacon; *Rhinos:* Gary Connolly.
Penalty count: 8-6; **Half-time:** 8-6;
Referee: Steve Ganson (St Helens); **Attendance:** 21,102.

ROUND 27

Friday 12th September 2003

HUDDERSFIELD GIANTS 12 WARRINGTON WOLVES 25

GIANTS: 1 Paul Reilly (C); 2 Hefin O'Hare; 26 Jamie Bloem; 4 Julian Bailey; 34 Marcus St Hilaire; 13 Steve McNamara; 9 Paul March; 25 Darren Fleary; 15 Darren Turner; 10 Jim Gannon; 16 Eorl Crabtree; 23 Ben Roarty; 7 Jarrod O'Doherty. Subs (all used): 8 Mick Slicker; 5 Matt Whitaker; 19 Iain Morrison; 21 Paul White.
Tries: O'Doherty (38), Bloem (77);
Goals: McNamara 2/3.
Sin bin: Roarty (19) - interference; Bloem (26) - fighting; Reilly (29) - foul in tackle; March (73) - offside.
On report: Brawl (26).
WOLVES: 28 Daryl Cardiss; 3 Brent Grose; 4 Ben Westwood; 11 Darren Burns; 20 Dean Gaskell; 5 Graham

Appo; 7 Nathan Wood (C); 10 Mark Hilton; 9 Jon Clarke; 8 Nick Fozzard; 23 Mike Wainwright; 16 Paul Wood; 13 Sid Domic. Subs (all used): 19 Gary Hulse; 14 Mark Gleeson; 18 Paul Noone; 15 Jerome Guisset.
Tries: Cardiss (11), P Wood (21);
Goals: Appo 7/8, Cardiss 1/1; **Field goal:** N Wood.
Sin bin: N Wood (26) - fighting;
Westwood (26) - fighting.
On report: Hilton (4) - high tackle; Brawl (26).
Rugby Leaguer & League Express Men of the Match: *Giants:* Iain Morrison; *Wolves:* Daryl Cardiss.
Penalty count: 11-16; **Half-time:** 6-16;
Referee: Russell Smith (Castleford); **Attendance:** 4,443.

LEEDS RHINOS 30 ST HELENS 20

RHINOS: 21 Richard Mathers; 2 Mark Calderwood; 18 Gary Connolly; 4 Keith Senior; 1 Francis Cummins; 14 Andrew Dunemann; 7 Rob Burrow; 17 Wayne McDonald; 9 Matt Diskin; 10 Barrie McDermott; 11 David Furner; 3 Chris McKenna; 13 Kevin Sinfield (C). Subs (all used): 8 Danny Ward; 15 Chris Feather; 6 Danny McGuire; 16 Willie Poching.
Tries: Burrow (63), Calderwood (65), Connolly (71), Mathers (73), Poching (79); **Goals:** Sinfield 5/5.
SAINTS: 1 Paul Wellens; 5 Darren Albert; 3 Martin Gleeson; 4 Paul Newlove; 19 Ade Gardner; 6 Jason Hooper; 7 Sean Long (C); 26 Keith Mason; 9 Keiron Cunningham; 10 Barry Ward; 32 Willie Talau; 12 John Stankevitch; 16 Darren Smith. Subs (all used): 14 Mick Higham; 15 Tim Jonkers; 2 Anthony Stewart; 22 Stuart Jones.
Tries: Smith (7), Cunningham (14), Stewart (44);
Goals: Long 4/4.
Rugby Leaguer & League Express Men of the Match: *Rhinos:* Richard Mathers; *Saints:* Sean Long.
Penalty count: 7-4; **Half-time:** 0-12; **Referee:** Richard Silverwood (Dewsbury); **Attendance:** 15,273.

WIGAN WARRIORS 28 HULL FC 6

WARRIORS: 1 Kris Radlinski; 5 Brian Carney; 18 Martin Aspinwall; 14 David Hodgson; 2 Brett Dallas; 15 Sean O'Loughlin; 20 Luke Robinson; 10 Craig Smith; 9 Terry Newton; 30 Quentin Pongia; 11 Mick Cassidy; 12 Danny Tickle; 13 Andy Farrell (C). Subs (all used): 4 Paul Johnson; 8 Terry O'Connor; 17 Mark Smith; 23 Gareth Hock.
Tries: Hodgson (10, 19), Tickle (26), Hock (65);
Goals: Tickle 5/5, Robinson 1/1.
Sin bin: Newton (3) - holding down.
HULL: 6 Richard Horne; 2 Colin Best; 24 Kirk Yeaman; 3 Richie Barnett; 32 Alex Wilkinson; 16 Paul Cooke; 13 Jason Smith (C); 8 Craig Greenhill; 9 Dean Treister; 10 Paul King; 33 Shayne McMenemy; 14 Sean Ryan; 17 Chris Chester. Subs (all used): 30 Ewan Dowes; 18 Warren Jowitt (D); 12 Scott Logan; 31 Peter Lupton.
Try: Yeaman (80); **Goals:** Cooke 1/2.
Sin bin: Jowitt (40) - pushing;
Chester (73) - obstruction.
Rugby Leaguer & League Express Men of the Match: *Warriors:* Luke Robinson; *Hull:* Richie Barnett.
Penalty count: 6-4; **Half-time:** 18-2;
Referee: Steve Ganson (St Helens); **Attendance:** 11,115.

Saturday 13th September 2003

WIDNES VIKINGS 0 LONDON BRONCOS 40

VIKINGS: 2 Paul Devlin; 29 John Robinson (D); 28 Aled James; 5 Jason Demetriou; 24 Chris Giles; 13 Daniel

Frame; 30 Stephen Myler; 8 Robert Relf (C); 9 Shane Millard; 10 Julian O'Neill (NZ); 11 Andy Hay; 25 Simon Finnigan; 3 Deon Bird. Subs (all used): 17 Anthony Farrell; 23 David Mills; 22 Phil Cantillon; 4 Adam Hughes.
BRONCOS: 1 Paul Sykes; 33 Joel Caine; 4 Tony Martin; 3 Nigel Roy; 25 Andrew King; 23 Chris Thorman; 7 Dennis Moran; 8 Francis Stephenson; 9 Bill Peden; 24 Russell Bawden; 11 Mat Toshack; 12 Steele Retchless; 13 Jim Dymock (C). Subs (all used): 32 Steve Trindall; 34 Dave McConnell; 31 Joe Mbu; 6 Rob Purdham.
Tries: Caine (48, 55, 68), Moran (61), Peden (72), Thorman (77); **Goals:** Thorman 8/8.
Rugby Leaguer & League Express Men of the Match: *Vikings:* Stephen Myler; *Broncos:* Jim Dymock.
Penalty count: 6-4; **Half-time:** 0-2; **Referee:** Karl Kirkpatrick (Warrington); **Attendance:** 5,009.

Sunday 14th September 2003

WAKEFIELD TRINITY WILDCATS 68 HALIFAX 6

WILDCATS: 1 Martyn Holland; 22 Matthew Wray; 3 Gareth Ellis (C); 30 Sylvain Houles; 24 Colum Halpenny; 16 Jamie Rooney; 7 Brad Davis; 18 Michael Korkidas; 9 David March; 25 Darrell Griffin; 10 Dallas Hood; 20 David Wrench; 12 Jamie Field. Subs (all used): 14 Paul Handforth; 21 Steve Snitch; 15 Ian Knott; 17 Richard Newlove.
Tries: Rooney (3, 14, 65), Griffin (6), Wrench (10), March (18), Korkidas (37), Newlove (43), Halpenny (48, 60, 79), Knott (53), Snitch (58);
Goals: Rooney 7/8, Davis 1/1.
HALIFAX: 5 Lee Finnerty; 2 Lee Greenwood; 27 Chris Maye; 21 Chris Norman; 30 Rikki Sheriffe; 14 Liam Finn; 7 Sean Penkywicz; 25 Neil Harmon; 9 Johnny Lawless (C); 29 Byron Smith; 18 Jaymes Chapman; 12 Andrew Brocklehurst; 15 Ryan Clayton. Subs (all used): 8 Andy Hobson; 10 Paul Davidson; 23 Ged Corcoran; 22 Simon Grix.
Try: Hobson (23); **Goals:** Finn 1/1.
Sin bin: Hobson (28) - holding down;
G Corcoran (58) - alleged striking.
Rugby Leaguer & League Express Men of the Match: *Wildcats:* Jamie Rooney; *Halifax:* Lee Finnerty.
Penalty count: 12-3; **Half-time:** 32-6;
Referee: Robert Connolly (Wigan); **Attendance:** 3,112.

BRADFORD BULLS 14 CASTLEFORD TIGERS 28

BULLS: 17 Stuart Reardon; 2 Tevita Vaikona; 20 Scott Naylor; 14 Lee Gilmour; 4 Shontayne Hape; 3 Leon Pryce; 7 Paul Deacon; 8 Joe Vagana; 9 James Lowes (C); 10 Paul Anderson; 11 Daniel Gartner; 12 Jamie Peacock; 19 Jamie Langley. Subs (all used): 15 Karl Pratt; 13 Mike Forshaw; 27 Robert Parker; 30 Richard Moore.
Tries: Hape (29), L Pryce (73); **Goals:** Deacon 3/4.
TIGERS: 20 Tom Saxton; 2 Waine Pryce; 4 Paul Mellor; 3 Michael Eagar; 5 Darren Rogers; 6 Danny Orr; 7 Mitch Healey; 8 Nathan Sykes; 13 Ryan Hudson (C); 10 Andy Lynch; 23 Michael Smith; 12 Dale Fritz; 24 Adrian Vowles. Subs (all used): 19 Wayne Godwin; 26 Craig Huby; 21 Richard Blakeway; 14 Andy Johnson.
Tries: Orr (13), Godwin (49), Lynch (54), Saxton (60);
Goals: Orr 6/6.
Sin bin: Fritz (68) - holding down.
Rugby Leaguer & League Express Men of the Match: *Bulls:* Paul Deacon; *Tigers:* Danny Orr.
Penalty count: 13-4; **Half-time:** 6-8;
Referee: Ashley Klein (London); **Attendance:** 13,628.

ROUND 27 - Andy Lynch swamped by Castleford teammates after scoring against Bradford

ROUND 28 - Leeds' Rob Burrow all wrapped up by Hull's Craig Greenhill

ROUND 28

Friday 19th September 2003

ST HELENS 18 BRADFORD BULLS 22

SAINTS: 1 Paul Wellens; 5 Darren Albert; 3 Martin Gleeson; 4 Paul Newlove; 19 Ade Gardner; 6 Jason Hooper; 7 Sean Long (C); 26 Keith Mason; 9 Keiron Cunningham; 10 Barry Ward; 32 Willie Talau; 12 John Stankevitch; 16 Darren Smith. Subs (all used): 2 Anthony Stewart; 15 Tim Jonkers; 14 Mick Higham; 18 Mark Edmondson.
Tries: Hooper (9), Albert (23), Smith (52); **Goals:** Long 3/5.
BULLS: 17 Stuart Reardon; 2 Tevita Vaikona; 3 Leon Pryce; 4 Shontayne Hape; 5 Lesley Vainikolo; 15 Karl Pratt; 7 Paul Deacon; 29 Stuart Fielden; 9 James Lowes (C); 10 Paul Anderson; 20 Scott Naylor; 14 Lee Gilmour; 13 Mike Forshaw. Subs (all used): 22 Karl Pryce (D); 23 Vinny Myler (D); 27 Robert Parker; 30 Richard Moore.
Tries: Hape (18), Vaikona (38), Vainikolo (43), L Pryce (55); **Goals:** Deacon 3/5.
Rugby Leaguer & League Express Men of the Match: *Saints:* Darren Smith; *Bulls:* Stuart Reardon.
Penalty count: 10-7; **Half-time:** 12-10; **Referee:** Russell Smith (Castleford); **Attendance:** 8,432.

Saturday 20th September 2003

HULL FC 12 LEEDS RHINOS 28

HULL: 6 Richard Horne; 2 Colin Best; 31 Peter Lupton; 24 Kirk Yeaman; 28 Gareth Raynor; 16 Paul Cooke; 13 Jason Smith (C); 8 Craig Greenhill; 9 Dean Treister; 10 Paul King; 33 Shayne McMenemy; 14 Sean Ryan; 17 Chris Chester. Subs (all used): 22 Andy Last; 30 Ewan Dowes; 18 Warren Jowitt; 12 Scott Logan.
Tries: Cooke (13), Raynor (46); **Goals:** Cooke 2/3.
RHINOS: 21 Richard Mathers; 2 Mark Calderwood; 18 Gary Connolly; 4 Keith Senior; 1 Francis Cummins; 14 Andrew Dunemann; 7 Rob Burrow; 12 Matt Adamson; 9 Matt Diskin; 10 Barrie McDermott; 11 David Furner; 3 Chris McKenna; 13 Kevin Sinfield (C). Subs (all used): 17 Wayne McDonald; 15 Chris Feather; 6 Danny McGuire; 16 Willie Poching.
Tries: Senior (20), Calderwood (28), Poching (36), Burrow (55); **Goals:** Sinfield 6/6.
Rugby Leaguer & League Express Men of the Match: *Hull:* Richard Horne; *Rhinos:* Richard Mathers.
Penalty count: 9-3; **Half-time:** 8-18; **Referee:** Karl Kirkpatrick (Warrington); **Attendance:** 14,706.

Sunday 21st September 2003

HALIFAX 20 WIDNES VIKINGS 48

HALIFAX: 5 Lee Finnerty; 30 Rikki Sheriffe; 21 Chris Norman; 22 Simon Grix; 2 Lee Greenwood; 14 Liam Finn; 32 Danny Jones (D); 25 Neil Harmon; 9 Johnny Lawless (C); 8 Andy Hobson; 23 Ged Corcoran; 12 Andrew Brocklehurst; 24 Wayne Corcoran. Subs (all used): 7 Sean Penkywicz; 10 Paul Davidson; 18 Jaymes Chapman; 29 Byron Smith.

Tries: Greenwood (23, 67), Norman (44), Brocklehurst (63); **Goals:** Finn 2/4.
VIKINGS: 1 Stuart Spruce (C); 2 Paul Devlin; 5 Jason Demetriou; 4 Adam Hughes; 24 Chris Giles; 26 Julian O'Neill (A); 30 Stephen Myler; 8 Robert Relf; 9 Shane Millard; 10 Julian O'Neill (NZ); 11 Andy Hay; 13 Daniel Frame; 3 Deon Bird. Subs (all used): 17 Anthony Farrell; 25 Simon Finnigan; 22 Phil Cantillon; 23 David Mills.
Tries: Spruce (2), Bird (13), Myler (20, 76), O'Neill (A) (26), Hughes (30), Cantillon (37, 57), Millard (73); **Goals:** Myler 4/7, Farrell 1/1, Demetriou 1/1.
Rugby Leaguer & League Express Men of the Match: *Halifax:* Wayne Corcoran; *Vikings:* Julian O'Neill (A).
Penalty count: 7-5; **Half-time:** 4-32; **Referee:** Ashley Klein (London); **Attendance:** 2,088.

LONDON BRONCOS 22 HUDDERSFIELD GIANTS 12

BRONCOS: 1 Paul Sykes; 33 Joel Caine; 5 Steve Hall; 3 Nigel Roy; 25 Andrew King; 23 Chris Thorman; 7 Dennis Moran; 12 Steele Retchless; 14 Neil Budworth; 8 Francis Stephenson; 11 Mat Toshack; 24 Russell Bawden; 13 Jim Dymock (C). Subs (all used): 32 Steve Trindall; 9 Bill Peden; 34 Dave McConnell; 6 Rob Purdham.
Tries: Sykes (17), Moran (31), Thorman (62); **Goals:** Thorman 5/6.
GIANTS: 1 Paul Reilly; 2 Hefin O'Hare; 26 Jamie Bloem; 4 Julian Bailey; 34 Marcus St Hilaire; 13 Steve McNamara (C); 9 Paul March; 8 Mick Slicker; 15 Darren Turner; 10 Jim Gannon; 23 Ben Roarty; 19 Iain Morrison; 7 Jarrod O'Doherty. Subs (all used): 5 Matt Whitaker; 21 Paul White; 11 Eorl Crabtree; 3 Ben Cooper.
Tries: White (38), Bailey (46); **Goals:** McNamara 2/3.
Rugby Leaguer & League Express Men of the Match: *Broncos:* Francis Stephenson; *Giants:* Paul March.
Penalty count: 7-9; **Half-time:** 14-6; **Referee:** Richard Silverwood (Dewsbury); **Attendance:** 3,286.

WARRINGTON WOLVES 52 WAKEFIELD TRINITY WILDCATS 12

WOLVES: 28 Daryl Cardiss; 4 Ben Westwood; 3 Brent Grose; 13 Sid Domic; 20 Dean Gaskell; 5 Graham Appo; 7 Nathan Wood (C); 8 Nick Fozzard; 9 Jon Clarke; 16 Paul Wood; 18 Paul Noone; 23 Mike Wainwright; 11 Darren Burns. Subs (all used): 19 Gary Hulse; 14 Mark Gleeson; 15 Jerome Guisset; 17 Warren Stevens.
Tries: Domic (4, 79), Appo (13, 22, 55), Noone (33), Westwood (39, 60); **Goals:** Appo 10/10.
WILDCATS: 1 Martyn Holland; 24 Colum Halpenny; 3 Gareth Ellis (C); 30 Sylvain Houles; 23 Robert Spicer; 16 Jamie Rooney; 6 Ben Jeffries; 18 Michael Korkidas; 9 David March; 25 Darrell Griffin; 10 Dallas Hood; 20 David Wrench; 12 Jamie Field. Subs (all used): 7 Brad Davis; 14 Paul Handforth; 21 Steve Snitch; 15 Ian Knott.
Tries: Spicer (41), Korkidas (66); **Goals:** Rooney 2/2.
Rugby Leaguer & League Express Men of the Match: *Wolves:* Graham Appo; *Wildcats:* Michael Korkidas.
Penalty count: 5-4; **Half-time:** 32-0; **Referee:** Robert Connolly (Wigan); **Attendance:** 9,261.

CASTLEFORD TIGERS 16 WIGAN WARRIORS 23

TIGERS: 20 Tom Saxton; 2 Waine Pryce; 1 Damian Gibson; 3 Michael Eagar; 5 Darren Rogers; 6 Danny Orr; 7 Mitch Healey; 8 Nathan Sykes; 13 Ryan Hudson (C); 10 Andy Lynch; 14 Andy Johnson; 12 Dale Fritz; 24 Adrian Vowles. Subs (all used): 21 Richard Blakeway; 22 Mark Lennon; 26 Craig Huby; 19 Wayne Godwin.
Tries: Pryce (6), Johnson (12), Orr (74); **Goals:** Orr 2/4.
WARRIORS: 1 Kris Radlinski; 5 Brian Carney; 18 Martin Aspinwall; 14 David Hodgson; 2 Brett Dallas; 15 Sean O'Loughlin; 20 Luke Robinson; 8 Terry O'Connor; 17 Mark Smith; 10 Craig Smith; 11 Mick Cassidy; 12 Danny Tickle; 13 Andy Farrell (C). Subs (all used): 7 Adrian Lam; 4 Paul Johnson; 16 Danny Sculthorpe; 23 Gareth Hock.
Tries: O'Connor (4), Dallas (62), Hodgson (64), Tickle (79); **Goals:** Farrell 3/4; **Field goal:** Lam.
Rugby Leaguer & League Express Men of the Match: *Tigers:* Wayne Godwin; *Warriors:* Adrian Lam.
Penalty count: 6-2; **Half-time:** 12-6; **Referee:** Steve Ganson (St Helens); **Attendance:** 7,886.

Wigan's Martin Aspinwall takes on Leeds' Danny McGuire during the Final Eliminator

Bradford's Stuart Reardon dragged down to the ground by Wigan's Craig Smith during the Super League Grand Final

PLAY-OFFS

Friday 26th September 2003

ELIMINATION PLAY-OFF

ST HELENS 24 LONDON BRONCOS 6

SAINTS: 1 Paul Wellens; 5 Darren Albert; 3 Martin Gleeson; 4 Paul Newlove; 19 Ade Gardner; 13 Paul Sculthorpe; 7 Sean Long (C); 11 Chris Joynt; 9 Keiron Cunningham; 10 Barry Ward; 32 Willie Talau; 12 John Stankevitch; 16 Darren Smith. Subs (all used): 6 Jason Hooper; 14 Mick Higham; 17 Mike Bennett; 18 Mark Edmondson.
Tries: Long (13, 28), Talau (38), Smith (74);
Goals: Long 4/5.
On report: Talau, Edmondson (50) - alleged lifting in the tackle on Dymock.
BRONCOS: 1 Paul Sykes; 33 Joel Caine; 4 Tony Martin; 3 Nigel Roy; 25 Andrew King; 23 Chris Thorman; 7 Dennis Moran; 24 Russell Bawden; 14 Neil Budworth; 8 Francis Stephenson; 11 Mat Toshack; 12 Steele Retchless; 13 Jim Dymock (C). Subs (all used): 32 Steve Trindall; 22 Andrew Hamilton; 34 Dave McConnell; 6 Rob Purdham.
Try: King (32); **Goals:** Thorman 1/3.
On report: Moran, Purdham (58) - alleged lifting in the tackle on Joynt.
Rugby Leaguer & League Express Men of the Match:
Saints: Sean Long; *Broncos:* Jim Dymock.
Penalty count: 7-6; **Half-time:** 20-6; **Referee:** Karl Kirkpatrick (Warrington); **Attendance:** 7,188.

Saturday 27th September 2003

ELIMINATION PLAY-OFF

WIGAN WARRIORS 25 WARRINGTON WOLVES 12

WARRIORS: 1 Kris Radlinski; 5 Brian Carney; 18 Martin Aspinwall; 14 David Hodgson; 2 Brett Dallas; 15 Sean O'Loughlin; 7 Adrian Lam; 10 Craig Smith; 9 Terry Newton; 30 Quentin Pongia; 11 Mick Cassidy; 12 Danny Tickle; 13 Andy Farrell (C). Subs (all used): 4 Paul Johnson; 8 Terry O'Connor; 20 Luke Robinson; 23 Gareth Hock.
Tries: Lam (26), Tickle (47), Dallas (66), C Smith (79);
Goals: Farrell 1/1, Tickle 2/3, Robinson 1/1;
Field goal: Robinson.
Sin bin: Pongia (10) - holding down;
Johnson (35) - obstruction.
WOLVES: 28 Daryl Cardiss; 4 Ben Westwood; 3 Brent Grose; 13 Sid Domic; 20 Dean Gaskell; 5 Graham Appo; 7 Nathan Wood (C); 8 Nick Fozzard; 14 Mark Gleeson; 16 Paul Wood; 18 Paul Noone; 23 Mike Wainwright; 11 Darren Burns. Subs (all used): 19 Gary Hulse; 12 Ian Sibbit; 15 Jerome Guisset; 17 Warren Stevens.
Tries: Burns (15), N Wood (39); **Goals:** Appo 2/3.
Rugby Leaguer & League Express Men of the Match:
Warriors: Kris Radlinski; *Wolves:* Nathan Wood.
Penalty count: 4-6; **Half-time:** 6-12;
Referee: Steve Ganson (St Helens); **Attendance:** 14,154.

Friday 3rd October 2003

ELIMINATION SEMI-FINAL

WIGAN WARRIORS 40 ST HELENS 24

WARRIORS: 1 Kris Radlinski; 5 Brian Carney; 18 Martin Aspinwall; 14 David Hodgson; 2 Brett Dallas; 15 Sean O'Loughlin; 7 Adrian Lam; 30 Quentin Pongia; 9 Terry Newton; 10 Craig Smith; 11 Mick Cassidy; 12 Danny Tickle; 13 Andy Farrell (C). Subs (all used): 4 Paul Johnson; 8 Terry O'Connor; 20 Luke Robinson; 23 Gareth Hock.
Tries: Tickle (6), Lam (9, 32), Cassidy (18), O'Loughlin (35), Carney (40), Radlinski (61);
Goals: Tickle 4/4, Lam 1/2, Robinson 1/1.
SAINTS: 1 Paul Wellens; 2 Anthony Stewart; 3 Martin Gleeson; 4 Paul Newlove; 19 Ade Gardner; 13 Paul Sculthorpe; 7 Sean Long (C); 10 Barry Ward; 9 Keiron Cunningham; 32 Willie Talau; 12 John Stankevitch; 16 Darren Smith. Subs (all used): 6 Jason Hooper; 14 Mick Higham; 17 Mike Bennett; 11 Chris Joynt.
Tries: Hooper (26), Smith (52, 80), Cunningham (69), Newlove (75); **Goals:** Long 2/5.
Rugby Leaguer & League Express Men of the Match:
Warriors: Terry Newton; *Saints:* Darren Smith.
Penalty count: 7-4; **Half-time:** 34-6; **Referee:** Karl Kirkpatrick (Warrington); **Attendance:** 21,790.

Saturday 4th October 2003

QUALIFYING SEMI-FINAL

BRADFORD BULLS 30 LEEDS RHINOS 14

BULLS: 17 Stuart Reardon; 2 Tevita Vaikona; 6 Michael Withers; 4 Shontayne Hape; 5 Lesley Vainikolo; 15 Karl Pratt; 7 Paul Deacon; 29 Stuart Fielden; 9 James Lowes (C); 8 Joe Vagana; 11 Daniel Gartner; 12 Jamie Peacock; 13 Mike Forshaw. Subs (all used): 14 Lee Gilmour; 3 Leon Pryce; 10 Paul Anderson; 18 Lee Radford.
Tries: Vainikolo (9), L Pryce (67), Forshaw (71, 76);
Goals: Deacon 7/7.
RHINOS: 21 Richard Mathers; 2 Mark Calderwood; 18 Gary Connolly; 4 Keith Senior; 1 Francis Cummins; 14 Andrew Dunemann; 7 Rob Burrow; 12 Matt Adamson; 9 Matt Diskin; 10 Barrie McDermott; 11 David Furner; 3 Chris McKenna; 13 Kevin Sinfield (C). Subs (all used): 17 Wayne McDonald; 15 Chris Feather; 6 Danny McGuire; 16 Willie Poching.
Tries: Cummins (32), Calderwood (47), Furner (64);
Goals: Sinfield 1/3.
On report: Diskin & Sinfield (52) - high tackle.
Rugby Leaguer & League Express Men of the Match:
Bulls: Mike Forshaw; *Rhinos:* David Furner.
Penalty count: 10-6; **Half-time:** 8-4; **Referee:** Russell Smith (Castleford); **Attendance:** 19,786.

Friday 10th October 2003

FINAL ELIMINATOR

LEEDS RHINOS 22 WIGAN WARRIORS 23

RHINOS: 6 Danny McGuire; 21 Richard Mathers; 18 Gary Connolly; 4 Keith Senior; 1 Francis Cummins; 14 Andrew Dunemann; 7 Rob Burrow; 12 Matt Adamson; 9 Matt Diskin; 10 Barrie McDermott; 11 David Furner; 3 Chris McKenna; 13 Kevin Sinfield (C). Subs (all used): 17 Wayne McDonald; 15 Chris Feather; 8 Danny Ward; 16 Willie Poching.
Tries: McGuire (13), Burrow (26, 49);
Goals: Sinfield 5/6.
WARRIORS: 1 Kris Radlinski; 5 Brian Carney; 18 Martin Aspinwall; 14 David Hodgson; 2 Brett Dallas; 15 Sean O'Loughlin; 20 Luke Robinson; 30 Quentin Pongia; 9 Terry Newton; 10 Craig Smith; 11 Mick Cassidy; 12 Danny Tickle; 13 Andy Farrell (C). Subs (all used): 8 Terry O'Connor; 4 Paul Johnson; 23 Gareth Hock; 17 Mark Smith.
Tries: Carney (6, 62), O'Loughlin (36, 55);
Goals: Tickle 0/1, Farrell 3/3; **Field goal:** Tickle.
Rugby Leaguer & League Express Men of the Match:
Rhinos: Danny McGuire; *Warriors:* Brian Carney.
Penalty count: 7-4; **Half-time:** 14-10;
Referee: Steve Ganson (St Helens); **Attendance:** 17,264.

Saturday 18th October 2003

GRAND FINAL

BRADFORD BULLS 25 WIGAN WARRIORS 12

BULLS: 17 Stuart Reardon; 2 Tevita Vaikona; 6 Michael Withers; 4 Shontayne Hape; 5 Lesley Vainikolo; 15 Karl Pratt; 7 Paul Deacon; 8 Joe Vagana; 9 James Lowes; 29 Stuart Fielden; 11 Daniel Gartner; 12 Jamie Peacock; 13 Mike Forshaw. Subs (all used): 10 Paul Anderson; 18 Lee Radford; 3 Leon Pryce; 1 Robbie Paul (C).
Tries: Reardon (51), Hape (59), Lowes (75);
Goals: Deacon 6/6; **Field goal:** Deacon.
WARRIORS: 1 Kris Radlinski; 5 Brian Carney; 18 Martin Aspinwall; 14 David Hodgson; 2 Brett Dallas; 15 Sean O'Loughlin; 20 Luke Robinson; 30 Quentin Pongia; 9 Terry Newton; 10 Craig Smith; 11 Mick Cassidy; 12 Danny Tickle; 13 Andy Farrell (C). Subs (all used): 4 Paul Johnson; 8 Terry O'Connor; 23 Gareth Hock; 17 Mark Smith.
Tries: Tickle (17), Radlinski (72); **Goals:** Farrell 2/3.
Rugby Leaguer & League Express Men of the Match:
Bulls: Stuart Reardon; *Warriors:* Kris Radlinski.
Penalty count: 7-6; **Half-time:** 4-6;
Referee: Karl Kirkpatrick (Warrington);
Attendance: 65,537 *(at Old Trafford, Manchester).*

SUPER LEAGUE VIII
Opta Index Analysis

SUPER LEAGUE VIII TOP PERFORMERS *(BY CATEGORY)*

TACKLES
Shane Millard	Widnes	856
Steele Retchless	London	843
David March	Wakefield	770
Neil Budworth	London	709
Paul Cooke	Hull	696
Johnny Lawless	Halifax	695
Matt Diskin	Leeds	681
Kevin Sinfield	Leeds	680
James Lowes	Bradford	666
Daniel Frame	Widnes	665

TACKLES MADE *(% Success)*
Lee Radford	Bradford	96.7%
Nick Graham	Wigan	96.3%
Jarrod O'Doherty	Huddersfield	96.1%
Paul March	Huddersfield	95.3%
Mike Bennett	St Helens	95.3%
Sean Ryan	Hull	95.2%
Mark Smith	Wigan	95.1%
Craig Smith	Wigan	94.9%
Darren Burns	Warrington	94.9%
Steve McNamara	Huddersfield	94.9%

CARRIES
Craig Greenhill	Hull	531
Steele Retchless	London	508
Richard Horne	Hull	492
Shane Millard	Widnes	488
Andy Lynch	Castleford	470
Paul Wellens	St Helens	445
Robert Relf	Widnes	431
Lesley Vainikolo	Bradford	431
James Lowes	Bradford	428
Stanley Gene	Huddersfield	417

AVERAGE GAIN PER CARRY
Jamie Ainscough	Wigan	10.0
Brett Dallas	Wigan	9.9
Mark Calderwood	Leeds	9.6
Brian Carney	Wigan	9.2
Adam Hughes	Widnes	9.2
Chev Walker	Leeds	9.2
Hefin O'Hare	Huddersfield	9.2
Ben Westwood	Warrington	9.0
Matt Adamson	Leeds	8.9
Keith Senior	Leeds	8.9

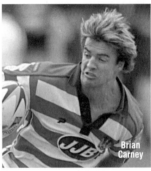

METRES
Lesley Vainikolo	Bradford	3677
Craig Greenhill	Hull	3594
Steele Retchless	London	3369
Brian Carney	Wigan	3359
Shane Millard	Widnes	3274
Richard Horne	Hull	3270
Stanley Gene	Huddersfield	3228
Andy Lynch	Castleford	3172
Nigel Roy	London	3129
Terry O'Connor	Wigan	3091

CLEAN BREAKS
Dennis Moran	London	49
Graham Appo	Warrington	40
Colin Best	Hull	38
Danny Orr	Castleford	38
Danny McGuire	Leeds	37
Lesley Vainikolo	Bradford	35
Richard Horne	Hull	35
Adrian Lam	Wigan	34
Keith Senior	Leeds	34
Mark Calderwood	Leeds	34

OFFLOADS
Andy Lynch	Castleford	90
Michael Smith	Castleford	78
Jamie Field	Wakefield	75
Tevita Vaikona	Bradford	59
Daniel Frame	Widnes	58
Mike Forshaw	Bradford	57
Russell Bawden	London	56
Keiron Cunningham	St Helens	55
Nathan Wood	Warrington	54
Sean Ryan	Hull	51

Brian Carney

TACKLE BUSTS
Brian Carney	Wigan	149
Lesley Vainikolo	Bradford	146
Colin Best	Hull	139
Richard Horne	Hull	126
Michael Smith	Castleford	112
Stanley Gene	Huddersfield	111
Tevita Vaikona	Bradford	109
Jamie Peacock	Bradford	107
Graham Appo	Warrington	99
Dennis Moran	London	91

MARKER TACKLES
James Lowes	Bradford	112
Shane Millard	Widnes	110
David March	Wakefield	109
Steele Retchless	London	108
Kevin Sinfield	Leeds	104
Matt Diskin	Leeds	99
Nathan Sykes	Castleford	99
Ryan Hudson	Castleford	94
Paul Cooke	Hull	93
Nick Graham	Wigan	84

TRY ASSISTS
James Lowes	Bradford	32
Paul Deacon	Bradford	30
Kevin Sinfield	Leeds	27
Sean Long	St Helens	26
Andrew Dunemann	Leeds	19
Chris Thorman	London	19
Paul Sculthorpe	St Helens	18
Brent Grose	Warrington	16
Mitch Healey	Castleford	16
Jim Dymock	London	16

40/20s
Paul Deacon	Bradford	8
Sean Long	St Helens	7
Lee Briers	Warrington	5
Mitch Healey	Castleford	4
Adrian Lam	Wigan	4
Ryan Sheridan	Widnes	3
Brad Davis	Wakefield	3

Paul Anderson shows his delight at scoring for Bradford, Super League VIII's leading team for tries scored

SUPER LEAGUE VIII AVERAGES PER MATCH

TACKLES		CARRIES		CLEAN BREAKS		TACKLE BUSTS	
London Broncos	276	Bradford Bulls	196	Bradford Bulls	11.4	Bradford Bulls	43
St Helens	267	St Helens	191	St Helens	11.4	Wigan Warriors	34
Wigan Warriors	251	Wigan Warriors	187	Leeds Rhinos	11.0	Hull FC	31
Leeds Rhinos	248	Hull FC	186	Wigan Warriors	11.0	Warrington Wolves	30
Widnes Vikings	247	Leeds Rhinos	186	London Broncos	10.6	Leeds Rhinos	29
Castleford Tigers	246	London Broncos	183	Widnes Vikings	10.0	St Helens	28
Halifax	244	Widnes Vikings	181	Warrington Wolves	9.9	London Broncos	27
Hull FC	241	Castleford Tigers	176	Hull FC	9.8	Castleford Tigers	26
Wakefield T Wildcats	239	Warrington Wolves	175	Huddersfield Giants	9.3	Wakefield T Wildcats	25
Warrington Wolves	238	Wakefield T Wildcats	169	Castleford Tigers	8.4	Widnes Vikings	24
Huddersfield Giants	234	Huddersfield Giants	163	Wakefield T Wildcats	7.1	Huddersfield Giants	23
Bradford Bulls	231	Halifax	158	Halifax	5.5	Halifax	19

MISSED TACKLES		METRES		OFFLOADS		RUNS FROM DUMMY HALF	
Halifax	42	Bradford Bulls	1380	Bradford Bulls	16.9	Bradford Bulls	37
Wakefield T Wildcats	37	Leeds Rhinos	1374	Castleford Tigers	16.6	St Helens	36
Widnes Vikings	34	Wigan Warriors	1340	Leeds Rhinos	15.5	London Broncos	33
Castleford Tigers	31	St Helens	1279	Huddersfield Giants	15.1	Warrington Wolves	31
London Broncos	31	Hull FC	1274	Wigan Warriors	14.7	Wigan Warriors	30
Warrington Wolves	29	London Broncos	1244	Hull FC	14.5	Castleford Tigers	28
St Helens	28	Widnes Vikings	1244	Widnes Vikings	13.5	Huddersfield Giants	27
Bradford Bulls	26	Warrington Wolves	1211	Warrington Wolves	12.6	Hull FC	27
Hull FC	26	Huddersfield Giants	1187	Wakefield T Wildcats	12.3	Widnes Vikings	24
Wigan Warriors	25	Castleford Tigers	1181	London Broncos	11.7	Wakefield T Wildcats	23
Huddersfield Giants	23	Wakefield T Wildcats	1138	St Helens	11.6	Leeds Rhinos	21
Leeds Rhinos	23	Halifax	938	Halifax	10.3	Halifax	20

SUPER LEAGUE VIII TRIES SCORED/CONCEDED

TOTAL TRIES SCORED		TOTAL TRIES CONCEDED		TRIES SCORED *(KICKS)*		TRIES CONCEDED *(KICKS)*	
Bradford Bulls	151	Halifax	213	Bradford Bulls	33	Halifax	27
St Helens	150	Wakefield T Wildcats	134	Wigan Warriors	30	Warrington Wolves	22
London Broncos	129	Widnes Vikings	125	Leeds Rhinos	22	Wigan Warriors	21
Warrington Wolves	126	Huddersfield Giants	119	London Broncos	19	Widnes Vikings	21
Wigan Warriors	126	London Broncos	118	Huddersfield Giants	18	Bradford Bulls	19
Castleford Tigers	115	Warrington Wolves	106	St Helens	18	Huddersfield Giants	18
Huddersfield Giants	108	Castleford Tigers	100	Castleford Tigers	17	London Broncos	17
Hull FC	106	Hull FC	90	Wakefield T Wildcats	16	Leeds Rhinos	17
Widnes Vikings	105	Wigan Warriors	88	Hull FC	13	St Helens	15
Wakefield T Wildcats	100	St Helens	88	Warrington Wolves	12	Hull FC	15
Leeds Rhinos	79	Leeds Rhinos	88	Halifax	9	Castleford Tigers	14
Halifax	61	Bradford Bulls	87	Widnes Vikings	9	Wakefield T Wildcats	10

BRADFORD BULLS

Robbie Paul

TEAM TOTALS

Tackles	6478
Missed Tackles	715
Carries	5501
Metres	38652
Clean Breaks	318
Offloads	473
Handling Errors	307
Penalties Conceded	163
Tackle Busts	1210
Runs From Dummy Half	1027
40/20s	12

TOP 5 OPTA INDEX PERFORMERS

	Paul	Vainikolo	Peacock	Vaikona	Lowes
Tackles	124	86	409	70	666
Misses	37	20	53	15	65
Carries	260	431	350	397	428
Metres	1755	3677	3038	2956	1838
Clean Breaks	22	35	12	27	13
Offloads	14	26	31	59	25
Tackle Busts	61	146	107	109	41

TACKLES

James Lowes	666
Mike Forshaw	587
Lee Radford	465
Daniel Gartner	437
Robert Parker	431

CARRIES

Lesley Vainikolo	431
James Lowes	428
Tevita Vaikona	397
Jamie Peacock	350
Mike Forshaw	325

METRES

Lesley Vainikolo	3677
Jamie Peacock	3038
Tevita Vaikona	2956
Paul Anderson	2756
Shontayne Hape	2345

OFFLOADS

Tevita Vaikona	59
Mike Forshaw	57
Shontayne Hape	36
Jamie Peacock	31
Stuart Fielden	29

CLEAN BREAKS

Lesley Vainikolo	35
Paul Deacon	30
Tevita Vaikona	27
Leon Pryce	25
Shontayne Hape	24

TACKLE BUSTS

Lesley Vainikolo	146
Tevita Vaikona	109
Jamie Peacock	107
Paul Deacon	72
Joe Vagana	71

MARKER TACKLES

James Lowes	112
Mike Forshaw	84
Scott Naylor	69
Lee Radford	69
Daniel Gartner	68

AVERAGE SEASON INDEX

Robbie Paul	1028
Lesley Vainikolo	943
Jamie Peacock	853
Tevita Vaikona	832
James Lowes	798

CASTLEFORD TIGERS

Andy Lynch

TEAM TOTALS

Tackles	6886
Missed Tackles	880
Carries	4915
Metres	33079
Clean Breaks	235
Offloads	464
Handling Errors	259
Penalties Conceded	219
Tackle Busts	734
Runs From Dummy Half	791
40/20s	4

TOP 5 OPTA INDEX PERFORMERS

	Lynch	Smith	Orr	Hudson	Saxton
Tackles	637	353	337	654	82
Misses	36	39	55	53	17
Carries	470	392	261	282	283
Metres	3172	3000	1643	1858	1872
Clean Breaks	8	12	38	17	11
Offloads	90	78	41	24	28
Tackle Busts	39	112	43	33	58

TACKLES

Nathan Sykes	665
Ryan Hudson	654
Andy Lynch	637
Dale Fritz	463
Andy Johnson	396

CARRIES

Andy Lynch	470
Michael Smith	392
Waine Pryce	386
Nathan Sykes	301
Darren Rogers	292

METRES

Andy Lynch	3172
Michael Smith	3000
Waine Pryce	2817
Darren Rogers	2089
Nathan Sykes	2049

OFFLOADS

Andy Lynch	90
Michael Smith	78
Danny Orr	41
Tom Saxton	28
Lee Harland	24

CLEAN BREAKS

Danny Orr	38
Darren Rogers	22
Michael Eagar	21
Waine Pryce	18
Ryan Hudson	17

TACKLE BUSTS

Michael Smith	112
Waine Pryce	76
Tom Saxton	58
Damian Gibson	49
Danny Orr	43

MARKER TACKLES

Nathan Sykes	99
Ryan Hudson	94
Andy Lynch	72
Wayne Godwin	58
Dale Fritz	56

AVERAGE SEASON INDEX

Andy Lynch	834
Michael Smith	822
Danny Orr	757
Ryan Hudson	609
Tom Saxton	607

HALIFAX

Lee
Finnerty

TEAM TOTALS
Tackles...........................6829
Missed Tackles 1169
Carries 4417
Metres 26274
Clean Breaks 154
Offloads 287
Handling Errors 307
Penalties Conceded 211
Tackle Busts..................525
Runs From Dummy Half..567
40/20s 0

TOP 5 OPTA INDEX PERFORMERS

	Moana	Finnerty	Frew	Dorahy	Greenwood
Tackles	279	163	145	278	230
Misses	40	48	30	46	30
Carries	201	250	204	197	225
Metres	955	1493	1490	878	1781
Clean Breaks	7	21	12	12	17
Offloads	29	9	9	9	12
Tackle Busts	23	65	32	33	29

TACKLES
Johnny Lawless..............695
Ryan Clayton 547
Andrew Brocklehurst......509
Heath Cruckshank 413
Andy Hobson 393

METRES
Andy Hobson 2028
Paul Davidson 1963
Lee Greenwood 1781
Andrew Brocklehurst....1687
Lee Finnerty 1493

TACKLE BUSTS
Lee Finnerty 65
Daryl Cardiss 39
Dane Dorahy 33
Andrew Frew 32
Sean Penkywicz...............32

CARRIES
Andy Hobson 288
Sean Penkywicz..............274
Andrew Brocklehurst......268
Johnny Lawless..............264
Lee Finnerty 250

OFFLOADS
Paul Davidson 36
Sean Penkywicz...............35
Martin Moana 29
Neil Harmon 22
Heath Cruckshank 22

MARKER TACKLES
Johnny Lawless................80
Ryan Clayton 75
Heath Cruckshank 61
Andrew Brocklehurst........57
Sean Penkywicz................56

CLEAN BREAKS
Lee Finnerty 21
Lee Greenwood 17
Daryl Cardiss 13
Dane Dorahy 12
Andrew Frew 12

AVERAGE SEASON INDEX
Martin Moana 600
Lee Finnerty 527
Andrew Frew 520
Dane Dorahy 465
Lee Greenwood 449

Stanley
Gene

HUDDERSFIELD GIANTS

TEAM TOTALS
Tackles...........................6546
Missed Tackles 651
Carries 4553
Metres 33231
Clean Breaks 260
Offloads 423
Handling Errors 283
Penalties Conceded 642
Tackle Busts...................642
Runs From Dummy Half..766
40/20s 2

TOP 5 OPTA INDEX PERFORMERS

	Gene	Costin	Reilly	O'Hare	O'Doherty
Tackles	327	330	77	176	511
Misses	32	48	14	26	21
Carries	417	280	304	282	290
Metres	3228	2038	2062	2585	2082
Clean Breaks	29	33	15	26	8
Offloads	20	32	10	19	42
Tackle Busts	111	69	54	70	31

TACKLES
Mick Slicker...................556
Jim Gannon 526
Jarrod O'Doherty 511
Paul March 467
Darren Turner 460

OFFLOADS
Jarrod O'Doherty 42
Ben Roarty......................42
Julian Bailey 39
Jim Gannon 33
Brandon Costin 32

MARKER TACKLES
Jamie Bloem 63
Jarrod O'Doherty 58
Paul March 58
Mick Slicker.....................53
Julian Bailey 51

CARRIES
Stanley Gene 417
Paul Reilly 304
Jim Gannon 304
Jarrod O'Doherty 290
Hefin O'Hare 282

CLEAN BREAKS
Brandon Costin 33
Stanley Gene 29
Marcus St Hilaire 28
Paul March 27
Julian Bailey 26

AVERAGE SEASON INDEX
Stanley Gene 978
Brandon Costin 777
Paul Reilly 748
Hefin O'Hare 582
Jarrod O'Doherty 569

METRES
Stanley Gene 3228
Hefin O'Hare 2585
Marcus St Hilaire 2324
Jarrod O'Doherty 2082
Paul Reilly 2062

TACKLE BUSTS
Stanley Gene 111
Hefin O'Hare 70
Brandon Costin 69
Marcus St Hilaire 59
Paul Reilly 54

Richard Horne

HULL F.C.

HULL FC
Est. 1865

TEAM TOTALS

Tackles	6740
Missed Tackles	739
Carries	5201
Metres	35668
Clean Breaks	273
Offloads	405
Handling Errors	293
Penalties Conceded	201
Tackle Busts	859
Runs From Dummy Half	761
40/20s	5

TOP 5 OPTA INDEX PERFORMERS

	R Horne	Best	Greenhill	Prescott	McMenemy
Tackles	319	184	543	78	86
Misses	46	16	50	19	7
Carries	492	369	531	205	62
Metres	3270	2934	3594	1486	385
Clean Breaks	35	38	6	17	2
Offloads	25	42	34	13	11
Tackle Busts	126	139	73	55	9

TACKLES

Paul Cooke	696
Sean Ryan	562
Craig Greenhill	543
Adam Maher	488
Chris Chester	398

OFFLOADS

Sean Ryan	51
Colin Best	42
Paul Cooke	34
Craig Greenhill	34
Richie Barnett	31

MARKER TACKLES

Paul Cooke	93
Adam Maher	72
Sean Ryan	70
Chris Chester	60
Dean Treister	55

CARRIES

Craig Greenhill	531
Richard Horne	492
Colin Best	369
Sean Ryan	364
Paul King	358

CLEAN BREAKS

Colin Best	38
Richard Horne	35
Richie Barnett	32
Steve Prescott	17
Kirk Yeaman	17

AVERAGE SEASON INDEX

Richard Horne	855
Colin Best	854
Craig Greenhill	753
Steve Prescott	708
Shayne McMenemy	707

METRES

Craig Greenhill	3594
Richard Horne	3270
Colin Best	2934
Sean Ryan	2624
Paul King	2606

TACKLE BUSTS

Colin Best	139
Richard Horne	126
Craig Greenhill	73
Steve Prescott	55
Richie Barnett	54

LEEDS RHINOS

TEAM TOTALS

Tackles	6952
Missed Tackles	637
Carries	5208
Metres	38461
Clean Breaks	307
Offloads	434
Handling Errors	289
Penalties Conceded	198
Tackle Busts	807
Runs From Dummy Half	597
40/20s	1

TOP 5 OPTA INDEX PERFORMERS

	Dunemann	Senior	Sinfield	Adamson	Poching
Tackles	538	350	680	331	481
Misses	50	27	56	34	47
Carries	362	317	357	310	303
Metres	2174	2809	1806	2759	2484
Clean Breaks	18	34	17	13	25
Offloads	33	45	46	13	41
Tackle Busts	45	76	29	61	89

TACKLES

Matt Diskin	681
Kevin Sinfield	680
David Furner	595
Andrew Dunemann	538
Willie Poching	481

METRES

Wayne McDonald	2934
Keith Senior	2809
Barrie McDermott	2793
Matt Adamson	2759
Gary Connolly	2622

TACKLE BUSTS

Willie Poching	89
Keith Senior	76
Matt Adamson	61
Danny McGuire	50
Mark Calderwood	47

CARRIES

Barrie McDermott	378
Gary Connolly	370
Andrew Dunemann	362
Kevin Sinfield	357
Wayne McDonald	335

OFFLOADS

Kevin Sinfield	46
Barrie McDermott	46
Keith Senior	45
David Furner	44
Willie Poching	41

MARKER TACKLES

Kevin Sinfield	104
Matt Diskin	99
Willie Poching	81
David Furner	76
Chris McKenna	68

CLEAN BREAKS

Danny McGuire	37
Keith Senior	34
Mark Calderwood	34
Willie Poching	25
Rob Burrow	24

AVERAGE SEASON INDEX

Andrew Dunemann	836
Keith Senior	797
Kevin Sinfield	737
Matt Adamson	723
Willie Poching	715

Andrew Dunemann

LONDON BRONCOS

TEAM TOTALS
Tackles...........................7993
Missed Tackles 908
Carries 5295
Metres 36066
Clean Breaks 306
Offloads..........................338
Handling Errors 324
Penalties Conceded 189
Tackle Busts..................792
Runs From Dummy Half..951
40/20s 4

TOP 5 OPTA INDEX PERFORMERS

	Thorman	Moran	Retchless	Peden	Roy
Tackles	469	292	843	549	380
Misses	63	111	75	63	38
Carries	411	283	508	300	412
Metres	2065	2206	3369	2305	3129
Clean Breaks	22	49	7	24	22
Offloads	30	27	28	31	14
Tackle Busts	64	91	35	54	51

Chris Thorman

TACKLES
Steele Retchless 843
Neil Budworth 709
Bill Peden 549
Rob Purdham 497
Jim Dymock 495

METRES
Steele Retchless 3369
Nigel Roy 3129
Russell Bawden 2537
Bill Peden 2305
Dennis Moran 2206

TACKLE BUSTS
Dennis Moran 91
Russell Bawden 71
Chris Thorman.................64
Andrew King 57
Bill Peden 54

CARRIES
Steele Retchless 508
Nigel Roy........................412
Chris Thorman................411
Jim Dymock 340
Bill Peden 300

OFFLOADS
Russell Bawden 56
Bill Peden 31
Jim Dymock 30
Chris Thorman.................30
Steele Retchless 28

MARKER TACKLES
Steele Retchless 108
Neil Budworth 72
Rob Purdham 67
Bill Peden 58
Francis Stephenson 57

CLEAN BREAKS
Dennis Moran 49
Tony Martin 32
Andrew King 26
Bill Peden 24
Chris Thorman................22

AVERAGE SEASON INDEX
Chris Thorman................817
Dennis Moran 785
Steele Retchless 751
Bill Peden 735
Nigel Roy.......................707

ST HELENS

Paul Sculthorpe

TEAM TOTALS
Tackles...........................7741
Missed Tackles 814
Carries 5547
Metres 37096
Clean Breaks 332
Offloads..........................336
Handling Errors 383
Penalties Conceded 190
Tackle Busts...................801
Runs From Dummy Half..1058
40/20s 8

TOP 5 OPTA INDEX PERFORMERS

	Sculthorpe	Cunningham	Long	Wellens	Albert
Tackles	332	465	302	321	192
Misses	34	44	53	60	27
Carries	300	332	410	445	283
Metres	1834	2084	2511	2781	2277
Clean Breaks	24	14	30	18	33
Offloads	16	55	29	12	7
Tackle Busts	56	82	55	71	53

TACKLES
Mick Higham 636
Tim Jonkers 587
Mike Bennett 507
Jason Hooper 499
John Stankevitch 468

OFFLOADS
Keiron Cunningham..........55
Sean Long 29
Darren Britt 24
John Stankevitch 23
Anthony Stewart 21

MARKER TACKLES
Mick Higham 73
Tim Jonkers....................72
Mike Bennett 68
Chris Joynt 64
Jason Hooper 57

CARRIES
Paul Wellens 445
Sean Long 410
Keiron Cunningham........332
Anthony Stewart 310
Darren Britt 303

CLEAN BREAKS
Darren Albert 33
Sean Long 30
Ade Gardner 25
Jason Hooper 25
Paul Sculthorpe 24

AVERAGE SEASON INDEX
Paul Sculthorpe 923
Keiron Cunningham........853
Sean Long 804
Paul Wellens 748
Darren Albert 713

METRES
Paul Wellens 2781
Sean Long 2511
Darren Albert 2277
Darren Britt 2242
Keiron Cunningham......2084

TACKLE BUSTS
Keiron Cunningham..........82
Paul Wellens 71
Paul Sculthorpe 56
Sean Long 55
Darren Albert 53

WAKEFIELD T WILDCATS

Jamie
Rooney

TEAM TOTALS
Tackles...........................6697
Missed Tackles 1026
Carries 4736
Metres 31850
Clean Breaks 199
Offloads 343
Handling Errors 261
Penalties Conceded 203
Tackle Busts...................708
Runs From Dummy Half..630
40/20s 5

TOP 5 OPTA INDEX PERFORMERS

	Rooney	Ellis	Korkidas	Field	March
Tackles	247	439	425	583	770
Misses	29	56	53	104	70
Carries	162	313	393	370	246
Metres	944	2290	3063	2046	1596
Clean Breaks	21	22	5	3	12
Offloads	6	26	28	75	29
Tackle Busts	44	73	50	40	47

TACKLES
David March 770
Jamie Field 583
Gareth Ellis 439
Michael Korkidas 425
Ian Knott 393

OFFLOADS
Jamie Field 75
Dallas Hood 41
David March 29
Michael Korkidas 28
Gareth Ellis 26

MARKER TACKLES
David March 109
Jamie Field 74
Ian Knott 69
Gareth Ellis 64
Paul Handforth 51

CARRIES
Michael Korkidas 393
Jamie Field 370
Gareth Ellis 313
Colum Halpenny 283
Dallas Hood 256

CLEAN BREAKS
Gareth Ellis 22
Jamie Rooney 21
Colum Halpenny 20
Ben Jeffries 15
Richard Newlove 14

AVERAGE SEASON INDEX
Jamie Rooney 659
Gareth Ellis 636
Michael Korkidas 612
Jamie Field 609
David March 581

METRES
Michael Korkidas 3063
Gareth Ellis 2290
Jamie Field 2046
Colum Halpenny 1993
Jon Wells.....................1909

TACKLE BUSTS
Gareth Ellis 73
Michael Korkidas 50
Colum Halpenny 48
Jon Wells........................47
David March 47

Opta
opta stats

Darren
Burns

WARRINGTON WOLVES

TEAM TOTALS
Tackles...........................6898
Missed Tackles 836
Carries 5070
Metres 35110
Clean Breaks 286
Offloads 364
Handling Errors 291
Penalties Conceded 197
Tackle Busts...................858
Runs From Dummy Half..890
40/20s 8

TOP 5 OPTA INDEX PERFORMERS

	Burns	Appo	N Wood	Domic	Grose
Tackles	494	154	425	316	404
Misses	28	56	88	38	68
Carries	389	302	329	322	269
Metres	2782	2491	2033	2354	1864
Clean Breaks	15	40	32	12	27
Offloads	38	25	54	11	28
Tackle Busts	59	99	79	62	51

TACKLES
Jon Clarke 584
Mike Wainwright 498
Darren Burns.................494
Jerome Guisset 446
Paul Wood 442

METRES
Darren Burns 2782
Graham Appo 2491
Sid Domic 2354
Nick Fozzard 2352
Mark Hilton 2090

TACKLE BUSTS
Graham Appo 99
Nathan Wood 79
Dean Gaskell 73
Sid Domic 62
Darren Burns 59

CARRIES
Darren Burns.................389
Nathan Wood.................329
Sid Domic 322
Nick Fozzard 322
Graham Appo 302

OFFLOADS
Nathan Wood...................54
Mike Wainwright 46
Darren Burns 38
Brent Grose 28
Graham Appo 25

MARKER TACKLES
Mike Wainwright 75
Paul Wood 65
Jon Clarke 65
Darren Burns 62
Paul Noone 61

Opta
opta stats

CLEAN BREAKS
Graham Appo 40
Nathan Wood...................32
Brent Grose 27
Rob Smyth 19
Ben Westwood.................18

AVERAGE SEASON INDEX
Darren Burns 726
Graham Appo 673
Nathan Wood.................671
Sid Domic 649
Brent Grose 591

WIDNES VIKINGS

TEAM TOTALS
Tackles...........................6912
Missed Tackles 941
Carries 5068
Metres 34844
Clean Breaks 280
Offloads 379
Handling Errors 302
Penalties Conceded 197
Tackle Busts..................661
Runs From Dummy Half..661
40/20s 4

TOP 5 OPTA INDEX PERFORMERS

	Millard	Frame	Julian O'Neill (NZ)	Lawford	Devlin
Tackles	856	665	582	206	79
Misses	62	107	52	54	10
Carries	488	396	387	163	208
Metres	3274	3003	2876	639	1587
Clean Breaks	29	28	4	11	19
Offloads	29	58	37	16	3
Tackle Busts	44	70	35	23	46

Shane Millard

TACKLES
Shane Millard 856
Daniel Frame 665
Julian O'Neill (NZ) 582
Andy Hay 474
Robert Relf 468

METRES
Shane Millard 3274
Robert Relf 3009
Daniel Frame 3003
Julian O'Neill (NZ) 2876
Jason Demetriou 2215

TACKLE BUSTS
Daniel Frame 70
Jason Demetriou 59
Paul Devlin 46
Shane Millard 44
Anthony Farrell 41

CARRIES
Shane Millard 488
Robert Relf 431
Daniel Frame 396
Julian O'Neill (NZ) 387
Andy Hay 301

OFFLOADS
Daniel Frame 58
Robert Relf 42
Julian O'Neill (NZ) 37
Adam Hughes 36
Shane Millard 29

MARKER TACKLES
Shane Millard 110
Julian O'Neill (NZ) 75
Daniel Frame 75
Simon Finnigan 53
Steve McCurrie 41

opta stats

CLEAN BREAKS
Adam Hughes 31
Shane Millard 29
Daniel Frame 28
Jason Demetriou 24
Paul Devlin 19

AVERAGE SEASON INDEX
Shane Millard 905
Daniel Frame 738
Julian O'Neill (NZ) 621
Dean Lawford 592
Paul Devlin 584

Andy Farrell

WIGAN WARRIORS

TEAM TOTALS
Tackles...........................7284
Missed Tackles 720
Carries 5416
Metres 38870
Clean Breaks 320
Offloads 426
Handling Errors 306
Penalties Conceded 187
Tackle Busts..................990
Runs From Dummy Half..857
40/20s 7

TOP 5 OPTA INDEX PERFORMERS

	Farrell	Carney	C Smith	Graham	Lam
Tackles	314	102	416	412	321
Misses	23	11	19	16	44
Carries	339	363	356	187	303
Metres	2178	3359	2959	1022	1817
Clean Breaks	16	26	11	6	34
Offloads	33	24	39	15	6
Tackle Busts	74	149	59	29	64

TACKLES
Sean O'Loughlin 541
Danny Tickle 499
Terry Newton 490
Terry O'Connor 472
Craig Smith 416

OFFLOADS
Danny Sculthorpe 43
Craig Smith 39
Terry Newton 36
Andy Farrell 33
Gareth Hock....................29

MARKER TACKLES
Nick Graham 84
Sean O'Loughlin 82
Danny Tickle 74
Terry Newton 69
Martin Aspinwall 63

CARRIES
Brian Carney 363
Terry O'Connor 361
Craig Smith 356
Andy Farrell 339
Adrian Lam 303

CLEAN BREAKS
Adrian Lam 34
Brian Carney 26
David Hodgson 26
Gareth Hock 20
Brett Dallas 19

AVERAGE SEASON INDEX
Andy Farrell 983
Brian Carney 865
Craig Smith 819
Nick Graham 782
Adrian Lam 750

METRES
Brian Carney 3359
Terry O'Connor 3091
Craig Smith 2959
Andy Farrell 2178
David Hodgson 2103

TACKLE BUSTS
Brian Carney 149
Andy Farrell 74
Adrian Lam 64
Craig Smith 59
David Hodgson 59

opta stats

251

NATIONAL LEAGUE ONE 2003
Club by Club

BATLEY BULLDOGS

DATE	FIXTURE	RESULT	SCORERS	LGE	ATT
19/1/03	Hunslet (h) (NLC)	W16-8	t:Spink,Rourke,Horsley g:Eaton(2)	2nd(NLC-C)	801
26/1/03	West Bowling (a) (CCR3) ●	W12-34	t:Toohey(3),Spurr,A Gibbons,Lingard g:Eaton(5)	N/A	1,047
8/2/03	Wath Brow (a) (CCR4)	W6-18	t:Eaton,Lewis,Harrison g:Eaton(3)	N/A	1,333
16/2/03	Keighley (a) (NLC)	W12-30	t:Lingard(3),Cartledge,Spurr g:Eaton(5)	1st(NLC-C)	1,209
23/2/03	London Skolars (h) (NLC)	W82-4	t:Booth(2),D Gibbons(2),North(2),Lewis,Bramald,Lingard,Toohey,Swinson, Spurr,Horsley,Harrison,Beard g:Eaton(11)	1st(NLC-C)	577
28/2/03	St Helens (a) (CCR5)	L38-12	t:A Gibbons,Harrison g:Eaton(2)	N/A	5,002
5/3/03	Sheffield (a) (NLC)	L18-8	t:Booth g:Eaton(2)	1st(NLC-C)	732
9/3/03	Dewsbury (a) (NLC)	L22-18	t:Toohey,A Gibbons,Harrison g:Eaton(3)	2nd(NLC-C)	1,432
16/3/03	Sheffield (h) (NLC)	W62-12	t:Spurr(4),Lingard(4),Horsley,Spink,Sibson g:Eaton(9)	1st(NLC-C)	639
23/3/03	Hunslet (a) (NLC)	L30-24	t:Sibson,Lingard,Swinson,Toohey g:Eaton(4)	3rd(NLC-C)	658
30/3/03	Dewsbury (h) (NLC)	L16-21	t:Sibson(2),Toohey g:Eaton(2)	3rd(NLC-C)	952
6/4/03	London Skolars (a) (NLC)	W12-56	t:Lingard(3),Lewis(2),Bramald,Sibson,A Gibbons,Harrison,Hough g:Eaton(8)	2nd(NLC-C)	307
13/4/03	Keighley (h) (NLC)	W40-16	t:Spink,Sibson,Lewis,Toohey,Horsley,Lingard g:Eaton(8)	2nd(NLC-C)	737
18/4/03	Dewsbury (h)	W28-10	t:Lingard,Spink,Horsley,Bramald,Maun g:Eaton(4)	2nd	1,245
21/4/03	Salford (h)	L54-12	t:Maun,Bramald g:Eaton(2)	6th	2,074
4/5/03	Leigh (h)	L12-38	t:Williamson,Lingard g:Eaton(2)	8th	1,034
11/5/03	Hull KR (a)	L16-10	t:Williamson(2) g:Eaton	10th	1,000
18/5/03	Hull KR (a) (NLCQF)	W12-16	t:Lythe,Sibson g:Eaton(4)	N/A	1,100
25/5/03	Whitehaven (h)	L31-12	t:Sibson,Harrison g:Eaton(2)	9th	1,444
1/6/03	Rochdale (h)	L16-43	t:Spurr,Cartledge,Williamson g:Eaton(2)	9th	728
8/6/03	Salford (a) (NLCSF)	L68-6	t:Eaton g:Eaton	N/A	1,379
15/6/03	Featherstone (a)	L34-18	t:Maun(2),A Gibbons(2) g:Eaton	9th	1,182
22/6/03	Oldham (h)	D20-20	t:Bramald,Toohey,Maun g:Eaton(4)	9th	821
29/6/03	Dewsbury (a)	W23-36	t:Thomas(2),Sibson,Lingard,Harrison g;Eaton(7) fg:Thomas,Cass	9th	1,123
13/7/03	Doncaster (a)	L32-25	t:Sibson,Maun,Horsley,Lingard g:Eaton(4) fg:Thomas	9th	858
20/7/03	Salford (h)	L16-54	t:Thomas,Sibson g:Eaton(4)	9th	835
27/7/03	Leigh (a)	L54-30	t:Maun(2),Thomas,Spurr,Bramald g:Eaton(5)	9th	2,283
3/8/03	Hull KR (h)	W27-13	t:Sibson,Cartledge,Toohey,Harrison g:Eaton(5) fg:Eaton	9th	926
10/8/03	Whitehaven (h)	W26-16	t:Maun,Cartledge,Harrison,Spink g:Eaton(5)	9th	604
17/8/03	Rochdale (a)	L38-32	t:Bramald,Eaton,Thomas,Harrison,A Gibbons g:Eaton(6)	9th	820
24/8/03	Featherstone (h)	W18-10	t:Horsley(2),Eaton g:Eaton(3)	8th	1,156
31/8/03	Oldham (a)	L36-10	t:Bramald,Toohey g:Eaton	8th	1,451
6/9/03	Doncaster (h)	L18-21	t:Spurr(2),Williamson g:Eaton(3)	9th	741
21/9/03	Doncaster (a) (NL1QPO)	L45-12	t:Williamson,Eaton g:Eaton(2)	N/A	887
11/10/03	Sheffield (h) (NL1QF)	W36-14	t:Lingard(2),Evans,Berry,Toohey,Cartledge g:Eaton(6)	N/A	1,040

● Played at Mount Pleasant

		APP		TRIES		GOALS		FG		PTS	
	D.O.B.	ALL	NL1	ALL	NL1	ALL	NL1	ALL	NL1	ALL	NL1
Steve Beard	21/6/79	2(7)	1(7)	1	0	0	0	0	0	4	0
Joe Berry	7/5/74	8(18)	5(7)	1	1	0	0	0	0	4	4
Craig Booth	28/10/70	20(8)	11(4)	3	0	0	0	0	0	12	0
Matt Bramald	6/2/73	21(2)	16(2)	8	6	0	0	0	0	32	24
Will Cartledge	11/9/79	25(3)	18(1)	5	4	0	0	0	0	20	16
Mark Cass	17/11/71	10(15)	5(9)	0	0	0	0	1	1	1	1
Jeremy Dyson	15/2/72	1(2)	0	0	0	0	0	0	0	0	0
Barry Eaton	30/9/73	35	20	5	3	138	69	1	1	297	151
Danny Evans	15/10/74	10(1)	10(1)	1	1	0	0	0	0	4	4
Anthony Gibbons	18/1/76	23(1)	13	7	3	0	0	0	0	28	12
David Gibbons	18/1/76	14	4	2	0	0	0	0	0	8	0
Paul Harrison	24/9/70	3(31)	2(17)	10	5	0	0	0	0	40	20
Steve Hill	17/11/76	15(6)	14(3)	0	0	0	0	0	0	0	0
Ryan Horsley	21/8/78	35	20	8	4	0	0	0	0	32	16
Chris Hough	30/8/81	1	0	1	0	0	0	0	0	4	0
Simon Lewis	5/9/80	12(4)	5(2)	5	0	0	0	0	0	20	0
Craig Lingard	11/12/77	29	16	20	6	0	0	0	0	80	24
Kris Lythe	29/3/83	10(1)	5	1	0	0	0	0	0	4	0
Danny Maun	5/1/81	29(4)	20	9	9	0	0	0	0	36	36
Ryan McDonald	24/2/78	2(2)	2(2)	0	0	0	0	0	0	0	0
Joe Naidole	23/12/67	14(7)	6(4)	0	0	0	0	0	0	0	0
Chris North	6/1/76	1	0	2	0	0	0	0	0	8	0
David Rourke	12/3/81	17(1)	3(1)	1	0	0	0	0	0	4	0
Mark Sibson	20/10/76	23(2)	12(2)	12	5	0	0	0	0	48	20
Andy Spink	12/1/79	17(13)	7(10)	5	2	0	0	0	0	20	8
Chris Spurr	7/7/80	14(3)	7(1)	11	4	0	0	0	0	44	16
Gavin Swinson	21/3/78	8(2)	4(1)	2	0	0	0	0	0	8	0
Danny Thomas	21/12/83	11(1)	11(1)	5	5	0	0	2	2	22	22
Mark Toohey	16/6/82	23(4)	12(3)	12	4	0	0	0	0	48	16
Leon Williamson	22/8/74	22(2)	11(2)	6	6	0	0	0	0	24	24

Craig Lingard

LEAGUE RECORD
P18-W5-D1-L12
(9th, NL1/NL1 Qualifying Final Winners)
F366, A543, Diff-177
11 points.

CHALLENGE CUP
Round Five

NATIONAL LEAGUE CUP
Semi Finalists/2nd, Central Division

ATTENDANCES
Best - v Dewsbury (NL1 - 1,245)
Worst - v London Skolars (NLC - 577)
Total (NL1, inc QF, & NLC only) - 12,836
Average (NL1, inc QF, & NLC only) - 856
(Down by 123 on 2002)

DEWSBURY RAMS

DATE	FIXTURE	RESULT	SCORERS	LGE	ATT
19/1/03	London Skolars (a) (NLC)	W10-22	t:Rhodes,Wainwright,Benn g:Benn(5)	1st(NLC-C)	820
26/1/03	Woolston (a) (CCR3)	W12-34	t:Elston,Chapman,Brough,Watene,Waddell,Wainwright g:Benn(4),Brough	N/A	685
2/2/03	Keighley (h) (NLC)	W12-6	t:Kershaw,Watene g:Benn(2)	1st(NLC-C)	954
9/2/03	Widnes (a) (CCR4)	L48-6	t:Elston g:Benn	N/A	3,196
16/2/03	Hunslet (h) (NLC)	L24-26	t:Kershaw(2),Chapman,Brough g:Benn(4)	3rd(NLC-C)	869
23/2/03	York (a) (NLC)	W18-38	t:Redfearn,Fella,Benn,Kershaw,Mack,Hicks g:Benn(7)	2nd(NLC-C)	1,231
9/3/03	Batley (h) (NLC)	W22-18	t:Wainwright(2),Elston,Hicks g:Brough(3)	1st(NLC-C)	1,432
16/3/03	Keighley (a) (NLC)	L22-2	g:Brough	2nd(NLC-C)	1,111
23/3/03	London Skolars (h) (NLC)	W35-33	t:Slater,Barlow,Walker,Dyson,Kershaw,Thewliss g:Brough(4),Dyson fg:Thewliss	2nd(NLC-C)	449
30/3/03	Batley (a) (NLC)	W16-21	t:Steele(2),Kershaw,Brough g:Brough(2) fg:Brough	1st(NLC-C)	952
6/4/03	York (h) (NLC)	L24-28	t:Thewliss(2),Wood,Batty g:Brough(4)	1st(NLC-C)	654
13/4/03	Hunslet (a) (NLC)	W31-32	t:Wainwright(2),Watene,Batty,Miles,Elston g:Wood(4)	1st(NLC-C)	599
18/4/03	Batley (a)	L28-10	t:Miles,Fella g:Wood	9th	1,245
21/4/03	Featherstone (h)	W26-20	t:Wainwright(2),Mack,Batty,Oldfield g:Brough(2) fg:Heptinstall,Brough	5th	1,247
4/5/03	Oldham (a)	L41-21	t:Heptinstall,Wood,Barlow,Wainwright g:Wood(2) fg:Heptinstall	7th	1,198
11/5/03	Doncaster (h)	L12-16	t:Elston,Waddell g:Wood(2)	7th	929
18/5/03	Whitehaven (a) (NLCQF)	L54-10	t:Hardy,Heptinstall g:Wood	N/A	1,503
25/5/03	Rochdale (h)	L6-60	t:Barlow g:Wood	10th	668
1/6/03	Salford (a)	L76-4	t:Kershaw	10th	1,698
15/6/03	Leigh (h)	L12-31	t:Batty,Watene g:Wood(2)	10th	971
22/6/03	Hull KR (a)	L35-12	t:Crouthers(2) g:Thaler(2)	10th	1,402
29/6/03	Batley (h)	L23-36	t:Gleadhill,Law,Watene,Crouthers g:Thaler(3) fg:Thaler	10th	1,123
13/7/03	Whitehaven (h)	D18-18	t:Wainwright(2) g:Benn(5)	10th	777
20/7/03	Featherstone (a)	L26-13	t:Wainwright,Redfearn g:Benn(2) fg:Benn	10th	1,536
27/7/03	Oldham (h)	L26-32	t:Houles(2),Hicks,Miles g:Benn(4) fg:Benn(2)	10th	1,098
3/8/03	Doncaster (a)	W16-31	t:Batty(2),Law,Wainwright g:Benn(7) fg:Benn	10th	726
10/8/03	Rochdale (a)	L52-14	t:Watene,Houles,Elston g:Benn	10th	732
17/8/03	Salford (h)	L18-58	t:Miles,Kershaw,Crouthers g:Benn(3)	10th	972
24/8/03	Leigh (a)	L78-18	t:Elston,Thewliss,Barlow g:Benn(3)	10th	1,763
31/8/03	Hull KR (h)	L8-60	t:Batty g:Benn(2)	10th	1,150
7/9/03	Whitehaven (a)	L68-12	t:Miles,Redfearn g:Law(2)	10th	1,234

		APP		TRIES		GOALS		FG		PTS	
	D.O.B.	ALL	NL1	ALL	NL1	ALL	NL1	ALL	NL1	ALL	NL1
Mark Barlow	16/2/84	9(7)	4(4)	4	3	0	0	0	0	16	12
Nathan Batty	20/5/82	23	17	7	5	0	0	0	0	28	20
Jamie Benn	4/5/77	14	8	2	0	50	27	4	4	112	58
Danny Brough	15/1/83	10(2)	2	3	0	17	2	2	1	48	5
Jim Cain	16/10/79	(2)	(2)	0	0	0	0	0	0	0	0
Chris Chapman	25/10/80	9	0	2	0	0	0	0	0	8	0
Kevin Crouthers	3/1/76	9	9	4	4	0	0	0	0	16	16
Jeremy Dyson	15/2/72	1	0	1	0	1	0	0	0	6	0
Jimmy Elston	8/12/79	11(18)	7(10)	7	3	0	0	0	0	28	12
Danny Evans	15/10/74	11(6)	1(3)	0	0	0	0	0	0	0	0
Gary Fahey	14/12/76	1(2)	0	0	0	0	0	0	0	0	0
Andrew Fawkes	29/9/83	1(1)	0	0	0	0	0	0	0	0	0
Tony Fella	18/12/71	10(9)	1(7)	2	1	0	0	0	0	8	4
Andy Fisher	17/11/67	2	1	0	0	0	0	0	0	0	0
Paul Gleadhill	2/2/76	2	2	1	1	0	0	0	0	4	4
Ryan Hardy	12/2/74	10(5)	7(2)	1	0	0	0	0	0	4	0
Andy Heptinstall	28/4/76	9(4)	3(1)	2	1	0	0	2	2	10	6
Paul Hicks	22/6/77	27(2)	18	3	1	0	0	0	0	12	4
Sylvain Houles	3/8/81	6	6	3	3	0	0	0	0	12	12
Billy Kershaw	22/11/78	29(1)	18	8	2	0	0	0	0	32	8
Ian Kirke	26/12/80	6(1)	5(1)	0	0	0	0	0	0	0	0
Graham Law	24/7/79	9(1)	9(1)	2	2	2	2	0	0	12	12
Scott MacDougall	20/6/81	2(1)	2(1)	0	0	0	0	0	0	0	0
George Mack	8/10/80	13	5	2	1	0	0	0	0	8	4
Neil Mears	9/1/79	(1)	0	0	0	0	0	0	0	0	0
Craig Miles	8/7/81	14	11	5	4	0	0	0	0	20	16
David Mycoe	1/5/72	6(2)	6(2)	0	0	0	0	0	0	0	0
Craig Nipperess	27/10/76	8	7	0	0	0	0	0	0	0	0
David Oldfield	22/3/78	4(2)	(1)	1	1	0	0	0	0	4	4
Chris Parker	9/9/78	3(1)	(1)	0	0	0	0	0	0	0	0
Paul Philpot	26/6/79	1(1)	1(1)	0	0	0	0	0	0	0	0
Chris Redfearn	4/12/80	21(6)	11(4)	3	2	0	0	0	0	12	8
Scott Rhodes	21/6/80	9	0	1	0	0	0	0	0	4	0
Leigh Riddell	28/9/75	1	1	0	0	0	0	0	0	0	0
Carl Sayer	23/1/82	1(3)	1	0	0	0	0	0	0	0	0
Andrew Senior	31/8/75	2(6)	2(6)	0	0	0	0	0	0	0	0
Richard Slater	29/8/70	2(1)	2(1)	1	0	0	0	0	0	4	0
Paul Smith	31/5/84	5(8)	5(8)	0	0	0	0	0	0	0	0
Glenn Spedding	5/5/83	3(6)	2(5)	0	0	0	0	0	0	0	0
Paul Steele	9/12/81	9(1)	2(1)	2	0	0	0	0	0	8	0
Graham Summerscales	21/7/68	(2)	0	0	0	0	0	0	0	0	0
Adam Thaler	3/9/83	14(1)	14(1)	0	0	5	5	1	1	11	11
Anthony Thewliss	22/6/85	9(7)	6(4)	4	1	0	0	1	0	17	4
Jon Waddell	6/1/84	2(5)	(3)	2	1	0	0	0	0	8	4
Michael Wainwright	4/11/80	29	18	13	7	0	0	0	0	52	28
Michael Walker	20/4/77	1(4)	0	1	0	0	0	0	0	4	0
Frank Watene	15/2/77	20(5)	11(2)	6	3	0	0	0	0	24	12
Danny Wood	8/10/77	11	8	2	1	13	8	0	0	34	20
Jon Wray	19/5/70	1(1)	(1)	0	0	0	0	0	0	0	0

Michael Wainwright

LEAGUE RECORD
P18-W2-D1-L15
(10th, NL1)
F284, A751, Diff-467
5 points.

CHALLENGE CUP
Round Four

NATIONAL LEAGUE CUP
Quarter Finalists/1st, Central Division

ATTENDANCES
Best - v Batley (NLC - 1,432)
Worst - v London Skolars (NLC - 449)
Total (NL1 & NLC only) - 13,293
Average (NL1 & NLC only) - 950
(Down by 184 on 2002)

DONCASTER DRAGONS

DATE	FIXTURE	RESULT	SCORERS	LGE	ATT
19/1/03	Keighley (a) (NLC)	L21-14	t:M Walker,Ross g:W Green(3)	3rd(NLC-E)	1,337
26/1/03	Redhill (h) (CCR3)	W64-2	t:Lee(3),Ross(2),J Walker,Lawton,M Walker,Colton,P Green,Gleadhill,Moxon g:Woodcock(5),Ross(2),Irving	N/A	944
2/2/03	York (h) (NLC)	W24-4	t:Irving(2),J Walker,Hepi,Ross g:Irving(2)	2nd(NLC-E)	1,029
9/2/03	York (a) (CCR4)	W20-21	t:Lee,Lawton,Gleadhill,Irving g:Irving(2) fg:Moxon	N/A	1,511
16/2/03	Sheffield (a) (NLC)	W4-26	t:Edwards,Ross,J Walker,Lawton,Irving g:Irving(3)	2nd(NLC-E)	1,053
23/2/03	Featherstone (a) (NLC)	W24-37	t:Lee(2),Edwards,Mansson,P Green,Irving,Handford g:Irving(4) fg:Ross	2nd(NLC-E)	2,075
2/3/03	Wigan (h) (CCR5)	L10-50	t:Lee,M Walker g:Irving	N/A	3,653
9/3/03	Hull KR (a) (NLC)	W8-21	t:M Walker,Mansson,Ross g:Irving(4) fg:Moxon	1st(NLC-E)	1,553
16/3/03	York (a) (NLC)	L34-20	t:Gleadhill,P Green,Golden g:Irving(4)	2nd(NLC-E)	1,133
23/3/03	Keighley (h) (NLC)	W42-12	t:Mansson(2),Colton,Irving,M Walker,Golden,Horne,Leafe g:Irving(5)	2nd(NLC-E)	985
30/3/03	Hull KR (h) (NLC)	L32-34	t:Mansson,Horne,Leafe,Irving,Golden g:Woodcock(6)	3rd(NLC-E)	1,127
6/4/03	Featherstone (h) (NLC)	W26-24	t:Horne,Irving,Colton,J Walker g:Woodcock(5)	2nd(NLC-E)	1,291
13/4/03	Sheffield (h) (NLC)	W38-30	t:Ross(3),Gleadhill(2),P Green,Irving g:Irving(5)	3rd(NLC-E)	909
18/4/03	Featherstone (a)	L44-18	t:Irving,Ross,Mansson g:Irving(3)	10th	1,540
4/5/03	Rochdale (h)	L28-44	t:Hemmings(2),Gleadhill,Mansson,P Green g:Woodcock(4)	9th	805
11/5/03	Dewsbury (a)	W12-16	t:Mansson,Hepi,Colton g:Woodcock(2)	8th	929
18/5/03	Oldham (h)	W52-24	t:Mansson(3),Horne(2),Hepi(2),Gleadhill,Fielden g:Woodcock(8)	4th	860
25/5/03	Salford (h)	L24-34	t:Woodcock,Mansson,Edwards g:Woodcock(6)	6th	1,069
1/6/03	Leigh (a)	L55-14	t:P Green,Irving,Hepi g:Woodcock	8th	1,988
15/6/03	Hull KR (h)	L22-43	t:P Green,Handford,David,Lawton g:J Walker(2),Lee	8th	1,124
22/6/03	Whitehaven (a)	W18-24	t:Grix,Sykes,Mansson,Irving g:Irving(4)	8th	1,461
27/6/03	Featherstone (h)	W30-19	t:David(2),Mansson(2),Irving g:Irving(5)	7th	1,008
13/7/03	Batley (h)	W32-25	t:Edwards(2),Seuseu,Lawton,Irving g:Irving(6)	6th	858
20/7/03	Oldham (a)	L31-20	t:Lloyd,P Green,Solomon,Edwards g:Grix(2)	6th	1,254
27/7/03	Rochdale (a)	L50-34	t:Grix(2),J Walker,Solomon,Greenwood,Lee g:Holroyd(5)	8th	623
3/8/03	Dewsbury (h)	L16-31	t:Handford,Moxon,Colton g:Holroyd(2)	8th	726
10/8/03	Salford (a)	L72-0	No Scorers	8th	1,620
17/8/03	Leigh (h)	L18-46	t:Holroyd(3) g:Holroyd(3)	8th	901
24/8/03	Hull KR (a)	L32-26	t:P Green(2),Handford,Woodcock g:Holroyd(5)	9th	1,522
31/8/03	Whitehaven (h)	D34-34	t:Lee(3),Ostler,Holroyd,Lawton g:Holroyd(5)	9th	677
6/9/03	Batley (a)	W18-21	t:Colton(2),Golden g:Holroyd(4) fg:Holroyd	8th	741
21/9/03	Batley (h) (NL1QPO)	W45-12	t:Lee(3),Solomon,Colton,Ostler,Holroyd,Moxon g:Holroyd(6) fg:Holroyd	N/A	887

		APP		TRIES		GOALS		FG		PTS	
	D.O.B.	ALL	NL1	ALL	NL1	ALL	NL1	ALL	NL1	ALL	NL1
Austin Aggrie	12/5/79	1(1)	1(1)	0	0	0	0	0	0	0	0
Shaun Archer	29/6/83	1	1	0	0	0	0	0	0	0	0
Tony Atter	6/1/79	1	0	0	0	0	0	0	0	0	0
Tom Buckenham	15/8/84	(5)	(3)	0	0	0	0	0	0	0	0
Andy Burland	5/11/77	(2)	0	0	0	0	0	0	0	0	0
Dean Colton	18/2/83	12(14)	8(5)	8	5	0	0	0	0	32	20
Craig Cook	26/5/83	1(2)	1(2)	0	0	0	0	0	0	0	0
Maea David	27/2/72	7(9)	4(4)	3	3	0	0	0	0	12	12
Jason Eagle	21/9/84	(1)	(1)	0	0	0	0	0	0	0	0
Peter Edwards	4/7/69	21(2)	11(1)	6	4	0	0	0	0	24	16
Gareth Everton	16/6/82	(2)	0	0	0	0	0	0	0	0	0
Jamie Fielden	9/5/78	1(4)	1(3)	1	1	0	0	0	0	4	4
David Ford	15/12/84	1(1)	1(1)	0	0	0	0	0	0	0	0
Craig Forsyth	24/10/70	5(10)	(2)	0	0	0	0	0	0	0	0
Wayne Frost	17/2/85	(2)	(2)	0	0	0	0	0	0	0	0
Paul Gleadhill	2/2/76	14(1)	4	7	2	0	0	0	0	28	8
Marvin Golden	21/12/76	14	3	4	1	0	0	0	0	16	4
Peter Green	2/12/81	32	19	10	6	0	0	0	0	40	24
Wayne Green	1/1/83	1(3)	(2)	0	0	3	0	0	0	6	0
Gareth Greenwood	14/1/83	11(1)	11(1)	1	1	0	0	0	0	4	4
Scott Grix	1/5/84	9	9	3	3	2	2	0	0	16	16
Gareth Handford	22/4/80	27(2)	14(2)	4	3	0	0	0	0	16	12
Chris Hemmings	24/12/83	4(5)	4(5)	2	2	0	0	0	0	8	8
Brad Hepi	11/2/68	6(2)	5	5	4	0	0	0	0	20	16
Graham Holroyd	25/10/75	8	8	5	5	30	30	2	2	82	82
Craig Horne	20/5/78	12	5	5	2	0	0	0	0	20	8
Simon Irving	22/3/67	23	11	14	5	49	18	0	0	154	56
Craig Lawton	17/2/81	27(4)	18(1)	6	3	0	0	0	0	24	12
Shaun Leafe	10/2/84	5(8)	2(1)	2	0	0	0	0	0	8	0
Jason Lee	16/1/71	23	11	14	7	1	1	0	0	58	30
Gareth Lloyd	12/8/75	5(6)	5(6)	1	1	0	0	0	0	4	4
Paul Mansson	13/3/72	20	11	15	10	0	0	0	0	60	40
Mark Moxon	22/8/80	28(2)	15(2)	3	2	0	0	2	0	14	8
Alex Muff	17/8/82	10(3)	10(3)	0	0	0	0	0	0	0	0
Martin Ostler	21/6/80	9(3)	9(3)	2	2	0	0	0	0	8	8
Chris Ross	23/8/78	14	3	10	1	2	0	1	0	45	4
Anthony Seuseu	24/3/79	1(2)	1(2)	1	1	0	0	0	0	4	4
PJ Solomon	17/8/76	11	11	3	3	0	0	0	0	12	12
Martin Sykes	28/12/76	5(3)	5(3)	1	1	0	0	0	0	4	4
James Walker	15/4/77	14(18)	9(10)	5	1	2	2	0	0	24	8
Matt Walker	23/11/78	19(10)	6(10)	5	0	0	0	0	0	20	0
Johnny Woodcock	5/2/81	13	10	2	2	37	21	0	0	82	50

Jason Lee

LEAGUE RECORD
P18-W6-D1-L11
(8th, NL1/NL1 Qualifying
Play Off Winners)
F429, A632, Diff-203
13 points.

CHALLENGE CUP
Round Five

NATIONAL LEAGUE CUP
3rd, East Division

ATTENDANCES
Best - v Wigan (CC - 3,653)
Worst - v Whitehaven (NL1 - 677)
Total (NL1, inc QPO,
& NLC only) - 14,256
Average (NL1, inc QPO,
& NLC only) - 950
(Down by 131 on 2002)

255

FEATHERSTONE ROVERS

DATE	FIXTURE	RESULT	SCORERS	LGE	ATT
19/1/03	Sheffield (h) (NLC)	W30-12	t:Seal(2),Graham,O'Meara,Stokes,Archibald g:Dickens(3)	1st(NLC-E)	1,595
26/1/03	Villeneuve (h) (CCR3)	W26-22	t:Brown,Molyneux,Flynn g:Dickens(6) fg:Briggs(2)	N/A	1,441
2/2/03	Hull KR (a) (NLC)	L20-0	No Scorers	3rd(NLC-E)	1,540
9/2/03	Leigh (h) (CCR4)	W28-22	t:Seal(2),Brown,Stokes g:Dickens(5) fg:Briggs(2)	N/A	2,257
16/2/03	York (h) (NLC)	W36-22	t:Chapman(2),Stokes(2),Seal,Agar,Briggs g:Dickens(2),Briggs(2)	3rd(NLC-E)	1,728
23/2/03	Doncaster (h) (NLC)	L24-37	t:Seal(2),Stokes,Flynn g:Dickens(2),Briggs(2)	3rd(NLC-E)	2,075
2/3/03	Swinton (a) (CCR5)	L32-10	t:O'Meara,Brown g:Dickens	N/A	1,092
9/3/03	Hunslet (a) (NLC)	W4-42	t:Stokes(3),Brown(2),Flynn(2),Dooler g:Dickens(3),Briggs fg:Agar,Briggs	3rd(NLC-E)	793
16/3/03	Hull KR (h) (NLC)	W44-20	t:Stokes(3),Graham,Brown,Briggs,Rice,Seal,Flynn g:Briggs(3),Dickens	1st(NLC-E)	1,712
21/3/03	Sheffield (a) (NLC)	W8-27	t:Brown(2),Stokes,Seal g:Dickens(4),Briggs fg:Agar	1st(NLC-E)	856
30/3/03	Hunslet (h) (NLC)	W50-10	t:O'Meara(2),Stokes(2),Tonks(2),Brown,Graham,Dooler g:Dickens(6),Briggs	1st(NLC-E)	1,212
6/4/03	Doncaster (a) (NLC)	L26-24	t:Flynn(2),Brown,Dooler g:Dickens(3),Briggs	1st(NLC-E)	1,291
13/4/03	York (a) (NLC)	W14-32	t:Seal(2),Graham,Brown,Chapman,Agar g:Dickens(2),Briggs(2)	1st(NLC-E)	1,415
18/4/03	Doncaster (h)	W44-18	t:Flynn(2),Seal(2),Tonks,O'Meara,Graham,Bailey g:Dickens(3),Briggs(3)	1st	1,540
21/4/03	Dewsbury (a)	L26-20	t:Chapman,Graham,Stokes,Briggs g:Briggs(2)	4th	1,247
4/5/03	Salford (h)	W18-16	t:Chapman,Langley g:Dickens(4),Briggs	3rd	1,616
11/5/03	Leigh (a)	L50-12	t:Dooler,Rice g:Briggs(2)	4th	2,073
18/5/03	Leigh (a) (NLCQF)	L26-6	t:Flynn g:Dickens	N/A	1,668
25/5/03	Hull KR (h)	W14-12	t:Flynn,Dooler g:Dickens(3)	4th	1,200
1/6/03	Whitehaven (a)	L46-6	t:Brown g:Briggs	5th	1,698
15/6/03	Batley (h)	W34-18	t:Dooler,Whiting,Flynn,Seal,Brown,Presley g:Dickens(5)	5th	1,182
22/6/03	Rochdale (h)	W30-16	t:Stokes(2),Chapman g:Dickens(8) fg:Briggs(2)	4th	1,359
27/6/03	Doncaster (a)	L30-19	t:Langley(2),Briggs g:Dickens(3) fg:Briggs	4th	1,008
13/7/03	Oldham (a)	L35-24	t:Stokes,Briggs,Chapman,Seal g:Dickens(2),Whiting(2)	5th	1,235
20/7/03	Dewsbury (h)	W26-13	t:Chapman(2),Presley,Stokes g:Dickens(5)	4th	1,536
27/7/03	Salford (a)	L36-20	t:Dickens,Presley,Flynn g:Dickens(4)	4th	2,025
3/8/03	Leigh (h)	L32-58	t:Seal,Dooler,Whiting,Brown,Houston,Chapman g:Whiting(4)	4th	1,747
10/8/03	Hull KR (a)	L13-0	No Scorers	5th	1,559
17/8/03	Whitehaven (h)	W52-12	t:O'Meara(2),Stokes(2),Graham(2),Darley,Flynn,Seal g:Briggs(6),Dickens(2)	5th	1,116
24/8/03	Batley (a)	L18-10	t:Dooler,Stokes g:Dickens	5th	1,156
31/8/03	Rochdale (a)	L42-12	t:O'Meara,Flynn g:Briggs,Dickens	5th	948
7/9/03	Oldham (h)	L14-19	t:Houston,Langley,Presley g:Dickens	7th	1,504

		APP		TRIES		GOALS		FG		PTS	
	D.O.B.	ALL	NL1	ALL	NL1	ALL	NL1	ALL	NL1	ALL	NL1
Richard Agar	20/1/72	10(2)	2(2)	2	0	0	0	2	0	10	0
Ben Archibald	21/10/82	1(5)	1(1)	1	0	0	0	0	0	4	0
Andy Bailey	15/10/82	6(19)	4(7)	1	1	0	0	0	0	4	4
Carl Briggs	27/9/74	30	16	5	3	29	16	8	3	86	47
Ian Brown	27/1/74	24(1)	10(1)	14	3	0	0	0	0	56	12
Richard Chapman	5/9/75	24(6)	13(5)	10	7	0	0	0	0	40	28
Paul Darley	26/1/74	6(10)	5(10)	1	1	0	0	0	0	4	4
Stuart Dickens	23/3/80	31(1)	18	1	1	81	42	0	0	166	88
Steve Dooler	31/12/77	30	18	8	5	0	0	0	0	32	20
Adrian Flynn	9/9/74	32	18	15	7	0	0	0	0	60	28
James Ford	29/9/82	4(1)	4(1)	0	0	0	0	0	0	0	0
Nathan Graham	23/11/71	31	17	8	4	0	0	0	0	32	16
James Houston	28/12/82	2(8)	2(8)	2	2	0	0	0	0	8	8
Andy Jarrett	26/4/83	1(2)	1(1)	0	0	0	0	0	0	0	0
Robin Jowitt	10/6/77	1(11)	(4)	0	0	0	0	0	0	0	0
Chris Langley	11/10/80	9(2)	8(2)	4	4	0	0	0	0	16	16
Andy McNally	9/1/82	4(6)	0	0	0	0	0	0	0	0	0
Chris Molyneux	5/5/80	7(23)	2(14)	1	0	0	0	0	0	4	0
Brendan O'Meara	26/5/72	31	17	8	4	0	0	0	0	32	16
Danny Patrickson	21/5/82	1(3)	1	0	0	0	0	0	0	0	0
Jonathan Presley	8/7/84	5(8)	3(6)	4	4	0	0	0	0	16	16
Andy Rice	9/6/80	26(6)	12(6)	2	1	0	0	0	0	8	4
Danny Seal	15/3/76	31	17	17	6	0	0	0	0	68	24
Kevin Spink	1/4/81	(1)	0	0	0	0	0	0	0	0	0
Jamie Stokes	13/8/79	32	18	22	8	0	0	0	0	88	32
Jamie Tennant	15/11/80	(1)	(1)	0	0	0	0	0	0	0	0
Ian Tonks	13/2/76	26(4)	16(1)	3	1	0	0	0	0	12	4
Richard Whiting	20/12/84	11(7)	11(2)	2	2	6	6	0	0	20	20

Danny Seal

LEAGUE RECORD
P18-W7-D0-L11
(7th, NL1)
F387, A478, Diff-91
14 points.

CHALLENGE CUP
Round Five

NATIONAL LEAGUE CUP
Quarter Finalists/1st, East Division

ATTENDANCES
Best - v Leigh (CC - 2,257)
Worst - v Whitehaven (NL1 - 1,116)
Total (NL1 & NLC only) - 21,122
Average (NL1 & NLC only) - 1,509
(Up by 27 on 2002)

HULL KINGSTON ROVERS

DATE	FIXTURE	RESULT	SCORERS	LGE	ATT
19/1/03	York (a) (NLC)	W26-36	t:Walker(2),Murdock,Poucher,Aston,Farrell,Cochran g:Murdock(4)	2nd(NLC-E)	3,105
26/1/03	Siddal (h) (CCR3)	W28-0	t:Pinkney(2),Poucher,Pickering g:Poucher(6)	N/A	1,526
2/2/03	Featherstone (h) (NLC)	W20-0	t:Pickering,Parker,McClarron g:Stott(4)	1st(NLC-E)	1,540
9/2/03	Rochdale (a) (CCR4)	W20-27	t:Stott,Bovill,McClarron,Parker g:Stott(5) fg:Stott	N/A	1,300
16/2/03	London Skolars (a) (NLC)	W8-24	t:McClarron(2),Pinkney,Parker,Blanchard g:Stott(2)	1st(NLC-E)	712
23/2/03	Sheffield (h) (NLC)	W30-24	t:Pinkney(2),Stott,Blanchard,Cochran g:Stott(5)	1st(NLC-E)	1,553
28/2/03	Salford (h) (CCR5)	L2-12	g:Stott	N/A	2,533
9/3/03	Doncaster (h) (NLC)	L8-21	t:Pickering g:Stephenson(2)	2nd(NLC-E)	1,553
16/3/03	Featherstone (a) (NLC)	L44-20	t:Parker,Pickering,Poucher g:Stott(4)	3rd(NLC-E)	1,712
23/3/03	York (h) (NLC)	W32-14	t:Pinkney(2),Pickering,Andrews,Poucher,Bell g:Stephenson(4)	3rd(NLC-E)	1,580
30/3/03	Doncaster (a) (NLC)	W32-34	t:Farrell(2),Aston,Tawhai,Stephenson,Pickering g:Stephenson(5)	2nd(NLC-E)	1,127
6/4/03	Sheffield (a) (NLC)	L33-26	t:Bovill,Poucher,Aston,McClarron,Parker g:Stephenson(3)	3rd(NLC-E)	1,150
13/4/03	London Skolars (h) (NLC)	W86-0	t:Smith(2),Pickering(2),Bell(2),Stephenson,Parker,Sullivan,McClarron,Fletcher, Seibold,Howard,Pinkney,Poucher g:Stephenson(13)	2nd(NLC-E)	1,175
18/4/03	Leigh (h)	L17-28	t:McClarron(3) g:Stephenson(2) fg:Tawhai	8th	2,030
21/4/03	Rochdale (a)	L29-18	t:Seibold(2),Pinkney,McClarron g:Tawhai	9th	1,097
4/5/03	Whitehaven (a)	L26-2	g:Stephenson	10th	1,315
11/5/03	Batley (h)	W16-10	t:Pinkney(2),Howard g:Stott(2)	9th	1,000
18/5/03	Batley (h) (NLCQF)	L12-16	t:Cooke,Aston g:Cooke(2)	N/A	1,100
25/5/03	Featherstone (a)	L14-12	t:Stott,Aston g:Stott(2)	8th	1,200
1/6/03	Oldham (h)	W23-10	t:Pinkney,Busby,Pickering,Seibold g:Stott(3) fg:Tawhai	6th	1,300
15/6/03	Doncaster (a)	W22-43	t:Blanchard(3),Howard,Poucher,Tawhai,Stott g:Stott(7) fg:Stott	6th	1,124
22/6/03	Dewsbury (h)	W35-12	t:Cooke,Tawhai,Pickering,Parker,Pinkney,Aizue g:Stott(5) fg:Tawhai	6th	1,402
29/6/03	Leigh (a)	L54-4	t:Aston	6th	2,363
13/7/03	Salford (a)	L24-12	t:Pickering,Smith g:Stott(2)	7th	2,063
20/7/03	Rochdale (h)	L18-33	t:Andrews,Aizue,McClarron g:Stott(3)	8th	1,750
27/7/03	Whitehaven (h)	W36-10	t:Poucher(2),Bovill,Mansson,Tawhai,Aizue g:Stephenson(5),Tawhai	7th	1,612
3/8/03	Batley (a)	L27-13	t:Mansson(2) g:Hall(2) fg:Tawhai	7th	926
10/8/03	Featherstone (h)	W13-0	t:Mansson,McClarron g:Stott(2) fg:Stott	4th	1,559
17/8/03	Oldham (a)	W24-29	t:Farrell,Seibold,Pickering,Poucher,McClarron g:Stott(4) fg:Stott	4th	1,414
24/8/03	Doncaster (h)	W32-26	t:Sullivan,Fletcher,Aston,Smith,Seibold g:Stott(5),Tawhai	4th	1,522
31/8/03	Dewsbury (a)	W8-60	t:McClarron(2),Tawhai(2),Fletcher,Pickering,Poucher,Andrews,Stephenson,Farrell g:Stott(7),Stephenson(3)	4th	1,150
7/9/03	Salford (h)	W18-16	t:Ellis,McClarron,Mansson g:Stott(3)	4th	2,060
14/9/03	Oldham (h) (EPO)	W38-24	t:Mansson,Tawhai,Parker,Poucher,McClarron,Pinkney g:Stott(7)	N/A	2,250
21/9/03	Rochdale (a) (ESF)	W26-30	t:McClarron,Poucher,Stott,Mansson,Andrews,Parker g:Stott(3)	N/A	1,710
28/9/03	Leigh (a) (FE)	L42-12	t:Mansson,Parker,McClarron	N/A	2,901

		APP		TRIES		GOALS		FG		PTS	
	D.O.B.	ALL	NL1	ALL	NL1	ALL	NL1	ALL	NL1	ALL	NL1
Makali Aizue	30/12/77	4(12)	4(12)	3	3	0	0	0	0	12	12
Dean Andrews	1/6/79	2(22)	1(12)	4	3	0	0	0	0	16	12
Jon Aston	5/6/76	34(1)	20(1)	7	3	0	0	0	0	28	12
Ian Bell	28/1/83	4	1	3	0	0	0	0	0	12	0
Mark Blanchard	11/7/82	19(4)	12(1)	5	3	0	0	0	0	20	12
Jamie Bovill	21/3/83	17(9)	5(8)	3	1	0	0	0	0	12	4
Dean Busby	1/2/73	6(4)	6(4)	1	1	0	0	0	0	4	4
Steve Cochran	2/12/82	1(9)	1(1)	2	0	0	0	0	0	8	0
Shaun Cooke	24/4/83	8	7	2	1	2	0	0	0	12	4
Andy Ellis	15/12/84	2	2	1	1	0	0	0	0	4	4
Matt Emmerson	31/1/85	(1)	0	0	0	0	0	0	0	0	0
Craig Farrell	8/10/81	26	13	5	2	0	0	0	0	20	8
Paul Fletcher	17/3/70	1(34)	(21)	3	2	0	0	0	0	12	8
Mike Hall	15/9/81	3	1	0	0	2	2	0	0	4	4
Craig Henry	9/7/81	(1)	(1)	0	0	0	0	0	0	0	0
Harvey Howard	25/3/69	10(7)	9(3)	3	2	0	0	0	0	12	8
Paul Mansson	13/3/72	9	9	8	8	0	0	0	0	32	32
Alasdair McClarron	19/6/73	29	17	19	13	0	0	0	0	76	52
Craig Murdock	24/10/73	6(3)	3(1)	1	0	4	0	0	0	12	0
Paul Parker	13/2/79	28	16	10	4	0	0	0	0	40	16
Paul Pickering	16/12/82	23(5)	11(5)	13	5	0	0	0	0	52	20
Nick Pinkney	6/12/70	24(3)	10(3)	14	6	0	0	0	0	56	24
Craig Poucher	12/9/80	23(1)	13(1)	13	7	6	0	0	0	64	28
Anthony Seibold	3/10/74	20(3)	20(1)	6	5	0	0	0	0	24	20
Andy Smith	4/1/76	29(1)	17(1)	4	2	0	0	0	0	16	8
Chris Stephenson	4/9/81	9(2)	3(1)	3	1	38	11	0	0	88	26
Lynton Stott	9/5/71	23(4)	16(1)	5	3	76	55	4	3	176	125
Adam Sullivan	14/11/82	19(6)	5(6)	2	1	0	0	0	0	8	4
Latham Tawhai	23/8/71	25(1)	19	7	6	3	3	4	4	38	34
Andy Taylor	15/12/82	(1)	0	0	0	0	0	0	0	0	0
Jimmy Walker	22/11/73	10(5)	6	2	0	0	0	0	0	8	0
David Wilson	30/9/84	6(1)	5	0	0	0	0	0	0	0	0
Richard Wilson	5/2/75	35	21	0	0	0	0	0	0	0	0

Lynton Stott

LEAGUE RECORD
P18-W10-D0-L8
(4th, NL1/Final Eliminator)
F401, A373, Diff+28
20 points.

CHALLENGE CUP
Round Five

NATIONAL LEAGUE CUP
Quarter Finalists/2nd, East Division

ATTENDANCES
Best - v Salford (CC - 2,533)
Worst - v Batley (NL1 - 1,000)
Total (NL1, inc play-offs,
& NLC, inc QF, only) - 24,986
Average (NL1, inc play-offs,
& NLC, inc QF, only) - 1,562
(Down by 226 on 2002)

LEIGH CENTURIONS

DATE	FIXTURE	RESULT	SCORERS	LGE	ATT
19/1/03	Oldham (h) (NLC)	W22-14	t:Munro(2),Hamilton,Alstead g:Sanderson(3)	3rd(NLC-W)	3,070
25/1/03	Locomotiv Moscow (h) (CCR3)	W62-0	t:Rowley(2),Cardoza(2),Munro(2),Hadcroft,Alstead,Richardson,Nickle,Holdstock g:Sanderson(8),Duffy	N/A	2,641
2/2/03	Swinton (a) (NLC)	W10-24	t:Cardoza(3),Munro,Rivett g:Duffy(2)	1st(NLC-W)	950
9/2/03	Featherstone (a) (CCR4)	L28-22	t:Munro(2),Cardoza,Alstead g:Sanderson(3)	N/A	2,257
16/2/03	Salford (h) (NLC)	D20-20	t:Richardson,Bristow,Duffy g:Duffy(4)	1st(NLC-W)	4,445
23/2/03	Chorley (h) (NLC)	W38-20	t:Rivett(2),Cardoza,Rowley,Duffy,Swann,Henare g:Duffy(5)	1st(NLC-W)	1,871
9/3/03	Rochdale (a) (NLC)	W32-34	t:Rowley(2),Munro,Rivett,Bristow,Sanderson g:Turley(5)	1st(NLC-W)	1,251
16/3/03	Oldham (a) (NLC)	W26-31	t:Weisner,Rowley,Turley,Andrews g:Turley(7) fg:Turley	1st(NLC-W)	1,945
23/3/03	Swinton (h) (NLC)	W62-6	t:Turley(5),Bristow(2),Bradbury,Rowley,Richardson,Munro g:Turley(9)	1st(NLC-W)	2,026
30/3/03	Salford (a) (NLC)	L22-10	t:Weisner,Munro g:Duffy	2nd(NLC-W)	3,099
6/4/03	Chorley (a) (NLC)	L31-22	t:Bristow,Turley,Sanderson,Weisner g:Turley(3)	2nd(NLC-W)	736
13/4/03	Rochdale (h) (NLC)	W58-30	t:Turley(3),Munro(2),Bristow,Cardoza,Rowley,Duffy,Swann g:Turley(7),Duffy(2)	2nd(NLC-W)	1,365
18/4/03	Hull KR (a)	W17-28	t:Holdstock(2),Hadcroft,Alstead,Kendrick g:Duffy(3) fg:Duffy(2)	3rd	2,030
21/4/03	Whitehaven (h)	W19-12	t:Henare,Rowley,Holdstock,Alstead g:Sanderson fg:Weisner	1st	1,996
4/5/03	Batley (a)	W12-38	t:Kendrick,Bristow,Duffy,Alstead,Nickle,Rowley,Norman g:Weisner(5)	1st	1,034
11/5/03	Featherstone (h)	W50-12	t:Munro(3),Kendrick(2),Richardson,Bristow,Rowley,Rivett g:Weisner(7)	1st	2,073
18/5/03	Featherstone (h) (NLCQF)	W26-6	t:Munro(2),Cardoza(2),Duffy g:Weisner(3)	N/A	1,668
25/5/03	Oldham (a)	L12-10	t:Rivett,Cardoza g:Weisner	2nd	1,691
1/6/03	Doncaster (h)	W55-14	t:Turley(3),Rivett(2),Bristow(2),Swann,Bradbury g:Turley(9) fg:Turley	1st	1,988
8/6/03	Whitehaven (a) (NLCSF)	W39-15	t:Norman,Munro,Kendrick,Hadcroft,Holdstock,Bradbury g:Turley(7) fg:Weisner	N/A	2,687
15/6/03	Dewsbury (a)	W12-31	t:Munro(2),Swann,Hadcroft,Duffy g:Weisner(5) fg:Weisner	1st	971
22/6/03	Salford (h)	L12-32	t:Richardson,Munro g:Weisner(2)	2nd	4,000
29/6/03	Hull KR (h)	W54-4	t:Rivett(3),Munro(2),Duffy(2),Bristow,Weisner,Holdstock g:Turley(5),Weisner(2)	2nd	2,363
6/7/03	Salford (NLCF) ●	L19-36	t:Rivett,Swann,Munro,Turley g:Turley fg:Turley	N/A	6,486
13/7/03	Rochdale (a)	W12-19	t:Rowley,Kendrick,Bristow g:Turley(3) fg:Turley	2nd	1,331
20/7/03	Whitehaven (a)	W8-20	t:Munro,Richardson,Nickle,Henare g:Turley(2)	2nd	1,750
27/7/03	Batley (a)	W54-30	t:Hadcroft(2),Rowley(2),Cardoza(2),Watts,Weisner,Swann,Rivett g:Turley(7)	2nd	2,283
3/8/03	Featherstone (a)	W32-58	t:Cardoza(3),Bristow(2),Martyn,Turley,Duffy,Rivett,Munro g:Turley(9)	2nd	1,747
10/8/03	Oldham (h)	W38-2	t:Martyn(2),Turley,Munro,Duffy,Weisner g:Turley(7)	2nd	2,287
17/8/03	Doncaster (a)	W18-46	t:Bradbury(2),Halliwell(2),Richardson,Martyn,Turley,Munro,Cardoza g:Turley(5)	2nd	901
24/8/03	Dewsbury (h)	W78-18	t:Rowley(3),Munro(2),Cardoza(2),Turley(2),Halliwell,Swann,Martyn,Holdstock,Sanderson g:Turley(11)	2nd	1,763
31/8/03	Salford (a)	L46-24	t:Cardoza,Bristow,Munro,Weisner g:Turley(4)	2nd	4,121
7/9/03	Rochdale (h)	W68-16	t:Rowley(3),Weisner(2),Sanderson,Holdstock,Rivett,Alstead,Bristow,Duffy,Nickle g:Turley(10)	2nd	2,782
21/9/03	Salford (a) (QSF)	L26-18	t:Duffy,Bristow,Alstead g:Turley(3)	N/A	3,660
28/9/03	Hull KR (h) (FE)	W42-12	t:Rivett(2),Halliwell,Weisner,Bradbury,Munro g:Turley(8),Sanderson	N/A	2,901
5/10/03	Salford (GF) ●●	L14-31	t:Richardson,Halliwell,Swann g:Turley	N/A	9,186

● Played at Spotland, Rochdale
●● Played at Halton Stadium, Widnes

		APP		TRIES		GOALS		FG		PTS	
	D.O.B.	ALL	NL1	ALL	NL1	ALL	NL1	ALL	NL1	ALL	NL1
David Alstead	18/2/82	18(3)	11(1)	8	5	0	0	0	0	32	20
Eric Andrews	11/2/82	3(2)	0	1	0	0	0	0	0	4	0
Rob Ball	22/3/76	11(12)	3(7)	0	0	0	0	0	0	0	0
Ricky Bibey	22/9/81	1(9)	1(9)	0	0	0	0	0	0	0	0
Anthony Blackwood	13/9/82	1(3)	(1)	0	0	0	0	0	0	0	0
David Bradbury	16/3/72	13(20)	9(11)	6	4	0	0	0	0	24	16
Adam Bristow	24/6/73	36	21	17	11	0	0	0	0	68	44
Dale Cardoza	13/9/79	18(5)	6(3)	20	10	0	0	0	0	80	40
John Duffy	2/7/80	23(6)	12(4)	12	8	18	3	2	2	86	40
Alan Hadcroft	31/3/77	29(1)	18	6	4	0	0	0	0	24	16
Danny Halliwell	23/3/81	8(1)	8(1)	5	5	0	0	0	0	20	20
John Hamilton	18/10/79	1(6)	(1)	1	0	0	0	0	0	4	0
Bryan Henare	24/9/74	26(3)	16(2)	3	2	0	0	0	0	12	8
Dale Holdstock	2/8/79	4(16)	3(9)	8	6	0	0	0	0	32	24
Phil Kendrick	31/10/77	16(4)	10	6	5	0	0	0	0	24	20
Keiron Maddocks	26/10/84	(1)	(1)	0	0	0	0	0	0	0	0
Tommy Martyn	4/6/71	9	9	5	5	0	0	0	0	20	20
Damian Munro	6/10/76	30(2)	16(1)	32	16	0	0	0	0	128	64
Sonny Nickle	4/5/69	28(2)	18	4	3	0	0	0	0	16	12
Paul Norman	25/3/74	15(10)	11(9)	2	1	0	0	0	0	8	4
Sean Richardson	20/8/73	35(1)	20(1)	8	5	0	0	0	0	32	20
Leroy Rivett	17/12/76	23(4)	13(2)	17	12	0	0	0	0	68	48
Paul Rowley	12/3/75	31	17	20	12	0	0	0	0	80	48
Lee Sanderson	16/12/81	7(15)	2(10)	4	2	16	2	0	0	48	12
Willie Swann	25/2/74	15(12)	9(8)	8	5	0	0	0	0	32	20
Neil Turley	15/3/80	22	14	19	8	123	84	4	2	326	202
Michael Watts	23/9/76	14(3)	8(1)	1	1	0	0	0	0	4	4
Patrick Weisner	17/3/82	31(2)	18(1)	10	7	25	22	3	2	93	74

Damian Munro

LEAGUE RECORD
P18-W15-D0-L3
(2nd, NL1/Grand Final Runners Up)
F702, A309, Diff+393
30 points.

CHALLENGE CUP
Round Four

NATIONAL LEAGUE CUP
Runners Up/2nd, West Division

ATTENDANCES
Best - v Salford (NLC - 4,445)
Worst - v Rochdale (NLC - 1,365)
Total (NL1, inc play-offs,
& NLC, inc QF & SF, only) - 41,568
Average (NL1, inc play-offs,
& NLC, inc QF & SF, only) - 2,445
(Down by 97 on 2002)

OLDHAM

DATE	FIXTURE	RESULT	SCORERS	LGE	ATT
19/1/03	Leigh (a) (NLC)	L22-14	t:Dodd,Farrell g:Svabic(2),Barber	4th(NLC-W)	3,070
26/1/03	East Hull (h) (CCR3)	W32-6	t:Campbell(2),Dodd,Farrell,Anderson,McNicholas,Roden g:Barber,Svabic	N/A	1,270
2/2/03	Rochdale (h) (NLC)	D22-22	t:Doran,Barber,Farrell,Morley g:Barber(3)	4th(NLC-W)	2,050
9/2/03	London (a) (CCR4)	L42-12	t:Dodd,Stazicker g:Barber,Svabic	N/A	1,514
23/2/03	Swinton (a) (NLC)	W16-24	t:Doran,Goddard,Hough,Barber g:Svabic(4)	3rd(NLC-W)	923
2/3/03	Barrow (h) (NLC)	W50-11	t:Dodd(2),Morgan,Farrell,Murray,Goddard,Barber,Anderson g:Svabic(9)	3rd(NLC-W)	1,280
9/3/03	Salford (h) (NLC)	L4-62	t:Irwin	3rd(NLC-W)	2,839
16/3/03	Leigh (h) (NLC)	L26-31	t:Hough,Barber,Irwin,Brennan,Dodd g:Barber(3)	4th(NLC-W)	1,945
23/3/03	Rochdale (a) (NLC)	L34-25	t:Stazicker,Anderson,Goddard,Brennan g:Barber(4) fg:Roden	4th(NLC-W)	1,314
30/3/03	Barrow (a) (NLC)	W16-23	t:I Marsh,Irwin,Doran g:Svabic(5) fg:Roden	4th(NLC-W)	781
6/4/03	Swinton (h) (NLC)	W68-14	t:I Marsh(2),Dodd(2),Svabic,Hough,Morgan,Roden,Anderson,McNicholas,Irwin, Brennan g:Svabic(10)	3rd(NLC-W)	1,032
13/4/03	Salford (a) (NLC)	L54-12	t:Svabic,Hough g:Svabic(2)	3rd(NLC-W)	2,162
17/4/03	Rochdale (h)	L28-33	t:Norton,Stazicker,Campbell,Doran g:Svabic(4),Barber(2)	7th	1,754
4/5/03	Dewsbury (h)	W41-21	t:Anderson(2),Morley,Molloy,Morgan,Stazicker,Barber g:Barber(6) fg:Roden	6th	1,198
10/5/03	Salford (a)	L44-12	t:Morgan,Barber g:Barber(2)	6th	1,657
18/5/03	Doncaster (a)	L52-24	t:Campbell(2),Dodd,Doran,Barber g:Barber(2)	9th	860
25/5/03	Leigh (h)	W12-10	t:Dodd g:Svabic(4)	7th	1,691
1/6/03	Hull KR (a)	L23-10	t:Farrell,Anderson g:Svabic	7th	1,300
15/6/03	Whitehaven (h)	D22-22	t:Molloy,Potter,Barber,Goddard g:Barber(3)	7th	1,096
22/6/03	Batley (a)	D20-20	t:Dodd(2),Potter,Barber g:Svabic(2)	7th	821
29/6/03	Rochdale (a)	L58-14	t:Brennan,Barber g:Barber(3)	8th	1,425
13/7/03	Featherstone (h)	W35-24	t:Doran(2),Roden(2),Cowell,Anderson g:Svabic(5) fg:Svabic	8th	1,235
20/7/03	Doncaster (h)	W31-20	t:Doran(3),Svabic,Dodd g:Svabic(5) fg:Svabic	7th	1,254
27/7/03	Dewsbury (a)	W26-32	t:Doran(2),Brennan,Morley,Dodd,Roden g:Svabic(4)	5th	1,098
3/8/03	Salford (h)	L22-32	t:Farrell,Doran,Barber,Morley g:Svabic(3)	5th	1,765
10/8/03	Leigh (a)	L38-2	g:Svabic	6th	2,287
17/8/03	Hull KR (h)	L24-29	t:Farrell,McLoughlin,Doran,Morgan g:Svabic(4)	6th	1,414
24/8/03	Whitehaven (a)	L24-20	t:Goddard(2),N Johnson,Barber g:Svabic(2)	7th	1,132
31/8/03	Batley (h)	W36-10	t:N Johnson(2),Roden(2),Svabic,Barber g:Svabic(6)	6th	1,451
7/9/03	Featherstone (a)	W14-19	t:I Marsh,Farrell,Morgan g:Svabic(2),Barber fg:Brennan	5th	1,504
14/9/03	Hull KR (a) (EPO)	L38-24	t:N Johnson,Hough,Svabic,Percival g:Svabic(4)	N/A	2,250

		APP		TRIES		GOALS		FG		PTS	
	D.O.B.	ALL	NL1	ALL	NL1	ALL	NL1	ALL	NL1	ALL	NL1
Paul Anderson	2/4/77	15(7)	7(4)	8	4	0	0	0	0	32	16
Gareth Barber	15/12/80	11(15)	6(11)	13	9	32	19	0	0	116	74
Keith Brennan	31/10/73	10(11)	8(5)	5	2	0	0	1	1	21	9
Chris Campbell	2/12/80	9	4	5	3	0	0	0	0	20	12
Jason Clegg	24/3/71	(3)	(1)	0	0	0	0	0	0	0	0
Will Cowell	31/12/79	11(1)	8(1)	1	1	0	0	0	0	4	4
Gavin Dodd	28/2/81	27(2)	16(2)	14	6	0	0	0	0	56	24
Lee Doran	23/3/81	31	19	14	11	0	0	0	0	56	44
Phil Farrell	14/2/80	25	18	8	4	0	0	0	0	32	16
Jon Goddard	21/6/82	24(1)	15(1)	6	3	0	0	0	0	24	12
Danny Guest	20/4/77	3(16)	2(12)	0	0	0	0	0	0	0	0
John Hough	14/4/76	25(2)	17	5	1	0	0	0	0	20	4
Chris Irwin	11/3/82	12	4	4	0	0	0	0	0	16	0
Gavin Johnson	18/12/80	1(4)	1(3)	0	0	0	0	0	0	0	0
Nicky Johnson	16/4/83	4	4	4	4	0	0	0	0	16	16
Iain Marsh	6/10/80	24(1)	14	4	1	0	0	0	0	16	4
Lee Marsh	5/3/83	5	5	0	0	0	0	0	0	0	0
Craig McDowell	5/11/81	4	4	0	0	0	0	0	0	0	0
Martin McLoughlin	2/8/80	5(16)	1(12)	1	1	0	0	0	0	4	4
Joe McNicholas	26/12/78	8(1)	2	2	0	0	0	0	0	8	0
Steve Molloy	11/3/69	26(3)	16(2)	2	2	0	0	0	0	8	8
Dane Morgan	30/1/79	17(8)	14(5)	6	4	0	0	0	0	24	16
Chris Morley	22/9/73	20(7)	13(3)	4	3	0	0	0	0	16	12
Anthony Murray	25/5/77	4(1)	0	1	0	0	0	0	0	4	0
Paul Norton	29/11/72	9(1)	5	1	1	0	0	0	0	4	4
Chris Percival	25/12/79	3	3	1	1	0	0	0	0	4	4
Dan Potter	8/11/78	4	4	2	2	0	0	0	0	8	8
Neil Roden	9/4/80	22(5)	12(5)	7	5	0	0	3	1	31	21
Adam Sharples	19/4/85	(1)	0	0	0	0	0	0	0	0	0
Darren Shaw	5/10/71	10(3)	8	0	0	0	0	0	0	0	0
Ryan Stazicker	28/7/79	12(6)	4(3)	4	2	0	0	0	0	16	8
Simon Svabic	18/1/80	20(10)	13(5)	5	3	81	47	2	2	184	108

Steve Molloy

LEAGUE RECORD
P18-W7-D2-L9
(5th, NL1/Elimination Play Off)
F404, A500, Diff-96
16 points.

CHALLENGE CUP
Round Four

NATIONAL LEAGUE CUP
3rd, West Division

ATTENDANCES
Best - v Salford (NLC - 2,839)
Worst - v Swinton (NLC - 1,032)
Total (NL1 & NLC only) - 22,004
Average (NL1 & NLC only) - 1,572
(Up by 422 on 2002)

ROCHDALE HORNETS

DATE	FIXTURE	RESULT	SCORERS	LGE	ATT
19/1/03	Workington (h) (NLC)	W32-8	t:Nanyn,Owen,Larder,Mayberry,Pachniuk g:Nanyn(6)	2nd(NLC-W)	778
26/1/03	Oldham St Annes (a) (CCR3) ●	W18-62	t:Smith(3),Owen(3),Ayres,Nanyn,Wood,Bunyan,Long g:Nanyn(9)	N/A	861
2/2/03	Oldham (a) (NLC)	D22-22	t:Bunyan,Long,Roper,Pachniuk g:Nanyn(3)	2nd(NLC-W)	2,050
9/2/03	Hull KR (h) (CCR4)	L20-27	t:Owen(2),Price,Nanyn g:Nanyn(2)	N/A	1,300
23/2/03	Salford (a) (NLC)	L58-16	t:Roper,Nanyn,Long g:Nanyn,Watson	4th(NLC-W)	2,346
9/3/03	Leigh (h) (NLC)	L32-34	t:Owen(3),Billy,Nanyn,Mayberry g:Watson(4)	4th(NLC-W)	1,251
16/3/03	Workington (a) (NLC)	W10-44	t:Southern(2),Larder,Leigh,Watson,Smith,Pachniuk,Nanyn g:Watson(6)	3rd(NLC-W)	336
19/3/03	Swinton (h) (NLC)	W24-14	t:Nanyn,Smith,Long,Owen g:Watson(4)	3rd(NLC-W)	727
23/3/03	Oldham (h) (NLC)	W34-25	t:Roper(2),Larder,Nanyn,Owen g:Watson(7)	3rd(NLC-W)	1,314
30/3/03	Swinton (a) (NLC)	L26-22	t:Smith,Billy,Nanyn,Roper g:Watson(3)	3rd(NLC-W)	391
6/4/03	Salford (h) (NLC)	L16-44	t:Billy(2),Bunyan g:Watson(2)	4th(NLC-W)	1,067
13/4/03	Leigh (a) (NLC)	L58-30	t:Leigh,Ball,Cooper,Roper,Wilson,Wallace g:Nanyn(3)	4th(NLC-W)	1,365
17/4/03	Oldham (a)	W28-33	t:Bunyan(2),Roper(2),Long,Larder g:Nanyn(4) fg:Watson	4th	1,754
21/4/03	Hull KR (h)	W29-18	t:Smith(2),Ball,Billy,Pachniuk g:Nanyn(4) fg:Watson	2nd	1,097
4/5/03	Doncaster (a)	W28-44	t:Roper(3),Owen,Pachniuk,Bowker,Watson,Leigh g:Nanyn(6)	2nd	805
25/5/03	Dewsbury (a)	W6-60	t:Ball(2),Pachniuk(2),Bowker,Owen,Price,Roper,Watson,Larder g:Nanyn(10)	1st	668
1/6/03	Batley (a)	W16-43	t:Smith(4),Nanyn(2),Larder,Ball g:Nanyn(5) fg:Watson	2nd	728
15/6/03	Salford (h)	L16-32	t:Smith,Nanyn,Price g:Nanyn(2)	3rd	1,571
22/6/03	Featherstone (a)	L30-16	t:Bowker,Hamilton,Nanyn g:Nanyn(2)	3rd	1,359
29/6/03	Oldham (h)	W58-14	t:Ball(2),Price(2),Smith(2),Long(2),Hamilton,Irwin g:Nanyn(9)	3rd	1,425
5/7/03	Whitehaven (h)	W43-26	t:Nanyn(2),Bowker(2),Ball,Long,Leigh,Southern g:Nanyn(5) fg:Ball	3rd	822
13/7/03	Leigh (h)	L12-19	t:Larder,Owen g:Nanyn(2)	3rd	1,331
20/7/03	Hull KR (a)	W18-33	t:Watson(2),Larder,Bowker,Nanyn,Billy g:Nanyn(4) fg:Watson	3rd	1,750
27/7/03	Doncaster (h)	W50-34	t:Larder(2),Bowker(2),Smith,Billy,Hamilton,Nanyn,Owen g:Nanyn(7)	3rd	623
3/8/03	Whitehaven (a)	W24-44	t:Nanyn(2),Irwin,Rogers,Roper,Bowker,Billy g:Watson(2)	3rd	1,282
10/8/03	Dewsbury (h)	W52-14	t:McHugh(2),Nanyn(2),Irwin(2),Larder,Pachniuk,Bunyan,Billy g:Nanyn(6)	3rd	732
17/8/03	Batley (h)	W38-32	t:Larder(2),Roper,Smith,McHugh,Leigh,Nanyn,Pachniuk g:Nanyn(3)	3rd	820
24/8/03	Salford (a)	L58-18	t:Nanyn,Billy,Smith g:Nanyn(3)	3rd	2,204
31/8/03	Featherstone (h)	W42-12	t:Southern(2),Irwin,Smith,Bowker,Watson,Nanyn g:Nanyn(7)	3rd	948
7/9/03	Leigh (a)	L68-16	t:Blake,Larder,Roper g:Nanyn(2)	3rd	2,782
14/9/03	Whitehaven (h) (EPO)	W40-38	t:Roper(2),Nanyn,Watson,Southern,Billy,Larder g:Nanyn(6)	N/A	779
21/9/03	Hull KR (h) (ESF)	L26-30	t:Bunyan,Nanyn,Larder,Calland g:Nanyn(5)	N/A	1,710

● Played at Spotland

		APP		TRIES		GOALS		FG		PTS	
	D.O.B.	ALL	NL1	ALL	NL1	ALL	NL1	ALL	NL1	ALL	NL1
Warren Ayres	11/12/78	6(8)	(5)	1	0	0	0	0	0	4	0
Damian Ball	14/7/75	28(2)	20	8	7	0	0	1	1	33	29
Marlon Billy	22/11/73	23	18	11	7	0	0	0	0	44	28
Ryan Blake	11/7/81	1(1)	1(1)	1	1	0	0	0	0	4	4
Radney Bowker	5/2/79	18	18	10	10	0	0	0	0	40	40
James Bunyan	2/11/77	29(2)	18(1)	7	4	0	0	0	0	28	16
Matt Calland	20/8/71	1(3)	1(3)	1	1	0	0	0	0	4	4
Sean Cooper	29/12/70	7(1)	(1)	1	0	0	0	0	0	4	0
Stephen Doherty	8/3/78	4(2)	0	0	0	0	0	0	0	0	0
Andy Grundy	19/1/77	9(10)	3(5)	0	0	0	0	0	0	0	0
John Hamilton	18/10/79	(8)	(8)	3	3	0	0	0	0	12	12
Chris Irwin	11/3/82	8(6)	8(6)	5	5	0	0	0	0	20	20
David Larder	5/6/76	29(1)	20	16	13	0	0	0	0	64	52
Matthew Leigh	24/2/78	8(17)	2(16)	5	3	0	0	0	0	20	12
Matthew Long	24/5/74	(28)	(17)	8	4	0	0	0	0	32	16
Casey Mayberry	19/12/81	10	0	2	0	0	0	0	0	8	0
Wayne McHugh	1/2/80	3(1)	2(1)	3	3	0	0	0	0	12	12
Mick Nanyn	3/6/82	28(4)	20	26	17	123	99	0	0	350	266
Paul Owen	15/8/78	22	12	15	4	0	0	0	0	60	16
Richard Pachniuk	24/3/71	31	20	9	6	0	0	0	0	36	24
Gareth Price	28/6/80	17(15)	15(5)	5	4	0	0	0	0	20	16
Wes Rogers	3/11/77	1(7)	(6)	1	1	0	0	0	0	4	4
Jon Roper	5/5/76	30	20	17	11	0	0	0	0	68	44
Paul Smith	17/5/77	31	20	19	13	0	0	0	0	76	52
Paul Southern	18/3/76	27(2)	20	6	4	0	0	0	0	24	16
David Stephenson	6/10/72	11(3)	2(3)	0	0	0	0	0	0	0	0
Andy Wallace	1/12/81	1(2)	0	1	0	0	0	0	0	4	0
Ian Watson	27/10/76	32	20	7	6	27	0	6	6	88	30
Lee Wilson	31/12/79	1	0	1	0	0	0	0	0	4	0
Danny Wood	8/10/77	(2)	0	1	0	0	0	0	0	4	0

Paul Smith

LEAGUE RECORD
P18-W13-D0-L5
(3rd, NL1/Elimination Semi Finalists)
F647, A477, Diff+170
26 points.

CHALLENGE CUP
Round Four

NATIONAL LEAGUE CUP
4th, West Division

ATTENDANCES
Best - v Hull KR (ESF - 1,710)
Worst - v Doncaster (NL1 - 623)
Total (NL1, inc play-offs,
& NLC only) - 16,995
Average (NL1, inc play-offs,
& NLC only) - 1,062
(Down by 127 on 2002)

SALFORD CITY REDS

DATE	FIXTURE	RESULT	SCORERS	LGE	ATT
19/1/03	Swinton (h) (NLC)	W58-6	t:Hunte(2),Flowers(2),Blakeley,Baldwin,Coley,Clinch,Marsh,Beverley,Littler g:Clinch(3),Blakeley(2),Marsh(2)	1st(NLC-W)	3,334
26/1/03	Toulouse (h) (CCR3)	W26-10	t:Flowers(2),Hunte,Littler,Beverley g:Clinch(2),Marsh	N/A	1,590
9/2/03	Barrow (a) (CCR4)	W6-22	t:Littler,Alker,Bowker,Baldwin g:Clinch(3)	N/A	1,392
16/2/03	Leigh (a) (NLC)	D20-20	t:Littler(2),Baynes,Hunte g:Marsh(2)	2nd(NLC-W)	4,445
23/2/03	Rochdale (h) (NLC)	W58-16	t:Beverley(2),Kirk(2),Flowers(2),Alker(2),Coley,D Highton,Clinch g:Marsh(5),Clinch(2)	2nd(NLC-W)	2,346
28/2/03	Hull KR (a) (CCR5)	W2-12	t:Hunte,Littler g:Clinch(2)	N/A	2,533
9/3/03	Oldham (a) (NLC)	W4-62	t:Charles(3),Alker(2),Littler(2),Beverley,Flowers,D Highton,Kirk g:Clinch(5),Blakeley(4)	2nd(NLC-W)	2,839
16/3/03	St Helens (h) (CCQF)	L6-54	t:Hunte g:Charles	N/A	5,717
19/3/03	Gateshead (a) (NLC)	W8-90	t:Alker(2),Blakeley(2),Lowe(2),Hunte(2),Beverley(2),Arnold(2),Kirk,Charles, D Highton,Marsh g:Blakeley(13)	2nd(NLC-W)	172
23/3/03	Gateshead (h) (NLC)	W100-12	t:Fitzpatrick(3),Beverley(2),Hunte(2),Flowers(2),Littler(2),Lowe,P Highton,Alker, Bowker,Kirk,Clough,Marsh g:Blakeley(14)	2nd(NLC-W)	1,653
30/3/03	Leigh (h) (NLC)	W22-10	t:Beverley(2),Platt,Kirk,Hunte g:Blakeley	1st(NLC-W)	3,099
2/4/03	Swinton (a) (NLC)	W0-72	t:Alker(4),Beverley(3),Kirk(2),Platt,Flowers,D Highton,Fitzpatrick g:Blakeley(10)	1st(NLC-W)	954
6/4/03	Rochdale (a) (NLC)	W16-44	t:Hunte(2),Clinch(2),Blakeley,Charles,D Highton,Kirk g:Blakeley(6)	1st(NLC-W)	1,067
13/4/03	Oldham (h) (NLC)	W54-12	t:Beverley(2),Hunte,Baldwin,Kirk,Arnold,Marsh,Coley,D Highton,Haggerty g:Marsh(7)	1st(NLC-W)	2,162
18/4/03	Whitehaven (a)	D22-22	t:Platt(2),Lowe,Littler g:Marsh(2),Charles	5th	2,136
21/4/03	Batley (h)	W54-12	t:Beverley(3),Charles(3),Kirk(2),Littler,Hunte g:Charles(7)	3rd	2,074
4/5/03	Featherstone (a)	L18-16	t:Arnold,Alker,Beverley g:Charles,Blakeley	4th	1,616
10/5/03	Oldham (h)	W44-12	t:Hunte(3),Alker(2),Marsh,Lowe,Baldwin g:Charles(5),Blakeley	3rd	1,657
18/5/03	Barrow (a) (NLCQF)	W20-40	t:Beverley(2),Littler,Charles,Lowe,Baldwin,Kirk g:Charles(6)	N/A	936
25/5/03	Doncaster (a)	W24-34	t:Kirk(2),Littler,Baldwin,Clinch,Coley g:Charles(3),Blakeley(2)	3rd	1,069
1/6/03	Dewsbury (h)	W76-4	t:Hunte(5),Beverley(3),Coley(2),Alker(2),Berne,Flowers g:Charles(10)	3rd	1,698
8/6/03	Batley (h) (NLCSF)	W68-6	t:Coley(3),Littler(2),Alker,Baldwin,Berne,Beverley,Bowker,P Highton,Hunte g:Charles(7),Blakeley(3)	N/A	1,379
15/6/03	Rochdale (a)	W16-32	t:Beverley(2),D Highton,Arnold,Littler g:Charles(3),Blakeley(3)	2nd	1,571
22/6/03	Leigh (a)	W12-32	t:Beverley,Clinch,Hunte,Arnold,Flowers g:Charles(4),Blakeley(2)	1st	4,000
29/6/03	Whitehaven (h)	D26-26	t:Kirk(2),Beverley,Arnold,Littler g:Charles(2),Blakeley	1st	2,056
6/7/03	Leigh (NLCF) ●	W19-36	t:Haggerty,Coley,Littler,Kirk,Arnold,Hunte g:Blakeley(5),Charles	N/A	6,486
13/7/03	Hull KR (h)	W24-12	t:Littler(2),Alker,Beverley,Hunte g:Charles(2)	1st	2,063
20/7/03	Batley (a)	W16-54	t:Kirk(2),Baynes,Arnold,Flowers,Beverley,Charles,Baldwin,P Highton g:Blakeley(7),Charles(2)	1st	835
27/7/03	Featherstone (h)	W36-20	t:Baynes,Kirk,Coley,Flowers,Littler,Alker g:Charles(5),Clinch	1st	2,025
3/8/03	Oldham (a)	W22-32	t:Baldwin,Hunte,Coley,Beverley,Alker,Littler g:Charles(4)	1st	1,765
10/8/03	Doncaster (h)	W72-0	t:Flowers(2),Kirk(2),D Highton(2),Haggerty,P Highton,Littler,Clinch,Lowe, Beverley,Coley g:Blakeley(10)	1st	1,620
17/8/03	Dewsbury (a)	W18-58	t:Clinch(2),D Highton,Baldwin,Flowers,P Highton,Beverley,Blakeley,Baynes,Coley g:Charles(5),Blakeley(3),Hunte	1st	972
24/8/03	Rochdale (h)	W58-18	t:Clinch(3),Littler(2),Davies(2),Hunte,Baldwin,Beverley g:Charles(6),Blakeley(3)	1st	2,204
31/8/03	Leigh (h)	W46-24	t:Littler(2),Baldwin,P Highton,Beverley,Alker,Hunte,Kirk g:Blakeley(6),Hunte	1st	4,121
7/9/03	Hull KR (a)	L18-16	t:Davies,Beverley,Baldwin g:Clinch(2)	1st	2,060
21/9/03	Leigh (h) (QSF)	W26-18	t:Littler,Baldwin,Arnold,Moana g:Charles(5)	N/A	3,660
5/10/03	Leigh (GF) ●●	W14-31	t:Hunte(2),Beverley,Littler g:Charles(6),Blakeley fg:Blakeley	N/A	9,186

● Played at Spotland, Rochdale
●● Played at Halton Stadium, Widnes

	D.O.B.	APP		TRIES		GOALS		FG		PTS	
		ALL	NL1	ALL	NL1	ALL	NL1	ALL	NL1	ALL	NL1
Malcolm Alker	4/11/78	35(2)	18(2)	22	9	0	0	0	0	88	36
Danny Arnold	15/4/77	28	15	10	6	0	0	0	0	40	24
Simon Baldwin	31/3/75	36	20	14	9	0	0	0	0	56	36
Danny Barton	7/9/83	(2)		0		0	0	0	0	0	0
Neil Baynes	14/9/77	28(5)	18	4	3	0	0	0	0	16	12
Mick Berne	5/10/81	4(2)	3(2)	2	1	0	0	0	0	8	4
Cliff Beverley	25/3/77	37	20	39	20	0	0	0	0	156	80
Steve Blakeley	26/10/72	9(19)	4(13)	5	1	98	40	1	1	217	85
Radney Bowker	5/2/79	4(2)		3	0	0	0	0	0	12	0
Chris Charles	7/3/76	30(2)	16(1)	10	4	86	71	0	0	212	158
Gavin Clinch	13/9/74	34	19	12	8	20	3	0	0	88	38
John Clough	13/9/84	(1)	0	1	0	0	0	0	0	4	0
Andy Coley	7/7/78	30(6)	17(3)	14	7	0	0	0	0	56	28
Wes Davies	20/1/78	10	10	3	3	0	0	0	0	12	12
Karl Fitzpatrick	13/9/80	1(5)	(2)	4	0	0	0	0	0	16	0
Jason Flowers	30/1/75	34	19	17	7	0	0	0	0	68	28
Andy Gorski	31/3/81	(9)	(3)	0	0	0	0	0	0	0	0
Gareth Haggerty	8/9/81	3(22)	1(14)	3	1	0	0	0	0	12	4
David Highton	31/1/80	4(32)	3(17)	10	4	0	0	0	0	40	16
Paul Highton	10/11/76	26(11)	16(4)	6	4	0	0	0	0	24	16
Alan Hunte	11/7/70	28(3)	14(3)	32	16	2	2	0	0	132	68
Andy Kirk	2/8/82	25(2)	15(2)	24	12	0	0	0	0	96	48
Stuart Littler	19/2/79	34	19	30	16	0	0	0	0	120	64
Neil Lowe	20/12/78	18(8)	5(6)	7	3	0	0	0	0	28	12
Lee Marsh	5/3/83	9(6)	3(1)	5	1	19	2	0	0	58	8
Martin Moana	13/8/73	1(7)	1(7)	1	1	0	0	0	0	4	4
Michael Platt	23/3/84	13	4	4	2	0	0	0	0	16	8

Cliff Beverley

LEAGUE RECORD
P18-W14-D2-L2
(1st, NL1/Grand Final Winners,
Champions)
F732, A294, Diff+438
30 points.

CHALLENGE CUP
Quarter Finalists

NATIONAL LEAGUE CUP
Winners/1st, West Division

ATTENDANCES
Best - v St Helens (CC - 5,717)
Worst - v Batley (NLCSF - 1,379)
Total (NL1, inc play-offs,
& NLC, inc SF, only) - 37,151
Average (NL1, inc play-offs,
& NLC, inc SF, only) - 2,322
(Down by 1,877 on 2002, SL)

WHITEHAVEN

DATE	FIXTURE	RESULT	SCORERS	LGE	ATT
19/1/03	Gateshead (h) (NLC)	W42-6	t:Jackson(2),Morton,Broadbent,Lester,L Smith,Lebbon g:Holt(7)	1st(NLC-N)	1,342
26/1/03	Cottingham (h) (CCR3)	W66-6	t:Seeds(3),Hill(3),Holt,McKinney,L Smith,Sherwen,Miller,Fatialofa,Kiddie g:Holt(5),O'Neil(2)	N/A	1,001
2/2/03	Chorley (a) (NLC)	W2-28	t:Kiddie(2),Miller,Seeds,O'Neil g:Holt(4)	1st(NLC-N)	383
9/2/03	Leeds (a) (CCR4)	L46-6	t:Morton g:Holt	N/A	7,535
23/2/03	Barrow (a) (NLC)	W18-30	t:Joe(2),O'Neil,Seeds,Morton g:Holt(5)	1st(NLC-N)	1,436
2/3/03	Workington (h) (NLC)	W36-14	t:Lester(2),Hill,Kiddie,Morton,Cunningham,O'Neil g:O'Neil(4)	1st(NLC-N)	1,479
9/3/03	Swinton (h) (NLC)	W38-6	t:Joe(4),Stenhouse,Holt,Lester g:Holt(5)	1st(NLC-N)	1,060
16/3/03	Gateshead (a) (NLC)	W20-34	t:O'Neil(2),Hill(2),Joe,Vaughan g:Holt(5)	1st(NLC-N)	272
23/3/03	Chorley (h) (NLC)	W28-20	t:Joe(2),Holt,O'Neil,McKinney g:Holt(4)	1st(NLC-N)	1,007
30/3/03	Workington (a) (NLC)	W10-39	t:Morton(2),Wallace,Stenhouse,Chambers,McKinney g:Holt(7) fg:Holt	1st(NLC-N)	1,004
4/4/03	Barrow (h) (NLC)	W44-14	t:Wallace(2),Seeds(2),McKinney,Kiddie,Joe,Lester g:Seeds(2),Jackson(2),Holt,Wood	1st(NLC-N)	1,047
13/4/03	Swinton (a) (NLC)	D22-22	t:Joe(3),Wood g:Holt(2),Wood	1st(NLC-N)	339
18/4/03	Salford (h)	D22-22	t:Chambers(2),Seeds,Wood g:Holt(3)	6th	2,136
21/4/03	Leigh (a)	L19-12	t:Stenhouse(2) g:Holt(2)	7th	1,996
4/5/03	Hull KR (h)	W26-2	t:Wallace(2),Joe,Wood,Jackson g:Holt(3)	5th	1,315
18/5/03	Dewsbury (h) (NLCQF)	W54-10	t:Hutton(2),Hill(2),Joe,Jackson,Lester,Fatialofa,Wood g:Holt(9)	N/A	1,503
25/5/03	Batley (h)	W31-12	t:Joe,Hill,Wood,Jackson,Campbell g:Holt(5) fg:Joe	5th	1,444
1/6/03	Featherstone (h)	W46-6	t:Joe(3),Seeds(2),Hill(2),Campbell g:Holt(7)	4th	1,698
8/6/03	Leigh (a) (NLCSF)	L39-18	t:Whitehead,Morton,Broadbent g:Holt(3)	N/A	2,687
15/6/03	Oldham (a)	D22-22	t:Fatialofa,Wood,Lester,Wallace g:Holt(3)	4th	1,096
22/6/03	Doncaster (h)	L18-24	t:Lester,Hill g:Holt(5)	5th	1,461
29/6/03	Salford (a)	D26-26	t:Miller,Whitehead,Joe,Frazer g:Holt(5)	5th	2,056
5/7/03	Rochdale (a)	L43-26	t:Seeds(2),Broadbent,Joe,Miller g:Holt(3)	5th	822
13/7/03	Dewsbury (a)	D18-18	t:Walsh(3),Morton g:Holt	4th	777
20/7/03	Leigh (h)	L8-20	t:Hill g:Holt(2)	5th	1,750
27/7/03	Hull KR (a)	L36-10	t:Wood,Joe g:Kirkbride	6th	1,612
3/8/03	Rochdale (h)	L24-44	t:O'Neil(2),Broadbent,Lester g:Kirkbride(4)	6th	1,282
10/8/03	Batley (a)	L26-16	t:Joe,Kirkbride,O'Neil g:Kirkbride(2)	7th	604
17/8/03	Featherstone (a)	L52-12	t:Morton(2) g:Kirkbride(2)	7th	1,116
24/8/03	Oldham (h)	W24-20	t:O'Neil(2),Lester,Seeds g:Kirkbride(4)	6th	1,132
31/8/03	Doncaster (a)	D34-34	t:Seeds(2),Lebbon,Wood,Hill,Chambers g:Kirkbride(5)	7th	677
7/9/03	Dewsbury (h)	W68-12	t:Lester(3),Seeds(2),Hill(2),Cunningham,Joe,Chambers,Broadbent,G Smith g:Kirkbride(10)	6th	1,234
14/9/03	Rochdale (a) (EPO)	L40-38	t:Joe(2),Broadbent,Wood,Sice,Lester g:Kirkbride(7)	N/A	779

		APP		TRIES		GOALS		FG		PTS	
	D.O.B.	ALL	NL1	ALL	NL1	ALL	NL1	ALL	NL1	ALL	NL1
Gary Broadbent	31/10/76	30	18	6	4	0	0	0	0	24	16
Dean Burgess	11/10/84	(1)	0	0	0	0	0	0	0	0	0
Ryan Campbell	23/9/81	(11)	(7)	2	2	0	0	0	0	8	8
Craig Chambers	25/4/73	11	6	5	4	0	0	0	0	20	16
Tony Cunningham	4/7/74	(16)	(12)	2	1	0	0	0	0	8	4
David Fatialofa	11/6/74	27(4)	19	3	1	0	0	0	0	12	4
Neil Frazer	7/3/76	6	6	1	1	0	0	0	0	4	4
Howard Hill	16/1/75	32	19	16	8	0	0	0	0	64	32
Darren Holt	21/9/76	23(2)	11	3	3	97	39	1	0	207	78
Glen Hutton	17/8/74	5	2	2	0	0	0	0	0	8	0
Marc Jackson	21/8/79	6(17)	5(7)	5	2	2	0	0	0	24	8
Leroy Joe	31/12/74	29(1)	17	26	12	0	0	1	1	105	49
Lee Kiddie	2/1/75	6(19)	2(9)	5	0	0	0	0	0	20	0
Darren King	9/3/82	1	0	0	0	0	0	0	0	0	0
Steve Kirkbride	10/1/81	8(3)	8(3)	1	1	35	35	0	0	74	74
John Lebbon	30/12/84	4	3	2	1	0	0	0	0	8	4
Aaron Lester	16/5/73	31	19	14	8	0	0	0	0	56	32
Danny Lockhart	16/6/82	1	1	0	0	0	0	0	0	0	0
Chris McKinney	12/11/76	23(1)	12(1)	4	0	0	0	0	0	16	0
Spencer Miller	27/2/80	17(9)	9(7)	4	2	0	0	0	0	16	8
Graeme Morton	15/1/73	18(2)	9(1)	10	3	0	0	0	0	40	12
Paul O'Neil	23/11/79	13	5	11	5	6	0	0	0	56	20
Garry Purdham	20/10/78	19	14	0	0	0	0	0	0	0	0
David Seeds	23/6/74	25	14	17	10	2	0	0	0	72	40
Phil Sherwen	4/11/78	3(2)	(1)	1	0	0	0	0	0	4	0
Carl Sice	13/4/80	(10)	(9)	1	1	0	0	0	0	4	4
Gary Smith	29/3/82	4(10)	(7)	1	1	0	0	0	0	4	4
Leigh Smith	1/9/75	3(2)	0	2	0	0	0	0	0	8	0
Jamie Stenhouse	9/10/80	10(1)	1	4	2	0	0	0	0	16	8
Matt Sturm	13/12/72	2	2	0	0	0	0	0	0	0	0
Dean Vaughan	9/2/78	18(5)	8(4)	1	0	0	0	0	0	4	0
Mark Wallace	21/2/78	12	7	6	3	0	0	0	0	24	12
Craig Walsh	19/9/78	3(2)	3(2)	3	3	0	0	0	0	12	12
Mike Whitehead	25/8/78	8(10)	3(6)	2	1	0	0	0	0	8	4
Wesley Wilson	30/5/77	6	6	0	0	0	0	0	0	0	0
Steven Wood	28/1/77	24(4)	18	9	7	2	0	0	0	40	28

Leroy Joe

LEAGUE RECORD
P18-W5-D5-L8
(6th, NL1/Elimination Play Off)
F443, A438, Diff+5
15 points.

CHALLENGE CUP
Round Four

NATIONAL LEAGUE CUP
Semi Finalists/1st, North Division

ATTENDANCES
Best - v Salford (NL1 - 2,136)
Worst - v Cottingham (CC - 1,001)
Total (NL1 & NLC, inc QF, only) - 20,890
Average (NL1 & NLC, inc QF, only) - 1,393
(Up by 164 on 2002)

NATIONAL LEAGUE TWO 2003
Club by Club

BARROW RAIDERS

DATE	FIXTURE	RESULT	SCORERS	LGE	ATT
19/1/03	Chorley (h) (NLC)	D18-18	t:P Jones,Henderson,Marshall g:Atkinson(3)	2nd(NLC-N)	817
26/1/03	Embassy (h) (CCR3)	W70-6	t:Gardner(3),P Jones(2),Bower,Archer,Stainton,Pate,Marshall,Irabor,Pugh g:Atkinson(4),Pate(4),Pugh(2),Evans	N/A	617
2/2/03	Workington (a) (NLC)	W10-20	t:Henderson,Marshall,W Jones g:Atkinson(4)	2nd(NLC-N)	578
9/2/03	Salford (h) (CCR4)	L6-22	t:Marshall g:Atkinson	N/A	1,392
23/2/03	Whitehaven (h) (NLC)	L18-30	t:Marshall(3) g:Evans(3)	2nd(NLC-N)	1,436
2/3/03	Oldham (a) (NLC)	L50-11	t:Marshall,McClure g:Evans fg:Evans	3rd(NLC-N)	1,280
9/3/03	Gateshead (a) (NLC)	W24-28	t:Evans,Pate,Irabor,King,Marshall g:Evans(3),Atkinson	3rd(NLC-N)	232
16/3/03	Chorley (a) (NLC)	W22-28	t:McClure,Atkinson,Clark,Evans,Irabor g:Atkinson(4)	2nd(NLC-N)	258
23/3/03	Workington (h) (NLC)	W44-18	t:Bower(2),Marshall,Henderson,Evans,P Jones,McClure g:Evans(8)	2nd(NLC-N)	788
30/3/03	Oldham (h) (NLC)	L16-23	t:Marshall(2),P Jones g:Evans(2)	2nd(NLC-N)	781
4/4/03	Whitehaven (a) (NLC)	L44-14	t:Bower,Marshall g:Evans(3)	3rd(NLC-N)	1,047
13/4/03	Gateshead (h) (NLC)	W34-24	t:Marshall(2),Dancer,W Jones,Bower,Lockhart g:Evans(4),Atkinson	2nd(NLC-N)	557
18/4/03	Workington (h)	W32-16	t:McClure(2),Lupton,Pugh,P Jones,Marshall g:Manihera(2),Atkinson fg:Manihera,Marshall	4th	953
21/4/03	Gateshead (a)	W22-30	t:P Jones(2),Jackson,Gardner,Atkinson g:Manihera(5)	3rd	316
4/5/03	Sheffield (h)	L12-30	t:P Jones,Marshall g:Manihera(2)	4th	911
11/5/03	London Skolars (a)	W10-41	t:King(2),P Jones,Marshall,Henderson g:Manihera(10) fg:Manihera	3rd	464
18/5/03	Salford (h) (NLCQF)	L20-40	t:Luxon,P Jones,Pate,Marshall g:Manihera(2)	N/A	936
25/5/03	York (h)	L20-27	t:Archer,Smith,King g:Manihera(4)	4th	742
1/6/03	Keighley (a)	L28-15	t:Smith(2) g:Manihera(3) fg:Manihera	4th	1,106
15/6/03	Swinton (h)	W42-20	t:Manihera(2),Smith,Archer,Henderson,Lupton,King,Liku g:Manihera(5)	5th	574
22/6/03	Chorley (h)	W22-16	t:P Jones,Henderson,Bower,Marshall g:Manihera(3)	4th	687
29/6/03	Hunslet (a)	W17-18	t:Smith,Marshall,Bower g:Manihera(3)	3rd	422
13/7/03	London Skolars (h)	W54-12	t:P Jones(3),Irabor(2),Bower,Smith,Marshall,Atkinson,Lupton g:Manihera(7)	2nd	681
20/7/03	Sheffield (a)	L43-42	t:Manihera(2),Marshall,P Jones,King,Irabor,Henderson g:Manihera(7)	5th	1,037
27/7/03	Gateshead (h)	W48-16	t:Smith(2),Irabor(2),Bower(2),Henderson,Atkinson,P Jones,Pate g:Manihera(4)	4th	660
3/8/03	Workington (a)	W20-24	t:Manihera,King,Henderson,McClure,Marshall g:Manihera(2)	3rd	534
10/8/03	York (a)	L28-16	t:Smith,Pate g:Pate(4)	4th	1,063
17/8/03	Keighley (h)	L16-18	t:Marshall,Smith g:Atkinson(3),Pate	5th	826
24/8/03	Chorley (a)	L52-24	t:McClure,Smith,King,Dancer g:Pate(4)	6th	424
31/8/03	Hunslet (h)	W52-10	t:Pate(2),McClure(2),Atkinson(2),Smith,King,Clark,Bower g:Pate(6)	6th	763
7/9/03	Swinton (a)	W34-38	t:Lupton,Liku,McClure,Archer,Wilcock,W Jones g:Pate(7)	5th	455
14/9/03	York (a) (EPO)	W30-50	t:P Jones(2),Pate(2),Henderson,Marshall,Bower,Clark g:Pate(9)	N/A	1,299
21/9/03	Keighley (a) (ESF)	L35-26	t:Pate(2),Bower,King,P Jones g:Pate(3)	N/A	1,332

Jamie Marshall

			APP		TRIES		GOALS		FG		PTS	
	D.O.B.	ALL	NL2	ALL	NL2	ALL	NL2	ALL	NL2	ALL	NL2	
Chris Archer	18/9/83	23(3)	12(3)	4	3	0	0	0	0	16	12	
Phil Atkinson	25/9/74	29(1)	19(1)	6	5	22	4	0	0	68	28	
Craig Bower	1/5/80	26(1)	14(1)	13	8	0	0	0	0	52	32	
Dave Byrne	27/12/82	1		0	0	0	0	0	0	0	0	
Dave Clark	6/4/71	9(2)	6(1)	3	2	0	0	0	0	12	8	
Stuart Dancer	9/10/74	6(22)	3(16)	2	1	0	0	0	0	8	4	
Paul Dean	3/2/68	(3)	0	0	0	0	0	0	0	0	0	
Ian Devlin	20/4/73	(5)	(5)	0	0	0	0	0	0	0	0	
Paul Evans	21/4/79	12(4)	2(3)	3	0	25	0	1	0	63	0	
Paul Gardner	22/11/77	5(4)	1(2)	4	1	0	0	0	0	16	4	
Andy Henderson	17/6/79	33	20	10	7	0	0	0	0	40	28	
Anthony Horton	11/9/79	1(1)	0	0	0	0	0	0	0	0	0	
Shane Irabor	14/1/82	23	12	8	5	0	0	0	0	32	20	
Steve Jackson	2/1/81	23(2)	11(2)	1	1	0	0	0	0	4	4	
Paul Jones	1/2/79	25	16	20	14	0	0	0	0	80	56	
Wayne Jones	20/10/74	7(18)	2(11)	3	1	0	0	0	0	12	4	
James King	12/12/80	28(1)	19(1)	10	9	0	0	0	0	40	36	
Tau Liku	21/2/71	27(1)	20	2	2	0	0	0	0	8	8	
Danny Lockhart	16/6/82	9(1)	5	1	0	0	0	0	0	4	0	
Paul Lupton	12/2/81	24(3)	15(2)	4	4	0	0	0	0	16	16	
Geoff Luxon	2/6/71	5(19)	3(12)	1	0	0	0	0	0	4	0	
Tane Manihera	6/8/74	18	16	5	5	59	57	3	3	141	137	
Jamie Marshall	17/7/78	32	19	26	10	0	0	1	1	105	41	
Andy McClure	30/9/77	25(7)	13(6)	10	7	0	0	0	0	40	28	
Adam Pate	19/8/83	13(10)	9(3)	11	8	38	34	0	0	120	100	
Barry Pugh	17/10/84	2(6)	2(2)	2	1	2	0	0	0	12	4	
Paul Salmon	6/3/81	3	3	0	0	0	0	0	0	0	0	
Jamie Smith	2/10/76	17	16	12	12	0	0	0	0	48	48	
James Stainton	28/4/81	1(14)	(6)	1	0	0	0	0	0	4	0	
Paul Wilcock	9/12/79	2(3)	2(3)	1	1	0	0	0	0	4	4	

LEAGUE RECORD
P18-W11-D0-L7
(5th, NL2/Elimination Semi Finalists)
F546, A419, Diff+127
22 points.

CHALLENGE CUP
Round Four

NATIONAL LEAGUE CUP
Quarter Finalists/2nd, North Division

ATTENDANCES
Best - v Whitehaven (NLC - 1,436)
Worst - v Gateshead (NLC - 557)
Total (NL2 & NLC, inc QF, only) - 12,112
Average (NL2 & NLC, inc QF, only) - 807
(Down by 121 on 2002)

CHORLEY LYNX

DATE	FIXTURE	RESULT	SCORERS	LGE	ATT
19/1/03	Barrow (a) (NLC)	D18-18	t:McCully,Garcia,Briggs g:Braddish(3)	2nd(NLC-N)	817
24/1/03	Leigh Miners Rangers (h) (CCR3)	W36-14	t:Redford(2),Ramsdale,Whittle,Street,Garcia,McConnell g:Braddish(4)	N/A	809
2/2/03	Whitehaven (h) (NLC)	L2-28	g:Braddish	3rd(NLC-N)	383
9/2/03	Swinton (h) (CCR4)	L16-32	t:Coates(2),Whittle g:Coates(2)	N/A	572
16/2/03	Gateshead (a) (NLC)	W18-24	t:Redford(2),McConnell,Kilgannon g:Braddish(4)	3rd(NLC-N)	308
23/2/03	Leigh (a) (NLC)	L38-20	t:Smith,Street,Briggs,Miller g:Braddish(2)	3rd(NLC-N)	1,871
9/3/03	Workington (h) (NLC)	W22-16	t:Ingram,Whittle,Briggs,Bretherton g:Braddish(3)	2nd(NLC-N)	251
16/3/03	Barrow (h) (NLC)	L22-28	t:McConnell,Bloor,Briggs,Hodson g:Braddish(2),McCully	3rd(NLC-N)	258
23/3/03	Whitehaven (a) (NLC)	L28-20	t:Redford,McConnell,Bretherton g:McCully(4)	3rd(NLC-N)	1,007
30/3/03	Gateshead (h) (NLC)	W54-24	t:Gambles(3),Braddish(2),Kilgannon(2),G Johnson,Garcia,Patel g:McCully(7)	3rd(NLC-N)	213
6/4/03	Leigh (h) (NLC)	W31-22	t:Gambles(3),Briggs,McCully g:McCully(5) fg:Braddish	2nd(NLC-N)	736
13/4/03	Workington (a) (NLC)	L24-22	t:Hodson,Patel,Gambles,Garcia g:McCully(2),Braddish	3rd(NLC-N)	355
18/4/03	Swinton (a)	L31-12	t:Briggs,Gambles g:McCully(2)	9th	446
21/4/03	Hunslet (h)	L18-24	t:Garcia(2),Rowley g:McCully(3)	9th	404
4/5/03	Keighley (h)	L22-23	t:McCully,Gambles,Garcia g:McCully(4) fg:Braddish(2)	10th	501
11/5/03	Workington (a)	W10-28	t:Redford,Stenhouse,Coates,Andrews g:McCully(5) fg:Braddish,Coates	7th	545
25/5/03	Gateshead (h)	W33-18	t:Andrews(2),Parker,Garcia,Stenhouse,Coates g:McCully(4) fg:Coates	6th	280
1/6/03	Sheffield (a)	W16-19	t:Garcia(2),Andrews(2) g:Dean fg:Dean	5th	747
15/6/03	London Skolars (h)	W64-8	t:Coates(2),Garcia,Newall,Hodson,Whittle,Andrews,Gambles,Ingram, McCully,Rowley g:McCully(10)	4th	252
22/6/03	Barrow (a)	L22-16	t:Andrews,Smith,Dean g:McCully(2)	6th	687
29/6/03	York (h)	W29-14	t:Andrews(2),McCully,McConnell,Stenhouse,Garcia g:McCully(2) fg:Dean	5th	450
13/7/03	Workington (h)	W56-18	t:McConnell,Hodson,McCully,Newall,Redford,Coates,Wingfield,Andrews, Ingram,Garcia g:McCully(8)	5th	302
20/7/03	Keighley (a)	W20-23	t:Andrews(2),Stenhouse g:McCully(5) fg:Coates	4th	1,028
27/7/03	Hunslet (a)	W36-49	t:Newall(2),McConnell(2),Andrews,McCully,Garcia,Hodson g:McCully(8) fg:Coates	3rd	475
3/8/03	Swinton (h)	W41-22	t:Campbell(2),Andrews(2),Coates,Briggs,Smith g:McCully(6) fg:Coates	2nd	465
10/8/03	Gateshead (a)	W14-22	t:Andrews(2),Hodson,Campbell g:McCully(3)	2nd	181
17/8/03	Sheffield (h)	W30-14	t:Campbell,Andrews,Hodson,Coates,McConnell g:McCully(4) fg:McConnell,Dean	1st	502
24/8/03	Barrow (h)	W52-24	t:Garcia(2),Newall(2),Andrews(2),Dean(2),Redford g:McCully(8)	1st	424
31/8/03	York (a)	L36-32	t:Briggs(2),Dean,Stenhouse,Newall,Andrews g:McCully(4)	2nd	1,077
7/9/03	London Skolars (a)	W12-38	t:Blackwood(2),Stenhouse(2),Andrews,Smith,Newall g:McCully(5)	2nd	257
21/9/03	Sheffield (a) (QSF)	L31-14	t:Braddish,Redford g:McCully(3)	N/A	732
28/9/03	Keighley (h) (FE)	L12-45	t:McCully(2) g:McCully(2)	N/A	1,085

		APP		TRIES		GOALS		FG		PTS	
	D.O.B.	ALL	NL2	ALL	NL2	ALL	NL2	ALL	NL2	ALL	NL2
Eric Andrews	11/2/82	20	20	22	22	0	0	0	0	88	88
Paul Bamber	25/12/81	(1)	(1)	0	0	0	0	0	0	0	0
Anthony Blackwood	13/9/82	6(4)	6(4)	2	2	0	0	0	0	8	8
Wayne Bloor	4/11/73	11	0	1	0	0	0	0	0	4	0
John Braddish	25/1/81	18(9)	8(8)	3	1	20	0	4	3	56	7
Liam Bretherton	20/6/79	7(1)	3	2	0	0	0	0	0	8	0
Mike Briggs	6/10/79	17(9)	8(7)	9	4	0	0	0	0	36	16
Dave Byrne	27/12/82	2(2)	(1)	0	0	0	0	0	0	0	0
Chris Campbell	2/12/80	9	9	4	4	0	0	0	0	16	16
Mick Coates	8/3/80	21(4)	16(3)	9	7	2	0	5	5	45	33
Craig Dean	20/10/76	12(2)	12(2)	4	4	1	1	3	3	21	21
Martin Gambles	8/3/80	8(3)	2(2)	10	3	0	0	0	0	40	12
Anton Garcia	7/9/79	32	20	16	12	0	0	0	0	64	48
Ian Hodson	23/10/81	30(1)	19	7	5	0	0	0	0	28	20
David Ingram	4/1/75	11(3)	5(3)	3	2	0	0	0	0	12	8
Gavin Johnson	18/12/80	7(2)	3(1)	1	0	0	0	0	0	4	0
Jason Johnson	12/11/78	2(1)	2(1)	0	0	0	0	0	0	0	0
Liam Jones	13/11/79	3	0	0	0	0	0	0	0	0	0
Eddie Kilgannon	4/12/77	11(10)	2(7)	3	0	0	0	0	0	12	0
Dave McConnell	25/3/81	26	14	9	5	0	0	1	1	37	21
Mark McCully	24/10/79	27	20	9	7	107	88	0	0	250	204
Marlon Miller	28/10/78	5	0	1	0	0	0	0	0	4	0
Chris Newall	30/11/76	13(2)	13(2)	8	8	0	0	0	0	32	32
Dave Newton	22/12/81	(4)	0	0	0	0	0	0	0	0	0
Ian Parry	2/4/81	3(10)	1(3)	0	0	0	0	0	0	0	0
Andy Parker	22/4/79	3	3	1	1	0	0	0	0	4	4
Safraz Patel	20/10/76	1(6)	(1)	2	0	0	0	0	0	8	0
Dave Radley	9/7/81	1(2)	0	0	0	0	0	0	0	0	0
Chris Ramsdale	25/4/82	4(2)	0	1	0	0	0	0	0	4	0
Mick Redford	24/6/81	27(2)	16(2)	9	4	0	0	0	0	36	16
Martin Roden	26/12/79	18(6)	18	0	0	0	0	0	0	0	0
Lee Rowley	3/2/83	6(9)	5(5)	2	2	0	0	0	0	8	8
Simon Smith	23/7/74	4(17)	2(11)	4	3	0	0	0	0	16	12
Jamie Stenhouse	9/10/80	16	16	7	7	0	0	0	0	28	28
Tim Street	29/6/68	21(7)	12(7)	2	0	0	0	0	0	8	0
David Whittle	22/9/76	10(3)	1(3)	4	1	0	0	0	0	16	4
Craig Wingfield	6/9/80	4(6)	4(6)	1	1	0	0	0	0	4	4

Eric Andrews

LEAGUE RECORD
P18-W13-D0-L5
(2nd, NL2/Final Eliminator)
F584, A362, Diff+222
26 points.

CHALLENGE CUP
Round Four

NATIONAL LEAGUE CUP
3rd, North Division

ATTENDANCES
Best - v Keighley (FE - 1,085)
Worst - v Gateshead (NLC - 213)
Total (NL2, inc play-offs,
& NLC only) - 6,506
Average (NL2, inc play-offs,
& NLC only) - 434
(Down by 60 on 2002)

GATESHEAD THUNDER

DATE	FIXTURE	RESULT	SCORERS	LGE	ATT
19/1/03	Whitehaven (a) (NLC)	L42-6	t:Mackay g:Fisher	5th(NLC-N)	1,342
26/1/03	Union Treiziste Catalane (h) (CCR3)	L4-38	t:Janan Billings	N/A	315
16/2/03	Chorley (h) (NLC)	L18-24	t:Neighbour,Janan Billings,MacDougall g:Fisher(3)	5th(NLC-N)	308
23/2/03	Workington (a) (NLC)	L31-24	t:Judd Billings(2),Neighbour(2),Rutherford g:Fisher(2)	5th(NLC-N)	503
9/3/03	Barrow (h) (NLC)	L24-28	t:Barnett(2),Fletcher,Bates,N Thorman g:N Thorman(2)	5th(NLC-N)	232
16/3/03	Whitehaven (h) (NLC)	L20-34	t:Reid(2),Peers,Neighbour g:N Thorman(2)	5th(NLC-N)	272
19/3/03	Salford (h) (NLC)	L8-90	t:Iwenofu,Reid	5th(NLC-N)	172
23/3/03	Salford (a) (NLC)	L100-12	t:Reid,Brown g:N Thorman(2)	5th(NLC-N)	1,653
30/3/03	Chorley (a) (NLC)	L54-24	t:Reid(2),Bates,Lyons,Iwenofu g:N Thorman(2)	5th(NLC-N)	213
6/4/03	Workington (h) (NLC)	W42-12	t:Reid(3),Barnett(2),Fletcher,MacDougall g:N Thorman(4),P Thorman(3)	5th(NLC-N)	208
13/4/03	Barrow (a) (NLC)	L34-24	t:N Thorman(2),MacDougall,Reid g:N Thorman(3),P Thorman	5th(NLC-N)	557
18/4/03	York (a)	W12-29	t:MacDougall(2),Neighbour,Firth,Barnett g:P Thorman(4) fg:P Thorman	3rd	1,271
21/4/03	Barrow (h) ●	L22-30	t:Lauriston,Fletcher,Reid,Peers g:P Thorman(3)	5th	316
4/5/03	Swinton (a)	W35-38	t:Neighbour(2),Doherty,Rutherford,Firth,Reid,N Thorman g:P Thorman(5)	3rd	418
11/5/03	Hunslet (a)	L28-14	t:MacDougall(2) g:P Thorman(3)	6th	417
25/5/03	Chorley (a)	L33-18	t:Thornton,MacDougall,A Walker g:P Thorman(3)	7th	280
31/5/03	Workington (h) ●●	D18-18	t:Janan Billings,Bates,Lyons g:P Thorman(3)	7th	287
15/6/03	Keighley (a)	L52-6	t:Thornton g:P Thorman	8th	992
22/6/03	London Skolars (h) ●●	W50-20	t:A Walker(5),P Thorman,Morton,Peers g:P Thorman(9)	8th	226
29/6/03	Sheffield (a)	L58-24	t:Bates(2),Oshagbemi,Thornton g:P Thorman(4)	8th	1,022
13/7/03	Hunslet (h) ●●●	L6-55	t:Oshagbemi g:P Thorman	8th	285
20/7/03	Swinton (h)	L30-39	t:A Walker,N Thorman,Lyons,Thornton,Gibson g:P Thorman(5)	8th	388
27/7/03	Barrow (a)	L48-16	t:Reid(2),Barnett g:P Thorman(2)	8th	660
3/8/03	York (h)	L8-64	t:Neighbour,Thornton	8th	413
10/8/03	Chorley (h)	L14-22	t:A Walker,N Thorman g:P Thorman(3)	8th	181
17/8/03	Workington (a)	L32-18	t:Bradley,A Walker,Reid g:P Thorman(3)	9th	406
24/8/03	London Skolars (a)	L48-14	t:Sozi,Morton g:P Thorman(3)	9th	307
31/8/03	Sheffield (h)	L24-48	t:Barnett(2),Morton,Reid g:P Thorman(4)	9th	263
7/9/03	Keighley (h)	L16-21	t:Sozi,Janan Billings,Reid g:P Thorman(2)	9th	349

● Played at Hedley Lawson Park
●● Played at Monkton Stadium, Jarrow
●●● Played at Preston Avenue, North Shields

	D.O.B.	APP ALL	APP NL2	TRIES ALL	TRIES NL2	GOALS ALL	GOALS NL2	FG ALL	FG NL2	PTS ALL	PTS NL2
Richie Barnett	26/4/81	21	13	8	4	0	0	0	0	32	16
David Bates	23/10/80	12(10)	4(8)	5	3	0	0	0	0	20	12
Janan Billings	27/1/82	12(9)	10(8)	4	2	0	0	0	0	16	8
Judd Billings	4/4/79	2	0	2	0	0	0	0	0	8	0
Steven Bradley	27/7/81	25(3)	16(2)	1	1	0	0	0	0	4	4
Clint Brown	27/9/75	24(3)	16(1)	1	0	0	0	0	0	4	0
Mark Cherry	8/5/74	1	0	0	0	0	0	0	0	0	0
Jermaine Coleman	17/6/82	17(1)	11(1)	0	0	0	0	0	0	0	0
John Coutts	9/1/79	1(2)	0	0	0	0	0	0	0	0	0
Nick Cowburn	5/10/81	2	0	0	0	0	0	0	0	0	0
Tony Doherty	3/8/83	(4)	(1)	1	1	0	0	0	0	4	4
Craig Firth	4/11/82	8(2)	4	2	2	0	0	0	0	8	8
Craig Fisher	16/9/77	5	0	0	0	6	0	0	0	12	0
Chris Fletcher	21/6/83	21(4)	11(4)	3	1	0	0	0	0	12	4
Mark Gibson	16/9/74	(2)	(2)	1	1	0	0	0	0	4	4
Scott Harrison	22/1/83	(12)	(12)	0	0	0	0	0	0	0	0
James Hartley	--/--/--	(1)	0	0	0	0	0	0	0	0	0
Scott Houston	27/1/84	7(2)	4(2)	0	0	0	0	0	0	0	0
Olu Iwenofu	28/9/81	2(1)	0	2	0	0	0	0	0	8	0
Dave Jessey	12/5/81	2(1)	2(1)	0	0	0	0	0	0	0	0
Tom Lauriston	18/5/72	4(5)	2(2)	1	1	0	0	0	0	4	4
Michael Lyons	15/9/82	5(6)	4(5)	3	2	0	0	0	0	12	8
Scott MacDougall	20/6/81	6(2)	3(1)	8	5	0	0	0	0	32	20
James Mackay	21/7/78	3(3)	0	1	0	0	0	0	0	4	0
Steve Morton	10/5/69	11	11	3	3	0	0	0	0	12	12
Kevin Neighbour	10/7/83	29	18	8	4	0	0	0	0	32	16
Peter Oshagbemi	26/1/81	9	9	2	2	0	0	0	0	8	8
Robin Peers	18/1/82	12(2)	6(2)	3	2	0	0	0	0	12	8
Damien Reid	14/3/84	26(1)	15(1)	17	7	0	0	0	0	68	28
Ryan Robinson	22/10/83	1(1)	1(1)	0	0	0	0	0	0	0	0
Steve Rutherford	24/8/81	24	16	2	1	0	0	0	0	8	4
PJ Solomon	17/8/76	5	0	0	0	0	0	0	0	0	0
Yusuf Sozi	20/12/81	18(9)	16(1)	2	2	0	0	0	0	8	8
Neil Thorman	4/6/84	9(14)	4(9)	6	3	0	0	0	0	24	12
Paul Thorman	28/9/82	27	18	1	1	73	58	1	1	151	121
Adam Thornton	21/7/81	8	8	5	5	0	0	0	0	20	20
Sam Turnell	21/8/80	(1)	(1)	0	0	0	0	0	0	0	0
Andy Walker	19/5/83	14(13)	12(5)	9	9	0	0	0	0	36	36
Nick Walker	1/5/82	2	0	0	0	0	0	0	0	0	0
Shaun Weatherall	31/10/81	2	0	0	0	0	0	0	0	0	0

Steve Rutherford

LEAGUE RECORD
P18-W3-D1-L14
(9th, NL2)
F365, A663, Diff-298
7 points.

CHALLENGE CUP
Round Three

NATIONAL LEAGUE CUP
5th, North Division

ATTENDANCES
Best - v York (NL2 - 413)
Worst - v Salford (NLC - 172)
Total (NL2 & NLC only) - 3,900
Average (NL2 & NLC only) - 279
(Down by 231 on 2002)

HUNSLET HAWKS

DATE	FIXTURE	RESULT	SCORERS	LGE	ATT
19/1/03	Batley (a) (NLC)	L16-8	t:Bastow g:Bastow(2)	4th(NLC-C)	801
26/1/03	Pia (h) (CCR3)	W28-18	t:Naylor(3),Fearon,Rayner g:Bastow(3),Liddell	N/A	524
2/2/03	London Skolars (h) (NLC)	W30-6	t:Naylor(2),McGibbon,W Freeman,Seal g:Liddell(5)	2nd(NLC-C)	434
9/2/03	Huddersfield (h) (CCR4)	W18-14	t:Powell,Lockwood,Briggs g:Liddell(3)	N/A	1,256
16/2/03	Dewsbury (a) (NLC)	W24-26	t:Naylor(2),Powell,Rayner,Brain g:Liddell(3)	2nd(NLC-C)	869
23/2/03	Keighley (h) (NLC)	W16-4	t:Rayner(2),Higgins g:Liddell(2)	3rd(NLC-C)	610
2/3/03	Bradford (h) (CCR5) ●	L0-82	No Scorers	N/A	5,685
9/3/03	Featherstone (h) (NLC)	L4-42	t:McGibbon	3rd(NLC-C)	793
16/3/03	London Skolars (a) (NLC)	W18-42	t:Hasty(2),Baker,Coyle,Naylor,Rayner,Powell g:Hasty(7)	3rd(NLC-C)	380
23/3/03	Batley (h) (NLC)	W30-24	t:Powell(2),C Ibbetson,Baker,W Freeman g:Liddell(5)	1st(NLC-C)	658
30/3/03	Featherstone (a) (NLC)	L50-10	t:Jackson,Powell g:Liddell	2nd(NLC-C)	1,212
6/4/03	Keighley (a) (NLC)	L21-8	t:Fearon g:Liddell(2)	4th(NLC-C)	1,170
13/4/03	Dewsbury (h) (NLC)	L31-32	t:Powell(2),Hasty,Fearon,Coyle g:Liddell(5) fg:Hasty	4th(NLC-C)	599
18/4/03	Keighley (h)	L12-20	t:Powell,Higgins g:Liddell,Hasty	6th	607
21/4/03	Chorley (a)	W18-24	t:W Freeman,Powell,Brent,Seal g:Hasty(4)	6th	404
4/5/03	Workington (h)	W43-38	t:McGibbon(2),Burton(2),Jakeman,Rayner,Hasty,Seal g:Hasty(3),Liddell(2) fg:Hasty	5th	393
11/5/03	Gateshead (h)	W28-14	t:Hasty,W Freeman,Seal,Rayner,Fearon g:Hasty(4)	4th	417
25/5/03	Sheffield (h)	W27-26	t:Rayner(2),Seal,Brent g:Hasty(5) fg:Hasty	2nd	553
1/6/03	London Skolars (a)	W6-36	t:Wray,Rayner,Powell,Hasty,Doherty,W Freeman g:Hasty(6)	2nd	482
15/6/03	York (h)	L18-40	t:Hasty,McGibbon,Parker g:Hasty(3)	2nd	649
22/6/03	Swinton (a)	D10-10	t:Wray g:Hasty(3)	2nd	503
29/6/03	Barrow (h)	L17-18	t:Coyle,Higgins,Hasty g:Hasty(2) fg:Bastow	4th	422
13/7/03	Gateshead (a)	W6-55	t:Powell(4),Liddell(2),Jakeman,Wray,Baker,Higgins g:Liddell(7) fg:Bastow	3rd	285
20/7/03	Workington (a)	W18-22	t:Powell(3),Higgins g:Liddell(3)	2nd	505
27/7/03	Chorley (h)	L36-49	t:Hasty,Bastow,Powell,Lockwood,Doherty g:Liddell(3),Hasty(3)	5th	475
3/8/03	Keighley (a)	W18-35	t:Hasty(2),Higgins,Bastow,Powell,Seal g:Hasty(5) fg:Hasty	5th	1,035
10/8/03	Sheffield (a)	L32-14	t:Rayner,Brook g:Hasty(3)	6th	1,002
17/8/03	London Skolars (h)	W64-14	t:Hasty(3),Pryce(2),W Freeman(2),Powell(2),Liddell,Burton,Jakeman g:Hasty(8)	4th	342
24/8/03	Swinton (h)	W46-14	t:Powell(2),Pryce,Lockwood,W Freeman,Bastow,Rayner,Fearon g:Hasty(7)	4th	621
31/8/03	Barrow (a)	L52-10	t:Lockwood,Doherty g:Hasty	5th	763
5/9/03	York (a)	L32-16	t:Rayner,W Freeman,Liddell g:Hasty,Liddell	6th	1,642
14/9/03	Keighley (a) (EPO)	L25-12	t:Doherty,W Freeman g:Hasty(2)	N/A	1,150

● Played at Headingley Stadium, Leeds

		APP		TRIES		GOALS		FG		PTS	
	D.O.B.	ALL	NL2	ALL	NL2	ALL	NL2	ALL	NL2	ALL	NL2
Richard Baker	26/1/75	16(1)	8	3	1	0	0	0	0	12	4
Andy Bastow	25/5/78	17(2)	12(2)	4	3	5	0	2	2	28	14
Steve Beard	21/6/79	(3)	(2)	0	0	0	0	0	0	0	0
Gareth Brain	19/12/81	4(2)	3	1	0	0	0	0	0	4	0
Andy Brent	1/5/76	15(11)	8(8)	2	2	0	0	0	0	8	8
Dan Briggs	15/7/79	(8)	(3)	1	0	0	0	0	0	4	0
David Brook	4/2/71	(4)	(3)	1	1	0	0	0	0	4	4
Danny Burton	17/5/75	15(3)	14	3	3	0	0	0	0	12	12
Billy Conway	31/1/67	(1)	0	0	0	0	0	0	0	0	0
Mick Coyle	5/3/71	15(9)	7(4)	3	1	0	0	0	0	12	4
Stephen Doherty	8/3/78	9(5)	9(5)	4	4	0	0	0	0	16	16
Danny Fearon	13/3/79	19(6)	8(5)	5	2	0	0	0	0	20	8
Glen Freeman	9/4/72	5(7)	5(7)	0	0	0	0	0	0	0	0
Lee Freeman	21/9/79	(1)	(1)	0	0	0	0	0	0	0	0
Wayne Freeman	30/4/74	30(1)	19	10	8	0	0	0	0	40	32
Chris Hall	23/5/79	1	1	0	0	0	0	0	0	0	0
Phil Hasty	28/5/80	29(2)	16(2)	15	12	68	61	4	3	200	173
Joe Hawley	11/2/85	9(2)	5(1)	0	0	0	0	0	0	0	0
Iain Higgins	14/9/76	25(4)	13(4)	6	5	0	0	0	0	24	20
Tony Howcroft	31/5/79	(3)	0	0	0	0	0	0	0	0	0
Ian Hughes	13/3/72	(1)	0	0	0	0	0	0	0	0	0
Craig Ibbetson	18/7/83	12(4)	1(3)	1	0	0	0	0	0	4	0
Shaun Ibbetson	13/4/85	5(2)	5(1)	0	0	0	0	0	0	0	0
Simon Jackson	4/2/77	5(2)	0	1	0	0	0	0	0	4	0
Steve Jakeman	30/7/79	8(5)	7(4)	3	3	0	0	0	0	12	12
Jon Liddell	25/8/82	24(1)	13	4	4	44	17	0	0	104	50
Jonlee Lockwood	18/3/78	10(14)	7(7)	4	3	0	0	0	0	16	12
Michael Lyons	15/9/82	2(2)	0	0	0	0	0	0	0	0	0
Wes McGibbon	13/1/79	25	14	5	3	0	0	0	0	20	12
Gareth Naylor	18/12/80	8(2)	0	8	0	0	0	0	0	32	0
Chris North	6/1/76	(3)	(2)	0	0	0	0	0	0	0	0
Chris Parker	9/9/78	1(6)	1(6)	1	1	0	0	0	0	4	4
Bryn Powell	5/9/79	32	19	24	16	0	0	0	0	96	64
Steve Pryce	12/5/69	12(1)	12(1)	3	3	0	0	0	0	12	12
George Rayner	19/9/80	29	17	13	8	0	0	0	0	52	32
Paul Seal	21/4/78	25(2)	15	6	5	0	0	0	0	24	20
Craig Taylor	21/11/82	(2)	(2)	0	0	0	0	0	0	0	0
Jamaine Wray	15/3/84	8(3)	8(3)	3	3	0	0	0	0	12	12

Phil Hasty

LEAGUE RECORD
P18-W10-D1-L7
(6th, NL2/Elimination Play-Off)
F513, A425, Diff+88
21 points.

CHALLENGE CUP
Round Five

NATIONAL LEAGUE CUP
4th, Central Division

ATTENDANCES
Best - v Huddersfield (CC - 1,256)
Worst - v London Skolars (NL2 - 342)
Total (NL2 & NLC only) - 7,573
Average (NL2 & NLC only) - 541
(Down by 75 on 2002)

KEIGHLEY COUGARS

DATE	FIXTURE	RESULT	SCORERS	LGE	ATT
19/1/03	Doncaster (h) (NLC)	W21-14	t:Robinson,Ashton,Helliwell g:Ashton(4) fg:Ashton	3rd(NLC-C)	1,337
26/1/03	Thornhill (h) (CCR3)	W33-10	t:Ashton(2),Hoyle,Firth,Smith g:Ashton(6) fg:Ashton	N/A	1,135
2/2/03	Dewsbury (a) (NLC)	L12-6	t:Rushforth g:Ashton	4th(NLC-C)	954
9/2/03	Sheffield (a) (CCR4)	L25-24	t:Hoyle,Smith,Sinfield,Wainwright,Rushforth g:Ashton(2)	N/A	1,235
16/2/03	Batley (h) (NLC)	L12-30	t:Smith,Rushforth g:Mitchell(2)	4th(NLC-C)	1,209
23/2/03	Hunslet (a) (NLC)	L16-4	g:Ashton(2)	4th(NLC-C)	610
9/3/03	London Skolars (h) (NLC)	W78-18	t:Firth(4),Ramshaw(2),M Foster(2),Smith(2),Wilkes,Mervill,Hoyle,Robinson g:Ashton(8),Wilkes(3)	4th(NLC-C)	732
16/3/03	Dewsbury (h) (NLC)	W22-2	t:Firth,Robinson,Mitchell,Wainwright g:Mitchell(3)	4th(NLC-C)	1,111
23/3/03	Doncaster (a) (NLC)	L42-12	t:Firth(2) g:Mitchell(2)	4th(NLC-C)	985
30/3/03	London Skolars (a) (NLC)	W18-48	t:Hewitt(2),Patterson,Stephenson,Helliwell,Wilkes,Wainwright,Durham g:Mitchell(8)	4th(NLC-C)	310
6/4/03	Hunslet (h) (NLC)	W21-8	t:D Foster,Hoyle,Robinson g:Mitchell(4) fg:Firth	3rd(NLC-C)	1,170
13/4/03	Batley (a) (NLC)	L40-16	t:M Foster,Rushforth,Wilkes g:Mitchell(2)	3rd(NLC-C)	737
18/4/03	Hunslet (a)	W12-20	t:Hewitt,D Foster,Wainwright g:Mitchell(4)	5th	607
21/4/03	London Skolars (h)	W68-6	t:Rushforth(4),Patterson(2),Wilkes(2),Ekis(2),Smith,Tomlinson,Firth g:Ashton(7),Wilkes	1st	963
4/5/03	Chorley (a)	W22-23	t:Hewitt(2),M Foster(2) g:Mitchell(3) fg:Firth	1st	501
11/5/03	York (h)	W38-26	t:M Foster(2),D Foster,Rushforth,Hoyle,Hewitt g:Mitchell(7)	1st	1,077
25/5/03	Workington (a)	W8-44	t:Robinson(2),M Foster(2),Ramshaw,D Foster,Hoyle g:Mitchell(8)	1st	610
1/6/03	Barrow (h)	W28-15	t:Wilkes,D Foster,Robinson,Firth,Wainwright g:Mitchell(4)	1st	1,106
15/6/03	Gateshead (h)	W52-6	t:Firth(3),M Foster(2),Hoyle(2),Ramshaw(2),Mitchell g:Mitchell(4),Ashton(2)	1st	992
22/6/03	Sheffield (a)	L33-6	t:Ramshaw g:Wilkes	1st	1,126
29/6/03	Swinton (h)	W18-15	t:Wilkes,Tomlinson,M Foster g:Mitchell(2),Ashton	1st	1,129
13/7/03	York (a)	L48-28	t:Rushforth,Mitchell,Robinson,M Foster,D Foster g:Ashton(3),Mitchell	1st	1,835
20/7/03	Chorley (h)	L20-23	t:M Foster,Mitchell,Firth g:Mitchell(3) fg:Firth(2)	1st	1,028
27/7/03	London Skolars (a)	W14-22	t:M Foster(2),Wilkes,Wainwright g:Ashton(3)	1st	304
3/8/03	Hunslet (a)	L18-35	t:Hoyle,Firth,Robinson g:Ashton(3)	4th	1,035
10/8/03	Workington (h)	W35-6	t:D Foster,Wilkes,Wainwright,Helliwell,Mitchell,Sinfield,M Foster g:Mitchell(2),Ashton fg:Ashton	3rd	844
17/8/03	Barrow (a)	W16-18	t:Robinson(2),Ramshaw,D Foster g:Mitchell	2nd	826
24/8/03	Sheffield (h)	L10-22	t:M Foster g:Mitchell(3)	3rd	1,468
31/8/03	Swinton (a)	W17-19	t:Sinfield(2),Robinson g:Ashton(3) fg:Ashton	3rd	507
7/9/03	Gateshead (a)	W16-21	t:Smith(2),D Foster,Wilkes g:Ashton(2) fg:Ashton	3rd	349
14/9/03	Hunslet (h) (EPO)	W25-12	t:Mervill,Sinfield g:Ashton(8) fg:Ashton	N/A	1,150
21/9/03	Barrow (h) (ESF)	W35-26	t:Ashton(2),Ramshaw,Rushforth g:Ashton(9) fg:Ashton	N/A	1,332
28/9/03	Chorley (a) (FE)	W12-45	t:Ashton(2),Tomlinson,Stephenson,Ekis,Robinson,Mervill g:Ashton(8) fg:Ashton	N/A	1,085
5/10/03	Sheffield (GF) ●	W13-11	t:M Foster,Robinson g:Ashton(2) fg:Firth	N/A	N/A

● Played at Halton Stadium, Widnes

		APP		TRIES		GOALS		FG		PTS	
	D.O.B.	ALL	NL2	ALL	NL2	ALL	NL2	ALL	NL2	ALL	NL2
Paul Ashton	17/6/79	16(5)	10(4)	7	4	75	52	8	6	186	126
Mick Durham	18/11/75	2(13)	2(12)	1	0	0	0	0	0	4	0
Danny Ekis	17/1/82	20(11)	12(7)	3	3	0	0	0	0	12	12
Matt Firth	19/2/81	34	22	15	7	0	0	5	4	65	32
David Foster	8/4/81	34	22	9	8	0	0	0	0	36	32
Matt Foster	10/6/76	23(1)	20	19	16	0	0	0	0	76	64
Phil Guck	10/5/80	2	0	0	0	0	0	0	0	0	0
Chris Hannah	22/11/71	7(12)	5(4)	0	0	0	0	0	0	0	0
Ricky Helliwell	14/2/78	11(11)	4(8)	3	1	0	0	0	0	12	4
Gareth Hewitt	5/1/79	13(4)	6(1)	6	4	0	0	0	0	24	16
Simeon Hoyle	18/9/79	32	20	9	5	0	0	0	0	36	20
Lee Kelly	18/3/75	2(2)	1	0	0	0	0	0	0	0	0
Richard Mervill	24/6/81	3(20)	3(15)	3	2	0	0	0	0	12	8
Adam Mitchell	7/8/81	18(1)	12(1)	5	4	63	42	0	0	146	100
Scott Parkin	2/11/75	2(1)	2(1)	0	0	0	0	0	0	0	0
Lee Patterson	5/7/81	8(13)	6(11)	3	2	0	0	0	0	12	8
Jason Ramshaw	23/7/69	28(4)	18(4)	8	6	0	0	0	0	32	24
Andy Robinson	15/11/78	31	20	14	10	0	0	0	0	56	40
James Rushforth	9/2/77	31(2)	19(2)	11	7	0	0	0	0	44	28
Ian Sinfield	7/4/77	27(5)	19(3)	5	4	0	0	0	0	20	16
Karl Smith	28/5/77	20(1)	9(1)	8	3	0	0	0	0	32	12
Matthew Steel	5/10/84	1(2)	0	0	0	0	0	0	0	0	0
Phil Stephenson	17/6/72	29	17	2	1	0	0	0	0	8	4
Max Tomlinson	12/4/70	10	10	3	3	0	0	0	0	12	12
Chris Wainwright	18/10/79	7(20)	5(11)	7	4	0	0	0	0	28	16
Oliver Wilkes	2/5/80	31(3)	22	10	7	5	2	0	0	50	32

Matt Firth

LEAGUE RECORD
P18-W13-D0-L5
(3rd, NL2/Grand Final Winners,
Champions)
F448, A340, Diff+148
26 points.

CHALLENGE CUP
Round Four

NATIONAL LEAGUE CUP
3rd, Central Division

ATTENDANCES
Best - v Sheffield (NL2 - 1,468)
Worst - v London Skolars (NLC - 732)
Total (NL2, inc play-offs,
& NLC only) - 17,683
Average (NL2, inc play-offs,
& NLC only) - 1,105
(Up by 33 on 2002)

LONDON SKOLARS

DATE	FIXTURE	RESULT	SCORERS	LGE	ATT
19/1/03	Dewsbury (h) (NLC)	L10-22	t:Wotherspoon,Pollard g:Thair	5th(NLC-C)	820
26/1/03	Halton Simms Cross (a) (CCR3)	L15-8	t:Johnstone g:Johnstone(2)	N/A	750
2/2/03	Hunslet (a) (NLC)	L30-6	t:Wotherspoon g:Johnstone	5th(NLC-C)	434
16/2/03	Hull KR (h) (NLC)	L8-24	t:Pollard g:Johnstone(2)	5th(NLC-C)	712
23/2/03	Batley (a) (NLC)	L82-4	t:Bennett	5th(NLC-C)	577
9/3/03	Keighley (a) (NLC)	L78-18	t:Bennett,Mushiso,Wotherspoon g:Johnstone(3)	5th(NLC-C)	732
16/3/03	Hunslet (h) (NLC)	L18-42	t:McKeown,McCroary,Henare g:Johnstone(3)	5th(NLC-C)	380
23/3/03	Dewsbury (a) (NLC)	L35-33	t:Mushiso(2),Bennett,McCroary,Solomon g:McKeown(6) fg:McKeown	5th(NLC-C)	449
30/3/03	Keighley (h) (NLC)	L18-48	t:Henare,Ijeoma,McKeown g:Johnstone(2),McKeown	5th(NLC-C)	310
6/4/03	Batley (h) (NLC)	L12-56	t:Johnstone(2) g:Johnstone(2)	5th(NLC-C)	307
13/4/03	Hull KR (a) (NLC)	L86-0	No Scorers	5th(NLC-C)	1,175
18/4/03	Sheffield (h)	L2-48	g:Johnstone	10th	643
21/4/03	Keighley (a)	L68-6	t:Henare g:McKeown	10th	963
4/5/03	York (a)	D16-16	t:Henare,Roberts,Ijeoma g:Johnstone(2)	9th	1,012
11/5/03	Barrow (h)	L10-41	t:Oyebade(2) g:McKeown	10th	464
1/6/03	Hunslet (a)	L6-36	t:Dougherty g:Johnstone	10th	482
8/6/03	Swinton (h)	L8-31	t:Jonker g:Johnstone(2)	10th	278
15/6/03	Chorley (a)	L64-8	t:Oyebade g:Johnstone(2)	10th	252
22/6/03	Gateshead (a)	L50-20	t:Jonker(2),Pollard g:Johnstone(4)	10th	226
29/6/03	Workington (h)	L6-52	t:Leef g:Johnstone	10th	324
13/7/03	Barrow (a)	L54-12	t:Tito,Leef g:Johnstone(2)	10th	681
20/7/03	York (h)	L6-66	t:Mushiso g:Johnstone	10th	425
27/7/03	Keighley (h)	L14-22	t:Henare(2) g:Osborn(3)	10th	304
3/8/03	Sheffield (a)	L98-4	t:Du Toit	10th	854
10/8/03	Swinton (a)	L34-12	t:Janes,Le g:Johnstone,Osborn	10th	289
17/8/03	Hunslet (a)	L64-14	t:Jonker(2),Le g:Johnstone	10th	342
24/8/03	Gateshead (h)	W48-14	t:Jonker(2),Mushiso(2),Smits,Janes,Leef g:Johnstone(10)	10th	307
31/8/03	Workington (a)	L80-18	t:Baxter,Okwusogu,Leef g:Johnstone(2),Baxter	10th	451
7/9/03	Chorley (h)	L12-38	t:Jonker,Okwusogu g:Osborn(2)	10th	257

	D.O.B.	ALL	NL2	ALL	NL2	ALL	NL2	ALL	NL2	ALL	NL2
				TRIES		**GOALS**		**FG**		**PTS**	
Jason Asplet	12/10/76	1	0	0	0	0	0	0	0	0	0
Ben Baxter	13/5/75	2	2	1	1	1	0	0	0	6	6
Keir Bell	14/6/85	(1)	(1)	0	0	0	0	0	0	0	0
Cory Bennett	11/3/76	12(5)	7(2)	3	0	0	0	0	0	12	0
Janan Billings	27/1/82	2(1)	0	0	0	0	0	0	0	0	0
Judd Billings	4/4/79	2	0	0	0	0	0	0	0	0	0
Richard Brantingham	22/6/79	(2)	0	0	0	0	0	0	0	0	0
Robert Brown	9/11/62	(1)	(1)	0	0	0	0	0	0	0	0
John Clarke	3/1/83	(3)	(3)	0	0	0	0	0	0	0	0
Andy Craig	29/3/76	6(1)	6	0	0	0	0	0	0	0	0
Jimmy Daines	18/3/82	1(1)	0	0	0	0	0	0	0	0	0
Anthony Dellar	15/4/74	4(5)	3(1)	0	0	0	0	0	0	0	0
Gareth Desmond	21/2/76	(1)	0	0	0	0	0	0	0	0	0
Nick Dodinski	12/1/77	1(1)	0	0	0	0	0	0	0	0	0
Troy Dougherty	12/5/77	9(6)	7(3)	1	1	0	0	0	0	4	4
Mario Du Toit	27/10/81	7(1)	7(1)	1	1	0	0	0	0	4	4
Michael Fitzgibbon	26/4/76	4(1)	3(1)	0	0	0	0	0	0	0	0
Mark Foster	3/3/74	(1)	(1)	0	0	0	0	0	0	0	0
Neil Foster	13/8/80	10(2)	9(1)	0	0	0	0	0	0	0	0
Gavin Gordon	28/2/78	2	0	0	0	0	0	0	0	0	0
Steve Hainey	8/2/74	4(3)	0	0	0	0	0	0	0	0	0
Kahu Henare	22/4/75	23	14	6	4	0	0	0	0	24	16
Ryan Hermanson	26/10/80	2(2)	2(2)	0	0	0	0	0	0	0	0
James Hersey	10/8/82	2(1)	0	0	0	0	0	0	0	0	0
Andy Himsley	29/7/80	(1)	(1)	0	0	0	0	0	0	0	0
Glen Hoare	29/11/76	4(1)	(1)	0	0	0	0	0	0	0	0
Gareth Honor	1/10/81	6(2)	6(2)	0	0	0	0	0	0	0	0
Graham Hughes	5/6/79	3(1)	3(1)	0	0	0	0	0	0	0	0
Steffan Hughes	11/2/81	5(1)	5(1)	0	0	0	0	0	0	0	0
Obi Ijeoma	31/10/71	12(3)	7(1)	2	1	0	0	0	0	8	4
Gareth Janes	13/5/73	7(7)	7(3)	2	2	0	0	0	0	8	8
Leon John	7/7/80	1	0	0	0	0	0	0	0	0	0
Jake Johnstone	6/12/77	23(1)	14	3	0	45	30	0	0	102	60
Rubert Jonker	7/1/79	16	13	8	8	0	0	0	0	32	32
Kirk King	18/9/80	1	1	0	0	0	0	0	0	0	0
Paul Koloi	25/12/72	3	3	0	0	0	0	0	0	0	0
Donny Lam	4/8/77	(2)	(2)	0	0	0	0	0	0	0	0
Huy Le	2/2/80	4(2)	4(2)	2	2	0	0	0	0	8	8
Paul Leef	20/3/76	14(1)	14(1)	4	4	0	0	0	0	16	16
Brett McCroary	30/1/74	16(1)	10(1)	2	0	0	0	0	0	8	0
Grayson McDonald	29/10/80	2(1)	2(1)	0	0	0	0	0	0	0	0
Jason McDonald	6/5/72	1	0	0	0	0	0	0	0	0	0
Rob McKeown	13/5/76	13(6)	5(6)	2	0	9	2	1	0	27	4
David Mossop	7/6/80	3(2)	3(2)	0	0	0	0	0	0	0	0

	D.O.B.	ALL	NL2	ALL	NL2	ALL	NL2	ALL	NL2	ALL	NL2
				TRIES		**GOALS**		**FG**		**PTS**	
Ronald Mushiso	12/8/81	11(3)	8(2)	6	3	0	0	0	0	24	12
Gerald Nkrumah	3/9/76	2(2)	1	0	0	0	0	0	0	0	0
Mike Okwusogu	28/4/73	13(2)	8(1)	2	2	0	0	0	0	8	8
Glenn Osborn	17/8/83	17(3)	8(3)	0	0	6	6	0	0	12	12
Charlie Oyebade	28/11/74	22	16	3	3	0	0	0	0	12	12
Wayne Parillon	27/11/80	1(3)	(3)	0	0	0	0	0	0	0	0
Dominic Peters	11/12/78	2	2	0	0	0	0	0	0	0	0
Richard Pollard	20/8/77	8(1)	1(1)	3	1	0	0	0	0	12	4
Peter Rawson	4/3/78	2(1)	0	0	0	0	0	0	0	0	0
Daniel Reeds	22/12/80	2(6)	1(4)	0	0	0	0	0	0	0	0
Pat Rich	25/6/78	1(1)	0	0	0	0	0	0	0	0	0
Scott Roberts	25/7/82	15(3)	5(2)	1	1	0	0	0	0	4	4
Bow Robertson	14/10/77	1	0	0	0	0	0	0	0	0	0
Keri Ryan	4/10/70	2(1)	0	0	0	0	0	0	0	0	0
Matt Shaw	20/2/77	1	1	0	0	0	0	0	0	0	0
Duncan Simpson	11/6/79	(1)	0	0	0	0	0	0	0	0	0
Alex Smits	8/8/74	9	9	1	1	0	0	0	0	4	4
PJ Solomon	17/8/76	11(1)	7	1	0	0	0	0	0	4	0
Al Stewart	28/12/74	2	1	0	0	0	0	0	0	0	0
Roger Teau	24/10/77	(3)	(3)	0	0	0	0	0	0	0	0
Chris Thair	4/6/77	2	0	0	0	0	0	1	0	2	0
Allan Tito	1/8/77	18	9	1	1	0	0	0	0	4	4
Ben Wakeley	23/11/80	(1)	(1)	0	0	0	0	0	0	0	0
Matt Walker	16/9/71	1(2)	1(2)	0	0	0	0	0	0	0	0
Bobby Wallis	7/1/83	(1)	(1)	0	0	0	0	0	0	0	0
John Warner	27/2/81	(2)	(2)	0	0	0	0	0	0	0	0
Tim Williams	12/10/72	(1)	0	0	0	0	0	0	0	0	0
Kirk Wotherspoon	16/8/76	6	0	3	0	0	0	0	0	12	0

LEAGUE RECORD
P18-W1-D1-L16
(10th, NL2)
F222, A876, Diff-654
3 points.

CHALLENGE CUP
Round Three

NATIONAL LEAGUE CUP
5th, Central Division

ATTENDANCES
Best - v Dewsbury (NLC - 820)
Worst - v Chorley (NL2 - 257)
Total (NL2 & NLC only) - 6,013
Average (NL2 & NLC only) - 430

Rubert Jonker

SHEFFIELD EAGLES

DATE	FIXTURE	RESULT	SCORERS	LGE	ATT
19/1/03	Featherstone (a) (NLC)	L30-12	t:Thompson,Tillyer g:G Brown(2)	5th(NLC-E)	1,595
24/1/03	Oulton (a) (CCR3)	W8-22	t:C Brown(2),Flynn,Thompson g:G Brown(3)	N/A	759
9/2/03	Keighley (h) (CCR4)	W25-24	t:Goddard(2),Poynter,G Brown g:G Brown(4) fg:Goddard	N/A	1,235
16/2/03	Doncaster (h) (NLC)	L4-26	g:G Brown(2)	4th(NLC-E)	1,053
23/2/03	Hull KR (a) (NLC)	L30-24	t:Poynter(2),G Brown,Whitter g:G Brown(4)	4th(NLC-E)	1,553
2/3/03	Hull (h) (CCR5) ●	L0-88	No Scorers	N/A	11,729
5/3/03	Batley (h) (NLC)	W18-8	t:Hurst,Reilly,Breakingbury g:G Brown(3)	4th(NLC-E)	732
9/3/03	York (h) (NLC)	L12-32	t:Wells,Raleigh g:G Brown(2)	5th(NLC-E)	730
16/3/03	Batley (a) (NLC)	L62-12	t:Breakingbury,Stringer g:G Brown(2)	5th(NLC-E)	639
21/3/03	Featherstone (h) (NLC)	L8-27	t:Stringer g:G Brown(2)	5th(NLC-E)	856
30/3/03	York (a) (NLC)	L32-18	t:Weller(2),G Brown,C Brown g:G Brown	5th(NLC-E)	978
6/4/03	Hull KR (h) (NLC)	W33-26	t:Weller,Turnbull,G Brown,Thompson g:G Brown(7) fg:G Brown(3)	5th(NLC-E)	1,150
13/4/03	Doncaster (a) (NLC)	L38-30	t:G Brown,Raleigh,Hurst,Stringer,Tillyer,Thompson g:G Brown(3)	5th(NLC-E)	909
18/4/03	London Skolars (a)	W2-48	t:Weller(3),C Brown(2),Reilly,Hurst,Poynter,G Brown g:Aston(4),G Brown(2)	1st	643
21/4/03	York (h)	W30-24	t:Weller,Poynter,Hurst,Thompson,Tillyer,Kite g:G Brown(2),Aston	2nd	897
4/5/03	Barrow (a)	W12-30	t:Raleigh,Kite,Flynn,Poynter,Hurst,Turnbull g:G Brown(3)	2nd	911
9/5/03	Swinton (h)	L18-23	t:Poynter,C Brown,Weller g:G Brown(3)	2nd	903
25/5/03	Hunslet (a)	L27-26	t:Poynter(2),Weller(2),Hurst g:G Brown(3)	3rd	553
1/6/03	Chorley (h)	L16-19	t:Stringer,Aston,Kite g:G Brown(2)	3rd	747
15/6/03	Workington (a)	W16-29	t:Poynter(2),Thompson(2),Stringer g:G Brown(4) fg:G Brown	3rd	487
22/6/03	Keighley (h)	W33-6	t:Turnbull,O'Reilly,Stanley,Weller,Raleigh g:G Brown(6) fg:Aston	3rd	1,126
29/6/03	Gateshead (h)	W58-24	t:Turnbull(3),Raleigh(2),G Brown,Weller,O'Reilly,Flynn,Hurst,Bruce g:G Brown(7)	2nd	1,022
13/7/03	Swinton (a)	L20-18	t:Poynter(2),Weller g:G Brown(3)	4th	496
20/7/03	Barrow (h)	W43-42	t:Flynn,Hurst,Kite,Bruce,G Brown,Weller,Tillyer,C Brown g:G Brown(5) fg:Goddard	3rd	1,037
27/7/03	York (a)	W18-25	t:Poynter(2),O'Reilly(2) g:G Brown(4) fg:G Brown	2nd	1,301
3/8/03	London Skolars (h)	W98-4	t:Poynter(4),Hurst(3),Stringer(2),Raleigh(2),Flynn(2),O'Reilly,Goddard,C Brown,Tillyer,Robinson g:G Brown(13)	1st	854
10/8/03	Hunslet (h)	W32-14	t:Robinson(3),Turnbull,Raleigh g:G Brown(6)	1st	1,002
17/8/03	Chorley (a)	L30-14	t:Poynter,Raleigh g:G Brown(3)	3rd	502
24/8/03	Keighley (a)	W10-22	t:Poynter,Reilly,Goddard g:G Brown(5)	2nd	1,468
31/8/03	Gateshead (a)	W24-48	t:Flynn(2),Reilly(2),O'Reilly,De Chenu,Raleigh,Goddard,Bruce g:G Brown(6)	1st	263
6/9/03	Workington (h)	W56-11	t:O'Reilly(2),Weller(2),Raleigh(2),Goddard,Breakingbury,G Brown,Aston,Reilly g:G Brown(6)	1st	1,011
21/9/03	Chorley (h) (QSF)	W31-14	t:Goddard,Poynter,Raleigh,G Brown,O'Reilly g:G Brown(4) fg:G Brown(2),Aston	N/A	732
5/10/03	Keighley (GF) ●●	L13-11	t:O'Reilly g:G Brown(3) fg:Reilly	N/A	N/A
11/10/03	Batley (a) (NL1QF)	L36-14	t:James,Hurst,Carroll g:G Brown	N/A	1,040

● Played at KC Stadium, Hull
●● Played at Halton Stadium, Widnes

		APP		TRIES		GOALS		FG		PTS	
	D.O.B.	ALL	NL2	ALL	NL2	ALL	NL2	ALL	NL2	ALL	NL2
Guy Adams	1/9/76	7(2)	1(1)	0	0	0	0	0	0	0	0
Ryan Angus	12/2/82	1(4)	0	0	0	0	0	0	0	0	0
Mark Aston	27/9/67	14(6)	14(6)	2	2	5	5	2	2	20	20
Lee Bettinson	22/7/81	13(3)	6	0	0	0	0	0	0	0	0
Sam Bibb	23/12/80	2(4)	0	0	0	0	0	0	0	0	0
Jon Breakingbury	5/10/82	13	2	3	1	0	0	0	0	12	4
Craig Brown	2/12/80	32(1)	21	8	5	0	0	0	0	32	20
Gavin Brown	18/9/77	34	21	10	5	126	91	7	4	299	206
Jon Bruce	30/10/71	24(5)	18	3	3	0	0	0	0	12	12
Adam Carroll	14/2/84	3(2)	(1)	1	1	0	0	0	0	4	4
Carl De Chenu	18/6/82	2	2	1	1	0	0	0	0	4	4
Wayne Flynn	19/11/76	24(2)	18	8	7	0	0	0	0	32	28
Richard Goddard	28/4/74	15(6)	7(5)	7	5	0	0	2	1	30	21
Jack Howieson	28/7/81	31	20	0	0	0	0	0	0	0	0
Greg Hurst	22/6/80	16(8)	12(7)	12	10	0	0	0	0	48	40
Jordan James	24/5/80	(2)	(2)	1	1	0	0	0	0	4	4
Neil Kite	9/9/78	17(4)	7(3)	4	4	0	0	0	0	16	16
Dale Laughton	10/1/71	1(4)	1(4)	0	0	0	0	0	0	0	0
Simon Morton	4/10/82	(3)	(2)	0	0	0	0	0	0	0	0
Tom O'Reilly	25/11/75	15	15	10	10	0	0	0	0	40	40
Andy Poynter	24/10/78	32	21	22	19	0	0	0	0	88	76
Andy Raleigh	17/3/81	28(2)	21	14	12	0	0	0	0	56	48
Peter Reilly	24/7/81	10(10)	3(6)	6	5	0	0	1	1	25	21
Pat Rich	25/6/78	3	0	0	0	0	0	0	0	0	0
Darren Robinson	28/5/79	3(1)	3(1)	4	4	0	0	0	0	16	16
Richard Singleton	12/5/78	(1)	0	0	0	0	0	0	0	0	0
Gareth Stanley	20/5/81	23(4)	16(3)	1	1	0	0	0	0	4	4
Mitchell Stringer	1/11/83	3(26)	2(19)	7	4	0	0	0	0	28	16
Ian Thompson	6/2/78	17	10	7	3	0	0	0	0	28	12
Simon Tillyer	9/5/80	7(27)	3(18)	5	3	0	0	0	0	20	12
Nick Turnbull	22/11/82	20(6)	11(5)	7	6	0	0	0	0	28	24
Tony Weller	9/5/79	21(1)	18	16	13	0	0	0	0	64	52
Paul Wells	21/2/81	5	0	1	0	0	0	0	0	4	0
Damien Whitter	25/11/76	6(1)	(1)	1	0	0	0	0	0	4	0

Jon Bruce

LEAGUE RECORD
P18-W13-D0-L5
(1st, NL2/Grand Final Runners Up,
NL1 Qualifying Final Runners Up)
F644, A326, Diff+318
26 points.

CHALLENGE CUP
Round Five

NATIONAL LEAGUE CUP
5th, East Division

ATTENDANCES
Best - v Keighley (CC - 1,235)
Worst - v York (NLC - 730)
Total (NL2, inc play-offs,
& NLC only) - 15,087
Average (NL2, inc play-offs,
& NLC only) - 943
(Down by 81 on 2002)

SWINTON LIONS

DATE	FIXTURE	RESULT	SCORERS	LGE	ATT
19/1/03	Salford (a) (NLC)	L58-6	t:Wingfield g:Hough	5th(NLC-W)	3,334
26/1/03	Shaw Cross (h) (CCR3)	W46-0	t:Thorpe(3),Cannon(2),English,Smith,Tassell,Cheetham g:Hough(5)	N/A	315
2/2/03	Leigh (h) (NLC)	L10-24	t:Wingfield,Thorpe g:Smith	5th(NLC-W)	950
9/2/03	Chorley (a) (CCR4)	W16-32	t:Tassell(3),Ellison,Thorpe,Hudson g:Wingfield(4)	N/A	572
23/2/03	Oldham (h) (NLC)	L16-24	t:Barraclough,Roach,Cannon g:Hough(2)	5th(NLC-W)	923
2/3/03	Featherstone (h) (CCR5)	W32-10	t:Hassan,English,Johnson,Thorpe,Knox,Cushion g:Hough(3) fg:Hough(2)	N/A	1,092
9/3/03	Whitehaven (a) (NLC)	L38-6	t:Bithel g:Wingfield	5th(NLC-W)	1,060
16/3/03	Wigan (h) (CCQF) ●	L12-70	t:Russell,Leathem g:Hough(2)	N/A	5,114
19/3/03	Rochdale (a) (NLC)	L24-14	t:Hough,Bithel g:Hough(3)	5th(NLC-W)	727
23/3/03	Leigh (a) (NLC)	L62-6	t:Hassan g:Hough	5th(NLC-W)	2,026
30/3/03	Rochdale (h) (NLC)	W26-22	t:Roach,Hudson,Hough,Ellison,Cannon g:Hough(3)	5th(NLC-W)	391
2/4/03	Salford (a) (NLC)	L0-72	No Scorers	5th(NLC-W)	954
6/4/03	Oldham (a) (NLC)	L68-14	t:Mead,Hudson,Russell g:Russell	5th(NLC-W)	1,032
13/4/03	Whitehaven (h) (NLC)	D22-22	t:Hudson(2),Knox,English g:Hough(3)	5th(NLC-W)	339
18/4/03	Chorley (h)	W31-12	t:Roach,Hudson,Smith,Tassell,Hough g:Hough(5) fg:Hough	2nd	446
21/4/03	Workington (a)	L8-4	t:Loughlin	4th	511
4/5/03	Gateshead (h)	L35-38	t:Roach(2),Cheetham(2),WIngfield,English g:Hough(4),Wingfield fg:Hough	6th	418
9/5/03	Sheffield (a)	W18-23	t:English,Cheetham,Loughlin g:Hough(5) fg:Hough	5th	903
1/6/03	York (h)	L40-2	g:Hough	8th	1,003
8/6/03	London Skolars (a)	W8-31	t:Knox(2),Roach,Ellison,Cannon g:Hough(5) fg:Hough	6th	278
15/6/03	Barrow (a)	L42-20	t:Roach,Hough,Tassell,Hassan g:Russell,Hough	7th	574
22/6/03	Hunslet (h)	D10-10	t:Ellison g:Hough(2) fg:Hough(2)	7th	503
29/6/03	Keighley (a)	L18-15	t:Tassell(2),Knox g:Hough fg:Hough	7th	1,129
13/7/03	Sheffield (h)	W20-18	t:Cannon,Hudson,Roach g:Hough(4)	7th	496
20/7/03	Gateshead (a)	W30-39	t:Hudson(3),Roach(2),Ellison g:Hough(7) fg:Patel	7th	388
27/7/03	Workington (h)	W56-12	t:Bithel(2),Thorpe,Tassell,Roach,Patel,English,Roe,Loughlin g:Hough(8),Gallagher(2)	7th	369
3/8/03	Chorley (a)	L41-22	t:Lomax,Thorpe,English g:Hough(5)	7th	465
10/8/03	London Skolars (h)	W34-12	t:Bithel,Gallagher,Knox,Roach,Hough,English g:Hough(4),Gallagher	7th	289
17/8/03	York (h)	W38-16	t:Roach(3),Hudson(2),Tassell,Loughlin g:Hough(4) fg:Hough(2)	7th	551
24/8/03	Hunslet (a)	L46-14	t:Gorski,Thorpe g:Hough(3)	7th	621
31/8/03	Keighley (h)	L17-19	t:Cannon,Tassell,Roach g:Hough(2) fg:Hough	7th	507
7/9/03	Barrow (h)	L34-38	t:Barton,Bithel,Barraclough,Roach,Hudson,Tassell,Hough g:Hough(2),Russell	7th	455

● Played at JJB Stadium, Wigan

	D.O.B.	APP		TRIES		GOALS		FG		PTS	
		ALL	NL2	ALL	NL2	ALL	NL2	ALL	NL2	ALL	NL2
Mark Ashton	1/10/84	1(2)	1	0	0	0	0	0	0	0	0
Rob Barraclough	27/9/78	20(3)	9(3)	2	1	0	0	0	0	8	4
Danny Barton	7/9/83	4	4	1	1	0	0	0	0	4	4
Grant Bithel	10/5/80	8(8)	4(5)	6	4	0	0	0	0	24	16
Danny Butler	16/6/80	(2)	(2)	0	0	0	0	0	0	0	0
Peter Cannon	22/3/74	29	17	7	3	0	0	0	0	28	12
Andy Cheetham	25/1/75	8(7)	3(2)	4	3	0	0	0	0	16	12
Phil Cushion	15/6/78	11(2)	3(1)	1	0	0	0	0	0	4	0
Mick Durham	18/11/75	3(1)	2(1)	0	0	0	0	0	0	0	0
Dave Ellison	2/4/82	18(3)	7(1)	5	3	0	0	0	0	20	12
Wayne English	8/3/80	30	16	8	5	0	0	0	0	32	20
Rob Gallagher	17/4/82	13(2)	9(1)	1	1	3	3	0	0	10	10
Andy Gorski	31/3/81	4	4	1	1	0	0	0	0	4	4
Lee Hansen	23/7/68	3(1)	3(1)	0	0	0	0	0	0	0	0
Phil Hassan	18/8/74	21(2)	11(2)	3	1	0	0	0	0	12	4
Chris Hough	30/8/81	28(1)	17(1)	6	4	86	63	12	10	208	152
Lee Hudson	4/1/78	25(4)	17	13	8	0	0	0	0	52	32
Mark Hudspith	20/2/72	(1)	0	0	0	0	0	0	0	0	0
Jason Johnson	12/11/78	2(6)	0	1	0	0	0	0	0	4	0
Simon Knox	14/10/72	32	18	6	4	0	0	0	0	24	16
Andy Leathem	30/3/77	16	3	1	0	0	0	0	0	4	0
James Lomax	20/10/81	5(1)	5(1)	1	1	0	0	0	0	4	4
Mike Loughlin	23/9/81	3(11)	3(11)	4	4	0	0	0	0	16	16
Greg McAvoy	18/10/83	1	1	0	0	0	0	0	0	0	0
Adrian Mead	6/4/76	5(1)	0	1	0	0	0	0	0	4	0
David Ogden	18/10/77	(1)	0	0	0	0	0	0	0	0	0
Liam Owen	16/9/83	(2)	(2)	0	0	0	0	0	0	0	0
Safraz Patel	20/10/76	3(7)	3(7)	1	0	0	0	1	1	5	5
Jason Roach	2/5/71	23(2)	15(2)	17	15	0	0	0	0	68	60
Chris Roe	13/7/84	11(14)	10(5)	1	1	0	0	0	0	4	4
Wes Rogers	3/11/77	2	2	0	0	0	0	0	0	0	0
Robert Russell	12/3/79	17(4)	9(2)	2	0	3	2	0	0	14	4
Mike Saunders	20/3/85	3(1)	3(1)	0	0	0	0	0	0	0	0
Alan Shea	29/11/80	3(4)	2	0	0	0	0	0	0	0	0
Kris Smith	20/8/78	7(10)	1(9)	2	1	1	0	0	0	10	4
Kris Tassell	16/9/73	20(2)	14(1)	12	8	0	0	0	0	48	32
Hugh Thorpe	19/12/78	19(5)	10(3)	9	3	0	0	0	0	36	12
Danny Turner	5/9/81	(3)	0	0	0	0	0	0	0	0	0
Daniel Tyres	13/5/76	4(4)	4(4)	0	0	0	0	0	0	0	0
Craig Wingfield	6/9/80	14(7)	4(3)	3	1	6	1	0	0	24	6

Peter Cannon

LEAGUE RECORD
P18-W8-D1-L9
(7th, NL2)
F445, A426, Diff+19
17 points.

CHALLENGE CUP
Quarter Finalists

NATIONAL LEAGUE CUP
5th, West Division

ATTENDANCES
Best - v Featherstone (CC - 1,092)
Worst - v London Skolars (NL2 - 289)
Total (NL2 & NLC only) - 7,591
Average (NL2 & NLC only) - 542
(Down by 5 on 2002)

WORKINGTON TOWN

DATE	FIXTURE	RESULT	SCORERS	LGE	ATT
19/1/03	Rochdale (a) (NLC)	L32-8	t:Heaney g:Hetherington(2)	4th(NLC-N)	778
24/1/03	Wath Brow (a) (CCR3)	L13-12	t:Williamson,Smith g:Hetherington,Heaney	N/A	3,017
2/2/03	Barrow (h) (NLC)	L10-20	t:Wright,Smith g:Heaney	4th(NLC-N)	578
23/2/03	Gateshead (h) (NLC)	W31-24	t:Tunstall,Hetherington,Johnson,Lewthwaite g:Hetherington(7) fg:Hetherington	4th(NLC-N)	503
2/3/03	Whitehaven (a) (NLC)	L36-14	t:Sharp,Wright g:Hetherington(3)	4th(NLC-N)	1,479
9/3/03	Chorley (a) (NLC)	L22-16	t:Smith,Pettit,Hetherington g:Smith,Hetherington	4th(NLC-N)	251
16/3/03	Rochdale (h) (NLC)	L10-44	t:Johnson,D Burns g:Hetherington	4th(NLC-N)	336
23/3/03	Barrow (a) (NLC)	L44-18	t:D Burns,Lewthwaite,Sice g:Hetherington(3)	4th(NLC-N)	788
30/3/03	Whitehaven (h) (NLC)	L10-39	t:Sice,Lewthwaite g:Hetherington	4th(NLC-N)	1,004
6/4/03	Gateshead (a) (NLC)	L42-12	t:Blackburn,Sice g:Smith(2)	4th(NLC-N)	208
13/4/03	Chorley (h) (NLC)	W24-22	t:Wright(2),Beaumont,Sharp g:Hetherington(4)	4th(NLC-N)	355
18/4/03	Barrow (a)	L32-16	t:Long,Sharp,Lewthwaite g:Fisher(2)	7th	953
21/4/03	Swinton (h)	W8-4	t:Lewthwaite g:Hetherington fg:Hetherington(2)	7th	511
4/5/03	Hunslet (a)	L43-38	t:Long(3),Beaumont(2),Lewthwaite,Tunstall,Coulson g:Fisher(3)	7th	393
11/5/03	Chorley (h)	L10-28	t:McDermott,Beaumont g:Fisher	8th	545
25/5/03	Keighley (h)	L8-44	t:Lewthwaite,Tunstall	9th	610
31/5/03	Gateshead (a)	D18-18	t:McDermott(2),Blackburn,Lewthwaite g:Stoddart	9th	287
15/6/03	Sheffield (h)	L16-29	t:Lewthwaite,Tunstall,Fisher g:Stoddart,Fisher	9th	487
22/6/03	York (h)	L14-33	t:McDermott,Murray g:Fisher(3)	9th	539
29/6/03	London Skolars (a)	W6-52	t:Pettit(3),Tunstall(2),Boylan,McDermott,Smith,Beaumont g:Fisher(6),Smith(2)	9th	324
13/7/03	Chorley (a)	L56-18	t:Dean(2),McDermott g:Fisher(3)	9th	302
20/7/03	Hunslet (h)	L18-22	t:Chilton(2),Fisher g:Fisher(3)	9th	505
27/7/03	Swinton (a)	L56-12	t:Horton(2),Johnson	9th	369
3/8/03	Barrow (h)	L20-24	t:Johnson(2),Dean g:Alexander(4)	9th	534
10/8/03	Keighley (a)	L35-6	t:Dean g:Alexander	9th	844
17/8/03	Gateshead (h)	W32-18	t:Johnson(2),Boylan(2),Lewthwaite,Tunstall g:Alexander(4)	8th	406
24/8/03	York (a)	L36-16	t:Chilton,Hutton,Murray g:Alexander(2)	8th	1,106
31/8/03	London Skolars (h)	W80-18	t:Lewthwaite(5),Boylan,Okesene(2),Hutton(2),McDermott,Dean,Alexander, Beaumont,King g:Alexander(7),Robinson	8th	451
6/9/03	Sheffield (a)	L56-11	t:Beaumont,Robinson g:Alexander fg:Alexander	8th	1,011

		APP		TRIES		GOALS		FG		PTS	
	D.O.B.	ALL	NL2	ALL	NL2	ALL	NL2	ALL	NL2	ALL	NL2
Neil Alexander	18/2/77	6	6	1	1	19	19	1	1	43	43
John Allen	16/6/72	1	0	0	0	0	0	0	0	0	0
Craig Barker	1/9/75	7(8)	1(6)	0	0	0	0	0	0	0	0
Jamie Beaumont	22/1/75	22(3)	16(2)	7	6	0	0	0	0	28	24
William Blackburn	26/8/72	14(1)	7	2	1	0	0	0	0	8	4
Shaun Boylan	16/10/80	10(1)	10(1)	5	5	0	0	0	0	20	20
Danny Burns	12/3/75	5	0	2	0	0	0	0	0	8	0
Willie Burns	4/10/71	7(1)	4	0	0	0	0	0	0	0	0
Gary Charlton	5/3/67	7(4)	6(2)	0	0	0	0	0	0	0	0
Scott Chilton	26/10/80	16(3)	12(3)	3	3	0	0	0	0	12	12
Adam Coulson	14/2/83	6(1)	4	1	1	0	0	0	0	4	4
Gareth Dean	31/3/81	13(1)	13(1)	5	5	0	0	0	0	20	20
Jon-Paul Doherty	6/1/77	(3)	(3)	0	0	0	0	0	0	0	0
Lee Dutton	3/11/80	1(6)	1(6)	0	0	0	0	0	0	0	0
Tony Dymtrowski	28/4/78	(2)	0	0	0	0	0	0	0	0	0
Andrew Fearon	21/9/74	1(2)	1(2)	0	0	0	0	0	0	0	0
Craig Fisher	16/9/77	11(4)	11(1)	2	2	22	22	0	0	52	52
Neil Frazer	7/3/76	(2)	0	0	0	0	0	0	0	0	0
Jonathan Heaney	30/10/79	8(1)	0	1	0	2	0	0	0	8	0
Kevin Hetherington	7/6/76	10(2)	1(1)	2	2	24	1	3	2	59	4
Anthony Horton	11/9/79	(7)	(7)	2	2	0	0	0	0	8	8
Anthony Huddart	17/3/81	8	0	0	0	0	0	0	0	0	0
Glen Hutton	17/8/74	8(1)	8(1)	3	3	0	0	0	0	12	12
Matthew Johnson	18/3/82	23(2)	12(2)	7	5	0	0	0	0	28	20
Darren King	9/3/82	7(4)	7(4)	1	1	0	0	0	0	4	4
Graeme Lewthwaite	5/7/72	23(4)	18	15	12	0	0	0	0	60	48
Karl Long	18/11/80	4	4	4	4	0	0	0	0	16	16
Brett McDermott	10/9/78	26	15	7	7	0	0	0	0	28	28
Stephen Milnes	10/2/68	(1)	0	0	0	0	0	0	0	0	0
Barrie Murdock	16/11/82	(2)	0	0	0	0	0	0	0	0	0
Anthony Murray	25/5/77	14(1)	13(1)	2	2	0	0	0	0	8	8
Hitro Okesene	22/9/71	24(4)	16(1)	2	2	0	0	0	0	8	8
David Pettit	23/10/79	6(15)	1(12)	4	3	0	0	0	0	16	12
Stewart Rhodes	16/1/72	(2)	(2)	0	0	0	0	0	0	0	0
James Robinson	4/3/79	13(6)	11(3)	1	1	1	1	0	0	6	6
Lokeni Savelio	24/11/69	2	0	0	0	0	0	0	0	0	0
Dean Sharp	23/7/76	18(1)	10(1)	3	1	0	0	0	0	12	4
Carl Sice	13/4/80	13	2	3	0	0	0	0	0	12	0
Brett Smith	17/10/77	13(4)	6(2)	4	1	5	2	0	0	26	8
Steve Stoddart	22/10/76	2(1)	2(1)	0	0	2	2	0	0	4	4
Alan Telford	5/7/77	(1)	0	0	0	0	0	0	0	0	0
Matthew Tunstall	7/9/77	18(9)	13(4)	7	6	0	0	0	0	28	24
Owen Williamson	30/10/80	3	0	1	0	0	0	0	0	4	0
Ricky Wright	15/3/77	6(1)	2	4	0	0	0	0	0	16	0
John Young	21/9/78	(1)	0	0	0	0	0	0	0	0	0

Graeme Lewthwaite

LEAGUE RECORD
P18-W4-D1-L13
(8th, NL2)
F393, A558, Diff-165
9 points.

CHALLENGE CUP
Round Three

NATIONAL LEAGUE CUP
4th, North Division

ATTENDANCES
Best - v Whitehaven (NLC - 1,004)
Worst - v Rochdale (NLC - 336)
Total (NL2 & NLC only) - 7,364
Average (NL2 & NLC only) - 526
(Down by 494 on 2002)

YORK CITY KNIGHTS

DATE	FIXTURE	RESULT	SCORERS	LGE	ATT
19/1/03	Hull KR (h) (NLC)	L26-36	t:A Godfrey,Callaghan,Yeaman,C Smith g:Hallas(5)	4th(NLC-E)	3,105
26/1/03	Skirlaugh (a) (CCR3)	W8-20	t:Yeaman(2),Callaghan g:Hallas(4)	N/A	943
2/2/03	Doncaster (a) (NLC)	L24-4	g:Cain(2)	5th(NLC-E)	1,029
9/2/03	Doncaster (h) (CCR4)	L20-21	t:Molloy(2),Jackson g:Hallas(4)	N/A	1,511
16/2/03	Featherstone (a) (NLC)	L36-22	t:Krause(2),Fletcher,Callaghan,C Smith g:Hallas	5th(NLC-E)	1,728
23/2/03	Dewsbury (h) (NLC)	L18-38	t:C Smith,Cain,Callaghan g:Robinson(2),Yeaman	5th(NLC-E)	1,231
9/3/03	Sheffield (a) (NLC)	W12-32	t:Ramsden,Callaghan,Molloy,C Smith g:Hallas(8)	4th(NLC-E)	730
16/3/03	Doncaster (h) (NLC)	W34-20	t:Hallas,Broadbent,Fletcher,Cain,Callaghan,Krause g:Hallas(5)	4th(NLC-E)	1,133
23/3/03	Hull KR (a) (NLC)	L32-14	t:Cain(2) g:Robinson(2),Hallas	4th(NLC-E)	1,580
30/3/03	Sheffield (h) (NLC)	W32-18	t:Cain,Rhodes,Ramsden,Krause,C Smith,Lloyd g:Thaler(4)	4th(NLC-E)	978
6/4/03	Dewsbury (a) (NLC)	W24-28	t:Thaler,C Smith,A Godfrey,Krause g:Thaler(6)	4th(NLC-E)	654
13/4/03	Featherstone (h) (NLC)	L14-32	t:Krause(2),Robinson g:Thaler	4th(NLC-E)	1,415
18/4/03	Gateshead (h)	L12-29	t:Lloyd,Sheriffe g:Thaler(2)	8th	1,271
21/4/03	Sheffield (a)	L30-24	t:Hallas(2),Sheriffe,Blaymire g:Thaler(4)	8th	897
4/5/03	London Skolars (h)	D16-16	t:Sheriffe,Brough,Cain g:Hallas,Brough	8th	1,012
11/5/03	Keighley (a)	L38-26	t:Law(2),Deakin,Cain,Krause g:Brough(3)	9th	1,077
25/5/03	Barrow (a)	W20-27	t:Law(2),Callaghan,Brough,Fletcher g:Brough(3) fg:Brough	8th	742
1/6/03	Swinton (h)	W40-2	t:C Smith(2),Blaymire(2),Law,A Godfrey,Hallas g:Brough(6)	6th	1,003
15/6/03	Hunslet (a)	W18-40	t:Krause,Jackson,Deakin,Brough,C Smith,Callaghan,Cain g:Brough(6)	6th	649
22/6/03	Workington (a)	W14-33	t:C Smith,Rhodes,Hallas,Law,A Godfrey g:Brough(6) fg:Brough	5th	539
29/6/03	Chorley (a)	L29-14	t:Law,Cain g:Brough(3)	6th	450
13/7/03	Keighley (a)	W48-28	t:A Godfrey(2),Law(2),Jackson,Spink,Rhodes,Woodcock g:Brough(8)	6th	1,835
20/7/03	London Skolars (a)	W6-66	t:Cain(3),Woodcock(2),Brough,Callaghan,Law,A Godfrey,Kama,Krause g:Brough(11)	6th	425
27/7/03	Sheffield (h)	L18-25	t:Kama,A Godfrey,Law g:Brough(3)	6th	1,301
3/8/03	Gateshead (a)	W8-64	t:Woodcock(3),Callaghan(2),Cain,Molloy,Brough,A Godfrey,Hughes,Krause g:Brough(10)	6th	413
10/8/03	Barrow (h)	W28-16	t:Woodcock,Krause,Jackson,Callaghan g:Brough(6)	5th	1,063
17/8/03	Swinton (a)	L38-16	t:Kama(2),Hughes g:Brough(2)	6th	551
24/8/03	Workington (h)	W36-16	t:Krause,A Godfrey,Hallas,Kama,Callaghan,Spink g:Brough(6)	5th	1,106
31/8/03	Chorley (h)	W36-32	t:Stewart(2),Kama,Hallas,Okul,A Godfrey g:Brough(6)	4th	1,077
5/9/03	Hunslet (h)	W32-16	t:Hallas(2),A Godfrey,Hughes,S Godfrey g:Brough(6)	4th	1,642
14/9/03	Barrow (h) (EPO)	L30-50	t:Hughes,Krause,Callaghan,S Godfrey,A Godfrey g:Brough(5)	N/A	1,299

		APP		TRIES		GOALS		FG		PTS	
	D.O.B.	ALL	NL2	ALL	NL2	ALL	NL2	ALL	NL2	ALL	NL2
Chris Beever	18/2/81	10(2)	1	0	0	0	0	0	0	0	0
Matt Blaymire	10/6/82	4(2)	4(2)	3	3	0	0	0	0	12	12
David Bolus	29/3/80	3(12)	(4)	0	0	0	0	0	0	0	0
Dan Briggs	15/7/79	(3)	(3)	0	0	0	0	0	0	0	0
Paul Broadbent	24/5/68	9(8)	3(7)	1	0	0	0	0	0	4	0
Danny Brough	15/1/83	17	17	5	5	91	91	2	2	204	204
James Brown	27/9/79	1(2)	1(2)	0	0	0	0	0	0	0	0
Andy Burland	5/11/77	3(10)	3(7)	0	0	0	0	0	0	0	0
Mark Cain	3/5/76	21(2)	12(1)	13	8	2	0	0	0	56	32
Darren Callaghan	6/8/76	24(5)	12(5)	14	8	0	0	0	0	56	32
Sam Clarke	19/3/80	1(1)	1	0	0	0	0	0	0	0	0
Jermaine Coleman	17/6/82	1(1)	0	0	0	0	0	0	0	0	0
Leigh Deakin	27/12/72	7(4)	7(4)	2	2	0	0	0	0	8	8
Mick Embleton	17/10/81	2(3)	(1)	0	0	0	0	0	0	0	0
Jonathan Firth	10/6/80	5	0	0	0	0	0	0	0	0	0
Scott Fletcher	7/2/75	17(1)	5(1)	3	1	0	0	0	0	12	4
Craig Forsyth	24/10/70	6(8)	6(8)	0	0	0	0	0	0	0	0
Tommy Gallagher	10/9/83	1(1)	0	0	0	0	0	0	0	0	0
Alex Godfrey	2/12/78	21	14	13	11	0	0	0	0	52	44
Stuart Godfrey	19/11/78	1(1)	1(1)	2	2	0	0	0	0	8	8
Graeme Hallas	27/2/71	20(2)	13(2)	9	8	29	1	0	0	94	34
Richard Hayes	21/2/70	31	19	0	0	0	0	0	0	0	0
Joe Helme	1/4/84	7(1)	7(1)	0	0	0	0	0	0	0	0
Carl Hughes	30/11/82	4(3)	4(3)	4	4	0	0	0	0	16	16
Lee Jackson	12/3/69	20(1)	14(1)	4	3	0	0	0	0	16	12
Rob Kama	5/8/76	11(1)	11(1)	6	6	0	0	0	0	24	24
Damian Kennedy	2/6/83	3(2)	0	0	0	0	0	0	0	0	0
Trevor Krause	17/11/72	31	19	14	7	0	0	0	0	56	28
Neil Law	23/10/74	12	12	11	11	0	0	0	0	44	44
Gareth Lloyd	12/8/75	5(6)	2	2	1	0	0	0	0	8	4
George Mack	8/10/80	1	1	0	0	0	0	0	0	0	0
Lee McTigue	24/7/78	1	0	0	0	0	0	0	0	0	0
Neil Mears	9/1/79	(3)	(3)	0	0	0	0	0	0	0	0
Gavin Molloy	3/3/80	12(8)	1(8)	4	1	0	0	0	0	16	4
John Okul	24/11/72	(2)	(2)	1	1	0	0	0	0	4	4
Mick Ramsden	13/11/71	27(1)	17	2	2	0	0	0	0	8	8
Scott Rhodes	21/6/80	15	13	3	2	0	0	0	0	12	8
Leigh Riddell	28/9/75	1(3)	1(3)	0	0	0	0	0	0	0	0
Darren Robinson	28/5/79	4(5)	1	1	0	4	0	0	0	12	0
Rikki Sheriffe	5/5/84	4	3	3	3	0	0	0	0	12	12
Chris Smith	31/10/75	20	8	10	4	0	0	0	0	40	16
Dave Smith	13/9/72	2	0	0	0	0	0	0	0	0	0
Kevin Spink	1/4/81	1(4)	1(4)	2	2	0	0	0	0	8	8
Carl Stannard	22/3/79	1(4)	(1)	0	0	0	0	0	0	0	0
Mark Stewart	11/2/81	4	4	2	2	0	0	0	0	8	8
Adam Thaler	3/9/83	5	2	1	0	17	6	0	0	38	12
Craig Westmoreland	8/2/83	(4)	0	0	0	0	0	0	0	0	0
Johnny Woodcock	5/2/81	5	5	7	7	0	0	0	0	28	28
Scott Yeaman	25/2/82	3(3)	0	3	0	1	0	0	0	14	0

Danny Brough

LEAGUE RECORD
P18-W11-D1-L6
(4th, NL2/Elimination Play Off)
F576, A381, Diff+195
23 points.

CHALLENGE CUP
Round Four

NATIONAL LEAGUE CUP
4th, East Division

ATTENDANCES
Best - v Hull KR (NLC - 3,105)
Worst - v Sheffield (NLC - 978)
Total (NL2, inc play-offs,
& NLC only) - 20,471
Average (NL2, inc play-offs,
& NLC only) - 1,365
(Up by 696 on 2002, York Wasps)

273

NATIONAL LEAGUE ONE 2003
Round by Round

WEEK 1

Thursday 17th April 2003

OLDHAM 28 ROCHDALE HORNETS 33

OLDHAM: 1 Gavin Dodd; 2 Chris Irwin; 3 Paul Anderson; 4 Iain Marsh; 5 Chris Campbell; 6 Simon Svabic; 7 Neil Roden; 8 Steve Molloy; 9 John Hough; 10 Paul Norton; 11 Lee Doran; 12 Ryan Stazicker; 13 Chris Morley. Subs (all used): 14 Keith Brennan; 15 Gareth Barber; 16 Danny Guest; 17 Dane Morgan.
Tries: Norton (21), Stazicker (34), Campbell (39), Doran (74); **Goals:** Svabic 4, Barber 2.
HORNETS: 1 Paul Owen; 2 Mick Nanyn; 3 James Bunyan; 4 Jon Roper; 5 Marlon Billy; 6 Radney Bowker; 7 Ian Watson; 8 Paul Southern; 9 Richard Pachniuk; 10 Andy Grundy; 11 David Larder; 12 Paul Smith; 13 Damian Ball. Subs: 14 Sean Cooper (not used); 15 Matthew Leigh; 16 Gareth Price; 17 Matthew Long.
Tries: Bunyan (11, 24), Roper (16, 41), Long (51), Larder (69); **Goals:** Nanyn 4; **Field goal:** Watson.
Rugby Leaguer & League Express Men of the Match: *Oldham:* Neil Roden; *Hornets:* Jon Roper.
Penalty count: 11-11; **Half-time:** 20-18; **Referee:** Ronnie Laughton (Barnsley); **Attendance:** 1,754.

Friday 18th April 2003

WHITEHAVEN 22 SALFORD CITY REDS 22

WHITEHAVEN: 1 Gary Broadbent; 2 Steven Wood; 3 David Seeds; 4 Howard Hill; 5 Mark Wallace; 6 Leroy Joe; 7 Darren Holt; 8 Dean Vaughan; 9 Aaron Lester; 10 David Fatialofa; 11 Craig Chambers; 12 Chris McKinney; 13 Garry Purdham. Subs (all used): 14 Lee Kiddie; 15 Spencer Miller; 16 Tony Cunningham; 17 Phil Sherwen.
Tries: Chambers (20, 66), Seeds (32), Wood (63); **Goals:** Holt 3.
CITY REDS: 1 Jason Flowers; 2 Michael Platt; 3 Stuart Littler; 4 Andy Kirk; 5 Danny Arnold; 6 Cliff Beverley; 7 Gavin Clinch; 8 Neil Baynes; 9 Malcolm Alker; 10 Andy Coley; 11 Simon Baldwin; 12 Neil Lowe; 13 Chris Charles. Subs (all used): 14 David Highton; 15 Paul Highton; 16 Lee Marsh; 17 Andy Gorski.
Tries: Lowe (6), Platt (9, 53 - penalty try), Littler (79); **Goals:** Marsh 2, Charles.
Rugby Leaguer & League Express Men of the Match: *Whitehaven:* Aaron Lester; *City Reds:* Andy Coley.
Penalty count: 4-7; **Half time:** 10-8; **Referee:** Robert Connolly (Wigan); **Attendance:** 2,136.

HULL KINGSTON ROVERS 17 LEIGH CENTURIONS 28

ROVERS: 1 Craig Poucher; 2 Nick Pinkney; 3 Ian Bell; 4 Craig Farrell; 5 Alasdair McClarron; 6 Chris Stephenson; 7 Latham Tawhai; 8 Richard Wilson; 9 Paul Pickering; 10 Jamie Bovill; 11 Adam Sullivan; 12 Jon Aston; 13 Andy Smith. Subs (all used): 14 Dean Andrews; 15 Anthony Seibold; 16 Harvey Howard; 17 Paul Fletcher.
Tries: McClarron (14, 20, 46); **Goals:** Stephenson 2; **Field goal:** Tawhai.
CENTURIONS: 1 David Alstead; 2 Leroy Rivett; 3 Alan Hadcroft; 4 Phil Kendrick; 5 Michael Watts; 6 Patrick Weisner; 7 John Duffy; 8 Sonny Nickle; 9 Paul Rowley; 10 Paul Norman; 11 Sean Richardson; 12 Bryan Henare; 13 Adam Bristow. Subs (all used): 14 Dale Holdstock; 15 Willie Swann; 16 Lee Sanderson; 17 David Bradbury.
Tries: Hadcroft (25), Holdstock (34, 71), Alstead (52), Kendrick (56); **Goals:** Duffy 3; **Field goals:** Duffy 2.
Rugby Leaguer & League Express Men of the Match: *Rovers:* Alasdair McClarron; *Centurions:* John Duffy.
Penalty count: 2-6; **Half-time:** 11-10; **Referee:** Peter Taberner (Wigan); **Attendance:** 2,030.

BATLEY BULLDOGS 28 DEWSBURY RAMS 10

BULLDOGS: 1 Craig Lingard; 2 Mark Sibson; 3 Simon Lewis; 4 Danny Maun; 5 Matt Bramald; 6 Mark Toohey; 7 Barry Eaton; 8 Craig Booth; 9 Gavin Swinson; 10 Andy Spink; 11 David Rourke; 12 Will Cartledge; 13 Ryan Horsley. Subs (all used): 14 Mark Cass; 15 Paul Harrison; 16 Joe Berry; 17 Joe Naidole.
Tries: Lingard (2), Spink (15), Horsley (25), Bramald (44), Maun (65); **Goals:** Eaton 4.
RAMS: 1 Nathan Batty; 2 Michael Wainwright; 3 Paul Steele; 4 Danny Wood; 5 Craig Miles; 6 Danny Brough; 7 Craig Nipperess; 8 Frank Watene; 9 Andy Heptinstall; 10 Paul Hicks; 11 Anthony Thewliss; 12 Billy Kershaw; 13 Chris Redfearn. Subs (all used): 14 Jimmy Elston; 15 Danny Evans; 16 Tony Fella; 17 Glen Spedding.
Tries: Miles (10), Fella (65); **Goal:** Wood.
Sin bin: Steele (23) - interference.
Rugby Leaguer & League Express Men of the Match: *Bulldogs:* Barry Eaton; *Rams:* Frank Watene.
Penalty count: 8-10; **Half time:** 20-4; **Referee:** Steve Nicholson (Whitehaven); **Attendance:** 1,245.

FEATHERSTONE ROVERS 44 DONCASTER DRAGONS 18

ROVERS: 1 Nathan Graham; 2 Jamie Stokes; 3 Brendan O'Meara; 4 Ian Brown; 5 Adrian Flynn; 6 Richard Agar; 7 Carl Briggs; 8 Ian Tonks; 9 Richard Chapman; 10 Stuart Dickens; 11 Steve Dooler; 12 Andy Rice; 13 Danny Seal. Subs (all used): 14 Richard Whiting; 15 Andy Bailey; 16 Robin Jowitt; 17 Chris Molyneux.
Tries: Flynn (14, 45), Tonks (21), O'Meara (24), Seal (42, 57), Graham (68), Bailey (75); **Goals:** Dickens 3, Briggs 3.
Sin bin: Rice (39) - fighting.
DRAGONS: 1 Chris Ross; 2 Paul Gleadhill; 3 Craig Horne; 4 Simon Irving; 5 Jason Lee; 6 Paul Mansson; 7 Mark Moxon; 8 Gareth Handford; 9 Peter Edwards; 10 Jamie Fielden; 11 Peter Green; 12 Craig Lawton; 13 Matt Walker. Subs (all used): 14 James Walker; 15 Craig Forsyth; 16 Chris Hemmings; 17 Dean Colton.
Tries: Irving (11), Ross (70), Mansson (72); **Goals:** Irving 3.
Sin bin: Mansson (39) - fighting.
Rugby Leaguer & League Express Men of the Match: *Rovers:* Adrian Flynn; *Dragons:* Paul Mansson.
Penalty count: 8-6; **Half-time:** 18-6; **Referee:** Mike Dawber (Wigan); **Attendance:** 1,540.

WEEK 2

Monday 21st April 2003

DEWSBURY RAMS 26 FEATHERSTONE ROVERS 20

RAMS: 1 Nathan Batty; 2 Michael Wainwright; 3 Ryan Hardy; 4 Danny Wood; 5 George Mack; 6 Mark Barlow; 7 Danny Brough; 8 Frank Watene; 9 Andy Heptinstall; 10 Carl Sayer; 11 Paul Hicks; 12 Billy Kershaw; 13 Chris Redfearn. Subs (all used): 14 David Oldfield; 15 Tony Fella; 16 Glen Spedding; 17 Paul Steele.
Tries: Wainwright (3, 17), Mack (11), Batty (44), Oldfield (75); **Goals:** Brough 2; **Field goals:** Heptinstall, Brough.
ROVERS: 1 Nathan Graham; 2 Jamie Stokes; 3 Brendan O'Meara; 4 Ian Brown; 5 Adrian Flynn; 6 Richard Agar; 7 Carl Briggs; 8 Ian Tonks; 9 Richard Chapman; 10 Stuart Dickens; 11 Steve Dooler; 12 Andy Rice; 13 Danny Seal. Subs (all used): 14 Richard Whiting; 15 Paul Darley; 16 Andy Bailey; 17 Robin Jowitt.
Tries: Chapman (40), Graham (47), Stokes (50), Briggs (66); **Goals:** Briggs 2.
Rugby Leaguer & League Express Men of the Match: *Rams:* Frank Watene; *Rovers:* Ian Tonks.
Penalty count: 5-7; **Half-time:** 16-6; **Referee:** Colin Morris (Huddersfield); **Attendance:** 1,247.

ROCHDALE HORNETS 29 HULL KINGSTON ROVERS 18

HORNETS: 1 Paul Owen; 2 Mick Nanyn; 3 James Bunyan; 4 Jon Roper; 5 Marlon Billy; 6 Radney Bowker; 7 Ian Watson; 8 Paul Southern; 9 Richard Pachniuk; 10 Andy Grundy; 11 David Larder; 12 Paul Smith; 13 Damian Ball. Subs (all used): 14 Sean Cooper; 15 Matthew Leigh; 16 Gareth Price; 17 Matthew Long.
Tries: Ball (17), Billy (20), Smith (32, 75), Pachniuk (63); **Goals:** Nanyn 4; **Field goal:** Watson.
ROVERS: 1 Craig Poucher; 2 Nick Pinkney; 3 Mark Blanchard; 4 Craig Farrell; 5 Alasdair McClarron; 6 Jimmy Walker; 7 Latham Tawhai; 8 Richard Wilson; 9 Paul Pickering; 10 Harvey Howard; 11 Anthony Seibold; 12 Jon Aston; 13 Andy Smith. Subs (all used): 14 Steve Cochran; 15 Dean Andrews; 16 Adam Sullivan; 17 Paul Fletcher.
Tries: Seibold (12, 72), Pinkney (23), McClarron (70); **Goal:** Tawhai.
Rugby Leaguer & League Express Men of the Match: *Hornets:* Richard Pachniuk; *Rovers:* Paul Fletcher.
Penalty count: 5-10; **Half-time:** 14-10; **Referee:** Karl Kirkpatrick (Warrington); **Attendance:** 1,097.

SALFORD CITY REDS 54 BATLEY BULLDOGS 12

CITY REDS: 1 Jason Flowers; 2 Alan Hunte; 3 Stuart Littler; 4 Andy Kirk; 5 Danny Arnold; 6 Cliff Beverley; 7 Gavin Clinch; 8 Neil Baynes; 9 Malcolm Alker; 10 Andy Coley; 11 Simon Baldwin; 12 Lee Marsh; 13 Chris Charles. Subs (all used): 14 David Highton; 15 Paul Highton; 16 Karl Fitzpatrick; 17 Andy Gorski.
Tries: Beverley (1, 23, 47), Charles (3, 61, 65), Littler (10), Kirk (26, 33), Hunte (58); **Goals:** Charles 7.
BULLDOGS: 1 Craig Lingard; 2 Mark Sibson; 3 Gavin Swinson; 4 Danny Maun; 5 Matt Bramald; 6 Mark Toohey; 7 Barry Eaton; 8 Craig Booth; 9 Kris Lythe; 10 Joe Naidole; 11 David Rourke; 12 Will Cartledge; 13 Ryan Horsley. Subs (all used): 14 Leon Williamson; 15 Paul Harrison; 16 Joe Berry; 17 Steve Hill.
Tries: Maun (37), Bramald (40); **Goals:** Eaton 2.
Rugby Leaguer & League Express Men of the Match: *City Reds:* Cliff Beverley; *Bulldogs:* Danny Maun.
Penalty count: 7-7; **Half-time:** 32-12; **Referee:** Steve Nicholson (Whitehaven); **Attendance:** 2,074.

LEIGH CENTURIONS 19 WHITEHAVEN 12

CENTURIONS: 1 David Alstead; 2 Michael Watts; 3 Dale Holdstock; 4 Phil Kendrick; 5 Alan Hadcroft; 6 Lee Sanderson; 7 John Duffy; 8 Sonny Nickle; 9 Paul Rowley; 10 Paul Norman; 11 Sean Richardson; 12 Bryan Henare; 13 Adam Bristow. Subs (all used): 14 Willie Swann; 15 Patrick Weisner; 16 John Hamilton; 17 David Bradbury.
Tries: Henare (14), Rowley (51), Holdstock (59), Alstead (69); **Goal:** Sanderson; **Field goal:** Weisner.
WHITEHAVEN: 1 Gary Broadbent; 2 Steven Wood; 3 David Seeds; 4 Howard Hill; 5 Jamie Stenhouse; 6 Leroy Joe; 7 Darren Holt; 8 Dean Vaughan; 9 Aaron Lester; 10 David Fatialofa; 11 Chris McKinney; 12 Graeme Morton; 13 Garry Purdham. Subs (all used): 14 Lee Kiddie; 15 Spencer Miller; 16 Mike Whitehead; 17 Tony Cunningham.
Tries: Stenhouse (62, 80); **Goals:** Holt 2.
Rugby Leaguer & League Express Men of the Match: *Centurions:* Paul Rowley; *Whitehaven:* Gary Broadbent.
Penalty count: 8-10; **Half-time:** 6-2; **Referee:** Richard Silverwood (Dewsbury); **Attendance:** 1,996.

WEEK 3

Sunday 4th May 2003

BATLEY BULLDOGS 12 LEIGH CENTURIONS 38

BULLDOGS: 1 Craig Lingard; 2 Matt Bramald; 3 Simon Lewis; 4 Danny Maun; 5 Leon Williamson; 6 David Gibbons; 7 Barry Eaton; 8 Andy Spink; 9 Will Cartledge; 10 Steve Hill; 11 Paul Harrison; 12 Joe Berry; 13 Ryan Horsley. Subs (all used): 14 Mark Sibson; 15 Mark Cass; 16 Craig Booth; 17 Joe Naidole.
Tries: Williamson (45), Lingard (66); **Goals:** Eaton 2.
CENTURIONS: 1 David Alstead; 2 Michael Watts; 3 Dale Cardoza; 4 Phil Kendrick; 5 Damian Munro; 6 Patrick Weisner; 7 John Duffy; 8 Sonny Nickle; 9 Paul Rowley; 10 Paul Norman; 11 Sean Richardson; 12 Bryan Henare; 13 Adam Bristow. Subs (all used): 14 Willie Swann; 15 Dale Holdstock; 16 Lee Sanderson; 17 David Bradbury.
Tries: Kendrick (10), Bristow (35), Duffy (40), Alstead (64), Nickle (74), Rowley (76), Norman (79); **Goals:** Weisner 5.
Rugby Leaguer & League Express Men of the Match: *Bulldogs:* Barry Eaton; *Centurions:* John Duffy.
Penalty count: 11-5; **Half-time:** 0-12; **Referee:** Steve Nicholson (Whitehaven); **Attendance:** 1,034.

DONCASTER DRAGONS 28 ROCHDALE HORNETS 44

DRAGONS: 1 Chris Ross; 2 Johnny Woodcock; 3 Shaun Archer; 4 Simon Irving; 5 Paul Gleadhill; 6 Paul Mansson; 7 Mark Moxon; 8 Gareth Handford; 9 Peter Edwards; 10 Chris Hemmings; 11 Peter Green; 12 Craig Lawton; 13 Brad Hepi. Subs (all used): 14 James Walker; 15 Dean Colton; 16 Jamie Fielden; 17 Alex Muff.
Tries: Hemmings (4, 49), Gleadhill (38), Mansson (73), P Green (79); **Goals:** Woodcock 4.
HORNETS: 1 Paul Owen; 2 Mick Nanyn; 3 James Bunyan; 4 Jon Roper; 5 Marlon Billy; 6 Radney Bowker; 7 Ian Watson; 8 Paul Southern; 9 Richard Pachniuk; 10 David Stephenson; 11 David Larder; 12 Paul Smith; 13 Damian Ball. Subs (all used): 14 Warren Ayres; 15 Matthew Leigh; 16 Gareth Price; 17 Andy Grundy.
Tries: Roper (1, 25, 31), Owen (22), Pachniuk (47), Bowker (67), Watson (76), Leigh (80); **Goals:** Nanyn 6.
Rugby Leaguer & League Express Men of the Match: *Dragons:* Chris Hemmings; *Hornets:* Jon Roper.
Penalty count: 6-9; **Half-time:** 12-18; **Referee:** Peter Taberner (Wigan); **Attendance:** 805.

FEATHERSTONE ROVERS 18 SALFORD CITY REDS 16

ROVERS: 1 Nathan Graham; 2 Jamie Stokes; 6 Chris Langley; 4 Ian Brown; 5 Adrian Flynn; 3 Brendan O'Meara; 7 Carl Briggs; 8 Ian Tonks; 9 Richard Chapman; 10 Stuart Dickens; 11 Steve Dooler; 12 Andy Rice; 13 Danny Seal. Subs (all used): 14 Paul Darley; 15 Andy Bailey; 16 Robin Jowitt; 17 Chris Molyneux.
Tries: Chapman (9), Langley (72); **Goals:** Dickens 4, Briggs.
CITY REDS: 1 Jason Flowers; 2 Michael Platt; 3 Alan Hunte; 4 Stuart Littler; 5 Danny Arnold; 6 Cliff Beverley; 7 Gavin Clinch; 8 Andy Coley; 9 Malcolm Alker; 10 Paul Highton; 11 Simon Baldwin; 12 Lee Marsh; 13 Chris Charles. Subs (all used): 14 David Highton; 15 Steve Blakeley; 16 Neil Lowe; 17 Gareth Haggerty.
Tries: Arnold (38), Alker (49), Beverley (79); **Goals:** Charles, Blakeley.
Rugby Leaguer & League Express Men of the Match: *Rovers:* Stuart Dickens; *City Reds:* Neil Lowe.
Penalty count: 9-9; **Half-time:** 8-6; **Referee:** Julian King (St Helens)/Robert Hicks (Oldham); **Attendance:** 1,616.

OLDHAM 41 DEWSBURY RAMS 21

OLDHAM: 1 Gavin Dodd; 2 Chris Irwin; 3 Paul Anderson; 4 Lee Doran; 5 Joe McNicholas; 6 Gareth Barber; 7 Neil Roden; 8 Steve Molloy; 9 John Hough; 10 Paul Norton; 11 Chris Morley; 12 Ryan Stazicker; 13 Phil Farrell. Subs (all used): 14 Keith Brennan; 15 Simon Svabic; 16 Danny Guest; 17 Dane Morgan.
Tries: Anderson (7, 19), Morley (22), Molloy (26), Morgan (37), Stazicker (55), Barber (58); **Goals:** Barber 6; **Field goal:** Roden.
RAMS: 1 Nathan Batty; 2 Michael Wainwright; 3 Paul Steele; 4 Danny Wood; 5 George Mack; 6 Adam Thaler; 7 Craig Nipperess; 8 Paul Hicks; 9 Andy Heptinstall; 10 Tony Fella; 11 Anthony Thewliss; 12 Billy Kershaw; 13 Chris Redfearn. Subs (all used): 14 Jimmy Elston; 15 Mark Barlow; 16 Danny Evans; 17 Glen Spedding.
Tries: Heptinstall (13), Wood (48), Barlow (66), Wainwright (69); **Goals:** Wood 2; **Field goal:** Heptinstall.
Sin bin: Evans (34) - deliberate offside.
Rugby Leaguer & League Express Men of the Match: *Oldham:* Neil Roden; *Rams:* Jimmy Elston.
Penalty count: 10-11; **Half-time:** 29-7; **Referee:** Ashley Klein (London); **Attendance:** 1,198.

WHITEHAVEN 26 HULL KINGSTON ROVERS 2

WHITEHAVEN: 1 Gary Broadbent; 2 Steven Wood; 3 David Seeds; 4 Howard Hill; 5 Mark Wallace; 6 Leroy Joe; 7 Darren Holt; 8 Dean Vaughan; 9 Aaron Lester; 10 David Fatialofa; 11 Chris McKinney; 12 Spencer Miller; 13 Garry Purdham. Subs (all used): 14 Lee Kiddie; 15 Marc Jackson; 16 Carl Sice; 17 Ryan Campbell.
Tries: Wallace (19, 40), Joe (32), Wood (66), Jackson (80); **Goals:** Holt 3.
ROVERS: 1 Craig Poucher; 2 Nick Pinkney; 3 Mark Blanchard; 4 Craig Farrell; 5 Alasdair McClarron; 6 Chris Stephenson; 7 Craig Murdock; 8 Richard Wilson; 9 Paul Pickering; 10 Harvey Howard; 11 Anthony Seibold; 12 Jon Aston; 13 Andy Smith. Subs (all used): 14 Lynton Stott; 15 Adam Sullivan; 16 Dean Busby; 17 Paul Fletcher.
Goal: Stephenson.
Rugby Leaguer & League Express Men of the Match: *Whitehaven:* David Fatialofa; *Rovers:* Paul Pickering.
Penalty count: 3-5; **Half-time:** 16-2; **Referee:** Colin Morris (Huddersfield); **Attendance:** 1,315.

Saturday 10th May 2003

SALFORD CITY REDS 44 OLDHAM 12

CITY REDS: 1 Jason Flowers; 2 Michael Platt; 3 Stuart Littler; 4 Lee Marsh; 5 Alan Hunte; 6 Cliff Beverley; 7 Gavin Clinch; 8 Neil Baynes; 9 Malcolm Alker; 10 Paul Highton; 11 Simon Baldwin; 12 Neil Lowe; 13 Chris Charles. Subs (all used): 14 David Highton; 15 Steve Blakeley; 16 Andy Coley; 17 Gareth Haggerty.
Tries: Alker (2, 5), Marsh (17), Lowe (20), Hunte (33, 37, 70), Baldwin (40); **Goals:** Charles 5, Blakeley.
OLDHAM: 1 Gavin Dodd; 2 Chris Irwin; 3 Paul Anderson; 4 Lee Doran; 5 Chris Campbell; 6 Gareth Barber; 7 Neil Roden; 8 Steve Molloy; 9 John Hough; 10 Paul Norton; 11 Chris Morley; 12 Ryan Stazicker; 13 Phil Farrell. Subs (all used): 14 Jon Goddard; 15 Simon Svabic; 16 Danny Guest; 17 Dane Morgan.
Tries: Morgan (17), Barber (61); **Goals:** Barber 2.
Rugby Leaguer & League Express Men of the Match: *City Reds:* Chris Charles; *Oldham:* Gareth Barber.
Penalty count: 7-5; **Half-time:** 38-6;
Referee: Robert Connolly (Wigan); **Attendance:** 1,657.

WEEK 4

Sunday 11th May 2003

DEWSBURY RAMS 12 DONCASTER DRAGONS 16

RAMS: 1 Nathan Batty; 2 Michael Wainwright; 3 Ryan Hardy; 4 Danny Wood; 5 George Mack; 6 Adam Thaler; 7 Craig Nipperess; 8 Paul Hicks; 9 Jimmy Elston; 10 Glen Spedding; 11 Ian Kirke; 12 Billy Kershaw; 13 Richard Slater. Subs (all used): 14 Andy Heptinstall; 15 John Waddell; 16 Tony Fella; 17 Danny Evans.
Tries: Elston (21), Waddell (72); **Goals:** Wood 2.
DRAGONS: 1 Johnny Woodcock; 2 Alex Muff; 3 Craig Horne; 4 Simon Irving; 5 Paul Gleadhill; 6 Paul Mansson; 7 Dean Colton; 8 Chris Hemmings; 9 Brad Hepi; 10 James Walker; 11 Peter Green; 12 Peter Edwards; 13 Chris Ross. Subs (all used): 14 Gareth Handford; 15 Matt Walker; 16 Jamie Fielden; 17 Craig Lawton.
Tries: Mansson (63), Hepi (69), Colton (78);
Goals: Woodcock 2.
Rugby Leaguer & League Express Men of the Match: *Rams:* Jimmy Elston; *Dragons:* Paul Mansson.
Penalty count: 4-3; **Half-time:** 8-0;
Referee: Colin Morris (Huddersfield); **Attendance:** 929.

LEIGH CENTURIONS 50 FEATHERSTONE ROVERS 12

CENTURIONS: 1 David Alstead; 2 Damian Munro; 3 Dale Cardoza; 4 Phil Kendrick; 5 Alan Hadcroft; 6 Patrick Weisner; 7 John Duffy; 8 Sonny Nickle; 9 Paul Rowley; 10 Paul Norman; 11 Sean Richardson; 12 Bryan Henare; 13 Adam Bristow. Subs (all used): 14 Dale Holdstock; 15 Willie Swann; 16 Leroy Rivett; 17 David Bradbury.
Tries: Kendrick (2, 15), Richardson (9), Bristow (16), Munro (33, 46, 61), Rowley (58), Rivett (74);
Goals: Weisner 7.
ROVERS: 1 Nathan Graham; 2 Jamie Stokes; 3 Chris Langley; 4 Ian Brown; 5 Adrian Flynn; 6 Brendan O'Meara; 7 Carl Briggs; 8 Ian Tonks; 9 Richard Chapman; 10 Stuart Dickens; 11 Steve Dooler; 12 Andy Rice; 13 Danny Seal. Subs (all used): 14 Paul Darley; 15 Andy Bailey; 16 Robin Jowitt; 17 Chris Molyneux.
Tries: Dooler (67), Rice (78); **Goals:** Briggs 2.
Rugby Leaguer & League Express Men of the Match: *Centurions:* Patrick Weisner; *Rovers:* Jamie Stokes.
Penalty count: 12-7; **Half-time:** 26-0;
Referee: Ashley Klein (London); **Attendance:** 2,073.

HULL KINGSTON ROVERS 16 BATLEY BULLDOGS 10

ROVERS: 1 Lynton Stott; 2 Nick Pinkney; 3 Mark Blanchard; 4 Craig Poucher; 5 Alasdair McClarron; 6 Craig Murdock; 7 Latham Tawhai; 8 Richard Wilson; 9 Paul Pickering; 10 Harvey Howard; 11 Anthony Seibold; 12 Jon Aston; 13 Dean Busby. Subs (all used): 14 Andy Smith; 15 Adam Sullivan; 16 Jamie Bovill; 17 Paul Fletcher.
Tries: Howard (14), Pinkney (28, 37 - penalty try);
Goals: Stott 2.
BULLDOGS: 1 Craig Lingard; 2 Matt Bramald; 3 Simon Lewis; 4 Danny Maun; 5 Leon Williamson; 6 David Gibbons; 7 Barry Eaton; 8 Andy Spink; 9 Mark Cass; 10 Steve Hill; 11 Will Cartledge; 12 Joe Berry; 13 Ryan Horsley. Subs (all used): 14 Chris Spurr; 15 Paul Harrison; 16 Joe Naidole; 17 Craig Booth.
Tries: Williamson (25, 64); **Goal:** Eaton.
Rugby Leaguer & League Express Men of the Match: *Rovers:* Paul Fletcher; *Bulldogs:* Craig Lingard.
Penalty count: 4-6; **Half-time:** 16-6;
Referee: Mike Dawber (Wigan); **Attendance:** 1,000.

WEEK 5

Sunday 18th May 2003

DONCASTER DRAGONS 52 OLDHAM 24

DRAGONS: 1 Johnny Woodcock; 2 Paul Gleadhill; 3 Craig Horne; 4 Simon Irving; 5 Alex Muff; 6 Paul Mansson; 7 Dean Colton; 8 Gareth Handford; 9 Brad Hepi; 10 Matt Walker; 11 Peter Green; 12 Craig Lawton; 13 Peter Edwards. Subs (all used): 14 James Walker; 15 Martin Sykes; 16 Jamie Fielden; 17 Craig Forsyth.
Tries: Mansson (9, 25, 66), Horne (12, 72), Hepi (22, 69), Gleadhill (32), Fielden (51); **Goals:** Woodcock 8.
OLDHAM: 1 Gavin Dodd; 2 Chris Irwin; 3 Paul Anderson; 4 Jon Goddard; 5 Chris Campbell; 6 Gareth Barber; 7 Neil Roden; 8 Steve Molloy; 9 John Hough; 10 Paul Norton; 11 Lee Doran; 12 Chris Morley; 13 Phil Farrell. Subs (all used): 14 Gavin Johnson; 15 Simon Svabic; 16 Danny Guest; 17 Dane Morgan.
Tries: Campbell (1, 37), Dodd (28), Doran (49), Barber (76); **Goals:** Barber 2.
Rugby Leaguer & League Express Men of the Match: *Dragons:* Peter Green; *Oldham:* Jon Goddard.
Penalty count: 13-8; **Half-time:** 26-14;
Referee: Ben Thaler (Wakefield); **Attendance:** 860.

WEEK 6

Sunday 25th May 2003

DEWSBURY RAMS 6 ROCHDALE HORNETS 60

RAMS: 1 Nathan Batty; 2 Michael Wainwright; 3 Ryan Hardy; 4 Danny Wood; 5 George Mack; 6 Adam Thaler; 7 Chris Redfearn; 8 Paul Hicks; 9 Jimmy Elston; 10 Glen Spedding; 11 Ian Kirke; 12 Billy Kershaw; 13 Richard Slater. Subs (all used): 14 Mark Barlow; 15 Anthony Thewliss; 16 Tony Fella; 17 Chris Parker.
Try: Barlow (23); **Goal:** Wood.
HORNETS: 1 Paul Owen; 2 Mick Nanyn; 3 James Bunyan; 4 Jon Roper; 5 Marlon Billy; 6 Radney Bowker; 7 Ian Watson; 8 Paul Southern; 9 Richard Pachniuk; 10 David Stephenson; 11 David Larder; 12 Paul Smith; 13 Damian Ball. Subs (all used): 14 Warren Ayres; 15 Matthew Leigh; 16 Gareth Price; 17 Matthew Long.
Tries: Ball (10, 61), Bowker (13), Pachniuk (46, 77), Owen (48), Price (51), Roper (55), Watson (67), Larder (71); **Goals:** Nanyn 10.
Rugby Leaguer & League Express Men of the Match: *Rams:* Michael Wainwright; *Hornets:* Damian Ball.
Penalty count: 8-4; **Half-time:** 6-14;
Referee: Peter Taberner (Wigan); **Attendance:** 668.

DONCASTER DRAGONS 24 SALFORD CITY REDS 34

DRAGONS: 1 Craig Horne; 2 Johnny Woodcock; 3 Martin Sykes; 4 Simon Irving; 5 Jason Lee; 6 Paul Mansson; 7 Mark Moxon; 8 Gareth Handford; 9 Brad Hepi; 10 Maea David; 11 Peter Green; 12 Craig Lawton; 13 Peter Edwards. Subs (all used): 14 James Walker; 15 Matt Walker; 16 Alex Muff; 17 Dean Colton.
Tries: Woodcock (18), Mansson (38), Edwards (60);
Goals: Woodcock 6.
CITY REDS: 1 Jason Flowers; 2 Michael Platt; 3 Stuart Littler; 4 Andy Kirk; 5 Alan Hunte; 6 Cliff Beverley; 7 Gavin Clinch; 8 Neil Baynes; 9 Malcolm Alker; 10 Paul Highton; 11 Simon Baldwin; 12 Neil Lowe; 13 Chris Charles. Subs (all used): 14 Steve Blakeley; 15 David Highton; 16 Andy Coley; 17 Gareth Haggerty.
Tries: Littler (4), Kirk (29, 74), Baldwin (52), Clinch (69), Coley (78); **Goals:** Charles 3, Blakeley 2.
Rugby Leaguer & League Express Men of the Match: *Dragons:* Peter Edwards; *City Reds:* Steve Blakeley.
Penalty count: 8-11; **Half-time:** 16-12; **Referee:** Ronnie Laughton (Barnsley); **Attendance:** 1,069.

FEATHERSTONE ROVERS 14
HULL KINGSTON ROVERS 12

ROVERS: 1 Nathan Graham; 2 Jamie Stokes; 3 Chris Langley; 4 Ian Brown; 5 Adrian Flynn; 6 Brendan O'Meara; 7 Carl Briggs; 8 Ian Tonks; 9 Paul Darley; 10 Stuart Dickens; 11 Steve Dooler; 12 Andy Rice; 13 Danny Seal. Subs (all used): 14 Richard Agar; 15 Richard Chapman; 16 Andy Bailey; 17 Chris Molyneux.
Tries: Flynn (51), Dooler (79); **Goals:** Dickens 3.
ROBINS: 1 Lynton Stott; 2 Nick Pinkney; 3 Mark Blanchard; 4 Paul Parker; 5 David Wilson; 6 Shaun Cooke; 7 Craig Murdock; 8 Richard Wilson; 9 Steve Cochran; 10 Harvey Howard; 11 Anthony Seibold; 12 Jon Aston; 13 Andy Smith. Subs (all used): 14 Dean Andrews; 15 Dean Busby; 16 Jamie Bovill; 17 Paul Fletcher.
Tries: Stott (24), Aston (35); **Goals:** Stott 2.
Rugby Leaguer & League Express Men of the Match: *Rovers:* Steve Dooler; *Robins:* Lynton Stott.
Penalty count: 7-7; **Half-time:** 2-12;
Referee: Colin Morris (Huddersfield); **Attendance:** 1,200.

OLDHAM 12 LEIGH CENTURIONS 10

OLDHAM: 1 Jon Goddard; 2 Chris Campbell; 3 Paul Anderson; 4 Dan Potter; 5 Gavin Dodd; 6 Simon Svabic; 7 Neil Roden; 8 Steve Molloy; 9 John Hough; 10 Paul Norton; 11 Chris Morley; 12 Lee Doran; 13 Phil Farrell. Subs (all used): 14 Keith Brennan; 15 Gareth Barber; 16 Danny Guest; 17 Dane Morgan.
Try: Dodd (35); **Goals:** Svabic 4.
CENTURIONS: 1 David Alstead; 2 Damian Munro; 3 Dale Cardoza; 4 Phil Kendrick; 5 Alan Hadcroft; 6 Patrick Weisner; 7 John Duffy; 8 Sonny Nickle; 9 Paul Rowley; 10 Rob Ball; 11 Sean Richardson; 12 Bryan Henare; 13 Adam Bristow. Subs (all used): 14 Paul Norman; 15 Willie Swann; 16 Leroy Rivett; 17 David Bradbury.
Tries: Rivett (64), Cardoza (72); **Goal:** Weisner.
On report: Cardoza (60) - use of the elbow.
Rugby Leaguer & League Express Men of the Match: *Oldham:* Simon Svabic; *Centurions:* Paul Rowley.
Penalty count: 6-10; **Half-time:** 10-0;
Referee: Mike Dawber (Wigan); **Attendance:** 1,691.

WHITEHAVEN 31 BATLEY BULLDOGS 12

WHITEHAVEN: 1 Gary Broadbent; 2 Glen Hutton; 3 David Seeds; 4 Howard Hill; 5 Steven Wood; 6 Leroy Joe; 7 Darren Holt; 8 Dean Vaughan; 9 Aaron Lester; 10 David Fatialofa; 11 Chris McKinney; 12 Spencer Miller; 13 Garry Purdham. Subs (all used): 14 Lee Kiddie; 15 Marc Jackson; 16 Ryan Campbell; 17 Gary Smith.
Tries: Joe (14), Hill (18), Wood (65), Jackson (68), Campbell (75); **Goals:** Holt 5; **Field goal:** Joe.
BULLDOGS: 1 Craig Lingard; 2 Mark Sibson; 3 Chris Spurr; 4 Danny Maun; 5 Leon Williamson; 6 David Gibbons; 7 Barry Eaton; 8 Andy Spink; 9 Kris Lythe; 10 Joe Naidole; 11 David Rourke; 12 Will Cartledge; 13 Ryan Horsley. Subs (all used): 14 Matt Bramald; 15 Paul Harrison; 16 Steve Beard; 17 Simon Lewis.
Tries: Sibson (39), Harrison (78); **Goals:** Eaton 2.
Rugby Leaguer & League Express Men of the Match: *Whitehaven:* Garry Purdham; *Bulldogs:* Barry Eaton.
Penalty count: 8-5; **Half-time:** 10-6;
Referee: Ashley Klein (London); **Attendance:** 1,444.

WEEK 7

Sunday 1st June 2003

BATLEY BULLDOGS 16 ROCHDALE HORNETS 43

BULLDOGS: 1 Craig Lingard; 2 Mark Sibson; 3 Chris Spurr; 4 Danny Maun; 5 Leon Williamson; 6 David Gibbons; 7 Barry Eaton; 8 Andy Spink; 9 Kris Lythe; 10 Craig Booth; 11 Mark Toohey; 12 Will Cartledge; 13 Ryan Horsley. Subs (all used): 14 Matt Bramald; 15 Paul Harrison; 16 Steve Beard; 17 Ryan McDonald.
Tries: Spurr (10), Cartledge (32), Williamson (79);
Goals: Eaton 2.
HORNETS: 1 Paul Owen; 2 Mick Nanyn; 3 James Bunyan; 4 Jon Roper; 5 Marlon Billy; 6 Radney Bowker; 7 Ian Watson; 8 Paul Southern; 9 Richard Pachniuk; 10 Andy Grundy; 11 David Larder; 12 Paul Smith; 13 Damian Ball. Subs (all used): 14 Warren Ayres; 15 Matthew Leigh; 16 Gareth Price; 17 Matthew Long.
Tries: Larder (1), Ball (17), Nanyn (22, 54), Smith (28, 61, 65, 74); **Goals:** Nanyn 5; **Field goal:** Watson.
Rugby Leaguer & League Express Men of the Match: *Bulldogs:* Will Cartledge; *Hornets:* Ian Watson.
Penalty count: 7-2; **Half-time:** 10-23;
Referee: Julian King (St Helens); **Attendance:** 728.

LEIGH CENTURIONS 55 DONCASTER DRAGONS 14

CENTURIONS: 1 Neil Turley; 2 Damian Munro; 3 Alan Hadcroft; 4 Phil Kendrick; 5 Leroy Rivett; 6 Patrick Weisner; 7 Willie Swann; 8 Sonny Nickle; 9 Paul Rowley; 10 Paul Norman; 11 Sean Richardson; 12 Bryan Henare; 13 Adam Bristow. Subs (all used): 14 Rob Ball; 15 Lee Sanderson; 16 David Alstead; 17 David Bradbury.
Tries: Rivett (2, 50), Turley (13, 32, 41), Swann (29), Bristow (37, 60), Bradbury (54); **Goals:** Turley 9;
Field goal: Turley.
Sin bin: Sanderson (76) - fighting.
DRAGONS: 1 Jason Lee; 2 Johnny Woodcock; 3 Martin Sykes; 4 Simon Irving; 5 Alex Muff; 6 Paul Mansson; 7 Mark Moxon; 8 Gareth Handford; 9 Brad Hepi; 10 Maea David; 11 Peter Green; 12 Craig Lawton; 13 Peter Edwards. Subs (all used): 14 James Walker; 15 Matt Walker; 16 Gareth Lloyd; 17 Dean Colton.
Tries: P Green (40), Irving (44), Hepi (68);
Goal: Woodcock.
Sin bin: M Walker (76) - fighting.
Rugby Leaguer & League Express Men of the Match: *Centurions:* Neil Turley; *Dragons:* Paul Mansson.
Penalty count: 8-6; **Half-time:** 31-4;
Referee: Russell Smith (Castleford); **Attendance:** 1,988.

SALFORD CITY REDS 76 DEWSBURY RAMS 4

CITY REDS: 1 Jason Flowers; 2 Danny Arnold; 3 Alan Hunte; 4 Andy Kirk; 5 Mick Berne; 6 Cliff Beverley; 7 Gavin Clinch; 8 Andy Coley; 9 Malcolm Alker; 10 Paul Highton; 11 Simon Baldwin; 12 Neil Lowe; 13 Chris Charles. Subs (all used): 14 Steve Blakeley; 15 David Highton; 16 Andy Gorski; 17 Gareth Haggerty.
Tries: Hunte (1, 17, 34, 40, 58), Berne (7), Beverley (10, 14, 42), Flowers (28), Coley (53, 61), Alker (62, 70);
Goals: Charles 10.
RAMS: 1 Nathan Batty; 2 Michael Wainwright; 3 Billy Kershaw; 4 Danny Wood; 5 Craig Miles; 6 Graham Law; 7 Craig Nipperess; 8 Frank Watene; 9 Jimmy Elston; 10 Paul Hicks; 11 Ian Kirke; 12 Danny Evans; 13 Leigh Riddell. Subs (all used): 14 Adam Thaler; 15 John Waddell; 16 Glen Spedding; 17 Paul Smith.
Try: Kershaw (78).
Rugby Leaguer & League Express Men of the Match: *City Reds:* Alan Hunte; *Rams:* Leigh Riddell.
Penalty count: 2-1; **Half-time:** 40-0; **Referee:** Steve Nicholson (Whitehaven); **Attendance:** 1,698.

WHITEHAVEN 46 FEATHERSTONE ROVERS 6

WHITEHAVEN: 1 Gary Broadbent; 2 Glen Hutton; 3 David Seeds; 4 Howard Hill; 5 Steven Wood; 6 Leroy Joe; 7 Darren Holt; 8 Dean Vaughan; 9 Aaron Lester; 10 David Fatialofa; 11 Chris McKinney; 12 Mike Whitehead; 13 Garry Purdham. Subs (all used): 14 Lee Kiddie; 15 Marc Jackson; 16 Ryan Campbell; 17 Gary Smith.
Tries: Seeds (4, 39), Joe (7, 51, 61), Hill (16, 71), Campbell (66); **Goals:** Holt 7.
Dismissal: Jackson (57) - punching.
ROVERS: 1 Nathan Graham; 2 Jamie Stokes; 3 Chris Langley; 4 Ian Brown; 5 Adrian Flynn; 6 Brendan O'Meara; 7 Carl Briggs; 8 Ian Tonks; 9 Paul Darley; 10 Stuart Dickens; 11 Steve Dooler; 12 Andy Rice; 13 Danny Seal. Subs (all used): 14 Richard Agar; 15 Richard Chapman; 16 Andy Bailey; 17 Chris Molyneux.
Try: Brown (74); **Goal:** Briggs.
Sin bin: Briggs (47) - dissent.
Rugby Leaguer & League Express Men of the Match: *Whitehaven:* Leroy Joe; *Rovers:* Andy Rice.
Penalty count: 9-8; **Half-time:** 22-0;
Referee: Steve Ganson (St Helens); **Attendance:** 1,698.

HULL KINGSTON ROVERS 23 OLDHAM 10

ROVERS: 1 Lynton Stott; 2 Nick Pinkney; 3 Mark Blanchard; 4 Paul Parker; 5 David Wilson; 6 Shaun Cooke; 7 Latham Tawhai; 8 Richard Wilson; 9 Paul Pickering; 10 Jamie Bovill; 11 Anthony Seibold; 12 Jon Aston; 13 Andy Smith. Subs (all used): 14 Makali Aizue; 15 Dean Busby; 16 Harvey Howard; 17 Paul Fletcher.
Tries: Pinkney (25), Busby (30), Pickering (37), Seibold (67); **Goals:** Stott 3; **Field goal:** Tawhai.
OLDHAM: 1 Jon Goddard; 2 Iain Marsh; 3 Paul Anderson; 4 Dan Potter; 5 Gavin Dodd; 6 Simon Svabic; 7 Neil Roden; 8 Steve Molloy; 9 John Hough; 10 Dane Morgan; 11 Lee Doran; 12 Chris Morley; 13 Phil Farrell. Subs (all used): 14 Keith Brennan; 15 Gareth Barber; 16 Ryan Stazicker; 17 Martin McLoughlin.
Tries: Farrell (55), Anderson (72); **Goal:** Svabic.
Rugby Leaguer & League Express Men of the Match: *Rovers:* Paul Pickering; *Oldham:* John Hough.
Penalty count: 10-8; **Half-time:** 16-0; **Referee:** Ronnie Laughton (Barnsley); **Attendance:** 1,300.

WEEK 8

Sunday 15th June 2003

DEWSBURY RAMS 12 LEIGH CENTURIONS 31

RAMS: 1 Nathan Batty; 2 Michael Wainwright; 3 Ryan Hardy; 4 Kevin Crouthers; 5 Craig Miles; 6 Danny Wood; 7 Craig Nipperess; 8 Paul Smith; 9 Adam Thaler; 10 Paul Hicks; 11 Anthony Thewliss; 12 Billy Kershaw; 13 Graham Law. Subs (all used): 14 Jimmy Elston; 15 Ian Kirke; 16 Glen Spedding; 17 Frank Watene.
Tries: Batty (58), Watene (73); **Goals:** Wood 2.
CENTURIONS: 1 David Alstead; 5 Michael Watts; 4 Phil Kendrick; 3 Alan Hadcroft; 2 Damian Munro; 6 Patrick Weisner; 7 Willie Swann; 8 Paul Norman; 9 Paul Rowley; 10 David Bradbury; 11 Sean Richardson; 12 Bryan Henare; 13 Adam Bristow. Subs: 14 Rob Ball; 15 John Duffy; 16 Leroy Rivett (not used); 17 Dale Holdstock.
Tries: Munro (17, 38), Swann (48), Hadcroft (51), Duffy (63); **Goals:** Weisner 5; **Field goal:** Weisner.
Sin bin: Henare (67) - obstruction.
Rugby Leaguer & League Express Men of the Match: *Rams:* Jimmy Elston; *Centurions:* Patrick Weisner.
Penalty count: 8-3; **Half-time:** 0-15; **Referee:** Steve Nicholson (Whitehaven); **Attendance:** 971.

DONCASTER DRAGONS 22
HULL KINGSTON ROVERS 43

DRAGONS: 1 Scott Grix; 2 Alex Muff; 3 Shaun Leafe; 4 Gareth Lloyd; 5 Jason Lee; 6 Paul Mansson; 7 Mark Moxon; 8 Gareth Handford; 9 Gareth Greenwood; 10 James Walker; 11 Peter Green; 12 Craig Lawton; 13 Maea David. Subs (all used): 14 Tom Buckenham; 15 Matt Walker; 16 Martin Sykes; 17 Martin Ostler.
Tries: P Green (13), Handford (40), David (59), Lawton (78); **Goals:** J Walker 2, Lee.
ROVERS: 1 Lynton Stott; 2 David Wilson; 3 Paul Parker; 4 Craig Poucher; 5 Mark Blanchard; 6 Shaun Cooke; 7 Latham Tawhai; 8 Richard Wilson; 9 Paul Pickering; 10 Harvey Howard; 11 Anthony Seibold; 12 Andy Smith; 13 Dean Busby. Subs (all used): 14 Makali Aizue; 15 Dean Andrews; 16 Jon Aston; 17 Paul Fletcher.
Tries: Howard (2), Blanchard (6, 30, 56), Poucher (35), Tawhai (48), Stott (65); **Goals:** Stott 7; **Field goal:** Stott.
Rugby Leaguer & League Express Men of the Match: *Dragons:* Craig Lawton; *Rovers:* Latham Tawhai.
Penalty count: 10-6; **Half-time:** 12-24;
Referee: Peter Taberner (Wigan); **Attendance:** 1,124.

FEATHERSTONE ROVERS 34 BATLEY BULLDOGS 18

ROVERS: 1 Ben Archibald; 2 Jamie Stokes; 3 Brendan O'Meara; 4 Ian Brown; 5 Adrian Flynn; 6 Richard Whiting; 7 Carl Briggs; 8 Ian Tonks; 9 Richard Chapman; 10 Stuart Dickens; 11 Steve Dooler; 12 Andy Rice; 13 Danny Seal. Subs (all used): 14 Jonathan Presley; 15 Chris Langley; 16 Paul Darley; 17 Chris Molyneux.
Tries: Dooler (28), Whiting (34), Flynn (40), Seal (56), Brown (61), Presley (75); **Goals:** Dickens 5.
BULLDOGS: 1 Matt Bramald; 2 Simon Lewis; 3 Chris Spurr; 4 Danny Maun; 5 Leon Williamson; 6 Ryan Horsley; 7 Barry Eaton; 8 Craig Booth; 9 Gavin Swinson; 10 Steve Hill; 11 Joe Berry; 12 Will Cartledge; 13 Anthony Gibbons. Subs (all used): 14 Mark Sibson; 15 Paul Harrison; 16 Joe Naidole; 17 Ryan McDonald.
Tries: Maun (6, 80), A Gibbons (19, 48); **Goal:** Eaton.
Rugby Leaguer & League Express Men of the Match: *Rovers:* Danny Seal; *Bulldogs:* Joe Berry.
Penalty count: 4-4; **Half-time:** 20-10;
Referee: Colin Morris (Huddersfield); **Attendance:** 1,182.

OLDHAM 22 WHITEHAVEN 22

OLDHAM: 1 Jon Goddard; 2 Iain Marsh; 3 Paul Anderson; 4 Dan Potter; 5 Gavin Dodd; 6 Gareth Barber; 7 Keith Brennan; 8 Steve Molloy; 9 John Hough; 10 Dane Morgan; 11 Lee Doran; 12 Darren Shaw; 13 Phil Farrell. Subs: 14 Simon Svabic (not used); 15 Neil Roden; 16 Chris Morley; 17 Martin McLoughlin.
Tries: Molloy (5), Potter (27), Barber (60), Goddard (65); **Goals:** Barber 3.
WHITEHAVEN: 1 Gary Broadbent; 2 Neil Frazer; 3 David Seeds; 4 Steven Wood; 5 Mark Wallace; 6 Lee Kiddie; 7 Darren Holt; 8 Chris McKinney; 9 Aaron Lester; 10 David Fatialofa; 11 Howard Hill; 12 Graeme Morton; 13 Garry Purdham. Subs (all used): 14 Steve Kirkbride; 15 Ryan Campbell; 16 Mike Whitehead; 17 Tony Cunningham.
Tries: Fatialofa (38), Wood (49), Lester (55), Wallace (73); **Goals:** Holt 3.
Rugby Leaguer & League Express Men of the Match: *Oldham:* Jon Goddard; *Whitehaven:* David Fatialofa.
Penalty count: 8-5; **Half-time:** 10-6; **Referee:** Ronnie Laughton (Barnsley); **Attendance:** 1,096.

ROCHDALE HORNETS 16 SALFORD CITY REDS 32

HORNETS: 1 Paul Owen; 2 Mick Nanyn; 3 James Bunyan; 4 Jon Roper; 5 Marlon Billy; 6 Paul Smith; 7 Ian Watson; 8 Paul Southern; 9 Richard Pachniuk; 10 Gareth Price; 11 David Larder; 12 Matthew Leigh; 13 Damian Ball. Subs: 14 Warren Ayres (not used); 15 Andy Grundy; 16 John Hamilton; 17 Matthew Long.
Tries: Smith (15), Nanyn (28), Price (51);
Goals: Nanyn 2.
Sin bin: Larder (76) - fighting.
CITY REDS: 1 Jason Flowers; 2 Danny Arnold; 3 Stuart Littler; 4 Alan Hunte; 5 Mick Berne; 6 Cliff Beverley; 7 Gavin Clinch; 8 Neil Baynes; 9 Malcolm Alker; 10 Andy Coley; 11 Simon Baldwin; 12 Chris Charles; 13 David Highton. Subs (all used): 14 Steve Blakeley; 15 Andy Kirk; 16 Paul Highton; 17 Gareth Haggerty.
Tries: D Highton (8), Beverley (18, 79), Arnold (63), Littler (69); **Goals:** Charles 3, Blakeley 3.
Sin bin: Hunte (76) - fighting.
Rugby Leaguer & League Express Men of the Match: *Hornets:* Ian Watson; *City Reds:* Gavin Clinch.
Penalty count: 5-12; **Half-time:** 12-14;
Referee: Julian King (St Helens); **Attendance:** 1,571.

WEEK 9

Sunday 22nd June 2003

BATLEY BULLDOGS 20 OLDHAM 20

BULLDOGS: 1 Mark Sibson; 2 Matt Bramald; 3 Anthony Gibbons; 4 Danny Maun; 5 Leon Williamson; 6 Danny Thomas; 7 Barry Eaton; 8 Craig Booth; 9 Mark Cass; 10 Ryan McDonald; 11 Danny Evans; 12 Will Cartledge; 13 Ryan Horsley. Subs (all used): 14 Mark Toohey; 15 Paul Harrison; 16 Andy Spink; 17 Steve Hill.
Tries: Bramald (18), Toohey (43), Maun (78);
Goals: Eaton 4.
Sin bin: Cass (23) - dissent.
OLDHAM: 1 Jon Goddard; 2 Will Cowell; 3 Iain Marsh; 4 Dan Potter; 5 Gavin Dodd; 6 Gareth Barber; 7 Keith Brennan; 8 Steve Molloy; 9 John Hough; 10 Dane Morgan; 11 Lee Doran; 12 Darren Shaw; 13 Phil Farrell. Subs (all used): 14 Simon Svabic; 15 Neil Roden; 16 Danny Guest; 17 Gavin Johnson.
Tries: Potter (23), Dodd (51, 55), Barber (74);
Goals: Svabic 2.
Sin bin: Marsh (37) - holding down.
Rugby Leaguer & League Express Men of the Match: *Bulldogs:* Andy Spink; *Oldham:* Dane Morgan.
Penalty count: 6-8; **Half time:** 8-4;
Referee: Steve Ganson (St Helens); **Attendance:** 821.

FEATHERSTONE ROVERS 30 ROCHDALE HORNETS 16

ROVERS: 1 Nathan Graham; 2 Jamie Stokes; 3 Brendan O'Meara; 4 Ian Brown; 5 Adrian Flynn; 6 Richard Whiting; 7 Carl Briggs; 8 Chris Molyneux; 9 Richard Chapman; 10 Stuart Dickens; 11 Andy Rice; 12 Steve Dooler; 13 Danny Seal. Subs (all used): 14 Ben Archibald; 15 Chris Langley; 16 Paul Darley; 17 James Houston.
Tries: Stokes (26, 65), Chapman (41); **Goals:** Dickens 8;
Field goals: Briggs 2.
Sin bin: Darley (70) - fighting;
Rice (79) - professional foul.
HORNETS: 1 Paul Owen; 2 Mick Nanyn; 3 James Bunyan; 4 Jon Roper; 5 Marlon Billy; 6 Radney Bowker; 7 Ian Watson; 8 Paul Southern; 9 Richard Pachniuk; 10 Gareth Price; 11 David Larder; 12 Paul Smith; 13 Damian Ball. Subs (all used): 14 John Hamilton; 15 Andy Grundy; 16 Chris Irwin; 17 Matthew Long.
Tries: Bowker (22), Hamilton (49), Nanyn (58);
Goals: Nanyn 2.
Sin bin: Owen (36, 54) - both professional fouls; Larder (70) - fighting.
Rugby Leaguer & League Express Men of the Match: *Rovers:* Stuart Dickens; *Hornets:* Radney Bowker.
Penalty count: 18-6; **Half-time:** 13-6;
Referee: Robert Connolly (Wigan); **Attendance:** 1,359.

LEIGH CENTURIONS 12 SALFORD CITY REDS 32

CENTURIONS: 1 David Alstead; 2 Damian Munro; 3 Alan Hadcroft; 4 Phil Kendrick; 5 Michael Watts; 6 Patrick Weisner; 7 Willie Swann; 8 Sonny Nickle; 9 John Duffy; 10 Paul Norman; 11 Sean Richardson; 12 Bryan Henare; 13 Adam Bristow. Subs (all used): 14 Rob Ball; 15 Lee Sanderson; 16 Dale Holdstock; 17 David Bradbury.
Tries: Richardson (32), Munro (40); **Goals:** Weisner 2.
CITY REDS: 1 Jason Flowers; 2 Danny Arnold; 3 Stuart Littler; 4 Alan Hunte; 5 Mick Berne; 6 Cliff Beverley; 7 Gavin Clinch; 8 Neil Baynes; 9 Malcolm Alker; 10 Andy Coley; 11 Simon Baldwin; 12 Paul Highton; 13 Chris Charles. Subs (all used): 14 Steve Blakeley; 15 David Highton; 16 Andy Kirk; 17 Gareth Haggerty.
Tries: Beverley (14), Clinch (18), Hunte (21), Arnold (29), Flowers (69); **Goals:** Charles 4, Blakeley 2.
Rugby Leaguer & League Express Men of the Match: *Centurions:* Adam Bristow; *City Reds:* Gavin Clinch.
Penalty count: 8-5; **Half-time:** 12-20; **Referee:** Colin Morris (Huddersfield); **Attendance:** 4,000.

WHITEHAVEN 18 DONCASTER DRAGONS 24

WHITEHAVEN: 1 Gary Broadbent; 2 Neil Frazer; 3 David Seeds; 4 Steven Wood; 5 Mark Wallace; 6 Lee Kiddie; 7 Darren Holt; 8 Dean Vaughan; 9 Aaron Lester; 10 David Fatialofa; 11 Graeme Morton; 12 Howard Hill; 13 Mike Whitehead. Subs (all used): 14 Steve Kirkbride; 15 Gary Smith; 16 Carl Sice; 17 Tony Cunningham.
Tries: Lester (24), Hill (44); **Goals:** Holt 5.
DRAGONS: 1 Scott Grix; 2 Alex Muff; 3 Simon Irving; 4 Martin Sykes; 5 Jason Lee; 6 Paul Mansson; 7 Mark Moxon; 8 James Walker; 9 Gareth Greenwood; 10 Matt Walker; 11 Peter Green; 12 Martin Ostler; 13 Craig Lawton. Subs (all used): 14 Tom Buckenham; 15 Maea David; 16 Wayne Frost; 17 Austin Aggrie.
Tries: Grix (14), Sykes (26), Mansson (68), Irving (71);
Goals: Irving 4.
Rugby Leaguer & League Express Men of the Match: *Whitehaven:* Aaron Lester; *Dragons:* Paul Mansson.
Penalty count: 9-7; **Half time:** 8-10;
Referee: Russell Smith (Castleford); **Attendance:** 1,461.

HULL KINGSTON ROVERS 35 DEWSBURY RAMS 12

ROVERS: 1 Lynton Stott; 2 Nick Pinkney; 3 Paul Parker; 4 Mark Blanchard; 5 David Wilson; 6 Shaun Cooke; 7 Latham Tawhai; 8 Richard Wilson; 9 Jon Aston; 10 Harvey Howard; 11 Anthony Seibold; 12 Andy Smith; 13 Dean Busby. Subs (all used): 14 Makali Aizue; 15 Jamie Bovill; 16 Paul Pickering; 17 Paul Fletcher.
Tries: Cooke (7), Tawhai (17), Pickering (33), Parker (61), Pinkney (64), Aizue (75); **Goals:** Stott 5;
Field goal: Tawhai.
RAMS: 1 George Mack; 2 Michael Wainwright; 3 Ryan Hardy; 4 Kevin Crouthers; 5 Chris Redfearn; 6 Danny Wood; 7 Craig Nipperess; 8 Frank Watene; 9 Adam Thaler; 10 Paul Hicks; 11 Ian Kirke; 12 Billy Kershaw; 13 Graham Law. Subs (all used): 14 Jimmy Elston; 15 Paul Smith; 16 Tony Fella; 17 Andrew Senior.
Tries: Crouthers (55, 69); **Goals:** Thaler 2.
Rugby Leaguer & League Express Men of the Match: *Rovers:* Lynton Stott; *Rams:* Kevin Crouthers.
Penalty count: 7-6; **Half-time:** 18-0; **Referee:** Ronnie Laughton (Barnsley); **Attendance:** 1,402.

Friday 27th June 2003

DONCASTER DRAGONS 30 FEATHERSTONE ROVERS 19

DRAGONS: 1 Martin Sykes; 2 Austin Aggrie; 3 Simon Irving; 4 PJ Solomon; 5 Alex Muff; 6 Paul Mansson; 7 Mark Moxon; 8 James Walker; 9 Gareth Greenwood; 10 Matt Walker; 11 Peter Green; 12 Martin Ostler; 13 Craig Lawton. Subs (all used): 14 Anthony Seuseu; 15 Peter Edwards; 16 Maea David; 17 Gareth Lloyd.
Tries: David (23, 50), Mansson (58, 80), Irving (62);
Goals: Irving 5.
ROVERS: 1 Nathan Graham; 2 Jamie Stokes; 3 Chris Langley; 4 Andy Bailey; 5 Adrian Flynn; 6 Richard Whiting; 7 Carl Briggs; 8 Chris Molyneux; 9 Richard Chapman; 10 Stuart Dickens; 11 Steve Dooler; 12 Andy Rice; 13 Danny Seal. Subs (all used): 14 Jonathan Presley; 15 James Houston; 16 Paul Darley; 17 Ian Tonks.
Tries: Langley (11, 26), Briggs (41); **Goals:** Dickens 3;
Field goal: Briggs.
Rugby Leaguer & League Express Men of the Match: *Dragons:* Maea David; *Rovers:* Ian Tonks.
Penalty count: 10-9; **Half-time:** 8-12; **Referee:** Richard Silverwood (Dewsbury); **Attendance:** 1,008.

WEEK 10

Sunday 29th June 2003

DEWSBURY RAMS 23 BATLEY BULLDOGS 36

RAMS: 1 Nathan Batty; 2 Michael Wainwright; 3 Graham Law; 4 Kevin Crouthers; 5 Paul Gleadhill; 6 Mark Barlow; 7 Adam Thaler; 8 Paul Hicks; 9 Jimmy Elston; 10 Andy Fisher; 11 Anthony Thewliss; 12 Ian Kirke; 13 Billy Kershaw. Subs (all used): 14 Chris Redfearn; 15 Paul Smith; 16 Andrew Senior; 17 Frank Watene.
Tries: Gleadhill (4), Law (19), Watene (28), Crouthers (69); **Goals:** Thaler 3; **Field goal:** Thaler.
BULLDOGS: 1 Craig Lingard; 2 Mark Sibson; 3 Anthony Gibbons; 4 Danny Maun; 5 Simon Lewis; 6 Danny Thomas; 7 Barry Eaton; 8 Craig Booth; 9 Mark Cass; 10 Ryan McDonald; 11 Danny Evans; 12 Will Cartledge; 13 Ryan Horsley. Subs (all used): 14 Mark Toohey; 15 Paul Harrison; 16 Andy Spink; 17 Steve Hill.
Tries: Thomas (16, 80), Sibson (37), Lingard (42), Harrison (65); **Goals:** Eaton 7; **Field goals:** Thomas, Cass.
Rugby Leaguer & League Express Men of the Match: *Rams:* Kevin Crouthers; *Bulldogs:* Danny Thomas.
Penalty count: 9-5; **Half-time:** 19-17;
Referee: Ashley Klein (London); **Attendance:** 1,123.

LEIGH CENTURIONS 54 HULL KINGSTON ROVERS 4

CENTURIONS: 1 Neil Turley; 2 Leroy Rivett; 3 Damian Munro; 4 Phil Kendrick; 5 David Alstead; 6 Patrick Weisner; 7 Willie Swann; 8 Sonny Nickle; 9 John Duffy; 10 Rob Ball; 11 Sean Richardson; 12 Bryan Henare; 13 Adam Bristow. Subs (all used): 14 Paul Norman; 15 Lee Sanderson; 16 Dale Holdstock; 17 David Bradbury.
Tries: Munro (4, 49), Duffy (15, 71), Rivett (24, 29, 68), Bristow (35), Weisner (42), Holdstock (75);
Goals: Turley 5, Weisner 2.
ROVERS: 1 Lynton Stott; 2 David Wilson; 3 Mark Blanchard; 4 Craig Farrell; 5 Alasdair McClarron; 6 Shaun Cooke; 7 Latham Tawhai; 8 Richard Wilson; 9 Jon Aston; 10 Harvey Howard; 11 Anthony Seibold; 12 Jamie Bovill; 13 Andy Smith. Subs (all used): 14 Makali Aizue; 15 Dean Andrews; 16 Paul Pickering; 17 Paul Fletcher.
Try: Aston (57).
Rugby Leaguer & League Express Men of the Match: *Centurions:* Leroy Rivett; *Rovers:* Paul Pickering.
Penalty count: 7-6; **Half-time:** 28-0;
Referee: Peter Taberner (Wigan); **Attendance:** 2,363.

ROCHDALE HORNETS 58 OLDHAM 14

HORNETS: 1 Paul Owen; 2 Mick Nanyn; 3 James Bunyan; 4 Jon Roper; 5 Marlon Billy; 6 Radney Bowker; 7 Ian Watson; 8 Paul Southern; 9 Richard Pachniuk; 10 Gareth Price; 11 David Larder; 12 Paul Smith; 13 Damian Ball. Subs (all used): 14 John Hamilton; 15 Matthew Leigh; 16 Chris Irwin; 17 Matthew Long.
Tries: Ball (9, 71), Price (16, 65), Smith (32, 49), Long (34, 73), Hamilton (52), Irwin (80); **Goals:** Nanyn 9.
OLDHAM: 1 Jon Goddard; 2 Will Cowell; 3 Iain Marsh; 4 Lee Doran; 5 Gavin Dodd; 6 Gareth Barber; 7 Keith Brennan; 8 Martin McLoughlin; 9 John Hough; 10 Dane Morgan; 11 Chris Morley; 12 Darren Shaw; 13 Phil Farrell. Subs (all used): 14 Paul Anderson; 15 Simon Svabic; 16 Ryan Stazicker; 17 Steve Molloy.
Tries: Brennan (19), Barber (54); **Goals:** Barber 3.
Rugby Leaguer & League Express Men of the Match: *Hornets:* Damian Ball; *Oldham:* John Hough.
Penalty count: 10-9; **Half time:** 24-8;
Referee: Mike Dawber (Wigan); **Attendance:** 1,425.

SALFORD CITY REDS 26 WHITEHAVEN 26

CITY REDS: 1 Wes Davies; 2 Danny Arnold; 3 Stuart Littler; 4 Alan Hunte; 5 Andy Kirk; 6 Cliff Beverley; 7 Gavin Clinch; 8 Neil Baynes; 9 Malcolm Alker; 10 Andy Coley; 11 Simon Baldwin; 12 Paul Highton; 13 Chris Charles. Subs (all used): 14 Steve Blakeley; 15 David Highton; 16 Mick Berne; 17 Gareth Haggerty.
Tries: Kirk (19, 65), Beverley (26), Arnold (30), Littler (72); **Goals:** Charles 2, Blakeley.
WHITEHAVEN: 1 Gary Broadbent; 2 Neil Frazer; 3 David Seeds; 4 Steven Wood; 5 Mark Wallace; 6 Leroy Joe; 7 Darren Holt; 8 Dean Vaughan; 9 Aaron Lester; 10 David Fatialofa; 11 Graeme Morton; 12 Spencer Miller; 13 Howard Hill. Subs (all used): 14 Lee Kiddie; 15 Craig Walsh; 16 Mike Whitehead; 17 Tony Cunningham.
Tries: Miller (16), Whitehead (36), Joe (50), Frazer (78); **Goals:** Holt 5.
Rugby Leaguer & League Express Men of the Match: *City Reds:* Andy Kirk; *Whitehaven:* Darren Holt.
Penalty count: 9-8; **Half-time:** 14-12; **Referee:** Karl Kirkpatrick (Warrington); **Attendance:** 2,056.

Saturday 5th July 2003

ROCHDALE HORNETS 43 WHITEHAVEN 26

HORNETS: 1 Paul Owen; 2 Mick Nanyn; 3 James Bunyan; 4 Jon Roper; 5 Marlon Billy; 6 Radney Bowker; 7 Ian Watson; 8 Paul Southern; 9 Richard Pachniuk; 10 Gareth Price; 11 David Larder; 12 Paul Smith; 13 Damian Ball. Subs (all used): 14 John Hamilton; 15 Matthew Leigh; 16 Chris Irwin; 17 Matthew Long.
Tries: Nanyn (12, 64), Ball (15), Bowker (27, 39), Long (47), Leigh (71), Southern (79); **Goals:** Nanyn 5;
Field goal: Ball.
WHITEHAVEN: 1 Gary Broadbent; 5 Mark Wallace; 4 Howard Hill; 3 David Seeds; 2 Steven Wood; 6 Leroy Joe; 7 Darren Holt; 8 Dean Vaughan; 9 Aaron Lester; 10 David Fatialofa; 11 Spencer Miller; 12 Graeme Morton; 13 Garry Purdham. Subs (all used): 14 Lee Kiddie; 15 Marc Jackson; 16 Craig Walsh; 17 Mike Whitehead.
Tries: Seeds (7, 18), Broadbent (44), Joe (68), Miller (75); **Goals:** Holt 3.
Sin bin: Jackson (47) - dissent.
Rugby Leaguer & League Express Men of the Match: *Hornets:* Paul Southern; *Whitehaven:* Gary Broadbent.
Penalty count: 6-8; **Half-time:** 25-12;
Referee: Ben Thaler (Wakefield); **Attendance:** 822.

WEEK 11

Sunday 13th July 2003

DEWSBURY RAMS 18 WHITEHAVEN 18

RAMS: 1 Nathan Batty; 2 Michael Wainwright; 3 Ryan Hardy; 4 Kevin Crouthers; 5 Paul Gleadhill; 6 Jamie Benn; 7 Craig Nipperess; 8 Frank Watene; 9 Adam Thaler; 10 Paul Smith; 11 Paul Hicks; 12 Billy Kershaw; 13 Graham Law. Subs (all used): 14 Jimmy Elston; 15 Chris Redfearn; 16 Tony Fella; 17 Andrew Senior.
Tries: Wainwright (22, 74); **Goals:** Benn 5.
WHITEHAVEN: 1 Gary Broadbent; 2 Neil Frazer; 3 Craig Walsh; 4 Howard Hill; 5 Mark Wallace; 6 Leroy Joe; 7 Darren Holt; 8 Chris McKinney; 9 Aaron Lester; 10 David Fatialofa; 11 Mike Whitehead; 12 Graeme Morton; 13 Garry Purdham. Subs (all used): 14 Steve Kirkbride; 15 Spencer Miller; 16 Dean Vaughan; 17 Tony Cunningham.
Tries: Walsh (1, 28, 36), Morton (68); **Goal:** Holt.
Rugby Leaguer & League Express Men of the Match: *Rams:* Frank Watene; *Whitehaven:* Leroy Joe.
Penalty count: 7-6; **Half-time:** 8-14;
Referee: Ronnie Laughton (Barnsley); **Attendance:** 777.

DONCASTER DRAGONS 32 BATLEY BULLDOGS 25

DRAGONS: 1 Scott Grix; 2 Gareth Lloyd; 3 Simon Irving; 4 PJ Solomon; 5 Craig Horne; 6 Paul Mansson; 7 Mark Moxon; 8 James Walker; 9 Gareth Greenwood; 10 Matt Walker; 11 Peter Green; 12 Craig Lawton; 13 Peter Edwards. Subs (all used): 14 Gareth Handford; 15 Maea David; 16 Anthony Seuseu; 17 Martin Sykes.
Tries: Edwards (6, 75), Seuseu (44), Lawton (56), Irving (68); **Goals:** Irving 6.
BULLDOGS: 1 Craig Lingard; 2 Mark Sibson; 3 Anthony Gibbons; 4 Danny Maun; 5 Chris Spurr; 6 Danny Thomas; 7 Barry Eaton; 8 Craig Booth; 9 Mark Cass; 10 Steve Hill; 11 Mark Toohey; 12 Will Cartledge; 13 Ryan Horsley. Subs (all used): 14 Steve Beard; 15 Paul Harrison; 16 Andy Spink; 17 Joe Berry.
Tries: Sibson (1), Maun (11), Horsley (26), Lingard (50); **Goals:** Eaton 4; **Field goal:** Thomas.
Rugby Leaguer & League Express Men of the Match: *Dragons:* Peter Edwards; *Bulldogs:* Barry Eaton.
Penalty count: 8-7; **Half-time:** 6-19;
Referee: Karl Kirkpatrick (Warrington); **Attendance:** 858.

OLDHAM 35 FEATHERSTONE ROVERS 24

OLDHAM: 1 Jon Goddard; 2 Will Cowell; 3 Iain Marsh; 4 Lee Doran; 5 Gavin Dodd; 6 Simon Svabic; 7 Keith Brennan; 8 Steve Molloy; 9 John Hough; 10 Dane Morgan; 11 Chris Morley; 12 Darren Shaw; 13 Phil Farrell. Subs (all used): 14 Paul Anderson; 15 Neil Roden; 16 Martin McLoughlin; 17 Danny Guest.
Tries: Doran (2, 79), Cowell (34), Roden (40, 70), Anderson (66); **Goals:** Svabic 5; **Field goal:** Svabic.
Sin bin: Doran (49) - professional foul.
ROVERS: 1 Nathan Graham; 2 Jamie Stokes; 3 Chris Langley; 4 Brendan O'Meara; 5 Adrian Flynn; 6 Richard Whiting; 7 Carl Briggs; 8 Ian Tonks; 9 Richard Chapman; 10 Stuart Dickens; 11 Steve Dooler; 12 Andy Bailey; 13 Danny Seal. Subs (all used): 14 Jamie Tennant; 15 Andy Jarrett; 16 Andy Rice; 17 Chris Molyneux.
Tries: Stokes (19), Briggs (50), Chapman (57), Seal (61); **Goals:** Dickens 2, Whiting 2.
Rugby Leaguer & League Express Men of the Match: *Oldham:* Neil Roden; *Rovers:* Danny Seal.
Penalty count: 5-5; **Half-time:** 19-8;
Referee: Ben Thaler (Wakefield); **Attendance:** 1,235.

ROCHDALE HORNETS 12 LEIGH CENTURIONS 19

HORNETS: 1 Paul Owen; 2 Mick Nanyn; 3 James Bunyan; 4 Jon Roper; 5 Marlon Billy; 6 Radney Bowker; 7 Ian Watson; 8 Paul Southern; 9 Richard Pachniuk; 10 Gareth Price; 11 David Larder; 12 Paul Smith; 13 Damian Ball. Subs (all used): 14 John Hamilton; 15 Matthew Leigh; 16 Chris Irwin; 17 Andy Grundy.
Tries: Larder (1), Owen (13); **Goals:** Nanyn 2.
Sin bin: Southern (65) - off the ball tackle.
CENTURIONS: 1 Neil Turley; 2 Leroy Rivett; 3 Alan Hadcroft; 4 Phil Kendrick; 5 Damian Munro; 6 Patrick Weisner; 7 Willie Swann; 8 Sonny Nickle; 9 Paul Rowley; 10 David Bradbury; 11 Sean Richardson; 12 Bryan Henare; 13 Adam Bristow. Subs (all used): 14 Dale Holdstock; 15 Rob Ball; 16 Michael Watts; 17 Paul Norman.
Tries: Rowley (10), Kendrick (21), Bristow (38); **Goals:** Turley 3; **Field goal:** Turley.
Rugby Leaguer & League Express Men of the Match: *Hornets:* Paul Owen; *Centurions:* Adam Bristow.
Penalty count: 4-6; **Half-time:** 10-16;
Referee: Colin Morris (Huddersfield); **Attendance:** 1,331.

SALFORD CITY REDS 24 HULL KINGSTON ROVERS 12

CITY REDS: 1 Jason Flowers; 2 Danny Arnold; 3 Stuart Littler; 4 Andy Kirk; 5 Wes Davies; 6 Cliff Beverley; 7 Steve Blakeley; 8 Neil Baynes; 9 Malcolm Alker; 10 Andy Coley; 11 Simon Baldwin; 12 Paul Highton; 13 Chris Charles. Subs (all used): 14 Alan Hunte; 15 David Highton; 16 Mick Berne; 17 Gareth Haggerty.
Tries: Littler (15, 68), Alker (48), Beverley (57), Hunte (66); **Goals:** Charles 2.
ROVERS: 1 Lynton Stott; 2 Nick Pinkney; 3 Paul Parker; 4 Mark Blanchard; 5 Alasdair McClarron; 6 Shaun Cooke; 7 Latham Tawhai; 8 Richard Wilson; 9 Paul Pickering; 10 Harvey Howard; 11 Anthony Seibold; 12 Jon Aston; 13 Andy Smith. Subs (all used); 14 Makali Aizue; 15 Dean Andrews; 16 Jamie Bovill; 17 Paul Fletcher.
Tries: Pickering (10), Smith (22); **Goals:** Stott 2.
Rugby Leaguer & League Express Men of the Match: *City Reds:* Stuart Littler; *Rovers:* Latham Tawhai.
Penalty count: 8-3; **Half-time:** 4-12;
Referee: Julian King (St Helens); **Attendance:** 2,063.

WEEK 12

Sunday 20th July 2003

BATLEY BULLDOGS 16 SALFORD CITY REDS 54

BULLDOGS: 1 Craig Lingard; 2 Mark Sibson; 3 Anthony Gibbons; 4 Danny Maun; 5 Matt Bramald; 6 Danny Thomas; 7 Barry Eaton; 8 Craig Booth; 9 Mark Cass; 10 Steve Hill; 11 Will Cartledge; 12 Mark Toohey; 13 Ryan Horsley. Subs (all used): 14 Andy Spink; 15 Paul Harrison; 16 Danny Evans; 17 Joe Berry.
Tries: Thomas (44), Sibson (48); **Goals:** Eaton 4.
CITY REDS: 1 Jason Flowers; 2 Danny Arnold; 3 Cliff Beverley; 4 Andy Kirk; 5 Wes Davies; 6 Steve Blakeley; 7 Gavin Clinch; 8 Neil Baynes; 9 Malcolm Alker; 10 Andy Coley; 11 Simon Baldwin; 12 Stuart Littler; 13 Paul Highton. Subs (all used): 14 Alan Hunte; 15 David Highton; 16 Chris Charles; 17 Gareth Haggerty.
Tries: Baynes (16), Arnold (22), Flowers (34), Beverley (38), Kirk (55, 73), Charles (60), Baldwin (68), P Highton (77); **Goals:** Blakeley 7, Charles 2.
Rugby Leaguer & League Express Men of the Match: *Bulldogs:* Andy Spink; *City Reds:* Gavin Clinch.
Penalty count: 10-9; **Half-time:** 4-24;
Referee: Ronnie Laughton (Barnsley); **Attendance:** 835.

FEATHERSTONE ROVERS 26 DEWSBURY RAMS 13

ROVERS: 1 Nathan Graham; 2 Jamie Stokes; 3 Chris Langley; 4 Brendan O'Meara; 5 Adrian Flynn; 6 Richard Whiting; 7 Jonathan Presley; 8 Ian Tonks; 9 Richard Chapman; 10 Stuart Dickens; 11 Steve Dooler; 12 Andy Bailey; 13 Danny Seal. Subs (all used): 14 James Ford; 15 James Houston; 16 Andy Rice; 17 Chris Molyneux.
Tries: Presley (2), Stokes (60), Chapman (62, 67); **Goals:** Dickens 5.
RAMS: 1 Nathan Batty; 2 Michael Wainwright; 3 Sylvain Houles; 4 Kevin Crouthers; 5 Craig Miles; 6 Jamie Benn; 7 David Mycoe; 8 Frank Watene; 9 Scott MacDougall; 10 Andrew Senior; 11 Paul Hicks; 12 Billy Kershaw; 13 Graham Law. Subs (all used): 14 Jimmy Elston; 15 Chris Redfearn; 16 Paul Smith; 17 Tony Fella.
Tries: Wainwright (42), Redfearn (79); **Goals:** Benn 2; **Field goal:** Benn.
Rugby Leaguer & League Express Men of the Match: *Rovers:* Richard Chapman; *Rams:* Jimmy Elston.
Penalty count: 6-3; **Half-time:** 8-2;
Referee: Colin Morris (Huddersfield); **Attendance:** 1,536.

HULL KINGSTON ROVERS 18 ROCHDALE HORNETS 33

ROVERS: 1 Lynton Stott; 2 Nick Pinkney; 3 Paul Parker; 4 Dean Andrews; 5 Alasdair McClarron; 6 Shaun Cooke; 7 Latham Tawhai; 8 Richard Wilson; 9 Paul Pickering; 10 Harvey Howard; 11 Anthony Seibold; 12 Jon Aston; 13 Andy Smith. Subs (all used): 14 Makali Aizue; 15 Dean Busby; 16 Jamie Bovill; 17 Paul Fletcher.
Tries: Andrews (44), Aizue (47), McClarron (64); **Goals:** Stott 3.
HORNETS: 1 Paul Owen; 2 Mick Nanyn; 3 James Bunyan; 4 Jon Roper; 5 Marlon Billy; 6 Radney Bowker; 7 Ian Watson; 8 Paul Southern; 9 Richard Pachniuk; 10 Gareth Price; 11 David Larder; 12 Paul Smith; 13 Damian Ball. Subs (all used): 14 John Hamilton; 15 Matthew Leigh; 16 Chris Irwin; 17 Andy Grundy.
Tries: Larder (11), Bowker (20), Nanyn (37), Watson (59, 77), Billy (61); **Goals:** Nanyn 4; **Field goal:** Watson.
Rugby Leaguer & League Express Men of the Match: *Rovers:* Makali Aizue; *Hornets:* Ian Watson.
Penalty count: 10-10; **Half-time:** 0-16;
Referee: Ben Thaler (Wakefield); **Attendance:** 1,750.

OLDHAM 31 DONCASTER DRAGONS 20

OLDHAM: 1 Jon Goddard; 2 Will Cowell; 3 Iain Marsh; 4 Lee Doran; 5 Gavin Dodd; 6 Simon Svabic; 7 Keith Brennan; 8 Steve Molloy; 9 John Hough; 10 Dane Morgan; 11 Chris Morley; 12 Darren Shaw; 13 Phil Farrell. Subs (all used): 14 Paul Anderson; 15 Neil Roden; 16 Martin McLoughlin; 17 Danny Guest.
Tries: Svabic (15), Doran (23, 47, 71), Dodd (28); **Goals:** Svabic 5; **Field goal:** Svabic.
DRAGONS: 1 Scott Grix; 2 Gareth Lloyd; 3 Craig Lawton; 4 PJ Solomon; 5 Alex Muff; 6 Paul Mansson; 7 Mark Moxon; 8 Gareth Handford; 9 Gareth Greenwood; 10 Anthony Seuseu; 11 Peter Green; 12 Martin Ostler; 13 Peter Edwards. Subs (all used): 14 James Walker; 15 Matt Walker; 16 Tom Buckenham; 17 Wayne Frost.
Tries: Lloyd (39), P Green (62), Solomon (68), Edwards (79); **Goals:** Grix 2.
Rugby Leaguer & League Express Men of the Match: *Oldham:* Simon Svabic; *Dragons:* Mark Moxon.
Penalty count: 8-9; **Half-time:** 17-6; **Referee:** Steve Nicholson (Whitehaven); **Attendance:** 1,254.

WHITEHAVEN 8 LEIGH CENTURIONS 20

WHITEHAVEN: 1 Gary Broadbent; 2 Steven Wood; 3 David Seeds; 4 Craig Walsh; 5 Neil Frazer; 6 Leroy Joe; 7 Darren Holt; 8 Chris McKinney; 9 Aaron Lester; 10 David Fatialofa; 11 Spencer Miller; 12 Howard Hill; 13 Garry Purdham. Subs (all used): 14 Carl Sice; 15 Dean Vaughan; 16 Mike Whitehead; 17 Gary Smith.
Try: Hill (80); **Goal:** Holt 2.
Sin bin: Joe (65) - fighting.
CENTURIONS: 1 Michael Watts; 2 Leroy Rivett; 3 Alan Hadcroft; 4 Damian Munro; 5 David Alstead; 6 Neil Turley; 7 Willie Swann; 8 Sonny Nickle; 9 Paul Rowley; 10 David Bradbury; 11 Sean Richardson; 12 Bryan Henare; 13 Adam Bristow. Subs (all used): 14 Keiron Maddocks; 15 Anthony Blackwood; 16 Rob Ball; 17 Paul Norman.
Tries: Munro (18), Richardson (48), Nickle (56), Henare (60); **Goals:** Turley 2.
Sin bin: Rowley (65) - fighting.
Rugby Leaguer & League Express Men of the Match: *Whitehaven:* David Seeds; *Centurions:* Neil Turley.
Penalty count: 13-9; **Half-time:** 2-4;
Referee: Mike Dawber (Wigan); **Attendance:** 1,750.

WEEK 13

Sunday 27th July 2003

DEWSBURY RAMS 26 OLDHAM 32

RAMS: 1 Nathan Batty; 2 Michael Wainwright; 3 Sylvain Houles; 4 Kevin Crouthers; 5 Craig Miles; 6 Jamie Benn; 7 David Mycoe; 8 Frank Watene; 9 Adam Thaler; 10 Paul Hicks; 11 Scott MacDougall; 12 Billy Kershaw; 13 Chris Redfearn. Subs (all used): 14 Jimmy Elston; 15 Ryan Hardy; 16 Anthony Thewliss; 17 Paul Smith.
Tries: Hicks (13), Houles (29, 44), Miles (50);
Goals: Benn 4; **Field goals:** Benn 2.
OLDHAM: 1 Jon Goddard; 2 Will Cowell; 3 Iain Marsh; 4 Lee Doran; 5 Gavin Dodd; 6 Simon Svabic; 7 Keith Brennan; 8 Steve Molloy; 9 John Hough; 10 Dane Morgan; 11 Chris Morley; 12 Darren Shaw; 13 Phil Farrell. Subs (all used): 14 Neil Roden; 15 Gareth Barber; 16 Martin McLoughlin; 17 Danny Guest.
Tries: Doran (2, 39), Brennan (8), Morley (57), Dodd (68), Roden (71); **Goals:** Svabic 4.
Rugby Leaguer & League Express Men of the Match: *Rams:* Frank Watene; *Oldham:* Jon Goddard.
Penalty count: 5-6; **Half-time:** 12-16;
Referee: Robert Connolly (Wigan); **Attendance:** 1,098.

HULL KINGSTON ROVERS 36 WHITEHAVEN 10

ROVERS: 1 Chris Stephenson; 2 Mark Blanchard; 3 Paul Parker; 4 Craig Poucher; 5 Alasdair McClarron; 6 Paul Mansson; 7 Latham Tawhai; 8 Richard Wilson; 9 Jimmy Walker; 10 Makali Aizue; 11 Anthony Seibold; 12 Jon Aston; 13 Dean Busby. Subs (all used): 14 Dean Andrews; 15 Jamie Bovill; 16 Harvey Howard; 17 Paul Fletcher.
Tries: Poucher (17, 54), Bovill (24), Mansson (29), Tawhai (59), Aizue (64); **Goals:** Stephenson 5, Tawhai.
WHITEHAVEN: 1 Paul O'Neil; 2 Neil Frazer; 3 Wesley Wilson; 4 Howard Hill; 5 Steven Wood; 6 Leroy Joe; 7 Steve Kirkbride; 8 Chris McKinney; 9 Aaron Lester; 10 David Fatialofa; 11 Spencer Miller; 12 Marc Jackson; 13 Garry Purdham. Subs (all used): 14 Carl Sice; 15 Ryan Campbell; 16 Dean Vaughan; 17 Gary Smith.
Tries: Wood (36), Joe (67); **Goal:** Kirkbride.
Rugby Leaguer & League Express Men of the Match: *Rovers:* Makali Aizue; *Whitehaven:* Steve Kirkbride.
Penalty count: 9-8; **Half-time:** 20-6;
Referee: Ashley Klein (London); **Attendance:** 1,612.

LEIGH CENTURIONS 54 BATLEY BULLDOGS 30

CENTURIONS: 1 Neil Turley; 2 Leroy Rivett; 3 Alan Hadcroft; 4 Damian Munro; 5 Michael Watts; 6 Patrick Weisner; 7 Tommy Martyn; 8 Sonny Nickle; 9 Paul Rowley; 10 David Bradbury; 11 Sean Richardson; 12 Bryan Henare; 13 Adam Bristow. Subs (all used): 14 Paul Norman; 15 Dale Cardoza; 16 Willie Swann; 17 Ricky Bibey.
Tries: Watts (13), Hadcroft (21, 78), Weisner (25), Rowley (29, 55), Swann (35), Rivett (37), Cardoza (57, 74); **Goals:** Turley 7.
BULLDOGS: 1 Mark Sibson; 2 Chris Spurr; 3 Anthony Gibbons; 4 Danny Maun; 5 Matt Bramald; 6 Danny Thomas; 7 Barry Eaton; 8 Andy Spink; 9 Will Cartledge; 10 Steve Hill; 11 Danny Evans; 12 Steve Beard; 13 Ryan Horsley. Subs (all used): 14 Mark Cass; 15 Simon Lewis; 16 Mark Toohey; 17 Craig Booth.
Tries: Maun (6, 66), Thomas (45), Spurr (53), Bramald (64); **Goals:** Eaton 5.
Rugby Leaguer & League Express Men of the Match: *Centurions:* Paul Rowley; *Bulldogs:* Danny Thomas.
Penalty count: 5-3; **Half-time:** 34-6; **Referee:** Steve Nicholson (Whitehaven); **Attendance:** 2,283.

ROCHDALE HORNETS 50 DONCASTER DRAGONS 34

HORNETS: 1 Paul Owen; 2 Mick Nanyn; 3 James Bunyan; 4 Jon Roper; 5 Marlon Billy; 6 Radney Bowker; 7 Ian Watson; 8 Paul Southern; 9 Richard Pachniuk; 10 Gareth Price; 11 David Larder; 12 Paul Smith; 13 Damian Ball. Subs (all used): 14 John Hamilton; 15 Matthew Leigh; 16 Chris Irwin; 17 Matthew Long.
Tries: Smith (9), Larder (15, 22), Bowker (25, 41), Billy (33), Hamilton (37), Nanyn (47), Owen (50);
Goals: Nanyn 7.
Dismissal: Price (70) - kicking.
Sin bin: Roper (60) - interference.
DRAGONS: 1 Scott Grix; 2 Martin Sykes; 3 Simon Irving; 4 PJ Solomon; 5 Jason Lee; 6 Graham Holroyd; 7 Mark Moxon; 8 Gareth Handford; 9 Gareth Greenwood; 10 Maea David; 11 Peter Green; 12 Craig Lawton; 13 Peter Edwards. Subs (all used): 14 James Walker; 15 Matt Walker; 16 Martin Ostler; 17 Gareth Lloyd.
Tries: J Walker (40), Grix (64, 66), Solomon (71), Greenwood (73), Lee (80); **Goals:** Holroyd 5.
Rugby Leaguer & League Express Men of the Match: *Hornets:* David Larder; *Dragons:* Jason Lee.
Penalty count: 7-13; **Half-time:** 34-8;
Referee: Ronnie Laughton (Barnsley); **Attendance:** 623.

SALFORD CITY REDS 36 FEATHERSTONE ROVERS 20

CITY REDS: 1 Jason Flowers; 2 Danny Arnold; 3 Stuart Littler; 4 Andy Kirk; 5 Wes Davies; 6 Cliff Beverley; 7 Gavin Clinch; 8 Neil Baynes; 9 Malcolm Alker; 10 Gareth Haggerty; 11 Simon Baldwin; 12 Paul Highton; 13 Chris Charles. Subs (all used): 14 Steve Blakeley; 15 David Highton; 16 Alan Hunte; 17 Andy Coley.
Tries: Baynes (19), Kirk (26), Coley (34), Flowers (44), Littler (59), Alker (71); **Goals:** Charles 5, Clinch.
Sin bin: Charles (8) - late tackle; Baldwin (50) - fighting.
ROVERS: 1 Nathan Graham; 2 Jamie Stokes; 3 Brendan O'Meara; 4 Ian Brown; 5 Adrian Flynn; 6 Richard Whiting; 7 Jonathan Presley; 8 Ian Tonks; 9 Richard Chapman; 10 Stuart Dickens; 11 Steve Dooler; 12 Andy Bailey; 13 Danny Seal. Subs (all used): 14 Paul Darley; 15 James Houston; 16 Andy Rice; 17 Chris Molyneux.
Tries: Dickens (55), Presley (65), Flynn (76);
Goals: Dickens 4.
Sin bin: Chapman (50) - fighting;
Darley (68) - obstruction.
Rugby Leaguer & League Express Men of the Match: *City Reds:* Malcolm Alker; *Rovers:* Stuart Dickens.
Penalty count: 9-12; **Half-time:** 20-2;
Referee: Mike Dawber (Wigan); **Attendance:** 2,025.

WEEK 14

Sunday 3rd August 2003

BATLEY BULLDOGS 27 HULL KINGSTON ROVERS 13

BULLDOGS: 1 Craig Lingard; 2 Mark Sibson; 3 Anthony Gibbons; 4 Danny Maun; 5 Matt Bramald; 6 Danny Thomas; 7 Barry Eaton; 8 Craig Booth; 9 Will Cartledge; 10 Steve Hill; 11 Danny Evans; 12 Mark Toohey; 13 Ryan Horsley. Subs (all used): 14 Mark Cass; 15 Paul Harrison; 16 Andy Spink; 17 Steve Beard.
Tries: Sibson (40), Cartledge (44), Toohey (55), Harrison (72); **Goals:** Eaton 5; **Field goal:** Eaton.
ROVERS: 1 Mike Hall; 2 Craig Farrell; 3 Paul Parker; 4 Craig Poucher; 5 Alasdair McClarron; 6 Paul Mansson; 7 Latham Tawhai; 8 Richard Wilson; 9 Jimmy Walker; 10 Makali Aizue; 11 Anthony Seibold; 12 Jon Aston; 13 Andy Smith. Subs (all used): 14 Craig Murdock; 15 Adam Sullivan; 16 Jamie Bovill; 17 Paul Fletcher.
Tries: Mansson (30, 77); **Goals:** Hall 2;
Field goal: Tawhai.
Sin bin: Wilson (59) - interference.
Rugby Leaguer & League Express Men of the Match: *Bulldogs:* Will Cartledge; *Rovers:* Paul Mansson.
Penalty count: 8-8; **Half-time:** 6-7;
Referee: Steve Presley (Castleford); **Attendance:** 926.

DONCASTER DRAGONS 16 DEWSBURY RAMS 31

DRAGONS: 1 Jason Lee; 2 Scott Grix; 3 Simon Irving; 4 PJ Solomon; 5 Alex Muff; 6 Graham Holroyd; 7 Mark Moxon; 8 Gareth Handford; 9 Peter Edwards; 10 Matt Walker; 11 Peter Green; 12 Martin Ostler; 13 Craig Lawton. Subs (all used): 14 James Walker; 15 Gareth Greenwood; 16 Maea David; 17 Dean Colton.
Tries: Handford (4), Moxon (22), Colton (70);
Goals: Holroyd 2.
RAMS: 1 Nathan Batty; 2 Michael Wainwright; 3 Sylvain Houles; 4 Graham Law; 5 Craig Miles; 6 Jamie Benn; 7 David Mycoe; 8 Frank Watene; 9 Adam Thaler; 10 Paul Hicks; 11 Kevin Crouthers; 12 Billy Kershaw; 13 Chris Redfearn. Subs (all used): 14 Jimmy Elston; 15 Scott MacDougall; 16 Anthony Thewliss; 17 Paul Smith.
Tries: Batty (13, 24), Law (18), Wainwright (66);
Goals: Benn 7; **Field goal:** Benn.
Rugby Leaguer & League Express Men of the Match: *Dragons:* Jason Lee; *Rams:* Jamie Benn.
Penalty count: 9-14; **Half-time:** 12-22;
Referee: Peter Taberner (Wigan); **Attendance:** 726.

FEATHERSTONE ROVERS 32 LEIGH CENTURIONS 58

ROVERS: 1 Nathan Graham; 2 Jamie Stokes; 3 Richard Whiting; 4 Brendan O'Meara; 5 Adrian Flynn; 6 Carl Briggs; 7 Jonathan Presley; 8 Ian Tonks; 9 Richard Chapman; 10 Stuart Dickens; 11 Steve Dooler; 12 Andy Rice; 13 Danny Seal. Subs (all used): 14 Ian Brown; 15 Paul Darley; 16 James Houston; 17 Chris Molyneux.
Tries: Seal (10), Dooler (30), Whiting (35), Brown (42), Houston (61), Chapman (69); **Goals:** Whiting 4.
CENTURIONS: 1 Neil Turley; 2 Leroy Rivett; 3 Alan Hadcroft; 4 Dale Cardoza; 5 Michael Watts; 6 Patrick Weisner; 7 Tommy Martyn; 8 Rob Ball; 9 John Duffy; 10 Paul Norman; 11 Sean Richardson; 12 Dale Holdstock; 13 Adam Bristow. Subs (all used): 14 Lee Sanderson; 15 Ricky Bibey; 16 Danny Halliwell; 17 Damian Munro.
Tries: Bristow (6, 14), Martyn (27), Turley (44), Duffy (47), Rivett (51), Munro (58), Cardoza (66, 72, 77);
Goals: Turley 9.
Rugby Leaguer & League Express Men of the Match: *Rovers:* Richard Whiting; *Centurions:* Neil Turley.
Penalty count: 10-7; **Half-time:** 16-20;
Referee: Ian Smith (Oldham); **Attendance:** 1,747.

OLDHAM 22 SALFORD CITY REDS 32

OLDHAM: 1 Jon Goddard; 2 Will Cowell; 3 Iain Marsh; 4 Lee Doran; 5 Gavin Dodd; 6 Simon Svabic; 7 Neil Roden; 8 Steve Molloy; 9 John Hough; 10 Dane Morgan; 11 Chris Morley; 12 Darren Shaw; 13 Phil Farrell. Subs (all used): 14 Gareth Barber; 15 Ryan Stazicker; 16 Martin McLoughlin; 17 Danny Guest.
Tries: Farrell (13), Doran (39), Barber (63), Morley (71);
Goals: Svabic 3.
CITY REDS: 1 Jason Flowers; 2 Danny Arnold; 3 Stuart Littler; 4 Alan Hunte; 5 Wes Davies; 6 Cliff Beverley; 7 Gavin Clinch; 8 Neil Baynes; 9 Malcolm Alker; 10 Andy Coley; 11 Simon Baldwin; 12 Paul Highton; 13 Chris Charles. Subs (all used): 14 Steve Blakeley; 15 David Highton; 16 Martin Moana; 17 Neil Lowe.
Tries: Baldwin (4), Hunte (20), Coley (29), Beverley (31), Alker (50), Littler (67); **Goals:** Charles 4.
Rugby Leaguer & League Express Men of the Match: *Oldham:* Phil Farrell; *City Reds:* David Highton.
Penalty count: 10-7; **Half-time:** 12-24; **Referee:** Steve Nicholson (Whitehaven); **Attendance:** 1,765.

WHITEHAVEN 24 ROCHDALE HORNETS 44

WHITEHAVEN: 1 Gary Broadbent; 2 Paul O'Neil; 3 Danny Lockhart; 4 Howard Hill; 5 Steven Wood; 6 Leroy Joe; 7 Steve Kirkbride; 8 Matt Sturm; 9 Aaron Lester; 10 David Fatialofa; 11 Chris McKinney; 12 Spencer Miller; 13 Garry Purdham. Subs (all used): 14 Carl Sice; 15 Marc Jackson; 16 Ryan Campbell; 17 Dean Vaughan.
Tries: Broadbent (19), Lester (23), O'Neil (28, 70);
Goals: Kirkbride 4.
HORNETS: 1 Chris Irwin; 2 Mick Nanyn; 3 Damian Ball; 4 Jon Roper; 5 Marlon Billy; 6 Radney Bowker; 7 Ian Watson; 8 Paul Southern; 9 Richard Pachniuk; 10 Gareth Price; 11 David Larder; 12 Matthew Leigh; 13 Paul Smith. Subs (all used): 14 Warren Ayres; 15 Wes Rogers; 16 John Hamilton; 17 Matthew Long.
Tries: Irwin (4), Rogers (31), Nanyn (35, 66), Roper (48), Bowker (60), Billy (74); **Goals:** Nanyn 7;
Field goals: Watson 2.
Rugby Leaguer & League Express Men of the Match: *Whitehaven:* Gary Broadbent; *Hornets:* Radney Bowker.
Penalty count: 1-6; **Half-time:** 20-18; **Referee:** Colin Morris (Huddersfield); **Attendance:** 1,282.

WEEK 15

Sunday 10th August 2003

BATLEY BULLDOGS 26 WHITEHAVEN 16

BULLDOGS: 1 Craig Lingard; 2 Mark Sibson; 3 Anthony Gibbons; 4 Danny Maun; 5 Matt Bramald; 6 Danny Thomas; 7 Barry Eaton; 8 Joe Naidole; 9 Will Cartledge; 10 Steve Hill; 11 Danny Evans; 12 Mark Toohey; 13 Ryan Horsley. Subs (all used): 14 Mark Cass; 15 Paul Harrison; 16 Andy Spink; 17 Steve Beard.
Tries: Maun (51), Cartledge (59), Harrison (68), Spink (78); **Goals:** Eaton 5.
Sin bin: Maun (37) - dissent.
WHITEHAVEN: 1 Gary Broadbent; 2 Steven Wood; 3 Craig Walsh; 4 Howard Hill; 5 Paul O'Neil; 6 Leroy Joe; 7 Steve Kirkbride; 8 Chris McKinney; 9 Aaron Lester; 10 David Fatialofa; 11 Matt Sturm; 12 Spencer Miller; 13 Garry Purdham. Subs (all used): 14 Marc Jackson; 15 Carl Sice; 16 Graeme Morton; 17 Tony Cunningham.
Tries: Joe (10), Kirkbride (37), O'Neil (73);
Goals: Kirkbride 2.
Sin bin: McKinney (78) - illegal use of elbow.
Rugby Leaguer & League Express Men of the Match: *Bulldogs:* Joe Naidole; *Whitehaven:* Leroy Joe.
Penalty count: 9-4; **Half-time:** 2-12;
Referee: Peter Taberner (Wigan); **Attendance:** 604.

HULL KINGSTON ROVERS 13 FEATHERSTONE ROVERS 0

ROBINS: 1 Lynton Stott; 2 Craig Farrell; 3 Paul Parker; 4 Mark Blanchard; 5 Alasdair McClarron; 6 Paul Mansson; 7 Latham Tawhai; 8 Richard Wilson; 9 Jimmy Walker; 10 Makali Aizue; 11 Anthony Seibold; 12 Jon Aston; 13 Andy Smith. Subs (all used): 14 Paul Pickering; 15 Jamie Bovill; 16 Adam Sullivan; 17 Paul Fletcher.
Tries: Mansson (5), McClarron (76); **Goals:** Stott 2;
Field goal: Stott.
Dismissal: Bovill (34) - high tackle.
ROVERS: 1 Nathan Graham; 2 Jamie Stokes; 3 Brendan O'Meara; 4 Ian Brown; 5 Adrian Flynn; 6 Richard Whiting; 7 Carl Briggs; 8 Ian Tonks; 9 Richard Chapman; 10 Stuart Dickens; 11 Steve Dooler; 12 Andy Rice; 13 Danny Seal. Subs (all used): 14 Paul Darley; 15 James Houston; 16 Andy Bailey; 17 Chris Molyneux.
Rugby Leaguer & League Express Men of the Match: *Robins:* Jimmy Walker; *Rovers:* Richard Chapman.
Penalty count: 4-6; **Half-time:** 6-0; **Referee:** Colin Morris (Huddersfield); **Attendance:** 1,559.

LEIGH CENTURIONS 38 OLDHAM 2

CENTURIONS: 1 Neil Turley; 2 Leroy Rivett; 3 Alan Hadcroft; 4 Danny Halliwell; 5 Damian Munro; 6 Patrick Weisner; 7 Tommy Martyn; 8 Paul Norman; 9 Paul Rowley; 10 David Bradbury; 11 Sean Richardson; 12 Bryan Henare; 13 Adam Bristow. Subs (all used): 14 Rob Ball; 15 Dale Cardoza; 16 John Duffy; 17 Ricky Bibey.
Tries: Turley (17), Martyn (24, 38), Munro (58), Duffy (62), Weisner (76); **Goals:** Turley 7.
Sin bin: Rowley (55) - holding down;
Munro (71) - holding down.
OLDHAM: 1 Gavin Dodd; 2 Will Cowell; 3 Gavin Johnson; 4 Lee Doran; 5 Joe McNicholas; 6 Simon Svabic; 7 Neil Roden; 8 Steve Molloy; 9 Darren Shaw; 10 Dane Morgan; 11 Chris Morley; 12 Ryan Stazicker; 13 Phil Farrell. Subs (all used): 14 Gareth Barber; 15 Martin McLoughlin; 16 Paul Anderson; 17 Danny Guest.
Goal: Svabic.
Sin bin: Anderson (43) - holding down.
Rugby Leaguer & League Express Men of the Match: *Centurions:* Damian Munro; *Oldham:* Joe McNicholas.
Penalty count: 13-12; **Half-time:** 20-2; **Referee:** Ronnie Laughton (Barnsley); **Attendance:** 2,287.

ROCHDALE HORNETS 52 DEWSBURY RAMS 14

HORNETS: 1 Chris Irwin; 2 Mick Nanyn; 3 Wayne McHugh; 4 Jon Roper; 5 Marlon Billy; 6 Radney Bowker; 7 Ian Watson; 8 Paul Southern; 9 Richard Pachniuk; 10 Gareth Price; 11 David Larder; 12 Paul Smith; 13 Damian Ball. Subs (all used): 14 James Bunyan; 15 Matthew Leigh; 16 Wes Rogers; 17 Matthew Long.
Tries: McHugh (3, 35), Larder (8), Nanyn (14, 21), Pachniuk (51), Irwin (54, 75), Bunyan (72), Billy (80);
Goals: Nanyn 6.
RAMS: 1 Nathan Batty; 2 Michael Wainwright; 3 Sylvain Houles; 4 Graham Law; 5 Craig Miles; 6 Jamie Benn; 7 David Mycoe; 8 Frank Watene; 9 Adam Thaler; 10 Paul Hicks; 11 Kevin Crouthers; 12 Billy Kershaw; 13 Chris Redfearn. Subs (all used): 14 Jimmy Elston; 15 Anthony Thewliss; 16 Ryan Hardy; 17 Paul Smith.
Tries: Watene (18), Houles (27), Elston (62); **Goal:** Benn.
Rugby Leaguer & League Express Men of the Match: *Hornets:* Wayne McHugh; *Rams:* Jimmy Elston.
Penalty count: 8-10; **Half-time:** 22-8;
Referee: Steve Presley (Castleford); **Attendance:** 732.

SALFORD CITY REDS 72 DONCASTER DRAGONS 0

CITY REDS: 1 Jason Flowers; 2 Danny Arnold; 3 Stuart Littler; 4 Andy Kirk; 5 Wes Davies; 6 Cliff Beverley; 7 Gavin Clinch; 8 Neil Baynes; 9 David Highton; 10 Andy Coley; 11 Simon Baldwin; 12 Paul Highton; 13 Steve Blakeley. Subs (all used): 14 Malcolm Alker; 15 Neil Lowe; 16 Martin Moana; 17 Gareth Haggerty.
Tries: Flowers (5, 45), Kirk (7, 70), D Highton (15, 41), Haggerty (21), P Highton (30), Littler (35), Clinch (40), Lowe (48), Beverley (67), Coley (74); **Goals:** Blakeley 10.
DRAGONS: 1 Alex Muff; 2 Gareth Lloyd; 3 David Ford; 4 PJ Solomon; 5 Dean Colton; 6 Scott Grix; 7 Graham Holroyd; 8 James Walker; 9 Gareth Greenwood; 10

Martin Ostler; 11 Peter Green; 12 Craig Lawton; 13 Peter Edwards. Subs (all used): 14 Chris Hemmings; 15 Mark Moxon; 16 Jason Eagle; 17 Wayne Green.
Sin bin: Lawton (29) - holding down.
Rugby Leaguer & League Express Men of the Match: *City Reds:* Andy Coley; *Dragons:* Gareth Greenwood.
Penalty count: 15-8; **Half-time:** 38-0;
Referee: Steve Ganson (St Helens); **Attendance:** 1,620.

WEEK 16

Sunday 17th August 2003

DEWSBURY RAMS 18 SALFORD CITY REDS 58

RAMS: 1 Nathan Batty; 2 Michael Wainwright; 3 Sylvain Houles; 4 Kevin Crouthers; 5 Craig Miles; 6 Jamie Benn; 7 David Mycoe; 8 Frank Watene; 9 Adam Thaler; 10 Paul Hicks; 11 Chris Redfearn; 12 Billy Kershaw; 13 Graham Law. Subs (all used): 14 Jimmy Elston; 15 Mark Barlow; 16 Andrew Senior; 17 Paul Smith.
Tries: Miles (63), Kershaw (75), Crouthers (79);
Goals: Benn 3.
CITY REDS: 1 Jason Flowers; 2 Wes Davies; 3 Stuart Littler; 4 Alan Hunte; 5 Andy Kirk; 6 Cliff Beverley; 7 Gavin Clinch; 8 Neil Baynes; 9 David Highton; 10 Andy Coley; 11 Simon Baldwin; 12 Neil Lowe; 13 Chris Charles. Subs (all used): 14 Steve Blakeley; 15 Malcolm Alker; 16 Martin Moana; 17 Paul Highton.
Tries: D Highton (9), Baldwin (12), Clinch (18, 51), Flowers (25), P Highton (34), Beverley (48), Blakeley (57), Baynes (69), Coley (71);
Goals: Charles 5, Blakeley 3, Hunte.
Rugby Leaguer & League Express Men of the Match: *Rams:* Jimmy Elston; *City Reds:* Gavin Clinch.
Penalty count: 4-4; **Half-time:** 0-30;
Referee: Steve Presley (Castleford); **Attendance:** 972.

DONCASTER DRAGONS 18 LEIGH CENTURIONS 46

DRAGONS: 1 Scott Grix; 2 Dean Colton; 3 Alex Muff; 4 PJ Solomon; 5 Johnny Woodcock; 6 Graham Holroyd; 7 Mark Moxon; 8 Gareth Handford; 9 Gareth Greenwood; 10 Chris Hemmings; 11 Peter Green; 12 Gareth Lloyd; 13 Craig Lawton. Subs (all used): 14 James Walker; 15 Martin Ostler; 16 David Ford; 17 Wayne Green.
Tries: Holroyd (21, 31, 63); **Goals:** Holroyd 3.
CENTURIONS: 1 Neil Turley; 2 Leroy Rivett; 3 Alan Hadcroft; 4 Danny Halliwell; 5 Damian Munro; 6 Patrick Weisner; 7 Tommy Martyn; 8 Sonny Nickle; 9 Paul Rowley; 10 David Bradbury; 11 Sean Richardson; 12 Bryan Henare; 13 Adam Bristow. Subs (all used): 14 Paul Norman; 15 John Duffy; 16 Dale Cardoza; 17 Ricky Bibey.
Tries: Richardson (4), Bradbury (10, 51), Martyn (16), Turley (45), Munro (57), Halliwell (59, 72), Cardoza (77);
Goals: Turley 5.
Rugby Leaguer & League Express Men of the Match: *Dragons:* Graham Holroyd; *Centurions:* Tommy Martyn.
Penalty count: 7-4; **Half-time:** 12-14;
Referee: Peter Taberner (Wigan); **Attendance:** 901.

FEATHERSTONE ROVERS 52 WHITEHAVEN 12

ROVERS: 1 Nathan Graham; 2 Jamie Stokes; 3 Brendan O'Meara; 4 Adrian Flynn; 5 James Ford; 6 Richard Whiting; 7 Carl Briggs; 8 Ian Tonks; 9 Paul Darley; 10 Stuart Dickens; 11 Steve Dooler; 12 James Houston; 13 Danny Seal. Subs (all used): 14 Jonathan Presley; 15 Richard Chapman; 16 Andy Rice; 17 Chris Molyneux.
Tries: Darley (1), O'Meara (22, 62), Stokes (24, 69), Graham (46, 48), Flynn (51), Seal (55);
Goals: Dickens 2, Briggs 6.
WHITEHAVEN: 1 Gary Broadbent; 2 Steven Wood; 3 Wesley Wilson; 4 Howard Hill; 5 Paul O'Neil; 6 Leroy Joe; 7 Steve Kirkbride; 8 Chris McKinney; 9 Aaron Lester; 10 David Fatialofa; 11 Craig Chambers; 12 Graeme Morton; 13 Spencer Miller. Subs (all used): 14 Marc Jackson; 15 Carl Sice; 16 Ryan Campbell; 17 Tony Cunningham.
Tries: Morton (67, 74); **Goals:** Kirkbride 2.
Sin bin: Sice (60) - holding down.
Rugby Leaguer & League Express Men of the Match: *Rovers:* Nathan Graham; *Whitehaven:* Howard Hill.
Penalty count: 11-5; **Half-time:** 16-2; **Referee:** Ronnie Laughton (Barnsley); **Attendance:** 1,116.

OLDHAM 24 HULL KINGSTON ROVERS 29

OLDHAM: 1 Jon Goddard; 2 Will Cowell; 3 Iain Marsh; 4 Lee Doran; 5 Gavin Dodd; 6 Simon Svabic; 7 Neil Roden; 8 Steve Molloy; 9 John Hough; 10 Dane Morgan; 11 Chris Morley; 12 Lee Marsh; 13 Phil Farrell. Subs (all used): 14 Gareth Barber; 15 Martin McLoughlin; 16 Gavin Johnson; 17 Danny Guest.
Tries: Farrell (2), McLoughlin (27), Doran (41), Morgan (70); **Goals:** Svabic 4.
ROVERS: 1 Lynton Stott; 2 Craig Farrell; 3 Paul Parker; 4 Mark Blanchard; 5 Alasdair McClarron; 6 Anthony Seibold; 7 Latham Tawhai; 8 Richard Wilson; 9 Jimmy Walker; 10 Jamie Bovill; 11 Adam Sullivan; 12 Jon Aston; 13 Andy Smith. Subs (all used): 14 Paul Pickering; 15 Craig Poucher; 16 Makali Aizue; 17 Paul Fletcher.
Tries: Farrell (19), Seibold (34), Pickering (37), Poucher (45), McClarron (72); **Goals:** Stott 4; **Field goal:** Stott.
Rugby Leaguer & League Express Men of the Match: *Oldham:* Gareth Barber; *Rovers:* Anthony Seibold.
Penalty count: 9-8; **Half-time** 12-16;
Referee: Mike Dawber (Wigan); **Attendance:** 1,414.

ROCHDALE HORNETS 38 BATLEY BULLDOGS 32

HORNETS: 1 Chris Irwin; 2 Mick Nanyn; 3 James Bunyan; 4 Jon Roper; 5 Wayne McHugh; 6 Radney Bowker; 7 Ian Watson; 8 Paul Southern; 9 Richard Pachniuk; 10 Gareth Price; 11 David Larder; 12 Paul Smith; 13 Damian Ball. Subs (all used): 14 Matt Calland; 15 Matthew Leigh; 16 Wes Rogers; 17 Matthew Long.
Tries: Larder (4, 73), Roper (21), Smith (25), McHugh (40), Leigh (42), Nanyn (55), Pachniuk (59);
Goals: Nanyn 3.
BULLDOGS: 1 Craig Lingard; 2 Mark Sibson; 3 Anthony Gibbons; 4 Danny Maun; 5 Matt Bramald; 6 Danny Thomas; 7 Barry Eaton; 8 Joe Naidole; 9 Gavin Swinson; 10 Steve Hill; 11 Danny Evans; 12 Mark Toohey; 13 Ryan Horsley. Subs (all used): 14 Leon Williamson; 15 Paul Harrison; 16 Steve Beard; 17 Craig Booth.
Tries: Bramald (8), Eaton (11), Thomas (37), Harrison (62), A Gibbons (80); **Goals:** Eaton 6.
Rugby Leaguer & League Express Men of the Match: *Hornets:* David Larder; *Bulldogs:* Barry Eaton.
Penalty count: 5-8; **Half-time:** 18-20;
Referee: Julian King (St Helens); **Attendance:** 820.

WEEK 17

Sunday 24th August 2003

BATLEY BULLDOGS 18 FEATHERSTONE ROVERS 10

BULLDOGS: 1 Craig Lingard; 2 Matt Bramald; 3 Chris Spurr; 4 Danny Maun; 5 Leon Williamson; 6 Danny Thomas; 7 Barry Eaton; 8 Craig Booth; 9 Will Cartledge; 10 Steve Hill; 11 Danny Evans; 12 Mark Toohey; 13 Ryan Horsley. Subs (all used): 14 Gavin Swinson; 15 Paul Harrison; 16 Joe Berry; 17 Andy Spink.
Tries: Eaton (32), Horsley (40, 70); **Goals:** Eaton 3.
Sin bin: Evans (47) - interference.
ROVERS: 1 Nathan Graham; 2 Jamie Stokes; 3 Brendan O'Meara; 4 Adrian Flynn; 5 James Ford; 6 Danny Patrickson; 7 Carl Briggs; 8 Ian Tonks; 9 Paul Darley; 10 Stuart Dickens; 11 Steve Dooler; 12 Andy Rice; 13 Danny Seal. Subs (all used): 14 Jonathan Presley; 15 Richard Chapman; 16 James Houston; 17 Chris Molyneux.
Tries: Dooler (9), Stokes (48); **Goal:** Dickens.
Rugby Leaguer & League Express Men of the Match: *Bulldogs:* Barry Eaton; *Rovers:* Ian Tonks.
Penalty count: 7-3; **Half-time:** 12-6; **Referee:** Steve Nicholson (Whitehaven); **Attendance:** 1,156.

HULL KINGSTON ROVERS 32 DONCASTER DRAGONS 26

ROVERS: 1 Lynton Stott; 2 Craig Farrell; 3 Paul Parker; 4 Craig Poucher; 5 Alasdair McClarron; 6 Paul Mansson; 7 Latham Tawhai; 8 Richard Wilson; 9 Jimmy Walker; 10 Makali Aizue; 11 Anthony Seibold; 12 Jon Aston; 13 Andy Smith. Subs (all used): 14 Paul Pickering; 15 Mark Blanchard; 16 Adam Sullivan; 17 Paul Fletcher.
Tries: Sullivan (22), Fletcher (26), Aston (29), Smith (37), Seibold (51); **Goals:** Stott 5, Tawhai.
DRAGONS: 1 Johnny Woodcock; 2 Dean Colton; 3 Scott Grix; 4 PJ Solomon; 5 Jason Lee; 6 Graham Holroyd; 7 Mark Moxon; 8 Gareth Handford; 9 Gareth Greenwood; 10 James Walker; 11 Peter Green; 12 Martin Ostler; 13 Craig Lawton. Subs (all used): 14 Chris Hemmings; 15 Matt Walker; 16 Craig Cook; 17 Alex Muff.
Tries: Handford (5), P Green (9, 53), Woodcock (16);
Goals: Holroyd 5.
Sin bin: M Walker (50) - punching;
Handford (76) - dissent.
On report: Solomon (43) - late tackle.
Rugby Leaguer & League Express Men of the Match: *Rovers:* Anthony Seibold; *Dragons:* Graham Holroyd.
Penalty count: 12-8; **Half-time:** 24-18; **Referee:** Ronnie Laughton (Barnsley); **Attendance:** 1,522.

LEIGH CENTURIONS 78 DEWSBURY RAMS 18

CENTURIONS: 1 Neil Turley; 2 Damian Munro; 3 Dale Cardoza; 4 Danny Halliwell; 5 Alan Hadcroft; 6 John Duffy; 7 Tommy Martyn; 8 Sonny Nickle; 9 Paul Rowley; 10 David Bradbury; 11 Sean Richardson; 12 Adam Bristow; 13 Willie Swann. Subs (all used): 14 Rob Ball; 15 Lee Sanderson; 16 Dale Holdstock; 17 Ricky Bibey.
Tries: Halliwell (3), Swann (15), Munro (24, 59), Martyn (28), Holdstock (36), Cardoza (43, 73), Rowley (46, 56, 61), Turley (54, 65), Sanderson (75); **Goals:** Turley 11.
RAMS: 1 Jamie Benn; 2 Michael Wainwright; 3 Sylvain Houles; 4 Nathan Batty; 5 Craig Miles; 6 Mark Barlow; 7 Jimmy Elston; 8 Paul Hicks; 9 Adam Thaler; 10 Paul Smith; 11 Anthony Thewliss; 12 Billy Kershaw; 13 Chris Redfearn. Subs (all used): 14 David Mycoe; 15 Paul Philpot; 16 Jim Cain; 17 Andrew Senior.
Tries: Elston (8), Thewliss (19), Barlow (46);
Goals: Benn 3.
Rugby Leaguer & League Express Man of the Match: *Centurions:* Paul Rowley; *Rams:* Mark Barlow.
Penalty count: 7-3; **Half-time:** 28-12;
Referee: Robert Hicks (Oldham); **Attendance:** 1,763.

SALFORD CITY REDS 58 ROCHDALE HORNETS 18

CITY REDS: 1 Jason Flowers; 2 Wes Davies; 3 Stuart Littler; 4 Alan Hunte; 5 Andy Kirk; 6 Cliff Beverley; 7 Gavin Clinch; 8 Neil Baynes; 9 Malcolm Alker; 10 Andy Coley; 11 Simon Baldwin; 12 Paul Highton; 13 Chris Charles. Subs (all used): 14 Steve Blakeley; 15 David Highton; 16 Martin Moana; 17 Neil Lowe.
Tries: Hunte (3), Littler (14, 53), Clinch (23, 47, 78), Baldwin (32), Davies (50, 70), Beverley (58);
Goals: Charles 6, Blakeley 3.
On report: Brawl (57).
HORNETS: 1 Chris Irwin; 2 Mick Nanyn; 3 James Bunyan; 4 Matt Calland; 5 Marlon Billy; 6 Jon Roper; 7 Ian Watson; 8 Paul Southern; 9 Richard Pachniuk; 10 Gareth Price; 11 David Larder; 12 Paul Smith; 13 Damian Ball. Subs (all used): 14 Wayne McHugh; 15 Matthew Leigh; 16 Wes Rogers; 17 Matthew Long.
Tries: Nanyn (6), Billy (27), Smith (73); **Goals:** Nanyn 3.
Dismissal: Rogers (57) - striking.
On report: Brawl (57).
Rugby Leaguer & League Express Men of the Match: *City Reds:* Gavin Clinch; *Hornets:* Ian Watson.
Penalty count: 8-4; **Half-time:** 24-12;
Referee: Peter Taberner (Wigan); **Attendance:** 2,204.

WHITEHAVEN 24 OLDHAM 20

WHITEHAVEN: 1 Gary Broadbent; 2 Steven Wood; 3 David Seeds; 4 Wesley Wilson; 5 Paul O'Neil; 6 Leroy Joe; 7 Steve Kirkbride; 8 Marc Jackson; 9 Aaron Lester; 10 David Fatialofa; 11 Craig Chambers; 12 Graeme Morton; 13 Howard Hill. Subs (all used): 14 Lee Kiddie; 15 Gary Smith; 16 Spencer Miller; 17 Tony Cunningham.
Tries: Lester (22), O'Neil (26, 65), Seeds (43);
Goals: Kirkbride 4.
OLDHAM: 1 Jon Goddard; 2 Gavin Dodd; 3 Iain Marsh; 4 Lee Doran; 5 Nicky Johnson; 6 Simon Svabic; 7 Neil Roden; 8 Danny Guest; 9 John Hough; 10 Dane Morgan; 11 Lee Marsh; 12 Craig McDowell; 13 Phil Farrell. Subs (all used): 14 Gareth Barber; 15 Will Cowell; 16 Martin McLoughlin; 17 Jason Clegg.
Tries: N Johnson (13), Goddard (33, 73), Barber (75);
Goals: Svabic 2.
Rugby Leaguer & League Express Men of the Match: *Whitehaven:* Aaron Lester; *Oldham:* Phil Farrell.
Penalty count: 11-13; **Half-time:** 16-10;
Referee: Steve Presley (Castleford); **Attendance:** 1,132.

WEEK 18

Sunday 31st August 2003

DEWSBURY RAMS 8 HULL KINGSTON ROVERS 60

RAMS: 1 Jamie Benn; 2 Michael Wainwright; 3 Nathan Batty; 4 Paul Philpot; 5 Craig Miles; 6 Mark Barlow; 7 Jimmy Elston; 8 Andrew Senior; 9 Adam Thaler; 10 Paul Smith; 11 Paul Hicks; 12 Anthony Thewliss; 13 Billy Kershaw. Subs (all used): 14 David Mycoe; 15 Jim Cain; 16 Chris Redfearn; 17 John Waddell.
Try: Batty (53); **Goals:** Benn 2.
Dismissal: Smith (47) - high tackle.
ROVERS: 1 Lynton Stott; 2 Craig Farrell; 3 Paul Parker; 4 Craig Poucher; 5 Alasdair McClarron; 6 Paul Mansson; 7 Latham Tawhai; 8 Richard Wilson; 9 Paul Pickering; 10 Adam Sullivan; 11 Anthony Seibold; 12 Jon Aston; 13 Andy Smith. Subs (all used): 14 Chris Stephenson; 15 Dean Andrews; 16 Makali Aizue; 17 Paul Fletcher.
Tries: McClarron (3, 37), Fletcher (26), Pickering (39), Tawhai (44, 71), Poucher (49), Andrews (56), Stephenson (75), Farrell (79);
Goals: Stott 7, Stephenson 3.
Rugby Leaguer & League Express Men of the Match: *Rams:* Nathan Batty; *Rovers:* Latham Tawhai.
Penalty count: 4-6; **Half-time:** 2-26; **Referee:** Steve Nicholson (Whitehaven); **Attendance:** 1,150.

DONCASTER DRAGONS 34 WHITEHAVEN 34

DRAGONS: 1 Johnny Woodcock; 2 Dean Colton; 3 Marvin Golden; 4 PJ Solomon; 5 Jason Lee; 6 Graham Holroyd; 7 Mark Moxon; 8 Gareth Handford; 9 Gareth Greenwood; 10 Chris Hemmings; 11 Peter Green; 12 Martin Ostler; 13 Craig Lawton. Subs (all used): 14 James Walker; 15 Matt Walker; 16 Gareth Lloyd; 17 Craig Cook.
Tries: Lee (12, 77, 79), Ostler (27), Holroyd (70), Lawton (74); **Goals:** Holroyd 5.
WHITEHAVEN: 1 Gary Broadbent; 2 Steven Wood; 3 David Seeds; 4 Wesley Wilson; 5 John Lebbon; 6 Leroy Joe; 7 Steve Kirkbride; 8 Marc Jackson; 9 Aaron Lester; 10 David Fatialofa; 11 Craig Chambers; 12 Graeme Morton; 13 Howard Hill. Subs (all used): 14 Lee Kiddie; 15 Spencer Miller; 16 Mike Whitehead; 17 Tony Cunningham.
Tries: Lebbon (4), Seeds (15, 38), Wood (30), Hill (34), Chambers (62); **Goals:** Kirkbride 5.
Rugby Leaguer & League Express Men of the Match: *Dragons:* Craig Lawton; *Whitehaven:* Leroy Joe.
Penalty count: 8-4; **Half-time:** 12-28;
Referee: Ben Thaler (Wakefield); **Attendance:** 677.

OLDHAM 36 BATLEY BULLDOGS 10

OLDHAM: 1 Jon Goddard; 2 Chris Percival; 3 Iain Marsh; 4 Lee Doran; 5 Nicky Johnson; 6 Simon Svabic; 7 Neil Roden; 8 Danny Guest; 9 John Hough; 10 Dane Morgan; 11 Craig McDowell; 12 Lee Marsh; 13 Phil Farrell. Subs (all used): 14 Gareth Barber; 15 Keith Brennan; 16 Martin McLoughlin; 17 Steve Molloy.
Tries: N Johnson (8, 57), Svabic (21), Roden (25, 71), Barber (61); **Goals:** Svabic 6.
On report: Farrell (39) - off-the-ball incident.
BULLDOGS: 1 Craig Lingard; 2 Matt Bramald; 3 Anthony Gibbons; 4 Danny Mann; 5 Leon Williamson; 6 Danny Thomas; 7 Barry Eaton; 8 Joe Berry; 9 Will Cartledge; 10 Steve Hill; 11 Danny Evans; 12 Mark Toohey; 13 Ryan Horsley. Subs (all used): 14 Mark Cass; 15 Paul Harrison; 16 Andy Spink; 17 Steve Beard.
Tries: Bramald (37), Toohey (69); **Goal:** Eaton.
On report: Lingard (39) - off-the-ball incident.
Rugby Leaguer & League Express Men of the Match: *Oldham:* Nicky Johnson; *Bulldogs:* Mark Cass.
Penalty count: 5-4; **Half-time:** 18-4; **Referee:** Ronnie Laughton (Barnsley); **Attendance:** 1,451.

Hull KR's Jon Aston held up by Salford duo Martin Moana and Andy Coley

ROCHDALE HORNETS 42 FEATHERSTONE ROVERS 12

HORNETS: 1 Chris Irwin; 2 Mick Nanyn; 3 James Bunyan; 4 Jon Roper; 5 Marlon Billy; 6 Radney Bowker; 7 Ian Watson; 8 Paul Southern; 9 Richard Pachniuk; 10 Gareth Price; 11 David Larder; 12 Paul Smith; 13 Damian Ball. Subs (all used): 14 Ryan Blake; 15 Matthew Leigh; 16 Wes Rogers; 17 Matthew Long. **Tries:** Irwin (7), Smith (14), Southern (27, 66), Bowker (37), Watson (60), Nanyn (75); **Goals:** Nanyn 7.
Sin bin: Watson (78) - professional foul.
ROVERS: 1 Nathan Graham; 2 Jamie Stokes; 3 Brendan O'Meara; 4 Adrian Flynn; 5 James Ford; 6 Richard Whiting; 7 Carl Briggs; 8 Ian Tonks; 9 Paul Darley; 10 Stuart Dickens; 11 Steve Dooler; 12 Andy Jarrett; 13 Danny Seal. Subs (all used): 14 Neil Lowe; 15 Richard Chapman; 16 Andy Rice; 17 James Houston.
Tries: O'Meara (20), Flynn (54); **Goals:** Briggs, Dickens.
Dismissal: Dickens (50) - punching.
Rugby Leaguer & League Express Men of the Match: *Hornets:* Ian Watson; *Rovers:* Carl Briggs.
Penalty count: 10-7; **Half-time:** 22-6;
Referee: Julian King (St Helens); **Attendance:** 948.

SALFORD CITY REDS 46 LEIGH CENTURIONS 24

CITY REDS: 1 Jason Flowers; 2 Wes Davies; 3 Stuart Littler; 4 Alan Hunte; 5 Andy Kirk; 6 Cliff Beverley; 7 Gavin Clinch; 8 Neil Baynes; 9 Malcolm Alker; 10 Andy Coley; 11 Simon Baldwin; 12 Paul Highton; 13 Steve Blakeley. Subs (all used): 14 Neil Lowe; 15 David Highton; 16 Martin Moana; 17 Gareth Haggerty.
Tries: Baldwin (17), P Highton (26), Littler (28, 70), Beverley (34), Alker (43), Hunte (62), Kirk (80);
Goals: Blakeley 6, Hunte.
CENTURIONS: 1 Neil Turley; 2 Damian Munro; 3 Dale Cardoza; 4 Danny Halliwell; 5 Alan Hadcroft; 6 Patrick Weisner; 7 Tommy Martyn; 8 Sonny Nickle; 9 Paul Rowley; 10 David Bradbury; 11 Sean Richardson; 12 Bryan Henare; 13 Adam Bristow. Subs (all used): 14 Paul Norman; 15 Willie Swann; 16 John Duffy; 17 Ricky Bibey.
Tries: Cardoza (8), Bristow (21), Munro (36), Weisner (49); **Goals:** Turley 4.
Rugby Leaguer & League Express Men of the Match: *City Reds:* Andy Coley; *Centurions:* David Bradbury.
Penalty count: 4-4; **Half-time:** 24-18; **Referee:** Colin Morris (Huddersfield); **Attendance:** 4,121.

Saturday 6th September 2003

BATLEY BULLDOGS 18 DONCASTER DRAGONS 21

BULLDOGS: 1 Anthony Gibbons; 2 Matt Bramald; 3 Chris Spurr; 4 Danny Maun; 5 Leon Williamson; 6 Danny Thomas; 7 Barry Eaton; 8 Craig Booth; 9 Kris Lythe; 10 Steve Hill; 11 Will Cartledge; 12 Mark Toohey; 13 Ryan Horsley. Subs (all used): 14 Mark Cass; 15 Paul Harrison; 16 Joe Berry; 17 Andy Spink.
Tries: Williamson (8), Spurr (29, 70); **Goals:** Eaton 3.

Dismissal: Booth (78) - dissent.
Sin bin: Booth (15) - dissent.
DRAGONS: 1 Johnny Woodcock; 2 Dean Colton; 3 PJ Solomon; 4 Marvin Golden; 5 Jason Lee; 6 Graham Holroyd; 7 Shaun Leafe; 8 Gareth Handford; 9 Gareth Greenwood; 10 James Walker; 11 Peter Green; 12 Martin Ostler; 13 Craig Lawton. Subs (all used): 14 Gareth Lloyd; 15 Matt Walker; 16 Chris Hemmings; 17 Mark Moxon.
Tries: Colton (58, 78), Golden (66);
Goals: Holroyd 4; **Field goal:** Holroyd.
Rugby Leaguer & League Express Men of the Match: *Bulldogs:* Andy Spink; *Dragons:* Graham Holroyd.
Penalty count: 9-4; **Half-time:** 12-0;
Referee: Colin Morris (Huddersfield); **Attendance:** 741.

WEEK 19

Sunday 7th September 2003

FEATHERSTONE ROVERS 14 OLDHAM 19

ROVERS: 1 Nathan Graham; 2 Jamie Stokes; 3 Brendan O'Meara; 4 Adrian Flynn; 5 James Ford; 6 Richard Whiting; 7 Carl Briggs; 8 Ian Tonks; 9 Richard Chapman; 10 Stuart Dickens; 11 Steve Dooler; 12 James Houston; 13 Chris Langley. Subs (all used): 14 Jonathan Presley; 15 Paul Darley; 16 Andy Rice; 17 Chris Molyneux.
Tries: Houston (2), Langley (60), Presley (62);
Goal: Dickens.
Sin bin: Chapman (19) - dissent; Flynn (59) - fighting.
OLDHAM: 1 Jon Goddard; 2 Chris Percival; 3 Iain Marsh; 4 Lee Doran; 5 Nicky Johnson; 6 Simon Svabic; 7 Neil Roden; 8 Steve Molloy; 9 Keith Brennan; 10 Dane Morgan; 11 Lee Marsh; 12 Craig McDowell; 13 Phil Farrell. Subs (all used): 14 Gareth Barber; 15 Gavin Dodd; 16 Chris Morley; 17 Martin McLoughlin.
Tries: I Marsh (20), Farrell (37), Morgan (73);
Goals: Barber, Svabic 2; **Field goal:** Brennan.
Sin bin: Percival (26) - dissent; I Marsh (59) - fighting.
Rugby Leaguer & League Express Men of the Match: *Rovers:* Nathan Graham; *Oldham:* Phil Farrell.
Penalty count: 10-9; **Half-time:** 4-12;
Referee: Peter Taberner (Wigan); **Attendance:** 1,504.

HULL KINGSTON ROVERS 18 SALFORD CITY REDS 16

ROVERS: 1 Lynton Stott; 2 Craig Farrell; 3 Paul Parker; 4 Nick Pinkney; 5 Alasdair McClarron; 6 Paul Mansson; 7 Latham Tawhai; 8 Richard Wilson; 9 Andy Ellis; 10 Adam Sullivan; 11 Craig Poucher; 12 Jon Aston; 13 Anthony Seibold. Subs (all used): 14 Craig Henry; 15 Dean Andrews; 16 Makali Aizue; 17 Paul Fletcher.
Tries: Ellis (23), McClarron (32), Mansson (44);
Goals: Stott 3.
CITY REDS: 1 Jason Flowers; 2 Wes Davies; 3 Stuart

Littler; 4 Andy Kirk; 5 Danny Arnold; 6 Cliff Beverley; 7 Gavin Clinch; 8 Neil Baynes; 9 Malcolm Alker; 10 Andy Coley; 11 Simon Baldwin; 12 Paul Highton; 13 Martin Moana. Subs (all used): 14 Karl Fitzpatrick; 15 David Highton; 16 Neil Lowe; 17 Gareth Haggerty.
Tries: Davies (6), Beverley (16), Baldwin (49);
Goals: Clinch 2.
Rugby Leaguer & League Express Men of the Match: *Rovers:* Andy Ellis; *City Reds:* Gavin Clinch.
Penalty count: 11-7; **Half-time:** 12-12;
Referee: Mike Dawber (Wigan); **Attendance:** 2,060.

LEIGH CENTURIONS 68 ROCHDALE HORNETS 16

CENTURIONS: 1 Neil Turley; 2 Leroy Rivett; 3 Dale Holdstock; 4 Danny Halliwell; 5 David Alstead; 6 John Duffy; 7 Lee Sanderson; 8 Sonny Nickle; 9 Paul Rowley; 10 Ricky Bibey; 11 Patrick Weisner; 12 Bryan Henare; 13 Adam Bristow. Subs (all used): 14 Paul Norman; 15 Willie Swann; 16 Sean Richardson; 17 David Bradbury.
Tries: Sanderson (9), Holdstock (20), Rivett (24), Weisner (27, 70), Rowley (34, 56, 76), Alstead (38), Bristow (51), Duffy (65), Nickle (67); **Goals:** Turley 10.
HORNETS: 1 Chris Irwin; 2 Mick Nanyn; 3 James Bunyan; 4 Jon Roper; 5 Ryan Blake; 6 Radney Bowker; 7 Ian Watson; 8 Paul Southern; 9 Richard Pachniuk; 10 Gareth Price; 11 David Larder; 12 Paul Smith; 13 Damian Ball. Subs (all used): 14 Warren Ayres; 15 Matthew Leigh; 16 David Stephenson; 17 Matthew Long.
Tries: Blake (2), Larder (43), Roper (46); **Goals:** Nanyn 2.
Rugby Leaguer & League Express Men of the Match: *Centurions:* John Duffy; *Hornets:* Ryan Blake.
Penalty count: 7-6; **Half-time:** 32-6;
Referee: Robert Connolly (Wigan); **Attendance:** 2,782.

WHITEHAVEN 68 DEWSBURY RAMS 12

WHITEHAVEN: 1 Gary Broadbent; 2 Steven Wood; 3 David Seeds; 4 Wesley Wilson; 5 John Lebbon; 6 Leroy Joe; 7 Steve Kirkbride; 8 Marc Jackson; 9 Aaron Lester; 10 David Fatialofa; 11 Craig Chambers; 12 Howard Hill; 13 Garry Purdham. Subs (all used): 14 Carl Sice; 15 Spencer Miller; 16 Gary Smith; 17 Tony Cunningham.
Tries: Seeds (13, 69), Lester (22, 26, 79), Cunningham (34), Joe (39), Chambers (42), Hill (59, 66), Broadbent (72), G Smith (76); **Goals:** Kirkbride 10.
RAMS: 1 Nathan Batty; 2 Michael Wainwright; 3 Chris Redfearn; 4 Ryan Hardy; 5 Craig Miles; 6 David Mycoe; 7 Jimmy Elston; 8 Frank Watene; 9 Adam Thaler; 10 Paul Smith; 11 Paul Hicks; 12 Billy Kershaw; 13 Graham Law. Subs (all used): 14 Mark Barlow; 15 Andrew Senior; 16 Richard Slater; 17 Jon Wray.
Tries: Miles (5), Redfearn (50); **Goals:** Law 2.
Rugby Leaguer & League Express Men of the Match: *Whitehaven:* Steve Kirkbride; *Rams:* Paul Hicks.
Penalty count: 7-4; **Half time:** 30-6; **Referee:** Ronnie Laughton (Barnsley); **Attendance:** 1,234.

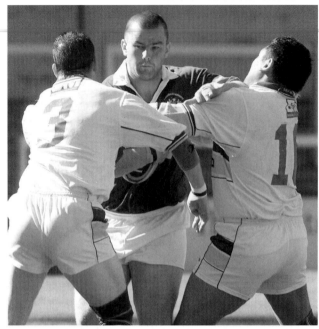

Rochdale's Paul Southern meets Whitehaven's David Seeds and David Fatialofa

PLAY-OFFS

Sunday 14th September 2003

ELIMINATION PLAY-OFFS

HULL KINGSTON ROVERS 38 OLDHAM 24

ROVERS: 1 Lynton Stott; 2 Craig Farrell; 3 Paul Parker; 4 Craig Poucher; 5 Alasdair McClarron; 6 Paul Mansson; 7 Latham Tawhai; 8 Richard Wilson; 9 Paul Pickering; 10 Adam Sullivan; 11 Anthony Seibold; 12 Jon Aston; 13 Andy Smith. Subs (all used): 14 Nick Pinkney; 15 Dean Andrews; 17 Paul Fletcher. **Tries:** Mansson (3), Tawhai (17), Parker (34), Poucher (37), McClarron (54), Pinkney (71); **Goals:** Stott 7. **Sin bin:** Stott (77) - fighting.
OLDHAM: 1 Jon Goddard; 2 Chris Percival; 3 Iain Marsh; 4 Lee Doran; 5 Nicky Johnson; 6 Simon Svabic; 7 Keith Brennan; 8 Steve Molloy; 9 John Hough; 10 Dane Morgan; 11 Lee Marsh; 12 Craig McDowell; 13 Phil Farrell. Subs (all used): 14 Gareth Barber; 15 Gavin Dodd; 16 Chris Morley; 17 Martin McLoughlin. **Tries:** N Johnson (10), Hough (23), Svabic (64), Percival (74); **Goals:** Svabic 4. **Sin bin:** Doran (44) - dissent; Barber (77) - fighting.
Rugby Leaguer & League Express Men of the Match: *Rovers:* Paul Mansson; *Oldham:* Simon Svabic. **Penalty count:** 10-10; **Half-time:** 26-12; **Referee:** Peter Taberner (Wigan); **Attendance:** 2,250.

ROCHDALE HORNETS 40 WHITEHAVEN 38

HORNETS: 1 Chris Irwin; 2 Mick Nanyn; 3 James Bunyan; 4 Jon Roper; 5 Marlon Billy; 6 Radney Bowker; 7 Ian Watson; 8 Paul Southern; 9 Richard Pachniuk; 10 Gareth Price; 11 David Larder; 12 Paul Smith; 13 Damian Ball. Subs (all used): 14 Matt Calland; 15 Matthew Leigh; 16 David Stephenson; 17 Matthew Long. **Tries:** Roper (10, 26), Nanyn (22), Watson (47), Southern (56), Billy (60), Larder (75); **Goals:** Nanyn 6.
WHITEHAVEN: 1 Gary Broadbent; 2 Steven Wood; 3 David Seeds; 4 Wesley Wilson; 5 John Lebbon; 6 Leroy Joe; 7 Steve Kirkbride; 8 Marc Jackson; 9 Aaron Lester; 10 David Fatialofa; 11 Craig Chambers; 12 Howard Hill; 13 Garry Purdham. Subs (all used): 14 Carl Sice; 15 Spencer Miller; 16 Chris McKinney; 17 Tony Cunningham. **Tries:** Broadbent (15), Joe (32, 79), Wood (50), Sice (65), Lester (70); **Goals:** Kirkbride 7.
Rugby Leaguer & League Express Men of the Match: *Hornets:* Radney Bowker; *Whitehaven:* Carl Sice. **Penalty count:** 9-13; **Half-time:** 18-14; **Referee:** Ian Smith (Oldham); **Attendance:** 779.

Sunday 21st September 2003

QUALIFYING SEMI-FINAL

SALFORD CITY REDS 26 LEIGH CENTURIONS 18

CITY REDS: 1 Jason Flowers; 2 Danny Arnold; 3 Stuart Littler; 4 Alan Hunte; 5 Andy Kirk; 6 Cliff Beverley; 7 Gavin Clinch; 8 Neil Baynes; 9 Malcolm Alker; 10 Andy Coley; 11 Simon Baldwin; 12 Paul Highton; 13 Chris Charles. Subs (all used): 14 Steve Blakeley; 15 David Highton; 16 Martin Moana; 17 Gareth Haggerty. **Tries:** Littler (2), Baldwin (7), Arnold (55), Moana (79); **Goals:** Charles 5.
CENTURIONS: 1 Neil Turley; 2 Leroy Rivett; 3 Alan Hadcroft; 4 Danny Halliwell; 5 David Alstead; 6 John Duffy; 7 Tommy Martyn; 8 Sonny Nickle; 9 Paul Rowley; 10 David Bradbury; 11 Sean Richardson; 12 Adam Bristow; 13 Patrick Weisner. Subs (all used): 14 Ricky Bibey; 15 Bryan Henare; 16 Lee Sanderson; 17 Paul Norman. **Tries:** Duffy (21), Bristow (60), Alstead (80); **Goals:** Turley 3. **Dismissals:** Bibey (41) - tripping; Rowley (42) - high tackle. **Sin bin:** Bristow (38) - high tackle.
Rugby Leaguer & League Express Men of the Match: *City Reds:* Neil Baynes; *Centurions:* John Duffy. **Penalty count:** 8-4; **Half-time:** 12-8; **Referee:** Ian Smith (Oldham); **Attendance:** 3,660.

ELIMINATION SEMI-FINAL

ROCHDALE HORNETS 26 HULL KINGSTON ROVERS 30

HORNETS: 1 Chris Irwin; 2 Mick Nanyn; 3 James Bunyan; 4 Jon Roper; 5 Marlon Billy; 6 Radney Bowker; 7 Ian Watson; 8 Paul Southern; 9 Richard Pachniuk; 10 Gareth Price; 11 David Larder; 12 Paul Smith; 13 Damian Ball. Subs (all used): 14 Matt Calland; 15 Wes Rogers; 16 David Stephenson; 17 Matthew Long. **Tries:** Bunyan (21), Nanyn (25), Larder (39), Calland (65); **Goals:** Nanyn 5.
ROVERS: 1 Lynton Stott; 2 Craig Farrell; 3 Paul Parker; 4 Craig Poucher; 5 Alasdair McClarron; 6 Paul Mansson; 7 Latham Tawhai; 8 Richard Wilson; 9 Paul Pickering; 10 Jon Aston; 11 Anthony Seibold; 12 Dean Busby; 13 Andy Smith. Subs (all used): 14 Nick Pinkney; 15 Dean Andrews; 16 Makali Aizue; 17 Paul Fletcher. **Tries:** McClarron (14), Poucher (29), Stott (35), Mansson (46), Andrews (58), Parker (80); **Goals:** Stott 3.
Rugby Leaguer & League Express Men of the Match: *Hornets:* Radney Bowker; *Rovers:* Paul Mansson. **Penalty count:** 6-5; **Half-time:** 18-16; **Referee:** Peter Taberner (Wigan); **Attendance:** 1,710.

QUALIFYING PLAY-OFF

DONCASTER DRAGONS 45 BATLEY BULLDOGS 12

DRAGONS: 1 Johnny Woodcock; 2 Dean Colton; 3 PJ Solomon; 4 Marvin Golden; 5 Jason Lee; 6 Graham Holroyd; 7 Mark Moxon; 8 Gareth Handford; 9 Craig Cook; 10 James Walker; 11 Peter Green; 12 Martin Ostler; 13 Craig Lawton. Subs (all used): 14 Chris Hemmings; 15 Mark Walker; 16 Gareth Lloyd; 17 Shaun Leafe. **Tries:** Lee (6, 71, 74), Solomon (11), Colton (21), Ostler (24), Holroyd (50), Moxon (65); **Goals:** Holroyd 6; **Field goal:** Holroyd. **Dismissal:** P Green (56) - punching.
BULLDOGS: 1 Craig Lingard; 2 Matt Bramald; 3 Anthony Gibbons; 4 Danny Maun; 5 Leon Williamson; 6 Ryan Horsley; 7 Barry Eaton; 8 Joe Naidole; 9 Kris Lythe; 10 Steve Hill; 11 Danny Evans; 12 Will Cartledge; 13 Paul Harrison. Subs (all used): 14 Mark Cass; 15 Danny Thomas; 16 Joe Berry; 17 Andy Spink. **Tries:** Williamson (3), Eaton (68); **Goals:** Eaton 2. **On report:** Naidole (5) - alleged spear tackle.
Rugby Leaguer & League Express Men of the Match: *Dragons:* Graham Holroyd; *Bulldogs:* Danny Evans. **Penalty count:** 9-11; **Half-time:** 22-6; **Referee:** Steve Presley (Castleford); **Attendance:** 887.

Leigh's Neil Turley looks for a gap against Hull KR in the Final Eliminator

Leigh's Sean Richardson brings down Salford's Alan Hunte during the National League One Grand Final

Sunday 28th September 2003

FINAL ELIMINATOR

LEIGH CENTURIONS 42 HULL KINGSTON ROVERS 12

CENTURIONS: 1 Neil Turley; 2 Damian Munro; 3 Alan Hadcroft; 4 Danny Halliwell; 5 Leroy Rivett; 6 Patrick Weisner; 7 Tommy Martyn; 8 Sonny Nickle; 9 Paul Rowley; 10 Paul Norman; 11 Sean Richardson; 12 Adam Bristow; 13 Willie Swann. Subs (all used): 14 David Bradbury; 15 Lee Sanderson; 16 Dale Holdstock; 17 Ricky Bibey.
Tries: Halliwell (12), Rivett (18, 29), Weisner (26), Bradbury (36), Munro (78); **Goals:** Turley 8, Sanderson.
Sin bin: Rivett (42) - interference at the play-the-ball.
ROVERS: 1 Lynton Stott; 2 Craig Farrell; 3 Paul Parker; 4 Craig Poucher; 5 Alasdair McClarron; 6 Paul Mansson; 7 Latham Tawhai; 8 Richard Wilson; 9 Andy Ellis; 10 Jamie Bovill; 11 Anthony Seibold; 12 Jon Aston; 13 Dean Busby. Subs (all used): 14 Nick Pinkney; 15 Dean Andrews; 16 Makali Aizue; 17 Paul Fletcher.
Tries: Mansson (19), Parker (62), McClarron (66).
Rugby Leaguer & League Express Men of the Match:
Centurions: Paul Rowley; *Rovers:* Paul Mansson.
Penalty count: 9-7; **Half-time:** 32-4;
Referee: Russell Smith (Castleford); **Attendance:** 2,901.

Sunday 5th October 2003

GRAND FINAL

LEIGH CENTURIONS 14 SALFORD CITY REDS 31

CENTURIONS: 1 Neil Turley; 2 Damian Munro; 3 Alan Hadcroft; 4 Danny Halliwell; 5 Leroy Rivett; 6 John Duffy; 7 Tommy Martyn; 8 Sonny Nickle; 9 Paul Weisner; 10 Paul Norman; 11 Sean Richardson; 12 Willie Swann; 13 Adam Bristow. Subs (all used): 14 David Bradbury; 15 Lee Sanderson; 16 Bryan Henare; 17 Ricky Bibey.
Tries: Richardson (33), Halliwell (38), Swann (65);
Goal: Turley.
On report: Nickle (60) - late tackle on Clinch.
CITY REDS: 1 Jason Flowers; 2 Danny Arnold; 3 Stuart Littler; 4 Alan Hunte; 5 Andy Kirk; 6 Cliff Beverley; 7 Gavin Clinch; 8 Neil Baynes; 9 Malcolm Alker; 10 Andy Coley; 11 Simon Baldwin; 12 Paul Highton; 13 Chris Charles. Subs (all used): 14 Steve Blakeley; 15 David Highton; 16 Martin Moana; 17 Gareth Haggerty.
Tries: Hunte (3, 52), Beverley (23), Littler (73);
Goals: Charles 6, Blakeley; **Field goal:** Blakeley.
Rugby Leaguer & League Express Men of the Match:
Centurions: Willie Swann; *City Reds:* Gavin Clinch.
Penalty count: 10-10; **Half-time:** 10-16;
Referee: Richard Silverwood (Dewsbury);
Attendance: 9,186 *(at Halton Stadium, Widnes).*

Saturday 11th October 2003

QUALIFYING FINAL

BATLEY BULLDOGS 36 SHEFFIELD EAGLES 14

BULLDOGS: 1 Craig Lingard; 2 Matt Bramald; 3 Anthony Gibbons; 4 Danny Maun; 5 Leon Williamson; 6 Mark Toohey; 7 Barry Eaton; 8 Joe Naidole; 9 Joe Berry; 10 Steve Hill; 11 Danny Evans; 12 Andy Spink; 13 Ryan Horsley. Subs (all used): 14 Mark Cass; 15 Paul Harrison; 16 Will Cartledge; 17 David Rourke.
Tries: Evans (19), Lingard (30, 61), Berry (33), Toohey (43), Cartledge (69); **Goals:** Eaton 6.
EAGLES: 1 Andy Poynter; 2 Tony Weller; 3 Richard Goddard; 4 Tom O'Reilly; 5 Greg Hurst; 6 Gavin Brown; 7 Mark Aston; 8 Jack Howieson; 9 Lee Bettinson; 10 Mitchell Stringer; 11 Andy Raleigh; 12 Craig Brown; 13 Simon Tillyer. Subs (all used): 14 Adam Carroll; 15 Simon Morton; 16 Nick Turnbull; 17 Jordan James.
Tries: James (24), Hurst (65), Carroll (73);
Goal: G Brown.
Sin bin: Poynter (28) - holding down.
Rugby Leaguer & League Express Men of the Match:
Bulldogs: Andy Spink; *Eagles:* Richard Goddard.
Penalty count: 4-6; **Half-time:** 18-6;
Referee: Ian Smith (Oldham); **Attendance:** 1,040.

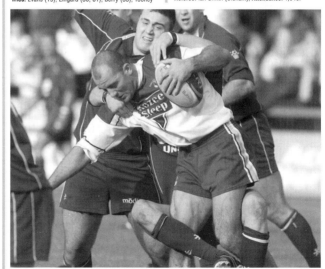

Batley's Andy Spink in the thick of the action against Sheffield in the National League One Qualifying Final

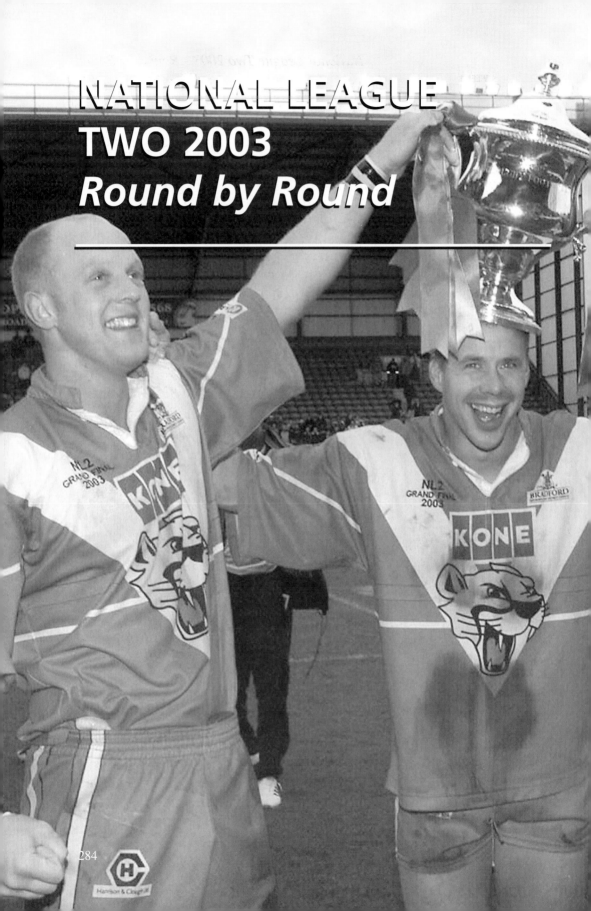

NATIONAL LEAGUE TWO 2003
Round by Round

WEEK 1

Friday 18th April 2003

BARROW RAIDERS 32 WORKINGTON TOWN 16

RAIDERS: 1 Craig Bower; 2 Danny Lockhart; 3 Andy McClure; 4 Paul Jones; 5 Shane Irabor; 6 Tane Manihera; 7 Jamie Marshall; 8 Tau Liku; 9 Andy Henderson; 10 Stuart Dancer; 11 Steve Jackson; 12 Paul Lupton; 13 Phil Atkinson. Subs (all used): 14 Barry Pugh; 15 James King; 16 Paul Gardner; 17 Wayne Jones.
Tries: Lupton (12), McClure (37, 44), Pugh (47), P Jones (58), Marshall (73); **Goals:** Manihera 2, Atkinson; **Field goals:** Manihera, Marshall.
TOWN: 1 Dean Sharp; 2 Scott Chilton; 3 Karl Long; 4 Matthew Johnson; 5 Graeme Lewthwaite; 6 Brett Smith; 7 Anthony Murray; 8 Hitro Okesene; 9 Carl Sice; 10 Willie Burns; 11 Jamie Beaumont; 12 William Blackburn; 13 Ricky Wright. Subs (all used): 14 Craig Fisher; 15 Matthew Tunstall; 16 Stewart Rhodes; 17 Gary Charlton.
Tries: Long (33), Sharp (52), Lewthwaite (70);
Goals: Fisher 2.
Rugby Leaguer & League Express Men of the Match: *Raiders:* Andy Henderson; *Town:* Karl Long.
Penalty count: 7-7; **Half-time:** 11-6;
Referee: Julian King (St Helens); **Attendance:** 953.

LONDON SKOLARS 2 SHEFFIELD EAGLES 48

SKOLARS: 1 Anthony Dellar; 2 Charlie Oyebade; 3 PJ Solomon; 4 Scott Roberts; 5 Mike Okwusogu; 6 Jake Johnstone; 7 Rob McKeown; 8 Glenn Osborn; 9 Kahu Henare; 10 Obi Ijeoma; 11 Brett McCroary; 12 Rubert Jonker; 13 Allan Tito. Subs (all used): 14 Paul Leef; 15 Troy Dougherty; 16 Wayne Parillon; 17 Bobby Wallis.
Goal: Johnstone.
Sin bin: Solomon (40) - sledging.
EAGLES: 1 Andy Poynter; 2 Tony Weller; 3 Nick Turnbull; 4 Neil Kite; 5 Ian Thompson; 6 Gavin Brown; 7 Lee Bettinson; 8 Jack Howieson; 9 Gareth Stanley; 10 Jon Bruce; 11 Andy Raleigh; 12 Craig Brown; 13 Simon Tillyer. Subs (all used): 14 Mark Aston; 15 Greg Hurst; 16 Peter Reilly; 17 Mitchell Stringer.
Tries: Weller (11, 66, 71), C Brown (29, 41), Reilly (44), Hurst (54), Poynter (57), G Brown (78);
Goals: Aston 4, G Brown 2.
Rugby Leaguer & League Express Men of the Match: *Skolars:* Obi Ijeoma; *Eagles:* Mark Aston.
Penalty count: 11-8; **Half-time:** 2-10;
Referee: Steve Presley (Castleford); **Attendance:** 643.

SWINTON LIONS 31 CHORLEY LYNX 12

LIONS: 1 Wayne English; 2 Jason Roach; 3 Kris Tassell; 4 Phil Hassan; 5 Lee Hudson; 6 Chris Hough; 7 Peter Cannon; 8 Andy Leathem; 9 Rob Barraclough; 10 Simon Knox; 11 Alan Shea; 12 Craig Wingfield; 13 Mick Durham. Subs (all used): 14 Robert Russell; 15 Kris Smith; 16 Chris Roe; 17 James Lomax.
Tries: Roach (28), Hudson (34), Smith (42 - penalty try), Tassell (56), Hough (63); **Goals:** Hough 5;
Field goal: Hough.
LYNX: 1 Mark McCully; 2 Anton Garcia; 3 David Ingram; 4 Eddie Kilgannon; 5 Eric Andrews; 6 John Braddish; 7 Martin Gambles; 8 Martin Roden; 9 Mike Briggs; 10 David Whittle; 11 Gavin Johnson; 12 Mick Redford; 13 Dave McConnell. Subs (all used): 14 Mick Coates; 15 Jason Johnson; 16 Dave Byrne; 17 Tim Street.
Tries: Briggs (24), Gambles (38); **Goals:** McCully 2.
Rugby Leaguer & League Express Men of the Match: *Lions:* Wayne English; *Lynx:* Mike Briggs.
Penalty count: 8-5; **Half-time:** 10-12;
Referee: Ben Thaler (Wakefield); **Attendance:** 446.

YORK CITY KNIGHTS 12 GATESHEAD THUNDER 29

CITY KNIGHTS: 1 Chris Smith; 2 Chris Beever; 3 Gareth Lloyd; 4 Sam Clarke; 5 Rikki Sheriffe; 6 Adam Thaler; 7 Scott Rhodes; 8 Paul Broadbent; 9 Trevor Krause; 10 Richard Hayes; 11 Mick Ramsden; 12 Scott Fletcher; 13 Darren Robinson. Subs (all used): 14 Matt Blaymire; 15 Gavin Molloy; 16 Andy Burland; 17 David Bolus.
Tries: Lloyd (22), Sheriffe (63); **Goals:** Thaler 2.
THUNDER: 1 Kevin Neighbour; 2 Robin Peers; 3 Damien Reid; 4 Craig Firth; 5 Richie Barnett; 6 Jermaine Coleman; 7 Paul Thorman; 8 Yusuf Sozi; 9 Scott MacDougall; 10 David Bates; 11 Clint Brown; 12 Steve Rutherford; 13 Andy Walker. Subs (all used): 14 Steven Bradley; 15 Janan Billings; 16 Tom Lauriston; 17 Neil Thorman.
Tries: Neighbour (27), Firth (33), Barnett (38), MacDougall (56, 70); **Goals:** P Thorman 4;
Field goal: P Thorman.
Rugby Leaguer & League Express Men of the Match: *City Knights:* Trevor Krause; *Thunder:* Paul Thorman.
Penalty count: 11-7; **Half-time:** 6-18;
Referee: Steve Addy (Huddersfield); **Attendance:** 1,271.

HUNSLET HAWKS 12 KEIGHLEY COUGARS 20

HAWKS: 1 George Rayner; 2 Bryn Powell; 3 Iain Higgins; 4 Wes McGibbon; 5 Gareth Brain; 6 Jon Liddell; 7 Phil Hasty; 8 Danny Burton; 9 Joe Hawley; 10 Andy Brent; 11 Wayne Freeman; 12 Paul Seal; 13 Mick Coyle. Subs (all used): 14 Craig Ibbetson; 15 Jonlee Lockwood; 16 Steve Beard; 17 Chris North.
Tries: Powell (46), Higgins (61); **Goals:** Liddell, Hasty.
COUGARS: 1 James Rushforth; 2 Karl Smith; 3 David Foster; 4 Gareth Hewitt; 5 Andy Robinson; 6 Adam Mitchell; 7 Matt Firth; 8 Chris Hannah; 9 Simeon Hoyle; 10 Danny Ekis; 11 Oliver Wilkes; 12 Ricky Helliwell; 13 Jason Ramshaw. Subs: 14 Chris Wainwright; 15 Lee Patterson (not used); 16 Richard Mervill; 17 Ian Sinfield.
Tries: Hewitt (2), D Foster (43), Wainwright (76);
Goals: Mitchell 4.
Dismissal: Hannah (70) – retaliation.
Rugby Leaguer & League Express Men of the Match: *Hawks:* Iain Higgins; *Cougars:* Ricky Helliwell.
Penalty count: 12-9; **Half time:** 0-8;
Referee: Ashley Klein (London); **Attendance:** 607.

WEEK 2

Monday 21st April 2003

CHORLEY LYNX 18 HUNSLET HAWKS 24

LYNX: 1 Mark McCully; 2 Anton Garcia; 3 Mick Redford; 4 David Ingram; 5 Eric Andrews; 6 John Braddish; 7 Mick Coates; 8 Tim Street; 9 Mike Briggs; 10 Martin Roden; 11 Ian Hodson; 12 Dave McConnell; 13 Jason Johnson. Subs (all used): 14 Gavin Johnson; 15 Ian Parry; 16 Lee Rowley; 17 Eddie Kilgannon.
Tries: Garcia (17, 63), Rowley (34); **Goals:** McCully 3.
Sin bin: Redford (69) - punching.
HAWKS: 1 George Rayner; 2 Bryn Powell; 3 Iain Higgins; 4 Wes McGibbon; 5 Gareth Brain; 6 Danny Fearon; 7 Phil Hasty; 8 Danny Burton; 9 Joe Hawley; 10 Andy Brent; 11 Wayne Freeman; 12 Craig Ibbetson; 13 Paul Seal. Subs (all used): 14 Jonlee Lockwood; 15 Steve Jakeman; 16 Chris North; 17 Dan Briggs.
Tries: W Freeman (24), Powell (38), Brent (73), Seal (79); **Goals:** Hasty 4.
Rugby Leaguer & League Express Men of the Match: *Lynx:* Anton Garcia; *Hawks:* Danny Fearon.
Penalty count: 9-12; **Half-time:** 12-12;
Referee: Julian King (St Helens); **Attendance:** 404.

KEIGHLEY COUGARS 68 LONDON SKOLARS 6

COUGARS: 1 James Rushforth; 2 Karl Smith; 3 David Foster; 4 Chris Wainwright; 5 Max Tomlinson; 6 Paul Ashton; 7 Matt Firth; 8 Chris Hannah; 9 Simeon Hoyle; 10 Lee Kelly; 11 Oliver Wilkes; 12 Lee Patterson; 13 Jason Ramshaw. Subs (all used): 14 Gareth Hewitt; 15 Ian Sinfield; 16 Danny Ekis; 17 Richard Mervill.
Tries: Rushforth (2, 16, 39, 65), Patterson (8, 14), Smith (11), Wilkes (20, 36), Ekis (26, 49), Tomlinson (42), Firth (67); **Goals:** Ashton 7, Wilkes.
Sin bin: Ashton (56) - dissent.
SKOLARS: 1 Anthony Dellar; 2 Neil Foster; 3 Paul Leef; 4 Scott Roberts; 5 Mario Du Toit; 6 Jake Johnstone; 7 Al Stewart; 8 Obi Ijeoma; 9 Kahu Henare; 10 Allan Tito; 11 Steffan Hughes; 12 Gerald Nkrumah; 13 PJ Solomon. Subs (all used): 14 Rob McKeown; 15 Mike Okwusogu; 16 Brett McCroary; 17 Ronald Mushiso.
Try: Henare (76); **Goal:** McKeown.
Sin bin: Leef (7) - professional foul; Ijeoma (36) - dissent.
Rugby Leaguer & League Express Men of the Match: *Cougars:* Jason Ramshaw; *Skolars:* Ronald Mushiso.
Penalty count: 9-5; **Half-time:** 46-0;
Referee: Steve Addy (Huddersfield); **Attendance:** 963.

WORKINGTON TOWN 8 SWINTON LIONS 4

TOWN: 1 Dean Sharp; 2 Matthew Johnson; 3 Adam Coulson; 4 Karl Long; 5 Graeme Lewthwaite; 6 Kevin Hetherington; 7 Craig Fisher; 8 Willie Burns; 9 Carl Sice; 10 Hitro Okesene; 11 Jamie Beaumont; 12 William Blackburn; 13 Gary Charlton. Subs (all used): 14 David Pettit; 15 Matthew Tunstall; 16 James Robinson; 17 Craig Barker.
Try: Lewthwaite (26); **Goal:** Hetherington;
Field goals: Hetherington 2.
LIONS: 1 Wayne English; 2 Jason Roach; 3 Kris Tassell; 4 James Lomax; 5 Lee Hudson; 6 Kris Smith; 7 Chris Hough; 8 Andy Leathem; 9 Rob Barraclough; 10 Simon Knox; 11 Alan Shea; 12 Craig Wingfield; 13 Peter Cannon. Subs (all used): 14 Mick Durham; 15 Mike Loughlin; 16 Andy Cheetham; 17 Chris Roe.
Try: Loughlin (75).
Rugby Leaguer & League Express Men of the Match: *Town:* William Blackburn; *Lions:* Peter Cannon.
Penalty count: 10-10; **Half-time:** 6-0;
Referee: Steve Presley (Castleford); **Attendance:** 511.

SHEFFIELD EAGLES 30 YORK CITY KNIGHTS 24

EAGLES: 1 Andy Poynter; 2 Carl de Chenu; 3 Tony Weller; 4 Neil Kite; 5 Ian Thompson; 6 Gavin Brown; 7 Peter Reilly; 8 Jack Howieson; 9 Gareth Stanley; 10 Jon Bruce; 11 Andy Raleigh; 12 Craig Brown; 13 Simon Tillyer. Subs (all used): 14 Mark Aston; 15 Nick Turnbull; 16 Greg Hurst; 17 Mitchell Stringer.
Tries: Weller (16), Poynter (41), Hurst (48), Thompson (58), Tillyer (61), Kite (65); **Goals:** G Brown 2, Aston.
CITY KNIGHTS: 1 Matt Blaymire; 2 Chris Smith; 3 Gareth Lloyd; 4 Graeme Hallas; 5 Rikki Sheriffe; 6 Adam Thaler; 7 Scott Rhodes; 8 Richard Hayes; 9 Trevor Krause; 10 Andy Burland; 11 Gavin Molloy; 12 Scott Fletcher; 13 Mick Ramsden. Subs (all used): 14 Mick Embleton; 15 Paul Broadbent; 16 Carl Stannard; 17 David Bolus.
Tries: Sheriffe (3), Hallas (35, 45), Blaymire (54);
Goals: Thaler 4.
Rugby Leaguer & League Express Men of the Match: *Eagles:* Tony Weller; *City Knights:* Trevor Krause.
Penalty count: 10-5; **Half-time:** 6-12;
Referee: Mike Dawber (Wigan); **Attendance:** 897.

GATESHEAD THUNDER 22 BARROW RAIDERS 30

THUNDER: 1 Kevin Neighbour; 2 Robin Peers; 3 Damien Reid; 4 Craig Firth; 5 Tom Lauriston; 6 Jermaine Coleman; 7 Paul Thorman; 8 Yusuf Sozi; 9 Scott MacDougall; 10 David Bates; 11 Clint Brown; 12 Steve Rutherford; 13 Andy Walker. Subs (all used): 14 Steven Bradley; 15 Janan Billings; 16 Chris Fletcher; 17 Neil Thorman.
Tries: Lauriston (33), Fletcher (36), Reid (66), Peers (75); **Goals:** P Thorman 3.
Sin bin: Bates (19) - dissent.
RAIDERS: 1 Danny Lockhart; 2 Adam Pate; 3 Andy McClure; 4 Paul Jones; 5 Paul Gardner; 6 Tane Manihera; 7 Jamie Marshall; 8 Tau Liku; 9 Andy Henderson; 10 Steve Jackson; 11 James King; 12 Paul Lupton; 13 Phil Atkinson. Subs (all used): 14 Paul Evans; 15 James Stainton; 16 Stuart Dancer; 17 Wayne Jones.
Tries: Jackson (11), Gardner (27), P Jones (43, 79), Atkinson (45); **Goals:** Manihera 5.
Sin bin: Dancer (23) - persistent fouling.
Rugby Leaguer & League Express Men of the Match: *Thunder:* Paul Thorman; *Raiders:* Paul Jones.
Penalty count: 12-7; **Half-time:** 14-14;
Referee: Ben Thaler (Wakefield);
Attendance: 316 *(at Hedley Lawson Park).*

WEEK 3

Sunday 4th May 2003

BARROW RAIDERS 12 SHEFFIELD EAGLES 30

RAIDERS: 1 Danny Lockhart; 2 Jamie Marshall; 3 Andy McClure; 4 Paul Jones; 5 Shane Irabor; 6 Tane Manihera; 7 Paul Evans; 8 Tau Liku; 9 Andy Henderson; 10 Steve Jackson; 11 James King; 12 Paul Lupton; 13 Phil Atkinson. Subs (all used): 14 Paul Gardner; 15 Stuart Dancer; 16 Ian Devlin; 17 Wayne Jones.
Tries: P Jones (11), Marshall (23); **Goals:** Manihera 2.
EAGLES: 1 Andy Poynter; 2 Tony Weller; 3 Nick Turnbull; 4 Neil Kite; 5 Ian Thompson; 6 Gavin Brown; 7 Peter Reilly; 8 Jack Howieson; 9 Gareth Stanley; 10 Jon Bruce; 11 Andy Raleigh; 12 Craig Brown; 13 Wayne Flynn. Subs (all used): 14 Mark Aston; 15 Simon Tillyer; 16 Greg Hurst; 17 Mitchell Stringer.
Tries: Raleigh (3), Kite (27), Flynn (32), Poynter (42), Hurst (50), Turnbull (77); **Goals:** G Brown 3.
Rugby Leaguer & League Express Men of the Match: *Raiders:* Phil Atkinson; *Eagles:* Gavin Brown.
Penalty count: 6-10; **Half-time:** 12-14;
Referee: Ben Thaler (Wakefield); **Attendance:** 911.

CHORLEY LYNX 22 KEIGHLEY COUGARS 23

LYNX: 1 Mark McCully; 2 Anton Garcia; 3 Mick Redford; 4 Liam Bretherton; 5 Eric Andrews; 6 John Braddish; 7 Martin Gambles; 8 Tim Street; 9 Mike Briggs; 10 Martin Roden; 11 Gavin Johnson; 12 Dave McConnell; 13 Ian Hodson. Subs (all used): 14 Safraz Patel; 15 Lee Rowley; 16 Ian Parry; 17 Eddie Kilgannon.
Tries: McCully (2), Gambles (16), Garcia (80);
Goals: McCully 4; **Field goals:** Braddish 2.
Sin bin: Street (37) - punching.
COUGARS: 1 James Rushforth; 2 Karl Smith; 3 David Foster; 4 Matt Foster; 5 Gareth Hewitt; 6 Adam Mitchell; 7 Matt Firth; 8 Phil Stephenson; 9 Simeon Hoyle; 10 Danny Ekis; 11 Oliver Wilkes; 12 Ricky Helliwell; 13 Jason Ramshaw. Subs (all used): 14 Paul Ashton; 15 Lee Patterson; 16 Ian Sinfield; 17 Richard Mervill.
Tries: Hewitt (23, 49), M Foster (61, 70);
Goals: Mitchell 3; **Field goal:** Firth.
Rugby Leaguer & League Express Men of the Match: *Lynx:* Mark McCully; *Cougars:* Gareth Hewitt.
Penalty count: 13-7; **Half-time:** 16-6;
Referee: Mike Dawber (Wigan); **Attendance:** 501.

SWINTON LIONS 35 GATESHEAD THUNDER 38

LIONS: 1 Wayne English; 2 Jason Roach; 3 Kris Tassell; 4 Phil Hassan; 5 Lee Hudson; 6 Robert Russell; 7 Chris Hough; 8 Andy Leathem; 9 Rob Barraclough; 10 Simon Knox; 11 Mick Durham; 12 James Lomax; 13 Peter Cannon. Subs (all used): 14 Andy Cheetham; 15 Kris Smith; 16 Craig Wingfield; 17 Lee Hansen.
Tries: Roach (8, 76), Wingfield (35), Cheetham (55, 68), English (65); **Goals:** Hough 4, Wingfield;
Field goal: Hough.
THUNDER: 1 Kevin Neighbour; 2 Michael Lyons; 3 Damien Reid; 4 Craig Firth; 5 Richie Barnett; 6 Jermaine Coleman; 7 Paul Thorman; 8 David Bates; 9 Chris Fletcher; 10 Steven Bradley; 11 Clint Brown; 12 Steve Rutherford; 13 Andy Walker. Subs (all used): 14 Scott Harrison; 15 Janan Billings; 16 Tony Doherty; 17 Neil Thorman.
Tries: Doherty (23), Rutherford (29), Neighbour (33, 46), Firth (41), Reid (44), N Thorman (61);
Goals: P Thorman 5.
Rugby Leaguer & League Express Men of the Match: *Lions:* Simon Knox; *Thunder:* Steven Bradley.
Penalty count: 6-9; **Half-time:** 13-16;
Referee: Steve Presley (Castleford); **Attendance:** 418.

YORK CITY KNIGHTS 16 LONDON SKOLARS 16

CITY KNIGHTS: 1 Chris Smith; 2 Neil Law; 3 Graeme Hallas; 4 Darren Callaghan; 5 Rikki Sheriffe; 6 Danny Brough; 7 Scott Rhodes; 8 Paul Broadbent; 9 Trevor Krause; 10 Richard Hayes; 11 Mick Ramsden; 12 Scott Fletcher; 13 Mark Cain. Subs (all used): 14 Matt Blaymire; 15 Leigh Deakin; 16 Andy Burland; 17 David Bolus.
Tries: Sheriffe (10), Brough (18), Cain (35);
Goals: Hallas, Brough.
SKOLARS: 1 Ronald Mushiso; 2 Charlie Oyebade; 3 Paul Leef; 4 Jake Johnstone; 5 Mario Du Toit; 6 Cory Bennett; 7 Rob McKeown; 8 Obi Ijeoma; 9 Kahu Henare; 10 Allan Tito; 11 Steffan Hughes; 12 Dominic Peters; 13 PJ Solomon. Subs (all used): 14 Scott Roberts; 15 Troy

Dougherty; 16 Wayne Parillon; 17 Matt Walker.
Tries: Henare (4), Roberts (70), Ijeoma (79);
Goals: Johnstone 2.
Sin bin: S Hughes (66) - dissent.
Rugby Leaguer & League Express Men of the Match: *City Knights:* Danny Brough; *Skolars:* Obi Ijeoma.
Penalty count: 14-8; **Half-time:** 14-8; **Referee:** Gareth Hewer (Whitehaven); **Attendance:** 1,012.

HUNSLET HAWKS 43 WORKINGTON TOWN 38

HAWKS: 1 Richard Baker; 2 Bryn Powell; 3 Iain Higgins; 4 Steve Jakeman; 5 George Rayner; 6 Wes McGibbon; 7 Stephen Doherty; 8 Jonlee Lockwood; 9 Jon Liddell; 10 Andy Brent; 11 Wayne Freeman; 12 Danny Burton; 13 Paul Seal. Subs (all used): 14 Danny Fearon; 15 Steve Beard; 16 Dan Briggs; 17 Phil Hasty.
Tries: Jakeman (8), McGibbon (16, 26), Burton (44, 72), Rayner (50), Hasty (55), Seal (57);
Goals: Hasty 3, Liddell 2; **Field goal:** Hasty.
TOWN: 1 Dean Sharp; 2 Matthew Johnson; 3 Adam Coulson; 4 Brett McDermott; 5 Graeme Lewthwaite; 6 Karl Long; 7 Craig Fisher; 8 Willie Burns; 9 Darren King; 10 Hitro Okesene; 11 Jamie Beaumont; 12 William Blackburn; 13 Gary Charlton. Subs: 14 Scott Chilton; 15 Matthew Tunstall; 16 James Robinson (not used); 17 David Pettit.
Tries: Beaumont (22, 30), Lewthwaite (35), Long (41, 63, 78), Tunstall (60), Coulson (62); **Goals:** Fisher 3.
Rugby Leaguer & League Express Men of the Match: *Hawks:* Phil Hasty; *Town:* Karl Long.
Penalty count: 7-4; **Half-time:** 16-18;
Referee: Steve Addy (Huddersfield); **Attendance:** 393.

Friday 9th May 2003

SHEFFIELD EAGLES 18 SWINTON LIONS 23

EAGLES: 1 Andy Poynter; 2 Greg Hurst; 3 Tony Weller; 4 Neil Kite; 5 Ian Thompson; 6 Gavin Brown; 7 Lee Bettinson; 8 Jack Howieson; 9 Gareth Stanley; 10 Jon Bruce; 11 Andy Raleigh; 12 Craig Brown; 13 Wayne Flynn. Subs (all used): 14 Mark Aston; 15 Simon Tillyer; 16 Simon Morton; 17 Mitchell Stringer.
Tries: Poynter (1), C Brown (8), Weller (38);
Goals: G Brown 3.
LIONS: 1 Wayne English; 2 Jason Roach; 3 Kris Tassell; 4 Andy Cheetham; 5 Lee Hudson; 6 Chris Hough; 7 Peter Cannon; 8 Lee Hansen; 9 Rob Barraclough; 10 Simon Knox; 11 Craig Wingfield; 12 Dave Ellison; 13 Robert Russell. Subs (all used): 14 Hugh Thorpe; 15 Kris Smith; 16 Mike Loughlin; 17 Chris Roe.
Tries: English (13), Cheetham (24), Loughlin (57);
Goals: Hough 5; **Field goal:** Hough.
Rugby Leaguer & League Express Men of the Match: *Eagles:* Andy Poynter; *Lions:* Rob Barraclough.
Penalty count: 11-10; **Half-time:** 16-14;
Referee: Steve Addy (Huddersfield); **Attendance:** 903.

WEEK 4

Sunday 11th May 2003

KEIGHLEY COUGARS 38 YORK CITY KNIGHTS 26

COUGARS: 1 James Rushforth; 2 Gareth Hewitt; 3 David Foster; 4 Matt Foster; 5 Andy Robinson; 6 Adam Mitchell; 7 Matt Firth; 8 Phil Stephenson; 9 Simeon Hoyle; 10 Danny Ekis; 11 Oliver Wilkes; 12 Ian Sinfield; 13 Jason Ramshaw. Subs (all used): 14 Chris Wainwright; 15 Ricky Helliwell; 16 Richard Mervill; 17 Chris Hannah.
Tries: D Foster (21), M Foster (27, 38), Rushforth (35), Hoyle (52), Hewitt (73); **Goals:** Mitchell 7.
Sin bin: Hoyle (14) - punching.
CITY KNIGHTS: 1 Chris Smith; 2 Matt Blaymire; 3 Neil Law; 4 Darren Callaghan; 5 Leigh Deakin; 6 Scott Rhodes; 7 Danny Brough; 8 Paul Broadbent; 9 Trevor Krause; 10 Richard Hayes; 11 Mick Ramsden; 12 Scott Fletcher; 13 Mark Cain. Subs: 14 Graeme Hallas (not used); 15 Gavin Molloy; 16 Andy Burland; 17 David Bolus.
Tries: Deakin (43), Cain (62), Law (70, 76), Krause (79);
Goals: Brough 3.
Rugby Leaguer & League Express Men of the Match: *Cougars:* Jason Ramshaw; *City Knights:* Neil Law.
Penalty count: 12-11; **Half-time:** 26-0; **Referee:** Steve Nicholson (Whitehaven); **Attendance:** 1,077.

LONDON SKOLARS 10 BARROW RAIDERS 41

SKOLARS: 1 Andy Craig; 2 Charlie Oyebade; 3 Dominic Peters; 4 Scott Roberts; 5 Paul Leef; 6 Ronald Mushiso; 7 Rob McKeown; 8 Obi Ijeoma; 9 Kahu Henare; 10 Allan Tito; 11 Steffan Hughes; 12 Rubert Jonker; 13 PJ Solomon. Subs (all used): 14 Michael Fitzgibbon; 15 Troy Dougherty; 16 Wayne Parillon; 17 Glenn Osborn.
Tries: Oyebade (40, 47); **Goal:** McKeown.
RAIDERS: 1 Danny Lockhart; 2 Jamie Marshall; 3 Andy McClure; 4 Paul Jones; 5 Shane Irabor; 6 Tane Manihera; 7 Chris Archer; 8 Tau Liku; 9 Andy Henderson; 10 Stuart Dancer; 11 James King; 12 Steve Jackson; 13 Phil Atkinson. Subs (all used): 14 Barry Pugh; 15 Geoff Luxon; 16 James Stainton; 17 Wayne Jones.
Tries: P Jones (8), Marshall (22), King (49, 51), Henderson (56); **Goals:** Manihera 10;
Field goal: Manihera.
Sin bin: Dancer (79) - dissent.
Rugby Leaguer & League Express Men of the Match: *Skolars:* Charlie Oyebade; *Raiders:* Tane Manihera.
Penalty count: 9-9; **Half-time:** 6-18;
Referee: Steve Presley (Castleford); **Attendance:** 464.

WORKINGTON TOWN 10 CHORLEY LYNX 28

TOWN: 1 Dean Sharp; 2 Matthew Johnson; 3 Adam Coulson; 4 Brett McDermott; 5 Graeme Lewthwaite; 6 Karl Long; 7 Craig Fisher; 8 Willie Burns; 9 Darren King; 10 Hitro Okesene; 11 Jamie Beaumont; 12 William Blackburn; 13 Gary Charlton. Subs (all used): 14 Kevin Hetherington; 15 Matthew Tunstall; 16 Scott Chilton; 17 Stewart Rhodes.
Tries: McDermott (10), Beaumont (36); **Goal:** Fisher.
Dismissal: Long (72) - head-butt.
Sin bin: Burns (52) - persistent interference.
LYNX: 1 Mark McCully; 2 Anton Garcia; 3 Mick Redford; 4 Jamie Stenhouse; 5 Eric Andrews; 6 Liam Bretherton; 7 John Braddish; 8 Tim Street; 9 Martin Roden; 10 Lee Rowley; 11 Gavin Johnson; 12 Dave McConnell; 13 Ian Hodson. Subs (all used): 14 Simon Smith; 15 Chris Newall; 16 David Whittle; 17 Mick Coates.
Tries: Redford (19), Stenhouse (70), Coates (74), Andrews (76); **Goals:** McCully 5;
Field goals: Braddish, Coates.
Dismissal: Whittle (39) - head-butt.
Rugby Leaguer & League Express Men of the Match: *Town:* Graeme Lewthwaite; *Lynx:* Ian Hodson.
Penalty count: 9-11; **Half-time:** 10-9;
Referee: Clive Walker (Oldham); **Attendance:** 545.

HUNSLET HAWKS 28 GATESHEAD THUNDER 14

HAWKS: 1 Richard Baker; 2 Bryn Powell; 3 Iain Higgins; 4 Paul Seal; 5 George Rayner; 6 Wes McGibbon; 7 Phil Hasty; 8 Jonlee Lockwood; 9 Joe Hawley; 10 Andy Brent; 11 Wayne Freeman; 12 Shaun Ibbetson; 13 Danny Burton. Subs (all used): 14 Craig Ibbetson; 15 Dan Briggs; 16 Danny Fearon; 17 David Brook.
Tries: Hasty (7), W Freeman (10), Seal (22), Rayner (34), Fearon (62); **Goals:** Hasty 4.
THUNDER: 1 Kevin Neighbour; 2 Michael Lyons; 3 Craig Firth; 4 Damien Reid; 5 Richie Barnett; 6 Jermaine Coleman; 7 Paul Thorman; 8 Steven Bradley; 9 Chris Fletcher; 10 David Bates; 11 Clint Brown; 12 Steve Rutherford; 13 Andy Walker. Subs (all used): 14 Yusuf Sozi; 15 Janan Billings; 16 Scott MacDougall; 17 Neil Thorman.
Tries: MacDougall (38, 42); **Goals:** P Thorman 3.
Sin bin: MacDougall (64) - professional foul.
Rugby Leaguer & League Express Men of the Match: *Hawks:* Phil Hasty; *Thunder:* Paul Thorman.
Penalty count: 14-10; **Half-time:** 18-8;
Referee: Gareth Hewer (Whitehaven); **Attendance:** 417.

WEEK 5

Sunday 25th May 2003

BARROW RAIDERS 20 YORK CITY KNIGHTS 27

RAIDERS: 1 Danny Lockhart; 2 Jamie Marshall; 3 Jamie Smith; 4 Andy McClure; 5 Adam Pate; 6 Tane Manihera; 7 Chris Archer; 8 Tau Liku; 9 Andy Henderson; 10 Steve Jackson; 11 James King; 12 Geoff Luxon; 13 Phil Atkinson. Subs (all used): 14 Paul Evans; 15 Stuart Dancer; 16 Paul Lupton; 17 Ian Devlin.
Tries: Archer (10), Smith (16), King (36);
Goals: Manihera 4.
CITY KNIGHTS: 1 Chris Smith; 2 Matt Blaymire; 3 Graeme Hallas; 4 Neil Law; 5 Leigh Deakin; 6 Scott Rhodes; 7 Danny Brough; 8 Andy Burland; 9 Trevor Krause; 10 Richard Hayes; 11 Mick Ramsden; 12 Scott Fletcher; 13 Mark Cain. Subs (all used): 14 Lee Jackson; 15 Darren Callaghan; 16 Gavin Molloy; 17 Paul Broadbent.
Tries: Callaghan (22), Law (39, 44), Brough (50), Fletcher (65); **Goals:** Brough 3; **Field goal:** Brough.
Rugby Leaguer & League Express Men of the Match: *Raiders:* Jamie Smith; *City Knights:* Scott Fletcher.
Penalty count: 4-5; **Half-time:** 18-10;
Referee: Steve Addy (Huddersfield); **Attendance:** 742.

CHORLEY LYNX 33 GATESHEAD THUNDER 18

LYNX: 1 Mark McCully; 2 Andy Parker; 3 Anton Garcia; 4 Jamie Stenhouse; 5 Eric Andrews; 6 Liam Bretherton; 7 John Braddish; 8 Tim Street; 9 Martin Roden; 10 Lee Rowley; 11 Ian Hodson; 12 Dave McConnell; 13 Jason Johnson. Subs (all used): 14 Mick Coates; 15 Chris Newall; 16 Ian Parry; 17 Paul Bamber.
Tries: Parker (6), Andrews (8, 42), Garcia (33), Stenhouse (45), Coates (78); **Goals:** McCully 4;
Field goal: Coates.
THUNDER: 1 Kevin Neighbour; 2 Michael Lyons; 3 Damien Reid; 4 Adam Thornton; 5 Richie Barnett; 6 Jermaine Coleman; 7 Paul Thorman; 8 Yusuf Sozi; 9 Chris Fletcher; 10 Steven Bradley; 11 Clint Brown; 12 Steve Rutherford; 13 Scott MacDougall. Subs (all used): 14 David Bates; 15 Andy Walker; 16 Scott Harrison; 17 Janan Billings.
Tries: Thornton (38), MacDougall (53), A Walker (60);
Goals: Thorman 3.
Rugby Leaguer & League Express Men of the Match: *Lynx:* Jamie Stenhouse; *Thunder:* Adam Thornton.
Penalty count: 7-7; **Half-time:** 16-6;**Referee:** Steve Nicholson (Whitehaven); **Attendance:** 280.

WORKINGTON TOWN 8 KEIGHLEY COUGARS 44

TOWN: 1 Dean Sharp; 2 Scott Chilton; 3 Adam Coulson; 4 Brett McDermott; 5 Graeme Lewthwaite; 6 Craig Fisher; 7 Anthony Murray; 8 Matthew Tunstall; 9 Darren King; 10 Hitro Okesene; 11 David Pettit; 12 William Blackburn; 13 Jamie Beaumont. Subs (all used): 14 Brett Smith; 15 Gareth Dean; 16 Lee Dutton; 17 Craig Barker.
Tries: Lewthwaite (15), Tunstall (73).
COUGARS: 1 James Rushforth; 2 Gareth Hewitt; 3 David Foster; 4 Matt Foster; 5 Andy Robinson; 6 Adam Mitchell; 7 Matt Firth; 8 Phil Stephenson; 9 Simeon Hoyle; 10 Danny Ekis; 11 Oliver Wilkes; 12 Ian Sinfield; 13 Jason Ramshaw. Subs (all used): 14 Chris Wainwright; 15 Lee Patterson; 16 Richard Mervill; 17 Mick Durham.
Tries: Robinson (8, 64), Ramshaw (46), M Foster (51, 68), D Foster (62), Hoyle (79); **Goals:** Mitchell 8.
Rugby Leaguer & League Express Men of the Match: *Town:* William Blackburn; *Cougars:* Adam Mitchell.
Penalty count: 8-7; **Half-time:** 4-10;
Referee: Julian King (St Helens); **Attendance:** 610.

HUNSLET HAWKS 27 SHEFFIELD EAGLES 26

HAWKS: 1 Richard Baker; 2 Bryn Powell; 3 Paul Seal; 4 Wes McGibbon; 5 George Rayner; 6 Stephen Doherty; 7 Phil Hasty; 8 Danny Burton; 9 Joe Hawley; 10 Andy Brent; 11 Wayne Freeman; 12 Shaun Ibbetson; 13 Iain Higgins. Subs (all used): 14 Craig Ibbetson; 15 Danny Fearon; 16 Steve Pryce; 17 Jonlee Lockwood.
Tries: Rayner (6, 75), Seal (44), Brent (66);
Goals: Hasty 5; **Field goal:** Hasty.
Sin bin: McGibbon (56) - fighting.
On report: Freeman (54) - alleged striking.
EAGLES: 1 Andy Poynter; 2 Greg Hurst; 3 Tony Weller; 4 Neil Kite; 5 Ian Thompson; 6 Gavin Brown; 7 Lee Bettinson; 8 Jack Howieson; 9 Gareth Stanley; 10 Jon Bruce; 11 Andy Raleigh; 12 Craig Brown; 13 Wayne Flynn. Subs (all used): 14 Mark Aston; 15 Guy Adams; 16 Simon Tillyer; 17 Mitchell Stringer.
Tries: Poynter (11, 22), Weller (39, 59), Hurst (62);
Goals: G Brown 3.
Rugby Leaguer & League Express Men of the Match: *Hawks:* Danny Burton; *Eagles:* Gavin Brown.
Sin bin: Aston (56) - fighting.
Penalty count: 9-6; **Half-time:** 9-16;
Referee: Ben Thaler (Wakefield); **Attendance:** 553.

Saturday 31st May 2003

GATESHEAD THUNDER 18 WORKINGTON TOWN 18

THUNDER: 1 Kevin Neighbour; 2 Michael Lyons; 3 Damien Reid; 4 Adam Thornton; 5 Richie Barnett; 6 Jermaine Coleman; 7 Paul Thorman; 8 Yusuf Sozi; 9 Janan Billings; 10 Steven Bradley; 11 Clint Brown; 12 Steve Rutherford; 13 Chris Fletcher. Subs (all used): 14 Neil Thorman; 15 Andy Walker; 16 Tom Lauriston; 17 David Bates.
Tries: Janan Billings (9), Bates (28), Lyons (32);
Goals: P Thorman 3.
TOWN: 1 Steve Stoddart; 2 Scott Chilton; 3 Brett McDermott; 4 Jamie Beaumont; 5 Graeme Lewthwaite; 6 Craig Fisher; 7 Anthony Murray; 8 Matthew Tunstall; 9 Darren King; 10 Hitro Okesene; 11 Gareth Dean; 12 William Blackburn; 13 Gary Charlton. Subs (all used): 14 James Robinson; 15 David Pettit; 16 Lee Dutton; 17 Craig Barker.
Tries: Blackburn (23), McDermott (45, 73), Lewthwaite (58); **Goal:** Stoddart.
Rugby Leaguer & League Express Men of the Match: *Thunder:* David Bates; *Town:* Gareth Dean.
Penalty count: 6-10; **Half-time:** 18-4;
Referee: Steve Addy (Huddersfield);
Attendance: 287 *(at Monkton Stadium, Jarrow).*

WEEK 6

Sunday 1st June 2003

KEIGHLEY COUGARS 28 BARROW RAIDERS 15

COUGARS: 1 James Rushforth; 2 Karl Smith; 3 David Foster; 4 Matt Foster; 5 Andy Robinson; 6 Adam Mitchell; 7 Matt Firth; 8 Phil Stephenson; 9 Simeon Hoyle; 10 Danny Ekis; 11 Oliver Wilkes; 12 Ian Sinfield; 13 Jason Ramshaw. Subs (all used): 14 Chris Wainwright; 15 Lee Patterson; 16 Richard Mervill; 17 Mick Durham.
Tries: Wilkes (16), D Foster (25), Robinson (27), Firth (35), Wainwright (71); **Goals:** Mitchell 4.
RAIDERS: 1 Adam Pate; 2 Jamie Marshall; 3 Jamie Smith; 4 Andy McClure; 5 Shane Irabor; 6 Tane Manihera; 7 Chris Archer; 8 Tau Liku; 9 Andy Henderson; 10 James King; 11 Phil Atkinson; 12 Geoff Luxon; 13 Barry Pugh. Subs (all used): 14 Ian Devlin; 15 Stuart Dancer; 16 Paul Wilcock; 17 Wayne Jones.
Tries: Smith (42, 78); **Goals:** Manihera 3;
Field goal: Manihera.
Sin bin: Pate (16) - dissent;
Henderson (69) - holding down.
On report: Liku (48) - alleged off the ball tackle.
Rugby Leaguer & League Express Men of the Match: *Cougars:* Oliver Wilkes; *Raiders:* James King.
Penalty count: 6-11; **Half-time:** 22-3;
Referee: Steve Presley (Castleford); **Attendance:** 1,106.

LONDON SKOLARS 6 HUNSLET HAWKS 36

SKOLARS: 1 Andy Craig; 2 Paul Koloi; 3 Paul Leef; 4 Jake Johnstone; 5 Charlie Oyebade; 6 Cory Bennett; 7 Troy Dougherty; 8 Brett McCroary; 9 Kahu Henare; 10 Allan Tito; 11 Steffan Hughes; 12 Michael Fitzgibbon; 13 PJ Solomon. Subs (all used): 14 Rob McKeown; 15 Scott Roberts; 16 Gareth Janes; 17 Glenn Osborn.
Try: Dougherty (6); **Goal:** Johnstone.
Sin bin: Henare (40) - punching.
HAWKS: 1 Richard Baker; 2 Bryn Powell; 3 Paul Seal; 4 Wes McGibbon; 5 George Rayner; 6 Stephen Doherty; 7 Phil Hasty; 8 Steve Pryce; 9 Jamaine Wray; 10 Andy Brent; 11 Wayne Freeman; 12 Danny Burton; 13 Iain Higgins. Subs (all used): 14 Andy Bastow; 15 Jonlee

Lockwood; 16 Shaun Ibbetson; 17 Lee Freeman.
Tries: Wray (10), Rayner (16), Powell (40), Hasty (41), Doherty (63), W Freeman (75); **Goals:** Hasty 6.
Rugby Leaguer & League Express Men of the Match: *Skolars:* Allan Tito; *Hawks:* Phil Hasty.
Penalty count: 10-12; **Half-time:** 6-16;
Referee: Mike Dawber (Wigan); **Attendance:** 482.

YORK CITY KNIGHTS 40 SWINTON LIONS 2

CITY KNIGHTS: 1 Chris Smith; 2 Matt Blaymire; 3 Graeme Hallas; 4 Neil Law; 5 Alex Godfrey; 6 Scott Rhodes; 7 Danny Brough; 8 Andy Burland; 9 Lee Jackson; 10 Richard Hayes; 11 Mick Ramsden; 12 Mark Cain; 13 Trevor Krause. Subs (all used): 14 Darren Callaghan; 15 Leigh Deakin; 16 Craig Forsyth; 17 Paul Broadbent.
Tries: Law (58), A Godfrey (60), Hallas (63), C Smith (66, 70), Blaymire (75, 77); **Goals:** Brough 6.
LIONS: 1 Wayne English; 2 Jason Roach; 3 Kris Tassell; 4 Phil Hassan; 5 Lee Hudson; 6 Chris Hough; 7 Peter Cannon; 8 Lee Hansen; 9 Rob Barraclough; 10 Simon Knox; 11 Craig Wingfield; 12 Dave Ellison; 13 Robert Russell. Subs (all used): 14 Hugh Thorpe; 15 Danny Butler; 16 Phil Cushion; 17 Mike Loughlin.
Goal: Hough.
Sin bin: Knox (24) – interference; Hudson (63) - dissent.
Rugby Leaguer & League Express Men of the Match: *City Knights:* Lee Jackson; *Lions:* Simon Knox.
Penalty count: 9-7; **Half-time:** 4-0;
Referee: Ben Thaler (Wakefield); **Attendance:** 1,003.

SHEFFIELD EAGLES 16 CHORLEY LYNX 19

EAGLES: 1 Andy Poynter; 2 Greg Hurst; 3 Tony Weller; 4 Neil Kite; 5 Ian Thompson; 6 Gavin Brown; 7 Lee Bettinson; 8 Jack Howieson; 9 Gareth Stanley; 10 Guy Adams; 11 Andy Raleigh; 12 Craig Brown; 13 Wayne Flynn. Subs (all used): 14 Mark Aston; 15 Simon Tillyer; 16 Nick Turnbull; 17 Mitchell Stringer.
Tries: Stringer (36), Aston (39), Kite (65);
Goals: G Brown 2.
LYNX: 1 Mark McCully; 2 Andy Parker; 3 Anton Garcia; 4 Jamie Stenhouse; 5 Eric Andrews; 6 John Braddish; 7 Mick Coates; 8 Ian Parry; 9 Dave McConnell; 10 Lee Rowley; 11 Chris Newall; 12 Martin Roden; 13 Ian Hodson. Subs (all used): 14 Craig Dean; 15 Tim Street; 16 Simon Smith; 17 Eddie Kilgannon.
Tries: Garcia (19, 50), Andrews (25, 78); **Goal:** Dean;
Field goal: Dean.
Rugby Leaguer & League Express Men of the Match: *Eagles:* Mitchell Stringer; *Lynx:* Tim Street.
Penalty count: 8-4; **Half-time:** 10-8;
Referee: Ashley Klein (London); **Attendance:** 747.

WEEK 7

Sunday 8th June 2003

LONDON SKOLARS 8 SWINTON LIONS 31

SKOLARS: 1 Andy Craig; 2 Paul Leef; 3 Paul Koloi; 4 PJ Solomon; 5 Charlie Oyebade; 6 Jake Johnstone; 7 Troy Dougherty; 8 Brett McCroary; 9 Kahu Henare; 10 Allan Tito; 11 Steffan Hughes; 12 Rubert Jonker; 13 Michael Fitzgibbon. Subs (all used): 14 Rob McKeown; 15 Cory Bennett; 16 Gareth Janes; 17 Glenn Osborn.
Try: Jonker (46); **Goals:** Johnstone 2.
Dismissal: McCroary (66) - fighting.
Sin bin: Bennett (54) - interference;
Fitzgibbon (60) - off the ball tackle.
LIONS: 1 Wayne English; 2 Jason Roach; 3 Andy Cheetham; 4 Phil Hassan; 5 Lee Hudson; 6 Kris Tassell; 7 Chris Hough; 8 Lee Hansen; 9 Peter Cannon; 10 Chris Roe; 11 Simon Knox; 12 Phil Cushion; 13 Robert Russell. Subs (all used): 14 Grant Bithel; 15 Liam Owen; 16 Craig Wingfield; 17 Dave Ellison.
Tries: Knox (3, 12), Roach (27), Ellison (39), Cannon (78); **Goals:** Hough 5; **Field goal:** Hough.
Dismissals: Russell (66) - fighting;
English (66) - fighting.
Rugby Leaguer & League Express Men of the Match: *Skolars:* Troy Dougherty; *Lions:* Phil Cushion.
Penalty count: 13-12; **Half-time:** 2-23;
Referee: Steve Presley (Castleford); **Attendance:** 278.

WEEK 8

Sunday 15th June 2003

BARROW RAIDERS 42 SWINTON LIONS 20

RAIDERS: 1 Paul Salmon; 2 Jamie Marshall; 3 Jamie Smith; 4 Paul Jones; 5 Shane Irabor; 6 Tane Manihera; 7 Andy Henderson; 8 Tau Liku; 9 Chris Archer; 10 Steve Jackson; 11 James King; 12 Paul Lupton; 13 Phil Atkinson. Subs (all used): 14 Andy McClure; 15 Geoff Luxon; 16 Craig Bower; 17 Paul Wilcock.
Tries: Smith (7), Archer (19), Manihera (27, 75), Henderson (30), Lupton (33), King (46), Liku (60);
Goals: Manihera 5.
Sin bin: King (27) - fighting.
LIONS: 1 Wayne English; 2 Jason Roach; 3 Andy Cheetham; 4 Phil Hassan; 5 Lee Hudson; 6 Kris Tassell; 7 Chris Hough; 8 Chris Roe; 9 Peter Cannon; 10 Phil Cushion; 11 Simon Knox; 12 Dave Ellison; 13 Robert Russell. Subs (all used): 14 Hugh Thorpe; 15 Grant Bithel; 16 Liam Owen; 17 Craig Wingfield.
Tries: Roach (40), Hough (52), Tassell (65), Hassan (71); **Goals:** Russell, Hough.
Sin bin: Knox (27) - fighting.

Rugby Leaguer & League Express Men of the Match: *Raiders:* Tane Manihera; *Lions:* Chris Hough.
Penalty count: 9-11; **Half-time:** 24-6;
Referee: Clive Walker (Oldham); **Attendance:** 574.

CHORLEY LYNX 64 LONDON SKOLARS 8

LYNX: 1 Mark McCully; 2 David Ingram; 3 Anton Garcia; 4 Jamie Stenhouse; 5 Eric Andrews; 6 Mick Coates; 7 Craig Dean; 8 Tim Street; 9 Dave McConnell; 10 Martin Roden; 11 Anthony Blackwood; 12 Chris Newall; 13 Ian Hodson. Subs (all used): 14 David Whittle; 15 Lee Rowley; 16 Mick Redford; 17 Martin Gambles.
Tries: Garcia (3), Newall (17), Hodson (30), Coates (33, 56), Whittle (38), Andrews (40), Gambles (66), Ingram (69), McCully (76), Rowley (80); **Goals:** McCully 10.
SKOLARS: 1 Andy Craig; 2 Paul Leef; 3 Paul Koloi; 4 PJ Solomon; 5 Charlie Oyebade; 6 Jake Johnstone; 7 Troy Dougherty; 8 Glenn Osborn; 9 Cory Bennett; 10 Gareth Janes; 11 Matt Shaw; 12 Rubert Jonker; 13 Michael Fitzgibbon. Subs: 14 Rob McKeown; 15 Grayson McDonald; 16 Mark Croston (not used); 17 Graham Hughes.
Try: Oyebade (48); **Goals:** Johnstone 2.
Rugby Leaguer & League Express Men of the Match: *Lynx:* Mark McCully; *Skolars:* Charlie Oyebade.
Penalty count: 7-11; **Half-time:** 36-2;
Referee: Steve Addy (Huddersfield); **Attendance:** 252.

KEIGHLEY COUGARS 52 GATESHEAD THUNDER 6

COUGARS: 1 James Rushforth; 2 Karl Smith; 3 David Foster; 4 Matt Foster; 5 Andy Robinson; 6 Adam Mitchell; 7 Matt Firth; 8 Phil Stephenson; 9 Simeon Hoyle; 10 Danny Ekis; 11 Oliver Wilkes; 12 Ian Sinfield; 13 Jason Ramshaw. Subs (all used): 14 Paul Ashton; 15 Lee Patterson; 16 Mick Durham; 17 Chris Hannah.
Tries: Mitchell (12), M Foster (16, 79), Hoyle (20, 64), Firth (31, 51, 75), Ramshaw (47, 72);
Goals: Mitchell 4, Ashton 2.
THUNDER: 1 Kevin Neighbour; 2 Robin Peers; 3 Tom Lauriston; 4 Adam Thornton; 5 Richie Barnett; 6 Jermaine Coleman; 7 Paul Thorman; 8 Yusuf Sozi; 9 Janan Billings; 10 Steven Bradley; 11 Clint Brown; 12 Steve Rutherford; 13 Chris Fletcher. Subs (all used): 14 Neil Thorman; 15 Andy Walker; 16 Scott Harrison; 17 David Bates.
Try: Thornton (36); **Goal:** P Thorman.
Rugby Leaguer & League Express Men of the Match: *Cougars:* Simeon Hoyle; *Thunder:* Kevin Neighbour.
Penalty count: 12-10; **Half-time:** 22-6;
Referee: Ben Thaler (Wakefield); **Attendance:** 992.

WORKINGTON TOWN 16 SHEFFIELD EAGLES 29

TOWN: 1 Dean Sharp; 2 Matthew Johnson; 3 Brett McDermott; 4 Jamie Beaumont; 5 Graeme Lewthwaite; 6 Steve Stoddart; 7 Craig Fisher; 8 Matthew Tunstall; 9 Anthony Murray; 10 Hitro Okesene; 11 Gareth Dean; 12 William Blackburn; 13 Gary Charlton. Subs (all used): 14 Darren King; 15 James Robinson; 16 David Pettit; 17 Lee Dutton.
Tries: Lewthwaite (38), Tunstall (51), Fisher (78);
Goals: Stoddart, Fisher.
EAGLES: 1 Andy Poynter; 2 Tony Weller; 3 Nick Turnbull; 4 Tom O'Reilly; 5 Ian Thompson; 6 Gavin Brown; 7 Mark Aston; 8 Jack Howieson; 9 Gareth Stanley; 10 Jon Bruce; 11 Andy Raleigh; 12 Craig Brown; 13 Wayne Flynn. Subs (all used): 14 Neil Kite; 15 Darren Robinson; 16 Simon Tillyer; 17 Mitchell Stringer.
Tries: Poynter (5, 21), Thompson (12, 63), Stringer (29); **Goals:** G Brown 4; **Field goal:** G Brown.
Rugby Leaguer & League Express Men of the Match: *Town:* Matthew Tunstall; *Eagles:* Tom O'Reilly.
Penalty count: 10-6; **Half-time:** 4-24;
Referee: Steve Presley (Castleford); **Attendance:** 487.

HUNSLET HAWKS 18 YORK CITY KNIGHTS 40

HAWKS: 1 George Rayner; 2 Bryn Powell; 3 Paul Seal; 4 Wes McGibbon; 5 Steve Jakeman; 6 Stephen Doherty; 7 Phil Hasty; 8 Steve Pryce; 9 Jamaine Wray; 10 Danny Burton; 11 Wayne Freeman; 12 Shaun Ibbetson; 13 Iain Higgins. Subs (all used); 14 Andy Bastow; 15 Danny Fearon; 16 Jonlee Lockwood; 17 Chris Parker.
Tries: Hasty (45), McGibbon (70), Parker (79);
Goals: Hasty 3.
CITY KNIGHTS: 1 Chris Smith; 2 Alex Godfrey; 3 Graeme Hallas; 4 Neil Law; 5 Leigh Deakin; 6 Scott Rhodes; 7 Danny Brough; 8 Richard Hayes; 9 Lee Jackson; 10 Craig Forsyth; 11 Mick Ramsden; 12 Mark Cain; 13 Trevor Krause. Subs (all used): 14 Rob Kama; 15 Darren Callaghan; 16 Andy Burland; 17 Paul Broadbent.
Tries: Krause (6), Jackson (10), Deakin (26), Brough (32), C Smith (41), Callaghan (51), Cain (55);
Goals: Brough 6.
Rugby Leaguer & League Express Men of the Match: *Hawks:* Jamaine Wray; *City Knights:* Danny Brough.
Penalty count: 11-11; **Half-time:** 0-24;
Referee: Andrew Leonard (Leeds); **Attendance:** 649.

WEEK 9

Sunday 22nd June 2003

BARROW RAIDERS 22 CHORLEY LYNX 16

RAIDERS: 1 Craig Bower; 2 Jamie Marshall; 3 Jamie Smith; 4 Paul Jones; 5 Paul Salmon; 6 Tane Manihera; 7 Andy Henderson; 8 Tau Liku; 9 Chris Archer; 10 Paul Wilcock; 11 James King; 12 Paul Lupton; 13 Phil Atkinson. Subs (all used): 14 Andy McClure; 15 Geoff Luxon; 16 Steve Jackson; 17 Stuart Dancer.

Tries: P Jones (43), Henderson (50), Bower (72), Marshall (79); **Goals:** Manihera 3.
LYNX: 1 Mark McCully; 2 Anton Garcia; 3 Mick Redford; 4 Jamie Stenhouse; 5 Eric Andrews; 6 Mick Coates; 7 Craig Dean; 8 Tim Street; 9 Dave McConnell; 10 Martin Roden; 11 Anthony Blackwood; 12 Chris Newall; 13 Ian Hodson. Subs (all used): 14 David Whittle; 15 Simon Smith; 16 Lee Rowley; 17 Eddie Kilgannon.
Tries: Andrews (17), Smith (31), Dean (35);
Goals: McCully 2.
Rugby Leaguer & League Express Men of the Match: *Raiders:* Chris Archer; *Lynx:* Craig Dean.
Penalty count: 8-9; **Half-time:** 0-14;
Referee: Steve Presley (Castleford); **Attendance:** 687.

SWINTON LIONS 10 HUNSLET HAWKS 10

LIONS: 1 Mike Saunders; 2 Jason Roach; 3 Mark Ashton; 4 Phil Hassan; 5 Lee Hudson; 6 Kris Tassell; 7 Chris Hough; 8 Chris Roe; 9 Safraz Patel; 10 Phil Cushion; 11 Dave Ellison; 12 Simon Knox; 13 Peter Cannon. Subs (all used): 14 Rob Gallagher; 15 Danny Butler; 16 Mike Loughlin; 17 Daniel Tyres.
Try: Ellison (13); **Goals:** Hough 2; **Field goals:** Hough 2.
Dismissal: Ashton (80) - high tackle.
Sin bin: Roe (22) - high tackle.
HAWKS: 1 Richard Baker; 2 Bryn Powell; 3 Paul Seal; 4 Wes McGibbon; 5 George Rayner; 6 Andy Bastow; 7 Phil Hasty; 8 Steve Pryce; 9 Joe Hawley; 10 Danny Fearon; 11 Wayne Freeman; 12 Danny Burton; 13 Jon Liddell. Subs (all used): 14 Jamaine Wray; 15 Chris Parker; 16 Iain Higgins; 17 Glen Freeman.
Try: Wray (65); **Goals:** Hasty 3.
Rugby Leaguer & League Express Men of the Match: *Lions:* Jason Roach; *Hawks:* Jamaine Wray.
Penalty count: 9-12; **Half-time:** 7-0;
Referee: Ben Thaler (Wakefield); **Attendance:** 503.

WORKINGTON TOWN 14 YORK CITY KNIGHTS 33

TOWN: 1 Dean Sharp; 2 Matthew Johnson; 3 Brett McDermott; 4 Jamie Beaumont; 5 Graeme Lewthwaite; 6 Shaun Boylan; 7 Craig Fisher; 8 Matthew Tunstall; 9 Anthony Murray; 10 Gareth Dean; 11 James Robinson; 12 William Blackburn; 13 Gary Charlton. Subs (all used): 14 Darren King; 15 Steve Stoddart; 16 David Pettit; 17 Lee Dutton.
Tries: McDermott (25), Murray (58); **Goals:** Fisher 3.
On report: Charlton (65) - incident.
CITY KNIGHTS: 1 Chris Smith; 2 Alex Godfrey; 3 Graeme Hallas; 4 Neil Law; 5 Leigh Deakin; 6 Scott Rhodes; 7 Danny Brough; 8 Richard Hayes; 9 Lee Jackson; 10 Craig Forsyth; 11 Mick Ramsden; 12 Mark Cain; 13 Trevor Krause. Subs (all used): 14 Darren Callaghan; 15 Gavin Molloy; 16 Andy Burland; 17 Paul Broadbent.
Tries: C Smith (11), Rhodes (32), Hallas (51), Law (74), A Godfrey (77); **Goals:** Brough 6; **Field goal:** Brough.
Sin bin: Brough (45) - persistent interference at the play-the-ball.
On report: Biting incident.
Rugby Leaguer & League Express Men of the Match: *Town:* Shaun Boylan; *City Knights:* Danny Brough.
Penalty count: 8-8; **Half-time:** 8-14;
Referee: Mike Dawber (Wigan); **Attendance:** 539.

SHEFFIELD EAGLES 33 KEIGHLEY COUGARS 6

EAGLES: 1 Andy Poynter; 2 Tony Weller; 3 Nick Turnbull; 4 Tom O'Reilly; 5 Ian Thompson; 6 Gavin Brown; 7 Mark Aston; 8 Jack Howieson; 9 Gareth Stanley; 10 Jon Bruce; 11 Andy Raleigh; 12 Craig Brown; 13 Wayne Flynn. Subs (all used): 14 Peter Reilly; 15 Simon Tillyer; 16 Greg Hurst; 17 Mitchell Stringer.
Tries: Turnbull (9), O'Reilly (13), Stanley (26), Weller (31), Raleigh (79); **Goals:** G Brown 6; **Field goal:** Aston.
Sin bin: Flynn (2) - fighting; Stanley (50) - holding down, (80) - ungentlemanly conduct.
COUGARS: 1 James Rushforth; 2 Gareth Hewitt; 3 David Foster; 4 Andy Robinson; 5 Matt Foster; 6 Adam Mitchell; 7 Matt Firth; 8 Phil Stephenson; 9 Simeon Hoyle; 10 Danny Ekis; 11 Oliver Wilkes; 12 Ian Sinfield; 13 Jason Ramshaw. Subs (all used): 14 Chris Wainwright; 15 Lee Patterson; 16 Ricky Helliwell; 17 Richard Mervill.
Try: Ramshaw (64); **Goal:** Wilkes.
Sin bin: Wilkes (2) - fighting;
Stephenson (7) - holding down.
Rugby Leaguer & League Express Men of the Match: *Eagles:* Andy Raleigh; *Cougars:* Matt Firth.
Penalty count: 6-11; **Half-time:** 24-0;
Referee: Julian King (St Helens); **Attendance:** 1,126.

GATESHEAD THUNDER 50 LONDON SKOLARS 20

THUNDER: 1 Kevin Neighbour; 2 Robin Peers; 3 Steve Morton; 4 Adam Thornton; 5 Peter Oshagbemi; 6 Paul Thorman; 7 Neil Thorman; 8 Yusuf Sozi; 9 Chris Fletcher; 10 Steven Bradley; 11 Clint Brown; 12 Steve Rutherford; 13 Andy Walker. Subs (all used): 14 Janan Billings; 15 Michael Lyons; 16 Scott Harrison; 17 David Bates.
Tries: Walker (5, 23, 25, 35, 59), P Thorman (9), Morton (28), Peers (51); **Goals:** P Thorman 9.
Sin bin: Bates (33) – professional foul.
SKOLARS: 1 Andy Craig; 2 Paul Leef; 3 Jake Johnstone; 4 Scott Roberts; 5 Richard Pollard; 6 Grayson McDonald; 7 Troy Dougherty; 8 Graham Hughes; 9 Rob McKeown; 10 Gareth Janes; 11 Obi Ijeoma; 12 Rubert Jonker; 13 Ryan Hermanson. Subs: 14 Gareth Honor; 15 Anthony Dellar; 16 Mark Croston (not used); 17 Mark Foster.
Tries: Jonker (16, 66), Pollard (69); **Goals:** Johnstone 4.
Rugby Leaguer & League Express Men of the Match: *Thunder:* Andy Walker; *Skolars:* Rubert Jonker.
Penalty count: 9-11; **Half-time:** 38-8;
Referee: Steve Nicholson (Whitehaven);
Attendance: 226 *(at Monkton Stadium, Jarrow).*

National League Two 2003 - Round by Round

WEEK 10

Sunday 29th June 2003

CHORLEY LYNX 29 YORK CITY KNIGHTS 14

LYNX: 1 Mark McCully; 2 Andy Parker; 3 Anton Garcia; 4 Jamie Stenhouse; 5 Eric Andrews; 6 Mick Coates; 7 Craig Dean; 8 Simon Smith; 9 Dave McConnell; 10 Martin Roden; 11 Anthony Blackwood; 12 Chris Newall; 13 Ian Hodson. Subs (all used): 14 Tim Street; 15 Mike Briggs; 16 Mick Redford; 17 Craig Wingfield.
Tries: Andrews (6, 46), McCully (18), McConnell (24), Stenhouse (27), Garcia (35); **Goals:** McCully 2;
Field goal: Dean.
CITY KNIGHTS: 1 Alex Godfrey; 2 Rob Kama; 3 Graeme Hallas; 4 Neil Law; 5 Leigh Deakin; 6 Scott Rhodes; 7 Danny Brough; 8 Richard Hayes; 9 Lee Jackson; 10 Craig Forsyth; 11 Mick Ramsden; 12 Mark Cain; 13 Trevor Krause. Subs (all used): 14 Darren Callaghan; 15 Scott Fletcher; 16 Andy Burland; 17 Paul Broadbent.
Tries: Law (30), Cain (55); **Goals:** Brough 3.
Dismissal: Hallas (78) - stamping.
Sin bin: Fletcher (26) - persistent interference at the play-the-ball; Rhodes (33) - offside.
Rugby Leaguer & League Express Men of the Match:
Lynx: Eric Andrews; *City Knights:* Scott Rhodes.
Penalty count: 11-9; **Half-time:** 24-8;
Referee: Steve Addy (Huddersfield); **Attendance:** 450.

KEIGHLEY COUGARS 18 SWINTON LIONS 15

COUGARS: 1 James Rushforth; 2 Max Tomlinson; 3 David Foster; 4 Matt Foster; 5 Andy Robinson; 6 Adam Mitchell; 7 Matt Firth; 8 Phil Stephenson; 9 Simeon Hoyle; 10 Ian Sinfield; 11 Oliver Wilkes; 12 Ricky Helliwell; 13 Jason Ramshaw. Subs (all used): 14 Paul Ashton; 15 Mick Durham; 16 Danny Ekis; 17 Chris Hannah.
Tries: Wilkes (10), Tomlinson (25), M Foster (77);
Goals: Mitchell 2, Ashton.
On report: Stephenson (17) - fighting.
LIONS: 1 Mike Saunders; 2 Hugh Thorpe; 3 Kris Tassell; 4 Phil Hassan; 5 Lee Hudson; 6 Rob Gallagher; 7 Chris Hough; 8 Chris Roe; 9 Safraz Patel; 10 Wes Rogers; 11 Dave Ellison; 12 Simon Knox; 13 Peter Cannon. Subs (all used): 14 Grant Bithel; 15 Kris Smith; 16 Mike Loughlin; 17 Daniel Tyres.
Tries: Tassell (3, 42), Knox (31); **Goal:** Hough;
Field goal: Hough.
Dismissal: Roe (79) - fighting.
Sin bin: Knox (17) - fighting.
Rugby Leaguer & League Express Men of the Match:
Cougars: Simeon Hoyle; *Lions:* Kris Tassell.
Penalty count: 12-12; **Half-time:** 12-10;
Referee: Clive Walker (Oldham); **Attendance:** 1,129.

LONDON SKOLARS 6 WORKINGTON TOWN 52

SKOLARS: 1 Andy Craig; 2 Paul Leef; 3 Jake Johnstone; 4 Scott Roberts; 5 Charlie Oyebade; 6 Grayson McDonald; 7 Troy Dougherty; 8 Graham Hughes; 9 Kahu Henare; 10 Brett McCroary; 11 Allan Tito; 12 Rubert Jonker; 13 Rob McKeown. Subs (all used): 14 Gareth Honor; 15 Richard Pollard; 16 Steffan Hughes; 17 Ronald Mushiso.
Try: Leef (71); **Goal:** Johnstone.
Sin bin: McCroary (25) - professional foul;
G McDonald (61) - punching.
TOWN: 1 Dean Sharp; 2 Scott Chilton; 3 Brett McDermott; 4 Jamie Beaumont; 5 Graeme Lewthwaite; 6 Shaun Boylan; 7 Craig Fisher; 8 Matthew Tunstall; 9 Anthony Murray; 10 Lee Dutton; 11 James Robinson; 12 Gareth Dean; 13 Brett Smith. Subs (all used): 14 Matthew Johnson; 15 David Pettit; 16 Jon-Paul Doherty; 17 Hitro Okesene.
Tries: Boylan (2), Pettit (26, 32, 67), McDermott (29), Smith (35), Beaumont (44), Tunstall (54, 76);
Goals: Fisher 6, Smith 2.
Rugby Leaguer & League Express Men of the Match:
Skolars: Kahu Henare; *Town:* Craig Fisher.
Penalty count: 6-15; **Half-time:** 0-30;
Referee: Ben Thaler (Wakefield); **Attendance:** 324.

SHEFFIELD EAGLES 58 GATESHEAD THUNDER 24

EAGLES: 1 Andy Poynter; 2 Tony Weller; 3 Nick Turnbull; 4 Tom O'Reilly; 5 Ian Thompson; 6 Gavin Brown; 7 Mark Aston; 8 Jack Howieson; 9 Gareth Stanley; 10 Jon Bruce; 11 Andy Raleigh; 12 Craig Brown; 13 Wayne Flynn. Subs (all used): 14 Greg Hurst; 15 Simon Tillyer; 16 Damien Whitter; 17 Mitchell Stringer.
Tries: G Brown (22), Turnbull (28, 76, 80), Weller (37), Raleigh (42, 52), O'Reilly (46), Flynn (49), Hurst (55), Bruce (59); **Goals:** G Brown 7.
Sin bin: Stringer (15) - persistent offside.
THUNDER: 1 Kevin Neighbour; 2 Robin Peers; 3 Steve Morton; 4 Adam Thornton; 5 Peter Oshagbemi; 6 Paul Thorman; 7 Neil Thorman; 8 Yusuf Sozi; 9 Chris Fletcher; 10 Steven Bradley; 11 Clint Brown; 12 Steve Rutherford; 13 Andy Walker. Subs (all used): 14 Janan Billings; 15 Damien Reid; 16 Scott Harrison; 17 David Bates.
Tries: Oshagbemi (4), Thornton (11), Bates (66, 71);
Goals: P Thorman 4.
Rugby Leaguer & League Express Men of the Match:
Eagles: Andy Raleigh; *Thunder:* Neil Thorman.
Penalty count: 1-7; **Half-time:** 16-12;
Referee: Steve Presley (Castleford); **Attendance:** 1,022.

HUNSLET HAWKS 17 BARROW RAIDERS 18

HAWKS: 1 Richard Baker; 2 Bryn Powell; 3 Paul Seal; 4 Wes McGibbon; 5 George Rayner; 6 Andy Bastow; 7 Phil Hasty; 8 Steve Pryce; 9 Jamaine Wray; 10 Danny Burton; 11 Wayne Freeman; 12 Glen Freeman; 13 Jon Liddell. Subs (all used): 14 Danny Fearon; 15 Andy Brent; 16 Iain Higgins; 17 Mick Coyle.
Tries: Coyle (39), Higgins (60), Hasty (65);
Goals: Hasty 2; **Field goal:** Bastow.
RAIDERS: 1 Craig Bower; 2 Jamie Marshall; 3 Jamie Smith; 4 Paul Jones; 5 Paul Salmon; 6 Tane Manihera; 7 Andy Henderson; 8 Tau Liku; 9 Chris Archer; 10 Paul Wilcock; 11 James King; 12 Paul Lupton; 13 Phil Atkinson. Subs (all used): 14 Andy McClure; 15 Geoff Luxon; 16 Steve Jackson; 17 Stuart Dancer.
Tries: Smith (3), Marshall (50), Bower (75);
Goals: Manihera 3.
Rugby Leaguer & League Express Men of the Match:
Hawks: Phil Hasty; *Raiders:* Jamie Marshall.
Penalty count: 10-2; **Half-time:** 6-6;
Referee: Julian King (St Helens); **Attendance:** 422.

WEEK 11

Sunday 13th July 2003

BARROW RAIDERS 54 LONDON SKOLARS 12

RAIDERS: 1 Craig Bower; 2 Jamie Marshall; 3 Jamie Smith; 4 Paul Jones; 5 Shane Irabor; 6 Tane Manihera; 7 Andy Henderson; 8 Tau Liku; 9 Chris Archer; 10 Steve Jackson; 11 James King; 12 Paul Lupton; 13 Phil Atkinson. Subs (all used): 14 Dave Clark; 15 Geoff Luxon; 16 Stuart Dancer; 17 Ian Devlin.
Tries: Bower (11), Smith (20), Marshall (33), Atkinson (39), Lupton (42), P Jones (45, 50, 68), Irabor (72, 78);
Goals: Manihera 7.
SKOLARS: 1 Kirk King; 2 Ronald Mushiso; 3 Paul Leef; 4 Jake Johnstone; 5 Charlie Oyebade; 6 Troy Dougherty; 7 Gareth Honor; 8 Obi Ijeoma; 9 Kahu Henare; 10 Alex Smits; 11 Brett McCroary; 12 Ryan Hermanson; 13 Allan Tito. Subs (all used): 14 Neil Foster; 15 David Mossop; 16 John Warner; 17 Rob McKeown.
Tries: Tito (55), Leef (60); **Goals:** Johnstone 2.
Rugby Leaguer & League Express Men of the Match:
Raiders: Paul Jones; *Skolars:* Kirk King.
Penalty count: 4-9; **Half-time:** 22-0;
Referee: Mike Dawber (Wigan); **Attendance:** 681.

CHORLEY LYNX 56 WORKINGTON TOWN 18

LYNX: 1 Mark McCully; 2 David Ingram; 3 Anton Garcia; 4 Jamie Stenhouse; 5 Eric Andrews; 6 Mick Coates; 7 Craig Dean; 8 Simon Smith; 9 Dave McConnell; 10 Martin Roden; 11 Mick Redford; 12 Chris Newall; 13 Ian Hodson. Subs (all used): 14 Tim Street; 15 John Braddish; 16 Mike Briggs; 17 Craig Wingfield.
Tries: McConnell (9), Hodson (20), McCully (24), Newall (29), Redford (35), Coates (45), Wingfield (49), Andrews (52), Ingram (60), Garcia (74); **Goals:** McCully 8.
TOWN: 1 Dean Sharp; 2 Scott Chilton; 3 Brett McDermott; 4 Glen Hutton; 5 Graeme Lewthwaite; 6 Shaun Boylan; 7 Craig Fisher; 8 Matthew Tunstall; 9 Anthony Murray; 10 Hitro Okesene; 11 James Robinson; 12 Gareth Dean; 13 Brett Smith. Subs (all used): 14 Jon-Paul Doherty; 15 David Pettit; 16 Jamie Beaumont; 17 Lee Dutton.
Tries: Dean (6, 77), McDermott (65); **Goals:** Fisher 3.
Rugby Leaguer & League Express Men of the Match:
Lynx: Mark McCully; *Town:* Gareth Dean.
Penalty count: 8-13; **Half-time:** 30-8;
Referee: Peter Taberner (Wigan); **Attendance:** 302.

SWINTON LIONS 20 SHEFFIELD EAGLES 18

LIONS: 1 Wayne English; 2 Hugh Thorpe; 3 Robert Russell; 4 Phil Hassan; 5 Lee Hudson; 6 Rob Gallagher; 7 Chris Hough; 8 Chris Roe; 9 Safraz Patel; 10 Wes Rogers; 11 Simon Knox; 12 Dave Ellison; 13 Peter Cannon. Subs: 14 Grant Bithel (not used); 15 Jason Roach; 16 Mike Loughlin; 17 Daniel Tyres.
Tries: Cannon (30), Hudson (34), Roach (67);
Goals: Hough 4.
Sin bin: Russell (10) - obstruction.
EAGLES: 1 Andy Poynter; 2 Tony Weller; 3 Nick Turnbull; 4 Tom O'Reilly; 5 Ian Thompson; 6 Gavin Brown; 7 Mark Aston; 8 Jack Howieson; 9 Gareth Stanley; 10 Jon Bruce; 11 Andy Raleigh; 12 Craig Brown; 13 Wayne Flynn. Subs (all used): 14 Greg Hurst; 15 Simon Tillyer; 16 Richard Goddard; 17 Mitchell Stringer.
Tries: Poynter (12, 20), Weller (75); **Goals:** G Brown 3.
Sin bin: Aston (58) - dissent.
On report: Aston (71) - incident in a tackle.
Rugby Leaguer & League Express Men of the Match:
Lions: Peter Cannon; *Eagles:* Gavin Brown.
Penalty count: 8-10; **Half-time:** 14-12; **Referee:** Steve Nicholson (Whitehaven); **Attendance:** 496.

YORK CITY KNIGHTS 48 KEIGHLEY COUGARS 28

CITY KNIGHTS: 1 Johnny Woodcock; 2 Alex Godfrey; 3 Mark Cain; 4 Neil Law; 5 Rob Kama; 6 Scott Rhodes; 7 Danny Brough; 8 Richard Hayes; 9 Lee Jackson; 10 Craig Forsyth; 11 Mick Ramsden; 12 Darren Callaghan; 13 Trevor Krause. Subs (all used): 14 Gavin Molloy; 15 Leigh Riddell; 16 Kevin Spink; 17 Paul Broadbent.
Tries: A Godfrey (32, 47), Law (34, 51), Jackson (43), Spink (54), Rhodes (65), Woodcock (76); **Goals:** Brough 8.
COUGARS: 1 James Rushforth; 2 Gareth Hewitt; 3 Chris Wainwright; 4 Matt Foster; 5 Andy Robinson; 6 Adam Mitchell; 7 Matt Firth; 8 Chris Hannah; 9 Simeon Hoyle; 10 Ian Sinfield; 11 Oliver Wilkes; 12 David Foster; 13 Jason Ramshaw. Subs (all used): 14 Paul Ashton; 15 Lee Patterson; 16 Richard Mervill; 17 Danny Ekis.
Tries: Rushforth (7), Mitchell (12), Robinson (62), M Foster (71), D Foster (80); **Goals:** Mitchell, Ashton 3.
Rugby Leaguer & League Express Men of the Match:
City Knights: Scott Rhodes; *Cougars:* Jason Ramshaw.
Penalty count: 5-4; **Half-time:** 14-10;
Referee: Steve Presley (Castleford); **Attendance:** 1,835.

GATESHEAD THUNDER 6 HUNSLET HAWKS 55

THUNDER: 1 Kevin Neighbour; 2 Steve Morton; 3 Damien Reid; 4 Adam Thornton; 5 Peter Oshagbemi; 6 Paul Thorman; 7 Neil Thorman; 8 Yusuf Sozi; 9 Janan Billings; 10 Steven Bradley; 11 Clint Brown; 12 Steve Rutherford; 13 Andy Walker. Subs (all used): 14 Robin Peers; 15 Mark Gibson; 16 Sam Turnell; 17 Scott Harrison.
Try: Oshagbemi (79); **Goal:** P Thorman.
HAWKS: 1 Richard Baker; 2 Bryn Powell; 3 Paul Seal; 4 Iain Higgins; 5 George Rayner; 6 Andy Bastow; 7 Stephen Doherty; 8 Danny Burton; 9 Jon Liddell; 10 Andy Brent; 11 Wayne Freeman; 12 Danny Fearon; 13 Mick Coyle. Subs (all used): 14 Glen Freeman; 15 Chris Parker; 16 Jamaine Wray; 17 Steve Jakeman.
Tries: Powell (2, 35, 39, 47), Liddell (7, 75), Jakeman (50), Wray (54), Baker (59), Higgins (65);
Goals: Liddell 7; **Field goal:** Bastow.
Rugby Leaguer & League Express Men of the Match:
Thunder: Yusuf Sozi; *Hawks:* Bryn Powell.
Penalty count: 8-9; **Half-time:** 0-23;
Referee: Steve Addy (Huddersfield);
Attendance: 285 *(at Preston Avenue, North Shields).*

WEEK 12

Sunday 20th July 2003

KEIGHLEY COUGARS 20 CHORLEY LYNX 23

COUGARS: 1 James Rushforth; 2 Karl Smith; 3 David Foster; 4 Matt Foster; 5 Andy Robinson; 6 Adam Mitchell; 7 Matt Firth; 8 Chris Hannah; 9 Simeon Hoyle; 10 Ian Sinfield; 11 Oliver Wilkes; 12 Lee Patterson; 13 Jason Ramshaw. Subs (all used): 14 Chris Wainwright; 15 Mick Durham; 16 Ricky Helliwell; 17 Richard Mervill.
Tries: M Foster (9), Mitchell (25), Firth (45);
Goals: Mitchell 3; **Field goals:** Firth 2.
On report: Wilkes (34) - fighting.
LYNX: 1 Mark McCully; 2 David Ingram; 3 Anton Garcia; 4 Jamie Stenhouse; 5 Eric Andrews; 6 Mick Coates; 7 Craig Dean; 8 Lee Rowley; 9 Mike Briggs; 10 Martin Roden; 11 Mick Redford; 12 Chris Newall; 13 Ian Hodson. Subs (all used): 14 Craig Wingfield; 15 Eddie Kilgannon; 16 John Braddish; 17 Martin Gambles.
Tries: Stenhouse (33), Andrews (60, 76);
Goals: McCully 5; **Field goal:** Coates.
On report: Dean (34) - fighting.
Rugby Leaguer & League Express Men of the Match:
Cougars: Matt Firth; *Lynx:* Mick Coates.
Penalty count: 3-4; **Half-time:** 13-8;
Referee: Julian King (St Helens); **Attendance:** 1,028.

LONDON SKOLARS 6 YORK CITY KNIGHTS 66

SKOLARS: 1 Ronald Mushiso; 2 Neil Foster; 3 Paul Leef; 4 Jake Johnstone; 5 Charlie Oyebade; 6 Troy Dougherty; 7 Gareth Honor; 8 Gareth Janes; 9 Kahu Henare; 10 Alex Smits; 11 Brett McCroary; 12 Obi Ijeoma; 13 Allan Tito. Subs (all used): 14 Cory Bennett; 15 Ryan Hermanson; 16 Roger Teau; 17 Rob McKeown.
Try: Mushiso (3); **Goal:** Johnstone.
Sin bin: Teau (34) - flopping.
CITY KNIGHTS: 1 Johnny Woodcock; 2 Alex Godfrey; 3 Mark Cain; 4 Neil Law; 5 Rob Kama; 6 Scott Rhodes; 7 Danny Brough; 8 Richard Hayes; 9 Lee Jackson; 10 Craig Forsyth; 11 Mick Ramsden; 12 Darren Callaghan; 13 Trevor Krause. Subs (all used): 14 Joe Helme; 15 Graeme Hallas; 16 Kevin Spink; 17 Leigh Riddell.
Tries: Brough (1), Callaghan (11), Law (29), Cain (35, 43, 62), A Godfrey (37), Woodcock (47, 79), Kama (69), Krause (76); **Goals:** Brough 11.
Sin bin: Riddell (49) - play-the-ball offence.
Rugby Leaguer & League Express Men of the Match:
Skolars: Alex Smits; *City Knights:* Danny Brough.
Penalty count: 9-8; **Half-time:** 6-30;
Referee: Steve Addy (Huddersfield); **Attendance:** 425.

WORKINGTON TOWN 18 HUNSLET HAWKS 22

TOWN: 1 Dean Sharp; 2 Scott Chilton; 3 Brett McDermott; 4 Jamie Beaumont; 5 Graeme Lewthwaite; 6 Shaun Boylan; 7 Craig Fisher; 8 Matthew Tunstall; 9 Anthony Murray; 10 Hitro Okesene; 11 James Robinson; 12 Gareth Dean; 13 Brett Smith. Subs (all used): 14 Glen Hutton; 15 David Pettit; 16 Anthony Horton; 17 Jon-Paul Doherty.
Tries: Chilton (36, 57), Fisher (43); **Goals:** Fisher 3.
HAWKS: 1 Richard Baker; 2 Bryn Powell; 3 Paul Seal; 4 Iain Higgins; 5 George Rayner; 6 Andy Bastow; 7 Stephen Doherty; 8 Steve Pryce; 9 Jon Liddell; 10 Danny Burton; 11 Wayne Freeman; 12 Glen Freeman; 13 Mick Coyle. Subs (all used): 14 Andy Brent; 15 Chris Parker; 16 Phil Hasty; 17 Steve Jakeman.
Tries: Higgins (8), Powell (29, 70, 79); **Goals:** Liddell 3.
Rugby Leaguer & League Express Men of the Match:
Town: Scott Chilton; *Hawks:* Bryn Powell.
Penalty count: 8-6; **Half-time:** 6-12;
Referee: Steve Presley (Castleford); **Attendance:** 505.

SHEFFIELD EAGLES 43 BARROW RAIDERS 42

EAGLES: 1 Andy Poynter; 2 Tony Weller; 3 Neil Kite; 4 Tom O'Reilly; 5 Greg Hurst; 6 Gavin Brown; 7 Mark Aston; 8 Jack Howieson; 9 Gareth Stanley; 10 Jon Bruce; 11 Andy Raleigh; 12 Craig Brown; 13 Wayne Flynn. Subs (all used): 14 Nick Turnbull; 15 Simon Tillyer; 16 Richard Goddard; 17 Mitchell Stringer.
Tries: Flynn (2), Hurst (4), Kite (40), Bruce (45),

G Brown (47), Weller (60), Tillyer (66), C Brown (78);
Goals: G Brown 5; **Field goal:** Goddard.
RAIDERS: 1 Craig Bower; 2 Jamie Marshall; 3 Jamie Smith; 4 Paul Jones; 5 Shane Irabor; 6 Tane Manihera; 7 Andy Henderson; 8 Tau Liku; 9 Dave Clark; 10 James King; 11 Steve Jackson; 12 Paul Lupton; 13 Phil Atkinson. Subs (all used): 14 Andy McClure; 15 Geoff Luxon; 16 Stuart Dancer; 17 Ian Devlin.
Tries: Marshall (10), Manihera (19, 51), P Jones (24), King (29), Irabor (70), Henderson (75); **Goals:** Manihera 7.
Rugby Leaguer & League Express Men of the Match: *Eagles:* Jon Bruce; *Raiders:* Andy Henderson.
Penalty count: 10-7; **Half-time:** 16-24; **Referee:** Gareth Hewer (Whitehaven); **Attendance:** 1,037.

GATESHEAD THUNDER 30 SWINTON LIONS 39

THUNDER: 1 Kevin Neighbour; 2 Robin Peers; 3 Steve Morton; 4 Adam Thornton; 5 Peter Oshagbemi; 6 Damien Reid; 7 Paul Thorman; 8 Yusuf Sozi; 9 Janan Billings; 10 Steven Bradley; 11 Clint Brown; 12 Steve Rutherford; 13 Andy Walker. Subs (all used): 14 Neil Thorman; 15 Mark Gibson; 16 Michael Lyons; 17 Scott Harrison.
Tries: Walker (5), N Thorman (56), Lyons (63), Thornton (68), Gibson (74); **Goals:** P Thorman 5.
LIONS: 1 Wayne English; 2 Hugh Thorpe; 3 Jason Roach; 4 Phil Hassan; 5 Lee Hudson; 6 Rob Gallagher; 7 Chris Hough; 8 Chris Roe; 9 Rob Barraclough; 10 Simon Knox; 11 Dave Ellison; 12 Mike Loughlin; 13 Peter Cannon. Subs (all used): 14 Kris Tassell; 15 Safraz Patel; 16 Robert Russell; 17 Daniel Tyres.
Tries: Hudson (18, 34, 53), Ellison (36), Roach (45, 59);
Goals: Hough 7; **Field goal:** Patel.
Rugby Leaguer & League Express Men of the Match: *Thunder:* Neil Thorman; *Lions:* Chris Hough.
Penalty count: 8-8; **Half-time:** 10-16;
Referee: Andrew Leonard (Leeds); **Attendance:** 388.

WEEK 13

Sunday 27th July 2003

BARROW RAIDERS 48 GATESHEAD THUNDER 16

RAIDERS: 1 Craig Bower; 2 Jamie Marshall; 3 Jamie Smith; 4 Paul Jones; 5 Shane Irabor; 6 Tane Manihera; 7 Chris Archer; 8 Tau Liku; 9 Dave Clark; 10 James King; 11 Phil Atkinson; 12 Steve Jackson; 13 Andy Henderson. Subs (all used): 14 Andy McClure; 15 Geoff Luxon; 16 Stuart Dancer; 17 Adam Pate.
Tries: Smith (12, 48), Henderson (18), Irabor (29, 37), Atkinson (32), Bower (42, 59), P Jones (57), Pate (76);
Goals: Manihera 4.
THUNDER: 1 Kevin Neighbour; 2 Peter Oshagbemi; 3 Andy Walker; 4 Steve Morton; 5 Richie Barnett; 6 Damien Reid; 7 Paul Thorman; 8 Yusuf Sozi; 9 Janan Billings; 10 Steven Bradley; 11 Clint Brown; 12 Steve Rutherford; 13 Chris Fletcher. Subs (all used): 14 Scott Harrison; 15 Robin Peers; 16 Michael Lyons; 17 Neil Thorman.
Tries: Barnett (8), Reid (39, 56); **Goals:** P Thorman 2.
Rugby Leaguer & League Express Men of the Match: *Raiders:* Andy Henderson; *Thunder:* Damien Reid.
Penalty count: 4-6; **Half-time:** 24-10;
Referee: Steve Presley (Castleford); **Attendance:** 660.

LONDON SKOLARS 14 KEIGHLEY COUGARS 22

SKOLARS: 1 Charlie Oyebade; 2 Neil Foster; 3 Paul Leef; 4 Ronald Mushiso; 5 Mike Okwusogu; 6 Cory Bennett; 7 Gareth Honor; 8 Gareth Janes; 9 Kahu Henare; 10 Alex Smits; 11 Rubert Jonker; 12 Glenn Osborn; 13 Brett McCroary. Subs (all used): 14 Huy Le; 15 Ryan Hermanson; 16 Matt Walker; 17 Roger Teau.
Tries: Henare (46, 63); **Goals:** Osborn 3.
Sin bin: Smits (19) - dissent.
COUGARS: 1 James Rushforth; 2 Karl Smith; 3 David Foster; 4 Matt Foster; 5 Andy Robinson; 6 Paul Ashton; 7 Matt Firth; 8 Chris Hannah; 9 Simeon Hoyle; 10 Danny Ekis; 11 Oliver Wilkes; 12 Ian Sinfield; 13 Jason Ramshaw. Subs (all used): 14 Chris Wainwright; 15 Lee Patterson; 16 Ricky Helliwell; 17 Richard Mervill.
Tries: Wilkes (22), M Foster (35, 80), Wainwright (48);
Goals: Ashton 3.
Rugby Leaguer & League Express Men of the Match: *Skolars:* Glenn Osborn; *Cougars:* Matt Foster.
Penalty count: 7-9; **Half-time:** 8-10;
Referee: Ben Thaler (Wakefield); **Attendance:** 304.

SWINTON LIONS 56 WORKINGTON TOWN 12

LIONS: 1 Wayne English; 2 Hugh Thorpe; 3 Jason Roach; 4 Kris Tassell; 5 Lee Hudson; 6 Rob Gallagher; 7 Chris Hough; 8 Chris Roe; 9 Rob Barraclough; 10 Simon Knox; 11 James Lomax; 12 Robert Russell; 13 Peter Cannon. Subs (all used): 14 Grant Bithel; 15 Safraz Patel; 16 Mike Loughlin; 17 Kris Smith.
Tries: Thorpe (3), Tassell (12), Roach (19), Patel (29), Bithel (44, 57), English (47), Roe (63), Loughlin (68);
Goals: Hough 8, Gallagher 2.
Sin bin: Barraclough (52) - holding down.
TOWN: 1 Scott Chilton; 2 Glen Hutton; 3 Brett McDermott; 4 Jamie Beaumont; 5 Graeme Lewthwaite; 6 Shaun Boylan; 7 Craig Fisher; 8 Matthew Tunstall; 9 Anthony Murray; 10 Hitro Okesene; 11 James Robinson; 12 Gareth Dean; 13 Brett Smith. Subs: (all used): 14 Matthew Johnson; 15 David Pettit; 16 Anthony Horton; 17 Lee Dutton.
Tries: Johnson (61), Horton (70, 77).
Sin bin: Murray (24) - holding down.
Rugby Leaguer & League Express Men of the Match: *Lions:* Safraz Patel; *Town:* Gareth Dean.
Penalty count: 12-10; **Half-time:** 26-0;
Referee: Steve Addy (Huddersfield); **Attendance:** 369.

YORK CITY KNIGHTS 18 SHEFFIELD EAGLES 25

CITY KNIGHTS: 1 Johnny Woodcock; 2 Alex Godfrey; 3 Mark Cain; 4 Neil Law; 5 Rob Kama; 6 Scott Rhodes; 7 Danny Brough; 8 Richard Hayes; 9 Lee Jackson; 10 Craig Forsyth; 11 Mick Ramsden; 12 Darren Callaghan; 13 Trevor Krause. Subs (all used): 14 Graeme Hallas; 15 Dan Briggs; 16 Andy Burland; 17 Leigh Riddell.
Tries: Kama (27), A Godfrey (36), Law (45);
Goals: Brough 3.
Sin bin: Godfrey (39) - interference.
EAGLES: 1 Andy Poynter; 2 Tony Weller; 3 Nick Turnbull; 4 Tom O'Reilly; 5 Greg Hurst; 6 Gavin Brown; 7 Mark Aston; 8 Jack Howieson; 9 Gareth Stanley; 10 Jon Bruce; 11 Andy Raleigh; 12 Craig Brown; 13 Wayne Flynn. Subs (all used): 14 Richard Goddard; 15 Simon Tillyer; 16 Neil Kite; 17 Mitchell Stringer.
Tries: Poynter (4, 66), O'Reilly (10, 32);
Goals: G Brown 4; **Field goal:** G Brown.
Rugby Leaguer & League Express Men of the Match: *City Knights:* Neil Law; *Eagles:* Gavin Brown.
Penalty count: 13-8; **Half-time:** 12-14;
Referee: Andrew Leonard (Leeds); **Attendance:** 1,301.

HUNSLET HAWKS 36 CHORLEY LYNX 49

HAWKS: 1 George Rayner; 2 Bryn Powell; 3 Paul Seal; 4 Wes McGibbon; 5 Gareth Brain; 6 Andy Bastow; 7 Phil Hasty; 8 Steve Pryce; 9 Jamaine Wray; 10 Danny Burton; 11 Wayne Freeman; 12 Glen Freeman; 13 Jon Liddell. Subs (all used): 14 Mick Coyle; 15 Jonlee Lockwood; 16 Stephen Doherty; 17 Andy Brent.
Tries: Bastow (17), Hasty (54, 77), Powell (62), Lockwood (71), Doherty (78); **Goals:** Liddell 3, Hasty 3.
LYNX: 1 Mark McCully; 2 Chris Campbell; 3 Anton Garcia; 4 Jamie Stenhouse; 5 Eric Andrews; 6 Mick Coates; 7 Craig Dean; 8 Lee Rowley; 9 Dave McConnell; 10 Craig Wingfield; 11 Mick Redford; 12 Chris Newall; 13 Ian Hodson. Subs (all used): 14 Tim Street; 15 Eddie Kilgannon; 16 John Braddish; 17 Mike Briggs.
Tries: Newall (5, 52), Andrews (22), McCully (41), Garcia (45), McConnell (47, 69), Hodson (75);
Goals: McCully 8; **Field goal:** Coates.
Rugby Leaguer & League Express Men of the Match: *Hawks:* Jamaine Wray; *Lynx:* Craig Dean.
Penalty count: 12-5; **Half-time:** 10-13;
Referee: Gareth Hewer (Whitehaven); **Attendance:** 475.

WEEK 14

Sunday 3rd August 2003

CHORLEY LYNX 41 SWINTON LIONS 22

LYNX: 1 Mark McCully; 2 Chris Campbell; 3 Anton Garcia; 4 Jamie Stenhouse; 5 Eric Andrews; 6 Mick Coates; 7 John Braddish; 8 Craig Wingfield; 9 Dave McConnell; 10 Martin Roden; 11 Mick Redford; 12 Chris Newall; 13 Ian Hodson. Subs (all used): 14 Tim Street; 15 Simon Smith; 16 Anthony Blackwood; 17 Mike Briggs.
Tries: Campbell (2, 77), Andrews (16, 59), Coates (67), Briggs (70), Smith (80); **Goals:** McCully 6;
Field goal: Coates.
LIONS: 1 Wayne English; 2 Hugh Thorpe; 3 Jason Roach; 4 Phil Hassan; 5 Lee Hudson; 6 Rob Gallagher; 7 Chris Hough; 8 Chris Roe; 9 Rob Barraclough; 10 Daniel Tyres; 11 James Lomax; 12 Simon Knox; 13 Peter Cannon. Subs (all used): 14 Grant Bithel; 15 Safraz Patel; 16 Mike Loughlin; 17 Kris Smith.
Tries: Lomax (43), Thorpe (54), English (73);
Goals: Hough 5.
On report: English (77) - high tackle.
Rugby Leaguer & League Express Men of the Match: *Lynx:* Mick Coates; *Lions:* Simon Knox.
Penalty count: 9-11; **Half-time:** 14-6;
Referee: Mike Dawber (Wigan); **Attendance:** 465.

KEIGHLEY COUGARS 18 HUNSLET HAWKS 35

COUGARS: 1 James Rushforth; 2 Karl Smith; 3 David Foster; 4 Matt Foster; 5 Andy Robinson; 6 Paul Ashton; 7 Matt Firth; 8 Phil Stephenson; 9 Simeon Hoyle; 10 Scott Parkin; 11 Oliver Wilkes; 12 Ian Sinfield; 13 Jason Ramshaw. Subs (all used): 14 Chris Wainwright; 15 Ricky Helliwell; 16 Danny Ekis; 17 Chris Hannah.
Tries: Hoyle (17), Firth (34), Robinson (63);
Goals: Ashton 3.
On report: Ramshaw & Hoyle (30) - spear tackle.
HAWKS: 1 Wes McGibbon; 2 Bryn Powell; 3 Paul Seal; 4 Iain Higgins; 5 Chris Hall; 6 Andy Bastow; 7 Phil Hasty; 8 Steve Pryce; 9 Jamaine Wray; 10 Jonlee Lockwood; 11 Wayne Freeman; 12 Danny Burton; 13 Mick Coyle. Subs (all used): 14 Stephen Doherty; 15 Glen Freeman; 16 Chris Parker; 17 Andy Brent.
Tries: Higgins (23), Hasty (27, 59), Bastow (40), Powell (67), Seal (77); **Goals:** Hasty 5; **Field goal:** Hasty.
Sin bin: Bastow (13) - professional foul.
Rugby Leaguer & League Express Men of the Match: *Cougars:* Karl Smith; *Hawks:* Phil Hasty.
Penalty count: 8-9; **Half-time:** 14-16;
Referee: Andrew Leonard (Leeds); **Attendance:** 1,035.

WORKINGTON TOWN 20 BARROW RAIDERS 24

TOWN: 1 Scott Chilton; 2 Glen Hutton; 3 Brett McDermott; 4 Matthew Johnson; 5 Graeme Lewthwaite; 6 Shaun Boylan; 7 Neil Alexander; 8 Matthew Tunstall; 9 Darren King; 10 Hitro Okesene; 11 James Robinson; 12 Gareth Dean; 13 Jamie Beaumont. Subs (all used): 14 Brett Smith; 15 David Pettit; 16 Anthony Horton; 17 Craig Barker.
Tries: Johnson (2, 77), Dean (13); **Goals:** Alexander 4.
RAIDERS: 1 Craig Bower; 2 Jamie Marshall; 3 Jamie Smith; 4 Paul Jones; 5 Shane Irabor; 6 Tane Manihera; 7 Andy Henderson; 8 Tau Liku; 9 Chris Archer; 10 Stuart Dancer; 11 James King; 12 Paul Lupton; 13 Phil Atkinson. Subs (all used): 14 Adam Pate; 15 Geoff Luxon; 16 Andy McClure; 17 Wayne Jones.
Tries: Manihera (5), King (34), Henderson (45), McClure (59), Marshall (65); **Goals:** Manihera 2.
Sin bin: Dancer (30) - holding down.
Rugby Leaguer & League Express Men of the Match: *Town:* Gareth Dean; *Raiders:* Andy Henderson.
Penalty count: 14-12; **Half-time:** 16-8;
Referee: Ben Thaler (Wakefield); **Attendance:** 534.

GATESHEAD THUNDER 8 YORK CITY KNIGHTS 64

THUNDER: 1 Kevin Neighbour; 2 Steve Morton; 3 Damien Reid; 4 Adam Thornton; 5 Richie Barnett; 6 Paul Thorman; 7 Neil Thorman; 8 Yusuf Sozi; 9 Janan Billings; 10 Steven Bradley; 11 Clint Brown; 12 Dave Jessey; 13 Andy Walker. Subs (all used): 14 David Bates; 15 Scott Houston; 16 Scott Harrison; 17 Chris Fletcher.
Tries: Neighbour (18), Thornton (63).
CITY KNIGHTS: 1 Johnny Woodcock; 2 Alex Godfrey; 3 Darren Callaghan; 4 Neil Law; 5 Rob Kama; 6 Mark Cain; 7 Danny Brough; 8 Richard Hayes; 9 Lee Jackson; 10 Joe Helme; 11 Mick Ramsden; 12 Dave Smith; 13 Trevor Krause. Subs (all used): 14 Carl Hughes; 15 Gavin Molloy; 16 Kevin Spink; 17 Craig Forsyth.
Tries: Cain (6), Woodcock (23, 39, 78), Molloy (25), Callaghan (45, 66), Brough (50), A Godfrey (53), Hughes (71), Krause (75); **Goals:** Brough 10.
Sin bin: Cain (55) - dissent.
Rugby Leaguer & League Express Men of the Match: *Thunder:* Scott Houston; *City Knights:* Danny Brough.
Penalty count: 11-8; **Half-time:** 4-22;
Referee: Paul Carr (Castleford); **Attendance:** 413.

SHEFFIELD EAGLES 98 LONDON SKOLARS 4

EAGLES: 1 Andy Poynter; 2 Nick Turnbull; 3 Richard Goddard; 4 Tom O'Reilly; 5 Greg Hurst; 6 Gavin Brown; 7 Mark Aston; 8 Mitchell Stringer; 9 Darren Robinson; 10 Jon Bruce; 11 Andy Raleigh; 12 Craig Brown; 13 Wayne Flynn. Subs (all used): 14 Neil Kite; 15 Simon Tillyer; 16 Jordan James; 17 Gareth Stanley.
Tries: Poynter (3, 55, 61, 67), Stringer (6, 70), O'Reilly (15), Hurst (18, 44, 73), Raleigh (21, 37), Goddard (34), Flynn (39, 51), C Brown (65), Tillyer (75), Robinson (78); **Goals:** G Brown 13.
SKOLARS: 1 Charlie Oyebade; 2 Mario Du Toit; 3 Rubert Jonker; 4 Neil Foster; 5 Mike Okwusogu; 6 Huy Le; 7 Cory Bennett; 8 Graham Hughes; 9 Anthony Dellar; 10 Alex Smits; 11 Matt Walker; 12 David Mossop; 13 Glenn Osborn. Subs (all used): 14 John Clarke; 15 John Warner; 16 Daniel Reeds; 17 Andy Himsley.
Try: Du Toit (31).
Rugby Leaguer & League Express Men of the Match: *Eagles:* Andy Poynter; *Skolars:* Charlie Oyebade.
Penalty count: 6-3; **Half-time:** 44-4;
Referee: Craig Halloran (Dewsbury); **Attendance:** 854.

WEEK 15

Sunday 10th August 2003

KEIGHLEY COUGARS 35 WORKINGTON TOWN 6

COUGARS: 1 Matt Foster; 2 Karl Smith; 3 David Foster; 4 Chris Wainwright; 5 Andy Robinson; 6 Paul Ashton; 7 Matt Firth; 8 Phil Stephenson; 9 Simeon Hoyle; 10 Scott Parkin; 11 Oliver Wilkes; 12 Ian Sinfield; 13 Jason Ramshaw. Subs (all used): 14 Adam Mitchell; 15 Ricky Helliwell; 16 Mick Durham; 17 Richard Mervill.
Tries: D Foster (3), Wilkes (9), Wainwright (22), Helliwell (31), Mitchell (60), Sinfield (74), M Foster (80);
Goals: Ashton, Mitchell 2; **Field goal:** Ashton.
TOWN: 1 Scott Chilton; 2 Glen Hutton; 3 Jamie Beaumont; 4 Matthew Johnson; 5 Graeme Lewthwaite; 6 Shaun Boylan; 7 Neil Alexander; 8 Matthew Tunstall; 9 Darren King; 10 Hitro Okesene; 11 James Robinson; 12 Gareth Dean; 13 Brett Smith. Subs: 14 Anthony Murray; 15 Anthony Horton; 16 Ricky Wright (not used); 17 Craig Barker.
Try: Dean (64); **Goal:** Alexander.
Sin bin: Alexander (30) - holding down,
Murray (79) - dissent.
Rugby Leaguer & League Express Men of the Match: *Cougars:* Richard Mervill; *Town:* Gareth Dean.
Penalty count: 15-7; **Half-time:** 19-0;
Referee: Ben Thaler (Wakefield); **Attendance:** 844.

SWINTON LIONS 34 LONDON SKOLARS 12

LIONS: 1 Wayne English; 2 Hugh Thorpe; 3 Jason Roach; 4 Mike Saunders; 5 Lee Hudson; 6 Rob Gallagher; 7 Grant Bithel; 8 Chris Roe; 9 Peter Cannon; 10 Daniel Tyres; 11 James Lomax; 12 Mike Loughlin; 13 Simon Knox. Subs (all used): 14 Kris Smith; 15 Safraz Patel; 16 Rob Barraclough; 17 Chris Hough.
Tries: Bithel (6), Gallagher (18), Knox (25), Roach (43), Hough (62), English (80); **Goals:** Gallagher, Hough 4.
Sin bin: Knox (52) - obstruction.
SKOLARS: 1 Charlie Oyebade; 2 Mario Du Toit; 3 Jake Johnstone; 4 Neil Foster; 5 Mike Okwusogu; 6 Huy Le; 7 Gareth Honor; 8 Glenn Osborn; 9 Kahu Henare; 10 Alex Smits; 11 Rubert Jonker; 12 David Mossop; 13 Brett McCroary. Subs: 14 Gareth Janes; 15 Daniel Reeds; 16 John Clarke; 17 Mark Croston (not used).
Tries: Janes (11), Le (68); **Goals:** Johnstone, Osborn.
Rugby Leaguer & League Express Men of Match: *Lions:* Wayne English; *Skolars:* Kahu Henare.
Penalty count: 11-4; **Half-time:** 16-6; **Referee:** Steve Nicholson (Whitehaven); **Attendance:** 289.

YORK CITY KNIGHTS 28 BARROW RAIDERS 16

CITY KNIGHTS: 1 Johnny Woodcock; 2 Alex Godfrey; 3 Graeme Hallas; 4 Neil Law; 5 Rob Kama; 6 Mark Cain; 7 Danny Brough; 8 Richard Hayes; 9 Lee Jackson; 10 Joe Helme; 11 Mick Ramsden; 12 Darren Callaghan; 13 Trevor Krause. Subs (all used): 14 Carl Hughes; 15 Gavin Molloy; 16 Kevin Spink; 17 Craig Forsyth.
Tries: Woodcock (22), Krause (36), Jackson (42), Callaghan (59); **Goals:** Brough 6.
RAIDERS: 1 Craig Bower; 2 Jamie Marshall; 3 Jamie Smith; 4 Paul Jones; 5 Shane Irabor; 6 Adam Pate; 7 Andy Henderson; 8 Tau Liku; 9 Chris Archer; 10 Steve Jackson; 11 James King; 12 Andy McClure; 13 Phil Atkinson. Subs (all used): 14 Paul Lupton; 15 Stuart Dancer; 16 James Stainton; 17 Wayne Jones.
Tries: Smith (27), Pate (40); **Goals:** Pate 4.
Rugby Leaguer & League Express Men of the Match:
City Knights: Trevor Krause; *Raiders:* Adam Pate.
Penalty count: 8-6; **Half-time:** 16-14;
Referee: Julian King (St Helens); **Attendance:** 1,063.

SHEFFIELD EAGLES 32 HUNSLET HAWKS 14

EAGLES: 1 Andy Poynter; 2 Nick Turnbull; 3 Richard Goddard; 4 Tom O'Reilly; 5 Greg Hurst; 6 Gavin Brown; 7 Mark Aston; 8 Jack Howieson; 9 Darren Robinson; 10 Jon Bruce; 11 Andy Raleigh; 12 Craig Brown; 13 Wayne Flynn. Subs (all used): 14 Gareth Stanley; 15 Simon Tillyer; 16 Dale Laughton; 17 Mitchell Stringer.
Tries: Turnbull (10), Robinson (15, 74, 77), Raleigh (53); **Goals:** G Brown 6.
HAWKS: 1 Jon Liddell; 2 Bryn Powell; 3 Paul Seal; 4 Iain Higgins; 5 George Rayner; 6 Andy Bastow; 7 Phil Hasty; 8 Steve Pryce; 9 Steve Doherty; 10 Jonlee Lockwood; 11 Wayne Freeman; 12 Chris Parker; 13 Mick Coyle. Subs (all used): 14 Glen Freeman; 15 Andy Brent; 16 David Brook; 17 Steve Jakeman.
Tries: Rayner (62), Brook (72); **Goals:** Hasty 3.
Sin bin: Pryce (37) - late, high challenge on G Brown.
On report: Pryce (37) - late, high challenge on G Brown.
Rugby Leaguer & League Express Men of the Match:
Eagles: Wayne Flynn; *Hawks:* Andy Bastow.
Penalty count: 10-5; **Half-time:** 14-2;
Referee: Mike Dawber (Wigan); **Attendance:** 1,002.

GATESHEAD THUNDER 14 CHORLEY LYNX 22

THUNDER: 1 Kevin Neighbour; 2 Peter Oshagbemi; 3 Damien Reid; 4 Steve Morton; 5 Richie Barnett; 6 Jermaine Coleman; 7 Paul Thorman; 8 Yusuf Sozi; 9 Janan Billings; 10 Steven Bradley; 11 Clint Brown; 12 Scott Houston; 13 Andy Walker. Subs (all used): 14 David Bates; 15 Chris Fletcher; 16 Dave Jessey; 17 Neil Thorman.
Tries: Walker (45), N Thorman (53); **Goals:** P Thorman 3.
LYNX: 1 Mark McCully; 2 Chris Campbell; 3 Anton Garcia; 4 Jamie Stenhouse; 5 Eric Andrews; 6 Mick Coates; 7 Craig Dean; 8 Craig Wingfield; 9 Dave McConnell; 10 Martin Roden; 11 Mick Redford; 12 Eddie Kilgannon; 13 Ian Hodson. Subs (all used): 14 John Braddish; 15 Simon Smith; 16 Tim Street; 17 Mike Briggs.
Tries: Hodson (24), Andrews (60, 64), Campbell (70); **Goals:** McCully 3.
Sin bin: Dean (50) - dissent.
Rugby Leaguer & League Express Men of the Match:
Thunder: Neil Thorman; *Lynx:* Dave McConnell.
Penalty count: 10-9; **Half-time:** 4-8;
Referee: Steve Addy (Huddersfield); **Attendance:** 181.

WEEK 16

Sunday 17th August 2003

BARROW RAIDERS 16 KEIGHLEY COUGARS 18

RAIDERS: 1 Craig Bower; 2 Jamie Marshall; 3 Jamie Smith; 4 Paul Jones; 5 Shane Irabor; 6 Phil Atkinson; 7 Andy Henderson; 8 Tau Liku; 9 Chris Archer; 10 Steve Jackson; 11 James King; 12 Andy McClure; 13 Paul Lupton. Subs (all used): 14 Adam Pate; 15 Geoff Luxon; 16 Stuart Dancer; 17 Wayne Jones.
Tries: Marshall (17), Smith (48); **Goals:** Atkinson 3, Pate.
Sin bin: Luxon (34) - fighting.
COUGARS: 1 Matt Foster; 2 Max Tomlinson; 3 David Foster; 4 Chris Wainwright; 5 Andy Robinson; 6 Adam Mitchell; 7 Matt Firth; 8 Phil Stephenson; 9 Ricky Helliwell; 10 Richard Mervill; 11 Oliver Wilkes; 12 Ian Sinfield; 13 Jason Ramshaw. Subs (all used): 14 James Rushforth; 15 Lee Patterson; 16 Mick Durham; 17 Danny Ekis.
Tries: Robinson (10, 79), Ramshaw (23), D Foster (75); **Goal:** Mitchell.
Dismissal: Ramshaw (74) - punching.
Sin bin: Wilkes (34) - fighting.
Rugby Leaguer & League Express Men of the Match:
Raiders: Andy Henderson; *Cougars:* Adam Mitchell.
Penalty count: 11-9; **Half-time:** 6-10;
Referee: Clive Walker (Oldham); **Attendance:** 826.

CHORLEY LYNX 30 SHEFFIELD EAGLES 14

LYNX: 1 Mark McCully; 2 Chris Campbell; 3 Anton Garcia; 4 Jamie Stenhouse; 5 Eric Andrews; 6 Mick Coates; 7 Craig Dean; 8 Tim Street; 9 Dave McConnell; 10 Martin Roden; 11 Mick Redford; 12 Chris Newall; 13 Ian Hodson. Subs (all used): 14 Craig Wingfield; 15 Simon Smith; 16 Anthony Blackwood; 17 Mike Briggs.
Tries: Campbell (1), Andrews (17), Hodson (32), Coates (50), McConnell (73); **Goals:** McCully 4;
Field goal: McConnell, Dean.
Sin bin: Redford (23) - fighting.
EAGLES: 1 Andy Poynter; 2 Nick Turnbull; 3 Richard

Goddard; 4 Tom O'Reilly; 5 Greg Hurst; 6 Gavin Brown; 7 Mark Aston; 8 Jack Howieson; 9 Darren Robinson; 10 Jon Bruce; 11 Andy Raleigh; 12 Craig Brown; 13 Wayne Flynn. Subs (all used): 14 Gareth Stanley; 15 Simon Tillyer; 16 Dale Laughton; 17 Mitchell Stringer.
Tries: Poynter (59), Raleigh (63); **Goals:** G Brown 3.
Sin bin: Aston (23) - fighting; G Brown (30) - punching.
Rugby Leaguer & League Express Men of the Match:
Lynx: Dave McConnell; *Eagles:* Mark Aston.
Penalty count: 7-10; **Half-time:** 17-2;
Referee: Ben Thaler (Wakefield); **Attendance:** 502.

SWINTON LIONS 38 YORK CITY KNIGHTS 16

LIONS: 1 Wayne English; 2 Hugh Thorpe; 3 Jason Roach; 4 Kris Tassell; 5 Lee Hudson; 6 Chris Hough; 7 Grant Bithel; 8 Daniel Tyres; 9 Peter Cannon; 10 Simon Knox; 11 Andy Gorski; 12 Darren Barton; 13 Rob Gallagher. Subs (all used): 14 Mike Saunders; 15 Kris Smith; 16 Chris Roe; 17 Mike Loughlin.
Tries: Hudson (8, 80), Tassell (19), Roach (23, 33, 62), Loughlin (54); **Goals:** Hough 4; **Field goal:** Hough 2.
CITY KNIGHTS: 1 James Brown; 2 Alex Godfrey; 3 Graeme Hallas; 4 Darren Callaghan; 5 Rob Kama; 6 Carl Hughes; 7 Danny Brough; 8 Richard Hayes; 9 Lee Jackson; 10 Joe Helme; 11 Mick Ramsden; 12 Dave Smith; 13 Trevor Krause. Subs (all used): 14 Leigh Deakin; 15 Gavin Molloy; 16 Mark Cain; 17 Craig Forsyth.
Tries: Hughes (2), Kama (65, 73); **Goals:** Brough 2.
Sin bin: Brown (32) - obstruction.
Rugby Leaguer & League Express Men of the Match:
Lions: Wayne English; *City Knights:* Carl Hughes.
Penalty count: 7-6; **Half-time:** 22-6;
Referee: Steve Addy (Huddersfield); **Attendance:** 551.

WORKINGTON TOWN 32 GATESHEAD THUNDER 18

TOWN: 1 Scott Chilton; 2 Glen Hutton; 3 Brett McDermott; 4 Matthew Johnson; 5 Graeme Lewthwaite; 6 Neil Alexander; 7 Anthony Murray; 8 Matthew Tunstall; 9 Darren King; 10 Hitro Okesene; 11 James Robinson; 12 Gareth Dean; 13 Ricky Wright. Subs (all used): 14 Shaun Boylan; 15 Jamie Beaumont; 16 Anthony Horton; 17 Gary Charlton.
Tries: Lewthwaite (2), Tunstall (30), Johnson (35, 72), Boylan (37, 78); **Goals:** Alexander 4.
THUNDER: 1 Kevin Neighbour; 2 Steve Morton; 3 Andy Walker; 4 Damien Reid; 5 Richie Barnett; 6 Jermaine Coleman; 7 Paul Thorman; 8 Yusuf Sozi; 9 Chris Fletcher; 10 Steven Bradley; 11 Scott Houston; 12 Dave Jessey; 13 Steve Rutherford. Subs (all used): 14 David Bates; 15 Janan Billings; 16 Scott Harrison; 17 Neil Thorman.
Tries: Bradley (43), Walker (47), Reid (60);
Goals: P Thorman 3.
Dismissal: Houston (67) - serious foul play.
On report: N Thorman (56) - high tackle.
Rugby Leaguer & League Express Men of the Match:
Town: Hitro Okesene; *Thunder:* Paul Thorman.
Penalty count: 6-5; **Half-time:** 22-2;
Referee: Craig Halloran (Dewsbury); **Attendance:** 406.

HUNSLET HAWKS 64 LONDON SKOLARS 14

HAWKS: 1 Jon Liddell; 2 Bryn Powell; 3 Paul Seal; 4 Steve Jakeman; 5 George Rayner; 6 Andy Bastow; 7 Phil Hasty; 8 Steve Pryce; 9 Jamaine Wray; 10 Jonlee Lockwood; 11 Wayne Freeman; 12 Danny Burton; 13 Danny Fearon. Subs (all used): 14 Andy Brent; 15 Glen

Freeman; 16 David Brook; 17 Stephen Doherty.
Tries: Liddell (5), Pryce (7, 20), Burton (12), W Freeman (18, 61), Powell (36, 71), Hasty (47, 57, 68), Jakeman (55); **Goals:** Hasty 8.
Sin bin: Brent (66) - fighting.
SKOLARS: 1 Charlie Oyebade; 2 Mario Du Toit; 3 Jake Johnstone; 4 Neil Foster; 5 Mike Okwusogu; 6 Huy Le; 7 Gareth Honor; 8 Gareth Janes; 9 Kahu Henare; 10 Alex Smits; 11 Glenn Osborn; 12 Rubert Jonker; 13 Ronald Mushiso. Subs (all used): 14 Donny Lam; 15 Roger Teau; 16 Daniel Reeds; 17 John Clarke.
Tries: Jonker (26, 50), Le (42); **Goal:** Johnstone.
Rugby Leaguer & League Express Men of the Match:
Hawks: Steve Pryce; *Skolars:* Rubert Jonker.
Penalty count: 8-7; **Half-time:** 30-4;
Referee: Paul Carr (Castleford); **Attendance:** 342.

WEEK 17

Sunday 24th August 2003

CHORLEY LYNX 52 BARROW RAIDERS 24

LYNX: 1 Mark McCully; 2 Chris Campbell; 3 Anton Garcia; 4 Jamie Stenhouse; 5 Eric Andrews; 6 Mick Coates; 7 Craig Dean; 8 Tim Street; 9 Mike Briggs; 10 Martin Roden; 11 Mick Redford; 12 Chris Newall; 13 Ian Hodson. Subs (all used): 14 Simon Smith; 15 Anthony Blackwood; 16 John Braddish; 17 Eddie Kilgannon.
Tries: Garcia (3, 18), Newall (30, 33), Andrews (36, 56), Dean (49, 80), Redford (53); **Goals:** McCully 8.
RAIDERS: 1 Craig Bower; 2 Jamie Marshall; 3 Jamie Smith; 4 Andy McClure; 5 Paul Jones; 6 Adam Pate; 7 Paul Evans; 8 Tau Liku; 9 Chris Archer; 10 James King; 11 Paul Lupton; 12 Steve Jackson; 13 Andy Henderson. Subs (all used): 14 Phil Atkinson; 15 Stuart Dancer; 16 Wayne Jones; 17 James Stainton.
Tries: McClure (13), Smith (23), King (39), Dancer (62); **Goals:** Pate 4.
Rugby Leaguer & League Express Men of the Match:
Lynx: Chris Newall; *Raiders:* James King.
Penalty count: 4-7; **Half-time:** 28-18;
Referee: Mike Dawber (Wigan); **Attendance:** 424.

KEIGHLEY COUGARS 10 SHEFFIELD EAGLES 22

COUGARS: 1 Matt Foster; 2 Max Tomlinson; 3 David Foster; 4 Chris Wainwright; 5 Andy Robinson; 6 Adam Mitchell; 7 Matt Firth; 8 Phil Stephenson; 9 Mick Durham; 10 Richard Mervill; 11 Oliver Wilkes; 12 Ian Sinfield; 13 Jason Ramshaw. Subs (all used): 14 James Rushforth; 15 Lee Patterson; 16 Ricky Helliwell; 17 Danny Ekis.
Try: M Foster (14); **Goals:** Mitchell 3.
EAGLES: 1 Andy Poynter; 2 Tony Weller; 3 Nick Turnbull; 4 Tom O'Reilly; 5 Greg Hurst; 6 Gavin Brown; 7 Mark Aston; 8 Jack Howieson; 9 Gareth Stanley; 10 Jon Bruce; 11 Andy Raleigh; 12 Craig Brown; 13 Wayne Flynn. Subs (all used): 14 Peter Neilly; 15 Simon Tillyer; 16 Richard Goddard; 17 Mitchell Stringer.
Tries: Poynter (44), Reilly (54), Goddard (71);
Goals: G Brown 5.
Sin bin: Goddard (34) - interference.
Rugby Leaguer & League Express Men of the Match:
Cougars: Ian Sinfield; *Eagles:* Jon Bruce.
Penalty count: 13-13; **Half-time:** 10-2;
Referee: Steve Addy (Huddersfield); **Attendance:** 1,468.

Sheffield's Jon Bruce takes on Keighley duo Phil Stephenson and Ian Sinfield

LONDON SKOLARS 48 GATESHEAD THUNDER 14

SKOLARS: 1 Charlie Oyebade; 2 Mike Okwusogu; 3 Paul Leef; 4 Neil Foster; 5 Ronald Mushiso; 6 Jake Johnstone; 7 Gareth Honor; 8 Gareth Janes; 9 Kahu Henare; 10 Alex Smits; 11 Brett McCroary; 12 Rubert Jonker; 13 Glenn Osborn. Subs (all used): 14 Donny Lam; 15 Huy Le; 16 Mario Du Toit; 17 David Mossop.
Tries: Smits (12), Jonker (32, 50), Janes (37), Mushiso (44, 61), Leef (69); **Goals:** Johnstone 10.
THUNDER: 1 Kevin Neighbour; 2 Peter Oshagbemi; 3 Steve Morton; 4 Damien Reid; 5 Richie Barnett; 6 Jermaine Coleman; 7 Paul Thorman; 8 Yusuf Sozi; 9 Janan Billings; 10 Steven Bradley; 11 Clint Brown; 12 Scott Houston; 13 Steve Rutherford. Subs (all used): 14 Scott Harrison; 15 Andy Walker; 16 Chris Fletcher; 17 Neil Thorman.
Tries: Sozi (15), Morton (65); **Goals:** P Thorman 3.
Rugby Leaguer & League Express Men of the Match:
Skolars: Jake Johnstone; *Thunder:* Yusuf Sozi.
Penalty count: 11-10; **Half-time:** 18-8;
Referee: Ben Thaler (Wakefield); **Attendance:** 307.

YORK CITY KNIGHTS 36 WORKINGTON TOWN 16

CITY KNIGHTS: 1 George Mack; 2 Alex Godfrey; 3 Graeme Hallas; 4 Mark Stewart; 5 Rob Kama; 6 Carl Hughes; 7 Danny Brough; 8 Richard Hayes; 9 Lee Jackson; 10 Joe Helme; 11 Kevin Spink; 12 Darren Callaghan; 13 Trevor Krause. Subs (all used): 14 Leigh Deakin; 15 John Okul; 16 James Brown; 17 Craig Forsyth.
Tries: Krause (10), A Godfrey (31), Hallas (42), Kama (59), Callaghan (74), Spink (77); **Goals:** Brough 6.
TOWN: 1 Scott Chilton; 2 Glen Hutton; 3 Brett McDermott; 4 Matthew Johnson; 5 Graeme Lewthwaite; 6 Shaun Boylan; 7 Neil Alexander; 8 Matthew Tunstall; 9 Anthony Murray; 10 Hitro Okesene; 11 James Robinson; 12 Gareth Dean; 13 Jamie Beaumont. Subs: 14 Darren King; 15 Anthony Horton; 16 Andrew Fearon; 17 Craig Barker (not used).
Tries: Chilton (3), Hutton (22), Murray (52);
Goals: Alexander 2.
Rugby Leaguer & League Express Men of the Match:
City Knights: Darren Callaghan; *Town:* Scott Chilton.
Penalty count: 9-9; **Half-time:** 12-10;
Referee: Andrew Leonard (Leeds); **Attendance:** 1,106.

HUNSLET HAWKS 46 SWINTON LIONS 14

HAWKS: 1 Jon Liddell; 2 Bryn Powell; 3 Wes McGibbon; 4 Steve Jakeman; 5 George Rayner; 6 Andy Bastow; 7 Phil Hasty; 8 Steve Pryce; 9 Jamaine Wray; 10 Jonlee Lockwood; 11 Wayne Freeman; 12 Glen Freeman; 13 Danny Fearon. Subs (all used): 14 Andy Brent; 15 Stephen Doherty; 16 Mick Coyle; 17 Iain Higgins.
Tries: Pryce (4), Lockwood (11), Powell (15, 39), W Freeman (20), Bastow (52), Rayner (70), Fearon (74);
Goals: Hasty 7.
Sin bin: Fearon (34) - kicking the ball away.
LIONS: 1 Wayne English; 2 Hugh Thorpe; 3 Jason Roach; 4 Kris Tassell; 5 Greg McAvoy; 6 Chris Hough; 7 Grant Bithel; 8 Danny Tyres; 9 Rob Barraclough; 10 Simon Knox; 11 Andy Gorski; 12 Danny Barton; 13 Rob Gallagher. Subs (all used): 14 Kris Smith; 15 Mike Loughlin; 16 Safraz Patel; 17 Chris Roe.
Tries: Gorski (26), Thorpe (41); **Goals:** Hough 3.
Rugby Leaguer & League Express Men of the Match:
Hawks: Wayne Freeman; *Lions:* Safraz Patel.
Penalty count: 9-15; **Half-time:** 28-8;
Referee: Clive Walker (Oldham); **Attendance:** 621.

WEEK 18

Sunday 31st August 2003

BARROW RAIDERS 52 HUNSLET HAWKS 10

RAIDERS: 1 Craig Bower; 2 Jamie Marshall; 3 Jamie Smith; 4 Andy McClure; 5 Adam Pate; 6 Tane Manihera; 7 Andy Henderson; 8 Tau Liku; 9 Dave Clark; 10 Wayne Jones; 11 James King; 12 Paul Lupton; 13 Phil Atkinson. Subs (all used): 14 Paul Evans; 15 Geoff Luxon; 16 Stuart Dancer; 17 James Stainton.
Tries: Smith (4), Pate (8, 77), McClure (12, 45), King (22), Clark (47), Atkinson (60, 65), Bower (74);
Goals: Pate 6.
HAWKS: 1 Jon Liddell; 2 Bryn Powell; 3 Wes McGibbon; 4 Steve Jakeman; 5 George Rayner; 6 Andy Bastow; 7 Phil Hasty; 8 Steve Pryce; 9 Jamaine Wray; 10 Jonlee Lockwood; 11 Wayne Freeman; 12 Glen Freeman; 13 Danny Fearon. Subs (all used): 14 Stephen Doherty; 15 Mick Coyle; 16 Ian Higgins; 17 Chris Parker.
Tries: Lockwood (50), Doherty (54); **Goal:** Hasty.
Rugby Leaguer & League Express Men of the Match:
Raiders: Dave Clark; *Hawks:* Phil Hasty.
Penalty count: 6-3; **Half-time:** 20-0;
Referee: Peter Taberner (Wigan); **Attendance:** 763.

SWINTON LIONS 17 KEIGHLEY COUGARS 19

LIONS: 1 Wayne English; 2 Lee Hudson; 3 Kris Tassell; 4 Phil Hassan; 5 Hugh Thorpe; 6 Rob Gallagher; 7 Chris Hough; 8 Chris Roe; 9 Peter Cannon; 10 Simon Knox; 11 Andy Gorski; 12 Danny Barton; 13 Robert Russell. Subs (all used): 14 Safraz Patel; 15 Jason Roach; 16 Mike Loughlin; 17 Rob Barraclough.
Tries: Cannon (43), Tassell (71), Roach (79);
Goals: Hough 2; **Field goal:** Hough.
COUGARS: 1 Matt Foster; 2 Max Tomlinson; 3 David Foster; 4 James Rushforth; 5 Andy Robinson; 6 Paul Ashton; 7 Matt Firth; 8 Phil Stephenson; 9 Simeon Hoyle; 10 Richard Mervill; 11 Oliver Wilkes; 12 Ian Sinfield; 13

Jason Ramshaw. Subs (all used): 14 Lee Patterson; 15 Mick Durham; 16 Ricky Helliwell; 17 Scott Parkin.
Tries: Sinfield (13, 22), Robinson (25); **Goals:** Ashton 3;
Field goal: Ashton.
On report: Biting incident (60).
Rugby Leaguer & League Express Men of the Match:
Lions: Andy Gorski; *Cougars:* Matt Firth.
Penalty count: 14-8; **Half-time:** 3-18;
Referee: Mike Dawber (Wigan); **Attendance:** 507.

WORKINGTON TOWN 80 LONDON SKOLARS 18

TOWN: 1 Scott Chilton; 2 Glen Hutton; 3 Brett McDermott; 4 Matthew Johnson; 5 Graeme Lewthwaite; 6 Shaun Boylan; 7 Neil Alexander; 8 Matthew Tunstall; 9 Anthony Murray; 10 Hitro Okesene; 11 James Robinson; 12 Gareth Dean; 13 Jamie Beaumont. Subs (all used): 14 Darren King; 15 David Pettit; 16 Andrew Fearon; 17 Craig Barker.
Tries: McDermott (1), Dean (4), Lewthwaite (7, 11, 37, 40, 62), Boylan (15, 76), Alexander (22), Beaumont (30), Okesene (53, 74), Hutton (56, 65), King (59);
Goals: Alexander 7, Robinson.
SKOLARS: 1 Charlie Oyebade; 2 Mike Okwusogu; 3 Paul Leef; 4 Neil Foster; 5 Mario Du Toit; 6 Jake Johnstone; 7 Cory Bennett; 8 Gareth Janes; 9 Ben Baxter; 10 Alex Smits; 11 David Mossop; 12 Rubert Jonker; 13 Daniel Reeds. Subs: 14 Ben Wakeley; 15 Glen Hoare; 16 Robert Brown; 17 Mark Croston (not used).
Tries: Baxter (27), Okwusogu (47), Leef (64);
Goals: Johnstone 2, Baxter.
Rugby Leaguer & League Express Men of the Match:
Town: Graeme Lewthwaite; *Skolars:* Ben Baxter.
Penalty count: 9-5; **Half-time:** 46-6;
Referee: Clive Walker (Oldham); **Attendance:** 451.

YORK CITY KNIGHTS 36 CHORLEY LYNX 32

CITY KNIGHTS: 1 Alex Godfrey; 2 Leigh Deakin; 3 Graeme Hallas; 4 Mark Stewart; 5 Rob Kama; 6 Carl Hughes; 7 Danny Brough; 8 Richard Hayes; 9 Lee Jackson; 10 Joe Helme; 11 Darren Callaghan; 12 Leigh Riddell; 13 Trevor Krause. Subs (all used): 14 James Brown; 15 Neil Mears; 16 John Okul; 17 Craig Forsyth.
Tries: Kama (1), Stewart (11, 35), Hallas (44), Okul (51), A Godfrey (63);
LYNX: 1 Mark McCully; 2 Chris Campbell; 3 Anton Garcia; 4 Jamie Stenhouse; 5 Eric Andrews; 6 Mick Coates; 7 Craig Dean; 8 Tim Street; 9 Mike Briggs; 10 Martin Roden; 11 Mick Redford; 12 Chris Newall; 13 Ian Hodson. Subs (all used): 14 Simon Smith; 15 Anthony Blackwood; 16 Lee Rowley; 17 John Braddish.
Tries: Briggs (7, 29), Dean (19), Stenhouse (21), Newall (41), Andrews (66); **Goals:** McCully 4.
Rugby Leaguer & League Express Men of the Match:
City Knights: Danny Brough; *Lynx:* Mick Coates.
Penalty count: 6-6; **Half-time:** 18-22;
Referee: Steve Addy (Huddersfield); **Attendance:** 1,077.

GATESHEAD THUNDER 24 SHEFFIELD EAGLES 48

THUNDER: 1 Kevin Neighbour; 2 Peter Oshagbemi; 3 Steve Morton; 4 Damien Reid; 5 Richie Barnett; 6 Ryan Robinson; 7 Paul Thorman; 8 Yusuf Sozi; 9 Janan Billings; 10 Steven Bradley; 11 Steve Rutherford; 12 Scott Houston; 13 Chris Fletcher. Subs (all used): 14 Scott Harrison; 15 Jermaine Coleman; 16 Clint Brown; 17 Neil Thorman.
Tries: Morton (11), Barnett (32, 53), Reid (72);

Chorley's Craig Dean skips past York's Darren Callaghan to score

Goals: P Thorman 4.
EAGLES: 1 Andy Poynter; 2 Greg Hurst; 3 Tony Weller; 4 Tom O'Reilly; 5 Carl De Chenu; 6 Gavin Brown; 7 Peter Reilly; 8 Jack Howieson; 9 Lee Bettinson; 10 Jon Bruce; 11 Andy Raleigh; 12 Craig Brown; 13 Wayne Flynn. Subs (all used): 14 Richard Goddard; 15 Simon Tillyer; 16 Dale Laughton; 17 Mitchell Stringer.
Tries: Flynn (2, 28), O'Reilly (8), De Chenu (22), Reilly (25, 65), Raleigh (37), Goddard (47), Bruce (75);
Goals: G Brown 6.
Rugby Leaguer & League Express Men of the Match:
Thunder: Steve Morton; *Eagles:* Peter Reilly.
Penalty count: 8-14; **Half-time:** 14-30;
Referee: Andrew Leonard (Leeds); **Attendance:** 263.

Friday 5th September 2003

YORK CITY KNIGHTS 32 HUNSLET HAWKS 16

CITY KNIGHTS: 1 Alex Godfrey; 2 Leigh Deakin; 3 Graeme Hallas; 4 Mark Stewart; 5 Rob Kama; 6 Carl Hughes; 7 Danny Brough; 8 Richard Hayes; 9 Lee Jackson; 10 Joe Helme; 11 Mick Ramsden; 12 Darren Callaghan; 13 Trevor Krause. Subs (all used): 14 Stuart Godfrey; 15 Neil Mears; 16 Dan Briggs; 17 Craig Forsyth.
Tries: A Godfrey (30), Hallas (44, 70), Hughes (64), S Godfrey (78); **Goals:** Brough 6.
Dismissal: Kama (11) - stamping.
Sin bin: Krause (23) - fighting.
HAWKS: 1 Jon Liddell; 2 Bryn Powell; 3 Steve Jakeman; 4 Iain Higgins; 5 George Rayner; 6 Andy Bastow; 7 Phil Hasty; 8 Danny Fearon; 9 Stephen Doherty; 10 Andy Brent; 11 Wayne Freeman; 12 Shaun Ibbetson; 13 Mick Coyle. Subs (all used): 14 Jonlee Lockwood; 15 Glen Freeman; 16 Craig Taylor; 17 Joe Hawley.
Tries: Rayner (13), W Freeman (40), Liddell (76);
Goals: Hasty, Liddell.
Dismissal: S Ibbetson (23) - violent conduct.
Sin bin: Coyle (23) - fighting; Hasty (48) - holding down.
Rugby Leaguer & League Express Men of the Match:
City Knights: Alex Godfrey; *Hawks:* Stephen Doherty.
Penalty count: 7-8; **Half-time:** 10-10; **Referee:** Steve Nicholson (Whitehaven); **Attendance:** 1,642.

Saturday 6th September 2003

SHEFFIELD EAGLES 56 WORKINGTON TOWN 11

EAGLES: 1 Andy Poynter; 2 Tony Weller; 3 Richard Goddard; 4 Tom O'Reilly; 5 Jon Breakingbury; 6 Gavin Brown; 7 Mark Aston; 8 Jack Howieson; 9 Gareth Stanley; 10 Jon Bruce; 11 Andy Raleigh; 12 Craig Brown; 13 Wayne Flynn. Subs (all used): 14 Peter Reilly; 15 Simon Tillyer; 16 Dale Laughton; 17 Mitchell Stringer.
Tries: O'Reilly (2, 14), Goddard (6), Weller (31, 46), Raleigh (40, 64), Breakingbury (41), G Brown (51), Aston (67), Reilly (73); **Goals:** G Brown 6.
TOWN: 1 Andrew Fearon; 2 Glen Hutton; 3 Brett McDermott; 4 Matthew Johnson; 5 Graeme Lewthwaite; 6 Shaun Boylan; 7 Neil Alexander; 8 Craig Barker; 9 Anthony Murray; 10 Hitro Okesene; 11 James Robinson; 12 Gareth Dean; 13 Jamie Beaumont. Subs (all used): 14 Dean Sharp; 15 David Petitt; 16 Scott Chilton; 17 Anthony Horton.
Tries: Beaumont (30), Robinson (51); **Goal:** Alexander;
Field goal: Alexander.
Rugby Leaguer & League Express Men of the Match:
Eagles: Gavin Brown; *Town:* Neil Alexander.
Penalty count: 9-7; **Half-time:** 26-4;
Referee: Ben Thaler (Wakefield); **Attendance:** 1,011.

York's Joe Helme halted against Hunslet

WEEK 19

Sunday 7th September 2003

LONDON SKOLARS 12 CHORLEY LYNX 38

SKOLARS: 1 Charlie Oyebade; 2 Ronald Mushiso; 3 Paul Leef; 4 Neil Foster; 5 Mario Du Toit; 6 Huy Le; 7 Ben Baxter; 8 Glenn Osborn; 9 Kahu Henare; 10 Alex Smits; 11 Brett McCroary; 12 Rubert Jonker; 13 Mike Okwusogu. Subs (all used): 14 Cory Bennett; 15 Keir Bell; 16 Daniel Reeds; 17 Obi Ijeoma.
Tries: Jonker (35), Okwusogu (70); **Goals:** Osborn 2.
Dismissal: Jonker (43) – use of elbow.
LYNX: 1 Mark McCully; 2 Chris Campbell; 3 Anton Garcia; 4 Jamie Stenhouse; 5 Eric Andrews; 6 Mick Coates; 7 Craig Dean; 8 Tim Street; 9 Mike Briggs; 10 Mick Redford; 11 Anthony Blackwood; 12 Chris Newall; 13 Ian Hodson. Subs (all used): 14 Simon Smith; 15 Craig Wingfield; 16 John Braddish; 17 David Ingram.
Tries: Blackwood (8, 24), Stenhouse (20, 62), Andrews (39), Smith (64), Newall (74); **Goals:** McCully 5.
Rugby Leaguer & League Express Men of the Match:
Skolars: Alex Smits; *Lynx:* Jamie Stenhouse.
Penalty count: 9-8; **Half-time:** 6-22;
Referee: Julian King (St Helens); **Attendance:** 257.

SWINTON LIONS 34 BARROW RAIDERS 38

LIONS: 1 Wayne English; 2 Hugh Thorpe; 3 Jason Roach; 4 Kris Tassell; 5 Lee Hudson; 6 Grant Bithel; 7 Chris Hough; 8 Simon Knox; 9 Peter Cannon; 10 Andy Gorski; 11 Mike Loughlin; 12 Danny Barton; 13 Robert Russell. Subs (all used, three subs only): 14 Safraz Patel; 15 Phil Hassan; 16 Rob Barraclough.
Tries: Barton (39), Bithel (15), Barraclough (52), Roach (56), Hudson (65), Tassell (68), Hough (72);
Goals: Hough 2, Russell.
Dismissal: Cannon (47) - dissent, following sin-binning.
RAIDERS: 1 Craig Bower; 2 Shane Irabor; 3 Jamie Smith; 4 Andy McClure; 5 Adam Pate; 6 Phil Atkinson; 7 Andy Henderson; 8 Tau Liku; 9 Dave Clark; 10 Wayne Jones; 11 James King; 12 Paul Lupton; 13 Barry Pugh. Subs (all used): 14 Chris Archer; 15 Stuart Dancer; 16 James Stainton; 17 Paul Wilcock.
Tries: Lupton (2), Liku (11), McClure (28), Archer (37), Wilcock (40), W Jones (61); **Goals:** Pate 7.
Rugby Leaguer & League Express Men of the Match:
Lions: Simon Knox; *Raiders:* Adam Pate.
Penalty count: 6-5; **Half-time:** 10-32;
Referee: Steve Presley (Castleford); **Attendance:** 455.

GATESHEAD THUNDER 16 KEIGHLEY COUGARS 21

THUNDER: 1 Kevin Neighbour; 2 Peter Oshagbemi; 3 Steve Morton; 4 Damien Reid; 5 Richie Barnett; 6 Jermaine Coleman; 7 Paul Thorman; 8 Yusuf Sozi; 9 Janan Billings; 10 Steven Bradley; 11 Clint Brown; 12 Steve Rutherford; 13 Chris Fletcher. Subs (all used): 14 Scott Houston; 15 Ryan Robinson; 16 Andy Walker; 17 Neil Thorman.

Tries: Sozi (2), Janan Billings (23), Reid (36);
Goals: P Thorman 2.
COUGARS: 1 Matt Foster; 2 Max Tomlinson; 3 David Foster; 4 James Rushforth; 5 Andy Robinson; 6 Paul Ashton; 7 Matt Firth; 8 Phil Stephenson; 9 Simeon Hoyle; 10 Mick Durham; 11 Oliver Wilkes; 12 Ian Sinfield; 13 Jason Ramshaw. Subs: 14 Karl Smith; 15 Lee Patterson; 16 Danny Ekis; 17 Scott Parkin (not used).
Tries: D Foster (7), Wilkes (43), Smith (49, 55);
Goals: Ashton 2; **Field goal:** Ashton.
Rugby Leaguer & League Express Men of the Match:
Thunder: Yusuf Sozi; *Cougars:* Oliver Wilkes.
Penalty count: 8-7; **Half-time:** 16-6;
Referee: Steve Addy (Huddersfield); **Attendance:** 349.

PLAY-OFFS

Sunday 14th September 2003

ELIMINATION PLAY-OFFS

KEIGHLEY COUGARS 25 HUNSLET HAWKS 12

COUGARS: 1 Matt Foster; 2 Max Tomlinson; 3 David Foster; 4 James Rushforth; 5 Andy Robinson; 6 Paul Ashton; 7 Matt Firth; 8 Phil Stephenson; 9 Simeon Hoyle; 10 Danny Ekis; 11 Oliver Wilkes; 12 Ian Sinfield; 13 Lee Patterson. Subs (all used): 14 Chris Wainwright; 15 Jason Ramshaw; 16 Mick Durham; 17 Richard Mervill.
Tries: Mervill (36), Sinfield (55); **Goals:** Ashton 8;
Field goal: Ashton.
HAWKS: 1 Jon Liddell; 2 Bryn Powell; 3 Wes McGibbon; 4 Steve Jakeman; 5 Iain Higgins; 6 Andy Bastow; 7 Phil Hasty; 8 Steve Pryce; 9 Stephen Doherty; 10 Danny Fearon; 11 Wayne Freeman; 12 Shaun Ibbetson; 13 Mick Coyle. Subs (all used): 14 Jamaine Wray; 15 Craig Taylor; 16 Glen Freeman; 17 Andy Brent.
Tries: Doherty (47), W Freeman (75); **Goals:** Hasty 2.
Sin bin: Hasty (28) - professional foul.
Rugby Leaguer & League Express Men of the Match:
Cougars: Richard Mervill; *Hawks:* Mick Coyle.
Penalty count: 10-11; **Half-time:** 12-4; **Referee:** Ronnie Laughton (Barnsley); **Attendance:** 1,150.

YORK CITY KNIGHTS 30 BARROW RAIDERS 50

CITY KNIGHTS: 1 Alex Godfrey; 2 Stuart Godfrey; 3 Graeme Hallas; 4 Mark Stewart; 5 Rob Kama; 6 Scott Rhodes; 7 Danny Brough; 8 Richard Hayes; 9 Lee Jackson; 10 Joe Helme; 11 Mick Ramsden; 12 Darren Callaghan; 13 Trevor Krause. Subs (all used): 14 Carl Hughes; 15 Dan Briggs; 16 Neil Mears; 17 Craig Forsyth.
Tries: Hughes (26), Krause (33), Callaghan (63), S Godfrey (78), A Godfrey (80); **Goals:** Brough 5.
Dismissal: Hallas (55) - punching.
RAIDERS: 1 Craig Bower; 2 Jamie Marshall; 3 Jamie Smith; 4 Paul Jones; 5 Adam Pate; 6 Tane Manihera; 7 Andy Henderson; 8 Tau Liku; 9 Dave Clark; 10 James King; 11 Andy McClure; 12 Paul Lupton; 13 Phil Atkinson. Subs (all used): 14 Chris Archer; 15 Geoff Luxon; 16 Wayne Jones; 17 Stuart Dancer.
Tries: P Jones (20, 75), Henderson (24), Marshall (37), Pate (43, 50), Bower (65), Clark (70); **Goals:** Pate 9.
Sin bin: Smith (53) - throwing ball at opponent.
Rugby Leaguer & League Express Men of the Match:
City Knights: Rob Kama; *Raiders:* Andy Henderson.
Penalty count: 3-6; **Half-time:** 12-20; **Referee:** Colin Morris (Huddersfield); **Attendance:** 1,299.

Sheffield's Richard Goddard collars Chorley's Jamie Stenhouse
during the Qualifying Semi Final

Keighley's Phil Stephenson offloads to Simeon Hoyle under heavy Sheffield pressure during the National League Two Grand Final

Sunday 21st September 2003

ELIMINATION SEMI-FINAL

KEIGHLEY COUGARS 35 BARROW RAIDERS 26

COUGARS: 1 Matt Foster; 2 Max Tomlinson; 3 David Foster; 4 James Rushforth; 5 Andy Robinson; 6 Paul Ashton; 7 Matt Firth; 8 Phil Stephenson; 9 Simeon Hoyle; 10 Danny Ekis; 11 Oliver Wilkes; 12 Ian Sinfield; 13 Lee Patterson. Subs: 14 Chris Wainwright (not used); 15 Richard Mervill; 16 Mick Durham; 17 Jason Ramshaw.
Tries: Ashton (27, 49), Ramshaw (64), Rushforth (70); **Goals:** Ashton 9; **Field goal:** Ashton.
RAIDERS: 1 Craig Bower; 2 Jamie Marshall; 3 Jamie Smith; 4 Paul Jones; 5 Adam Pate; 6 Tane Manihera; 7 Andy Henderson; 8 Tau Liku; 9 Dave Clark; 10 James King; 11 Paul Lupton; 12 Andy McClure; 13 Phil Atkinson. Subs (all used): 14 Chris Archer; 15 Geoff Luxon; 16 Wayne Jones; 17 Stuart Dancer.
Tries: Pate (59, 78), Bower (75), King (79), P Jones (80); **Goals:** Pate 3.
Sin bin: King (10) - professional foul.
Rugby Leaguer & League Express Men of the Match: *Cougars:* Paul Ashton; *Raiders:* Tane Manihera.
Penalty count: 8-5; **Half-time:** 13-0; **Referee:** Ronnie Laughton (Barnsley); **Attendance:** 1,332.

QUALIFYING SEMI-FINAL

SHEFFIELD EAGLES 31 CHORLEY LYNX 14

EAGLES: 1 Andy Poynter; 2 Tony Weller; 3 Richard Goddard; 4 Tom O'Reilly; 5 Jon Breakingbury; 6 Gavin Brown; 7 Mark Aston; 8 Jack Howieson; 9 Gareth Stanley; 10 Jon Bruce; 11 Andy Raleigh; 12 Craig Brown; 13 Wayne Flynn. Subs (all used): 14 Peter Reilly; 15 Simon Tillyer; 16 Greg Hurst; 17 Mitchell Stringer.
Tries: Goddard (2), Poynter (15), Raleigh (22), G Brown (69), O'Reilly (74); **Goals:** G Brown 4;
Field goals: Aston, G Brown 2.
LYNX: 1 Mark McCully; 2 Chris Campbell; 3 Anton Garcia; 4 Jamie Stenhouse; 5 Eric Andrews; 6 Mick Coates; 7 Craig Dean; 8 Tim Street; 9 Mike Briggs; 10 Martin Roden; 11 Mick Redford; 12 Anthony Blackwood; 13 Ian Hodson. Subs (all used): 14 Simon Smith; 15 Craig Wingfield; 16 David Ingram; 17 John Braddish.
Tries: Braddish (35), Redford (72); **Goals:** McCully 3.
Sin bin: Street (35) - dissent.
Rugby Leaguer & League Express Men of the Match: *Eagles:* Gavin Brown; *Lynx:* Mick Coates.
Penalty count: 4-8; **Half-time:** 17-8;
Referee: Colin Morris (Huddersfield); **Attendance:** 732.

Sunday 28th September 2003

FINAL ELIMINATOR

CHORLEY LYNX 12 KEIGHLEY COUGARS 45

LYNX: 1 Mark McCully; 2 Chris Campbell; 3 Anton Garcia; 4 Anthony Blackwood; 5 Eric Andrews; 6 Mick Coates; 7 John Braddish; 8 Tim Street; 9 Martin Roden; 10 Craig Wingfield; 11 Mick Redford; 12 Chris Newall; 13 Ian Hodson. Subs (all used): 14 Simon Smith; 15 Mike Briggs; 16 David Ingram; 17 Craig Dean.
Tries: McCully (11, 77); **Goals:** McCully 2.
Dismissal: Redford (65) - tripping.
Sin bin: Briggs (62) - punching.
COUGARS: 1 Matt Foster; 2 Max Tomlinson; 3 David Foster; 4 James Rushforth; 5 Andy Robinson; 6 Paul Ashton; 7 Matt Firth; 8 Phil Stephenson; 9 Simeon Hoyle; 10 Danny Ekis; 11 Oliver Wilkes; 12 Ian Sinfield; 13 Lee Patterson. Subs (all used): 14 Chris Wainwright; 15 Richard Mervill; 16 Mick Durham; 17 Jason Ramshaw.
Tries: Tomlinson (7), Stephenson (15), Ekis (18), Robinson (66), Mervill (70), Ashton (72, 80); **Goals:** Ashton 8; **Field goal:** Ashton.
Rugby Leaguer & League Express Men of the Match: *Lynx:* Ian Hodson; *Cougars:* Paul Ashton.
Penalty count: 5-14; **Half-time:** 6-19; **Referee:** Richard Silverwood (Dewsbury); **Attendance:** 1,085.

Sunday 5th October 2003

GRAND FINAL

KEIGHLEY COUGARS 13 SHEFFIELD EAGLES 11

COUGARS: 1 Matt Foster; 2 Max Tomlinson; 3 David Foster; 4 James Rushforth; 5 Andy Robinson; 6 Paul Ashton; 7 Matt Firth; 8 Phil Stephenson; 9 Simeon Hoyle; 10 Danny Ekis; 11 Oliver Wilkes; 12 Ian Sinfield; 13 Lee Patterson. Subs (all used): 14 Chris Wainwright; 15 Richard Mervill; 16 Mick Durham; 17 Jason Ramshaw.
Tries: M Foster (7), Robinson (74); **Goals:** Foster 2;
Field goal: Firth.
EAGLES: 1 Andy Poynter; 2 Tony Weller; 3 Richard Goddard; 4 Tom O'Reilly; 5 Greg Hurst; 6 Gavin Brown; 7 Mark Aston; 8 Jack Howieson; 9 Gareth Stanley; 10 Dale Laughton; 11 Andy Raleigh; 12 Craig Brown; 13 Wayne Flynn. Subs (all used): 14 Peter Reilly; 15 Simon Tillyer; 16 Nick Turnbull; 17 Mitchell Stringer.
Try: O'Reilly (51); **Goals:** G Brown 3; **Field goal:** Reilly.
Rugby Leaguer & League Express Men of the Match: *Cougars:* Simeon Hoyle; *Eagles:* Andy Raleigh.
Penalty count: 6-8; **Half-time:** 9-4;
Referee: Peter Taberner (Wigan).
(At Halton Stadium, Widnes).

Saturday 11th October 2003

NATIONAL LEAGUE ONE QUALIFYING FINAL

BATLEY BULLDOGS 36 SHEFFIELD EAGLES 14

BULLDOGS: 1 Craig Lingard; 2 Matt Bramald; 3 Anthony Gibbons; 4 Danny Maun; 5 Leon Williamson; 6 Mark Toohey; 7 Barry Eaton; 8 Joe Naidole; 9 Joe Berry; 10 Steve Hill; 11 Danny Evans; 12 Andy Spink; 13 Ryan Horsley. Subs (all used): 14 Mark Cass; 15 Paul Harrison; 16 Will Cartledge; 17 David Rourke.
Tries: Evans (19), Lingard (30, 61), Berry (33), Toohey (43), Cartledge (69); **Goals:** Eaton 6.
EAGLES: 1 Andy Poynter; 2 Tony Weller; 3 Richard Goddard; 4 Tom O'Reilly; 5 Greg Hurst; 6 Gavin Brown; 7 Mark Aston; 8 Jack Howieson; 9 Lee Bettinson; 10 Mitchell Stringer; 11 Andy Raleigh; 12 Craig Brown; 13 Simon Tillyer. Subs (all used): 14 Adam Carroll; 15 Simon Morton; 16 Nick Turnbull; 17 Jordan James.
Tries: James (24), Hurst (65), Carroll (73);
Goal: G Brown.
Sin bin: Poynter (28) - holding down.
Rugby Leaguer & League Express Men of the Match: *Bulldogs:* Andy Spink; *Eagles:* Richard Goddard.
Penalty count: 4-6; **Half-time:** 18-6;
Referee: Ian Smith (Oldham); **Attendance:** 1,040.

Sheffield's Jordan James
brought down against Batley during the
National League One Qualifying Final

NATIONAL LEAGUE CUP 2003
Round by Round

WEEK 1

Sunday 19th January 2003

NORTH

BARROW RAIDERS 18 CHORLEY LYNX 18

RAIDERS: 1 Anthony Horton; 2 Jamie Marshall; 3 Andy McClure; 4 Craig Bower; 5 Shane Irabor; 6 Paul Jones; 7 Chris Archer; 8 Wayne Jones; 9 Andy Henderson; 10 Steve Jackson; 11 James King; 12 Dave Byrne; 13 Phil Atkinson. Subs (all used): 14 Danny Lockhart; 15 Geoff Luxon; 16 Paul Dean; 17 Paul Lupton.
Tries: P Jones (10), Henderson (58), Marshall (63); **Goals:** Atkinson 3.
On report: King (29) - alleged high tackle on Smith.
LYNX: 1 Mark McCully; 2 Eddie Kilgannon; 3 David Ingram; 4 Anton Garcia; 5 Liam Jones; 6 John Braddish; 7 Martin Gambles; 8 Tim Street; 9 Mike Briggs; 10 David Whittle; 11 Wayne Bloor; 12 Dave McConnell; 13 Ian Hodson. Subs (all used): 14 Ian Parry; 15 Simon Smith; 16 Martin Roden; 17 Chris Ramsdale.
Tries: McCully (3), Garcia (39), Briggs (47); **Goals:** Braddish 3.
Rugby Leaguer & League Express Men of the Match: *Raiders:* James King; *Lynx:* John Braddish.
Penalty count: 8-8; **Half-time:** 8-12; **Referee:** Steve Nicholson (Whitehaven); **Attendance:** 817.

WHITEHAVEN 42 GATESHEAD THUNDER 6

WHITEHAVEN: 1 Gary Broadbent; 2 John Lebbon; 3 Jamie Stenhouse; 4 Howard Hill; 5 Leigh Smith; 6 Leroy Joe; 7 Darren Holt; 8 Dean Vaughan; 9 Aaron Lester; 10 David Fatialofa; 11 Graeme Morton; 12 Chris McKinney; 13 Mike Whitehead. Subs (all used): 14 Marc Jackson; 15 Lee Kiddie; 16 Gary Smith; 17 Spencer Miller.
Tries: Morton (16), Broadbent (20), Lester (45), L Smith (50), Jackson (61, 70), Lebbon (76); **Goals:** Holt 7.
THUNDER: 1 Kevin Neighbour; 2 Richie Barnett; 3 Damien Reid; 4 PJ Solomon; 5 Robin Peers; 6 Paul Thorman; 7 Craig Fisher; 8 Yusuf Sozi; 9 Chris Fletcher; 10 Steven Bradley; 11 Scott Houston; 12 James Mackay; 13 Steve Rutherford. Subs (all used): 14 Neil Thorman; 15 Andy Walker; 16 Clint Brown; 17 David Bates.
Try: Mackay (79); **Goal:** Fisher.
Rugby Leaguer & League Express Men of the Match: *Whitehaven:* Gary Broadbent; *Thunder:* Craig Fisher.
Penalty count: 4-8; **Half-time:** 12-0;
Referee: Colin Morris (Huddersfield); **Attendance:** 1,342.

EAST

FEATHERSTONE ROVERS 30 SHEFFIELD EAGLES 12

ROVERS: 1 Nathan Graham; 2 Jamie Stokes; 3 Brendan O'Meara; 4 Ian Brown; 5 Adrian Flynn; 6 Andy McNally; 7 Carl Briggs; 8 Chris Molyneux; 9 Danny Seal; 10 Stuart Dickens; 11 Steve Dooler; 12 Ian Tonks; 13 Andy Rice. Subs (all used): 14 Danny Patrickson; 15 Ben Archibald; 16 Andy Bailey; 17 Robin Jowitt.
Tries: Seal (18, 36), Graham (41), O'Meara (44), Stokes (53), Archibald (64); **Goals:** Dickens 3.
EAGLES: 1 Andy Poynter; 2 Jon Breakingbury; 3 Neil Kite; 4 Wayne Flynn; 5 Ian Thompson; 6 Lee Bettinson; 7 Gavin Brown; 8 Damien Whitter; 9 Gareth Stanley; 10 Jack Howieson; 11 Guy Adams; 12 Craig Brown; 13 Richard Goddard. Subs (all used): 14 Peter Reilly; 15 Sam Bibb; 16 Simon Tillyer; 17 Jon Bruce.
Tries: Thompson (28), Tillyer (69); **Goals:** G Brown 2.
Sin bin: G Brown (33) - holding down.
Rugby Leaguer & League Express Men of the Match: *Rovers:* Carl Briggs; *Eagles:* Lee Bettinson.
Penalty count: 10-11; **Half-time:** 12-6;
Referee: Mike Dawber (Wigan); **Attendance:** 1,595.

YORK CITY KNIGHTS 26 HULL KINGSTON ROVERS 36

CITY KNIGHTS: 1 Chris Beever; 2 Alex Godfrey; 3 Graeme Hallas; 4 Chris Smith; 5 Gavin Molloy; 6 Mark Cain; 7 Trevor Krause; 8 David Bolus; 9 Lee Jackson; 10 Richard Hayes; 11 Mick Ramsden; 12 Scott Fletcher; 13 Darren Callaghan. Subs (all used): 14 Scott Yeaman; 15 Gareth Lloyd; 16 Carl Stannard; 17 Damian Kennedy.
Tries: A Godfrey (19), Callaghan (33), Yeaman (54), C Smith (65); **Goals:** Hallas 5.
Sin bin: Molloy (70) - off the ball tackle.
ROVERS: 1 Craig Poucher; 2 Nick Pinkney; 3 Paul Parker; 4 Craig Farrell; 5 Alasdair McClarron; 6 Jimmy Walker; 7 Craig Murdock; 8 Richard Wilson; 9 Paul Pickering; 10 Jamie Bovill; 11 Adam Sullivan; 12 Jon Aston; 13 Andy Smith. Subs (all used): 14 Mark Blanchard; 15 Dean Andrews; 16 Steve Cochran; 17 Paul Fletcher.
Tries: Murdock (16), Walker (23, 46), Poucher (42), Aston (72), Farrell (74), Cochran (78); **Goals:** Murdock 4.
Sin bin: Sullivan (65) - off the ball tackle.
Rugby Leaguer & League Express Men of the Match: *City Knights:* Scott Fletcher; *Rovers:* Craig Murdock.
Penalty count: 10-9; **Half-time:** 14-12;
Referee: Steve Presley (Castleford); **Attendance:** 3,105.

WEST

LEIGH CENTURIONS 22 OLDHAM 14

CENTURIONS: 1 David Alstead; 2 Michael Watts; 3 Damian Munro; 4 Dale Cardoza; 5 Alan Hadcroft; 6 John Duffy; 7 Lee Sanderson; 8 Sonny Nickle; 9 Paul Rowley; 10 David Bradbury; 11 Sean Richardson; 12 Phil Kendrick; 13 Adam Bristow. Subs (all used): 14 Anthony Blackwood; 15 John Hamilton; 16 Patrick Weisner; 17 Rob Ball.
Tries: Munro (3, 63), Hamilton (58), Alstead (80); **Goals:** Sanderson 3.
Sin bin: Rowley (77) - fighting.
OLDHAM: 1 Gavin Dodd; 2 Iain Marsh; 3 Jon Goddard; 4 Paul Anderson; 5 Joe McNicholas; 6 Simon Svabic; 7 Neil Roden; 8 Steve Molloy; 9 John Hough; 10 Martin McLoughlin; 11 Lee Doran; 12 Chris Morley; 13 Phil Farrell. Subs (all used): 14 Gareth Barber; 15 Gavin Johnson; 16 Ryan Stazicker; 17 Danny Guest.
Tries: Dodd (44), Farrell (78); **Goals:** Svabic 2, Barber.
Sin bin: Doran (29) - holding down; Molloy (77) - fighting.
Rugby Leaguer & League Express Men of the Match: *Centurions:* Damian Munro; *Oldham:* Paul Anderson.
Penalty count: 11-9; **Half-time:** 8-4;
Referee: Peter Taberner (Wigan); **Attendance:** 3,070.

SALFORD CITY REDS 58 SWINTON LIONS 6

CITY REDS: 1 Jason Flowers; 2 Alan Hunte; 3 Stuart Littler; 4 Cliff Beverley; 5 Danny Arnold; 6 Steve Blakeley; 7 Gavin Clinch; 8 Andy Coley; 9 Malcolm Alker; 10 Paul Highton; 11 Simon Baldwin; 12 Neil Lowe; 13 Lee Marsh. Subs (all used): 14 Radney Bowker; 15 David Highton; 16 Andy Gorski; 17 Neil Baynes.
Tries: Blakeley (8), Baldwin (28), Hunte (33, 78), Flowers (36, 73), Coley (43), Clinch (47), Marsh (63), Beverley (66), Littler (75); **Goals:** Blakeley 2, Clinch 3, Marsh 2.
LIONS: 1 Wayne English; 2 Hugh Thorpe; 3 Andy Cheetham; 4 Phil Hassan; 5 Lee Hudson; 6 Jason Johnson; 7 Chris Hough; 8 Andy Leathem; 9 Peter Cannon; 10 Simon Knox; 11 Phil Cushion; 12 Dave Ellison; 13 Kris Smith. Subs (all used): 14 Rob Gallagher; 15 Danny Turner; 16 Chris Roe; 17 Craig Wingfield.
Try: Wingfield (57); **Goal:** Hough.
Rugby Leaguer & League Express Men Of the Match: *City Reds:* Gavin Clinch; *Lions:* Peter Cannon.
Penalty count: 7-11; **Half-time:** 20-2;
Referee: Ashley Klein (London); **Attendance:** 3,334.

CENTRAL

BATLEY BULLDOGS 16 HUNSLET HAWKS 8

BULLDOGS: 1 Craig Lingard; 2 Simon Lewis; 3 Anthony Gibbons; 4 Danny Maun; 5 Leon Williamson; 6 David Gibbons; 7 Barry Eaton; 8 Craig Booth; 9 Kris Lythe; 10 Joe Naidole; 11 David Rourke; 12 Mark Toohey; 13 Ryan Horsley. Subs (all used): 14 Mark Cass; 15 Paul Harrison; 16 Joe Berry; 17 Andy Spink.
Tries: Spink (35), Rourke (57), Horsley (67); **Goals:** Eaton 2.
HAWKS: 1 Simon Jackson; 2 Bryn Powell; 3 Iain Higgins; 4 Wes McGibbon; 5 George Rayner; 6 Andy Bastow; 7 Phil Hasty; 8 Craig Ibbetson; 9 Gareth Naylor; 10 Andy Brent; 11 Mick Coyle; 12 Wayne Freeman; 13 Danny Fearon. Subs (all used): 14 Paul Seal; 15 Jonlee Lockwood; 16 Jon Liddell; 17 Billy Conway.
Try: Bastow (19); **Goal:** Bastow 2.
Rugby Leaguer & League Express Men of the Match: *Bulldogs:* Barry Eaton; *Hawks:* Danny Fearon.
Penalty count: 12-5; **Half-time:** 6-8;
Referee: Ronnie Laughton (Barnsley); **Attendance:** 801.

LONDON SKOLARS 10 DEWSBURY RAMS 22

SKOLARS: 1 Kirk Wotherspoon; 2 Mike Okwusogu; 3 Scott Roberts; 4 Jake Johnstone; 5 Charlie Oyebade; 6 Richard Pollard; 7 Bow Robertson; 8 Jason Asplet; 9 Kahu Henare; 10 Allan Tito; 11 Rubert Jonker; 12 Mike Fitzgibbon; 13 Chris Thair. Subs (all used): 14 Steve Hainey; 15 Peter Rawson; 16 Obi Ijeoma; 17 Jimmy Daines.
Tries: Wotherspoon (28), Pollard (72); **Goal:** Thair.
Sin bin: Okwusogu (39) - interference.
RAMS: 1 Jamie Benn; 2 Michael Wainwright; 3 Chris Chapman; 4 Chris Redfearn; 5 Paul Steele; 6 Scott Rhodes; 7 Danny Brough; 8 Paul Hicks; 9 David Oldfield; 10 Tony Fella; 11 Danny Evans; 12 Billy Kershaw; 13 Chris Parker. Subs (all used): 14 Jimmy Elston; 15 Ryan Hardy; 16 Frank Watene; 17 Carl Sayer.
Tries: Rhodes (35), Wainwright (39), Benn (42); **Goals:** Benn 5.
Sin bin: Evans (48) - interference.
Rugby Leaguer & League Express Men of the Match: *Skolars:* Richard Pollard; *Rams:* Scott Rhodes.
Penalty count: 11-11; **Half-time:** 6-14;
Referee: Steve Addy (Huddersfield); **Attendance:** 820.

CENTRAL v EAST

KEIGHLEY COUGARS 21 DONCASTER DRAGONS 14

COUGARS: 1 James Rushforth; 2 Karl Smith; 3 David Foster; 4 Gareth Hewitt; 5 Andy Robinson; 6 Paul Ashton; 7 Matt Firth; 8 Phil Stephenson; 9 Simeon Hoyle; 10 Danny Ekis; 11 Ian Sinfield; 12 Ricky Helliwell; 13 Jason Ramshaw. Subs: 14 Chris Wainwright; 15 Lee Patterson (not used); 16 Oliver Wilkes; 17 Chris Hannah.
Tries: Robinson (17), Ashton (22), Helliwell (45); **Goals:** Ashton 4; **Field goal:** Ashton.
Sin bin: Helliwell (14) - holding down.
On report: Brawl (2).
DRAGONS: 1 Craig Horne; 2 Wayne Green; 3 Marvin Golden; 4 Paul Gleadhill; 5 Jason Lee; 6 Chris Ross; 7 Mark Moxon; 8 Gareth Handford; 9 Peter Green; 10 Craig Forsyth; 11 Tony Atter; 12 Craig Lawton; 13 Matt Walker. Subs (all used): 14 James Walker; 15 Dean Colton; 16 Shaun Leafe; 17 Gareth Everton.
Tries: M Walker (30), Ross (63); **Goals:** W Green 3.
Sin bin: Gleadhill (21) - holding down.
On report: Brawl (2).
Rugby Leaguer & League Express Men of the Match: *Cougars:* Jason Ramshaw; *Dragons:* Chris Ross.
Penalty count: 15-16; **Half-time:** 12-10;
Referee: Steve Ganson (St Helens); **Attendance:** 1,337.

WEST v NORTH

ROCHDALE HORNETS 32 WORKINGTON TOWN 8

HORNETS: 1 Paul Owen; 2 Sean Cooper; 3 Mick Nanyn; 4 James Bunyan; 5 Casey Mayberry; 6 Warren Ayres; 7 Ian Watson; 8 Paul Southern; 9 Richard Pachniuk; 10 David Stephenson; 11 David Larder; 12 Paul Smith; 13 Damian Ball. Subs (all used): 14 Danny Wood; 15 Andy Grundy; 16 Gareth Price; 17 Matthew Long.
Tries: Nanyn (12), Owen (21), Larder (38), Mayberry (50), Pachniuk (70); **Goals:** Nanyn 6.
TOWN: 1 Anthony Huddart; 2 Matthew Johnson; 3 Brett McDermott; 4 Jonathan Heaney; 5 Graeme Lewthwaite; 6 Kevin Hetherington; 7 Owen Williamson; 8 William Blackburn; 9 Carl Sice; 10 Hitro Okesene; 11 Jamie Beaumont; 12 Lokeni Savelio; 13 Brett Smith. Subs (all used): 14 Craig Barker; 15 Matthew Tunstall; 16 Barrie Murdock; 17 Gary Charlton.
Try: Heaney (8); **Goals:** Hetherington 2.
Rugby Leaguer & League Express Men of the Match: *Hornets:* Paul Smith; *Town:* Carl Sice.
Penalty count: 6-7; **Half-time:** 20-6;
Referee: Ben Thaler (Wakefield); **Attendance:** 778.

WEEK 2

Sunday 2nd February 2003

NORTH

CHORLEY LYNX 2 WHITEHAVEN 28

LYNX: 1 Chris Ramsdale; 2 Marlon Miller; 3 Mick Redford; 4 Anton Garcia; 5 Eddie Kilgannon; 6 John Braddish; 7 Mick Coates; 8 Tim Street; 9 Mike Briggs; 10 Simon Smith; 11 Wayne Bloor; 12 Dave McConnell; 13 Ian Hodson. Subs (all used): 14 Safraz Patel; 15 Martin Roden; 16 Ian Parry; 17 Dave Radney.
Goal: Braddish.
WHITEHAVEN: 1 Gary Broadbent; 2 Paul O'Neil; 4 Howard Hill; 3 David Seeds; 5 Steven Wood; 6 Leroy Joe; 7 Darren Holt; 8 Phil Sherwen; 9 Aaron Lester; 10 Dean Vaughan; 11 Chris McKinney; 12 Graeme Morton; 13 Spencer Miller. Subs (all used): 14 Marc Jackson; 15 Lee Kiddie; 16 Mike Whitehead; 17 Jamie Stenhouse.
Tries: Miller (13), Kiddie (47, 62), Seeds (53), O'Neil (66); **Goals:** Holt 4.
Rugby Leaguer & League Express Men of the Match: *Lynx:* Wayne Bloor; *Whitehaven:* Lee Kiddie.
Penalty count: 7-8; **Half-time:** 2-6;
Referee: Steve Addy (Huddersfield); **Attendance:** 383.

WORKINGTON TOWN 10 BARROW RAIDERS 20

TOWN: 1 Dean Sharp; 2 Matthew Johnson; 3 Brett McDermott; 4 Jonathan Heaney; 5 Scott Chilton; 6 Anthony Huddart; 7 Owen Williamson; 8 Craig Barker; 9 Carl Sice; 10 Matthew Tunstall; 11 Ricky Wright; 12 William Blackburn; 13 Brett Smith. Subs (all used): 14 Kevin Hetherington; 15 Graeme Lewthwaite; 16 Neil Frazer; 17 Hitro Okesene.
Tries: Wright (12), Smith (49); **Goal:** Heaney.
RAIDERS: 1 Craig Bower; 2 Jamie Marshall; 3 Andy McClure; 4 Paul Jones; 5 Shane Irabor; 6 Paul Evans; 7 Chris Archer; 8 Wayne Jones; 9 Andy Henderson; 10 Stuart Dancer; 11 Steve Jackson; 12 Paul Gardner; 13 Phil Atkinson. Subs (all used): 14 Adam Pate; 15 Geoff Luxon; 16 Paul Dean; 17 James Stainton.
Tries: Henderson (9), Marshall (15), W Jones (19); **Goals:** Atkinson 4.
Rugby Leaguer & League Express Men of the Match: *Town:* Ricky Wright; *Raiders:* Andy Henderson.
Penalty count: 11-8; **Half-time:** 4-18;
Referee: Julian King (St Helens); **Attendance:** 578.

EAST

DONCASTER DRAGONS 24 YORK CITY KNIGHTS 4

DRAGONS: 1 Chris Ross; 2 Paul Gleadhill; 3 Marvin Golden; 4 Simon Irving; 5 Jason Lee; 6 Shaun Leafe; 7 Mark Moxon; 8 Gareth Handford; 9 Dean Colton; 10 Craig Forsyth; 11 Peter Green; 12 Craig Lawton; 13 Matt Walker. Subs (all used): 14 James Walker; 15 Peter Edwards; 16 Maea David; 17 Brad Hepi.
Tries: Irving (23, 74), J Walker (50), Hepi (66), Ross (69); **Goals:** Irving 2.
Sin bin: Ross (14) – deliberate obstruction.
CITY KNIGHTS: 1 Chris Beever; 2 Alex Godfrey; 3 Chris Smith; 4 Jermaine Coleman; 5 Gavin Molloy; 6 Mark Cain; 7 Trevor Krause; 8 Richard Hayes; 9 Lee Jackson; 10 David Bolus; 11 Mick Ramsden; 12 Scott Fletcher; 13 Darren Callaghan. Subs (all used): 14 Scott Yeaman; 15 Mick Embleton; 16 Carl Stannard; 17 Damian Kennedy.
Goals: Cain 2.
Rugby Leaguer & League Express Men of the Match: *Dragons:* Chris Ross; *City Knights:* Mark Cain.
Penalty count: 7-7; **Half-time:** 4-4; **Referee:** Steve Nicholson (Whitehaven); **Attendance:** 1,029.

HULL KINGSTON ROVERS 20 FEATHERSTONE ROVERS 0

ROBINS: 1 Mike Hall; 2 Nick Pinkney; 3 Lynton Stott; 4 Craig Farrell; 5 Alasdair McClarron; 6 Paul Parker; 7 Latham Tawhai; 8 Richard Wilson; 9 Paul Pickering; 10 Jamie Bovill; 11 Adam Sullivan; 12 Jon Aston; 13 Andy

Smith. Subs (all used): 14 Jimmy Walker; 15 Mark Blanchard; 16 Steve Cochran; 17 Paul Fletcher.
Tries: Pickering (15), Parker (64), McClarron (73);
Goals: Stott 4.
ROVERS: 1 Nathan Graham; 2 Jamie Stokes; 3 Brendan O'Meara; 4 Ian Brown; 5 Adrian Flynn; 6 Andy McNally; 7 Carl Briggs; 8 Chris Molyneux; 9 Richard Chapman; 10 Stuart Dickens; 11 Steve Dooler; 12 Andy Rice; 13 Danny Seal. Subs (all used): 14 Danny Patrickson; 15 Ben Archibald; 16 Andy Bailey; 17 Robin Jowitt.
Rugby Leaguer & League Express Men of the Match: *Robins:* Latham Tawhai; *Rovers:* Danny Seal.
Penalty count: 7-9; **Half-time:** 10-0;
Referee: Ashley Klein (London); **Attendance:** 1,540.

WEST

OLDHAM 22 ROCHDALE HORNETS 22

OLDHAM: 1 Gavin Dodd; 2 Chris Irwin; 3 Paul Anderson; 4 Jon Goddard; 5 Will Cowell; 6 Gareth Barber; 7 Neil Roden; 8 Steve Molloy; 9 Anthony Murray; 10 Martin McLoughlin; 11 Lee Doran; 12 Ryan Stazicker; 13 Phil Farrell. Subs (all used): 14 John Hough; 15 Simon Svabic; 16 Chris Morley; 17 Darren Shaw.
Tries: Doran (21), Barber (44), Farrell (57), Morley (61);
Goals: Barber 3.
Sin bin: Dodd (32) - interference.
HORNETS: 1 Paul Owen; 2 Sean Cooper; 3 Mick Nanyn; 4 Jon Roper; 5 Casey Mayberry; 6 Warren Ayres; 7 Ian Watson; 8 Paul Southern; 9 Richard Pachniuk; 10 David Stephenson; 11 David Larder; 12 James Bunyan; 13 Paul Smith. Subs: 14 Stephen Doherty (not used); 15 Andy Grundy; 16 Gareth Price; 17 Matthew Long.
Tries: Bunyan (16), Long (32), Roper (64), Pachniuk (67); **Goals:** Nanyn 3.
Rugby Leaguer & League Express Men of the Match: *Oldham:* Phil Farrell; *Hornets:* Richard Pachniuk.
Penalty count: 9-8; **Half-time:** 6-10; **Referee:** Colin Morris (Huddersfield); **Attendance:** 2,050.

SWINTON LIONS 10 LEIGH CENTURIONS 24

LIONS: 1 Wayne English; 2 Jason Roach; 3 Andy Cheetham; 4 Robert Russell; 5 Hugh Thorpe; 6 Rob Gallagher; 7 Chris Hough; 8 Andy Leathem; 9 Peter Cannon; 10 Simon Knox; 11 Craig Wingfield; 12 Dave Ellison; 13 Kris Smith. Subs (all used): 14 Lee Hudson; 15 Jason Johnson; 16 Danny Turner; 17 Chris Roe.
Tries: Wingfield (26), Thorpe (46); **Goal:** Smith.
Sin bin: English (57) - holding down.
CENTURIONS: 1 Michael Watts; 2 Eric Andrews; 3 Damian Munro; 4 Dale Cardoza; 5 Leroy Rivett; 6 Patrick Weisner; 7 John Duffy; 8 Sonny Nickle; 9 Paul Rowley; 10 Rob Ball; 11 Sean Richardson; 12 Dale Holdstock; 13 Adam Bristow. Subs (all used): 14 Phil Kendrick; 15 Lee Sanderson; 16 John Hamilton; 17 David Bradbury.
Tries: Munro (22), Cardoza (37, 54, 78), Rivett (79);
Goals: Duffy 2.
Rugby Leaguer & League Express Men of the Match: *Lions:* Simon Knox; *Centurions:* Dale Cardoza.
Penalty count: 10-9; **Half-time:** 6-10;
Referee: Steve Presley (Castleford); **Attendance:** 950.

CENTRAL

DEWSBURY RAMS 12 KEIGHLEY COUGARS 6

RAMS: 1 Jamie Benn; 2 Michael Wainwright; 3 Chris Chapman; 4 Paul Steele; 5 Mark Barlow; 6 Danny Brough; 7 Scott Rhodes; 8 Paul Hicks; 9 Jimmy Elston; 10 Danny Evans; 11 Gary Fahey; 12 Billy Kershaw; 13 Chris Parker. Subs (all used): 14 Andy Heptinstall; 15 Chris Redfearn; 16 Frank Watene; 17 Tony Fella.
Tries: Kershaw (17), Watene (24); **Goals:** Benn 2.
Sin bin: Parker (6) - interference;
Chapman (60) - fighting.
COUGARS: 1 James Rushforth; 2 Phil Guck; 3 Chris Wainwright; 4 Gareth Hewitt; 5 Andy Robinson; 6 Paul Ashton; 7 Matt Firth; 8 Phil Stephenson; 9 Simeon Hoyle; 10 Chris Hannah; 11 David Foster; 12 Ricky Helliwell; 13 Jason Ramshaw. Subs (all used): 14 Matthew Steel; 15 Oliver Wilkes; 16 Lee Kelly; 17 Danny Ekis.
Try: Rushforth (42); **Goal:** Ashton.
Rugby Leaguer & League Express Men of the Match: *Rams:* Tony Fella; *Cougars:* Simeon Hoyle.
Penalty count: 14-11; **Half-time:** 12-0;
Referee: Peter Taberner (Wigan); **Attendance:** 954.

HUNSLET HAWKS 30 LONDON SKOLARS 6

HAWKS: 1 Simon Jackson; 2 Bryn Powell; 3 Iain Higgins; 4 Wes McGibbon; 5 George Rayner; 6 Jon Liddell; 7 Phil Hasty; 8 Craig Ibbetson; 9 Joe Hawley; 10 Andy Brent; 11 Danny Fearon; 12 Paul Seal; 13 Gareth Naylor. Subs (all used): 14 Michael Lyons; 15 Wayne Freeman; 16 Ian Hughes; 17 Mick Coyle.
Tries: McGibbon (3), Naylor (13, 21), W Freeman (63), Seal (65); **Goals:** Liddell 5.
SKOLARS: 1 Kirk Wotherspoon; 2 Charlie Oyebade; 3 Jake Johnstone; 4 Scott Roberts; 5 Mike Okwusogu; 6 Peter Rawson; 7 Richard Pollard; 8 Glenn Osborn; 9 Kahu Henare; 10 Gerald Nkrumah; 11 Allan Tito; 12 Steve Hainey; 13 Pat Rich. Subs (all used): 14 Anthony Dellar; 15 Cory Bennett; 16 Bobby Wallis; 17 Duncan Simpson.
Try: Wotherspoon (32); **Goal:** Johnstone.
Rugby Leaguer & League Express Men of the Match: *Hawks:* Gareth Naylor; *Skolars:* Richard Pollard.
Penalty count: 12-8; **Half-time:** 18-6;
Referee: Mike Dawber (Wigan); **Attendance:** 434.

WEEK 3

Sunday 16th February 2003

NORTH

GATESHEAD THUNDER 18 CHORLEY LYNX 24

THUNDER: 1 Kevin Neighbour; 2 Judd Billings; 3 Nick Cowburn; 4 PJ Solomon; 5 Damien Reid; 6 Scott MacDougall; 7 Craig Fisher; 8 Shaun Weatherall; 9 Chris Fletcher; 10 Nick Walker; 11 Mark Cherry; 12 Scott Houston; 13 Steve Rutherford. Subs (all used); 14 Yusuf Sozi; 15 Andy Walker; 16 Clint Brown; 17 Janan Billings.
Tries: Neighbour (34), Janan Billings (51), MacDougall (63); **Goals:** Fisher 3.
LYNX: 1 David Ingram; 2 Marlon Miller; 3 Mick Redford; 4 Eddie Kilgannon; 5 Anton Garcia; 6 Mick Coates; 7 John Braddish; 8 Tim Street; 9 Mike Briggs; 10 Ian Parry; 11 Wayne Bloor; 12 Dave McConnell; 13 Ian Hodson. Subs (all used): 14 Safraz Patel; 15 Simon Smith; 16 Dave Byrne; 17 Martin Roden.
Tries: McConnell (17), Redford (30, 60), Kilgannon (39);
Goals: Braddish 4.
Sin bin: Briggs (26) - persistent interference at play-the-ball.
Rugby Leaguer & League Express Men of the Match: *Thunder:* Nick Cowburn; *Lynx:* Mick Coates.
Penalty count: 11-5; **Half-time:** 6-18;
Referee: Colin Morris (Huddersfield); **Attendance:** 308.

EAST

FEATHERSTONE ROVERS 36 YORK CITY KNIGHTS 22

ROVERS: 1 Nathan Graham; 2 Jamie Stokes; 3 Brendan O'Meara; 4 Ian Brown; 5 Adrian Flynn; 6 Richard Agar; 7 Carl Briggs; 8 Chris Molyneux; 9 Richard Chapman; 10 Stuart Dickens; 11 Steve Dooler; 12 Andy Rice; 13 Danny Seal. Subs (all used): 14 Andy McNally; 15 Andy Bailey; 16 Ian Tonks; 17 Robin Jowitt.
Tries: Chapman (18, 69), Seal (39), Stokes (42, 63), Agar (51), Briggs (55); **Goals:** Dickens 2, Briggs 2.
CITY KNIGHTS: 1 Chris Beever; 2 Chris Smith; 3 Graeme Hallas; 4 Darren Callaghan; 5 Gavin Molloy; 6 Jonathan Firth; 7 Scott Yeaman; 8 Richard Hayes; 9 Trevor Krause; 10 David Bolus; 11 Damian Kennedy; 12 Scott Fletcher; 13 Mark Cain. Subs (all used): 14 Tommy Gallagher; 15 Craig Westmoreland; 16 Carl Stannard; 17 Darren Robinson.
Tries: Krause (6, 34), Fletcher (58), Callaghan (72), C Smith (77); **Goal:** Hallas.
Rugby Leaguer & League Express Men Of the Match: *Rovers:* Ian Tonks; *City Knights:* Trevor Krause.
Penalty count: 5-3; **Half-time:** 10-10; **Referee:** Steve Nicholson (Whitehaven); **Attendance:** 1,728.

SHEFFIELD EAGLES 4 DONCASTER DRAGONS 26

EAGLES: 1 Andy Poynter; 2 Jon Breakingbury; 3 Nick Turnbull; 4 Neil Kite; 5 Ian Thompson; 6 Gavin Brown; 7 Lee Bettinson; 8 Jack Howieson; 9 Adam Carroll; 10 Damien Whitter; 11 Sam Bibb; 12 Craig Brown; 13 Richard Goddard. Subs (all used): 14 Peter Reilly; 15 Guy Adams; 16 Simon Tillyer; 17 Mitchell Stringer.
Goals: G Brown 2.
DRAGONS: 1 Chris Ross; 2 Craig Horne; 3 Marvin Golden; 4 Simon Irving; 5 Jason Lee; 6 Paul Mansson; 7 Mark Moxon; 8 Gareth Handford; 9 Peter Edwards; 10 James Walker; 11 Peter Green; 12 Craig Lawton; 13 Matt Walker. Subs (all used): 14 Dean Colton; 15 Brad Hepi; 16 Maea David; 17 Craig Forsyth.
Tries: Edwards (25), Ross (49), J Walker (57), Lawton (70), Irving (79); **Goals:** Irving 3.
Rugby Leaguer & League Express Men of the Match: *Eagles:* Damien Whitter; *Dragons:* Mark Moxon.
Penalty count: 14-4; **Half-time:** 0-8;
Referee: Julian King (St Helens); **Attendance:** 1,053.

WEST

LEIGH CENTURIONS 20 SALFORD CITY REDS 20

CENTURIONS: 1 David Alstead; 2 Leroy Rivett; 3 Damian Munro; 4 Dale Cardoza; 5 Alan Hadcroft; 6 Patrick Weisner; 7 John Duffy; 8 Sonny Nickle; 9 Paul Rowley; 10 Rob Ball; 11 Sean Richardson; 12 Bryan Henare; 13 Adam Bristow. Subs (all used): 14 David Bradbury; 15 Michael Watts; 16 John Hamilton; 17 Phil Kendrick.
Tries: Richardson (7), Bristow (23), Duffy (50);
Goals: Duffy 4.
Sin bin: Kendrick (78) - holding down.
CITY REDS: 1 Jason Flowers; 2 Alan Hunte; 3 Stuart Littler; 4 Cliff Beverley; 5 Michael Platt; 6 Radney Bowker; 7 Gavin Clinch; 8 Neil Baynes; 9 Malcolm Alker; 10 Andy Coley; 11 Simon Baldwin; 12 Neil Lowe; 13 Chris Charles. Subs (all used): 14 Lee Marsh; 15 David Highton; 16 Andy Gorski; 17 Paul Highton.
Tries: Baynes (3), Littler (55, 74), Hunte (57);
Goals: Marsh 2.
Sin bin: Charles (30) - holding down.
Rugby Leaguer & League Express Men of the Match: *Centurions:* Adam Bristow; *City Reds:* Stuart Littler.
Penalty count: 10-12; **Half-time:** 12-4; **Referee:** Ronnie Laughton (Barnsley); **Attendance:** 4,445.

CENTRAL

DEWSBURY RAMS 24 HUNSLET HAWKS 26

RAMS: 1 Jamie Benn; 2 Michael Wainwright; 3 Chris Chapman; 4 Ryan Hardy; 5 Jon Wray; 6 Chris Redfearn; 7 Scott Rhodes; 8 Frank Watene; 9 Andy Heptinstall; 10 Paul Hicks; 11 Danny Evans; 12 Billy Kershaw; 13 Michael Walker. Subs (all used): 14 Jimmy Elston; 15 Tony Fella; 16 Danny Brough; 17 Carl Sayer.
Tries: Chapman (21), Kershaw (67, 73), Brough (77);
Goals: Benn 4.
HAWKS: 1 Richard Baker; 2 Bryn Powell; 3 Michael Lyons; 4 Wes McGibbon; 5 George Rayner; 6 Jon Liddell; 7 Phil Hasty; 8 Craig Ibbetson; 9 Gareth Naylor; 10 Mick Coyle; 11 Wayne Freeman; 12 Danny Fearon; 13 Paul Seal. Subs (all used): 14 Joe Hawley; 15 Gareth Brain; 16 Jonlee Lockwood; 17 David Brook.
Tries: Powell (7), Naylor (10, 12), Rayner (44), Brain (52); **Goals:** Liddell 3.
Rugby Leaguer & League Express Men of the Match: *Rams:* Billy Kershaw; *Hawks:* Phil Hasty.
Penalty count: 12-9; **Half-time:** 6-16;
Referee: Ashley Klein (London); **Attendance:** 869.

KEIGHLEY COUGARS 12 BATLEY BULLDOGS 30

COUGARS: 1 James Rushforth; 2 Karl Smith; 3 David Foster; 4 Matthew Steel; 5 Phil Guck; 6 Adam Mitchell; 7 Matt Firth; 8 Phil Stephenson; 9 Simeon Hoyle; 10 Lee Kelly; 11 Oliver Wilkes; 12 Ian Sinfield; 13 Lee Patterson. Subs (all used): 14 Paul Ashton; 15 Chris Wainwright; 16 Danny Ekis; 17 Chris Hannah.
Tries: Smith (69), Rushforth (72); **Goals:** Mitchell 2.
Sin bin: Wainwright (32) - interference.
BULLDOGS: 1 Craig Lingard; 2 Mark Sibson; 3 Anthony Gibbons; 4 Chris Spurr; 5 Leon Williamson; 6 David Gibbons; 7 Barry Eaton; 8 Joe Naidole; 9 Mark Cass; 10 Andy Spink; 11 David Rourke; 12 Will Cartledge; 13 Ryan Horsley. Subs (all used): 14 Jeremy Dyson; 15 Paul Harrison; 16 Joe Berry; 17 Craig Booth.
Tries: Lingard (33, 37, 75), Cartledge (54), Spurr (80);
Goals: Eaton 5.
Dismissal: Booth (44) - illegal use of the elbow.
On report: D Gibbons (68) - high tackle.
Rugby Leaguer & League Express Men of the Match: *Cougars:* David Foster; *Bulldogs:* Craig Lingard.
Penalty count: 8-7; **Half-time:** 14-4;
Referee: Steve Presley (Castleford); **Attendance:** 1,209.

CENTRAL v EAST

LONDON SKOLARS 8 HULL KINGSTON ROVERS 24

SKOLARS: 1 Kirk Wotherspoon; 2 Mike Okwusogu; 3 Jake Johnstone; 4 Scott Roberts; 5 Gavin Gordon; 6 Richard Pollard; 7 Rob McKeown; 8 Glenn Osborn; 9 Kahu Henare; 10 Obi Ijeoma; 11 Allan Tito; 12 Brett McCroary; 13 Steve Hainey. Subs (all used): 14 Anthony Dellar; 15 Cory Bennett; 16 Tim Williams; 17 Richard Brantingham.
Try: Pollard (32); **Goals:** Johnstone 2.
ROBINS: 1 Lynton Stott; 2 Nick Pinkney; 3 Mark Blanchard; 4 Craig Farrell; 5 Alasdair McClarron; 6 Paul Parker; 7 Craig Stephenson; 8 Richard Wilson; 9 Paul Pickering; 10 Jamie Bovill; 11 Adam Sullivan; 12 Jon Aston; 13 Jimmy Walker. Subs (all used): 14 Steve Cochran; 15 Andy Taylor; 16 Dean Andrews; 17 Paul Fletcher.
Tries: Pinkney (10), Parker (24), Blanchard (54), McClarron (66, 72); **Goals:** Stott 2.
Rugby Leaguer & League Express Men of the Match: *Skolars:* Richard Pollard; *Robins:* Jon Aston.
Penalty count: 5-6; **Half-time:** 6-10;
Referee: Ben Thaler (Wakefield); **Attendance:** 712.

WEEK 4

Sunday 23rd February 2003

NORTH

BARROW RAIDERS 18 WHITEHAVEN 30

RAIDERS: 1 Craig Bower; 2 Jamie Marshall; 3 Danny Lockhart; 4 Andy McClure; 5 Shane Irabor; 6 Paul Evans; 7 Chris Archer; 8 Wayne Jones; 9 Andy Henderson; 10 Steve Jackson; 11 Paul Lupton; 12 Paul Gardner; 13 Dave Clark. Subs (all used): 14 Adam Pate; 15 Geoff Luxon; 16 Tau Liku; 17 James Stainton.
Tries: Marshall (43, 50, 79); **Goals:** Evans 3.
Sin bin: Luxon (76) - holding down.
WHITEHAVEN: 1 Gary Broadbent; 2 Paul O'Neil; 3 David Seeds; 4 Howard Hill; 5 Jamie Stenhouse; 6 Leroy Joe; 7 Darren Holt; 8 Phil Sherwen; 9 Aaron Lester; 10 Dean Vaughan; 11 Chris McKinney; 12 Graeme Morton; 13 Spencer Miller. Subs (all used): 14 Lee Kiddie; 15 Marc Jackson; 16 Ryan Campbell; 17 David Fatialofa.
Tries: O'Neil (4), Seeds (10), Morton (20), Joe (54, 60);
Goals: Holt 5.
Rugby Leaguer & League Express Men of the Match: *Raiders:* Jamie Marshall; *Whitehaven:* Leroy Joe.
Penalty count: 10-8; **Half-time:** 2-18;
Referee: Ashley Klein (London); **Attendance:** 1,436.

WORKINGTON TOWN 31 GATESHEAD THUNDER 24

TOWN: 1 Dean Sharp; 2 Matthew Johnson; 3 Brett McDermott; 4 Anthony Huddart; 5 Scott Chilton; 6 Brett Smith; 7 Kevin Hetherington; 8 Craig Barker; 9 Carl Sice; 10 Matthew Tunstall; 11 Ricky Wright; 12 William Blackburn; 13 Jamie Beaumont. Subs (all used): 14 David Pettit; 15 Neil Frazer; 16 Graeme Lewthwaite; 17 Hitro Okesene.
Tries: Tunstall (2), Hetherington (41), Johnson (60), Lewthwaite (79); **Goals:** Hetherington 7;
Field goal: Hetherington.
THUNDER: 1 Kevin Neighbour; 2 Judd Billings; 3 Nick Cowburn; 4 PJ Solomon; 5 Damien Reid; 6 Paul Thorman; 7 Craig Fisher; 8 Shaun Weatherall; 9 Janan Billings; 10 Steven Bradley; 11 Nick Walker; 12 Clint

Brown; 13 Steve Rutherford. Subs (all used): 14 Yusuf Sozi; 15 Andy Walker; 16 David Bates; 17 Neil Thorman.
Tries: Rutherford (5), Judd Billings (23, 47), Neighbour (44, 74); **Goals:** Fisher 2.
Sin bin: Bates (68) - off the ball challenge;
Brown (71) - persistent holding down.
On report: Bates (68) - off the ball challenge.
Rugby Leaguer & League Express Men of the Match: *Town:* Kevin Hetherington; *Thunder:* Janan Billings.
Penalty count: 16-8; **Half-time:** 12-8;
Referee: Gareth Hewer (Whitehaven); **Attendance:** 503.

EAST

FEATHERSTONE ROVERS 24 DONCASTER DRAGONS 37

ROVERS: 1 Nathan Graham; 2 Jamie Stokes; 3 Brendan O'Meara; 4 Ian Brown; 5 Adrian Flynn; 6 Richard Agar; 7 Carl Briggs; 8 Ian Tonks; 9 Richard Chapman; 10 Stuart Dickens; 11 Andy Bailey; 12 Andy Rice; 13 Danny Seal. Subs (all used): 14 Andy McNally; 15 Ben Archibald; 16 Chris Molyneux; 17 Robin Jowitt.
Tries: Stokes (4), Flynn (6), Seal (44, 79);
Goals: Dickens 2, Briggs 2.
DRAGONS: 1 Chris Ross; 2 Paul Gleadhill; 3 Marvin Golden; 4 Simon Irving; 5 Jason Lee; 6 Paul Mansson; 7 Mark Moxon; 8 Gareth Handford; 9 Peter Edwards; 10 James Walker; 11 Peter Green; 12 Craig Lawton; 13 Matt Walker. Subs (all used): 14 Dean Colton; 15 Craig Forsyth; 16 Maea David; 17 Gareth Everton.
Tries: Lee (13, 78), Edwards (24), Mansson (26), P Green (60), Irving (65), Handford (72);
Goals: Irving 4; **Field goal:** Ross.
On report: Golden (50) - high tackle.
Rugby Leaguer & League Express Men of the Match: *Rovers:* Nathan Graham; *Dragons:* Paul Mansson.
Penalty count: 11-4; **Half-time:** 14-18; **Referee:** Ronnie Laughton (Barnsley); **Attendance:** 2,075.

HULL KINGSTON ROVERS 30 SHEFFIELD EAGLES 24

ROVERS: 1 Craig Poucher; 2 Nick Pinkney; 3 Lynton Stott; 4 Craig Farrell; 5 Mark Blanchard; 6 Paul Parker; 7 Latham Tawhai; 8 Richard Wilson; 9 Jimmy Walker; 10 Paul Fletcher; 11 Adam Sullivan; 12 Jon Aston; 13 Andy Smith. Subs (all used): 14 Craig Murdock; 15 Steve Cochran; 16 David Wilson; 17 Dean Andrews.
Tries: Stott (11), Pinkney (29, 71), Blanchard (36), Cochran (52); **Goals:** Stott 5.
EAGLES: 1 Andy Poynter; 2 Jon Breakingbury; 3 Neil Kite; 4 Nick Turnbull; 5 Greg Hurst; 6 Gavin Brown; 7 Peter Reilly; 8 Mitchell Stringer; 9 Gareth Stanley; 10 Damien Whitter; 11 Guy Adams; 12 Andy Raleigh; 13 Wayne Flynn. Subs (all used): 14 Richard Goddard; 15 Sam Bibb; 16 Simon Tillyer; 17 Jon Bruce.
Tries: G Brown (26), Poynter (49, 74), Whitter (65);
Goals: G Brown 4.
Sin bin: Bruce (32) - ball stealing.
Rugby Leaguer & League Express Men of the Match: *Rovers:* Paul Parker; *Eagles:* Gavin Brown.
Penalty count: 11-7; **Half-time:** 20-6;
Referee: Steve Addy (Huddersfield); **Attendance:** 1,553.

WEST

SALFORD CITY REDS 58 ROCHDALE HORNETS 16

CITY REDS: 1 Jason Flowers; 2 Michael Platt; 3 Stuart Littler; 4 Andy Kirk; 5 Alan Hunte; 6 Cliff Beverley; 7 Gavin Clinch; 8 Neil Baynes; 9 Malcolm Alker; 10 Andy Coley; 11 Simon Baldwin; 12 Lee Marsh; 13 Chris Charles. Subs (all used): 14 David Highton; 15 Karl Fitzpatrick; 16 Paul Highton; 17 Neil Lowe.
Tries: Beverley (3, 26), Kirk (10, 72), Coley (13), Flowers (15, 63), Alker (17, 42), D Highton (44), Clinch (54);
Goals: Marsh 5, Clinch 2.
HORNETS: 1 Paul Owen; 2 Sean Cooper; 3 Mick Nanyn; 4 Jon Roper; 5 Casey Mayberry; 6 Stephen Doherty; 7 Ian Watson; 8 Paul Southern; 9 Richard Pachniuk; 10 David Stephenson; 11 Paul Smith; 12 James Bunyan; 13 Damian Ball. Subs (all used): 14 Warren Ayres; 15 David Larder; 16 Gareth Price; 17 Matthew Long.
Tries: Roper (7), Nanyn (22), Long (50);
Goals: Nanyn, Watson.
Rugby Leaguer & League Express Men of the Match: *City Reds:* Cliff Beverley; *Hornets:* Ian Watson.
Penalty count: 12-6; **Half-time:** 30-10;
Referee: Ben Thaler (Wakefield); **Attendance:** 2,346.

SWINTON LIONS 16 OLDHAM 24

LIONS: 1 Wayne English; 2 Jason Roach; 3 Kris Tassell; 4 Phil Hassan; 5 Hugh Thorpe; 6 Rob Gallagher; 7 Chris Hough; 8 Andy Leathem; 9 Rob Barraclough; 10 Simon Knox; 11 Craig Wingfield; 12 Phil Cushion; 13 Peter Cannon. Subs (all used): 14 Chris Roe; 15 Grant Bithel; 16 Andy Cheetham; 17 Dave Ellison.
Tries: Barraclough (10), Roach (31), Cannon (54);
Goals: Hough 2.
OLDHAM: 1 Jon Goddard; 2 Chris Irwin; 3 Paul Anderson; 4 Iain Marsh; 5 Joe McNicholas; 6 Simon Svabic; 7 Neil Roden; 8 Steve Molloy; 9 John Hough; 10 Martin McLoughlin; 11 Lee Doran; 12 Ryan Stazicker; 13 Phil Farrell. Subs (all used): 14 Gareth Barber; 15 Keith Brennan; 16 Chris Morley; 17 Jason Clegg.
Tries: Doran (6), Goddard (16), Hough (23), Barber (73); **Goals:** Svabic 4.
Rugby Leaguer & League Express Men of the Match: *Lions:* Wayne English; *Oldham:* Simon Svabic.
Penalty count: 10-7; **Half-time:** 10-18;
Referee: Steve Presley (Castleford); **Attendance:** 923.

CENTRAL

BATLEY BULLDOGS 82 LONDON SKOLARS 4

BULLDOGS: 1 Craig Lingard; 2 Chris North; 3 Chris Spurr; 4 Simon Lewis; 5 Matt Bramald; 6 David Gibbons; 7 Barry Eaton; 8 Craig Booth; 9 Kris Lythe; 10 Joe Berry; 11 Steve Beard; 12 Mark Toohey; 13 Ryan Horsley. Subs (all used): 14 Danny Maun; 15 Paul Harrison; 16 Andy Spink; 17 Gavin Swinson.
Tries: Booth (9, 58), Lewis (13), Bramald (18), Lingard (20), D Gibbons (25, 65), Toohey (32), North (40, 68), Swinson (52), Spurr (63), Horsley (70), Harrison (72), Beard (77); **Goals:** Eaton 11.
SKOLARS: 1 Kirk Wotherspoon; 2 Charlie Oyebade; 3 Scott Roberts; 4 Jake Johnstone; 5 Leon John; 6 Richard Pollard; 7 Rob McKeown; 8 Obi Ijeoma; 9 Cory Bennett; 10 Glenn Osborn; 11 Allan Tito; 12 Mike Okwusogu; 13 Steve Hainey. Subs (all used): 14 Troy Dougherty; 15 Neil Foster; 16 Gareth Janes; 17 Richard Brantingham.
Try: Bennett (60).
Rugby Leaguer & League Express Men of the Match: *Bulldogs:* Craig Booth; *Skolars:* Allan Tito.
Penalty count: 10-6; **Half-time:** 38-0;
Referee: Peter Taberner (Wigan); **Attendance:** 577.

HUNSLET HAWKS 16 KEIGHLEY COUGARS 4

HAWKS: 1 Richard Baker; 2 Bryn Powell; 3 Iain Higgins; 4 Michael Lyons; 5 George Rayner; 6 Jon Liddell; 7 Phil Hasty; 8 Craig Ibbetson; 9 Gareth Naylor; 10 Mick Coyle; 11 Wayne Freeman; 12 Danny Fearon; 13 Paul Seal. Subs (all used): 14 Gareth Brain; 15 Simon Jackson; 16 Jonlee Lockwood; 17 Andy Brent.
Tries: Higgins (13), Rayner (37, 70); **Goals:** Liddell 2.
Sin bin: Coyle (38) - fighting.
COUGARS: 1 James Rushforth; 2 Karl Smith; 3 David Foster; 4 Chris Wainwright; 5 Andy Robinson; 6 Paul Ashton; 7 Matt Firth; 8 Phil Stephenson; 9 Simeon Hoyle; 10 Danny Ekis; 11 Oliver Wilkes; 12 Ian Sinfield; 13 Jason Ramshaw. Subs (all used): 14 Lee Patterson; 15 Richard Mervill; 16 Lee Kelly; 17 Chris Hannah.
Goals: Ashton 2.
Rugby Leaguer & League Express Men of the Match: *Hawks:* George Rayner; *Cougars:* Jason Ramshaw.
Penalty count: 12-10; **Half-time:** 10-4;
Referee: Julian King (St Helens); **Attendance:** 610.

WEST v NORTH

LEIGH CENTURIONS 38 CHORLEY LYNX 20

CENTURIONS: 1 Michael Watts; 2 Leroy Rivett; 3 Damian Munro; 4 Dale Cardoza; 5 Alan Hadcroft; 6 Patrick Weisner; 7 John Duffy; 8 Sonny Nickle; 9 Paul Rowley; 10 Rob Ball; 11 Sean Richardson; 12 Bryan Henare; 13 Adam Bristow. Subs (all used): 14 Willie Swann; 15 Lee Sanderson; 16 John Hamilton; 17 Dale Holdstock.
Tries: Rivett (7, 57), Cardoza (11), Rowley (15), Duffy (28), Swann (35), Henare (53); **Goals:** Duffy 5.
LYNX: 1 Chris Ramsdale; 2 Marlon Miller; 3 Mick Redford; 4 Eddie Kilgannon; 5 Anton Garcia; 6 Mick Coates; 7 John Braddish; 8 Tim Street; 9 Mike Briggs; 10 Simon Smith; 11 Wayne Bloor; 12 Dave McConnell; 13 Ian Hodson. Subs (all used): 14 Ian Parry; 15 Dave Newton; 16 Lee Rowley; 17 Martin Roden.
Tries: Smith (23), Street (63), Briggs (66), Miller (70);
Goals: Braddish 2.
Rugby Leaguer & League Express Men of the Match: *Centurions:* John Duffy; *Lynx:* Simon Smith.
Penalty count: 4-12; **Half-time:** 28-6; **Referee:** Steve Nicholson (Whitehaven); **Attendance:** 1,871.

EAST v CENTRAL

YORK CITY KNIGHTS 18 DEWSBURY RAMS 38

CITY KNIGHTS: 1 Gavin Molloy; 2 Chris Smith; 3 Jonathan Firth; 4 Darren Callaghan; 5 Chris Beever; 6 Scott Yeaman; 7 Trevor Krause; 8 Richard Hayes; 9 Lee Jackson; 10 Tommy Gallagher; 11 Damian Kennedy; 12 Scott Fletcher; 13 Mark Cain. Subs (all used): 14 Darren Robinson; 15 Gareth Lloyd; 16 Mick Ramsden; 17 Paul Broadbent.
Tries: C Smith (46), Cain (62), Callaghan (69);
Goals: Yeaman, Robinson 2.
RAMS: 1 Jamie Benn; 2 George Mack; 3 Chris Chapman; 4 Billy Kershaw; 5 Chris Redfearn; 6 Danny Brough; 7 Scott Rhodes; 8 Frank Watene; 9 Andy Heptinstall; 10 Tony Fella; 11 Paul Hicks; 12 Danny Evans; 13 Richard Slater. Subs (all used): 14 Jimmy Elston; 15 Mark Barlow; 16 Anthony Thewliss; 17 Carl Sayer.
Tries: Redfearn (4), Fella (31), Benn (52), Kershaw (66), Mack (76), Hicks (79); **Goals:** Benn 7.
Rugby Leaguer & League Express Men of the Match: *City Knights:* Chris Smith; *Rams:* Frank Watene.
Penalty count: 13-9; **Half-time:** 0-12;
Referee: Mike Dawber (Wigan); **Attendance:** 1,231.

WEEK 5

Sunday 2nd March 2003

NORTH

WHITEHAVEN 36 WORKINGTON TOWN 14

WHITEHAVEN: 1 Gary Broadbent; 2 Paul O'Neil; 4 Howard Hill; 3 David Seeds; 5 Jamie Stenhouse; 6 Leroy Joe; 7 Lee Kiddie; 8 Dean Vaughan; 9 Aaron Lester; 10 David Fatialofa; 11 Chris McKinney; 12 Graeme Morton; 13 Spencer Miller. Subs (all used): 14 Darren Holt; 15 Marc Jackson; 16 Tony Cunningham; 17 Steven Wood.
Tries: Hill (4), Kiddie (19), Morton (30), Cunningham (49), Lester (60, 65), O'Neil (67); **Goals:** O'Neil 4.
TOWN: 1 Dean Sharp; 2 Matthew Johnson; 3 Brett McDermott; 4 Anthony Huddart; 5 Graeme Lewthwaite; 6 Brett Smith; 7 Kevin Hetherington; 8 Matthew Tunstall; 9 Carl Sice; 10 Craig Barker; 11 Jamie Beaumont; 12 William Blackburn; 13 Ricky Wright. Subs (all used, three subs only): 14 Hitro Okesene; 15 David Pettit; 16 Jonathan Heaney.
Tries: Sharp (12), Wright (35); **Goals:** Hetherington 3.
Rugby Leaguer & League Express Men of the Match: *Whitehaven:* Aaron Lester; *Town:* Ricky Wright.
Penalty count: 9-8; **Half-time:** 12-14;
Referee: Mike Dawber (Wigan); **Attendance:** 1,479.

WEST v NORTH

OLDHAM 50 BARROW RAIDERS 11

OLDHAM: 1 Gavin Dodd; 2 Chris Campbell; 3 Iain Marsh; 4 Jon Goddard; 5 Joe McNicholas; 6 Simon Svabic; 7 Keith Brennan; 8 Steve Molloy; 9 Anthony Murray; 10 Dane Morgan; 11 Lee Doran; 12 Ryan Stazicker; 13 Phil Farrell. Subs (all used): 14 Gareth Barber; 15 Paul Anderson; 16 Adam Sharples; 17 Darren Shaw.
Tries: Morgan (8), Farrell (25), Murray (36), Goddard (51), Dodd (65, 79), Barber (68), Anderson (71);
Goals: Svabic 9.
RAIDERS: 1 Adam Pate; 2 Jamie Marshall; 3 Danny Lockhart; 4 Andy McClure; 5 Shane Irabor; 6 Craig Bower; 7 Paul Evans; 8 Tau Liku; 9 Andy Henderson; 10 Stuart Dancer; 11 Paul Lupton; 12 Steve Jackson; 13 Geoff Luxon. Subs (all used): 14 Barry Pugh; 15 Paul Dean; 16 Wayne Jones; 17 James Stainton.
Tries: Marshall (15), McClure (46);
Goal: Evans; **Field goal:** Evans.
Rugby Leaguer & League Express Men of the Match: *Oldham:* Simon Svabic; *Raiders:* Andy Henderson.
Penalty count: 9-12; **Half-time:** 18-7;
Referee: Steve Addy (Huddersfield); **Attendance:** 1,280.

Wednesday 5th March 2003

EAST v CENTRAL

SHEFFIELD EAGLES 18 BATLEY BULLDOGS 8

EAGLES: 1 Greg Hurst; 2 Jon Breakingbury; 3 Neil Kite; 4 Nick Turnbull; 5 Paul Wells; 6 Peter Reilly; 7 Gavin Brown; 8 Jon Bruce; 9 Lee Bettinson; 10 Jack Howieson; 11 Craig Brown; 12 Andy Raleigh; 13 Richard Goddard. Subs (all used): 14 Mitchell Stringer; 15 Wayne Flynn; 16 Simon Tillyer; 17 Ryan Angus.
Tries: Hurst (8), Reilly (41), Breakingbury (62);
Goals: G Brown 3.
BULLDOGS: 1 Craig Lingard; 2 Jeremy Dyson; 3 Anthony Gibbons; 4 Danny Maun; 5 Matt Bramald; 6 David Gibbons; 7 Barry Eaton; 8 Joe Naidole; 9 Kris Lythe; 10 Joe Berry; 11 David Rourke; 12 Will Cartledge; 13 Ryan Horsley. Subs (all used): 14 Chris Spurr; 15 Paul Harrison; 16 Mark Toohey; 17 Craig Booth.
Try: Booth (58); **Goals:** Eaton 2.
Rugby Leaguer & League Express Men of the Match: *Eagles:* Peter Reilly; *Bulldogs:* Barry Eaton.
Penalty count: 10-9; **Half-time:** 4-2;
Referee: Ben Thaler (Wakefield); **Attendance:** 732.

WEEK 6

Sunday 9th March 2003

NORTH

CHORLEY LYNX 22 WORKINGTON TOWN 16

LYNX: 1 Mark McCully; 2 Marlon Miller; 3 Mick Redford; 4 David Ingram; 5 Anton Garcia; 6 Ian Hodson; 7 John Braddish; 8 Tim Street; 9 Mike Briggs; 10 David Whittle; 11 Wayne Bloor; 12 Dave Byrne; 13 Dave McConnell. Subs (all used): 14 Eddie Kilgannon; 15 Liam Bretherton; 16 Dave Newton; 17 Ian Parry.
Tries: Ingram (13), Whittle (31), Briggs (45), Bretherton (73); **Goals:** Braddish 3.
Sin bin: Whittle (55) - dissent.
TOWN: 1 Dean Sharp; 2 Matthew Johnson; 3 Jonathan Heaney; 4 Kevin Hetherington; 5 Anthony Huddart; 6 Brett Smith; 7 Danny Burns; 8 Craig Barker; 9 Carl Sice; 10 Hitro Okesene; 11 Jamie Beaumont; 12 David Pettit; 13 Brett McDermott. Subs (all used): 14 James Robinson; 15 Matthew Tunstall; 16 Tony Dymtrowski; 17 Graeme Lewthwaite.
Tries: Smith (9), Pettit (24), Hetherington (35);
Goals: Smith, Hetherington.
Rugby Leaguer & League Express Men of the Match: *Lynx:* Mike Briggs; *Town:* Carl Sice.
Penalty count: 8-7; **Half-time:** 12-14;
Referee: Ben Thaler (Wakefield); **Attendance:** 251.

GATESHEAD THUNDER 24 BARROW RAIDERS 28

THUNDER: 1 Kevin Neighbour; 2 Robin Peers; 3 Damien Reid; 4 PJ Solomon; 5 Richie Barnett; 6 Paul Thorman; 7 Craig Fisher; 8 Steven Bradley; 9 Chris Fletcher; 10 David Bates; 11 Clint Brown; 12 Craig Firth; 13 Jermaine Coleman. Subs (all used): 14 Yusuf Sozi; 15 Tom Lauriston; 16 James Mackay; 17 Neil Thorman.
Tries: Fletcher (20), Barnett (36, 48), Bates (63), N Thorman (72); **Goals:** N Thorman 2.
RAIDERS: 1 Adam Pate; 2 Jamie Marshall; 3 Craig Bower; 4 Andy McClure; 5 Shane Irabor; 6 Paul Evans; 7 Chris Archer; 8 Tau Liku; 9 Andy Henderson; 10 Steve Jackson; 11 James King; 12 Paul Lupton; 13 Phil Atkinson. Subs (all used): 14 Paul Gardner; 15 Geoff

Luxon; 16 Stuart Dancer; 17 James Stainton.
Tries: Evans (7), Pate (28), Irabor (31), King (46), Marshall (66); **Goals:** Atkinson, Evans 3.
Rugby Leaguer & League Express Men of the Match: *Thunder:* Richie Barnett; *Raiders:* Chris Archer.
Penalty count: 8-9; **Half-time:** 8-14;
Referee: Julian King (St Helens); **Attendance:** 232.

EAST

HULL KINGSTON ROVERS 8 DONCASTER DRAGONS 21

ROVERS: 1 Craig Poucher; 2 Nick Pinkney; 3 Mark Blanchard; 4 Craig Farrell; 5 Alasdair McClarron; 6 Paul Parker; 7 Chris Stephenson; 8 Richard Wilson; 9 Paul Pickering; 10 Jamie Bovill; 11 Adam Sullivan; 12 Dean Andrews; 13 Jon Aston. Subs (all used): 14 Jimmy Walker; 15 Steve Cochran; 16 Matt Emmerson; 17 Paul Fletcher.
Try: Pickering (9); **Goals:** Stephenson 2.
Sin bin: Bovill (22) - fighting; Pinkney (30) - dissent.
DRAGONS: 1 Chris Ross; 2 Paul Gleadhill; 3 Marvin Golden; 4 Simon Irving; 5 Dean Colton; 6 Paul Mansson; 7 Mark Moxon; 8 Gareth Handford; 9 Peter Edwards; 10 Maea David; 11 Peter Green; 12 Matt Walker; 13 Brad Hepi. Subs (all used): 14 James Walker; 15 Shaun Leafe; 16 Craig Lawton; 17 Craig Forsyth.
Tries: M Walker (15), Mansson (30), Ross (51);
Goals: Irving 4; **Field goal:** Moxon.
Sin bin: Handford (22) - fighting;
Edwards (32) - striking.
Rugby Leaguer & League Express Men of the Match: *Rovers:* Paul Pickering; *Dragons:* Paul Mansson.
Penalty count: 11-8; **Half-time:** 8-14;
Referee: Steve Presley (Castleford); **Attendance:** 1,553.

SHEFFIELD EAGLES 12 YORK CITY KNIGHTS 32

EAGLES: 1 Andy Poynter; 2 Jon Breakingbury; 3 Neil Kite; 4 Pat Rich; 5 Paul Wells; 6 Peter Reilly; 7 Gavin Brown; 8 Jack Howieson; 9 Guy Adams; 10 Jon Bruce; 11 Richard Goddard; 12 Simon Tillyer; 13 Wayne Flynn. Subs (all used): 14 Lee Bettinson; 15 Ryan Angus; 16 Andy Raleigh; 17 Craig Brown.
Tries: Wells (22), Raleigh (57); **Goals:** G Brown 2.
CITY KNIGHTS: 1 Chris Beever; 2 Chris Smith; 3 Graeme Hallas; 4 Darren Callaghan; 5 Gavin Molloy; 6 Jonathan Firth; 7 Trevor Krause; 8 Paul Broadbent; 9 Lee Jackson; 10 Richard Hayes; 11 Mick Ramsden; 12 Scott Fletcher; 13 Mark Cain. Subs (all used): 14 Darren Robinson; 15 Gareth Lloyd; 16 Mick Embleton; 17 David Bolus.
Tries: Ramsden (17), Callaghan (30), Molloy (34), C Smith (74); **Goals:** Hallas 8.
Rugby Leaguer & League Express Men of the Match: *Eagles:* Peter Reilly; *City Knights:* Graeme Hallas.
Penalty count: 11-11; **Half-time:** 6-22;
Referee: Ashley Klein (London); **Attendance:** 730.

WEST

OLDHAM 4 SALFORD CITY REDS 62

OLDHAM: 1 Gavin Dodd; 2 Chris Irwin; 3 Paul Anderson; 4 Iain Marsh; 5 Chris Campbell; 6 Simon Svabic; 7 Keith Brennan; 8 Steve Molloy; 9 Anthony Murray; 10 Darren Shaw; 11 Lee Doran; 12 Chris Morley; 13 Phil Farrell. Subs (all used): 14 Gareth Barber; 15 Martin McLoughlin; 16 Ryan Stazicker; 17 Dane Morgan.
Try: Irwin (25).
CITY REDS: 1 Jason Flowers; 2 Michael Platt; 3 Stuart Littler; 4 Andy Kirk; 5 Danny Arnold; 6 Cliff Beverley; 7 Gavin Clinch; 8 Andy Coley; 9 Malcolm Alker; 10 Paul Highton; 11 Simon Baldwin; 12 Neil Lowe; 13 Chris Charles. Subs (all used): 14 Steve Blakeley; 15 David Highton; 16 Gareth Haggerty; 17 Andy Gorski.
Tries: Charles (1, 37, 67), Beverley (31), Flowers (44), Alker (53, 58), D Highton (55), Littler (63, 77), Kirk (71);
Goals: Clinch 5, Blakeley 4.
Rugby Leaguer & League Express Men of the Match: *Oldham:* Keith Brennan; *City Reds:* Gavin Clinch.
Penalty count: 8-5; **Half-time:** 4-18;
Referee: Peter Taberner (Wigan; **Attendance:** 2,839.

ROCHDALE HORNETS 32 LEIGH CENTURIONS 34

HORNETS: 1 Paul Owen; 2 Casey Mayberry; 3 James Bunyan; 4 Jon Roper; 5 Marlon Billy; 6 Warren Ayres; 7 Ian Watson; 8 Andy Grundy; 9 Richard Pachniuk; 10 Gareth Price; 11 David Larder; 12 Matthew Leigh; 13 Paul Smith. Subs (all used): 14 Damian Ball; 15 Paul Southern; 16 Mick Nanyn; 17 Matthew Long.
Tries: Owen (12, 57 ,61), Billy (35), Nanyn (75), Mayberry (80); **Goals:** Watson 4.
CENTURIONS: 1 Neil Turley; 2 Leroy Rivett; 3 Damian Munro; 4 Dale Cardoza; 5 Alan Hadcroft; 6 Willie Swann; 7 John Duffy; 8 Sonny Nickle; 9 Paul Rowley; 10 David Bradbury; 11 Sean Richardson; 12 Bryan Henare; 13 Adam Bristow. Subs (all used): 14 Phil Kendrick; 14 Michael Watts; 16 Lee Sanderson; 17 Rob Ball.
Tries: Rowley (15, 72), Munro (17), Rivett (40), Bristow (53), Sanderson (79); **Goals:** Turley 5.
Rugby Leaguer & League Express Men of the Match: *Hornets:* Paul Owen; *Centurions:* Adam Bristow.
Penalty count: 3-4; **Half-time:** 10-16; **Referee:** Colin Morris (Huddersfield); **Attendance:** 1,251.

CENTRAL

DEWSBURY RAMS 22 BATLEY BULLDOGS 18

RAMS: 1 Nathan Batty; 2 Michael Wainwright; 3 Chris Chapman; 4 Billy Kershaw; 5 George Mack; 6 Danny Brough; 7 Scott Rhodes; 8 Frank Watene; 9 Jimmy Elston; 10 Tony Fella; 11 Danny Evans; 12 Paul Hicks; 13 Chris Redfearn. Subs (all used): 14 John Waddell; 15 Ryan Hardy; 16 Andrew Fawkes; 17 Graham Summerscales.
Tries: Elston (9), Hicks (24), Wainwright (47, 75);
Goals: Brough 3.
BULLDOGS: 1 Craig Lingard; 2 Mark Sibson; 3 Anthony Gibbons; 4 Danny Maun; 5 Leon Williamson; 6 David Gibbons; 7 Barry Eaton; 8 Craig Booth; 9 Mark Cass; 10 Andy Spink; 11 David Rourke; 12 Mark Toohey; 13 Ryan Horsley. Subs (all used): 14 Simon Lewis; 15 Paul Harrison; 16 Joe Berry; 17 Will Cartledge.
Tries: Toohey (5), A Gibbons (34), Harrison (79);
Goals: Eaton 3.
Rugby Leaguer & League Express Men of the Match: *Rams:* Paul Hicks; *Bulldogs:* Craig Booth.
Penalty count: 9-15; **Half-time:** 10-12; **Referee:** Ronnie Laughton (Barnsley); **Attendance:** 1,432.

KEIGHLEY COUGARS 78 LONDON SKOLARS 18

COUGARS: 1 James Rushforth; 2 Karl Smith; 3 David Foster; 4 Matt Foster; 5 Andy Robinson; 6 Paul Ashton; 7 Matt Firth; 8 Phil Stephenson; 9 Simeon Hoyle; 10 Danny Ekis; 11 Oliver Wilkes; 12 Ian Sinfield; 13 Jason Ramshaw. Subs (all used): 14 Chris Wainwright; 15 Gareth Hewitt; 16 Richard Mervill; 17 Ricky Helliwell.
Tries: Firth (2, 15, 71, 76), Wilkes (8), Ramshaw (13, 57), M Foster (27, 37), Smith (34, 73), Mervill (48), Hoyle (55), Robinson (78); **Goals:** Ashton 8, Wilkes 3.
SKOLARS: 1 Kirk Wotherspoon; 2 Neil Foster; 3 Jake Johnstone; 4 Ronald Mushiso; 5 Charlie Oyebade; 6 Richard Pollard; 7 Rob McKeown; 8 Glenn Osborn; 9 Kahu Henare; 10 Obi Ijeoma; 11 Brett McCroary; 12 Allan Tito; 13 Cory Bennett. Subs (all used): 14 Scott Roberts; 15 James Hersey; 16 Keri Ryan; 17 Gareth Janes.
Tries: Bennett (45), Mushiso (66), Wotherspoon (79);
Goals: Johnstone 3.
Sin bin: Mushiso (39) - high tackle.
Rugby Leaguer & League Express Men of the Match: *Cougars:* Matt Firth; *Skolars:* Rob McKeown.
Penalty count: 3-7; **Half-time:** 38-0;
Referee: Steve Addy (Huddersfield); **Attendance:** 732.

NORTH v WEST

WHITEHAVEN 38 SWINTON LIONS 6

WHITEHAVEN: 1 Paul O'Neil; 2 Steven Wood; 3 Howard Hill; 4 David Seeds; 5 Jamie Stenhouse; 6 Leroy Joe; 7 Darren Holt; 8 Gary Smith; 9 Aaron Lester; 10 David Fatialofa; 11 Spencer Miller; 12 Graeme Morton; 13 Garry Purdham. Subs (all used): 14 Lee Kiddie; 15 Ryan Campbell; 16 Tony Cunningham; 17 Mike Whitehead.
Tries: Stenhouse (11), Holt (16), Joe (27, 36, 39, 75), Lester (55); **Goals:** Holt 5.
LIONS: 1 Wayne English; 2 Adrian Mead; 3 Andy Cheetham; 4 Phil Hassan; 5 Lee Hudson; 6 Grant Bithel; 7 Chris Hough; 8 Simon Knox; 9 Rob Barraclough; 10 Phil Cushion; 11 Craig Wingfield; 12 Dave Ellison; 13 Peter Cannon. Subs (all used): 14 Hugh Thorpe; 15 Jason Johnson; 16 Mark Ashton; 17 Alan Shea.
Try: Bithel (72); **Goal:** Wingfield.
Sin bin: Cannon (45) - holding down.
Rugby Leaguer & League Express Men of the Match: *Whitehaven:* Aaron Lester; *Lions:* Rob Barraclough.
Penalty count: 10-6; **Half-time:** 26-0;
Referee: Mike Dawber (Wigan); **Attendance:** 1,060.

CENTRAL v EAST

HUNSLET HAWKS 4 FEATHERSTONE ROVERS 42

HAWKS: 1 Richard Baker; 2 Bryn Powell; 3 Iain Higgins; 4 Wes McGibbon; 5 George Rayner; 6 Jon Liddell; 7 Phil Hasty; 8 Craig Ibbetson; 9 Gareth Naylor; 10 Mick Coyle; 11 Wayne Freeman; 12 Danny Fearon; 13 Paul Seal. Subs (all used): 14 Tony Howcroft; 15 Jonlee Lockwood; 16 Andy Brent; 17 Shaun Ibbetson.
Try: McGibbon (67).
ROVERS: 1 Nathan Graham; 2 Jamie Stokes; 3 Brendan O'Meara; 4 Ian Brown; 5 Adrian Flynn; 6 Richard Agar; 7 Carl Briggs; 8 Ian Tonks; 9 Richard Chapman; 10 Stuart Dickens; 11 Steve Dooler; 12 Andy Rice; 13 Danny Seal. Subs (all used): 14 Andy McNally; 15 Andy Bailey; 16 Chris Molyneux; 17 Robin Jowitt.
Tries: Brown (4, 79), Flynn (25, 74), Stokes (42, 48, 56), Dooler (54); **Goals:** Briggs, Dickens 3;
Field goals: Agar, Briggs.
Sin bin: Chapman (30) - dissent; Tonks (61) - dissent.
Rugby Leaguer & League Express Men of the Match: *Hawks:* Phil Hasty; *Rovers:* Richard Chapman.
Penalty count: 12-8; **Half-time:** 0-11; **Referee:** Steve Nicholson (Whitehaven); **Attendance:** 793.

WEEK 7

Sunday 16th March 2003

NORTH

CHORLEY LYNX 22 BARROW RAIDERS 28

LYNX: 1 Mark McCully; 2 Marlon Miller; 3 Mick Redford; 4 David Ingram; 5 Anton Garcia; 6 Liam Bretherton; 7 John Braddish; 8 Tim Street; 9 Mike Briggs; 10 David Whittle; 11 Wayne Bloor; 12 Dave Byrne; 13 Dave McConnell. Subs (all used): 14 Gavin Johnson; 15 Eddie Kilgannon; 16 Martin Gambles; 17 Ian Hodson.
Tries: McConnell (33), Bloor (38), Briggs (71), Hodson (75); **Goals:** Braddish 2, McCully.
RAIDERS: 1 Craig Bower; 2 Jamie Marshall; 3 Phil Atkinson; 4 Andy McClure; 5 Shane Irabor; 6 Paul Evans; 7 Chris Archer; 8 Tau Liku; 9 Dave Clark; 10 Steve Jackson; 11 James King; 12 Paul Lupton; 13 Andy Henderson. Subs: 14 Geoff Luxon; 15 James Stainton (not used); 16 Stuart Dancer; 17 Wayne Jones.
Tries: McClure (11), Atkinson (24), Clark (28), Evans (48), Irabor (52); **Goals:** Atkinson 4.
Rugby Leaguer & League Express Men of the Match: *Lynx:* Mick Redford; *Raiders:* Dave Clark.
Penalty count: 6-11; **Half-time:** 12-18;
Referee: Ashley Klein (London); **Attendance:** 258.

GATESHEAD THUNDER 20 WHITEHAVEN 34

THUNDER: 1 Kevin Neighbour; 2 Robin Peers; 3 Damien Reid; 4 Andy Walker; 5 Richie Barnett; 6 Paul Thorman; 7 Neil Thorman; 8 Steven Bradley; 9 Chris Fletcher; 10 David Bates; 11 Steve Rutherford; 12 James Mackay; 13 Jermaine Coleman. Subs (all used): 14 James Hartley; 15 Olu Iwenofu; 16 Tony Doherty; 17 John Coutts.
Tries: Reid (18, 63), Peers (45), Neighbour (79);
Goals: N Thorman 2.
WHITEHAVEN: 1 Gary Broadbent; 2 Paul O'Neil; 3 David Seeds; 4 Jamie Stenhouse; 5 Leigh Smith; 6 Leroy Joe; 7 Darren Holt; 8 Gary Smith; 9 Marc Jackson; 10 David Fatialofa; 11 Chris McKinney; 12 Craig Chambers; 13 Howard Hill. Subs (all used): 14 Lee Kiddie; 15 Steven Wood; 16 Mike Whitehead; 17 Dean Vaughan.
Tries: Joe (5), O'Neil (8, 70), Hill (31, 48), Vaughan (60);
Goals: Holt 5.
Sin bin: Whitehead (53) - persistent offside.
Rugby Leaguer & League Express Men of the Match: *Thunder:* Damien Reid; *Whitehaven:* Howard Hill.
Penalty count: 11-6; **Half-time:** 4-18;
Referee: Steve Addy (Huddersfield); **Attendance:** 272.

EAST

FEATHERSTONE ROVERS 44 HULL KINGSTON ROVERS 20

ROVERS: 1 Nathan Graham; 2 Jamie Stokes; 3 Brendan O'Meara; 4 Ian Brown; 5 Adrian Flynn; 6 Richard Agar; 7 Carl Briggs; 8 Ian Tonks; 9 Richard Chapman; 10 Stuart Dickens; 11 Steve Dooler; 12 Andy Rice; 13 Danny Seal. Subs (all used): 14 Jonathan Presley; 15 Andy McNally; 16 Andy Bailey; 17 Chris Molyneux.
Tries: Stokes (5, 35, 67), Graham (20), Brown (29), Briggs (31), Rice (44), Seal (78), Flynn (79);
Goals: Dickens, Briggs 3.
ROBINS: 1 Craig Poucher; 2 Nick Pinkney; 3 Lynton Stott; 4 Craig Farrell; 5 Alasdair McClarron; 6 Paul Parker; 7 Chris Stephenson; 8 Richard Wilson; 9 Paul Pickering; 10 Jamie Bovill; 11 Adam Sullivan; 12 Jon Aston; 13 Andy Smith. Subs (all used): 14 Jimmy Walker; 15 Steve Cochran; 16 Dean Andrews; 17 Paul Fletcher.
Tries: Parker (15), Pickering (58), Poucher (72);
Goals: Stott 4.
Sin bin: Smith (24) - professional foul.
Rugby Leaguer & League Express Men of the Match: *Rovers:* Ian Tonks; *Robins:* Chris Stephenson.
Penalty count: 11-4; **Half-time:** 24-8;
Referee: Mike Dawber (Wigan); **Attendance:** 1,712.

YORK CITY KNIGHTS 34 DONCASTER DRAGONS 20

CITY KNIGHTS: 1 Chris Smith; 2 Alex Godfrey; 3 Graeme Hallas; 4 Darren Callaghan; 5 Gavin Molloy; 6 Jonathan Firth; 7 Trevor Krause; 8 Paul Broadbent; 9 Darren Robinson; 10 Richard Hayes; 11 Mick Ramsden; 12 Scott Fletcher; 13 Mark Cain. Subs: 14 Chris Beever (not used); 15 Gareth Lloyd; 16 Mick Embleton (not used); 17 David Bolus.
Tries: Hallas (29), Broadbent (50), Fletcher (56), Cain (61), Callaghan (69), Krause (72); **Goals:** Hallas 5.
DRAGONS: 1 Chris Ross; 2 Paul Gleadhill; 3 Marvin Golden; 4 Simon Irving; 5 Jason Lee; 6 Paul Mansson; 7 Mark Moxon; 8 Gareth Handford; 9 Peter Edwards; 10 Craig Forsyth; 11 Peter Green; 12 Craig Lawton; 13 Matt Walker. Subs (all used): 14 James Walker; 15 Dean Colton; 16 Andy Burland; 17 Shaun Leafe.
Tries: Gleadhill (23), P Green (32), Golden (45);
Goals: Irving 4.
Dismissal: Ross (39) - punching.
Rugby Leaguer & League Express Men of the Match: *City Knights:* Scott Fletcher; *Dragons:* Paul Mansson.
Penalty count: 8-9; **Half-time:** 8-14;
Referee: Ben Thaler (Wakefield); **Attendance:** 1,133.

WEST

OLDHAM 26 LEIGH CENTURIONS 31

OLDHAM: 1 Gavin Dodd; 2 Chris Irwin; 3 Paul Anderson; 4 Iain Marsh; 5 Will Cowell; 6 Gareth Barber; 7 Neil Roden; 8 Steve Molloy; 9 John Hough; 10 Darren Shaw; 11 Lee Doran; 12 Ryan Stazicker; 13 Chris Morley. Subs (all used): 14 Keith Brennan; 15 Simon Svabic; 16 Martin McLoughlin; 17 Paul Norton.
Tries: Hough (6), Barber (36), Irwin (68), Brennan (75), Dodd (78); **Goals:** Barber 3.
CENTURIONS: 1 Neil Turley; 2 Leroy Rivett; 3 Damian Munro; 4 Dale Cardoza; 5 Michael Watts; 6 Patrick Weisner; 7 John Duffy; 8 Rob Ball; 9 Paul Rowley; 10 Bryan Henare; 11 Sean Richardson; 12 Adam Bristow; 13 Willie Swann. Subs (all used): 14 Dale Holdstock; 15 Eric Andrews; 16 David Alstead; 17 Phil Kendrick.
Tries: Weisner (22), Rowley (27), Turley (49), Andrews (71); **Goals:** Turley 7; **Field goal:** Turley.
Sin bin: Duffy (57) - persistent offside.
Rugby Leaguer & League Express Men of the Match: *Oldham:* Lee Doran; *Centurions:* Paul Rowley.
Penalty count: 15-12; **Half-time:** 12-12; **Referee:** Ronnie Laughton (Barnsley); **Attendance:** 1,945.

CENTRAL

KEIGHLEY COUGARS 22 DEWSBURY RAMS 2

COUGARS: 1 James Rushforth; 2 Karl Smith; 3 David Foster; 4 Matt Foster; 5 Andy Robinson; 6 Adam Mitchell; 7 Matt Firth; 8 Phil Stephenson; 9 Simeon Hoyle; 10 Danny Ekis; 11 Oliver Wilkes; 12 Ian Sinfield; 13 Jason Ramshaw. Subs (all used): 14 Chris Wainwright; 15 Gareth Hewitt; 16 Ricky Helliwell; 17 Richard Mervill.
Tries: Firth (13), Robinson (49), Mitchell (62), Wainwright (76); **Goals:** Mitchell 3.
RAMS: 1 Nathan Batty; 2 Michael Wainwright; 3 Andrew Fawkes; 4 Billy Kershaw; 5 George Mack; 6 Danny Brough; 7 Scott Rhodes; 8 Frank Watene; 9 Jimmy Elston; 10 Tony Fella; 11 Danny Evans; 12 Paul Hicks; 13 Chris Redfearn. Subs (all used): 14 Michael Walker; 15 Ryan Hardy; 16 John Waddell; 17 Graham Summerscales.
Goal: Brough.
Rugby Leaguer & League Express Men of the Match: *Cougars:* Matt Firth; *Rams:* Frank Watene.
Penalty count: 8-6; **Half-time:** 8-0;
Referee: Peter Taberner (Wigan); **Attendance:** 1,111.

LONDON SKOLARS 18 HUNSLET HAWKS 42

SKOLARS: 1 Richard Pollard; 2 Glen Hoare; 3 Jake Johnstone; 4 Scott Roberts; 5 Mike Okwusogu; 6 Cory Bennett; 7 Rob McKeown; 8 Glenn Osborn; 9 Kahu Henare; 10 Allan Tito; 11 Brett McCroary; 12 Keri Ryan; 13 James Hersey. Subs (all used): 14 Troy Dougherty; 15 Gareth Janes; 16 Obi Ijeoma; 17 PJ Solomon.
Tries: McKeown (56), McCroary (61), Henare (68); **Goals:** Johnstone 3.
HAWKS: 1 Richard Baker; 2 Bryn Powell; 3 Iain Higgins; 4 Wes McGibbon; 5 George Rayner; 6 Andy Bastow; 7 Phil Hasty; 8 Jonlee Lockwood; 9 Joe Hawley; 10 Andy Brent; 11 Wayne Freeman; 12 Craig Ibbetson; 13 Paul Seal. Subs (all used): 14 Mick Coyle; 15 Danny Burton; 16 Tony Howcroft; 17 Gareth Naylor.
Tries: Baker (14), Hasty (18, 48), Coyle (43), Naylor (63), Rayner (75), Powell (79); **Goals:** Hasty 7.
Rugby Leaguer & League Express Men of the Match: *Skolars:* Brett McCroary; *Hawks:* Phil Hasty.
Penalty count: 6-5; **Half-time:** 0-14;
Referee: Colin Morris (Huddersfield); **Attendance:** 380.

CENTRAL v EAST

BATLEY BULLDOGS 62 SHEFFIELD EAGLES 12

BULLDOGS: 1 Craig Lingard; 2 Mark Sibson; 3 Chris Spurr; 4 Danny Maun; 5 Leon Williamson; 6 Mark Toohey; 7 Barry Eaton; 8 Craig Booth; 9 Gavin Swinson; 10 Andy Spink; 11 David Rourke; 12 Paul Harrison; 13 Ryan Horsley. Subs (all used): 14 Mark Cass; 15 Anthony Gibbons; 16 Joe Berry; 17 Joe Naidole.
Tries: Spurr (5, 22, 60, 68), Horsley (20), Lingard (27, 42, 57, 64), Spink (36), Sibson (39); **Goals:** Eaton 9.
EAGLES: 1 Andy Poynter; 2 Jon Breakingbury; 3 Neil Kite; 4 Pat Rich; 5 Paul Wells; 6 Peter Reilly; 7 Gavin Brown; 8 Guy Adams; 9 Gareth Stanley; 10 Jon Bruce; 11 Craig Brown; 12 Andy Raleigh; 13 Simon Tillyer. Subs (all used): 14 Lee Bettinson; 15 Nick Turnbull; 16 Simon Morton; 17 Mitchell Stringer.
Tries: Breakingbury (73), Stringer (79);
Goals: G Brown 2.
Sin bin: Stringer (12) - interference.
Rugby Leaguer & League Express Men of the Match: *Bulldogs:* Andy Spink; *Eagles:* Andy Raleigh.
Penalty count: 9-6; **Half-time:** 32-0; **Referee:** Steve Nicholson (Whitehaven); **Attendance:** 639.

NORTH v WEST

WORKINGTON TOWN 10 ROCHDALE HORNETS 44

TOWN: 1 Dean Sharp; 2 Matthew Johnson; 3 Jonathan Heaney; 4 John Allen; 5 Anthony Huddart; 6 Kevin Hetherington; 7 Danny Burns; 8 Craig Barker; 9 Carl Sice; 10 Hitro Okesene; 11 James Robinson; 12 David Pettit; 13 Brett McDermott. Subs (all used): 14 John Young; 15 Tony Dymtrowski; 16 Alan Telford; 17 Stephen Milnes.
Tries: Johnson (43), D Burns (64); **Goal:** Hetherington.
HORNETS: 1 Paul Owen; 2 Casey Mayberry; 3 James Bunyan; 4 Jon Roper; 5 Marlon Billy; 6 Stephen Doherty; 7 Ian Watson; 8 Andy Grundy; 9 Richard Pachniuk; 10 David Stephenson; 11 David Larder; 12 Matthew Leigh; 13 Paul Smith. Subs (all used): 14 Damian Ball; 15 Paul Southern; 16 Gareth Price; 17 Mick Nanyn.
Tries: Southern (25, 47), Larder (37), Leigh (40), Watson (55), Smith (57), Pachniuk (68), Nanyn (73);
Goals: Watson 6.
Sin bin: Larder (63) - professional foul, holding down.
Rugby Leaguer & League Express Men of the Match: *Town:* Brett McDermott; *Hornets:* Richard Pachniuk.
Penalty count: 9-5; **Half-time:** 0-18;
Referee: Julian King (St Helens); **Attendance:** 336.

Wednesday 19th March 2003

WEST

ROCHDALE HORNETS 24 SWINTON LIONS 14

HORNETS: 1 Paul Owen; 2 Sean Cooper; 3 James Bunyan; 4 Jon Roper; 5 Mick Nanyn; 6 Stephen Doherty; 7 Ian Watson; 8 Paul Southern; 9 Richard Pachniuk; 10 David Stephenson; 11 Damian Ball; 12 Matthew Leigh; 13 Paul Smith. Subs (all used): 14 Andy Wallace; 15 Andy Grundy; 16 Gareth Price; 17 Matthew Long.
Tries: Nanyn (13), Smith (20), Long (48), Owen (66);
Goals: Watson 4.
Sin bin: Roper (28) - use of elbow;
Southern (61) - fighting.
LIONS: 1 Wayne English; 2 Lee Hudson; 3 Kris Tassell; 4 Phil Hassan; 5 Adrian Mead; 6 Grant Bithel; 7 Chris Hough; 8 Andy Leathem; 9 Rob Barraclough; 10 Simon Knox; 11 Craig Wingfield; 12 Dave Ellison; 13 Peter Cannon. Subs (all used): 14 Mark Ashton; 15 Andy Cheetham; 16 Robert Russell; 17 Alan Shea.
Tries: Hough (28), Bithel (42); **Goals:** Hough 3.
Sin bin: Russell (56) - professional foul;
Knox (61) - fighting.
Rugby Leaguer & League Express Men of the Match: *Hornets:* Ian Watson; *Lions:* Wayne English.
Penalty count: 12-17; **Half-time:** 14-8;
Referee: Ben Thaler (Wakefield); **Attendance:** 727.

NORTH v WEST

GATESHEAD THUNDER 8 SALFORD CITY REDS 90

THUNDER: 1 Kevin Neighbour; 2 Olu Iwenofu; 3 Damien Reid; 4 Tom Lauriston; 5 Richie Barnett; 6 John Coutts; 7 Neil Thorman; 8 Steven Bradley; 9 Chris Fletcher; 10 David Bates; 11 Clint Brown; 12 Steve Rutherford; 13 Jermaine Coleman. Subs (all used): 14 Yusuf Sozi; 15 Craig Firth; 16 James Mackay; 17 Andy Walker.
Tries: Iwenofu (37), Reid (74).
CITY REDS: 1 Cliff Beverley; 2 Alan Hunte; 3 Andy Kirk; 4 Stuart Littler; 5 Danny Arnold; 6 Steve Blakeley; 7 Gavin Clinch; 8 Gareth Haggerty; 9 Malcolm Alker; 10 Paul Highton; 11 Simon Baldwin; 12 Neil Lowe; 13 Chris Charles. Subs (all used): 14 David Highton; 15 Lee Marsh; 16 Andy Coley; 17 Neil Baynes.
Tries: Alker (1, 50), Blakeley (2, 52), Lowe (8, 19), Kirk (10), Hunte (12, 66), Beverley (15, 48), Arnold (25, 77), Charles (46), D Highton (62), Marsh (69);
Goals: Blakeley 13.
Rugby Leaguer & League Express Men of the Match: *Thunder:* Neil Thorman; *City Reds:* Gareth Haggerty.
Penalty count: 4-7; **Half-time:** 4-46;
Referee: Ronnie Laughton (Barnsley); **Attendance:** 172.

Friday 21st March 2003

EAST

SHEFFIELD EAGLES 8 FEATHERSTONE ROVERS 27

EAGLES: 1 Andy Poynter; 2 Jon Breakingbury; 3 Neil Kite; 4 Pat Rich; 5 Paul Wells; 6 Peter Reilly; 7 Gavin Brown; 8 Jack Howieson; 9 Gareth Stanley; 10 Ryan Angus; 11 Andy Raleigh; 12 Craig Brown; 13 Richard Goddard. Subs (all used): 14 Lee Bettinson; 15 Simon Tillyer; 16 Tony Weller; 17 Mitchell Stringer.
Try: Stringer (47); **Goals:** G Brown 2.
Sin bin: Poynter (27) - holding down.
ROVERS: 1 Nathan Graham; 2 Jamie Stokes; 3 Brendan O'Meara; 4 Ian Brown; 5 Adrian Flynn; 6 Richard Agar; 7 Carl Briggs; 8 Ian Tonks; 9 Richard Chapman; 10 Stuart Dickens; 11 Steve Dooler; 12 Andy Rice; 13 Danny Seal. Subs (all used): 14 Jonathan Presley; 15 Richard Whiting; 16 Andy Bailey; 17 Chris Molyneux.
Tries: Brown (35, 40), Stokes (60), Seal (75);
Goals: Dickens 4, Briggs; **Field goal:** Agar.
Rugby Leaguer & League Express Men of the Match: *Eagles:* Jack Howieson; *Rovers:* Carl Briggs.
Penalty count: 8-9; **Half-time:** 4-14;
Referee: Steve Addy (Huddersfield); **Attendance:** 856.

WEEK 8

Sunday 23rd March 2003

NORTH

BARROW RAIDERS 44 WORKINGTON TOWN 18

RAIDERS: 1 Craig Bower; 2 Jamie Marshall; 3 Paul Jones; 4 Andy McClure; 5 Shane Irabor; 6 Paul Evans; 7 Chris Archer; 8 Tau Liku; 9 Dave Clark; 10 Steve Jackson; 11 James King; 12 Paul Lupton; 13 Andy Henderson. Subs (all used): 14 Adam Pate; 15 Stuart Dancer; 16 James Stainton; 17 Wayne Jones.
Tries: Bower (10, 27), Marshall (30), Henderson (32), Evans (43), P Jones (60), McClure (77); **Goals:** Evans 8.
Sin bin: Marshall (52) - dissent.
TOWN: 1 Dean Sharp; 2 Anthony Huddart; 3 Jonathan Heaney; 4 Matthew Johnson; 5 Graeme Lewthwaite; 6 Kevin Hetherington; 7 Danny Burns; 8 Craig Barker; 9 Carl Sice; 10 Hitro Okesene; 11 James Robinson; 12 David Pettit; 13 Brett McDermott. Subs (all used): 14 Adam Coulson; 15 Matthew Tunstall; 16 Brett Smith; 17 Willie Burns.
Tries: D Burns (39), Lewthwaite (55), Sice (73);
Goals: Hetherington 3.
Rugby Leaguer & League Express Men of the Match: *Raiders:* Craig Bower; *Town:* Carl Sice.
Penalty count: 4-5; **Half-time:** 28-6;
Referee: Mike Dawber (Wigan); **Attendance:** 788.

WHITEHAVEN 28 CHORLEY LYNX 20

WHITEHAVEN: 1 Gary Broadbent; 2 Paul O'Neil; 3 David Seeds; 4 Howard Hill; 5 Mark Wallace; 6 Leroy Joe; 7 Darren Holt; 8 Dean Vaughan; 9 Aaron Lester; 10 Chris McKinney; 11 Graeme Morton; 12 Craig Chambers; 13 Spencer Miller. Subs (all used): 14 Lee Kiddie; 15 Leigh Smith; 16 Gary Smith; 17 David Fatialofa.
Tries: Joe (8, 61), Holt (33), O'Neil (35), McKinney (71);
Goals: Holt 4.
LYNX: 1 Mark McCully; 2 Chris Ramsdale; 3 Mick Redford; 4 Eddie Kilgannon; 5 Anton Garcia; 6 Liam Bretherton; 7 Martin Gambles; 8 Tim Street; 9 Dave McConnell; 10 David Whittle; 11 Wayne Bloor; 12 Gavin Johnson; 13 Ian Hodson. Subs (all used): 14 Safraz Patel; 15 John Braddish; 16 Lee Rowley; 17 Ian Parry.
Tries: Redford (19), McConnell (52), Bretherton (77);
Goals: McCully 4.
Rugby Leaguer & League Express Men of the Match: *Whitehaven:* Leroy Joe; *Lynx:* Liam Bretherton.
Penalty count: 8-9; **Half-time:** 16-8;
Referee: Julian King (St Helens); **Attendance:** 1,007.

EAST

HULL KINGSTON ROVERS 32 YORK CITY KNIGHTS 14

ROVERS: 1 Craig Poucher; 2 Nick Pinkney; 3 Ian Bell; 4 Craig Farrell; 5 Alasdair McClarron; 6 Chris Stephenson; 7 Latham Tawhai; 8 Richard Wilson; 9 Paul Pickering; 10 Jamie Bovill; 11 Adam Sullivan; 12 Jon Aston; 13 Andy Smith. Subs (all used): 14 Lynton Stott; 15 Dean Andrews; 16 Harvey Howard; 17 Paul Fletcher.
Tries: Pickering (17), Pinkney (29, 38), Andrews (56), Poucher (59), Bell (74); **Goals:** Stephenson 4.
CITY KNIGHTS: 1 Chris Smith; 2 Alex Godfrey; 3 Graeme Hallas; 4 Darren Callaghan; 5 Gavin Molloy; 6 Jonathan Firth; 7 Trevor Krause; 8 Paul Broadbent; 9 Darren Robinson; 10 Richard Hayes; 11 Mick Ramsden; 12 Scott Fletcher; 13 Mark Cain. Subs (all used): 14 Chris Beever; 15 Gareth Lloyd; 16 Craig Westmoreland; 17 David Bolus.
Tries: Cain (41, 77); **Goals:** Hallas, Robinson 2.
Rugby Leaguer & League Express Men of the Match: *Rovers:* Craig Poucher; *City Knights:* Mark Cain.
Penalty count: 12-8; **Half-time:** 18-2; **Referee:** Steve Nicholson (Whitehaven); **Attendance:** 1,580.

WEST

LEIGH CENTURIONS 62 SWINTON LIONS 6

CENTURIONS: 1 Neil Turley; 2 Leroy Rivett; 3 Damian Munro; 4 Dale Cardoza; 5 David Alstead; 6 Patrick Weisner; 7 John Duffy; 8 Rob Ball; 9 Paul Rowley; 10 Bryan Henare; 11 Sean Richardson; 12 Adam Bristow; 13 Willie Swann. Subs (all used): 14 Dale Holdstock; 15 Eric Andrews; 16 Lee Sanderson; 17 David Bradbury.
Tries: Turley (9, 13, 47, 68, 78), Bristow (19, 60), Bradbury (39), Rowley (56), Richardson (62), Munro (66); **Goals:** Turley 9.
LIONS: 1 Wayne English; 2 Adrian Mead; 3 Andy Cheetham; 4 Phil Hassan; 5 Lee Hudson; 6 Jason Johnson; 7 Chris Hough; 8 Andy Leathem; 9 Rob Barraclough; 10 Simon Knox; 11 Craig Wingfield; 12 Dave Ellison; 13 Robert Russell. Subs (all used): 14 Hugh Thorpe; 15 Grant Bithel; 16 Alan Shea; 17 Chris Roe.
Try: Hassan (35); **Goal:** Hough.
Rugby Leaguer & League Express Men of the Match: *Centurions:* Neil Turley; *Lions:* Phil Hassan.
Penalty count: 7-7; **Half-time:** 20-6;
Referee: Peter Taberner (Wigan); **Attendance:** 2,026.

ROCHDALE HORNETS 34 OLDHAM 25

HORNETS: 1 Paul Owen; 2 Casey Mayberry; 3 James Bunyan; 4 Jon Roper; 5 Marlon Billy; 6 Paul Smith; 7 Ian Watson; 8 Paul Southern; 9 Richard Pachniuk; 10 David Stephenson; 11 David Larder; 12 Matthew Leigh; 13 Damian Ball. Subs (all used): 14 Mick Nanyn; 15 Andy Grundy; 16 Gareth Price; 17 Matthew Long.
Tries: Roper (33, 53), Larder (55), Nanyn (60), Owen (78); **Goals:** Watson 7.
OLDHAM: 1 Gavin Dodd; 2 Iain Marsh; 3 Paul Anderson; 4 Jon Goddard; 5 Joe McNicholas; 6 Gareth Barber; 7 Neil Roden; 8 Paul Norton; 9 John Hough; 10 Dane Morgan; 11 Lee Doran; 12 Ryan Stazicker; 13 Chris Morley. Subs (all used): 14 Simon Svabic; 15 Martin McLoughlin; 16 Keith Brennan; 17 Jason Clegg.
Tries: Stazicker (1), Anderson (10), Goddard (28), Brennan (45); **Goals:** Barber 4; **Field goal:** Roden.
Rugby Leaguer & League Express Men of the Match: *Hornets:* Damian Ball; *Oldham:* Neil Roden.
Penalty count: 12-6; **Half-time:** 12-18;
Referee: Robert Connolly (Wigan); **Attendance:** 1,314.

CENTRAL

DEWSBURY RAMS 35 LONDON SKOLARS 33

RAMS: 1 Nathan Batty; 2 Michael Wainwright; 3 Jeremy Dyson; 4 Billy Kershaw; 5 George Mack; 6 Mark Barlow; 7 Scott Rhodes; 8 Frank Watene; 9 Andy Heptinstall; 10 Paul Hicks; 11 Danny Evans; 12 Andy Fisher; 13 Richard Slater. Subs (all used): 14 Michael Walker; 15 Jimmy Elston; 16 Anthony Thewliss; 17 Danny Brough.
Tries: Slater (24), Barlow (25), Walker (45), Dyson (60), Kershaw (62), Thewliss (63); **Goals:** Dyson, Brough 4;
Field goal: Thewliss.
SKOLARS: 1 Glen Hoare; 2 Ronald Mushiso; 3 PJ Solomon; 4 Scott Roberts; 5 Judd Billings; 6 Cory Bennett; 7 Rob McKeown; 8 Glenn Osborn; 9 Kahu Henare; 10 Allan Tito; 11 Brett McCroary; 12 Keri Ryan; 13 James Hersey. Subs (all used): 14 Troy Dougherty; 15 Gareth Janes; 16 Bobby Wallis; 17 Janan Billings.
Tries: Mushiso (8, 47), Bennett (20), McCroary (35), Solomon (38); **Goals:** McKeown 6; **Field goal:** McKeown.
Rugby Leaguer & League Express Men of the Match: *Rams:* Danny Brough; *Skolars:* Rob McKeown.
Penalty count: 4-8; **Half-time:** 10-26;
Referee: Steve Presley (Castleford); **Attendance:** 449.

HUNSLET HAWKS 30 BATLEY BULLDOGS 24

HAWKS: 1 Richard Baker; 2 Bryn Powell; 3 Iain Higgins; 4 Wes McGibbon; 5 George Rayner; 6 Andy Bastow; 7

Phil Hasty; 8 Jonlee Lockwood; 9 Jon Liddell; 10 Andy Brent; 11 Wayne Freeman; 12 Craig Ibbetson; 13 Paul Seal. Subs (all used): 14 Gareth Naylor; 15 Mick Coyle; 16 Danny Burton; 17 Danny Fearon.
Tries: C Ibbetson (14), Powell (23, 49), Baker (39), W Freeman (52); **Goals:** Liddell 5.
BULLDOGS: 1 Craig Lingard; 2 Mark Sibson; 3 Anthony Gibbons; 4 Chris Spurr; 5 Leon Williamson; 6 David Gibbons; 7 Barry Eaton; 8 Craig Booth; 9 Gavin Swinson; 10 Andy Spink; 11 David Rourke; 12 Mark Toohey; 13 Ryan Horsley. Subs (all used): 14 Mark Cass; 15 Paul Harrison; 16 Joe Berry; 17 Danny Maun.
Tries: Sibson (5), Lingard (17), Swinson (33), Toohey (64); **Goals:** Eaton 4.
Rugby Leaguer & League Express Men of the Match: *Hawks:* Phil Hasty; *Bulldogs:* Barry Eaton.
Penalty count: 7-9; **Half-time:** 16-18;
Referee: Ashley Klein (London); **Attendance:** 658.

EAST v CENTRAL

DONCASTER DRAGONS 42 KEIGHLEY COUGARS 12

DRAGONS: 1 Craig Horne; 2 Dean Colton; 3 Marvin Golden; 4 Simon Irving; 5 Jason Lee; 6 Paul Mansson; 7 Mark Moxon; 8 Gareth Handford; 9 Peter Edwards; 10 Craig Forsyth; 11 Peter Green; 12 Matt Walker; 13 Chris Ross. Subs (all used): 14 James Walker; 15 Shaun Leafe; 16 Paul Gleadhill; 17 Andy Burland.
Tries: Colton (25), Mansson (31, 62), Irving (48), M Walker (56), Golden (72), Horne (75), Leafe (79); **Goals:** Irving 5.
COUGARS: 1 James Rushforth; 2 Karl Smith; 3 David Foster; 4 Gareth Hewitt; 5 Andy Robinson; 6 Adam Mitchell; 7 Matt Firth; 8 Phil Stephenson; 9 Simeon Hoyle; 10 Danny Ekis; 11 Oliver Wilkes; 12 Ian Sinfield; 13 Jason Ramshaw. Subs (all used): 14 Chris Wainwright; 15 Ricky Helliwell; 16 Richard Mervill; 17 Chris Hannah.
Tries: Firth (28, 35); **Goals:** Mitchell 2.
Sin bin: Ramshaw (69) - punching.
Rugby Leaguer & League Express Men of the Match: *Dragons:* Matt Walker; *Cougars:* Matt Firth.
Penalty count: 5-7; **Half-time:** 10-12;
Referee: Colin Morris (Huddersfield); **Attendance:** 985.

WEST v NORTH

SALFORD CITY REDS 100 GATESHEAD THUNDER 12

CITY REDS: 1 Jason Flowers; 2 Alan Hunte; 3 Stuart Littler; 4 Cliff Beverley; 5 Andy Kirk; 6 Steve Blakeley; 7 Karl Fitzpatrick; 8 Gareth Haggerty; 9 Malcolm Alker; 10 Paul Highton; 11 Simon Baldwin; 12 Neil Lowe; 13 Radney Bowker. Subs (all used): 14 John Clough; 15 Lee Marsh; 16 Andy Gorski; 17 Neil Baynes.
Tries: Fitzpatrick (1, 28, 72), Beverley (4, 36), Lowe (12), P Highton (14), Hunte (19, 55), Alker (30), Flowers (43, 66), Littler (50, 70), Bowker (57), Kirk (64), Clough (75), Marsh (79); **Goals:** Blakeley 14.
THUNDER: 1 Kevin Neighbour; 2 Robin Peers; 3 Damien Reid; 4 Craig Firth; 5 Richie Barnett; 6 Paul Thorman; 7 Neil Thorman; 8 Steven Bradley; 9 Chris Fletcher; 10 David Bates; 11 Clint Brown; 12 James Mackay; 13 Jermaine Coleman. Subs (all used): 14 Andy Walker; 15 Tony Doherty; 16 Tom Lauriston; 17 Yusuf Sozi.
Tries: Reid (24), Brown (61); **Goals:** N Thorman 2.
Rugby Leaguer & League Express Men of the Match: *City Reds:* Cliff Beverley; *Thunder:* Jermaine Coleman.
Penalty count: 5-1; **Half-time:** 38-6;
Referee: Ben Thaler (Wakefield); **Attendance:** 1,653.

WEEK 9

Sunday 30th March 2003

NORTH

CHORLEY LYNX 54 GATESHEAD THUNDER 24

LYNX: 1 Mark McCully; 2 Eddie Kilgannon; 3 Mick Redford; 4 Liam Bretherton; 5 Anton Garcia; 6 John Braddish; 7 Martin Gambles; 8 Lee Rowley; 9 Dave McConnell; 10 David Whittle; 11 Wayne Bloor; 12 Gavin Johnson; 13 Ian Hodson. Subs (all used): 14 Dave Newton; 15 Mike Briggs; 16 Safraz Patel; 17 Ian Parry.
Tries: Braddish (13, 48), Gambles (19, 31, 80), Kilgannon (27, 68), G Johnson (58), Garcia (63), Patel (73); **Goals:** McCully 7.
Sin bin: Redford (76).
THUNDER: 1 Kevin Neighbour; 2 Olu Iwenofu; 3 Damien Reid; 4 Scott MacDougall; 5 Michael Lyons; 6 Paul Thorman; 7 Neil Thorman; 8 Steven Bradley; 9 Chris Fletcher; 10 David Bates; 11 Clint Brown; 12 Steve Rutherford; 13 Jermaine Coleman. Subs (all used): 14 Yusuf Sozi; 15 Andy Walker; 16 Tom Lauriston; 17 Craig Firth.
Tries: Reid (8, 41), Bates (40), Lyons (52), Iwenofu (77); **Goals:** N Thorman 2.
Rugby Leaguer & League Express Men of the Match: *Lynx:* Martin Gambles; *Thunder:* Damien Reid.
Penalty count: 7-7; **Half-time:** 24-12;
Referee: Steve Presley (Castleford); **Attendance:** 213.

WORKINGTON TOWN 10 WHITEHAVEN 39

TOWN: 1 Adam Coulson; 2 Matthew Johnson; 3 Brett McDermott; 4 Jonathan Heaney; 5 Graeme Lewthwaite; 6 Kevin Hetherington; 7 Danny Burns; 8 Matthew Tunstall; 9 Carl Sice; 10 Hitro Okesene; 11 Willie Burns; 12 David Pettit; 13 Brett Smith. Subs (all used): 14 Craig Fisher; 15 James Robinson; 16 William Blackburn; 17 Craig Barker.
Tries: Sice (52), Lewthwaite (58); **Goal:** Hetherington.
Sin bin: Tunstall (9) - holding down; McDermott (38) - pushing.
WHITEHAVEN: 1 Gary Broadbent; 2 Steven Wood; 3 Jamie Stenhouse; 4 Howard Hill; 5 Mark Wallace; 6 Leroy Joe; 7 Darren Holt; 8 Dean Vaughan; 9 Aaron Lester; 10 Chris McKinney; 11 Craig Chambers; 12 Graeme Morton; 13 Garry Purdham. Subs (all used): 14 Lee Kiddie; 15 Marc Jackson; 16 Leigh Smith; 17 David Fatialofa.
Tries: Wallace (17), Stenhouse (24), Morton (28, 41), Chambers (36), McKinney (76); **Goals:** Holt 7;
Field goal: Holt.
Sin bin: Fatialofa (52) - holding down.
Rugby Leaguer & League Express Men of the Match: *Town:* Carl Sice; *Whitehaven:* Graeme Morton.
Penalty count: 11-17; **Half-time:** 0-27;
Referee: Steve Addy (Huddersfield); **Attendance:** 1,004.

EAST

**DONCASTER DRAGONS 32
HULL KINGSTON ROVERS 34**

DRAGONS: 1 Craig Horne; 2 Johnny Woodcock; 3 Marvin Golden; 4 Simon Irving; 5 Jason Lee; 6 Paul Mansson; 7 Mark Moxon; 8 Gareth Handford; 9 Peter Edwards; 10 James Walker; 11 Peter Green; 12 Matt Walker; 13 Maea David. Subs (all used): 14 Shaun Leafe; 15 Craig Forsyth; 16 Craig Lawton; 17 Dean Colton.
Tries: Mansson (16), Horne (41), Leafe (61), Irving (65), Golden (78); **Goals:** Woodcock 6.
ROVERS: 1 Craig Poucher; 2 Nick Pinkney; 3 Ian Bell; 4 Craig Farrell; 5 Alasdair McClarron; 6 Paul Parker; 7 Latham Tawhai; 8 Richard Wilson; 9 Paul Pickering; 10 Jamie Bovill; 11 Adam Sullivan; 12 Jon Aston; 13 Andy Smith. Subs (all used): 14 Lynton Stott; 15 Chris Stephenson; 16 Harvey Howard; 17 Paul Fletcher.
Tries: Aston (8), Tawhai (10), Farrell (31, 52), Stephenson (34), Pickering (46); **Goals:** Stephenson 5.
Rugby Leaguer & League Express Men of the Match: *Dragons:* Paul Mansson; *Rovers:* Chris Stephenson.
Penalty count: 12-10; **Half-time:** 10-20; **Referee:** Richard Silverwood (Dewsbury); **Attendance:** 1,127.

YORK CITY KNIGHTS 32 SHEFFIELD EAGLES 18

CITY KNIGHTS: 1 Chris Smith; 2 Chris Beever; 3 Gareth Lloyd; 4 Darren Callaghan; 5 Gavin Molloy; 6 Adam Thaler; 7 Scott Rhodes; 8 Paul Broadbent; 9 Trevor Krause; 10 Richard Hayes; 11 Mick Ramsden; 12 Scott Fletcher; 13 Mark Cain. Subs (all used): 14 Darren Robinson; 15 Craig Westmoreland; 16 Andy Burland; 17 David Bolus.
Tries: Cain (2), Rhodes (5), Ramsden (39), Krause (55), Smith (60), Lloyd (74); **Goals:** Thaler 4.
EAGLES: 1 Andy Poynter; 2 Greg Hurst; 3 Tony Weller; 4 Nick Turnbull; 5 Ian Thompson; 6 Peter Reilly; 7 Gavin Brown; 8 Jack Howieson; 9 Gareth Stanley; 10 Jon Bruce; 11 Richard Goddard; 12 Craig Brown; 13 Simon Tillyer. Subs (all used): 14 Wayne Flynn; 15 Andy Raleigh; 16 Ryan Angus; 17 Mitchell Stringer.
Tries: Weller (41, 50), G Brown (69), C Brown (80); **Goal:** G Brown.
Rugby Leaguer & League Express Men of the Match: *City Knights:* Trevor Krause; *Eagles:* Tony Weller.
Penalty count: 9-7; **Half-time:** 16-0;
Referee: Mike Dawber (Wigan); **Attendance:** 978.

WEST

SALFORD CITY REDS 22 LEIGH CENTURIONS 10

CITY REDS: 1 Jason Flowers; 2 Michael Platt; 3 Stuart Littler; 4 Andy Kirk; 5 Alan Hunte; 6 Cliff Beverley; 7 Gavin Clinch; 8 Neil Baynes; 9 Malcolm Alker; 10 Andy Coley; 11 Simon Baldwin; 12 Neil Lowe; 13 Chris Charles. Subs (all used): 14 David Highton; 15 Steve Blakeley; 16 Paul Highton; 17 Gareth Haggerty.
Tries: Platt (10), Kirk (46), Beverley (69, 80), Hunte (76); **Goal:** Blakeley.
CENTURIONS: 1 Neil Turley; 2 Leroy Rivett; 3 Damian Munro; 4 David Alstead; 5 Alan Hadcroft; 6 Lee Sanderson; 7 John Duffy; 8 Rob Ball; 9 Paul Rowley; 10 Bryan Henare; 11 Sean Richardson; 12 Adam Bristow; 13 Patrick Weisner. Subs (all used): 14 Dale Holdstock; 15 Willie Swann; 16 Dale Cardoza; 17 David Bradbury.
Tries: Weisner (57), Munro (67); **Goal:** Duffy.
Rugby Leaguer & League Express Men of the Match: *City Reds:* Cliff Beverley; *Centurions:* Patrick Weisner.
Penalty count: 6-3; **Half-time:** 4-0;
Referee: Ian Smith (Oldham); **Attendance:** 3,099.

SWINTON LIONS 26 ROCHDALE HORNETS 22

LIONS: 1 Wayne English; 2 Jason Roach; 3 Robert Russell; 4 Phil Hassan; 5 Lee Hudson; 6 Grant Bithel; 7 Chris Hough; 8 Andy Leathem; 9 Rob Barraclough; 10 Simon Knox; 11 Phil Cushion; 12 Dave Ellison; 13 Peter Cannon. Subs: 14 Hugh Thorpe (not used); 15 Chris Roe; 16 Craig Wingfield; 17 Kris Smith.
Tries: Roach (7), Hudson (14), Hough (50), Ellison (62), Cannon (79); **Goals:** Hough 3.
HORNETS: 1 Paul Owen; 2 Casey Mayberry; 3 James Bunyan; 4 Jon Roper; 5 Marlon Billy; 6 Warren Ayres; 7 Ian Watson; 8 Andy Grundy; 9 Richard Pachniuk; 10 David Stephenson; 11 David Larder; 12 Matthew Leigh; 13 Paul Smith. Subs (all used): 14 Stephen Doherty; 15 Mick Nanyn; 16 Gareth Price; 17 Matthew Long.
Tries: Smith (26), Billy (44), Nanyn (65), Roper (71); **Goals:** Watson 3.
Rugby Leaguer & League Express Men of the Match: *Lions:* Simon Knox; *Hornets:* Paul Smith.
Penalty count: 10-5; **Half-time:** 10-10;
Referee: Ashley Klein (London); **Attendance:** 391.

CENTRAL

BATLEY BULLDOGS 16 DEWSBURY RAMS 21

BULLDOGS: 1 Craig Lingard; 2 Mark Sibson; 3 Anthony Gibbons; 4 Danny Maun; 5 Leon Williamson; 6 David Gibbons; 7 Barry Eaton; 8 Craig Booth; 9 Mark Cass; 10 Andy Spink; 11 David Rourke; 12 Mark Toohey; 13 Ryan Horsley. Subs (all used): 14 Chris Spurr; 15 Paul Harrison; 16 Joe Berry; 17 Joe Naidole.
Tries: Sibson (2, 63), Toohey (25); **Goals:** Eaton 2.
RAMS: 1 Nathan Batty; 2 George Mack; 3 Chris Chapman; 4 Paul Steele; 5 Michael Wainwright; 6 Mark Barlow; 7 Danny Brough; 8 Tony Fella; 9 Andy Heptinstall; 10 Paul Hicks; 11 Anthony Thewliss; 12 Billy Kershaw; 13 Chris Redfearn. Subs (all used): 14 Jimmy Elston; 15 Frank Watene; 16 Michael Walker; 17 Danny Evans.
Tries: Kershaw (35), Steele (58, 68), Brough (75);
Goals: Brough 2; **Field goal:** Brough.
Rugby Leaguer & League Express Men of the Match: *Bulldogs:* Paul Harrison; *Rams:* Paul Hicks.
Penalty count: 8-3; **Half-time:** 12-4;
Referee: Ben Thaler (Wakefield); **Attendance:** 952.

LONDON SKOLARS 18 KEIGHLEY COUGARS 48

SKOLARS: 1 Glen Hoare; 2 Charlie Oyebade; 3 PJ Solomon; 4 Scott Roberts; 5 Judd Billings; 6 Troy Dougherty; 7 Rob McKeown; 8 Glenn Osborn; 9 Kahu Henare; 10 Obi Ijeoma; 11 Allan Tito; 12 Rubert Jonker; 13 Janan Billings. Subs (all used): 14 Jake Johnstone; 15 Ronald Mushiso; 16 Daniel Reeds; 17 Steve Hainey.
Tries: Henare (28), Ijeoma (33), McKeown (49);
Goals: McKeown, Johnstone 2.
COUGARS: 1 James Rushforth; 2 Karl Smith; 3 David Foster; 4 Gareth Hewitt; 5 Andy Robinson; 6 Adam Mitchell; 7 Matt Firth; 8 Phil Stephenson; 9 Simeon Hoyle; 10 Danny Ekis; 11 Oliver Wilkes; 12 Ricky Helliwell; 13 Lee Patterson. Subs (all used): 14 Chris Wainwright; 15 Ian Sinfield; 16 Mick Durham; 17 Chris Hannah.
Tries: Patterson (11), Hewitt (13, 80), Stephenson (16), Helliwell (55), Wilkes (65), Wainwright (71), Durham (75); **Goals:** Mitchell 8.
Sin bin: Robinson (58) - professional foul.
Rugby Leaguer & League Express Men of the Match: *Skolars:* Rob McKeown; *Cougars:* James Rushforth.
Penalty count: 9-7; **Half-time:** 10-20;
Referee: Julian King (St Helens); **Attendance:** 310.

NORTH v WEST

BARROW RAIDERS 16 OLDHAM 23

RAIDERS: 1 Craig Bower; 2 Jamie Marshall; 3 Andy McClure; 4 Paul Jones; 5 Shane Irabor; 6 Paul Evans; 7 Chris Archer; 8 Tau Liku; 9 Andy Henderson; 10 Steve Jackson; 11 James King; 12 Paul Lupton; 13 Phil Atkinson. Subs (all used): 14 Adam Pate; 15 Stuart Dancer; 16 Barry Pugh; 17 Wayne Jones.
Tries: Marshall (7, 33), P Jones (72); **Goals:** Evans 2.
OLDHAM: 1 Gavin Dodd; 2 Chris Irwin; 3 Iain Marsh; 4 Jon Goddard; 5 Chris Campbell; 6 Simon Svabic; 7 Neil Roden; 8 Paul Norton; 9 John Hough; 10 Dane Morgan; 11 Lee Doran; 12 Ryan Stazicker; 13 Chris Morley. Subs (all used): 14 Keith Brennan; 15 Joe McNicholas; 16 Steve Molloy; 17 Danny Guest.
Tries: I Marsh (22), Irwin (46), Doran (69);
Goals: Svabic 5; **Field goal:** Roden.
Dismissal: Hough (57) - high tackle.
Sin bin: Goddard (15) - holding down.
Rugby Leaguer & League Express Men of the Match: *Raiders:* James King; *Oldham:* Lee Doran.
Penalty count: 9-4; **Half-time:** 10-10; **Referee:** Steve Nicholson (Whitehaven); **Attendance:** 781.

EAST v CENTRAL

FEATHERSTONE ROVERS 50 HUNSLET HAWKS 10

ROVERS: 1 Nathan Graham; 2 Jamie Stokes; 3 Brendan O'Meara; 4 Ian Brown; 5 Adrian Flynn; 6 Carl Briggs; 7 Jonathan Presley; 8 Ian Tonks; 9 Danny Seal; 10 Stuart Dickens; 11 Steve Dooler; 12 Andy Bailey; 13 Andy Rice. Subs (all used): 14 Kevin Spink; 15 Richard Chapman; 16 Richard Whiting; 17 Chris Molyneux.
Tries: O'Meara (5, 72), Stokes (13, 39), Brown (35), Graham (38), Dooler (53), Tonks (64, 79);
Goals: Dickens 6, Briggs.
HAWKS: 1 Simon Jackson; 2 Bryn Powell; 3 Iain Higgins; 4 Wes McGibbon; 5 George Rayner; 6 Andy Bastow; 7 Phil Hasty; 8 Jonlee Lockwood; 9 Jon Liddell; 10 Andy Brent; 11 Wayne Freeman; 12 Craig Ibbetson; 13 Danny Fearon. Subs (all used): 14 Mick Coyle; 15 Danny Burton; 16 Dan Briggs; 17 Chris North.
Tries: Jackson (47), Powell (49); **Goal:** Liddell.
Rugby Leaguer & League Express Men of the Match: *Rovers:* Stuart Dickens; *Hawks:* Mick Coyle.
Penalty count: 7-3; **Half-time:** 30-0;
Referee: Colin Morris (Huddersfield); **Attendance:** 1,212.

Wednesday 2nd April 2003

WEST

SWINTON LIONS 0 SALFORD CITY REDS 72

LIONS: 1 Wayne English; 2 Jason Roach; 3 Robert Russell; 4 Hugh Thorpe; 5 Lee Hudson; 6 Grant Bithel; 7 Peter Cannon; 8 Andy Leathem; 9 Rob Barraclough; 10 Simon Knox; 11 Craig Wingfield; 12 Dave Ellison; 13 Kris Smith. Subs (all used): 14 Adrian Mead; 15 Mark Hudspith; 16 David Ogden; 17 Chris Roe.

CITY REDS: 1 Jason Flowers; 2 Michael Platt; 3 Stuart Littler; 4 Andy Kirk; 5 Danny Arnold; 6 Cliff Beverley; 7 Steve Blakeley; 8 Neil Baynes; 9 Malcolm Alker; 10 Andy Coley; 11 Lee Marsh; 12 Neil Lowe; 13 Chris Charles. Subs (all used): 14 David Highton; 15 Karl Fitzpatrick; 16 Danny Barton; 17 Paul Highton.
Tries: Alker (1, 3, 8, 73), Platt (7), Beverley (17, 39, 52), Kirk (25, 65), Flowers (42), D Highton (50), Fitzpatrick (68); **Goals:** Blakeley 10.
Rugby Leaguer & League Express Men of the Match: *Lions:* None; *City Reds:* Malcolm Alker.
Penalty count: 13-6; **Half-time:** 0-38;
Referee: Julian King (St Helens); **Attendance:** 954.

Friday 4th April 2003

NORTH

WHITEHAVEN 44 BARROW RAIDERS 14

WHITEHAVEN: 1 Gary Broadbent; 2 Mark Wallace; 3 David Seeds; 4 Jamie Stenhouse; 5 Glen Hutton; 6 Lee Kiddie; 7 Darren Holt; 8 Mike Whitehead; 9 Aaron Lester; 10 David Fatialofa; 11 Craig Chambers; 12 Chris McKinney; 13 Howard Hill. Subs (all used): 14 Leroy Joe; 15 Marc Jackson; 16 Tony Cunningham; 17 Steven Wood.
Tries: McKinney (25), Wallace (28, 70), Seeds (30, 35), Kiddie (39), Joe (62), Lester (80);
Goals: Holt, Seeds 2, Jackson 2, Wood.
RAIDERS: 1 Craig Bower; 2 Jamie Marshall; 3 Andy McClure; 4 Paul Jones; 5 Shane Irabor; 6 Paul Evans; 7 Chris Archer; 8 James Stainton; 9 Andy Henderson; 10 Steve Jackson; 11 James King; 12 Paul Lupton; 13 Phil Atkinson. Subs (all used): 14 Adam Pate; 15 Paul Gardner; 16 Stuart Dancer; 17 Wayne Jones.
Tries: Bower (17), Marshall (53); **Goals:** Evans 3.
Rugby Leaguer & League Express Men of the Match: *Whitehaven:* Chris McKinney; *Raiders:* Paul Evans.
Penalty count: 12-6; **Half time:** 28-8;
Referee: Mike Dawber (Wigan); **Attendance:** 1,047.

WEEK 10

Sunday 6th April 2003

NORTH

GATESHEAD THUNDER 42 WORKINGTON TOWN 12

THUNDER: 1 Kevin Neighbour; 2 Robin Peers; 3 Damien Reid; 4 Craig Firth; 5 Richie Barnett; 6 Jermaine Coleman; 7 Paul Thorman; 8 Yusuf Sozi; 9 Chris Fletcher; 10 David Bates; 11 Steve Rutherford; 12 Clint Brown; 13 Andy Walker. Subs (all used): 14 Steven Bradley; 15 Michael Lyons; 16 Scott MacDougall; 17 Neil Thorman.
Tries: Fletcher (3), Barnett (13, 60), Reid (28, 62, 78), MacDougall (66); **Goals:** N Thorman 4, P Thorman 3.
TOWN: 1 Dean Sharp; 2 Matthew Johnson; 3 Adam Coulson; 4 Jonathan Heaney; 5 Scott Chilton; 6 Brett Smith; 7 Danny Burns; 8 Willie Burns; 9 Carl Sice; 10 Hitro Okesene; 11 David Pettit; 12 William Blackburn; 13 Brett McDermott. Subs (all used): 14 Craig Fisher; 15 Matthew Tunstall; 16 James Robinson; 17 Jamie Beaumont.
Tries: Blackburn (22), Sice (72); **Goals:** Smith 2.
Rugby Leaguer & League Express Men of the Match: *Thunder:* Steven Bradley; *Town:* Carl Sice.
Penalty count: 14-11; **Half-time:** 18-6;
Referee: Ashley Klein (London);
Attendance: 208 *(at Hedley Lawson Park).*

EAST

DONCASTER DRAGONS 26 FEATHERSTONE ROVERS 24

DRAGONS: 1 Craig Horne; 2 Johnny Woodcock; 3 Paul Gleadhill; 4 Simon Irving; 5 Jason Lee; 6 Paul Mansson; 7 Mark Moxon; 8 Gareth Handford; 9 Peter Edwards; 10 Matt Walker; 11 Peter Green; 12 Craig Lawton; 13 Shaun Leafe. Subs (all used): 14 Jimmy Walker; 15 Tom Buckenham; 16 Craig Forsyth; 17 Dean Colton.
Tries: Horne (28), Irving (50), Colton (61), J Walker (68); **Goals:** Woodcock 5.
ROVERS: 1 Nathan Graham; 2 Jamie Stokes; 3 Brendan O'Meara; 4 Ian Brown; 5 Adrian Flynn; 6 Carl Briggs; 7 Jonathan Presley; 8 Ian Tonks; 9 Richard Chapman; 10 Stuart Dickens; 11 Steve Dooler; 12 Andy Rice; 13 Danny Seal. Subs (all used): 14 Andy McNally; 15 Richard Whiting; 16 Andy Bailey; 17 Chris Molyneux.
Tries: Brown (40), Flynn (57, 65), Dooler (77);
Goals: Dickens 3, Briggs.
Rugby Leaguer & League Express Men of the Match: *Dragons:* Craig Horne; *Rovers:* Nathan Graham.
Penalty count: 7-12; **Half-time:** 10-10; **Referee:** Ronnie Laughton (Barnsley); **Attendance:** 1,291.

SHEFFIELD EAGLES 33 HULL KINGSTON ROVERS 26

EAGLES: 1 Andy Poynter; 2 Jon Breakingbury; 3 Tony Weller; 4 Nick Turnbull; 5 Ian Thompson; 6 Gavin Brown; 7 Lee Bettinson; 8 Jack Howieson; 9 Gareth Stanley; 10 Jon Bruce; 11 Andy Raleigh; 12 Craig Brown; 13 Wayne Flynn. Subs (all used): 14 Adam Carroll; 15 Simon Tillyer; 16 Neil Kite; 17 Mitchell Stringer.
Tries: Weller (2), Turnbull (19), G Brown (27), Thompson (40); **Goals:** G Brown 7; **Field goals:** G Brown 3.
Sin bin: Breakingbury (51) - holding down.
ROVERS: 1 Craig Poucher; 2 Nick Pinkney; 3 Mark Blanchard; 4 Craig Farrell; 5 Alasdair McClarron; 6 Paul Parker; 7 Chris Stephenson; 8 Richard Wilson; 9 Lynton Stott; 10 Jamie Bovill; 11 Adam Sullivan; 12 Jon Aston; 13 Andy Smith. Subs (all used): 14 Dean Andrews; 15 Anthony Seibold; 16 Harvey Howard; 17 Paul Fletcher.
Tries: Bovill (8), Poucher (32), Aston (50), McClarron (68), Parker (72, pen); **Goals:** Stephenson 3.
Rugby Leaguer & League Express Men of the Match: *Eagles:* Gavin Brown; *Rovers:* Craig Poucher.
Penalty count: 13-11; **Half-time:** 28-10;
Referee: Steve Presley (Castleford); **Attendance:** 1,150.

WEST

OLDHAM 68 SWINTON LIONS 14

OLDHAM: 1 Gavin Dodd; 2 Chris Irwin; 3 Iain Marsh; 4 Jon Goddard; 5 Joe McNicholas; 6 Simon Svabic; 7 Neil Roden; 8 Steve Molloy; 9 John Hough; 10 Paul Norton; 11 Lee Doran; 12 Ryan Stazicker; 13 Chris Morley. Subs (all used): 14 Keith Brennan; 15 Paul Anderson; 16 Danny Guest; 17 Dane Morgan.
Tries: Svabic (12), I Marsh (16, 48), Hough (18), Dodd (28, 52), Morgan (40), Roden (42), Anderson (55), McNicholas (60), Irwin (67), Brennan (77);
Goals: Svabic 10.
Sin bin: Doran (34) - offside.
LIONS: 1 Wayne English; 2 Adrian Mead; 3 Robert Russell; 4 Hugh Thorpe; 5 Lee Hudson; 6 Kris Smith; 7 Peter Cannon; 8 Andy Leathem; 9 Rob Barraclough; 10 Chris Roe; 11 Phil Cushion; 12 Dave Ellison; 13 Simon Knox. Subs: 14 Grant Bithel; 15 Craig Wingfield; 16 Alan Shea; 17 Andy Cheetham (not used).
Tries: Mead (20), Hudson (35), Russell (73);
Goal: Russell.
Sin bin: Cannon (9) - offside.
Rugby Leaguer & League Express Men of the Match: *Oldham:* John Hough; *Lions:* Simon Knox.
Penalty count: 12-6; **Half-time:** 34-10;
Referee: Steve Addy (Huddersfield); **Attendance:** 1,032.

ROCHDALE HORNETS 16 SALFORD CITY REDS 44

HORNETS: 1 Casey Mayberry; 2 Mick Nanyn; 3 James Bunyan; 4 Jon Roper; 5 Marlon Billy; 6 Stephen Doherty; 7 Ian Watson; 8 Andy Grundy; 9 Richard Pachniuk; 10 Wes Rogers; 11 David Larder; 12 Paul Smith; 13 Damian Ball. Subs (all used): 14 Warren Ayres; 15 Andy Wallace; 16 Gareth Price; 17 Matthew Long.
Tries: Billy (13, 66), Bunyan (70); **Goals:** Watson 2.
CITY REDS: 1 Jason Flowers; 2 Alan Hunte; 3 Andy Kirk; 4 Cliff Beverley; 5 Danny Arnold; 6 Steve Blakeley; 7 Gavin Clinch; 8 Neil Baynes; 9 Malcolm Alker; 10 Paul Highton; 11 Simon Baldwin; 12 Lee Marsh; 13 Chris Charles. Subs (all used): 14 David Highton; 15 Neil Lowe; 16 Andy Coley; 17 Gareth Haggerty.
Tries: Hunte (22, 42), Blakeley (29), Clinch (34, 76), Charles (52), D Highton (60), Kirk (63);
Goals: Blakeley 6.
Rugby Leaguer & League Express Men of the Match: *Hornets:* James Bunyan; *City Reds:* Gavin Clinch.
Penalty count: 4-9; **Half-time:** 6-16;
Referee: Steve Ganson (St Helens); **Attendance:** 1,067.

CENTRAL

KEIGHLEY COUGARS 21 HUNSLET HAWKS 8

COUGARS: 1 James Rushforth; 2 Karl Smith; 3 David Foster; 4 Gareth Hewitt; 5 Andy Robinson; 6 Adam Mitchell; 7 Matt Firth; 8 Phil Stephenson; 9 Simeon Hoyle; 10 Danny Ekis; 11 Oliver Wilkes; 12 Ricky Helliwell; 13 Jason Ramshaw. Subs (all used): 14 Chris Wainwright; 15 Matt Foster; 16 Ian Sinfield; 17 Chris Hannah.
Tries: D Foster (9), Hoyle (26), Robinson (62);
Goals: Mitchell 4; **Field goal:** Firth.
Sin bin: Wilkes (74) - fighting.
HAWKS: 1 Simon Jackson; 2 Bryn Powell; 3 Iain Higgins; 4 Wes McGibbon; 5 Richard Baker; 6 Jon Liddell; 7 Phil Hasty; 8 Danny Burton; 9 Joe Hawley; 10 Mick Coyle; 11 Wayne Freeman; 12 Danny Fearon; 13 Paul Seal. Subs (all used): 14 Tony Howcroft; 15 Jonlee Lockwood; 16 Dan Briggs; 17 Steve Jakeman.
Try: Fearon (43); **Goals:** Liddell 2.
Dismissal: Fearon (69) - high tackle.
Sin bin: Howcroft (60) - professional foul; Seal (74) - fighting.
Rugby Leaguer & League Express Men of the Match: *Cougars:* Matt Firth; *Hawks:* Jon Liddell.
Penalty count: 7-7; **Half-time:** 16-2;
Referee: Ben Thaler (Wakefield); **Attendance:** 1,170.

LONDON SKOLARS 12 BATLEY BULLDOGS 56

SKOLARS: 1 Ronald Mushiso; 2 Troy Dougherty; 3 Jake Johnstone; 4 Scott Roberts; 5 Glen Hoare; 6 Cory Bennett; 7 Rob McKeown; 8 Glenn Osborn; 9 Kahu Henare; 10 Obi Ijeoma; 11 Brett McCroary; 12 Rubert Jonker; 13 PJ Solomon. Subs (all used): 14 Nick Dodinski; 15 Anthony Dellar; 16 Daniel Reeds; 17 Gerald Nkrumah.
Tries: Johnstone (56, 73); **Goals:** Johnstone 2.
BULLDOGS: 1 Craig Lingard; 2 Mark Sibson; 3 Anthony Gibbons; 4 Simon Lewis; 5 Matt Bramald; 6 Chris Hough; 7 Barry Eaton; 8 Joe Naidole; 9 Mark Cass; 10 Andy Spink; 11 David Rourke; 12 Will Cartledge; 13 Ryan Horsley. Subs (all used): 14 Danny Maun; 15 Paul Harrison; 16 Craig Booth; 17 Steve Hill.
Tries: Lewis (2, 59), Lingard (4, 35, 42), Bramald (29), Sibson (37), A Gibbons (49), Harrison (73), Hough (77);
Goals: Eaton 8.
Rugby Leaguer & League Express Men of the Match: *Skolars:* Jake Johnstone; *Bulldogs:* Barry Eaton.
Penalty count: 7-9; **Half-time:** 0-28;
Referee: Clive Walker (Oldham); **Attendance:** 307.

NORTH v WEST

CHORLEY LYNX 31 LEIGH CENTURIONS 22

LYNX: 1 Mark McCully; 2 Eddie Kilgannon; 3 Mick Redford; 4 Liam Bretherton; 5 Anton Garcia; 6 John Braddish; 7 Martin Gambles; 8 Wayne Bloor; 9 Mike Briggs; 10 David Whittle; 11 Gavin Johnson; 12 Dave McConnell; 13 Ian Hodson. Subs (all used): 14 Lee Rowley; 15 Ian Parry; 16 Safraz Patel; 17 Simon Smith.
Tries: Gambles (15, 46, 73), Briggs (62), McCully (67);
Goals: McCully 5; **Field goal:** Braddish.
CENTURIONS: 1 Neil Turley; 2 Eric Andrews; 3 Damian Munro; 4 Dale Cardoza; 5 Michael Watts; 6 Patrick Weisner; 7 Lee Sanderson; 8 Paul Norman; 9 Paul Rowley; 10 Bryan Henare; 11 Sean Richardson; 12 Adam Bristow; 13 Willie Swann. Subs (all used): 14 Sonny Nickle; 15 Alan Hadcroft; 16 Leroy Rivett; 17 David Bradbury.
Tries: Bristow (28), Turley (44), Sanderson (60), Weisner (77); **Goals:** Turley 3.
Dismissal: Cardoza (72) - punching.
Rugby Leaguer & League Express Men of the Match: *Lynx:* Martin Gambles; *Centurions:* Paul Rowley.
Penalty count: 5-13; **Half-time:** 8-4;
Referee: Julian King (St Helens); **Attendance:** 736.

CENTRAL v EAST

DEWSBURY RAMS 24 YORK CITY KNIGHTS 28

RAMS: 1 Nathan Batty; 2 Michael Wainwright; 3 Chris Chapman; 4 Paul Steele; 5 Craig Miles; 6 Danny Wood; 7 Danny Brough; 8 Frank Watene; 9 Andy Heptinstall; 10 Tony Fella; 11 Anthony Thewliss; 12 Billy Kershaw; 13 Chris Redfearn. Subs (all used): 14 Jimmy Elston; 15 Mark Barlow; 16 Danny Evans; 17 Michael Walker.
Tries: Wood (4), Thewliss (14, 32), Batty (70);
Goals: Brough 4.
CITY KNIGHTS: 1 Chris Smith; 2 Alex Godfrey; 3 Gareth Lloyd; 4 Darren Callaghan; 5 Gavin Molloy; 6 Adam Thaler; 7 Trevor Krause; 8 Paul Broadbent; 9 Darren Robinson; 10 Richard Hayes; 11 Mick Embleton; 12 Scott Fletcher; 13 Mick Ramsden. Subs: 14 Chris Beever; 15 Craig Westmoreland (not used); 16 Andy Burland; 17 David Bolus.
Tries: Thaler (19), C Smith (37), A Godfrey (39), Krause (61); **Goals:** Thaler 6.
Rugby Leaguer & League Express Men of the Match: *Rams:* Danny Brough; *City Knights:* Trevor Krause.
Penalty count: 8-11; **Half-time:** 18-16;
Referee: Russell Smith (Castleford); **Attendance:** 654.

WEEK 11

Sunday 13th April 2003

NORTH

BARROW RAIDERS 34 GATESHEAD THUNDER 24

RAIDERS: 1 Craig Bower; 2 Danny Lockhart; 3 Andy McClure; 4 Paul Jones; 5 Adam Pate; 6 Paul Evans; 7 Jamie Marshall; 8 Tau Liku; 9 Andy Henderson; 10 Steve Jackson; 11 James King; 12 Paul Lupton; 13 Phil Atkinson. Subs (all used): 14 Anthony Horton; 15 Stuart Dancer; 16 James Stainton; 17 Wayne Jones.
Tries: Marshall (4, 47), Dancer (30), W Jones (44), Bower (57), Lockhart (66); **Goals:** Evans 4, Atkinson.
THUNDER: 1 Kevin Neighbour; 2 Robin Peers; 3 Damien Reid; 4 Craig Firth; 5 Richie Barnett; 6 Paul Thorman; 7 Neil Thorman; 8 David Bates; 9 Chris Fletcher; 10 Steven Bradley; 11 Clint Brown; 12 Steve Rutherford; 13 Scott MacDougall. Subs (all used): 14 Yusuf Sozi; 15 Andy Walker; 16 Tony Doherty; 17 John Coutts.
Tries: N Thorman (11, 20), MacDougall (61), Reid (76);
Goals: N Thorman 3, P Thorman.
Rugby Leaguer & League Express Men of the Match: *Raiders:* Jamie Marshall; *Thunder:* Neil Thorman.
Penalty count: 12-5; **Half-time:** 12-12;
Referee: Craig Halloran (Dewsbury); **Attendance:** 557.

WORKINGTON TOWN 24 CHORLEY LYNX 22

TOWN: 1 Dean Sharp; 2 Scott Chilton; 3 Brett McDermott; 4 Matthew Johnson; 5 Graeme Lewthwaite; 6 Kevin Hetherington; 7 Anthony Murray; 8 Willie Burns; 9 Carl Sice; 10 Hitro Okesene; 11 Jamie Beaumont; 12 William Blackburn; 13 Ricky Wright. Subs (all used): 14 Craig Fisher; 15 Matthew Tunstall; 16 David Pettit; 17 Gary Charlton.
Tries: Wright (18, 68), Beaumont (43), Sharp (50);
Goals: Hetherington 4.
On report: Wright (72) - high tackle.
LYNX: 1 Mark McCully; 2 Safraz Patel; 3 Mick Redford; 4 Eddie Kilgannon; 5 Anton Garcia; 6 John Braddish; 7 Martin Gambles; 8 Ian Parry; 9 Mike Briggs; 10 David Whittle; 11 Gavin Johnson; 12 Dave McConnell; 13 Ian Hodson. Subs (all used): 14 Lee Rowley; 15 Dave Newton; 16 Mick Coates; 17 Simon Smith.
Tries: Hodson (12), Patel (37), Gambles (39), Garcia (55); **Goals:** McCully 2, Braddish.
Dismissal: McCully (63) - headbutt.
Sin bin: Patel (43) - off-the-ball tackle.
Rugby Leaguer & League Express Men of the Match: *Town:* Ricky Wright; *Lynx:* Ian Hodson.
Penalty count: 7-4; **Half-time:** 6-16;
Referee: Colin Morris (Huddersfield); **Attendance:** 355.

EAST

DONCASTER DRAGONS 38 SHEFFIELD EAGLES 30

DRAGONS: 1 Craig Horne; 2 Paul Gleadhill; 3 Simon Irving; 4 Shaun Leafe; 5 Jason Lee; 6 Paul Mansson; 7

Mark Moxon; 8 Gareth Handford; 9 Peter Edwards; 10 Craig Forsyth; 11 Peter Green; 12 Matt Walker; 13 Chris Ross. Subs (all used): 14 James Walker; 15 Jamie Fielden; 16 Dean Colton; 17 Craig Lawton.
Tries: P Green (1), Ross (12, 40, 58), Gleadhill (19, 37), Irving (54); **Goals:** Irving 5.
EAGLES: 1 Tony Weller; 2 Jon Breakingbury; 3 Neil Kite; 4 Nick Turnbull; 5 Ian Thompson; 6 Gavin Brown; 7 Lee Bettinson; 8 Jack Howieson; 9 Gareth Stanley; 10 Jon Bruce; 11 Andy Raleigh; 12 Craig Brown; 13 Simon Tillyer. Subs (all used): 14 Peter Reilly; 15 Ryan Angus; 16 Greg Hurst; 17 Mitchell Stringer.
Tries: G Brown (28), Raleigh (42), Hurst (45), Stringer (50), Tillyer (71), Thompson (78); **Goals:** G Brown 3.
Rugby Leaguer & League Express Men of the Match: *Dragons:* Chris Ross; *Eagles:* Gavin Brown.
Penalty count: 10-6; **Half-time:** 28-6; **Referee:** Steve Nicholson (Whitehaven); **Attendance:** 909.

YORK CITY KNIGHTS 14 FEATHERSTONE ROVERS 32

CITY KNIGHTS: 1 Chris Smith; 2 Chris Beever; 3 Gareth Lloyd; 4 Darren Callaghan; 5 Rikki Sheriffe; 6 Adam Thaler; 7 Scott Rhodes; 8 Paul Broadbent; 9 Trevor Krause; 10 Richard Hayes; 11 Mick Embleton; 12 Scott Fletcher; 13 Mick Ramsden. Subs (all used): 14 Sam Clarke; 15 Darren Robinson; 16 Andy Burland; 17 David Bolus.
Tries: Krause (28, 63), Robinson (58); **Goal:** Thaler.
ROVERS: 1 James Graham; 2 Jamie Stokes; 3 Brendan O'Meara; 4 Ian Brown; 5 Adrian Flynn; 6 Richard Agar; 7 Carl Briggs; 8 Ian Tonks; 9 Richard Chapman; 10 Stuart Dickens; 11 Steve Dooler; 12 Andy Rice; 13 Danny Seal. Subs: 14 Richard Whiting (not used); 15 Andy Bailey; 16 Robin Jowitt; 17 Chris Molyneux.
Tries: Graham (2), Seal (5, 40), Brown (11), Chapman (46), Agar (73); **Goals:** Dickens 2, Briggs 2.
Rugby Leaguer & League Express Men of the Match: *City Knights:* Chris Smith; *Rovers:* Richard Chapman.
Penalty count: 7-5; **Half-time:** 4-22;
Referee: Julian King (St Helens); **Attendance:** 1,415.

WEST

LEIGH CENTURIONS 58 ROCHDALE HORNETS 30

CENTURIONS: 1 Neil Turley; 2 Leroy Rivett; 3 Dale Cardoza; 4 Phil Kendrick; 5 Alan Hadcroft; 6 Patrick Weisner; 7 John Duffy; 8 Sonny Nickle; 9 Paul Rowley; 10 Paul Norman; 11 Sean Richardson; 12 Bryan Henare; 13 Adam Bristow. Subs (all used): 14 Willie Swann; 15 Damian Munro; 16 David Alstead; 17 David Bradbury.
Tries: Bristow (11), Cardoza (34), Munro (37, 43), Rowley (57), Turley (60, 65, 70), Duffy (76), Swann (77); **Goals:** Turley 7, Duffy 2.
HORNETS: 1 Wayne McHugh; 2 Sean Cooper; 3 Mick Nanyn; 4 Jon Roper; 5 Lee Wilson; 6 Warren Ayres; 7 Ian Watson; 8 Paul Southern; 9 Andy Wallace; 10 Andy Grundy; 11 Matthew Leigh; 12 Gareth Price; 13 Damian Ball. Subs (all used): 14 Stephen Doherty; 15 Wes Rogers; 16 James Bunyan; 17 Matthew Long.
Tries: Leigh (5), Ball (15), Cooper (30), Roper (30), Wilson (50), Wallace (68); **Goals:** Nanyn 3.
Rugby Leaguer & League Express Men of the Match: *Centurions:* Paul Rowley; *Hornets:* Gareth Price.
Penalty count: 7-9; **Half-time:** 16-18; **Referee:** Richard Silverwood (Dewsbury); **Attendance:** 1,365.

SALFORD CITY REDS 54 OLDHAM 12

CITY REDS: 1 Alan Hunte; 2 Michael Platt; 3 Andy Kirk; 4 Lee Marsh; 5 Danny Arnold; 6 Cliff Beverley; 7 Gavin Clinch; 8 Neil Baynes; 9 Malcolm Alker; 10 Andy Coley; 11 Simon Baldwin; 12 Neil Lowe; 13 Chris Charles. Subs (all used): 14 David Highton; 15 Karl Fitzpatrick; 16 Paul Highton; 17 Gareth Haggerty.
Tries: Hunte (2), Baldwin (5), Kirk (15), Beverley (25, 64), Arnold (30), Marsh (45), Coley (70), D Highton (76), Haggerty (79); **Goals:** Marsh 7.
OLDHAM: 1 Gavin Dodd; 2 Chris Irwin; 3 Iain Marsh; 4 Jon Goddard; 5 Chris Campbell; 6 Simon Svabic; 7 Neil Roden; 8 Steve Molloy; 9 John Hough; 10 Paul Norton; 11 Lee Doran; 12 Ryan Stazicker; 13 Chris Morley. Subs (all used): 14 Keith Brennan; 15 Paul Anderson; 16 Danny Guest; 17 Dane Morgan.
Tries: Svabic (33), Hough (78); **Goals:** Svabic 2.
Rugby Leaguer & League Express Men of the Match: *City Reds:* Cliff Beverley; *Oldham:* Steve Molloy.
Penalty count: 7-5; **Half-time:** 26-6; **Referee:** Ronnie Laughton (Barnsley); **Attendance:** 2,162.

CENTRAL

BATLEY BULLDOGS 40 KEIGHLEY COUGARS 16

BULLDOGS: 1 Craig Lingard; 2 Mark Sibson; 3 Simon Lewis; 4 Danny Maun; 5 Leon Williamson; 6 Mark Toohey; 7 Barry Eaton; 8 Joe Naidole; 9 Gavin Swinson; 10 Andy Spink; 11 David Rourke; 12 Will Cartledge; 13 Ryan Horsley. Subs (all used): 14 Mark Cass; 15 Paul Harrison; 16 Joe Berry; 17 Steve Hill.
Tries: Spink (32), Sibson (39), Lewis (53), Toohey (74), Horsley (76), Lingard (80); **Goals:** Eaton 8.
COUGARS: 1 James Rushforth; 2 Karl Smith; 3 David Foster; 4 Matt Foster; 5 Andy Robinson; 6 Adam Mitchell; 7 Matt Firth; 8 Phil Stephenson; 9 Simeon Hoyle; 10 Chris Hannah; 11 Oliver Wilkes; 12 Ricky Helliwell; 13 Jason Ramshaw. Subs: 14 Lee Patterson (not used); 15 Richard Mervill; 16 Gareth Hewitt; 17 Danny Ekis.
Tries: M Foster (9), Rushforth (27), Wilkes (36); **Goals:** Mitchell 2.
Rugby Leaguer & League Express Men of the Match: *Bulldogs:* Paul Harrison; *Cougars:* Oliver Wilkes.

Penalty count: 10-6; **Half-time:** 16-10;
Referee: Ashley Klein (London); **Attendance:** 737.

HUNSLET HAWKS 31 DEWSBURY RAMS 32

HAWKS: 1 George Rayner; 2 Bryn Powell; 3 Iain Higgins; 4 Steve Jakeman; 5 Gareth Brain; 6 Jon Liddell; 7 Phil Hasty; 8 Andy Brent; 9 Joe Hawley; 10 Mick Coyle; 11 Wayne Freeman; 12 Paul Seal; 13 Danny Fearon. Subs: 14 Craig Ibbetson; 15 Dan Briggs; 16 Steve Beard; 17 Chris North (not used).
Tries: Hasty (22), Fearon (28), Coyle (31), Powell (34, 38); **Goals:** Liddell 5; **Field goal:** Hasty.
RAMS: 1 Nathan Batty; 2 Michael Wainwright; 3 Paul Steele; 4 Ryan Hardy; 5 Craig Miles; 6 Danny Wood; 7 Mark Barlow; 8 Frank Watene; 9 Andy Heptinstall; 10 Tony Fella; 11 Anthony Thewliss; 12 Billy Kershaw; 13 Chris Redfearn. Subs (all used): 14 Jimmy Elston; 15 Danny Evans; 16 Glenn Spedding; 17 David Oldfield.
Tries: Wainwright (12, 17), Watene (26), Batty (44), Miles (55), Elston (75); **Goals:** Wood 4.
On report: Watene (7) - striking.
Rugby Leaguer & League Express Men of the Match: *Hawks:* Phil Hasty; *Rams:* Frank Watene.
Penalty count: 10-8; **Half-time:** 30-18;
Referee: Mike Dawber (Wigan); **Attendance:** 599.

EAST v CENTRAL

HULL KINGSTON ROVERS 86 LONDON SKOLARS 0

ROVERS: 1 Craig Poucher; 2 Nick Pinkney; 3 Ian Bell; 4 Craig Farrell; 5 Alasdair McClarron; 6 Paul Parker; 7 Chris Stephenson; 8 Richard Wilson; 9 Paul Pickering; 10 Jamie Bovill; 11 Adam Sullivan; 12 Jon Aston; 13 Andy Smith. Subs (all used): 14 Mark Blanchard; 15 Anthony Seibold; 16 Harvey Howard; 17 Paul Fletcher.
Tries: Stephenson (2), Smith (7, 16), Parker (11), Sullivan (18), Pickering (23, 70), McClarron (25), Fletcher (32), Seibold (38), Howard (41), Bell (50, 73), Pinkney (55), Poucher (67); **Goals:** Stephenson 13.
SKOLARS: 1 Anthony Dellar; 2 Jason McDonald; 3 Jake Johnstone; 4 Scott Roberts; 5 Nick Dodinski; 6 Rob McKeown; 7 Al Stewart; 8 Daniel Reeds; 9 Janan Billings; 10 Bobby Wallis; 11 Wayne Parrilon; 12 Brett McCroary; 13 PJ Solomon. Subs (all used): 14 Andy Craig; 15 Gareth Desmond; 16 Gerald Nkrumah; 17 Steve Hainey.
Rugby Leaguer & League Express Men of the Match: *Rovers:* Andy Smith; *Skolars:* Rob McKeown.
Penalty count: 11-5; **Half-time:** 52-0; **Referee:** Gareth Hewer (Whitehaven); **Attendance:** 1,175.

WEST v NORTH

SWINTON LIONS 22 WHITEHAVEN 22

LIONS: 1 Wayne English; 2 Adrian Mead; 3 Robert Russell; 4 Phil Hassan; 5 Lee Hudson; 6 Kris Smith; 7 Chris Hough; 8 Andy Leathem; 9 Rob Barraclough; 10 Simon Knox; 11 Phil Cushion; 12 Alan Shea; 13 Wayne Durham. Subs: 14 Grant Bithel (not used); 15 Kris Tassell; 16 Craig Wingfield; 17 Chris Roe.
Tries: Knox (20), Hudson (33, 59), English (68); **Goals:** Hough 3.
WHITEHAVEN: 1 Steven Wood; 2 Glen Hutton; 3 Jamie Stenhouse; 4 Howard Hill; 5 Mark Wallace; 6 Leroy Joe; 7 Lee Kiddie; 8 Gary Smith; 9 Darren King; 10 Mike Whitehead; 11 Craig Chambers; 12 Spencer Miller; 13 Garry Purdham. Subs (all used): 14 Darren Holt; 15 Ryan Campbell; 16 Tony Cunningham; 17 Dean Burgess.
Tries: Wood (30), Joe (44, 45, 73); **Goals:** Wood, Holt 2.
Rugby Leaguer & League Express Men of the Match: *Lions:* Simon Knox; *Whitehaven:* Craig Chambers.
Penalty count: 10-10; **Half-time:** 12-6;
Referee: Clive Walker (Oldham); **Attendance:** 339.

QUARTER FINALS

Sunday 18th May 2003

BARROW RAIDERS 20 SALFORD CITY REDS 40

RAIDERS: 1 Danny Lockhart; 2 Jamie Marshall; 3 Jamie Smith; 4 Paul Jones; 5 Adam Pate; 6 Tane Manihera; 7 Chris Archer; 8 Stuart Dancer; 9 Andy Henderson; 10 James King; 11 Geoff Luxon; 12 Paul Lupton; 13 Phil Atkinson. Subs (all used): 14 Barry Pugh; 15 Paul Evans; 16 Andy McClure; 17 Wayne Jones.
Tries: Luxon (6), P Jones (37), Pate (48), Marshall (69); **Goals:** Manihera 2.
CITY REDS: 1 Jason Flowers; 2 Michael Platt; 3 Stuart Littler; 4 Andy Kirk; 5 Danny Arnold; 6 Cliff Beverley; 7 Gavin Clinch; 8 Neil Baynes; 9 Malcolm Alker; 10 Paul Highton; 11 Simon Baldwin; 12 Neil Lowe; 13 Chris Charles. Subs (all used): 14 David Highton; 15 Steve Blakeley; 16 Lee Marsh; 17 Andy Coley.
Tries: Beverley (11, 59), Littler (17), Charles (21), Lowe (24), Baldwin (27), Kirk (31); **Goals:** Charles 6.
Rugby Leaguer & League Express Men of the Match: *Raiders:* Andy Henderson; *City Reds:* Cliff Beverley.
Penalty count: 5-3; **Half-time:** 10-34;
Referee: Colin Morris (Huddersfield); **Attendance:** 936.

LEIGH CENTURIONS 26 FEATHERSTONE ROVERS 6

CENTURIONS: 1 David Alstead; 2 Damian Munro; 3 Dale Cardoza; 4 Phil Kendrick; 5 Alan Hadcroft; 6 Patrick Weisner; 7 John Duffy; 8 Sonny Nickle; 9 Jim Hamilton; 10 Paul Norman; 11 Sean Richardson; 12 Adam Bristow; 13 Willie Swann. Subs (all used): 14 Rob Ball; 15 Bryan Henare; 16 Leroy Rivett; 17 David Bradbury.
Tries: Munro (5, 73), Cardoza (17, 51), Duffy (69); **Goals:** Weisner 3.

Whitehaven's Dean Vaughan clings on to Leigh's Willie Swann as the Centurions reach the National League Cup Final

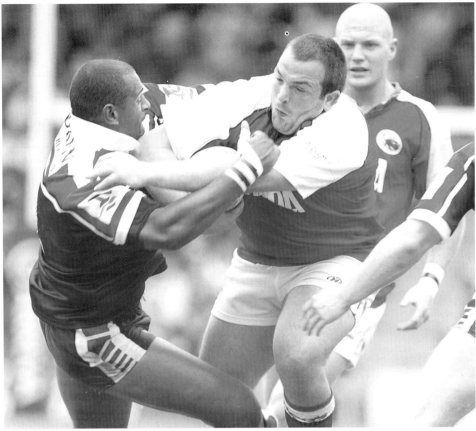

Salford's Neil Baynes tries to break free from Leigh's Sean Richardson during the National League Cup Final

ROVERS: 1 Nathan Graham; 2 Jamie Stokes; 3 Chris Langley; 4 Ian Brown; 5 Adrian Flynn; 6 Brendan O'Meara; 7 Carl Briggs; 8 Ian Tonks; 9 Paul Darley; 10 Stuart Dickens; 11 Steve Dooler; 12 Andy Rice; 13 Danny Seal. Subs (all used): 14 Richard Whiting; 15 Andy Jarrett; 16 Andy Bailey; 17 Chris Molyneux.
Try: Flynn (59); **Goal:** Dickens.
Rugby Leaguer & League Express Men of the Match: *Centurions:* Adam Bristow; *Rovers:* Carl Briggs.
Penalty count: 7-7; **Half-time:** 8-2; **Referee:** Steve Nicholson (Whitehaven); **Attendance:** 1,668.

WHITEHAVEN 54 DEWSBURY RAMS 10

WHITEHAVEN: 1 Gary Broadbent; 2 Steven Wood; 3 David Seeds; 4 Howard Hill; 5 Glen Hutton; 6 Leroy Joe; 7 Darren Holt; 8 Gary Smith; 9 Aaron Lester; 10 David Fatialofa; 11 Dean Vaughan; 12 Spencer Miller; 13 Garry Purdham. Subs (all used): 14 Lee Kiddie; 15 Marc Jackson; 16 Carl Sice; 17 Ryan Campbell.
Tries: Hutton (9, 69), Joe (23), Jackson (30), Lester (49), Fatialofa (52), Hill (55, 66), Wood (78); **Goals:** Holt 9.
RAMS: 1 George Mack; 2 Craig Miles; 3 Danny Wood; 4 Ryan Hardy; 5 Paul Steele; 6 Mark Barlow; 7 Craig Nipperess; 8 Paul Hicks; 9 David Oldfield; 10 Glen Spedding; 11 Ian Kirke; 12 Chris Parker; 13 Danny Evans. Subs (all used): 14 Chris Redfearn; 15 Andy Heptinstall; 16 Neil Mears; 17 Anthony Thewliss.
Tries: Hardy (16), Heptinstall (42); **Goal:** Wood.
Rugby Leaguer & League Express Men of the Match: *Whitehaven:* Howard Hill; *Rams:* Ian Kirke.
Penalty count: 12-9; **Half-time:** 16-6; **Referee:** Karl Kirkpatrick (Warrington); **Attendance:** 1,503.

HULL KINGSTON ROVERS 12 BATLEY BULLDOGS 16

ROVERS: 1 Mike Hall; 2 David Wilson; 3 Nick Pinkney; 4 Mark Blanchard; 5 Alasdair McClarron; 6 Shaun Cooke; 7 Latham Tawhai; 8 Richard Wilson; 9 Paul Pickering; 10 Harvey Howard; 11 Adam Sullivan; 12 Jon Aston; 13 Andy Smith. Subs (all used): 14 Craig Murdock; 15 Dean Andrews; 16 Jamie Bovill; 17 Paul Fletcher.
Tries: Cooke (7), Aston (64); **Goals:** Cooke 2.
On report: Aston (78) – alleged punch on Spink.
BULLDOGS: 1 Mark Sibson; 2 Matt Bramald; 3 Chris Spurr; 4 Danny Maun; 5 Leon Williamson; 6 David Gibbons; 7 Barry Eaton; 8 Andy Spink; 9 Will Cartledge;

10 Steve Hill; 11 David Rourke; 12 Joe Berry; 13 Ryan Horsley. Subs (all used): 14 Kris Lythe; 15 Paul Harrison; 16 Joe Naidole; 17 Craig Booth.
Tries: Lythe (41), Sibson (60); **Goals:** Eaton 4.
Rugby Leaguer & League Express Men of the Match: *Rovers:* Latham Tawhai; *Bulldogs:* Barry Eaton.
Penalty count: 11-12; **Half-time:** 8-0;
Referee: Russell Smith (Castleford); **Attendance:** 1,100.

SEMI FINALS

Sunday 8th June 2003

LEIGH CENTURIONS 39 WHITEHAVEN 18

CENTURIONS: 1 Neil Turley; 2 Damian Munro; 3 Alan Hadcroft; 4 Phil Kendrick; 5 Leroy Rivett; 6 Patrick Weisner; 7 Willie Swann; 8 Sonny Nickle; 9 Paul Rowley; 10 Paul Norman; 11 Sean Richardson; 12 Bryan Henare; 13 Adam Bristow. Subs (all used): 14 Rob Ball; 15 Lee Sanderson; 16 Dale Holdstock; 17 David Bradbury.
Tries: Norman (9), Munro (36), Kendrick (41), Hadcroft (50), Holdstock (60), Bradbury (77); **Goals:** Turley 7;
Field goal: Weisner.
WHITEHAVEN: 1 Gary Broadbent; 2 Steven Wood; 3 David Seeds; 4 Howard Hill; 5 Mark Wallace; 6 Leroy Joe; 7 Darren Holt; 8 Dean Vaughan; 9 Aaron Lester; 10 David Fatialofa; 11 Chris McKinney; 12 Mike Whitehead; 13 Garry Purdham. Subs (all used): 14 Lee Kiddie; 15 Marc Jackson; 16 Gary Smith; 17 Graeme Morton.
Tries: Whitehead (24), Morton (63), Broadbent (65);
Goals: Holt 3.
Rugby Leaguer & League Express Men of the Match: *Centurions:* Willie Swann; *Whitehaven:* Aaron Lester.
Penalty count: 5-6; **Half-time:** 16-8; **Referee:** Karl Kirkpatrick (Warrington); **Attendance:** 2,687.

SALFORD CITY REDS 68 BATLEY BULLDOGS 6

CITY REDS: 1 Jason Flowers; 2 Danny Arnold; 3 Stuart Littler; 4 Alan Hunte; 5 Mick Berne; 6 Cliff Beverley; 7 Gavin Clinch; 8 Andy Coley; 9 Malcolm Alker; 10 Paul Highton; 11 Simon Baldwin; 12 Chris Charles; 13 David Highton. Subs (all used): 14 Steve Blakeley; 15 Danny Barton; 16 Radney Bowker; 17 Gareth Haggerty.
Tries: Coley (18, 45, 57), Alker (21), Baldwin (27), Berne

(33), Beverley (37), Littler (39, 42), Bowker (60), P Highton (72), Hunte (78); **Goals:** Charles 7, Blakeley 3.
BULLDOGS: 1 Mark Sibson; 2 Simon Lewis; 3 Chris Spurr; 4 Danny Maun; 5 Leon Williamson; 6 Mark Toohey; 7 Barry Eaton; 8 Andy Spink; 9 Kris Lythe; 10 Joe Naidole; 11 David Rourke; 12 Will Cartledge; 13 Ryan Horsley. Subs (all used): 14 Mark Cass; 15 Paul Harrison; 16 Joe Berry; 17 Steve Hill.
Try: Eaton (49); **Goal:** Eaton.
Rugby Leaguer & League Express Men of the Match: *City Reds:* Andy Coley; *Bulldogs:* Barry Eaton.
Penalty count: 14-4; **Half-time:** 34-0; **Referee:** Ronnie Laughton (Barnsley); **Attendance:** 1,379.

FINAL

Sunday 6th July 2003

LEIGH CENTURIONS 19 SALFORD CITY REDS 36

CENTURIONS: 1 Neil Turley; 2 Damian Munro; 3 Alan Hadcroft; 4 Phil Kendrick; 5 Leroy Rivett; 6 Patrick Weisner; 7 John Duffy; 8 Sonny Nickle; 9 Paul Rowley; 10 Rob Ball; 11 Sean Richardson; 12 Bryan Henare; 13 Adam Bristow. Subs (all used): 14 David Bradbury; 15 Dale Cardoza; 16 Willie Swann; 17 Paul Norman.
Tries: Rivett (13), Swann (45), Munro (57), Turley (73);
Goal: Turley. **Field goal:** Turley.
Dismissal: Kendrick (78) - late tackle.
Sin bin: Nickle (70) - fighting.
On report: Brawl (70).
CITY REDS: 1 Jason Flowers; 2 Danny Arnold; 3 Stuart Littler; 4 Alan Hunte; 5 Andy Kirk; 6 Cliff Beverley; 7 Gavin Clinch; 8 Neil Baynes; 9 Malcolm Alker; 10 Andy Coley; 11 Simon Baldwin; 12 Paul Highton; 13 Chris Charles. Subs: 14 Steve Blakeley; 15 David Highton; 16 Mick Berne (not used); 17 Gareth Haggerty.
Tries: Haggerty (24), Coley (30), Littler (34), Kirk (37), Arnold (48), Hunte (64); **Goals:** Charles, Blakeley 5.
Sin bin: Hunte (70) - fighting.
On report: Brawl (70).
Rugby Leaguer & League Express Men of the Match: *Centurions:* Neil Turley; *City Reds:* Gavin Clinch.
Penalty count: 10-8; **Half-time:** 5-20;
Referee: Peter Taberner (Wigan).
Attendance: 6,486 *(at Spotland, Rochdale).*

CHALLENGE CUP 2003
Round by Round

ROUND 3

Friday 24th January 2003

WATH BROW HORNETS 13 WORKINGTON TOWN 12

HORNETS: 1 Gary Elliott; 2 Craig Calvert; 3 Ian Rooney; 4 Gary Clarke; 5 Gavin Curwen; 6 Craig Johnstone; 7 Andrew Hocking; 8 Mark Deans; 9 Scott Anderson; 10 Mark Troughton; 11 Paul Davidson; 12 Graeme Mattinson; 13 Carl Rudd. Subs (all used): 14 Stewart Sanderson; 15 Neil Stewart; 16 Mickey McAllister; 17 Scott Teare.
Tries: Troughton (46); **Goals:** Curwen 4;
Field goal: Rudd.
Sin bin: Teare (64) - late tackle.
TOWN: 1 Anthony Huddart; 2 Matthew Johnson; 3 Brett McDermott; 4 Jamie Beaumont; 5 Jonathan Heaney; 6 Kevin Hetherington; 7 Owen Williamson; 8 William Blackburn; 9 Carl Sice; 10 Hitro Okesene; 11 Matthew Tunstall; 12 Lokeni Savelio; 13 Gary Charlton. Subs (all used): 14 Ricky Wright; 15 Graeme Lewthwaite; 16 Barrie Murdock; 17 Brett Smith.
Tries: Williamson (29), Smith (59);
Goals: Hetherington, Heaney.
Rugby Leaguer & League Express Men of the Match: *Hornets:* Andrew Hocking; *Town:* Carl Sice.
Penalty count: 12-12; **Half-time:** 4-6;
Referee: Steve Presley (Castleford); **Attendance:** 3,017
(at The Recreation Ground, Whitehaven).

OULTON RAIDERS 8 SHEFFIELD EAGLES 22

RAIDERS: 1 Danny Coward; 2 David Wilkin; 3 Dan Nicol; 4 Steve Jakeman; 5 Geoff Hick; 6 Stephen Doherty; 7 Scott Goodall; 8 Rob Ward; 9 Matt White; 10 Mark Longley; 11 Carlos Sanchez; 12 Sasch Brook; 13 Gavin Wood. Subs: 14 Neil Horton (not used); 15 Jason Longstaff; 16 Rob Palmer; 17 Andy Siddons.
Tries: Doherty (24), White (62).
Sin bin: White (39) - holding down.
EAGLES: 1 Andy Poynter; 2 Jon Breakingbury; 3 Neil Kite; 4 Nick Turnbull; 5 Ian Thompson; 6 Gavin Brown; 7 Lee Bettinson; 8 Damien Whitter; 9 Adam Carroll; 10 Jack Howieson; 11 Guy Adams; 12 Craig Brown; 13 Wayne Flynn. Subs (all used): 14 Peter Reilly; 15 Sam Bibb; 16 Simon Tillyer; 17 Jon Bruce.
Tries: Flynn (4), C Brown (15, 32), Thompson (19);
Goals: G Brown 3.
Rugby Leaguer & League Express Men of the Match: *Raiders:* Stephen Doherty; *Eagles:* Guy Adams.
Penalty count: 13-19; **Half time:** 4-22;
Referee: Gareth Hewer (Whitehaven); **Attendance:** 759
(at South Leeds Stadium, Hunslet).

CHORLEY LYNX 36 LEIGH MINERS RANGERS 14

LYNX: 1 David Ingram; 2 Chris Ramsdale; 3 Mick Redford; 4 Anton Garcia; 5 Liam Jones; 6 John Braddish; 7 Mick Coates; 8 Tim Street; 9 Mike Briggs; 10 David Whittle; 11 Wayne Bloor; 12 Dave McConnell; 13 Ian Hodson. Subs (all used): 14 Simon Smith; 15 Dave Radley; 16 Martin Roden; 17 Eddie Kilgannon.
Tries: Ramsdale (19), Whittle (28), Street (39), Redford (53, 72), Garcia (61), McConnell (66); **Goals:** Braddish 4.
Sin bin: Ingram (11) - lying on; Braddish (11) - dissent.
MINERS RANGERS: 1 Darren Pilkington; 2 Glen Bracek; 3 Lee Patterson; 4 Alan Reddicliffe; 5 Craig Graham; 6 Aaron Beath; 7 Sean Phoenix; 8 Danny Flannery; 9 Roy Stott; 10 Jon Light; 11 Richard Varkulis; 12 Steve Flannery; 13 Tom Goulden. Subs (all used): 14 Matt Jones; 15 Steve Houghton; 16 Lee Lomax; 17 Dean Balmer.
Tries: Reddicliffe (15), Patterson (80); **Goals:** Beath 3.
Rugby Leaguer & League Express Men of the Match: *Lynx:* Mike Briggs; *Miners Rangers:* Jon Light.
Penalty count: 10-14; **Half-time:** 16-8;
Referee: Steve Ganson (St Helens); **Attendance:** 809.

Saturday 25th January 2003

LEIGH CENTURIONS 62 LOCOMOTIV MOSCOW 0

CENTURIONS: 1 David Alstead; 2 Eric Andrews; 3 Damian Munro; 4 Dale Cardoza; 5 Alan Hadcroft; 6 Patrick Weisner; 7 Lee Sanderson; 8 Rob Ball; 9 Paul Rowley; 10 David Bradbury; 11 Sean Richardson; 12 Anthony Blackwood; 13 Adam Bristow. Subs (all used): 14 Dale Holdstock; 15 John Hamilton; 16 John Duffy; 17 Sonny Nickle.
Tries: Hadcroft (7), Rowley (11, 79), Cardoza (28, 39), Munro (30, 38), Alstead (33), Richardson (43), Nickle (52), Holdstock (71); **Goals:** Sanderson 8, Duffy.
MOSCOW: 1 Phillipe Romanov; 2 Andrei Postnikov; 3 Igor Gavriline; 4 Vladimir Ouchinnikov; 5 Denis Mechov; 6 Viktor Nechaev; 7 Denis Nikolski; 8 Petr Sokolov; 9 Roman Ouchinnikov; 10 Aleksandr Lysenkov; 11 Robert Ilyasov; 12 Andrei Doumalkis; 13 Evgueni Bozgukov. Subs (all used): 14 Oleg Logumov; 15 Rouslan Izmailov; 16 Andrei Koltyklov; 17 Dmitri Jivorykine.
Rugby Leaguer & League Express Men of the Match: *Centurions:* Dale Cardoza; *Moscow:* Robert Ilyasov.
Penalty count: 8-11; **Half-time:** 38-0; **Referee:** Steve Nicholson (Whitehaven); **Attendance:** 2,641.

Sunday 26th January 2003

OLDHAM ST ANNES 18 ROCHDALE HORNETS 62

ST ANNES: 1 Ryan Blake; 2 Graeme Sykes; 3 Warren Druggitt; 4 Chris Worth; 5 Danny Tyrell; 6 Richard Badby; 7 Lee Charlesworth; 8 Jason Akeroyd; 9 Phil Russell; 10 Martin Taylor; 11 David Best; 12 Jason Best; 13 Michael Deakin. Subs (all used): 14 Josh Brady; 15 Andy Sands; 16 Kevin McCormack; 17 Craig Milner.
Tries: J Best (50), Sands (63), Milner (72);
Goals: Badby 3.
HORNETS: 1 Paul Owen; 2 Sean Cooper; 3 Mick Nanyn; 4 James Bunyan; 5 Casey Mayberry; 6 Warren Ayres; 7 Ian Watson; 8 Andy Grundy; 9 Richard Pachniuk; 10 David Stephenson; 11 David Larder; 12 Paul Smith; 13 Damian Ball. Subs (all used): 14 Danny Wood; 15 Matthew Leigh; 16 Gareth Price; 17 Matthew Long.
Tries: Smith (5, 36, 43), Owen (23, 46, 53), Ayres (39), Nanyn (41), Wood (60), Bunyan (67), Long (80);
Goals: Nanyn 9.
Rugby Leaguer & League Express Men of the Match: *St Annes:* Martin Taylor; *Hornets:* Ian Watson.
Penalty count: 10-6; **Half-time:** 20-0;
Referee: Richard Frileux (France); **Attendance:** 861
(at Spotland, Rochdale).

SKIRLAUGH 8 YORK CITY KNIGHTS 20

SKIRLAUGH: 1 Carl Wiles; 2 Paul Hannath; 3 Phil Elbourne; 4 Alex Bloom; 5 Phil Thacker; 6 Paul Garner; 7 Colin Brown; 8 Tim Last; 9 Chris Batty; 10 Steve Robson; 11 Phil Crane; 12 Gary Smith; 13 Sean Wildbore. Subs (all used): 14 Danny Wilson; 15 Simon Kilby; 16 Shaun Hill; 17 Kevin Sumpton.
Try: Brown (75); **Goals:** Brown 2.
CITY KNIGHTS: 1 Chris Beever; 2 Alex Godfrey; 3 Graeme Hallas; 4 Chris Smith; 5 Gavin Molloy; 6 Mark Cain; 7 Trevor Krause; 8 Richard Hayes; 9 Lee Jackson; 10 Damian Kennedy; 11 Mick Ramsden; 12 Scott Fletcher; 13 Darren Callaghan. Subs (all used): 14 Scott Yeaman; 15 Gareth Lloyd; 16 Jermaine Coleman; 17 David Bolus.
Tries: Callaghan (4), Yeaman (48, 52); **Goals:** Hallas 4.
Dismissal: Smith (70) - use of elbow.
Sin bin: Fletcher (65) - interference.
Rugby Leaguer & League Express Men of the Match: *Skirlaugh:* Colin Brown; *City Knights:* Trevor Krause.
Penalty count: 8-8; **Half-time:** 2-6;
Referee: Steve Addy (Huddersfield); **Attendance:** 943
(at The Boulevard, Hull).

BARROW RAIDERS 70 EMBASSY 6

RAIDERS: 1 Craig Bower; 2 Jamie Marshall; 3 Andy McClure; 4 Paul Jones; 5 Shane Irabor; 6 Paul Evans; 7 Chris Archer; 8 Wayne Jones; 9 Andy Henderson; 10 Steve Jackson; 11 James King; 12 Paul Gardner; 13 Phil Atkinson. Subs (all used): 14 Barry Pugh; 15 Geoff Luxon; 16 Adam Pate; 17 James Stainton.
Tries: P Jones (5, 35), Bower (14), Gardner (42, 68, 79), Archer (47), Stainton (52), Pate (67), Marshall (70), Irabor (76), Pugh (78);
Goals: Atkinson 4, Pate 4, Pugh 2, Evans.
EMBASSY: 1 Glen Ellerby; 2 Ben Green; 3 Mark Dawson; 4 Craig Barker; 5 Martin Hardy; 6 Danny Sharkett; 7 Glen Matsell; 8 Andy Spencley; 9 Chris Heslop; 10 Dave Holdstock; 11 Mark Sawyers; 12 Matthew Green; 13 Dale Blakeley. Subs (all used): 14 Danny Macklin; 15 Mike Able; 16 Chris Green; 17 Paul Smith.
Try: Sharkett (18); **Goal:** Dawson.
Rugby Leaguer & League Express Men of the Match: *Raiders:* Andy Henderson; *Embassy:* Glen Matsell.
Penalty count: 8-4; **Half-time:** 20-6;
Referee: Craig Halloran (Dewsbury); **Attendance:** 617.

DONCASTER DRAGONS 64 REDHILL 2

DRAGONS: 1 Johnny Woodcock; 2 Paul Gleadhill; 3 Marvin Golden; 4 Simon Irving; 5 Jason Lee; 6 Chris Ross; 7 Mark Moxon; 8 Gareth Handford; 9 Dean Colton; 10 James Walker; 11 Peter Green; 12 Craig Lawton; 13 Matt Walker. Subs (all used): 14 Shaun Leafe; 15 Wayne Green; 16 Maea David; 17 Craig Forsyth.
Tries: Lee (2, 41, 61), Ross (6, 50), J Walker (12), Lawton (13), M Walker (22), Colton (28), P Green (32), Gleadhill (34), Moxon (69);
Goals: Woodcock 5, Ross 2, Irving.
REDHILL: 1 Steve Embling; 2 Paul Baxter; 3 Craig Brookes; 4 Neil Bennett; 5 Jason Deveraux; 6 Wayne Appleby; 7 Dave Horner; 8 Dave Spears; 9 Tony Handford; 10 Colin Handford; 11 Steve Handford; 12 Shaun Goodway; 13 Danny Bolton. Subs (all used): 14 Danny Huby; 15 Mick Huby; 16 Adam Dickinson; 17 Lee Partridge.
Goal: Embling.
Rugby Leaguer & League Express Men of the Match: *Dragons:* Chris Ross; *Redhill:* Tony Handford.
Penalty count: 7-6; **Half-time:** 46-0;
Referee: Ben Thaler (Wakefield); **Attendance:** 944.

FEATHERSTONE ROVERS 26 VILLENEUVE LEOPARDS 22

ROVERS: 1 Nathan Graham; 2 Jamie Stokes; 3 Brendan O'Meara; 4 Ian Brown; 5 Adrian Flynn; 6 Andy McNally; 7 Carl Briggs; 8 Ian Tonks; 9 Richard Chapman; 10 Stuart Dickens; 11 Steve Dooler; 12 Andy Rice; 13 Danny Seal. Subs (all used): 14 Danny Patrickson; 15 Ben Archibald; 16 Andy Bailey; 17 Chris Molyneux.
Tries: Brown (35), Molyneux (45), Flynn (79);
Goals: Dickens 6; **Field goals:** Briggs 2.
LEOPARDS: 1 David Despin; 2 Jérôme Hermet; 3 Jason Webber; 4 Freddy Banquet; 5 Michael Van Snick; 6 Laurent Frayssinous; 7 Julien Rinaldi; 8 Quentin Pongia; 9 Vincent Wulf; 10 Romain Gagliazzo; 11 Artie Shead; 12 Djamel Fakir; 13 Laurent Carrasco. Subs: 14 Sébastien Gauffre; 15 Gilles Cornut (not used); 16 Phil Shead; 17 Pierre Sabatié.
Tries: Banquet (40), Carrasco (59), Webber (66), Despin (68); **Goals:** Frayssinous 3.
Sin bin: Webber (7) - interference;
Wulf (26) - interference.
On report: Pongia (14) - high tackle on Bailey.
Rugby Leaguer & League Express Men of the Match: *Rovers:* Stuart Dickens; *Leopards:* Laurent Carrasco.
Penalty count: 17-5; **Half-time:** 15-6;
Referee: Peter Taberner (Wigan); **Attendance:** 1,441.

HALTON SIMMS CROSS 15 LONDON SKOLARS 8

SIMMS CROSS: 1 Brian Capewell; 2 Kevin O'Neill; 3 David Percival; 4 Paul Walsh; 5 Darren O'Brien; 6 Neil Percival; 7 Paul Roberts; 8 Mike Donnelly; 9 Matt Carmichael; 10 Peter Grady; 11 Keith Newton; 12 Andy O'Neill; 13 Peter Hodson. Subs (all used): 14 Keiron Kavanagh; 15 Gary Middlehurst; 16 Lee Swain; 17 John Bowles.
Tries: Walsh (39), Capewell (57); **Goals:** Capewell 3;
Field goal: Roberts.
SKOLARS: 1 Kirk Wotherspoon; 2 Charlie Oyebade; 3 Scott Roberts; 4 Jake Johnstone; 5 Gavin Gordon; 6 Peter Rawson; 7 Richard Pollard; 8 Allan Tito; 9 Kahu Henare; 10 Glenn Osborn; 11 Jimmy Daines; 12 Steve Hainey; 13 Chris Thair. Subs (all used): 14 Anthony Dellar; 15 Pat Rich; 16 Cory Bennett; 17 Mike Okwusogu.
Try: Johnstone (19); **Goals:** Johnstone 2.
Rugby Leaguer & League Express Men of the Match: *Simms Cross:* Brian Capewell; *Skolars:* Glenn Osborn.
Penalty count: 6-4; **Half-time:** 8-7;
Referee: Julian King (St Helens); **Attendance:** 750
(at Halton Stadium, Widnes).

HULL KINGSTON ROVERS 28 SIDDAL 0

ROVERS: 1 Craig Poucher; 2 Nick Pinkney; 3 Paul Parker; 4 Craig Farrell; 5 Alasdair McClarron; 6 Jimmy Walker; 7 Craig Murdock; 8 Richard Wilson; 9 Paul Pickering; 10 Jamie Bovill; 11 Adam Sullivan; 12 Jon Aston; 13 Andy Smith. Subs (all used): 14 Lynton Stott; 15 Latham Tawhai; 16 Dean Andrews; 17 Paul Fletcher.
Tries: Pinkney (13, 36), Poucher (52), Pickering (58);
Goals: Poucher 6.
Dismissal: Sullivan (70) - fighting.
SIDDAL: 1 Darren Phillips; 2 Jason Blackburn; 3 Steven Lewis; 4 James Simeunovich; 5 Anthony Sawyer; 6 Craig Turner; 7 Liam Walsh; 8 Gary Lewis; 9 Martin Scrimshaw; 10 Jamie Wrigley; 11 Vaughan Uttley; 12 Nicky Shaw; 13 Mick Shaw. Subs (all used): 14 Paul Phillips; 15 Gareth Hooson; 16 Shaun Blackburn; 17 Wayne Graham.
Dismissals: Walsh (70) - fighting; Uttley (70) - fighting.
Rugby Leaguer & League Express Men of the Match: *Rovers:* Craig Poucher; *Siddal:* Liam Walsh.
Penalty count: 11-5; **Half-time:** 14-0;
Referee: Paul Carr (Castleford); **Attendance:** 1,526.

KEIGHLEY COUGARS 33 THORNHILL TROJANS 10

COUGARS: 1 James Rushforth; 2 Karl Smith; 3 David Foster; 4 Gareth Hewitt; 5 Andy Robinson; 6 Paul Ashton; 7 Matt Firth; 8 Phil Stephenson; 9 Simeon Hoyle; 10 Danny Ekis; 11 Ian Sinfield; 12 Ricky Helliwell; 13 Jason Ramshaw. Subs (all used): 14 Chris Wainwright; 15 Lee Patterson; 16 Oliver Wilkes; 17 Chris Hannah.
Tries: Ashton (7, 32), Hoyle (22), Firth (46), Smith (73);
Goals: Ashton 6; **Field goal:** Ashton.
TROJANS: 1 Craig Holmes; 2 Robert Copley; 3 Richard Bainton; 4 Danny Howley; 5 Scott Redgwick; 6 Martin Fox; 7 Alex Bretherton; 8 Steve Naylor; 9 Anthony Broadhead; 10 Lee Schofield; 11 Matt Roberts; 12 Phil Hepworth; 13 Jason Firth. Subs (all used): 14 Rob Hoyle; 15 Adam Hoyle; 16 Richard Williams; 17 James Folan.
Tries: Firth (70), Howley (80); **Goal:** Holmes.
Rugby Leaguer & League Express Men of the Match: *Cougars:* Paul Ashton; *Trojans:* Jason Firth.
Penalty count: 8-8; **Half-time:** 20-0;
Referee: Ashley Klein (London); **Attendance:** 1,135.

OLDHAM 32 EAST HULL 6

OLDHAM: 1 Gavin Dodd; 2 Chris Campbell; 3 Paul Anderson; 4 Jon Goddard; 5 Joe McNicholas; 6 Gareth Barber; 7 Neil Roden; 8 Steve Molloy; 9 Anthony Murray; 10 Danny Guest; 11 Lee Doran; 12 Chris Morley; 13 Phil Farrell. Subs (all used): 14 John Hough; 15 Simon Svabic; 16 Iain Marsh; 17 Martin McLoughlin.
Tries: Campbell (3, 6), Dodd (22), Farrell (37), Anderson (47), McNicholas (54), Roden (66);
Goals: Barber, Svabic.
Sin bin: Farrell (12) - fighting.
EAST HULL: 1 Jason Abdul; 2 Graham Clark; 3 Gary Noble; 4 John McCracken; 5 Danny Lakeman; 6 Jordan Precious; 7 Chris Windass; 8 Lee Brown; 9 Gary Weymes; 10 James Aramayo; 11 Paul Roberts; 12 Mark Woodcock; 13 Michael Docherty. Subs (all used): 14 Lee Roberts; 15 Phil Batty; 16 Gary Blanchard; 17 Lee Cator.
Try: Aramayo (76); **Goal:** Docherty.
Sin bin: P Roberts (12) - fighting.
Rugby Leaguer & League Express Men of the Match: *Oldham:* Paul Anderson; *East Hull:* Lee Brown.
Penalty count: 10-15; **Half-time:** 18-0;
Referee: Thierry Alibert (France); **Attendance:** 1,270.

SALFORD CITY REDS 26 TOULOUSE SPACERS 10

CITY REDS: 1 Jason Flowers; 2 Alan Hunte; 3 Stuart Littler; 4 Cliff Beverley; 5 Danny Arnold; 6 Radney Bowker; 7 Gavin Clinch; 8 Andy Coley; 9 Malcolm Alker; 10 Paul Highton; 11 Simon Baldwin; 12 Neil Lowe; 13 Lee Marsh. Subs (all used): 14 Chris Charles; 15 David Highton; 16 Andy Gorski; 17 Neil Baynes.
Tries: Flowers (3, 76), Hunte (16), Littler (30), Beverley (72); **Goals:** Marsh, Clinch 2.
Sin bin: Marsh (65) - interference;
Baynes (79) - fighting.
On report: Brawl (79).

Hunslet's Paul Seal takes on Julian Bailey as the Hawks dump Huddersfield out of the Challenge Cup in Round Four

SPACERS: 1 Dave Mulholland; 2 Ludovic Perolari; 3 Frederic Zitter; 4 Brad Kelly; 5 Damien Couturier; 6 Julien Gerin; 7 James Wynne; 8 Olivier Pramil; 9 Thibaud Leib; 10 Cedric Rodriguez; 11 Sebastien Amigas; 12 Sebastien Raguin; 13 Trent Robinson. Subs (all used): 14 Cedric Gay; 15 David Delpoux; 16 Eric Frayssinet; 17 Cedric Estebanez.
Tries: Perolari (8), Mulholland (66); **Goal:** Gerin.
Sin bin: Wynne (62) - holding down;
Pramil (79) - fighting.
On report: Brawl (79).
Rugby Leaguer & League Express Men of the Match:
City Reds: Gavin Clinch; *Spacers:* Olivier Pramil.
Penalty count: 10-9; **Half-time:** 14-4; **Referee:** Colin Morris (Huddersfield); **Attendance:** 1,590.

SWINTON LIONS 46 SHAW CROSS SHARKS 0

LIONS: 1 Wayne English; 2 Jason Roach; 3 Andy Cheetham; 4 Kris Tassell; 5 Hugh Thorpe; 6 Rob Gallagher; 7 Chris Hough; 8 Andy Leathem; 9 Peter Cannon; 10 Simon Knox; 11 Craig Wingfield; 12 Dave Ellison; 13 Kris Smith. Subs (all used): 14 Jason Johnson; 15 Chris Roe; 16 Robert Russell; 17 Danny Turner.
Tries: English (4), Cannon (18, 34), Thorpe (37, 62, 73), Smith (40), Tassell (46), Cheetham (69); **Goals:** Hough 5.
SHARKS: 1 Mark Land; 2 Richard Patnelli; 3 Craig Simons; 4 Craig Lilley; 5 Mark Brown; 6 Joe Dickinson; 7 Mick Senior; 8 Graham Summerscales; 9 Paul Fishburn; 10 Lenny Steele; 11 John Raithby; 12 John Bates; 13 Ashley Lindsay. Subs (all used): 14 Rob Hinchcliffe; 15 Jamie Spence; 16 Ashley Fothergill; 17 Mark Hirst.
Rugby Leaguer & League Express Men of the Match:
Lions: Peter Cannon; *Sharks:* Joe Dickinson.
Penalty count: 8-10; **Half-time:** 24-0;
Referee: Clive Walker (Oldham); **Attendance:** 315.

WEST BOWLING 12 BATLEY BULLDOGS 34

WEST BOWLING: 1 Peter Simpson; 2 Justin Hunter; 3 Martin Tordorff; 4 Mark Dunning; 5 Paul Gardner; 6 Scott Pendlebury; 7 Steve Illingworth; 8 Richard Greenwood; 9 Glen Barraclough; 10 Lee Hutchinson; 11 John Metcalfe; 12 Simon Owen; 13 Nigel Halmshaw. Subs (all used): 14 Shaun Fallon; 15 Ian Wormald; 16 Daniel Lang; 17 Phil Chappell.
Tries: Illingworth (40), Hunter (74); **Goals:** Simpson 2.
BULLDOGS: 1 Craig Lingard; 2 Chris Spurr; 3 Anthony Gibbons; 4 Danny Maun; 5 Matt Bramald; 6 Mark Toohey; 7 Barry Eaton; 8 Craig Booth; 9 Kris Lythe; 10 Joe Naidole; 11 David Rourke; 12 Will Cartledge; 13 Ryan Horsley. Subs (all used): 14 Simon Lewis; 15 Paul

Harrison; 16 Joe Berry; 17 Andy Spink.
Tries: Spurr (17), Toohey (32, 41, 45), A Gibbons (52), Lingard (78); **Goals:** Eaton 5.
Rugby Leaguer & League Express Men of the Match:
West Bowling: Nigel Halmshaw; *Bulldogs:* Mark Toohey.
Penalty count: 10-8; **Half-time:** 8-10;
Referee: Ian Smith (Oldham); **Attendance:** 1,047
(at Mount Pleasant, Batley).

WHITEHAVEN 66 COTTINGHAM TIGERS 6

WHITEHAVEN: 1 Gary Broadbent; 2 Paul O'Neil; 3 David Seeds; 4 Howard Hill; 5 Leigh Smith; 6 Leroy Joe; 7 Darren Holt; 8 Dean Vaughan; 9 Aaron Lester; 10 David Fatialofa; 11 Chris McKinney; 12 Graeme Morton; 13 Mike Whitehead. Subs (all used): 14 Lee Kiddie; 15 Marc Jackson; 16 Phil Sherwen; 17 Spencer Miller.
Tries: Seeds (3, 62, 72), Holt (7), McKinney (10), L Smith (27), Sherwen (35), Hill (44, 54, 58), Miller (50), Fatialofa (76), Kiddie (79); **Goals:** Holt 5, O'Neil 2.
TIGERS: 1 Ian Robinson; 2 Paul Baker; 3 Alex Benson; 4 Mike Mallinson; 5 John Pritchard; 6 Craig Adams; 7 Lee Craig; 8 Scott Jackson; 9 Andy Ellis; 10 Dave Wilkinson; 11 Jimmy Heazberg; 12 Phil Musgrave; 13 Richard Anderson. Subs (all used): 14 Mike Fry; 15 Ray Morris; 16 James Finch; 17 Barry Sowerby.
Try: Craig (16); **Goal:** Benson.
Rugby Leaguer & League Express Men of the Match:
Whitehaven: Graeme Morton; *Tigers:* Phil Musgrave.
Penalty count: 9-6; **Half-time:** 26-6; **Referee:** Richard Silverwood (Dewsbury); **Attendance:** 1,001.

WOOLSTON ROVERS 12 DEWSBURY RAMS 34

ROVERS: 1 Mark Wallington; 2 Mark Cosgrove; 3 Steve Warburton; 4 Jon Cole; 5 Kris Buckley; 6 Chris Mellor; 7 Liam McCarthy; 8 Mark Shephard; 9 Shane Williams; 10 Dave Powlesland; 11 Lee Rushton; 12 Danny Heaton; 13 Phil Dermott. Subs (all used): 14 Dave Kelly; 15 Matt Patterson; 16 Sean Geritas; 17 Andy James.
Tries: Shephard (16), Cole (77); **Goals:** Mellor 2.
RAMS: 1 Jamie Benn; 2 Michael Wainwright; 3 Chris Chapman; 4 Paul Steele; 5 George Mack; 6 Scott Rhodes; 7 Danny Brough; 8 Frank Watene; 9 David Oldfield; 10 Tony Fella; 11 Danny Evans; 12 John Waddell; 13 Chris Redfearn. Subs (all used): 14 Jimmy Elston; 15 Paul Hicks; 16 Gary Fahey; 17 Billy Kershaw.
Tries: Elston (27), Chapman (37), Brough (42), Watene (51), Waddell (60), Wainwright (66);
Goals: Benn 4, Brough.
Rugby Leaguer & League Express Men of the Match:
Rovers: Mark Wallington; *Rams:* Jimmy Elston.
Penalty count: 6-6; **Half-time:** 6-12;

Referee: Robert Connolly (Wigan); **Attendance:** 685
(at Wilderspool, Warrington).

GATESHEAD THUNDER 4
UNION TREIZISTE CATALANE 38

THUNDER: 1 Kevin Neighbour; 2 Richie Barnett; 3 Damien Reid; 4 PJ Solomon; 5 Tom Lauriston; 6 Paul Thorman; 7 Craig Fisher; 8 David Bates; 9 Janan Billings; 10 Steven Bradley; 11 Scott Houston; 12 Clint Brown; 13 Chris Fletcher. Subs (all used): 14 Yusuf Sozi; 15 Andy Walker; 16 James Mackay; 17 Neil Thorman.
Try: Janan Billings (21).
UTC: 1 Renaud Guigue; 2 Gilles Mendez; 3 Bruno Verges; 4 Phil Howlett; 5 Patrice Gomez; 6 Thomas Bosc; 7 Brett Trudgett; 8 Troy Perkins; 9 David Berthezene; 10 Pascal Jampy; 11 Phillip Leuluai; 12 Said Tamghart; 13 Aurelien Cologni. Subs (all used): 14 Aaron Smith; 15 Lionel Teixido; 16 Justin Dooley; 17 Mathias Garrabe.
Tries: Howlett (13), Mendez (18, 60), Berthezene (35), Trudgett (41), Teixido (79); **Goals:** Bosc 6, Gomez.
Dismissal: Cologni (75) - punching.
Sin bin: Garrabe (73) - fighting.
Rugby Leaguer & League Express Men of the Match:
Thunder: Yusuf Sozi; *UTC:* Brett Trudgett.
Penalty count: 15-7; **Half-time:** 4-20;
Referee: Mike Dawber (Wigan); **Attendance:** 315.

HUNSLET HAWKS 28 PIA 18

HAWKS: 1 Simon Jackson; 2 Bryn Powell; 3 Iain Higgins; 4 Wes McGibbon; 5 George Rayner; 6 Andy Bastow; 7 Phil Hasty; 8 Craig Ibbetson; 9 Jon Liddell; 10 Andy Brent; 11 Wayne Freeman; 12 Danny Fearon; 13 Gareth Naylor. Subs (all used): 14 Mick Coyle; 15 Paul Seal; 16 Richard Baker; 17 Michael Lyons.
Tries: Naylor (21, 36, 43), Fearon (28), Rayner (76); **Goals:** Bastow 3, Liddell.
Sin bin: Coyle (63) - interference.
PIA: 1 Sebastian Terrado; 2 Moussa Loukili; 3 Lawrence Raleigh; 4 Tom O'Reilly; 5 Patrick Noguera; 6 Adam Nable; 7 Craig Field; 8 Karl Jaavou; 9 Eric Van Brussel; 10 Tim Maddison; 11 Talite Liava'a; 12 Frank Ravira; 13 David Romero. Subs (all used): 14 Jean-Pascal Pellicier; 15 Nanu Bansept; 16 Anthony Nartrette; 17 Laurent Nicholas.
Tries: Nable (10), O'Reilly (59), Bansept (79);
Goals: Terrado 3.
Sin bin: Jaavou (26) - holding down.
Rugby Leaguer & League Express Men of the Match:
Hawks: Gareth Naylor; *Pia:* Tim Maddison.
Penalty count: 9-11; **Half-time:** 16-6;
Referee: Ronnie Laughton (Barnsley); **Attendance:** 524.

ROUND 4

Saturday 8th February 2003

WAKEFIELD TRINITY WILDCATS 20 CASTLEFORD TIGERS 18

WILDCATS: 1 Martyn Holland; 5 Jon Wells (D); 3 Gareth Ellis; 4 Matt Seers (D); 24 Colum Halpenny (D); 6 Ben Jeffries (D); 7 Brad Davis; 8 Clinton O'Brien (D); 9 David March; 18 Michael Korkidas (D); 10 Dallas Hood (D); 15 Ian Knott; 13 Adrian Vowles (C). Subs (all used): 14 Paul Handforth; 2 Waisale Sovatabua; 11 Troy Slattery; 20 David Wrench.
Tries: Ellis (35), Jeffries (63), Sovatabua (75);
Goals: Knott 4.
Sin bin: Seers (19) - fighting.
TIGERS: 22 Mark Lennon; 2 Waine Pryce; 1 Damian Gibson (D); 3 Michael Eagar; 5 Darren Rogers; 6 Danny Orr (C); 7 Mitch Healey; 8 Nathan Sykes; 9 Wayne Bartrim; 10 Andy Lynch; 23 Michael Smith; 12 Dale Fritz; 13 Ryan Hudson. Subs: 11 Lee Harland; 17 Paul Jackson (D); 18 Jamie Thackray (D); 20 Tom Saxton (not used).
Tries: Lennon (2, 68), Orr (48); **Goals:** Bartrim 3.
Dismissal: Hudson (19) - fighting.
Rugby Leaguer & League Express Men of the Match: *Wildcats:* Ben Jeffries; *Tigers:* Mark Lennon.
Penalty count: 12-9; **Half-time:** 6-6;
Referee: Ian Smith (Oldham); **Attendance:** 4,125.

WARRINGTON WOLVES 12 BRADFORD BULLS 38

WOLVES: 1 Lee Penny; 2 Rob Smyth; 12 Ian Sibbit (D2); 4 Ben Westwood; 3 Brent Grose (D); 6 Lee Briers (C); 7 Nathan Wood; 8 Nick Fozzard; 9 Jon Clarke; 10 Mark Hilton; 11 Darren Burns; 23 Mike Wainwright (D2); 13 Sid Domic. Subs (all used): 14 Mark Gleeson (D2); 5 Graham Appo; 16 Paul Wood; 17 Warren Stevens.
Try: Burns (11); **Goal:** Briers 4.
Sin bin: Appo (39) - professional foul; Domic (52) - dissent; Briers (72) - dissent.
BULLS: 3 Leon Pryce; 15 Karl Pratt (D); 20 Scott Naylor; 4 Shontayne Hape (D); 5 Lesley Vainikolo; 1 Robbie Paul (C); 7 Paul Deacon; 8 Joe Vagana; 9 James Lowes; 29 Stuart Fielden; 11 Daniel Gartner; 12 Jamie Peacock; 13 Mike Forshaw. Subs (all used): 14 Lee Gilmour; 18 Lee Radford; 27 Robert Parker; 10 Paul Anderson.
Tries: Paul (35), Vainikolo (43, 59), L Pryce (54), Naylor (69), Hape (74); **Goals:** Deacon 7.
Rugby Leaguer & League Express Men of the Match: *Wolves:* Mark Hilton; *Bulls:* Stuart Fielden.
Penalty count: 9-12; **Half-time:** 12-12;
Referee: Robert Connolly (Wigan); **Attendance:** 5,869.

WATH BROW HORNETS 6 BATLEY BULLDOGS 18

HORNETS: 1 Gary Elliott; 2 Craig Calvert; 3 Ian Rooney; 4 Gary Clarke; 5 Gavin Curwen; 6 Craig Johnstone; 7 Andrew Hocking; 8 Mark Deans; 9 Neil McCartney; 10 Mark Troughton; 11 Paul Davidson; 12 Graeme Mattinson; 13 Carl Rudd. Subs (all used): 14 Stewart Sanderson; 15 Neil Stewart; 16 Mickey McAllister; 17 Scott Teare.
Try: Curwen (75); **Goal:** Curwen.
BULLDOGS: 1 Craig Lingard; 2 Mark Sibson; 3 Anthony Gibbons; 4 Simon Lewis; 5 Leon Williamson; 6 David Gibbons; 7 Barry Eaton; 8 Craig Booth; 9 Gavin Swinson; 10 Andy Spink; 11 David Rourke; 12 Mark Toohey; 13 Ryan Horsley. Subs (all used): 14 Mark Cass; 15 Paul Harrison; 16 Joe Berry; 17 Jeremy Dyson.
Tries: Eaton (18), Lewis (60), Harrison (73);
Goals: Eaton 3.
Rugby Leaguer & League Express Men of the Match: *Hornets:* Paul Davidson; *Bulldogs:* Andy Spink.
Penalty count: 6-4; **Half-time:** 0-8;
Referee: Julian King (St Helens); **Attendance:** 1,333 *(at The Recreation Ground, Whitehaven).*

UNION TREIZISTE CATALANE 6 ST HELENS 70

UTC: 1 Renaud Guigue; 2 Gilles Mendez; 3 Bruno Verges; 4 Phil Howlett; 5 Patrice Gomez; 6 Thomas Bosc; 7 Brett Trudgett; 8 Troy Perkins; 9 David Berthezene; 10 Pascal Jampy; 11 Philip Leuluai; 12 Said Tamghart; 13 Aurelien Cologni. Subs (all used): 14 Aaron Smith; 15 Lionel Teixido; 16 Justin Dooley; 17 David Dos Reis.
Try: Cologni (72); **Goal:** Trudgett.
SAINTS: 5 Darren Albert; 19 Ade Gardner; 3 Martin Gleeson; 4 Paul Newlove; 2 Anthony Stewart; 20 Tommy Martyn; 7 Sean Long; 8 Darren Britt; 14 Mick Higham; 12 John Stankevitch; 11 Chris Joynt (C); 16 Darren Smith (D); 15 Tim Jonkers. Subs (all used): 6 Jason Hooper (D); 10 Barry Ward; 18 Mark Edmondson; 17 Mike Bennett.
Tries: Stewart (2, 36), Gardner (4), Long (10, 57, 68, 78), Gleeson (20), Hooper (30, 41), Smith (45), Stankevitch (56), Albert (65); **Goals:** Long 9.
Rugby Leaguer & League Express Men of the Match: *UTC:* Pascal Jampy; *Saints:* Sean Long.
Penalty count: 5-11; **Half-time:** 0-32; **Referee:** Karl Kirkpatrick (Warrington); **Attendance:** 2,700 (est) *(at Stade Aime Giral, Perpignan).*

Sunday 9th February 2003

BARROW RAIDERS 6 SALFORD CITY REDS 22

RAIDERS: 1 Craig Bower; 2 Jamie Marshall; 3 Andy McClure; 4 Paul Jones; 5 Shane Irabor; 6 Tane Manihera; 7 Chris Archer; 8 Tau Liku; 9 Andy Henderson; 10 Wayne Jones; 11 Steve Jackson; 12 Paul Gardner; 13 Phil Atkinson. Subs (all used): 14 Adam Pate; 15 Geoff Luxon; 16 Dave Clark; 17 James Stainton.
Try: Marshall (72); **Goal:** Atkinson.
CITY REDS: 1 Jason Flowers; 2 Alan Hunte; 3 Stuart Littler; 4 Cliff Beverley; 5 Danny Arnold; 6 Radney Bowker; 7 Gavin Clinch; 8 Andy Coley; 9 Malcolm Alker; 10 Paul Highton; 11 Simon Baldwin; 12 Neil Lowe; 13 Chris Charles. Subs (all used): 14 Lee Marsh; 15 David Highton; 16 Gareth Haggerty; 17 Neil Baynes.
Tries: Littler (30), Alker (32), Bowker (54), Baldwin (78);
Goals: Clinch 3.
Rugby Leaguer & League Express Men of the Match: *Raiders:* Chris Archer; *City Reds:* Malcolm Alker.
Penalty count: 3-4; **Half-time:** 2-12;
Referee: Peter Taberner (Wigan); **Attendance:** 1,392.

CHORLEY LYNX 16 SWINTON LIONS 32

LYNX: 1 David Ingram; 2 Eddie Kilgannon; 3 Mick Redford; 4 Anton Garcia; 5 Liam Jones; 6 Mick Coates; 7 Martin Gambles; 8 Tim Street; 9 Dave McConnell; 10 David Whittle; 11 Wayne Bloor; 12 Dave Radley; 13 Ian Hodson. Subs (all used): 14 Simon Smith; 15 Chris Ramsdale; 16 Martin Roden; 17 Mike Briggs.
Tries: Coates (12, 32), Whittle (77); **Goals:** Coates 2.
LIONS: 1 Wayne English; 2 Jason Roach; 3 Kris Tassell; 4 Phil Hassan; 5 Hugh Thorpe; 6 Rob Gallagher; 7 Peter Cannon; 8 Andy Leathem; 9 Rob Barraclough; 10 Simon Knox; 11 Craig Wingfield; 12 Dave Ellison; 13 Phil Cushion. Subs (all used): 14 Lee Hudson; 15 Jason Johnson; 16 Andy Cheetham; 17 Chris Roe.
Tries: Ellison (7), Tassell (22, 40, 73), Thorpe (43), Hudson (79); **Goals:** Wingfield 4.
Sin bin: Cheetham (76) - dissent.
On report: Roe (76) - high tackle on Jones.
Rugby Leaguer & League Express Men of the Match: *Lynx:* Mick Coates; *Lions:* Kris Tassell.
Penalty count: 8-7; **Half time:** 10-18;
Referee: Ben Thaler (Wakefield); **Attendance:** 572.

FEATHERSTONE ROVERS 28 LEIGH CENTURIONS 22

ROVERS: 1 Nathan Graham; 2 Jamie Stokes; 3 Brendan O'Meara; 4 Ian Brown; 5 Adrian Flynn; 6 Richard Agar; 7 Carl Briggs; 8 Chris Molyneux; 9 Richard Chapman; 10 Stuart Dickens; 11 Steve Dooler; 12 Andy Rice; 13 Danny Seal. Subs (all used): 14 Andy McNally; 15 Andy Bailey; 16 Ian Tonks; 17 Robin Jowitt.
Tries: Brown (11), Seal (17, 44), Stokes (21);
Goals: Dickens 5; **Field goals:** Briggs 2.
Sin bin: Briggs (51) - interference; Chapman (78) - fighting.
CENTURIONS: 1 David Alstead; 2 Michael Watts; 3 Damian Munro; 4 Dale Cardoza; 5 Alan Hadcroft; 6 Patrick Weisner; 7 Lee Sanderson; 8 Sonny Nickle; 9 Paul Rowley; 10 David Bradbury; 11 Sean Richardson; 12 Phil Kendrick; 13 Adam Bristow. Subs (all used): 14 Dale Holdstock; 15 John Duffy; 16 Anthony Blackwood; 17 Rob Ball.
Tries: Munro (5, 79), Cardoza (70), Alstead (75);
Goals: Sanderson 3.
Sin bin: Bristow (42) - interference; Munro (64) - interference; Bristow (65) - interference; Bradbury (78) - fighting.
Rugby Leaguer & League Express Men of the Match: *Rovers:* Danny Seal; *Centurions:* Patrick Weisner.
Penalty count: 12-11; **Half-time:** 16-8;
Referee: Russell Smith (Castleford); **Attendance:** 2,257.

LEEDS RHINOS 46 WHITEHAVEN 6

RHINOS: 18 Gary Connolly (D); 2 Mark Calderwood; 3 Chris McKenna (D); 4 Keith Senior; 1 Francis Cummins; 14 Andrew Dunemann (D); 7 Rob Burrow; 17 Wayne McDonald; 9 Matt Diskin; 19 Ryan Bailey; 11 David Furner (D); 12 Matt Adamson; 13 Kevin Sinfield (C). Subs (all used): 15 Chris Feather (D); 24 Ewan Dowes; 5 Chev Walker; 6 Danny McGuire.
Tries: Burrow (6, 51), McDonald (16), McKenna (19), Sinfield (38), Furner (41), Cummins (48), Connolly (71), Calderwood (73); **Goals:** Furner 5.
WHITEHAVEN: 1 Gary Broadbent; 2 Paul O'Neil; 3 David Seeds; 4 Howard Hill; 5 Jamie Stenhouse; 6 Lee Kiddie; 7 Darren Holt; 8 Phil Sherwen; 9 Aaron Lester; 10 Dean Vaughan; 11 Chris McKinney; 12 Graeme Morton; 13 Spencer Miller. Subs (all used): 14 Marc Jackson; 15 Mike Whitehead; 16 Steven Wood; 17 David Fatialofa.
Try: Morton (26); **Goal:** Holt.
Rugby Leaguer & League Express Men of the Match: *Rhinos:* Rob Burrow; *Whitehaven:* Aaron Lester.
Penalty count: 10-8; **Half-time:** 22-6; **Referee:** Ronnie Laughton (Barnsley); **Attendance:** 7,535.

LONDON BRONCOS 42 OLDHAM 12

BRONCOS: 3 Nigel Roy; 5 Steve Hall; 4 Tony Martin; 21 Rob Jackson; 2 Dominic Peters; 6 Rob Purdham; 23 Chris Thorman (D); 15 Mark Cox (D); 14 Neil Budworth; 10 Richard Marshall; 17 Tommy Haughey (D); 12 Steele Retchless; 13 Jim Dymock (C). Subs (all used): 16 Jamie Fielden (D); 22 Andrew Hamilton (D2); 19 Nick Johnson (D); 24 Russell Bawden.
Tries: Hall (4, 34), Jackson (12, 64), Peters (19), Thorman (37), Roy (61), Martin (74); **Goals:** Martin 5.
OLDHAM: 1 Gavin Dodd; 2 Chris Irwin; 3 Paul Anderson; 4 Iain Marsh; 5 Will Cowell; 6 Gareth Barber; 7 Neil Roden; 8 Steve Molloy; 9 John Hough; 10 Martin McLoughlin; 11 Lee Doran; 12 Ryan Stazicker; 13 Phil Farrell. Subs (all used): 14 Anthony Murray; 15 Simon Svabic; 16 Chris Morley; 17 Darren Shaw.
Tries: Dodd (27), Stazicker (67); **Goals:** Barber, Svabic.
Sin bin: Roden (58) - interference.
Rugby Leaguer & League Express Men of the Match: *Broncos:* Rob Jackson; *Oldham:* Chris Morley.
Penalty count: 10-10; **Half-time:** 24-6;
Referee: Mike Dawber (Wigan); **Attendance:** 1,514.

ROCHDALE HORNETS 20 HULL KINGSTON ROVERS 27

HORNETS: 1 Paul Owen; 2 Sean Cooper; 3 Mick Nanyn; 4 Jon Roper; 5 Casey Mayberry; 6 Paul Smith; 7 Ian Watson; 8 Paul Southern; 9 Richard Pachniuk; 10 David Stephenson; 11 David Larder; 12 James Bunyan; 13 Damian Ball. Subs (all used): 14 Warren Ayres; 15 Andy Grundy; 16 Gareth Price; 17 Matthew Long.
Tries: Price (30), Owen (44, 77), Nanyn (79);
Goals: Nanyn 2.
ROVERS: 1 Lynton Stott; 2 Nick Pinkney; 3 Mark Blanchard; 4 Craig Farrell; 5 Alasdair McClarron; 6 Paul Parker; 7 Latham Tawhai; 8 Richard Wilson; 9 Paul Pickering; 10 Jamie Bovill; 11 Adam Sullivan; 12 Jon Aston; 13 Andy Smith. Subs (all used): 14 Jimmy Walker; 15 Steve Cochran; 16 Dean Andrews; 17 Paul Fletcher.
Tries: Stott (8), Bovill (13), McClarron (69), Parker (71);
Goals: Stott 5; **Field goal:** Stott.
Rugby Leaguer & League Express Men of the Match: *Hornets:* David Larder; *Rovers:* Latham Tawhai.
Penalty count: 8-7; **Half-time:** 6-16; **Referee:** Richard Silverwood (Dewsbury); **Attendance:** 1,300.

WIDNES VIKINGS 48 DEWSBURY RAMS 6

VIKINGS: 1 Stuart Spruce; 5 Jason Demetriou; 3 Deon Bird (D); 4 Adam Hughes; 21 Chris Percival; 18 Dean Lawford (D); 7 Ryan Sheridan (C) (D); 8 Robert Relf; 9 Shane Millard (D); 10 Julian O'Neill (NZ); 11 Andy Hay (D); 12 Steve McCurrie; 13 Daniel Frame. Subs (all used): 20 Dan Potter; 15 Ryan McDonald; 22 Phil Cantillon; 17 Anthony Farrell.
Tries: Lawford (8), Percival (13, 48), Hay (24), Hughes (27), Cantillon (54), Potter (57), Sheridan (62), Demetriou (80); **Goals:** Hughes 6.
RAMS: 1 Jamie Benn; 2 Michael Wainwright; 3 Chris Chapman; 4 John Waddell; 5 George Mack; 6 Scott Rhodes; 7 Jimmy Elston; 8 Frank Watene; 9 David Oldfield; 10 Tony Fella; 11 Danny Evans; 12 Billy Kershaw; 13 Chris Redfearn. Subs (all used): 14 Andy Heptinstall; 15 Mark Barlow; 16 Paul Hicks; 17 Gary Fahey.
Try: Elston (73); **Goal:** Benn.
Rugby Leaguer & League Express Men of the Match: *Vikings:* Ryan Sheridan; *Rams:* Jimmy Elston.
Penalty count: 4-7; **Half-time:** 24-2; **Referee:** Steve Nicholson (Whitehaven); **Attendance:** 3,196.

WIGAN WARRIORS 82 HALTON SIMMS CROSS 3

WARRIORS: 1 Kris Radlinski; 5 Brian Carney; 14 David Hodgson; 18 Martin Aspinwall; 3 Jamie Ainscough; 6 Julian O'Neill; 7 Adrian Lam; 16 Danny Sculthorpe; 9 Terry Newton; 10 Craig Smith; 11 Mick Cassidy; 12 Danny Tickle; 13 Andy Farrell (C). Subs (all used): 15 Sean O'Loughlin; 17 Mark Smith; 19 Stephen Wild; 21 Ricky Bibey.
Tries: Newton (9, 26), Radlinski (16, 40, 55), Aspinwall (18), Farrell (22, 58), Hodgson (30), O'Loughlin (38, 68), Ainscough (51), Bibey (66), Wild (72), Carney (79);
Goals: Farrell 11.
SIMMS CROSS: 1 Brian Capewell; 2 Kevin O'Neill; 3 David Percival; 4 Paul Walsh; 5 Darren O'Brien; 6 Neil Percival; 7 Paul Roberts; 8 Peter Grady; 9 Matt Carmichael; 10 Andy O'Neill; 11 John Bowles; 12 Peter Hodson; 13 Gary Middlehurst. Subs (all used): 14 Keiron Kavanagh; 15 Lee Swain; 16 Anthony Elwell; 17 Mike Donnelly.
Goal: Capewell; **Field goal:** Capewell.
Rugby Leaguer & League Express Men of the Match: *Warriors:* Andy Farrell; *Simms Cross:* Matt Carmichael.
Penalty count: 5-6; **Half-time:** 44-3;
Referee: Ashley Klein (London); **Attendance:** 3,790.

YORK CITY KNIGHTS 20 DONCASTER DRAGONS 21

CITY KNIGHTS: 1 Chris Beever; 2 Alex Godfrey; 3 Graeme Hallas; 4 Chris Smith; 5 Gavin Molloy; 6 Scott Yeaman; 7 Trevor Krause; 8 Richard Hayes; 9 Lee Jackson; 10 Lee McTigue; 11 Mick Ramsden; 12 Scott Fletcher; 13 Darren Callaghan. Subs (all used): 14 Mark Cain; 15 Craig Westmoreland; 16 Carl Stannard; 17 David Bolus.
Tries: Jackson (32), Molloy (73, 78); **Goals:** Hallas 4.
Sin bin: Godfrey (40) - fighting; Yeaman (40) - fighting.
DRAGONS: 1 Craig Horne; 2 Paul Gleadhill; 3 Marvin Golden; 4 Simon Irving; 5 Jason Lee; 6 Chris Ross; 7 Mark Moxon; 8 Gareth Handford; 9 Peter Edwards; 10 James Walker; 11 Peter Green; 12 Craig Lawton; 13 Matt Walker. Subs (all used): 14 Dean Colton; 15 Craig Forsyth; 16 Maea David; 17 Tom Buckenham.
Tries: Lee (10), Lawton (12), Gleadhill (43), Irving (65);
Goals: Irving 2; **Field goal:** Moxon.
Sin bin: Horne (40) - fighting; Handford (55) – head-butt.
Rugby Leaguer & League Express Men of the Match: *City Knights:* Mick Ramsden; *Dragons:* Peter Edwards.
Penalty count: 7-3; **Half-time:** 6-10; **Referee:** Colin Morris (Huddersfield); **Attendance:** 1,511.

HULL FC 24 HALIFAX 16

HULL: 1 Steve Prescott; 2 Colin Best (D); 3 Richie Barnett (D); 4 Toa Kohe-Love; 5 Matt Crowther; 6 Richard Horne; 7 Tony Smith; 8 Craig Greenhill; 22 Andy Last; 12 Scott Logan; 11 Adam Maher; 19 Richard Fletcher; 13 Jason Smith (C). Subs (all used): 15 Steve Craven; 16 Paul Cooke; 21 Dwayne West (D); 10 Paul King.
Tries: Best (6), Barnett (37), Kohe-Love (41);
Goals: Crowther 6.
Dismissals: J Smith (1) – high tackle; Fletcher (48) – high tackle.
HALIFAX: 5 Lee Finnerty (D); 2 Lee Greenwood; 3 Stuart Donlan; 4 Danny Halliwell; 21 Chris Norman (D); 6 Martin Moana (D2); 20 Dane Dorahy (D); 8 Andy Hobson; 9 Johnny Lawless (C); 16 Chris Birchall; 11 Heath

Cruckshank (D); 12 Andrew Brocklehurst; 13 Shayne McMenemy. Subs (all used): 14 Liam Finn; 7 Sean Penkywicz; 10 Paul Davidson; 17 Anthony Seuseu (D).
Tries: Dorahy (14), Greenwood (45); **Goals:** Dorahy 4.
On report: Moana (19) - high tackle.
Rugby Leaguer & League Express Men of the Match: *Hull:* Steve Prescott; *Halifax:* Dane Dorahy.
Penalty count: 10-6; **Half-time:** 16-10;
Referee: Steve Ganson (St Helens); **Attendance:** 15,310.

SHEFFIELD EAGLES 25 KEIGHLEY COUGARS 24

EAGLES: 1 Andy Poynter; 2 Paul Wells; 3 Wayne Flynn; 4 Nick Turnbull; 5 Ian Thompson; 6 Gavin Brown; 7 Lee Bettinson; 8 Jack Howieson; 9 Adam Carroll; 10 Damien Whitter; 11 Sam Bibb; 12 Craig Brown; 13 Richard Goddard. Subs: 14 Mitchell Stringer (not used); 15 Simon Tillyer; 16 Richard Singleton; 17 Jon Bruce.
Tries: Poynter (9), Goddard (16, 42), G Brown (46);
Goals: G Brown 4; **Field goal:** Goddard.
COUGARS: 1 James Rushforth; 2 Karl Smith; 3 David Foster; 4 Gareth Hewitt; 5 Andy Robinson; 6 Paul Ashton; 7 Matt Firth; 8 Phil Stephenson; 9 Simeon Hoyle; 10 Oliver Wilkes; 11 Ian Sinfield; 12 Ricky Helliwell; 13 Jason Ramshaw. Subs (all used): 14 Chris Wainwright; 15 Danny Ekis; 16 Matthew Steel; 17 Chris Hannah.
Tries: Hoyle (2), Smith (35), Sinfield (61), Wainwright (64), Rushforth (73); **Goals:** Ashton 2.
Sin bin: Sinfield (22) - persistent lying on.
Rugby Leaguer & League Express Men of the Match: *Eagles:* Gavin Brown; *Cougars:* Paul Ashton.
Penalty count: 8-10; **Half-time:** 12-8;
Referee: Steve Addy (Huddersfield); **Attendance:** 1,235.

HUNSLET HAWKS 18 HUDDERSFIELD GIANTS 14

HAWKS: 1 Richard Baker; 2 Bryn Powell; 3 Iain Higgins; 4 Wes McGibbon; 5 George Rayner; 6 Jon Liddell; 7 Phil Hasty; 8 Craig Ibbetson; 9 Gareth Naylor; 10 Mick Coyle; 11 Wayne Freeman; 12 Danny Fearon; 13 Paul Seal. Subs: 14 Gareth Brain (not used); 15 Joe Hawley (not used); 16 Jonlee Lockwood; 17 Dan Briggs.
Tries: Powell (5), Lockwood (32), Briggs (36);
Goals: Liddell 3.
GIANTS: 3 Ben Cooper; 2 Hefin O'Hare; 4 Julian Bailey (D); 20 Matt Calland (D); 34 Marcus St Hilaire; 6 Brandon Costin (C) (D2); 21 Paul White; 8 Mick Slicker; 9 Paul March; 25 Darren Fleary (D); 11 Eorl Crabtree; 10 Jim Gannon (D); 7 Jarrod O'Doherty (D). Subs (all used): 5 Matthew Whitaker; 15 Darren Turner; 32 Jeff Wittenberg; 19 Iain Morrison (D).
Tries: Costin (2, 49), St Hilaire (24); **Goal:** Costin.
Rugby Leaguer & League Express Men of the Match: *Hawks:* Danny Fearon; *Giants:* Darren Fleary.
Penalty count: 10-11; **Half-time:** 16-8;
Referee: Steve Presley (Castleford); **Attendance:** 1,256.

ROUND 5

Friday 28th February 2003

HULL KINGSTON ROVERS 2 SALFORD CITY REDS 12

ROVERS: 1 Craig Poucher; 2 Nick Pinkney; 3 Lynton Stott; 4 Craig Farrell; 5 Mark Blanchard; 6 Paul Parker; 7 Craig Murdock; 8 Richard Wilson; 9 Paul Pickering; 10 Jamie Bovill; 11 Adam Sullivan; 12 Jon Aston; 13 Andy Smith. Subs (all used): 14 Jimmy Walker; 15 Steve Cochran; 16 Dean Andrews; 17 Paul Fletcher.
Goal: Stott.
CITY REDS: 1 Jason Flowers; 2 Michael Platt; 3 Stuart Littler; 4 Alan Hunte; 5 Danny Arnold; 6 Cliff Beverley; 7 Gavin Clinch; 8 Neil Baynes; 9 Malcolm Alker; 10 Andy Coley; 11 Simon Baldwin; 12 Neil Lowe; 13 Chris Charles. Subs (all used): 14 Paul Highton; 15 David Highton; 16 Gareth Haggerty; 17 Andy Gorski.
Tries: Hunte (39), Littler (75); **Goals:** Clinch 2.
Rugby Leaguer & League Express Men of the Match: *Rovers:* Craig Poucher; *City Reds:* Gavin Clinch.
Penalty count: 8-10; **Half-time:** 2-6; **Referee:** Richard Silverwood (Dewsbury); **Attendance:** 2,533.

ST HELENS 38 BATLEY BULLDOGS 12

SAINTS: 21 John Kirkpatrick; 26 Steve Rowlands (D); 19 Ade Gardner; 4 Paul Newlove; 24 Steve Maden; 20 Tommy Martyn; 7 Sean Long; 10 Barry Ward; 14 Mick Higham; 12 John Stankevitch; 15 Tim Jonkers; 16 Darren Smith; 18 Mark Edmondson. Subs (all used): 11 Chris Joynt (C); 17 Mike Bennett; 22 Stuart Jones; 23 Jon Wilkin (D).
Tries: Martyn (19), Jonkers (24, 60), Ward (30), Maden (34), Edmondson (44), Kirkpatrick (51);
Goals: Long 4, Martyn.
Sin bin: Kirkpatrick (15) - holding down.
BULLDOGS: 1 Craig Lingard; 2 Mark Sibson; 3 Anthony Gibbons; 4 Simon Lewis; 5 Leon Williamson; 6 David Gibbons; 7 Barry Eaton; 8 Craig Booth; 9 Mark Cass; 10 Joe Naidole; 11 David Rourke; 12 Mark Toohey; 13 Ryan Horsley. Subs (all used): 14 Danny Maun; 15 Paul Harrison; 16 Joe Berry; 17 Will Cartledge.
Tries: A Gibbons (2), Harrison (47); **Goals:** Eaton 2.
Rugby Leaguer & League Express Men of the Match: *Saints:* Sean Long; *Bulldogs:* David Gibbons.
Penalty count: 3-2; **Half-time:** 22-6;
Referee: Robert Connolly (Wigan); **Attendance:** 5,002.

Saturday 1st March 2003

LEEDS RHINOS 21 LONDON BRONCOS 12

RHINOS: 18 Gary Connolly; 2 Mark Calderwood; 3 Chris McKenna; 4 Keith Senior; 1 Francis Cummins; 14 Andrew Dunemann; 7 Rob Burrow; 17 Wayne McDonald; 9 Matt Diskin; 19 Ryan Bailey; 11 David Furner; 12 Matt Adamson; 13 Kevin Sinfield (C). Subs (all used): 5 Chev Walker; 10 Barrie McDermott; 8 Danny Ward; 6 Danny McGuire.
Tries: Senior (31), Calderwood (37), Sinfield (49);
Goals: Furner 4; **Field goal:** Sinfield.
BRONCOS: 3 Nigel Roy; 5 Steve Hall; 4 Tony Martin; 21 Rob Jackson; 17 Tommy Haughey; 6 Rob Purdham; 23 Chris Thorman; 8 Francis Stephenson; 14 Neil Budworth; 10 Richard Marshall; 9 Bill Peden; 12 Steele Retchless; 13 Jim Dymock (C). Subs (all used): 11 Mat Toshack; 24 Russell Bawden; 22 Andrew Hamilton; 19 Nick Johnson.
Tries: Peden (26), Dymock (42); **Goals:** Martin 2.
Rugby Leaguer & League Express Men of the Match: *Rhinos:* Kevin Sinfield; *Broncos:* Rob Purdham.
Penalty count: 9-7; **Half-time:** 12-6;
Referee: Steve Ganson (St Helens); **Attendance:** 6,717.

Sunday 2nd March 2003

WAKEFIELD TRINITY WILDCATS 12 WIDNES VIKINGS 22

WILDCATS: 1 Martyn Holland; 5 Jon Wells; 3 Gareth Ellis; 17 Richard Newlove; 24 Colum Halpenny; 6 Ben Jeffries; 7 Brad Davis; 18 Michael Korkidas; 9 David March; 10 Dallas Hood; 11 Troy Slattery; 15 Ian Knott; 13 Adrian Vowles (C). Subs (all used): 8 Clinton O'Brien; 14 Paul Handforth; 19 Olivier Elima; 20 David Wrench.
Try: Ellis (37); **Goals:** Knott 4.
VIKINGS: 1 Stuart Spruce; 21 Chris Percival; 4 Adam Hughes; 3 Deon Bird; 5 Jason Demetriou; 18 Dean Lawford; 7 Ryan Sheridan (C); 8 Robert Relf; 9 Shane Millard; 10 Julian O'Neill (NZ); 12 Steve McCurrie; 11 Andy Hay; 13 Daniel Frame. Subs (all used): 17 Anthony Farrell; 19 Paul Atcheson; 23 David Mills; 22 Phil Cantillon.
Tries: Hughes (17, 54), Lawford (26), McCurrie (79);
Goals: Hughes 3.
Sin bin: Bird (66) - holding down.
Rugby Leaguer & League Express Men of the Match: *Wildcats:* David March; *Vikings:* Adam Hughes.
Penalty count: 12-8; **Half-time:** 12-12;
Referee: Russell Smith (Castleford); **Attendance:** 2,625.

DONCASTER DRAGONS 10 WIGAN WARRIORS 50

DRAGONS: 1 Chris Ross; 2 Paul Gleadhill; 3 Marvin Golden; 4 Simon Irving; 5 Jason Lee; 6 Paul Mansson; 7 Mark Moxon; 8 Gareth Handford; 9 Peter Edwards; 10 Maea David; 11 Peter Green; 12 Craig Lawton; 13 Matt Walker. Subs (all used): 14 James Walker; 15 Craig Forsyth; 16 Shaun Leafe; 17 Dean Colton.
Tries: Lee (61), M Walker (64); **Goal:** Irving.
WARRIORS: 1 Kris Radlinski; 2 Brett Dallas; 14 David Hodgson; 3 Jamie Ainscough; 5 Brian Carney; 6 Julian O'Neill; 7 Adrian Lam (C); 10 Craig Smith; 17 Mark Smith; 16 Danny Sculthorpe; 12 Danny Tickle; 11 Mick Cassidy; 15 Sean O'Loughlin. Subs (all used): 9 Terry Newton; 19 Stephen Wild; 23 Gareth Hock (D); 18 Martin Aspinwall.
Tries: Carney (3, 28, 31), Ainscough (23), Hodgson (39), O'Neill (42), Hock (45, 47), Newton (57);
Goals: O'Neill 7.
Rugby Leaguer & League Express Men of the Match: *Dragons:* Gareth Handford; *Warriors:* Craig Smith.
Penalty count: 8-6; **Half-time:** 0-28;
Referee: Ian Smith (Oldham); **Attendance:** 3,653.

SWINTON LIONS 32 FEATHERSTONE ROVERS 10

LIONS: 1 Wayne English; 2 Jason Roach; 3 Kris Tassell; 4 Phil Hassan; 5 Hugh Thorpe; 6 Chris Hough; 7 Peter Cannon; 8 Andy Leathem; 9 Rob Barraclough; 10 Simon Knox; 11 Craig Wingfield; 12 Dave Ellison; 13 Robert Russell. Subs (all used): 14 Lee Hudson; 15 Jason Johnson; 16 Andy Cheetham; 17 Phil Cushion.
Tries: Hassan (9), English (28), Johnson (53), Thorpe (60), Knox (68), Cushion (78); **Goals:** Hough 3;
Field goals: Hough 2.
Sin bin: Knox (19) - fighting.
ROVERS: 1 Nathan Graham; 2 Jamie Stokes; 3 Brendan O'Meara; 4 Andy McNally; 5 Adrian Flynn; 6 Richard Agar; 7 Carl Briggs; 8 Chris Molyneux; 9 Richard Chapman; 10 Robin Jowitt; 11 Ian Brown; 12 Andy Rice; 13 Danny Seal. Subs (all used): 14 Richard Whiting; 15 Andy Bailey; 16 Stuart Dickens; 17 Ian Tonks.
Tries: O'Meara (35), Brown (63); **Goal:** Dickens.
Sin bin: Graham (19) - fighting.
Rugby Leaguer & League Express Men of the Match: *Lions:* Peter Cannon; *Rovers:* Ian Tonks.
Penalty count: 8-10; **Half-time:** 11-4;
Referee: Peter Taberner (Wigan); **Attendance:** 1,092.

SHEFFIELD EAGLES 0 HULL FC 88

EAGLES: 1 Andy Poynter; 2 Jon Breakingbury; 3 Neil Kite; 4 Nick Turnbull; 5 Greg Hurst; 6 Peter Reilly; 7 Gavin Brown; 8 Jack Howieson; 9 Guy Adams; 10 Damien Whitter; 11 Craig Brown; 12 Andy Raleigh; 13 Richard Goddard. Subs (all used): 14 Gareth Stanley; 15 Simon Tillyer; 16 Sam Bibb; 17 Jon Bruce.
HULL: 1 Steve Prescott; 2 Colin Best; 3 Richie Barnett (C); 4 Toa Kohe-Love; 5 Matt Crowther; 16 Paul Cooke; 6 Richard Horne; 15 Steve Craven; 22 Andy Last; 10 Paul King; 12 Scott Logan; 14 Sean Ryan; 17 Chris Chester. Subs (all used): 8 Craig Greenhill; 20 Garreth Carvell; 26 Graeme Horne (D); 11 Adam Maher.
Tries: Crowther (4), Cooke (6), Prescott (13, 63, 68), Kohe-Love (15), Barnett (18, 26, 33, 56), R Horne (37), Ryan (53), G Horne (66, 79), Best (75);
Goals: Crowther 14.
Rugby Leaguer & League Express Men of the Match: *Eagles:* Nick Turnbull; *Hull:* Steve Prescott.
Penalty count: 1-2; **Half-time:** 0-48; **Referee:** Colin Morris (Huddersfield); **Attendance:** 11,729
(at Kingston Communications Stadium, Hull).

HUNSLET HAWKS 0 BRADFORD BULLS 82

HAWKS: 1 Richard Baker; 2 Bryn Powell; 3 Iain Higgins; 4 Wes McGibbon; 5 George Rayner; 6 Jon Liddell; 7 Phil Hasty; 8 Craig Ibbetson; 9 Gareth Naylor; 10 Mick Coyle; 11 Wayne Freeman; 12 Danny Fearon; 13 Paul Seal. Subs (all used): 14 Simon Jackson; 15 Jonlee Lockwood; 16 Andy Brent; 17 Dan Briggs.
BULLS: 3 Leon Pryce; 2 Tevita Vaikona; 20 Scott Naylor; 4 Shontayne Hape; 5 Lesley Vainikolo; 1 Robbie Paul (C); 7 Paul Deacon; 8 Joe Vagana; 15 Karl Pratt; 29 Stuart Fielden; 12 Jamie Peacock; 11 Daniel Gartner; 13 Mike Forshaw. Subs (all used): 14 Lee Gilmour; 18 Lee Radford; 27 Robert Parker; 10 Paul Anderson.
Tries: Fielden (5), Vainikolo (8, 48, 74), Pratt (11, 24), Gartner (14), L Pryce (32, 76), Parker (34), Gilmour (52), Radford (56), Vaikona (60, 70), Hape (62);
Goals: Deacon 11.
Rugby Leaguer & League Express Men of the Match: *Hawks:* Richard Baker; *Bulls:* Leon Pryce.
Penalty count: 3-7; **Half-time:** 0-36; **Referee:** Karl Kirkpatrick (Warrington); **Attendance:** 5,685
(at Headingley Stadium, Leeds).

QUARTER FINALS

Saturday 15th March 2003

WIDNES VIKINGS 28 BRADFORD BULLS 38

VIKINGS: 1 Stuart Spruce (C); 2 Paul Devlin; 20 Dan Potter; 4 Adam Hughes; 5 Jason Demetriou; 13 Daniel Frame; 18 Dean Lawford; 8 Robert Relf; 9 Shane Millard; 10 Julian O'Neill (NZ); 11 Andy Hay; 12 Steve McCurrie; 3 Deon Bird. Subs (all used): 23 David Mills; 19 Paul Atcheson; 22 Phil Cantillon; 17 Anthony Farrell.
Tries: Demetriou (16), Spruce (20), Lawford (32), Hughes (40), Cantillon (77);
Goals: Hughes 3/4, Lawford 1/1.
BULLS: 6 Michael Withers; 17 Stuart Reardon; 20 Scott Naylor; 4 Shontayne Hape; 5 Lesley Vainikolo; 3 Leon Pryce; 7 Paul Deacon; 27 Robert Parker; 15 Karl Pratt; 29 Stuart Fielden; 11 Daniel Gartner; 14 Lee Gilmour; 13 Mike Forshaw. Subs (all used): 1 Robbie Paul (C); 19 Jamie Langley; 18 Lee Radford; 30 Richard Moore.
Tries: Hape (7), L Pryce (24), Forshaw (41, 63), Paul (67), Naylor (80); **Goals:** Deacon 7/8.
Rugby Leaguer & League Express Men of the Match: *Vikings:* Dean Lawford; *Bulls:* Mike Forshaw.
Penalty count: 6-5; **Half-time:** 22-12;
Referee: Steve Ganson (St Helens); **Attendance:** 4,129.

Sunday 16th March 2003

LEEDS RHINOS 41 HULL FC 18

RHINOS: 18 Gary Connolly; 2 Mark Calderwood; 5 Chev Walker; 4 Keith Senior; 1 Francis Cummins; 14 Andrew Dunemann; 7 Rob Burrow; 17 Wayne McDonald; 9 Matt Diskin; 19 Ryan Bailey; 11 David Furner; 12 Matt Adamson; 13 Kevin Sinfield (C). Subs (all used): 10 Barrie McDermott; 15 Chris Feather; 16 Willie Poching; 6 Danny McGuire.
Tries: Furner (17, 73), Senior (20), McDermott (24), Calderwood (50), Cummins (70), McGuire (78);
Goals: Furner 6/9; **Field goal:** Sinfield.
On report: Walker & Burrow (29) - tackle on Barnett; Connolly (54) - high tackle on Prescott.
HULL: 1 Steve Prescott; 2 Colin Best; 3 Richie Barnett; 4 Toa Kohe-Love; 5 Matt Crowther; 6 Richard Horne; 7 Tony Smith; 8 Craig Greenhill; 22 Andy Last; 10 Paul King; 12 Scott Logan; 19 Richard Fletcher; 13 Jason Smith (C). Subs (all used): 14 Sean Ryan; 17 Chris Chester; 27 Liam Higgins (D); 16 Paul Cooke.
Tries: Prescott (43, 62), T Smith (79);
Goals: Crowther 2/3, Prescott 1/1.
Rugby Leaguer & League Express Men of the Match: *Rhinos:* Matt Diskin; *Hull:* Steve Prescott.
Penalty count: 11-9; **Half time:** 18-2;
Referee: Ian Smith (Oldham); **Attendance:** 11,420.

SALFORD CITY REDS 6 ST HELENS 54

CITY REDS: 1 Jason Flowers; 2 Michael Platt; 3 Stuart Littler; 4 Alan Hunte; 5 Danny Arnold; 6 Cliff Beverley; 7 Gavin Clinch; 8 Neil Baynes; 9 Malcolm Alker; 10 Andy Coley; 11 Simon Baldwin; 12 Neil Lowe; 13 Chris Charles. Subs: 14 Steve Blakeley; 15 Paul Highton; 16 Andy Gorski (not used); 17 David Highton.
Try: Hunte (2); **Goals:** Clinch 0/2, Charles 1/2.
Sin bin: Clinch (36) - holding down.
SAINTS: 1 Paul Wellens; 5 Darren Albert; 16 Darren Smith; 4 Paul Newlove; 2 Anthony Stewart; 13 Paul Sculthorpe; 7 Sean Long; 8 Darren Britt; 14 Mick Higham; 12 John Stankevitch; 11 Chris Joynt (C); 15 Tim Jonkers; 6 Jason Hooper. Subs (all used): 19 Ade Gardner; 17 Mike Bennett; 10 Barry Ward; 18 Mark Edmondson.
Tries: Sculthorpe (33, 56), Newlove (42), Smith (45, 61), Stewart (48), Albert (53), Long (58), Britt (77), Gardner (80); **Goals:** Long 7/10.
Sin bin: Ward (27) - holding down.
Rugby Leaguer & League Express Men of the Match: *City Reds:* Malcolm Alker; *Saints:* Paul Sculthorpe.
Penalty count: 10-10; **Half-time:** 6-6;
Referee: Russell Smith (Castleford); **Attendance:** 5,717.

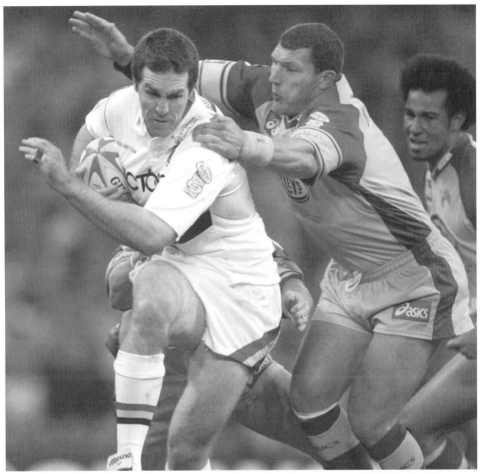

Bradford's Daniel Gartner ducks under the challenge of Leeds' Barrie McDermott during the Challenge Cup Final

SWINTON LIONS 12 WIGAN WARRIORS 70

LIONS: 1 Wayne English; 2 Jason Roach; 3 Kris Tassell; 4 Phil Hassan; 5 Hugh Thorpe; 6 Chris Hough; 7 Peter Cannon; 8 Andy Leathem; 9 Rob Barraclough; 10 Simon Knox; 11 Craig Wingfield; 12 Phil Cushion; 13 Robert Russell. Subs (all used): 14 Andy Cheetham; 15 Jason Johnson; 16 Lee Hudson; 17 Dave Ellison.
Tries: Russell (9), Leathem (74); **Goals:** Hough 2/2.
WARRIORS: 1 Kris Radlinski; 2 Brett Dallas; 18 Martin Aspinwall; 14 David Hodgson; 3 Jamie Ainscough; 20 Luke Robinson; 7 Adrian Lam (C); 16 Danny Sculthorpe; 9 Terry Newton; 10 Craig Smith; 23 Gareth Hock; 4 Paul Johnson; 15 Sean O'Loughlin. Subs (all used): 21 Ricky Bibey; 17 Mark Smith; 19 Stephen Wild; 6 Julian O'Neill.
Tries: Hodgson (23, 79), Dallas (26, 49), Robinson (27), Hock (32), Johnson (35), Ainscough (39), Bibey (42), M Smith (57), Lam (63), Aspinwall (65), O'Loughlin (67);
Goals: Robinson 2/3, O'Neill 7/10.
Rugby Leaguer & League Express Men of the Match: *Lions:* Rob Barraclough; *Warriors:* Sean O'Loughlin.
Penalty count: 3-6; **Half-time:** 6-30;
Referee: Karl Kirkpatrick (Warrington);
Attendance: 5,114 *(at JJB Stadium, Wigan).*

SEMI FINALS

Saturday 12th April 2003

LEEDS RHINOS 33 ST HELENS 26
(After extra time, 26-26 after 80 minutes)

RHINOS: 18 Gary Connolly; 2 Mark Calderwood; 3 Chris McKenna; 4 Keith Senior; 13 Kevin Sinfield (C); 14 Andrew Dunemann; 10 Barrie McDermott; 9 Matt Diskin; 19 Ryan Bailey; 5 Chev Walker; 12 Matt Adamson; 11 David Furner. Subs (all used): 6 Danny McGuire; 8 Danny Ward; 16 Willie Poching; 17 Wayne McDonald.

Tries: Calderwood (14, 18), Cummins (25), McGuire (79, 98); **Goals:** Sinfield 6/8; **Field goal:** Sinfield.
SAINTS: 1 Paul Wellens; 2 Anthony Stewart; 3 Martin Gleeson; 4 Paul Newlove; 5 Darren Albert; 6 Jason Hooper; 13 Paul Sculthorpe; 8 Darren Britt; 14 Mick Higham; 12 John Stankevitch; 11 Chris Joynt (C); 15 Tim Jonkers; 16 Darren Smith. Subs (all used): 7 Sean Long; 17 Mike Bennett; 18 Mark Edmondson; 10 Barry Ward.
Tries: Smith (7, 75), Newlove (38), Sculthorpe (51);
Goals: Sculthorpe 5/6.
Rugby Leaguer & League Express Men of the Match: *Rhinos:* Danny McGuire; *Saints:* Paul Sculthorpe.
Penalty count: 12-7; **Referee:** Russell Smith (Castleford); **Half-time:** 18-12; **Attendance:** 19,118 *(at McAlpine Stadium, Huddersfield).*

Sunday 13th April 2003

BRADFORD BULLS 36 WIGAN WARRIORS 22

BULLS: 6 Michael Withers; 2 Tevita Vaikona; 3 Leon Pryce; 4 Shontayne Hape; 5 Lesley Vainikolo; 1 Robbie Paul (C); 7 Paul Deacon; 8 Joe Vagana; 9 James Lowes; 29 Stuart Fielden; 18 Lee Radford; 12 Jamie Peacock; 13 Mike Forshaw. Subs (all used): 15 Karl Pratt; 14 Lee Gilmour; 27 Robert Parker; 10 Paul Anderson.
Tries: Lowes (18), Radford (25, 53), Hape (44), Deacon (56), Vaikona (64); **Goals:** Deacon 6/8.
WARRIORS: 1 Kris Radlinski; 5 Brian Carney; 18 Martin Aspinwall; 14 David Hodgson; 22 Shaun Briscoe; 4 Paul Johnson; 7 Adrian Lam (C); 8 Terry O'Connor; 9 Terry Newton; 10 Craig Smith; 21 Ricky Bibey; 12 Danny Tickle; 23 Gareth Hock. Subs (all used): 16 Danny Sculthorpe; 17 Mark Smith; 20 Luke Robinson; 15 Sean O'Loughlin.
Tries: Newton (33), Sculthorpe (39), Carney (71);
Goals: Tickle 5/5.
Rugby Leaguer & League Express Men of the Match: *Bulls:* James Lowes; *Warriors:* Danny Tickle.
Penalty count: 7-6; **Half-time:** 12-16;
Referee: Steve Ganson (St Helens); **Attendance:** 15,359 *(at McAlpine Stadium, Huddersfield).*

FINAL

Saturday 26th April 2003

BRADFORD BULLS 22 LEEDS RHINOS 20

BULLS: 1 Robbie Paul (C); 2 Tevita Vaikona; 20 Scott Naylor; 4 Shontayne Hape; 5 Lesley Vainikolo; 3 Leon Pryce; 7 Paul Deacon; 8 Joe Vagana; 9 James Lowes; 11 Daniel Gartner; 18 Lee Radford; 12 Jamie Peacock; 13 Mike Forshaw. Subs: 10 Paul Anderson for Vagana (21); 14 Lee Gilmour for Radford (31); 27 Robert Parker for Gartner (31); 15 Karl Pratt for Lowes (48); Vagana for Anderson (50); Gartner for Vagana (61); Radford for Parker (65); Parker for Vainikolo (75).
Tries: Paul (6), Vainikolo (39), Peacock (43);
Goals: Deacon 5/5.
RHINOS: 18 Gary Connolly; 2 Mark Calderwood; 3 Chris McKenna; 4 Keith Senior; 1 Francis Cummins; 13 Kevin Sinfield (C); 14 Andrew Dunemann; 19 Ryan Bailey; 9 Matt Diskin; 10 Barrie McDermott; 5 Chev Walker; 12 Matt Adamson; 11 David Furner. Subs: 8 Danny Ward for McDermott (19); 17 Wayne McDonald for Bailey (19); 7 Rob Burrow for Diskin (33); 16 Willie Poching for Bailey (54); McDermott for McDonald (33); Bailey for Ward (33); Diskin for Burrow (39); Ward for McDermott (54); McDonald for Adamson (54); McDermott for McDonald (57); Bailey for Ward (71); Adamson for McDermott (71).
Tries: Connolly (10), McKenna (22), Furner (60);
Goals: Sinfield 4/4.
Rugby Leaguer & League Express Men of the Match: *Bulls:* Jamie Peacock; *Rhinos:* Gary Connolly.
Penalty count: 9-5; **Half time:** 14-14;
Referee: Russell Smith (Castleford); **Attendance:** 71,212 *(at The Millennium Stadium, Cardiff).*

Amateur round-up 2003

NATIONAL LEAGUE THREE

WEEK 1
Saturday 3rd May 2003
Coventry 16 Warrington-Woolston 13; Hemel Hempstead 6 Bradford-Dudley Hill 58; Sheffield-Hillsborough 38 Manchester 0; South London 24 Huddersfield-Underbank 16; St Albans 16 Teesside 20

WEEK 2
Saturday 10th May 2003
Bradford-Dudley Hill 42 South London 0; Huddersfield-Underbank 21 Sheffield-Hillsborough 20; Manchester 44 Coventry 14; Warrington-Woolston 46 St Albans 10
Postponed - Teesside v Hemel Hempstead
(awarded to Teesside, 24-0)

WEEK 3
Saturday 17th May 2003
Coventry 20 South London 14; Manchester 22 Teesside 28; Sheffield-Hillsborough 42 Hemel Hempstead 16; St Albans 28 Huddersfield-Underbank 22; Warrington-Woolston 11 Bradford-Dudley Hill 21

WEEK 4
Saturday 31st May 2003
Bradford-Dudley Hill 42 Huddersfield-Underbank 15; Coventry 18 St Albans 40; Hemel Hempstead 24 Manchester 30; South London 28 Sheffield-Hillsborough 22; Teesside 26 Warrington-Woolston 16

WEEK 5
Saturday 7th June 2003
Bradford-Dudley Hill 16 St Albans 8; Huddersfield-Underbank 55 Hemel Hempstead 20; Manchester 2 South London 42; Teesside 34 Coventry 8; Warrington-Woolston 20 Sheffield-Hillsborough 16

WEEK 6
Saturday 14th June 2003
Bradford-Dudley Hill 48 Manchester 16; Hemel Hempstead 4 Coventry 19; Huddersfield-Underbank 23 Warrington-Woolston 44; St Albans 38 South London 18; Teesside 26 Sheffield-Hillsborough Hawks 25

WEEK 7
Saturday 21st June 2003
Huddersfield-Underbank 20 Bradford-Dudley Hill 44; Manchester 36 Hemel Hempstead 16; Sheffield-Hillsborough 36 South London 10; St Albans 24 Coventry 14; Warrington-Woolston 26 Teesside 26

WEEK 8
Saturday 28th June 2003
Coventry 18 Bradford-Dudley Hill 36; Manchester 16 Warrington-Woolston 54; South London 26 Hemel Hempstead 8; St Albans 36 Sheffield-Hillsborough 30; Teesside 16 Huddersfield-Underbank 28

WEEK 9
Saturday 5th July 2003
Coventry 48 Hemel Hempstead 14; Manchester 10 Bradford-Dudley Hill 68; Sheffield-Hillsborough 20 Teesside 23; South London 6 St Albans 28; Warrington-Woolston 56 Huddersfield-Underbank 8

WEEK 10
Saturday 12th July 2003
Coventry 24 Huddersfield-Underbank 30; Hemel Hempstead 12 Warrington-Woolston 46; Sheffield-Hillsborough 22 Bradford-Dudley Hill 16; South London 32 Teesside 36; St Albans 40 Manchester 10

WEEK 11
Saturday 19th July 2003
Bradford-Dudley Hill 40 Coventry 8; Hemel Hempstead 16 South London 22; Huddersfield-Underbank 4 Teesside 28; Sheffield-Hillsborough 18 St Albans 6; Warrington-Woolston 60 Manchester 14

WEEK 12
Saturday 26th July 2003
Coventry 32 Sheffield-Hillsborough 32; Hemel Hempstead 6 St Albans 58; Manchester 14 Huddersfield-Underbank 80; South London 4 Warrington-Woolston 32; Teesside 16 Bradford-Dudley Hill 37

WEEK 13
Saturday 2nd August 2003
Bradford-Dudley Hill 38 Warrington-Woolston 12; Hemel Hempstead 0 Sheffield-Hillsborough 48; Huddersfield-Underbank 42 St Albans 22; South London 34 Coventry 22
Postponed - Teesside v Manchester
(awarded to Teesside, 24-0)

WEEK 14
Saturday 9th August 2003
Bradford-Dudley Hill 39 Teesside 16; Huddersfield-Underbank 48 Manchester 14; St Albans 56 Hemel Hempstead 18; Sheffield-Hillsborough 26 Coventry 12; Warrington-Woolston 44 South London 14

FINAL TABLE

	P	W	D	L	F	A	Diff	PTS
B'ford-Dudley Hill	14	13	0	1	545	178	367	26
Teesside	14	10	1	3	343	273	70	21
Warr-Woolston	14	9	1	4	480	244	236	19
St Albans	14	9	0	5	410	284	126	18
Sheff-Hillsborough	14	7	1	6	395	246	149	15
Hudds-Underbank	14	7	0	7	412	396	16	14
South London	14	6	0	8	274	362	-88	12
Coventry	14	4	1	9	273	385	-112	9
Manchester	14	3	0	11	228	584	-356	6
Hemel Hempstead	14	0	0	14	160	568	-408	0

PLAY-OFFS

Saturday 16th August 2003
QUALIFYING SEMI-FINAL
Bradford-Dudley Hill 8 Teesside 10
ELIMINATION PLAY-OFFS
St Albans 20 Sheffield-Hillsborough 8
Warrington-Woolston 18 Huddersfield-Underbank 10

Saturday 23rd August 2003
ELIMINATION SEMI-FINAL
Warrington-Woolston 24 St Albans 10

Saturday 30th August 2003
FINAL ELIMINATOR
Bradford-Dudley Hill 12 Warrington-Woolston 34

Sunday 14th September 2003
GRAND FINAL
Teesside 6 Warrington-Woolston 42
(at Winnington Park, Northwich)

TOTALRL.COM CONFERENCE

WEEK 1
Saturday 3rd May 2003
NORTH MIDLANDS: Mansfield Storm 34 Crewe Wolves 18; Nottingham Outlaws 34 Derby City 14; Rotherham Giants 78 Worksop Sharks 1
NORTH WEST: Blackpool Sea Eagles 20 Bolton le Moors 40; Carlisle Centurions 56 Lancaster 6; Liverpool Buccaneers 22 Chester Wolves 24
WEST: Bristol Sonics 72 Worcestershire Saints 22; Oxford Cavaliers 20 Cardiff Demons 64; Somerset Vikings 14 Gloucestershire Warriors 48
EAST: Essex Eels 60 Cambridge Eagles 20; South Norfolk Saints 20 Ipswich Rhinos 38; St Ives Roosters 4 Luton Vipers 78
SOUTH MIDLANDS: Leicester Phoenix 36 Bedford Swifts 22; Telford Raiders 10 Birmingham Bulldogs 58; Wolverhampton Wizards 33 Coventry Bears 'A' 28
NORTH EAST: Bridlington Bulls 78 Sunderland City 4; Durham Tigers 14 Newcastle Knights 44; Leeds Akademiks 58 Whitley Bay Barbarians 12; Yorkshire Coast Tigers 0 Gateshead Storm 60
LONDON & SOUTH: Gosport & Fareham Vikings 80 South London Storm 'A' 6; Greenwich Admirals 18 Crawley Jets 34; Hemel Stags 'A' 0 North London Skolars 'A' 48; Kingston Warriors 20 West London Sharks 26
Sunday 4th May 2003
WALES: Bridgend Blue Bulls 56 Aberavon Fighting Irish 16; Cynon Valley Cougars 25 Torfaen Tigers 28; Rumney Rhinos 74 Swansea Bulls 16

WEEK 2
Saturday 10th May 2003
NORTH MIDLANDS: Crewe Wolves 46 Derby City 10; Rotherham Giants 28 Mansfield Storm 38; Worksop Sharks 0 Nottingham Outlaws 82
NORTH WEST: Chester Wolves 74 Blackpool Sea Eagles 14; Liverpool Buccaneers 18 Carlisle Centurions 48
WEST: Cardiff Demons 90 Bristol Sonics 0; Gloucestershire Warriors 78 Worcester Saints 6; Oxford Cavaliers 16 Somerset Vikings 12
EAST: Cambridge Eagles 6 Luton Vipers 82; Ipswich Rhinos 62 Essex Eels 10; South Norfolk Saints 64 St Ives Roosters 14
SOUTH MIDLANDS: Bedford Swifts 20 Wolverhampton Wizards 47; Birmingham Bulldogs 42 Leicester Phoenix 12; Coventry Bears 'A' 34 Telford Raiders 28
NORTH EAST: Gateshead Storm 12 Bridlington Bulls 6; Newcastle Knights 52 Yorkshire Coast Tigers 18; Sunderland City 14 Leeds Akademiks 64
LONDON & SOUTH: Crawley Jets 49 Gosport & Fareham Vikings 32; North London Skolars 'A' 40 Kingston Warriors 10; South London Storm 'A' 16 Greenwich Admirals 40; West London Sharks 52 Hemel Stags 'A' 26
Sunday 11th May 2003
NORTH EAST: Durham Tigers 68 Whitley Bay Barbarians 10
WALES: Aberavon Fighting Irish 68 Swansea Bulls 38; Cynon Valley Cougars 22 Bridgend Blue Bulls 66; Torfaen Tigers 34 Rumney Rhinos 50

WEEK 3
Saturday 17th May 2003
NORTH MIDLANDS: Derby City 38 Rotherham Giants 30; Mansfield Storm 22 Worksop Sharks 0; Nottingham Outlaws 28 Crewe Wolves 6
NORTH WEST: Blackpool Sea Eagles 8 Liverpool Buccaneers 20; Carlisle Centurions 52 Bolton le Moors 12; Lancaster 28 Chester Wolves 38
WEST: Bristol Sonics 20 Oxford Cavaliers 50; Gloucestershire Warriors 2 Cardiff Demons 26; Somerset Vikings 24 Worcester Saints 0
EAST: Essex Eels 24 South Norfolk Saints 34; Luton Vipers 14 Ipswich Rhinos 19; St Ives Roosters 24 Cambridge Eagles 0
SOUTH MIDLANDS: Birmingham Bulldogs 50 Bedford Swifts 11; Leicester Phoenix 48 Coventry Bears 'A' 8; Telford Raiders 13 Wolverhampton Wizards 6
NORTH EAST: Bridlington Bulls 48 Newcastle Knights 10; Durham Tigers 22 Sunderland City 28; Leeds Akademiks 34 Gateshead Storm 4; Yorkshire Coast Tigers 42 Whitley Bay Barbarians 2
LONDON & SOUTH: Crawley Jets 78 Kingston Warriors 6; Gosport & Fareham Vikings 16 West London Sharks 30; Greenwich Admirals 30 North London Skolars 'A' 30; South London Storm 'A' 18 Hemel Stags 'A' 12

Sunday 18th May 2003
WALES: Bridgend Blue Bulls 80 Torfaen Tigers 21; Rumney Rhinos 18 Aberavon Fighting Irish 46; Swansea Bulls 40 Cynon Valley Cougars 40
Wednesday 21st May 2003
NORTH WEST: Bolton le Moors 14 Lancaster 6

WEEK 4
Saturday 31st May 2003
NORTH MIDLANDS: Crewe Wolves 28 Rotherham Giants 24; Nottingham Outlaws 20 Mansfield Storm 26; Worksop Sharks 16 Derby City 42
NORTH WEST: Blackpool Sea Eagles 16 Carlisle Centurions 76; Bolton le Moors 38 Chester Wolves 44
WEST: Oxford Cavaliers 26 Gloucestershire Warriors 40; Somerset Vikings 46 Bristol Sonics 12; Worcestershire Saints 17 Cardiff Demons 58
EAST: Cambridge Eagles 0 Ipswich Rhinos 86; St Ives Roosters 14 Essex Eels 64
SOUTH MIDLANDS: Birmingham Bulldogs 62 Coventry Bears 'A' 18; Telford Raiders 24 Bedford Swifts 0
NORTH EAST: Gateshead Storm 25 Durham Tigers 13; Newcastle Knights 10 Leeds Akademiks 23; Sunderland City 36 Yorkshire Coast Tigers 35; Whitley Bay Barbarians 12 Bridlington Bulls 102
LONDON & SOUTH: Gosport & Fareham Vikings 40 Greenwich Admirals 24; Hemel Stags 'A' 24 Kingston Warriors 27; North London Skolars 'A' 18 West London Sharks 24; South London Storm 'A' 0 Crawley Jets 88
WALES: Aberavon Fighting Irish 32 Bridgend Blue Bulls 50; Swansea Bulls 24 Rumney Rhinos 0; Torfaen Tigers 44 Cynon Valley Cougars 12
Sunday 1st June 2003
NORTH WEST: Liverpool Buccaneers 38 Lancaster 10

WEEK 5
Saturday 7th June 2003
NORTH MIDLANDS: Derby City 12 Mansfield Storm 34; Rotherham Giants 34 Nottingham Outlaws 36; Worksop Sharks 14 Crewe Wolves 41
NORTH WEST: Bolton le Moors 52 Liverpool Buccaneers 12; Lancaster 20 Blackpool Sea Eagles 38
WEST: Cardiff Demons 38 Somerset Vikings 22; Gloucestershire Warriors 60 Bristol Sonics 18; Worcester Saints 13 Oxford Cavaliers 6
EAST: Ipswich Rhinos 102 St Ives Roosters 4; Luton Vipers 40 Essex Eels 38; South Norfolk Saints 72 Cambridge Eagles 14
SOUTH MIDLANDS: Coventry Bears 'A' 24 Bedford Swifts 0; Leicester Phoenix 52 Telford Raiders 16; Wolverhampton Wizards 4 Birmingham Bulldogs 54
NORTH EAST: Gateshead Storm 18 Newcastle Knights 34; Leeds Akademiks 27 Bridlington Bulls 12; Sunderland City 86 Whitley Bay Barbarians 14; Yorkshire Coast Tigers 92 Durham Tigers 4
LONDON & SOUTH: Crawley Jets 80 Greenwich Admirals 18; North London Skolars 'A' 50 Hemel Stags 'A' 14; South London Storm 'A' 14 Gosport & Fareham Vikings 24; West London Sharks 52 Kingston Warriors 12
WALES: Aberavon Fighting Irish 66 Cynon Valley Cougars 14; Rumney Rhinos 14 Bridgend Blue Bulls 28; Swansea Bulls 32 Torfaen Tigers 48
Sunday 8th June 2003
NORTH WEST: Chester Wolves 6 Carlisle Centurions 30

WEEK 6
Saturday 14th June 2003
NORTH MIDLANDS: Crewe Wolves 24 Mansfield Storm 18; Derby City 0 Nottingham Outlaws 52; Worksop Sharks 16 Rotherham Giants 62
NORTH WEST: Bolton le Moors 40 Blackpool Sea Eagles 24; Chester Wolves 64 Liverpool Buccaneers 16; Lancaster 7 Carlisle Centurions 52
WEST: Cardiff Demons 38 Oxford Cavaliers 10; Gloucestershire Warriors 12 Somerset Vikings 26; Worcester Saints 19 Bristol Sonics 16
EAST: Cambridge Eagles 0 Essex Eels 74; Ipswich Rhinos 25 South Norfolk Saints 42; Luton Vipers 94 St Ives Roosters 10
SOUTH MIDLANDS: Birmingham Bulldogs 68 Telford Raiders 6; Coventry Bears 'A' 46 Wolverhampton Wizards 22; Bedford Swifts withdrew from Division
NORTH EAST: Bridlington Bulls 42 Yorkshire Coast Tigers 8; Durham Tigers 16 Leeds Akademiks 44; Newcastle Knights 80 Whitley Bay Barbarians 10; Sunderland City 10 Gateshead Storm 46
LONDON & SOUTH: Hemel Stags 'A' 18 Greenwich Admirals 46; Kingston Warriors 28 Gosport & Fareham Vikings 42; North London Skolars 'A' 10 Crawley Jets 40; West London Sharks 88 South London Storm 'A' 12
WALES: Aberavon Fighting Irish 38 Torfaen Tigers 31; Cynon Valley Cougars 54 Rumney Rhinos 34
Sunday 15th June 2003
WALES: Swansea Bulls 17 Bridgend Blue Bulls 48

WEEK 7
Saturday 28th June 2003
NORTH MIDLANDS: Derby City 16 Crewe Wolves 25; Mansfield Storm 21 Rotherham Giants 16; Nottingham Outlaws 64 Worksop Sharks 10
NORTH WEST: Blackpool Sea Eagles 22 Chester Wolves 40; Carlisle Centurions 72 Liverpool Buccaneers 4; Lancaster 25 Bolton le Moors 38
WEST: Bristol Sonics 8 Cardiff Demons 100; Somerset Vikings 46 Oxford Cavaliers 17; Worcester Saints 10 Gloucestershire Warriors 80
EAST: Essex Eels 44 Ipswich Rhinos 16; Luton Vipers 94 Cambridge Eagles 18; St Ives Roosters 4 South Norfolk Saints 90
SOUTH MIDLANDS: Leicester Phoenix 20 Birmingham Bulldogs 47; Telford Raiders 38 Coventry Bears 'A' 30
NORTH EAST: Gateshead Storm 58 Sunderland City 24; Leeds Akademiks 42 Durham Tigers 11; Whitley Bay Barbarians 28 Newcastle Knights 68; Yorkshire Coast

Tigers 0 Bridlington Bulls 66
LONDON & SOUTH: Gosport & Fareham Vikings 52 Crawley Jets 16; Greenwich Admirals 62 South London Storm 'A' 8; Hemel Stags 'A' 0 West London Sharks 56; Kingston Warriors 28 North London Skolars 'A' 32
WALES: Bridgend Blue Bulls 72 Cynon Valley Cougars 26; Rumney Rhinos 24 Torfaen Tigers 55; Swansea Bulls 26 Aberavon Fighting Irish 48

WEEK 8
Saturday 5th July 2003
NORTH MIDLANDS: Crewe Wolves 25 Nottingham Outlaws 16; Rotherham Giants 20 Derby City 16; Worksop Sharks 0 Mansfield Storm 58
NORTH WEST: Carlisle Centurions 26 Bolton le Moors 24; Chester Wolves 58 Lancaster 8; Liverpool Buccaneers 42 Blackpool Sea Eagles 26
WEST: Cardiff Demons 28 Gloucestershire Warriors 6; Oxford Cavaliers 50 Bristol Sonics 28; Somerset Vikings 64 Worcester Saints 0
EAST: Ipswich Rhinos 48 Luton Vipers 0; South Norfolk Saints 36 Essex Eels 24; St Ives Roosters 34 Cambridge Eagles 12
SOUTH MIDLANDS: Coventry Bears 'A' 28 Leicester Phoenix 40; Wolverhampton Wizards 10 Telford Raiders 2
NORTH EAST: Bridlington Bulls 26 Leeds Akademiks 27; Durham Tigers 14 Yorkshire Coast Tigers 52; Gateshead Storm 14 Newcastle Knights 16; Whitley Bay Barbarians 24 Sunderland City 26
LONDON & SOUTH: Crawley Jets 55 Hemel Stags 'A' 19; Gosport & Fareham Vikings 21 North London Skolars 'A' 16; Greenwich Admirals 20 West London Sharks 66; South London Storm 'A' 16 Kingston Warriors 26
WALES: Aberavon Fighting Irish 76 Rumney Rhinos 18; Cynon Valley Cougars 40 Swansea Bulls 28; Torfaen Tigers 22 Bridgend Blue Bulls 52

WEEK 9
Saturday 12th July 2003
NORTH MIDLANDS: Derby City 42 Worksop Sharks 14; Mansfield Storm 12 Nottingham Outlaws 28; Rotherham Giants 24 Crewe Wolves 22
NORTH WEST: Carlisle Centurions 98 Blackpool Sea Eagles 1; Chester Wolves 40 Bolton le Moors 36; Lancaster 26 Liverpool Buccaneers 20
WEST: Bristol Sonics 48 Somerset Vikings 44; Cardiff Demons 52 Worcester Saints 12; Gloucestershire Warriors 98 Oxford Cavaliers 20
EAST: Essex Eels 84 St Ives 22; Ipswich Rhinos 64 Cambridge Eagles 0; Luton Vipers 20 South Norfolk Saints 28
SOUTH MIDLANDS: Coventry Bears 'A' 4 Birmingham Bulldogs 58; Leicester Phoenix 32 Wolverhampton Wizards 30
NORTH EAST: Bridlington Bulls 46 Durham Tigers 4; Gateshead Storm 38 Whitley Bay Barbarians 12; Leeds Akademiks 22 Yorkshire Coast Tigers 10; Sunderland City 20 Newcastle Knights 28
LONDON & SOUTH: Hemel Stags 'A' 32 Gosport & Fareham Vikings 66; Kingston Warriors 28 Greenwich Admirals 20; North London Skolars 'A' 82 South London Storm 'A' 8; West London Sharks 20 Crawley Jets 29
WALES: Aberavon Fighting Irish 88 Cynon Valley Cougars 8; Bridgend Blue Bulls 72 Rumney Rhinos 26; Swansea Bulls 22 Torfaen Tigers 54

WEEK 10
Saturday 19th July 2003
NORTH MIDLANDS: Crewe Wolves 72 Worksop Sharks 6; Mansfield Storm 26 Derby City 24; Nottingham Outlaws 42 Rotherham Giants 16
NORTH WEST: Blackpool Sea Eagles 31 Lancaster 26; Carlisle Centurions 44 Chester Wolves 10; Liverpool Buccaneers 18 Bolton le Moors 41
WEST: Bristol Sonics 4 Gloucestershire Warriors 44; Somerset Vikings 26 Cardiff Demons 16; Worcester Saints 34 Oxford Cavaliers 32
EAST: Cambridge Eagles 0 South Norfolk Saints 60; Essex Eels 110 Luton Vipers 12; St Ives Roosters 28 Ipswich Rhinos 52
SOUTH MIDLANDS: Birmingham Bulldogs 64 Wolverhampton Wizards 6; Telford Raiders 24 Leicester Phoenix 0
NORTH EAST: Durham Tigers 6 Bridlington Bulls 82; Gateshead Storm 82 Whitley Bay Barbarians 2; Newcastle Knights 60 Sunderland City 5; Yorkshire Coast Tigers 6 Leeds Akademiks 6
LONDON & SOUTH: Crawley Jets 94 South London Storm 'A' 4; Greenwich Admirals 20 Gosport & Fareham Vikings 30; Kingston Warriors 54 Hemel Stags 'A' 12; West London Sharks 24 North London Skolars 'A' 32
WALES: Rumney Rhinos 86 Cynon Valley Cougars 6; Swansea Bulls 1 Bridgend Blue Bulls 84; Torfaen Tigers 26 Aberavon Fighting Irish 22

WEEK 11
Saturday 26th July 2003
EAST: South Norfolk Saints 49 Luton Vipers 18
SOUTH MIDLANDS: Wolverhampton Wizards 24 Leicester Phoenix 0
RLC SHIELD QUALIFYING PLAY-OFFS
NORTH EAST: Sunderland City 48 Whitley Bay Barbarians 0; Yorkshire Coast Tigers 24 Durham Tigers 0
LONDON & SOUTH: Greenwich Admirals 54 South London Storm 'A' 16; Kingston Warriors 24 Hemel Stags 'A' 0

FINAL TABLES

NORTH MIDLANDS

	P	W	D	L	F	A	Diff	PTS
Nottingham O'laws	10	8	0	2	402	143	259	16
Mansfield Storm	10	8	0	2	289	170	119	16
Crewe Wolves	10	7	0	3	307	190	117	14
Rotherham Giants	10	4	0	6	332	258	74	8
Derby City	10	3	0	7	214	297	-83	6
Worksop Sharks	10	0	0	10	77	563	-486	0

NORTH WEST

	P	W	D	L	F	A	Diff	PTS
Carlisle Centurions	10	10	0	0	554	104	450	20
Chester Wolves	10	8	0	2	398	258	140	16
Bolton le Moors	10	6	0	4	335	267	68	12
Liverpool B'caneers	10	3	0	7	210	371	-161	6
Blackpool S Eagles	10	2	0	8	200	476	-276	4
Lancaster	10	1	0	9	162	383	-221	2

WEST

	P	W	D	L	F	A	Diff	PTS
Cardiff Demons	10	9	0	1	510	123	387	18
Gloucestershire W	10	7	0	3	468	178	290	14
Somerset Vikings	10	6	0	4	324	207	117	12
Oxford Cavaliers	10	3	0	7	247	393	-146	6
Worcestershire Sts	10	3	0	7	133	482	-349	6
Bristol Sonics	10	2	0	8	226	525	-299	4

EAST

	P	W	D	L	F	A	Diff	PTS
South Norfolk Sts	10	9	0	1	495	181	314	18
Ipswich Rhinos	10	8	0	2	512	162	350	16
Essex Eels	10	6	0	4	532	258	274	12
Luton Vipers	10	5	0	5	452	330	122	10
St Ives Roosters	10	2	0	8	158	640	-482	4
Cambridge Eagles	10	0	0	10	72	650	-578	0

SOUTH MIDLANDS

	P	W	D	L	F	A	Diff	PTS
Birmingham B'dogs	8	8	0	0	453	80	373	16
Leicester Phoenix	8	4	0	4	204	219	-15	8
Wolverhampton W	8	3	0	5	135	239	-104	6
Telford Raiders	8	3	0	5	137	258	-121	6
Coventry Bears 'A'	8	2	0	6	196	329	-133	4

Bedford Swifts record expunged

NORTH EAST

	P	W	D	L	F	A	Diff	PTS
Leeds Akademiks	10	9	1	0	347	121	226	19
Newcastle Knights	10	8	0	2	402	198	204	16
Bridlington Bulls	10	7	0	3	508	110	398	14
Gateshead Storm	10	7	0	3	357	151	206	14
Sunderland City	10	4	0	6	253	429	-176	8
Yorkshire Coast T	10	3	1	6	263	304	-41	7
Durham Tigers	10	1	0	9	172	465	-293	2
Whitley Bay Barb'	10	0	0	10	126	650	-524	0

LONDON & SOUTH

	P	W	D	L	F	A	Diff	PTS
Crawley Jets	10	9	0	1	563	179	384	18
West London S	10	8	0	2	438	185	253	16
Gosport Vikings	10	8	0	2	403	233	170	16
North London S 'A'	10	6	1	3	358	199	159	13
Kingston Warriors	10	4	0	6	239	342	-103	8
Greenwich Admirals	10	3	1	6	298	350	-52	7
South London S 'A'	10	1	0	9	100	596	-496	2
Hemel Stags 'A'	10	0	0	10	157	472	-315	0

WALES

	P	W	D	L	F	A	Diff	PTS
Bridgend Blue Bulls	10	10	0	0	608	197	411	20
Aberavon Fighting I	10	7	0	3	500	285	215	14
Torfaen Tigers	10	6	0	4	363	357	6	12
Rumney Rhinos	10	3	0	7	344	411	-67	6
Cynon V'ey Cougars	10	2	1	7	247	552	-305	5
Swansea Bulls	10	1	1	8	244	504	-260	3

PLAY-OFFS

Friday 1st August 2003
HARRY JEPSON TROPHY - QUALIFYING PLAY-OFF: Bridgend Blue Bulls 38 Cardiff Demons 16
Saturday 2nd August 2003
HARRY JEPSON TROPHY - QUALIFYING PLAY-OFFS: Birmingham Bulldogs 33 Nottingham Outlaws 22; Carlisle Centurions 68 Leeds Akademiks 2; Crawley Jets 44 South Norfolk Saints 28
HARRY JEPSON TROPHY - ELIMINATION PLAY-OFFS: Aberavon Fighting Irish 58 Gloucestershire Warriors 30; Chester Wolves 50 Newcastle Knights 22; Ipswich Rhinos 42 West London Sharks 28; Mansfield Storm 36 Leicester Phoenix 30
RLC SHIELD - PLAY-OFFS ROUND 1: Bolton le Moors 32 Yorkshire Coast Tigers 16; Bridlington Bulls 44 Lancaster 12; Essex Eels 18 Greenwich Admirals 26; Gateshead Storm 52 Blackpool Sea Eagles 10; Gosport & Fareham Vikings 78 Cambridge Eagles 0; Liverpool Buccaneers 38 Sunderland City 36; Luton Vipers 18 Kingston Warriors 34; North London Skolars 'A' 86 St Ives Roosters 10; Rotherham Giants 24 Coventry Bears 'A' 0; Rumney Rhinos 88 Worcester Saints 6; Telford Raiders 8 Derby City 54; Torfaen Tigers 82 Bristol Sonics 12; Wolverhampton Wizards 26 Worksop Sharks 0; Byes - Crewe Wolves, Oxford Cavaliers, Somerset Vikings

Saturday 9th August 2003
HARRY JEPSON TROPHY - QUARTER FINALS: Cardiff Demons 21 Aberavon Fighting Irish 47; Leeds Akademiks 25 Chester Wolves 20; Nottingham Outlaws 16 Mansfield Storm 24; South Norfolk Saints 20 Ipswich Rhinos 44
RLC SHIELD - PLAY-OFFS ROUND 2: Bolton le Moors 31 Gateshead Storm 18; Bridlington Bulls 24 Liverpool Buccaneers 0; Crewe Wolves 36 Derby City 12; Gosport & Fareham Vikings 38 Kingston Warriors 8; North London Skolars 'A' 17 Greenwich Admirals 26; Somerset Vikings 24 Rumney Rhinos 0; Torfaen Tigers 82 Oxford Cavaliers 12; Wolverhampton Wizards 13 Rotherham Giants 54

Thursday 14th August 2003
HARRY JEPSON TROPHY - MINOR SEMI-FINAL: Bridgend Blue Bulls 42 Aberavon Fighting Irish 8

Saturday 16th August 2003
HARRY JEPSON TROPHY - MINOR SEMI-FINALS: Carlisle Centurions 60 Leeds Akademiks 0; Crawley Jets 22 Ipswich Rhinos 27; Birmingham Bulldogs 30 Mansfield Storm 16
RLC SHIELD - QUARTER FINALS: Bridlington Bulls 30 Bolton le Moors 24; Crewe Wolves 16 Rotherham Giants 20; Gosport & Fareham Vikings 40 Greenwich Admirals 16; Torfaen Tigers 50 Somerset Vikings 18

Sunday 24th August 2003
HARRY JEPSON TROPHY - SEMI FINALS: Bridgend Blue Bulls 44 Ipswich Rhinos 24 *(at Broad Street RFC, Coventry)*; Birmingham Bulldogs 2 Carlisle Centurions 44 *(at Hillsborough Arena, Sheffield)*
RLC SHIELD - SEMI FINALS: Gosport & Fareham Vikings 26 Torfaen Tigers 36 *(at Broad Street RFC, Coventry)*; Bolton le Moors 38 Rotherham Giants 14 *(at Hillsborough Arena, Sheffield)*

Saturday 6th September 2003
HARRY JEPSON TROPHY - GRAND FINAL:
Bridgend Blue Bulls 33 Carlisle Centurions 26
(at Wilderspool, Warrington)
RLC SHIELD - GRAND FINAL:
Bolton le Moors 28 Torfaen Tigers 21
(at Wilderspool, Warrington)

NATIONAL CONFERENCE

FINAL TABLES

PREMIER DIVISION

	P	W	D	L	F	A	Diff	PTS
Siddal	26	19	1	6	629	384	245	39
West Hull *	26	20	1	5	694	400	294	37
West Bowling	26	16	1	9	567	411	156	33
Leigh Miners	26	15	1	10	611	442	169	31
Skirlaugh	26	14	2	10	500	480	20	30
Lock Lane	26	15	0	11	492	488	4	30
Leigh East	26	13	1	12	493	505	-12	27
Wigan St Patricks	26	11	1	14	485	428	57	23
Thornhill	26	11	0	15	399	409	-10	22
Ideal Isberg	26	10	1	15	382	526	-144	21
Oulton Raiders	26	10	0	16	390	624	-234	20
Oldham St Annes	26	9	0	17	424	495	-71	18
Woolston	26	8	1	17	502	671	-169	17
East Leeds	26	6	0	20	348	653	-305	12

** Denotes four points deducted*

DIVISION ONE

	P	W	D	L	For	Agst	Diff	Pts
Thatto Heath	24	18	2	4	792	319	473	38
Featherstone Lions	24	18	0	6	607	360	247	36
Walney Central	24	18	0	6	420	297	123	36
Wigan St Judes	24	15	2	7	493	362	131	32
Dudley Hill	24	13	1	10	521	439	82	27
Hull Dockers	24	11	1	12	492	533	-41	23
Shaw Cross Sharks	24	10	2	12	321	409	-88	22
Hunslet Warriors	24	10	1	13	355	434	-79	21
Crosfields	24	9	1	14	426	543	-117	19
Saddleworth	24	8	2	14	424	568	-144	18
Eccles	24	7	1	16	353	441	-88	15
Askam	24	7	1	16	410	541	-131	15
Waterhead	24	5	0	19	315	683	-368	10

Redhill record expunged

DIVISION TWO

	P	W	D	L	For	Agst	Diff	Pts
Wath Brow Hornets	22	20	1	1	936	228	708	41
Milford Marlins	22	16	2	4	640	249	391	34
Heworth	22	15	0	7	456	354	102	30
Castleford Panthers	22	12	2	8	484	368	116	26
Eastmoor Dragons	22	11	2	9	434	447	-13	24
Hudds Syngenta	22	9	2	11	435	528	-93	20
Widnes St Maries	22	9	0	13	471	488	-17	18
Cottingham Tigers	22	8	1	13	333	435	-102	17
Normanton Knights	22	8	0	14	530	544	-14	16
York Acorn	22	8	0	14	350	538	-188	16
Mayfield	22	7	0	15	283	617	-334	14
Millom	22	4	0	18	239	795	-556	8

Sheffield Hillsborough Hawks & Dewsbury Moor records expunged

PLAY-OFFS

Saturday 3rd May 2003
QUALIFYING PLAY-OFF: West Hull 27 West Bowling 19
ELIMINATION PLAY-OFF: Leigh Miners Rangers 24 Skirlaugh 6

Saturday 10th May 2003
QUALIFYING SEMI-FINAL: Siddal 46 West Hull 6
ELIMINATION SEMI-FINAL: West Bowling 19 Leigh Miners Rangers 12

Saturday 17th May 2003
FINAL ELIMINATOR: West Hull 18 West Bowling 2

Saturday 31st May 2003
GRAND FINAL: Siddal 19 West Hull 14
(at Mount Pleasant, Batley)

GMB UNION NATIONAL CUP FINAL
Saturday 24th May 2003
Oldham St Annes 15 West Hull 14
(at Bloomfield Road, Blackpool)

SUPER LEAGUE
2004 FIXTURES

ROUND 1

FRIDAY 20 FEBRUARY 2004
Bradford Bulls v Wigan Warriors 8:00
St Helens v Hull FC 8:00
SATURDAY 21 FEBRUARY 2004
Warrington Wolves
v Wakefield Trinity Wildcats..................6:00
SUNDAY 22 FEBRUARY 2004
Huddersfield Giants
v Castleford Tigers.................................3:00
Leeds Rhinos v London Broncos..........3:00
Salford City Reds v Widnes Vikings......3:00

SUNDAY 29 FEBRUARY 2004
POWERGEN CHALLENGE CUP
- FOURTH ROUND

ROUND 2

FRIDAY 5 MARCH 2004
Widnes Vikings v Huddersfield Giants..8:00
SATURDAY 6 MARCH 2004
London Broncos v St Helens 6:00
SUNDAY 7 MARCH 2004
Castleford Tigers v Leeds Rhinos 3:30
Hull FC v Warrington Wolves................3:15
Wakefield Trinity Wildcats
v Bradford Bulls...................................3:30
Wigan Warriors v Salford City Reds 3:00

SUNDAY 14 MARCH 2004
POWERGEN CHALLENGE CUP
- FIFTH ROUND

ROUND 3

FRIDAY 19 MARCH 2004
Leeds Rhinos v Wigan Warriors 8:00
St Helens v Widnes Vikings..................8:00
SATURDAY 20 MARCH 2004
Salford City Reds
vWakefield Trinity Wildcats..................6:00
SUNDAY 21 MARCH 2004
Huddersfield Giants v Bradford Bulls....3:00
Hull FC v London Broncos...................3:15
Warrington Wolves
v Castleford Tigers...............................3:00

SUNDAY 28 MARCH 2004
POWERGEN CHALLENGE CUP
- QUARTER FINALS

ROUND 4

FRIDAY 2 APRIL 2004
Castleford Tigers v St Helens...............8:00
SATURDAY 3 APRIL 2004
Wakefield Trinity Wildcats v Hull FC 6:00
SUNDAY 4 APRIL 2004
Bradford Bulls v Salford City Reds 6:00
London Broncos v Warrington Wolves...3:00
Widnes Vikings v Leeds Rhinos 3:00
Wigan Warriors v Huddersfield Giants..3:00

ROUND 5

THURSDAY 8 APRIL 2004
Leeds Rhinos v Bradford Bulls..............TBC
London Broncos
v Wakefield Trinity Wildcats..................8:00
GOOD FRIDAY, 9 APRIL 2004
Huddersfield Giants
v Salford City Reds 7:30
Hull FC v Castleford Tigers 7:30
St Helens v Wigan Warriors ....TBC
Warrington Wolves v Widnes Vikings ..7:30

ROUND 6

EASTER MONDAY, 12 APRIL 2004
Bradford Bulls v St Helens ....TBC
Castleford Tigers v London Broncos 7:30
Salford City Reds v Leeds Rhinos 6:00
Wakefield Trinity Wildcats
v Huddersfield Giants 3:30
Widnes Vikings v Hull FC.....................7:30
Wigan Warriors v Warrington Wolves ..3:00
TUESDAY 13 APRIL 2004
Match to be selected from Round 6

ROUND 7

FRIDAY 16 APRIL 2004
Leeds Rhinos v Huddersfield Giants 8:00
St Helens v Salford City Reds 8:00

SUNDAY 18 APRIL 2004
POWERGEN CHALLENGE CUP
- SEMI FINAL 1

SUNDAY 18 APRIL 2004
Castleford Tigers
v Wakefield Trinity Wildcats..................3:30
Hull FC v Wigan Warriors 3:15
London Broncos v Widnes Vikings 3:00
Warrington Wolves v Bradford Bulls 3:00
(Round 7 Friday & Saturday
games to be selected when Challenge Cup
semi-finalists known)

ROUND 8

FRIDAY 23 APRIL 2004
Wakefield Trinity Wildcats
v Leeds Rhinos 8:00

SUNDAY 25 APRIL 2004
POWERGEN CHALLENGE CUP
- SEMI FINAL 2

SUNDAY 25 APRIL 2004
Bradford Bulls v Hull FC 6:00
Huddersfield Giants v St Helens 3:00
Salford City Reds v Warrington Wolves ..3:00
Widnes Vikings v Castleford Tigers 3:00
Wigan Warriors v London Broncos 3:00
(Round 8 Friday & Saturday
games to be selected when Challenge Cup
semi-finalists known)

ROUND 9

FRIDAY 30 APRIL 2004
St Helens v Leeds Rhinos 8:00
SATURDAY 1 MAY 2004
Castleford Tigers v Wigan Warriors......6:00
SUNDAY 2 MAY 2004
Hull FC v Salford City Reds 3:15
Wakefield Trinity Wildcats
v Widnes Vikings 3:30
Warrington Wolves
v Huddersfield Giants 3:00
MONDAY 3 MAY 2004
London Broncos v Bradford Bulls ....TBC

ROUND 10

FRIDAY 7 MAY 2004
Huddersfield Giants v Hull FC 8:00
Leeds Rhinos v Warrington Wolves......8:00
St Helens v Wakefield Trinity Wildcats..8:00
Wigan Warriors v Widnes Vikings 8:00
SATURDAY 8 MAY 2004
Salford City Reds v London Broncos....6:00
SUNDAY 9 MAY 2004
Bradford Bulls v Castleford Tigers........6:00

SATURDAY 15 MAY 2004
POWERGEN CHALLENGE CUP FINAL

ROUND 11

FRIDAY 21 MAY 2004
Hull FC v Leeds Rhinos 8:00
SATURDAY 22 MAY 2004
Warrington Wolves v St Helens 6:00
SUNDAY 23 MAY 2004
Castleford Tigers v Salford City Reds ..3:30
London Broncos
v Huddersfield Giants 3:00
Wakefield Trinity Wildcats
v Wigan Warriors 3:30
Widnes Vikings v Bradford Bulls 3:00

ROUND 12

FRIDAY 28 MAY 2004
Leeds Rhinos v Salford City Reds 8:00
Warrington Wolves v Wigan Warriors ..8:00
SATURDAY 29 MAY 2004
St Helens v Bradford Bulls...................6:00
SUNDAY 30 MAY 2004
Huddersfield Giants
v Wakefield Trinity Wildcats..................5:30
London Broncos v Castleford Tigers 3:00
MONDAY 31 MAY 2004
Hull FC v Widnes Vikings ....TBC

ROUND 13

FRIDAY 4 JUNE 2004
Wigan Warriors v St Helens..................8:00
SATURDAY 5 JUNE 2004
Bradford Bulls v Leeds Rhinos 6:00
SUNDAY 6 JUNE 2004
Castleford Tigers v Hull FC 3:30
Salford City Reds
v Huddersfield Giants 3:00
Wakefield Trinity Wildcats
v London Broncos 3:30
Widnes Vikings v Warrington Wolves ..3:00

ROUND 14

FRIDAY 11 JUNE 2004
Leeds Rhinos v Widnes Vikings 8:00
St Helens v Castleford Tigers...............8:00
SATURDAY 12 JUNE 2004
Huddersfield Giants v Wigan Warriors..6:00
SUNDAY 13 JUNE 2004
Hull FC v Wakefield Trinity Wildcats 3:15
Salford City Reds v Bradford Bulls 3:00
Warrington Wolves v London Broncos 3:00

ROUND 15

FRIDAY 18 JUNE 2004
Widnes Vikings v St Helens..................8:00
SATURDAY 19 JUNE 2004
Wigan Warriors v Leeds Rhinos 6:00
SUNDAY 20 JUNE 2004
Bradford Bulls v Huddersfield Giants....6:00
Castleford Tigers v Warrington Wolves ..3:30
London Broncos v Hull FC.....................3:00
Wakefield Trinity Wildcats
v Salford City Reds 3:30

ROUND 16

FRIDAY 25 JUNE 2004
St Helens v Warrington Wolves 8:00
Wigan Warriors
v Wakefield Trinity Wildcats..................8:00
SATURDAY 26 JUNE 2004
Leeds Rhinos v Hull FC 6:00
SUNDAY 27 JUNE 2004
Bradford Bulls v Widnes Vikings 6:00
Huddersfield Giants v London Broncos..5:30
Salford City Reds v Castleford Tigers ..3:00

ROUND 17

SATURDAY 3 JULY 2004
Widnes Vikings v Wigan Warriors 6:00
SUNDAY 4 JULY 2004
Castleford Tigers v Bradford Bulls........3:30
Hull FC v Huddersfield Giants 3:15
London Broncos v Salford City Reds....3:00
Wakefield Trinity Wildcats v St Helens..3:30
Warrington Wolves v Leeds Rhinos......3:00

ROUND 18

FRIDAY 9 JULY 2004
Leeds Rhinos v Castleford Tigers 8:00
SATURDAY 10 JULY 2004
St Helens v London Broncos.................6:00
SUNDAY 11 JULY 2004
Bradford Bulls
v Wakefield Trinity Wildcats..................6:00
Huddersfield Giants v Widnes Vikings..5:30
Salford City Reds v Wigan Warriors 3:00
Warrington Wolves v Hull FC................3:00

ROUND 19

FRIDAY 16 JULY 2004
Wigan Warriors v Bradford Bulls..........8:00
SATURDAY 17 JULY 2004
Hull FC v St Helens 6:00
SUNDAY 18 JULY 2004
Castleford Tigers v Huddersfield Giants ..3:30
London Broncos v Leeds Rhinos..........3:00
Wakefield Trinity Wildcats
v Warrington Wolves 3:30
Widnes Vikings v Salford City Reds......3:00

ROUND 20

FRIDAY 23 JULY 2004
Leeds Rhinos v St Helens 8:00
Wigan Warriors v Castleford Tigers......8:00
SATURDAY 24 JULY 2004
Huddersfield Giants
v Warrington Wolves 6:00
SUNDAY 25 JULY 2004
Bradford Bulls v London Broncos 6:00
Salford City Reds v Hull FC 3:00
Widnes Vikings
v Wakefield Trinity Wildcats..................3:00

ROUND 21

FRIDAY 30 JULY 2004
Hull FC v Bradford Bulls 8:00
St Helens v Huddersfield Giants 8:00
SATURDAY 31 JULY 2004
Castleford Tigers v Widnes Vikings 6:00
SUNDAY 1 AUGUST 2004
Leeds Rhinos
v Wakefield Trinity Wildcats..................3:00
London Broncos v Wigan Warriors 3:00
Warrington Wolves v Salford City Reds ..3:00

ROUND 22

FRIDAY 6 AUGUST 2004
Wigan Warriors v Hull FC 8:00
SUNDAY 8 AUGUST 2004
Bradford Bulls v Warrington Wolves 6:00
Huddersfield Giants v Leeds Rhinos 5:30
Salford City Reds v St Helens 3:00
Wakefield Trinity Wildcats
v Castleford Tigers...............................3:30
Widnes Vikings v London Broncos 3:00

ROUND 23

FRIDAY 13 AUGUST 2004
St Helens v London Broncos................8:00
SUNDAY 15 AUGUST 2004
Bradford Bulls v Wigan Warriors..........6:00
Huddersfield Giants v Castleford Tigers ..5:30
Hull FC v Wakefield Trinity Wildcats 3:15
Salford City Reds v Widnes Vikings......3:00
Warrington Wolves v Leeds Rhinos......3:00

ROUND 24

FRIDAY 20 AUGUST 2004
Leeds Rhinos v Bradford Bulls 8:00
Wigan Warriors v St Helens..................8:00
SUNDAY 22 AUGUST 2004
Castleford Tigers v Hull FC 3:30
London Broncos v Warrington Wolves..3:00
Wakefield Trinity Wildcats
v Salford City Reds 3:30
Widnes Vikings v Huddersfield Giants..3:00

ROUND 25

FRIDAY 27 AUGUST 2004
Leeds Rhinos v Castleford Tigers 8:00
St Helens v Huddersfield Giants 8:00
SUNDAY 29 AUGUST 2004
London Broncos
v Wakefield Trinity Wildcats..................3:00
Salford City Reds v Warrington Wolves ..3:00
Widnes Vikings v Wigan Warriors 3:00
MONDAY 30 AUGUST 2004
Hull FC v Bradford Bulls ....TBC

ROUND 26

FRIDAY 3 SEPTEMBER 2004
Wigan Warriors v Leeds Rhinos 8:00
SUNDAY 5 SEPTEMBER 2004
Bradford Bulls v London Broncos 6:00
Castleford Tigers v Salford City Reds ..3:30
Huddersfield Giants v Hull FC 5:30
Wakefield Trinity Wildcats
v Widnes Vikings 3:30
Warrington Wolves v St Helens 3:00

ROUND 27

FRIDAY 10 SEPTEMBER 2004
St Helens v Leeds Rhinos 8:00
SUNDAY 12 SEPTEMBER 2004
London Broncos v Wigan Warriors 3:00
Salford City Reds v Hull FC 3:00
Wakefield Trinity Wildcats
v Huddersfield Giants 3:30
Warrington Wolves v Bradford Bulls 3:00
Widnes Vikings v Castleford Tigers 3:00

ROUND 28

FRIDAY 17 SEPTEMBER 2004
Leeds Rhinos v London Broncos..........8:00
Wigan Warriors v Warrington Wolves ..8:00
SUNDAY 19 SEPTEMBER 2004
Bradford Bulls v St Helens....................6:00
Castleford Tigers
v Wakefield Trinity Wildcats..................3:30
Huddersfield Giants
v Salford City Reds 5:30
Hull FC v Widnes Vikings.....................3:15

PLAY-OFFS

FRIDAY 24 SEPTEMBER 2004
ELIMINATION PLAY-OFF
SATURDAY 25 SEPTEMBER 2004
ELIMINATION PLAY-OFF

FRIDAY 1 OCTOBER 2004/
SATURDAY 2 OCTOBER 2004
ELIMINATION SEMI-FINAL
QUALIFYING SEMI-FINAL

FRIDAY 8 OCTOBER 2004
FINAL ELIMINATOR

SATURDAY 16 OCTOBER 2004
TETLEY'S SUPER LEAGUE
- GRAND FINAL 2004

313

NATIONAL LEAGUE
2004 FIXTURES

NATIONAL LEAGUE ONE

EASTER MONDAY, 12 APRIL 2004
Batley Bulldogs v Rochdale Hornets 3:00
Halifax v Doncaster Dragons 3:00
Hull Kingston Rovers v Keighley Cougars ..3:00
Oldham v Featherstone Rovers 3:00
Whitehaven v Leigh Centurions 3:00

SUNDAY 18 APRIL 2004
Doncaster Dragons v Hull Kingston Rovers ..3:00
Halifax v Oldham 3:00
Keighley Cougars v Batley Bulldogs 3:00
Leigh Centurions v Featherstone Rovers ..3:00
Rochdale Hornets v Whitehaven 3:00

SUNDAY 2 MAY 2004
Batley Bulldogs v Doncaster Dragons 3:00
Featherstone Rovers v Rochdale Hornets ..3:00
Hull Kingston Rovers v Halifax 3:00
Oldham v Leigh Centurions 3:00
Whitehaven v Keighley Cougars 3:00

SUNDAY 9 MAY 2004
Doncaster Dragons v Whitehaven 3:00
Halifax v Batley Bulldogs 3:00
Hull Kingston Rovers v Oldham 3:00
Keighley Cougars v Featherstone Rovers ..3:00
Rochdale Hornets v Leigh Centurions 3:00

SUNDAY 23 MAY 2004
Batley Bulldogs v Hull Kingston Rovers 3:00
Featherstone Rovers v Doncaster Dragons ..3:00
Leigh Centurions v Keighley Cougars 3:00
Oldham v Rochdale Hornets 3:00
Whitehaven v Halifax 3:00

SUNDAY 30 MAY 2004
Doncaster Dragons v Leigh Centurions 3:00
Halifax v Featherstone Rovers 3:00
Hull Kingston Rovers v Whitehaven 3:00
Keighley Cougars v Rochdale Hornets 3:00
Oldham v Batley Bulldogs 3:00

SUNDAY 13 JUNE 2004
Featherstone Rovers v Hull Kingston Rovers ..3:00
Keighley Cougars v Oldham 3:00
Leigh Centurions v Halifax 3:00
Rochdale Hornets v Doncaster Dragons ..3:00
Whitehaven v Batley Bulldogs 3:00

SUNDAY 20 JUNE 2004
Batley Bulldogs v Featherstone Rovers 3:00
Doncaster Dragons v Keighley Cougars 3:00
Halifax v Rochdale Hornets 3:00
Hull Kingston Rovers v Leigh Centurions ..3:00
Oldham v Whitehaven 3:00

SUNDAY 4 JULY 2004
Doncaster Dragons v Oldham 3:00
Featherstone Rovers v Whitehaven 3:00
Keighley Cougars v Halifax 3:00
Leigh Centurions v Batley Bulldogs 3:00
Rochdale Hornets v Hull Kingston Rovers ..3:00

SUNDAY 11 JULY 2004
Batley Bulldogs v Keighley Cougars 3:00
Featherstone Rovers v Leigh Centurions ..3:00
Hull Kingston Rovers v Doncaster Dragons ..3:00
Oldham v Halifax 3:00
Whitehaven v Rochdale Hornets 3:00

SUNDAY 25 JULY 2004
Doncaster Dragons v Batley Bulldogs 3:00
Halifax v Hull Kingston Rovers 3:00
Keighley Cougars v Whitehaven 3:00
Leigh Centurions v Oldham 3:00
Rochdale Hornets v Featherstone Rovers ..3:00

SUNDAY 1 AUGUST 2004
Batley Bulldogs v Halifax 3:00
Featherstone Rovers v Keighley Cougars ..3:00
Leigh Centurions v Rochdale Hornets 3:00
Oldham v Hull Kingston Rovers 3:00
Whitehaven v Doncaster Dragons 3:00

SUNDAY 8 AUGUST 2004
Doncaster Dragons v Featherstone Rovers ..3:00
Halifax v Whitehaven 3:00
Hull Kingston Rovers v Batley Bulldogs 3:00
Keighley Cougars v Leigh Centurions 3:00
Rochdale Hornets v Oldham 3:00

SUNDAY 15 AUGUST 2004
Batley Bulldogs v Oldham 3:00
Featherstone Rovers v Halifax 3:00
Leigh Centurions v Doncaster Dragons 3:00
Rochdale Hornets v Keighley Cougars 3:00
Whitehaven v Hull Kingston Rovers 3:00

SUNDAY 22 AUGUST 2004
Batley Bulldogs v Whitehaven 3:00
Doncaster Dragons v Rochdale Hornets ..3:00
Halifax v Leigh Centurions 3:00
Hull Kingston Rovers v Featherstone Rovers ..3:00
Oldham v Keighley Cougars 3:00

SUNDAY 29 AUGUST 2004
Featherstone Rovers v Batley Bulldogs 3:00
Keighley Cougars v Doncaster Dragons 3:00
Leigh Centurions v Hull Kingston Rovers ..3:00
Rochdale Hornets v Halifax 3:00
Whitehaven v Oldham 3:00

SUNDAY 5 SEPTEMBER 2004
Doncaster Dragons v Halifax 3:00
Featherstone Rovers v Oldham 3:00
Keighley Cougars v Hull Kingston Rovers ..3:00
Leigh Centurions v Whitehaven 3:00
Rochdale Hornets v Batley Bulldogs 3:00

SUNDAY 12 SEPTEMBER 2004
Batley Bulldogs v Leigh Centurions 3:00
Halifax v Keighley Cougars 3:00
Hull Kingston Rovers v Rochdale Hornets ..3:00
Oldham v Doncaster Dragons 3:00
Whitehaven v Featherstone Rovers 3:00

SUNDAY 19 SEPTEMBER 2004
NATIONAL LEAGUE ONE PLAY-OFFS

SUNDAY 26 SEPTEMBER 2004
NATIONAL LEAGUE ONE PLAY-OFFS

SUNDAY 3 OCTOBER 2004
NATIONAL LEAGUE ONE PLAY-OFFS

SUNDAY 10 OCTOBER 2004
NATIONAL LEAGUE ONE GRAND FINAL

SUNDAY 17 OCTOBER 2004
*NATIONAL LEAGUE ONE & TWO
PROMOTION/RELEGATION PLAY-OFF*

NATIONAL LEAGUE TWO

GOOD FRIDAY, 9 APRIL 2004
London Skolars v Sheffield Eagles 7:30

EASTER MONDAY, 12 APRIL 2004
Barrow Raiders v Dewsbury Rams 3:00
Hunslet Hawks v Workington Town 3:30
Swinton Lions v Gateshead Thunder 3:00
York City Knights v Chorley Lynx 3:00

SUNDAY 18 APRIL 2004
Chorley Lynx v Sheffield Eagles 3:00
Dewsbury Rams v Swinton Lions 3:00
Gateshead Thunder v London Skolars 3:30
Hunslet Hawks v York City Knights 3:30
Workington Town v Barrow Raiders 3:00

SATURDAY 1 MAY 2004
London Skolars v Dewsbury Rams 3:00

SUNDAY 2 MAY 2004
Barrow Raiders v Hunslet Hawks 3:00
Chorley Lynx v Gateshead Thunder 3:00
Swinton Lions v Workington Town 3:00
York City Knights v Sheffield Eagles 3:00

SUNDAY 9 MAY 2004
Barrow Raiders v York City Knights 3:00
Dewsbury Rams v Chorley Lynx 3:00
Gateshead Thunder v Sheffield Eagles 3:30
Hunslet Hawks v Swinton Lions 3:30
Workington Town v London Skolars 3:00

FRIDAY 21 MAY 2004
Sheffield Eagles v Dewsbury Rams 8:00

SUNDAY 23 MAY 2004
Chorley Lynx v Workington Town 3:00
Hunslet Hawks v London Skolars 3:30
Swinton Lions v Barrow Raiders 3:00
York City Knights v Gateshead Thunder 3:00

SUNDAY 30 MAY 2004
Barrow Raiders v London Skolars 3:00
Chorley Lynx v Hunslet Hawks 3:00
Dewsbury Rams v Gateshead Thunder 3:00
Workington Town v Sheffield Eagles 3:00
York City Knights v Swinton Lions 3:00

FRIDAY 4 JUNE 2004
Sheffield Eagles v Workington Town 8:00
(subject to Arriva Train Cup commitments)

SUNDAY 13 JUNE 2004
Barrow Raiders v Chorley Lynx 3:00
Dewsbury Rams v York City Knights 3:00
Gateshead Thunder v Workington Town ...3:30
Hunslet Hawks v Sheffield Eagles 3:30
London Skolars v Swinton Lions 3:00

SUNDAY 20 JUNE 2004
Hunslet Hawks v Gateshead Thunder 3:30
Sheffield Eagles v Barrow Raiders 3:15
Swinton Lions v Chorley Lynx 3:00
Workington Town v Dewsbury Rams 3:00
York City Knights v London Skolars 3:00

314

FRIDAY 2 JULY 2004
Sheffield Eagles v Swinton Lions 8:00

SUNDAY 4 JULY 2004
Chorley Lynx v London Skolars 3:00
Dewsbury Rams v Hunslet Hawks 3:00
Gateshead Thunder v Barrow Raiders 3:30
Workington Town v York City Knights 3:00

SUNDAY 11 JULY 2004
Barrow Raiders v Workington Town 3:00
London Skolars v Gateshead Thunder 3:00
Sheffield Eagles v Chorley Lynx 3:15
Swinton Lions v Dewsbury Rams 3:00
York City Knights v Hunslet Hawks 3:00

FRIDAY 23 JULY 2004
Sheffield Eagles v York City Knights 8:00

SUNDAY 25 JULY 2004
Dewsbury Rams v London Skolars 3:00
Gateshead Thunder v Chorley Lynx 3:30
Hunslet Hawks v Barrow Raiders 3:30
Workington Town v Swinton Lions 3:00

FRIDAY 30 JULY 2004
Sheffield Eagles v Gateshead Thunder 8:00

SUNDAY 1 AUGUST 2004
Chorley Lynx v Dewsbury Rams 3:00
London Skolars v Workington Town 3:00
Swinton Lions v Hunslet Hawks 3:00
York City Knights v Barrow Raiders 3:00

SUNDAY 8 AUGUST 2004
Barrow Raiders v Swinton Lions 3:00
Dewsbury Rams v Sheffield Eagles 3:00
Gateshead Thunder v York City Knights 3:30
London Skolars v Hunslet Hawks 3:00
Workington Town v Chorley Lynx 3:00

SUNDAY 15 AUGUST 2004
Gateshead Thunder v Dewsbury Rams ...3:30
Hunslet Hawks v Chorley Lynx 3:30
London Skolars v Barrow Raiders 3:00
Swinton Lions v York City Knights 3:00

FRIDAY 20 AUGUST 2004
Sheffield Eagles v Hunslet Hawks 8:00

SUNDAY 22 AUGUST 2004
Chorley Lynx v Barrow Raiders 3:00
Swinton Lions v London Skolars 3:00
Workington Town v Gateshead Thunder 3:00
York City Knights v Dewsbury Rams 3:00

SUNDAY 29 AUGUST 2004
Barrow Raiders v Sheffield Eagles 3:00
Chorley Lynx v Swinton Lions 3:00
Dewsbury Rams v Workington Town 3:00
Gateshead Thunder v Hunslet Hawks 3:30
London Skolars v York City Knights 3:00

SUNDAY 5 SEPTEMBER 2004
Barrow Raiders v Gateshead Thunder 3:00
Hunslet Hawks v Dewsbury Rams 3:30
London Skolars v Chorley Lynx 3:00
Swinton Lions v Sheffield Eagles 3:00
York City Knights v Workington Town 3:00

FRIDAY 10 SEPTEMBER 2004
Sheffield Eagles v London Skolars 8:00

SUNDAY 12 SEPTEMBER 2004
Chorley Lynx v York City Knights 3:00
Dewsbury Rams v Barrow Raiders 3:00
Gateshead Thunder v Swinton Lions 3:30
Workington Town v Hunslet Hawks 3:00

SUNDAY 19 SEPTEMBER 2004
NATIONAL LEAGUE TWO PLAY-OFFS

SUNDAY 26 SEPTEMBER 2004
NATIONAL LEAGUE TWO PLAY-OFFS

SUNDAY 3 OCTOBER 2004
NATIONAL LEAGUE TWO PLAY-OFFS

SUNDAY 10 OCTOBER 2004
NATIONAL LEAGUE TWO GRAND FINAL

SUNDAY 17 OCTOBER 2004
*NATIONAL LEAGUE ONE & TWO
PROMOTION/RELEGATION PLAY-OFF*

ARRIVA TRAINS CUP

SUNDAY 1 FEBRUARY 2004
Barrow Raiders v Whitehaven 2:00
Dewsbury Rams v Featherstone Rovers 3:00
Doncaster Dragons v London Skolars........3:00
Halifax v Keighley Cougars 3:00
Hull Kingston Rovers v Sheffield Eagles ...3:00
Hunslet Hawks v Rochdale Hornets 3:30
Oldham v Chorley Lynx 3:00
Swinton Lions v Leigh Centurions 3:00
Workington Town v Gateshead Thunder 3:00
York City Knights v Batley Bulldogs 3:00

SUNDAY 15 FEBRUARY 2004
Batley Bulldogs v Doncaster Dragons 3:00
Chorley Lynx v Barrow Raiders 3:00
Featherstone Rovers v Hull Kingston Rovers ..3:00
Gateshead Thunder v York City Knights 3:30
Keighley Cougars v Workington Town 3:00
Leigh Centurions v Oldham 3:00
London Skolars v Hunslet Hawks 3:00
Rochdale Hornets v Halifax 3:00
Sheffield Eagles v Dewsbury Rams 3:15
Whitehaven v Swinton Lions 3:00

SUNDAY 22 FEBRUARY 2004
Dewsbury Rams v York City Knights 3:00
Featherstone Rovers v Batley Bulldogs 3:00
Gateshead Thunder v Whitehaven 3:00
Hull Kingston Rovers v Doncaster Dragons ..3:00
Hunslet Hawks v Halifax 3:30
Leigh Centurions v Chorley Lynx 3:00
Rochdale Hornets v Keighley Cougars 3:00
Sheffield Eagles v London Skolars 3:15
Swinton Lions v Oldham 3:00
Workington Town v Barrow Raiders 3:00

SUNDAY 7 MARCH 2004
Barrow Raiders v Gateshead Thunder 2:00
Batley Bulldogs v Dewsbury Rams 3:00
Doncaster Dragons v Sheffield Eagles 3:00
Halifax v Rochdale Hornets 3:00
Hull Kingston Rovers v London Skolars 3:00
Hunslet Hawks v Keighley Cougars 3:30
Oldham v Leigh Centurions 3:00
Swinton Lions v Chorley Lynx 3:00
Whitehaven v Workington Town 3:00
York City Knights v Featherstone Rovers ..3:00

SUNDAY 14 MARCH 2004
London Skolars v Sheffield Eagles 3:00
(subject to Powergen Challenge Cup commitments)

FRIDAY 19 MARCH 2004
Sheffield Eagles v Hull Kingston Rovers ..8:00

SATURDAY 20 MARCH 2004
London Skolars v Doncaster Dragons 3:00

SUNDAY 21 MARCH 2004
Batley Bulldogs v York City Knights 3:00
Chorley Lynx v Oldham 3:00
Featherstone Rovers v Dewsbury Rams 3:00
Gateshead Thunder v Workington Town 3:30
Keighley Cougars v Halifax 3:00
Leigh Centurions v Swinton Lions 3:00
Rochdale Hornets v Hunslet Hawks 3:00
Whitehaven v Barrow Raiders 3:00

SUNDAY 28 MARCH 2004
Barrow Raiders v Chorley Lynx 2:00
Dewsbury Rams v Sheffield Eagles 3:00
Doncaster Dragons v Batley Bulldogs 3:00
Halifax v Leigh Centurions 3:00
Hull Kingston Rovers v Featherstone Rovers ..3:00
Hunslet Hawks v London Skolars 3:30
Oldham v Rochdale Hornets 3:00
Swinton Lions v Whitehaven 3:00
Workington Town v Keighley Cougars 3:00
York City Knights v Gateshead Thunder 3:00

FRIDAY 2 APRIL 2004
Sheffield Eagles v Doncaster Dragons 8:00

SATURDAY 3 APRIL 2004
London Skolars v Hull Kingston Rovers 3:00

SUNDAY 4 APRIL 2004
Barrow Raiders v Workington Town 3:00
Batley Bulldogs v Featherstone Rovers 3:00
Chorley Lynx v Leigh Centurions 3:00
Halifax v Hunslet Hawks 3:00
Keighley Cougars v Rochdale Hornets 3:00
Oldham v Swinton Lions 3:00
Whitehaven v Gateshead Thunder 3:00
York City Knights v Dewsbury Rams 3:00

GOOD FRIDAY, 9 APRIL 2004
Chorley Lynx v Swinton Lions 3:00
Dewsbury Rams v Batley Bulldogs 7:30
Doncaster Dragons v Hull Kingston Rovers ..7:30
Featherstone Rovers v York City Knights ..7:30
Gateshead Thunder v Barrow Raiders 3:00
Keighley Cougars v Hunslet Hawks 7:30
Leigh Centurions v Halifax 3:00
Rochdale Hornets v Oldham 7:30
Workington Town v Whitehaven 3:00

SUNDAY 25 APRIL 2004
ARRIVA TRAINS CUP - PLAY-OFFS

SUNDAY 6 JUNE 2004
ARRIVA TRAINS CUP - QUARTER FINALS

SUNDAY 27 JUNE 2004
ARRIVA TRAINS CUP - SEMI-FINALS

SUNDAY 18 JULY 2004
ARRIVA TRAINS CUP - FINAL

2003 AWARD WINNERS

SUPER LEAGUE AWARDS

MAN OF STEEL
Jamie Peacock (Bradford Bulls)

COACH OF THE YEAR
Brian Noble (Bradford Bulls)
Nominees:
Tony Rea (London Broncos),
Mike Gregory (Wigan Warriors),
Paul Cullen (Warrington Wolves)

YOUNG PLAYER OF THE YEAR
Gareth Hock (Wigan Warriors)
Nominees:
Luke Robinson (Wigan Warriors),
Danny McGuire (Leeds Rhinos)

RLPA PLAYER OF THE YEAR
Jamie Peacock (Bradford Bulls)
Nominees:
Brandon Costin (Huddersfield Giants),
Shane Millard (Widnes Vikings)

REFEREE OF THE YEAR
Karl Kirkpatrick (Warrington)

TOP TRY SCORER
Dennis Moran (London Broncos)

OPTA INDEX HITMAN
Shane Millard (Widnes Vikings)

OPTA INDEX TOP METRE MAKER
Lesley Vainikolo (Bradford Bulls)

NATIONAL LEAGUE AWARDS

YOUNG PLAYERS OF THE YEAR
National League One: Richard Whiting
(Featherstone Rovers)
National League Two:
Danny Brough (York City Knights)
National League Three:
Tom Sibley (Teesside Steelers)

COACHES OF THE YEAR
National League One:
Martin Hall (Rochdale Hornets)
National League Two:
Darren Abram (Chorley Lynx)
National League Three:
Peter Tonkin (St Albans Centurions)

PLAYERS OF THE YEAR
National League One:
Gavin Clinch (Salford City Reds)
National League Two:
Phil Hasty (Hunslet Hawks)
National League Three:
Dave Patterson
(Warrington Woolston Rovers)

REFEREE OF THE YEAR:
Peter Taberner (Wigan)
COMMUNITY CLUB OF THE YEAR:
Whitehaven
**NATIONAL LEAGUE
CLUB OF THE YEAR**
York City Knights
RLPA PLAYER OF THE YEAR:
Gavin Clinch (Salford City Reds)

Bradford's Jamie Peacock shows off his awards double

RUGBY LEAGUE WORLD DREAM TEAMS

NATIONAL LEAGUE ONE
1 Gary Broadbent (Whitehaven)
2 Damian Munro (Leigh Centurions)
3 Alan Hunte (Salford City Reds)
4 Danny Maun (Batley Bulldogs)
5 Alasdair McClarron
(Hull Kingston Rovers)
6 Cliff Beverley (Salford City Reds)
7 Gavin Clinch (Salford City Reds)
8 Paul Southern (Rochdale Hornets)
9 Paul Rowley (Leigh Centurions)
10 Andy Coley (Salford City Reds)
11 Paul Smith (Rochdale Hornets)
12 David Larder (Rochdale Hornets)
13 Adam Bristow (Leigh Centurions)

NATIONAL LEAGUE TWO
1 Andy Poynter (Sheffield Eagles)
2 Bryn Powell (Hunslet Hawks)
3 Damien Reid (Gateshead Thunder)
4 Matt Foster (Keighley Cougars)
5 Eric Andrews (Chorley Lynx)
6 Mick Coates (Chorley Lynx)
7 Phil Hasty (Hunslet Hawks)
8 Simon Knox (Swinton Lions)
9 Andy Henderson (Barrow Raiders)
10 Jon Bruce (Sheffield Eagles)
11 Andy Raleigh (Sheffield Eagles)
12 Oliver Wilkes (Keighley Cougars)
13 Trevor Krause (York City Knights)

NATIONAL LEAGUE THREE
1 Issi Fa
(Huddersfield Underbank Rangers)
2 Phil Pitt (Teesside Steelers)
3 Dene Miller (St Albans Centurions)
4 Tom Sibley (Teesside Steelers)
5 Steve Toon (St Albans Centurions)
6 Tom Eisenhuth
(St Albans Centurions)
7 Liam Jarvis (Bradford Dudley Hill)
8 Richard Bingley
(Bradford Dudley Hill)
9 Peter Rousso
(Sheffield Hillsborough Hawks)
10 Koben Katipa
(South London Storm)
11 Dave Patterson
(Warrington Woolston Rovers)
12 Chris Mellor
(Warrington Woolston Rovers)
13 Sean Dickinson
(Bradford Dudley Hill)

SUPER LEAGUE

(Play-offs in brackets, inc. in totals)

TRIES

1 Dennis Moran
  London 24 (0)
2 Graham Appo
  Warrington 23 (0)
3 Lesley Vainikolo
  Bradford 22 (1)
4 Mark Calderwood
  Leeds 20 (1)
5 Brandon Costin
  Huddersfield ....19 (-)
  Colin Best
  Hull ....19 (-)
7 Leon Pryce
  Bradford 18 (1)
8 Darren Albert
  St Helens 17 (0)
9 David Hodgson
  Wigan 16 (0)

GOALS

1 Paul Deacon
  Bradford 137 (13)
2 Kevin Sinfield
  Leeds 112 (6)
3 Sean Long
  St Helens 98 (6)
4 Julian O'Neill (A) *
  Widnes ....95 (-)
5 Andy Farrell
  Wigan 88 (6)
6 Chris Thorman
  London 81 (1)
7 Steve Prescott
  Hull ....71 (-)
8 Steve McNamara
  Huddersfield ....68 (-)
9 Jamie Rooney
  Wakefield ....64 (-)
10 Graham Appo
  Warrington 62 (2)

* includes 11 for Wigan

POINTS

1 Paul Deacon
  Bradford 313 (27)
2 Sean Long
  St Helens 249 (20)
3 Kevin Sinfield
  Leeds 242 (12)
4 Graham Appo
  Warrington 216 (4)
  Julian O'Neill (A) *
  Widnes ....216 (-)
6 Andy Farrell
  Wigan 205 (12)
7 Steve Prescott
  Hull ....194 (-)
8 Chris Thorman
  London 191 (2)
9 Jamie Rooney
  Wakefield ....172 (-)
10 Lee Briers
  Warrington 152 (0)

* includes 26 for Wigan

NATIONAL LEAGUE 1

(Play-offs in brackets, inc. in totals)

TRIES

1 Cliff Beverley
  Salford 20 (1)
2 Paul Mansson *
  Hull KR 18 (3)
3 Mick Nanyn
  Rochdale 17 (2)
4 Damian Munro
  Leigh 16 (1)
  Alan Hunte
  Salford 16 (2)
  Stuart Littler
  Salford 16 (2)
7 Alasdair McClarron
  Hull KR 13 (3)
  David Larder
  Rochdale 13 (2)
  Paul Smith
  Rochdale 13 (0)

* includes 10 for Doncaster

GOALS

1 Mick Nanyn
  Rochdale 99 (11)
2 Neil Turley
  Leigh 84 (12)
3 Chris Charles
  Salford 71 (11)
4 Barry Eaton
  Batley 69 (8)
5 Lynton Stott
  Hull KR 55 (10)
6 Simon Svabic
  Oldham 47 (4)
7 Stuart Dickens
  Featherstone ....42 (-)
8 Steve Blakeley
  Salford 40 (1)
9 Darren Holt
  Whitehaven 39 (0)
10 Steve Kirkbride
  Whitehaven 35 (7)

POINTS

1 Mick Nanyn
  Rochdale 266 (30)
2 Neil Turley
  Leigh 202 (24)
3 Chris Charles
  Salford 158 (22)
4 Barry Eaton
  Batley 151 (20)
5 Lynton Stott
  Hull KR 125 (24)
6 Simon Svabic
  Oldham 108 (12)
7 Stuart Dickens
  Featherstone ....88 (-)
8 Steve Blakeley
  Salford 85 (3)
9 Graham Holroyd
  Doncaster 82 (17)
10 Cliff Beverley
  Salford 80 (4)

NATIONAL LEAGUE 2

(Play-offs in brackets, inc. in totals)

TRIES

1 Eric Andrews
  Chorley 22 (0)
2 Andy Poynter
  Sheffield 19 (1)
3 Bryn Powell
  Hunslet 16 (0)
  Matt Foster
  Keighley 16 (1)
5 Jason Roach
  Swinton ....15 (-)
6 Paul Jones
  Barrow 14 (3)
7 Tony Weller
  Sheffield 13 (0)
8 Jamie Smith
  Barrow 12 (0)
  Anton Garcia
  Chorley 12 (0)
  Phil Hasty
  Hunslet 12 (0)
  Andy Raleigh
  Sheffield 12 (1)
  Graeme Lewthwaite
  Workington ....12 (-)

GOALS

1 Danny Brough
  York 91 (5)
  Gavin Brown
  Sheffield 91 (8)
3 Mark McCully
  Chorley 88 (5)
4 Chris Hough
  Swinton ....63 (-)
5 Phil Hasty
  Hunslet 61 (2)
6 Paul Thorman
  Gateshead ....58 (-)
7 Tane Manihera
  Barrow 57 (0)
8 Paul Ashton
  Keighley 52 (27)
9 Adam Mitchell
  Keighley 42 (0)
10 Adam Pate
  Barrow 34 (12)

POINTS

1 Gavin Brown
  Sheffield 206 (22)
2 Danny Brough
  York 204 (10)
  Mark McCully
  Chorley 204 (18)
4 Phil Hasty
  Hunslet 173 (4)
5 Chris Hough
  Swinton ....152 (-)
6 Tane Manihera
  Barrow 137 (0)
7 Paul Ashton
  Keighley 126 (73)
8 Paul Thorman
  Gateshead ....121 (-)
9 Adam Mitchell
  Keighley 100 (0)
  Adam Pate
  Barrow 100 (40)

Dennis Moran

Cliff Beverley

Eric Andrews

NAT LEAGUE CUP

TRIES
1 Cliff Beverley
  Salford 18
2 Jamie Marshall
  Barrow 14
  Leroy Joe
  Whitehaven 14
4 Craig Lingard
  Batley 13
  Jamie Stokes
  Featherstone 13
  Alan Hunte
  Salford 13
7 Damian Munro
  Leigh 12
  Malcolm Alker
  Salford 12
  Andy Kirk
  Salford 12
  Neil Turley
  Leigh 11
  Stuart Littler
  Salford 11

GOALS
1 Barry Eaton
  Batley 59
2 Steve Blakeley
  Salford 58
3 Darren Holt
  Whitehaven 52
4 Neil Turley
  Leigh 39
5 Simon Svabic
  Oldham 32
6 Gavin Brown
  Sheffield 28
7 Stuart Dickens
  Featherstone 27
  Simon Irving
  Doncaster 27
  Chris Stephenson
  Hull KR 27
  Ian Watson
  Rochdale 27

POINTS
1 Steve Blakeley
  Salford 132
2 Neil Turley
  Leigh 124
3 Barry Eaton
  Batley 122
4 Darren Holt
  Whitehaven 113
5 Simon Irving
  Doncaster 86
6 Gavin Brown
  Sheffield 75
7 Cliff Beverley
  Salford 72
  Simon Svabic
  Oldham 72
9 Chris Stephenson
  Hull KR 62
10 Paul Evans
  Barrow 61

CHALLENGE CUP

TRIES
1 Lesley Vainikolo
  Bradford 6
2 Jason Lee
  Doncaster 5
  Richie Barnett
  Hull 5
  Steve Prescott
  Hull 5
  Mark Calderwood
  Leeds 5
  Paul Owen
  Rochdale 5
  Sean Long
  St Helens 5
  Darren Smith
  St Helens 5
  Hugh Thorpe
  Swinton 5
  Brian Carney
  Wigan 5

GOALS
1 Paul Deacon
  Bradford 36
2 Matt Crowther
  Hull 22
3 Sean Long
  St Helens 20
4 David Furner
  Leeds 15
5 Julian O'Neill
  Wigan 14
6 Stuart Dickens
  Featherstone 12
  Adam Hughes
  Widnes 12
8 Andy Farrell
  Wigan 11
  Mick Nanyn
  Rochdale 11
  Lee Sanderson
  Leigh 11

POINTS
1 Paul Deacon
  Bradford 76
2 Sean Long
  St Helens 60
3 Matt Crowther
  Hull 48
4 David Furner
  Leeds 46
5 Adam Hughes
  Widnes 40
6 Julian O'Neill
  Wigan 32
7 Kevin Sinfield
  Leeds 31
8 Andy Farrell
  Wigan 30
  Mick Nanyn
  Rochdale 30
10 Paul Ashton
  Keighley 25

ALL COMPETITIONS

TRIES
1 Cliff Beverley
  Salford 39
2 Damian Munro
  Leigh 32
  Alan Hunte
  Salford 32
4 Stuart Littler
  Salford 30
5 Lesley Vainikolo
  Bradford 28
6 Jamie Marshall
  Barrow 26
  Mick Nanyn
  Rochdale 26
  Leroy Joe
  Whitehaven 26
9 Mark Calderwood
  Leeds 25
10 Bryn Powell
  Hunslet 24
  Dennis Moran
  London 24
  Andy Kirk
  Salford 24

GOALS
1 Paul Deacon
  Bradford 173
2 Barry Eaton
  Batley 138
3 Gavin Brown
  Sheffield 126
4 Mick Nanyn
  Rochdale 123
  Neil Turley
  Leigh 123
6 Kevin Sinfield
  Leeds 122
7 Sean Long
  St Helens 118
8 Julian O'Neill (A) *
  Widnes 109
9 Danny Brough **
  York 108
10 Mark McCully
  Chorley 107
  * includes 25 for Wigan
  ** includes 17 for Dewsbury

POINTS
1 Paul Deacon
  Bradford 389
2 Mick Nanyn
  Rochdale 350
3 Neil Turley
  Leigh 326
4 Sean Long
  St Helens 309
5 Gavin Brown
  Sheffield 299
6 Barry Eaton
  Batley 297
7 Kevin Sinfield
  Leeds 273
8 Danny Brough **
  York 252
9 Mark McCully
  Chorley 250
10 Julian O'Neill (A) *
  Widnes 248
  * includes 58 for Wigan
  ** includes 48 for Dewsbury

Steve Blakeley

Lesley Vainikolo

Paul Deacon

2003 Season - Stats round-up

FINAL TABLES

SUPER LEAGUE

	P	W	D	L	F	A	D	PTS
Bradford	28	22	0	6	878	529	349	44
Leeds	28	19	3	6	751	555	196	41
Wigan	28	19	2	7	776	512	264	40
St Helens *	28	16	1	11	845	535	310	31
London	28	14	2	12	643	696	-53	30
Warrington	28	14	1	13	748	619	129	29
Hull *	28	13	3	12	701	577	124	27
Castleford	28	12	1	15	612	633	-21	25
Widnes	28	12	1	15	640	727	-87	25
H'dersfield	28	11	1	16	628	715	-87	23
Wakefield	28	7	1	20	505	774	-269	15
Halifax *	28	1	0	27	372	1227	-855	0

two points deducted for 2002 salary cap breach

NATIONAL LEAGUE ONE

	P	W	D	L	F	A	D	PTS
Salford	18	14	2	2	732	294	438	30
Leigh	18	15	0	3	702	309	393	30
Rochdale	18	13	0	5	647	477	170	26
Hull KR	18	10	0	8	401	373	28	20
Oldham	18	7	2	9	404	500	-96	16
Whitehaven	18	5	5	8	443	438	5	15
F'therstone	18	7	0	11	387	478	-91	14
Doncaster	18	6	1	11	429	632	-203	13
Batley	18	5	1	12	366	543	-177	11
Dewsbury	18	2	1	15	284	751	-467	5

NATIONAL LEAGUE TWO

	P	W	D	L	F	A	D	PTS
Sheffield	18	13	0	5	644	326	318	26
Chorley	18	13	0	5	584	362	222	26
Keighley	18	13	0	5	488	340	148	26
York	18	11	1	6	576	381	195	23
Barrow	18	11	0	7	546	419	127	22
Hunslet	18	10	1	7	513	425	88	21
Swinton	18	8	1	9	445	426	19	17
Workington	18	4	1	13	393	558	-165	9
Gateshead	18	3	1	14	365	663	-298	7
London S	18	1	1	16	222	876	-654	3

FIELD GOALS

1	Chris Hough Swinton	12
2	Carl Briggs Featherstone	8
	Paul Ashton Keighley	8
4	Gavin Brown Sheffield	7
5	Ian Watson Rochdale	6
6	Mick Coates Chorley	5
	Matt Firth Keighley	5
	Kevin Sinfield Leeds	5
	Adrian Lam Wigan	5
10	John Braddish Chorley	4
	Jamie Benn Dewsbury	4
	Lynton Stott Hull KR	4
	Latham Tawhai Hull KR	4
	Phil Hasty Hunslet	4
	Neil Turley Leigh	4
	Jamie Rooney Wakefield	4
	Lee Briers Warrington	4
	Dean Lawford Widnes	4

ATTENDANCES

SUPER LEAGUE

	2003 Avg	2002 Avg	Diff
Bradford	15,259	11,524	+3,735
Leeds	13,143	12,192	+951
Hull	11,598	6,928	+4,670
Wigan	11,217	10,480	+737
St Helens	9,643	10,580	-937
Castleford	7,199	6,914	+285
Warrington	7,031	6,153	+878
Widnes	6,511	6,584	-73
Huddersfield	4,722	2,570	+2,152
Wakefield	4,017	3,890	+127
London	3,546	3,760	-214
Halifax	2,977	4,080	-1,103

'03 Avg 8,188 / **'02 Avg** 7,377 / **Diff** +811

BEST CROWDS

65,537	Bradford v Wigan (GF)	18/10/03
23,035	Leeds v Bradford (R22)	8/8/03
21,790	Wigan v St Helens (ESF)	3/10/03
21,784	Bradford v Leeds (R11)	23/5/03
21,102	Bradford v Leeds (R26)	7/9/03
20,283	Bradford v Wakefield (R2)	9/3/03
19,786	Bradford v Leeds (QSF)	4/10/03
19,549	Hull v Bradford (R13)	8/6/03
17,264	Leeds v Wigan (FE)	10/10/03
15,732	Bradford v Wigan (R15)	21/6/03

WORST CROWDS

1,276	Halifax v London (R24)	22/8/03
1,781	Halifax v London (R16)	28/6/03
1,919	Halifax v Widnes (R14)	14/6/03
2,088	Halifax v Widnes (R28)	21/9/03
2,274	Halifax v Wakefield (R21)	1/8/03
2,415	Wakefield v London (R22)	10/8/03
2,473	Halifax v Huddersfield (R23)	15/8/03
2,543	Halifax v Wigan (R25)	31/8/03
2,679	London v Huddersfield (R15)	22/7/03
2,806	Wakefield v Halifax (R10)	16/5/03

NATIONAL LEAGUE ONE

	2003 Avg	2002 Avg	Diff
Leigh	2,445	2,542	-97
Salford	2,322	4,199	-1,877
Oldham	1,572	1,150	+422
Hull KR	1,562	1,788	-226
Featherstone	1,509	1,482	+27
Whitehaven	1,393	1,229	+164
Rochdale	1,062	1,189	-127
Dewsbury	950	1,134	-184
Doncaster	950	1,081	-131
Batley	856	979	-123

2003 Avg 1,462

NFP 2002 Avg 1,179

BEST CROWDS

9,186	Leigh v Salford (GF)	5/10/03
4,121	Salford v Leigh (W18)	31/8/03
4,000	Leigh v Salford (W9)	22/6/03
3,660	Salford v Leigh (QSF)	21/9/03
2,901	Leigh v Hull KR (FE)	28/9/03
2,782	Leigh v Rochdale (W19)	7/9/03
2,363	Leigh v Hull KR (W10)	29/6/03
2,287	Leigh v Oldham (W15)	10/8/03
2,283	Leigh v Batley (W13)	27/7/03
2,250	Hull KR v Oldham (EPO)	14/9/03

WORST CROWDS

604	Batley v Whitehaven (W15)	10/8/03
623	Rochdale v Doncaster (W13)	27/7/03
668	Dewsbury v Rochdale (W6)	25/5/03
677	Doncaster v Whitehaven (W18)	31/8/03
726	Doncaster v Dewsbury (W14)	3/8/03
728	Batley v Rochdale (W7)	1/6/03
732	Rochdale v Dewsbury (W15)	10/8/03
741	Batley v Doncaster (W18)	6/9/03
777	Dewsbury v Whitehaven (W11)	13/7/03
779	Rochdale v Whitehaven (EPO)	14/9/03

NATIONAL LEAGUE TWO

	2003 Avg	2002 Avg	Diff
York	1,365	669	+696
Keighley	1,105	1,072	+33
Sheffield	943	1,024	-81
Barrow	807	928	-121
Swinton	542	547	-5
Hunslet	541	616	-75
Workington	526	1,020	-494
Chorley	434	494	-60
London S	430	N/A	N/A
Gateshead	279	510	-231

2003 Avg 697

NFP 2002 Avg 1,179

BEST CROWDS

(Attendance figure unavailable for GF)

1,835	York v Keighley (W11)	13/7/03
1,642	York v Hunslet (W18)	5/9/03
1,468	Keighley v Sheffield (W17)	24/8/03
1,332	Keighley v Barrow (ESF)	21/9/03
1,301	York v Sheffield (W13)	27/7/03
1,299	York v Barrow (EPO)	14/9/03
1,271	York v Gateshead (W1)	18/4/03
1,150	Keighley v Hunslet (EPO)	14/9/03
1,129	Keighley v Swinton (W10)	29/6/03
1,126	Sheffield v Keighley (W9)	22/6/03

WORST CROWDS

181	Gateshead v Chorley (W15)	10/8/03
226	Gateshead v London Skolars (W9)	22/6/03
252	Chorley v London Skolars (W8)	15/6/03
257	London Skolars v Chorley (W19)	7/9/03
263	Gateshead v Sheffield (W18)	31/8/03
278	London Skolars v Swinton (W7)	8/6/03
280	Chorley v Gateshead (W5)	25/5/03
285	Gateshead v Hunslet (W11)	13/7/03
287	Gateshead v Workington (W5)	31/5/03
289	Swinton v London Skolars (W15)	10/8/03

NATIONAL LEAGUE CUP

BEST CROWDS

6,486	Leigh v Salford (F)	6/7/03
4,445	Leigh v Salford (W3)	16/2/03
3,334	Salford v Swinton (W1)	19/1/03
3,105	York v Hull KR (W1)	19/1/03
3,099	Salford v Leigh (W9)	30/3/03
3,070	Leigh v Oldham (W1)	19/1/03
2,839	Oldham v Salford (W6)	9/3/03
2,687	Leigh v Whitehaven (SF)	8/6/03
2,346	Salford v Rochdale (W4)	23/2/03
2,162	Salford v Oldham (W11)	13/4/03

WORST CROWDS

172	Gateshead v Salford (W7)	19/3/03
208	Gateshead v Workington (W10)	6/4/03
213	Chorley v Gateshead (W9)	30/3/03
232	Gateshead v Barrow (W6)	9/3/03
251	Chorley v Workington (W6)	9/3/03
258	Chorley v Barrow (W7)	16/3/03
272	Gateshead v Whitehaven (W7)	16/3/03
307	London Skolars v Batley (W10)	6/4/03
308	Gateshead v Chorley (W3)	16/2/03
310	London Skolars v Keighley (W9)	30/3/03

CHALLENGE CUP

BEST CROWDS

71,212	Bradford v Leeds (F)	26/4/03
19,118	Leeds v St Helens (SF)	12/4/03
15,359	Bradford v Wigan (SF)	13/4/03
15,310	Hull v Halifax (R4)	9/2/03
11,729	Sheffield v Hull (R5)	2/3/03
	at KC Stadium	
11,420	Leeds v Hull (R3)	16/3/03
7,535	Leeds v Whitehaven (R4)	9/2/03
6,717	Leeds v London (R5)	1/3/03
5,869	Warrington v Bradford (R4)	8/2/03
5,717	Salford v St Helens (QF)	16/3/03

WORST CROWDS

315	Gateshead v UTC (R3)	26/1/03
315	Swinton v Shaw Cross (R3)	26/1/03
524	Hunslet v Pia (R3)	26/1/03
572	Chorley v Swinton (R4)	9/2/03
617	Barrow v Embassy (R3)	26/1/03
685	Woolston v Dewsbury (R3)	26/1/03
750	Halton Simms Cross v London Skolars (R3)	26/1/03
759	Oulton v Sheffield (R3)	24/1/03
809	Chorley v Leigh Miners Rangers (R3)	24/1/03
861	Oldham St Annes v Rochdale (R3)	26/1/03